SO-BZL-732

Advance Praise for
Transatlantic Romanticism

Transatlantic Romanticism promises to fulfill the long-felt need for an intelligent anthology of eighteenth- to nineteenth-century transatlantic materials. The range and organization of texts, and the invaluable headnotes, make it a must have.

—Elizabeth Fay
University of Massachusetts, Boston

This masterpiece of an introduction . . . manages to communicate the complexity of the subject at the same time it demonstrates the profound interconnections of cultural, political and social forces. It manages to do all that in language that [students will] find comprehensible and compelling. Bravo! I'd adopt it for this alone.

—Nancy Cirillo
University of Illinois, Chicago

The excellently written introduction moves purposefully between Anglo and North American perspectives and effectively contextualizes the wide-ranging selection of texts.

—Martin Halliwell
University of Leicester

The anthology has a wonderfully complete representation of both major and minor writers of the Romantic period. . . . The selections give the reader a much fuller picture of the Romantic cast of thought, political and social approach, and philosophy than other anthologies have done.

—Brad Strickland
Gainesville College

[This] comprehensive anthology . . . is of immeasurable value to those of us who must currently cobble course packs together, and to our students!

—Miranda Burgess
The University of British Columbia

Transatlantic Romanticism provides a unique, comprehensive, and imaginative answer to a crying need. This splendid new anthology truly advances the study of British, Canadian, and American literature.

—Richard E. Brantley
University of Florida

The large cultural, historical, and aesthetic resonances and differences between America and Britain during this period provide an excellent means of (re)reading and thinking about the authors [included in] this anthology. The anthology offers provocative texts and contexts for a wide variety of crucial concerns of the period including science, religion, art, and politics.

—Ron Broglio
Georgia Tech

[This book] meets the growing demand for a transatlantic Romantic reader, presents texts not otherwise readily available to students, and includes contemporary (Romantic) material specifically addressing transatlantic issues. . . . It is a pioneer in its field. There simply isn't any relevant competition in a single anthology.

—Susan Manning
University of Edinburgh

Transatlantic Romanticism

An Anthology of British, American, and Canadian Literature 1767–1867

Lance Newman
California State University, San Marcos

Joel Pace
University of Wisconsin, Eau Claire

Chris Koenig-Woodyard
University of Toronto at Mississauga

PEARSON
Longman

New York   Boston   San Francisco
London   Toronto   Sydney   Tokyo   Singapore   Madrid
Mexico City   Munich   Paris   Cape Town   Hong Kong   Montreal

Transatlantic Romanticism

An Anthology of British, American, and Canadian Literature 1767–1867

Lance Newman
California State University, San Marcos

Joel Pace
University of Wisconsin, Eau Claire

Chris Koenig-Woodyard
University of Toronto at Mississauga

New York   Boston   San Francisco
London   Toronto   Sydney   Tokyo   Singapore   Madrid
Mexico City   Munich   Paris   Cape Town   Hong Kong   Montreal

For Willow, Caldwell, and Adrienne

Acquisitions Editor: *Erika Berg*
Development Editor: *Barbara Santoro*
Marketing Manager: *Ann Stypuloski*
Production Coordinator: *Virginia Riker*
Senior Supplements Editor: *Donna Campion*
Project Coordination, Text Design, and Page Makeup: *Dianne Hall*
Cover Designer/Manager: *Wendy Ann Fredericks*
Cover Art: *T. Hustwick*, Liverpool Harbor. *Oil on canvas. Photograph by Sexton/Dykes*.
   © *Peabody Essex Museum*.
Manufacturing Buyer: *Roy L. Pickering, Jr.*
Printer and Binder: *Quebecor World Taunton*
Cover Printer: *Phoenix Color*

For permission to use copyrighted material, grateful acknowledgment is made to the copyright holders on page 1300, which is hereby made part of this copyright page.

Library of Congress Cataloging-in-Publication Data
CIP data is on file.

Copyright © 2006 by Pearson Education, Inc.

All rights reserved. No part of this publication may be reproduced, stored in a retrieval system, or transmitted, in any form or by any means, electronic, mechanical, photocopying, recording, or otherwise, without the prior written permission of the publisher. Printed in the United States.

Please visit us at www.ablongman.com

ISBN: 0-321-21712-8

1 2 3 4 5 6 7 8 9 0—QWT—08 07 06 05

CONTENTS

~ TRANSATLANTIC EXCHANGES ~
Religion and Revivalism 544

⟶ TRANSATLANTIC EXCHANGES ⟵
Civilization and Nature   1072

PREFACE

ARCHIBALD LAMPMA
The City at the End of Things
The Frogs
The Railway Station
Voices of Earth
Dimaun
DUNCAN CAMPBELL SCOTT (1862-1947)
The Onondaga Madonna
Night Hymns on Lake Nipigon

This anthology is designed to meet the needs of teachers and students of an exciting
new field, Transatlantic Romanticism, the study of literary and cultural exchanges
between Britain, the United States, and Canada during the Romantic period. The
chronological scope of the collection matches its broad geographic reach. Our selections span what we define as the long Romantic century, 1767–1867, a century of literary and political revolutions that gave birth to the modern world.

Scholars are only now beginning to understand the ways in which these three
nations influenced each other culturally. Until recently, literatures were studied separately by nation; however, compelling recent scholarship has shed light on the many
transnational connections that were formative for literatures on both sides of the
Atlantic. But the lack of a teachable textbook kept this thrilling new research out of
the classroom. Previously, it was necessary to assign one expensive anthology per
nation studied. *Transatlantic Romanticism* promises to be lighter on both the bank
account and the backpack. In addition to combining the literatures of three nations
into one book, we provide what the separate single-nation anthologies lack—a comparative framework that establishes transatlantic links and encourages students and
professors to make more of their own.

In short, while existing collections of Romantic literature focus narrowly on
short periods in single nations, *Transatlantic Romanticism* provides a comprehensive
and wide-ranging survey of Romantic literature written in English on both sides of
the Atlantic. We juxtapose texts by the most significant writers in the British
Empire's center at London with those produced in peripheral but rapidly growing
cities like Philadelphia, New York, Boston, Toronto, and Ottawa, as well as in remote
frontier towns across North America. Our goal is to give readers a fresh perspective
on one of the most stirring and challenging periods in literary history, a period during which many of our own most urgent ways of thinking and writing first took form.

Approach and Organization

Transatlantic Romanticism is organized to help readers make connections not only
between national literatures but also between texts and their contexts, recognizing
that literature is defined by culture and vice versa. In order to reflect clearly the inte-
gration of transatlantic Romanticism and to give a sense of the sweep of history, the
selections in this anthology are organized by the authors' birthdates. At the same time,
several topical sections called "Transatlantic Exchanges" punctuate this chronological
sequence. These "exchanges" gather texts that demonstrate a range of competing
responses to key political and cultural debates and restore what other anthologies

represent as single-nation movements, such as abolition, to the transatlantic conversation of which they were a part. Each of these sections is inserted immediately after a major author to whose work it is especially relevant. In addition, several brief "Contemporary Responses" have been included; these feature direct commentary, usually from the opposite side of the Atlantic, about the work and influence of one of the period's major authors. These "Transatlantic Exchanges" and "Contemporary Responses" translate well into the classroom. They can serve as the foundation of topical units and provide the basis for rhetorical analysis of more familiar texts (even serving as frameworks for course assignments, written or oral). At the same time, they encourage comparative readings by suggestion, rather than by prescription.

Overall, the volume's structure emphasizes the powerful role that openly polemical writing played in the period's inspiring movements for human equality and liberation, including native resistance to westward expansion, revolutionary republicanism, working-class radicalism, and the struggles to abolish slavery and win women's rights. *Transatlantic Romanticism* shows that even seemingly apolitical literary texts responded, if sometimes obliquely, to the period's rich international atmosphere of idealism and dissent.

Selections

Transatlantic Romanticism showcases canonical texts that focus on transatlantic themes (such as William Blake's *America* and the Canadian Oliver Goldsmith's *The Rising Village*, to name a few). Well-known public documents like these are supplemented with a sampling of private ones: excerpts from unpublished and published letters and journals of authors writing to or about one another (such as William Wordsworth, William Atkinson, and Lydia Huntley Sigourney). We include public texts by several lesser-known writers now entering the canon (e.g., Orestes Brownson's *The Laboring Classes*), and cover a wide range of genres as we strive for a balanced exchange of North American and British authors. We also include texts by authors who have been underrepresented in the study of Romanticism but played important roles in its national and transnational dimensions and are only recently reclaiming the place they held in their time: Olaudah Equiano, Margaret Fuller, and Samson Occom, to name a few. Often, these writers question and redefine Romantic sensibilities (with regard to gender and race) from the periphery, causing readers then and now to rethink the center. In expanding the range of texts and authors, we recover a more historically accurate picture of the various manifestations of and reactions to Romanticism(s). We more sharply define the field by restoring marginalized figures without trying to subsume them. For instance, this anthology includes several writers of the "black Atlantic," a term Paul Gilroy coined to describe writers of African descent who lived and traveled on the Atlantic Rim. Their inclusion forces reconsideration of the geographic as well as cultural influences working in the Romantic period.

With a few exceptions, *Transatlantic Romanticism* focuses on literature written (or spoken) in English in Britain, Canada, and North America. Spain and France were shaping presences in North America during the eighteenth and nineteenth centuries, but to include only the most important texts of French and Spanish Romanticism (not to mention German and Portuguese) would require at least an additional volume.

Also, because we feel that the practice of excerpting novels and plays creates a jarring reading experience, we have limited ourselves to a few exceptional cases, where portions of novels connect elementally to Romantic and transatlantic issues.

Pedagogical Features

Transatlantic Romanticism is designed to be streamlined and accessible, to provide students with the information they need to understand each text, but not to overwhelm them with minute details.

- **An accessible introduction** places the period and its writers in context, using a set of emblematic writers and texts to sketch a rounded picture of the Romantic century as a whole. At the same time, it identifies and explains major cultural, aesthetic, and political issues and trends. Finally, the introduction defines several central "keywords of Romanticism": *reform*, *nature*, *individual*, *imagination*, and *literature*.

- **Clear and lively headnotes** provide basic biographical and bibliographical information for the writers, while emphasizing their transatlantic interests, influences, exchanges, and travels. The headnotes benefit students and teachers by suggesting approaches and interpretive strategies for the selections that follow.

- **"Transatlantic Exchanges"** feature representative sets of literary and historical documents relevant to central cultural debates:
  - Revolutionary Republicanism
  - Slavery and Abolition
  - Women's Rights
  - Wordsworth in Britain and America
  - Religion and Revivalism
  - Utopianism and Socialism
  - Civilization and Nature

  The documents gathered under these headings provide materials for contextual analysis. They encourage comparative readings (even structuring comparison-based assignments and exercises), allowing readers the opportunity to explore the unfolding of key social and political debates and issues from a range of perspectives. Each "Transatlantic Exchange" section is introduced by a note that helps students place the topic in a historical and transatlantic context.

- **"Contemporary Responses"** include excerpted reviews, letters, and other texts in which authors discuss one another's work, directly demonstrating how key texts shaped the transatlantic nature of literary culture during the period. These materials deepen our understanding of how authors from either side of the Atlantic read and influenced each other—in some cases, documenting the exchange and transmission of specific ideas and ideals, poetical and political.

- **"A Sheaf of Poems"** by Canadian poets of Confederation concludes the volume by collecting representative poets born during the 1860s, the decade of Canadian

Confederation. Rarely included in discussions of American and British Romanticism, these Canadian romantics offer a fresh perspective to the influence of Romantic ideas and literature in a newly forged country.

- **A glossary** provides definitions of key literary and cultural terms specific to the history, culture, and literature of Britain, America, and Canada during the transatlantic Romantic century.

- **A selected bibliography** gathers landmark critical sources and studies on transatlantic literature and Romanticism.

- **A Web Companion** at <http://transatlanticromanticism.net> offers supplementary material on authors in the anthology and on the transatlantic period. Teaching and research resources include sample syllabi for transatlantic Romantic courses, a comprehensive bibliography, and links to valuable on-line transatlantic Romantic and nineteenth-century literary and cultural resources.

Acknowledgments

This anthology began with a conversation with Linda Schlesinger, a Pearson sales representative, about the lack of a teaching text for transatlantic Romanticism. Many thanks are owed to Linda for her early encouragement of this project. Our deepest debt of gratitude is to Barbara Santoro and Erika Berg, whose excellent suggestions, sage advice and guidance, patience, and tireless enthusiasm have helped us move from proposal to finished product. Dianne Hall and Chrysta Meadowbrooke transformed our massive manuscript into a sleek and readable book. David Damrosch's *Longman Anthology of British Literature* provided an important model for our approach to representing cultural debates and contexts.

Lance Newman would like to thank his co-editors for their passionate dedication to this project. The students in my courses in transatlantic Romanticism at the State University of West Georgia and Cal State San Marcos field-tested and refined many of the ideas and approaches found in this collection. Lisa Crafton first proved to me that such a course could not only be imagined but taught brilliantly as well. Helen Gunn provided invaluable assistance with archival work. Finally, I wish to thank my colleagues and families for their infinite patience.

Joel Pace would like to thank his co-editors as well as to acknowledge several others to whom he is grateful: Joselyn Almeida-Beveridge, Richard Brantley, James Butler, Don Christian, Jeff Cowton, Valerie A. Dodd, Bernard Duyfhuizen, Michael Eberle-Sinatra, Chris Gair, Max Garland, Stephen Gill, Bruce Graver, Richard Gravil, Jennifer Hamm, Cole Heinowitz, Clive Hurst, David Jones, Karen Karbiener, Sohui Lee, Allyson and Jon Loomis, Susan Manning, Robert Nowlan, Seamus Perry, Matthew Scott, David and Robin Shih, Fiona Stafford, Stacy Thompson, Michael Turner, Astrid Wind, Marty Wood, Robert and Pamela Woof, Jonathan and Jessica Wordsworth, and Duncan Wu. John Rykhus provided invaluable editorial assistance. For love, support, and friendship: Sharon and Joseph Pace, Frank and Amy Pace, Isaac Castillo, Michael Darigan, Curtis Odom, Omni, Machiste Rankin, Babatunde Thomas, Christopher J. Williams, Leslie and Raymond Camero and their family, and last but certainly not least Caldwell Camero, to whom this book is dedicated.

Chris Koenig-Woodyard would like to thank Joel and Lance for their energy, enthusiasm, and friendship. I am indebted to the influence and inspiration of a number of colleagues and friends: Alan Bewell, Jane Campbell, Angela Esterhammer, Stephen Gill, Dolan Hubbard, J. Douglas Kneale, Lucy Newlyn, Jarrett Rudy, Kathryn Sutherland, and Leslie Thomson. I am also grateful to the students of the 2004–2005 session of English 435, Studies in Transatlantic Romanticism (Trent University), who helped to shape and sharpen the contents of this anthology: Penka Bogatinov, Amanda Janus, Cristina Keen, Kim Kerr, Amie Kurianowicz, Catherine McCormick, Lisa Seabrook, Vanessa Spicer, Jennifer Webb, Sophie Wells, and Lauren Zakoor. For their support, patience, and good humour, I am indebted to the Koenig and Woodyard families, and to my wife, Adrienne, to whom this book is dedicated.

Finally, our thanks go to the many reviewers of *Transatlantic Romanticism* who provided extremely helpful feedback and advice: Joselyn M. Almeida, Boston University; Stephen C. Behrendt, University of Nebraska; Elizabeth Bolton, Swarthmore College; Richard Brantley, University of Florida; Ron Broglio, Georgia Institute of Technology; Miranda Burgess, University of British Columbia; Nancy Cirillo, University of Illinois at Chicago; Stuart Curran, University of Pennsylvania; Mary Agnes Favret, Indiana University; Elizabeth Fay, University of Massachusetts, Boston; Dan Fraustino, University of Scranton; Robert Gemmett, SUNY Brockport; Bruce Graver, Providence College; Martin Halliwell, University of Leicester; Steven F. Klepetar, Saint Cloud State University; Scott A. Leonard, Youngstown State University; Heidi Macpherson, University of Central Lancashire, UK; Laura Mandell, University of Miami at Ohio; Susan Manning, University of Edinburgh; Larry H. Peer, Brigham Young University; Geraldine Pittman de Batlle, Marlboro College; Laura Quinney, Brandeis University; Jeffrey Robinson, University of Colorado; Mark Trevor Smith, Southwest Missouri State University; David Stout, Luzerne County Community College; Brad Strickland, Gainesville College; Verne Underwood, Rogue Community College; and Paul Yoder, University of Alabama Little Rock.

—*Lance Newman*
Joel Pace
Chris Koenig-Woodyard

Additional Titles of Interest

Any of these Penguin-Putnam, Inc., titles can be packaged with *Transatlantic Romanticism* at a special discount. Please contact your local Longman sales representative for details on how to create a value pack.

Jane Austen, *Emma*
Jane Austen, *Persuasion*
Jane Austen, *Pride and Prejudice*
Jane Austen, *Sense and Sensibility*
Charlotte Brontë, *Jane Eyre*
Charlotte Brontë, *Villette*
Emily Brontë, *Wuthering Heights*
Edmund Burke, *Reflections on the Revolution in France*
Alexis de Tocqueville, *Democracy in America*
Charles Dickens, *Bleak House*
Charles Dickens, *Great Expectations*
Charles Dickens, *Hard Times*
Charles Dickens, *Nicholas Nickleby*
Frederick Douglass, *My Bondage and My Freedom*
Frederick Douglass, *Narrative of the Life of Frederick Douglass: An American Slave*
Olaudah Equiano, *The Interesting Narrative and Other Writings*
Benjamin Franklin, *The Autobiography and Other Writings*
Alexander Hamilton, *The Federalist Papers*
Nathaniel Hawthorne, *The Scarlet Letter; A Romance*
Harriet Jacobs, *Incidents in the Life of a Slave Girl*
Thomas Jefferson, *Notes on the State of Virginia*
Karl Marx, *The Communist Manifesto*
Herman Melville, *Moby Dick*
John Stuart Mill, *On Liberty*
Thomas Paine, *Common Sense*
Jean-Jacques Rousseau, *The Social Contract*
Mary Shelley, *Frankenstein*
Harriet Beecher Stowe, *Uncle Tom's Cabin*
Whitney Terrell, *The Huntsman*
Henry David Thoreau, *Walden and Civil Disobedience*
Sojourner Truth, *The Narrative of Sojourner Truth*
Horace Walpole, *The Castle of Otranto*

THE
POLITICAL FAMILY:

OR A

DISCOURSE,

POINTING OUT THE

RECIPROCAL ADVANTAGES,

Which flow from an uninterrupted Union between
GREAT-BRITAIN and her AMERICAN COLONIES.

By ISAAC HUNT, Esquire.
NUMB. I.

IF WE STRIKE, WE BREAK.

PHILADELPHIA:
PRINTED, BY JAMES HUMPHREYS, JUNIOR.

M DCC LXXV.

Figure 1. Isaac Hunt, title page of *The Political Family* (1775).

Figure 2. Olaudah Equiano, frontispiece to *The Interesting Narrative of the Life of Olaudah Equiano* (1789).

Figure 3. William Blake, "The Tyger," *Songs of Innocence and Experience* (1794).

Figure 4. William Blake, frontispiece to *America* (1793).

Figure 5. Albert Bierstadt, *Emigrants Crossing the Plains* (1867).

Figure 6. John Constable, *Branch Hill Pond, Hampstead* (1828).

Figure 7. J. M. W. Turner, *Slaves Throwing Overboard the Dead and the Dying* (1840).

Introduction

A MEETING OF ROMANTIC MINDS
IN THE WILDERNESS

American educator, editor, and writer Margaret Fuller spent the first week of June 1843 at Niagara Falls, on the border between the United States of America and the British colony of Upper Canada (now the province of Ontario). Although at Niagara the U.S.–Canadian border had not been in dispute, along much of its length its location had been definitively established only by the Webster-Ashburton Treaty, which had been signed less than a year previously. During her stay at the Falls, Fuller wrote to her good friend, Massachusetts philosopher Ralph Waldo Emerson, about the book she was reading: *Past and Present* by the Scottish political essayist Thomas Carlyle. Emerson had overseen the U.S. publication of Carlyle's books. And Emerson's good friend, Boston socialist George Ripley, had predicted that the Scotsman would "find his warmest admirers in old Massachusetts." What New England readers most admired was the candor and passion of Carlyle's writings on the most pressing social questions of the day:

> With unabated bounty the land of England blooms and grows; waving with yellow harvests; thick-studded with workshops, industrial implements, with fifteen millions of workers . . . and behold, some baleful fiat as of Enchantment has gone forth, saying, "Touch it not, ye workers . . . no man of you shall be the better for it; this is enchanted fruit!"

Carlyle was among the first to say unequivocally that modernity amounted to a broken promise, that the much vaunted progress of the preceding century had borne no better fruit than "the bitter discontent grown fierce and mad . . . of the Working Classes of England."

During the late eighteenth and early nineteenth centuries, England was the workshop of the world. With the most technologically advanced industrial system in human history, it had conquered an empire that spanned the globe. Such breakneck growth and expansion required intense exploitation of workers at home and violent oppression of native populations in the far-flung colonies. As a result, the empire was repeatedly shaken by social upheavals inspired by the republican creed stated in the U.S. Declaration of Independence (1776): "All men are created equal." First, revolutionary militias in British North American colonies defied the army of George III, the most powerful monarch on the planet. Then in 1789, the people of Paris stormed the political prison, the Bastille, bringing down a hated symbol of repression and aristocratic power. The French Revolution gave renewed confidence to radicals across England, inspiring fresh interrogation of the monarchy and other social institutions by figures like William Godwin, Mary Wollstonecraft, William Wordsworth, and

1

Samuel Taylor Coleridge. Then, in the French colony of Saint Domingue, free blacks rebelled when they were denied citizenship rights guaranteed by the "Declaration of the Rights of Man." Under the leadership of Toussaint L'Ouverture, they defeated French and British expeditionary armies, freed the colony's slaves, and established the first black republic, Haiti, on January 1, 1804.

Before long, radicalism had taken root in the industrial cities of England, where hundreds of thousands of desperately poor workers adopted egalitarian ideas and built mass movements demanding the realization of their rights to "Life, Liberty and the pursuit of Happiness." No event more clearly exemplified working-class discontent and radicalism than the "Peterloo Massacre" of 1819. On August 16, tens of thousands, perhaps as many as 150,000, gathered in St. Peter's Field in Manchester to rally in support of a broad range of reforms, including universal male suffrage. Conservative local magistrates brought in a large militia. Under the pretext of preserving order, they commanded their soldiers to attack the crowd. At least fifteen demonstrators were shot, stabbed, or trampled to death. Percy Bysshe Shelley's great political satire, "The Mask of Anarchy," describes the scene with mordant humor and driving chant-like meter, urging English workers to overthrow their oppressors:

> Rise like Lions after slumber
> In unvanquishable number,
> Shake your chains to earth like dew
> Which in sleep had fallen on you—
> Ye are many—they are few.

Outraged reformers sarcastically named the massacre after the infamous battle at Waterloo during which the French emperor Napoleon's imperial ambitions were finally defeated. Peterloo became the central example of the extreme means the powerful would use to protect their interests.

At Niagara, Margaret Fuller was reading Carlyle's *Past and Present* for ideas about how to resolve the social conflicts that had inflamed such intense passions. But she was disappointed to find that Carlyle could only call for renewed authoritarianism. In her letter to Emerson, she writes: "There is no valuable doctrine in [the] book. . . . He ends as he began. . . . Everything is very bad. You are fools and hypocrites, or you would make it better." Why then was she interested in Carlyle at all? Fuller's sarcasm masks a grave recognition that the disease he had diagnosed, the disorder racking the social body of England, might well spread to the United States. After all, New England was rapidly traveling the mother country's path into the capitalist future, building its first large-scale factories and gathering its first urban working class.

Ironically, Fuller's week at Niagara had been made possible by the very process of international modernization against which Carlyle thundered. The construction of regional networks of canals, roads, and railroads had allowed easy access to this hinterland spot. As a result, in 1818 entrepreneur Thomas Barnett saw enough traffic to warrant construction of a staircase to the foot of the Falls. By 1827 a tourist could follow a newly laid path that wound behind Horseshoe Falls and then visit a museum Barnett had built on Table Rock. Before long Niagara Falls had developed into an internationally famous tourist destination. Hundreds of descriptions and images of the place circulated in the press on both sides of the Atlantic, and it became a symbol both of the uncorrupted nature of North America and of nature's transformative power.

For many visitors, like Canadian poet John Breakenridge, Niagara provoked deeply spiritual experiences:

> Like thunder on my startled ear, thine everlasting roar
> Hath broken, and reverberates from shore to echoing shore. . . .
> Voluminous and ceaseless still, forever swift descend
> Thy waters, in their headlong course—then, turning, heaven-ward wend;
> Now, disenthralled, their essence hath its spirit shape resumed,
> Bright, bodiless, and pure, its flight to yon empyrean plumed!

Breakenridge's pounding fourteen-syllable lines evoke the rhythmic din of falling water, and his ceremonial diction and reverential tone reveal the depth of his conviction that the Falls are a gateway to the supernatural, a place where the sacred breaks through into this mundane world.

But the Falls were so popular by the 1840s that the purity Breakenridge valued had been badly polluted. British novelist Charles Dickens, in his travelogue *American Notes* (1842), complained not only that it was possible to buy cheap "little relics of the place" at the guide's cottage on Table Rock but also that the caretakers kept on display several volumes of "poetical effusions" scribbled by tourists over the years. Dickens fumed: "It is humiliating . . . to know that there are among men brutes so obscene and worthless, that they can delight in laying their miserable profanations upon the very steps of Nature's greatest altar." No doubt he would have been even more chagrined to learn that selections of the visitor book entries were published in 1848 in the *Table Rock Album and Sketches of the Falls and Scenery Adjacent*. The contents of this book range widely. There are pithy mottos: "Roar away, mighty Fall / I am done—that is all." And there is a doodled chiasmus by one "Bryant," presumably a New York banker:

> I came from Wall Street,
> To see this water sheet;
> Having seen this water sheet,
> I return to Wall Street.

This kind of flat verse dominates the collection. But Dickens would have found at least one equally disgusted companion, an anonymous author who scolds:

> Ye prosing poets, who dull rhymes indite,
> Why in this place your leaden nonsense write?
> Can scenes like these no nobler strain inspire
> Than vulgar slang and wit whose jokes miss fire?

The problem was more than just mawkish doggerel. For Dickens, the triviality and cheapness of the typical tourist's response spoiled Niagara Falls as an object of reverence and awe.

If Dickens recorded his disgust at the fledgling tourist industry's sentimentality, Fuller worked to recover for herself what she thought of as an authentic experience of nature. In *Summer on the Lakes in 1843*, she writes of her disappointment on first seeing the Falls: "When I first came here I felt nothing but a quiet satisfaction. I found that the drawings, the panorama, &c. had given me a clear notion of the position and proportions of all objects here; I knew where to look for everything, and everything looked as I thought it would." Despite her self-conscious disenchantment, she stayed a week. And her feelings began to change once she felt that she had managed to see the place for herself, rather than through the eyes of previous visitors. By crossing the river to the Canadian side, Fuller found what she felt was a better perspective: "As a picture, the falls can only be seen from the British side. There they are seen in their veils, and at sufficient distance to appreciate the magical effects of these, and the light and shade." Thus, paradoxically, it was only when she found a vantage point far enough away to allow her to see the Falls in all their immensity that she began to feel threatened by their power:

> After awhile it so drew me into itself as to inspire an undefined dread, such as I never knew before, such as may be felt when death is about to usher us into a new existence. The perpetual trampling of the waters seized my senses. I felt that no other sound, however near, could be heard, and would start and look behind me for a foe. I realized the identity of that mood of nature in which these waters were poured down with such absorbing force, with that in which the Indian was shaped on the same soil. For continually upon my mind came, unsought and unwelcome, images, such as had never haunted it before, of naked savages stealing behind me with uplifted tomahawks.

This unsettling image—a Native American defending the symbolic center of the New World against her intrusion—lingers until Fuller descends to a viewpoint on a stone outcrop at the fall's base: "What I liked best was to sit on Table Rock close to the great fall; there all power of observing details, all separate consciousness was quite lost." In order to escape the association of nature with the threat of death, Fuller must advance further into the scene, until the roar is so loud that it obliterates "all separate consciousness"; the Falls erase her self.

Romantic writers and artists struck such exaggerated poses in nature because they were so deeply anxious to demonstrate that it was meaningful. Fuller implies as much when she recalls her summer in the West while reviewing a travelogue, *America and the American People* (1845), by the German author Frederick Von Raumer:

> Though the scenery which I beheld throughout a large extent of the United States was very much inferior to that of Europe, it must be admitted that the old world can offer nothing to equal Niagara—Such an accumulation of splendors would certainly well repay a voyage across the ocean.

Fuller worried that North America lacked a deep human history, that it was empty of the cultural traditions and rich historical landscapes needed to nourish and inspire young writers. Similarly, Canadian writer Catherine Parr Traill, who emigrated from Suffolk at the age of 30, describes her new home as a blank slate in her settler narrative, *The Backwoods of Canada* (1836): "Here there are no historical associations, no legendary tales of those that came before us. . . . We have neither fay nor fairy, ghost nor bogle, satyr or wood-nymph. . . ." But Traill, like Fuller, reassures herself that the New World holds compensations for its seeming emptiness: "If its volume of history is yet blank, that of Nature is open, and eloquently marked by the finger of God. . . ." Failing the presence of a rich cultural history, the raw materials of artistic creation might be found in the continent's spectacular natural scenes.

At the same time that Fuller was trying to have a specifically New World experience of nature at Niagara Falls, she was also participating in a cultural tradition that she had helped import from the Old World. The New England Transcendentalists were among the first Americans to seek out opportunities to admire natural beauty, and they did so through the lens of borrowed theories of the sublime. In *Philosophical Enquiry into the Origin of Our Ideas of the Sublime and the Beautiful* (1757), English statesman Edmund Burke writes,

> The passion caused by the great and sublime in nature is astonishment, and astonishment is that state of the soul in which all its motions are suspended, with some degree of horror. The mind is so entirely filled with its object that it cannot entertain any other, nor reason on that object which fills it.

This is the breathless experience Fuller was so carefully cultivating at Niagara. Similarly, in his *Critique of Judgement* (1790), the German philosopher Immanuel Kant describes the sublime as "a feeling of displeasure" that "may be compared with vibration, i.e., with a rapidly alternating repulsion and attraction produced by one and the same object. The point of excess for the imagination [is] like an abyss in which it fears to lose itself." Just so, when Fuller loses herself in the sublime splash of Niagara Falls, it is because she is overwhelmed simultaneously by reverence and fear, by mutually canceling feelings of attraction and repulsion.

New England painter Frederic Edwin Church offers dramatic pictorial representations of Kant's sublime in two canvasses depicting the Falls. Church's Niagara paintings, completed in 1857 and 1867, were transatlantic successes—immediate hits when displayed in New York and London. The first captures the Canadian view of the falls—the view Fuller writes of in *Summer on the Lakes*. The composition is broodingly powerful. It divides in two at the horizon—with sky filling the top half, and the Falls the bottom. The viewer looks down one wall of the gorge toward the foot of the Falls, where a wall of white water plunges to the unseen river below. We seem to be dangerously close to the Falls, and there is a sense of precariousness that suggests the power of the water Fuller describes as "pour[ing] down with such absorbing force." The tremendous torrent seems to threaten to pull the viewer with it and triggers a kind of Kantian "astonishment."

The effect on viewers is no less powerful in Church's 1867 canvas, but the painter achieves the sublime through a different approach (see Figure 8). The later canvas offers a more inviting perspective than the awful grandeur of the earlier work. However, about one third of the way down from the top left corner of the 1867 canvas, a lone figure sits on a small wooden platform on stilts. This tourist is minuscule against the backdrop of the falls, and a rising drizzle of mist partially obscures the figure. By encouraging viewers to measure themselves against this tiny shape, Church's canvas offers an opportunity to experience the Kantian sublime vicariously, to feel both awed and comforted by the divine spectacle. Bright colors, clear sky, and a rainbow evoke reverence for the majesty of the Falls and the creator of it. For Church, as for Fuller, Breakenridge, Dickens, and innumerable others, Niagara Falls had come to stand as the central emblem of one of the most influential Romantic ideas, the correspondence between humanity and sublime

Figure 8. Frederic Edwin Church, *Niagara Falls, from the American Side* (1867).

F. M. Fuller

From the original painting by Chappel in the possession of the publishers

Johnson, Wilson & Co., Publishers, New York.

Figure 9. Margaret Fuller, from *Portrait Gallery of Eminent Men and Women of Europe and America. . . . with Biographies.* By E. A. D. (1872–1874).

nature. Niagara was both the site and sign of a primeval communion that was at once terrifying, spirit-renewing, and vulnerable to despoliation.

Ironically, Niagara also offered an image for articulating the dizzying pace of political and economic modernization. Carlyle, for instance, repeatedly employs the Falls in metaphors that capture his ambivalence toward the period's radical movements for social change. In an 1867 article titled "Shooting Niagara: and After?" he complains about a recent political reform, claiming that its main value is that it "accelerates notably what I have long looked upon as inevitable;—pushes us at once into the Niagara Rapids." The Falls here symbolize sudden and irreversible democratization, a prospect that the conservative Carlyle contemplated with deep worry at first and later with bitter resignation. He was convinced that "England would have to take the Niagara leap of completed Democracy one day. . . ." In the end, it was seeing an analogy between two sublime terrors, wild landscapes and political equality, that inspired Carlyle to praise the comforts of authority in *Past and Present*.

Fuller saw the same parallel between nature and politics but responded to it oppositely. Rather than take refuge in tradition, she sought her identity by getting lost in something larger than herself. Thus, her moment of self-annihilation comes at the beginning of *Summer on the Lakes* specifically because it demonstrates her credentials as a Romantic traveler and writer. It reveals her faith that, as British poet William Wordsworth argues in "Tintern Abbey," sublime nature can transform selves degraded by modernity:

> . . . For I have learned
> To look on nature, not as in the hour
> Of thoughtless youth, but hearing oftentimes
> The still, sad music of humanity,
> Not harsh or grating, though of ample power
> To chasten and subdue. And I have felt
> A presence that disturbs me with the joy
> Of elevated thoughts; a sense sublime
> Of something far more deeply interfused,
> Whose dwelling is the light of setting suns,
> And the round ocean, and the living air,
> And the blue sky, and in the mind of man,
> A motion and a spirit, that impels
> All thinking things, all objects of all thought,
> And rolls through all things.

Wordsworth puts this point more plainly in *The Prelude* (1850), where he describes his experience climbing Mt. Helvellyn as an example of the "Love of Nature Leading to Love of Man."

Time and again, Romantic writers describe in rapturous tones the experience of becoming immersed in, lost in, even swallowed up by nature. Always they feel they have been reformed, even redeemed by its power; they feel charged with a new seriousness of moral purpose. Canadian poet George Menzies, for instance, describes the Falls in terms appropriate to religious conversion in his Wordsworthian poem, "Written at the Table Rock During a Thunder Storm," a piece that appears in the *Table Rock Album* (1848):

This is the shrine at which the soul
    Is tutored to forget
The weakness and the earthliness
    That cling around it yet.

Who that hath ever lingered here
    A little hour or twain,
Can think as he hath thought, or be
    What he hath been again?

Experiences of the sublime like this one were pursued not just for their own sake but also as badges of sensitivity and creativity, of spiritual fitness to write the kind of literature that could redeem a society wracked by poverty, oppression, and violence.

This Romantic way of thinking about how nature, which bore the record of a primeval human nature, could inspire social change received one of its most powerful statements in Percy Bysshe Shelley's famous address to Mont Blanc, an emblematic peak in the French Alps:

Thou hast a voice, great Mountain, to repeal
Large codes of fraud and woe; not understood
By all, but which the wise, and great, and good
Interpret, or make felt, or deeply feel.

Shelley suggests that the truths nature tells have the potential to set society free of the stifling weight of centuries of class oppression and economic exploitation. Elsewhere, he calls the poets and writers who can hear nature's voice "the unacknowledged legislators of the world," for it is through them, "the wise, and great, and good," that the laws of nature and of human nature will be discovered. Knowledge of those laws would enable them to lead their young nations into a better future, for with its help they could articulate the natural hunger for liberty that in Carlyle's England seemed inevitably to call forth bloody repression.

TRANSATLANTIC ROMANTICISM AND EMPIRE

When Fuller left behind her acculturated self to become one with primeval nature, she was participating deeply in the culture of her time, in an international community of thought and feeling we now call Romanticism. Romanticism was a tremendously diverse, multilingual phenomenon. It spanned the entire Atlantic Rim from the Scottish Hebrides to Africa's Cape of Good Hope and from Canada's Newfoundland to Tierra del Fuego at the tip of South America. However it also existed in a world structured by sharp hierarchies of political, economic, and cultural power.

The landscape of Romanticism centered above all on London, the sparkling capital of the aggressively expanding British Empire. London had entered the nineteenth century with a staggering population of just over one million, making it the largest city on earth. William Wordsworth described it, in *The Prelude*, as a "monstrous ant-hill on the plain / Of a too busy world!" It seemed to present an astonishing spectacle of anonymous humanity, frantically pursuing the day-to-day commerce of life—an "endless stream of men and moving things!" Not all Romantics, though, were so unsettled by the sublime metropolis. Essayist Charles

Lamb wrote to Wordsworth in 1801 to pay him a back-handed compliment: "Separate from the pleasure of your company, I don't much care if I never see a mountain in my life. . . ." To make the point that he was an urban-dweller at heart, Lamb scribbled a loving sketch of London:

> The lighted shops of the Strand and Fleet Street, the innumerable trades, tradesmen and customers, coaches, wagons, playhouses, all the bustle and wickedness round about Covent Garden, the very women of the town, the watchmen, drunken scenes, rattles; life awake, if you awake, at all hours of the night, the impossibility of being dull in Fleet Street, the crowds, the very dirt and mud, the sun shining upon houses and pavements, the print shops, the old book stalls, parsons cheapening books, coffee-houses, steams of soups from kitchens, the pantomimes—London itself a pantomime and a masquerade: all these things work themselves into my mind and feed me without a power of satiating me.

Similar scenes of London's vital street life would be captured decades later in sketches by French illustrator Gustave Doré (see Figure 10).

As the capital of a growing world empire, London was the most multicultural spot on the face of the planet. People of all kinds arrived on political and personal missions and as refugees. After Boston printers refused to release her work, African American poet Phillis Wheatley traveled to London along with her master's son to find a publisher. Frederick Douglass took refuge here from the fugitive slave laws that threatened to return him to bondage. His speaking tour of the British Isles raised the funds with which he later founded the influential abolitionist newspaper, the *North Star*. As Wordsworth records in *The Prelude*, the city's population included

> . . . all specimens of man,
> Through all the colours which the sun bestows,
> And every character of form and face:
> The Swede, the Russian; from the genial south,
> The Frenchman and the Spaniard; from remote
> America, the Hunter-Indian; Moors,
> Malays, Lascars, the Tartar, the Chinese,
> And Negro Ladies in white muslin gowns.

Along with such diverse people, London imported their cultural traditions and carried on a brisk trade in their ideas. The city's readers collected the latest philosophical and literary texts from European capitals like Jena, Heidelberg, and Paris, along with sacred books from living and ancient societies throughout Africa, the Middle East, and Asia.

At the same time that the imperial fleet brought the world to London, it also exported English culture. London, that is, attempted to dictate to its colonies, protectorates, allies, and rivals not only the terms of trade but also the terms of thought and creativity. Its most effective tool for the exercise of cultural power was a burgeoning publishing industry. Tens of thousands of books, newspapers, and magazines issued from the city's presses. While these presses usually operated in the service of king and country, they were sometimes controlled by more politically and socially forward-thinking members of society. For instance, in the 1780s and early 1790s, the reform-minded publisher Joseph Johnson issued Thomas Paine's *Rights of Man*, Mary Wollstonecroft's *Vindication of the Rights of Man* and *Vindication of the Rights of Woman*, and William Godwin's *Political Justice*, as well as revolutionary books of poems by William Blake, Anna Laetitia Barbauld, William Wordsworth,

LUDGATE HILL.

Figure 10. Gustave Doré, "Ludgate Hill," *London: A Pilgrimage* (1872).

and Samuel Taylor Coleridge. Johnson's offices were a meeting place for intellectuals who supported the French revolution and advocated universal suffrage and parliamentary reform at home.

The Crown set out to break up such organizing centers of radicalism, and in 1794 the Treasonable and Seditious Practices Act was imposed, extending the definition of treason to any spoken or written utterance that maligned or undermined the King or the government. This law was the centerpiece of a campaign of intimidation and censorship that sought to reestablish royal control over the circulation of ideas. Radical intellectuals, including Thomas Paine and Joseph Priestley, fled the country or retired from public life. And London publishers were forced to exercise self-censorship to avoid prosecution.

Given the resulting climate of political repression in the capital, alternative centers of cultural production sprung up in provincial cities across the English-speaking world. The *Edinburgh Review*, for instance, was founded by Francis Jeffrey in 1802 as a mouthpiece for liberal Whigs (and was printed continuously until 1929). Sir Walter Scott writes of its influence: "no genteel family can pretend to be without the *Edinburgh Review*; because, independent of its politics, it gives the only valuable literary criticisms that can be met with." It was widely read in North America, for as soon as a copy arrived in New York City by transatlantic vessel, it was reproduced and distributed by the printer and publisher, Theodore Foster. Similarly, Joseph Dennie's *Port-Folio*, founded in Philadelphia in 1801, published works by Charles Brockden Brown and John Quincy Adams, but also reprinted and championed the poetry of Wordsworth, Thomas Moore, and the young Leigh Hunt. The international influence of such provincial periodicals was powerful enough that conservative Tory alternatives were founded to parry their thrusts: Lord Byron's publisher John Murray launched the *Quarterly Review* in London (1809–1962), and *Blackwood's Magazine* appeared in Edinburgh (1817–1980). The latter established its reputation early in its print history by lambasting Romantic poet Leigh Hunt and what its reviewer called the "Cockney school of poetry."

Magazines, then, were the communications infrastructure of a transatlantic cultural network within which there was intense debate, but also fundamental agreement on which social, literary, and political issues mattered. The operations of this Romantic network could be quite circuitous. For instance, the English poet and philosopher Samuel Taylor Coleridge wrote extensively in his *Aids to Reflection* (1825) about the Transcendentalist philosophy of Immanuel Kant. *Aids to Reflection* was republished in the United States in 1829, and the minister and intellectual Frederick Henry Hedge reviewed the book in Boston's *Christian Examiner* in March 1833. Hedge praised Kant's notion that "consciousness [is] an active and not a passive state," that the human mind and our perceptions are structured by fundamental ideas, such as the categories of space and time, that were implanted by God. Kant had originally meant to make a conservative religious critique of Enlightenment empiricism and radicalism, but Hedge teased out some rather radical implications of his ideas: "It is not a skeptical philosophy; it seeks not to overthrow, but to build up; it wars not with the common opinions and general experience of mankind, but aims to place these on a scientific basis, and to verify them by scientific demonstration." For Hedge, all human beings shared a basic set of mental equipment, a "common sense" of the world and how it works. This conviction empowered a fundamental faith in human equality. Hedge's friend, the philosopher Ralph Waldo Emerson, agreed strongly, and thus the transatlantic perspective that Hedge offered of Kant became the point of origin for New England Transcendentalism, the most influential form of Romanticism in North America.

Not only were the writers, artists, and intellectuals who made up the transatlantic community of Romanticism aware of one another's concerns, they also routinely made the transatlantic voyage to visit one another's homes and homelands. Their relationships were sometimes marked by rivalry and competition, but more often they felt themselves engaged in shared social and artistic endeavors. Indeed, these transatlantic interactions showed the full measure of human emotional depth and complexity. For instance, in 1818, a fifteen-year-old Ralph Waldo Emerson writes in his journal about William Wordsworth, one of Britain's most internationally influential poets: "I have thirsted to abuse the poetical character of Mr. Wordsworth whose poems have lately been read to me." This was the inauspicious beginning of a lifelong intellectual relationship marked by shifting tides of admiration and resentment. The adult Emerson would recognize in 1840 that "the fame of Wordsworth is a leading fact in modern literature," but would qualify his estimation by remarking that "more than any other poet [Wordsworth's] success has not been his own, but that of the idea which he shared with his coevals, and which he has rarely succeeded in adequately expressing." That idea was "democracy," for Emerson admired what he would have called Wordsworth's naturalness of sentiment and expression, his apparent lack of artificiality and aristocratic pretense. Again in his journal, Emerson writes that "some divine savage like Webster, Wordsworth, & Reed whom neither the town nor the college ever made shall say that [which] we shall all believe. How we thirst for a natural thinker." The tone here is openly reverential: Wordsworth is a great man, a natural genius.

Emerson's reverence was to be tested, though, on the morning of August 28, 1833, when he paid a visit to Wordsworth's home at Rydal Mount. He was taken aback to find that the author of the radically optimistic *Lyrical Ballads* was a "plain, elderly, white-haired man—disfigured by green goggles." And when Wordsworth sat down and held forth on one of his favorite topics, America, he turned out to be quite conservative. Americans were "too much given to the making of money; and secondly, to politics. . . ." He felt that "they needed a civil war in America, to teach the necessity of knitting social ties stronger." Despite his skepticism, Wordsworth eagerly received over one hundred visitors from the young republic during his lifetime. Inevitably, he turned the conversation, as with Emerson, to the subject of American reforms—political, social, economic, poetical, and religious. In fact, he informed one visitor that although his fame was founded on the popularity of his writings, he "had given twelve hours thought to the conditions of society, for one to poetry." For Wordsworth, then, the ongoing republican experiment in America was a central intellectual concern. He not only followed its progress closely but also made sure that his poetry, with its central focus on "social ties," circulated widely there. Wordsworth was convinced that, as he wrote to his U.S. editor, Henry Reed, "a vast field is there open to the English mind, acting through our noble language!" So, despite Emerson's disappointment in the great English poet, he was forced to conclude in August 1837 that "Wordsworth now act[s] out of England on us. . . ." However, it was just as true that Americans and their radical ideas had acted and continued to act reciprocally on

Wordsworth. In short, transatlantic cultural exchange was multidirectional, with writers of all nationalities influencing one another, but that exchange took place within the defining structure of Britain's imperial and cultural dominance.

Romanticism's transatlantic nature, then, is the starting point for this anthology, which seeks to broaden traditional definitions of the field. *Transatlantic Romanticism* surveys the cultural transactions that occurred between the British imperial center and its North American periphery, offering a selection of texts written between 1767 and 1867 in what are now Britain, the United States, and Canada. These borders are somewhat arbitrary, simultaneously accommodating and defining reality, as all borders do. After all, Romanticism in English was constantly fertilized by developments in all the other languages and cultures of the Atlantic Rim, including French, German, Spanish, Portuguese, and several West African, Native American, and Creole languages. The wider than usual, but necessarily still limited, focus of this collection offers a representative sample of that greater, perhaps infinite, complexity.

The Romantic Century as defined here is similarly heuristic: It is a provisional formulation designed as a starting point for investigation. The year 1767 saw the implementation of the Townshend Acts in the colonies, a series of sweeping measures designed to strengthen and consolidate the British government's control over its unruly possessions. New taxes were imposed on imported goods, including tea, glass, paint, oil, lead, and paper, and a new customs bureaucracy was created to collect them. The colonial legislature of New York was suspended for its refusal to quarter British troops. And colonial officials were now to be paid directly by the Crown, effectively removing them from local oversight. Taken together, these Acts were a bold assertion of imperial power, and the anger they produced culminated in the Declaration of Independence in 1776. The Revolution that followed both enacted the Enlightenment belief in human reason as the basis for social equality and began a process of transformation and adaptation of those ideas to a new historical situation.

On the other hand, 1867 saw the confederation of the colonies of Ontario, Quebec, New Brunswick, and Nova Scotia into the Dominion of Canada, as part of the now truly global British Empire. This same year, in the wake of the American Civil War, Howard University and Atlanta University were established for the education of freed slaves from the defeated Confederacy. No longer entrenched in war at home, the U.S. federal government at Washington claimed the Midway Islands in the South Pacific and purchased Alaska from Russia for $7.2 million, signaling its desire to build its own empire beyond the Lower 48 to which it had long claimed a "manifest destiny." In other words, these dates mark, first, the coming into self-consciousness of the British Empire, and second, the beginning of its displacement by its rebellious offspring. Transatlantic Romanticism coincides, that is, with the period during which, despite constant and intensifying centrifugal forces, Britain maintained imperial power sufficient to hold together an integrated cultural community in those places—the British Isles and Eastern North America—where English was the dominant language.

TRANSATLANTIC ROMANTICISM AND CAPITALISM

What common ideas and experiences unified the members of the transatlantic Romantic community? Above all, a feeling of historical vertigo. The final year of the

Romantic Century, 1867, saw the publication of the first volume of Karl Marx's *Capital*. Written in London, *Capital* was the most thorough analysis to date of the economic system that had transformed the city into the center of a world empire. Marx set out to offer a scientific explanation of the functioning of the society around him: "The first premise of all human history is, of course, the existence of living human individuals. Thus the first fact to be established is the physical organization of these individuals and their consequent relation to the rest of nature." He argued that more and more society was dividing itself into two main classes, the owners of capital and those who worked for them. Their relationship to one another was based on a fundamental reality that the English conservative political philosopher Edmund Burke described briskly: "Labour is a commodity like any other . . . an article of trade." In order to survive, workers competed for opportunities to sell their labor. It was purchased from them by the "bourgeoisie," or the owners of the factories, tools, land, and other resources needed to make the food, clothing, and shelter on which all depended. Dizzying growth was driven by constant competition for profits between capitalists. In order to win an advantage over rivals, entrepreneurs constantly strove to innovate, spurring fantastically rapid advances in science and technology. At the same time, as Marx observed, periodic stagnation drove capitalist nations both to look beyond their own borders for new markets and to transform the most fundamental habits of life within their borders:

> Hence the exploration of the whole of nature in order to discover new useful properties of things; the universal exchange of the products coming from the most diverse climates and lands[;] hence the development of the natural sciences to their highest point; the discovery, creation and satisfaction of new needs arising from society itself; cultivating all the qualities of social man and producing him in a form as rich as possible in needs because rich in qualities and relations—producing man as the most total and universal product possible (for in order to enjoy many different kinds of things he must be capable of enjoyment, that is[,] he must be cultivated to a high degree)—all these are new branches of production based on capital.

In short, capitalism stimulated human creativity and productivity to a fever pitch. At the same time, it created new and intense forms of oppression and misery. And finally, it sought irresistibly to internationalize itself, incorporating wider and wider regions of the globe into its circuits of exchange and domination. It was this total transformation of the world by capitalism that structured Romanticism. The transatlantic Romantic community was unified above all else, then, by feelings of newness, strangeness, and urgency as Britain, the United States, and Canada rushed together into modernity.

The rise of capitalism, after all, had been staggeringly rapid in historical terms. One necessary if not sufficient cause had been advances in naval and military technology that allowed western European explorers to cross the Atlantic in the sixteenth century and pillage the cities of Central and South America. Hundreds of shiploads of plundered Aztec and Inca gold and silver overflowed the coffers of European monarchs, financing new rounds of exploration, conquest, and colonization. In many areas of the New World, disease, starvation, and genocide reduced native populations by as much as 95% within a few decades of contact. This produced a problem for colonists bent on profit: a shortage of workers. Their solution was to enslave millions of Africans and transport them to the colonies, where their labor was used to extract raw materials and to produce agricultural goods for export home to Europe. By the eighteenth century, British merchant-seamen had mastered this set of brutal exchanges, and they built huge fortunes out of what came to be called the Triangle Trade. Ships from British ports like Liverpool, Bristol, and Glasgow carried manufactured goods like weapons and cloth to the West African coast, using them to purchase human beings, who were then transported to the Americas, where they were traded for loads of tobacco, sugar, or cotton for the journey home.

The enormous profits of the Triangle Trade stoked the already smoldering fires of economic development in Britain, stimulating and even financing the modernization of the agricultural system and the industrial revolution. Where once tenants had worked small plots of land owned by a feudal lord, delivering part of their crop to him for his own use, now agriculture became a profit-driven enterprise shaped by a market increasingly reliant upon mass production. Small farms were consolidated into large ones. The commons, lands once used by all, were "enclosed" by Parliamentary decree and placed in the hands of agricultural businessmen. The farm worker and poet John Clare bitterly denounces this legal theft of the traditional privileges of rural workers in "The Mores": "Inclosure came & trampled on the grave / Of labours rights & made the poor a slave." Moreover, Clare makes an explicit connection between the oppression of the poor and the destruction of the land for the sake of profit:

> Accursed wealth o'erbounding human laws
> Of every evil thou remainst the cause
> Victims of want those wretches such as me
> Too truly lay their wretchedness to thee
> Thou art the bar that keeps from being fed
> And thine our loss of labor and of bread
> Thou art the cause that levels every tree
> And woods bow down to clear a way for thee

At the same time that rural communities were being disrupted by enclosure, new factories, mills, and mines demanded thousands of workers. As a result, much of the rural population was displaced to new centers of production in Britain, such as Birmingham, Liverpool, and Manchester. These new industrial cities mounted spectacular displays of technological sophistication, but at the same time they were ringed with slums that were desperately poor and violent, as well as horribly polluted. William Blake measured the reality of life for the urban poor against the ideals of the Christian faith in the verse preface to his long poem, "Milton." Condemning England's "dark Satanic mills," he vows, "I will not cease from mental fight, / Nor shall my sword sleep in my hand / Till we have built Jerusalem / In England's green and pleasant land."

Massive shifts of population occurred not only within the British Isles but also across the Atlantic. Already squeezed by absentee English landlords, Irish tenant farmers were ruined by potato blight during the 1840s. In short order, they were evicted from their farms in droves. As many as one million starved to death, while another million emigrated, many to the United States and Canada, where they were forced to take on the worst-paying jobs. Henry David Thoreau imagines the plight of one such immigrant as follows:

> I am the little Irish boy
>> That lives in the shanty
> I am four years old today
>> And shall soon be one and twenty
> I shall grow up and be a great man
>> And shovel all day
>> As hard as I can . . .

Even as immigrants crossed the ocean to escape modernizing Britain, they were followed by the very historical forces that had driven them from their homes. Capitalists in the United States and Canada were enthusiastically following England's lead, building textile mills and factories wherever reliable sources of water power existed. The resulting contrast between imperial London and bleak Massachusetts mill towns like Lowell, Lynn, and Lawrence informed the industrial gothic of Herman Melville's paired stories "The Paradise of Bachelors" and "The Tartarus of Maids" (1855).

Not surprisingly, these wholesale economic changes produced corresponding ideological and cultural trends. The fabulously wealthy merchants, traders, manufacturers, and financiers who had built this new world were eager to win political and cultural power to match their newly central economic position in society. This necessarily brought them into conflict with the established dominant class, the aristocracy, in whose interests the entire legal and political apparatus of British society had evolved over centuries of feudalism. Faced with the entrenched, inherited power of aristocracy, the bourgeoisie had articulated a set of radical philosophical and political ideas over the course of the eighteenth century, a period that has come to be called the Enlightenment. For instance, in *The First Principles of Government and the Nature of Political, Civil and Religious Liberty* (1768), the English scientist, philosopher, and dissenting minister Joseph Priestley writes that "the good and happiness of the members, that is the majority of the members of the state, is the great standard by which every thing relating to that state must finally be determined." This seemingly innocuous claim amounted to a declaration of war against the entrenched power of the tiny English aristocracy, whose "good and happiness" seemed to be the state's sole concern. Like Priestley, the bourgeois philosophers of the Enlightenment set out to question, and eventually to overthrow, a hidebound feudal social order that obstructed their development as a class. The most fundamental idea that they articulated was that human reason was equal to the task of reorganizing society along more just and equal lines.

At the beginning of the Romantic period, this Enlightenment philosophy was a vibrant revolutionary creed. The British aristocracy and their allies saw it as a threat to the foundations of state power, and they used all means at their disposal to crush it out along with its advocates. In 1791, for example, when it was suspected that Priestley planned to participate in the second anniversary celebration of Bastille Day, a Loyalist mob burned his Birmingham church, home, and laboratory. He fled the city, and eventually the country. Coleridge, in "Religious Musings," laments Priestley's persecution and immigration: "Him from his native land / Statesmen blood-stain'd and Priests idolatrous / By dark lies mad'ning the blind multitude /

Drove with vain hate." Priestley did not stop with criticizing the state. After settling in Pennsylvania, he took part in a broad movement of rational inquiry into Christianity, becoming one of the founders of a new faith, Unitarianism. Unitarians rejected the Holy Trinity and insisted on the humanity of the historical Jesus Christ—a figure whose kindness and spirit were to be emulated but not worshipped. Many also applied this rational, human-centered habit of thought to contemporary political and social questions: The appalling social inequality afflicting both Old and New Worlds was not a form of justice doled out by an angry God but was created by man and could be repaired.

Romanticism is most often described as a reaction against the Enlightenment. If the Enlightenment stood for reason, empiricism, and materialism, then Romanticism is said to have favored emotion, intuition, and spiritualism. Thus, Ralph Waldo Emerson called Priestley's Unitarianism "corpse-cold" and complained that it emphasized arcane theological disputes instead of religious emotions. But at the same time that Emerson rejected its rationalism, he extended its faith in the individual's ability to contact the divine immediately without the help of ministers. In the end, he dispensed with church-going altogether, seeking religious experience in a nature he saw as infused with spirit.

In other words, Romanticism was not a simple programmatic rejection of the Enlightenment but a selective and organic transformation of it to suit new circumstances. Rather than an episode of reaction, the Romantic period was one of ideological experimentation and of persistent struggles for control of the key words or central concepts according to which people understood their lives and the world around them. During its early decades, the insurgent bourgeoisie deployed rationalist philosophy to undermine the authority of the declining but still powerful aristocracy, who in turn often appealed to emotionalism, mysticism, and tradition to defend themselves. Once it had acceded to power, that same bourgeoisie had now to explain to a growing working class its failure to create the just society it had held up for so long as an ideal. It frequently did so by displacing that ideal, attempting to convince its attackers that true justice was a matter of spiritual rather than economic or political equality. At the same time, bourgeois radicals, such as many New England abolitionists, maintained their commitment to Enlightenment ideals but rearticulated them in spiritualist, rather than materialist, terms. Thus, throughout the period, a core set of interlocking ideas were used as tools, even as weapons, both to attack and defend the successive ruling classes and the arguments they used to shore up their power.

SOME KEYWORDS OF TRANSATLANTIC ROMANTICISM

Reform: If large-scale and continuous social change was the governing reality of the Romantic period, then the center of gravity of its ideological system was the idea of reform, the conviction that society was changing (or needed to be changed) for the better. Reform might be envisioned as a process of gradual and moderate social evolution; radicals, however, called for more rapid and thorough-going change; meanwhile, revolutionaries demanded an immediate overthrow of the established order. Reform might be imagined as forward progress toward a more advanced future, or a return to a more natural prior state.

In a passage composed in 1804 and intended for inclusion in *The Prelude*, Wordsworth described the passion for reform felt by London radicals during the early years of the French revolution: "Bliss was it in that dawn to be alive, / But to be young was very heaven!" After the revolutionaries in Paris began executing aristocrats, including the king and queen, an intense reaction occurred. Conservatives accused reformers, radicals, and revolutionaries of inviting anarchy by following reason beyond the bounds of common sense. Many advocates of reform retreated into passivity or confusion, but the power of the idea was such that it remained active and deeply influential, undergoing gradual evolution.

Some defended the revolutionary tradition. In an 1839 review, Boston minister and editor Orestes Brownson accuses Wordsworth of political cowardice for abandoning his support of the French Revolution, arguing that it was "a great, though terrible, effort of Humanity to gain possession of those rights which Christianity had taught her to regard as her inalienable patrimony. . . ." Brownson was defiant: "That Revolution needs no apology. . . . Its excesses will be forgotten much sooner than . . . the murders, the soul-destroying tyrannies, of kings and aristocracies." But such uncompromising defense of revolutionary principles became increasingly uncommon as the Romantic century progressed.

Instead, as the bourgeoisie consolidated its hold on political and cultural power, its attention shifted from social revolution to self-reform, from changing the world to changing the lives of individuals. Religious revivals, campaigns for temperance, movements to improve conditions in prisons and asylums, and many other causes absorbed the energies of tens of thousands of crusaders. The most significant of these were the movements for women's equality and for the abolition of slavery. (See the introductions to the relevant sections titled "Transatlantic Exchanges" for full treatments of these movements.) And as the industrial working class grew, reform energies poured into the organization of benevolent societies and the first unions. Finally, there were many utopians, among them figures such as Robert Owen, Fanny Wright, and George Ripley, who planned and founded socialist communities, hoping that their example would lead to a peaceful revolution in which society as a whole would be reorganized according to the principle of cooperation instead of competition.

One of the most famous of these socialist communities is the never-realized "Pantisocracy" of Robert Southey and Samuel Taylor Coleridge. Coleridge saw in the wilds of America an environment for social and intellectual repose: "O'er the Ocean Swell / Sublime of Hope I seek the cottag'd Dell, / Where Virtue calm with careless step may stray. . . ." Ideologically, the plan was informed by the political writings of Joseph Priestley and William Godwin. Godwin wrote in his *Enquiry Concerning the Principles of Political Justice* (1793) that in the future "there will be no war, no crimes, no administration of justice, as it is called, and no government." Pantisocracy (meaning an all-equal society) would be a self-sustaining community on the banks of the Susquehanna River in Pennsylvania. A dozen families would own and work the land in common, sharing the produce and profits of their cooperative labor. Southey imagined that "when Coleridge and I are sawing down a tree we shall discuss metaphysics; criticise poetry when hunting a buffalo, and write sonnets whilst following the plough." Not all utopian schemes were as quaintly visionary as

Pantisocracy. During the mid-1790s alone, some two thousand people left England for more practical cooperative societies in America, including Gilbert Imlay's in Kentucky and Thomas Cooper's in Pennsylvania.

Moreover, the fundamental rejection of British cultural, economic, and political institutions that Coleridge and Southey envisioned was shared broadly outside the socialist movement. Even Emerson believed that an economy founded on industrial capitalism subverted the virtues of humanity and required wholesale reform. In a lecture delivered to the Mechanics' Apprentices' Library Association in Boston on January 25, 1841, and published as "Man the Reformer," Emerson observed that "the general system of our trade . . . is a system of selfishness; is not dictated by the high sentiments of human nature; is not measured by the exact law of reciprocity; much less by the sentiments of love and heroism, but is a system of distrust, of concealment, of superior keenness, not of giving but of taking advantage." In such a world, he asked, "What is a man born for but to be a Reformer, a Remaker of what man has made; a renouncer of lies; a restorer of truth and good, imitating that great Nature which embosoms us all? . . ."

Nature: In his *Notes on the State of Virginia* (1787), Thomas Jefferson celebrates the undeveloped state of commerce and industry in the young nation he had helped to found:

> Those who labour in the earth are the chosen people of God, if ever he had a chosen people, whose breasts he has made his peculiar deposit for substantial and genuine virtue. It is the focus in which he keeps alive that sacred fire, which otherwise might escape from the face of the earth. Corruption of morals in the mass of cultivators is a phenomenon of which no age nor nation has furnished an example.

This characteristically Romantic way of writing about nature, known as agrarianism, started from the idea that farmwork produces everything of economic value in society and allowed agricultural capitalists like Jefferson to mount a moral critique of what they saw as the parasitism of both aristocrats and urban-based merchants.

In a closely related usage characteristic of Enlightenment rationalism, nature was also the object of scientific investigation. It was a complex machine that operated according to laws established by the creator. Thus, it was possible to appeal to nature as a benchmark of perfection: the social world that was the object of reformers' plans called for remaking because it had degenerated, had fallen away from the state of nature. If civilization had been deformed by the weight of centuries of superstition, avarice, and greed, then the way to redeem it was to recreate it in the image of nature. Finally, in a kind of semantic slippage, the classically Romantic spiritualization of nature occurred when the moral virtue that people associated with the philosophical state of nature was extended to physical nature, to mountains, woods, and streams. This Romantic conflation of philosophical and material natures led Wordsworth, in one of history's first environmental campaigns, to protest the extension of a railway through his beloved Lake District. He was inspired, perhaps, by a letter from Sarah P. Green, founder of Rydal Mount Seminary, that pictures economic development as an assault on the ideal: "Utilitarian enterprise and mercenary speculation have converted the mighty Ocean into a highway of venal profit and wealth; and transmuted the ancient temples of Nature into fire-wood for steam-ships and rail-roads. . . ."

For Jefferson, nature was a field for moral labor that made the laborer independent. For Green, nature was a realm of spiritual purity threatened by the crass greed of capital. Such flexibility meant that it was possible for appeals to nature to be made from all points on the political spectrum. At the same time that revolutionaries could defend the French Revolution as restoring natural democracy, Edmund Burke could attack them for their unnatural insensitivity to the bonds of human sympathy and respect. As an imagined alternative to modernity, nature could operate as a utopian ideal that awakened radical political energies. Just as easily, it could focus conservative nostalgia for a world in which peasants naturally respected their betters.

Individual: Though they were responding as a community to a collective history, many Romantics felt that their experiences were most authentic and powerful when they seemed to interact with the world as free and independent individuals. After all, the goal of reform was the realization of the natural rights that belonged to every human being: the right to live and to choose how to do so, and freedom from unreasonable interference by others, including the government. Moreover, if they were given the liberty to develop according to their own natural tendencies, human beings would become generous and decent, but as members of complex societies they tended instead to become selfish and mean.

Since the social world was so irretrievably corrupt, one should at all times rely on one's self. Henry David Thoreau stated this idea influentially in his essay, "Resistance to Civil Government" (1848):

> Must the citizen ever for a moment, or in the least degree, resign his conscience to the legislator? Why has every man a conscience, then? I think that we should be men first, and subjects afterward. It is not desirable to cultivate a respect for the law, so much as for the right. The only obligation which I have a right to assume is to do at any time what I think right.

Thoreau carried this self-reliance over into his practice as a writer, opening *Walden* (1854) by warning his reader wryly that while "In most books, the I, or first person, is omitted; in this it will be retained. . . . I should not talk so much about myself if there were anybody else whom I knew as well." Many Romantic writers similarly felt that their own experiences and their responses to them formed their most compelling subject matter. The poet John Keats dismissively labeled this the "egotistical sublime." But Romantic readers took as much interest in a writer's persona as in his or her text. Writers were seen as far more than makers of books. Poets or bards were promethean figures who, at their best, shone the light of divinely inspired truth onto a benighted world.

Since they commanded such power, poets could be quite dangerous—as a reviewer for Boston's *Christian Examiner* suggests, writing of three central Romantic poets:

> At a period in which Byron, goaded by disappointed ambition to fierce misanthropy and a scorn of all that is divine in heaven or on earth, was polluting not a few by covert blasphemy, and when Shelley, embittered by the bigotry of the Church, and swayed by a gloomy temperament, was making poetry the vehicle of skepticism, Wordsworth employed his pen in a steady philosophic defense of religious truth.

If on the one hand, writers seemed to be superhuman figures, on the other, their experience was often felt to be definitively human; the writer's life was emblematic, embodying the experience of thousands, even millions of ordinary people. So, for instance, when the great abolitionist orator Frederick Douglass published his autobiography, he gave it the full title, *The Narrative of the Life of Frederick Douglass, an American Slave, Written by Himself* (1845). This was the life story of a particular individual, but it was also, to use Emerson's phrase, a parable about a "representative man," and for that very reason it was all the more important to remind readers of its authenticity.

Imagination: If reason was a faculty held in common by all, and if through the exercise of it, one arrived at objective, verifiable facts, then the Romantic individual, especially the poet, exercised the different power of imagination, by means of which higher truths might be perceived behind or beyond the material world. In his *Biographia Literaria* (1817), Coleridge distinguishes imagination from fancy:

> The IMAGINATION, then, I consider either as primary, or secondary. The primary IMAGINA-
> TION I hold to be the living power and prime agent of all human perception, and as a rep-
> etition in the finite mind of the eternal act of creation in the infinite I AM. The secondary
> I consider as an echo of the former, co-existing with the conscious will, yet still as identi-
> cal with the primary in the *kind* of its agency, and differing only in *degree*, and in the *mode*
> of its operation. It dissolves, diffuses, dissipates, in order to recreate; or where this process
> is rendered impossible, yet still, at all events, it struggles to idealize and to unify. It is
> essentially *vital*, even as all objects (*as* objects) are essentially fixed and dead.

Imagination was a radical mode of perception, a way to break through the stale conformity and limited concerns of everyday life to a more fulfilling order of experience, whether spiritual, intellectual, moral, or aesthetic. It allowed the poet or the individual to transcend the tawdry world of the market and gain access to ideal truths in nature that could then inspire reform.

It was possible, though, for imagination to become its own end. Coleridge's division of the faculty into primary and secondary elements reflects the increasing limitation of the term, through the period, to creative thought as the primary tool of artistic production whose goal was no longer to reform this place but simply to envision another one. One conventional marker of imaginative power was, paradoxically, the poet's inability to control the process. Thus Romantic poetry is full of deliberate fragments, like Coleridge's "Kubla Khan" and "Christabel," that hint at unplumbed depths. Likewise, imagination was often imagined as a spontaneous inrush of sensation or emotion, and this produced a strong interest in ephemera. Finally, it often seemed as though authentic imaginative truths could not be captured in overly rational literary devices, so many writers favored what they thought of as organic as opposed to mechanical forms. They felt, in other words, that a text should take its shape from the intuitive truths it was attempting to communicate, rather than thinking of form as an ideal pattern to which artists should make truth correspond.

Literature: Just as the word *imagination* saw a narrowing over the Romantic century, so too did *literature*, from the sense of important books of all kinds to the sense of creative or imaginative writing. This reflected changes in the way that writing was made and consumed. Early in the period, bourgeois radicals saw and harnessed the power of the press to circulate ideas to mass audiences. Thomas Paine's revolutionary pamphlet, *Common Sense* (1776), which argued for complete and immediate independence from England, sold as many as half a million copies. Many Romantic writers saw their work as a deeply serious responsibility, since literature was so intricately concerned with the most pressing political and social questions of the day.

Increasingly, though, writers had to contend with the reality that the production of literature was a business. James Humphreys, for instance, was a Loyalist printer who, during the British occupation of Philadelphia, issued a daily newspaper that bore the King's arms in the title. He was forced to leave and eventually settled in Canada, opening a printing house in Shelburne where he published *The Nova Scotia Packet*. After the newspaper failed, he returned to post-Revolutionary Philadelphia. There, in an attempt to change his own political loyalties and cater to his patriotic audience, he published the first American edition of Wordsworth and Coleridge's book of radical poems, *Lyrical Ballads* (1798), on paper watermarked with a U.S. Federalist eagle.

As expanding literacy increased the demand for books and magazines, and as copyright laws and technological advances in printing created the potential for large profits in the burgeoning publishing industry, many writers acquired a sense of themselves as literary professionals producing a commodity for market. This induced considerable anxiety about the relation between exalted notions of literature's function as moral education and its increasing tendency to cater to the demand for entertainment. Thus, Nathaniel Hawthorne's lurid stories of witch trials and adultery in the distant past were never merely evasions of the present; they addressed contemporary matters obliquely through the use of exotic materials. This kind of displacement is characteristic of the period's innumerable gothic novels, historical romances, and pastorals. Nevertheless, Hawthorne wryly imagined his ancestors complaining that he was "A writer of story-books! What kind of a business in life,—what mode of glorifying God, or being serviceable to mankind in his day and generation,—may that be? Why, the degenerate fellow might as well have been a fiddler!"

We hope that this story-book will prove serviceable to you, that it will allow you to explore a richer and more varied version of Romanticism than has been easily accessible before. Its contents are organized chronologically by the author's birth date in order to represent the evolution of ideas and styles over the long Romantic century. However, emplaced within the chronological table of contents, there are sets of texts grouped thematically to allow for more focused examination of the ways of thinking and writing that developed around several of the period's most central political and social questions, such as slavery and abolition, and sexism and women's rights. The section introductions provide more detailed historical context for these debates than can be offered here. And the headnotes for individual authors emphasize anecdotes and information that demonstrate the transatlantic character of Romantic literary and cultural production. Footnotes and textual glosses have been kept to a bare minimum in order to make space for as many primary texts as possible. In the end, the texts speak for themselves, articulating an urgent, powerful range of responses to the turbulent century during which the modern world was born.

Benjamin Franklin
1706–1790

Ben Franklin was one of thirteen children in a devout Boston Congregationalist family. His father, a candle and soap maker, apprenticed him at age twelve to his older brother James, printer and publisher of the *New-England Courant*. Franklin's famous *Autobiography* (Paris, 1791; London, 1793; New York, 1794) narrates his rise to eminence from these humble beginnings. The newspaper trade gave Franklin a quick, intense education as a writer, and at sixteen he published his first pieces of political satire. Under the pen name Silence Dogood, he defended freedom of speech and attacked religious insincerity, fancy clothes, and other irrational conventions. After running away at seventeen, Franklin traveled first to New York and Philadelphia, then to London, where he worked as a printer.

In London, he published a radical Deist pamphlet in which he explained his "thoughts of the general state of things in the universe." Deism advocates a rationalist approach to God, viewing the universe as one vast machine that He designed and set in motion; accordingly, Franklin argued that in a world created and controlled by an omnipotent, omniscient, and benevolent God, "Evil doth not exist." He also maintained that since pleasure and pain are equally balanced in this world, there can be no need of an afterlife where punishments and rewards are given out. Franklin later called the book one of the main "errata" of his life and renounced the religious skepticism that he had voiced there. Nevertheless, he went on to apply the same kind of rational inquiry to topics ranging from ethics and entrepreneurship to scientific discovery and the politics of republicanism. In doing so, he came to typify the Enlightenment ways of thinking that Romanticism would both extend and transform.

Upon returning to the colonies, Franklin worked in Philadelphia, then North America's most cosmopolitan city, as a shopkeeper, newspaper editor, and publisher of almanacs. By the 1750s, his success in business had won him a political career, and he spent much of the rest of his life on diplomatic missions to England and France, beginning in 1757 as a representative of the colony of Pennsylvania, and after 1776 of the United States. Throughout his long public career, Franklin wrote satirical and polemical essays in response to contemporary events. One of his most effective travesties was "Rules by Which a Great Empire May Be Reduced to a Small One," published in London's *Gentleman's Magazine* in September 1773, as the tensions between Britain and its colonies began to approach the point of no return. In the essay, Franklin adopts the persona of "a modern simpleton" (p. 26) or wise fool; he lists the policies that had sparked unrest in the colonies, showing how together they will soon relieve the imperial government of "the trouble of governing" (p. 31). Franklin's most common rhetorical strategy in his essays, though, is to embody cool-headed, good-humored common sense. For instance, "Information to Those Who Would Remove to America" insists that the new nation is a "Land of Labour" and ridicules the "wild Imaginations" of Europeans who dream that across the sea lies a land of limitless plenty, a place where "the Fowls fly about ready roasted, crying, *Come eat me!*" (p. 33). Immediately after its 1782 publication, this open letter was translated into several languages and circulated widely, sometimes being put to uses Franklin could not have foreseen. For instance, Mary Wollstonecraft's opportunistic lover, Gilbert Imlay, printed Franklin's essay as an appendix to his pseudo-scientific book, *A Topographical Description of the Western Territory of North America* (1797), which was in fact a prospectus for a fraudulent

North American Land Company. Similarly, the 1784 pamphlet, "Remarks Concerning the Savages of North America," makes an even-tempered argument about cultural equality. It culminates in a disarming anecdote in which Franklin represents a native chieftain, Canassatego, as a latter-day Diogenes, the Greek philosopher who was said to have searched fruitlessly for years to find an honest man. By forcing the reader to see the world from a Native perspective, Franklin condemns the intensification of European-American racism in the post-Revolutionary era.

Franklin's last public act was to sign a petition demanding the abolition of the slave trade and emancipation of the slaves. He had followed his rationalist belief in human equality to its logical conclusion. He stood by that conclusion and, despite its political explosiveness, the petition was presented to Congress on December 12, 1790. Early in his long life as a practical man of letters, Franklin wrote the following epitaph for himself:

> The Body
> Of
> Benjamin Franklin,
> Printer,
> (Like the cover of an old book,
> Its contents torn out,
> And stript of its lettering and gilding,)
> Lies here, food for worms.
> But the work shall not be lost,
> For it will, as he believed, appear once more,
> In a new and more elegant edition,
> Revised and corrected
> By
> THE AUTHOR

Perhaps the corrected edition he imagined was his *Autobiography*, an act of textual self-creation in which Franklin constructs himself as a representative American, thus ensuring that his narrative would become the pattern for innumerable future life stories.

Rules by Which a Great Empire May Be Reduced to a Small One

Presented to a Late Minister,
When He Entered upon His Administration.

An ancient Sage boasted, that, tho' he could not fiddle, he knew how to make a *great city* of a *little one*. The science that I, a modern simpleton, am about to communicate, is the very reverse.

I address myself to all ministers who have the management of extensive dominions, which from their very greatness are become troublesome to govern, because the multiplicity of their affairs leaves no time for *fiddling*.

I. In the first place, gentlemen, you are to consider, that a great empire, like a great cake, is most easily diminished at the edges. Turn your attention, therefore, first to your *remotest* provinces; that, as you get rid of them, the next may follow in order.

II. That the possibility of this separation may always exist, take special care the provinces are never incorporated with the mother country; that they do not enjoy the same common rights, the same privileges in commerce; and that they are governed by *severer* laws, all of *your enacting*, without allowing them any share in the choice of the legislators. By carefully making and preserving such distinctions, you will (to keep to my simile of the cake) act like a wise gingerbread-baker, who, to facilitate a division, cuts his dough half through in those places where, when baked, he would have it *broken to pieces*.

III. Those remote provinces have perhaps been acquired, purchased, or conquered, at the *sole expence* of the settlers, or their ancestors, without the aid of the mother country. If this should happen to increase her *strength*, by their growing numbers, ready to join in her wars; her *commerce*, by their growing demand for her manufactures; or her *naval power*, by greater employment for her ships and seamen, they may probably suppose some merit in this, and that it entitles them to some favor; you are therefore to *forget it all, or resent it*, as if they had done you injury. If they happen to be zealous whigs, friends of liberty, nurtured in revolution principles, *remember all that* to their prejudice, and resolve to punish it; for such principles, after a revolution is thoroughly established, are of *no more use*; they are even *odious* and *abominable*.

IV. However peaceably your colonies have submitted to your government, shown their affection to your interests, and patiently borne their grievances; you are to *suppose* them always inclined to revolt, and treat them accordingly. Quarter troops among them, who by their insolence may *provoke* the rising of mobs, and by their bullets and bayonets *suppress* them. By this means, like the husband who uses his wife ill *from suspicion*, you may in time convert your *suspicions* into *realities*.

V. Remote provinces must have *Governors* and *Judges*, to represent the Royal Person, and execute everywhere the delegated parts of his office and authority. You ministers know, that much of the strength of government depends on the opinion of the people; and much of that opinion on the choice of rulers placed immediately over them. If you send them wise and good men for governors, who study the interest of the colonists, and advance their prosperity, they will think their King wise and good, and that he wishes the welfare of his subjects. If you send them learned and upright men for judges, they will think him a lover of justice. This may attach your provinces more to his government. You are therefore to be careful whom you recommend for those offices. If you can find prodigals, who have ruined their fortunes, broken gamesters or stockjobbers, these may do well as *governors*; for they will probably be rapacious, and provoke the people by their extortions. Wrangling proctors and pettifogging lawyers, too, are not amiss; for they will be for ever disputing and quarrelling with their little parliaments. If withal they should be ignorant, wrong-headed, and insolent, so much the better. Attorneys' clerks and Newgate[1] solicitors will do for *Chief Justices*, especially if they hold their places *during your pleasure*; and all will contribute to impress those ideas of your government, that are proper for a people *you would wish to renounce it*.

VI. To confirm these impressions, and strike them deeper, whenever the injured come to the capital with complaints of maladministration, oppression, or injustice, punish such suitors with long delay, enormous expense, and a final judgment in favor of the oppressor. This will have an admirable effect every way. The trouble of future complaints will be prevented, and Governors and Judges will be encouraged to farther acts of oppression and injustice; and thence the people may become more disaffected, and at length desperate.

VII. When such Governors have crammed their coffers, and made themselves so odious to the people that they can no longer remain among them, with safety to their persons, *recall and reward* them with pensions. You may make them *baronets* too, if that

---

1. A London prison.

respectable order should not think fit to resent it. All will contribute to encourage new governors in the same practice, and make the supreme government, *detestable*.

VIII. If, when you are engaged in war, your colonies should vie in liberal aids of men and money against the common enemy, upon your simple requisition, and give far beyond their abilities, reflect that a penny taken from them by your power is more honorable to you, than a pound presented by their benevolence; despise therefore their voluntary grants, and resolve to harass them with novel taxes. They will probably complain to your parliaments, that they are taxed by a body in which they have no representative, and that this is contrary to common right. They will petition for redress. Let the Parliaments flout their claims, reject their petitions, refuse even to suffer the reading of them, and treat the petitioners with the utmost contempt. Nothing can have a better effect in producing the alienation proposed; for though many can forgive injuries, *none ever forgave contempt.*

IX. In laying these taxes, never regard the heavy burthens those remote people already undergo, in defending their own frontiers, supporting their own provincial governments, making new roads, building bridges, churches, and other public edifices, which in old countries have been done to your lands by your ancestors, but which occasion constant calls and demands on the purses of a new people. Forget the *restraints* you lay on their trade for *your own* benefit, and the advantage a *monopoly* of this trade gives your exacting merchants. Think nothing of the wealth those merchants and your manufacturers acquire by the colony commerce; their increased ability thereby to pay taxes at home; their accumulating, in the price of their commodities, most of those taxes, and so levying them from their consuming customers; all this, and the employment and support of thousands of your poor by the colonists, you are *entirely to forget.* But remember to make your arbitrary tax more grievous to your provinces, by public declarations importing that your power of taxing them has *no limits;* so that when you take from them without their consent one shilling in the pound, you have a clear right to the other nineteen. This will probably weaken every idea of *security in their property,* and convince them, that under such a government they *have nothing they can call their own;* which can scarce fail of producing the *happiest consequences!*

X. Possibly, indeed, some of them might still comfort themselves, and say, "Though we have no property, we have yet *something* left that is valuable; we have constitutional *liberty,* both of person and of conscience. This King, these Lords, and these Commons, who it seems are too remote from us to know us, and feel for us, cannot take from us our *Habeas Corpus* right,[2] or our right of trial *by a jury of our neighbors;* they cannot deprive us of the exercise of our religion, alter our ecclesiastical constitution, and compel us to be Papists, if they please, or Mahometans." To annihilate this comfort, begin by laws to perplex their commerce with infinite regulations, impossible to be remembered and observed; ordain seizures of their property for every failure; take away the trial of such property by Jury, and give it to arbitrary Judges of your own appointing, and of the lowest characters in the country, whose salaries and emoluments are to arise out of the duties or condemnations, and whose appointments are *during pleasure.* Then let there be a formal declaration of both Houses, that opposition to your edicts is *treason*, and that any person suspected of treason in the provinces may, according to some obsolete law, be seized and sent to the metropolis of the empire for trial; and pass an act, that

---

2. Legal right to know the charges against one.

those there charged with certain other offenses, shall be sent away in chains from their friends and country to be tried in the same manner for felony. Then erect a new Court of Inquisition among them, accompanied by an armed force, with instructions to transport all such suspected persons, to be ruined by the expense, if they bring over evidences to prove their innocence, or be found guilty and hanged, if they cannot afford it. And, lest the people should think you cannot possibly go any farther, pass another solemn declaratory act, "that King, Lords, Commons had, hath, and of right ought to have, full power and authority to make statutes of sufficient force and validity to bind the unrepresented provinces IN ALL CASES WHATSOEVER." This will include *spiritual* with temporal, and, taken together, must operate wonderfully to your purpose; by convincing them, that they are at present under a power something like that spoken of in the scriptures, which can not only *kill their bodies*, but *damn their souls* to all eternity, by compelling them, if it pleases, *to worship the Devil*.

XI. To make your taxes more odious, and more likely to procure resistance, send from the capital a board of officers to superintend the collection, composed of the most *indiscreet, ill-bred,* and *insolent* you can find. Let these have large salaries out of the extorted revenue, and live in open, grating luxury upon the sweat and blood of the industrious; whom they are to worry continually with groundless and expensive prosecutions before the abovementioned arbitrary revenue Judges; *all at the cost of the party prosecuted,* tho' acquitted, because *the King is to pay no costs.* Let these men, *by your order,* be exempted from all the common taxes and burthens of the province, though they and their property are protected by its laws. If any revenue offices are *suspected* of the least tenderness for the people, discard them. If others are justly complained of, protect and reward them. If any of the under officers behave so as to provoke the people to drub them, promote those to better offices: this will encourage others to procure for themselves such profitable drubbings, by multiplying and enlarging such provocations, and *all will work towards the end you aim at.*

XII. Another way to make your tax odious, is to misapply the produce of it. If it was originally appropriated for the *defense* of the provinces, the better support of government, and the administration of justice, where it may be *necessary,* then apply none of it to that *defense,* but bestow it where it is *not necessary,* in augmented salaries or pensions to every governor, who has distinguished himself by his enmity to the people, and by calumniating them to their sovereign. This will make them pay it more unwillingly, and be more apt to quarrel with those that collect it and those that imposed it, who will quarrel again with them, and all shall contribute to your *main purpose,* of making them *weary of your government.*

XIII. If the people of any province have been accustomed to support their own Governors and Judges to satisfaction, you are to apprehend that such Governors and Judges may be thereby influenced to treat the people kindly, and to do them justice. This is another reason for applying part of that revenue in larger salaries to such Governors and Judges, given, as their commissions are, *during your pleasure* only; forbidding them to take any salaries from their provinces; that thus the people may no longer hope any kindness from their Governors, or (in Crown cases) any justice from their Judges. And, as the money thus misapplied in one province is extorted from all, probably *all will resent the misapplication.*

XIV. If the parliaments of your provinces should dare to claim rights, or complain of your administration, order them to be harrassed with *repeated dissolutions.* If the same men are continually returned by new elections, adjourn their meetings to some country village, where they cannot be accommodated, and there keep them *during pleasure*; for this, you know, is your PREROGATIVE; and an excellent one it is, as you may manage it to promote discontents among the people, diminish their respect, and *increase their disaffection*.

XV. Convert the brave, honest officers of your *navy* into pimping tide-waiters and colony officers of the *customs*. Let those, who in time of war fought gallantly in defense of the commerce of their countrymen, in peace be taught to prey upon it. Let them learn to be corrupted by great and real smugglers; but (to show their diligence) scour with armed boats every bay, harbor, river, creek, cove, or nook throughout the coast of your colonies; stop and detain every coaster, every wood-boat, every fisherman, tumble their cargoes and even their ballast inside out and upside down; and, if a penn'orth of pins is found unentered, let the whole be seized and confiscated. Thus shall the trade of your colonists suffer more from their friends in time of peace, than it did from their enemies in war. Then let these boats' crews land upon every farm in their way, rob the orchards, steal the pigs and the poultry, and insult the inhabitants. If the injured and exasperated farmers, unable to procure other justice, should attack the aggressors, drub them, and burn their boats; you are to call this *high treason and rebellion*, order fleets and armies into their country, and threaten to carry all the offenders three thousand miles to be hanged, drawn, and quartered. *O! this will work admirably!*

XVI. If you are told of discontents in your colonies, never believe that they are general, or that you have given occasion for them; therefore do not think of applying any remedy, or of changing any offensive measure. Redress no grievance, lest they should be encouraged to demand the redress of some other grievance. Grant no request that is just and reasonable, lest they should make another that is unreasonable. Take all your informations of the state of the colonies from your Governors and officers in enmity with them. Encourage and reward these *leasing-makers*[3]; secrete their lying accusations, lest they should be confuted; but act upon them as the clearest evidence; and believe nothing you hear from the friends of the people: suppose all *their* complaints to be invented and promoted by a few factious demagogues, whom if you could catch and hang, all would be quiet. Catch and hang a few of them accordingly; and the *blood of the Martyrs* shall *work miracles* in favor of your purpose.

XVII. If you see *rival nations* rejoicing at the prospect of your disunion with your provinces, and endeavoring to promote it; if they translate, publish, and applaud all the complaints of your discontented colonists, at the same time privately stimulating you to severer measures, let not that *alarm* or offend you. Why should it, since you all mean *the same thing*?

XVIII. If any colony should at their own charge erect a fortress to secure their port against the fleets of a foreign enemy, get your Governor to betray that fortress into your hands. Never think of paying what it cost the country, for that would look, at least, like some regard for justice; but turn it into a citadel to awe the inhabitants and curb their commerce. If they should have lodged in such fortress the very arms they bought and used to aid you in your conquests, seize them all; it will provoke like *ingratitude* added to *robbery*. One admirable effect of these operations will be, to discourage every other colony from erecting such defenses, and so your enemies may

---

3. Informers.

more easily invade them; to the great disgrace of your government, and of course *the furtherance of your project.*

XIX. Send armies into their country under pretense of protecting the inhabitants; but, instead of garrisoning the forts on their frontiers with those troops, to prevent incursions, demolish those forts, and order the troops into the heart of the country, that the savages may be encouraged to attack the frontiers, and that the troops may be protected by the inhabitants. This will seem to proceed from your ill will or your ignorance, and contribute farther to produce and strengthen an opinion among them, *that you are no longer fit to govern them.*

XX. Lastly, invest the General of your army in the provinces, with great and unconstitutional powers, and free him from the control of even your own Civil Governors. Let him have troops enow under his command, with all the fortresses in his possession; and who knows but (like some provincial Generals in the Roman empire, and encouraged by the universal discontent you have produced) he may take it into his head to set up for himself? If he should, and you have carefully practiced these few *excellent rules* of mine, take my word for it, all the provinces will immediately join him; and you will that day (if you have not done it sooner) get rid of the trouble of governing them, and all the *plagues* attending their *commerce* and connection from henceforth and for ever.   Q. E. D.

—1773

Information to Those Who Would Remove to America

Many Persons in Europe, having directly or by Letters, express'd to the Writer of this, who is well acquainted with North America, their Desire of transporting and establishing themselves in that Country; but who appear to have formed, thro' Ignorance, mistaken Ideas and Expectations of what is to be obtained there; he thinks it may be useful, and prevent inconvenient, expensive, and fruitless Removals and Voyages of improper Persons, if he gives some clearer and truer Notions of that part of the World, than appear to have hitherto prevailed.

He finds it is imagined by Numbers, that the Inhabitants of North America are rich, capable of rewarding, and dispos'd to reward, all sorts of Ingenuity; that they are at the same time ignorant of all the Sciences, and, consequently, that Strangers, possessing Talents in the Belles-Lettres, fine Arts, &c., must be highly esteemed, and so well paid, as to become easily rich themselves; that there are also abundance of profitable Offices to be disposed of, which the Natives are not qualified to fill; and that, having few Persons of Family among them, Strangers of Birth must be greatly respected, and of course easily obtain the best of those Offices, which will make all their Fortunes; that the Governments too, to encourage Emigrations from Europe, not only pay the Expence of personal Transportation, but give Lands gratis to Strangers, with Negroes to work for them, Utensils of Husbandry, and Stocks of Cattle. These are all wild Imaginations; and those who go to America with Expectations founded upon them will surely find themselves disappointed.

The Truth is, that though there are in that Country few People so miserable as the Poor of Europe, there are also very few that in Europe would be called rich; it is rather a general happy Mediocrity that prevails. There are few great Proprietors of the Soil, and few Tenants; most People cultivate their own Lands, or follow some Handicraft or Merchandise; very few rich enough to live idly upon their Rents or Incomes, or to pay the high Prices given in Europe for Paintings, Statues, Architecture, and the other Works of Art, that are more curious than useful. Hence the natural Geniuses, that have arisen in America with such Talents, have uniformly quitted that Country for Europe, where they can be more suitably rewarded. It is true, that Letters and Mathematical Knowledge are in Esteem there, but they are at the same time more common than is apprehended; there being already existing nine Colleges or Universities, viz. four in New England, and one in each of the Provinces of New York, New Jersey, Pennsilvania, Maryland, and Virginia, all furnish'd with learned Professors; besides a number of smaller Academies; these educate many of their Youth in the Languages, and those Sciences that qualify men for the Professions of Divinity, Law, or Physick. Strangers indeed are by no means excluded from exercising those Professions; and the quick Increase of Inhabitants everywhere gives them a Chance of Employ, which they have in common with the Natives. Of civil Offices, or Employments, there are few; no super-fluous Ones, as in Europe; and it is a Rule establish'd in some of the States, that no Office should be so profitable as to make it desirable. The 36th Article of the Constitution of Pennsylvania, runs expressly in these Words; "As every Freeman, to pre-serve his Independence, (if he has not a sufficient Estate) ought to have some Profession, Calling, Trade, or Farm, whereby he may honestly subsist, there can be no Necessity for, nor Use in, establishing Offices of Profit; the usual Effects of which are Dependence and Servility, unbecoming Freemen, in the Possessors and Expectants; Faction, Contention, Corruption, and Disorder among the People. Wherefore, when-ever an Office, thro' Increase of Fees or otherwise, becomes so profitable, as to occasion many to apply for it, the Profits ought to be lessened by the Legislature."

These Ideas prevailing more or less in all the United States, it cannot be worth any Man's while, who has a means of Living at home, to expatriate himself, in hopes of obtaining a profitable civil Office in America; and, as to military Offices, they are at an End with the War, the Armies being disbanded. Much less is it adviseable for a Person to go thither, who has no other Quality to recommend him but his Birth. In Europe it has indeed its Value; but it is a Commodity that cannot be carried to a worse Market than that of America, where people do not inquire concerning a Stranger, *What is he?* but, *What can he do?* If he has any useful Art, he is welcome; and if he exercises it, and behaves well, he will be respected by all that know him; but a mere Man of Quality, who, on that Account, wants to live upon the Public, by some Office or Salary, will be despis'd and disregarded. The Husbandman is in honor there, and even the Mechanic, because their Employments are useful. The People have a saying, that God Almighty is himself a Mechanic, the greatest in the Universe; and he is respected and admired more for the Variety, Ingenuity, and Utility of his Handyworks, than for the Antiquity of his Family. They are pleas'd with the Observation of a Negro, and frequently mention it, that *Boccarorra* (meaning the White men) *make de black man workee, make de Horse workee, make de Ox workee, make ebery ting workee; only de Hog. He, de hog, no workee; he eat, he drink, he walk about, he go to sleep when he please, he libb like a Gentleman.* According to these Opinions of the Americans, one of them would think himself more oblig'd to a Genealogist, who could prove for him that his Ancestors and Relations for ten Generations had been Ploughmen, Smiths, Carpenters, Turners, Weavers, Tanners, or even Shoemakers, and consequently that they were useful Members of Society; than if he could only prove that they were Gentlemen, doing nothing of Value, but living idly on the Labour of others, mere *fruges consumere nati*,[1] and otherwise *good for nothing*, till by their Death their Estates, like the Carcass of the Negro's Gentleman-Hog, come to be *cut up*.

With regard to Encouragements for Strangers from Government, they are really only what are derived from good Laws and Liberty. Strangers are welcome, because there is room enough for them all, and therefore the old Inhabitants are not jealous of them; the Laws protect them sufficiently, so that they have no need of the Patronage of Great Men; and every one will enjoy securely the Profits of his Industry. But, if he does not bring a Fortune with him, he must work and be industrious to live. One or two Years' residence gives him all the Rights of a Citizen; but the government does not at present, whatever it may have done in former times, hire People to become Settlers, by Paying their Passages, giving Land, Negroes, Utensils, Stock, or any other kind of Emolument whatsoever. In short, America is the Land of Labour, and by no means what the English call *Lubberland*, and the French *Pays de Cocagne*, where the streets are said to be pav'd with half-peck Loaves, the Houses til'd with Pancakes, and where the Fowls fly about ready roasted, crying, *Come eat me!*

Who then are the kind of Persons to whom an Emigration to America may be advantageous? And what are the Advantages they may reasonably expect?

Land being cheap in that Country, from the vast Forests still void of Inhabitants, and not likely to be occupied in an Age to come, insomuch that the Propriety of an hundred Acres of fertile Soil full of Wood may be obtained near the Frontiers, in many Places, for Eight or Ten Guineas, hearty young Labouring Men, who understand the Husbandry of Corn and Cattle, which is nearly the same in that Country as in Europe, may easily establish themselves there. A little Money sav'd of the good Wages they receive there, while they work for others, enables them to buy the Land and begin their Plantation, in which they are assisted by the Good-Will of their Neighbours, and some Credit. Multitudes of poor People from England, Ireland, Scotland, and Germany, have by this means in a few years become wealthy Farmers, who, in their own Countries, where all the Lands are fully occupied, and the Wages of Labour low, could never have emerged from the poor Condition wherein they were born.

From the salubrity of the Air, the healthiness of the Climate, the plenty of good Provisions, and the Encouragement to early Marriages by the certainty of Subsistence in cultivating the Earth, the Increase of Inhabitants by natural Generation is very rapid in America, and becomes still more so by the Accession of Strangers; hence there is a continual Demand for more Artisans of all the necessary and useful kinds, to supply those Cultivators of the Earth with Houses, and with Furniture and Utensils of the grosser sorts, which cannot so well be brought from Europe. Tolerably good Workmen in any of those mechanic Arts are sure to find Employ, and to be well paid for their Work, there being no Restraints preventing Strangers from exercising any Art they understand, nor any Permission necessary. If they are poor, they begin first as Servants or Journeymen; and if they are sober,

---

1. [Franklin's note] There are a number of us born
   Merely to eat up the corn.
                    —WATTS

industrious, and frugal, they soon become Masters, establish themselves in Business, marry, raise Families, and become respectable Citizens.

Also, Persons of moderate Fortunes and Capitals, who, having a Number of Children to provide for, are desirous of bringing them up to Industry, and to secure Estates for their Posterity, have Opportunities of doing it in America, which Europe does not afford. There they may be taught and practise profitable mechanic Arts, without incurring Disgrace on that Account, but on the contrary acquiring Respect by such Abilities. There small Capitals laid out in Lands, which daily become more valuable by the Increase of People, afford a solid Prospect of ample Fortunes thereafter for those Children. The Writer of this has known several Instances of large Tracts of Land, bought, on what was then the Frontier of Pennsilvania, for Ten Pounds per hundred Acres, which after 20 years, when the Settlements had been extended far beyond them, sold readily, without any Improvement made upon them, for three Pounds per Acre. The Acre in America is the same with the English Acre, or the Acre of Normandy.

Those, who desire to understand the State of Government in America, would do well to read the Constitutions of the several States, and the Articles of Confederation that bind the whole together for general Purposes, under the Direction of one Assembly, called the Congress. These Constitutions have been printed, by order of Congress, in America; two Editions of them have also been printed in London; and a good Translation of them into French has lately been published at Paris.

Several of the Princes of Europe having of late years, from an Opinion of Advantage to arise by producing all Commodities and Manufactures within their own Dominions, so as to diminish or render useless their Importations, have endeavoured to entice Workmen from other Countries by high Salaries, Privileges, &c. Many Persons, pretending to be skilled in various great Manufactures, imagining that America must be in Want of them, and that the Congress would probably be dispos'd to imitate the Princes above mentioned, have proposed to go over, on Condition of having their Passages paid, Lands given, Salaries appointed, exclusive Privileges for Terms of years, &c. Such Persons, on reading the Articles of Confederation, will find, that the Congress have no Power committed to them, or Money put into their Hands, for such purposes; and that if any such Encouragement is given, it must be by the Government of some separate State. This, however, has rarely been done in America; and, when it has been done, it has rarely succeeded, so as to establish a Manufacture, which the Country was not yet so ripe for as to encourage private Persons to set it up; Labour being generally too dear there, and Hands difficult to be kept together, every one desiring to be a Master, and the Cheapness of Lands inclining many to leave Trades for Agriculture. Some indeed have met with Success, and are carried on to Advantage; but they are generally such as require only a few Hands, or wherein great Part of the Work is performed by Machines. Things that are bulky, and of so small Value as not well to bear the Expence of Freight, may often be made cheaper in the Country than they can be imported; and the Manufacture of such Things will be profitable wherever there is a sufficient Demand. The Farmers in America produce indeed a good deal of Wool and Flax; and none is exported, it is all work'd up; but it is in the Way of domestic Manufacture, for the Use of the Family. The buying up Quantities of Wool and Flax, with the Design to employ Spinners, Weavers, &c., and form great Establishments, producing Quantities of Linen and Woollen Goods for

Sale, has been several times attempted in different Provinces; but those Projects have generally failed, goods of equal Value being imported cheaper. And when the Governments have been solicited to support such Schemes by Encouragements, in Money, or by imposing Duties on Importation of such Goods, it has been generally refused, on this Principle, that, if the Country is ripe for the Manufacture, it may be carried on by private Persons to Advantage; and if not, it is a Folly to think of forcing Nature. Great Establishments of Manufacture require great Numbers of Poor to do the Work for small Wages; these Poor are to be found in Europe, but will not be found in America, till the Lands are all taken up and cultivated, and the Excess of People, who cannot get Land, want Employment. The Manufacture of Silk, they say, is natural in France, as that of Cloth in England, because each Country produces in Plenty the first Material; but if England will have a Manufacture of Silk as well as that of Cloth, and France one of Cloth as well as of Silk, these unnatural Operations must be supported by mutual Prohibitions, or high Duties on the Importation of each other's Goods; by which means the Workmen are enabled to tax the home Consumer by greater Prices, while the higher Wages they receive makes them neither happier nor richer, since they only drink more and work less. Therefore the Governments in America do nothing to encourage such Projects. The People, by this Means, are not impos'd on, either by the Merchant or Mechanic. If the Merchant demands too much Profit on imported Shoes, they buy of the Shoemaker; and if he asks too high a Price, they take them of the Merchant; thus the two Professions are checks on each other. The Shoemaker, however, has, on the whole, a considerable Profit upon his Labour in America, beyond what he had in Europe, as he can add to his Price a Sum nearly equal to all the Expences of Freight and Commission, Risque or Insurance, &c., necessarily charged by the Merchant. And the Case is the same with the Workmen in every other Mechanic Art. Hence it is, that Artisans generally live better and more easily in America than in Europe; and such as are good Œconomists make a comfortable Provision for Age, and for their Children. Such may, therefore, remove with Advantage to America.

In the long-settled Countries of Europe, all Arts, Trades, Professions, Farms, &c., are so full, that it is difficult for a poor Man, who has Children, to place them where they may gain, or learn to gain, a decent Livelihood. The Artisans, who fear creating future Rivals in Business, refuse to take Apprentices, but upon Conditions of Money, Maintenance, or the like, which the Parents are unable to comply with. Hence the Youth are dragg'd up in Ignorance of every gainful Art, and oblig'd to become Soldiers, or Servants, or Thieves, for a Subsistence. In America, the rapid Increase of Inhabitants takes away that Fear of Rivalship, and Artisans willingly receive Apprentices from the hope of Profit by their Labour, during the Remainder of the Time stipulated, after they shall be instructed. Hence it is easy for poor Families to get their Children instructed; for the Artisans are so desirous of Apprentices, that many of them will even give Money to the Parents, to have Boys from Ten to Fifteen Years of Age bound Apprentices to them till the Age of Twenty-one; and many poor Parents have, by that means, on their Arrival in the Country, raised Money enough to buy Land sufficient to establish themselves, and to subsist the rest of their Family by Agriculture. These Contracts for Apprentices are made before a Magistrate, who regulates the Agreement according to Reason and Justice, and, having in view the Formation of a future useful Citizen, obliges the Master to engage by a written

Indenture, not only that, during the time of Service stipulated, the Apprentice shall be duly provided with Meat, Drink, Apparel, washing, and Lodging, and, at its Expiration, with a compleat new Suit of Cloaths, but also that he shall be taught to read, write, and cast Accompts; and that he shall be well instructed in the Art or Profession of his Master, or some other, by which he may afterwards gain a Livelihood, and be able in his turn to raise a Family. A Copy of this Indenture is given to the Apprentice or his Friends, and the Magistrate keeps a Record of it, to which recourse may be had, in case of Failure by the Master in any Point of Performance. This desire among the Masters, to have more Hands employ'd in working for them, induces them to pay the Passages of young Persons, of both Sexes, who, on their Arrival, agree to serve them one, two, three, or four Years; those, who have already learnt a Trade, agreeing for a shorter Term, in proportion to their Skill, and the consequent immediate Value of their Service; and those, who have none, agreeing for a longer Term, in consideration of being taught an Art their Poverty would not permit them to acquire in their own Country.

The almost general Mediocrity of Fortune that prevails in America obliging its People to follow some Business for subsistence, those Vices, that arise usually from Idleness, are in a great measure prevented. Industry and constant Employment are great preservatives of the Morals and Virtue of a Nation. Hence bad Examples of Youth are more rare in America, which must be a comfortable Consideration to Parents. To this may be truly added, that serious Religion, under its various Denominations, is not only tolerated, but respected and practised. Atheism is unknown there; Infidelity rare and secret; so that persons may live to a great Age in that Country, without having their Piety shocked by meeting with either an Atheist or an Infidel. And the Divine Being seems to have manifested his Approbation of the mutual Forbearance and Kindness with which the different Sects treat each other, by the remarkable Prosperity with which He has been pleased to favour the whole Country.

—1784

Remarks Concerning the Savages of North America

Savages we call them, because their Manners differ from ours, which we think the Perfection of Civility; they think the same of theirs.

Perhaps, if we could examine the Manners of different Nations with Impartiality, we should find no People so rude, as to be without any Rules of Politeness; nor any so polite, as not to have some Remains of Rudeness.

The Indian Men, when young, are Hunters and Warriors; when old, Counsellors; for all their Government is by Counsel of the Sages; there is no Force, there are no Prisons, no Officers to compel Obedience, or inflict Punishment. Hence they generally study Oratory, the best Speaker having the most Influence. The Indian Women till the Ground, dress the Food, nurse and bring up the Children, and preserve and hand down to Posterity the Memory of public Transactions. These Employments of Men and Women are accounted natural and honourable. Having few artificial Wants, they have abundance of Leisure for Improvement by Conversation. Our laborious Manner of Life, compared with theirs, they esteem slavish and base; and the Learning, on which we value ourselves, they regard as frivolous and useless. An Instance of this occurred at the Treaty of Lancaster, in Pennsylvania, *anno* 1744, between the Government of Virginia and the Six Nations.[1] After the principal Business was settled, the Commissioners from Virginia acquainted the Indians by a Speech, that there was at Williamsburg a College, with a Fund for Educating Indian youth; and that, if the Six Nations would send down half a dozen of their young Lads to that College, the Government would take care that they should be well provided for, and instructed in all the Learning of the White People. It is one of the Indian Rules of Politeness not to answer a public Proposition the same day that it is made; they think it would be treating it as a light matter, and that they show it Respect by taking time to consider it, as of a Matter important. They therefore deferr'd their Answer till the Day following; when their Speaker began, by expressing their deep Sense of the kindness of the Virginia Government, in making them that Offer; for we know, says he, that you highly esteem the kind of Learning taught in those Colleges, and that the Maintenance of our young Men, while with you, would be very expensive to you. We are convinc'd, therefore, that you mean to do us Good by your Proposal; and we thank you heartily. But you, who are wise, must know that different Nations have different Conceptions of things; and you will therefore not take it amiss, if our Ideas of this kind of Education happen not to be the same with yours. We have had some Experience of it; several of our young People were formerly brought up at the Colleges of the Northern Provinces; they were instructed in all your Sciences; but, when they came back to us, they were bad Runners, ignorant of every means of living in the Woods, unable to bear either Cold or Hunger, knew neither how to build a Cabin, take a Deer, or kill an Enemy, spoke our Language imperfectly, were therefore neither fit for Hunters, Warriors, nor Counsellors; they were totally good for nothing. We are however not the less oblig'd by your kind Offer, tho' we decline accepting it; and, to show our grateful Sense of it, if the Gentlemen of Virginia will send us a Dozen of their Sons, we will take great Care of their Education, instruct them in all we know, and make *Men* of them.

Having frequent Occasions to hold public Councils, they have acquired great Order and Decency in conducting them. The old Men sit in the foremost Ranks, the Warriors in the next, and the Women and Children in the hindmost. The Business of the Women is to take exact Notice of what passes, imprint it in their Memories (for they have no Writing), and communicate it to their Children. They are the Records of the Council, and they preserve Traditions of the Stipulations in Treaties 100 Years back; which, when we compare with our Writings, we always find exact. He that would speak, rises. The rest observe a profound Silence. When he has finish'd and sits down, they leave him 5 to 6 Minutes to recollect, that, if he has omitted anything he intended to say, or has any thing to add, he may rise again and deliver it. To interrupt another, even in common Conversation, is reckon'd highly indecent. How different this is from the conduct of a polite British House of Commons, where scarce a day passes without some Confusion, that makes the Speaker hoarse in calling *to Order;* and how different from the Mode of Conversation in many polite Companies of Europe, where, if you do not deliver your Sentence with great Rapidity, you are cut off in the middle of it by the Impatient Loquacity of those you converse with, and never suffer'd to finish it!

---

1. The Iroquois Confederacy of Seneca, Oneida, Cayuga, Mohawk, Onondaga, and Tuscarora tribes.

The Politeness of these Savages in Conversation is indeed carried to Excess, since it does not permit them to contradict or deny the Truth of what is asserted in their Presence. By this means they indeed avoid Disputes; but then it becomes difficult to know their Minds, or what Impression you make upon them. The Missionaries who have attempted to convert them to Christianity, all complain of this as one of the great Difficulties of their Mission. The Indians hear with Patience the Truths of the Gospel explain'd to them, and give their usual Tokens of Assent and Approbation; you would think they were convinc'd. No such matter. It is mere Civility.

A Swedish Minister, having assembled the chiefs of the Susquehanah Indians, made a Sermon to them, acquainting them with the principal historical Facts on which our Religion is founded; such as the Fall of our first Parents by eating an Apple, the coming of Christ to repair the Mischief, his Miracles and Suffering, &c. When he had finished, an Indian Orator stood up to thank him. "What you have told us," says he, "is all very good. It is indeed bad to eat Apples. It is better to make them all into Cyder. We are much oblig'd by your kindness in coming so far, to tell us these Things which you have heard from your Mothers. In return, I will tell you some of those we had heard from ours. In the Beginning, our Fathers had only the Flesh of Animals to subsist on; and if their Hunting was unsuccessful, they were starving. Two of our young Hunters, having kill'd a Deer, made a Fire in the Woods to broil some Part of it. When they were about to satisfy their Hunger, they beheld a beautiful young Woman descend from the Clouds, and seat herself on that Hill, which you see yonder among the blue Mountains. They said to each other, it is a Spirit that has smelt our broiling Venison, and wishes to eat of it; let us offer some to her. They presented her with the Tongue; she was pleas'd with the Taste of it, and said, 'Your kindness shall be rewarded; come to this Place after thirteen Moons, and you shall find something that will be of great Benefit in nourishing you and your Children to the latest Generations.' They did so, and, to their Surprise, found Plants they had never seen before; but which, from that ancient time, have been constantly cultivated among us, to our great Advantage. Where her right Hand had touched the Ground, they found Maize; where her left hand had touch'd it, they found Kidney-Beans; and where her Backside had sat on it, they found Tobacco." The good Missionary, disgusted with this idle Tale, said, "What I delivered to you were sacred Truths; but what you tell me is mere Fable, Fiction, and Falsehood." The Indian, offended, reply'd, "My brother, it seems your Friends have not done you Justice in your Education; they have not well instructed you in the Rules of common Civility. You saw that we, who understand and practise those Rules, believ'd all your stories; why do you refuse to believe ours?"

When any of them come into our Towns, our People are apt to crowd round them, gaze upon them, and incommode them, where they desire to be private; this they esteem great Rudeness, and the Effect of the Want of Instruction in the Rules of Civility and good Manners. "We have," say they, "as much Curiosity as you, and when you come into our Towns, we wish for Opportunities of looking at you; but for this purpose we hide ourselves behind Bushes, where you are to pass, and never intrude ourselves into your Company."

Their Manner of entering one another's village has likewise its Rules. It is reckon'd uncivil in travelling Strangers to enter a Village abruptly, without giving Notice of their Approach. Therefore, as soon as they arrive within hearing, they stop and halloo, remaining there till invited to enter. Two old Men usually come out to them, and lead them in. There is in every Village a vacant Dwelling, called *the Strangers' House*. Here they are plac'd, while the old Men go round from Hut to Hut, acquainting the Inhabitants, that Strangers are arriv'd, who are probably hungry and weary; and every one sends them what he can spare of Victuals, and Skins to repose on. When the Strangers are refresh'd, Pipes and Tobacco are brought; and then, but not before, Conversation begins, with Enquiries who they are, whither bound, what News, &c.; and it usually ends with offers of Service, if the Strangers have occasion of Guides, or any Necessaries for continuing their journey; and nothing is exacted for the Entertainment.

The same Hospitality, esteem'd among them as a principal Virtue, is practis'd by private Persons; of which Conrad Weiser, our Interpreter, gave me the following Instance. He had been naturaliz'd among the Six Nations, and spoke well the Mohock Language. In going thro' the Indian Country, to carry a Message from our Governor to the Council at Onondaga, he call'd at the Habitation of Canassatego, an old Acquaintance, who embrac'd him, spread Furs for him to sit on, plac'd before him some boil'd Beans and Venison, and mix'd some Rum and Water for his Drink. When he was well refresh'd, and had lit his Pipe, Canassatego began to converse with him; ask'd how he had far'd the many Years since they had seen each other; whence he then came; what occasion'd the journey, &c. Conrad answered all his Questions; and when the Discourse began to flag, the Indian, to continue it, said, "Conrad, you have lived long among the white People, and know something of their Customs; I have been sometimes at Albany, and have observed, that once in Seven Days they shut up their Shops, and assemble all in the great House; tell me what it is for? What do they do there?" "They meet there," says Conrad, "to hear and learn *good Things*." "I do not doubt," says the Indian, "that they tell you so; they have told me the same; but I doubt the Truth of what they say, and I will tell you my Reasons. I went lately to Albany to sell my Skins and buy Blankets, Knives, Powder, Rum, &c. You know I us'd generally to deal with Hans Hanson; but I was a little inclin'd this time to try some other Merchant. However, I call'd first upon Hans, and asked him what he would give for Beaver. He said he could not give any more than four Shillings a Pound; 'but,' says he, 'I cannot talk on Business now; this is the Day when we meet together to learn *Good Things*, and I am going to the Meeting.' So I thought to myself, 'Since we cannot do any Business to-day, I may as well go to the meeting too,' and I went with him. There stood up a Man in Black, and began to talk to the People very angrily. I did not understand what he said; but, perceiving that he look'd much at me and at Hanson, I imagin'd he was angry at seeing me there; so I went out, sat down near the House, struck Fire, and lit my Pipe, waiting till the Meeting should break up. I thought too, that the Man had mention'd something of Beaver, and I suspected it might be the Subject of their Meeting. So, when they came out, I accosted my Merchant. 'Well, Hans,' says I, 'I hope you have agreed to give more than four Shillings a Pound.' 'No,' says he, 'I cannot give so much; I cannot give more than three shillings and sixpence.' I then spoke to several other Dealers, but they all sung the same song,—Three and sixpence,—Three and sixpence. This made it clear to me, that my Suspicion was right; and, that whatever they pretended of meeting to learn *good Things*, the real purpose was to consult how to cheat Indians in the Price of Beaver. Consider but a little, Conrad, and you must be of my Opinion. If they met so often to learn *good Things*, they would certainly have learnt some before this time. But they are still ignorant. You know our Practice. If a white Man, in travelling thro' our Country, enters one of our Cabins, we all treat him as I treat you; we dry him if he is wet, we warm him if he is cold, we give him Meat and Drink, that he may allay his Thirst and Hunger; and we spread soft Furs for him to rest and sleep on; we demand nothing in return. But, if I go into a white Man's House at Albany, and ask for Victuals and Drink, they say, 'Where is your Money?' and if I have none, they say, 'Get out, you Indian Dog.' You see they have not yet learned those little *Good Things*, that we need no Meetings to be instructed in, because our Mothers taught them to us when we were Children; and therefore it is impossible their Meetings should be, as they say, for any such purpose, or have any such Effect; they are only to contrive *the Cheating of Indians in the Price of Beaver*."

—1784

Samson Occom
1723–1792

The first two Native American printed texts were Samson Occom's *A Sermon Preached at the Execution of Moses Paul, an Indian* (1772) and *A Choice Collection of Spiritual Hymns and Songs* (1774). Occom was born in a Connecticut Mohegan village at a time when encroachment by colonists was making it impossible for the tribe to maintain its traditional lifeways. He followed his mother's decision to convert to Christianity and entered Eleazar Wheelock's school in Lebanon, New Hampshire (the forerunner of Dartmouth College). After four years of study, during which he learned to read and write English, Occom began a career as a teacher and minister, working in the Native American communities of New England. He moved to Long Island, where for eleven years he kept a school for the children of thirty-two Montauk families who were able to support him only with donations of food and labor. In 1765, on the suggestion of the great evangelist George Whitefield, Occom set out on a tour of England, where he preached before more than 300 congregations and collected as much as £12,000 for Wheelock's Indian Charity School.

On his return to the colonies, having been lionized abroad, Occom was newly outraged at the treatment of Native Americans, and he dedicated himself to pursuing better conditions for his people. For the last two decades of his life, he worked to found a settlement in Brothertown, New York, where converted New England Indians could unite. He continued to work tirelessly to teach literacy, which he saw as the most important tool for survival in colonial society.

Occom's narrative of his life, dated September 17, 1768, was written in response to a slander campaign mounted by enemies who hoped to retaliate for his involvement in a Mohegan suit for the return of stolen land. More than two centuries passed before the manuscript was published for the first time after a researcher found it in the collections of Dartmouth University. Occom's work was immediately recognized as a deeply significant document, for it is one of the earliest examples of a text by a person of color that accuses racist Christians of hypocrisy. Moreover, Occom's years of experience as a preacher are clearly reflected in his masterful control of the tone and structure of his argument and in his use of vivid anecdotes to establish a warm rapport with his audience before he delivers an adamant, soul-stinging conclusion.

S. Occom's Account of Himself Written Sept. 17, 1768

Having seen and heard Several Representations in England and Scotland, by Some gentlemen in America, Concerning me, and finding many gross mistakes in their Account, I thought it my Duty to give a Short, Plain, and Honest Account of my Self, that those, who may hereafter see it may know the truth Concerning me.

That it is against my mind to give a History of myself whilst I am alive. Yet to do Justice to myself and to those who may desire to know Some thing concerning me, and for the Honor of Religion, I will venture to give a Short Narrative of my Life.

From my Birth till I received the Christian Religion

I was Born a Heathen and Brought up In Heathenism, till I was between 16 & 17 years of age, at a Place Calld *Mohegan*, in New London, Connecticut, in New England. My Parents Livd a wandering life, as did all the Indians at Mohegan, they Chiefly Depended upon Hunting, Fishing, & Fowling for their Living and had no Connection with the English, excepting to Traffic with them in their small Trifles; and they Strictly maintained and followed their Heathenish Ways, Customs & Religion, though there was Some Preaching among them. Once a Fortnight, in ye Summer Season, a Minister from New London used to come up, and the Indians to attend; not that they regarded the Christian Religion, but they had Blankets given to them every Fall of the Year and for these things they would attend and there was a Sort of School kept, when I was quite young, but I believe there never was one that ever Learnt to read any thing,—and when I was about 10 Years of age there was a man who went about among the Indian Wigwams, and wherever he Could find the Indian Children, would make them read; but the Children Used to take Care to keep out of his way;—and he used to Catch me Some times and make me Say over my Letters; and I believe I learnt Some of them. But this was Soon over too; and all this Time there was not one amongst us, that made a Profession of Christianity—Neither did we Cultivate our Land, nor kept any Sort of Creatures except Dogs, which we used in Hunting; and we Dwelt in Wigwams. These are a Sort of Tents, Covered with Matts, made of Flags. And to this Time we were unaquainted with the English Tongue in general though there were a few, who understood a little of it.

From the Time of our Reformation till I left Mr. Wheelock's

When I was 16 years of age, we heard a Strange Rumor among the English, that there were Extraordinary Ministers Preaching from Place to Place and a Strange Concern among the White People. This was in the Spring of the Year. But we Saw nothing of these things, till Some Time in the Summer, when Some Ministers began to visit us and Preach the Word of God; and the Common People all Came frequently and exhorted us to the things of God, which it pleased the Lord, as I humbly hope, to Bless and accompany with Divine Influences to the Conviction and Saving Conversion of a Number of us; amongst whom I was one that was Imprest with the things we had heard. These Preachers did not only come to us, but we frequently went to their meetings and Churches. After I was awakened, I went to all the meetings, I could come at; & Continued under Trouble of Mind about 6 months; at which time I began to Learn the English Letters; got me a Primmer, and used to go to my English Neighbours frequently for Assistance in Reading, but went to no School. And when I was 17 years of age, I had, as I trust, a Discovery of the way of Salvation through Jesus Christ, and was enabl'd to put my trust in him alone for Life & Salvation. From this Time the Distress and Burden of my mind was removed, and I found Serenity and Pleasure of Soul, in Serving God. By this time I just began to Read in the New Testament without Spelling,—and I had a Stronger Desire Still to Learn to read the Word of God, and at the Same Time had an uncommon Pity and Compassion to my Poor Brethren According to the Flesh. I used to wish I was capable of Instructing my poor Kindred. I used to think, if I Could once Learn to Read I would Instruct the poor Children in Reading,—and used frequently to talk with our Indians Concerning Religion. This continued till I was in my 19th year: by this Time I Could Read a bit in the Bible. At this Time my Poor Mother was going to Lebanon, and having had Some Knowledge of Mr. *Wheelock* and hearing he had a Number of English youth under his Tuition, I had a great Inclination to go to him and be with him a week or a Fortnight, and Desired my Mother to Ask Mr. Wheelock, Whether he would take me a little while to Instruct me in Reading. Mother did so; and when She Came Back, She Said Mr. Wheelock wanted to See me as Soon as possible. So I went up, thinking I Should be back again in a few Days; when I got up there, he received me With kindness and Compassion and in Stead of Staying a Forthnight or 3 Weeks, I Spent 4 Years with him.—After I had been with him Some Time, he began to acquaint his Friends of my being with him, and of his Intentions of Educating me, and my Circumstances. And the good People began to give Some Assistance to Mr. Wheelock, and gave me Some old and Some New Clothes. Then he represented the Case to the Honorable Commissioners at Boston, who were Commission'd by the Honourable Society in London for Propagating the gospel among the Indians in New England and parts adjacent, and they allowed him 60£ in old Tenor, which was about 6£ Sterling, and they Continu'd it 2 or 3 years, I can't tell exactly.—While I was at Mr. Wheelock's, I was very weakly and my Health much impaired, and at the End of 4 Years, I over Strained my Eyes to such a Degree, I Could not persue my Studies any Longer; and out of these 4 years I Lost Just about one year;—And was obliged to quit my Studies.

From the Time I left Mr. Wheelock till I went to Europe

As soon as I left Mr. Wheelock, I endeavored to find Some Employ among the Indians; went to Nahantuck, thinking they may want a School Master, but they had one; then went to Narraganset, and they were Indifferent about a School, and went back to Mohegan, and heard a number of our Indians were going to *Montauk*, on Long Island,—and I went with them, and the Indians there were very desirous to have me keep a School amongst them, and I Consented, and went back a while to Mohegan and Some time in November I went on the Island, I think it is 17 years ago last November. I agreed to keep School with them Half a Year, and left it with them to give me what they Pleased; and they took turns to Provide Food for me. I had near 30 Scholars this

winter; I had an evening School too for those that could not attend the Day School—
and began to Carry on their meetings, they had a Minister, one Mr. *Horton*, the Scotch
Society's Missionary; but he Spent, I think two thirds of his Time at Sheenecock, 30
Miles from Montauk. We met together 3 times for Divine Worship every Sabbath and
once on every Wednesday evening. I [used] to read the Scriptures to them and used to
expound upon Some particular Passages in my own Tongue. Visited the Sick and
attended their Burials.—When the half year expired, they Desired me to Continue
with them, which I complied with, for another half year, when I had fulfilled that, they
were urgent to have me Stay Longer, So I continued amongst them till I was Married,
which was about 2 years after I went there. And Continued to Instruct them in the
Same manner as I did before. After I was married a while, I found there was need of a
Support more than I needed while I was Single,—and I made my Case Known to Mr.
Buell and to Mr. *Wheelock* and also the Needy Circumstances and the Desires of these
Indians of my Continuence amongst them and Mr. *Wheelock* and other gentlemen
Represented my Circumstances and the Desires of these Indians of my Continuence
amongst them, and the Commissioners were so good as to grant £15 a year Sterling—
And I kept on in my Service as usual, yea I had additional Service; I kept School as I
did before and Carried on the Religious Meetings as often as ever, and attended the
Sick and their Funerals, and did what Writings they wanted, and often Sat as a judge
to reconcile and Decide their Matters Between them, and had visitors of Indians from
all Quarters; and, as our Custom is, we freely Entertain all Visitors. And was fetched
often from my Tribe and from others to see into their Affairs Both Religious,
Temporal,—Besides my Domestick Concerns. And it Pleased the Lord to Increase my
Family fast—and Soon after I was Married, Mr. *Horton* left these Indians and the
Shenecock Indians & after this I was licensed to preach and then I had the whole care
of these Indians at Montauk, and visited the Shenecock Indians often. Used to Set out
Saturdays towards Night and come back again Mondays. I have been obliged to Set out
from Home after Sun Set, and Ride 30 Miles in the Night, to Preach to these Indians.—
And Some Indians at Shenecock Sent their Children to my School at Montauk; I kept
one of them Some Time, and had a Young Man a half year from Mohegan, a Lad from
Nahantuck, who was with me almost a year; and had little or nothing for keeping them.

My Method in the School was, as Soon as the Children got together, and took
their proper Seats, I Prayed with them, then began to hear them. I generally began
(after some of them Could Spell and Read,) With those that were yet in their
Alphabets, So around, as they were properly Seated till I got through and I obliged
them to Study their Books, and to help one another. When they could not make
out a hard word they Brought it to me—and I usually heard them, in the Summer
Season 8 Times a Day 4 in the morning, and in ye after Noon.—In the Winter
Season 6 Times a Day, As Soon as they could Spell, they were obliged to Spell
when ever they wanted to go out. I concluded with Prayer; I generally heard my
Evening Scholars 3 Times Round, And as they go out the School, every one, that
Can Spell, is obliged to Spell a Word, and to go out Leisurely one after another. I
Catechised 3 or 4 Times a Week according to the Assembly's Shorter Catechism,
and many Times Proposed Questions of my own, and in my own Tongue. I found
Difficulty with Some Children, who were Some what Dull, most of these can soon
learn to Say over their Letters, they Distinguish the Sounds by the Ear, but their
Eyes can't Distinguish the Letters, and the way I took to cure them was by making

an Alphabet on Small bits of paper, and glued them on Small Chips of Cedar after this manner A B &c. I put these Letters in order on a Bench then point to one Letter and bid a Child to take notice of it, and then I order the Child to fetch me the Letter from the Bench; if he Brings the Letter, it is well, if not he must go again and again till he brings ye right Letter. When they can bring any Letters this way, then I just jumble them together, and bid them to set them in Alphabetical order, and it is a Pleasure to them; and they soon Learn their Letters this way.—I frequently Discussed or Exhorted my Scholars, in Religious matters.—My Method in our Religious Meetings was this; Sabbath Morning we Assemble together about 10 o'C and begin with Singing; we generally Sung Dr. Watt's Psalms or Hymns. I distinctly read the Psalm or Hymn first, and then gave the meaning of it to them, after that Sing, then Pray, and Sing again after Prayer. Then proceed to Read from Suitable portion of Scripture, and so just give the plain Sense of it in Familiar Discourse and apply it to them. So continued with Prayer and Singing. In the after Noon and Evening we Proceed in the Same Manner, and so in Wednesday Evening. Some Time after Mr. Horton left these Indians, there was a remarkable revival of religion among these Indians and many were hopefully converted to the Saving knowledge of God in Jesus. It is to be observed before Mr. Horton left these Indians they had Some Prejudices infused in their minds, by Some Enthusiastical Exhorters from New England, against Mr. Horton, and many of them had left him; by this means he was Discouraged; and Sued a Dismission and was dismissed from these Indians. And being acquainted with the Enthusiasts in New England: & the make and the Disposition of the Indians I took a mild way to reclaim them. I opposed them not openly but let them go on in their way, and whenever I had an opportunity, I would read Such pages of the Scriptures, and I thought would confound their Notions, and I would come to them with all Authority, Saying, "thus Saith the Lord"; and by this means, the Lord was pleased to Bless my poor Endeavours, and they were reclaimed, and Brought to hear almost any of the ministers.—I am now to give an Account of my Circumstances and manner of Living. I Dwelt in a Wigwam, a Small Hut with Small Poles and Covered with Matts made of Flags, and I was obliged to remove twice a Year, about 2 miles Distance, by reason of the Scarcity of wood, for in one Neck of Land they Planted their Corn, and in another, they had their wood, and I was obligd to have my Corn carted and my Hay also,— and I got my Ground Plow'd every year, which Cost me about 12 shillings an acre; and I kept a Cow and a Horse, for which I paid 21 shillings every year York currency, and went 18 miles to Mill for every Dust of meal we used in my family. I Hired or joined with my Neighbours to go to Mill, with a Horse or ox Cart, or on Horse Back, and Some time went myself. My Family Increasing fast, and my Visitors also. I was obliged to contrive every way to Support my Family; I took all opportunities, to get Some thing to feed my Family Daily. I Planted my own Corn, Potatoes, and Beans; I used to be out hoeing my Corn Some times before Sun Rise and after my School is Dismist, and by this means I was able to raise my own Pork, for I was allowed to keep 5 Swine. Some mornings & Evenings I would be out with my Hook and Line to Catch fish and in the Fall of Year and in the Spring, I used my gun, and fed my Family with Fowls. I Could more than pay for my Powder & Shot with Feathers. At other Times I Bound old Books for Easthampton People, made wooden Spoons and Ladles, Stocked Guns, & worked on Cedar to make

Pails, Piggins, and Churns &c. Besides all these Difficulties I met with adverse Providence. I bought a Mare, had it but a little while, and she fell into the Quick Sand and Died. After a while Bought another, I kept her about half year, and she was gone, and I never have heard of nor Seen her from that Day to this; it was Supposed Some Rogue Stole her. I got another and Died with a Distemper, and last of all I Bought a Young Mare, and kept her till She had one Colt, and She broke her Leg and Died, and Presently after the Colt Died also. In the whole I Lost 5 Horse Kind; all these Losses helped to pull me down; and by this Time I got greatly in Debt, and acquainted my Circumstances to Some of my Friends, and they Represented my Case to the Commissioners of Boston, and Interceded with them for me, and they were pleased to vote 15£ for my Help, and Soon after Sent a Letter to my good Friend at New London, acquainting him that they had Superseded their Vote; and my Friends were so good as to represent my Needy Circumstances Still to them, and they were so good at Last, as to Vote £15 and Sent it, for which I am very thankful; and the Revd Mr. *Buell* was so kind as to write in my behalf to the gentlemen of Boston; and he told me they were much Displeased with him, and heard also once again that they blamed me for being Extravagant; I Can't Conceive how these gentlemen would have me Live. I am ready to impute it to their Ignorance, and I would wish they had Changed Circumstances with me but one month, that they may know, by experience what my Case really was; but I am now fully convinced, that it was not Ignorance, For I believe it can be proved to the world that these Same Gentlemen gave a young Missionary a Single man, *one Hundred Pounds* for one year, and fifty Pounds for an Interpreter, and thirty Pounds for an Introducer; so it Cost them one Hundred & Eighty Pounds in one Single Year, and they Sent too where there was no Need of a Missionary.

Now you See what difference they made between me and other missionaries; they gave me 180 Pounds for 12 years Service, which they gave for one years Services in another Mission.—In my Service (I speak like a fool, but I am Constrained) I was my own Interpreter. I was both a School master and Minister to the Indians, yea I was their Ear, Eye & Hand, as Well as Mouth. I leave it with the World, as wicked as it is, to judge, whether I ought not to have had half as much, they gave a young man just mentioned which would have been but £50 a year; and if they ought to have given me that, I am not under obligations to them, I owe them nothing at all; what can be the Reason that they used me after this manner? I can't think of any thing, but this as a Poor Indian Boy Said, Who was Bound out to an English Family, and he used to Drive Plow for a young man, and he whipt and Beat him allmost every Day, and the young man found fault with him, and Complained of him to his master and the poor Boy was Called to answer for himself before his master, and he was asked, what it was he did, that he was So Complained of and beat almost every Day. He Said, he did not know, but he Supposed it was because he could not drive any better; but says he, I Drive as well as I know how; and at other Times he Beats me, because he is of a mind to beat me; but says he believes he Beats me for the most of the Time "because I am an Indian".

So I am *ready* to Say, they have used me thus, because I Can't Influence the Indians so well as other missionaries; but I can *assure them* I have endeavoured to teach them as well as I know how;—but I *must Say*, "I believe it is because I am a poor Indian". I Can't help that God has made me So; I did not make my self so.—

—1768

Frances Brooke
c. 1724–1789

As Canada's and North America's first novelist, Frances Brooke has the distinction of wearing twin laurels. Born in England, Brooke lived in Canada intermittently from 1763 to 1768 while her husband, a chaplain, was posted to the British garrison at Quebec. Before her arrival in Canada, Brooke had already established herself as a literary force in London, editing a weekly journal called *The Old Maid* under the pseudonym Mary Singleton, Spinster. She also had considerable literary connections, counting many prominent English writers among her friends, including Samuel Johnson, James Boswell, Anna Seward, Oliver Goldsmith, and Fanny Burney.

Born to an Anglican clergyman, Brooke was raised in small towns in rural Lincolnshire before moving to London at age twenty-four in 1748. By the mid-1750s, she was known for her efforts in contributions to *The Old Maid* and for forays into theater. An early drama, *Virginia* (1756), was rejected by Richard Garrick, the owner of London's Drury Lane Theatre, because the market was flooded with new productions about the New World. Undeterred, Brooke tried her hand at writing novels. Her first effort, the epistolary novel *The History of Julia Mandeville* (1763), may have been influenced by her own correspondence-shaped life: Until her departure for Canada in 1763 to join her husband, the two corresponded steadily after his settlement in Quebec in 1760. Brooke spent five years in Canada, and the active social life she enjoyed there, as well as her eye for natural and cultural detail, shaped the novel she published shortly after her return to permanent residence in England.

The History of Emily Montague (1769) is a true transatlantic novel—combining the literary forms of the Old World (the novel of sensibility) with the scenes and sounds of the New. In this epistolary novel set in Quebec, Brooke records the exchange between two lovers, Colonel Rivers and Emily Montague, as well as numerous political and cultural observations on life in the colony (on taxation, native Canadians, freedom of religion). She also addresses a series of balanced themes: man versus nature, male versus female, the urban versus the rural, and civilization versus savagery. *The History of Emily Montague* is characterized by Brooke's keen eye for geographic details and for the political climate of late eighteenth-century Quebec—the tension between the local French citizenry and the occupying British military and administrative force. These New World details, combined with the conventions of an established genre, the epistolary novel, are designed to appeal to the British audience Brooke has in mind. On the one hand, she can genuinely marvel at the natural splendor of the St. Lawrence River and Montmorenci Falls, yet, on the other, she can meet what she surely anticipates are the expectations of readers who have not seen such scenery for themselves. Brooke revels in the novelty of the season's extreme frigidity: "the cold is beyond all the thermometers here." Exaggeration quickly builds into playful hyperbole as she describes a climate that dulls the creative and physical senses: "the rigor of the climate suspends the very powers of the understanding; what then must become of the imagination." Matters become more serious though as she acknowledges that the winters are so sharp as to threaten life itself: "the cold is so amazingly intense as almost totally to stop respiration." The transatlantic appeal of Brooke's descriptions of the Canadian frontier was tremendous: Her novel ran through six editions in England and Ireland from 1769 to 1786.

from The History of Emily Montague

LETTER V.

To Miss Rivers, Clarges Street.

Quebec, July 4.

What an inconstant animal is man! do you know, Lucy, I begin to be tir'd of the lovely landscape round me? I have enjoy'd from it all the pleasure meer inanimate objects can give, and find 'tis a pleasure that soon satiates, if not relieved by others which are more lively. The scenery is to be sure divine, but one grows weary of meer scenery: the most enchanting prospect soon loses its power of pleasing, when the eye is accustom'd to it: we gaze at first transported on the charms of nature, and fancy they will please for ever; but, alas! it will not do; we sigh for society, the conversation of those dear to us; the more animated pleasures of the heart. There are fine women, and men of merit here; but, as the affections are not in our power, I have not yet felt my heart gravitate towards any of them. I must absolutely set in earnest about my set-tlement, in order to emerge from the state of vegetation into which I seem falling.

But to your last: you ask me a particular account of the convents here. Have you an inclination, my dear, to turn nun? if you have, you could not have applied to a properer person; my extreme modesty and reserve, and my speaking French, having made me already a great favourite with the older part of all the three com-munities, who unanimously declare colonel Rivers to be *un tres aimable homme*,[1] and have given me an unlimited liberty of visiting them whenever I please: they now and then treat *me* with a sight of some of the young ones, but this is a favor not allow'd to all the world.

There are three religious houses at Quebec, so you have choice; the Ursulines, the Hotel Dieu, and the General Hospital.[2] The first is the severest order in the Romish church, except that very cruel one which denies its fair votaries the ines-timable liberty of speech. The house is large and handsome, but has an air of gloomi-ness, with which the black habit, and the livid paleness of the nuns, extremely corresponds. The church is, contrary to the style of the rest of the convent, orna-mented and lively to the last degree. The superior is an English-woman of good fam-ily, who was taken prisoner by the savages when a child, and plac'd here by the generosity of a French officer. She is one of the most amiable women I ever knew, with a benevolence in her countenance which inspires all who see her with affection: I am very fond of her conversation, tho' sixty and a nun.

The Hotel Dieu is very pleasantly situated, with a view of the two rivers, and the entrance of the port: the house is chearful, airy, and agreeable; the habit extremely becoming, a circumstance a handsome woman ought by no means to overlook; 'tis white with a black gauze veil, which would shew your complexion to great advantage. The order is much less severe than the Ursulines, and I might add, much more use-ful, their province being the care of the sick: the nuns of this house are sprightly, and have a look of health which is wanting at the Ursulines.

---

1. A very likeable man.   2. Three orders of Catholic nuns.

The General Hospital, situated about a mile out of town, on the borders of the river St. Charles, is much the most agreeable of the three. The order and the habit are the same with the Hotel Dieu, except that to the habit is added the cross, generally worn in Europe by canonesses only: a distinction procur'd for them by their founder, St. Vallier, the second bishop of Quebec. The house is, without, a very noble building; and neatness, elegance and propriety reign within. The nuns, who are all of the noblesse, are many of them handsome, and all genteel, lively, and well bred; they have an air of the world, their conversation is easy, spirited, and polite: with them you almost forget the recluse in the woman of condition. In short, you have the best nuns at the Ursulines, the most agreeable women at the General Hospital: all however have an air of chagrin, which they in vain endeavour to conceal; and the general eagerness with which they tell you unask'd they are happy, is a strong proof of the contrary.

Tho' the most indulgent of all men to the follies of others, especially such as have their source in mistaken devotion; tho' willing to allow all the world to play the fool their own way, yet I cannot help being fir'd with a degree of zeal against an institution equally incompatible with public good, and private happiness; an institution which cruelly devotes beauty and innocence to slavery, regret, and wretchedness; to a more irksome imprisonment than the severest laws inflict on the worst of criminals.

Could any thing but experience, my dear Lucy, make it be believ'd possible that there should be rational beings, who think they are serving the God of mercy by inflicting on themselves voluntary tortures, and cutting themselves off from that state of society in which he has plac'd them, and for which they were form'd? by renouncing the best affections of the human heart, the tender names of friend, of wife, of mother? and, as far as in them lies, counterworking creation? by spurning from them every amusement however innocent, by refusing the gifts of that beneficent power who made us to be happy, and destroying his most precious gifts, health, beauty, sensibility, chearfulness, and peace!

My indignation is yet awake, from having seen a few days since at the Ursulines, an extreme lovely young girl, whose countenance spoke a soul form'd for the most lively, yet delicate, ties of love and friendship, led by a momentary enthusiasm, or perhaps by a childish vanity artfully excited, to the foot of those altars, which she will probably too soon bathe with the bitter tears of repentance and remorse.

The ceremony, form'd to strike the imagination, and seduce the heart of unguarded youth, is extremely solemn and affecting; the procession of the nuns, the sweetness of their voices in the choir, the dignified devotion with which the charming enthusiast received the veil, and took the cruel vow which shut her from the world for ever, struck my heart in spite of my reason, and I felt myself touch'd even to tears by a superstition I equally pity and despise.

I am not however certain it was the ceremony which affected me thus strongly; it was impossible not to feel for this amiable victim; never was there an object more interesting; her form was elegance itself; her air and motion animated and graceful; the glow of pleasure was on her cheek, the fire of enthusiasm in her eyes, which are the finest I ever saw: never did I see joy so livelily painted on the countenance of the happiest bride; she seem'd to walk in air; her whole person look'd more than human.

An enemy to every species of superstition, I must however allow it to be least destructive to true virtue in your gentle sex, and therefore to be indulg'd with least danger: the superstition of men is gloomy and ferocious; it lights the fire, and points the dagger of the assassin; whilst that of women takes its color from the sex; is soft, mild, and benevolent; exerts itself in acts of kindness and charity, and seems only substituting the love of God to that of man.

Who can help admiring, whilst they pity, the foundress of the Ursuline convent, Madame de la Peltrie, to whom the very colony in some measure owes its existence? young, rich and lovely; a widow in the bloom of life, mistress of her own actions, the world was gay before her, yet she left all the pleasures that world could give, to devote her days to the severities of a religion she thought the only true one: she dar'd the dangers of the sea, and the greater dangers of a savage people; she landed on an unknown shore, submitted to the extremities of cold and heat, of thirst and hunger, to perform a service she thought acceptable to the Deity. To an action like this, however mistaken the motive, bigotry alone will deny praise: the man of candor will only lament that minds capable of such heroic virtue are not directed to views more conducive to their own and the general happiness.

I am unexpectedly call'd this moment, my dear Lucy, on some business to Montreal, from whence you shall hear from me.

ADIEU!

ED. RIVERS.

LETTER VI

To Miss Rivers, Clarges Street.

Montreal, July 9.

I am arriv'd, my dear, and have brought my heart safe thro' such a continued fire as never poor knight errant was exposed to; waited on at every stage by blooming country girls, full of spirit and coquetry, without any of the village bashfulness of England, and dressed like the shepherdesses of romance. A man of adventure might make a pleasant journey to Montreal.

The peasants are ignorant, lazy, dirty, and stupid beyond all belief; but hospitable, courteous, civil; and, what is particularly agreeable, they leave their wives and daughters to do the honors of the house: in which obliging office they acquit themselves with an attention, which, amidst every inconvenience apparent (tho' I am told not real) poverty can cause, must please every guest who has a soul inclin'd to be pleas'd: for my part, I was charm'd with them, and eat my homely fare with as much pleasure as if I had been feasting on ortolans[3] in a palace. Their conversation is lively and amusing; all the little knowledge of Canada is confined to the sex; very few, even of the seigneurs, being able to write their own names.

The road from Quebec to Montreal is almost a continued street, the villages being numerous, and so extended along the banks of the river St. Lawrence as to leave scarce a space without houses in view; except where here or there a river, a wood, or mountain intervenes, as if to give a more pleasing variety to the scene. I don't remember ever having had a more agreeable journey; the fine prospects of the day so enliven'd by the gay chat of the evening, that I was really sorry when I approach'd Montreal.

The island of Montreal, on which the town stands, is a very lovely spot; highly cultivated, and tho' less wild and magnificent, more smiling than the country round

---

3. Small game birds.

Quebec: the ladies, who seem to make pleasure their only business, and most of whom I have seen this morning driving about the town in calashes,[4] and making what they call, the *tour de la ville*, attended by English officers, seem generally handsome, and have an air of sprightliness with which I am charm'd; I must be acquainted with them all, for tho' my stay is to be short, I see no reason why it should be dull. I am told they are fond of little rural balls in the country, and intend to give one as soon as I have paid my respects in form.

Six in the evening.

I am just come from dining with the ____ regiment, and find I have a visit to pay I was not aware of, to two English ladies who are a few miles out of town: one of them is wife to the major of the regiment, and the other just going to be married to a captain in it, Sir George Clayton, a young handsome baronet, just come to his title and a very fine estate, by the death of a distant relation: he is at present at New York, and I am told they are to be married as soon as he comes back.

Eight o'clock.

I have been making some flying visits to the French ladies; tho' I have not seen many beauties, yet in general the women are handsome; their manner is easy and obliging, they make the most of their charms by their vivacity, and I certainly cannot be displeas'd with their extreme partiality for the English officers; their own men, who indeed are not very attractive, have not the least chance for any share in their good graces.

Thursday morning.

I am just setting out with a friend for Major Melmoth's, to pay my compliments to the two ladies: I have no relish for this visit; I hate misses that are going to be married; they are always so full of the dear man, that they have not common civility to other people. I am told however both the ladies are agreeable.

14th. Eight in the evening.

Agreeable, Lucy! she is an angel: 'tis happy for me she is engag'd; nothing else could secure my heart, of which you know I am very tenacious: only think of finding beauty, delicacy, sensibility, all that can charm in woman, hid in a wood in Canada!

You say I am given to be enthusiastic in my approbations, but she is really charming. I am resolv'd not only to have a friendship for her myself, but that *you* shall, and have told her so; she comes to England as soon as she is married; you are form'd to love each other.

But I must tell you; Major Melmoth kept us a week at his house in the country, in one continued round of rural amusements; by which I do not mean hunting and shooting, but such pleasures as the ladies could share; little rustic balls and parties round the neighbouring country, in which parties we were joined by all the fine women at Montreal. Mrs. Melmoth is a very pleasing, genteel brunette, but Emily Montague—you will say I am in love with her if I describe her, and yet I declare to you I am not: knowing she loves another, to whom she is soon to be united, I see her charms with the same kind of pleasure I do yours; a pleasure, which, tho' extremely lively, is by our situation without the least mixture of desire.

I have said, she is charming; there are men here who do not think so, but to me she is loveliness itself. My ideas of beauty are perhaps a little out of the common road:

---

4. Small carriages.

I hate a woman of whom every man coldly says, *she is handsome*; I adore beauty, but it is not meer features or complexion to which I give that name; 'tis life, 'tis spirit, 'tis animation, 'tis—in one word, 'tis Emily Montague—without being regularly beautiful, she charms every sensible heart; all other women, however lovely, appear marble statues near her: fair; pale (a paleness which gives the idea of delicacy without destroying that of health), with dark hair and eyes, the latter large and languishing, she seems made to feel to a trembling excess the passion she cannot fail of inspiring: her elegant form has an air of softness and languor, which seizes the whole soul in a moment: her eyes, the most intelligent I ever saw, hold you enchain'd by their bewitching sensibility.

There are a thousand unspeakable charms in her conversation; but what I am most pleas'd with, is the attentive politeness of her manner, which you seldom see in a person in love; the extreme desire of pleasing one man generally taking off greatly from the attention due to all the rest. This is partly owing to her admirable understanding, and partly to the natural softness of her soul, which gives her the strongest desire of pleasing. As I am a philosopher in these matters, and have made the heart my study, I want extremely to see her with her lover, and to observe the gradual encrease of her charms in his presence; love, which embellishes the most unmeaning countenance, must give to her's a fire irresistible: what eyes! when animated by tenderness!

The very soul acquires a new force and beauty by loving; a woman of honor never appears half so amiable, or displays half so many virtues, as when sensible to the merit of a man who deserves her affection. Observe, Lucy, I shall never allow you to be handsome till I hear you are in love.

Did I tell you Emily Montague had the finest hand and arm in the world? I should however have excepted yours: her tone of voice too has the same melodious sweetness, a perfection without which the loveliest woman could never make the least impression on my heart: I don't think you are very unlike upon the whole, except that she is paler. You know, Lucy, you have often told me I should certainly have been in love with you if I had not been your brother: this resemblance is a proof you were right. You are really as handsome as any woman can be whose sensibility has never been put in motion.

I am to give a ball to-morrow; Mrs. Melmoth is to have the honors of it, but as she is with child, she does not dance. This circumstance has produc'd a dispute not a little flattering to my vanity: the ladies are making interest to dance with me; what a happy exchange have I made! what man of common sense would stay to be overlook'd in England, who can have rival beauties contend for him in Canada? This important point is not yet settled; the *etiquette* here is rather difficult to adjust; as to me, I have nothing to do in the consultation; my hand is destin'd to the longest pedigree; we stand prodigiously on our noblesse at Montreal.

Four o'clock.

After a dispute in which two French ladies were near drawing their husbands into a duel, the point of honor is yielded by both to Miss Montague; each insisting only that I should not dance with the other: for my part, I submit with a good grace, as you will suppose.

Saturday morning.

I never passed a more agreeable evening: we have our amusements here, I assure you: a set of fine young fellows, and handsome women, all well dress'd, and in humor with themselves, and with each other: my lovely Emily like Venus amongst the

Graces, only multiplied to about sixteen. Nothing is, in my opinion, so favorable to the display of beauty as a ball. A state of rest is ungraceful; all nature is most beautiful in motion; trees agitated by the wind, a ship under sail, a horse in the course, a fine woman dancing: never any human being had such an aversion to still life as I have.

I am going back to Melmoth's for a month; don't be alarm'd, Lucy! I see all her perfections, but I see them with the cold eye of admiration only: a woman engaged loses all her attractions as a woman; there is no love without a ray of hope: my only ambition is to be her friend; I want to be the confidant of her passion. With what spirit such a mind as hers must love!

ADIEU! MY DEAR!

YOURS,

ED. RIVERS.

* * *

LETTER X.

Silleri, August 24.

I have been a month arrived, my dear, without having seen your brother, who is at Montreal, but I am told is expected to-day. I have spent my time however very agreeably. I know not what the winter may be, but I am enchanted with the beauty of this country in summer; bold, picturesque, romantic, nature reigns here in all her wanton luxuriance, adorned by a thousand wild graces which mock the cultivated beauties of Europe. The scenery about the town is infinitely lovely; the prospect extensive, and diversified by a variety of hills, woods, rivers, cascades, intermingled with smiling farms and cottages, and bounded by distant mountains which seem to scale the very Heavens.

The days are much hotter here than in England, but the heat is more supportable from the breezes which always spring up about noon; and the evenings are charming beyond expression. We have much thunder and lightening, but very few instances of their being fatal: the thunder is more magnificent and aweful than in Europe, and the lightening brighter and more beautiful; I have even seen it of a clear pale purple, resembling the gay tints of the morning.

The verdure is equal to that of England, and in the evening acquires an unspeakable beauty from the lucid splendor of the fire-flies sparkling like a thousand little stars on the trees and on the grass.

There are two very noble falls of water near Quebec, la Chaudiere and Montmorenci: the former is a prodigious sheet of water, rushing over the wildest rocks, and forming a scene grotesque, irregular, astonishing: the latter, less wild, less irregular, but more pleasing and more majestic, falls from an immense height, down the side of a romantic mountain, into the river St. Lawrence, opposite the most smiling part of the island of Orleans, to the cultivated charms of which it forms the most striking and agreeable contrast.

The river of the same name, which supplies the cascade of Montmorenci, is the most lovely of all inanimate objects; but why do I call it inanimate? It almost breathes; I no longer wonder at the enthusiasm of Greece and Rome; 'twas from objects resembling this their mythology took its rise; it seems the residence of a thousand deities.

Paint to yourself a stupendous rock burst as it were in sunder by the hands of nature, to give passage to a small, but very deep and beautiful river; and forming on each side a regular and magnificent wall, crowned with the noblest woods that can be imagined; the sides of these romantic walls adorned with a variety of the gayest flowers, and in many places little streams of the purest water gushing through, and losing themselves in the river below: a thousand natural grottoes in the rock make you suppose yourself in the abode of the Nereids[5]; as a little island, covered with flowering shrubs, about a mile above the falls, where the river enlarges itself as if to give it room, seems intended for the throne of the river goddess. Beyond this, the rapids, formed by the irregular projections of the rock, which in some places seem almost to meet, rival in beauty, as they excel in variety, the cascade itself, and close this little world of enchantment.

In short, the loveliness of this fairy scene alone more than pays the fatigues of my voyage; and, if I ever murmur at having crossed the Atlantic, remind me that I have seen the river Montmorenci.

I can give you a very imperfect account of the people here; I have only examined the landscape about Quebec, and have given very little attention to the figures; the French ladies are handsome, but as to the beaux, they appear to me not at all dangerous, and one might safely walk in a wood by moonlight with the most agreeable Frenchman here. I am not surprized the Canadian ladies take such pains to seduce our men from us; but I think it a little hard we have no temptation to make reprisals.

I am at present at an extreme pretty farm on the banks of the river St. Lawrence; the house stands at the foot of a steep mountain covered with a variety of trees, forming a verdant sloping wall, which rises in a kind of regular confusion,
"Shade above shade, a woody theatre,"[6]
and has in front this noble river, on which the ships continually passing present to the delighted eye the most charming moving picture imaginable; I never saw a place so formed to inspire that pleasing lassitude, that divine inclination to saunter, which may not improperly be called, the luxurious indolence of the country. I intend to build a temple here to the charming goddess of laziness.

A gentleman is just coming down the winding path on the side of the hill, whom by his air I take to be your brother. Adieu! I must receive him: my father is at Quebec.

YOURS,

ARABELLA FERMOR.

* * *

LETTER XXI.

To John Temple, Esq; Pall Mall.

Montreal, Sept. 24.

What you say, my dear friend, is more true than I wish it was; our English women of character are generally too reserved; their manner is cold and forbidding; they seem to think it a crime to be too attractive; they appear almost afraid to please.

'Tis to this ill-judged reserve I attribute the low profligacy of too many of our young men; the grave faces and distant behaviour of the generality of virtuous women fright them from their acquaintance, and drive them into the society of those wretched votaries of vice, whose conversation debases every sentiment of their souls.

---

5. In Greek myth, sea nymphs who aid sailors.   6. John Milton (1608–1674), *Paradise Lost* (1667), 4.141.

With as much beauty, good sense, sensibility, and softness, at least, as any women on earth, no women please so little as the English: depending on their native charms, and on those really amiable qualities which envy cannot deny them, they are too careless in acquiring those enchanting nameless graces, which no language can define, which give resistless force to beauty, and even supply its place where it is wanting.

They are satisfied with being good, without considering that unadorned virtue may command esteem, but will never excite love; and both are necessary in marriage, which I suppose to be the state every woman of honor has in prospect; for I own myself rather incredulous as to the assertions of maiden aunts and cousins to the contrary. I wish my amiable country-women would consider one moment, that virtue is never so lovely as when dressed in smiles: the virtue of women should have all the softness of the sex; it should be gentle, it should be even playful, to please.

There is a lady here, whom I wish you to see, as the shortest way of explaining to you all I mean; she is the most pleasing woman I ever beheld, independently of her being one of the handsomest; her manner is irresistible: she has all the smiling graces of France, all the blushing delicacy and native softness of England.

Nothing can be more delicate, my dear Temple, than the manner in which you offer me your estate in Rutland, by way of anticipating your intended legacy: it is however impossible for me to accept it; my father, who saw me naturally more profuse than became my expectations, took such pains to counterwork it by inspiring me with the love of independence, that I cannot have such an obligation even to you.

Besides, your legacy is left on the supposition that you are not to marry, and I am absolutely determined you shall; so that, by accepting this mark of your esteem, I should be robbing your younger children.

I have not a wish to be richer whilst I am a batchelor, and the only woman I ever wished to marry, the only one my heart desires, will be in three weeks the wife of another; I shall spend less than my income here: shall I not then be rich? To make you easy, know I have four thousand pounds in the funds; and that, from the equality of living here, an ensign is obliged to spend near as much as I am; he is inevitably ruined, but I have money.

I pity you, my friend; I am hurt to hear you talk of happiness in the life you at present lead; of finding pleasure in possessing venal beauty; you are in danger of acquiring a habit which will vitiate your taste, and exclude you from that state of refined and tender friendship for which nature formed a heart like yours, and which is only to be found in marriage: I need not add, in a marriage of choice.

It has been said that love marriages are generally unhappy; nothing is more false; marriages of meer inclination will always be so: passion alone being concerned, when that is gratified, all tenderness ceases of course: but love, the gay child of sympathy and esteem, is, when attended by delicacy, the only happiness worth a reasonable man's pursuit, and the choicest gift of heaven: it is a softer, tenderer friendship, enlivened by taste, and by the most ardent desire of pleasing, which time, instead of destroying, will render every hour more dear and interesting.

If, as you possibly will, you should call me romantic, hear a man of pleasure on the subject, the Petronius[7] of the last age, the elegant, but voluptuous St. Evremond, who speaks in the following manner of the friendship between married persons:

---

7. Roman satirist of the first century A.D.

"I believe it is this pleasing intercourse of tenderness, this reciprocation of esteem, or, if you will, this mutual ardor of preventing each other in every endearing mark of affection, in which consists the sweetness of this second species of friendship.

"I do not speak of other pleasures, which are not so much in themselves as in the assurance they give of the intire possession of those we love: this appears to me so true, that I am not afraid to assert, the man who is by any other means certainly assured of the tenderness of her he loves, may easily support the privation of those pleasures; and that they ought not to enter into the account of friendship, but as proofs that it is without reserve.

"'Tis true, few men are capable of the purity of these sentiments, and 'tis for that reason we so very seldom see perfect friendship in marriage, at least for any long time: the object which a sensual passion has in view cannot long sustain a commerce so noble as that of friendship."

You see, the pleasures you so much boast are the least of those which true tenderness has to give, and this in the opinion of a voluptuary.

My dear Temple, all you have ever known of love is nothing to that sweet consent of souls in unison, that harmony of minds congenial to each other, of which you have not yet an idea.

You have seen beauty, and it has inspired a momentary emotion, but you have never yet had a real attachment; you yet know nothing of that irresistible tenderness, that delirium of the soul, which, whilst it refines, adds strength to passion.

I perhaps say too much, but I wish with ardor to see you happy; in which there is the more merit, as I have not the least prospect of being so myself.

I wish you to pursue the plan of life which I myself think most likely to bring happiness, because I know our souls to be of the same frame: we have taken different roads, but you will come back to mine. Awake to delicate pleasures, I have no taste for any other; there are no other for sensible minds. My gallantries have been few, rather (if it is allowed to speak thus of one's self even to a friend) from elegance of taste than severity of manners; I have loved seldom, because I cannot love without esteem.

Believe me, Jack, the meer pleasure of loving, even without a return, is superior to all the joys of sense where the heart is untouched: the French poet does not exaggerate when he says,

———Amour;
Tous les autres plaisirs ne valent pas tes peines.[8]

You will perhaps call me mad; I am just come from a woman who is capable of making all mankind so. Adieu!

                                              Yours,
                                              Ed. Rivers.

                                                     —1769

8. "Love, thy pains are worth more than all other pleasures."

Edmund Burke
1729–1797

Irish by birth, Burke called for abolishing restrictions imposed by the British government and the Church of England on the rights of Irish Catholics. A friend of Benjamin Franklin and other Americans, Burke also was an advocate for American independence. He used his considerable oratorical skills and his position as a Member of Parliament to champion American and Irish rights in a subtle way. It may come as a surprise, then, to learn that this champion of civil and national liberties abroad raised the ire of many Jacobins (English radicals who supported the French Revolution) at home, most notably feminist political philosopher Mary Wollstonecraft and poet William Wordsworth, who disagreed with his politics but greatly respected his skill as a rhetorician. The reason was Burke's *Reflections on the Revolution in France* (London, 1790; Philadelphia, 1792), a work that represented the French Revolution *not* as the outgrowth of freedoms sown by the American Revolution but as bloodthirsty anarchy that threatened the political and cultural traditions of England and its royalty. Burke feared that a violent English revolution by the people to establish a government of the people would result in barbaric mob rule, destroying the legacy of England's Glorious Revolution (1688) and its unwritten guarantee of civil liberties. He was also concerned that the French Revolution's initiatives in favor of women's rights would cross the Channel and destabilize England. According to Burke, the home is the microcosm of the nation, and if women leave the home, the domestic sphere—as well as its macrocosmic counterpart—will lose its center. This attitude explains why Wollstonecraft took issue with Burke in her famous *Vindication of the Rights of Woman* (1792).

Long before Burke attempted to bring gender to bear on politics, he brought it to bear on aesthetics and poetics. His first work was the widely influential *A Philosophical Enquiry into the Origin of Our Ideas of the Sublime and Beautiful* (London, 1757; Philadelphia, 1806). What embodied the sublime were great or terrible objects that simultaneously caused fear and admiration in the viewer. A large, rugged mountain, for instance, could be thought of as sublime. The beautiful, on the other hand, ultimately inspired love and was the opposite of the sublime: symmetrical, small, and pleasurable. Often, the sublime was seen in masculinity and the beautiful in femininity. Also, the sublime was often associated with racial otherness, creating an aesthetic that problematically naturalized whiteness and maleness. The Burkean sublime pervades British Romantic writing and landscape painting. Americans and Canadians also used Burke's terms, often modifying them to describe and depict the landscape of North America. For the traveler in search of picturesque views, a site like Niagara Falls, for instance, embodied sublimity and beauty on a scale unrivalled by European scenes.

After Burke's foray into the literary world with his work on the sublime and the beautiful, he set out on a political career, which began with his being made secretary to Lord Rockingham (1765–1782). As a Member of Parliament, Burke represented several areas in Britain: Wendover, Bristol, and Malton. Although Burke took up politics, he did not put down his pen, for he soon was using his considerable rhetorical skill to serve his political ends and allegiances. Among other works, he published *Speech of Edmund Burke, Esquire, on Moving His Resolutions for Conciliation with the Colonies* (London and New York, 1775). Though considerably more moderate in both politics and rhetoric than Thomas Paine's *Common Sense* (1776), Burke's speech does argue for the reform of Britain's finances and policies with regard to its American colonies. Clearly evoking the situation of his own people, the Irish, Burke tells

Parliament that the American colonies will never be content in a state of subordination and oppression. Peace can only be restored if Britain grants full civil rights to the colonists and acknowledges them as equals.

from A Philosophical Enquiry into the Origin of Our Ideas of the Sublime and Beautiful

The Sublime

Whatever is fitted in any sort to excite the ideas of pain and danger, that is to say, whatever is in any sort terrible, or is conversant about terrible objects, or operates in a manner analogous to terror, is a source of the *sublime*; that is, it is productive of the strongest emotion which the mind is capable of feeling. I say the strongest emotion, because I am satisfied the ideas of pain are much more powerful than those which enter on the part of pleasure. Without all doubt, the torments which we may be made to sufffer, are much greater in their effect on the body and mind, than any pleasures which the most learned voluptuary could suggest, or than the liveliest imagination, and the most sound and exquisitely sensible body, could enjoy. Nay I am in great doubt whether any man could be found who would earn a life of the most perfect satisfaction, at the price of ending it in the torments, which justice inflicted in a few hours on the late unfortunate regicide in France.[1] But as pain is stronger in its operation than pleasure, so death is in general a much more affecting idea than pain; because there are very few pains, however exquisite, which are not preferred to death; nay, what generally makes pain itself, if I may say so, more painful, is, that it is considered as an emissary of this king of terrors. When danger or pain press too nearly, they are incapable of giving any delight, and are simply terrible; but at certain distances, and with certain modifications, they may be, and they are delightful, as we every day experience. The cause of this I shall endeavour to investigate hereafter.

The passion caused by the Sublime

The passion caused by the great and sublime in *nature*, when those causes operate most powerfully, is astonishment; and astonishment is that state of the soul, in which all its motions are suspended, with some degree of horror. In this case the mind is so entirely filled with its object, that it cannot entertain any other, nor by consequence reason on that object which employs it. Hence arises the great power of the sublime, that, far from being produced by them, it anticipates our reasonings, and hurries us on by an irresistible force. Astonishment, as I have said, is the effect of the sublime in its highest degree; the inferior effects are admiration, reverence, and respect.

from Terror

No passion so effectually robs the mind of all its powers of acting and reasoning as fear. For fear being an apprehension of pain or death, it operates in a manner that resembles actual pain. Whatever therefore is terrible, with regard to sight, is sublime too,

---

1. Burke refers to the 1757 execution of Robert-François Damiens, who attempted to assassinate Louis XV.

whether this cause of terror be endued with greatness of dimensions or not; for it is impossible to look on any thing as trifling, or contemptible, that may be dangerous.

from Obscurity

To make any thing very terrible, obscurity seems in general to be necessary. When we know the full extent of any danger, when we can accustom our eyes to it, a great deal of the apprehension vanishes. Every one will be sensible of this, who considers how greatly night adds to our dread, in all cases of danger, and how much the notions of ghosts and goblins, of which none can form clear ideas, affect minds which give credit to the popular tales concerning such sorts of beings. . . . No person seems better to have understood the secret of heightening, or of setting terrible things, if I may use the expression, in their strongest light by the force of a judicious obscurity, than Milton. His description of Death in the second book is admirably studied; it is astonishing with what a gloomy pomp, with what a significant and expressive uncertainty of strokes and colouring, he has finished the portrait of the king of terrors:

> The other shape,
> If shape it might be call'd that shape had none
> Distinguishable, in member, joint, or limb;
> Or substance might be call'd that shadow seemed;
> For such seemed either; black he stood as night;
> Fierce as ten furies; terrible as hell;
> And shook a deadly dart. What seem'd his head
> The likeness of a kingly crown had on.[2]

In this description all is dark, uncertain, confused, terrible, and sublime to the last degree. . . .

In nature, dark, confused, uncertain images have a greater power on the fancy to form the grander passions, than those have which are more clear and determinate. . . . I am sensible that this idea has met with opposition, and is likely still to be rejected by several. But let it be considered that hardly any thing can strike the mind with its greatness, which does not make some sort of approach towards infinity; which nothing can do whilst we are able to perceive its bounds; but to see an object distinctly, and to perceive its bounds, is one and the same thing. A clear idea is therefore another name for a little idea.

from Power

Besides those things which directly suggest the idea of danger, and those which produce a similar effect from a mechanical cause, I know of nothing sublime, which is not some modification of power. And this branch rises as naturally as the other two branches, from terror, the common stock of every thing that is sublime. . . . Look at a man, or any other animal of prodigious strength, and what is your idea before reflection? Is it that this strength will be subservient to you, to your ease, to your pleasure, to your interest in any sense? No; the emotion you feel is, lest this enormous strength should be

---

2. John Milton, *Paradise Lost* (1667), 2.666–673.

employed to the purposes of rapine and destruction. That power derives all its sublimity from the terror with which it is generally accompanied, will appear evidently from its effect in the very few cases, in which it may be possible to strip a considerable degree of strength of its ability to hurt. When you do this, you spoil it of every thing sublime, and it immediately becomes contemptible. An ox is a creature of vast strength; but he is an innocent creature, extremely serviceable, and not at all dangerous; for which reason the idea of an ox is by no means grand. A bull is strong too; but his strength is of another kind; often very destructive, seldom (at least amongst us) of any use in our business; the idea of a bull is therefore great, and it has frequently a place in sublime descriptions, and elevating comparisons. Let us look at another strong animal in the two distinct lights in which we may consider him. The horse in the light of an useful beast, fit for the plough, the road, the draught; in every social useful light, the horse has nothing of the sublime; but it is thus that we are affected with him, *whose neck is cloathed with thunder, the glory of whose nostrils is terrible, who swalloweth the ground with fierceness and rage, neither believeth that it is the sound of the trumpet?*[3] In this description the useful character of the horse entirely disappears, and the terrible and the sublime blaze out together. . . . In short, wheresoever we find strength, and in what light soever we look upon power, we shall all along observe the sublime the concomitant of terror, and contempt the attendant on a strength that is subservient and innoxious. The race of dogs in many of their kinds, have generally a competent degree of strength and swiftness; and they exert these, and other valuable qualities which they possess, greatly to our convenience and pleasure. Dogs are indeed the most social, affectionate, and amiable animals of the whole brute creation; but love approaches much nearer to contempt than is commonly imagined; and accordingly, though we caress dogs, we borrow from them an appellation of the most despicable kind, when we employ terms of reproach; and this appellation is the common mark of the last vileness and contempt in every language.

from Vastness

Greatness of dimension is a powerful cause of the sublime. This is too evident, and the observation too common, to need any illustration; it is not so common, to consider in what ways greatness of dimension, vastness of extent, or quantity, has the most striking effect. Extension is either in length, height, or depth. Of these the length strikes least; an hundred yards of even ground will never work such an effect as a tower an hundred yards high, or a rock or mountain of that altitude. I am apt to imagine likewise, that height is less grand than depth; and that we are more struck at looking down from a precipice, than at looking up at an object of equal height: but of that I am not very positive. A perpendicular has more force in forming the sublime, than an inclined plane; and the effects of a rugged and broken surface seem stronger than where it is smooth and polished.

from Infinity

Another source of the sublime, is *Infinity*; if it does not rather belong to the last. Infinity has a tendency to fill the mind with that sort of delightful horror, which is the most genuine effect, and truest test of the sublime.

---

3. Book of Job, 39.19–24.

from Perfection not the cause of Beauty

There is another notion current, pretty closely allied to the former; that *Perfection* is the constituent cause of beauty. This opinion has been made to extend much farther than to sensible objects. But in these, so far is perfection, considered as such, from being the cause of beauty; that this quality, where it is highest, in the female sex, almost always carries with it an idea of weakness and imperfection. Women are very sensible of this; for which reason, they learn to lisp, to totter in their walk, to counterfeit weakness, and even sickness. In all this they are guided by nature. Beauty in distress is much the most affecting beauty. Blushing has little less power; and modesty in general, which is a tacit allowance of imperfection, is itself considered as an amiable quality, and certainly heightens every other that is so.

from Beautiful objects small

The most obvious point that presents itself to us in examining any object, is its extent or quantity. And what degree of extent prevails in bodies that are held beautiful, may be gathered from the usual manner of expression concerning it. I am told that, in most languages, the objects of love are spoken of under diminutive epithets. It is so in all the languages of which I have any knowledge.

from Smoothness

The next property constantly observable in such objects is *Smoothness*: A quality so essential to beauty, I do not now recollect any thing beautiful that is not smooth. In trees and flowers, smooth leaves are beautiful; smooth slopes of earth in gardens; smooth streams in the landscape; smooth coats of birds and beasts in animal beauties; in fine women, smooth skins; and in several sorts of ornamental furniture, smooth and polished surfaces.

from Gradual Variation

But as perfectly beautiful bodies are not composed of angular parts, so their parts never continue long in the same right line. They vary their direction every moment, and they change under the eye by a deviation continually carrying on, but for whose beginning or end you will find it difficult to ascertain a point. . . . Observe that part of a beautiful woman where she is perhaps the most beautiful, about the neck and breasts; the smoothness; the softness; the easy and insensible swell; the variety of the surface, which is never for the smallest space the same; the deceitful maze, through which the unsteady eye slides giddily, without knowing where to fix, or whither it is carried. Is not this a demonstration of that change of surface, continual, and yet hardly perceptible at any point, which forms one of the great constituents of beauty?

from The physical cause of Love

When we have before us such objects as excite love and competency, the body is affected, so far as I could observe, much in the following manner. The head reclines something on one side; the eyelids are more closed than usual, and the eyes roll gently with an inclination to the object, the mouth is a little opened, and the breath drawn slowly, with now and then a low sigh: the whole body is composed, and the hands fall idly to the sides. All this is accompanied with an inward sense of melting and languor. These appearances are always proportioned to the degree of beauty in the object, and of sensibility in the observer. And this gradation from the highest pitch of beauty and sensibility, even to the lowest of mediocrity and indifference, and their correspondent effects, ought to be kept in view, else this description will seem exaggerated, which it certainly is not. But from this description it is almost impossible not to conclude, that beauty acts by relaxing the solids of the whole system. There are all the appearances of such a relaxation; and a relaxation somewhat below the natural tone seems to me the cause of all positive pleasure.

from How Words influence the passions

In painting we may represent any fine figure we please; but we never can give it those enlivening touches which it may receive from words. To represent an angel in a picture, you can only draw a beautiful young man winged: but what painting can furnish any thing so grand as the addition of one word, "the angel of the *Lord?*" It is true, I have here no clear idea; but these words affect the mind more than the sensible image did; which is all I contend for. A picture of Priam dragged to the altar's foot, and there murdered, if it were well executed, would undoubtedly be very moving; but there are very aggravating circumstances which it could never represent:

> *Sanguine faedantem* quos ipse sacraverat *ignes.*[4]

As a further instance, let us consider those lines of Milton, where he describes the travels of the fallen angels through their dismal habitation,

> —O'er many a dark and dreary vale
> They pass'd, and many a region dolorous;
> O'er many a frozen, many a fiery Alp;
> Rocks, caves, lakes, fens, bogs, dens, and shades of death,
> A universe of death.[5]

Here is displayed the force of union in

> Rocks, caves, lakes, dens, bogs, fens, and shades—;

which yet would lose the greatest part of the effect, if they were not the

> *Rocks, caves, lakes, dens, bogs, fens, and shades*——
> ——*of* Death.

This idea or this affection caused by a word, which nothing but a word could annex to the others, raises a very great degree of the sublime; and this sublime is raised yet higher by what follows, a "*universe of Death.*" Here are again two ideas not presentable but by language; and an union of them great and amazing beyond conception; if they may properly be called ideas which present no distinct image to the mind:—but still it will be difficult to conceive how words can move the passions which belong to real objects, without representing those objects clearly. This is difficult to us, because

---

4. Virgil, *Aeneid*, 2.502. Priam's "blood polluting the very same fires he had made holy."   5. John Milton, *Paradise Lost* (1667), 2.618–622.

we do not sufficiently distinguish, in our observations upon language, between a clear expression, and a strong expression. These are frequently confounded with each other, though they are in reality extremely different. The former regards the understanding; the latter belongs to the passions. The one describes a thing as it is; the other describes it as it is felt. . . . The truth is, all verbal description, merely as naked description, though never so exact, conveys so poor and insufficient an idea of the thing described, that it could scarcely have the smallest effect, if the speaker did not call in to his aid those modes of speech that mark a strong and lively feeling in himself. Then by the contagion of our passions, we catch a fire already kindled in another, which probably might never have been struck out by the object described. Words, by strongly conveying the passions, by those means which we have already mentioned, fully compensate for their weakness in other respects.

—1757

from Speech of Edmund Burke, Esquire, on Moving His Resolutions for Conciliation with the Colonies

If, Sir, we incline to the side of conciliation, we are not at all embarrassed (unless we please to make ourselves so) by any incongruous mixture of coercion and restraint. We are therefore called upon, as it were by a superior warning voice, again to attend to America; to attend to the whole of it together; and to review the subject with an unusual degree of care and calmness. . . .

The proposition is peace. Not peace through the medium of war; not peace to be hunted through the labyrinth of intricate and endless negotiations; not peace to arise out of universal discord fomented from principle in all parts of the empire; not peace to depend on the juridical determination of perplexing questions, or the precise marking the shadowy boundaries of a complex government. It is simple peace, sought in its natural course and in its ordinary haunts. It is peace sought in the spirit of peace, and laid in principles purely pacific. I propose, by removing the ground of the difference, and by restoring the *former unsuspecting confidence of the colonies in the mother country*, to give permanent satisfaction to your people; and (far from a scheme of ruling by discord) to reconcile them to each other in the same act and by the bond of the very same interest which reconciles them to British government.

My idea is nothing more. Refined policy ever has been the parent of confusion; and ever will be so, as long as the world endures. Plain good intention, which is as easily discovered at the first view as fraud is surely detected at last, is, let me say, of no mean force in the government of mankind. Genuine simplicity of heart is an healing and cementing principle. My plan, therefore, being formed upon the most simple grounds imaginable, may disappoint some people when they hear it. . . . I mean to give peace. Peace implies reconciliation; and where there has been a material dispute, reconciliation does in a manner always imply concession on the one part or on the other. In this state of things I make no difficulty in affirming that the proposal ought to originate from us. Great and acknowledged force is not impaired, either in effect or in opinion, by an unwillingness to exert itself. The superior power may offer peace with honor and with safety. Such an offer from such a power will be attributed to magnanimity. But the concessions of the weak are the concessions of fear. When such a one is disarmed, he is wholly at the mercy of his superior; and he loses forever that time and those chances which, as they happen to all men, are the strength and resources of all inferior power.

The capital leading questions on which you must this day decide are these two: first, whether you ought to concede; and secondly, what your concession ought to be. On the first of these questions we have gained (as I have just taken the liberty of observing to you) some ground. But I am sensible that a good deal more is still to be done. Indeed, Sir, to enable us to determine both on the one and the other of these great questions with a firm and precise judgment, I think it may be necessary to consider distinctly the true nature and the peculiar circumstances of the object which we have before us: because after all our struggle, whether we will or not, we must govern America according to that nature and to those circumstances, and not according to our own imaginations, not according to abstract ideas of right; by no means according to mere general theories of government, the resort to which appears to me in our present situation no better than arrant trifling. I shall therefore endeavor, with your leave, to lay before you some of the most material of these circumstances in as full and as clear a manner as I am able to state them.

The first thing that we have to consider with regard to the nature of the object is the number of people in the colonies. I have taken for some years a good deal of pains on that point. I can by no calculation justify myself in placing the number below two millions of inhabitants of our own European blood and color; besides at least 500,000 others, who form no inconsiderable part of the strength and opulence of the whole. This, Sir, is, I believe, about the true number. There is no occasion to exaggerate where plain truth is of so much weight and importance. But whether I put the present numbers too high or too low is a matter of little moment. Such is the strength with which population shoots in that part of the world, that, state the numbers as high as we will, whilst the dispute continues, the exaggeration ends. Whilst we are discussing any given magnitude, they are grown to it. Whilst we spend our time in deliberating on the mode of governing two millions, we shall find we have millions more to manage. Your children do not grow faster from infancy to manhood than they spread from families to communities, and from villages to nations.

I put this consideration of the present and the growing numbers in the front of our deliberation; because, Sir, this consideration will make it evident to a blunter discernment than yours, that no partial, narrow, contracted, pinched, occasional system will be at all suitable to such an object. It will show you that it is not to be considered as one of those *minima*[1] which are out of the eye and consideration of the law; not a paltry excrescence of the state; not a mean dependent, who may be neglected with little damage and provoked with little danger. It will prove that some degree of care and caution is required in the handling of such an object; it will show that you ought not, in reason, to trifle with so large a mass of the interests and feelings of the human race. You could at no time do so without guilt; and be assured you will not be able to do it long with impunity.

But the population of this country, the great and growing population, though a very important consideration, will lose much of its weight, if not combined with other circumstances. The commerce of your colonies is out of all proportion beyond the numbers of the people. This ground of their commerce, indeed, has been trod

---

1. Small, trifling matters.

some days ago, and with great ability, by a distinguished person at your bar. This gentleman, after thirty-five years,—it is so long since he first appeared at the same place to plead for the commerce of Great Britain,—has come again before you to plead the same cause, without any other effect of time than that to the fire of imagination and extent of erudition, which even then marked him as one of the first literary characters of his age, he has added a consummate knowledge in the commercial interest of his country, formed by a long course of enlightened and discriminating experience.

Sir, I should be inexcusable in coming after such a person with any detail, if a great part of the members who now fill the House had not the misfortune to be absent when he appeared at your bar. Besides, Sir, I propose to take the matter at periods of time somewhat different from his. There is, if I mistake not, a point of view from whence, if you will look at this subject, it is impossible that it should not make an impression upon you. . . .

The trade with America alone is now within less than £500,000 of being equal to what this great commercial nation, England, carried on at the beginning of this century with the whole world! If I had taken the largest year of those on your table, it would rather have exceeded. But, it will be said, is not this American trade an unnatural protuberance that has drawn the juices from the rest of the body? The reverse. It is the very food that has nourished every other part into its present magnitude. Our general trade has been greatly augmented, and augmented more or less in almost every part to which it ever extended, but with this material difference: that of the six millions which in the beginning of the century constituted the whole mass of our export commerce, the colony trade was but one-twelfth part; it is now (as a part of sixteen millions) considerably more than a third of the whole. This is the relative proportion of the importance of the colonies at these two periods: and all reasoning concerning our mode of treating them must have this proportion as its basis; or it is a reasoning weak, rotten and sophistical. . . .

I am sensible, Sir, that all which I have asserted in my detail is admitted in the gross, but that quite a different conclusion is drawn from it. America, gentlemen say, is a noble object; it is an object well worth fighting for. Certainly it is, if fighting a people be the best way of gaining them. Gentlemen in this respect will be led to their choice of means by their complexions and their habits. Those who understand the military art will of course have some predilection for it. Those who wield the thunder of the state may have more confidence in the efficacy of arms. But I confess, possibly for want of this knowledge, my opinion is much more in favor of prudent management than of force,—considering force not as an odious, but a feeble, instrument for preserving a people so numerous, so active, so growing, so spirited as this, in a profitable and subordinate connection with us.

First, Sir, permit me to observe that the use of force alone is but *temporary*. It may subdue for a moment, but it does not remove the necessity of subduing again: and a nation is not governed which is perpetually to be conquered.

My next objection is its *uncertainty*. Terror is not always the effect of force; and an armament is not a victory. If you do not succeed, you are without resource: for conciliation failing, force remains; but force failing, no further hope of reconciliation is left. Power and authority are sometimes bought by kindness; but they can never be begged as alms by an impoverished and defeated violence.

A further objection to force is that you *impair the object* by your very endeavors to preserve it. The thing you fought for is not the thing which you recover; but depreciated, sunk, wasted and consumed in the contest. Nothing less will content me than *whole America*. I do not choose to consume its strength along with our own; because in all parts it is British strength that I consume. I do not choose to be caught by a foreign enemy at the end of this exhausting conflict; and still less in the midst of it. I may escape; but I can make no insurance against such an event. Let me add that I do not choose wholly to break the American spirit; because it is the spirit that has made the country.

Lastly, we have no sort of *experience* in favor of force as an instrument in the rule of our colonies. Their growth and their utility have been owing to methods altogether different. Our ancient indulgence has been said to be pursued to a fault. It may be so; but we know, if feeling is evidence, that our fault was more tolerable than our attempt to mend it, and our sin far more salutary than our penitence.

These, Sir, are my reasons for not entertaining that high opinion of untried force, by which many gentlemen, for whose sentiments in other particulars I have great respect, seem to be so greatly captivated. But there is still behind a third consideration concerning this object, which serves to determine my opinion on the sort of policy which ought to be pursued in the management of America, even more than its population and its commerce: I mean its *temper and character*.

In this character of the Americans a love of freedom is the predominating feature which marks and distinguishes the whole: and as an ardent is always a jealous affection, your colonies become suspicious, restive and untractable, whenever they see the least attempt to wrest from them by force or shuffle from them by chicane what they think the only advantage worth living for. This fierce spirit of liberty is stronger in the English colonies probably than in any other people of the earth; and this from a great variety of powerful causes, which, to understand the true temper of their minds and the direction which this spirit takes, it will not be amiss to lay open somewhat more largely.

First, the people of the colonies are descendants of Englishmen. England, Sir, is a nation which still, I hope, respects, and formerly adored, her freedom. The colonists emigrated from you when this part of your character was most predominant; and they took this bias and direction the moment they parted from your hands. They are therefore not only devoted to liberty, but to liberty according to English ideas and on English principles. . . .

The temper and character which prevail in our colonies are, I am afraid, unalterable by any human art. We cannot, I fear, falsify the pedigree of this fierce people and persuade them that they are not sprung from a nation in whose veins the blood of freedom circulates. The language in which they would hear you tell them this tale would detect the imposition; your speech would betray you. An Englishman is the unfittest person on earth to argue another Englishman into slavery.

I think it is nearly as little in our power to change their republican religion as their free descent, or to substitute the Roman Catholic as a penalty, or the Church of England as an improvement. The mode of inquisition and dragooning[2] is going out of fashion in the Old World; and I should not confide much to their efficacy in the New. The education of the Americans is also on the same unalterable bottom with their religion. You cannot persuade them to burn their books of curious science; to banish their lawyers from their courts of laws; or to quench the lights of their assemblies by refusing to choose those persons who are best read in their privileges. It would

---

2. Enforcing by military strength.

be no less impracticable to think of wholly annihilating the popular assemblies in which these lawyers sit. The army, by which we must govern in their place, would be far more chargeable to us; not quite so effectual; and perhaps in the end full as difficult to be kept in obedience.

With regard to the high aristocratic spirit of Virginia and the southern colonies, it has been proposed, I know, to reduce it by declaring a general enfranchisement of their slaves. This project has had its advocates and panegyrists[3]; yet I never could argue myself into any opinion of it. Slaves are often much attached to their masters. A general wild offer of liberty would not always be accepted. History furnishes few instances of it. It is sometimes as hard to persuade slaves to be free as it is to compel freemen to be slaves; and in this auspicious scheme we should have both these pleasing tasks on our hands at once. But when we talk of enfranchisement, do we not perceive that the American master may enfranchise too, and arm servile hands in defence of freedom?—a measure to which other people have had recourse more than once, and not without success, in a desperate situation of their affairs.

Slaves as these unfortunate black people are, and dull as all men are from slavery, must they not a little suspect the offer of freedom from that very nation which has sold them to their present masters? from that nation, one of whose causes of quarrel with those masters is their refusal to deal any more in that inhuman traffic? An offer of freedom from England would come rather oddly, shipped to them in an African vessel, which is refused an entry into the ports of Virginia or Carolina, with a cargo of three hundred Angola negroes. It would be curious to see the Guinea captain attempting at the same instant to publish his proclamation of liberty and to advertise his sale of slaves. . . .

In this situation, let us seriously and coolly ponder. What is it we have got by all our menaces, which have been many and ferocious? What advantage have we derived from the penal laws we have passed, and which, for the time, have been severe and numerous? What advances have we made towards our object, by the sending of a force which, by land and sea, is no contemptible strength? Has the disorder abated? Nothing less. When I see things in this situation, after such confident hopes, bold promises and active exertions, I cannot for my life avoid a suspicion that the plan itself is not correctly right.

If, then, the removal of the causes of this spirit of American liberty be for the greater part, or rather entirely, impracticable; if the ideas of criminal process be inapplicable, or if applicable, are in the highest degree inexpedient; what way yet remains? No way is open but the third and last,—to comply with the American spirit as necessary; or, if you please, to submit to it as a necessary evil.

If we adopt this mode, if we mean to conciliate and concede, let us see of what nature the concession ought to be. To ascertain the nature of our concession, we must look at their complaint. The colonies complain that they have not the characteristic mark and seal of British freedom. They complain that they are taxed in a Parliament in which they are not represented. If you mean to satisfy them at all, you must satisfy them with regard to this complaint. If you mean to please any people, you must give them the boon which they ask,—not what you may think better for them, but of a kind totally different. Such an act may be a wise regulation, but it is no concession; whereas our present theme is the mode of giving satisfaction. . . .

—1775

---

3. Speakers who praise a topic enthusiastically.

from Reflections on the Revolution in France

All circumstances taken together, the French Revolution is the most astonishing that has hitherto happened in the world. The most wonderful things are brought about in many instances by means the most absurd and ridiculous; in the most ridiculous modes; and, apparently, by the most contemptible instruments. Everything seems out of nature in this strange chaos of levity and ferocity, and of all sorts of crimes jumbled together with all sorts of follies. In viewing this monstrous tragicomic scene, the most opposite passions necessarily succeed, and sometimes mix with each other in the mind; alternate contempt and indignation; alternate laughter and tears; alternate scorn and horror.

It cannot however be denied, that to some this strange scene appeared in quite another point of view. Into them it inspired no other sentiments than those of exultation and rapture. They saw nothing in what has been done in France, but a firm and temperate exertion of freedom; so consistent, on the whole, with morals and with piety as to make it deserving not only of the secular applause of dashing Machiavelian politicians, but to render it a fit theme for all the devout effusions of sacred eloquence. . . .

The constituent parts of a state are obliged to hold their public faith with each other, and with all those who derive any serious interest under their engagements, as much as the whole state is bound to keep its faith with separate communities. Otherwise competence and power would soon be confounded, and no law be left but the will of a prevailing force. On this principle the succession of the crown has always been what it now is, an hereditary succession by law: in the old line it was a succession by the common law; in the new by the statute law, operating on the principles of the common law, not changing the substance, but regulating the mode, and describing the persons. Both these descriptions of law are of the same force, and are derived from an equal authority, emanating from the common agreement and original compact of the state, *communi sponsione reipublicae*,[1] and as such are equally binding on king and people too, as long as the terms are observed, and they continue the same body politic. . . .

You will observe, that from Magna Charta to the Declaration of Right, it has been the uniform policy of our constitution to claim and assert our liberties, as an *entailed inheritance* derived to us from our forefathers, and to be transmitted to our posterity; as an estate specially belonging to the people of this kingdom, without any reference whatever to any other more general or prior right. By this means our constitution preserves a unity in so great a diversity of its parts. We have an inheritable crown; an inheritable peerage; and a House of Commons and a people inheriting privileges, franchises, and liberties, from a long line of ancestors.

This policy appears to me to be the result of profound reflection; or rather the happy effect of following nature, which is wisdom without reflection, and above it. A spirit of innovation is generally the result of a selfish temper, and confined views. People will not look forward to posterity, who never look backward to their ancestors. Besides, the people of England well know, that the idea of inheritance furnishes a sure principle of conservation, and a sure principle of transmission;

---

1. "The common compact of the state."

without at all excluding a principle of improvement. It leaves acquisition free; but it secures what it acquires. Whatever advantages are obtained by a state proceeding on these maxims, are locked fast as in a sort of family settlement; grasped as in a kind of mortmain[2] for ever. By a constitutional policy, working after the pattern of nature, we receive, we hold, we transmit our government and our privileges, in the same manner in which we enjoy and transmit our property and our lives. The institutions of policy, the goods of fortune, the gifts of providence, are handed down to us, and from us, in the same course and order. Our political system is placed in a just correspondence and symmetry with the order of the world, and with the mode of existence decreed to a permanent body composed of transitory parts; wherein, by the disposition of a stupendous wisdom, moulding together the great mysterious incorporation of the human race, the whole, at one time, is never old, or middle-aged, or young, but, in a condition of unchangeable constancy, moves on through the varied tenor of perpetual decay, fall, renovation, and progression. Thus, by preserving the method of nature in the conduct of the state, in what we improve, we are never wholly new; in what we retain, we are never wholly obsolete. By adhering in this manner and on those principles to our forefathers, we are guided not by the superstition of antiquarians, but by the spirit of philosophic analogy. In this choice of inheritance we have given to our frame of polity the image of a relation in blood; binding up the constitution of our country with our dearest domestic ties; adopting our fundamental laws into the bosom of our family affections; keeping inseparable, and cherishing with the warmth of all their combined and mutually reflected charities, our state, our hearths, our sepulchres, and our altars.

Through the same plan of a conformity to nature in our artificial institutions, and by calling in the aid of her unerring and powerful instincts, to fortify the fallible and feeble contrivances of our reason, we have derived several other, and those no small benefits, from considering our liberties in the light of an inheritance. Always acting as if in the presence of canonized forefathers, the spirit of freedom, leading in itself to misrule and excess, is tempered with an awful gravity. This idea of a liberal descent inspires us with a sense of habitual native dignity, which prevents that upstart insolence almost inevitably adhering to and disgracing those who are the first acquirers of any distinction. By this means our liberty becomes a noble freedom. It carries an imposing and majestic aspect. It has a pedigree and illustrating ancestors. It has its bearings and its ensigns armorial. It has its gallery of portraits; its monumental inscriptions; its records, evidences, and titles. We procure reverence to our civil institutions on the principle upon which nature teaches us to revere individual men; on account of their age, and on account of those from whom they are descended. All your sophisters cannot produce anything better adapted to preserve a rational and manly freedom than the course that we have pursued, who have chosen our nature rather than our speculations, our breasts rather than our inventions, for the great conservatories and magazines of our rights and privileges. . . .

Your present confusion, like a palsy, has attacked the fountain of life itself. Every person in your country, in a situation to be actuated by a principle of honour,

---

2. French for "dead hand." Legal term for a corporation's continued possession of property despite deaths of stockholders.

is disgraced and degraded, and can entertain no sensation of life, except in a mortified and humiliated indignation. But this generation will quickly pass away. The next generation of the nobility will resemble the artificers and clowns, and money-jobbers, usurers, and Jews, who will be always their fellows, sometimes their masters. Believe me, Sir, those who attempt to level, never equalise. In all societies, consisting of various descriptions of citizens, some description must be uppermost. The levellers[3] therefore only change and pervert the natural order of things. . . .

Far am I from denying in theory, full as far is my heart from withholding in practice, (if I were of power to give or to withhold,) the *real* rights of men. In denying their false claims of right, I do not mean to injure those which are real, and are such as their pretended rights would totally destroy. If civil society be made for the advantage of man, all the advantages for which it is made become his right. It is an institution of beneficence; and law itself is only beneficence acting by a rule. Men have a right to live by that rule; they have a right to do justice, as between their fellows, whether their fellows are in public function or in ordinary occupation. They have a right to the fruits of their industry; and to the means of making their industry fruitful. They have a right to the acquisitions of their parents; to the nourishment and improvement of their offspring; to instruction in life, and to consolation in death. Whatever each man can separately do, without trespassing upon others, he has a right to do for himself; and he has a right to a fair portion of all which society, with all its combinations of skill and force, can do in his favour. In this partnership all men have equal rights; but not to equal things. He that has but five shillings in the partnership, has as good a right to it, as he that has five hundred pounds has to his larger proportion. But he has not a right to an equal dividend in the product of the joint stock; and as to the share of power, authority, and direction which each individual ought to have in the management of the state, that I must deny to be amongst the direct original rights of man in civil society. . . .

History will record, that on the morning of the 6th of October, 1789, the king and queen of France, after a day of confusion, alarm, dismay, and slaughter, lay down, under the pledged security of public faith, to indulge nature in a few hours of respite, and troubled, melancholy repose. From this sleep the queen was first startled by the voice of the sentinel at her door, who cried out to her to save herself by flight—that this was the last proof of fidelity he could give—that they were upon him, and he was dead. Instantly he was cut down. A band of cruel ruffians and assassins, reeking with his blood, rushed into the chamber of the queen, and pierced with a hundred strokes of bayonets and poniards the bed, from whence this persecuted woman had but just time to fly almost naked, and, through ways unknown to the murderers, had escaped to seek refuge at the feet of a king and husband, not secure of his own life for a moment.

This king, to say no more of him, and this queen, and their infant children, (who once would have been the pride and hope of a great and generous people,) were then forced to abandon the sanctuary of the most splendid palace in the world, which they left swimming in blood, polluted by massacre, and strewed with scattered limbs and mutilated carcases. Thence they were conducted into

---

3. Advocates of universal voting rights and legal equality.

the capital of their kingdom. Two had been selected from the unprovoked, unresisted, promiscuous slaughter, which was made of the gentlemen of birth and family who composed the king's body guard. These two gentlemen, with all the parade of an execution of justice, were cruelly and publicly dragged to the block, and beheaded in the great court of the palace. Their heads were stuck upon spears, and led the procession; whilst the royal captives who followed in the train were slowly moved along, amidst the horrid yells, and shrilling screams, and frantic dances, and infamous contumelies, and all the unutterable abominations of the furies of hell, in the abused shape of the vilest of women. After they had been made to taste, drop by drop, more than the bitterness of death, in the slow torture of a journey of twelve miles, protracted to six hours, they were, under a guard, composed of those very soldiers who had thus conducted them through this famous triumph, lodged in one of the old palaces of Paris, now converted into a bastile[4] for kings.

Is this a triumph to be consecrated at altars? to be commemorated with grateful thanksgiving? to be offered to the divine humanity with fervent prayer and enthusiastic ejaculation? . . .

Such treatment of any human creatures must be shocking to any but those who are made for accomplishing revolutions. But I cannot stop here. Influenced by the inborn feelings of my nature, and not being illuminated by a single ray of this new sprung modern light, I confess to you, Sir, that the exalted rank of the persons suffering, and particularly the sex, the beauty, and the amiable qualities of the descendant of so many kings and emperors, with the tender age of royal infants, insensible only through infancy and innocence of the cruel outrages to which their parents were exposed, instead of being a subject of exultation, adds not a little to my sensibility on that most melancholy occasion.

I hear that the august person, who was the principal object of our preacher's triumph,[5] though he supported himself, felt much on that shameful occasion. As a man, it became him to feel for his wife and his children, and the faithful guards of his person, that were massacred in cold blood about him; as a prince, it became him to feel for the strange and frightful transformation of his civilized subjects, and to be more grieved for them than solicitous for himself. It derogates little from his fortitude, while it adds infinitely to the honour of his humanity. I am very sorry to say it, very sorry indeed, that such personages are in a situation in which it is not becoming in us to praise the virtues of the great.

I hear, and I rejoice to hear, that the great lady, the other object of the triumph, has borne that day, (one is interested that beings made for suffering should suffer well,) and that she bears all the succeeding days, that she bears the imprisonment of her husband, and her own captivity, and the exile of her friends, and the insulting adulation of addresses, and the whole weight of her accumulated wrongs, with a serene patience, in a manner suited to her rank and race, and becoming the offspring of a sovereign distinguished for her piety and her courage: that, like her, she has lofty sentiments; that she feels with the dignity of a Roman matron; that in the last

---

4. Prison.   5. "August person": Louis XIV. "Preacher": Richard Price, whose *Discourse on the Love of Our Country* was a cry for equality to which Burke is responding.

extremity she will save herself from the last disgrace; and that, if she must fall, she will fall by no ignoble hand.[6]

It is now sixteen or seventeen years since I saw the queen of France, then the dauphiness [princess], at Versailles; and surely never lighted on this orb, which she hardly seemed to touch, a more delightful vision. I saw her just above the horizon, decorating and cheering the elevated sphere she just began to move in,—glittering like the morning-star, full of life, and splendour, and joy. Oh! what a revolution! and what a heart must I have to contemplate without emotion that elevation and that fall! Little did I dream when she added titles of veneration to those of enthusiastic, distant, respectful love, that she should ever be obliged to carry the sharp antidote[7] against disgrace concealed in that bosom; little did I dream that I should have lived to see such disasters fallen upon her in a nation of gallant men, in a nation of men of honour, and of cavaliers. I thought ten thousand swords must have leaped from their scabbards to avenge even a look that threatened her with insult. But the age of chivalry is gone. That of sophisters, economists, and calculators, has succeeded; and the glory of Europe is extinguished for ever. Never, never more shall we behold that generous loyalty to rank and sex, that proud submission, that dignified obedience, that subordination of the heart, which kept alive, even in servitude itself, the spirit of an exalted freedom. The unbought grace of life, the cheap defence of nations, the nurse of manly sentiment and heroic enterprise, is gone! It is gone, that sensibility of principle, that chastity of honour, which felt a stain like a wound, which inspired courage whilst it mitigated ferocity, which ennobled whatever it touched, and under which vice itself lost half its evil, by losing all its grossness.

This mixed system of opinion and sentiment had its origin in the ancient chivalry; and the principle, though varied in its appearance by the varying state of human affairs, subsisted and influenced through a long succession of generations, even to the time we live in. If it should ever be totally extinguished, the loss I fear will be great. It is this which has given its character to modern Europe. It is this which has distinguished it under all its forms of government, and distinguished it to its advantage, from the states of Asia, and possibly from those states which flourished in the most brilliant periods of the antique world. It was this, which, without confounding ranks, had produced a noble equality, and handed it down through all the gradations of social life. It was this opinion which mitigated kings into companions, and raised private men to be fellows with kings. Without force or opposition, it subdued the fierceness of pride and power; it obliged sovereigns to submit to the soft collar of social esteem, compelled stern authority to submit to elegance, and gave a dominating vanquisher of laws to be subdued by manners.

But now all is to be changed. All the pleasing illusions, which made power gentle and obedience liberal, which harmonized the different shades of life, and which, by a bland assimilation, incorporated into politics the sentiments which beautify and soften private society, are to be dissolved by this new conquering empire of light and reason. All the decent drapery of life is to be rudely torn off. All the super-added ideas, furnished from the wardrobe of a moral imagination, which the heart owns, and the understanding ratifies, as necessary to cover the defects of our naked, shivering nature, and to raise it to dignity in our own estimation, are to be exploded as a ridiculous, absurd, and antiquated fashion.

---

6. Queen Marie Antoinette was subsequently executed in 1793.   7. A dagger for committing suicide.

On this scheme of things, a king is but a man, a queen is but a woman; a woman is but an animal, and an animal not of the highest order. All homage paid to the sex in general as such, and without distinct views, is to be regarded as romance and folly. Regicide, and parricide, and sacrilege, are but fictions of superstition, corrupting jurisprudence by destroying its simplicity. The murder of a king, or a queen, or a bishop, or a father, are only common homicide; and if the people are by any chance, or in any way, gainers by it, a sort of homicide much the most pardonable, and into which we ought not to make too severe a scrutiny.

On the scheme of this barbarous philosophy, which is the offspring of cold hearts and muddy understandings, and which is as void of solid wisdom as it is destitute of all taste and elegance, laws are to be supported only by their own terrors, and by the concern which each individual may find in them from his own private speculations, or can spare to them from his own private interests. In the groves of *their* academy, at the end of every vista, you see nothing but the gallows. Nothing is left which engages the affections on the part of the commonwealth. On the principles of this mechanic philosophy, our institutions can never be embodied, if I may use the expression, in persons; so as to create in us love, veneration, admiration, or attachment. But that sort of reason which banishes the affections is incapable of filling their place. These public affections, combined with manners, are required sometimes as supplements, sometimes as correctives, always as aids to law. The precept given by a wise man, as well as a great critic, for the construction of poems, is equally true as to states:—*Non satis est pulchra esse poemata, dulcia sunto.*[8] There ought to be a system of manners in every nation, which a well-formed mind would be disposed to relish. To make us love our country, our country ought to be lovely.

But power, of some kind or other, will survive the shock in which manners and opinions perish; and it will find other and worse means for its support. The usurpation which, in order to subvert ancient institutions, has destroyed ancient principles, will hold power by arts similar to those by which it has acquired it. When the old feudal and chivalrous spirit of *fealty*, which, by freeing kings from fear, freed both kings and subjects from the precautions of tyranny, shall be extinct in the minds of men, plots and assassinations will be anticipated by preventive murder and preventive confiscation, and that long roll of grim and bloody maxims, which form the political code of all power, not standing on its own honour, and the honour of those who are to obey it. Kings will be tyrants from policy, when subjects are rebels from principle.

When ancient opinions and rules of life are taken away, the loss cannot possibly be estimated. From that moment we have no compass to govern us; nor can we know distinctly to what port we steer. Europe, undoubtedly, taken in a mass, was in a flourishing condition the day on which your revolution was completed. How much of that prosperous state was owing to the spirit of our old manners and opinions is not easy to say; but as such causes cannot be indifferent in their operation, we must presume, that, on the whole, their operation was beneficial.

We are but too apt to consider things in the state in which we find them, without sufficiently adverting to the causes by which they have been produced, and possibly may be upheld. Nothing is more certain, than that our manners, our civilization, and all the good things which are connected with manners and with civilization, have, in this European world of ours, depended for ages upon two principles; and were

---

8. Horace, *Ars Poetica*: "It is not sufficient that a poem be beautiful; it must be sweet as well."

indeed the result of both combined; I mean the spirit of a gentleman, and the spirit of religion. The nobility and the clergy, the one by profession, the other by patronage, kept learning in existence, even in the midst of arms and confusions, and whilst governments were rather in their causes, than formed. Learning paid back what it received to nobility and to priesthood; and paid it with usury, by enlarging their ideas, and by furnishing their minds. Happy if they had all continued to know their indissoluble union, and their proper place! Happy if learning, not debauched by ambition, had been satisfied to continue the instructor, and not aspired to be the master! Along with its natural protectors and guardians, learning will be cast into the mire, and trodden down under the hoofs of a swinish multitude. . . .

[W]hen kings are hurled from their thrones by the Supreme Director of this great drama, and become the objects of insult to the base, and of pity to the good, we behold such disasters in the moral, as we should behold a miracle in the physical, order of things. We are alarmed into reflection; our minds (as it has long since been observed) are purified by terror and pity; our weak, unthinking pride is humbled under the dispensations of a mysterious wisdom. Some tears might be drawn from me, if such a spectacle were exhibited on the stage. I should be truly ashamed of finding in myself that superficial, theatric sense of painted distress, whilst I could exult over it in real life. With such a perverted mind, I could never venture to show my face at a tragedy. People would think the tears that Garrick formerly, or that Siddons[9] not long since, have extorted from me, were the tears of hypocrisy; I should know them to be the tears of folly.

Indeed the theatre is a better school of moral sentiments than churches, where the feelings of humanity are thus outraged. Poets who have to deal with an audience not yet graduated in the school of the rights of men, and who must apply themselves to the moral constitution of the heart, would not dare to produce such a triumph as a matter of exultation. There, where men follow their natural impulses, they would not bear the odious maxims of a Machiavelian policy, whether applied to the attainment of monarchical or democratic tyranny. They would reject them on the modern, as they once did on the ancient stage, where they could not bear even the hypothetical proposition of such wickedness in the mouth of a personated tyrant, though suitable to the character he sustained. No theatric audience in Athens would bear what has been borne, in the midst of the real tragedy of this triumphal day; a principal actor weighing, as it were in scales hung in a shop of horrors,—so much actual crime against so much contingent advantage,—and after putting in and out weights, declaring that the balance was on the side of the advantages. They would not bear to see the crimes of new democracy posted as in a ledger against the crimes of old despotism, and the book-keepers of politics finding democracy still in debt, but by no means unable or unwilling to pay the balance. In the theatre, the first intuitive glance, without any elaborate process of reasoning, will show, that this method of political computation would justify every extent of crime. They would see, that on these principles, even where the very worst acts were not perpetrated, it was owing rather to the fortune of the conspirators, than to their parsimony in the expenditure of treachery and blood. They would soon see, that criminal means once tolerated are soon preferred. They present a shorter cut to the object than through the highway of the moral virtues. Justifying perfidy and murder for public benefit, public benefit

---

9. David Garrick (1717–1779) and Sarah Siddons (1755–1831) were London-based actors of Shakespearean tragedies.

would soon become the pretext, and perfidy and murder the end; until rapacity, malice, revenge, and fear more dreadful than revenge, could satiate their insatiable appetites. Such must be the consequences of losing, in the splendour of these triumphs of the rights of men, all natural sense of wrong and right.

—1790

Oliver Goldsmith
1730–1774

Oliver Goldsmith, as the saying goes, missed the boat. In 1749, frustrated and despondent at the end of his studies at Trinity College, Dublin, Goldsmith resolved to follow the path of many of his fellow Irishmen. He would go to America. The New World offered the promise of economic prosperity that Ireland did not: Depression, political and religious persecution, and crop failure left many scanning the horizon for new homes. Throughout the eighteenth century, a steadily increasing stream of immigrants left Ireland for the New World, and it is estimated that as many as 100,000 citizens arrived in America between 1775 and 1820. So, Goldsmith set out from Dublin to the West Coast of Ireland—to Cork—to book passage in a transatlantic ship. Passage was available, but Goldsmith grew restless during the three-week interval in which no sailing winds appeared. When sufficient wind arrived, Goldsmith was rambling in the countryside with friends and missed his ship.

Various biographical accounts record a career full of such misadventures. Born to a poor Anglican clergyman, Goldsmith was the fifth of eight children. He was talkative, fun-loving, slight in stature, and awkward in manner, and a childhood bout of small pox blemished his complexion. James Boswell presents Goldsmith in his *Life of Johnson* (1791) as buffoonish, vain and ridiculous in dress and behavior, yet kind and generous. While Goldsmith in person baffled many people, Goldsmith on paper met with great success. After trying his hand at several fields of study and careers—theology, law, medicine, and teaching—he turned to writing in 1756. Desperately poor, he established himself in London, translating, reviewing, and contributing political pieces to periodicals. Goldsmith's 1762 poem "The Citizen of the World" brought him to the attention of Samuel Johnson (one of many literary luminaries whom Goldsmith would befriend), and his reputation grew with the publication of "The Traveller" in 1764.

When "The Deserted Village" was published in 1770, it became an immediate hit. Goldsmith had labored on the poem for two years, and he continued to revise it after its first appearance. Six editions appeared in the poem's first year in print (including the revised fourth edition, which is reproduced here), with ten more by 1775 (including a translation into French). The poem is a complaint against luxury and the self-centered indulgence of an increasingly prosperous bourgeoisie; Goldsmith was especially angered by moneyed merchants who purchased and transformed agricultural land into game parks, displacing villagers and farmers. While the village of Auburn is fictional, Goldsmith treated a factual instance of this kind of depopulation in a June 1762 *Lloyd's Evening Post* piece, "The Revolution in Low Living." There he writes of a small community fifty miles outside of London that was purchased by a wealthy merchant, who destroyed the town to make way for a park for his pleasure. In the dedication of "The Deserted Village," Goldsmith positions himself within a longstanding pastoral tradition in which the countryside serves as a standpoint from which to criticize wealth and power:

For twenty or thirty years past, it has been the fashion to consider luxury as one of the greatest national advantages; and all the wisdom of antiquity in that particular, as erroneous. Still however, I must remain a professed ancient on that head, and continue to think those luxuries prejudicial to states, by which so many vices are introduced, and so many kingdoms have been undone.

Goldsmith's nostalgia is not limited to his longing for a simpler time and way of life; he also engages in a kind of formal pastoralism in his decision to write in heroic couplets (two rhyming lines of iambic pentameter) modeled on those used by Alexander Pope in his influential poem, "Windsor Forest" (1713).

During his most productive years in London, Goldsmith also wrote two theatrical comedies, *The Good-natur'd Man* (1768) and *She Stoops to Conquer* (1773); a novel, *The Vicar of Wakefield* (1766); and several popular historical works: *A History of England* (1764); *Roman History* (1769); *Grecian History* (1774); and a *History of the Earth, and Animated Nature* (1774). In short, he was a very successful working writer, operating in a wide variety of genres in response to the demands of the literary market.

from The Deserted Village

Sweet Auburn, loveliest village of the plain,
Where health and plenty cheered the laboring swain,
Where smiling spring its earliest visit paid,
And parting summer's lingering blooms delayed:
Dear lovely bowers of innocence and ease,   5
Seats of my youth, when every sport could please,
How often have I loitered o'er thy green,
Where humble happiness endeared each scene;
How often have I paused on every charm,
The sheltered cot,[1] the cultivated farm,   10
The never-failing brook, the busy mill,
The decent church that topped the neighboring hill,
The hawthorn bush, with seats beneath the shade,
For talking age and whispering lovers made.
How often have I blessed the coming day,   15
When toil remitting lent its turn to play,
And all the village train, from labor free,
Led up their sports beneath the spreading tree,
While many a pastime circled in the shade,
The young contending as the old surveyed;   20
And many a gambol[2] frolicked o'er the ground,
And sleights of art and feats of strength went round.
And still as each repeated pleasure tired,
Succeeding sports the mirthful band inspired;
The dancing pair that simply sought renown   25
By holding out to tire each other down;
The swain mistrustless of his smutted face,

1. Cottage.   2. Playful dance.

While secret laughter tittered round the place;
The bashful virgin's sidelong looks of love,
The matron's glance that would those looks reprove.   30
These were thy charms, sweet village; sports like these,
With sweet succession, taught even toil to please;
These round thy bowers their cheerful influence shed,
These were thy charms—But all these charms are fled.

    Sweet smiling village, loveliest of the lawn,   35
Thy sports are fled, and all thy charms withdrawn;
Amidst thy bowers the tyrant's hand is seen,
And desolation saddens all thy green:
One only master grasps the whole domain,
And half a tillage stints thy smiling plain;   40
No more thy glassy brook reflects the day,
But choked with sedges, works its weedy way.
Along thy glades, a solitary guest,
The hollow sounding bittern guards its nest;
Amidst thy desert walks the lapwing flies,   45
And tires their echoes with unvaried cries.
Sunk are thy bowers, in shapeless ruin all,
And the long grass o'ertops the mouldering wall,
And trembling, shrinking from the spoiler's hand,
Far, far away thy children leave the land.   50

    Ill fares the land, to hastening ills a prey,
Where wealth accumulates and men decay:
Princes and lords may flourish or may fade;
A breath can make them, as a breath has made;
But a bold peasantry, their country's pride,   55
When once destroyed, can never be supplied.

    A time there was, ere England's griefs began,
When every rood³ of ground maintained its man;
For him light labor spread her wholesome store,
Just gave what life required, but gave no more: 60
His best companions, innocence and health;
And his best riches, ignorance of wealth.

    But times are altered; trade's unfeeling train
Usurp the land and dispossess the swain;
Along the lawn,⁴ where scattered hamlets rose,   65
Unwieldy wealth and cumbrous pomp repose;
And every want to opulence allied,
And every pang that folly pays to pride.
These gentle hours that plenty bade to bloom,

---

3. One quarter of an acre.   4. Countryside.

Those calm desires that asked but little room,   70
Those healthful sports that graced the peaceful scene,
Lived in each look, and brightened all the green;
These far departing seek a kinder shore,
And rural mirth and manners are no more.

   Sweet Auburn! parent of the blissful hour,   75
Thy glades forlorn confess the tyrant's power.
Here as I take my solitary rounds,
Amidst thy tangling walks, and ruined grounds,
And, many a year elapsed, return to view
Where once the cottage stood, the hawthorn grew,   80
Remembrance wakes with all her busy train,
Swells at my breast, and turns the past to pain. . . .

   Near yonder copse, where once the garden smiled,
And still where many a garden flower grows wild;
There, where a few torn shrubs the place disclose,
The village preacher's modest mansion rose.   140
A man he was, to all the country dear,
And passing rich with forty pounds a year;
Remote from towns he ran his godly race,
Nor e'er had changed, nor wished to change his place;
Unpracticed he to fawn, or seek for power,   145
By doctrines fashioned to the varying hour;
Far other aims his heart had learned to prize,
More skilled to raise the wretched than to rise.
His house was known to all the vagrant train,
He chid their wanderings, but relieved their pain;   150
The long remembered beggar was his guest,
Whose beard descending swept his aged breast;
The ruined spendthrift, now no longer proud,
Claimed kindred there, and had his claims allowed;
The broken soldier, kindly bade to stay,   155
Sat by his fire, and talked the night away;
Wept o'er his wounds, or tales of sorrow done,
Shouldered his crutch, and showed how fields were won.
Pleased with his guests, the good man learned to glow,
And quite forgot their vices in their woe;   160
Careless their merits or their faults to scan,
His pity gave ere charity began.

   Thus to relieve the wretched was his pride,
And even his failings leaned to virtue's side;
But in his duty prompt at every call,   165
He watched and wept, he prayed and felt, for all.
And, as a bird each fond endearment tries,
To tempt its new fledged offspring to the skies,

He tried each art, reproved each dull delay,
Allured to brighter worlds, and led the way.   170

   Beside the bed where parting life was laid,
And sorrow, guilt, and pain by turns dismayed,
The reverend champion stood. At his control,
Despair and anguish fled the struggling soul;
Comfort came down the trembling wretch to raise,   175
And his last faltering accents whispered praise.

   At church, with meek and unaffected grace,
His looks adorned the venerable place;
Truth from his lips prevailed with double sway,
And fools, who came to scoff, remained to pray.   180
The service past, around the pious man,
With steady zeal each honest rustic ran;
Even children followed with endearing wile,
And plucked his gown, to share the good man's smile.
His ready smile a parent's warmth expressed,   185
Their welfare pleased him, and their cares distressed;
To them his heart, his love, his griefs were given,
But all his serious thoughts had rest in Heaven.
As some tall cliff that lifts its awful form,
Swells from the vale, and midway leaves the storm,   190
Though round its breast the rolling clouds are spread,
Eternal sunshine settles on its head.

   Beside yon straggling fence that skirts the way,
With blossomed furze[5] unprofitably gay,
There, in his noisy mansion, skilled to rule,   195
The village master taught his little school;
A man severe he was, and stern to view,
I knew him well, and every truant knew;
Well had the boding tremblers learned to trace
The day's disasters in his morning face;   200
Full well they laughed with counterfeited glee,
At all his jokes, for many a joke had he;
Full well the busy whisper circling round,
Conveyed the dismal tidings when he frowned;
Yet he was kind, or if severe in aught,   205
The love he bore to learning was in fault;
The village all declared how much he knew;
'Twas certain he could write, and cipher too;
Lands he could measure, terms and tides[6] presage,
And even the story ran that he could gauge.   210
In arguing too, the parson owned his skill,

---

5. A thorny shrub.   6. Days for payment of rent and holidays.

For even though vanquished, he could argue still;
While words of learned length, and thundering sound,
Amazed the gazing rustics ranged around;
And still they gazed, and still the wonder grew,   215
That one small head could carry all he knew.

    But past is all his fame. The very spot,
Where many a time he triumphed, is forgot.
Near yonder thorn, that lifts its head on high,
Where once the signpost caught the passing eye,   220
Low lies that house where nut-brown draughts inspired,
Where gray-beard mirth and smiling toil retired,
Where village statesmen talked with looks profound,
And news much older than their ale went round.
Imagination fondly stoops to trace   225
The parlor splendors of that festive place;
The whitewashed wall, the nicely sanded floor,
The varnished clock that clicked behind the door;
The chest contrived a double debt to pay,
A bed by night, a chest of drawers by day;   230
The pictures placed for ornament and use,
The twelve good rules, the royal game of goose[7];
The hearth, except when winter chilled the day,
With aspen boughs, and flowers, and fennel gay,
While broken teacups, wisely kept for show,   235
Ranged o'er the chimney, glistened in a row.

    Vain transitory splendors! Could not all
Reprieve the tottering mansion from its fall!
Obscure it sinks, nor shall it more impart
An hour's importance to the poor man's heart;   240
Thither no more the peasant shall repair
To sweet oblivion of his daily care;
No more the farmer's news, the barber's tale,
No more the woodman's ballad shall prevail;
No more the smith his dusky brow shall clear,   245
Relax his ponderous strength, and lean to hear;
The host himself no longer shall be found
Careful to see the mantling[8] bliss go round;
Nor the coy maid, half willing to be pressed,
Shall kiss the cup to pass it to the rest.   250

    Yes! let the rich deride, the proud disdain,
These simple blessings of the lowly train;
To me more dear, congenial to my heart,
One native charm, than all the gloss of art;

---

7. A game with cards and dice.   8. Foaming.

Spontaneous joys, where nature has its play,   255
The soul adopts, and owns their first born sway;
Lightly they frolic o'er the vacant mind,
Unenvied, unmolested, unconfined.
But the long pomp, the midnight masquerade,
With all the freaks of wanton wealth arrayed,   260
In these, ere triflers half their wish obtain,
The toiling pleasure sickens into pain;
And, even while fashion's brightest arts decoy,
The heart distrusting asks, if this be joy.

    Ye friends to truth, ye statesmen, who survey   265
The rich man's joys increase, the poor's decay,
'Tis yours to judge, how wide the limits stand
Between a splendid and an happy land.
Proud swells the tide with loads of freighted ore,
And shouting Folly hails them from her shore;   270
Hoards, even beyond the miser's wish abound,
And rich men flock from all the world around.
Yet count our gains. This wealth is but a name
That leaves our useful products still the same.
Not so the loss. The man of wealth and pride   275
Takes up a space that many poor supplied;
Space for his lake, his park's extended bounds,
Space for his horses, equipage, and hounds;
The robe that wraps his limbs in silken sloth
Has robbed the neighboring fields of half their growth;   280
His seat, where solitary sports are seen,
Indignant spurns the cottage from the green;
Around the world each needful product flies,
For all the luxuries the world supplies.
While thus the land adorned for pleasure all   285
In barren splendor feebly waits the fall. . . .

    Where then, ah where, shall poverty reside,
To scape the pressure of contiguous pride?
If to some common's fenceless limits strayed,   305
He drives his flock to pick the scanty blade,
Those fenceless fields the sons of wealth divide,
And even the bare-worn common is denied.

    If to the city sped—What waits him there?
To see profusion that he must not share;   310
To see ten thousand baneful arts combined
To pamper luxury, and thin mankind;
To see those joys the sons of pleasure know
Extorted from his fellow-creature's woe.
Here, while the courtier glitters in brocade,   315

There the pale artist plies the sickly trade;
Here, while the proud their long-drawn pomps display,
There the black gibbet glooms beside the way.
The dome where Pleasure holds her midnight reign,
Here, richly decked, admits the gorgeous train;   320
Tumultuous grandeur crowds the blazing square,
The rattling chariots clash, the torches glare.
Sure scenes like these no troubles e'er annoy!
Sure these denote one universal joy!
Are these thy serious thoughts?—Ah, turn thine eyes   325
Where the poor houseless shivering female lies.
She once, perhaps, in village plenty blest,
Has wept at tales of innocence distressed;
Her modest looks the cottage might adorn,
Sweet as the primrose peeps beneath the thorn;   330
Now lost to all; her friends, her virtue fled,
Near her betrayer's door she lays her head,
And pinched with cold, and shrinking from the shower,
With heavy heart deplores that luckless hour
When idly first, ambitious of the town,   335
She left her wheel and robes of country brown.

   Do thine, sweet Auburn, thine, the loveliest train,
Do thy fair tribes participate her pain?
Even now, perhaps, by cold and hunger led,
At proud men's doors they ask a little bread!   340

   Ah, no. To distant climes, a dreary scene,
Where half the convex world intrudes between,
Through torrid tracts with fainting steps they go,
Where wild Altama[9] murmurs to their woe.
Far different there from all that charmed before,   345
The various terrors of that horrid shore;
Those blazing suns that dart a downward ray,
And fiercely shed intolerable day;
Those matted woods where birds forget to sing,
But silent bats in drowsy clusters cling,   350
Those poisonous fields with rank luxuriance crowned,
Where the dark scorpion gathers death around;
Where at each step the stranger fears to wake
The rattling terrors of the vengeful snake;
Where crouching tigers wait their hapless prey,   355
And savage men, more murderous still than they;
While oft in whirls the mad tornado flies,
Mingling the ravaged landscape with the skies.
Far different these from every former scene,

9. Altamaha River in Georgia, U.S.

The cooling brook, the grassy vested green,   360
The breezy covert of the warbling grove,
That only sheltered thefts of harmless love.

   Good Heaven! what sorrows gloomed that parting day,
That called them from their native walks away;
When the poor exiles, every pleasure past,   365
Hung round their bowers, and fondly looked their last,
And took a long farewell, and wished in vain
For seats like these beyond the western main;
And shuddering still to face the distant deep,
Returned and wept, and still returned to weep.   370
The good old sire the first prepared to go
To new-found worlds, and wept for others' woe.
But for himself, in conscious virtue brave,
He only wished for worlds beyond the grave.
His lovely daughter, lovelier in her tears,   375
The fond companion of his helpless years,
Silent went next, neglectful of her charms,
And left a lover's for a father's arms.
With louder plaints the mother spoke her woes,
And blessed the cot where every pleasure rose;   380
And kissed her thoughtless babes with many a tear,
And clasped them close in sorrow doubly dear;
Whilst her fond husband strove to lend relief
In all the silent manliness of grief. . . .

   Even now the devastation is begun,   395
And half the business of destruction done;
Even now, methinks, as pondering here I stand,
I see the rural virtues leave the land.
Down where yon anchoring vessel spreads the sail,
That idly waiting flaps with every gale,   400
Downward they move, a melancholy band,
Pass from the shore, and darken all the strand.
Contented toil, and hospitable care,
And kind connubial tenderness are there;
And piety, with wishes placed above,   405
And steady loyalty, and faithful love:
And thou, sweet Poetry, thou loveliest maid,
Still first to fly where sensual joys invade;
Unfit, in these degenerate times of shame,
To catch the heart, or strike for honest fame;   410
Dear charming nymph, neglected and decried,
My shame in crowds, my solitary pride;
Thou source of all my bliss, and all my woe,
That found'st me poor at first, and keep'st me so;
Thou guide by which the nobler arts excel,   415

Thou nurse of every virtue, fare thee well.
Farewell, and O where'er thy voice be tried,
On Torno's cliffs, or Pambamarca's[10] side,
Whether where equinoctial fervors glow,
Or winter wraps the polar world in snow,   420
Still let thy voice, prevailing over time,
Redress the rigors of the inclement clime;
Aid slighted truth, with thy persuasive strain
Teach erring man to spurn the rage of gain;
Teach him that states of native strength possessed,   425
Though very poor, may still be very blest;
That trade's proud empire hastes to swift decay,
As ocean sweeps the labored mole[11] away;
While self-dependent power can time defy,
As rocks resist the billows and the sky.   430

—1770

❦

CONTEMPORARY RESPONSE

Oliver Goldsmith
1794–1861

The Canadian poet Oliver Goldsmith was named for his great uncle, the famous author of "The Deserted Village." Goldsmith was born to an English father and an American Loyalist mother on July 6, 1794, at St. Andrew's, New Brunswick. Nearly a decade earlier, in 1785, his parents had moved from New York to New Brunswick as a show of political support for the Crown. The senior Goldsmith had been wounded twice during the American Revolution and was urged—and encouraged with £6,000—by his wife's parents to leave the British service. He refused the offer and upon his arrival in New Brunswick began an administrative career in the military that culminated with his promotion to Assistant Commissary General, a rank his son would also achieve. The younger Goldsmith inherited from his father a sense of duty to the empire and distinguished himself during his long public career as an effective colonial administrator with an amiable personality.

Goldsmith's long poem, "The Rising Village," published in London by John Sharpe in 1825, was the first British-published poem by a Canadian-born author. (Goldsmith was also the first Canadian to publish an autobiography and to publish his work in both England and Canada.) The poem was reprinted in Montreal in the February 1826 issue of the *Canadian Review and Magazine* and was revised for an 1834 Canadian edition. "The Rising Village" details the settlement and development of a Loyalist village in embryonic Canada. In doing so, it continues the project of "The Deserted Village" (1770), by Goldsmith's great-uncle, which mentions that a number of British citizens are leaving for homes "beyond the western main"—beyond the Atlantic (p. 82). The Canadian Goldsmith picks up here, offering a portrait of the New World through the microcosm of a single village, the fictitious Auburn. The poem follows the establishment and development of various village buildings and institutions (a tavern, a church, a country store, and a school) and its citizens (the patient and industrious settler, the "half-bred" doctor

---

10. The Tornio River in Sweden and Mount Pambamarca in Ecuador.   11. Breakwater.

[p. 88], and the schoolmaster). The story of the community's and the country's development, with its attendant successes and woes, is paralleled in a love story of two young settlers.

There are interesting differences between the 1825 British and the 1834 Canadian versions that mark a shift in political and national sensibility. The British version—which is reproduced here—focuses on the rural and the wild. Its language is rustic and archaic, colloquially expressed through truncated vowels. It is also a poem of the colony, respectful of the British Christian missionary group, the Society for the Propagation of the Gospel in Foreign Parts, and of Lord Dalhousie's role in early Canadian development. In the Canadian edition, on the other hand, the elided vowels are restored, giving the poem a more sophisticated voice. Also, references to the Society for the Propagation of the Gospel and a tribute to Dalhousie are excised. By 1834, Canadian readers had become all too familiar with Dalhousie's heavy-handed policies. By erasing Dalhousie from the poem, Goldsmith not only makes a gesture of accommodation to his Canadian audience but also quietly criticizes his domineering superior. Thus the two versions cater to two different audiences, showing Nova Scotians as rural and charming to British readers in 1825 and as independent and sophisticated to Canadian readers in 1834—reflecting the changing times between the appearance of the two volumes.

Goldsmith spent thirty-four years in the Commissariat of the British Navy and was widely acclaimed for his devotion to the Crown and his active contributions to the military and civilian communities at a variety of posts around the world. According to one newspaper report, when he departed Halifax in 1844, bound for a post in China, some two thousand people crowded the docks to send him off. Although he held a variety of posts around the world and was shipwrecked twice, Goldsmith was no Robinson Crusoe. Indeed, the adventure of surviving two wrecks received little more than a passing glance in his *Autobiography*, first published posthumously in 1943.

from The Rising Village

Thou dear companion of my early years,
Partner of all my boyish hopes and fears,
To whom I oft addressed the youthful strain,
And sought no other praise than thine to gain;
Who oft hast bid me emulate his fame   5
Whose genius formed the glory of our name;
Say, when thou canst, in manhood's ripened age,
With judgment scan the more aspiring page,
Wilt thou accept this tribute of my lay,
By far too small thy fondness to repay?   10
Say, dearest Brother, wilt thou now excuse
This bolder flight of my adventurous muse?
    If, then, adown your cheek a tear should flow
For Auburn's Village, and its speechless woe;
If, while you weep, you think the "lowly train"   15
Their early joys can never more regain,
Come, turn with me where happier prospects rise,
Beneath the sternness of Acadian[1] skies.
And thou, dear spirit! whose harmonious lay
Didst lovely Auburn's piercing woes display,   20
Do thou to thy fond relative impart
Some portion of thy sweet poetic art;

1. Acadia, a French colony in Quebec.

Like thine, Oh! let my verse as gently flow,
While truth and virtue in my numbers glow:
And guide my pen with thy bewitching hand,   25
To paint the Rising Village of the land.
   How chaste and splendid are the scenes that lie
Beneath the circle of Britannia's sky!
What charming prospects there arrest the view,
How bright, how varied, and how boundless too!   30
Cities and plains extending far and wide,
The merchant's glory, and the farmer's pride.
Majestic palaces in pomp display
The wealth and splendour of the regal sway;
While the low hamlet and the shepherd's cot,   35
In peace and freedom mark the peasant's lot.
There nature's vernal bloom adorns the field,
And Autumn's fruits their rich luxuriance yield.
There men, in busy crowds, with men combine,
That arts may flourish, and fair science shine;   40
And thence, to distant climes their labours send,
As o'er the world their widening views extend.
Compar'd with scenes like these, how lone and drear
Did once Acadia's woods and wilds appear;
Where wandering savages, and beasts of prey,   45
Displayed, by turns, the fury of their sway.
What noble courage must their hearts have fired,
How great the ardour which their souls inspired,
Who leaving far behind their native plain,
Have sought a home beyond the Western main;   50
And braved the perils of the stormy seas,
In search of wealth, of freedom, and of ease!
Oh! none can tell but they who sadly share
The bosom's anguish, and its wild despair,
What dire distress awaits the hardy bands,   55
That venture first on bleak and desert lands.
How great the pain, the danger, and the toil,
Which mark the first rude culture of the soil.
When, looking round, the lonely settler sees
His home amid a wilderness of trees: 60
How sinks his heart in those deep solitudes,
Where not a voice upon his ear intrudes;
Where solemn silence all the waste pervades,
Heightening the horror of its gloomy shades;
Save where the sturdy woodman's strokes resound,   65
That strew the fallen forest on the ground.
See! from their heights the lofty pines descend,
And crackling, down their pond'rous lengths extend.
Soon from their boughs the curling flames arise,

Mount into air, and redden all the skies; 70
And where the forest once its foliage spread,
The golden corn triumphant waves its head.
   How blest, did nature's ruggedness appear
The only source of trouble or of fear;
How happy, did no hardship meet his view, 75
No other care his anxious steps pursue;
But, while his labour gains a short repose,
And hope presents a solace for his woes,
New ills arise, new fears his peace annoy,
And other dangers all his hopes destroy. 80
Behold the savage tribes in wildest strain,
Approach with death and terror in their train;
No longer silence o'er the forest reigns,
No longer stillness now her power retains;
But hideous yells announce the murderous band, 85
Whose bloody footsteps desolate the land;
He hears them oft in sternest mood maintain,
Their right to rule the mountain and the plain;
He hears them doom the *white man's* instant death,
Shrinks from the sentence, while he gasps for breath, 90
Then, rousing with one effort all his might,
Darts from his hut, and saves himself by flight.
Yet, what a refuge! Here a host of foes,
On every side, his trembling steps oppose;
Here savage beasts around his cottage howl, 95
As through the gloomy wood they nightly prowl,
Till morning comes, and then is heard no more
The shouts of man, or beast's appalling roar;
The wandering Indian turns another way,
And brutes avoid the first approach of day. 100
   Yet, tho' these threat'ning dangers round him roll,
Perplex his thoughts, and agitate his soul,
By patient firmness and industrious toil,
He still retains possession of the soil;
Around his dwelling scattered huts extend, 105
Whilst every hut affords another friend.
And now, behold! his bold aggressors fly,
To seek their prey beneath some other sky;
Resign the haunts they can maintain no more,
And safety in far distant wilds explore. 110
His perils vanished, and his fears o'ercome,
Sweet hope portrays a happy peaceful home.
On every side fair prospects charm his eyes,
And future joys in every thought arise.
His humble cot, built from the neighbouring trees, 115
Affords protection from each chilling breeze;

His rising crops, with rich luxuriance crowned,
In waving softness shed their freshness round;
By nature nourished, by her bounty blest,
He looks to Heaven, and lulls his cares to rest.   120
    The arts of culture now extend their sway,
And many a charm of rural life display.
Where once the pine upreared its lofty head,
The settlers' humble cottages are spread;
Where the broad firs once sheltered from the storm,   125
By slow degrees a neighbourhood they form;
And, as it bounds, each circling year, increase
In social life, prosperity, and peace,
New prospects rise, new objects too appear,
To add more comfort to its lowly sphere.   130
Where some rude sign or post the spot betrays,
The tavern first its useful front displays.
Here, oft the weary traveller at the close
Of evening, finds a snug and safe repose.
The passing stranger here, a welcome guest,   135
From all his toil enjoys a peaceful rest;
Unless the host, solicitous to please,
With care officious mar his hope of ease,
With flippant questions to no end confined,
Exhaust his patience, and perplex his mind.   140
    Yet, let no one condemn with thoughtless haste,
The hardy settler of the dreary waste,
Who, far removed from every busy throng,
And social pleasures that to life belong,
Whene'er a stranger comes within his reach,   145
Will sigh to learn whatever he can teach.
To this, must be ascribed in great degree,
That ceaseless, idle curiosity,
Which over all the Western world prevails,
And every breast, or more or less, assails;   150
Till, by indulgence, so o'erpowering grown,
It seeks to know all business but its own.
Here, oft when winter's dreary terrors reign,
And cold, and snow, and storm, pervade the plain,
Around the birch-wood blaze the settlers draw,   155
"To tell of all they felt, and all they saw."
When, thus in peace are met a happy few,
Sweet are the social pleasures that ensue.
What lively joy each honest bosom feels,
As o'er the past events his memory steals,   160
And to the listeners paints the dire distress,
That marked his progress in the wilderness;
The danger, trouble, hardship, toil, and strife,

Which chased each effort of his struggling life. . . .
    While now the Rising Village claims a name,
Its limits still increase, and still its fame.
The wandering Pedlar, who undaunted traced
His lonely footsteps o'er the silent waste;   200
Who traversed once the cold and snow-clad plain,
Reckless of danger, trouble, or of pain,
To find a market for his little wares,
The source of all his hopes, and all his cares,
Established here, his settled home maintains,   205
And soon a merchant's higher title gains.
Around his store, on spacious shelves arrayed,
Behold his great and various stock in trade.
Here, nails and blankets, side by side, are seen,
There, horses' collars, and a large tureen;   210
Buttons and tumblers, fish-hooks, spoons and knives,
Shawls for young damsels, flannel for old wives;
Woolcards and stockings, hats for men and boys,
Mill-saws and fenders, silks, and children's toys;
All useful things, and joined with many more,   215
Compose the well-assorted country store.
    The half-bred Doctor next then settles down,
And hopes the village soon will prove a town.
No rival here disputes his doubtful skill,
He cures, by chance, or ends each human ill;   220
By turns he physics, or his patient bleeds,
Uncertain in what case each best succeeds.
And if, from friends untimely snatched away,
Some beauty fall a victim to decay;
If some fine youth, his parents' fond delight,   225
Be early hurried to the shades of night,
Death bears the blame, 'tis his envenomed dart
That strikes the suffering mortal to the heart.
    Beneath the shelter of a log-built shed
The country school-house next erects its head.   230
No "man severe," with learning's bright display,
Here leads the opening blossoms into day;
No master here, in every art refined,
Through fields of science guides the aspiring mind;
But some poor wanderer of the human race,   235
Unequal to the task, supplies his place,
Whose greatest source of knowledge or of skill
Consists in reading, and in writing ill;
Whose efforts can no higher merit claim,
Than spreading Dilworth's[2] great scholastic fame.   240

---

2. Thomas Dilworth (d. 1780), author of popular school textbooks.

No modest youths surround his awful chair,
His frowns to deprecate, or smiles to share,
But all the terrors of his lawful sway
The proud despise, the fearless disobey;
The rugged urchins spurn at all control,   245
Which cramps the movements of the free-born soul,
Till, in their own conceit so wise they've grown,
They think their knowledge far exceeds his own.
   As thus the village each successive year
Presents new prospects, and extends its sphere,   250
While all around its smiling charms expand,
And rural beauties decorate the land. . . .
   Nor culture's arts, a nation's noblest friend,
Alone o'er Scotia's[3] fields their power extend;   520
From all her shores, with every gentle gale,
Commerce expands her free and swelling sail;
And all the land, luxuriant, rich, and gay,
Exulting owns the splendour of their sway.
These are thy blessings, Scotia, and for these,   525
For wealth, for freedom, happiness, and ease,
Thy grateful thanks to Britian's care are due,
Her power protects, her smiles past hopes renew,
Her valour guards thee, and her councils guide,
Then, may thy parent ever be thy pride!   530
   Happy Britannia! though thy history's page
In darkest ignorance shrouds thine infant age,
Though long thy childhood's years in error strayed,
And long in superstition's bands delayed;
Matur'd and strong, thou shin'st in manhood's prime,   535
The first and brightest star of Europe's clime.
The nurse of science, and the seat of arts,
The home of fairest forms and gentlest hearts;
The land of heroes, generous, free, and brave,
The noblest conquerors of the field and wave;   540
Thy flag, on every sea and shore unfurled,
Has spread thy glory, and thy thunder hurled.
When, o'er the earth, a tyrant would have thrown
His iron chain, and called the world his own,
Thine arm preserved it, in its darkest hour,   545
Destroyed his hopes, and crushed his dreaded power,
To sinking nations life and freedom gave,
'Twas thine to conquer, as 'twas thine to save.
   Then blest Acadia! ever may thy name,
Like hers, be graven on the rolls of fame;   550
May all thy sons, like hers, be brave and free,

---

3. Nova Scotia.

Possessors of her laws and liberty;
Heirs of her splendour, science, power, and skill,
And through succeeding years her children still.
And as the sun, with gentle dawning ray,   555
From night's dull bosom wakes, and leads the day,
His course majestic keeps, till in the height
He glows one blaze of pure exhaustless light;
So may thy years increase, thy glories rise,
To be the wonder of the Western skies;   560
And bliss and peace encircle all thy shore,
Till empires rise and sink, on earth, no more.

—1834

CONTEMPORARY RESPONSE
Timothy Dwight
1752–1817

At age four, Timothy Dwight was already able to read the Bible. A couple of years later, Dwight, a descendent of a family of conservative Congregationalists and a grandson of the famous American theologian and preacher Jonathan Edwards (1703–1758), was instructing local Native Americans in catechism. Devout belief in a puritanical Christianity shaped Dwight's life, but his Calvinist ministering and teaching were also influenced by his family's belief that individuals are responsible for their own actions and are not simply the inheritors of the sins of Adam and Eve. Dwight's theology, grounded as it is in the English Enlightenment belief in rational conduct, influenced generations of students at Yale University—an institution to which Dwight had a lifelong connection.

After studying theology at Yale from ages thirteen to seventeen, although he had met the university's admission standard by age eight, Dwight graduated in 1769 with highest honors. At Yale, he met Joel Barlow, who along with other students there, including David Humphreys and John Trumbull, became known as the Connecticut Wits. (For more on the Wits, see Joel Barlow, p. 160.) The Wits drew on the models of Samuel Butler's *Hudibras* (1663–1678) and Alexander Pope's *Dunciad* (1728) to satirize democracy and its advocates, especially Thomas Jefferson. The Wits also sought to create an American literature—a national literature based on New World subjects—and Dwight, along with Trumbull, argued for the introduction of contemporary English and American literature into the Yale curriculum.

Dwight's intense studies weakened his vision to the point that he could no longer see to write and routinely required an amanuensis. His failing eyes also led to his habit of speaking extemporaneously on public occasions. After graduation, he briefly pursued but abandoned a legal career, then returned to tutor at Yale from 1771 to 1777. After his teaching stint he accepted a position as chaplain at the military institution, West Point. He later went on to receive a Doctor of Divinity from Princeton and helped found the Andover Theological Seminary, the American Bible Society, the American Board of Commissioners for Foreign Missions, and the Missionary Society of Connecticut.

In 1783, Dwight moved his family to Greenfield, Connecticut, where he farmed, served as a pastor, and founded a highly respected school for boys and girls. During his twelve years in Greenfield, Dwight's literary output was prodigious. *The Conquest of Canaan* was published in 1785, dedicated to his friend, George Washington. This poem retells the story of Joshua's conquest of lands promised by God, allegorizing the colonization and settlement of the New World. Three years later, *The Triumph of Infidelity* appeared—a work in which Dwight employs Satan as a figure of destruction who attempts to overthrow the new republic of America. In *Greenfield Hill,* first published in 1794, Dwight responds to the elder Oliver Goldsmith's "The Deserted Village," by relocating the virtuous utopian society that Goldsmith laments to the New World. Dwight's didactic poem consistently contrasts a dystopian and corrupt Europe to an idyllic, enlightened America. But in order to do so, the poem must gloss over social realities in America that it is quick to damn in Europe, even suggesting that the life of a slave in Connecticut was far better than that of one in Europe. Dwight was able to apply this same tendentious logic in life as in poetry, attracting many southerners to Yale during his long tenure there as president. It is reflected perhaps most clearly in the terms of purchase for his slave Naomi (the receipt of her purchase survives in Yale's archives). Naomi was allowed to work for her freedom (to "refund" Dwight for the money he paid for her) so long as "she shall uniformly behave well, faithfully, and truly towards me and mine." Whether she was able to purchase her freedom is not known.

from Greenfield Hill
Part II
The Flourishing Village

Fair Verna![1] loveliest village of the west;
Of every joy, and every charm, possess'd;
How pleas'd amid thy varied walks I rove,
Sweet, cheerful walks of innocence, and love,
And o'er thy smiling prospects cast my eyes,   5
And see the seats of peace, and pleasure, rise,
And hear the voice of Industry resound,
And mark the smile of Competence, around!
Hail, happy village! O'er the cheerful lawns,
With earliest beauty, spring delighted dawns;   10
The northward sun begins his vernal smile;
The spring-bird carols o'er the cressy rill:
The shower, that patters in the ruffled stream,
The ploughboy's voice, that chides the lingering team,
The bee, industrious, with his busy song,   15
The woodman's axe, the distant groves among,
The wagon, rattling down the rugged steep,
The light wind, lulling every care to sleep,
All these, with mingled music, from below,
Deceive intruding sorrow, as I go.   20

How pleas'd, fond Recollection, with a smile,
Surveys the varied round of wintery toil!
How pleas'd, amid the flowers, that scent the plain,
Recalls the vanish'd frost, and sleeted rain;
The chilling damp, the ice-endangering street,   25
And treacherous earth that slump'd beneath the feet.

Yet even stern winter's glooms could joy inspire:
Then social circles grac'd the nutwood fire;
The axe resounded, at the sunny door;

---

1. A generic New England village.

The swain, industrious, trimm'd his flaxen store;   30
Or thresh'd, with vigorous flail, the bounding wheat,
His poultry round him pilfering for their meat;
Or slid his firewood on the creaking snow;
Or bore his produce to the main below;
Or o'er his rich returns exulting laugh'd;   35
Or pledg'd the healthful orchard's sparkling draught:
While, on his board, for friends and neighbors spread,
The turkey smok'd, his busy housewife fed;
And Hospitality look'd smiling round,
And Leisure told his tale, with gleeful sound.   40

   Then too, the rough road hid beneath the sleigh,
The distant friend despis'd a length of way,
And join'd the warm embrace, the mingling smile,
And told of all his bliss, and all his toil;
And, many a month elaps'd, was pleas'd to view   45
How well the household far'd, the children grew;
While tales of sympathy deceiv'd the hour,
And Sleep, amus'd, resign'd his wonted power.

   Yes! let the proud despise, the rich deride,
These humble joys, to Competence allied: 50
To me, they bloom, all fragrant to my heart,
Nor ask the pomp of wealth, nor gloss of art.
And as a bird, in prison long confin'd,
Springs from his open'd cage, and mounts the wind,
Thro' fields of flowers, and fragrance, gaily flies,   55
Or reassumes his birth-right, in the skies:
Unprison'd thus from artificial joys,
Where pomp fatigues, and fussful fashion cloys,
The soul, reviving, loves to wander free
Thro' native scenes of sweet simplicity;   60
Thro' Peace' low vale, where Pleasure lingers long,
And every songster tunes his sweetest song,
And Zephyr hastes, to breathe his first perfume,
And Autumn stays, to drop his latest bloom:
'Till grown mature, and gathering strength to roam,   65
She lifts her lengthen'd wings, and seeks her home.

   But now the wintery glooms are vanish'd all;
The lingering drift behind the shady wall;
The dark-brown spots, that patch'd the snowy field;
The surly frost, that every bud conceal'd;   70
The russet veil, the way with slime o'erspread,
And all the saddening scenes of March are fled.

   Sweet-smiling village! loveliest of the hills!
How green thy groves! How pure thy glassy rills!

With what new joy, I walk thy verdant streets!   75
How often pause, to breathe thy gale of sweets;
To mark thy well-built walls! thy budding fields!
And every charm, that rural nature yields;
And every joy, to Competence allied,
And every good, that Virtue gains from Pride!   80

   No griping landlord here alarms the door,
To halve, for rent, the poor man's little store.
No haughty owner drives the humble swain
To some far refuge from his dread domain;
Nor wastes, upon his robe of useless pride,   85
The wealth, which shivering thousands want beside;
Nor in one palace sinks a hundred cots;
Nor in one manor drowns a thousand lots;
Nor, on one table, spread for death and pain,
Devours what would a village well sustain.   90

   O Competence, thou bless'd by Heaven's decree,
How well exchang'd is empty pride for thee!
Oft to thy cot my feet delighted turn,
To meet thy cheerful smile, at peep of morn;
To join thy toils, that bid the earth look gay;   95
To mark thy sports, that hail the eve of May;
To see thy ruddy children, at thy board,
And share thy temperate meal, and frugal hoard;
And every joy, by winning prattlers giv'n,
And every earnest of a future Heaven.   100

   There the poor wanderer finds a table spread,
The fireside welcome, and the peaceful bed.
The needy neighbor, oft by wealth denied,
There finds the little aids of life supplied;
The horse, that bears to mill the hard-earn'd grain;   105
The day's work given, to reap the ripen'd plain;
The useful team, to house the precious food,
And all the offices of real good.

   There too, divine Religion is a guest,
And all the Virtues join the daily feast.   110
Kind Hospitality attends the door,
To welcome in the stranger and the poor;
Sweet Chastity, still blushing as she goes;
And Patience smiling at her train of woes;
And meek-eyed Innocence, and Truth refin'd,   115
And Fortitude, of bold, but gentle mind.

   Thou pay'st the tax, the rich man will not pay;
Thou feed'st the poor, the rich man drives away.

Thy sons, for freedom, hazard limbs, and life,
While pride applauds, but shuns the manly strife: 120
Thou prop'st religion's cause, the world around,
And show'st thy faith in works, and not in sound.

   Say, child of passion! while, with idiot stare,
Thou seest proud grandeur wheel her sunny car;
While kings, and nobles, roll bespangled by,   125
And the tall palace lessens in the sky;
Say, while with pomp thy giddy brain runs round,
What joys, like these, in splendor can be found?
Ah, yonder turn thy wealth-enchanted eyes,
Where that poor, friendless wretch expiring lies!   130
Hear his sad partner shriek, beside his bed,
And call down curses on her landlord's head,
Who drove, from yon small cot, her household sweet,
To pine with want, and perish in the street.
See the pale tradesman toil, the livelong day,   135
To deck imperious lords, who never pay!
Who waste, at dice, their boundless breadth of soil,
But grudge the scanty meed of honest toil.
See hounds and horses riot on the store,
By Heaven created for the hapless poor!   140
See half a realm one tyrant scarce sustain,
While meager thousands round him glean the plain!
See, for his mistress' robe, a village sold,
Whose matrons shrink from nakedness and cold!
See too the Farmer prowl around the shed,   145
To rob the starving household of their bread;
And seize, with cruel fangs, the helpless swain,
While wives, and daughters, plead, and weep, in vain;
Or yield to infamy themselves, to save
Their sire from prison, famine, and the grave.   150

   There too foul luxury taints the putrid mind,
And slavery there imbrutes the reasoning kind:
There humble worth, in damps of deep despair,
Is bound by poverty's eternal bar:
No motives bright the ethereal aim impart,   155
Nor one fair ray of hope allures the heart.

   But, O sweet Competence! how chang'd the scene,
Where thy soft footsteps lightly print the green!
Where Freedom walks erect, with manly port,
And all the blessings to his side resort,   160
In every hamlet, Learning builds her schools,
And beggars, children gain her arts, and rules;

And mild Simplicity o'er manners reigns,
And blameless morals Purity sustains.

From thee the rich enjoyments round me spring,   165
Where every farmer reigns a little king;
Where all to comfort, none to danger, rise;
Where pride finds few, but nature all supplies;
Where peace and sweet civility are seen,
And meek good-neighborhood endears the green.   170
Here every class (if classes those we call,
Where one extended class embraces all,
All mingling, as the rainbow's beauty blends,
Unknown where every hue begins or ends)
Each following, each, with uninvidious strife,   175
Wears every feature of improving life.
Each gains from other comeliness of dress,
And learns, with gentle mein to win and bless,
With welcome mild the stranger to receive,
And with plain, pleasing decency to live.   180
Refinement hence even humblest life improves;
Not the loose fair, that form and frippery loves;
But she, whose mansion is the gentle mind,
In thought, and action, virtuously refin'd.
Hence, wives and husbands act a lovelier part,   185
More just the conduct, and more kind the heart;
Hence brother, sister, parent, child, and friend,
The harmony of life more sweetly blend;
Hence labor brightens every rural scene;
Hence cheerful plenty lives along the green;   190
Still Prudence eyes her hoard, with watchful care,
And robes of thrift and neatness, all things wear.

—1794

Michel Guillaume Jean de Crèvecoeur
1735–1813

Born to an aristocratic family in Caen, France, Michel Guillaume Jean de Crèvecoeur became one of the most influential interpreters of the American Revolution for European audiences. Crèvecoeur emigrated at age nineteen first to London and then to New France, where he served under the Marquis de Montcalm during the war between France, Great Britain, and their allied native tribes for control of North America. During the war, he witnessed the 1757 massacre of

British soldiers at Fort William Henry, an incident that would later supply the basis for James Fenimore Cooper's *Last of the Mohicans* (1826). After he was wounded in the 1758 battle for Quebec, Crèvecoeur was discharged from the army and took up surveying in the British colonies. Soon, the Treaty of Paris confirmed the future of North America, and Crèvecoeur became a British subject, changing his name to J. Hector St. John, the name by which he became known to American literature. In 1769, as the colonies moved toward independence, he married, bought land in Orange County, New York, and began to farm and write. Crèvecoeur did not support the Revolution, and when Loyalists (those living in the colonies who remained loyal to George III) began to come under sustained attack, he took refuge in Europe with his eldest son, leaving his wife and two other children to maintain the farm. In 1781, he sold the manuscript for *Letters from an American Farmer* to a London publisher, then traveled to France to reclaim his inheritance. When he returned to the post-Revolutionary United States as French consul, his farm had been burned, his wife was dead, and his children had disappeared.

Letters from an American Farmer is an epistolary fiction—some would say North America's first novel—whose narrator, a Pennsylvania farmer named James, addresses a series of twelve letters to an English correspondent, F. B., describing life in the United States and Canada. The earlier letters give voice to the colonial ideology of agrarian republicanism. In North America, free (or at least cheap) land was available to those willing to cultivate it. This meant that those who in Europe would have been poor and despised could establish economic independence, which in turn allowed them self-respect and political independence. Moreover, agricultural labor put freeholders in touch with nature and its laws, where they learned a simple and vigorous morality. Letter III, "What is an American?," gives a compelling vision of a classless society of immigrants bound together as a nation by their dedication to hard work and liberty. But as the book progresses, Farmer James's optimistic faith in America comes under heavy attack. In Letter IX, he recounts his chilling discovery of the brutality of the slave system in the South. And by Letter XII, he has become a desperate man, hiding on his farm, awaiting a vindictive mob of revolutionaries whom he expects will massacre his family. Liberty has become anarchy, and the benign landscape of agrarianism has become a wilderness that reduces civilized people to savagery.

Letters was received enthusiastically in England. While in France, Crèvecoeur translated the book into his native language. He significantly expanded it in the process and had it published in Paris as *Lettres d'un cultivateur Americain* (1784). This new version was so successful and so laudatory of the New World that more than five hundred families left France to settle on the Ohio River, where most perished. In 1793, the great Philadelphia printer Matthew Carey republished the book in North America, where it met with similar acclaim.

Critics have proposed several alternative readings of this ambiguous text. For many years, it was seen as a bold declaration of faith, tempered by realism, in the Enlightenment project of rational government. Others argue that the text mounts a pacifist critique of the American Revolution, asking its readers to place their hopes for human progress in the simple virtue of agrarian yeomen like Farmer James. But most now regard the book as a deadpan satire of republican political ideology with a finally quite conservative political message.

from Letters from an American Farmer
from Letter III. What is an American?

I wish I could be acquainted with the feelings and thoughts which must agitate the heart and present themselves to the mind of an enlightened Englishman when he first lands on this continent. He must greatly rejoice that he lived at a time to see this fair country discovered and settled; he must necessarily feel a share of national pride when he views the chain of settlements which embellish these extended shores. When he says to himself, "This is the work of my countrymen, who, when convulsed by factions, afflicted by a variety of miseries and wants, restless and impatient, took refuge here. They brought along with them their national genius, to which they principally owe what liberty they enjoy and what substance they possess." Here he sees the industry of his native country displayed in a new manner and traces in their works the embryos of all the arts, sciences, and ingenuity which flourish in Europe. Here he beholds fair cities, substantial villages, extensive fields, an immense country filled with decent houses, good roads, orchards, meadows, and bridges where an hundred years ago all was wild, woody, and uncultivated! What a train of pleasing ideas this fair spectacle must suggest; it is a prospect which must inspire a good citizen with the most heart-felt pleasure. The difficulty consists in the manner of viewing so extensive a scene. He is arrived on a new continent; a modern society offers itself to his contemplation, different from what he had hitherto seen. It is not composed, as in Europe, of great lords who possess everything and of a herd of people who have nothing. Here are no aristocratical families, no courts, no kings, no bishops, no ecclesiastical dominion, no invisible power giving to a few a very visible one, no great manufactures employing thousands, no great refinements of luxury. The rich and the poor are not so far removed from each other as they are in Europe. Some few towns excepted, we are all tillers of the earth, from Nova Scotia to West Florida. We are a people of cultivators scattered over an immense territory, communicating with each other by means of good roads and navigable rivers, united by the silken bands of mild government, all respecting the laws without dreading their power, because they are equitable. We are all animated with the spirit of an industry which is unfettered and unrestrained, because each person works for himself. If he travels through our rural districts, he views not the hostile castle and the haughty mansion, contrasted with the clay-built hut and miserable cabin, where cattle and men help to keep each other warm and dwell in meanness, smoke, and indigence. A pleasing uniformity of decent competence appears throughout our habitations. The meanest of our log-houses is a dry and comfortable habitation. Lawyer or merchant are the fairest titles our towns afford; that of a farmer is the only appellation of the rural inhabitants of our country. It must take some time ere he can reconcile himself to our dictionary, which is but short in words of dignity and names of honour. There, on a Sunday, he sees a congregation of respectable farmers and their wives, all clad in neat homespun, well mounted, or riding in their own humble waggons. There is not among them an esquire, saving the unlettered magistrate. There he sees a parson as simple as his flock, a farmer who does not riot on the labour of others. We have no princes for whom we toil, starve, and bleed; we are the most perfect society now existing in the world. Here man is free as he ought to be, nor is this pleasing equality so transitory as many others are. Many ages will not see the shores of our great lakes replenished with inland nations, nor the unknown bounds of North America entirely peopled. Who can tell how far it extends? Who can tell the millions of men whom it will feed and contain? For no European foot has as yet travelled half the extent of this mighty continent!

    The next wish of this traveller will be to know whence came all these people. They are a mixture of English, Scotch, Irish, French, Dutch, Germans, and Swedes. From this promiscuous breed, that race now called Americans have arisen. The eastern provinces must indeed be excepted as being the unmixed descendants of Englishmen. I have heard many wish that they had been more intermixed also; for my part, I am no wisher and think it much better as it has happened. They exhibit a most conspicuous figure in this great and variegated picture; they too enter for a great share in the pleasing perspective displayed in these thirteen provinces. I know it is fashionable to reflect on them, but I respect them for what they have done; for the accuracy and wisdom with which they have settled their territory; for the decency of their manners; for their early love of letters; their ancient college, the first in this hemisphere; for their industry, which to me who am but a farmer is the criterion of everything. There never was a people, situated as they are, who with so ungrateful a soil have done more in so short a time. Do you think that the monarchical ingredients which are more prevalent in other governments have purged them from all foul stains? Their histories assert the contrary.

In this great American asylum, the poor of Europe have by some means met together, and in consequence of various causes; to what purpose should they ask one another what countrymen they are? Alas, two thirds of them had no country. Can a wretch who wanders about, who works and starves, whose life is a continual scene of sore affliction or pinching penury—can that man call England or any other kingdom his country? A country that had no bread for him, whose fields procured him no harvest, who met with nothing but the frowns of the rich, the severity of the laws, with jails and punishments, who owned not a single foot of the extensive surface of this planet? No! Urged by a variety of motives, here they came. Everything has tended to regenerate them: new laws, a new mode of living, a new social system; here they are become men: in Europe they were as so many useless plants, wanting vegetative mould and refreshing showers; they withered, and were mowed down by want, hunger, and war; but now, by the power of transplantation, like all other plants they have taken root and flourished! Formerly they were not numbered in any civil lists of their country, except in those of the poor; here they rank as citizens. By what invisible power hath this surprising metamorphosis been performed? By that of the laws and that of their industry. The laws, the indulgent laws, protect them as they arrive, stamping on them the symbol of adoption; they receive ample rewards for their labours; these accumulated rewards procure them lands; those lands confer on them the title of freemen, and to that title every benefit is affixed which men can possibly require. This is the great operation daily performed by our laws. Whence proceed these laws? From the government. Whence that government? It is derived from the original genius and strong desire of the people ratified and confirmed by the crown. This is the great chain which links us all, this is the picture which every province exhibits, Nova Scotia excepted. There the crown has done all; either there were no people who had genius or it was not much attended to; the consequence is that the province is very thinly inhabited indeed; the power of the crown in conjunction with the musketos has prevented men from settling there. Yet some parts of it flourished once, and it contained a mild, harmless set of people. But for the fault of a few leaders, the whole was banished. The greatest political error the crown ever committed in America was to cut off men from a country which wanted nothing but men!

What attachment can a poor European emigrant have for a country where he had nothing? The knowledge of the language, the love of a few kindred as poor as himself, were the only cords that tied him; his country is now that which gives him his land, bread, protection, and consequence. *Ubi panis ibi patria*[1] is the motto of all emigrants. What, then, is the American, this new man? He is either an European or the descendant of an European; hence that strange mixture of blood, which you will find in no

---

1. Where there is bread, there is the fatherland.

other country. I could point out to you a family whose grandfather was an Englishman, whose wife was Dutch, whose son married a French woman, and whose present four sons have now four wives of different nations. *He* is an American, who, leaving behind him all his ancient prejudices and manners, receives new ones from the new mode of life he has embraced, the new government he obeys, and the new rank he holds. He becomes an American by being received in the broad lap of our great Alma Mater. Here individuals of all nations are melted into a new race of men, whose labours and posterity will one day cause great changes in the world. Americans are the western pilgrims who are carrying along with them that great mass of arts, sciences, vigour, and industry which began long since in the East; they will finish the great circle. The Americans were once scattered all over Europe; here they are incorporated into one of the finest systems of population which has ever appeared, and which will hereafter become distinct by the power of the different climates they inhabit. The American ought therefore to love this country much better than that wherein either he or his forefathers were born. Here the rewards of his industry follow with equal steps the progress of his labour; his labour is founded on the basis of nature, self-interest; can it want a stronger allurement? Wives and children, who before in vain demanded of him a morsel of bread, now, fat and frolicsome, gladly help their father to clear those fields whence exuberant crops are to arise to feed and to clothe them all, without any part being claimed, either by a despotic prince, a rich abbot, or a mighty lord. Here religion demands but little of him: a small voluntary salary to the minister and gratitude to God; can he refuse these? The American is a new man, who acts upon new principles; he must therefore entertain new ideas and form new opinions. From involuntary idleness, servile dependence, penury, and useless labour, he has passed to toils of a very different nature, rewarded by ample subsistence. This is an American.

British America is divided into many provinces, forming a large association, scattered along a coast 1500 miles extent and about 200 wide. This society I would fain examine, at least such as it appears in the middle provinces; if it does not afford that variety of tinges and gradations which may be observed in Europe, we have colours peculiar to ourselves. For instance, it is natural to conceive that those who live near the sea, must be very different from those who live in the woods; the intermediate space will afford a separate and distinct class.

Men are like plants; the goodness and flavour of the fruit proceeds from the peculiar soil and exposition in which they grow. We are nothing but what we derive from the air we breathe, the climate we inhabit, the government we obey, the system of religion we profess, and the nature of our employment. Here you will find but few crimes; these have acquired as yet no root among us. I wish I were able to trace all my ideas; if my ignorance prevents me from describing them properly, I hope I shall be able to delineate a few of the outlines, which are all I propose.

Those who live near the sea, feed more on fish than on flesh, and often encounter that boisterous element. This renders them more bold and enterprising; this leads them to neglect the confined occupations of the land. They see and converse with a variety of people; their intercourse with mankind becomes extensive. The sea inspires them with a love of traffic, a desire of transporting produce from one place to another; and leads them to a variety of resources which supply the place of labour. Those who inhabit the middle settlements, by far the most numerous, must be very different; the simple cultivation of the earth purifies them, but the indulgences of the government, the soft remonstrances of religion, the rank of independent freeholders, must necessarily inspire them with sentiments, very little known in Europe among people of the same class. What do I say? Europe has no such class of men; the early knowledge they acquire, the early bargains they make, give them a great degree of sagacity. As freemen they will be litigious; pride and obstinacy are often the cause of law suits; the nature of our laws and governments may be another. As citizens it is easy to imagine, that they will carefully read the newspapers, enter into every political disquisition, freely blame or censure governors and others. As farmers they will be careful and anxious to get as much as they can, because what they get is their own. As northern men they will love the chearful cup. As Christians, religion curbs them not in their opinions; the general indulgence leaves every one to think for themselves in spiritual matters; the laws inspect our actions, our thoughts are left to God. Industry, good living, selfishness, litigiousness, country politics, the pride of freemen, religious indifference, are their characteristics. If you recede still farther from the sea, you will come into more modern settlements; they exhibit the same strong lineaments, in a ruder appearance. Religion seems to have still less influence, and their manners are less improved.

Now we arrive near the great woods, near the last inhabited districts; there men seem to be placed still farther beyond the reach of government, which in some measure leaves them to themselves. How can it pervade every corner; as they were driven there by misfortunes, necessity of beginnings, desire of acquiring large tracks of land, idleness, frequent want of œconomy, ancient debts; the re-union of such people does not afford a very pleasing spectacle. When discord, want of unity and friendship; when either drunkenness or idleness prevail in such remote districts; contention, inactivity, and wretchedness must ensue. There are not the same remedies to these evils as in a long established community. The few magistrates they have, are in general little better than the rest; they are often in a perfect state of war; that of man against man, sometimes decided by blows, sometimes by means of the law; that of man against every wild inhabitant of these venerable woods, of which they are come to dispossess them. There men appear to be no better than carnivorous animals of a superior rank, living on the flesh of wild animals when they can catch them, and when they are not able, they subsist on grain. He who would wish to see America in its proper light, and have a true idea of its feeble beginnings and barbarous rudiments, must visit our extended line of frontiers where the last settlers dwell, and where he may see the first labours of settlement, the mode of clearing the earth, in all their different appearances; where men are wholly left dependent on their native tempers, and on the spur of uncertain industry, which often fails when not sanctified by the efficacy of a few moral rules. There, remote from the power of example, and check of shame, many families exhibit the most hideous parts of our society. They are a kind of forlorn hope, preceding by ten or twelve years the most respectable army of veterans which come after them. In that space, prosperity will polish some, vice and the law will drive off the rest, who uniting again with others like themselves will recede still farther; making room for more industrious people, who will finish their improvements, convert the loghouse into a convenient habitation, and rejoicing that the first heavy labours are finished, will change in a few years that hitherto barbarous country into a fine fertile, well regulated district. Such is our progress, such is the march of the Europeans toward the interior parts of this continent. In all societies there are off-casts; this impure part serves as our precursors or pioneers; my father himself was one of that class, but he came upon honest principles, and was therefore one of the few who held fast; by good conduct and temperance, he transmitted to me his fair inheritance, when not above one in fourteen of his contemporaries had the same good fortune.

Forty years ago this smiling country was thus inhabited; it is now purged, a general decency of manners prevails throughout, and such has been the fate of our best countries.

Exclusive of those general characteristics, each province has its own, founded on the government, climate, mode of husbandry, customs, and peculiarity of circumstances. Europeans submit insensibly to these great powers, and become, in the course of a few generations, not only Americans in general, but either Pensylvanians, Virginians, or provincials under some other name. Whoever traverses the continent must easily observe those strong differences, which will grow more evident in time. The inhabitants of Canada, Massachuset, the middle provinces, the southern ones will be as different as their climates; their only points of unity will be those of religion and language. . . .

* * *

Letter IX. Description of Charles-Town; Thoughts on Slavery; On Physical Evil; A Melancholy Scene.

Charles-Town is, in the north, what Lima is in the south; both are Capitals of the richest provinces of their respective hemispheres: you may therefore conjecture, that both cities must exhibit the appearances necessarily resulting from riches. Peru abounding in gold, Lima is filled with inhabitants who enjoy all those gradations of pleasure, refinement, and luxury, which proceed from wealth. Carolina produces commodities, more valuable perhaps than gold, because they are gained by greater industry; it exhibits also on our northern stage, a display of riches and luxury, inferior indeed to the former, but far superior to what are to be seen in our northern towns. Its situation is admirable, being built at the confluence of two large rivers, which receive in their course a great number of inferior streams; all navigable in the spring, for flat boats. Here the produce of this extensive territory concentres; here therefore is the seat of the most valuable exportation; their wharfs, their docks, their magazines, are extremely convenient to facilitate this great commercial business. The inhabitants are the gayest in America; it is called the centre of our beau monde, and it always filled with the richest planters of the province, who resort hither in quest of health and pleasure. Here are always to be seen a great number of valetudinarians from the West-Indies, seeking for the renovation of health, exhausted by the debilitating nature of their sun, air, and modes of living. Many of these West-Indians have I seen, at thirty, loaded with the infirmities of old age; for nothing is more common in those countries of wealth, than for persons to lose the abilities of enjoying the comforts of life, at a time when we northern men just begin to taste the fruits of our labour and prudence. The round of pleasure, and the expences of those citizens' tables, are much superior to what you would imagine: indeed the growth of this town and province has been astonishingly rapid. It is pity that the narrowness of the neck on which it stands prevents it from increasing; and which is the reason why houses are so dear. The heat of the climate, which is sometimes very great in the interior parts of the country, is always temperate in Charles-Town; though sometimes when they have no sea breezes the sun is too powerful. The climate renders excesses of all kinds very dangerous, particularly those of the table; and yet, insensible or fearless of danger, they live on, and enjoy a short and a merry life: the rays of their sun seem to urge them irresistably to dissipation and pleasure: on the contrary, the women, from being abstemious, reach to a longer period of life, and seldom die without having had several husbands. An European at his first arrival must be greatly surprised when he sees the elegance of their houses, their sumptuous furniture, as well as the magnificence of their tables can he imagine himself in a country, the establishment of which is so recent?

The three principal classes of inhabitants are, lawyers, planters, and merchants; this is the province which has afforded to the first the richest spoils, for nothing can exceed their wealth, their power, and their influence. They have reached the *ne plus ultra*[2] of worldly felicity; no plantation is secured, no title is good, no will is valid, but what they dictate, regulate, and approve. The whole mass of provincial property is become tributary to this society; which, far above priests and bishops, disdain to be satisfied with the poor Mosaical portion of the tenth. I appeal to the many inhabitants, who, while contending perhaps for their right to a few hundred acres, have lost by the mazes of the law their whole patrimony. These men are more properly law givers than interpreters of the law; and have united here, as well as in most other provinces, the skill and dexterity of the scribe with the power and ambition of the prince: who can tell where this may lead in a future day? The nature of our laws, and the spirit of freedom, which often tends to make us litigious, must necessarily throw the greatest part of the property of the colonies into the hands of these gentlemen. In another century, the law will possess in the north, what now the church possesses in Peru and Mexico.

While all is joy, festivity, and happiness in Charles-Town, would you imagine that scenes of misery overspread in the country? Their ears by habit are become deaf, their hearts are hardened; they neither see, hear, nor feel for the woes of their poor slaves, from whose painful labours all their wealth proceeds. Here the horrors of slavery, the hardship of incessant toils, are unseen; and no one thinks with compassion of those showers of sweat and of tears which from the bodies of Africans, daily drop, and moisten the ground they till. The cracks of the whip urging these miserable beings to excessive labour, are far too distant from the gay Capital to be heard. The chosen race eat, drink, and live happy, while the unfortunate one grubs up the ground, raises indigo, or husks the rice; exposed to a sun full as scorching as their native one; without the support of good food, without the cordials of any chearing liquor. This great contrast has often afforded me subjects of the most afflicting meditation. On the one side, behold a people enjoying all that life affords most bewitching and pleasurable, without labour, without fatigue, hardly subjected to the trouble of wishing. With gold, dug from Peruvian mountains, they order vessels to the coasts of Guinea; by virtue of that gold, wars, murders, and devastations are committed in some harmless, peaceable African neighbourhood, where dwelt innocent people, who even knew not but that all men were black. The daughter torn from her weeping mother, the child from the wretched parents, the wife from the loving husband; whole families swept away and brought through storms and tempests to this rich metropolis! There, arranged like horses at a fair, they are branded like cattle, and then driven to toil, to starve, and to languish for a few years on the different plantations of

---

2. Limit or endpoint.

these citizens. And for whom must they work? For persons they know not, and who have no other power over them than that of violence; no other right than what this accursed metal has given them! Strange order of things! Oh, Nature, where are thou?—Are not these blacks thy children as well as we? On the other side, nothing is to be seen but the most diffusive misery and wretchedness, unrelieved even in thought or wish! Day after day they drudge on without any prospect of ever reaping for themselves; they are obliged to devote their lives, their limbs, their will, and every vital exertion to swell the wealth of masters; who look not upon them with half the kindness and affection with which they consider their dogs and horses. Kindness and affection are not the portion of those who till the earth, who carry the burdens, who convert the logs into useful boards. This reward, simple and natural as one would conceive it, would border on humanity; and planters must have none of it!

If negroes are permitted to become fathers, this fatal indulgence only tends to increase their misery: the poor companions of their scanty pleasures are likewise the companions of their labours; and when at some critical seasons they could wish to see them relieved, with tears in their eyes they behold them perhaps doubly oppressed, obliged to bear the burden of nature—a fatal present—as well as that of unabated tasks. How many have I seen cursing the irresistible propensity, and regretting, that by having tasted of those harmless joys, they had become the authors of double misery to their wives. Like their masters, they are not permitted to partake of those ineffable sensations with which nature inspires the hearts of fathers and mothers; they must repel them all, and become callous and passive. This unnatural state often occasions the most acute, the most pungent of their afflictions; they have no time, like us, tenderly to rear their help-less offspring, to nurse them on their knees, to enjoy the delight of being parents. Their paternal fondness is embittered by considering, that if their children live, they must live to be slaves like themselves; no time is allowed them to exercise their pious office, the mothers must fasten them on their backs, and, with this double load, follow their hus-bands in the fields, where they too often hear no other sound than that of the voice or whip of the task-master, and the cries of their infants, broiling in the sun. These unfor-tunate creatures cry and weep like their parents, without a possibility of relief; the very instinct of the brute, so laudable, so irresistible, runs counter here to their master's inter-est; and to that god, all the laws of nature must give way. Thus planters get rich; so raw, so inexperienced am I in this mode of life, that were I to be possessed of a plantation, and my slaves treated as in general they are here, never could I rest in peace; my sleep would be perpetually disturbed by a retrospect of the frauds committed in Africa, in order to entrap them; frauds surpassing in enormity every thing which a common mind can possibly conceive. I should be thinking of the barbarous treatment they meet with on ship-board; of their anguish, of the despair necessarily inspired by their situation, when torn from their friends and relations; when delivered into the hands of a people differ-ently coloured, whom they cannot understand; carried in a strange machine over an ever agitated element, which they had never seen before; and finally delivered over to the severities of the whippers, and the excessive labours of the field. Can it be possible that the force of custom should ever make me deaf to all these reflections, and as insensible to the injustice of that trade, and to their miseries, as the rich inhabitants of this town seem to be? What then is man; this being who boasts so much of the excellence and dig-nity of his nature, among that variety of unscrutable mysteries, of unsolvable problems, with which he is surrounded? The reason why man has been thus created, is not the least astonishing! It is said, I know that they are much happier here than in the West-Indies; because land being cheaper upon this continent than in those islands, the fields allowed them to raise their subsistence from, are in general more extensive. The only possible chance of any alleviation depends on the humour of the planters, who, bred in the midst of slaves, learn from the example of their parents to despise them; and seldom conceive either from religion or philosophy, any ideas that tend to make their fate less calamitous; except some strong native tenderness of heart, some rays of philanthropy, overcome the obduracy contracted by habit.

I have not resided here long enough to become insensible of pain for the objects which I every day behold. In the choice of my friends and acquaintance, I always endeavour to find out those whose dispositions are somewhat congenial with my own. We have slaves likewise in our northern provinces; I hope the time draws near when they will be all emancipated: but how different their lot, how different their situation, in every possible respect! They enjoy as much liberty as their masters, they are as well clad, and as well fed; in health and sickness they are tenderly taken care of; they live under the same roof, and are, truly speaking, a part of our families. Many of them are taught to read and write, and are well instructed in the principles of religion; they are the companions of our labours, and treated as such; they enjoy many perquisites, many established holidays, and are not obliged to work more than white people. They marry where inclination leads them; visit their wives every week; are as decently clad as the common people; they are indulged in educating, cherishing, and chastising their children, who are taught subordination to them as to their lawful parents: in short, they participate in many of the benefits of our society, without being obliged to bear any of its burthens. They are fat, healthy, and hearty, and far from repining at their fate; they think themselves happier than many of the lower class whites: they share with their masters the wheat and meat provision they help to raise; many of those whom the good Quakers have emancipated, have received that great benefit with tears of regret, and have never quitted, though free, their former masters and benefactors.

But is it really true, as I have heard it asserted here, that those blacks are incapable of feeling the spurs of emulation, and the chearful sound of encouragement? By no means; there are a thousand proofs existing of their gratitude and fidelity: those hearts in which such noble dispositions can grow, are then like ours, they are susceptible of every generous sentiment, of every useful motive of action; they are capable of receiving lights, of imbibing ideas that would greatly alleviate the weight of their miseries. But what methods have in general been made use of to obtain so desirable an end? None; the day in which they arrive and are sold, is the first of their labours; labours, which from that hour admit of no respite; for though indulged by law with relaxation on Sundays, they are obliged to employ that time which is intended for rest, to till their little plantations. What can be expected from wretches in such circumstances? Forced from their native country, cruelly treated when on board, and not less so on the plantations to which they are driven; is there any thing in this treatment but what must kindle all the passions, sow the seeds of inveterate resentment, and nourish a wish of perpetual revenge? They are left to the irresistible effects of those strong and natural propensities; the blows they receive are they conducive to extinguish them, or to win their affections? They are neither soothed by the hopes that their slavery will ever terminate but with their lives; or yet encouraged by the goodness of their food, or the mildness of their treatment. The very hopes held out to mankind by religion, that consolatory system, so useful to the miserable, are never presented to them; neither moral nor physical means are made use of to soften their chains; they are left in their original and untutored state; that very state where in the natural propensities of revenge and warm passions, are so soon kindled. Cheered by no one single motive that can impel the will, or excite their efforts; nothing but terrors and punishments are presented to them; death is denounced if they run away; horrid delaceration if they speak with their native freedom; perpetually awed by the terrible cracks of whips, or by the fear of capital punishments, while even those punishments often fail of their purpose.

A clergyman settled a few years ago at George-Town, and feeling as I do now, warmly recommended to the planters, from the pulpit, a relaxation of severity; he introduced the benignity of Christianity, and pathetically made use of the admirable precepts of that system to melt the hearts of his congregation into a greater degree of compassion toward their slaves than had been hitherto customary; "Sir" (said one of his hearers) "we pay you a genteel salary to read to us the prayers of the liturgy, and to explain to us such parts of the Gospel as the rule of the church directs; but we do not want you to teach us what we are to do with our blacks." The clergyman found it prudent to with-hold any farther admonition. Whence this astonishing right, or rather this barbarous custom, for most certainly we have no kind of right beyond that of force? We are told, it is true, that slavery cannot be so repugnant to human nature as we at first imagine, because it has been practised in all ages, and in all nations; the Lacedemonians themselves, those great assertors of liberty, conquered the Helotes with the design of making them their slaves[3]; the Romans, whom we consider as our masters in civil and military policy, lived in the exercise of the most horrid oppression; they conquered to plunder and to enslave. What a hideous aspect the face of the earth must then have exhibited! Provinces, towns, districts, often depopulated; their inhabitants driven to Rome, the greatest market in the world, and there sold by thousands! The Roman dominions were tilled by the hands of unfortunate people, who had once been, like their victors free, rich, and possessed of every benefit society can confer; until they became subject to the cruel right of war, and to lawless force. Is there then no superintending power who conducts the moral operations of the world, as well as the physical? The same sublime hand which guides the planets round the sun with so much exactness, which preserves the arrangement of the whole with such exalted wisdom and paternal care, and prevents the vast system from falling into confusion; doth it abandon mankind to all the errors, the follies, and the miseries, which their most frantic rage, and their most dangerous vices and passions can produce?

The history of the earth! doth it present any thing but crimes of the most heinous nature, committed from one end of the world to the other? We observe avarice, rapine, and murder, equally prevailing in all parts. History perpetually tells us, of millions of people abandoned to the caprice of the maddest princes, and of whole nations devoted to the blind fury of tyrants. Countries destroyed; nations alternately buried in ruins by other nations; some parts of the world beautifully cultivated, returned again to the pristine state; the fruits of ages of industry, the toil of thousands in a short time destroyed by a few! If one corner breathes in peace for a few years, it is, in turn subjected, torne, and levelled; one would almost believe the principles of action in man, considered as the first agent of this planet, to be poisoned in their most essential parts. We certainly are not

---

3. The Lacedaemonians, inhabitants of ancient Sparta, enslaved the inhabitants of Elos, giving rise to the term "helot," meaning slave, serf, or bondsman.

that class of beings which we vainly think ourselves to be; man an animal of prey, seems to have rapine and the love of bloodshed implanted in his heart; nay, to hold it the most honourable occupation in society: we never speak of a hero of mathematics, a hero of knowledge of humanity; no, this illustrious appellation is reserved for the most success-ful butchers of the world. If Nature has given us a fruitful soil to inhabit, she has refused us such inclinations and propensities as would afford us the full enjoyment of it. Extensive as the surface of this planet is, not one half of it is yet cultivated, not half replenished; she created man, and placed him either in the woods or plains, and provided him with passions which must for ever oppose his happiness; every thing is submitted to the power of the strongest; men, like the elements, are always at war; the weakest yield to the most potent; force, subtilty, and malice, always triumph over unguarded honesty, and simplicity. Benignity, moderation, and justice, are virtues adapted only to the hum-ble paths of life: we love to talk of virtue and to admire its beauty, while in the shade of solitude, and retirement; but when we step forth into active life, if it happen to be in competition with any passion or desire, do we observe it to prevail? Hence so many reli-gious impostors have triumphed over the credulity of mankind, and have rendered their frauds the creeds of succeeding generations, during the course of many ages; until worne away by time, they have been replaced by new ones. Hence the most unjust war, if sup-ported by the greatest force, always succeeds; hence the most just ones, when supported only by their justice, as often fail. Such is the ascendancy of power; the supreme arbiter of all the revolutions which we observe in this planet: so irresistible is power, that it often thwarts the tendency of the most forcible causes, and prevents their subsequent salutary effects, though ordained for the good of man by the Governor of the universe. Such is the perverseness of human nature; who can describe it in all its latitude?

In the moments of our philanthropy we often talk of an indulgent nature, a kind parent, who for the benefit of mankind has taken singular pains to vary the genera of plants, fruits, grain, and the different productions of the earth; and has spread peculiar blessings in each climate. This is undoubtedly an object of contemplation which calls forth our warmest gratitude; for so singularly benevolent have those parental intentions been, that where barrenness of soil or severity of climate prevail, there she has implanted in the heart of man, sentiments which over-balance every misery, and supply the place of every want. She has given to the inhabitants of these regions, an attachment to their savage rocks and wild shores, unknown to those who inhabit the fertile fields of the tem-perate zone. Yet if we attentively view this globe, will it not appear rather a place of pun-ishment, than of delight? And what misfortune! that those punishments should fall on the innocent, and its few delights be enjoyed by the most unworthy. Famine, diseases, elementary convulsions, human feuds, dissensions, &c. are the produce of every climate; each climate produces besides, vices, and miseries peculiar to its latitude. View the frigid sterility of the north, whose famished inhabitants hardly acquainted with the sun, live and fare worse than the bears they hunt: and to which they are superior only in the fac-ulty of speaking. View the arctic and antarctic regions, those huge voids, where nothing lives; regions of eternal snow: where winter in all his horrors has established his throne, and arrested every creative power of nature. Will you call the miserable stragglers in these countries by the name of men? Now contrast this frigid power of the north and south with that of the sun; examine the parched lands of the torrid zone, replete with sulphureous exhalations; view those countries of Asia subject to pestilential infections which lay nature waste; view this globe often convulsed both from within and without;

pouring forth from several mouths, rivers of boiling matter, which are imperceptibly leaving immense subterranean graves, wherein millions will one day perish! Look at the poisonous soil of the equator, at those putrid slimy tracks, teeming with horrid monsters, the enemies of the human race; look next at the sandy continent, scorched perhaps by the fatal approach of some ancient comet, now the abode of desolation. Examine the rains, the convulsive storms of those climates, where masses of sulphur, bitumen, and electrical fire, combining their dreadful powers, are incessantly hovering and bursting over a globe threatened with dissolution. On this little shell, how very few are the spots where man can live and flourish? even under those mild climates which seem to breathe peace and happiness, the poison of slavery, the fury of despotism, and the rage of superstition, are all combined against man! There only the few live and rule, whilst the many starve and utter ineffectual complaints: there, human nature appears more debased, perhaps than in the less favoured climates. The fertile plains of Asia, the rich low lands of Egypt and of Diarbeck,[4] the fruitful fields bordering on the Tigris and the Euphrates, the extensive country of the East-Indies in all its separate districts; all these must to the geographical eye, seem as if intended for terrestrial paradises: but though surrounded with the spontaneous riches of nature though her kindest favours seem to be shed on those beautiful regions with the most profuse hand; yet there in general we find the most wretched people in the world. Almost every where, liberty so natural to mankind, is refused, or rather enjoyed but by their tyrants; the word slave, is the appellation of every rank, who adore as a divinity, a being worse than themselves; subject to every caprice, and to every lawless rage which unrestrained power can give. Tears are shed, perpetual groans are heard, where only the accents of peace, alacrity, and gratitude should resound. There the very delirium of tyranny tramples on the best gifts of nature, and sports with the fate, the happiness, the lives of millions: there the extreme fertility of the ground always indicates the extreme misery of the inhabitants!

Every where one part of the human species are taught the art of shedding the blood of the other; of setting fire to their dwellings; of levelling the works of their industry: half of the existence of nations regularly employed in destroying other nations. What little political felicity is to be met with here and there, has cost oceans of blood to purchase; as if good was never to be the portion of unhappy man. Republics, kingdoms, monarchies, founded either on fraud or successful violence, increase by pursuing the steps of the same policy, until they are destroyed in their turn, either by the influence of their own crimes, or by more successful but equally criminal enemies.

If from this general review of human nature, we descend to the examination of what is called civilized society; there the combination of every natural and artifical want, makes us pay very dear for what little share of political felicity we enjoy. It is a strange heterogeneous assemblage of vices and virtues, and of a variety of other principles, for ever at war, for ever jarring for ever producing some dangerous, some distressing extreme. Where do you conceive then that nature intended we should be happy? Would you prefer the state of men in the woods, to that of men in a more improved situation? Evil preponderates in both; in the first they often eat each other for want of food, and in the other they often starve each other for want of room. For my part, I think the vices and miseries to be found in the latter, exceed those of the former; in which real evil is more scarce, more supportable, and less enormous. Yet

---

4. Historical name for Kurdish regions of the Middle East.

we wish to see the earth peopled; to accomplish the happiness of kingdoms, which is said to consist in numbers. Gracious God! to what end is the introduction of so many beings into a mode of existence in which they must grope amidst as many errors, commit as many crimes, and meet with as many diseases, wants, and sufferings!

The following scene will I hope account for these melancholy reflections, and apologize for the gloomy thoughts with which I have filled this letter: my mind is, and always has been, oppressed since I became a witness to it. I was not long since invited to dine with a planter who lived three miles from ———, where he then resided. In order to avoid the heat of the sun, I resolved to go on foot, sheltered in a small path, leading through a pleasant wood. I was leisurely travelling along, attentively examining some peculiar plants which I had collected, when all at once I felt the air strongly agitated; though the day was perfectly calm and sultry. I immediately cast my eyes toward the cleared ground, from which I was but at a small distance, in order to see whether it was not occasioned by a sudden shower; when at that instant a sound resembling a deep rough voice, uttered, as I thought, a few inarticulate monosyllables. Alarmed and surprized, I precipitately looked all round, when I perceived at about six rods distance something resembling a cage, suspended to the limbs of a tree; all the branches of which appeared covered with large birds of prey, fluttering about, and anxiously endeavouring to perch on the cage. Actuated by an involuntary motion of my hands, more than by any design of my mind, I fired at them; they all flew to a short distance, with a most hideous noise: when, horrid to think and painful to repeat, I perceived a negro, suspended in the cage, and left there to expire! I shudder when I recollect that the birds had already picked out his eyes, his cheek bones were bare; his arms had been attacked in several places, and his body seemed covered with a multitude of wounds. From the edges of the hollow sockets and from the lacerations with which he was disfigured, the blood slowly dropped, and tinged the ground beneath. No sooner were the birds flown, than swarms of insects covered the whole body of this unfortunate wretch, eager to feed on his mangled flesh and to drink his blood. I found myself suddenly arrested by the power of affright and terror; my nerves were convulsed; I trembled, I stood motionless, involuntarily contemplating the fate of this negro, in all its dismal latitude. The living spectre, though deprived of his eyes, could still distinctly hear, and in his uncouth dialect begged me to give him some water to allay his thirst. Humanity herself would have recoiled back with horror; she would have balanced whether to lessen such reliefless distress, or mercifully with one blow to end this dreadful scene of agonizing torture! Had I had a ball in my gun, I certainly should have despatched him; but finding myself unable to perform so kind an office, I sought, though trembling, to relieve him as well as I could. A shell ready fixed to a pole, which had been used by some negroes, presented itself to me; I filled it with water, and with trembling hands I guided it to the quivering lips of the wretched sufferer. Urged by the irresistible power of thirst, he endeavoured to meet it, as he instinctively guessed its approach by the noise it made in passing through the bars of the cage. "Tankè, you whitè man, tankè you, putè somè poyson and givè me." How long have you been hanging there? I asked him. "Two days, and me no die; the birds, the birds; aaah me!" Oppressed with the reflections which this shocking spectacle afforded me, I mustered strength enough to walk away, and soon reached the house at which I intended to dine. There I heard that the reason for this slave being thus punished, was on account of his having killed the overseer of the plantation. They told me that the laws of self-preservation rendered such executions necessary; and supported the doctrine of slavery with the arguments generally made use of to justify the practice; with the repetition of which I shall not trouble you at present.

Adieu.

—1770

Thomas Paine
1737–1809

On January 10, 1776, hawkers on Philadelphia's streets could be found selling a political pamphlet, *Common Sense*, that set out to invent American patriotism. The pamphlet, which sold over 500,000 copies in three months, argued in no uncertain terms for independence from England. Its author was Thomas Paine, who only two years earlier had crossed the Atlantic at the suggestion of his friend Benjamin Franklin to pursue a career that employed his considerable writing skills. Paine took the strongest arguments for American sovereignty, stripped them of high-flown rhetoric, and recast them in language accessible to a broad readership. He also familiarized himself with the most persuasive arguments against the American cause and stood them on their head. One popular argument among British opponents of American independence and American Tories (a term for Loyalists who continued to support George III) was that the colonies were behaving like unruly and disobedient children. Paine issued a sharp rebuttal in *Common Sense*: "Britain is the parent country, say some. Then the more shame upon her conduct. Even brutes do not devour their young" (p. 114). Despite (or perhaps because of) the heavy British opposition to the work, the book sold very well in England, going through eight British editions by 1800. It was reprinted in Europe in several different languages. Throughout the American Revolution, Paine continued to wage war with type rather than bullets by printing a series of tracts under the title *The American Crisis*. By General George Washington's decree, these pamphlets were read to all the American troops to bolster morale.

After inciting America to sever its ties to the Old World during the Revolution, Paine turned his ingenuity to engineering and developed an iron bridge that in 1787 he tried to sell in Europe. He was present for the French Revolution and built ideological bridges between France and the United States by publishing, under an assumed name, another incendiary pamphlet, *The Rights of Man* (1791). This was Paine's reply to Edmund Burke's archly conservative *Reflections on the Revolution in France* (1790), and it called for the establishment of people's rights by the forcible removal of royalty. The publication of Paine's new pamphlet resulted in his being outlawed by the English Court of King's Bench, which dealt with legal matters relating to the monarch. The work was incredibly popular in America and was published in fifteen separate editions between 1791 and 1794. In France, Paine was lionized and elected a member of the National Convention, the main legislative body of the revolutionary government. Ultimately, though, he proved too conservative for the French Jacobins, radicals who came to power during the later stages of the Revolution. He was imprisoned by Maximilien Robespierre, who ordered the execution of so many aristocrats and political opponents that his brief rule came to be called the Reign of Terror. Paine nearly lost his head while waiting for American friends to intervene. Eventually, through the efforts of James Monroe, then the American Minister to France, Paine regained his freedom and returned to America.

Revolutions were more than political events for Paine, they were cosmic ones as well. He had learned this by attending lectures in London that illustrated the revolutions of planets through the use of an orrery, a mechanism that represented, by means of clockwork, the orbits of heavenly bodies around the sun. The son of Quakers, Paine came to embrace Deism, a form of rational religion that viewed God as an absent clockmaker who had set the great timepiece of the universe in motion and then withdrawn. Inspired, perhaps, by the French Revolution's attacks on the church and established religion, Paine began writing a book that denounced the Bible and Christianity with the same kind of harsh invective he had employed in his political writing. Against the wishes of his friend and fellow religious dissenter, Benjamin Franklin, he published *The Age of Reason* (Boston, New York, London, and Paris, 1794), alienating many American and English admirers, as Franklin had warned. Despite his religious radicalism, Paine requested that his remains be buried either in a Quaker graveyard (a request the Quakers did not approve) or on his farm in New Rochelle, New York. Toward the end of his life, despite visits from a friend who was a Quaker clockmaker and several other Christians who were concerned for his soul, Paine remained true to his beliefs and did not seek atonement. Additionally, he asked that no words of religion be engraved on his tombstone, solely the words "Author of *Common Sense*." Ten years after his burial in New Rochelle in 1809, William Cobbett, one of Paine's former political enemies, attempted to honor him by having his remains exhumed and taken across the Atlantic one last time to be buried under a grand monument in England. Cobbett succeeded in removing Paine's bones to England, but the British government would not permit the monument to be erected, so the probate court assigned them to a receiver. Their whereabouts are still a mystery.

from Common Sense
Introduction

Perhaps the sentiments contained in the following pages, are not yet sufficiently fashionable to procure them general favor; a long habit of not thinking a thing *wrong*, gives it a superficial appearance of being *right*, and raises at first a formidable outcry in defence of custom. But tumult soon subsides. Time makes more converts than reason.

As a long and violent abuse of power is generally the Means of calling the right of it in question, (and in Matters too which might never have been thought of, had not the Sufferers been aggravated into the inquiry,) and as the King of England hath undertaken in his *own Right*, to support the parliament in what he calls *Theirs*, and as the good people of this country are grievously oppressed by the combination, they have an undoubted privilege to inquire into the pretensions of both, and equally to reject the usurpations of either.

In the following sheets, the author hath studiously avoided every thing which is personal among ourselves. Compliments as well as censure to individuals make no part thereof. The wise and the worthy need not the triumph of a pamphlet; and those whose sentiments are injudicious or unfriendly, will cease of themselves, unless too much pains are bestowed upon their conversion.

The cause of America is, in a great measure, the cause of all mankind. Many circumstances have, and will arise, which are not local, but universal, and through which the principles of all Lovers of Mankind are affected, and in the Event of which, their Affections are interested. The laying a Country desolate with Fire and Sword, declaring War against the natural rights of all Mankind, and extirpating the Defenders thereof from the Face of the Earth, is the Concern of every Man to whom Nature hath given the Power of feeling; of which Class, regardless of Party Censure, is the

AUTHOR

Philadelphia, Feb. 14, 1776.

Of the Origin and Design of Government in General. With Concise Remarks on the English Constitution

Some writers have so confounded society with government, as to leave little or no distinction between them; whereas they are not only different, but have different origins. Society is produced by our wants, and government by our wickedness; the former promotes our happiness *positively* by uniting our affections, the latter *negatively* by restraining our vices. The one encourages intercourse, the other creates distinctions. The first is a patron, the last a punisher. . . .

I know it is difficult to get over local or long standing prejudices, yet if we will suffer ourselves to examine the component parts of the English constitution, we shall find them to be the base remains of two ancient tyrannies, compounded with some new republican materials.

First.—The remains of monarchical tyranny in the person of the king.

Secondly.—The remains of aristocratical tyranny in the persons of the peers.

Thirdly.—The new republican materials, in the persons of the commons, on whose virtue depends the freedom of England.

The two first, by being hereditary, are independent of the people; wherefore in a *constitutional sense* they contribute nothing towards the freedom of the state.

To say that the constitution of England is a *union* of three powers reciprocally *checking* each other, is farcical, either the words have no meaning, or they are flat contradictions.

To say that the commons is a check upon the king, presupposes two things.

First.—That the king is not to be trusted without being looked after, or in other words, that a thirst for absolute power is the natural disease of monarchy.

Secondly.—That the commons, by being appointed for that purpose, are either wiser or more worthy of confidence than the crown.

But as the same constitution which gives the commons a power to check the king by withholding the supplies, gives afterwards the king a power to check the commons, by empowering him to reject their other bills; it again supposes that the king is wiser than those whom it has already supposed to be wiser than him. A mere absurdity!

There is something exceedingly ridiculous in the composition of monarchy; it first excludes a man from the means of information, yet empowers him to act in cases where the highest judgment is required. The state of a king shuts him from the world, yet the business of a king requires him to know it thoroughly; wherefore the different parts, unnaturally opposing and destroying each other, prove the whole character to be absurd and useless.

Some writers have explained the English constitution thus; the king, say they, is one, the people another; the peers are an house in behalf of the king; the commons in behalf of the people; but this hath all the distinctions of an house divided against itself; and though the expressions be pleasantly arranged, yet when examined they appear idle and ambiguous; and it will always happen, that the nicest construction that words are capable of, when applied to the description of something which either cannot exist, or is too incomprehensible to be within the compass of description, will be words of sound only, and though they may amuse the ear, they cannot inform the mind, for this explanation includes a previous question, viz. *How came the king by a power which the people are afraid to trust, and always obliged to check?* Such a power could not be the gift of a wise people, neither can any power, *which needs checking*, be from God; yet the provision, which the constitution makes, supposes such a power to exist.

But the provision is unequal to the task; the means either cannot or will not accomplish the end, and the whole affair is a felo de se[1]; for as the greater weight will always carry up the less, and as all the wheels of a machine are put in motion by one, it only remains to know which power in the constitution has the most weight, for that will govern; and though the others, or a part of them, may clog, or, as the phrase is, check the rapidity of its motion, yet so long as they cannot stop it, their endeavors will be ineffectual; the first moving power will at last have its way, and what it wants in speed is supplied by time.

That the crown is this overbearing part in the English constitution needs not be mentioned, and that it derives its whole consequence merely from being the giver of places and pensions is self evident, wherefore, though we have been wise enough to shut and lock a door against absolute monarchy, we at the same time have been foolish enough to put the crown in possession of the key.

The prejudice of Englishmen, in favor of their own government by king, lords, and commons, arises as much or more from national pride than reason. Individuals are undoubtedly safer in England than in some other countries, but the *will* of the king is as much the *law* of the land in Britain as in France, with this difference, that instead of proceeding directly from his mouth, it is handed to the people under the most formidable shape of an act of parliament. For the fate of Charles the First,[2] hath only made kings more subtle—not more just.

Wherefore, laying aside all national pride and prejudice in favor of modes and forms, the plain truth is, that *it is wholly owing to the constitution of the people, and not to the constitution of the government* that the crown is not as oppressive in England as in Turkey.

An inquiry into the *constitutional errors* in the English form of government is at this time highly necessary; for as we are never in a proper condition of doing justice to others, while we continue under the influence of some leading partiality, so neither are we capable of doing it to ourselves while we remain fettered by any obstinate prejudice. And as a man, who is attached to a prostitute, is unfitted to choose or judge of a wife, so any prepossession in favor of a rotten constitution of government will disable us from discerning a good one. . . .

Thoughts of the present state of American Affairs

In the following pages I offer nothing more than simple facts, plain arguments, and common sense; and have no other preliminaries to settle with the reader, than that he will divest himself of prejudice and prepossession, and suffer his reason and his feelings to determine for themselves; that he will put *on*, or rather that he will not put *off* the true character of a man, and generously enlarge his views beyond the present day.

Volumes have been written on the subject of the struggle between England and America. Men of all ranks have embarked in the controversy, from different motives, and with various designs; but all have been ineffectual, and the period of debate is

---

1. A self-destructive act.   2. Charles the First was dethroned and killed for abuse of power, resulting in the English Civil War of the 1640s.

closed. Arms, as the last resource, decide the contest; the appeal was the choice of the king, and the continent hath accepted the challenge.

It hath been reported of the late Mr. Pelham[3] (who tho' an able minister was not without his faults) that on his being attacked in the house of commons, on the score, that his measures were only of a temporary kind, replied, *"they will last my time."* Should a thought so fatal and unmanly possess the colonies in the present contest, the name of ancestors will be remembered by future generations with detestation.

The sun never shined on a cause of greater worth. 'Tis not the affair of a city, a country, a province, or a kingdom, but of a continent—of at least one eighth part of the habitable globe. 'Tis not the concern of a day, a year, or an age; posterity are virtually involved in the contest, and will be more or less affected, even to the end of time, by the proceedings now. Now is the seed time of continental union, faith and honor. The least fracture now will be like a name engraved with the point of a pin on the tender rind of a young oak; the wound will enlarge with the tree, and posterity read it in full grown characters.

By referring the matter from argument to arms, a new area for politics is struck; a new method of thinking hath arisen. All plans, proposals, &c. prior to the nineteenth of April, i.e., to the commencement of hostilities,[4] are like the almanacks of the last year; which, though proper then, are superseded and useless now. Whatever was advanced by the advocates on either side of the question then, terminated in one and the same point, viz., a union with Great Britain; the only difference between the parties was the method of effecting it; the one proposing force, the other friendship; but it hath so far happened that the first hath failed, and the second hath withdrawn her influence.

As much hath been said of the advantages of reconciliation, which, like an agreeable dream, hath passed away and left us as we were, it is but right, that we should examine the contrary side of the argument, and inquire into some of the many material injuries which these colonies sustain, and always will sustain, by being connected with, and dependant on Great Britain. To examine that connection and dependance, on the principles of nature and common sense, to see what we have to trust to, if separated, and what we are to expect, if dependant.

I have heard it asserted by some, that as America hath flourished under her former connection with Great Britain, that the same connection is necessary towards her future happiness, and will always have the same effect. Nothing can be more fallacious than this kind of argument. We may as well assert, that because a child has thrived upon milk, that it is never to have meat; or that the first twenty years of our lives is to become a precedent for the next twenty. But even this is admitting more than is true, for I answer roundly, that America would have flourished as much, and probably much more, had no European power had any thing to do with her. The commerce by which she hath enriched herself are the necessaries of life, and will always have a market while eating is the custom of Europe.

But she has protected us, say some. That she hath engrossed us is true, and defended the continent at our expense as well as her own is admitted, and she would have defended Turkey from the same motive, viz., the sake of trade and dominion.

Alas, we have been long led away by ancient prejudices and made large sacrifices to superstition. We have boasted the protection of Great Britain, without considering,

---

3. Thomas Pelham (1693–1768), England's prime minister from 1743 to 1754.   4. The Battle of Lexington and Concord in Massachusetts, April 19, 1775.

that her motive was *interest* not *attachment*; that she did not protect us from *our ene-mies* on *our account*, but from *her enemies* on *her own account*, from those who had no quarrel with us on any *other account*, and who will always be our enemies on the *same account*. Let Britain wave her pretensions to the continent, or the continent throw off the dependance, and we should be at peace with France and Spain were they at war with Britain. The miseries of Hanover last war,[5] ought to warn us against connections.

It hath lately been asserted in parliament, that the colonies have no relation to each other but through the parent country, *i.e.*, that Pennsylvania and the Jerseys, and so on for the rest, are sister colonies by the way of England; this is certainly a very roundabout way of proving relationship, but it is the nearest and only true way of proving enemyship, if I may so call it. France and Spain never were, nor perhaps ever will be our enemies as *Americans*, but as our being the subjects of *Great Britain*.

But Britain is the parent country, say some. Then the more shame upon her conduct. Even brutes do not devour their young; nor savages make war upon their families; where-fore the assertion, if true, turns to her reproach; but it happens not to be true, or only partly so, and the phrase *parent* or *mother country* hath been jesuitically adopted by the king and his parasites, with a low papistical design of gaining an unfair bias on the cred-ulous weakness of our minds. Europe, and not England, is the parent country of America. This new world hath been the asylum for the persecuted lovers of civil and religious lib-erty from *every part* of Europe. Hither have they fled, not from the tender embraces of the mother, but from the cruelty of the monster; and it is so far true of England, that the same tyranny which drove the first emigrants from home pursues their descendants still.

In this extensive quarter of the globe, we forget the narrow limits of three hun-dred and sixty miles (the extent of England) and carry our friendship on a larger scale; we claim brotherhood with every European Christian, and triumph in the generosity of the sentiment.

It is pleasant to observe by what regular gradations we surmount the force of local prejudice, as we enlarge our acquaintance with the world. A man born in any town in England divided into parishes, will naturally associate most with his fellow parishioners (because their interests in many cases will be common) and distinguish him by the name of *neighbor*; if he meet him but a few miles from home, he drops the narrow idea of a street, and salutes him by the name of *townsman*; if he travels out of the county, and meet him in any other, he forgets the minor divisions of street and town, and calls him *countryman; i.e., countyman*; but if in their foreign excursions they should associate in France or any other part of *Europe*, their local remembrance would be enlarged into that of *Englishmen*. And by a just parity of reasoning, all Europeans meeting in America, or any other quarter of the globe, are *countrymen*; for England, Holland, Germany, or Sweden, when compared with the whole, stand in the same places on the larger scale, which the divisions of street, town, and county do on the smaller ones; distinctions too limited for continental minds. Not one third of the inhabitants, even of this province, are of English descent. Wherefore, I reprobate the phrase of parent or mother country applied to England only, as being false, selfish, narrow and ungenerous.

But admitting that we were all of English descent, what does it amount to? Nothing. Britain, being now an open enemy, extinguishes every other name and title: And to say that reconciliation is our duty, is truly farcical. The first king of England,

---

5. Bloody battles during the Seven Year's War were fought in Hanover, which later became a German province.

of the present line (William the Conqueror) was a Frenchman, and half the Peers of England are descendants from the same country; wherefore by the same method of reasoning, England ought to be governed by France.

Much hath been said of the united strength of Britain and the colonies, that in conjunction they might bid defiance to the world. But this is mere presumption; the fate of war is uncertain, neither do the expressions mean anything; for this continent would never suffer itself to be drained of inhabitants to support the British arms in either Asia, Africa, or Europe.

Besides, what have we to do with setting the world at defiance? Our plan is commerce, and that, well attended to, will secure us the peace and friendship of all Europe; because it is the interest of all Europe to have America a *free* port. Her trade will always be a protection, and her barrenness of gold and silver secure her from invaders.

I challenge the warmest advocate for reconciliation, to show, a single advantage that this continent can reap, by being connected with Great Britain. I repeat the challenge, not a single advantage is derived. Our corn will fetch its price in any market in Europe, and our imported goods must be paid for buy them where we will.

But the injuries and disadvantages we sustain by that connection, are without number; and our duty to mankind at large, as well as to ourselves, instruct us to renounce the alliance: Because, any submission to, or dependance on Great Britain, tends directly to involve this continent in European wars and quarrels; and sets us at variance with nations, who would otherwise seek our friendship, and against whom, we have neither anger nor complaint. As Europe is our market for trade, we ought to form no partial connection with any part of it. It is the true interest of America to steer clear of European contentions, which she never can do, while by her dependance on Britain, she is made the make-weight in the scale of British politics.

Europe is too thickly planted with kingdoms to be long at peace, and whenever a war breaks out between England and any foreign power, the trade of America goes to ruin, *because of her connection with Britain.* The next war may not turn out like the Past, and should it not, the advocates for reconciliation now will be wishing for separation then, because, neutrality in that case, would be a safer convoy than a man of war. Every thing that is right or natural pleads for separation. The blood of the slain, the weeping voice of nature cries, 'TIS TIME TO PART. Even the distance at which the Almighty hath placed England and America, is a strong and natural proof, that the authority of the one, over the other, was never the design of Heaven. The time likewise at which the continent was discovered, adds weight to the argument, and the manner in which it was peopled increases the force of it. The reformation was preceded by the discovery of America, as if the Almighty graciously meant to open a sanctuary to the persecuted in future years, when home should afford neither friendship nor safety.

The authority of Great Britain over this continent, is a form of government, which sooner or later must have an end: And a serious mind can draw no true pleasure by looking forward, under the painful and positive conviction, that what he calls "the present constitution" is merely temporary. As parents, we can have no joy, knowing that *this government* is not sufficiently lasting to ensure any thing which we may bequeath to posterity: And by a plain method of argument, as we are running the next generation into debt, we ought to do the work of it, otherwise we use them meanly and pitifully. In order to discover the line of our duty rightly, we should take our children in our hand, and fix our station a few years farther into life; that eminence will present a prospect, which a few present fears and prejudices conceal from our sight.

Though I would carefully avoid giving unnecessary offence, yet I am inclined to believe, that all those who espouse the doctrine of reconciliation, may be included within the following descriptions: Interested men, who are not to be trusted; weak men who *cannot* see; prejudiced men who *will not* see; and a certain set of moderate men, who think better of the European world than it deserves; and this last class by an ill-judged deliberation, will be the cause of more calamities to this continent than all the other three.

It is the good fortune of many to live distant from the scene of sorrow; the evil is not sufficiently brought to *their* doors to make *them* feel the precariousness with which all American property is possessed. But let our imaginations transport us for a few moments to Boston, that seat of wretchedness will teach us wisdom, and instruct us for ever to renounce a power in whom we can have no trust. The inhabitants of that unfortunate city, who but a few months ago were in ease and affluence, have now no other alternative than to stay and starve, or turn out to beg. Endangered by the fire of their friends if they continue within the city, and plundered by the soldiery if they leave it. In their present condition they are prisoners without the hope of redemption, and in a general attack for their relief, they would be exposed to the fury of both armies.

Men of passive tempers look somewhat lightly over the offenses of Britain, and, still hoping for the best, are apt to call out, "*Come, come, we shall be friends again for all this.*" But examine the passions and feelings of mankind. Bring the doctrine of reconciliation to the touchstone of nature, and then tell me, whether you can hereafter love, honor, and faithfully serve the power that hath carried fire and sword into your land? If you cannot do all these, then are you only deceiving yourselves, and by your delay bringing ruin upon posterity. Your future connection with Britain, whom you can neither love nor honor, will be forced and unnatural, and being formed only on the plan of present convenience, will in a little time fall into a relapse more wretched than the first. But if you say, you can still pass the violations over, then I ask, Hath your house been burnt? Hath your property been destroyed before your face? Are your wife and children destitute of a bed to lie on, or bread to live on? Have you lost a parent or a child by their hands, and yourself the ruined and wretched survivor? If you have not, then are you not a judge of those who have. But if you have, and can still shake hands with the murderers, then are you unworthy the name of husband, father, friend, or lover, and whatever may be your rank or title in life, you have the heart of a coward, and the spirit of a sycophant.

This is not inflaming or exaggerating matters, but trying them by those feelings and affections which nature justifies, and without which, we should be incapable of discharging the social duties of life, or enjoying the felicities of it. I mean not to exhibit horror for the purpose of provoking revenge, but to awaken us from fatal and unmanly slumbers, that we may pursue determinately some fixed object. It is not in the power of Britain or of Europe to conquer America, if she do not conquer herself by *delay* and *timidity*. The present winter is worth an age if rightly employed, but if lost or neglected, the whole continent will partake of the misfortune; and there is no punishment which that man will not deserve, be he who, or what, or where he will, that may be the means of sacrificing a season so precious and useful.

'Tis repugnant to reason, to the universal order of things, to all examples from the former ages, to suppose, that this continent can longer remain subject to any external power. The most sanguine in Britain does not think so. The utmost stretch of human wisdom cannot, at this time compass a plan short of separation, which can promise the continent even a year's security. Reconciliation is *now* a fallacious dream. Nature hath deserted the connection, and Art cannot supply her place. For, as Milton wisely expresses, "never can true reconcilement grow where wounds of deadly hate have pierced so deep."[6]

Every quiet method for peace hath been ineffectual. Our prayers have been rejected with disdain; and only tended to convince us, that nothing flatters vanity, or confirms obstinacy in kings more than repeated petitioning—and nothing hath contributed more than that very measure to make the kings of Europe absolute: Witness Denmark and Sweden. Wherefore since nothing but blows will do, for God's sake, let us come to a final separation, and not leave the next generation to be cutting throats, under the violated unmeaning names of parent and child.

To say, they will never attempt it again is idle and visionary, we thought so at the repeal of the stamp act, yet a year or two undeceived us[7]; as well may we suppose that nations, which have been once defeated, will never renew the quarrel.

As to government matters, it is not in the powers of Britain to do this continent justice: The business of it will soon be too weighty, and intricate, to be managed with any tolerable degree of convenience, by a power, so distant from us, and so very ignorant of us; for if they cannot conquer us, they cannot govern us. To be always running three or four thousand miles with a tale or a petition, waiting four or five months for an answer, which when obtained requires five or six more to explain it in, will in a few years be looked upon as folly and childishness—there was a time when it was proper, and there is a proper time for it to cease.

Small islands not capable of protecting themselves, are the proper objects for kingdoms to take under their care; but there is something very absurd, in supposing a continent to be perpetually governed by an island. In no instance hath nature made the satellite larger than its primary planet, and as England and America, with respect to each Other, reverses the common order of nature, it is evident they belong to different systems: England to Europe—America to itself.

I am not induced by motives of pride, party, or resentment to espouse the doctrine of separation and independence; I am clearly, positively, and conscientiously persuaded that it is the true interest of this continent to be so; that every thing short of *that* is mere patchwork, that it can afford no lasting felicity,—that it is leaving the sword to our children, and shrinking back at a time, when, a little more, a little farther, would have rendered this continent the glory of the earth.

As Britain hath not manifested the least inclination towards a compromise, we may be assured that no terms can be obtained worthy the acceptance of the continent, or any ways equal to the expense of blood and treasure we have been already put to.

The object contended for, ought always to bear some just proportion to the expense. The removal of the North, or the whole detestable junto, is a matter unworthy the millions we have expended. A temporary stoppage of trade, was an inconvenience, which would have sufficiently balanced the repeal of all the acts complained of, had such repeals been obtained; but if the whole continent must take up arms, if

---

6. John Milton, *Paradise Lost* (1667), 4.98–99.   7. The Stamp Act was passed in 1765, then repealed in 1766. By 1767, new taxes were imposed on the colonies by the Townshend Act.

every man must be a soldier, it is scarcely worth our while to fight against a contemptible ministry only. Dearly, dearly, do we pay for the repeal of the acts, if that is all we fight for; for in a just estimation, it is as great a folly to pay a Bunker Hill price for law, as for land. As I have always considered the independency of this continent, as an event, which sooner or later must arrive, so from the late rapid progress of the continent to maturity, the event could not be far off. Wherefore, on the breaking out of hostilities, it was not worth the while to have disputed a matter, which time would have finally redressed, unless we meant to be in earnest; otherwise, it is like wasting an estate of a suit at law, to regulate the trespasses of a tenant, whose lease is just expiring. No man was a warmer wisher for reconciliation than myself, before the fatal nineteenth of April, 1775,[8] but the moment the event of that day was made known, I rejected the hardened, sullen tempered Pharaoh of England for ever; and disdain the wretch, that with the pretended title of FATHER OF HIS PEOPLE, can unfeelingly hear of their slaughter, and composedly sleep with their blood upon his soul.

But admitting that matters were now made up, what would be the event? I answer, the ruin of the continent. And that for several reasons:

First. The powers of governing still remaining in the hands of the king, he will have a negative over the whole legislation of this continent. And as he hath shown himself such an inveterate enemy to liberty, and discovered such a thirst for arbitrary power, is he, or is he not, a proper man to say to these colonies, *"You shall make no laws but what I please?"* And is there any inhabitants in America so ignorant, as not to know, that according to what is called the *present constitution*, that this continent can make no laws but what the king gives leave to? and is there any man so unwise, as not to see, that (considering what has happened) he will suffer no Law to be made here, but such as suit *his* purpose? We may be as effectually enslaved by the want of laws in America, as by submitting to laws made for us in England. After matters are made up (as it is called) can there be any doubt but the whole power of the crown will be exerted, to keep this continent as low and humble as possible? Instead of going forward we shall go backward, or be perpetually quarrelling or ridiculously petitioning. We are already greater than the king wishes us to be, and will he not hereafter endeavor to make us less? To bring the matter to one point. Is the power who is jealous of our prosperity, a proper power to govern us? Whoever says *No* to this question is an *independent*, for independency means no more, than, whether we shall make our own laws, or whether the king, the greatest enemy this continent hath, or can have, shall tell us, *"there shall be laws but such as I like."*

But the king you will say has a negative in England; the people there can make no laws without his consent. In point of right and good order, there is something very ridiculous, that a youth of twenty-one (which hath often happened) shall say to several millions of people, older and wiser than himself, I forbid this or that act of yours to be law. But in this place I decline this sort of reply, though I will never cease to expose the absurdity of it, and only answer, that England being the king's residence, and America not so, make quite another case. The king's negative *here* is ten times more dangerous and fatal than it can be in England, for *there* he will scarcely refuse his consent to a bill for putting England into as strong a state of defence as possible, and in America he would never suffer such a bill to be passed.

---

8. [Paine's note] Massacre at Lexington.

America is only a secondary object in the system of British politics—England consults the good of *this* country, no farther than it answers her *own* purpose. Wherefore, her own interest leads her to suppress the growth of *ours* in every case which doth not promote her advantage, or in the least interfere with it. A pretty state we should soon be in under such a second-hand government, considering what has happened! Men do not change from enemies to friends by the alteration of a name; and in order to show that reconciliation now is a dangerous doctrine, I affirm, *that it would be policy in the kingdom at this time, to repeal the acts for the sake of reinstating himself in the government of the provinces*; in order, that HE MAY ACCOMPLISH BY CRAFT AND SUBTLETY, IN THE LONG RUN, WHAT HE CANNOT DO BY FORCE AND VIOLENCE IN THE SHORT ONE. Reconciliation and ruin are nearly related.

Secondly. That as even the best terms, which we can expect to obtain, can amount to no more than a temporary expedient, or a kind of government by guardianship, which can last no longer than till the colonies come of age, so the general face and state of things, in the interim, will be unsettled and unpromising. Emigrants of property will not choose to come to a country whose form of government hangs but by a thread, and who is every day tottering on the brink of commotion and disturbance; and numbers of the present inhabitants would lay hold of the interval, to dispose of their effects, and quit the continent.

But the most powerful of all arguments, is, that nothing but independence, i.e., a continental form of government, can keep the peace of the continent and preserve it inviolate from civil wars. I dread the event of a reconciliation with Britain now, as it is more than probable, that it will be followed by a revolt somewhere or other, the consequences of which may be far more fatal than all the malice of Britain.

Thousands are already ruined by British barbarity; (thousands more will probably suffer the same fate). Those men have other feelings than us who have nothing suffered. All they *now* possess is liberty, what they before enjoyed is sacrificed to its service, and having nothing more to lose, they disdain submission. Besides, the general temper of the colonies, towards a British government, will be like that of a youth, who is nearly out of his time, they will care very little about her. And a government which cannot preserve the peace, is no government at all, and in that case we pay our money for nothing; and pray what is it that Britain can do, whose power will be wholly on paper, should a civil tumult break out the very day after reconciliation? I have heard some men say, many of whom I believe spoke without thinking, that they dreaded independence, fearing that it would produce civil wars. It is but seldom that our first thoughts are truly correct, and that is the case here; for there are ten times more to dread from a patched up connection than from independence. I make the sufferers' case my own, and I protest, that were I driven from house and home, my property destroyed, and my circumstances ruined, that as a man, sensible of injuries, I could never relish the doctrine of reconciliation, or consider myself bound thereby.

The colonies have manifested such a spirit of good order and obedience to continental government, as is sufficient to make every reasonable person easy and happy on that head. No man can assign the least pretence for his fears, on any other grounds, than such as are truly childish and ridiculous, viz., that one colony will be striving for superiority over another.

Where there are no distinctions there can be no superiority, perfect equality affords no temptation. The republics of Europe are all (and we may say always) in peace. Holland and Switzerland are without wars, foreign or domestic; monarchical governments, it is true, are never long at rest: the crown itself is a temptation to enterprising ruffians at *home*; and that degree of pride and insolence ever attendant on regal authority swells into a rupture with foreign powers, in instances where a republican government, by being formed on more natural principles, would negotiate the mistake.

If there is any true cause of fear respecting independence it is because no plan is yet laid down. Men do not see their way out—Wherefore, as an opening into that business I offer the following hints; at the same time modestly affirming, that I have no other opinion of them myself, than that they may be the means of giving rise to something better. Could the straggling thoughts of individuals be collected, they would frequently form materials for wise and able men to improve to useful matter.

Let the assemblies be annual, with a President only. The representation more equal. Their business wholly domestic, and subject to the authority of a continental congress.

Let each colony be divided into six, eight, or ten, convenient districts, each district to send a proper number of delegates to Congress, so that each colony send at least thirty. The whole number in Congress will be at least three hundred ninety. Each Congress to sit and to choose a president by the following method. When the delegates are met, let a colony be taken from the whole thirteen colonies by lot, after which let the whole Congress choose (by ballot) a president from out of the delegates of *that* province. In the next Congress, let a colony be taken by lot from twelve only, omitting that colony from which the president was taken in the former Congress, and so proceeding on till the whole thirteen shall have had their proper rotation. And in order that nothing may pass into a law but what is satisfactorily just, not less than three fifths of the Congress to be called a majority. He that will promote discord, under a government so equally formed as this, would join Lucifer in his revolt.

But as there is a peculiar delicacy, from whom, or in what manner, this business must first arise, and as it seems most agreeable and consistent, that it should come from some intermediate body between the governed and the governors, that is between the Congress and the people, let a CONTINENTAL CONFERENCE be held, in the following manner, and for the following purpose:

A committee of twenty-six members of Congress, viz., two for each colony. Two members for each House of Assembly, or Provincial Convention; and five representatives of the people at large, to be chosen in the capital city or town of each province, for, and in behalf of the whole province, by as many qualified voters as shall think proper to attend from all parts of the province for that purpose; or, if more convenient, the representatives may be chosen in two or three of the most populous parts thereof. In this conference, thus assembled, will be united, the two grand principles of business, *knowledge* and *power*. The members of Congress, Assemblies, or Conventions, by having had experience in national concerns, will be able and useful counsellors, and the whole, being empowered by the people will have a truly legal authority.

The conferring members being met, let their business be to frame a CONTINENTAL CHARTER, or Charter of the United Colonies; (answering to what is called the Magna Charta of England) fixing the number and manner of choosing members of Congress, members of Assembly, with their date of sitting, and drawing the line of business and jurisdiction between them: always remembering, that our strength is continental, not provincial: Securing freedom and property to all men, and above all things the free exercise of religion, according to the dictates of conscience; with such other matter as is necessary for a charter to contain. Immediately after which, the said Conference to dissolve, and the bodies which shall be chosen conformable to the said charter, to be the legislators and governors of this continent for the time being: Whose peace and happiness, may God preserve, Amen.

Should any body of men be hereafter delegated for this or some similar purpose, I offer them the following extracts from that wise observer on governments *Dragonetti*. "The science" says he, "of the politician consists in fixing the true point of happiness and freedom. Those men would deserve the gratitude of ages, who should discover a mode of government that contained the greatest sum of individual happiness, with the least national expense."—Dragonetti on Virtue and Rewards.[9]

But where says some is the king of America? I'll tell you Friend, he reigns above, and doth not make havoc of mankind like the Royal Brute of Britain. Yet that we may not appear to be defective even in earthly honors, let a day be solemnly set apart for proclaiming the charter; let it be brought forth placed on the divine law, the word of God; let a crown be placed thereon, by which the world may know, that so far as we approve of monarchy, that in America THE LAW IS KING. For as in absolute governments the King is law, so in free countries the law *ought* to be King; and there ought to be no other. But lest any ill use should afterwards arise, let the crown at the conclusion of the ceremony be demolished, and scattered among the people whose right it is.

A government of our own is our natural right: And when a man seriously reflects on the precariousness of human affairs, he will become convinced, that it is infinitely wiser and safer, to form a constitution of our own in a cool deliberate manner, while we have it in our power, than to trust such an interesting event to time and chance. If we omit it now, some Massenello[10] may hereafter arise, who laying hold of popular disquietudes, may collect together the desperate and the discontented, and by assuming to themselves the powers of government, may sweep away the liberties of the continent like a deluge. Should the government of America return again into the hands of Britain, the tottering situation of things, will be a temptation for some desperate adventurer to try his fortune; and in such a case, what relief can Britain give? Ere she could hear the news the fatal business might be done, and ourselves suffering like the wretched Britons under the oppression of the Conqueror. Ye that oppose independence now, ye know not what ye do; ye are opening a door to eternal tyranny, by keeping vacant the seat of government. There are thousands and tens of thousands; who would think it glorious to expel from the continent, that barbarous and hellish power, which hath stirred up the Indians and Negroes to destroy us; the cruelty hath a double guilt, it is dealing brutally by us, and treacherously by them.

To talk of friendship with those in whom our reason forbids us to have faith, and our affections, (wounded through a thousand pores) instruct us to detest, is madness and folly. Every day wears out the little remains of kindred between us and them, and can there be any reason to hope, that as the relationship expires, the affection will increase, or that we shall agree better, when we have ten times more and greater concerns to quarrel over than ever?

Ye that tell us of harmony and reconciliation, can ye restore to us the time that is past? Can ye give to prostitution its former innocence? Neither can ye reconcile Britain

---

9. Giacinto Dragonetti (1738–1818), *Trattorio delle virtù et de primi* (1765).   10. [Paine's note] Thomas Anello, otherwise Massanello, a fisherman of Naples, who after spiriting up his countrymen in the public market place, against the oppression of the Spaniards, to whom the place was then subject, prompted them to revolt, and in the space of a day became king.

and America. The last cord now is broken, the people of England are presenting addresses against us. There are injuries which nature cannot forgive; she would cease to be nature if she did. As well can the lover forgive the ravisher of his mistress, as the continent forgive the murders of Britain. The Almighty hath implanted in us these inextinguishable feelings for good and wise purposes. They are the guardians of his image in our hearts. They distinguish us from the herd of common animals. The social compact would dissolve, and justice be extirpated from the earth, or have only a casual existence were we callous to the touches of affection. The robber and the murderer, would often escape unpunished, did not the injuries which our tempers sustain, provoke us into justice.

O ye that love mankind! Ye that dare oppose, not only the tyranny, but the tyrant, stand forth! Every spot of the old world is overrun with oppression. Freedom hath been hunted round the globe. Asia, and Africa, have long expelled her.—Europe regards her like a stranger, and England hath given her warning to depart. O! receive the fugitive, and prepare in time an asylum for mankind. . . .

—1776

from The Rights of Man

Being an answer to Mr. Burke's attack on the French Revolution

There never did, there never will, and there never can, exist a Parliament, or any description of men, or any generation of men, in any country, possessed of the right or the power of binding and controuling posterity to the *"end of time."* . . . Every age and generation must be as free to act for itself *in all cases* as the ages and generations which preceded it. The vanity and presumption of governing beyond the grave is the most ridiculous and insolent of all tyrannies. Man has no property in man; neither has any generation a property in the generations which are to follow. The Parliament or the people of 1688,[1] or of any other period, had no more right to dispose of the people of the present day, or to bind or to controul them *in any shape whatever,* than the Parliament or the people of the present day have to dispose of, bind or controul those who are to live a hundred or a thousand years hence. Every generation is, and must be, competent to all the purposes which its occasions require. It is the living, and not the dead, that are to be accommodated. When man ceases to be, his power and his wants cease with him; and having no longer any participation in the concerns of this world, he has no longer any authority in directing who shall be its governors, or how its Government shall be organised, or how administered.

I am not contending for nor against any form of Government, nor for nor against any party, here or elsewhere. That which a whole Nation chooses to do, it has a right to do. Mr. Burke says, No. Where, then does the right exist? I am contending for the rights of the *living,* and against their being willed away, and controuled and contracted for, by the manuscript assumed authority of the dead; and Mr. Burke is contending for the authority of the dead over the rights and freedom of the living. There was a time when Kings disposed of their Crowns by will upon their death-beds, and consigned the people, like beasts of the field, to whatever successor they appointed. This is now so exploded as scarcely to be remembered, and so monstrous as hardly to be believed; but the Parliamentary clauses upon which Mr. Burke builds his political church are of the same nature.

---

1. England's Glorious Revolution of 1688 resulted in more power for Parliament and less for the Crown.

The laws of every country must be analogous to some common principle. In England no parent or master, nor all the authority of Parliament, omnipotent as it has called itself, can bind or controul the personal freedom even of an individual beyond the age of twenty-one years. On what ground of right, then, could the Parliament of 1688, or any other Parliament, bind all posterity for ever?

Those who have quitted the world, and those who are not yet arrived at it, are as remote from each other as the utmost stretch of mortal imagination can conceive. What possible obligation, then, can exist between them; what rule or principle can be laid down that of two non-entities, the one out of existence and the other not in, and who never can meet in this world, the one should controul the other to the end of time? . . . It is the nature of man to die, and he will continue to die as long as he continues to be born. But Mr. Burke has set up a sort of political Adam, in whom all posterity are bound for ever; he must, therefore, prove that his Adam possessed such a power, or such a right. . . . It requires but a very small glance of thought to perceive that altho' laws made in one generation often continue in force through succeeding generations, yet that they continue to derive their force from the consent of the living. A law not repealed continues in force, not because it *cannot* be repealed, but because it *is not* repealed; and the non-repealing passes for consent. . . .

If the mere name of antiquity is to govern in the affairs of life, the people who are to live an hundred or a thousand years hence, may as well take us for a precedent, as we make a precedent of those who lived an hundred or a thousand years ago. The fact is, that portions of antiquity, by proving everything, establish nothing. It is authority against authority all the way, till we come to the divine origin of the rights of man at the creation. Here our inquiries find a resting-place, and our reason finds a home. If a dispute about the rights of man had arisen at the distance of an hundred years from the creation, it is to this source of authority they must have referred, and it is to this same source of authority that we must now refer.

Though I mean not to touch upon any sectarian principle of religion, yet it may be worth observing, that the genealogy of Christ is traced to Adam. Why then not trace the rights of man to the creation of man? I will answer the question. Because there have been upstart Governments, thrusting themselves between and presumptuously working to *un-make* man.

If any generation of men ever possessed the right of dictating the mode by which the world should be governed for ever, it was the first generation that existed; and if that generation did it not, no succeeding generation can show any authority for doing it, nor can set any up. The illuminating and divine principle of the equal rights of man (for it has its origin from the Maker of man) relates, not only to the living individuals, but to generations of men succeeding each other. Every generation is equal in rights to the generations which preceded it, by the same rule that every individual is born equal in rights with his contemporary.

Every history of the creation, and every traditionary account, whether from the lettered or unlettered world, however they may vary in their opinion or belief of certain particulars, all agree in establishing one point, *the unity of man*; by which I mean that men are all of *one degree*, and consequently that all men are born equal, and with equal natural rights, in the same manner as if posterity had been continued by *creation* instead of *generation*, the latter being only the mode by which the former is carried forward; and consequently every child born into the world must be considered as deriving its existence from God. The world is as new to him as it was to the first man that existed, and his natural right in it is of the same kind.

The Mosaic account of the creation,[2] whether taken as divine authority or merely historical, is fully up to this point, *the unity or equality of man*. The expressions admit of no controversy. "And God said, Let us make man in our own image. In the image of God created he him; male and female created he them."[3] The distinction of sexes is pointed out, but no other distinction is even implied. If this be not divine authority, it is at least historical authority, and shows that the equality of man, so far from being a modern doctrine, is the oldest upon record. . . .

It is not among the least of the evils of the present existing Governments in all parts of Europe that man, considered as man, is thrown back to a vast distance from his Maker, and the artificial chasm filled up by a succession of barriers, or sort of turnpike gates, through which he has to pass. I will quote Mr. Burke's catalogue of barriers that he has set up between Man and his Maker. Putting himself in the character of a herald, he says: *We fear God—we look with* AWE *to kings—with affection to Parliaments—with duty to magistrates—with reverence to priests, and with respect to nobility.* Mr. Burke has forgotten to put in "*chivalry.*" He has also forgotten to put in Peter.[4]

The duty of man is not a wilderness of turnpike gates, through which he is to pass by tickets from one to the other. It is plain and simple, and consists but of two points. His duty to God, which every man must feel; and with respect to his neighbour, to do as he would be done by. If those to whom power is delegated do well, they will be respected; if not, they will be despised; and with regard to those to whom no power is delegated, but who assume it, the rational world can know nothing of them. . . .

When we survey the wretched condition of Man, under the monarchical and hereditary systems of Government, dragged from his home by one power, or driven by another, and impoverished by taxes more than by enemies, it becomes evident that those systems are bad, and that a general Revolution in the principle and construction of Governments is necessary.

What is Government more than the management of the affairs of a Nation? It is not, and from its nature cannot be, the property of any particular man or family, but of the whole community, at whose expence it is supported; and though by force and contrivance it has been usurped into an inheritance, the usurpation cannot alter the right of things. Sovereignty, as a matter of right, appertains to the Nation only, and not to any individual; and a Nation has at all times an inherent, indefeasible right to abolish any form of Government it finds inconvenient, and to establish such as accords with its interest, disposition, and happiness. The romantic and barbarous distinction of men into Kings and subjects, though it may suit the conditions of courtiers, cannot that of citizens; and is exploded by the principle upon which Governments are now founded. Every citizen is a member of the sovereignty, and, as such, can acknowledge no personal subjection: and his obedience can be only to the laws. . . .

In this view of Government, the Republican system, as established by America and France, operates to embrace the whole of a Nation. . . . What we formerly called Revolutions, were little more than a change of persons, or an alteration of local circumstances. They rose and fell like things of course, and had nothing in their existence or their fate that could influence beyond the spot that produced them. But what we now see in the world, from the Revolutions of America and France, are a renovation of the natural order of things, a system of principles as universal as truth and the existence of man, and combining moral with political happiness and national prosperity.

—1791

2. The biblical narrative of creation in the Book of Genesis was believed to have been written by Moses.   3. Genesis 1.26–27.   4. St. Peter was supposed to guard the gates of Heaven.

Thomas Jefferson
1743–1826

Thomas Jefferson's opening to the Declaration of Independence (1776) is famously rife with paradox. While this was America's most prominent avowal of the principles of liberty and equality, these rights were extended only to property-owning white males. Before drafting the Declaration, Jefferson had taken a ten-day vacation from the Continental Congress to oversee the enlargement of his estate; he now owned farms in three counties that together employed thirty-three white laborers and eighty-three black slaves. Nevertheless, his original draft included a passage condemning King George III's complicity in the slave trade: "He has waged cruel war against human nature itself, violating its most sacred rights of life and liberty in the persons of a distant people who never offended him, captivating and carrying them into slavery in another hemisphere" (p. 129). The Continental Congress removed this passage and refocused attention on Canada's role as a symbol of the British imperial yoke. Jefferson's condemnation of slavery was replaced with the demand that the King be held accountable "for abolishing the free system of English laws in a neighboring province, establishing therein an arbitrary government, and enlarging its boundaries, so as to render it at once an example and fit instrument for introducing the same absolute rule into these colonies" (p. 129). At issue here is the Quebec Act, one of the so-called Intolerable Acts of 1774. The Quebec Act reaffirmed Britain's political and legal presence in Canada and was viewed by many Americans as questionable, even contradictory. While it guaranteed the right of religious freedom to French-speaking, Roman Catholic Canadians, it simultaneously expanded the border of the province of Quebec south to the Ohio River and west to the Mississippi.

The Continental Congress's revision of Jefferson's Declaration speaks to a fundamental tension latent in the founding moments of the United States. The colonies had severed ties to imperial Britain for reasons that had everything to do with developing economic rivalry, but they justified this decision by reference to a philosophy of human rights that had its roots in the work of British and European Enlightenment thinkers. Likewise, Jefferson was a revolutionary spokesman who, during his education at the College of William and Mary, had been steeped in British law, philosophy, and literature. These traditions are not simply echoed in the Declaration; they are redefined, superseded, and sometimes subverted. Take, for instance, the phrase "E pluribus unum" (Out of many, one), which Jefferson helped select as the legend for America's seal. This phrase was adopted from the cover of the *Gentleman's Magazine*, an aristocratic British publication that had appropriated the words from the classical Roman poet Virgil. These words took on an entirely new meaning when applied to a republic instead of a monarchy.

After declaring America's independence from Britain, Jefferson, as governor of Virginia, went on to declare the independence of the church from the state with "An Act for Establishing Religious Freedom" (1786), noting that, "compulsion makes hypocrites, not converts." Unifying the secular and sacred in the governing of a people was a vestige of England's divine right of kings. Next, he served as an ambassador to pre-Revolutionary France. Writing to James Madison, Jefferson described the rule of the French Monarchy as a "government of wolves over sheep." He was asked by François Marbois, secretary to the French delegation in Philadelphia, to answer several detailed questions about Virginia, so he set about publishing his *Notes on the State of Virginia* in French in 1785 and in English in 1787, as a means of not only providing information about his home state but also disseminating republican sentiments. This work also served as a rebuttal to the great French naturalist Georges-Louis Leclerc, Comte de Buffon, who claimed that America's indigenous flora, fauna, and people had degenerated from those of Europe. Jefferson praises the landscape, plants, and people of Virginia, depicting Native Americans stereotypically as noble savages. On the other hand, *Notes* portrays African Americans in an unfavorable light and disparages the writing of Phillis Wheatley, whose poems Jefferson declared beneath the contempt of critics. Despite his opposition to the slave trade, Jefferson's views on race were informed by and contributed to contemporary racist pseudo-science that tried to classify races categorically and hierarchically with Anglo-Europeans at the top.

Despite his portrayal of Native Americans in *Notes*, Jefferson, when he became president, did not take measures to safeguard their rights as the new republic expanded westward. Indeed, his term in office saw the size of the United States double as a result of the Louisiana Purchase, which forced tribes to relocate west of the Mississippi. Jefferson's vision was to make America a strong republic of farmers, and he tried to pressure the Cherokee, among others, to assimilate, agreeing to grant them rights only if they gave up hunting and took up farming. Although he had lobbied successfully for the separation of church and state, his notion that those "who labor in the earth are the chosen people of God" had clear political consequences for those not deemed to be among the elect.

Jefferson wished to be remembered for his humanitarian efforts on behalf of the emerging nation, such as his words in honor of civil and religious liberty and his founding of the University of Virginia. And the egalitarian sentiments of the Declaration, despite their imperfection, remain relevant in an America that still suffers from the legacy of slavery and manifest destiny. Jefferson's words continue to be used as a benchmark of what America should *be* rather than simply represent. The ultimate question about the legacy of these words was posed by Reverend Dr. Martin Luther King, Jr.: "Was not Thomas Jefferson an extremist—'We hold these truths to be self-evident that all men are created equal.' So the question is not whether we will be extremist but what kind of extremist will we be. Will we be extremists for hate or will we be extremists for love?"

from Autobiography of Thomas Jefferson

(Declaration of Independence)

It appearing in the course of these debates,[1] that the colonies of New York, New Jersey, Pennsylvania, Delaware, Maryland, and South Carolina were not yet matured for falling from the parent stem, but that they were fast advancing to that state, it was thought most prudent to wait a while for them, and to postpone the final decision to July 1st; but, that this might occasion as little delay as possible, a committee was appointed to prepare a Declaration of Independence. The committee were John Adams, Dr. Franklin, Roger Sherman, Robert R. Livingston, and myself. Committees were also appointed, at the same time, to prepare a plan of confederation for the colonies, and to state the terms proper to be proposed for foreign alliance. The committee for drawing the Declaration of Independence, desired me to do it. It was accordingly done, and being approved by them, I reported it to the House on Friday, the 28th of June, when it was read, and ordered to lie on the table. On Monday, the 1st of July, the House resolved itself into a committee of the whole, and resumed the consideration of the original motion made by the delegates of Virginia, which, being again debated through the day, was carried in the affirmative by the votes of New Hampshire, Connecticut, Massachusetts, Rhode Island, New Jersey, Maryland, Virginia, North Carolina and Georgia. South Carolina and Pennsylvania voted against it. Delaware had but two members present, and they were divided. The delegates from New York declared they were for it themselves, and were assured their constituents were for it; but that their

---

1. At the Continental Congress.

instructions having been drawn near a twelve-month before, when reconciliation was still the general object, they were enjoined by them to do nothing which should impede that object. They, therefore, thought themselves not justifiable in voting on either side, and asked leave to withdraw from the question: which was given them. The committee rose and reported their resolution to the House. Mr. Edward Rutledge, of South Carolina, then requested the determination might be put off to the next day, as he believed his colleagues, though they disapproved of the resolution, would then join in it for the sake of unanimity. The ultimate question, whether the House would agree to the resolution of the committee, was accordingly postponed to the next day, when it was again moved, and South Carolina concurred in voting for it. In the meantime, a third member had come post from the Delaware counties, and turned the vote of that colony in favor of the resolution. Members of a different sentiment attending that morning from Pennsylvania also, her vote was changed, so that the whole twelve colonies who were authorized to vote at all, gave their voices for it; and, within a few days, the convention of New York approved of it, and thus supplied the void occasioned by the withdrawing of her delegates from the vote.

Congress proceeded the same day to consider the Declaration of Independence, which had been reported and lain on the table the Friday preceding, and on Monday referred to a committee of the whole. The pusillanimous idea that we had friends in England worth keeping terms with, still haunted the minds of many. For this reason, those passages which conveyed censures on the people of England were struck out, lest they should give them offense. The clause too, reprobating the enslaving the inhabitants of Africa, was struck out in complaisance to South Carolina and Georgia, who had never attempted to restrain the importation of slaves, and who, on the contrary, still wished to continue it. Our northern brethren also, I believe, felt a little tender under those censures; for though their people had very few slaves themselves, yet they had been pretty considerable carriers of them to others. The debates, having taken up the greater parts of the 2d, 3d, and 4th days of July, were, on the evening of the last, closed; the Declaration was reported by the committee, agreed to by the House, and signed by every member present, except Mr. Dickinson. As the sentiments of men are known not only by what they receive, but what they reject also, I will state the form of the Declaration as originally reported. The parts struck out by Congress shall be distinguished by a black line drawn under them, and those inserted by them shall be placed in the margin, or in a concurrent column.

A Declaration by the Representatives of the United States of America, in General Congress Assembled.

When, in the course of human events, it becomes necessary for one people to dissolve the political bands which have connected them with another, and to assume among the powers of the earth the separate & equal station to which the laws of nature and of nature's God entitle them, a decent respect to the opinions of mankind requires that they should declare the causes which impel them to the separation.

We hold these truths to be self evident: that all men are created equal; that they are endowed by their Creator with <u>inherent and</u> inalienable rights; that among these   certain
are life, liberty, and the pursuit of happiness; that to secure these rights, governments are instituted among men, deriving their just powers from the consent of the governed; that whenever any form of government becomes destructive of these ends, it

is the right of the people to alter or to abolish it, and to institute new government, laying its foundation on such principles, and organizing its powers in such form, as to them shall seem most likely to effect their safety and happiness. Prudence, indeed, will dictate that governments long established should not be changed for light and transient causes; and accordingly all experience hath shown that mankind are more disposed to suffer while evils are sufferable, than to right themselves by abolishing the forms to which they are accustomed. But when a long train of abuses and usurpations, begun at a distinguished period and pursuing invariably the same object, evinces a design to reduce them under absolute despotism, it is their right, it is their duty to throw off such government, and to provide new guards for their future security. Such has been the patient sufferance of these colonies; and such is now the necessity which constrains them to expunge their former systems of government. The history [alter] of the present king of Great Britain is a history of unremitting injuries and usurpa- [repeated] tions, among which appears no solitary fact to contradict the uniform tenor of the [all having] rest, but all have in direct object the establishment of an absolute tyranny over these states. To prove this, let facts be submitted to a candid world for the truth of which we pledge a faith yet unsullied by falsehood.

He has refused his assent to laws the most wholesome and necessary for the public good.

He has forbidden his governors to pass laws of immediate and pressing importance, unless suspended in their operation till his assent should be obtained; and, when so suspended, he has utterly neglected to attend to them.

He has refused to pass other laws for the accommodation of large districts of people, unless those people would relinquish the right of representation to the legislature, a right inestimable to them, and formidable to tyrants only.

He has called together legislative bodies at places unusual, uncomfortable, and distant from the depository of their public records, for the sole purpose of fatiguing them into compliance with his measures.

He has dissolved representative houses repeatedly and continually for opposing with manly firmness his invasions on the rights of the people.

He has refused for a long time after such dissolutions to cause others to be elected, whereby the legislative powers, incapable of annihilation, have returned to the people at large for their exercise, the state remaining, in the meantime, exposed to all the dangers of invasions from without and convulsions within.

He has endeavored to prevent the population of these states; for that purpose obstructing the laws for naturalization of foreigners, refusing to pass others to encourage their migrations hither, and raising the conditions of new appropriations of lands.

He has suffered the administration of justice totally to cease in some of these [obstructed] states refusing his assent to laws for establishing judiciary powers. [by]

He has made our judges dependent on his will alone for the tenure of their offices, and the amount and payment of their salaries.

He has erected a multitude of new offices, by a self-assumed power and sent hither swarms of new officers to harass our people and eat out their substance.

He has kept among us in times of peace standing armies and ships of war without the consent of our legislatures.

He has affected to render the military independent of, and superior to, the civil power.

He has combined with others to subject us to a jurisdiction foreign to our constitutions and unacknowledged by our laws, giving his assent to their acts of pretended legislation for quartering large bodies of armed troops among us; for protecting them by a mock trial from punishment for any murders which they should commit on the inhabitants of these states; for cutting off our trade with all parts of the world; for imposing taxes on us without our consent; for depriving us [   ] of the benefits of trial by jury; for transporting us beyond seas to be tried for pretended offenses; for abolishing the free system of English laws in a neighboring province, establishing therein an arbitrary government, and enlarging its boundaries, so as to render it at once an example and fit instrument for introducing the same absolute rule into these states; for taking away our charters, abolishing our most valuable laws, and altering fundamentally the forms of our governments; for suspending our own legislatures, and declaring themselves invested with power to legislate for us in all cases whatsoever.

[margin: in many cases]
[margin: colonies;]

He has abdicated government here withdrawing his governors, and declaring us out of his allegiance and protection.

[margin: by declaring us out of his protection, and waging war against us.]

He has plundered our seas, ravaged our coasts, burnt our towns, and destroyed the lives of our people.

He is at this time transporting large armies of foreign mercenaries to complete the works of death, desolation and tyranny already begun with circumstances of cruelty and perfidy [   ] unworthy the head of a civilized nation.

[margin: scarcely paralleled in the most barbarous ages, and totally]

He has constrained our fellow citizens taken captive on the high seas, to bear arms against their country, to become the executioners of their friends and brethren, or to fall themselves by their hands.

He has [   ] endeavored to bring on the inhabitants of our frontiers, the merciless Indian savages, whose known rule of warfare is an undistinguished destruction of all ages, sexes and conditions of existence.

[margin: excited domestic insurrection among us, and has]

He has incited treasonable insurrections of our fellow citizens, with the allurements of forfeiture and confiscation of our property.

He has waged cruel war against human nature itself, violating its most sacred rights of life and liberty in the persons of a distant people who never offended him, captivating and carrying them into slavery in another hemisphere, or to incur miserable death in their transportation thither. This piratical warfare, the opprobrium of INFIDEL powers, is the warfare of the CHRISTIAN king of Great Britain. Determined to keep open a market where MEN should be bought and sold, he has prostituted his negative for suppressing every legislative attempt to prohibit or to restrain this execrable commerce. And that this assemblage of horrors might want no fact of distinguished die, he is now exciting those very people to rise in arms among us, and to purchase that liberty of which he has deprived them, by murdering the people on whom he also obtruded them: thus paying off former crimes committed against the LIBERTIES of one people, with crimes which he urges them to commit against the LIVES of another.

[margin: obstructed by]

In every stage of these oppressions we have petitioned for redress in the most humble terms: our repeated petitions have been answered only by repeated injuries.

A prince whose character is thus marked by every act which may define a tyrant is unfit to be the ruler of a people who mean to be free. Future ages will scarcely believe that the hardiness of one man adventured, within the short compass of twelve years only, to lay a foundation so broad and so undisguised for tyranny over a people fostered and fixed in principles of freedom.

[margin: free]

Nor have we been wanting in attentions to our British brethren. We have warned them from time to time of attempts by their legislature to extend a jurisdiction over these our states. We have reminded them of the circumstances of our emigration and settlement here, no one of which could warrant so strange a pretension: that these were effected at the expense of our own blood and treasure, unassisted by the wealth or the strength of Great Britain: that in constituting indeed our several forms of government, we had adopted one common king,

[margin: an unwarrantable us]

thereby laying a foundation for perpetual league and amity with them: but that submission to their parliament was no part of our constitution, nor ever in idea, if history may be credited: and, we [   ] appealed to their native justice and magnanimity as well as to the ties of our common kindred to disavow these usurpations which were likely to interrupt our connection and correspondence. They too have been deaf to the voice of justice and of consanguinity, and when occasions have been given them, by the regular course of their laws, of removing from their councils the disturbers of our harmony, they have, by their free election, reestablished them in power. At this very time too, they are permitting their chief magistrate to send over not only soldiers of our common blood, but Scotch and foreign mercenaries to invade and destroy us. These facts have given the last stab of agonizing affection, and manly spirit bids us to renounce forever these unfeeling brethren. We must endeavor to forget our former love for them, and hold them as we hold the rest of mankind, enemies in war, in peace friends. We might have been a free and a great people together; but a communication of grandeur and of freedom, it seems, is below their dignity. Be it so, since they will have it. The road to happiness and to glory is open to us, too. We will tread it apart from them, and acquiesce in the necessity which denounces our eternal separation.

[margin notes: have and we have conjured them by would inevitably]

[margin notes: We must therefore]

[margin notes: and hold them as we hold the rest of mankind, enemies in war, in peace friends.]

We therefore the representatives of the United States of America in General Congress assembled, do in the name, and by the authority of the good people of these states reject and renounce all allegiance and subjection to the kings of Great Britain and all others who may hereafter claim by, through or under them; we utterly dissolve all political connection which may heretofore have subsisted between us and the people or parliament of Great Britain: and finally we do assert and declare these colonies to be free and independent states, and that as free and independent states, they have full power to levy war, conclude peace, contract alliances, establish commerce, and to do all other acts and things which independent states may of right do.

And for the support of this declaration, we mutually pledge to each other our lives, our fortunes, and our sacred honor.

We, therefore, the representatives of the United States of America in General Congress assembled, appealing to the supreme judge of the world for the rectitude of our intentions, do in the name, and by the authority of the good people of these colonies, solemnly publish and declare, that these united colonies are, and of right ought to be free and independent states; that they are absolved from all allegiance to the British crown, and that all political connection between them and the state of Great Britain is, and ought to be, totally dissolved; and that as free and independent states, they have full power to levy war, conclude peace, contract alliances, establish commerce, and to do all other acts and things which independent states may of right do.

And for the support of this declaration, with a firm reliance on the protection of divine providence, we mutually pledge to each other our lives, our fortunes, and our sacred honor.

The Declaration thus signed on the 4th, on paper, was engrossed on parchment, and signed again on the 2d of August.

—1821–1829

from Notes on the State of Virginia

from Query V. Its cascades and caverns?

Natural Bridge

The *Natural bridge*, the most sublime of Nature's works, though not comprehended under the present head, must not be pretermitted. It is on the ascent of a hill, which seems to have been cloven through its length by some great convulsion. The fissure, just at the bridge, is by some admeasurements, 270 feet deep, by others only 205. It is about 45 feet wide at the bottom, and 90 feet at the top; this of course determines the length of the bridge, and its height from the water. Its breadth in the middle, is about 60 feet, but more at the ends, and the thickness of the mass at the summit of the arch, about 40 feet. A part of this thickness is constituted by a coat of earth, which gives growth to many large trees. The residue, with the hill on both sides, is one solid rock of limestone. The arch approaches the semi-elliptical form; but the larger axis of the ellipsis, which would be the cord of the arch, is many times longer than the semi-axis which gives its height. Though the sides of this bridge are provided in some parts with a parapet of fixed rocks, yet few men have resolution to walk to them and look over into the abyss. You involuntarily fall on your hands and feet, creep to the parapet and peep over it. Looking down from this height about a minute gave me a violent headache. This painful sensation is relieved by a short, but pleasing view of the Blue ridge along the fissure downwards, and upwards by that of the Short hills, which, with the Purgatory mountain is a divergence from the North ridge; and, descending then to the valley below, the sensation becomes delightful in the extreme. It is impossible for the emotions, arising from the sublime, to be felt beyond what they are here: so beautiful an arch, so elevated, so light, and springing, as it were, up to heaven, the rapture of the Spectator is really indescribable! The fissure continues deep and narrow and, following the margin of the stream upwards about three eighths of a mile you arrive at a limestone cavern, less remarkable, however, for height and extent than those before described. Its entrance into the hill is but a few feet above the bed of the stream. This bridge is in the county of Rockbridge, to which it has given name, and affords a public and commodious passage over a valley, which cannot be crossed elsewhere for a considerable distance. The stream passing under it is called Cedar Creek. It is a water of James River, and sufficient in the driest seasons to turn a grist-mill, though its fountain is not more than two miles above.

from Query VI. A notice of the mines and other subterraneous riches; its trees, plants, fruits, etc.?

The opinion advanced by the Count de Buffon[1] is 1. That the animals common both to the old and new world are smaller in the latter. 2. That those peculiar to the new are on a smaller scale. 3. That those which have been domesticated in both have degenerated in America. and 4. That on the whole it exhibits fewer species. And the reason he thinks is that the heats of America are less; that more waters are spread over its surface by nature, and fewer of these drained off by the hand of man. In other words, that *heat* is friendly, and *moisture* adverse to the production and development of large quadrupeds. I will not meet this hypothesis on its first doubtful ground, whether the cli-

---

1. Georges-Louis Leclerc, Comte de Buffon (1707–1788).

mate of America be comparatively more humid? Because we are not furnished with observations sufficient to decide this question. And though, till it be decided, we are as free to deny, as others are to affirm, the fact, yet for a moment let it be supposed. The hypothesis, after this supposition, proceeds to another; that *moisture* is unfriendly to animal growth. The truth of this is inscrutable to us by reasonings a priori.[2] Nature has hidden from us her modus agendi.[3] Our only appeal on such questions is to experience; and I think that experience is against the supposition. It is by the assistance of *heat* and *moisture* that vegetables are elaborated from the elements of earth, air, water, and fire. We accordingly see the more humid climates produce the greater quantity of vegetables. Vegetables are mediately or immediately the food of every animal: and in proportion to the quantity of food, we see animals not only multiplied in their numbers, but improved in their bulk, as far as the laws of their nature will admit. Of this opinion is the Count de Buffon himself in another part of his work: "in general it seems that somewhat cold countries are better suited to our oxen than hot countries, and they are the heavier and bigger in proportion as the climate is damper and more abounding in pasture lands. The oxen of Denmark, of Podolie,[4] of the Ukraine, and of Tartary which is inhabited by the Calmouques,[5] are the largest of all." Here then a race of animals, and one of the largest too, has been increased in its dimensions by *cold* and *moisture*, in direct opposition to the hypothesis, which supposes that these two circumstances diminish animal bulk, and that it is their contraries *heat* and *dryness* which enlarge it. But when we appeal to experience, we are not to rest satisfied with a single fact. Let us therefore try our question on more general ground. Let us take our portions of the earth, Europe and America for instance, sufficiently extensive to give operation to general causes; let us consider the circumstances peculiar to each, and observe their effect on animal nature. America, running through the torrid as well as temperate zone, has more *heat*, collectively taken, than Europe. But Europe, according to our hypothesis, is the *dryest*. They are equally adapted then to animal productions; each being endowed with one of those causes which befriend animal growth, and with one which opposes it. If it be thought unequal to compare Europe with America, which is so much larger, I answer, not more so than to compare America with the whole world. Besides, the purpose of the comparison is to try an hypothesis, which makes the size of animals depend on the *heat* and *moisture* of climate. If therefore we take a region, so extensive as to comprehend a sensible distinction of climate, and so extensive too as that local accidents, or the intercourse of animals on its borders, may not materially affect the size of those in its interior parts, we shall comply with those conditions which the hypothesis may reasonably demand. The objection would be the weaker in the present case, because any intercourse of animals which may take place on the confines of Europe and Asia, is to the advantage of the former, Asia producing certainly larger animals than Europe. . . .

Hitherto I have considered this hypothesis as applied to brute animals only, and not in its extension to the man of America, whether aboriginal or transplanted. It is the opinion of Mons. de Buffon that the former furnishes no exception to it: "Although the savage of the new world is about the same height as man in our world, this does not suffice for him to constitute an exception to the general fact that all living nature has become smaller on that continent. The savage is feeble, and has small organs of gener-

---

2. Reasoning based on pure logic rather than experience.   3. Mode of accomplishing things.   4. A town in northeastern India.   5. Kalmuks, a tribe in Mongolia.

ation; he has neither hair nor beard, and no ardor whatever for his female; although swifter than the European because he is better accustomed to running, he is, on the other hand, less strong in body; he is also less sensitive, and yet more timid and cowardly; he has no vivacity, no activity of mind; the activity of his body is less an exercise, a voluntary motion, than a necessary action caused by want; relieve him of hunger and thirst, and you deprive him of the active principle of all his movements; he will rest stupidly upon his legs or lying down entire days. There is no need for seeking further the cause of the isolated mode of life of these savages and their repugnance for society: the most precious spark of the fire of nature has been refused to them; they lack ardor for their females, and consequently have no love for their fellow men: not knowing this stongest and most tender of all affections, their other feelings are also cold and languid; they love their parents and children but little; the most intimate of all ties, the family connection, binds them therefore but loosely together; between family and family there is no tie at all; hence they have no communion, no commonwealth, no state of society. Physical love constitutes their only morality; their heart is icy, their society cold, and their rule harsh. They look upon their wives only as servants for all work, or as beasts of burden, which they load without consideration with the burden of their hunting, and which they compel without mercy, without gratitude, to perform tasks which are often beyond their strength. They have only few children, and they take little care of them. Everywhere the original defect appears: they are indifferent because they have little sexual capacity, and this indifference to the other sex is the fundamental defect which weakens their nature, prevents its development, and—destroying the very germs of life—uproots society at the same time. Man is here no exception to the general rule. Nature, by refusing him the power of love, has treated him worse and lowered him deeper than any animal." An afflicting picture indeed, which, for the honor of human nature, I am glad to believe has no original. Of the Indian of South America I know nothing; for I would not honour with the appellation of knowledge, what I derive from the fables published of them. These I believe to be just as true as the fables of Aesop. This belief is founded on what I have seen of man, white, red, and black, and what has been written of him by authors, enlightened themselves, and writing admidst an enlightened people. The Indian of North America being more within our reach, I can speak of him somewhat from my own knowledge, but more from the information of others better acquainted with him, and on whose truth and judgment I can rely. From these sources I am able to say, in contradiction to this representation, that he is neither more defective in ardour, nor more impotent with his female, than the white reduced to the same diet and exercise: that he is brave, when an enterprise depends on bravery; education with him making the point of honor consist in the destruction of an enemy by stratagem, and in the preservation of his own person free from injury; or perhaps this is nature; while it is education which teaches us to honor force more than finesse; that he will defend himself against an host of enemies, always choosing to be killed, rather than to surrender, though it be to the whites, who he knows will treat him well: that in other situations also he meets death with more deliberation, and endures tortures with a firmness unknown almost to religious enthusiasm with us: that he is affectionate to his children, careful of them, and indulgent in the extreme: that his affections comprehend his other connexions, weakening, as with us, from circle to circle, as they recede from the center: that his friendships are strong and faithful to the uttermost extremity: that his sensibility is keen, even the warriors weeping most bitterly on the loss of their children, though in general they endeavor to appear superior to human events: that his vivacity and activity of mind is equal to ours in the same situation; hence his eagerness for hunting, and for games of chance. The women are submitted to unjust drudgery. This I believe is the case with every barbarous people. With such, force is law. The stronger sex therefore imposes on the weaker. It is civilization alone which replaces women in the enjoyment of their natural equality. That first teaches us to subdue the selfish passions, and to respect those rights in others which we value in ourselves. Were we in equal barbarism, our females would be equal drudges. The man with them is less strong than with us, but their woman stronger than ours; and both for the same obvious reason; because our man and their woman is habituated to labour, and formed by it. With both races the sex which is indulged with ease is least athletic. An Indian man is small in the hand and wrist for the same reason for which a sailor is large and strong in the arms and shoulders, and a porter in the legs and thighs. They raise fewer children than we do. The causes of this are to be found, not in a difference of nature, but of circumstance. The women are frequently attending the men in their parties of war and of hunting, childbearing becomes extremely inconvenient to them. It is said therefore, that they have learnt the practice of procuring abortion by the use of some vegetable; and that it even extends to prevent conception for a considerable time after. During these parties they are exposed to numerous hazards, to excessive exertions, to the greatest extremities of hunger. Even at their homes the nation depends for food, through a certain part of every year, on the gleanings of the forest; that is, they experience a famine once in every year. With all animals, if the female be badly fed, or not fed at all, her young perish: and if both male and female be reduced to like want, generation becomes less active, less productive. To the obstacles then of want and hazard, which nature has opposed to the multiplication of wild animals, for the purpose of restraining their numbers within certain bounds; those of labour and of voluntary abortion are added with the Indian. No wonder then if they multiply less than we do. Where food is regularly supplied, a single farm will shew more of cattle, than a whole country of forests can of buffaloes. The same Indian women, when married to white traders, who feed them and their children plentifully and regularly, who exempt them from excessive drudgery, who keep them stationary and unexposed to accident, produce and raise as many children as the white women. Instances are known, under these circumstances, of their rearing a dozen children. An inhuman practice once prevailed in this country of making slaves of the Indians. It is a fact well known with us, that the Indian women so enslaved produced and raised as numerous families as either the whites or blacks among whom they lived. It has been said, that Indians have less hair than the whites, except on the head. But this is a fact of which fair proof can scarcely be had. With them it is disgraceful to be hairy on the body. They say it likens them to hogs. They therefore pluck the hair as fast as it appears. But the traders who marry their women, and prevail on them to discontinue this practice, say, that nature is the same with them as with the whites. Nor, if the fact be true, is the consequence necessary which has been drawn from it. Negroes have notoriously less hair than the whites; yet they are more ardent. But if cold and moisture be the agents of nature for diminishing the races of animals, how comes she all at once to suspend their operation as to the physical man of the new world, whom the Count acknowledges to be "about the same size as the man of our hemisphere," and to let loose their influence on his moral faculties? How has this "combination of the elements and other physical causes, so contrary to the enlargement of animal nature in this new world, these obstacles to the development and formation of great germs," been arrested and suspended, so as to permit the human body to acquire its just dimensions, and by what inconceivable process has their action been directed on his mind alone? To judge of the truth of this, to form a just estimate of their genius and mental powers, more facts are wanting, and great allowance to be made for those circumstances of their situation which call for a display of particular talents only. This done, we shall probably find that they are formed in mind as well as in body, on the same module with the "Homo sapiens Europaeus."[6] The principles of their society forbidding all compulsion, they are to be led to duty and to enterprize by personal influence and persuasion. Hence eloquence in council, bravery and address in war, become the foundations of all consequence with them. To these acquirements all their faculties are directed. Of their bravery and address in war we have multiplied proofs, because we have been the subjects on which they were exercised. Of their eminence in oratory we have fewer examples, because it is displayed chiefly in their own councils. Some, however, we have of very superior luster. I may challenge the whole orations of Demosthenes and Cicero,[7] and of any more eminent orator, if Europe has furnished more eminent, to produce a single passage, superor to the speech of Logan, a Mingo chief, to Lord Dunmore, when governor of this state. And, as a testimony of their talents in this line, I beg leave to introduce it, first stating the incidents necessary for understanding it.

In the spring of the year 1774, a robbery was committed by some Indians on certain land-adventurers on the river Ohio. The whites in that quarter, according to their custom, undertook to punish this outrage in a summary way. Captain Michael Cresap, and a certain Daniel Great-house,[8] leading on these parties, surprised, at different times, traveling and hunting parties of the Indians, having their women and children with them, and murdered many. Among these were unfortunately the family of Logan, a chief celebrated in peace and war, and long distinguished as the friend of the whites. This unworthy return provoked his vengeance. He accordingly signalized himself in the war which ensued. In the autumn of the same year a decisive battle was fought at the mouth of the Great Kanhaway, between the collected forces of the Shawanese, Mingoes, and Delawares, and a detachment of the Virginia militia. The Indians were defeated, and sued for peace. Logan however disdained to be seen among the suppliants. But, lest the sincerity of a treaty should be distrusted, from which so distinguished a chief absented himself, he sent by a messenger the following speech to be delivered to Lord Dunmore.

"I appeal to any white man to say, if ever he entered Logan's cabin hungry, and he gave him not meat; if ever he came cold and naked, and he clothed him not. During the course of the last long and bloody war, Logan remained idle in his cabin, an advocate for peace. Such was my love for the whites, that my countrymen pointed as they passed, and said, 'Logan is the friend of white men.' I had even thought to have lived with you, but for the injuries of one man. Col. Cresap, the last spring, in cold blood, and unprovoked, murdered all the relations of Logan, not sparing even my women and children. There runs not a drop of my blood in the veins of any living creature. This called on me for revenge. I have sought it: I have killed many: I have fully glutted my vengeance. For my country, I rejoice at the

6. European humans.   7. Classical orators, Greek and Roman, respectively.   8. Michael Cresap (1742–1775), a Maryland land speculator, and Daniel Greathouse, a settler.

beams of peace. But do not harbor a thought that mine is the joy of fear. Logan never felt fear. He will not turn on his heel to save his life. Who is there to mourn for Logan?—Not one."

Before we condemn the Indians of this continent as wanting genius, we must consider that letters have not yet been introduced among them. Were we to compare them in their present state with the Europeans North of the Alps, when the Roman arms and arts first crossed those mountains, the comparison would be unequal, because, at that time, those parts of Europe were swarming with numbers; because numbers produce emulation, and multiply the chances of improvement, and one improvement begets another. Yet I may safely ask, How many good poets, how many able mathematicians, how many great inventors in arts or sciences had Europe, North of the Alps, then produced? And it was sixteen centuries after this before a Newton could be formed. I do not mean to deny, that there are varieties in the race of man, distinguished by their powers both of body and mind. I believe there are, as I see to be the case in the races of other animals. I only mean to suggest a doubt, whether the bulk and faculties of animals depend on the side of the Atlantic on which their food happens to grow, or which furnishes the elements of which they are compounded? Whether nature has enlisted herself as a Cis or Trans-Atlantic partisan? I am induced to suspect, there has been more eloquence than sound reasoning displayed in support of this theory; that it is one of those cases where the judgment has been seduced by a glowing pen: and whilst I render every tribute of honor and esteem to the celebrated zoologist, who has added, and is still adding, so many precious things to the treasures of science, I must doubt whether in this instance he has not cherished error also, by lending her for a moment his vivid imagination and bewitching language.

So far the Count de Buffon has carried his new theory of the tendency of nature to belittle her productions on this side the Atlantic. Its application to the race of whites, transplanted from Europe, remained for the Abbé Raynal.[9] 'On doit etre etonné (he says) que l'Amerique n'ait pas encore produit un bon poëte, un habile mathematicien, un homme de genie dans un seul art, ou une seule science.'[10] When we shall have existed as a people as long as the Greeks did before they produced a Homer, the Romans a Virgil, the French a Racine and Voltaire, the English a Shakespeare and Milton, should this reproach be still true, we will enquire from what unfriendly causes it has proceeded, that the other countries of Europe and quarters of the earth shall not have inscribed any name in the roll of poets. But neither has America produced 'one able mathematician, one man of genius in a single art or a single science.' In war we have produced a Washington, whose memory will be adored while liberty shall have votaries, whose name will triumph over time, and will in future ages assume its just station among the most celebrated worthies of the world, when that wretched philosophy shall be forgotten which would have arranged him among the degeneracies of nature. In physics we have produced a Franklin, than whom no one of the present age has made more important discoveries, nor has enriched philosophy with more, or more ingenious solutions of the phenomena of nature. We have supposed Mr. Rittenhouse[11] second to no astronomer living: that in genius he must be the first, because he is self-taught. As

9. Guillaume Thomas François Raynal (1713–1796), French historian.   10. [Jefferson's note] Hist. Philos. p. 92. ed. Maestricht. 1774. 'America has not yet produced one good poet.'   11. David Rittenhouse (1732–1796), designer of models of the solar system.

an artist he has exhibited as great a proof of mechanical genius as the world has ever produced. He has not indeed made a world; but he has by imitation approached nearer its Maker than any man who has lived from the creation to this day. As in philosophy and war, so in government, in oratory, in painting, in the plastic art, we might show that America, though but a child of yesterday, has already given hopeful proofs of genius, as well of the nobler kinds, which arouse the best feelings of man, which call him into action, which substantiate his freedom, and conduct him to happiness, as of the subordinate, which serve to amuse him only. We therefore suppose, that this reproach is as unjust as it is unkind; and that, of the geniuses which adorn the present age, America contributes its full share. For comparing it with those countries, where genius is most cultivated, where are the most excellent models for art, and scaffoldings for the attainment of science, as France and England for instance, we calculate thus: The United States contain three millions of inhabitants; France twenty millions; and the British islands ten. We produce a Washington, a Franklin, a Rittenhouse. France then should have half a dozen in each of these lines, and Great Britain half that number, equally eminent. It may be true, that France has: we are but just becoming acquainted with her, and our acquaintance so far gives us high ideas of the genius of her inhabitants. It would be injuring too many of them to name particularly a Voltaire, a Buffon, the constellation of Encyclopedists, the Abbé Raynal himself, &c. &c. We therefore have reason to believe she can produce her full quota of genius. The present war having so long cut off all communication with Great Britain, we are not able to make a fair estimate of the state of science in that country. The spirit in which she wages war, is the only sample before our eyes, and that does not seem the legitimate offspring either of science or of civilization. The sun of her glory is fast descending to the horizon. Her philosophy has crossed the channel, her freedom the Atlantic, and herself seems passing to that awful dissolution, whose issue is not given human foresight to scan. . . .

To this catalogue of our indigenous animals, I will add a short account of an anomaly of nature, taking place sometimes in the race of negroes brought from Africa, who, though black themselves, have, in rare instances, white children, called Albinos. I have known four of these myself, and have faithful accounts of three others. The circumstances in which all the individuals agree, are these. They are of a pallid cadaverous white, untinged with red, without any coloured spots or seams; their hair of the same kind of white, short, coarse and curled as is that of the negro; all of them well formed, strong, healthy, perfect in their senses, except that of sight, and born of parents who had no mixture of white blood. Three of these Albinos were sisters, having two other full sisters, who were black. The youngest of the three was killed by lightning, at twelve years of age. The eldest died at about 27 years of age, in child-bed, with her second child. The middle one is now alive in health, and has issue, as the eldest had, by a black man, which issue was black. They are uncommonly shrewd, quick in their apprehensions and in reply. Their eyes are in a perpetual tremulous vibration, very weak, and much affected by the sun: but they see much better in the night than we do. They are the property of Col. Skipwith, of Cumberland. The fourth is a negro woman, whose parents came from Guinea, and had three other children, who were of their own colour. She is freckled, her eye-sight so weak that she is obliged to wear a bonnet in the summer; but it is better in the night than day. She had an Albino child by a black man. It died at the age of a few weeks. These were the property of Col. Carter, of Albemarle. A sixth instance is a woman of the property of Mr. Butler, near Petersburg. She is stout and robust, has issue a daughter, jet black, by a black man. I am not informed as to her eye-sight. The seventh instance is of a male belonging to a Mr. Lee of Cumberland. His eyes are tremulous and weak. He is tall of stature, and now advanced in years. He is the only male of the Albinos which have come within my information. Whatever be the cause of the disease in the skin, or in its colouring matter, which produces this change, it seems more incident to the female than male sex. To these I may add the mention of a negro man within my own knowledge, born black, and of black parents; on whose chin, when a boy, a white spot appeared. This continued to increase till he became a man, by which time it had extended over his chin, lips, one cheek, the under jaw, and neck on that side. It is of the Albino white, without any mixture of red, and has for several years been stationary. He is robust and healthy, and the change of colour was not accompanied with any sensible disease, either general or topical.

from Query XI. A description of the Indians established in that state?

When the first effectual settlement of our colony was made, which was in 1607, the country from the sea-coast to the mountains, and from Patowmac to the most southern waters of James river, was occupied by upwards of forty different tribes of Indians. Of these the *Powhatans*, the *Mannahoacs*, and *Monacans*, were the most powerful. Those between the sea-coast and falls of the rivers, were in amity with one another, and attached to the *Powhatans* as their link of union. Those between the falls of the rivers and the mountains, were divided into two confederacies; the tribes inhabiting the head waters of Patowmac and Rappahanoc being attached to the *Mannahoacs*; and those on the upper parts of James river to the *Monacans*. But the *Monacans* and their friends were in amity with the *Mannahoacs* and their friends, and waged joint and perpetual war against the *Powhatans*. We are told that the *Powhatans*, *Mannahoacs*, and *Monacans*, spoke languages so radically different, that interpreters were necesary when they transacted business. Hence we may conjecture, that this was not the case between all the tribes, and probably that each spoke the language of the nation to which it was attached; which we know to have been the case in many particular instances. Very possibly there may have been anciently three different stocks, each of which multiplying in a long course of time, had separated into so many little societies. This practice results from the circumstance of their having never submitted themselves to any laws, any coercive power, any shadow of government. Their only controuls are their manners, and that moral sense of right and wrong, which, like the sense of tasting and feeling, in every man makes a part of his nature. An offence against these is punished by contempt, by exclusion from society, or, where the case is serious, as that of murder, by the individuals whom it concerns. Imperfect as this species of coercion may seem, crimes are very rare among them: insomuch that were it made a question, whether no law, as among the savage Americans, or too much law, as among the civilized Europeans, submits man to the greatest evil, one who has seen both conditions of existence would pronounce it to be the last: and that the sheep are happier of themselves, than under care of the wolves. It will be said, that great societies cannot exist without government. The Savages therefore break them into small ones. . . .

 I know of no such thing existing as an Indian monument: for I would not honour with that name arrow points, stone hatchets, stone pipes, and half-shapen images. Of labour on the large scale, I think there is no remain as respectable as would be a common ditch for the draining of lands: unless indeed it be the barrows, of which many are to be found all over this country. These are of different sizes, some of them constructed of earth, and some of loose stones. That they were repositories of the dead, has been obvious to all: but on what particular occasion constructed, was matter of doubt. Some have thought they covered the bones of those who have fallen in battles fought on the spot of interment. Some ascribed them to the custom, said to prevail among the Indians, of collecting, at certain periods, the bones of all their dead, wheresoever deposited at the time of death. Others again supposed them the general sepulchres for towns, conjectured to have been on or near these grounds; and this opinion was supported by the quality of the lands in which they are found, (those constructed of earth being generally in the softest and most fertile meadow-grounds on river sides) and by a tradition, said to be handed down from the aboriginal Indians, that, when they settled in a town, the first person who died was placed erect, and earth put about him, so as to cover and support him; that, when another died, a narrow passage was dug to the first, the second reclined against him, and the cover of earth replaced, and so on. There being one of these in my neighbourhood, I wished to satisfy myself whether any, and which of these opinions were just. For this purpose I determined to open and examine it thoroughly. It was situated on the low grounds of the Rivanna, about two miles above its principle fork, and opposite to some hills, on which had been an Indian town. It was of a spheroidical form, of about 40 feet in diameter at the base, and had been of about twelve feet altitude, though now reduced by the plough to seven and a half, having been under cultivation about a dozen years. Before this it was covered with trees of twelve inches diameter, and round the base was an excavation of five feet depth and width, from whence the earth had been taken of which the hillock was formed. I first dug superficially in several parts of it, and came to collections of human bones, at different depths, from six inches to three feet below the surface. These were lying in the utmost confusion, some vertical, some oblique, some horizontal, and directed to every point of the compass, entangled, and held together in clusters by the earth. Bones of the most distant parts were found together, as, for instance, the small bones of the foot in the hollow of a scull, many sculls would sometimes be in contact, lying on the face, on the side, on the back, top or bottom, so as, on the whole to give the idea of bones emptied promiscuously from a bag or basket, and covered over with earth, without any attention to their order. The bones of which the greatest numbers remained, were sculls, jaw-bones, teeth, the bones of the arms, thighs, legs, feet and hands. A few ribs remained, some vertebrae of the neck and spine, without their processes, and one instance only of the bone which serves as a base to the vertebral column. The sculls were so tender, that they generally fell to pieces on being touched. The other bones were stronger. There were some teeth which were judged to be smaller than those of an adult; a scull, which, on a slight view, appeared to be that of an infant, but it fell to pieces on being taken out, so as to prevent satisfactory examination; a rib, and a fragment of the under-jaw of a person about half grown; another rib of an infant; and part of the jaw of a child, which had not yet cut its teeth. This last furnishing the most decisive proof of the burial of children here, I was particular in my attention to it. It was part of the right-half of the under-jaw. The processes, by which it was articulated to the temporal bones, were entire; and the bone itself firm to where it had been broken off, which, as nearly as I could judge, was about the place of the eye-tooth. Its upper edge, wherein would have been the sockets of the teeth, was perfectly smooth. Measuring it with that of an adult, by placing their hinder processes together, its broken end extended to the penultimate grinder of the adult. This bone was white, all the others of a sand colour. The bones of infants being soft, they probably decay sooner, which might be the cause so few were found here. I proceeded then to make a perpendicular cut through the body of the barrow, that I might examine its internal structure. This passed about three feet from its center, was opened to the former surface of the earth, and was wide enough for a man to walk through and examine its sides. At the bottom, that is, on the level of the circumjacent plain, I found bones; above these a few stones, brought from a cliff a quarter of a mile off, and from the river one-eighth of a mile off; then a large interval of earth, then a stratum of bones, and so on. At one end of the section were four strata of bones plainly distinguishable; at the other, three; the strata in one part not ranging with those in another. The bones nearest the surface were least decayed. No holes were discovered in any of them, as if made with bullets, arrows, or other weapons. I conjectured that in this barrow might have been a thousand skeletons. Every one will readily seize the circumstances above related, which militate against the opinion, that it covered the bones only of persons fallen in battle; and against the tradition also, which would make it the common sepulchre of a town, in which the bodies were placed upright, and touching each other. Appearances certainly indicate that it has derived both origin and growth from the accustomary collection of bones, and deposition of them togther; that the first collection had been deposited on the common surface of the earth, a few stones put over it, and then a covering of earth, that the second had been laid on this, had covered more or less of it in proportion to the number of bones, and was then also covered with earth; and so on. The following are the particular circumstances which give it this aspect. 1. The number of bones. 2. Their confused position. 3. Their being in different strata. 4. The strata in one part having no correspondence with those in another. 5. The different states of decay in these strata, which seem to indicate a difference in the time of inhumation. 6. The existence of infant bones among them.

But on whatever occasion they may have been made, they are of considerable notoriety among the Indians: for a party passing, about thirty years ago, through the part of the country where this barrow is, went through the woods directly to it, without any instructions or enquiry, and having staid about it some time, with expressions which were construed to be those of sorrow, they returned to the high road, which they had left about half a dozen miles to pay this visit, and pursued their journey. There is another barrow, much resembling this in the low grounds of the South branch of Shenandoah, where it is crossed by the road leading from the Rockfish gap to Staunton. Both of these have, within these dozen years, been cleared of their trees and put under cultivation, are much reduced in their height, and spread in width, by the plough, and will probably disappear in time. There is another on a hill in the Blue ridge of mountains, a few miles North of Wood's gap, which is made up of small stones thrown together. This has been opened and found to contain human bones, as the others do. There are also many others in other parts of the country.

Great question has arisen from whence came those aboriginal inhabitants of America? Discoveries, long ago made, were sufficient to shew that a passage from Europe to America was always practicable, even to the imperfect navigation of ancient times. In going from Norway to Iceland, from Iceland to Groenland, from Groenland to Labrador, the first traject is the widest: and this having been practised from the earliest times of which we have any account of that part of the earth, it is not difficult to suppose that the subsequent trajects may have been sometimes passed. Again, the late discoveries of Captain Cook,[12] coasting from Kamschatka to California, have proved that, if the two continents of Asia and America be separated at all, it is only by a narrow streight. So that from this side also, inhabitants may have passed into America: and the resemblance between the Indians of America and the Eastern inhabitants of Asia, would induce us to conjecture, that the former are the descendants of the latter, or the latter of the former: excepting indeed the Eskimaux, who, from the same circumstance of resemblance, and from identity of language, must be derived from the Groenlanders, and these probably from some of the northern parts of the old continent. A knowledge of their several languages would be the most certain evidence of their derivation which could be produced. In fact, it is the best proof of the affinity of nations which ever can be referred to. How many ages have elapsed since the English, the Dutch, the Germans, the Swiss, the Norwegians, Danes and Swedes have separated from their common stock? Yet how many more must elapse before the proofs of their common origin, which exist in their several languages, will disappear? It is to be lamented then, very much to be lamented, that we have suffered so many of the Indian tribes already to extinguish, without our having previously collected and deposited in the records of literature, the general rudiments at least of the languages they spoke. Were vocabularies formed of all the languages spoken in North and South America, preserving their appellations of the most common objects in nature, of those which must be present to every nation barbarous or civilised, with the inflections of their nouns and verbs, their principles of regimen and concord, and these deposited in all the public libraries, it would furnish opportunities to those skilled in the languages of the old world to compare them with these, now, or at any future time, and hence to construct the best evidence of the derivation of this part of the human race.

But imperfect as is our knowledge of the tongues spoken in America, it suffices to discover the following remarkable fact. Arranging them under the radical ones to which they may be palpably traced, and doing the same by those of the red men of Asia, there will be found probably twenty in America, for one in Asia, of those radical languages, so called because, if they were ever the same they have lost all resemblance to one another. A separation into dialects may be the work of a few ages only, but for two dialects to recede from one another till they have lost all vestiges of their common origin, must require an immense course of time; perhaps not less than many people give to the age of the earth. A greater number of those radical changes of language having taken place among the red men of America, proves them of greater antiquity than those of Asia.

from Query XVIII. The particular customs and manners that may happen to be received in that state?

It is difficult to determine on the standard by which the manners of a nation may be tried, whether *catholic,* or *particular.* It is more difficult for a native to bring to that standard the manners of his own nation, familiarized to him by habit. There must doubtless be an unhappy influence on the manners of our people produced by the existence of slavery among us. The whole commerce between master and slave is a perpetual exercise of the most boisterous passions, the most unremitting despotism on the one part, and degrading submissions on the other. Our children see this, and learn

---

12. James Cook (1728–1779), British explorer of the Pacific Ocean.

to imitate it; for man is an imitative animal. This quality is the germ of all education in him. From his cradle to his grave he is learning to do what he sees others do. If a parent could find no motive either in his philanthropy or his self-love, for restraining the intemperance of passion towards his slave, it should always be a sufficient one that his child is present. But generally it is not sufficient. The parent storms, the child looks on, catches the lineaments of wrath, puts on the same airs in the circle of smaller slaves, gives a loose to his worst of passions, and thus nursed, educated, and daily exercised in tyranny, cannot but be stamped by it with odious peculiarities. The man must be a prodigy who can retain his manners and morals undepraved by such circumstances. And with what execration should the statesman be loaded, who permitting one half the citizens thus to trample on the rights of the other, transforms those into despots, and these into enemies, destroys the morals of the one part, and the amor patriæ[13] of the other. For if a slave can have a country in this world, it must be any other in preference to that in which he is born to live and labour for another: in which he must lock up the faculties of his nature, contribute as far as depends on his individual endeavours to the evanishment of the human race, or entail his own miserable condition on the endless generations proceeding from him. With the morals of the people, their industry also is destroyed. For in a warm climate, no man will labour for himself who can make another labour for him. This is so true, that of the proprietors of slaves a very small proportion indeed are ever seen to labour. And can the liberties of a nation be thought secure when we have removed their only firm basis, a conviction in the minds of the people that these liberties are of the gift of God? That they are not to be violated but with his wrath? Indeed I tremble for my country when I reflect that God is just: that his justice cannot sleep for ever: that considering numbers, nature and natural means only, a revolution of the wheel of fortune, an exchange of situation, is among possible events: that it may become probable by supernatural interference! The Almighty has no attribute which can take side with us in such a contest—But it is impossible to be temperate and to pursue this subject through the various considerations of policy, of morals, of history natural and civil. We must be contended to hope they will force their way into every one's mind. I think a change already perceptible, since the origin of the present revolution. The spirit of the master is abating, that of the slave rising from the dust, his condition mollifying, the way I hope preparing, under the auspices of heaven, for a total emancipation, and that this is disposed, in the order of events, to be with the consent of the masters, rather than by their extirpation.

—1787

⟳ TRANSATLANTIC EXCHANGES ⟲

Revolutionary Republicanism

In the United States today, the term "republican" denotes a member of the more conservative of the two mainstream political parties. During the Romantic period, a "republican" was a person who believed in citizens' right to govern themselves as opposed to being governed by a king

---

13. Love of country.

or queen. When the United States gained freedom from British rule, the country became a "republic," which in the words of James Madison is "a government which derives all its powers directly or indirectly from the great body of the people, and is administered by persons holding their offices . . . for a limited period, or during good behavior." In America, Britain, and Canada, republicans were radicals who valued the rights and liberties of the common people over those of the aristocracy, privileged, and wealthy.

The American Revolution began as a colonial revolt against taxes imposed by the imperial government in London but soon grew into a much broader political and ideological conflict. British taxes had always existed in the colonies but were rarely enforced, due to rampant corruption in the Colonial Customs Service. In 1764, though, this all changed: The Sugar or Revenue Act was introduced. It was a duplicitous measure, as it actually reduced the tax on molasses by 50% but enforced its payment with ruthless consistency. A year later, a special tax that applied only to Americans was levied—the Stamp Act. The colonial assemblies declared this duty to be egregiously unfair, since it forced the American colonies to pay vast sums of money to support a British government in which they had no say. "No taxation without representation" was both the chorus on the lips of rioters who burned stamps publicly and the refrain printed in American newspapers (which, by decree of the Act, had to be printed on stamped paper). As a result of this dissent, the Stamp Act was repealed. This reversal set a precedent that threatened the stability of British rule, for the colonies now realized that public and violent dissent could effectively counter the colonial policy of the home government.

When Britain sought to quell its angry subjects in Boston by increasing its military presence there, it was, in the words of Benjamin Franklin, setting up "a Smith's Forge in a Magazine of Gunpowder." British soldiers were pelted by snowballs thrown by a sixty-strong mob of Bostonians. Whether or not Captain Preston gave the order for the redcoats to return fire with muskets was never determined, but colonists were shot and killed, including an African American protester, Crispus Attucks. The soldiers responsible were acquitted of murder charges, and Samuel Adams dubbed the fight the "Boston Massacre." Paul Revere, who would later take his famous midnight ride to spread word of the coming British armies, stirred up the public's ire by capturing the event in an engraving, which circulated in countless copies throughout the colonies. The overwhelming response to the image exemplified the power the printing press wielded during the American Revolution.

In Philadelphia too, the Revolution was waged with both bullets and type. As the redcoats struggled to control the city militarily, their efforts were buttressed by the Loyalist publications of James Humphreys, who printed a newspaper with the King's arms displayed on the front page, along with Isaac Hunt's The Political Family (1775; see Figure 1) and Charles Inglis's The True Interest of America Impartially Stated in Certain Strictures on a Pamphlet Intitled Common Sense (1776). In the eyes of Loyalists, America was betraying a fundamental kinship through its actions. Such writers consistently represented the political and economic connections between the imperial center and the periphery by employing the metaphor of family ties. William Pitt, for instance, who campaigned actively in Parliament to improve relations with the colonies, nevertheless believed that the Americans "must be subordinate. This is the Mother Country. They are the children." Similarly, Isaac Hunt depicted England and America as tied together by family bonds, the severance of which would have dire consequences. Inglis took this trope (figure of speech) even further, arguing that the action that Paine wanted America to take against England "would resemble the conduct of a rash . . . stripling, who should call his mother a d-mn-d b—ch, swear he had no relation to her, and attempt to knock her down."

At the same time, hawkers on Philadelphia street corners sold Thomas Paine's Common Sense (1776), which was printed by the patriot publisher William Bradford. Paine saw things differently from the Loyalists and contested their central metaphor of the family; he argued that the colonies were in fact a multinational society and that "the phrase *parent* or *mother country* hath been jesuitically adopted by the king and his parasites, with a low papistical design of gaining an unfair bias on the credulous weakness of our minds. Europe, and not England, is the parent country of America" (p. 114). Paine addressed a largely Protestant audience with a combination of logic and passionate invective designed to appeal to anti-Catholic prejudices. He represented the King and Parliament not as heads of a family but as usurpers of authority. And he insisted not only on the illogicality of rule by a foreign government but also on its impracticality. As he put it, "the distance at which the Almighty hath placed England and America, is a strong and natural proof, that the authority of the one, over the other, was never the design of Heaven" (p. 115).

Tropes of the family haunted the transatlantic imagination long after American independence. William Wordsworth's poem "Ruth," which he composed in Goslar, Germany, in 1799 and published the next year in *Lyrical Ballads*, shows how imaginative links between the Revolution and the dissolution of kinship ties continued to find their way from political pamphlets into more belletristic texts. Wordsworth remarked that when he wrote "Ruth," which depicts a family being torn apart by political violence, "the war with America was fresh in my memory." Images of fractured families even entered into literary criticism: British journals of the time are filled with remarks on America's cultural dependence on Britain and with condemnations of its literature as England's illegitimate and dependent offspring. Anglo-American notions of family continue to operate in the present in related ways. Such figures of speech still appear in attempted justifications of military and cultural imperialism, representing powerful nations as parents who set out to benevolently guide distant cultures and nations out of "states of infancy."

British Parliament
1767

Named after Britain's Chancellor of the Exchequer, Charles Townshend (1725–1767), the Townshend Acts imposed new duties on paper, glass, lead, paint, and tea. Imported goods were popular in America, and paper was crucial to the functioning of the active presses in the colonies. Townshend's heavy taxes generated thousands of pounds in annual revenue, money that was meant to pay the salaries of British government officials in the colonies. But, like the Stamp Acts before them, the Townshend Acts were about more than money—they were also designed to make clear to the rebellious colonists that Parliament was firmly in command of their economic and political lives. Boston would not stand for such treatment, though, and became a center of protest, the site of violent attacks on customs officials and mob raids on customs warehouses and vice-admiralty courts. The colonies also boycotted British goods through the Nonimport Agreements, which succeeded in reducing British profit margins and led to the Parliamentary repeal of the Townshend Revenue Act in 1770. In order to retain the right to tax the colonies, the duty on tea was continued, an idea that did not go over well with the colonists. They expressed their anger in the Boston Tea Party (1773), during which Samuel Adams and other patriots dressed as Native Americans and raided British ships, throwing all of the tea they held into the harbor. These small-scale rebellions against British authority anticipated the all-out revolution that would erupt in the next decade.

from The Townshend Acts

An act for granting certain duties in the British colonies and plantations in America; for allowing a drawback of the duties of customs upon the exportation, from this kingdom, of coffee and cocoa nuts of the produce of the said colonies or plantations; for discontinuing the drawbacks payable on china earthen ware exported to America; and for more effectually preventing the clandestine running of goods in the colonies and plantations.

WHEREAS it is expedient that a revenue should be raised in your Majesty's dominions in America, for making a more certain and adequate provision for defraying the charge of the administration of justice, and the support of civil government, in such provinces where it shall be found necessary; and towards further defraying the expenses of defending, protecting, and securing, the said dominions; we, your Majesty's most dutiful and loyal subjects, the commons of Great Britain, in parliament assembled, have therefore resolved to give and grant unto your Majesty the several rates and duties herein after mentioned; and do most humbly beseech your Majesty that it may be enacted, and be it enacted by the King's most excellent majesty, by and with the advice of the lords spiritual and temporal, and commons, in this present parliament assembled, and by the authority of the same, That from and after the twentieth day of November, one thousand seven hundred and sixty seven, there shall be raised, levied, collected, and paid, unto his Majesty, his heirs, and successors, for and upon the respective goods herein after mentioned, which shall be imported from Great Britain into any colony or plantation in America which now is, or hereafter may be, under the dominion of his Majesty, his heirs, or successors, the several rates and duties following; that is to say,

For every hundred weight avoirdupois[1] of crown, plate, flint, and white glass, four shillings and eight pence.

For every hundred weight avoirdupois of green glass, one shilling and two pence.

For every hundred weight avoirdupois of red lead, two shillings.

For every hundred weight avoirdupois of white lead, two shillings.

For every hundred weight avoirdupois of painters colours, two shillings.

For every pound weight avoirdupois of tea, three pence.

For every ream of paper, usually called or known by the name of Atlas Fine, twelve shillings.

For every ream of paper called Atlas Ordinary, six shillings.

For every ream of paper called Bastard, or Double Copy, one shilling and six pence.

For every single ream of blue paper for sugar bakers, ten pence halfpenny.

For every ream of paper called Blue Royal, one shilling and six pence.

For every bundle of brown paper containing forty quires, not made in Great Britain, six pence.

For every ream of paper called Brown Cap, not made in Great Britain, nine pence.

For every ream of paper called Brown Large Cap, made in Great Britain, four pence halfpenny.

For every ream of paper called Small Ordinary Brown, made in Great Britain, three pence. . . .

---

1. Avoirdupois: goods sold by weight.

I. And for and upon all paper which shall be printed, painted, or stained, in Great Britain, to serve for hangings or other uses, three farthings for every yard square, over and above the duties payable for such paper by this act, if the same had not been printed, painted, or stained; and after those rates respectively for any greater or less quantity.

II. And it is hereby further enacted by the authority aforesaid, That all other paper (not being particularly rated and charged in this act) shall pay the several and respective duties that are charged by this act, upon such paper as is nearest above in size and goodness to such unrated paper.

III. And be it declared and enacted by the authority aforesaid, That a ream of paper, chargeable by this act, shall be understood to consist of twenty quires, and each quire of twenty four sheets.

IV. And it is hereby further enacted by the authority aforesaid, That the said rates and duties, charged by this act upon goods imported into any British American colony or plantation, shall be deemed, and are hereby declared to be, sterling money of Great Britain. . . .

V. And be it further enacted by the authority aforesaid, That his Majesty and his successors shall be, and are hereby, impowered, from time to time, by any warrant or warrants under his or their royal sign manual or sign manuals, countersigned by the high treasurer, or any three or more of the commissioners of the treasury for the time being, to cause such monies to be applied, out of the produce of the duties granted by this act, as his Majesty, or his successors, shall think proper or necessary, for defray-ing the charges of the administration of justice, and the support of the civil govern-ment, within all or any of the said colonies or plantations. . . .

IX. And for the more effectual preventing the clandestine running of goods in the British dominions in America, be it further enacted by the authority aforesaid, That from and after the said twentieth day of November, one thousand seven hun-dred and sixty seven, the master or other person having or taking the charge or com-mand of every ship or vessel arriving in any British colony or plantation in America shall, before he proceeds with his vessel to the place of unlading, come directly to the custom house for the port or district where he arrives, and make a just and true entry, upon oath, before the collector and comptroller, or other principal officer of the cus-toms there, of the burthen, contents, and lading of such ship or vessel, with the par-ticular marks, numbers, qualities, and contents, of every parcel of goods therein laden, to the best of his knowledge. . . .

X. And whereas . . . it is doubted whether such officers can legally enter houses and other places on land, to search for and seize goods, in the manner directed by the said recited acts: To obviate which doubts for the future, and in order to carry the intention of the said recited acts into effectual execution, be it enacted, and it is hereby enacted by the authority aforesaid, That from and after the said twentieth day of November, one thousand seven hundred and sixty seven, such writs of assistance, to authorize and impower the officer of his Majesty's customs to enter and go into any house, warehouse, shop, cellar, or other place, in the British colonies of plantations of America, to search for and seize prohibited or uncustomed goods, in the manner directed by the said recited acts, shall and may be granted by the said superior or supreme courts of justice having jurisdiction within such colony or plantation respectively.

—1767

James Madison
1751–1836

James Madison was born to one of Virginia's most prominent families and was prepared for a public career at the College of New Jersey (the forerunner of Princeton University). At Princeton, along with his classmate, Philip Freneau, he read widely in the philosophers of the Enlightenment, forming a strong intellectual commitment to their rationalist political principles. After graduating, Madison quickly found himself shaping the course of the Revolution and the new republic as a member of the Virginia Assembly and then of the Continental Congress. The main force behind the drafting of the Constitution in 1787, he went on to serve first in the House of Representatives and then as the fourth president. Throughout his long political career, he balanced, sometimes shakily, between his commitment to republicanism and the interests of his class. On one hand, he drafted the Bill of Rights, with its guarantees of freedom of religion, freedom from unreasonable search and seizure, and the right to a jury trial. On the other hand, he remained dedicated throughout his life to the Federalist idea that a powerful central government would be necessary to prevent the post-Revolutionary United States from degenerating into the chaos of mobocracy. Similarly, despite his commitment to human liberty, he owned at least one hundred slaves. And while he admitted that slavery was an "evil," he would only go so far as to embrace gradual emancipation, and then only on the condition that freed slaves be returned to Africa.

After the Constitution had been signed, Madison set out to help win its ratification by state assemblies. He collaborated with two other writers, Alexander Hamilton and John Jay, to write a series of newspaper essays published under the pen name Publius and later collected under the title *The Federalist* (1787–1788). The way of thinking about authorship that is reflected by this use of a collective pseudonym runs counter to the Romantic way of closely associating ideas and works with individual personalities. According to the conventions governing republican political discourse, persuasion should be accomplished with the power of rigorous logical argument, not force of character. The truth and clarity of ideas would be compromised by the introduction of personal opinions or considerations. As Madison puts it, "No man is allowed to be a judge in his own cause; because his interest would certainly bias his judgment, and, not improbably, corrupt his integrity" (p. 149). Of course, the stance of objectivity and public interest can often be a most effective disguise for private motivations. And Madison's personal reasons to "control the violence of faction" (p. 147) were quite strong. As a leading member of the colonial and then post-Revolutionary elite, he hoped that a strong executive would solidify the power of his class, the landowning gentry. He was especially concerned to contain the democratic radicalism of the small farmers, merchants, tradesmen, and other members of the middle classes. In the wake of a Revolution whose battles they had fought, they now demanded the actualization of rights they had been promised in the Declaration of Independence penned by Madison's closest friend, Thomas Jefferson.

The Federalist. Number 10

November 22, 1787
To the People of the State of New York.

Among the numerous advantages promised by a well constructed Union, none deserves to be more accurately developed than its tendency to break and control the violence of faction. The friend of popular governments, never finds himself so much alarmed for their character and fate, as when he contemplates their propensity to this dangerous vice. He will not fail therefore to set a due value on any plan which, without violating the principles to which he is attached, provides a proper cure for it. The instability, injustice and confusion introduced in the public councils, have in truth been the mortal diseases under which popular governments have every where perished; as they continue to be the favorite and fruitful topics from which the adversaries to liberty derive their most specious declamations. The valuable improvements made by the American constitutions on the popular models, both ancient and modern, cannot certainly be too much admired; but it would be an unwarrantable partiality, to contend that they have as effectually obviated the danger on this side as was wished and expected. Complaints are every where heard from our most considerate and virtuous citizens, equally the friends of public and private faith, and of public and personal liberty; that our governments are too unstable; that the public good is disregarded in the conflicts of rival parties; and that measures are too often decided, not according to the rules of justice, and the rights of the minor party; but by the superior force of an interested and over-bearing majority. However anxiously we may wish that these complaints had no foundation, the evidence of known facts will not permit us to deny that they are in some degree true. It will be found indeed, on a candid review of our situation, that some of the distresses under which we labor, have been erroneously charged on the operation of our governments; but it will be found, at the same time, that other causes will not alone account for many of our heaviest misfortunes; and particularly, for that prevailing and increasing distrust of public engagements, and alarm for private rights, which are echoed from one end of the continent to the other. These must be chiefly, if not wholly, effects of the unsteadiness and injustice, with which a factious spirit tainted our public administrations.

By a faction I understand a number of citizens, whether amounting to a majority or minority of the whole, who are united and actuated by some common impulse of passion, or of interest, adverse to the rights of other citizens, or to the permanent and aggregate interests of the community.

There are two methods of curing the mischiefs of faction: the one, by removing its causes; the other, by controling its effects.

There are again two methods of removing the causes of faction: the one by destroying the liberty which is essential to its existence; the other, by giving to every citizen the same opinions, the same passions, and the same interests.

It could never be more truly said than of the first remedy, that it is worse than the disease. Liberty is to faction, what air is to fire, an aliment without which it instantly expires. But it could not be a less folly to abolish liberty, which is essential to political life, because it nourishes faction, than it would be to wish the annihilation of air, which is essential to animal life, because it imparts to fire its destructive agency.

The second expedient is as impracticable, as the first would be unwise. As long as the reason of man continues fallible, and he is at liberty to exercise it, different opinions will be formed. As long as the connection subsists between his reason and his self-love, his opinions and his passions will have a reciprocal influence on each other; and the former will be objects to which the latter will attach themselves. The diversity in the faculties of men from which the rights of property originate, is not less an insuperable obstacle to a uniformity of interests. The protection of these faculties is the first object of Government. From the protection of different and unequal faculties of acquiring property, the possession of degrees and kinds of property immediately results; and from the influence of these on the sentiments and views of the respective proprietors, ensues a division of the society into different interests and parties.

The latent causes of faction are thus sown in the nature of man; and we see them every where brought into different degrees of activity, according to the different circumstances of civil society. A zeal for different opinions concerning religion, concerning Government and many other points, as well of speculation as of practice; an attachment to different leaders ambitiously contending for pre-eminence and power; or to persons of other descriptions whose fortunes have been interesting to the human passions, have in turn divided mankind into parties, inflamed them with mutual animosity, and rendered them much more disposed to vex and oppress each other, than to cooperate for their common good. So strong is this propensity of mankind to fall into mutual animosities, that where no substantial occasion presents itself, the most frivolous and fanciful distinctions have been sufficient to kindle their unfriendly passions, and excite their most violent conflicts. But the most common and durable source of factions, has been the various and unequal distribution of property. Those who hold, and those who are without property, have ever formed distinct interests in society. Those who are creditors, and those who are debtors, fall under a like discrimination. A landed interest, a manufacturing interest, a mercantile interest, a monied interest, with many lesser interests, grow up of necessity in civilized nations, and divide them into different classes, actuated by different sentiments and views. The regulation of these various and interfering interests forms the principal task of modern Legislation, and involves the spirit of party and faction in the necessary and ordinary operations of Government.

No man is allowed to be a judge in his own cause; because his interest would certainly bias his judgment, and, not improbably, corrupt his integrity. With equal, nay with greater reason, a body of men, are unfit to be both judges and parties, at the same time; yet, what are many of the most important acts of legislation, but so many judicial determinations, not indeed concerning the rights of single persons, but concerning the rights of large bodies of citizens; and what are the different classes of legislators, but advocates and parties to the causes which they determine? Is a law proposed concerning private debts? It is a question to which the creditors are parties on one side, and the debtors on the other. Justice ought to hold the balance between them. Yet the parties are and must be themselves the judges; and the most numerous party, or in other words, the most powerful faction must be expected to prevail. Shall domestic manufactures be encouraged, and in what degree, by restrictions on foreign manufactures? are questions which would be differently decided by the landed and the manufacturing classes; and probably by neither, with a sole regard to justice and the public good. The apportionment of taxes on the various descriptions of poverty, is an act which seems to require the most exact impartiality; yet, there is perhaps no legislative act in which greater opportunity and temptation are given to a predominant party, to trample on the rules of justice. Every shilling with which they overburden the inferior number, is a shilling saved to their own pockets.

It is in vain to say, that enlightened statesmen will be able to adjust these clashing interests, and render them all subservient to the public good. Enlightened statesmen will not always be at the helm: nor, in many cases, can such an adjustment be made at all, without taking into view indirect and remote considerations, which will rarely prevail over the immediate interest which one party may find in disregarding the rights of another, or the good of the whole.

The inference to which we are brought, is, that the causes of faction cannot be removed; and that relief is only to be sought in the means of controling its *effects*.

If a faction consists of less than a majority, relief is supplied by the republican principle, which enables the majority to defeat its sinister views by regular vote: it may clog the administration, it may convulse the society; but it will be unable to execute and mask its violence under the forms of the Constitution. When a majority is included in a faction, the form of popular government on the other hand enables it to sacrifice to its ruling passion or interest, both the public good and the rights of other citizens. To secure the public good, and private rights, against the danger of such a faction, and at the same time to preserve the spirit and the form of popular government, is then the great object to which our enquiries are directed: Let me add that it is the great desideratum, by which alone this form of government can be rescued from the opprobrium under which it has so long labored, and be recommended to the esteem and adoption of mankind.

By what means is this object attainable? Evidently by one of two only. Either the existence of the same passion or interest in a majority at the same time, must be prevented; or the majority, having such co-existent passion or interest, must be rendered, by their number and local situation, unable to concert and carry into effect schemes of oppression. If the impulse and the opportunity be suffered to coincide, we well know that neither moral nor religious motives can be relied on as an adequate control. They are not found to be such on the injustice and violence of individuals, and lose their efficacy in proportion to the numbers combined together; that is, in proportion as their efficacy becomes needful.

From this view of the subject, it may be concluded, that a pure Democracy, by which I mean, a Society, consisting of a small number of citizens, who assemble and administer the Government in person, can admit of no cure for the mischiefs of faction. A common passion or interest will, in almost every case, be felt by a majority of the whole; a communication and concern results from the form of Government itself; and there is nothing to check the inducements to sacrifice the weaker party, or an obnoxious individual. Hence it is, that such Democracies have ever been spectacles of turbulence and contention; have ever been found incompatible with personal security, or the rights of property; and have in general been as short in their lives, as they have been violent in their deaths. Theoretic politicians, who have patronized this species of Government, have erroneously supposed, that by reducing mankind to a perfect equality in their political rights, they would at the same time, be perfectly equalized and assimilated in their possessions, their opinions, and their passions.

A Republic, by which I mean a Government in which the scheme of representation takes place, opens a different prospect, and promises the cure for which we are seeking. Let us examine the points in which it varies from pure Democracy, and we shall comprehend both the nature of the cure, and the efficacy which it must derive from the Union.

The two great points of difference between a Democracy and a Republic are, first, the delegation of the Government, in the latter, to a small number of citizens elected by the rest: secondly, the greater number of citizens, and greater sphere of country, over which the latter may be extended.

The effect of the first difference is, on the one hand to refine and enlarge the public views, by passing them through the medium of a chosen body of citizens, whose wisdom may best discern the true interest of their country, and whose patriotism and love of justice, will be least likely to sacrifice it to temporary or partial considerations. Under such a regulation, it may well happen that the public voice pronounced by the representatives of the people, will be more consonant to the public good, than if pronounced by the people themselves convened for the purpose. On the other hand, the effect may be inverted. Men of factious tempers, of local prejudices, or of sinister designs, may by intrigue, by corruption or by other means, first obtain the suffrages, and then betray the interests of the people. The question resulting is, whether small or extensive Republics are most favorable to the election of proper guardians of the public weal; and it is clearly decided in favor of the latter by two obvious considerations.

In the first place it is to be remarked that however small the Republic may be, the Representatives must be raised to a certain number, in order to guard against the cabals of a few; and that however large it may be, they must be limited to a certain number, in order to guard against the confusion of a multitude. Hence the number of Representatives in the two cases, not being in proportion to that of the Constituents, and being proportionally greatest in the small Republic, it follows, that if the proportion of fit characters, be not less, in the large than in the small Republic, the former will present a greater option, and consequently a greater probability of a fit choice.

In the next place, as each Representative will be chosen by a greater number of citizens in the large than in the small Republic, it will be more difficult for unworthy candidates to practise with success the vicious arts, by which elections are too often carried; and the suffrages of the people being more free, will be more likely to centre on men who possess the most attractive merit, and the most diffusive and established characters.

It must be confessed, that in this, as in most other cases, there is a mean, on both sides of which inconveniencies will be found to lie. By enlarging too much the number of electors, you render the representative too little acquainted with all their local circumstances and lesser interests; as by reducing it too much, you render him unduly attached to these, and too little fit to comprehend and pursue great and national objects. The Federal Constitution forms a happy combination in this respect; the great and aggregate interests being referred to the national, the local and particular, to the state legislatures.

The other point of difference is, the greater number of citizens and extent of territory which may be brought within the compass of Republican, than of Democratic Government; and it is this circumstance principally which renders factious combinations less to be dreaded in the former, than in the latter. The smaller the society, the fewer probably will be the distinct parties and interests composing it; the fewer the distinct parties and interests, the more frequently will a majority be found of the same party; and the smaller the numbers of individuals composing a majority, and the smaller the compass within which they are placed, the more easily will they concert and execute their plans of oppression. Extend the sphere, and you take in a greater variety of parties and interests; you make it less probable that a majority of the whole will have a common motive to invade the rights of other citizens; or if such a common motive exists, it will be more difficult for all who feel it to discover their own strength, and to act in unison with each other. Besides other impediments, it may be remarked, that where there is a consciousness of unjust or dishonorable purposes, communication is always checked by distrust, in proportion to the number whose concurrence is necessary.

Hence it clearly appears, that the same advantage, which a Republic has over a Democracy, in controling the effects of faction, is enjoyed by a large over a small Republic—is enjoyed by the Union over the States composing it. Does this advantage consist in the substitution of Representatives, whose enlightened views and virtuous sentiments render them superior to local prejudices, and to schemes of injustice? It will not be denied, that the Representation of the Union will be most likely to possess these requisite endowments. Does it, in fine, consist in the greater security afforded by a greater variety of parties, against the event of any one party being able to outnumber and oppress the rest? In an equal degree does the increased variety of parties, comprised within the Union, increase this security? Does it, in fine, consist in the greater obstacles opposed to the concert and accomplishment of the secret wishes of an unjust and interested majority? Here, again, the extent of the Union gives it the most palpable advantage.

The influence of factious leaders may kindle a flame within their particular States but will be unable to spread a general conflagration through the other States: a religious sect, may degenerate into a political faction in a part of the confederacy; but the variety of sects dispersed over the entire face of it, must secure the national Councils against any danger from that source: a rage for paper money, for an abolition of debts, for an equal division of property, or for any other improper or wicked project, will be less apt to pervade the whole body of the Union, than a particular member of it; in the same proportion as such a malady is more likely to taint a particular county or district, than an entire State.

In the extent and proper structure of the Union, therefore, we behold a Republican remedy for the diseases most incident to Republican Government. And according to the degree of pleasure and pride, we feel in being Republicans, ought to be our zeal in cherishing the spirit, and supporting the character of Federalists.

PUBLIUS.

—1787

Isaac Hunt
1751–1809

Born in Barbados, Isaac Hunt moved to Philadelphia, where he was educated at what is now the University of Pennsylvania. His graduation speech was reported to have been so eloquent that he won the heart and hand of Mary Shewell, a member of a prominent Quaker family. After receiving his BA, he studied law and was admitted to the bar in 1765. This same year he applied to his alma mater for his MA; however, his application did not meet the criteria laid out in college statutes and decrees. He reapplied the following year, but by this time his writing of satirical tracts had caused him to fall into disfavor. The college authorities refused to grant the degree to the "author and publisher of several scurrilous and scandalous pieces," which included "A Humble Attempt at Scurrility" and "The Substance of an Exercise had this Morning at Scurrility Hall." His writing made him few friends at the college and would continue to make him enemies throughout his time in Philadelphia. For instance, in 1775, just as the pitch of patriotic fervor was rising, he published *The Political Family: or a Discourse, Pointing Out the Reciprocal Advantages, Which Flow from an Uninterrupted Union Between Great-Britain and Her American Colonies*. As the title indicates, this was a piece of Loyalist, or Tory, rhetoric. The book was published by James Humphreys, Jr., a known Tory who had raised the ire of patriots by printing the King's arms on the masthead of his newspaper. He also seized the opportunity to use the title page of Hunt's work to showcase a Loyalist image that illustrates revolution's potential damage to Anglo-American relations.

Consequently, Hunt was pulled out of bed one morning in 1775 by a mob of fifty armed men who dragged him through the city streets in an open cart. Hunt escaped tar and feathers but still found himself in prison, where he used his rhetorical skills and, perhaps, ready cash or a promissory note to secure his freedom. No sooner had he made his escape than he boarded a ship for Barbados, and then sailed on to England. There, following in the footsteps of his grandfather and father, he became a preacher, a low-paying job that landed him in debtor's prison as often as the pulpit. When Thomas Paine, his old American rival, attempted to bring the French Revolution to England by censuring Edmund Burke's *Reflections on the Revolution in France* (London, 1790; Philadelphia, 1792) in his *Rights of Man* (1791), Hunt published one last tract, a defense of Burke titled *Rights of Englishmen, an Antidote to the Poison Now Vending by the Transatlantic Republican Thomas Paine* (1791). Due to the Loyalist nature of Hunt's works, Philadelphians never received them as warmly as they did the publishing efforts of his sons, John and Leigh, who published radical newspapers: the *Indicator* and the *Liberal*. In fact, Leigh Hunt's poetry and prose were so popular in America that he complained about the lack of an international copyright agreement (not established until 1893), noting that American publishers did the English "so much honour in taking our books, and giving us nothing in exchange."

By referring to America and Britain as one "political family," Isaac Hunt is alluding to the literal kinship of the British and the Americans who had emigrated from Britain to the New World. Of course, in so doing, he is rhetorically erasing both Native Americans and vast numbers of Americans from other parts of the globe to create the political fiction of a homogeneous people who belong together. James Humphreys, the publisher, employs the anxious image of two earthen vessels floating dangerously close to each other in rough waters with the legend "IF WE STRIKE, WE BREAK" to depict the potential consequences of the American Revolution (Figure 1). If the patriots fomented a violent revolution, it would shatter America's as well as England's peace and prosperity, sinking both to the bottom of a stormy sea. Loyalists, like Humphreys and Hunt, believed that this delicate situation could be rectified only by diplomacy and negotiation, not violence. They felt that if Britain and America could maintain unity above all during a brief stretch of troubled times, smooth sailing would lie ahead.

The Political Family

The jealousies which at present unhappily subsist between *Great-Britain* and her *colonies*, render a discourse on this subject as delicate and hazardous, as the fatal consequences of a rupture between them make it weighty and important. But though the die be doubtful, yet in so interesting a cause I will venture a cast.

In this discourse I shall consider the *mother country* and her *colonies* as a body politic.

By *union* in a body politic I understand (with Baron Montesquieu[1]) such a harmony as makes all the particular parts, as opposite as they may seem, concur to the general welfare of the whole, as discords in music contribute to the melody of sounds.

Protection requires *dependence* in return. But to preserve that dependence, agreeable to the principles of an *English constitution*, it is necessary there should be a *union of laws and government*. And this union is necessary for the security of liberty, and the well conducting of commerce, on which the happiness of our political society is founded.

As in the *natural body* all the inferior springs of life depend upon the motion of the *heart*, so in the *body politic* all inferior jurisdictions should flow from *one superior fountain*. Two distinct *independent powers* in *one civil state* are as inconsistent as *two hearts* in the *same natural body*. Because if such a thing can be imagined, they must constantly interfere in their operations, so as to reduce the WHOLE to anarchy and confusion, and bring on a *dissolution* in the event. A due subordination of the less parts to the greater is therefore necessary to the *existence of* BOTH.

According to the great Mr. Locke[2]—that which constitutes a political society is nothing but the consent of any number of freemen, capable of a majority, to incorporate into such a society. This consent is either expressed or implied: expressed, when men in a state of nature for their mutual defence, agree upon certain rules for their government: Implied, when they come into and continue in a country where there is a civil state already settled, and receive the *benefit* and *protection* of the laws of that state.

The common law of England declares the original consent of the people, and may be stiled the constitution of their civil state. But as the affairs of all nations are in a continual fluctuation, by the common law, any part of it then declared may from time to time be altered by acts of parliament. Sage and reverend judges, ever since the emigration of the *American colonists*, have often solemnly determined that as they settled a part of the *British empire*, they tacitly agreed to be governed according to the common law of their parent country.

These colonies are of two kinds: Such as have been newly found out by the subjects of *Great-Britain*, and purchased from the natives by the authority of the crown, as Pennsylvania, &c. or such as have been conquered in open and just war, as Jamaica, Quebec, &c. In the first, the laws of England were in force immediately upon their discovery and settlement. In the other, the laws of England did not take place till declared so by the conqueror. But in both, acts of the *British parliament* bind the colonists *where they are specially named* according to the adjudications of able lawyers and judges throughout English America.

His Majesty's predecessors have granted to many of the colonies certain privileges by charters. The laws of England in force at the time of the settlement of new discovered colonies;—Acts of parliament made since, in which they are expressly named;—And laws enacted by themselves in pursuance of their charters, and approved and confirmed in England, seem then to be the constitutions of such colonies. This also is similar to the constitution of the *Roman colonies*. They received their laws from the people of *Rome*, or they enacted them by their inferior senates, or by the consent of the people of the *colonies*. Though every particular *colony* had laws distinct from the general laws of *Rome*, yet they were either dictated to them, or con-

---

1. Charles-Louis de Secondat, Baron de Montesquieu (1689–1753), French essayist.   2. John Locke (1632–1704), British philosopher.

firmed by the *Triumviri*.[3] They are of that sort of colonies which Baron Puffendorff mentions as united to the mother country by a kind of unequal confederacy.

The fires kindled by the late act of parliament imposing a duty of threepence in the pound on tea, have led me into this consideration of the nature of the governments of the British colonies. Far be it from me to determine the legality of imposing such duties. The subject has been so amply discussed by abler pens, both in England and America, as to make it unnecessary. But thus much I would observe, no government can be supported without great charge: And every one who enjoys a share of protection should pay his proportion for the maintenance of it in one way or other.

Much has been said about *external* and *internal* taxes. I know but little difference between them. Struggle and contrive as you will, says Mr. Locke; lay your taxes as you please, the traders will shift them off for their own gain; the merchant will bear the least part of them and grow poor last; things of necessity must still be had, and things of fashion will be had as long as men have money or credit. If the merchant pays a quarter more for his commodities he will sell them at a price proportionably raised. But though the duty may be legal, many things are lawful which are not expedient. A strenuous execution of the strict letter of the law is often the greatest injustice. It was a saying of the Emperor *Tiberius*, in relation to taxes, sheep should be fleeced not flead.[4] The Grand *Seignior*, according to the constitution of the Ottoman empire, may ordain a taxation; but the universal murmurs of his subjects make him sensible of the necessity of restricting this power. All mankind are liable to be deceived, and to err by misinformation and false appearances: And it is the glory of a man to acknowledge and correct an error when it is discovered: We find the *British Senate*, upon decent and legal applications, in the case of the stamp-act, did not think it unbecoming their dignity, to reconsider that act. The result of their deliberations was such as fully convinced us, justice and moderation were the noble principles which actuated that august body. They shewed us we may safely confide in them, not only as our protectors from foreign enemies, but as the grand conservators of liberty, throughout the wide extent of the British dominions. Let us then, on our part, convince them by our conduct, we are a sober, loyal, and grateful people, worthy of their highest favours.

Had the *colonists* on that occasion, or on occasion of the late acts of parliament concerning trade, been mad enough to have thrown off their *dependence on Great-Britain*, she must have looked upon it as a breach of the original compact, and that thereby the *constitutional union* in *legislation* and *government* was dissolved; the reciprocal advantages of which union will appear, if we consider the bad consequences of it's *dissolution*.

It is easy to believe, *Great-Britain* will not tamely give up her right of regulating the trade of *colonies*, which she has planted, raised, supported and protected at a vast expence of blood and treasure: Nor will she suffer the profits of that trade to fall into the hands of rival nations. And though she is able to crush them as a moth, yet her expences in sending fleets and armies to conquer her own subjects and maintain her *sovereignty* must be immense; besides the loss of the profits of their trade in the mean time; the advantages of which I shall mention hereafter. On the other hand, I will admit, for argument's sake, the *colonists* are able to protect themselves by land; yet this cannot be done without a *union* among themselves.

---

3. A ruling group of three officials.   4. Flayed.

How difficult a thorough *union* is to be effected in the *colonies* will appear, besides other instances, from the disputes about the quotas which the *continental colonies* should furnish for their own defence, when the common enemy were butchering and scalping many hundreds of the inhabitants, and laying waste their frontiers. The animosities which have long subsisted between some of them about settling their boundaries have not yet subsided. By their charters they have been used to different forms of internal government and laws. Different modes of worship have been established in many of them. It is, therefore, scarcely probable they ever can or will be *united* without being under the *sovereignty* of some superior state, whose *interest* it is to continue them so, and protect them. But admitting they may be *united*, and, as I said, they can protect themselves on the land side: Yet who would protect their many thousands of unarmed ships, their cities, and their long extended, and, at present, defenceless sea coasts, from the depredations of pirates and rovers, or the greater power of ambitious and aspiring states, who are watching for such an opportunity like vultures hovering o'er their prey? To whom, then, but *Great-Britain*, can they go for succour? Or, if they would withdraw their *dependence*, who can deliver them out of her hands? Not France or Spain. The British navy is superior to both *united*. If it were not, those powers would not consent to defend and protect them for nothing. They would divide them among themselves, and require not only *dependence*, but *absolute subjection*. There is no need of arguments to prove, it is more eligible to submit to laws made by a protestant British Sovereign, an august Assembly of right honorable and right reverend Nobles, the representatives of a free people, connected with them by the ties of blood, similarity of manners, and common interests, and by a President General appointed by the crown, at the head of delegates chosen by the colonies to sit in grand council, than by the arbitrary edicts of a French monarch, which his parliament is only to register; and it is better for a man to be at liberty to worship God in the manner he believes is most agreeable to him, by the toleration of a British government, than be forced to conform to the superstitious rites and ceremonies of the Romish church[5] by the racks and tortures of a Spanish inquisition. It seems, therefore, as much the *interest* of the *colonies* to avoid throwing off their *dependence* on *Great-Britain*, as it is her's to protect them from their enemies, support them in their liberties, and encourage them in their commerce;—the reciprocal advantages of which I am next to consider.

The British American dominions extend through such various climates that they can produce *most* of the commodities war or peace require. They can supply most of the delicacies as well as conveniences and necessaries of life. Yet nature hath poured forth her blessings, in a different manner, upon the different regions of the world, for the mutual intercourse and traffic of mankind, that thereby they may have a *dependence* upon one another, and be *united* by their common interest.

Every inhabitable country hath a superfluity of some kind of natural product, and no country can produce all the necessaries and conveniences of life. Hence arise the *reciprocal advantages* of commerce in general, as it carries out of a country what is superfluous, and returns what is wanting.

The power of a state consists in the multitude of it's subjects well employed, and the riches of it's treasury. Trade encourages the labourer to industry. Industry procures him property, by which he is encouraged to undertake the charge of a family, and to

---

5. The Catholic church, based in Rome.

propagate his species. If he cannot be industriously employed, he will scarcely venture to make himself, and a woman whom he loves, miserable, by seeing the tender pledges of their affection, whom they might be the means of bringing into the world, starving for want of bread. It is reckoned a million of the inhabitants of *Great-Britain* are daily employed in manufactures for the *American colonists*, most of whom cannot get other employment. Consequently many thousands are thereby induced to marry. Hence it is the number of her inhabitants is not decreased, notwithstanding many thousands have formerly come over to her *colonies*, or have been destroyed in her wars. The trade and population of the *colonies* have, therefore, a considerable tendency to increase the number of subjects in *Great-Britain*.

The enlargement of commerce increases the riches of a state. The riches of a nation are the sinews of war, and the establishment of peace. Power and strength are principally acquired by money. Money will procure arms and friends. Nothing else is wanting to obtain dominion, but wisdom and the permission of divine Providence. The ordinary customs upon merchandize in *England* which go into the treasury are now above forty times more than they were at the death of *Queen Elizabeth*,[6] when the *American colonies* began to be considerable. And Mr. Anderson observes the trade of *Great-Britain* with her *colonies* is equal in quantity, and more in profit than all the other commerce she has with the rest of the world. One half, therefore, of these additional riches of the treasury, arises from the *colony* trade. Hence it is the *British* navy is now double in number, of larger size, and carries heavier metal than at the *revolution*.[7] Many thousand ships are constantly employed in this trade, which is a perpetual nursery of seamen to fit out the King's ships. Besides the advantages *Great-Britain* receives from the trade of her *colonies*, in the increase of her subjects, the employment of her industrious poor in manufactures, the support of government by duties on merchandize, and the increase of her naval power, her landed interest is also greatly increased. This plainly appears from the country gentlemen and farmers having better household furniture, greater stocks of cattle, and lands better improved since she had *colonies*. The demand for, and consumption of what the farmer produces must be in proportion to the number of people employed in manufactures and navigation. *Great-Britain*, it is thought, may support sixteen millions of inhabitants more than she does at present, and the greater part of these will find employment in manufactures, which it will be the interest of the *colonies* to take off her hands, if they increase, as they are likely to do from their great extent of territory. The *continental colonies* abound in timber and iron ore. There are numberless symptoms of other valuable ore, which, doubtless, in the course of time, ingenious men, if encouraged, will discover. The land, in general, is very fit for tillage. Pennsylvania and New York in particular may be justly termed the granary of the West-India islands, which daily increase in the number of inhabitants. Besides, without mentioning the wheat which they send to Portugal and Spain, and their dominions, they ship great quantities up the Straits; and some few years ago they relieved Italy from famine; by which means they were enabled to make considerable remittances to *Great-Britain* they could not otherwise have done, *on account of the late restriction on their commerce*. While therefore the inhabitants can be advantageously employed in these branches of business, and in the fisheries along their coasts, it is not their interest to engage in manufactures which they can import from *Great-Britain* at a

---

6. Queen Elizabeth I (1533–1603).   7. The Glorious Revolution of 1688.

much cheaper rate than they can make them themselves. Woolen and linen they must have. Fine linen can not be made up, if the flax be not pulled before the seed is ripe. Flax seed brings in more to the farmer, if we consider the price of labour, than the flax itself. The flax-seed which New York and Pennsylvania ship to Ireland, I am well informed, overpays the fine linen which they import from thence. It is also idle to attempt to raise so many sheep as will produce wool enough for clothing while they import woolens at the price they now do from *Great-Britain*. On the frontiers the wolves and foxes destroy the sheep and lambs in such a manner, that few of the farmers attempt to raise them. In the interior parts the profits of the lands in tillage, and the fodder which the sheep require in the long winters, are such, that the farmers do not raise more than is sufficient to produce wool to employ their children and servants when they can be spared from agriculture, which is but seldom. Indeed, when a farmer's children are growing up and he must employ servants in the fields and meadows in the summer, it is better they should be employed in such manufactures than be idle in the winter. During the fishing season, most, if not all the tradesmen near the sea coasts in the *northern colonies* find their account in leaving off their trades and pursuing the fisheries. Manufactories in populous cities like Philadelphia for setting poor vagrants to work are very proper. Sturdy beggars, however, might be better employed in mending the highways, in clearing the rivers of the rocks, and thereby improving the communication between different parts of the country. But for the *colonists* to enter into manufactures in general, in the circumstances I have mentioned, must be greatly to their loss, as well as a prejudice to the trade, and of consequence to the wealth and power of *Great-Britain*. For manufactures are founded in poverty. Wherever there is a vast extent of territory to be settled and cultivated, and lands can be taken up, at an easy rate, especially in this province, under landlords so generous and indulgent to their tenants, as *our honourable Proprietaries*, people find it more beneficial to apply themselves to agriculture.

The West-India islands find the advantages so great which they receive from raising and making sugar, molasses, rum, ginger, pimento, coffee and drugs, that they make them the principal objects of their industry, and import provisions from the *continental colonies*, and their cloathing from *Great-Britain*: In return for which, they export their own products, which greatly augment his Majesty's customs, and employ many thousands of the manufacturers and seamen of Great-Britain, and, at the same time, have procured to the planters immense estates. A union, therefore, in commerce, is attended with these *reciprocal advantages*, that the *mother country* and the *colonies* are both more usefully employed in the products they exchange, than by raising or manufacturing *all* they stand in need of.

The importance of the *colonies* to *Great-Britain* will *ever* be greater, as they increase, which they will still do while they have such a vast extent of country to settle, and can so easily earn bread for the maintenance of a family. Ship timber, house timber, copper, hemp, iron, pitch, tar, turpentine, potash, fish, &c. which she imports from Norway, Sweden, and Russia, can all be supplied by her North American colonies. Virginia, Carolina, and the southern continental colonies produce not only tobacco, rice and indigo, but silk, as good in quality as and, very probably, will in time, as much in quantity, as she imports from Italy, Turkey, or the East-Indies. The *colonies* abound in fruits and drugs equal to Spain, Italy, or any other country. To receive all these articles from her own subjects, a great part of which she receives from foreign nations (who in a case of necessity may refuse to supply her, as Sweden did in the article of iron in this century) will enrich them, while, at the same time, it will increase her naval power, furnish her industrious people at home with employment, enable her to protect the trade of her *colonies*, continue their immunities, and procure others in the Mediterranean, and other foreign ports, which the powers to whom they belong cannot procure from one another, and render her the *Arbitress of Europe*. Besides, a time may come, when *Great-Britain* shall find it her interest to employ a much greater number of her people in manufactures, and upon the loss of a crop in an unfruitful season, may stand in need of bread, with which she can be abundantly supplied by her *American* subjects. On the other hand, as *America* will constantly increase in the number of inhabitants, and improvement of land, her trade in the manufactures of her mother country must increase in proportion, and, consequently, require a more *extensive protection* from the *British* flag. This *British* naval power will also prevent the inveterate enemies of both the *mother country* and her *colonies* from possessing hereafter any considerable tract of territory on the continent of North-America, and thereby having an opportunity of stirring up the Indian natives to massacre, and butcher the *colonists*: And while the emissaries of France and Spain are kept from amongst them, they will find their account in carrying on the fur and peltry trade with our people; the advantages of which to *Great-Britain* and the colonies are immense.

But, waving the protection of the *mother country*, with what state can the *colonists* carry on a trade to advantage equal to that with her. Most of the branches, before enumerated, are the leading articles of their commerce, which *Great-Britain* wants, and other parts of Europe produce in common with the *colonies*, and of which she would take from her *colonies* only, if they could, as they will in time, be able to furnish her with a sufficient quantity, duties will be imposed upon commodities of foreign growth or production, and, very probably, bounties given for the same produced in the *colonies*, as was lately proposed in the article of iron. These *reciprocal advantages* of a *union* must, therefore, be as long as *Great-Britain* continues mistress of the ocean; her industrious manufacturers multiply by being enabled to marry, and maintain their children, and the *American* seas abound in fish, the mines with ore, or the hills covered with timber, and the many millions of acres yet unplanted can produce any of the commodities before enumerated.

Let us now consider *Great-Britain* and her *American colonies* as a family, the establishment of which depends upon unity, friendship, and a *continued* series of mutual good offices.

Colonies, my Lord Bacon[8] observes, are the children of more ancient nations. Children receive nourishment from the milk of their mothers, till they are capable of digesting other food! And they receive from the hands of their parents, protection from the insults and injuries, to which their feeble, infant state is exposed. They ought, therefore, when they have attained the state of youth, or manhood, to evidence their gratitude, by a pious love and filial obedience. But though, obedience be due to parents, parents ought not to provoke their children to wrath. The state of minority is temporary. When that state ceases, the right of chastisement and absolute command ceases also. But honor, reverence, esteem and support, when wanted, in return for nourishment, education, and protection are *perpetually* due to the parent.

Great-Britain has been a nursing mother to her *colonies*. Her first embarkations to America, and her first conquests there, were attended with great expence, without any

8. Francis Bacon (1561–1626), English philosopher of science.

immediate return of profit; and, at the same time, drained her of many people useful at home. Her floating castles have protected and daily do protect their trade. Royal licences have been granted to collect money for the promotion of learning and virtue in the *colonies*; and the money was generously given by their brethren in *Great-Britain*. The inhabitants of *Great-Britain* have, above sixty years ago, nobly and generously established and supported, and still do support a venerable society, who send over gentlemen of piety, learning, and virtue, to publish the glad tidings of salvation in the *colonies*, which before were the haunts of wild beasts, and idolatrous savages: And she hath lately, at a great expence of blood, and millions of treasure, saved them from the butchering knife of the *Savage*, and the unjust encroachments of ambitious enemies.

On the other hand, the advantages which (as I mentioned before) she receives in the encouragement of her manufactures, the extension of her commerce, and the increase of power, by sea and land, from the trade of her industrious colonists, have already rendered her the Queen of nations; and in a short time, *Great-Britain* and her *American colonies*, if they continue *united*, must inevitably be the most powerful Empire in the world. The advantages of which are not only *reciprocal* to them, but to all the protestant and christian states of Europe. Because the love of virtue and liberty, which is predominant and peculiar in Englishmen, will diffuse itself wherever it can have INFLUENCE.

—1775

Joel Barlow
1754–1812

Born to a Connecticut family of farmers, Joel Barlow's love for poetry was fostered in his native state. His career as a public poet began when he was chosen to deliver the commencement poem for his 1775 graduation from the College in New Haven (the forerunner of Yale). Barlow's college experience was formative not only for his early poetics but for his early politics as well. While an undergraduate, he met many of the founding members of a group of writers later known as the Connecticut Wits: Noah Webster, John Trumbull, Timothy Dwight, Theodore Dwight, David Humphreys, Lemuel Hopkins, Richard Alsop, Dr. Mason F. Cogswell, and Elihu Hubbard Smith. Also known as the Hartford Wits, the members of this group of satirists were, with the exception of Barlow, wealthy and conservative men of letters. What Barlow had in common with them was a transatlantic poetic sensibility. The group members modeled themselves and their writing on the Augustan Wits, a group of eighteenth-century writers including Joseph Addison, Richard Steele, Alexander Pope, John Dryden, and William Congreve. Although aspects of their poetic mode may have been derivative, the group's politics, religion, and subject matter were not: Their orthodox Calvinism and Federalism could be found lurking in the background of many of their pieces, and they often versified American history, society, and political as well as literary independence. Among them they published the following works: *The Anarchiad* (1786–1787), a polemic against Shay's Rebellion, an uprising of impoverished farmers who had lost their land in the depression that followed the Revolutionary War; *The Echo* (1791–1805), a satire of contemporary newspaper and magazine writing as well as a censure on the politics of the French Revolution; and *American Poems* (1793), which included Barlow's commencement poem.

The grandest work undertaken by a member of the Wits was Barlow's epic poem *The Vision of Columbus* (1787), later revised and republished as *The Columbiad* (Philadelphia, 1807; London, 1809). As the "iad" ending of the title indicates, Barlow hoped this poem would take its place among the epic poems that catalog the great events of a great nation, as the *Iliad* and the *Aeneid* did for Greece and Rome, respectively. This poem sought to show the course of empire from ancient Greece and Rome through England and ultimately to America. In its opening lines, the 1807 version echoes both the Roman epic poet Virgil and the British Romantic balladeer Samuel Taylor Coleridge: "I sing the Mariner who first unfurl'd / An eastern banner o'er the western world."

The list of subscribers (those who ordered copies of the poem in advance of its publication) to the 1787 edition includes Benjamin Franklin, Alexander Hamilton, Thomas Paine, and George Washington. But much changed for Barlow in the twenty years between the printing of the 1787 and 1807 editions, and the political sentiments of the latter edition shocked the conservative Connecticut Wits. He prepared the 1807 edition in Paris after having witnessed firsthand the early stages of the French Revolution and after sympathizing, to a degree, with its anti-royalist politics. This was quite a significant change; the 1787 version had been dedicated to Louis XVI. Barlow had also spent 1791–1792 in England, where he published the anti-aristocratic *Advice to the Privileged Orders*, thereby winning the company of London radicals like Joseph Priestley and Horne Tooke as well as the enmity of Edmund Burke and the government. Barlow's political change is made manifest in the preface to the 1807 version, which notes that the poem's purpose is "to inculcate the love of national liberty, and to . . . show that on the basis of republican principles all . . . good government . . . must be founded." After publishing *The Columbiad*, Barlow lived the reclusive life of a scholar until being appointed minister to France. He died in Poland on a diplomatic mission to meet and negotiate a treaty with Napoleon. His attempt to make an epic poem about America inspired several later poets, most notably Walt Whitman.

from The Columbiad

Argument

Coast of France rises in vision. Louis, to humble the British power, forms an alliance with the American states. This brings France, Spain and Holland into the war, and rouses Hyder Ally[1] to attack the English in India. The vision returns to America, where the military operations continue with various success. Battle of Monmouth. Storming of Stonypoint by Wayne. Actions of Lincoln, and surrender of Charleston. Movements of Cornwallis. Actions of Greene, and battle of Eutaw. French army arrives, and joins the American. They march to besiege the English army of Cornwallis in York and Gloster. Naval battle of Degrasse and Graves. Two of their ships grappled and blown up. Progress of the siege. A citadel mined and blown up. Capture of Cornwallis and his army. Their banners furled and muskets piled on the field of battle.

from Book VII

Thus view'd the Pair; when lo, in eastern skies,
From glooms unfolding, Gallia's[2] coasts arise.
Bright o'er the scenes of state a golden throne,
Instarr'd with gems and hung with purple, shone;
Young Bourbon[3] there in royal splendor sat,   5
And fleets and moving armies round him wait.
For now the contest, with increased alarms,
Fill'd every court and roused the world to arms;
As Hesper's hand,[4] that light from darkness brings,

---

1. Hyder Ali (1722–1782), rebel fighter against the British occupation of India. 2. France's. 3. Louis XIV. 4. The evening star.

And good to nations from the scourge of kings,   10
In this dread hour bade broader beams unfold,
And the new world illuminate the old.
        In Europe's realms a school of sages trace
The expanding dawn that waits the Reasoning Race;
On the bright Occident[5] they fix their eyes,   15
Thro glorious toils where struggling nations rise;
Where each firm deed, each new illustrious name
Calls into light a field of nobler fame:
A field that feeds their hope, confirms the plan
Of well poized freedom and the weal of man.   20
They scheme, they theorise, expand their scope,
Glance o'er Hesperia[6] to her utmost cope;
Where streams unknown for other oceans stray,
Where suns unseen their waste of beams display,
Where sires of unborn nations claim their birth,   25
And ask their empires in those wilds of earth.
While round all eastern climes, with painful eye,
In slavery sunk they see the kingdoms lie,
Whole states exhausted to enrich a throne,
Their fruits untasted and their rights unknown;   30
Thro tears of grief that speak the well taught mind,
They hail the era that relieves mankind.
        Of these the first, the Gallic sages stand,
And urge their king to lift an aiding hand.
The cause of humankind their souls inspired,   35
Columbia's[7] wrongs their indignation fired;
To share her fateful deeds their counsel moved,
To base in practice what in theme they proved:
That no proud privilege from birth can spring,
No right divine, nor compact form a king;   40
That in the people dwells the sovereign sway,
Who rule by proxy, by themselves obey;
That virtues, talents are the test of awe,
And Equal Rights the only source of law.
Surrounding heroes wait the monarch's word,   45
In foreign fields to draw the patriot sword,
Prepared with joy to join those infant powers,
Who build republics on the western shores.
        By honest guile the royal ear they bend,
And lure him on, blest Freedom to defend;   50
That, once recognised, once establisht there,
The world might learn her profer'd boon to share.
But artful arguments their plan disguise,
Garb'd in the gloss that suits a monarch's eyes.

---

5. The West.   6. The New World.   7. America's.

By arms to humble Britain's haughty power,   55
From her to sever that extended shore,
Contents his utmost wish. For this he lends
His powerful aid, and calls the opprest his friends.
The league proposed, he lifts his arm to save,
And speaks the borrow'd language of the brave: 60
    Ye states of France, and ye of rising name
Who work those distant miracles of fame,
Hear and attend; let heaven the witness bear,
We wed the cause, we join the righteous war.
Let leagues eternal bind each friendly land,   65
Given by our voice, and stablisht by our hand;
Let that brave people fix their infant sway,
And spread their blessings with the bounds of day.
Yet know, ye nations; hear, ye Powers above,
Our purposed aid no views of conquest move;   70
In that young world revives no ancient claim
Of regions peopled by the Gallic name;
Our envied bounds, already stretch'd afar,
Nor ask the sword, nor fear encroaching war;
But virtue, coping with the tyrant power   75
That drenches earth in her best children's gore,
With nature's foes bids former compact cease;
We war reluctant, and our wish is peace;
For man's whole race the sword of France we draw;
Such is our will, and let our will be law.   80
    He spoke; his moving armies veil'd the plain,
His fleets rode bounding on the western main;
O'er lands and seas the loud applauses rung,
And war and union dwelt on every tongue.
    The other Bourbon caught the splendid strain,   85
To Gallia's arms he joins the powers of Spain;
Their sails assemble; Crillon lifts the sword,
Minorca bows and owns her ancient lord.[8]
But while dread Elliott[9] shakes the Midland wave,
They strive in vain the Calpian rock to brave.   90
Batavia's[10] states with equal speed prepare
Thro western isles to meet the naval war;
For Albion[11] there rakes rude the tortured main,
And foils the force of Holland, France and Spain.
    Where old Indostan[12] still perfumes the skies,   95
To furious strife his ardent myriads rise;
Fierce Hyder there, unconquerably bold,
Bids a new flag its horned moons unfold,

---

8. Minorca, the easternmost Balearic island, was conquered by the Duke de Crillon in 1781–1782.   9. General Elliot's British forces held Gibraltar despite the efforts of the Spanish and French militaries.   10. The Netherlands.   11. Britain.   12. India.

Spreads o'er Carnatic kings his splendid force,
And checks the Britons in their wasting course.   100
    Europe's pacific powers their counsels join,
The laws of trade to settle and define.
The imperial Moscovite around him draws
Each Baltic state to join the righteous cause;
Whose arm'd Neutrality the way prepares   105
To check the ravages of future wars;
Till by degrees the wasting sword shall cease,
And commerce lead to universal peace.
    Thus all the ancient world with anxious eyes
Enjoy the lights that gild Atlantic skies,   110
Wake to new life, assume a borrow'd flame,
Enlarge the lustre and partake the fame.
So mounts of ice, that polar heavens invade,
Tho piled unseen thro night's long wintry shade,
When morn at last illumes their glaring throne,   115
Give back the day and imitate the sun.
    But still Columbus, on his war-beat shore,
Sees Albion's fleets her new battalions pour;
The states unconquer'd still their terrors wield,
And stain with mingled gore the embattled field.   120
On Pennsylvania's various plains they move,
And adverse armies equal slaughter prove;
Columbia mourns her Nash[13] in combat slain,
Britons around him press the gory plain;
Skirmish and cannonade and distant fire   125
Each power diminish and each nation tire.
Till Howe[14] from fruitless toil demands repose,
And leaves despairing in a land of foes
His wearied host; who now, to reach their fleet,
O'er Jersey hills commence their long retreat,   130
Tread back the steps their chief had led before,
And ask in vain the late abandon'd shore,
Where Hudson meets the main; for on their rear
Columbia moves, and checks their swift career.
    But where green Monmouth lifts his grassy height,   135
They halt, they face, they dare the coming fight.
Howe's proud successor, Clinton,[15] hosting there,
To tempt once more the desperate chance of war,
Towers at their head, in hopes to work relief,
And mend the errors of his former chief.   140
Here shines his day; and here with loud acclaim
Begins and ends his little task of fame.
He vaults before them with his balanced blade,

13. General Francis Nash (1742–1777).   14. Sir William Howe (1729–1814).   15. Sir Henry Clinton (1738–1795).

Wheels the bright van, and forms the long parade;
Where Britons, Hessians crowd the glittering field,   145
And all their powers for ready combat wield.
As the dim sun, beneath the skirts of even,
Crimsons the clouds that sail the western heaven;
So, in red wavy rows, where spread the train
Of men and standards, shone the fateful plain.   150
    They shone, till Washington obscured their light,
And his long ranks roll'd forward to the fight.
He points the charge; the mounted thunders roar,
And rake the champaign to the distant shore.
Above the folds of smoke that veil the war,   155
His guiding sword illumes the fields of air;
And vollied flames, bright bursting o'er the plain,
Break the brown clouds, discovering far the slain:
Till flight begins; the smoke is roll'd away,
And the red standards open into day.   160
Britons and Germans hurry from the field,
Now wrapt in dust, and now to sight reveal'd;
Behind, swift Washington his falchion[16] drives,
Thins the pale ranks, but saves submissive lives.
Hosts captive bow and move behind his arm,   165
And hosts before him wing the sounding storm;
When the glad sea salutes their fainting sight,
And Albion's fleet wide thundering aids their flight;
They steer to sad Newyork their hasty way,
And rue the toils of Monmouth's[17] mournful day.   170
    But Hudson still, with his interior tide,
Laves a rude rock that bears Britannia's pride,
Swells round the headland with indignant roar,
And mocks her thunders from his murmuring shore;
When a firm cohort starts from Peekskill plain,   175
To crush the invaders and the post regain.
Here, gallant Hull, again thy sword is tried,
Meigs, Fleury, Butler, laboring side by side,
Wayne[18] takes the guidance, culls the vigorous band,
Strikes out the flint, and bids the nervous hand   180
Trust the mute bayonet and midnight skies,
To stretch o'er craggy walls the dark surprise.
With axes, handspikes on the shoulder hung,
And the sly watchword whisper'd from the tongue,
Thro different paths the silent march they take,   185
Plunge, climb the ditch, the palisado break,

---

16. Sword.   17. Battle of Monmouth, a stalemate.   18. General William Hull (1753–1825), Colonel Return Jonathon
Meigs (1734–1823), Colonel François de Fleury (1749–?), Thomas Butler (1754–1805), and General "Mad Anthony"
Wayne (1745–1796).

Secure each sentinel, each picket shun,
Grope the dim postern where the byways run.
Soon the roused garrison perceives its plight;
Small time to rally and no means of flight,   190
They spring confused to every post they know,
Point their poized cannon where they hear the foe,
Streak the dark welkin with the flames they pour,
And rock the mountain with convulsive roar.
    The swift assailants still no fire return,   195
But, tow'rd the batteries that above them burn,
Climb hard from crag to crag; and scaling higher
They pierce the long dense canopy of fire
That sheeted all the sky; then rush amain,
Storm every outwork, each dread summit gain,   200
Hew timber'd gates, the sullen drawbridge fall,
File thro and form within the sounding wall.
The Britons strike their flag, the fort forego,
Descend sad prisoners to the plain below.
A thousand veterans, ere the morning rose,   205
Received their handcuffs from five hundred foes;
And Stonypoint beheld, with dawning day,
His own starr'd standard on his rampart play.[19]
    From sack'd Savanna, whelm'd in hostile fires,
A few raw troops brave Lincoln now retires;   210
With rapid march to suffering Charleston goes,
To meet the myriads of concentring foes,
Who shade the pointed strand.[20] Each fluvial flood
Their gathering fleets and floating batteries load,
Close their black sails, debark the amphibious host,   215
And with their moony anchors fang the coast.
    The bold beleaguer'd post the hero gains,
And the hard siege with various fate sustains.
Cornwallis, towering at the British van,
In these fierce toils his wild career began;   220
He mounts the forky streams, and soon bestrides
The narrow neck that parts converging tides,
Sinks the deep trench, erects the mantling tower,
Lines with strong forts the desolated shore,
Hems on all sides the long unsuccour'd place,   225
With mines and parallels contracts the space;
Then bids the battering floats his labors crown,
And pour their bombard on the shuddering town.
    High from the decks the mortar's bursting fires

---

19. General Wayne captured Stony Point on the Hudson River, which had given the British access to the southern colonies.   20. General Benjamin Lincoln (1733–1810) was defeated at Charleston but eventually accepted Cornwallis's surrender, ending the Revolutionary War.

Sweep the full streets, and splinter down the spires.   230
Blaze-trailing fuses vault the night's dim round,
And shells and langrage lacerate the ground;
Till all the tented plain, where heroes tread,
Is torn with crags and cover'd with the dead.
Each shower of flames renews the townsmen's woe,   235
They wail the fight, they dread the cruel foe.
Matrons in crowds, while tears bedew their charms,
Babes at their sides and infants in their arms,
Press round their Lincoln and his hand implore,
To save them trembling from the tyrant's power.   240
He shares their anguish with a moistening eye,
And bids the balls rain thicker thro the sky;
Tries every aid that art and valor yield,
The sap, the countermine, the battling field,
The bold sortie, by famine urged afar,   245
That dreadful daughter of earth-wasting War.
But vain the conflict now; on all the shore,
The foes in fresh brigades around him pour;
He yields at last the well contested prize,
And freedom's banners quit the southern skies.   250
      The victor Britons soon the champaign tread,
And far anorth their fire and slaughter spread;
Thro fortless realms, where unarm'd peasants fly,
Cornwallis bears his bloody standard high;
O'er Carolina rolls his growing force,   255
And thousands fall and thousands aid his course;
While in his march athwart the wide domain,
Colonial dastards join his splendid train.
So mountain streams thro slopes of melting snow,
Swell their foul waves and flood the world below.   260
      Awhile the Patriarch saw, with heaving sighs,
These crimson flags insult the saddening skies,
Saw desolation whelm his favorite coast,
His children scatter'd and their vigor lost,
Dekalb in furious combat press the plain,   265
Morgan and Smallwood every shock sustain,
Gates, now no more triumphant, quit the field,
Indignant Davidson his lifeblood yield,
Blount, Gregory, Williamson, with souls of fire
But slender force, from hill to hill retire;   270
When Greene in lonely greatness takes the ground,
And bids at last the trump of vengeance sound.[21]

---

21. Baron John Dekalb (1721–1780), General Daniel Morgan (1736–1802), General William Smallwood (1732–1792), Horatio Gates (1728–1806), William Lee Davidson (1746–1781), William Blount (1749–1800), Hugh Williamson (1735–1819), and Nathaniel Greene (1742–1786).

A few firm patriots to the chief repair,
Raise the star standard and demand the war.
But o'er the regions as he turns his eyes,   275
What foes develop! and what forts arise!
Rawdon with rapid marches leads their course,
From state to state Cornwallis whirls their force,
Impetuous Tarleton like a torrent pours,
And fresh battalions land along the shores;   280
Where, now resurgent from his captive chain,
Phillips wide storming shakes the field again;
And traitor Arnold, lured by plunder o'er,
Joins the proud powers his valor foil'd before.[22]

    Greene views the tempest with collected soul,   285
And fates of empires in his bosom roll;
So small his force, where shall he lift the steel?
(Superior hosts o'er every canton wheel)
Or how behold their wanton carnage spread,
Himself stand idle and his country bleed?   290
Fixt in a moment's pause the general stood,
And held his warriors from the field of blood;
Then points the British legions where to steer,
Marks to their chief a rapid wild career,
Wide o'er Virginia lets him foeless roam,   295
To search for pillage and to find his doom,
With short-lived glory feeds his sateless flame,
But leaves the victory to a nobler name,
Gives to great Washington to meet his way,
Nor claims the honors of so bright a day.   300

from Book VIII

Hail, holy Peace, from thy sublime abode
Mid circling saints that grace the throne of God.
Before his arm, around our embryon earth,
Stretch'd the dim void, and gave to nature birth,
Ere morning stars his glowing chambers hung,   5
Or songs of gladness woke an angel's tongue,
Veil'd in the splendors of his beamful mind,
In blest repose thy placid form reclined,
Lived in his life, his inward sapience caught,
And traced and toned his universe of thought.   10
Borne thro the expanse with his creating voice
Thy presence bade the unfolding worlds rejoice,
Led forth the systems on their bright career,
Shaped all their curves and fashion'd every sphere,

---

22. Banastre Tarleton (1754–1833), William Phillips (1731–1781), and Benedict Arnold (1741–1801).

Spaced out their suns, and round each radiant goal,   15
Orb over orb, compell'd their train to roll,
Bade heaven's own harmony their force combine,
Taught all their host symphonious strains to join,
Gave to seraphic harps their sounding lays,
Their joys to angels, and to men their praise.   20
    From scenes of blood, these verdant shores that stain,
From numerous friends in recent battle slain,
From blazing towns that scorch the purple sky,
From houseless hordes, their smoking walls that fly,
From the black prison ships, those groaning graves,   25
From warring fleets that vex the gory waves,
From a storm'd world, long taught thy flight to mourn,
I rise, delightful Peace, and greet thy glad return.
    For now the untuneful trump shall grate no more;
Ye silver streams, no longer swell with gore,   30
Bear from your war-beat banks the guilty stain
With yon retiring navies to the main.
While other views, unfolding on my eyes,
And happier themes bid bolder numbers rise;
Bring, bounteous Peace, in thy celestial throng,   35
Life to my soul, and rapture to my song;
Give me to trace, with pure unclouded ray,
The arts and virtues that attend thy sway,
To see thy blissful charms, that here descend,
Thro distant realms and endless years extend.   40
    Too long the groans of death and battle's bray
Have rung discordant thro my turgid lay:
The drum's rude clang, the war wolf's hideous howl
Convulsed my nerves and agonised my soul,
Untuned the harp for all but misery's pains,   45
And chased the Muse from corse-encumber'd plains.
Let memory's balm its pious fragrance shed
On heroes' wounds and patriot warriors dead;
Accept, departed Shades, these grateful sighs,
Your fond attendants thro your homeward skies.   50

—1807

Milcah Martha Moore
1740–1829

Named after the biblical Milcah, the wife of Abraham's brother, Moore was descended from
Welsh settlers who in 1683 put down roots in Pennsylvania. She was part of a wealthy
Philadelphia Quaker community, until they disowned her for marrying without their permission.
Ostracized from one community, she soon found herself at the center of another, a Revolutionary-

era group of well-educated women whose areas of interests ranged far beyond the domestic to encompass politics, society, religion, mortality, and Anglo-American literature. She cultivated these friendships through letters that secure her a place among literature's foremost epistolarians. Available for the first time in a modern edition edited by Catherine La Courreye Blecki and Karin Wulf, Moore's commonplace book, which contains letters and poems by her correspondents, testifies to the rich exchange of ideas and creative works among her female friends. This community of women writers and readers rivals those across the Atlantic, such as the Bluestockings, and anticipates nineteenth-century American groups, such as the ones formed by Margaret Fuller in her "Conversations." Moore's poetry encouraged the women in her group to dissent in both politics and poetics, buttressing the Revolutionary cause through actions and words. Moore's writings were influential beyond her immediate circle of friends: She was an internationally known writer of didactic poetry. Her book, *Miscellanies, Moral and Instructive* (1787), was first published in Philadelphia and then reprinted in London in 1794 and Dublin in 1798.

The Female Patriots.
Address'd to the Daughters of Liberty in America, 1768

Since the men, from a party or fear of a frown,
Are kept by a sugar-plum quietly down,
Supinely asleep—and depriv'd of their sight,
Are stripp'd of their freedom, and robb'd of their right;
If the sons, so degenerate! the blessings despise,   5
Let the Daughters of Liberty nobly arise;
And though we've no voice but a negative here,
The use of the taxables, let us forbear:—
(Then merchants import till your stores are all full,
May the buyers be few, and your traffic be dull!)   10
Stand firmly resolv'd, and bid Grenville[1] to see,
That rather than freedom we part with our tea,
And well as we love the dear draught when a-dry,
As American Patriots our taste we deny—
Pennsylvania's gay meadows can richly afford   15
To pamper our fancy or furnish our board;
And paper sufficient at home still we have,
To assure the wiseacre, we will not sign slave;
When this homespun shall fail, to remonstrate our grief,
We can speak viva voce, or scratch on a leaf;   20
Refuse all their colors, though richest of dye,
When the juice of a berry our paint can supply,
To humor our fancy—and as for our houses,
They'll do without painting as well as our spouses;
While to keep out the cold of a keen winter morn,   25
We can screen the north-west with a well polished horn;
And trust me a woman, by honest invention,
Might give this state-doctor a dose of prevention.

---

1. George Grenville (1712–1770), British politician who taxed the American colonies, inciting revolution.

Join mutual in this—and but small as it seems,
We may jostle a Grenville, and puzzle his schemes;   30
But a motive more worthy our patriot pen,
Thus acting—we point out their duty to men;
And should the bound-pensioners tell us to hush,
We can throw back the satire, by biding them blush.

—1787

William Godwin
1756–1836

William Godwin earned his place at the center of a community of radical writers by publishing the widely influential book *Political Justice* (London, 1793; Philadelphia, 1796). This work
announced that humankind was evolving to the point when government would no longer be
needed, when reason would triumph over emotion and vice, ushering in a utopian future. The
book was published only weeks before the beheading of Louis XVI, the prelude to the French
Revolution's "Reign of Terror." Conservatives like Edmund Burke argued that events across the
channel contradicted the Revolution's announced principles, and many supporters in England
fell away. Because of Godwin's uncompromising Enlightenment optimism, his work became a
beacon of hope to British radicals who refused to abandon their faith in the Revolution.

    Political Justice was first issued in two large quarto volumes (a publisher's term for a book
made from large sheets of paper folded twice to give four approximately 9- × 12-inch pages per
sheet) whose 898 pages of political rhetoric and philosophy did not come cheap. Working-class
readers found ways around the high price, pooling their resources to purchase the books and
then reading them aloud in pubs across England. The work earned the early respect and admiration of many Romantic-era radical writers, such as William Wordsworth, Samuel Taylor
Coleridge, and above all Mary Wollstonecraft, whom Godwin later married. Godwin was frequently racked with debt and was often supported by his admirers, particularly the young poet
Percy Bysshe Shelley, who had written to Godwin addressing him as a friend of liberty. Shelley
soon found himself in love with Godwin and Wollstonecraft's daughter, who was later to marry
the poet and become famous as Mary Shelley, author of *Frankenstein* (London and New York,
1818). Both Percy's poetry and Mary's novel *Frankenstein*, the second edition of which Godwin
edited, show the influence of the radical egalitarian politics of *Political Justice*.

    Godwin's career was not limited to political philosophy but also included the publication of
six novels, the most famous of which is *Things as They Are, or, The Adventures of Caleb Williams*
(1794). The novel is named after its main character, a servant who discovers the crime of his aristocratic master. This master, though, is able to restrict Caleb's civil liberties with impunity because
of their relative class status. A caustic attack on the privileges of the nobility and a legal system
that enabled the rich to persecute the poor, this novel was widely read in England and America,
where it was reprinted in Philadelphia in 1795. Another work of Godwin's that was widely dissem-
inated on both sides of the Atlantic was a biography of Wollstonecraft, who died shortly after giving birth to their daughter Mary. In *Memoirs of the Author of Vindication of the Rights of Woman*
(London, 1798; Philadelphia, 1802), Godwin deemphasized Mary Wollstonecraft's monumental
intellectual achievements, choosing to focus instead on her chaotic emotional life. In so doing, he
sealed the fate of her legacy in a nineteenth-century England that was becoming increasingly dominated by Victorian pieties and sexist notions of gender and propriety. The selection printed here,
from *Letters of Advice to a Young American* (1818), similarly domesticates Godwin's early radicalism, articulating his ideas for a properly republican education.

from Letters of Advice to a Young American

My Dear Sir,

I have thought, at least twenty times since you left London, of the promise I made you, and was at first inclined to consider it, as you appear to have done, as wholly unconditional, and to be performed out of hand. And I should perhaps have proceeded in that way; but that my situation often draws me with an imperious summons in a thousand different directions, and thus the first heat of my engagement subsided. I then altered my mind, and made a resolution, that you should never have the thing you asked for, unless you wrote to remind me of my promise. I thought within myself, that if the advice was not worth that, it was not worth my trouble in digesting. From the first moment I saw you in this house, I conceived a partiality for you, founded on physiognomy in an extensive sense, as comprehending countenance, voice, figure, gesture, and demeanour; but if you forgot me as soon as I was out of your sight, I determined that this partiality should not prove a source of trouble to me.

And, now that you have discharged your part of the condition I secretly prescribed, I am very apprehensive that you have formed an exaggerated idea of what I can do for you in this respect. I am a man of very limited observation and enquiry, and know little but of such things as lie within those limits. If I wished to form a universal library, I should feel myself in conscience obliged to resort to those persons who knew more in one and another class of literature than I did, and to lay their knowledge in whatever they understood best, under contribution. But this I do not mean to undertake for you; I will reason but of what I know; and I shall leave you to learn of the professors themselves, as to the things to which I have never dedicated myself.

You will find many of my ideas of the studies to be pursued, and the books to be read, by young persons, in the Enquirer, and more to the same purpose in the Preface to a small book for children, entitled, "Scripture Histories, given in the words of the original," in two volumes, 18mo.[1]

It is my opinion, that the imagination is to be cultivated in education, more than the dry accumulation of science and natural facts. The noblest part of man is his moral nature; and I hold morality principally to depend, agreeably to the admirable maxim of Jesus, upon our putting ourselves in the place of another, feeling his feelings, and apprehending his desires; in a word, doing to others, as we would wish, were we they, to be done unto.

Another thing that may be a great and most esssential aid to our cultivating moral sentiments, will consist in our studying the best models, and figuring to ourselves the most excellent things of which human nature is capable. For this purpose there is nothing so valuable as the histories of Greece and Rome. There are certain cold-blooded reasoners who say, that the ancients were in nothing better than ourselves, that their stature of mind was no taller, and their feelings in nothing more elevated, and that human nature in all ages and countries is the same. I do not myself believe this. But, if it is so, certainly ancient history is the bravest and sublimest fiction that it ever entered into the mind of man to create. No poets, or romance-writers, or story-tellers, have ever been able to feign such models of an erect and generous and public-spirited and self-postponing mind, as are to be found in Livy and Dionysius of Halicarnassus. If the story be a falsehood, the emotions, and in many

---

1. In this essay, Godwin cites a wide range of classical and contemporary authors too numerous to identify individually.

readers the never-to-be-destroyed impressions it produces, are real: and I am firmly of opinion, that the man that has not been imbued with these tales in his earliest youth, can never be so noble a creature, as the man with whom they have made a part of his education stands a chance to be.

To study the Greek and Roman history it were undoubtedly best to read it in their own historians. To do this we must have a competent mastery of the Greek and Latin languages. But it would be a dangerous delusion to put off the study long, under the idea that a few years hence we will read these things in the originals. You will find the story told with a decent portion of congenial feeling in Rollin's Ancient History, and Vertot's Revolutions of Rome. You should also read Plutarch's Lives, and a translation into English or French, of Dionysius's Antiquities. Mitford for the History of Greece, and Hooke for that of Rome, are writers of some degree of critical judgment; but Hooke has a baleful scepticism about, and a pernicious lust to dispute, the virtues of illustrious men, and Mitford is almost frantic with the love of despotism and oppression. Middleton's Life of Cicero, and Blackwell's Court of Augustus, are books written in the right spirit. And, if you do not soon read Thucydides in the original, you will soon feel yourself disposed to read Sallust, and Livy, and perhaps Tacitus, in the genuine language in which these glorious men have clothed their thoughts.

The aim of my meditation at this moment is to devise that course of study, that shall make him who pursues it independent and generous. For a similar reason therefore to that which has induced me to recommend the histories of Greece and Rome, I would next call the attention of my pupil to the age of chivalry. This also is a generous age, though of a very different cast from that of the best period of ancient history. Each has its beauty. Considered in relation to man as a species of being divided into two sexes, the age of chivalry has greatly the advantage over the purest ages of antiquity. How far their several excellencies may be united and blended together in future time, may be a matter for after consideration. You may begin your acquaintance with the age of chivalry with Sᵗᵉ Palaye's Memoires sur l'Ancienne Chevalerie, and Southey's Chronicle of the Cid. Cervantes's admirable romance of Don Quixote, if read with a deep feeling of its contents, and that high veneration for and strong sympathy with its hero, which it is calculated to excite in every ingenuous mind, is one of the noblest records of the principles of chivalry. I am not anxious to recommend a complete cycle of the best writers on any subject. You cannot do better perhaps in that respect, than I have done before you. I always found one writer in his occasional remembrances and references leading to another, till I might, if I had chosen it, have collected a complete library of the best books on any given topic, without almost being obliged to recur to any one living counsellor for his advice.

We can never get at the sort of man that I am contemplating, and that I would, if I could, create, without making him also a reader and lover of Poetry. I require from him the glow of intellect and sentiment, as well as the glow of a social being. I would have him have his occasional moods of sublimity, and if I may so call it, literary tenderness, as well as a constant determination of mind to habits of philanthropy. You will find some good ideas on the value of poetry in Sir Philip Sidney's Defense of Poesy, and the last part of Sir William Temple's Miscellanies.

The subject of poetry is intimately connected with the last subject I mentioned, the age of chivalry. It is in the institutions of chivalry that the great characteristics, which distinguish ancient from modern poetry, originate. The soul of modern poetry, separately considered, lies in the importance which the spirit of chivalry has given to the female sex. The ancients pitted a man against a man, and thought much of his thews and sinews, and the graces and energy which nature has given to his corporeal frame. This was the state of things in the time of Homer. In a more refined age they added all those excellencies which grow out of the most fervid and entire love of country. Antiquity taught her men to love women, and that not in the purest sense; the age of chivalry taught hers to adore them. I think, quite contrary to the vulgar maxim on the subject, that love is never love in its best spirit, but among unequals. The love of parent and child is its highest model, and most permanent effect. It is therefore an excellent invention of modern times, that, while woman by the nature of things must look up to man, teaches us in our turn to regard woman, not merely as a convenience to be made use of, but as a being to be treated with courtship and consideration and fealty.

Agreeably to the difference between what we call the heroic times, and the times of chivalry, are the characteristic features of ancient and modern poetry. The ancient is simple and manly and distinct, full of severe graces and heroic enthusiasm. The modern excels more in tenderness, and the indulgence of a tone of magnificent obscurity. The ancient upon the whole had more energy; we have more of the wantoning of the imagination, and the conjuring up a fairy vision

> "Of some gay creatures of the element,
> That in the colours of the rainbow live,
> And play in the plighted clouds."[2]

It is not necessary to decide whether the ancient or the modern poetry is best; both are above all price; but it is certain that the excellencies that are all our own, have a grandeur and a beauty and a thrilling character, that nothing can surpass. The best English poets are Shakespear and Milton and Chaucer and Spenser. Ariosto is above all other the poet of chivalry. The Greek and Latin poets it is hardly necessary to enumerate. There is one book of criticism, and perhaps only one, that I would recommend to you, Schlegel's Lectures on Dramatic Literature. The book is deformed indeed with a pretty copious sprinkling of German mysticism, but it is fraught with a great multitude of admirable observations.

The mention of criticism leads me to a thought which I will immediately put down. I would advise a young person to be very moderate in his attention to new books. In all the world I think there is scarcely any thing more despicable, than the man that confines his reading to the publications of the day: he is next in rank to the boarding-school miss who devours every novel that is spawned forth from the press of the season. If you look into Reviews, let it be principally to wonder at the stolidity of your contemporaries who regard them as the oracles of learning.

One other course of reading I would earnestly recommend to you; and many persons would vehemently exclaim against me for doing so,—Metaphysics. It excels perhaps all other studies in the world, in the character of a practical logic, a disciplining and subtilising of the rational faculties. Metaphysics we are told, is a mere jargon, where men dispute for ever without gaining a single step; it is nothing but specious obscurity and ignorance. This is not my opinion. In the first place, metaphysics is the theoretical science of the human mind; and it would be strange if mind was the only science not

---

2. John Milton, *Comus* (1637), 11.298–300.

worth studying, or the only science in which real knowledge could not be acquired. Secondly, it is the theoretical science of the universe and of causation, and must settle, if ever they can be settled, the first principles of natural religion. As to its uncertainty, I cannot conceive that any one with an unprejudiced mind can read what has been best written on free-will and necessity, on self-love and benevolence, and other grand questions, and then say that nothing has been attained, and that all this is impertinent and senseless waste of words. I would particularly recommend Bishop Berkley, especially his Principles of Human Knowledge, and Hume's Treatise of Human Nature, and Hartley's Observations on Man. Your own Jonathan Edwards has written excellently on free-will; and Hutcheson and Hazlitt on self-love and benevolence. The title of Hutcheson's book is an Essay on the Nature and Conduct of the Passions and Affections, and of Hazlit's an Enquiry into the Principles of Human Action. No young man can read Andrew Baxter's Enquiry into the Nature of the Human Soul, without being the better for it.

It is time that I should now come to the consideration of Language. Language is as necessary an instrument for conducting the operations of the mind, as the hands are for conducting the operations of the body; and the most obvious way of acquiring the power of weighing and judging words aright, is by enabling ourselves to compare the words and forms of different languages. I therefore highly approve of classical education. It has often been said by the wise men of the world, What a miserable waste of time it is, that boys should be occupied for successive year after year, in acquiring the Greek and Latin tongues! How much more usefully would these years be employed, in learning the knowledge of things, and making a substantial acquaintance with the studies of men! I totally dissent from this. As to the knowledge of things, young men will soon enough be plunged in the mire of cold and sordid realities, such things as it is the calamity of man that he should be condemned to consume so much of his mature life upon; and I could wish that those who can afford the leisure of education, should begin with acquiring something a little generous and elevated. As to the studies of men, if boys begin with them before they are capable of weighing them, they will acquire nothing but prejudices, which it will be their greatest interest and highest happiness, with infinite labour to unlearn. Words are happily a knowledge, to the acquisition of which the faculties of boys are perfectly competent, and which can do them nothing but good. Nature has decreed that human beings should be so long in a state of nonage, that it demands some ingenuity to discover how the years of boys of a certain condition in life, may be employed innocently, in acquiring good habits, and none of that appearance of reason and wisdom, which in boys surpasses in nothing the instructions we bestow on parrots and monkies. One of the best maxims of the eloquent Rousseau, is where he says, The master-piece of a good education is to know how to lose time profitably.

Every man has a language that is peculiarly his own; and it should be a great object with him to learn whatever may give illustration to the genius of that. Our language is the English. For this purpose then, I would recommend to every young man who has leisure, to acquire some knowledge of the Saxon, and one or two other northern languages. Horne Tooke, in his Diversions of Purley, is the only man that has done much towards analysing the elements of the English tongue. But another, and perhaps still more important way to acquire a knowledge and true relish of the genius of the English tongue, is by studying its successive authors from age to age. It is an eminent happiness we possess, that our authors from generation to generation are so much worth studying. The first resplendent genius in our literary annals is Chaucer. From this age to that of

Elizabeth we have not much; but it will be good not entirely to drop any of the links of the chain. The period of Elizabeth is perfectly admirable. Roger Ascham, and Golding's version of Mornay's Trewnesse of Christian Religion, are among the best canonical books of genuine English. Next come the translators of the classics in that age, who are worthy to be studied day and night, by those who would perfectly feel the genius of our language. Among these, Phaer's Virgil, Chapman's Homer, and Sir Thomas North's Plutarch, are perhaps the best, and are in my opinion incomparably superior to the later translations of those authors. Of course I hardly need say, that Lord Bacon is one of the first writers that has appeared in the catalogue of human creatures, and one of those who is most worthy to be studied. I might have brought him in among the metaphysicians; but I preferred putting him here. Nothing can be more magnificent and impressive than his language: it is rather that of a God, than a man. I would also specially recommend Burton's Anatomy of Melancholy, and the writings of Sir Thomas Browne. No man I suppose is to be told, that the dramatic writers of the age of Elizabeth are among the most astonishing specimens of human intellect. Shakespear is the greatest, and stands at an immense distance from all the rest. But though he outshines them, he does not put out their light. Ben Jonson is himself a host: of Beaumont and Fletcher I cannot think without enthusiasm: and Ford, and Massinger well deserve to be studied. Even French literature was worthy of some notice in these times; and Montaigne is entitled to rank with some of the best English prose-writers his contemporaries.

In looking over what I have written, I think I have not said enough on the subject of Modern History. Your language is English; the frame of your laws and your lawcourts is essentially English. Therefore, and because the English moral and intellectual character ranks the first of modern times, I think English history is entitled to your preference. Whoever reads English history must take Hume for his text. The subtlety of his mind, the depth of his conceptions, and the surpassing graces of his composition, must always place him in the first class of writers. His work is tarnished with a worthless partiality to the race of kings that Scotland sent to reign over us; and is wofully destitute of that energetic moral and public feeling that distinguishes the Latin historians. Yet we have nothing else on the subject, that deserves the name of composition. I have already spoken of the emphatic attention that is due to the age of chivalry. The feudal system is one of the most extraordinary productions of the human mind. It is a great mistake to say, that these were dark ages. It was about this period that logic was invented: for I will venture to assert that the ancients knew nothing about close reasoning and an unbroken chain of argumentative deduction, in comparison with the moderns. For all the excellence we possess in this art we are indebted to the schoolmen, the monks and friars in the solitude of their cloisters. It is true, that they were too proud of their new acquisitions, and subtilised and refined till occasionally they became truly ridiculous. This does not extinguish their claim to our applause, though it has dreadfully tarnished the lustre of their memory in the vulgar eye. Hume passes over the feudal system and the age of chivalry, as if it were a dishonour to his pen to be employed on these subjects, while he enlarges with endless copiousness on the proofs of the sincerity of Charles the First, and the execrable public and private profligacies of Charles the Second.

Next to the age of feudality and chivalry the period of English history most worthy of our attention lies between the accession of Elizabeth and the Restoration. But let no man think that he learns any thing, particularly of modern history, by reading a single book. It fortunately happens, as far as the civil wars are concerned, that we have two excellent writers of the two opposite parties, Clarendon and Ludlow, beside many others worthy to be consulted. You should also have recourse to as many lives of eminent persons connected with the period then under your consideration, as you can conveniently procure. Letters of state, memorials, and public papers, are in this respect of inestimable value. They are, to a considerable degree, the principal actors in the scene writing their own history. He that would really understand history, should proceed in some degree as if he were composing a history. He should be surrounded with chronological tables and maps. He should compare one authority with another, and not put himself under the guidance of any. This is the difference I make between reading and study. He that confines himself to one book at a time, may be amused, but is no student. In order to study, I must sit in some measure in the middle of a library. Nor can any one truly study, without the perpetual use of a pen, to make notes, and abstracts, and arrangements of dates. The shorter the notes, and the more they can be looked through at a glance, the better. The only limit in this respect is that they should be so constructed, that if I do not look at them again till after an interval of seven years, I should understand them. Learn to read slow;—if you keep to your point, and do not suffer your thoughts, according to an old phrase, to go a wool-gathering, you will be in little danger of excess in this direction.

Accept in good part, my young friend, this attempt to answer your expectation, and be assured that, if I could have done better, it should not have been less at your service. Your dispositions appear to me to be excellent: and, as you will probably be enabled to make some figure, and, which is much better, to act the part of the real patriot and the friend of man, in your own country, you should resolve to bestow on your mind an assiduous cultivation. It is the truly enlightened man, that is best qualified to be truly useful; and, as Lord Bacon says, "It is almost without instance contradictory, that ever any government was disastrous, that was in the hands of learned governors. The wit of one man can no more countervail learning, than one man's means can hold way with a common purse."[3]

My best wishes attend you.

—1818

⟳ END OF TRANSATLANTIC EXCHANGES ⟲

Anna Laetitia Barbauld
1743–1825

Barbauld was born Anna Laetitia Aikin and from her earliest childhood exhibited a precocity that her father, a teacher in the Dissenting Academy at Warrington in Cheshire, England, indulged by tutoring her in a classical education. Joseph Priestley, her father's colleague at Warrington who was to immigrate to Pennsylvania, showed a keen interest in her early poetry and offered much encouragement. In 1773, she published two books: *Poems* (which ran through five editions in England and was reprinted in Boston in 1820) and, with her brother, John Aikin, *Miscellaneous Pieces in Prose*. Her poems won her such renown that she drew the admiration of literary critic Elizabeth

---

3. Sir Francis Bacon, *The Advancement of Learning* (1605).

Montagu, who asked for her help starting a Literary Academy for Ladies. Montagu was famous as a host of gatherings of Bluestockings—a derisive term meant to indicate the pedantic literary tastes of women who sought intellectual development and stimulation in conversation with each other. Barbauld, though, had come to believe that a woman should acquire education "from conversations with a father, a brother or friend, in the way of family intercourse and easy conversation, and by such a course of reading as they may recommend," and so she refused to take part in establishing the academy. In 1774, Anna married Rochemont Barbauld, a dissenting minister with whom she opened a boys' school in Sussex. During this time she published some of the books that were to win her recognition in England and a vast readership in America: *Lessons for Children* (1778) and *Hymns in Prose for Children* (1781). In 1785, the school closed and the couple moved to London, where Barbauld began publishing poetry in the *Monthly Magazine*.

Barbauld rebelled against her early conservatism during her later connection with the London radicals of the Johnson Circle. (Among the authors associated with the radical publisher Joseph Johnson were the revolutionary writers William Blake, William Godwin, William Wordsworth, and Mary Wollstonecraft.) And she went on to distinguish herself by publishing widely on education, abolition, and democracy and by editing a fifty-volume set of British novels. Her works were widely read in America, selling through more editions than those of any of her contemporaries. For example, *Hymns in Prose for Children* alone was reprinted in twenty-four editions in Massachusetts, Connecticut, and New York from 1786 to 1825.

Barbauld addresses Wollstonecraft directly in her poem titled "The Rights of Woman," a shortened version of the title of Wollstonecraft's famous manifesto, *A Vindication of the Rights of Woman* (1792). In her manifesto, Wollstonecraft had referred to Barbauld's poem, "To a Lady, with Some Painted Flowers," which states that women's "sweetest empire is—To Please." In reference to this poem, Wollstonecraft noted that "even women of superior sense" can "rob the sex of its dignity." Whether Barbauld's "The Rights of Woman" is answering Wollstonecraft by poking fun at her, endorsing her views, or upbraiding and satirizing them is a question worth discussing. When the poem notes that in marriage "separate rights are lost in mutual love" (p. 182), it could mean that in marriage both become one in utopian love, or it could imply that a woman loses her rights in marriage, as was legally the case at this time. Read in the context of her own failing marriage to Rochemont, whose fits of insanity were a threat to Barbauld's life and led to his suicide in 1808, and in the context of her poem "Washing-Day," with its biting exploration of the gender and class roles of domestic "duties," this question becomes more complex.

In "Washing-Day," Barbauld experiments playfully with the traditionally male-dominated verse forms of satire and epic in order to determine whether they are adaptable to the domestic sphere. She invokes the muse not to sing of wars and heroes as the classical poets Homer and Virgil did, nor to justify the ways of God to men, as John Milton sought to do in *Paradise Lost* (1667), but to "sing the dreaded Washing-Day" and of those "who beneath the yoke of wedlock bend" (p. 191). Here, she takes up a point that Wollstonecraft discusses as well: how men are as bound by the gender roles and separate spheres they prescribe as women, the spheres being signified in the poem by, on the one hand, the laundry-soap bubble and, on the other, the "silken ball" (p. 192) of one of the era's inventions, the hot-air balloon.

Barbauld's wry critique of rigid gender roles in her poetry was completely missed by the reviewer John Wilson Croker. Attacking her poem "Eighteen Hundred and Eleven" (1812), which ranges beyond the domestic to cover international politics and foreign policy, he upbraids her for writing beyond her sphere, noting "that she has wandered from the course in which she was respectable and useful, in exchanging the birchen for the satiric rod" and in throwing down her "spectacles and her knitting needles . . . to sally forth." He also takes issue with the fact that the poem foretells England's waning and America's waxing, assuring her that he "should not by any means impute it to want of taste or patriotism on her part, if, for her country, her fears were less confident, and for America her hopes less ardent." It is troubling to reflect that this poem was the last that Barbauld published, perhaps because of Croker's harsh review.

Epistle to William Wilberforce

Cease, Wilberforce,[1] to urge thy generous aim!
Thy Country knows the sin, and stands the shame!
The Preacher, Poet, Senator, in vain
Has rattled in her fight the Negro's chain;
With his deep groans assail'd her startled ear,   5
And rent the veil that hid his constant tear;
Forc'd her averted eyes his stripes to scan,
Beneath the bloody scourge laid bare the man,
Claim'd Pity's tear, urged Conscience' strong controul
And flash'd conviction on her shrinking soul.   10
The Muse, too soon awaked, with ready tongue
At Mercy's shrine applausive paeans rung;
And Freedom's eager sons, in vain foretold
A new Astrean reign, an age of gold:
She knows and she persists—Still Afric bleeds,   15
Unchecked, the human traffic still proceeds;
She stamps her infamy to future time,
And on her hardened forehead seals the crime.

    In vain, to thy white standard gathering round,
Wit, Worth, and Parts and Eloquence are found: 20
In vain, to push to birth thy great design,
Contending chiefs, and hostile virtues join;
All, from conflicting ranks, of power possest
To rouse, to melt, or to inform the breast.
Where seasoned tools of Avarice prevail,   25
A Nation's eloquence, combined, must fail:
Each flimsy sophistry by turns they try;
The plausive argument, the daring lye,
The artful gloss, that moral sense confounds,
Th' acknowledged thirst of gain that honour wounds: 30
Bane of ingenuous minds! th' unfeeling sneer,
Which, sudden, turns to stone the falling tear:
They search assiduous, with inverted skill,
For forms of wrong, and precedents of ill;
With impious mockery wrest the sacred page,   35
And glean up crimes from each remoter age:
Wrung Nature's tortures, shuddering, while you tell,
From scoffing fiends bursts forth the laugh of hell;
In Britain's senate, Misery's pangs give birth
To jests unseemly, and to horrid mirth——   40
Forbear!—thy virtues but provoke our doom,

---

1. William Wilberforce (1759–1833) successfully lobbied for an anti-slavery bill passed by the British Parliament in 1807.

And swell th' account of vengeance yet to come;
For, not unmarked in Heaven's impartial plan,
Shall man, proud worm, contemn his fellow-man?
And injured Afric, by herself redrest,   45
Darts her own serpents at her Tyrant's breast.
Each vice, to minds depraved by bondage known,
With sure contagion fastens on his own;
In sickly languors melts his nerveless frame,
And blows to rage impetuous Passion's flame: 50
Fermenting swift, the fiery venom gains
The milky innocence of infant veins;
There swells the stubborn will, damps learning's fire,
The whirlwind wakes of uncontrouled desire,
Sears the young heart to images of wo,   55
And blasts the buds of Virtue as they blow.

   Lo! where reclined, pale Beauty courts the breeze,
Diffused on sofas of voluptuous ease;
With anxious awe, her menial train around,
Catch her faint whispers of half-utter'd sound;   60
See her, in monstrous fellowship, unite
At once the Scythian, and the Sybarite[2];
Blending repugnant vices, misally'd,
Which *frugal* nature purposed to divide;
See her, with indolence to fierceness join'd,   65
Of body delicate, infirm of mind,
With languid tones imperious mandates urge;
With arm recumbent wield the household scourge;
And with unruffled mien, and placid sounds,
Contriving torture, and inflicting wounds.   70

   Nor, in their palmy walks and spicy groves,
The form benign of rural Pleasure roves;
No milk-maids' song, or hum of village talk,
Sooths the lone poet in his evening walk:
No willing arm the flail unwearyed plies,   75
Where the mixed sounds of chearful labour rise;
No blooming maids, and frolic swains are seen
To pay gay homage to their harvest queen:
No heart-expanding scenes their eyes must prove
Of thriving industry, and faithful love: 80
But shrieks and yells disturb the balmy air,
Dumb sullen looks of wo announce despair,   }
And angry eyes thro' dusky features glare.

---

2. Scythian: a supposedly androgynous or emasculated person from the region north of the Black Sea; Sybarite: a native of the ancient Greek city of Sybaris, supposed to be luxurious and hedonistic.

Far from the sounding lash the Muses fly,
And sensual riot drowns each finer joy.   85

   Nor less from the gay East; on essenced wings,
Breathing unnamed perfumes, Contagion springs;
The soft luxurious plague alike pervades
The marble palaces, and rural shades;
Hence throng'd Augusta builds her rosy bowers,   90
And decks in summer wreaths her smoky towers;
And hence, in summer bow'rs, Art's costly hand
Pours courtly splendours o'er the dazzled land:
The manners melt—One undistinguish'd blaze
O'erwhelms the sober pomp of elder days;   95
Corruption follows with gigantic stride,
And scarce vouchsafes his shameless front to hide:
The spreading leprosy taints ev'ry part,
Infects each limb, and sickens at the heart.
Simplicity! most dear of rural maids,   100
Weeping resigns her violated shades:
Stern Independence from his glebe[3] retires,
And anxious Freedom eyes her drooping fires;
By foreign wealth are British morals chang'd,
And Afric's sons, and India's, smile avenged.   105

   For you, whose temper'd ardour long has borne
Untired the labour, and unmoved the scorn;
In Virtue's fasti[4] be inscribed your fame,
And uttered yours with Howard's honour'd name,
Friends of the friendless—Hail, ye generous band!   110
Whose efforts yet arrest Heaven's lifted hand,
Around whose steady brows, in union bright,
The civic wreath, and Christian's palm unite:
Your merit stands, no greater and no less,
Without, or with the varnish of success;   115
But seek no more to break a Nation's fall,
For ye have sav'd yourselves—and that is all.
Succeeding times your struggles, and their fate,
With mingled shame and triumph shall relate,
While faithful History, in her various page,   120
Marking the features of this motley age,
To shed a glory, and to fix a stain,
Tells how you strove, and that you strove in vain.

The End.

—1791

---

3. Cultivated field.   4. A calendar of important historical events.

The Rights of Woman

Yes, injured Woman! rise, assert thy right!
Woman! too long degraded, scorned, opprest;
O born to rule in partial Law's despite,
Resume thy native empire o'er the breast!

Go forth arrayed in panoply divine;   5
That angel pureness which admits no stain;
Go, bid proud Man his boasted rule resign,
And kiss the golden sceptre of thy reign.

Go, gird thyself with grace; collect thy store
Of bright artillery glancing from afar;   10
Soft melting tones thy thundering cannon's roar,
Blushes and fears thy magazine of war.

Thy rights are empire: urge no meaner claim,—
Felt, not defined, and if debated, lost;
Like sacred mysteries, which withheld from fame,   15
Shunning discussion, are revered the most.

Try all that wit and art suggest to bend
Of thy imperial foe the stubborn knee;
Make treacherous Man thy subject, not thy friend:
Thou mayst command, but never canst be free.   20

Awe the licentious, and restrain the rude;
Soften the sullen, clear the cloudy brow:
Be, more than princes' gifts, thy favours sued;—
She hazards all, who will the least allow.

But hope not, courted idol of mankind,   25
On this proud eminence secure to stay;
Subduing and subdued, thou soon shalt find
Thy coldness soften, and thy pride give way.

Then, then, abandon each ambitious thought,
Conquest or rule thy heart shall feebly move,   30
In Nature's school, by her soft maxims taught,
That separate rights are lost in mutual love.

—1795

Eighteen Hundred and Eleven

Still the loud death-drum, thundering from afar,
O'er the vext nations pours the storm of war:
To the stern call still Britain bends her ear,
Feeds the fierce strife, the alternate hope and fear;

Bravely, though vainly, dares to strive with Fate,   5
And seeks by turns to prop each sinking state.
Colossal power with overwhelming force
Bears down each foot of Freedom in its course;
Prostrate she lies beneath the despot's sway,
While the hushed nations curse him—and obey.   10

Bounteous in vain, with frantic man at strife,
Glad Nature pours the means—the joys of life;
In vain with orange-blossoms scents the gale,
The hills with olives clothes, with corn the vale;
Man calls to Famine, nor invokes in vain,   15
Disease and Rapine follow in her train;
The tramp of marching hosts disturbs the plough,
The sword, not sickle, reaps the harvest now,
And where the soldier gleans the scant supply,
The helpless peasant but retires to die;   20
No laws his hut from licensed outrage shield,
And war's least horror is the ensanguined field.

Fruitful in vain, the matron counts with pride
The blooming youths that grace her honored side;
No son returns to press her widowed hand,   25
Her fallen blossoms strew a foreign strand.
—Fruitful in vain, she boasts her virgin race,
Whom cultured arts adorn and gentlest grace;
Defrauded of its homage, Beauty mourns
And the rose withers on its virgin thorns.   30
Frequent, some stream obscure, some uncouth name,
By deeds of blood is lifted into fame;
Oft o'er the daily page some soft one bends
To learn the fate of husband, brothers, friends,
Or the spread map with anxious eye explores,   35
Its dotted boundaries and pencilled shores,
Asks where the spot that wrecked her bliss is found,
And learns its name but to detest the sound.

And think'st thou, Britain, still to sit at ease,
An island queen amidst thy subject seas,   40
While the vext billows, in their distant roar,
But soothe thy slumbers, and but kiss thy shore?
To sport in wars, while danger keeps aloof,
Thy grassy turf unbruised by hostile hoof?
So sing thy flatterers;—but, Britain, know,   45
Thou who hast shared the guilt must share the woe.
Nor distant is the hour; low murmurs spread,
And whispered fears, creating what they dread;
Ruin, as with an earthquake shock, is here,

There, the heart-witherings of unuttered fear,   50
And that sad death, whence most affection bleeds,
Which sickness, only of the soul, precedes.
Thy baseless wealth dissolves in air away,
Like mists that melt before the morning ray:
No more on crowded mart or busy street   55
Friends, meeting friends, with cheerful hurry greet;
Sad, on the ground thy princely merchants bend
Their altered looks, and evil days portend,
And fold their arms, and watch with anxious breast
The tempest blackening in the distant West.   60

Yes, thou must droop; thy Midas[1] dream is o'er;
The golden tide of Commerce leaves thy shore,
Leaves thee to prove the alternate ills that haunt
Enfeebling Luxury and ghastly Want;
Leaves thee, perhaps, to visit distant lands,   65
And deal the gifts of Heaven with equal hands.

Yet, O my Country, name beloved, revered,
By every tie that binds the soul endeared,
Whose image to my infant senses came
Mixt with Religion's light and Freedom's holy flame!   70
If prayers may not avert, if 't is thy fate
To rank amongst the names that once were great,
Not like the dim, cold Crescent[2] shalt thou fade,
Thy debt to Science and the Muse unpaid;
Thine are the laws surrounding states revere,   75
Thine the full harvest of the mental year,
Thine the bright stars in Glory's sky that shine,
And arts that make it life to live are thine.
If westward streams the light that leaves thy shores,
Still from thy lamp the streaming radiance pours.   80
Wide spreads thy race from Ganges to the pole,
O'er half the Western world thy accents roll:
Nations beyond the Apalachian hills
Thy hand has planted and thy spirit fills:
Soon as their gradual progress shall impart   85
The finer sense of morals and of art,
Thy stores of knowledge the new states shall know,
And think thy thoughts, and with thy fancy glow;
Thy Lockes, thy Paleys,[3] shall instruct their youth,
Thy leading star direct their search for truth;   90
Beneath the spreading plantan's tent-like shade,
Or by Missouri's rushing waters laid,

---

1. King Midas of Phrygia, said to have the power to change matter to gold by his touch.   2. Symbol of the Islamic Ottoman Empire.   3. John Locke (1632–1704) and William Paley (1743–1805), British philosophers.

"Old Father Thames" shall be the poet's theme,
Of Hagley's woods the enamored virgin dream,
And Milton's tones the raptured ear enthrall,   95
Mixt with the roaring of Niagara's fall;
In Thomson's[4] glass the ingenuous youth shall learn
A fairer face of Nature to discern;
Nor of the bards that swept the British lyre
Shall fade one laurel, or one note expire.   100
Then, loved Joanna,[5] to admiring eyes
Thy storied groups in scenic pomp shall rise;
Their high-souled strains and Shakespeare's noble rage
Shall with alternate passion shake the stage.
Some youthful Basil from thy moral lay   105
With stricter hand his fond desires shall sway;
Some Ethwald, as the fleeting shadows pass,
Start at his likeness in the mystic glass;
The tragic Muse resume her just control,
With pity and with terror purge the soul,   110
While wide o'er transatlantic realms thy name
Shall live in light and gather all its fame.

Where wanders Fancy down the lapse of years,
Shedding o'er imaged woes untimely tears?
Fond, moody power! as hopes—as fears prevail,   115
She longs, or dreads, to lift the awful veil,
On visions of delight now loves to dwell,
Now hears the shriek of woe or Freedom's knell:
Perhaps, she says, long ages past away,
And set in western wave our closing day,   120
Night, Gothic night, again may shade the plains
Where Power is seated, and where Science reigns;
England, the seat of arts, be only known
By the gray ruin and the mouldering stone;
That Time may tear the garland from her brow,   125
And Europe sit in dust, as Asia now.

Yet then the ingenuous youth whom Fancy fires
With pictured glories of illustrious sires,
With duteous zeal their pilgrimage shall take
From the Blue Mountains, or Ontario's lake,   130
With fond, adoring steps to press the sod
By statesmen, sages, poets, heroes, trod;
On Isis' banks to draw inspiring air,
From Runnymede to send the patriot's prayer;
In pensive thought, where Cam's slow waters wind,   135

---

4. James Thomson (1700–1748), author of *The Seasons*, an influential poem of nature appreciation.   5. Joanna Baillie
(1762–1851), British poet and playwright.

To meet those shades that ruled the realms of mind;
In silent halls to sculptured marbles bow,
And hang fresh wreaths round Newton's awful brow.[6]
Oft shall they seek some peasant's homely shed,
Who toils, unconscious of the mighty dead,   140
To ask where Avon's winding waters stray,
And thence a knot of wild flowers bear away;
Anxious inquire where Clarkson, friend of man,
Or all-accomplished Jones his race began;
If of the modest mansion aught remains   145
Where Heaven and Nature prompted Cowper's strains;
Where Roscoe, to whose patriot breast belong
The Roman virtue and the Tuscan song,
Led Ceres to the black and barren moor
Where Ceres never gained a wreath before[7]:   150
With curious search their pilgrim steps shall rove
By many a ruined tower and proud alcove,
Shall listen for those strains that soothed of yore
Thy rock, stern Skiddaw, and thy fall, Lodore;
Feast with Dun Edin's classic brow their sight,   155
And "visit Melross by the pale moonlight."[8]

But who their mingled feelings shall pursue
When London's faded glories rise to view?
The mighty city, which by every road,
In floods of people poured itself abroad   160
Ungirt by walls, irregularly great,
No jealous drawbridge, and no closing gate;
Whose merchants (such the state which commerce brings)
Sent forth their mandates to dependent kings;
Streets, where the turbaned Moslem, bearded Jew,   165
And woolly Afric, met the brown Hindu;
Where through each vein spontaneous plenty flowed,
Where Wealth enjoyed, and Charity bestowed.
Pensive and thoughtful shall the wanderers greet
Each splendid square, and still, untrodden street;   170
Or of some crumbling turret, mined by time,
The broken stairs with perilous step shall climb,
Thence stretch their view the wide horizon round,
By scattered hamlets trace its ancient bound,
And, choked no more with fleets, fair Thames survey   175
Through reeds and sedge pursue his idle way.

---

6. The Isis and Runnymede are sections of the Thames River in England. The Cam flows past Cambridge University where a statue honors Sir Isaac Newton (1642–1727).   7. Thomas Clarkson (1760–1846), Sir William Jones (1746–1794), William Cowper (1731–1800), William Roscoe (1753–1831).   8. Skiddaw and Lodore are a peak and a waterfall in the English Lake district; Dun Edin is Edinburgh; Melross is Melrose Abbey as described in Sir Walter Scott's *The Lay of the Last Minstrel* (1805), 2.1–2.

With throbbing bosoms shall the wanderers tread
The hallowed mansions of the silent dead.
Shall enter the long aisle and vaulted dome
Where Genius and where Valor find a home;
Awe-struck 'midst chill sepulchral marbles breathe,   180
Where all above is still, as all beneath;
Bend at each antique shrine, and frequent turn
To clasp with fond delight some sculptured urn,
The ponderous mass of Johnson's form to greet,   185
Or breathe the prayer at Howard's sainted feet.[9]

Perhaps some Briton, in whose musing mind
Those ages live which Time has cast behind,
To every spot shall lead his wondering guests
On whose known site the beam of glory rests;   190
Here Chatham's eloquence in thunder broke,
Here Fox persuaded, or here Garrick spoke;
Shall boast how Nelson, fame and death in view,
To wonted victory led his ardent crew,
In England's name enforced, with loftiest tone,   195
Their duty,—and too well fulfilled his own:
How gallant Moore, as ebbing life dissolved,
But hoped his country had his fame absolved.[10]
Or call up sages whose capacious mind
Left in its course a track of light behind;   200
Point where mute crowds on Davy's lips reposed,
And Nature's coyest secrets were disclosed;
Join with their Franklin, Priestley's injured name,
Whom, then, each continent shall proudly claim.[11]

Oft shall the strangers turn their eager feet   205
The rich remains of ancient art to greet,
The pictured walls with critic eye explore,
And Reynolds be what Raphael was before.[12]
On spoils from every clime their eyes shall gaze,
Egyptian granites and the Etruscan vase;   210
And when 'midst fallen London they survey
The stone where Alexander's ashes lay,[13]
Shall own with humbled pride the lesson just
By Time's slow finger written in the dust.
There walks a Spirit o'er the peopled earth,   215
Secret his progress is, unknown his birth;

---

9. Statues of Samuel Johnson (1709–1784) and John Howard (1726–1790) are located in London's St. Paul's Cathedral, which this stanza describes.   10. William Pitt, Earl of Chatham (1708–1778), Charles James Fox (1749–1806), David Garrick (1717–1779), Admiral Horatio Nelson (1758–1805), and Sir John Moore (1761–1809).   11. Sir Humphrey Davy (1778–1829), Benjamin Franklin (1706–1790), and Joseph Priestley (1733–1804).   12. Sir Joshua Reynolds (1723–1792) and Raffaello Sanzio (1483–1520), both painters.   13. The Macedonian conqueror Alexander the Great's ashes were believed to be contained in a sarcophagus on display at the British Museum in London.

Moody and viewless as the changing wind,
No force arrests his foot, no chains can bind;
Where'er he turns, the human brute awakes,
And, roused to better life, his sordid hut forsakes: 220
He thinks, he reasons, glows with purer fires,
Feels finer wants, and burns with new desires:
Obedient Nature follows where he leads;
The steaming marsh is changed to fruitful meads;
The beasts retire from man's asserted reign,   225
And prove his kingdom was not given in vain.
Then from its bed is drawn the ponderous ore,
Then Commerce pours her gifts on every shore,
Then Babel's towers and terraced gardens rise,
And pointed obelisks invade the skies;   230
The prince commands, in Tyrian purple drest,
And Egypt's virgins weave the linen vest.
Then spans the graceful arch the roaring tide,
And stricter bounds the cultured fields divide.
Then kindles Fancy, then expands the heart,   235
Then blow the flowers of Genius and of Art;
Saints, heroes, sages, who the land adorn,
Seem rather to descend than to be born;
While History, 'midst the rolls consigned to fame,
With pen of adamant inscribes their name.   240

The Genius now forsakes the favored shore,
And hates, capricious, what he loved before;
Then empires fall to dust, then arts decay,
And wasted realms enfeebled despots sway;
Even Nature's changed; without his fostering smile   245
Ophir no gold, no plenty yields the Nile;
The thirsty sand absorbs the useless rill,
And spotted plagues from putrid fens distil.
In desert solitudes then Tadmor sleeps,
Stern Marius then o'er fallen Carthage weeps[14];   250
Then with enthusiast love the pilgrim roves
To seek his footsteps in forsaken groves,
Explores the fractured arch, the ruined tower,
Those limbs disjointed of gigantic power;
Still at each step he dreads the adder's sting,   255
The Arab's javelin, or the tiger's spring;
With doubtful caution treads the echoing ground,
And asks where Troy or Babylon is found.

---

14. Ophir was a region famed for gold. The Egyptian Nile overflows annually, irrigating its banks. Tadmor is the biblical name for the Syrian city of Palmyra. Gaius Marius unsuccessfully sought refuge in Carthage after being exiled from Rome.

And now the vagrant Power no more detains
The vale of Tempe or Ausonian plains[15];   260
Northward he throws the animating ray,
O'er Celtic nations bursts the mental day;
And, as some playful child the mirror turns,
Now here, now there, the moving lustre burns;
Now o'er his changeful fancy more prevail   265
Batavia's dykes than Arno's purple vale;
And stinted suns, and rivers bound with frost,
Than Enna's plains or Baia's viny coast;
Venice the Adriatic weds in vain,
And Death sits brooding o'er Campania's plain;   270
O'er Baltic shores and through Hercynian groves,[16]
Stirring the soul, the mighty impulse moves;
Art plies his tools, and Commerce spreads her sail,
And wealth is wafted in each shifting gale.
The sons of Odin tread on Persian looms,   275
And Odin's daughters breathe distilled perfumes;
Loud minstrel bards, in Gothic halls, rehearse
The Runic rhyme, and "build the lofty verse."[17]
The Muse, whose liquid notes were wont to swell
To the soft breathings of the Æolian shell,   280
Submits, reluctant, to the harsher tone,
And scarce believes the altered voice her own.
And now, where Cæsar saw with proud disdain
The wattled hut and skin of azure stain,
Corinthian columns rear their graceful forms,   285
And light verandas brave the wintry storms,
While British tongues the fading fame prolong
Of Tully's eloquence and Maro's song.
Where once Bonduca whirled the scythed car,[18]
And the fierce matrons raised the shriek of war,   290
Light forms beneath transparent muslins float,
And tutored voices swell the artful note.
Light-leaved acacias and the shady plane
And spreading cedar grace the woodland reign;
While crystal walls the tenderer plants confine,   295
The fragrant orange and the nectared pine;
The Syrian grape there hangs her rich festoons,
Nor asks for purer air or brighter noons:
Science and Art urge on the useful toil,

---

15. Tempe: a famed vale in Greece; Ausonia: Italy in the works of Virgil. 16. Batavia: The Netherlands. The Arno River flows through Florence, Italy. Enna:: Sicily. Baia: Naples. During an annual ceremony, Venice "weds" the Adriatic Sea; Italy's Campania was famous for outbreaks of malaria. 17. John Milton (1608–1674), *Lycidas* (1638). 18. Julius Caesar's *Gallic Wars* mentions that Scottish warriors painted their faces blue for battle. Tully: Marcus Tullius Cicero (106–43 BC); Publius Virgillus Maro (70–19 BC) is Virgil, author of the *Aeneid*. Boudicca, the Celtic queen, led many raids on Roman forts but was defeated in AD 61.

New mould a climate and create the soil,
Subdue the rigor of the Northern Bear,
O'er polar climes shed aromatic air,
On yielding Nature urge their new demands,
And ask not gifts, but tribute, at her hands.   300

London exults:—on London Art bestows   305
Her summer ices and her winter rose;
Gems of the East her mural crown adorn,
And Plenty at her feet pours forth her horn.
While even the exiles her just laws disclaim,
People a continent, and build a name: 310
August she sits, and with extended hands
Holds forth the book of life to distant lands.

But fairest flowers expand but to decay;
The worm is in thy core, thy glories pass away;
Arts, arms, and wealth destroy the fruits they bring;   315
Commerce, like beauty, knows no second spring.
Crime walks thy streets, Fraud earns her unblest bread,
O'er want and woe thy gorgeous robe is spread,
And angel charities in vain oppose:
With grandeur's growth the mass of misery grows.   320
For, see,—to other climes the Genius soars,
He turns from Europe's desolated shores;
And lo! even now, 'midst mountains wrapt in storm,
On Andes' heights he shrouds his awful form;
On Chimborazo's summits treads sublime,   325
Measuring in lofty thought the march of Time;
Sudden he calls: "'Tis now the hour!" he cries,
Spreads his broad hand, and bids the nations rise.
La Plata hears amidst her torrents' roar;
Potosi hears it, as she digs the ore[19]:   330
Ardent, the Genius fans the noble strife,
And pours through feeble souls a higher life,
Shouts to the mingled tribes from sea to sea,
And swears—Thy world, Columbus, shall be free.

—1812

Washing-Day

"... And their voice,
Turning again towards childish treble, pipes
And whistles in its sound."[1]

---

19. Chimborazo Mountain, Ecuador. La Plata, Argentina, and Potosi, Bolivia, were both famous for silver.

1. William Shakespeare, *As You Like It* (1623), 2.7.161–163.

The Muses are turned gossips; they have lost
The buskined step, and clear, high-sounding phrase,
Language of gods. Come, then, domestic Muse,
In slipshod measure loosely prattling on
Of farm or orchard, pleasant curds and cream,   5
Or drowning flies, or shoe lost in the mire
By little whimpering boy, with rueful face;
Come, Muse, and sing the dreaded Washing-day.
Ye who beneath the yoke of wedlock bend,
With bowed soul, full well ye ken the day   10
Which week, smooth sliding after week, brings on
Too soon;—for to that day nor peace belongs,
Nor comfort; ere the first gray streak of dawn,
The red-armed washers come and chase repose.
Nor pleasant smile, nor quaint device of mirth,   15
E'er visited that day: the very cat,
From the wet kitchen's scared and reeking hearth,
Visits the parlor,—an unwonted guest.
The silent breakfast-meal is soon despatched;
Uninterrupted, save by anxious looks   20
Cast at the lowering sky, if sky should lower.
From that last evil, O preserve us, heavens!
For should the skies pour down, adieu to all
Remains of quiet: then expect to hear
Of sad disasters,—dirt and gravel stains   25
Hard to efface, and loaded lines at once
Snapped short,—and linen-horse by dog thrown down,
And all the petty miseries of life.
Saints have been calm while stretched upon the rack,
And Guatimozin smiled on burning coals[2];   30
But never yet did housewife notable
Greet with a smile a rainy washing-day.
But grant the welkin fair, require not thou
Who call'st thyself perchance the master there,
Or study swept, or nicely dusted coat,   35
Or usual 'tendance,—ask not, indiscreet,
Thy stockings mended, though the yawning rents
Gape wide as Erebus[3]; nor hope to find
Some snug recess impervious: shouldst thou try
The 'customed garden-walks, thine eyes shall rue   40
The budding fragrance of thy tender shrubs,
Myrtle or rose, all crushed beneath the weight
Of coarse checked apron,—with impatient hand
Twitched off when showers impend: or crossing lines

---

2. Cuauhtémoc, Aztec emperor tortured by Hernán Cortés, the Spanish conquistador, in 1525.   3. The passage to Hades, the underworld of Greek mythology.

Shall mar thy musings, as the wet, cold sheet   45
Flaps in thy face abrupt. Woe to the friend
Whose evil stars have urged him forth to claim
On such a day the hospitable rites!
Looks, blank at best, and stinted courtesy,
Shall he receive. Vainly he feeds his hopes   50
With dinner of roast chicken, savory pie,
Or tart, or pudding:—pudding he nor tart
That day shall eat; nor, though the husband try,
Mending what can't be helped, to kindle mirth
From cheer deficient, shall his consort's brow   55
Clear up propitious: the unlucky guest
In silence dines, and early slinks away.
I well remember, when a child, the awe
This day struck into me; for then the maids,
I scarce knew why, looked cross, and drove me from them: 60
Nor soft caress could I obtain; nor hope
Usual indulgences; jelly or creams,
Relic of costly suppers, and set by
For me their petted one, or buttered toast,
When butter was forbid; or thrilling tale   65
Of ghost or witch or murder,—so I went
And sheltered me beside the parlor fire:
There my dear grandmother, eldest of forms,
Tended the little ones, and watched from harm,
Anxiously fond, though oft her spectacles   70
With elfin cunning hid, and oft the pins
Drawn from her ravelled stockings, might have soured
One less indulgent.—
At intervals my mother's voice was heard,
Urging despatch: briskly the work went on,   75
All hands employed to wash, to rinse, to wring,
To fold, and starch, and clap, and iron, and plait.
Then would I sit me down, and ponder much
Why washings were. Sometimes through hollow bowl
Of pipe amused we blew, and sent aloft   80
The floating bubbles; little dreaming then
To see, Montgolfier,[4] thy silken ball
Ride buoyant through the clouds,—so near approach
The sports of children and the toils of men.
Earth, air, and sky, and ocean hath its bubbles,   85
And verse is one of them,—this most of all.

—1797

---

4. The Montgolfier brothers launched the first successful hot air balloon in France in 1783.

The Hill of Science, a Vision.

In that season of the year when the serenity of the sky, the various fruits which cover the ground, the discoloured foliage of the trees, and all the sweet, but fading graces of inspiring autumn, open the mind to benevolence, and dispose it for contemplation; I was wandering in a beautiful and romantic country, till curiosity began to give way to weariness; and I sat me down on the fragment of a rock overgrown with moss, where the rustling of the falling leaves, the dashing of waters, and the hum of the distant city, soothed my mind into the most perfect tranquility, and sleep insensibly stole upon me, as I was indulging the agreeable reveries which the objects around me naturally inspired.

I immediately found myself in a vast extended plain, in the middle of which arose a mountain higher than I had before any conception of. It was covered with a multitude of people, chiefly youth; many of whom pressed forwards with the liveliest expression of ardor in their countenance, though the way was in many places steep and difficult. I observed, that those who had but just begun to climb the hill, thought themselves not far from the top; but as they proceeded, new hills were continually rising to their view, and the summit of the highest they could before discern, seemed but the foot of another, till the mountain at length appeared to lose itself in the clouds. As I was gazing on these things with astonishment, my good genius suddenly appeared. The mountain before thee, said he, is the HILL OF SCIENCE. On the top is the temple of Truth, whose head is above the clouds, and a veil of pure light covers her face. Observe the progress of her votaries; be silent, and attentive.

I saw that the only regular approach to the mountain was by a gate, called the gate of languages. It was kept by a woman of a pensive and thoughtful appearance, whose lips were continually moving, as though she repeated something to herself. Her name was MEMORY. On entering this first enclosure, I was stunned with a confused murmur of jarring voices, and dissonant sounds; which increased upon me to such a degree, that I was utterly confounded, and could compare the noise to nothing but the confusion of tongues at Babel. The road was also rough and stony; and rendered more difficult by heaps of rubbish, continually tumbled down from the higher parts of the mountain; and broken ruins of ancient buildings, which the travellers were obliged to climb over at every step; insomuch that many, disgusted with so rough a beginning, turned back and attempted the mountain no more: while others, having conquered this difficulty, had no spirits to ascend further, and sitting down on some fragment of the rubbish, harangued the multitude below with the greatest marks of importance and self-complacency.

About half way up the hill, I observed on each side of the path a thick forest covered with continual fogs, and cut out into labyrinths, cross alleys, and serpentine walks, entangled with thorns and briars. This was called the wood of error: and I heard the voices of many who were lost up and down in it, calling to one another, and endeavouring in vain to extricate themselves. The trees in many places shot their boughs over the path, and a thick mist often rested on it; yet never so much but that it was discernable by the light which beamed from the countenance of truth.

In the pleasantest part of the mountain were placed the bowers of the Muses, whose office it was to cheer the spirits of the travellers, and encourage their fainting steps with songs from their divine harps. Not far from hence were the fields of fiction, filled with a variety of wild flowers springing up in the greatest luxuriance, of richer scents and brighter colours than I had observed in any other climate. And near them was the *dark walk of allegory*, so artificially shaded, that the light at noon-day was never stronger than that of a bright moon-shine. This gave it a pleasingly romantic air for those who delighted in contemplation. The paths and alleys were perplexed with intricate windings, and were all terminated with the statue of a Grace, a Virtue, or a Muse.

After I had observed these things, I turned my eye towards the multitudes who were climbing the steep ascent, and observed amongst them a youth of a lively look, a piercing eye, and something fiery and irregular in all his motions. His name was GENIUS. He darted like an eagle up the mountain, and left his companions gazing after him with envy and admiration: but his progress was unequal, and interrupted by a thousand caprices. When Pleasure warbled in the valley he mingled in her train. When Pride beckoned towards the precipice he ventured to the tottering edge. He delighted in devious and untried paths; and made so many excursions from the road that his feebler companions often outstripped him. I observed that the Muses beheld him with partiality; but Truth often frowned and turned aside her face. While Genius was thus wasting his strength in excentric flights, I saw a person of a very different appearance named APPLICATION. He crept along with a slow and unremitting pace, his eyes fixed on the top of the mountain, patiently removing every stone that obstructed his way, till he saw most of those below him who had at first derided his slow and toilsome progress. Indeed there were few who ascended the hill with equal and uninterrupted steadiness; for beside the difficulties of the way, they were continually sollicited to turn aside by a numerous crowd of Appetites, Passions, and Pleasures, whose importunity, when they had once complied with, they became less and less able to resist; and though they often returned to the path, the asperities of the road were more severely felt, the hill appeared more steep and rugged, the fruits which were wholesome and refreshing seemed harsh and ill-tasted, their sight grew dim, and their feet tript at every little obstruction.

I saw, with some surprize, that the Muses, whose business was to cheer and encourage those who were toiling up the ascent, would often sing in the bowers of Pleasure, and accompany those who were enticed away at the call of the Passions. They accompanied them, however, but a little way, and always forsook them when they lost sight of the hill. The tyrants then doubled their chains upon the unhappy captives, and led them away without resistance to the cells of Ignorance, or the mansions of Misery. Amongst the unnumerable seducers, who were endeavouring to draw away the votaries of Truth from the path of Science, there was one, so little formidable in her appearance, and so gentle and languid in her attempts, that I should scarcely have taken notice of her, but for the numbers she had imperceptibly loaded with her chains. INDOLENCE (for so she was called) far from proceeding to open hostilities, did not attempt to turn their feet out of the path, but contented herself with retarding their progress; and the purpose she could not force them to abandon, she persuaded them to delay. Her touch had a power like that of the Torpedo,[1] which withered the strength of those who came within its influence. Her unhappy captives still turned their faces towards the temple, and always hoped to arrive there; but the ground seemed to slide from beneath their feet, and they found themselves at the bottom before they suspected they had changed their place. The placid serenity which at first appeared in their countenance, changed by degrees into a melancholy languor, which was tinged with deeper and deeper gloom as they glided down the *stream of insignificance*; a dark and sluggish water, which is curled by no breeze, and

---

1. A sting ray or electric ray.

enlivened by no murmur, till it falls into a dead sea, where the startled passengers are awakened by the shock, and the next moment buried in the gulph of oblivion.

Of all the unhappy deserters from the paths of Science, none seemed less able to return than the followers of Indolence. The captives of Appetite and Passion could often seize the moment when their tyrants were languid or asleep to escape from their enchantment; but the dominion of Indolence was constant and unremitted, and seldom resisted till resistance was in vain.

After contemplating these things, I turned my eyes towards the top of the mountain, where the air was always pure and exhilarating, the path shaded with laurels and other ever-greens, and the effulgence which beamed from the face of the Goddess seemed to shed a glory round her votaries. Happy, said I, are they who are permitted to ascend the mountain!—but while I was pronouncing this exclamation with uncommon ardour, I saw standing beside me a form of diviner features and a more benign radiance. Happier, said she, are those whom VIRTUE conducts to the mansions of Content! What, said I, does Virtue then reside in the vale? I am found, said she, in the vale, and I illuminate the mountain. I cheer the cottager at his toil, and inspire the sage at his meditation. I mingle in the crowd of cities, and bless the hermit in his cell. I have a temple in every heart that owns my influence; and to him that wishes for me I am already present. Science may raise you to eminence, but I alone can guide you to felicity! While the Goddess was thus speaking, I stretched out my arms towards her with a vehemence which broke my slumbers. The chill dews were falling around me, and the shades of evening stretched over the landscape. I hastened homeward, and resigned the night to silence and meditation.

—1775

The Female Choice. A Tale.

A YOUNG girl, having fatigued herself one hot day with running about the garden, sat herself down in a pleasant arbour, where she presently fell asleep. During her slumber, two female figures presented themselves before her. One was loosely habited in a thin robe of pink with light green trimmings. Her sash of silver gauze flowed to the ground. Her fair hair fell in ringlets down her neck; and her head-dress consisted of artificial flowers interwoven with feathers. She held in one hand a ball-ticket, and in the other a fancy dress all covered with spangles and knots of gay riband. She advanced smiling to the girl, and with a familiar air thus addressed her:—

My dearest Melissa, I am a kind genius, who have watched you from your birth, and have joyfully beheld all your beauties expand, till at length they have rendered you a companion worthy of me. See what I have brought you. This dress and this ticket will give you free access to all the ravishing delights of my palace. With me you will pass your days in a perpetual round of ever-varying amusements. Like the gay butterfly, you will have no other business than to flutter from flower to flower, and spread your charms before admiring spectators. No restraints, no toils, no dull tasks are to be found within my happy domains. All is pleasure, life, and good humour. Come, then, my dear! Let me put on you this dress, which will make you quite enchanting; and away, away, with me!

Melissa felt a strong inclination to comply with the call of this inviting nymph; but first she thought it would be prudent at least to ask her name.

My name, said she, is DISSIPATION.

The other female then advanced. She was clothed in a close habit of brown stuff, simply relieved with white. She wore her smooth hair under a plain cap. Her whole person was perfectly neat and clean. Her look was serious, but satisfied; and her air was staid and composed. She held in one hand a distaff[1]; on the opposite arm hung a work-basket; and the girdle round her waist was garnished with scissars, knitting needles, reels, and other implements of female labour. A bunch of keys hung at her side. She thus accosted the sleeping girl:—

Melissa, I am the genius who have ever been the friend and companion of your mother; and I now offer my protection to you. I have no allurements to tempt you with, like those of my gay rival. Instead of spending all your time in amusements, if you enter yourself of my train, you must rise early, and pass the long day in a variety of employments, some of them difficult, some laborious, and all requiring some exertion of body or mind. You must dress plainly, live mostly at home, and aim at being useful rather than shining. But in return I will ensure you content, even spirits, self-approbation, and the esteem of all who thoroughly know you. If these offers appear to your young mind less inviting than those of my rival, be assured, however, that they are more real. She has promised much more than she can ever make good. Perpetual pleasures are no more in the power of Dissipation, than of Vice or Folly, to bestow. Her delights quickly pall, and are inevitably succeeded by languor and disgust. She appears to you under a disguise, and what you see is not her real face. For myself, I shall never seem to you less amiable than I now do, but on the contrary, you will like me better and better. If I look grave to you now, you will hear me sing at my work; and when work is over, I can dance too. But I have said enough. It is time for you to choose whom you will follow, and upon that choice all your happiness depends. If you would know my name, it is HOUSEWIFERY.

Melissa heard her with more attention than delight; and though overawed by her manner, she could not help turning again to take another look at the first speaker. She beheld her still offering her presents with so bewitching an air, that she felt it scarcely possible to resist; when, by a lucky accident, the mask, with which Dissipation's face was so artfully covered, fell off. As soon as Melissa beheld, instead of the smiling features of youth and cheerfulness, a countenance wan and ghastly with sickness, and soured by fretfulness, she turned away with horror, and gave her hand unreluctantly to her sober and sincere companion.

—1778

Olaudah Equiano
c. 1745–1797

Anthologized separately in both American *and* British literature texts, Olaudah Equiano's narrative of his life, first published in 1789, is the perfect example of a work that defies canonization in a system based on classification by an author's nationality. Is Equiano an African writer, an Afro-Caribbean writer, an African American writer, or an Anglo-African writer? Present-

---

1. A forked stick used for spinning thread, often used as a symbol of women.

day scholar Paul Gilroy settles the matter when he accurately describes Equiano as a writer of the "black Atlantic." Gilroy does not classify Equiano according to a single nation's literary tradition but groups him with other writers of African descent who lived and traveled around the Atlantic Rim. The full title of Equiano's autobiography speaks to its multicultural roots: *The Interesting Narrative of the Life of Olaudah Equiano, or Gustavus Vassa, the African.* It is important to him that he retain the name given to him by his parents of the Ibo tribe of the Isseke (or Essaka) village in Nigeria, preserving his bond to his country and culture from which he was kidnapped and sold into slavery as a child of ten or eleven.

In 1789, Equiano published his autobiography, which would go through twenty-five printings before his death, including publication in America, Germany, Ireland, the Netherlands, Russia, and Scotland. After promoting the book in England and Ireland, where he sold nearly two thousand copies, he lived out the rest of his days in England, marrying an Englishwoman, Susanna Cullen, in 1792. Over the next three years they had two daughters, Anna Maria and Johanna. A few months after Johanna's birth in 1795, Susanna Cullen Vassa died, and Equiano died in London two years later.

Equiano's book lived on after his death, going through another fourteen printings by 1837, and was embraced by abolitionists on both sides of the Atlantic. He offers his life's story also as a testimony to the potential of people of African descent to participate fully in the European- and American-controlled worlds of business, trade, the military, science, exploration, classical music, professional writing, and theology. At the same time, he attacks the economic arguments that supported slavery and denied Africans access to literacy and advancement in the Atlantic Rim colonies and countries to which they were taken by force. In the *Narrative*, he is quick to point out the differences between slavery as it existed among African tribes and the cruel institution of the Atlantic Rim that trafficked in innocent human lives and promulgated race-based discrimination, torture, and rape in the name of financial profit.

Equiano's spiritual autobiography focuses closely on his learning to read and write as well as on his attainment of earthly and spiritual liberation from bondage. In doing so, it issues a challenge to the so-called Christians who support this institution based on false notions of European superiority. Equiano's *Narrative* documents a voyage of external and internal discovery; in addition to experimenting with Anglicanism, Judaism, the Muslim faith, and Methodism, Equiano also navigates the earthly realm, traveling to the Americas, the Caribbean Islands, Turkey, the North Pole, Italy, Spain, and Britain. He records the prejudice and abuse he encounters as a slave and a "free" black man in a world dominated by white supremacists, showing examples of the dehumanization of slaves and masters, revealing the latter as cruel, heartless hypocrites who disgrace the love they profess to practice as Christians. Equiano's text uses the language of the Enlightenment to show the dehumanization that underwrites a humanist movement and the lack of sense in what was deemed the age of sensibility.

from The Interesting Narrative of the Life of Olaudah Equiano, or Gustavus Vassa, the African

The first object that saluted my eyes when I arrived on the coast was the sea, and a slave ship, which was then riding at anchor, and waiting for its cargo. These filled me with astonishment, that was soon converted into terror, which I am yet at a loss to describe, and much more the then feelings of my mind when I was carried on board. I was immediately handled and tossed up to see if I was sound, by some of the crew; and I was now persuaded that I had got into a world of bad spirits, and that they were going to kill me. Their complexions too, differing so much from ours, their long hair, and the language they spoke, which was very different from any I had ever heard, united to confirm me in this belief. Indeed such were the horrors of my views and fears at the moment, that if ten thousand worlds had been my own, I would have freely parted with them all to have exchanged my condition with the meanest slave in my own country. When I looked round the ship too, and saw a large furnace or copper boiling and a multitude of black people, of every description, chained together, every one of their countenances expressing dejection and sorrow, I no longer doubted of my fate; and, quite overpowered with horror and anguish, I fell motionless on the deck, and fainted. When I recovered a little, I found some black people about me, who I believed were some of those who brought me on board, and had been receiving their pay: they talked to me in order to cheer me, but all in vain. I asked them if we were not to be eaten by those white men with horrible looks, red faces, and long hair. They told me I was not: and one of the crew brought me a small portion of spirituous liquor in a wine glass; but, being afraid of him, I would not take it out of his hand. One of the blacks therefore took it from him and gave it to me, and I took a little down my palate, which, instead of reviving me, as they thought it would, threw me into the greatest consternation at the strange feeling it produced, having never tasted any such liquor before.

Soon after this the blacks who brought me on board went off, and left me abandoned to despair. I now saw myself deprived of all chance of returning to my native country, or even the least glimpse of gaining the shore, which I now considered as friendly; and I even wished for my former slavery, in preference to my present situation, which was filled with horrors of every kind, still heightened by my ignorance of what I was to undergo. I was not long suffered to indulge my grief. I was soon put down under the decks, and there I received such a salutation in my nostrils as I had never experienced in my life: so that, with the loathsomeness of the stench, and with my crying together, I became so sick and low that I was not able to eat, nor had I the least desire to taste any thing. I now wished for the last friend, death, to relieve me; but soon, to my grief, two of the white men offered me eatables; and, on my refusing to eat, one of them held me fast by the hands, and laid me across, I think, the windlass, and tied my feet, while the other flogged me severely. I had never experienced any thing of this kind before, and although, not being used to the water, I naturally feared that element the first time I saw it, yet nevertheless, could I have got over the nettings, I would have jumped over the side, but I could not; and besides the crew used to watch us very closely, who were not chained down to the decks, lest we should leap into the water. I have seen some of these poor African prisoners most severely cut for attempting to do so, and hourly whipped for not eating. This indeed was often the case with myself. In a little time after, amongst the poor chained men, I found some of my own nation, which in a small degree gave ease to my mind. I inquired of these what was to be done with us. They gave me to understand we were to be carried to these white people's country to work for them. I was then a little revived, and thought if it were no worse than working, my situation was not so desperate. But still I feared I should be put to death, the white people looked and acted, as I thought, in so savage a manner; for I had never seen among any people such instances of brutal cruelty: and this is not only shewn towards us blacks, but also to some of the whites themselves. One white man in particular I saw, when we were permitted to be on deck, flogged so unmercifully with a large rope near the foremast, that he died in consequence of it; and they tossed him over the side as they would have done a brute. This made me fear these people the more; and I expected nothing less than to be treated in the same manner. I could not help expressing my fearful apprehensions to some of my countrymen; I asked them if these people had no country, but lived in this hollow place, the ship. They told me they did not, but came from a distant one. "Then," said I, "how comes it, that in all our country we never heard of them?" They told me, because they lived so very far off. I then asked, where their women were: had they any like themselves. I was told they had. "And why," said I, "do we not see them?" They answered, because they were left behind. I asked how the vessel could go. They told me they could not tell; but that there was cloth put upon the masts by the help of the ropes I saw, and then the vessel went on; and the white men had some spell or magic they put in the water, when they liked, in order to stop the vessel. I was exceedingly amazed at this account, and really thought they were spirits. I therefore wished much to be from amongst them, for I expected they would sacrifice me; but my wishes were in vain, for we were so quartered that it was impossible for any of us to make our escape. . . .[1]

One morning, when I got upon deck, I perceived it covered over with the snow that fell overnight. As I had never seen any thing of the kind before, I thought it was salt; so I immediately ran down to the mate and desired him, as well as I could, to come and see how somebody in the night had thrown salt all over the deck. He, knowing what it was, desired me to bring some of it down to him; accordingly I took up a handful of it, which I found very cold indeed; and when I brought it to him he desired me to taste it. I did so, and was surprised above measure. I then asked him what it was; he told me it was snow; but I could not by any means understand him. He asked me if we had no such thing in our country; and I told him "No." I then asked him the use of it, and who made it; he told me a great man in the heavens, called God: but here again I was to all intents and purposes at a loss to understand him; and the more so, when a little after I saw the air filled with it, in a heavy shower, which fell down on the same day.

After this I went to church; and having never been at such a place before, I was again amazed at seeing and hearing the service. I asked all I could about it; and they gave me to understand it was "worshiping God, who made us and all things." I was still at a loss, and soon got into an endless field of inquiries, as well as I was able to speak and ask about things. However, my dear little friend Dick used to be my best interpreter; for I could make free with him and he always instructed me with pleasure. And from what I could understand by him of this God, and in seeing that these white people did not sell one another as we did, I was much pleased: and in this I thought they were much happier than we Africans. I was astonished at the wisdom of the white people in all things which I beheld; but I was greatly amazed at their not sacrificing, not making any offerings, and at their eating with unwashen hands, and touching of the dead. I also could not help remarking the particular slenderness of their women, which I did not at first like, and I thought them not so modest and shamefaced as the African women.

I had often seen my master Dick employed in reading; and I had a great curiosity to talk to the books, as I thought they did; and so to learn how all things had a

---

1. After being taken first to Barbados, then to Virginia, Equiano is purchased by a lieutenant in the British Royal Navy, Michael Henry Pascal.

beginning. For that purpose I have often taken up a book and talked to it, and then put my ears to it, when alone, in hopes it would answer me; and I have been very much concerned when I found it remaining silent. . . . .

There was also one Daniel Queen, about forty years of age, a man very well educated, who messed[2] with me on board this ship, and he likewise dressed and attended the captain. Fortunately this man soon became very much attached to me, and took great pains to instruct me in many things. He taught me to shave, and dress hair a little, and also to read in the Bible, explaining many passages to me, which I did not comprehend. I was wonderfully surprised to see the laws and rules of my own country written almost exactly here; a circumstance which, I believe, tended to impress our manners and customs more deeply on my memory. I used to tell him of this resemblance, and many a time we have sat up the whole night together at this employment. In short, he was like a father to me; and some used even to call me after his name: they also styled me "the black Christian." Indeed I almost loved him with the affection of a son. Many things I have denied myself, that he might have them; and when I used to play at marbles or any other game, and won a few halfpence, or got some money for shaving any one, I used to buy him a little sugar or tobacco, as far as my stock of money would go. He used to say that he and I never should part, and that when our ship was paid off, as I was free as himself or any other man on board, he would instruct me in his business, by which I might gain a good livelihood. This gave me new life and spirits; and my heart burned within me, while I thought the time long till I obtained my freedom. For though my master had not promised it to me, yet, besides the assurances I had often received that he had no right to detain me, he always treated me with the greatest kindness, and reposed in me an unbounded confidence. He even paid attention to my morals, and would never suffer me to deceive him, or tell lies, of which he used to tell me the consequences; and that if I did so, God would not love me. So that from all this tenderness I had never once supposed, in all my dreams of freedom, that he would think of detaining me any longer than I wished.

In pursuance of our orders we sailed from Portsmouth for the Thames, and arrived at Deptford the 10th of December, where we cast anchor just as it was high water. The ship was up about half an hour, when my master ordered the barge to be manned; and, all in an instant, without having before given me the least reason to suspect any thing of the matter, he forced me into the barge, saying, I was going to leave him, but he would take care that I did not. I was so struck with the unexpectedness of this proceeding, that for some time I did not make a reply, only I made an offer to go for my books and chest of clothes, but he swore I should not move out of his sight; and if I did, he would cut my throat, at the same time taking out his hanger.[3] I told him that I was free, and he could not by law serve me so. But this only enraged him the more; and he continued to swear, and said he would soon let me know whether he would or not, and at that instant sprung himself into the barge, from the ship, to the astonishment and sorrow of all on board.

The tide, rather unluckily for me, had just turned downward, so that we quickly fell down the river along with it, till we came among some outwardbound West Indiamen; for he was resolved to put me on board the first vessel he could get to receive me. The boat's crew, who pulled against their will, became quite faint at different

---

2. Ate.   3. Sword.

times, and would have gone ashore, but he would not let them. Some of them strove then to cheer me, and told me he could not sell me, and that they would stand by me, which revived me a little, and I still entertained hopes; for as they pulled me along he asked some vessels to receive me, and they refused.

But, just as we had got a little below Gravesend, we came alongside of a ship going away the next tide for the West-Indies; her name was the Charming Sally, Captain James Doran. My master went on board and agreed with him for me; and in little time I was sent for into the cabin. When I came there Captain Doran asked me if I knew him; I answered I did not: "Then," said he, "you are now my slave." I told him my master could not sell me to him nor to any one else. "Why," said he, "did not your master buy you?" I confessed he did. "But I have served him," said I, "many years, and he has taken all my wages and prize-money, for I only got one sixpence during the war. Besides this I have been baptized; and, by the laws of the land, no man has a right to sell me." And I added, that I had heard a lawyer, and others, at different times tell my master so. They both then said, that those people who told me so, were not my friends: but I replied—it was very extraordinary that other people did not know the law as well as they. Upon this, Captain Doran said I talked too much English, and if I did not behave myself well and be quiet, he had a method on board to make me. I was too well convinced of his power over me to doubt what he said; and my former sufferings in the slave-ship presenting themselves to my mind, the recollection of them made me shudder. However, before I retired I told them, that as I could not get any right among men here, I hoped I should hereafter in Heaven, and I immediately left the cabin, filled with resentment and sorrow.

The only coat I had with me my master took away with him, and said, "if your prize-money had been £10,000, I had a right to it all, and would have taken it." I had about nine guineas, which, during my long sea-faring life, I had scraped together from trifling perquisites and little ventures; and I hid it that instant, lest my master should take that from me likewise, still hoping that, by some means or other, I should make my escape to the shore. Indeed some of my old shipmates told me not to despair, for they would get me back again; and that, as soon as they could get their pay, they would immediately come to Portsmouth to me, where this ship was going. But, alas, all my hopes were baffled, and the hour of my deliverance was, as yet, far off. My master, having soon concluded his bargain with the captain, came out of the cabin, and he and his people got into the boat and put off. I followed them with aching eyes as long as I could, and when they were out of sight I threw myself on the deck, with a heart ready to burst with sorrow and anguish. . . .

I have since often seen in Jamaica and other islands, free men, whom I have known in America, thus villainously trepanned and kept in bondage. I have heard of two similar practices even in Philadelphia: and were it not for the benevolence of the Quakers in that city, many of the sable race, who now breathe the air of liberty, would, I believe, be groaning under some planter's chains. These things opened my mind to a new scene of horror, to which I had been before a stranger. Hitherto I had thought only slavery dreadful; but the state of a free negro appeared to me now equally so at least, and in some respects even worse; for they live in constant alarm for their liberty, which is but nominal; and they are universally insulted and plundered without the possibility of redress; such being the equity of the West-Indian laws, that no free negro's evidence will be admitted in their courts of justice. . . .

I determined to make every exertion to obtain my freedom, and to return to Old England. For this purpose I thought a knowledge of Navigation might be of use to me; for, though I did not intend to run away unless I should be ill used, yet, in such a case, if I understood navigation, I might attempt my escape in our sloop, which was one of the swiftest sailing vessels in the West-Indies, and I could be at no loss for hands to join me. Had I made this attempt, I had intended to go in her to England; but this, as I said, was only to be in the event of my meeting with any ill usage. I therefore employed the mate of our vessel to teach me Navigation, for which I agreed to give him twenty-four dollars, and actually paid him part of the money down; though when the captain, some time after, came to know that the mate was to have such a sum for teaching me, he rebuked him, and said it was a shame for him to take any money from me. However, my progress in this useful art was much retarded by the constancy of our work.

Had I wished to run away I did not want opportunities, which frequently presented themselves; and particularly at one time, soon after this. When we were at the island of Guadaloupe there was a large fleet of merchantmen bound for Old France; and seamen then being very scarce, they gave from fifteen to twenty pounds a man for the run. Our mate and all the white sailors left our vessel on this account, and went aboard of the French ships. They would have had me also to go with them, for they regarded me, and swore to protect me, if I would go: and, as the fleet was to sail the next day, I really believe I could have got safe to Europe at that time. However, as my master was kind, I would not attempt to leave him; still remembering the old maxim, that *honesty is the best policy*, I suffered them to go without me. Indeed my captain was much afraid of my leaving him and the vessel at that time, as I had so fair an opportunity: but, I thank God, this fidelity of mine turned out much to my advantage hereafter, when I did not in the least think of it; and made me so much in favour with the captain, that he used now and then to teach me some parts of Navigation himself. But some of our passengers, and others, seeing this, found much fault with him for it, saying it was a very dangerous thing to let a negro know Navigation; and thus I was hindered again in my pursuits. . . .

When we had unladen the vessel, and I had sold my venture, finding myself master of about forty-seven pounds, I consulted my true friend, the Captain, how I should proceed in offering my master the money for my freedom. He told me to come on a certain morning, when he and my master would be at breakfast together. Accordingly, on that morning I went, and met the Captain there, as he had appointed. When I went in I made my obeisance to my master, and with my money in my hand, and many fears in my heart, I prayed him to be as good as his offer to me, when he was pleased to promise me my freedom as soon as I could purchase it. This speech seemed to confound him; he began to recoil; and my heart that instant sunk within me. "What," said he, "give you your freedom? Why, where did you get the money? Have you got forty pounds sterling?" "Yes, sir," I answered. "How did you get it?" replied he. I told him, "very honestly." The Captain then said he knew I got the money very honestly and with much industry, and that I was particularly careful. On which my master replied, I got money much faster than he did; and said he would not have made me the promise which he did, had he thought I should have got the money so soon. "Come, come," said my worthy Captain, clapping my master on the back, "Come, Robert, (which was his name) I think you must let him have his freedom. You have laid your money out very well; you have received good interest for it all this time, and here is now the principal at last. I know GUSTAVUS has earned you more than a hundred a year, and he will still save you money, as he will not leave you. Come, Robert, take the money." My master then said, he would not be worse than his promise; and, taking the money, told me to go to the Secretary at the Register Office, and get my manumission drawn up.

These words of my master were like a voice from heaven to me: in an instant all my trepidation was turned into unutterable bliss, and I most reverently bowed myself with gratitude, unable to express my feelings, but by the overflowing of my eyes, and a heart replete with thanks to God; while my true and worthy friend, the Captain, congratulated us both with a peculiar degree of heartfelt pleasure. As soon as the first transports of my joy were over, and that I had expressed my thanks to these my worthy friends in the best manner I was able, I rose with a heart full of affection and reverence, and left the room, in order to obey my master's joyful mandate of going to the Register Office. As I was leaving the house I called to mind the words of the Psalmist, in the 126th Psalm, and like him, "I glorified God in my heart, in whom I trusted." These words had been impressed on my mind from the very day I was forced from Deptford to the present hour, and I now saw them, as I thought, fulfilled and verified.

My imagination was all rapture as I flew to the Register Office; and in this respect, like the apostle Peter (whose deliverance from prison was so sudden and extraordinary, that he thought he was in a vision) I could scarcely believe I was awake. Heavens! who could do justice to my feelings at this moment? Not conquering heroes themselves, in the midst of a triumph—Not the tender mother who has just regained her long-lost infant, and presses it to her heart—Not the weary, hungry mariner, at the sight of the desired friendly port—Not the lover, when he once more embraces his beloved mistress, after she has been ravished from his arms!—All within my breast was tumult, wildness, and delirium! My feet scarcely touched the ground; for they were winged with joy, and, like Elijah, as he rose to Heaven, they "were with lightning sped as I went on." Every one I met I told of my happiness, and blazed about the virtue of my amiable master and Captain. . . .

In short, the fair as well as black people immediately styled me by a new appellation,—to me the most desirable in the world,—which was "Freeman," and, at the dances I gave, my Georgia superfine blue clothes made no indifferent appearance, as I thought. Some of the sable females, who formerly stood aloof, now began to relax and appear less coy; but my heart was still fixed on London, where I hoped to be ere long. So that my worthy Captain, and his owner, my late master, finding that the bent of my mind was towards London, said to me, "We hope you won't leave us, but that you will still be with the vessels." Here gratitude bowed me down; and none but the generous mind can judge of my feelings, struggling between inclination and duty. However, notwithstanding my wish to be in London, I obediently answered my benefactors that I would go in the vessel, and not leave them; and from that day I was entered on board as an able-bodied seaman, at thirty-six shillings per month, besides what perquisites I could make. My intention was to make a voyage or two, entirely to please these my honoured patrons; but I determined that the year following, if it pleased God, I would see Old England once more, and surprise my old master, Captain Pascal, who was hourly in my mind: for I still loved him, notwithstanding his usage to me, and I pleased myself with thinking of what he would say when he saw what the Lord had done for me in so short a time, instead of being, as he might perhaps suppose, under the cruel yoke of some planter.

—1789

Philip Morin Freneau
1752–1832

Philip Freneau's parents, successful New Yorkers of French Huguenot and Scotch Presbyterian descent, raised their bookish son with the expectation that he would join the ministry. Admitted at sixteen to what is now Princeton University, he roomed with James Madison, and the two remained friends for the rest of their lives. In collaboration with author and editor Hugh Henry Brackenridge, Freneau wrote and delivered commencement verses titled, "A Poem, on the Rising Glory of America" (1771). Despite his success at college, he soon rejected his training in Calvinist theology. Three years after graduation, he wrote in his journal that "the study of Divinity [is] in fact the study of Nothing!—and the profession of a priest is little better than that of a slothful Blockhead." Abandoning his career plans, Freneau spent two years as a common sailor in the Caribbean. When the Revolutionary War began, he returned to the colonies, where he joined the New Jersey militia and worked as a crewmember on blockade-running privateers. When his ship, the *Aurora*, was captured in 1780, Freneau was imprisoned on board the *Scorpion* in New York harbor, where he nearly died of starvation. He told his story in a bitterly anti-British poem, composed in heroic couplets (two rhyming lines of iambic pentameter), "The British Prison-Ship" (1781). For the rest of the war, he dedicated himself to writing verse that adapted the neoclassical tradition of Alexander Pope and Thomas Gray to the rhetorical demands of revolutionary republicanism. His many patriotic works, with titles like "On the Memorable Victory Obtained by the Gallant Captain Paul Jones of the *Good Man Richard* over the *Seraphis*," appeared either as broadside sheets that sold for a few pennies in the streets or in Brackenridge's *United States Magazine* and Francis Bailey's *Freeman's Journal*.

In 1791, Thomas Jefferson gave Freneau a position as a translator for the State Department. Freneau returned the favor by founding a republican political journal, *The National Gazette*, where he satirized his benefactor's opponents in the Hamiltonian Federalist party, provoking none other than George Washington to call him "that rascal Freneau." Despite his notoriety, he was frustrated in his desire to earn a living by his pen. At home in New Jersey, he served for a time as editor of the *Jersey Chronicle* and the *Time-Piece and Literary Companion*. But he was forced finally to return to sea, where he captained several merchant vessels, eventually dying poor and unknown in 1832.

Since called "the poet of the American revolution," Freneau was one of the most influential propagandists of the period. But for many decades, he has been regarded as a secondary or transitional figure because late Romantic and modern readers regarded the kind of polemical verse he wrote as inferior to lyric explorations of individual consciousness. Nevertheless, his bright voicings of radical faith in human perfectibility and natural law place him at the center of transatlantic Romanticism. Moreover, after national independence had been won, he applied his fearlessly rationalist mind and breezy style to a far broader range of subjects, including natural religion, Native American culture and its endangerment, and the beauty and solace of nature.

On the Emigration to America and Peopling the Western Country

To western woods, and lonely plains,
Palemon[1] from the crowd departs,

---

1. A conventional name for a young adventurer.

Where Nature's wildest genius reigns,
To tame the soil, and plant the arts—
What wonders there shall freedom show,
What mighty states successive grow!

From Europe's proud, despotic shores
Hither the stranger takes his way,
And in our new found world explores
A happier soil, a milder sway,
Where no proud despot holds him down,
No slaves insult him with a crown.

What charming scenes attract the eye,
On wild Ohio's savage stream!
There Nature reigns, whose works outvie
The boldest pattern art can frame;
There ages past have rolled away,
And forests bloomed but to decay.

From these fair plains, these rural seats,
So long concealed, so lately known,
The unsocial Indian far retreats,
To make some other clime his own,
Where other streams, less pleasing flow,
And darker forests round him grow.

Great sire of floods! whose varied wave
Through climes and countries takes its way,
To whom creating Nature gave
Ten thousand streams to swell thy sway!
No longer shall *they* useless prove,
Nor idly through the forests rove;

Nor longer shall your princely flood
From distant lakes be swelled in vain,
Nor longer through a darksome wood
Advance, unnoticed, to the main,
Far other ends, the heavens decree—
And commerce plans new freights for thee.

While virtue warms the generous breast,
There heaven-born freedom shall reside,
Nor shall the voice of war molest,
Nor Europe's all-aspiring pride—
There Reason shall new laws devise,
And order from confusion rise.

5

10

15

20

25

30

35

40

Forsaking kings and regal state,
With all their pomp and fancied bliss,
The traveler owns, convinced though late,   45
No realm so free, so blessed as this—
The east is half to slaves consigned,
Where kings and priests enchain the mind.

O come the time, and haste the day,
When man shall man no longer crush,   50
When Reason shall enforce her sway,
Nor these fair regions raise our blush,
Where still the *African* complains,
And mourns his yet unbroken chains.

Far brighter scenes a future age,   55
The muse predicts, these states will hail,
Whose genius may the world engage,
Whose deeds may over death prevail,
And happier systems bring to view,
Than all the eastern sages knew.   60

                                                —1785

Literary Importation

However we wrangled with Britain awhile
We think of her now in a different stile,
And many fine things we receive from her isle;
Among all the rest,
Some demon possessed   5
Our dealers in knowledge and sellers of sense
To have a good *bishop* imported from thence.

The words of *Sam Chandler*[1] were thought to be vain,
When he argued so often and proved it *so plain*
"That Satan must flourish till bishops should reign:"   10
Though he went to the wall
With his project and all,
Another bold Sammy,[2] in bishop's array,
Has got something more than his pains for his pay.

It seems we had spirit to humble a throne,   15
Have genius for science inferior to none,
But hardly encourage a plant of our own:
If a college be planned,

---

1. Advocate for the founding of an American Episcopacy, an administrative unit of the Church of England.   2. Bishop Samuel Seabury, first Anglican bishop in America.

'Tis all at a stand
'Till in Europe we send at a shameful expense,   20
To send us a book-worm to teach us some sense.

Can we never be thought to have learning or grace
Unless it be brought from that horrible place
Where tyranny reigns with her impudent face;
And popes and pretenders,   25
And sly faith-defenders
Have ever been hostile to reason and wit,
Enslaving a world that shall conquer them yet.

'Tis folly to fret at the picture I draw:
And I say what was said by a *Doctor Magraw*[3];   30
"If they give us their Bishops, they'll give us their law."
How that will agree
With such people as we,
Let us leave to the learned to reflect on awhile,
And say what they think in a handsomer stile.   35

—1788

The Wild Honey Suckle

Fair flower, that dost so comely grow,
Hid in this silent, dull retreat,
Untouched thy honied blossoms blow,
Unseen thy little branches greet:
    No roving foot shall crush thee here,   5
    No busy hand provoke a tear.

By Nature's self in white arrayed,
She bade thee shun the vulgar eye,
And planted here the guardian shade,
And sent soft waters murmuring by;   10
    Thus quietly thy summer goes,
    Thy days declining to repose.

Smit with those charms, that must decay,
I grieve to see your future doom;
They died—nor were those flowers more gay,   15
The flowers that did in Eden bloom;
    Unpitying frosts, and Autumn's power
    Shall leave no vestige of this flower.

---

3. [Freneau's note] A cynical Doctor of Physic, formerly of New York; a man, in his day, of considerable note in the political world.

From morning suns and evening dews
At first thy little being came:
If nothing once, you nothing lose,
For when you die you are the same;
    The space between, is but an hour,
    The frail duration of a flower.

—1786

The Indian Burying Ground

In spite of all the learned have said,
I still my old opinion keep;
The *posture*, that *we* give the dead,
Points out the soul's eternal sleep.

Not so the ancients of these lands—
The Indian, when from life released,
Again is seated with his friends,
And shares again the joyous feast.

His imaged birds, and painted bowl,
And venison, for a journey dressed,
Bespeak the nature of the soul,
ACTIVITY, that knows no rest.

His bow, for action ready bent,
And arrows, with a head of stone,
Can only mean that life is spent,
And not the old ideas gone.

Thou, stranger, that shalt come this way,
No fraud upon the dead commit—
Observe the swelling turf, and say
They do not *lie*, but here they *sit*.

Here still a lofty rock remains,
On which the curious eye may trace
(Now wasted, half, by wearing rains)
The fancies of a ruder race.

Here still an aged elm aspires,
Beneath whose far-projecting shade
(And which the shepherd still admires)
The children of the forest played!

There oft a restless Indian queen
(Pale *Shebah*, with her braided hair)

And many a barbarous form is seen
To chide the man that lingers there.

By midnight moons, o'er moistening dews;
In habit for the chase arrayed,
The hunter still the deer pursues,   35
The hunter and the deer, a shade.

And long shall timorous fancy see
The painted chief, and pointed spear,
And Reason's self shall bow the knee
To shadows and delusions here.   40

—1788

On Mr. Paine's Rights of Man

Thus briefly sketched the sacred RIGHTS OF MAN,
How inconsistent with the ROYAL PLAN!
Which for itself exclusive honour craves,
Where some are masters born, and millions slaves.
With what contempt must every eye look down   5
On that base, childish bauble called a *crown*,
The gilded bait, that lures the crowd, to come,
Bow down their necks, and meet a slavish doom;
The source of half the miseries men endure,
The quack that kills them, while it seems to cure.   10
     Roused by the REASON of his manly page,
Once more shall PAINE a listening world engage:
From Reason's source, a bold reform he brings,
In raising up *mankind*, he pulls down *kings*,
Who, source of discord, patrons of all wrong,   15
On blood and murder have been fed too long:
Hid from the world, and tutored to be base,
The curse, the scourge, the ruin of the race,
Their's was the task, a dull designing few,
To shackle beings that they scarcely knew,   20
Who made this globe the residence of slaves,
And built their thrones on systems formed by knaves
—Advance, bright years, to work their final fall,
And haste the period that shall crush them all.
     Who, that has read and scanned the historic page   25
But glows, at every line, with kindling rage,
To see by them the rights of men aspersed,
Freedom restrained, and Nature's law reversed,
Men, ranked with beasts, by monarchs *will'd* away,
And bound young fools, or madmen to obey: 30
Now driven to wars, and now oppressed at home,

Compelled in crowds o'er distant seas to roam,
From India's climes the plundered prize to bring
To glad the strumpet, or to glut the king.
    COLUMBIA,[1] hail! immortal be thy reign: 35
Without a king, we till the smiling plain;
Without a king, we trace the unbounded sea,
And traffic round the globe, through each degree;
Each foreign clime our honored flag reveres,
Which asks no monarch, to support the STARS: 40
Without a *king*, the laws maintain their sway,
While honor bids each generous heart obey.
Be ours the task the ambitious to restrain,
And this great lesson teach—that kings are vain;
That warring realms to certain ruin haste,   45
That kings subsist by war, and wars are waste:
So shall our nation, formed on Virtue's plan,
Remain the guardian of the Rights of Man,
A vast Republic, famed through every clime,
Without a king, to see the end of time.   50

—1791

On the Universality and Other Attributes of the God of Nature

All that we see, about, abroad,
What is it all, but nature's God?
In meaner works discover'd here
No less than in the starry sphere.

In seas, on earth, this God is seen;   5
All that exist, upon him lean;
He lives in all, and never stray'd
A moment from the works he made:

His system fix'd on general laws
Bespeaks a wise creating cause;   10
Impartially he rules mankind
And all that on this globe we find.

Unchanged in all that seems to change,
Unbounded space is his great range;
To one vast purpose always true,   15
No time, with him, is old or new.

---

1. America.

In all the attributes divine
Unlimited perfectings shine;
In these enwrapt, in these complete,
All virtues in that centre meet.   20

This power who doth all powers transcend,
To all intelligence a friend,
Exists, the *greatest and the best*
Throughout all worlds, to make them blest.

All that he did he first approved   25
He all things into *being* loved;
O'er all he made he still presides,
For them in life, or death provides.

—1815

On the Uniformity and Perfection of Nature

On one fix'd point all nature moves,
Nor deviates from the track she loves;
Her system, drawn from reason's source,
She scorns to change her wonted course.

Could she descend from that great plan   5
To work unusual things for man,
To suit the insect of an hour—
This would betray a want of power,

Unsettled in its first design
And erring, when it did combine   10
The parts that form the vast machine,
The figures sketch'd on nature's scene.

Perfections of the great first cause
Submit to no contracted laws,
But all-sufficient, all-supreme,   15
Include no trivial views in them.

Who looks through nature with an eye
That would the scheme of heaven descry,
Observes her constant, still the same,
In all her laws, through all her frame.   20

No imperfection can be found
In all that is, above, around,—

All, nature made, in reason's sight
Is order all, and *all is right*.

—1815

On the Religion of Nature

The power, that gives with liberal hand
   The blessings man enjoys, while here,
And scatters through a smiling land
   Abundant products of the year;
      That power of nature, ever blessed,   5
      Bestowed religion with the rest.

Born with ourselves, her early sway
   Inclines the tender mind to take
The path of right, fair virtue's way
   Its own felicity to make.   10
      This universally extends
      And leads to no mysterious ends.

Religion, such as nature taught,
   With all divine perfection suits;
Had all mankind this system sought   15
   Sophists would cease their vain disputes,
      And from this source would nations know
      All that can make their heaven below.

This deals not curses on mankind,
   Or dooms them to perpetual grief,   20
If from its aid no joys they find,
   It damns them not for unbelief;
      Upon a more exalted plan
      Creatress nature dealt with man—

Joy to the day, when all agree   25
   On such grand systems to proceed,
From fraud, design, and error free,
   And which to truth and goodness lead:
      Then persecution will retreat
      And man's religion be complete.   30

—1815

Phillis Wheatley
1753–1784

One of the greatest poets of the eighteenth-century Atlantic Rim, Phillis Wheatley was born in West Africa, kidnapped, and taken on board the slave ship *Phillis* to Massachusetts, where she became the slave of John and Susannah Wheatley of Boston in 1761. Her precocious intellect soon asserted itself: By the age of ten, she was reading the Bible. Soon she was also reading John Milton and Alexander Pope and becoming well versed in Roman literature as well. In 1767, her first poetry appeared in a Rhode Island newspaper. By the time she was nineteen or twenty, she was already famous for her elegy on the Reverend George Whitefield, whose sermons had spread the Great Awakening from England to America.

Several subsequent published elegies secured her reputation and led to her 1773 trip to England to have a book of her poems issued in London. Immediately after arrival, she was the guest of Selina, Countess of Huntingdon (who was converted to Methodism and a life of philanthropy by George Whitefield). Wheatley also spent time in the company of the British philanthropist and statesman Lord Dartmouth (who oversaw the colonies after 1772), as well as visiting Benjamin Franklin and Brooke Watson, Lord Mayor of London. *Poems on Various Subjects, Religious and Moral*, in which several of the selections in this anthology first appeared, was published simultaneously in London and Boston in September 1773. Before it appeared, Wheatley had returned to Massachusetts to attend to her ill mistress, Susannah, to whom she was very close. The same month that the book was published, Phillis obtained her freedom but remained with the Wheatleys, caring for them until Susannah's death in 1774 and John's four years later. On April 1, 1778, she married John Peters, also a free African American who advocated abolition.

During the years between her return to Boston and her marriage, America was in the early stages of revolution, a cause to which Wheatley devoted her poetry. Her 1775 poem to George Washington earned her an invitation to visit the general at his headquarters in Cambridge, Massachusetts, which she did during the following year. The poem was written in Providence, Rhode Island, the home state of her friend and correspondent Arbour Tanner and the place to which Wheatley moved during the British occupation of Boston. Until her death on December 5, 1784, she continued to show support for the American Revolution, praising it even in the posthumously published "Liberty and Peace" (1785). As her correspondence with Samson Occom, Mohegan tribesman and advocate for Native American freedom and equality, illustrates, Wheatley believed in extending Jeffersonian principles of rights to African Americans and Native Americans. Merely by writing verse she affronted Euro-American pseudo-science, which sought to justify slavery and colonialism by holding that all non-European peoples were inferior. So strong was this prejudice that *Poems on Various Subjects* was issued with a testimony, signed by John Hancock and eighteen other prominent figures, that she "had been examined and thought qualified to write them."

Wheatley's poems sparked debate on both sides of the Atlantic. Many Americans, such as Thomas Jefferson, sought to deny their achievement and contribution to literature: "Religion has produced a Phillis Whately [sic], but it could not produce a poet," wrote Jefferson in *Notes on the State of Virginia* (1787). Elsewhere he pronounces that "her poems were below the dignity of criticism." Dr. Samuel Smith retorted, demanding of "Mr. Jefferson, or any other man who is acquainted with American planters, how many of those masters could have written poems equal to those of Phillis Whately [sic]." Several other eminent thinkers on both sides of the Atlantic disagreed with Jefferson's assessment and published Wheatley's poems to buttress the cause of the New England abolitionists. To this day, Wheatley's poems are debated by scholars. Some believe her poems contain a tacit acceptance of racist poetics and politics of the time, while others understand the poems as subtly yet poignantly subversive of the racist limitations of religion, literature, and arts as practiced in her day. It is certain that her profound influence on American and Atlantic Rim literature, African American poetry, and, in the words of Henry Louis Gates, Jr., "the black woman's literary tradition" is only beginning to be acknowledged.

Liberty and Peace

Lo freedom comes. Th' prescient muse foretold,
All eyes th' accomplish'd prophecy behold:
Her port describ'd, "She moves divinely fair,
Olive and laurel bind her golden hair."
She, the bright progeny of Heaven, descends,   5
And every grace her sovereign step attends;
For now kind Heaven, indulgent to our prayer,
In smiling peace resolves the din of war.
Fix'd in Columbia her illustrious line,
And bids in thee her future council shine.   10
To every realm her portals open'd wide,
Receives from each the full commercial tide.
Each art and science now with rising charms,
Th' expanding heart with emulation warns.
E'en great Britannia sees with dread surprise,   15
And from the dazzling splendors turns her eyes.
Britain, whose navies swept th' Atlantic o'er,
And thunder sent to every distant shore;
E'en thou, in manners cruel as thou art,
The sword resign'd, resume the friendly part.   20
For Gallia's power espous'd Columbia's cause,
And new-born Rome shall give Britannia laws,
Nor unremember'd in the grateful strain,
Shall princely Louis' friendly deeds remain;
The generous prince th' impending vengeance eyes,   25
Sees the fierce wrong and to the rescue flies.
Perish that thirst of boundless power, that drew
On Albion's[1] head the curse to tyrants due.
But thou appeas'd submit to Heaven's decree,
That bids this realm of freedom rival thee.   30
Now sheathe the sword that bade the brave atone
With guiltless blood for madness not their own.
Sent from th' enjoyment of their native shore,
Ill-fated—never to behold her more.
From every kingdom on Europe's coast   35
Throng'd various troops, their glory, strength, and boast.
With heart-felt pity fair Hibernia[2] saw

---

1. Gallia: France. Louis: Louis XIV, King of France. Albion: England.   2. Ireland.

Columbia menac'd by the Tyrant's law:
On hostile fields fraternal arms engage,
And mutual deaths, all dealt with mutual rage: 40
The muse's ear hears mother earth deplore
Her ample surface smoke with kindred gore:
The hostile field destroys the social ties,
And everlasting slumber seals their eyes.
Columbia mourns, the haughty foes deride,   45
Her treasures plunder'd and her towns destroy'd:
Witness how Charlestown's curling smokes arise,
In sable columns to the clouded skies.
The ample dome, high-wrought with curious toil,
In one sad hour the savage troops despoil.   50
Descending peace the power of war confounds;
From every tongue celestial peace resounds:
As from the east th' illustrious king of day,
With rising radiance drives the shades away,
So freedom comes array'd with charmes divine,   55
And in her train commerce and plenty shine.
Britannia owns her independent reign,
Hibernia, Scotia³ and the realms of Spain;
And great Germania's ample coast admires
The generous spirit that Columbia fires.   60
Auspicious Heaven shall fill with fav'ring gales,
Where e'er Columbia spreads her swelling sails:
To every realm shall peace her charms display,
And heavenly freedom spread her golden ray.

—1784

Thoughts on the Works of Providence

Arise, my soul, on wings enraptur'd, rise
To praise the monarch of the earth and skies,
Whose goodness and beneficence appear
As round its center moves the rolling year,
Or when the morning glows with rosy charms,   5
Or the sun slumbers in the ocean's arms,
Of light divine be a rich portion lent
To guide my soul, and favour my intent.
Celestial muse, my arduous flight sustain,
And raise my mind to a seraphic strain!   10
    Ador'd forever be the God unseen,
Which round the sun revolves this vast machine,
Though to his eye its mass a point appears:

---

3. Scotland.

Ador'd the God that whirls surrounding spheres,
Which first ordain'd that mighty Sol should reign   15
The peerless monarch of th' ethereal train;
Of miles twice forty millions in his height,
And yet his radiance dazzles mortal sight
So far beneath—from him th' extended earth
Vigor derives, and ev'ry flow'ry birth: 20
Vast through her orb she moves with easy grace
Around her Phoebus[1] in unbounded space;
True to her course th' impetuous storm derides,
Triumphant o'er the winds and surging tides.
    Almighty, in these wond'rous works of thine,   25
What Pow'r, what Wisdom, and what Goodness shine?
And are thy wonders, Lord, by men explor'd,
And yet creating glory unador'd!
    Creation smiles in various beauty gay,
While day to night and night succeeds to day;   30
That Wisdom which attends Jehovah's ways,
Shines most conspicuous in the solar rays;
Without them, destitute of heat and light,
This world would be the reign of endless night;
In their excess how would our race complain,   35
Abhoring life! how hate its length'ned chain!
From air adust what num'rous ills would rise!
What dire contagion taint the burning skies;
What pestilential vapours, fraught with death,
Would rise, and overspread the lands beneath!   40
    Hail, smiling morn, that from the Orient main
Ascending dost adorn the heav'nly plain!
So rich, so various are thy beauteous dies,
That spread through all the circuit of the skies,
That, full of thee, my soul in rapture soars,   45
And thy great God, the cause of all adores.
    O'er beings infinite his love extends,
His wisdom rules them, and his Pow'r defends.
When tasks diurnal tire the human frame,
The spirit's faint, and dim the vital flame,   50
Then too that ever active bounty shines,
Which not infinity of space confines.
The sable veil, that Night in silence draws,
Conceals effects, but shows th' Almighty Cause;
Night seals in sleep the wide creation fair,   55
And all is peaceful but the brow of care.
Again, gay Phoebus, as the day before,
Wakes ev'ry eye, but what shall wake no more;

---

1. Greek god of music, poetry, and light.

Again the face of nature is renew'd,
Which still appears harmonious, fair, and good.   60
May grateful strains salute the smiling morn,
Before its beams the eastern hill adorn!
    Shall day to day, and night to night, conspire
To show the goodness of the Almighty Sire?
This mental voice shall man regardless hear,   65
And never, never raise the filial pray'r?
Today, O hearken, nor your folly mourn
For time misspent, that never will return.
    But see the sons of vegetation rise,
And spread their leafy banners to the skies.   70
All-wise Almighty Providence do ye trace
In trees, and plants, and all the flow'ry race;
As clear as in the nobler frame of man,
All lovely copies of the Maker's plan.
The pow'r the same that forms a ray of light,   75
That call'd creation from eternal night.
"Let there be light," he said; from his profound
Old Chaos heard, and trembled at the sound:
Swift as the word, inspir'd by pow'r divine,
Behold the light around its Maker shine,   80
The first fair product of th' omnific God
And now through all his works diffus'd abroad.
    As reason's pow'rs by day our God disclose,
So we may trace him in the night's repose:
Say what is sleep? and dreams how passing strange!   85
When action ceases, and ideas range
Licentious and unbounded o'er the plains,
Where Fancy's queen in giddy triumph reigns,
Hear in soft strains the dreaming lover sigh
To a kind fair, or rave in jealousy;   90
On pleasure now, and now on vengeance bent,
The lab'ring passions struggle for a vent.
What pow'r, O man! thy reason then restores,
So long suspended in nocturnal hours?
What secret hand returns the mental train,   95
And gives improv'd thine active pow'rs again?
From thee, O man, what gratitude should rise
And, when from balmy sleep thou op'st thine eyes,
Let thy first thoughts be praises to the skies.
How merciful our God who thus imparts   100
O'erflowing tides of joy to human hearts,
When wants and woes might be our righteous lot,
Our God forgetting, by our God forgot!
    Among the mental pow'rs a question rose,
"What most the image of th' Eternal shows?"   105

When thus to Reason (so let Fancy rove)
Her great companion spoke immortal Love:
  "Say, mighty pow'r, how long shall strife prevail,
"And with its murmurs load the whisp'ring gale?
"Refer the cause to Recollection's shrine,   110
"Who loud proclaims my origin divine,
"The cause whence heav'n and earth began to be,
"And is not man immortaliz'd by me?
"Reason, let this most causeless strife subside."
    Thus Love pronounc'd, and Reason thus repli'd: 115
  "Thy birth, celestial queen! 'tis mine to own,
"In thee resplendent is the Godhead shown;
"Thy words persuade, my soul enraptur'd feels
"Resistless beauty which thy smile reveals."
Ardent she spoke, and, kindling at her charms,   120
She clasp'd the blooming goddess in her arms.
  Infinite Love where'er we turn our eyes
Appears: this ev'ry creature's wants supplies;
This most is heard in Nature's constant voice,
This makes the morn, and this the eve rejoice;   125
This bids the fost'ring rains and dews descend
To nourish all, to serve one gen'ral end,
The good of man: yet man ungrateful pays
But little homage, and but little praise.
To him, whose works array'd with mercy shine,   130
What songs should rise, how constant, how divine!

—1773

On the Death of the Rev. Mr. George Whitefield.[1] 1770.

Hail, happy saint, on thine immortal throne,
Possest of glory, life, and bliss unknown;
We hear no more the music of thy tongue,
Thy wonted auditories cease to throng,
Thy sermons in unequall'd accents flow'd,   5
And ev'ry bosom with devotion glow'd;
Thou didst in strains of eloquence refin'd
Inflame the heart, and captivate the mind.
Unhappy we the setting sun deplore,
So glorious once, but ah! it shines no more.   10

  Behold the prophet in his tow'ring flight!
He leaves the earth for heav'n's unmeasur'd height,
And worlds unknown receive him from our sight.

---

1. George Whitefield (1714–1770), Anglican minister who led Methodist revival movements in England and the United States.

There *Whitefield* wings with rapid course his way,
And sails to *Zion* through vast seas of day.   15

Thy pray'rs, great saint, and thine incessant cries
Have pierc'd the bosom of thy native skies.
Thou moon hast seen, and all the stars of light,
How he has wrestled with his God by night.
He pray'd that grace in ev'ry heart might dwell,   20
He long'd to see *America* excel;
He charg'd its youth that ev'ry grace divine
Should with full lustre in their conduct shine;
That Saviour, which his soul did first receive,
The greatest gift that ev'n a God can give,   25
He freely offer'd to the num'rous throng,
That on his lips with list'ning pleasure hung.

"Take him, ye wretched, for your only good,
"Take him[,] ye starving sinners, for your food;
"Ye thirsty, come to this life-giving stream,   30
"Ye preachers, take him for your joyful theme;
"Take him[,] my dear *Americans*,["] he said,
"Be your complaints on his kind bosom laid:
"Take him, ye *Africans*, he longs for you,
"*Impartial Saviour* is his title due: 35
"Wash'd in the fountain of redeeming blood,
"You shall be son, and kings, and priests to God."

Great *Countess*,[2] we *Americans* revere
Thy name, and mingle in thy grief sincere;
New England deeply feels, the *Orphans* mourn,   40
Their more than father will no more return.

But, though arrested by the hand of death,
Whitefield no more exerts his lab'ring breath,
Yet let us view him in th'eternal skies,
Let ev'ry heart to this bright vision rise;   45
While the tomb safe retains its sacred trust,
Till life divine re-animates his dust.

                                                    —1770

On Being Brought from Africa to America

'Twas mercy brought me from my *Pagan* land,
Taught my benighted soul to understand
That there's a God, that there's a *Saviour* too:

---

2. Selina, Countess of Huntington (1707–1791), a Methodist leader.

Once I redemption neither sought nor knew.
Some view our sable race with scornful eye,   5
"Their colour is a diabolic die."
Remember, *Christians*, *Negros*, black as *Cain*,
May be refin'd, and join th'angelic train.

—1773

On Imagination

Thy various works, imperial queen, we see,
How bright their forms! how deck'd with pomp by thee!
Thy wond'rous acts in beauteous order stand,
And all attest how potent is thine hand.

    From *Helicon's*[1] refulgent heights attend,   5
Ye sacred choir, and my attempts befriend:
To tell her glories with a faithful tongue,
Ye blooming graces, triumph in my song.

    Now here, now there, the roving *Fancy* flies,
Till some lov'd object strikes her wand'ring eyes,   10
Whose silken fetters all the senses bind,
And soft captivity involves the mind.

    Imagination! who can sing thy force?
Or who describe the swiftness of thy course?
Soaring through air to find the bright abode,   15
Th' empyreal palace of the thund'ring God,
We on thy pinions can surpass the wind,
And leave the rolling universe behind:
From star to star the mental optics rove,
Measure the skies, and range the realms above.   20
There in one view we grasp the mighty whole,
Or with new worlds amaze th' unbounded soul.

    Though *Winter* frowns to *Fancy's* raptur'd eyes
The fields may flourish, and gay scenes arise;
The frozen deeps may break their iron bands,   25
And bid their waters murmur o'er the sands.
Fair *Flora*[2] may resume her fragrant reign,
And with her flow'ry riches deck the plain;
Sylvanus[3] may diffuse his honours round,
And all the forest may with leaves be crown'd: 30
Show'rs may descend, and dews their gems disclose,
And nectar sparkle on the blooming rose.

---

1. A mountain sacred to the poetic muses.   2. Roman goddess of flowers.   3. Roman god of forests.

Such is thy pow'r, nor are thine orders vain,
O thou the leader of the mental train:
In full perfection all thy works are wrought,   35
And thine the sceptre o'er the realms of thought.
Before thy throne the subject-passions bow,
Of subject-passions sov'reign ruler thou;
At thy command joy rushes on the heart,
And through the glowing veins the spirits dart.   40

Fancy might now her silken pinions try
To rise from earth, and sweep th' expanse on high:
From Tithon's bed now might Aurora rise,[4]
Her cheeks all glowing with celestial dies,
While a pure stream of light o'erflows the skies.   45
The monarch of the day I might behold,
And all the mountains tipt with radiant gold,
But I reluctant leave the pleasing views,
Which Fancy dresses to delight the Muse;
Winter austere forbids me to aspire,   50
And northern tempests damp the rising fire;
They chill the tides of Fancy's flowing sea,
Cease then, my song, cease the unequal lay.

—1773

To S.M. A Young African Painter, on Seeing His Works

To show the lab'ring bosom's deep intent,
And thought in living characters to paint,
When first thy pencil did those beauties give,
And breathing figures learnt from thee to live,
How did those prospects give my soul delight,   5
A new creation rushing on my sight?
Still, wond'rous youth! each noble path pursue,
On deathless glories fix thine ardent view:
Still may the painter's and the poet's fire
To aid thy pencil, and thy verse conspire!   10
And may the charms of each seraphic theme
Conduct thy footsteps to immortal fame!
High to the blissful wonders of the skies
Elate thy soul, and raise thy wishful eyes.
Thrice happy, when exalted to survey   15
That splendid city, crown'd with endless day,
Whose twice six gates on radiant hinges ring:
Celestial Salem blooms in endless spring.

---

4. Aurora, goddess of dawn, fell in love with the mortal, Tithonus, a prince of Troy, and convinced Jupiter to grant him immortality.

Calm and serene thy moments glide along,
And may the muse inspire each future song!   20
Still, with the sweets of contemplation bless'd,
May peace with balmy wings your soul invest!
But when these shades of time are chas'd away,
And darkness ends in everlasting day,
On what seraphic pinions shall we move,   25
And view the landscapes in the realms above?
There shall thy tongue in heav'nly murmurs flow,
And there my muse with heav'nly transport glow:
No more to tell of *Damon's* tender sighs,
Or rising radiance of *Aurora's* eyes,[1]   30
For nobler themes demand a nobler strain,
And purer language on th' ethereal plain.
Cease, gentle muse! the solemn gloom of night
Now seals the fair creation from my sight.

—1773

To His Excellency General Washington

SIR.

I Have taken the freedom to address your Excellency in the enclosed poem,
and entreat your acceptance, though I am not insensible of its inaccuracies.
Your being appointed by the Grand Continental Congress to be Generalissimo
of the armies of North America, together with the fame of your virtues, excite
sensations not easy to suppress. Your generosity, therefore, I presume, will pardon the attempt. Wishing your Excellency all possible success in the great cause
you are so generously engaged in. I am,

Your Excellency's most obedient humble servant,
PHILLIS WHEATLEY.

Providence, Oct. 26, 1775.
His Excellency Gen. Washington.

Celestial choir! enthron'd in realms of light,
   Columbia's scenes of glorious toils I write.
While freedom's cause her anxious breast alarms,
She flashes dreadful in refulgent arms.
See mother earth her offspring's fate bemoan,   5
And nations gaze at scenes before unknown!
See the bright beams of heaven's revolving light
Involved in sorrows and the veil of night!
   The goddess comes, she moves divinely fair,
Olive and laurel binds her golden hair: 10

---

1. Damon and Aurora, both minor Roman gods, stand here for trivial poetic subjects.

Wherever shines this native of the skies,
Unnumber'd charms and recent graces rise.
　Muse! bow propitious while my pen relates
How pour her armies through a thousand gates,
As when Eolus[1] heaven's fair face deforms,　　　　　　　15
Enwrapp'd in tempest and a night of storms;
Astonish'd ocean feels the wild uproar,
The refluent surges beat the sounding shore;
Or thick as leaves in Autumn's golden reign,
Such, and so many, moves the warrior's train.　　　　　20
In bright array they seek the work of war,
Where high unfurl'd the ensign waves in air.
Shall I to Washington their praise recite?
Enough thou know'st them in the fields of fight.
Thee, first in peace and honours,—we demand　　　　25
The grace and glory of thy martial band.
Fam'd for thy valour, for thy virtues more,
Hear every tongue thy guardian aid implore!
　One century scarce perform'd its destined round,
When Gallic powers Columbia's fury found;　　　　　30
And so may you, whoever dares disgrace
The land of freedom's heaven-defended race!
Fix'd are the eyes of nations on the scales,
For in their hopes Columbia's arm prevails.
Anon Britannia droops the pensive head,　　　　　　35
While round increase the rising hills of dead.
Ah! cruel blindness to Columbia's state!
Lament thy thirst of boundless power too late.
　Proceed, great chief, with virtue on thy side,
Thy ev'ry action let the goddess guide.　　　　　　　40
A crown, a mansion, and a throne that shine,
With gold unfading, WASHINGTON! be thine.

　　　　　　　　　　　　　　　　　　　　—1776

To a Lady on Her Coming to North America with Her Son, for the Recovery of Her Health

Indulgent muse! my grov'ling mind inspire,
And fill my bosom with celestial fire.
See from Jamaica's fervid shore she moves,
Like the fair mother of the blooming loves,
When from above the Goddess with her hand　　　　5
Fans the soft breeze, and lights upon the land;
Thus she on Neptune's wat'ry realm reclin'd
Appear'd, and thus invites the ling'ring wind.

----

1. Greek god of wind.

"Arise, ye winds, America explore,
"Waft me, ye gales, from this malignant shore;   10
"The Northern milder climes I long to greet,
"There hope that health will my arrival meet."
Soon as she spoke in my ideal view
The winds assented, and the vessel flew.
    Madam, your spouse bereft of wife and son,   15
In the grove's dark recesses pours his moan;
Each branch, wide-spreading to the ambient sky,
Forgets its verdure, and submits to die.
    From thence I turn, and leave the sultry plain,
And swift pursue thy passage o'er the main: 20
The ship arrives before the fav'ring wind,
And makes the Philadelphian port assign'd,
Thence I attend you to Bostonia's arms,
Where gen'rous friendship ev'ry bosom warms:
Thrice welcome here! may health revive again,   25
Bloom on thy cheek, and bound in ev'ry vein!
Then back return to gladden ev'ry heart,
And give your spouse his soul's far dearer part,
Receiv'd again with what a sweet surprise,
The tear in transport starting from his eyes!   30
While his attendant son with blooming grace
Springs to his father's ever dear embrace.
With shouts of joy Jamaica's rocks resound,
With shouts of joy the country rings around.

—1773

A Farewell to America. To Mrs. S. W.

I.

Adieu, New-England's smiling meads
Adieu, the flow'ry plain:
I leave thine op'ning charms, O spring
And tempt the roaring main.

II.

In vain for me the flow'rets rise,   5
And boast their gaudy pride,
While here beneath the Northern skies
I mourn for health deny'd.

III.

Celestial maid of rosy hue,
O let me feel thy reign!   10

I languish till thy face I view
Thy vanish'd joys regain.

IV.

Susannah mourns, nor can I bear
To see the crystal flow'r,
Or mark the tender falling tear   15
At sad departure's hour;

V.

Not unregarding can I see
Her soul with grief opprest
So let no sigh, nor groans for me
Steal from her pensive breast.   20

VI.

In vain the feather'd warblers sing,
In vain the garden blooms,
And on the bosom of the spring
Breathes out her sweet perfumes.

VII.

While for Britannia's distant shore   25
We sweep the liquid plain,
And with astonish'd eyes explore
The wide-extended main.

VIII.

Lo! Health appears! celestial dame!
Complacent and serene,   30
With Hebe's[1] mantle o'er her Frame,
With soul-delighting mein.

IX.

To mark the vale where London lies
With misty vapors crown'd
Which cloud Aurora's thousand dyes,   35
And veil her charms around.

X.

Why, Phoebus, moves thy car so slow?
So slow thy rising ray?

---

1. Greek goddess of youth.

Give us the famous town to view,
Thou glorious king of day!   40

XI.

For thee, Britannia, I resign
New-England's smiling fields;
To view again her charms divine,
What joy the prospect yields!

XII.

But thou! Temptation hence away,   45
With all thy fatal train
Nor once seduce my soul away,
By thine enchanting strain.

XIII.

Thrice happy they, whose heav'nly shield
Secures their souls from harms   50
And fell Temptation on the field
Of all its pow'r disarms!

—1773

Letter to Rev. Samson Occom, New London, Connecticut

Feb. 11, 1774

Reverend and honoured Sir,

I have this day received your obliging kind epistle, and am greatly satisfied with your reasons respecting the negroes, and think highly reasonable what you offer in vindication of their natural rights: Those that invade them cannot be insensible that the divine light is chasing away the thick darkness which broods over the land of Africa; and the chaos which has reigned so long, is converting into beautiful order, and reveals more and more clearly the glorious dispensation of civil and religious liberty, which are so inseparably united, that there is little or no enjoyment of one without the other: Otherwise, perhaps, the Israelites had been less solicitous for their freedom from Egyptian slavery; I do not say they would have been contented without it, by no means; for in every human breast God has implanted a principle, which we call love of freedom; it is impatient of oppression, and pants for deliverance; and by the leave of our modern Egyptians I will assert, that the same principle lives in us. God grant deliverance in his own way and time, and get him honour upon all those whose avarice impels them to countenance and help forward the calamities of their fellow creatures. This I desire not for their hurt, but to convince them of the strange absurdity of their conduct, whose words and actions are so diametrically opposite. How well the cry for liberty, and the reverse disposition for the exercise of oppressive power over others agree—I humbly think it does not require the penetration of a philosopher to determine.—

—1774

⌒TRANSATLANTIC EXCHANGES ⌒
Slavery and Abolition

On September 6, 1781, the slave ship *Zong* sailed away from the coast of Africa bound for Jamaica. The hold was packed with some 440 chained, suffering people, Africans who had been kidnapped. By November 27, the ship had completed "the middle passage" across the Atlantic to the Caribbean, but not without tragedy having struck. Sixty slaves died from the want of livable air, space, water, food, and sanitary conditions; many more were sick, too sick to be sold for what the slavers would deem a decent price. So, rather than pulling into port, Captain Luke Collingwood ran the ship off course to commit a deed telling of the atrocity of slavery: He ordered 133 slaves to be thrown overboard. If these slaves died from sickness, Collingwood would have to sustain the financial loss, but if they were thrown overboard, he thought he could collect the insurance on them. The underwriters refused to pay, and the case went to court, where it was heard as if no more than matters of finance were at stake.

The underpinnings of what came to be called the "triangular trade" were profit and greed. British merchants earned more than 100% profit on the ship voyages they financially backed. Ships left Bristol, England, for the coast of Africa, where they purchased kidnapped Africans and brought them across the Atlantic to the Caribbean. In the British West Indies and South America, the slaves were sold to work on sugar plantations or transported to the United States for work on cotton plantations and other forms of manual labor (and sometimes clerical or nautical work). These ships returned to Bristol and European ports heavily laden with colonial sugar, cotton, tobacco, rum, and molasses purchased cheaply in the New World and sold at a high price in the Old. Between 1518 and 1850, more than 11 million slaves were brought from Africa to America.

The inhumanity of the *Zong* proceedings spurred Granville Sharp and other abolitionists to action. Although Sharp failed to get Collingwood brought up on murder charges, he succeeded in attracting the attention of the newspapers and raising public awareness. Sharp was neither the last nor the first to point out the cruelties and injustices of slavery: As early as 1754, the Quaker John Woolman had written *Some Considerations on the Keeping of Negroes*. In 1789, Olaudah Equiano, who had told Sharp of the *Zong* massacre, published his abolitionist autobiography, *The Interesting Narrative of the Life of Olaudah Equiano, or Gustavus Vassa, the African*. That same year, Parliament decided to regulate, not end, the slave trade. Despite the Declaration of Independence's claim that all men are equal, many U.S. states did not take measures to stem the importation of slaves. Connecticut, Massachusetts, New York, and Pennsylvania did not bar their citizens from participation in the trade until 1781. It was not until 1807, considerably after the American Revolution, that Britain and America abolished the slave trade. Nevertheless, it continued. Between 1811 and 1820, 53,600 Africans were kidnapped and brought to the New World each year. Had America remained a colony of Britain, slavery would likely have been abolished in 1833, when the slaves of the British West Indies were emancipated. It took the Civil War (1861–1865) to bring slavery nominally to an end in the United States, though its legacy of both individual and institutional racism remains to be overcome.

Before its overthrow, slavery was predicated upon systematic repression and segregation enforced by intense physical and mental cruelty, not only from the crews of ships during Atlantic Rim journeys but also from the masters, mistresses, and overseers of plantations. Even the architects of American civil liberties, such as Thomas Jefferson, held slaves. And Jefferson, like others, placed advertisements in the local papers whenever a slave escaped. Every issue of the *Virginia Gazette*, even the ones from the month and year the Declaration of Independence was signed, has advertisements offering rewards for the return of runaway slaves: "RUN away from the Subscriber, a Negro man named BAGLEY, about 20 years of age, 5 feet 5 or 6 Inches high, black complexion, and well made. . . . Whoever delivers the said Slave to me in Williamsburg shall have TEN SHILLINGS Reward" (July 20, 1776). Other advertisements speak to the physical abuse of the slaves, unabashedly noting unjustly inflicted wounds as potential marks of identification:

RUN AWAY from the subscriber, viz. JUPITER, alias GIBB, a Negro fellow . . . has several scars on his back from a severe whipping he lately had at the Sussex court-house, having been tried there for stirring up the Negroes to an insurrection, being a great . . . preacher. Robin, . . . a stout fellow, has a film over one of his eyes . . . and is brother to Gibb. Dinah, an old wench, . . . has a remarkable stump of a thumb . . . and is mother to the two fellows. (September 28, 1767)

Such descriptions reduce bodies to texts of suffering, sometimes quite literally by noting that the master's initials were branded on the cheeks or chests of the slaves who had run away. The ads are informed by notions directly contradictory to the ideological foundations of the country in which they were issued. To change location for freedom, as the Pilgrims once did, was construed in this case as a crime; fighting for liberty was regarded as a punishable offense, not an inalienable right. These texts also contradict the racist assumptions of slavers, as in the example shown praising the eloquence of Jupiter while relying upon a system that denies his intelligence and humanity to keep him enslaved.

Many slaves who escaped from southern plantations began their journey to freedom in the North by first hiding in neighboring plantations among enslaved friends and family. Some were guided only by the North Star, while many others proceeded from safe house to safe house along the Underground Railroad, a network of slaves, free African Americans, and white abolitionists who facilitated the covert movements of slaves from the South to northeastern states. The terminus of the Railroad for many was Canada, where former slaves were beyond the reach of statutes like the Fugitive Slave Law (which legally obligated even citizens in the Northeast to return escaped slaves to their southern masters). Because of this migration, larger communities of free blacks formed in the Northeast and in Canada, becoming the audiences for early black abolitionist newspapers like Frederick Douglass's *North Star*. Cities like New York, Boston, and Halifax, Nova Scotia, had large congregations of African American and Afro-Canadian Christians led by great preachers like John Marrant and Boston King.

Community and identity, especially within the family, were anathema to the slave system. Husbands were separated from wives, mothers and fathers were separated from children through kidnapping in Africa or the auction block in the New World. Upon arrival, slaves were almost always renamed in an attempt to strip them of their tribal identities. As the present-day scholar Ira Berlin has pointed out, these names were often founded upon cruel irony: The slavers often gave those who were forced into the lowliest stations in life the names of historical heroes and gods, as exemplified by the name Jupiter (the Roman name for the Greek god of thunder and head of the divine pantheon). The names of slave ships also exemplified bitter irony and paradox. One famous slave ship, the subject of a 1997 Hollywood epic directed by Steven Spielberg, was called the *Amistad*, the Spanish word for friendship. Masters often named slaves for the ships that brought them to America, as is the case with Phillis Wheatley, who was purchased by the Wheatley family from the ship *Phillis*. Other slaves like Olaudah Equiano, who was given several names including Gustavus Vassa, reclaimed their African names as well and went by both names to exemplify their transnational cultural identity.

Equiano and Wheatley, like Quobna Ottobah Cugoano and many other slaves who published autobiographies, used writing to advocate for their fellow people of African descent who were enslaved on the Atlantic Rim. Many of these writers used their writing and their Christianity to redefine both. Equiano, writing in the autobiographical tradition of St. Augustine of North Africa, related not only a spiritual liberation from bondage but a physical one as well, as he recounts both his spiritual conversion and his manumission from slavery. Wheatley, Equiano, Cugoano, and others articulate a transnational theology of liberation (from slavery) that is at once an adaptation as well as a subversion of the theology of the Great Awakening that was being preached by George Whitefield and John Wesley.

Wesley and Whitefield traveled between Britain and America sharing their message of a religion infused with emotion and predicated on a belief in salvation and divine providence.

Wheatley and Equiano owe their conversion to Christianity to Whitefield, and yet they redefine their theology, which allowed for slavery. Despite the views of many racist Christians of the day who denied that slaves and free people of African descent had souls, Equiano, Marrant, Cugoano, and others told stories of how the presence of God and providence shaped their lives, souls, and views on the depraved institution of slavery. Eventually, Afro-Christianity began to spread among plantation slaves who made Christianity their own by mixing it with many customs and beliefs of their indigenous religions. Although these slaves lacked the "mobility in chains" of Wheatley and Equiano to travel across the Atlantic, they spiritually countered the racist institution from within its borders. As the spirituals (devotional songs of praise, redemption, and freedom) of slaves attest, these oppressed people found a powerful example in Christ and could relate in ways their oppressors could not to the Bible's notions of enduring physical and mental cruelty on earth to find salvation in heaven: "And with his stripes [wounds] we are healed." One hundred years after Lincoln issued the Emancipation Proclamation, the Reverend Dr. Martin Luther King, Jr. delivered his "I Have a Dream" speech at Washington, D.C.'s Lincoln Memorial and quoted a spiritual to emphasize that the movement for African American civil liberties would not cease until all were equal and "free at last!"

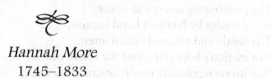

Hannah More
1745–1833

Viewed by her contemporaries as an authoritative voice on all matters moral, Hannah More's essays, poetry, and educational books are fueled by her concern with the social and moral well-being of England. Her father, a schoolmaster, saw that his five daughters were well educated. His three eldest founded a girls' school while still teenagers.

Born in Bristol in 1745, More's writing talent emerged early, and she wrote her first play, *The Search After Happiness*, at age sixteen. The play, published in 1773 and 1774 in England and America, signaled the start of a prolific transatlantic publishing career. Of the seventy-five works More published during her lifetime, forty were printed in America, if not during the same year they appeared in England, then shortly after. Her essays, plays, poetry, and fiction during the 1770s gave way to an increased interest in moral and ethical work by the end of that decade. Although her 1777 play *Percy* was a hit (with the help of her mentor, the famous actor David Garrick) that established her on the London literary scene, More began writing with greater moral purpose, addressing the need for moral laws in England and the working, social, and educational circumstances of the poor, women, and slaves.

Between 1794 and 1797, for instance, More composed fifty pamphlets in her *Cheap Repository Tracts*, a series that discussed such topics as sexual restraint and the dangers of alcohol. At times, her political conservatism was criticized, but the pamphlets were widely distributed, and More became one of the most successful Romantic writers. Some two million copies of the series were sold in the United States alone. More's mission to help the impoverished and disenfranchised was fueled by her association with the Bluestockings—a group of intelligent, artistic (and often socially minded) women and men who met to discuss and debate literary and political matters. More's poem "Das Bleu" (1786) gave the term increased currency as she argues for the importance of such interaction for women: "Our intellectual ore must shine, / Not slumber idly in the mine."

While More devoted much time to writing on the need for social and educational rights for women and the poor, the abolition of slavery was a central concern. She timed the appearance of "Slavery, A Poem" (London, 1788) to coincide with early Parliamentary debates on slavery. The same year it was printed in America in Philadelphia (by James Humphreys, the Loyalist-turned-patriot publisher who printed works by Thomas Paine and Joseph Priestley) and New York. Issued as a small pamphlet, the poem captured the public imagination as an unflinching, unequivocal condemnation of the slave trade. Poetically More was influenced by the pre-Romantic poet William Cowper, whose 1778 poems "Pity for Poor Africans" and "The Negro's Complaint" swayed many opinions, and politically by William Wilberforce, who for several years after his election to Parliament in 1780 focused most of his energy on the abolition of the slave trade. The poem is built on the philosophical argument that the soul is universal and that focusing on the body (that is, on skin color) runs counter to the Christian faith and to the values of a society that prides itself on cultivating civility and liberty.

Slavery, A Poem

IF heaven has into being deign'd to call
Thy light, O LIBERTY! to shine on all;
Bright intellectual Sun! why does thy ray
To earth distribute only partial day?
Since no resisting cause from spirit flows   5
Thy penetrating essence to opose;
No obstacles by Nature's hand imprest,
Thy subtle and ethereal beams arrest;
Nor motion's laws can speed thy active course,
Nor strong repulsion's pow'rs obstruct thy force;   10
Since there is no convexity in MIND,
Why are thy genial beams to parts confin'd?
While the chill North with thy bright ray is blest,
Why should fell darkness half the South invest?
Was it decreed, fair Freedom! at thy birth,   15
That thou shou'd'st ne'er irradiate all the earth?
While Britain basks in thy full blaze of light,
Why lies sad Afric quench'd in total night?
    Thee only, sober Goddess! I attest,
In smiles chastis'd, and decent graces drest.   20
Not that unlicens'd monster of the crowd,
Whose roar terrific bursts in peals so loud,
Deaf'ning the ear of Peace: fierce Faction's tool;
Of rash Sedition born, and mad Misrule;
Whose stubborn mouth, rejecting Reason's rein,   25
No strength can govern, and no skill restrain;
Whose magic cries the frantic vulgar draw
To spurn at Order, and to outrage Law;
To tread on grave Authority and Pow'r,
And shake the work of ages in an hour: 30
Convuls'd her voice, and pestilent her breath,
She raves of mercy, while she deals out death:
Each blast is fate; she darts from either hand
Red conflagration o'er th' astonish'd land;
Clamouring for peace, she rends the air with noise,   35
And to reform a part, the whole destroys.

O, plaintive Southerne![1] whose impassion'd strain
So oft has wak'd my languid Muse in vain!
Now, when congenial themes her cares engage,
She burns to emulate thy glowing page;   40
Her failing efforts mock her fond desires,
She shares thy feelings, not partakes thy fires.
Strange pow'r of song! the strain that warms the heart
Seems the same inspiration to impart;
Touch'd by the kindling energy alone,   45
We think the flame which melts us is our own;
Deceiv'd, for genius we mistake delight,
Charm'd as we read, we fancy we can write.
   Tho' not to me, sweet Bard, thy pow'rs belong
Fair Truth, a hallow'd guide! inspires my song.   50
Here Art wou'd weave her gayest flow'rs in vain,
For Truth the bright invention wou'd disdain.
For no fictitious ills these numbers flow,
But living anguish, and substantial woe;
No individual griefs my bosom melt,   55
For millions feel what Oronoko felt:
Fir'd by no single wrongs, the countless host
I mourn, by rapine dragg'd from Afric's coast.
   Perish th'illiberal thought which wou'd debase
The native genius of the sable race!   60
Perish the proud philosophy, which sought
To rob them of the pow'rs of equal thought!
Does then th' immortal principle within
Change with the casual colour of a skin?
Does matter govern spirit? or is mind   65
Degraded by the form to which 'tis join'd?
   No: they have heads to think, and hearts to feel,
And souls to act, with firm, tho' erring, zeal;
For they have keen affections, kind desires,
Love strong as death, and active patriot fires;   70
All the rude energy, the fervid flame,
Of high-soul'd passion, and ingenuous shame:
Strong, but luxuriant virtues boldly shoot
From the wild vigour of a savage root.
   Nor weak their sense of honour's proud control,   75
For pride is virtue in a Pagan soul;
A sense of worth, a conscience of desert,
A high, unbroken haughtiness of heart:
That self-same stuff which erst proud empires sway'd,
Of which the conquerers of the world were made.   80

---

1. [More's note] Author of the Tragedy of Oronoko. [Aphra Behn (1640–1689)]

Capricious fate of man! that very pride
In Afric scourg'd, in Rome was deify'd.
   No Muse, O Quashi![2] shall thy deeds relate,
No statue snatch thee from oblivious fate!
For thou wast born where never gentle Muse   85
On Valour's grave the flow'rs of Genius strews;
And thou wast born where no recording page
Plucks the fair deed from Time's devouring rage.
Had Fortune plac'd thee on some happier coast,
Where polish'd souls heroic virtue boast,   90
To thee, who sought'st a voluntary grave,
Th' uninjur'd honours of thy name to save,
Whose generous arm thy barbarous Master spar'd,
Altars had smok'd, and temples had been rear'd.
   Whene'er to Afric's shores I turn my eyes,   95
Horrors of deepest, deadliest guilt arise;
I see, by more than Fancy's mirror shewn,
The burning village, and the blazing town:
See the dire victim torn from social life,
The shrieking babe, the agonizing wife!   100
She, wretch forlorn! is dragg'd by hostile hands,
To distant tyrants sold, in distant lands!
Transmitted miseries, and successive chains,
The sole sad heritage her child obtains!
Ev'n this last wretched boon their foes deny,   105
To weep together, or together die.
By felon hands, by one relentless stroke,
See the fond links of feeling nature broke!
The fibres twisting round a parent's heart,
Torn from their grasp, and bleeding as they part.   110
   Hold, murderers, hold! not aggravate distress;
Respect the passions you yourselves possess;
Ev'n you, of ruffian heart, and ruthless hand,
Love your own offspring, love your native land.
Ah! leave them holy Freedom's cheering smile,   115
The heav'n-taught fondness for the parent soil;
Revere affections mingled with our frame,
In every nature, every clime the same;
In all, these feelings equal sway maintain;

2. [More's note] It is a point of honour among negroes of a high spirit to die rather than to suffer their glossy skin to bear the mark of the whip. Qua-shi had somehow offended his master, a young planter with whom he had been bred up in the endearing intimacy of a play-fellow. His services had been faithful; his attachment affectionate. The master resolved to punish him, and persued him for that purpose. In trying to escape Qua-shi stumbled and fell; the master fell upon him; they wrestled long with doubtful victory; at length Qua-shi got uppermost, and, being firmly seated on his master's breast, he secured his legs with one hand, and with the other drew a sharp knife; then said, "Master, I have been bred up with you from a child; I have loved you as myself: in return, you have condemned me to a punishment of which I must ever have borne the marks: thus only can I avoid them;" so saying, he drew the knife with all his strength across his own throat, and fell down dead, without a groan, on his master's body.
   —Ramsay's Essay on the Treatment of African Slaves.

In all the love of HOME and FREEDOM reign: 120
And Tempe's vale, and parch'd Angola's sand,
One equal fondness of their sons command.
Th' unconquer'd Savage laughs at pain and toil,
Basking in Freedom's beams which gild his native soil.
  Does thirst of empire, does desire of fame,   125
(For these are specious crimes) our rage inflame?
No: sordid lust of gold their fate controls,
The basest appetite of basest souls;
Gold, better gain'd, by what their ripening sky,
Their fertile fields, their arts[3] and mines supply.   130
  What wrongs, what injuries does Opression plead
To smooth the horror of th' unnatural deed?
What strange offence, what aggravated sin?
They stand convicted—of a darker skin!
Barbarians, hold! th' opprobious commerce spare,   135
Respect *his* sacred image which they bear:
Tho' dark and savage, ignorant and blind,
They claim the common privilege of kind;
Let Malice strip them of each other plea,
They still are men, and men shou'd still be free.   140
Insulted Reason, loaths th' inverted trade—
Dire change! the agent is the purchase made!
Perplex'd, the baffled Muse involves the tale;
Nature confounded, well may language fail!
The outrag'd Goddess with abhorrent eyes   145
Sees MAN the traffic, SOULS the merchandize!
  Plead not, in reason's palpable abuse,
Their sense of[4] feeling callous and obtuse:
From heads to hearts lies Nature's plain appeal,
Tho' few can reason, all mankind can feel.   150
Tho' wit may boast a livelier dread of shame,
A loftier sense of wrong refinement claim;
Tho' polished manners may fresh wants invent,
And nice distinctions nicer souls torment;
Tho' these on finer spirits heavier fall,   155
Yet natural evils are the same to all.
Tho' wounds there are which reason's force may heal,
There needs no logic sure to make us feel.
The nerve, howe'er untutor'd, can sustain
A sharp, unutterable sense of pain;   160
As exquisitely fashion'd in a slave,
As where unequal fate a sceptre gave.

---

3. [More's note] Besides many valuable productions of the soil, cloths and carpets of exquisite manufacture are brought from the coast of Guinea.   4. [More's note] Nothing is more frequent than this cruel and stupid argument, that they do not *feel* the miseries inflicted on them as Europeans would do.

Sense is as keen where Congo's sons preside,
As where proud Tiber rolls his classic tide.
Rhetoric or verse may point the feeling line,   165
They do not whet sensation, but define.
Did ever slave less feel the galling chain,
When Zeno[5] prov'd there was no ill in pain?
Their miseries philosophic quirks deride,
Slaves groan in pangs disown'd by Stoic[6] pride.   170
    When the fierce Sun darts vertical his beams,
And thirst and hunger mix their wild extremes;
When the sharp iron[7] wounds his inmost soul,
And his strain'd eyes in burning anguish roll;
Will the parch'd negro find, ere he expire,   175
No pain in hunger, and no heat in fire?
    For him, when fate his tortur'd frame destroys,
What hope of present fame, or future joys?
For *this*, have heroes shorten'd nature's date;
For *that*, have martyrs gladly met their fate;   180
But him, forlorn, no hero's pride sustains,
No martyr's blissful visions sooth his pains;
Sullen, he mingles with his kindred dust,
For he has learn'd to dread the Christian's trust;
To him what mercy can that Pow'r display,   185
Whose servants murder, and whose sons betray?
Savage! thy venial error I deplore,
They are *not* Christians who infest thy shore.
    O thou sad spirit, whose preposterous yoke
The great deliver Death, at length, has broke!   190
Releas'd from misery, and escap'd from care,
Go meet that mercy man deny'd thee here.
In thy dark home, sure refuge of th' opress'd,
The wicked vex not, and the weary rest.
And, if some notions, vague and undefin'd,   195
Of future terrors have assail'd thy mind;
If such thy masters have presum'd to teach,
As terrors only they are prone to preach;
(For shou'd they paint eternal Mercy's reign,
Where were th' oppressor's rod, the captive's chain?)   200
If, then, thy troubled soul has learn'd to dread
The dark unknown thy trembling footsteps tread;
On HIM, who made thee what thou art, depend;
HE, who withholds the means, accepts the end.
Not *thine* the reckoning dire of LIGHT abus'd,   205

---

5. Zeno (333–264 BC), Greek philosopher.   6. Stoicism, an ancient philosophy, advocated restraining emotions to attain happiness.   7. [More's note] This is not said figuratively. The writer of these lines has seen a complete set of chains, fitted to every separate limb of these unhappy, innocent men; together with instruments for wrenching open the jaws, contrived with such ingenious cruelty as would shock the humanity of an inquisitor.

KNOWLEDGE disgrac'd, and LIBERTY misus'd;
On *thee* no awful judge incens'd shall sit
For parts perverted, and dishonour'd wit.
Where ignorance will be found the surest plea,
How many learn'd and wise shall envy *thee*!   210
    And thou, WHITE SAVAGE! whether lust of gold,
Or lust of conquest, rule thee uncontrol'd!
Hero, or robber!—by whatever name
Thou plead thy impious claim to wealth or fame;
Whether inferior mischiefs be thy boast,   215
A petty tyrant rifling Gambia's coast:
Or bolder carnage track thy crimson way,
Kings disposses'd, and Provinces thy prey;
Panting to tame wide earth's remotest bound;
All Cortez[8] murder'd, all Columbus found;   220
O'er plunder'd realms to reign, detested Lord,
Make millions wretched, and thyself abhorr'd;——
In Reason's eye, in Wisdom's fair account,
Your sum of glory boasts a like amount;
The means may differ, but the end's the same;   225
Conquest is pillage with a nobler name.
Who makes the sum of human blessings less,
Or sinks the stock of general happiness,
No solid fame shall grace, no true renown,
His life shall blazon, or his memory crown.   230
    Had those advent'rous spirits who explore
Thro' ocean's trackless wastes, the far-sought shore;
Whether of wealth insatiate, or of pow'r,
Conquerors who waste, or ruffians who devour:
Had these possess'd, O COOK![9] thy gentle mind,   235
Thy love of arts, thy love of humankind;
Had these pursued thy mild and liberal plan,
DISCOVERERS had not been a curse to man!
The, bless'd Philanthropy! thy social hands
Had link'd dissever'd worlds in brothers bands;   240
Careless, if colour, or if clime divide;
Then, lov'd, and loving, man had liv'd, and died.
    The purest wreaths which hang on glory's shrine,
For empires founded, peaceful PENN![10] are thine;
No blood-stain'd laurels crown'd thy virtuous toil,   245
No slaughter'd natives drench'd thy fair-earn'd soil.
Still thy meek spirit in thy[11] flock survives,
Consistent still, *their* doctrines rule their lives;
Thy followers only have effac'd the shame

---

8. Hernán Cortés (1485–1547), Spanish conquistador.   9. Captain James Cook (1728–1779), British explorer.
10. William Penn (1644–1718), founder of Pennsylvania.   11. [More's note] The Quakers have emancipated all their slaves throughout America.

Inscrib'd by SLAVERY on the Christian name.   250
    Shall Britain, where the soul of freedom reigns,
Forge chains for others she herself disdains?
Forbid it, Heaven! O let the nations know
The liberty she loves she will bestow;
Not to herself the glorious gift confin'd,   255
She spreads the blessing wide as humankind;
And, scorning narrow views of time and place,
Bids all be free in earth's extended space.
    What page of human annals can record
A deed so bright as human rights restor'd?   260
O may that god-like deed, that shining page,
Redeem OUR fame, and consecrate OUR age!
    And see, the cherub Mercy from above,
Descending softly, quits the sphere of love!
On feeling hearts she sheds celestial dew,   265
And breathes her spirit o'er th' enlighten'd few;
From soul to soul the spreading influence steals,
Till every breast the soft contagion feels.
She bears, exulting, to the burning shore
The loveliest office Angel ever bore;   270
To vindicate the pow'r in Heaven ador'd,
To still the clank of chains, and sheathe the sword;
To cheer the mourner, and with soothing hands
From bursting hearts unbind th' Oppressor's bands;
To raise the lustre of the Christian name,   275
And clear the foulest blot that dims its fame.
    As the mild Spirit hovers o'er the coast,
A fresher hue the wither'd landscapes boast;
Her healing smiles the ruin'd scenes repair,
And blasted Nature wears a joyous air.   280
She spreads her blest commission from above,
Stamp'd with the sacred characters of love;
She tears the banner stain'd with blood and tears,
And, LIBERTY! thy shining standard rears!
As the bright ensign's glory she displays,   285
See pale OPPRESSION faints beneath the blaze!
The giant dies! no more his frown appals,
The chain untouch'd, drops off; the fetter falls.
Astonish'd echo tells the vocal shore,
Opression's fall'n, and Slavery is no more!   290
The dusky myriads crowd the sultry plain,
And hail that mercy long invok'd in vain.
Victorious Pow'r! she bursts their tow-fold bands,
And FAITH and FREEDOM spring from Mercy's hands.
FINIS.

—1788

Quobna Ottobah Cugoano
1757–c. 1801

At age thirteen, Quobna Ottobah Cugoano was kidnapped from his native region, the coast of present-day Ghana, and brought to Grenada to work. Eventually he became the servant of Alexander Campbell, who took him to England in 1772. In London, he was baptized and joined the Sons of Africa, a community of fellow black Christian abolitionists who numbered among their ranks Olaudah Equiano. These men used their literacy to lobby for the rights of slaves, and their letters to London newspapers and politicians (including King George III, the Prince of Wales, Edmund Burke, and Prime Minister Pitt) saved many lives. Their combined efforts, however, did not deter greedy businessmen from embezzling funds from the Sierra Leone Company, a government-funded project to settle London's black poor in the West African resettlement colony Sierra Leone. Encouraging each other and freely sharing their theological arguments in opposition to slavery, Cugoano and Equiano published books devoted to the relocation project. Some modern readers have deemed the abolitionist writing of Equiano and Phillis Wheatley too moderate, but Cugoano's *Thoughts and Sentiments on the Evil and Wicked Traffic of Slavery and Commerce of the Human Species* (1787) sharply condemned the hypocrisy of the Christian nations that ran the slave trade. The strong reaction Cugoano's work met with among conservative white readers is a telling commentary on the modes of discourse and rhetoric available to black abolitionists of the time. Aware of the reception of Cugoano's forthright polemic, Equiano chose to weave more of the details of his life into his anti-slavery arguments, letting the abuses he witnessed and suffered be their own testimonies against the horrors of slavery.

from Thoughts and Sentiments on the Evil and Wicked Traffic of Slavery and Commerce of the Human Species

> *One law, and one manner shall be for you, and for the stranger*
> *that sojourneth with you; and therefore, all things whatsoever*
> *ye would that men should do to you, do ye even so to them.*
>
> Numb. xv. 16.—Math. vii. 12.

As several learned gentlemen of distinguished abilities, as well as eminent for their great humanity, liberality and candour, have written various essays against that infamous traffic of the African Slave Trade, carried on with the West-India planters and merchants, to the great shame and disgrace of all Christian nations wherever it is admitted in any of their territories, or in any place or situation amongst them; it cannot be amiss that I should thankfully acknowledge these truly worthy and humane gentlemen with the warmest sense of gratitude, for their beneficent and laudable endeavours towards a total suppression of that infamous and iniquitous traffic of stealing, kid-napping, buying, selling, and cruelly enslaving men!

Those who have endeavoured to restore to their fellow-creatures the common rights of nature, of which especially the poor unfortunate Black People have been so unjustly deprived, cannot fail in meeting with the applause of all good men, and the approbation of that which will for ever redound to their honor; they have the warrant of that which is divine: *Open thy mouth, judge righteously, plead the cause of the poor and needy*[1]; *for the liberal deviseth liberal things, and by liberal things shall stand.*[2] And they can say with the pious Job, *Did not I weep for him that was in trouble; was not my soul grieved for the poor?*[3]

The kind exertions of many benevolent and humane gentlemen, against the iniquitous traffic of slavery and oppression, has been attended with much good to many, and must redound with great honor to themselves, to humanity and their country; their laudable endeavours have been productive of the most beneficent effects in preventing that savage barbarity from taking place in free countries at home. In this, as well as in many other respects, there is one class of people (whose virtues of probity and humanity are well known) who are worthy of universal approbation and imitation, because, like men of honor and humanity, they have jointly agreed to carry on no slavery and savage barbarity among them; and, since the last war, some mitigation of slavery has been obtained in some respective districts of America, though not in proportion to their own vaunted claims of freedom; but it is to be hoped, that they will yet go on to make a further and greater reformation. However, notwithstanding all that has been done and written against it, that brutish barbarity, and unparallelled injustice, is still carried on to a very great extent in the colonies, and with an avidity as insidious, cruel and oppressive as ever. The longer that men continue in the practice of evil and wickedness, they grow the more abandoned; for nothing in history can equal the barbarity and cruelty of the tortures and murders committed under various pretences in modern slavery, except the annals of the Inquisition and the bloody edicts of Popish massacres.[4]

It is therefore manifest, that something else ought yet to be done; and what is required, is evidently the incumbent duty of all men of enlightened understanding, and of every man that has any claim or affinity to the name of Christian, that the base treatment which the African Slaves undergo, ought to be abolished; and it is moreover evident, that the whole, or any part of that iniquitous traffic of slavery, can no where, or in any degree, be admitted, but among those who must eventually resign their own claim to any degree of sensibility and humanity, for that of barbarians and ruffians.

But it would be needless to arrange an history of all the base treatment which the African Slaves are subjected to, in order to shew the exceeding wickedness and evil of that insidious traffic, as the whole may easily appear in every part, and at every view, to be wholly and totally inimical to every idea of justice, equity, reason and humanity. What I intend to advance against that evil, criminal and wicked traffic of enslaving men, are only some Thoughts and Sentiments which occur to me, as being obvious from the Scriptures of Divine Truth, or such arguments as are chiefly deduced from thence, with other such observations as I have been able to collect. Some of these observations may lead into a larger field of consideration, than that of the African Slave Trade alone; but those causes from wherever they originate, and become the production of slavery, the evil effects produced by it, must shew that its origin and source is of a wicked and criminal nature.

No necessity, or any situation of men, however poor, pitiful and wretched they may be, can warrant them to rob others, or oblige them to become thieves, because they are poor, miserable and wretched: But the robbers of men, the kidnappers, ensnarers and slave-holders, who take away the common rights and privileges of others to support and enrich themselves, are universally those pitiful and detestable wretches; for the ensnar-

---

1. Proverbs 31.9.   2. Isaiah 32.8.   3. Job 30.25.   4. The Inquisition was an office of the Catholic Church (often called "Popish" by Protestants) that suppressed heresy, sometimes violently.

ing of others, and taking away their liberty by slavery and oppression, is the worst kind of robbery, as most opposite to every precept and injunction of the Divine Law, and contrary to that command which enjoins that *all men should love their neighbours as themselves, and that they should do unto others, as they would that men should do to them*.[5] As to any other laws that slave-holders may make among themselves, as respecting slaves, they can be of no better kind, nor give them any better character, than what is implied in the common report—that there may be some honesty among thieves. This may seem a harsh comparison, but the parallel is so coincident that, I must say, I can find no other way of expressing my Thoughts and Sentiments, without making use of some harsh words and comparisons against the carriers on of such abandoned wickedness. But, in this little undertaking, I must humbly hope the impartial reader will excuse such defects as may arise from want of better education; and as to the resentment of those who can lay their cruel lash upon the backs of thousands, for a thousand times less crimes than writing against their enormous wickedness and brutal avarice, is what I may be sure to meet with.

However, it cannot but be very discouraging to a man of my complexion in such an attempt as this, to meet with the evil aspersions of some men, who say, "That an African is not entitled to any competent degree of knowledge, or capable of imbibing any sentiments of probity; and that nature designed him for some inferior link in the chain, fitted only to be a slave."[6] But when I meet with those who make no scruple to deal with the human species, as with the beasts of the earth, I must think them not only brutish, but wicked and base; and that their aspersions are insidious and false: And if such men can boast of greater degrees of knowledge, than any African is entitled to, I shall let them enjoy all the advantages of it unenvied, as I fear it consists only in a greater share of infidelity, and that of a blacker kind than only skin deep. And if their complexion be not what I may suppose, it is at least the nearest in resemblance to an internal hue. A good man will neither speak nor do as a bad man will; but if a man is bad, it makes no difference whether he be a black or a white devil.

By some of such complexion, as whether black or white it matters not, I was early snatched away from my native country, with about eighteen or twenty more boys and girls, as we were playing in a field. We lived but a few days journey from the coast where we were kid-napped, and as we were decoyed and drove along, we were soon conducted to a factory, and from thence, in the fashionable way of traffic, consigned to Grenada. Perhaps it may not be amiss to give a few remarks, as some account of myself, in this transposition of captivity.

I was born in the city of Agimaque, on the coast of Fantyn; my father was a companion to the chief in that part of the country of Fantee, and when the old king died I was left in his house with his family; soon after I was sent for by his nephew, Ambro Accasa, who succeeded the old king in the chiefdom of that part of Fantee known by the name of Agimaque and Affinee.[7] I lived with his children, enjoying peace and tranquillity, about twenty moons, which, according to their way of reckoning time, is two years. I was sent for to visit an uncle, who lived at a considerable distance from Agimaque. The first day after we set out we arrived at Affinee, and the third day at my uncle's habitation, where I lived about three months, and was then thinking of returning to my father and young companion at Agimaque; but by this time I had got well acquainted with

---

5. Paraphrases Leviticus 19.18 and Matthew 7.12.   6. No source for this quotation can be identified. Cugoano is likely summarizing the increasingly influential pseudo-scientific racism of the eighteenth century.   7. Agimaque, Fantyn, Fantee, and Affinee are towns and regions of what is now Ghana.

some of the children of my uncle's hundreds of relations, and we were some days too venturesome in going into the woods to gather fruit and catch birds, and such amusements as pleased us. One day I refused to go with the rest, being rather apprehensive that something might happen to us; till one of my play-fellows said to me, because you belong to the great men, you are afraid to venture your carcase, or else of the *bounsam*, which is the devil. This enraged me so much, that I set a resolution to join the rest, and we went into the woods as usual; but we had not been above two hours before our troubles began, when several great ruffians came upon us suddenly, and said we had committed a fault against their lord, and we must go and answer for it ourselves before him. . . . This made me cry bitterly, but I was soon conducted to a prison, for three days, where I heard the groans and cries of many, and saw some of my fellow-captives. But when a vessel arrived to conduct us away to the ship, it was a most horrible scene; there was nothing to be heard but rattling of chains, smacking of whips, and the groans and cries of our fellow-men. Some would not stir from the ground, when they were lashed and beat in the most horrible manner. I have forgot the name of this infernal fort; but we were taken in the ship that came for us, to another that was ready to sail from Cape Coast. When we were put into the ship, we saw several black merchants coming on board, but we were all drove into our holes, and not suffered to speak to any of them. In this situation we continued several days in sight of our native land; but I could find no good person to give any information of my situation to Accasa at Agimaque. And when we found ourselves at last taken away, death was more preferable than life, and a plan was concerted amongst us, that we might burn and blow up the ship, and to perish all together in the flames; but we were betrayed by one of our own countrywomen, who slept with some of the head men of the ship, for it was common for the dirty filthy sailors to take the African women and lie upon their bodies; but the men were chained and pent up in holes. It was the women and boys which were to burn the ship, with the approbation and groans of the rest; though that was prevented, the discovery was likewise a cruel bloody scene.

But it would be needless to give a description of all the horrible scenes which we saw, and the base treatment which we met with in this dreadful captive situation, as the similar cases of thousands, which suffer by this infernal traffic, are well known. Let it suffice to say, that I was thus lost to my dear indulgent parents and relations, and they to me. All my help was cries and tears, and these could not avail; nor suffered long, till one succeeding woe, and dread, swelled up another. Brought from a state of innocence and freedom, and, in a barbarous and cruel manner, conveyed to a state of horror and slavery: This abandoned situation may be easier conceived than described. From the time that I was kid napped and conducted to a factory, and from thence in the brutish, base, but fashionable way of traffic, consigned to Grenada, the grievous thoughts which I then felt, still pant in my heart; though my fears and tears have long since subsided. And yet it is still grievous to think that thousands more have suffered in similar and greater distress, under the hands of barbarous robbers, and merciless taskmasters; and that many even now are suffering in all the extreme bitterness of grief and woe, that no language can describe. The cries of some, and the sight of their misery, may be seen and heard afar; but the deep sounding groans of thousands, and the great sadness of their misery and woe, under the heavy load of oppressions and calamities inflicted upon them, are such as can only be distinctly known to the ears of Jehovah Sabaoth.[8]

---

8. The God of the Hebrew scriptures.

This Lord of Hosts, in his great Providence, and in great mercy to me, made a way for my deliverance from Grenada.—Being in this dreadful captivity and horrible slavery, without any hope of deliverance, for about eight or nine months, beholding the most dreadful scenes of misery and cruelty, and seeing my miserable companions often cruelly lashed, and as it were cut to pieces, for the most trifling faults; this made me often tremble and weep, but I escaped better than many of them. For eating a piece of sugarcane, some were cruelly lashed, or struck over the face to knock their teeth out. Some of the stouter ones, I suppose often reproved, and grown hardened and stupid with many cruel beatings and lashings, or perhaps faint and pressed with hunger and hard labour, were often committing trespasses of this kind, and when detected, they met with exemplary punishment. Some told me they had their teeth pulled out to deter others, and to prevent them from eating any cane in future. Thus seeing my miserable companions and countrymen in this pitiful, distressed and horrible situation, with all the brutish baseness and barbarity attending it, could not but fill my little mind with horror and indignation. But I must own, to the shame of my own countrymen, that I was first kid-napped and betrayed by some of my own complexion, who were the first cause of my exile and slavery; but if there were no buyers there would be no sellers. So far as I can remember, some of the Africans in my country keep slaves, which they take in war, or for debt; but those which they keep are well fed, and good care taken of them, and treated well; and, as to their cloathing, they differ according to the custom of the country. But I may safely say, that all the poverty and misery that any of the inhabitants of Africa meet with among themselves, is far inferior to those inhospitable regions of misery which they meet with in the West-Indies, where their hard-hearted overseers have neither regard to the laws of God, nor the life of their fellow-men.

Thanks be to God, I was delivered from Grenada, and that horrid brutal slavery.—A gentleman coming to England, took me for his servant, and brought me away, where I soon found my situation become more agreeable. After coming to England, and seeing others write and read, I had a strong desire to learn, and getting what assistance I could, I applied myself to learn reading and writing, which soon became my recreation, pleasure, and delight; and when my master perceived that I could write some, he sent me to a proper school for that purpose to learn. Since, I have endeavoured to improve my mind in reading, and have sought to get all the intelligence I could, in my situation of life, towards the state of my brethren and countrymen in complexion, and of the miserable situation of those who are barbarously sold into captivity, and unlawfully held in slavery.

—1787

David Walker
1785–1830

David Walker's mother was a free black woman in Wilmington, North Carolina, and his father was a slave. According to the law of the South, Walker followed the condition of his mother. He exercised his freedom, traveling widely, and he may have met Denmark Vasey, the leader of a slave rebellion that was discovered and crushed before it could be launched in 1822. Walker relocated to Boston in 1825 and opened a used clothing store on Brattle Street. He quickly became an active member of a black abolitionist organization, the Massachusetts General Colored Association, and acted as Boston agent for *Freedom's Journal*, the first black newspaper in the United States.

In 1829, he published *An Appeal to the Colored Citizens of the World*. The pamphlet bitterly attacked pseudo-scientific theories of racial difference articulated by figures like Thomas Jefferson. It also refuted pro-slavery arguments based on the existence of the institution in Egypt, Rome, and elsewhere, maintaining that the American system of plantation slavery was something historically new and incomparably brutal. Walker rightly pointed out that the nation's wealth and power had been built with the "blood and tears" of black slaves, and therefore blacks had as strong a claim to America as whites did. He called on slaves to arm themselves and overthrow their masters with whatever violence was necessary. Walker's *Appeal* was widely distributed in the South, enraging the slavocracy. A bounty of $10,000 was offered for capture of the author. Georgia made circulating "pamphlets of evil tendency among our domestics" an offense punishable by execution. Walker did not relent. He published two more editions of the pamphlet at his own expense. Copies were discovered throughout the South. Three months after the third edition appeared, he died in what many believed was an assassination by poisoning. A year later, Nat Turner led a slave militia in a Virginia uprising that attempted to answer the demands of Walker's historic *Appeal*.

from An Appeal to the Colored Citizens of the World

Article I.
Our Wretchedness in Consequence of Slavery.

My beloved brethren: The Indians of North and of South America—the Greeks—the Irish subjected under the king of Great Britain—the Jews that ancient people of the Lord—the inhabitants of the islands of the sea—in fine, all the inhabitants of the earth, (except however, the sons of Africa) are called *men*, and of course are, and ought to be free. But we, (coloured people) and our childen are *brutes!!* and of course are and ought to be SLAVES to the American people and their children forever! to dig their mines and work their farms; and thus go on enriching them, from one generation to another with our blood and our tears!!

I promised in a preceding page to demonstrate to the satisfaction of the most incredulous, that we, (colored people of these United States of America) are the *most wretched, degraded* and abject set of beings that ever *lived* since the world began, and that the white Americans having reduced us to the wretched state of *slavery*, treat us in that condition *more cruel* (they being an enlightened and christian people) than any heathen nation did any people whom it had reduced to our condition. These affirmations are so well confirmed in the minds of all unprejudiced men who have taken the trouble to read histories, that they need no elucidation from me. But to put them beyond all doubt, I refer you in the first place to the children of Jacob, or of Israel in Egypt, under Pharaoh and his people. Some of my brethren do not know who Pharaoh and the Egyptians were—I know it to be a fact that some of them take the Egyptians to have been a gang of *devils*, not knowing any better, and that they (Egyptians) having got possession of the Lord's people, treated them *nearly* as cruel as *christian Americans* do us, at the present day. For the information of such, I would only mention that the Egyptians, were Africans or colored people, such as we are—some of them yellow and others dark—a mixture of Ethiopians and the natives of Egypt—

about the same as you see the colored people of the United States at the present day,—I say, I call your attention then, to the children of Jacob, while I point out particularly to you his son Joseph among the rest, in Egypt.

"And Pharaoh, said unto Joseph, thou shalt be over my house, and according unto thy word shall all my people be ruled; only in the throne will I be greater than thou."

"And Pharaoh said unto Joseph, see, I have set thee over all the land of Egypt."

"And Pharaoh said unto Joseph, I am Pharaoh, and without thee shall no man lift up his hand or foot in all the land of Egypt."[1]

Now I appeal to heaven and to earth, and particularly to the American people themselves who cease not to declare that our condition is not *hard*, and that we are comparatively satisfied to rest in wretchedness and misery, under them and their children. Not, indeed, to show me a colored President, a Governor, a Legislator, a Senator, a Mayor, or an Attorney at the Bar.—But to show me a man of color, who holds the low office of a Constable, or one who sits in a Juror Box, even on a case of one of his wretched brethren, throughout this great Republic!!—But let us pass Joseph the son of Israel a little further in review, as he existed with that heathen nation.

"And Pharaoh called Joseph's name Zaphnath-paaneah; and he gave him to wife Asenath the daughter of Potipherah priest of On. And Joseph went out over all the land of Egypt."[2]

Compare the above, with the American institutions. Do they not institute laws to prohibit us from marrying among the whites? I would wish, candidly, however, before the Lord, to be understood, that I would not give *a pinch of snuff* to be married to any white person I ever saw in all the days of my life. And I do say it, that the black man, or man of color, who will leave his own color (provided he can get one who is good for any thing) and marry a white woman, to be a double slave to her just because she is *white*, ought to be treated by her as he surely will be, viz; as a NIGER!!! It is not indeed what I care about intermarriages with the whites, which induced me to pass this subject in review; for the Lord knows, that there is a day coming when they will be glad enough to get into the company of the blacks, notwithstanding, we are, in this generation, levelled by them almost on a level with the brute creation; and some of us they treat even worse than they do the brutes that perish. I only made this extract to show how much lower we are held, and how much more cruel we are treated by the Americans, than were the children of Jacob, by the Egyptians. We will notice the sufferings of Israel some further, under *heathen Pharaoh*, compared with ours under the *enlightened christians of America*.

"And Pharaoh spake unto Joseph, saying, thy father and thy brethren are come unto thee."

"The land of Egypt is before thee: in the best of the land make thy father and brethren to dwell; in the land of Goshen let them dwell; and if thou knowest any men of activity among them, then make them rulers over my cattle."[3]

I ask those people who treat us so *well*, Oh! I ask them, where is the most barren spot of land which they have given unto us? Israel had the most fertile land in all Egypt. Need I mention the very notorious fact, that I have known a poor man of color, who labored night and day, to acquire a little money, and having acquired it, he vested it in a small piece of land, and got him a house erected thereon, and hav-

1. Genesis, 41.39–44.   2. Genesis, 41.45.   3. Genesis, 47.5–6.

ing paid for the whole, he moved his family into it, where he was suffered to remain but nine months, when he was cheated out of his property by a white man, and driven out of door!—And is not this the case generally? Can a man of color buy a piece of land and keep it peaceably? Will not some white man try to get it from him even if it is in a *mud hole?* I need not comment any farther on a subject, which all, both black and white, will readily admit. But I must, really, observe that in this very city, when a man of color dies, if he owned any real estate it must generally fall into the hands of some white person. The wife and children of the deceased may weep and lament if they please, but the estate will be kept snug enough by its white posessors.

But to prove farther that the condition of the Israelites was better under the Egyptians than ours is under the whites, I call upon the professing christians, I call upon the philanthropist, I call upon the very tyrant himself, to show me a page of history, either sacred or profane, on which a verse can be found, which maintains, that the Egyptians heaped the *insupportable insult* upon the children of Israel by telling them that they were not of the *human family.* Can the whites deny this charge? Have they not, after having reduced us to the deplorable condition of slaves under their feet, held us up as descending originally from the tribes of *Monkeys or Orang-Outangs?* O! my God! I appeal to every man of feeling—is not this insupportable? Is it not heaping the most gross insult upon our miseries, because they have got us under their feet and we cannot help ourselves? Oh! pity us we pray thee, Lord Jesus, Master.—Has Mr. Jefferson declared to the world, that we are inferior to the whites, both in the endowments of our bodies and of minds? It is indeed surprising, that a man of such great learning, combined with such excellent natural parts, should speak so of a set of men in chains. I do not know what to compare it to, unless, like putting one wild deer in an iron cage, where it will be secured, and hold another by the side of the same, then let it go, and expect the one in the cage to run as fast as the one at liberty. So far, my brethren, were the Egyptians from heaping these insults upon their slaves, that Pharaoh's daughter took Moses, a son of Israel, for her own, as will appear by the following.

"And Pharaoh's daughter said unto her, [Moses' mother] take this child away, and nurse it for me and I will pay thee thy wages. And the woman took the child [Moses] and nursed it.

"And the child grew, and she brought him unto Pharaoh's daughter and he became her son. And she called his name Moses: and she said because I drew him out of the water."[4]

In all probability, Moses would have become Prince Regent to the throne, and no doubt, in process of time but he would have been seated on the throne of Egypt. But he had rather suffer shame, with the people of God, than to enjoy pleasures with that wicked people for a season. O! that the colored people were long since of Moses' excellent disposition, instead of courting favor with, and telling news and lies to our *natural enemies,* against each other—aiding them to keep their hellish chains of slavery upon us. Would we not long before this time, have been respectable men, instead of such wretched victims of oppression as we are? Would they be able to drag our mothers, our fathers, our wives, our children and ourselves, around the world in chains and hand-cuffs as they do, to dig up gold and silver for them and theirs? This question, my brethren, I leave for you to digest; and may God Almighty force it home

---

4. [Walker's note] See Exodus, chap. ii, v. 9, 10.

to your hearts. Remember that unless you are united, keeping your tongues within your teeth, you will be afraid to trust your secrets to each other, and thus perpetuate our miseries under the *christians*!!!!! [ADDITION,—Remember, also to lay humble at the feet of our Lord and Master Jesus Christ, with prayers and fastings. Let our enemies go on with their butcheries, and at once fill up their cup. Never make an attempt to gain our freedom or *natural right*, from under our cruel oppressors and murderers, until you see your way clear; when that hour arrives and you move, be not afraid or dismayed; for be you assured that Jesus Christ the king of heaven and of earth who is the God of justice and of armies, will surely go before you. And those enemies who have for hundreds of years stolen our *rights*, and kept us ignorant of Him and His divine worship, he will remove. Millions of whom, are this day, so ignorant and avaricious, that they cannot conceive how God can have an attribute of justice, and show mercy to us because it pleased Him to make us black—which color, Mr. Jefferson calls unfortunate!!!!!! As though we are not as thankful to our God for having made us as it pleased himself, as they (the whites) are for having made them white. They think because they hold us in their infernal chains of slavery that we wish to be white, or of their color—but they are dreadfully deceived—we wish to be just as it pleased our Creator to have made us, and no avaricious and unmerciful wretches, have any business to make slaves of or hold us in slavery. How would they like for us to make slaves of, or hold them in cruel slavery, and murder them as they do us? But is Mr. Jefferson's assertion true? viz. "that it is unfortunate for us that our Creator has been pleased to make us black." We will not take his say so, for the fact. The world will have an opportunity to see whether it is unfortunate for us, that our Creator *has made us* darker than the *whites*.

Fear not the number and education of our *enemies*, against whom we shall have to contend for our lawful right; guaranteed to us by our Maker; for why should we be afraid, when God is, and will continue (if we continue humble) to be on our side?

The man who would not fight under our Lord and Master Jesus Christ, in the glorious and heavenly cause of freedom and of God—to be delivered from the most wretched, abject and servile slavery, that ever a people was afflicted with since the foundation of the world, to the present day—ought to be kept with all of his children or family, in slavery, or in chains, to be butchered by his *cruel enemies*.

I saw a paragraph, a few years since, in a South Carolina paper, which, speaking of the barbarity of the Turks it said: "The Turks are the most barbarous people in the world—they treat the Greeks more like *brutes* than human beings." And in the same paper was an advertisement, which said: "Eight well built Virginia and Maryland *Negro fellows* and four *wenches* will positively be *sold* this day *to the highest bidder!*" And what astonished me still more was, to see in this same *humane* paper!! the cuts[5] of three men, with clubs and budgets on their backs, and an advertisement offering a considerable sum of money for their apprehension and delivery. I declare it is really so *funny* to hear the Southerners and Westerners of this country talk about *barbarity*, that it is positively, enough to make a man *smile*.

The sufferings of the Helots[6] among the Spartans, were somewhat severe, it is true, but to say that theirs were as severe as ours among the Americans I do most

---

5. Engravings.   6. The helots were a class of peasants in ancient Sparta, also known as Lacedaemonia.

strenuously deny—for instance, can any man show me an article on a page of ancient history which specifies, that, the Spartans chained, and hand-cuffed the Helots, and dragged them from their wives and children, children from their parents, mothers from their sucking babes, wives from their husbands, driving them from one end of the country to the other? Notice the Spartans were heathens, who lived long before our Divine Master made his appearance in the flesh. Can Christian Americans deny these barbarous cruelties? Have you not Americans, having subjected us under you, added to these miseries, by insulting us in telling us to our face, because we are helpless that we are not of the human family? I ask you, O! Americans, I ask you, in the name of the Lord, can you deny these charges? Some perhaps may deny, by saying, that they never thought or said that we were not men. But do not actions speak louder than words?—have they not made provisions for the Greeks, and Irish? Nations who have never done the least thing for them, while we who have enriched their country with our blood and tears—have dug up gold and silver for them and their children, from generation to generation, and are in more miseries than any other people under heaven, are not seen, but by comparatively a handful of the American people? There are indeed, more ways to kill a dog besides choaking it to death with butter. Further. The Spartans or Lacedemonians, had some frivolous pretext for enslaving the Helots, for they (Helots) while being free inhabitants of Sparta, stirred up an intestine commotion, and were by the Spartans subdued, and made prisoners of war. Consequently they and their children were condemned to perpetual slavery.[7]

I have been for years troubling the pages of historians to find out what our fathers have done to the *white Christians of America*, to merit such condign punishment as they have inflicted on them, and do continue to inflict on us their children. But I must aver, that my researches have hitherto been to no effect. I have therefore come to the immovable conclusion, that they (Americans) have, and do continue to punish us for nothing else, but for enriching them and their country. For I cannot conceive of any thing else. Nor will I ever believe otherwise until the Lord shall convince me.

The world knows, that slavery as it existed among the Romans, (which was the primary cause of their destruction) was, comparatively speaking, no more than a *cypher*, when compared with ours under the Americans. Indeed, I should not have noticed the Roman slaves, had not the very learned and penetrating Mr. Jefferson said, "When a master was murdered, all his slaves in the same house or within hearing, were condemned to death."[8]—Here let me ask Mr. Jefferson, (but he is gone to answer at the bar of God, for the deeds done in his body while living,) I therefore ask the whole American people, had I not rather die, or be put to death than to be a slave to any tyrant, who takes not only my own, but my wife and children's lives by the inches? Yea, would I meet death with avidity far! far!! in preference to such *servile submission* to the murderous hands of tyrants. Mr. Jefferson's very severe remarks on us have been so extensively argued upon by men whose attainments in literature, I shall never be able to reach, that I would not have meddled with it, were it not to solicit each of my brethren, who has the spirit of a man, to buy a copy of

---

7. [Walker's note] See Dr. Goldsmith's History of Greece—page 9. See also Plutarch's lives. The Helots subdued by Agis, king of Sparta.   8. [Walker's note] See his notes on Virginia, page 210.

Mr. Jefferson's "Notes on Virginia," and put it in the hand of his son. For let no one of us suppose that the refutations which have been written by our white friends are enough—they are *whites*—we are *blacks*. We, and the world wish to see the charges of Mr. Jefferson refuted by the blacks *themselves*, according to their chance: for we must remember that what the whites have written respecting this subject, is other men's labors and did not emanate from the blacks. I know well, that there are some talents and learning among the coloured people of this country, which we have not a chance to develope, in consequence of oppression; but our oppression ought not to hinder us from acquiring all we can.—For we will have a chance to develope them by and by. God will not suffer us, always to be oppressed. Our sufferings will come to an *end*, in spite of all the Americans this side of *eternity*. Then we will want all the learning and talents among ourselves, and perhaps more, to govern ourselves.— "Every dog must have its day," the American's is coming to an end.

But let us review Mr. Jefferson's remarks respecting us some further. Comparing our miserable fathers, with the learned philosophers of Greece, he says: "Yet notwith-standing these and other discouraging circumstances among the Romans, their slaves were often their rarest artists. They excelled too in science, insomuch as to be usually employed as tutors to their master's children; Epictetus, Terence and Phaedrus, were slaves,—but they were of the race of whites. It is not their *condition* then, but *nature*, which has produced the distinction."[9] See this, my brethren!! Do you believe that this assertion is swallowed by millions of the whites? Do you know that Mr. Jefferson was one of as great characters as ever lived among the whites? See his writings for the world, and public labors for the United States of America. Do you believe that the assertions of such a man, will pass away into oblivion unobserved by this people and the world? If you do you are much mistaken—See how the American people treat us—have we souls in our bodies? are we men who have any spirits at all? I know that there are many *swell-bellied* fellows among us whose greatest object is to fill their stomachs. Such I do not mean—I am after those who know and feel, that we are MEN as well as other people; to them, I say, that unless we try to refute Mr. Jefferson's argu-ments respecting us, we will only establish them.

But the slaves among the Romans. Every body who has read history, knows, that as soon as a slave among the Romans obtained his freedom, he could rise to the great-est eminence in the State, and there was no law instituted to hinder a slave from buy-ing his freedom. Have not the Americans instituted laws to hinder us from obtaining our freedom. Do any deny this charge? Read the laws of Virginia, North Carolina, &c. Further: have not the Americans instituted laws to prohibit a man of colour from obtaining and holding any office whatever, under the government of the United States of America? Now, Mr. Jefferson tells us that our condition is not so hard, as the slaves were under the Romans!!!!

It is time for me to bring this article to a close. But before I close it, I must observe to my brethren that at the close of the first Revolution in this country with Great Britain, there were but thirteen States in the Union, now there are twenty-four, most of which are slave-holding States, and the whites are dragging us around in chains and hand-cuffs to their new States and Territories to work their mines and farms, to enrich them and their children, and millions of them believing firmly that

---

9. [Walker's note] See his notes on Virginia, page 211.

we being a little darker than they, were made by our creater to be an inheritance to them and their children forever—the same as a parcel of *brutes*!!

Are we MEN!!—I ask you, O my brethren! are we MEN? Did our creator make us to be slaves to dust and ashes like ourselves? Are they not dying worms as well as we? Have they not to make their appearance before the tribunal of heaven, to answer for the deeds done in the body, as well as we? Have we any other master but Jesus Christ alone? Is he not their master as well as ours?—What right then, have we to obey and call any other master, but Himself? How we could be so *submissive* to a gang of men, whom we cannot tell whether they are as *good* as ourselves or not, I never could conceive. However, this is shut up with the Lord and we cannot precisely tell—but I declare, we judge men by their works.

The whites have always been an unjust, jealous unmerciful, avaricious and blood thirsty set of beings, always seeking after power and authority.—We view them all over the confederacy of Greece, where they were first known to be any thing, (in consequence of education) we see them there, cutting each other's throats—trying to subject each other to wretchedness and misery, to effect which they used all kinds of deceitful, unfair and unmerciful means. We view them next in Rome, where the spirit of tyranny and deceit raged still higher.—We view them in Gaul, Spain and in Britain—in fine, we view them all over Europe, together with what were scattered about in Asia and Africa, as heathens, and we see them acting more like devils than accountable men. But some may ask, did not the blacks of Africa, and the mulattoes of Asia, go on in the same way as did the whites of Europe. I answer no—they never were half so avaricious, deceitful and unmerciful as the whites, according to their knowledge.

But we will leave the whites or Europeans as heathens and take a view of them as christians, in which capacity we see them as cruel, if not more so than ever. In fact, take them as a body, they are ten times more cruel avaricious and unmerciful than ever they were; for while they were heathens they were bad enough it is true, but it is positively a fact that there were not quite so audacious as to go and take vessel loads of men, women and children, and in cold blood and through devilishness, throw them into the sea, and murder them in all kinds of ways. While they were heathens, they were too ignorant for such barbarity. But being christians, enlightened and sensible, they are completely prepared for such hellish cruelties. Now suppose God were to give them more sense, what would they do. If it were possible would they not *dethrone* Jehovah and seat themselves upon his throne? I therefore, in the name and fear of the Lord God of heaven and of earth, divested of prejudice either on the side of my colour or that of the whites, advance my suspicion of them, whether they are *as good by nature* as we are or not. Their actions, since they were known as a people, have been the reverse, I do indeed suspect them, but this, as I before observed, is shut up with the Lord, we cannot exactly tell, it will be proved in succeeding generations.—The whites have had the essence of the gospel as it was preached by my master and his apostles—the Ethiopians have not, who are to have it in its meridian splendor—the Lord will give it to them to their satisfaction. I hope and pray my God, that they will make good use of it, that it may be well with them.

—1829

William Lloyd Garrison
1805–1879

William Lloyd Garrison's parents emigrated from Nova Scotia to Newburyport, Massachusetts, just before his birth. His first newspaper, the Newburyport *Free Press*, adopted a scornful editorial tone that alienated subscribers. The paper collapsed after little more than a year, but not before publishing the first poems of the Quaker poet John Greenleaf Whittier. Garrison did not relent; his subsequent papers became more radical, decrying all the "vices" of the day: alcohol, prostitution, gambling, Sabbath-breaking, and war. Increasingly, he was guided by the philosophy of "non-resistance," which held that social ills should be overcome not through political action or legislation but through direct appeals to the conscience and reason.

In the late 1820s, Garrison extended the scope of his activism to include opposition to slavery, and he applied the logic of non-resistance to this new crusade. As he put it in the American Anti-Slavery Society's 1833 manifesto, "Our measures shall be such only as the opposition of moral purity to moral corruption—the destruction of error by the potency of the truth—the overthrow of prejudice by the power of love—and the abolition of slavery by the spirit of repentance." On the strength of these principles, which he maintained throughout his life, Garrison later disapproved of the abolitionist movement's growing reliance on the electoral strategies of the Free Soil and Republican parties, and he condemned John Brown's raid on Harper's Ferry. Brown and his supporters attacked the Virginia town in the summer of 1859, with the hope of commandeering guns from a federal arsenal and establishing a base from which to strike slave-owners. Garrison, on the other hand, placed his faith in the transformative fire of the naked truth, applied to the public through the mechanism of the press. This way of thinking about the role of the journalist in society explains the scorching and obdurate tone of his prose.

Radicalism in thought, speech, and action was a constant in Garrison's life. At a time when most abolitionists felt that slaves should be freed gradually and repatriated to Africa, he called for immediate emancipation and no colonization. When he found that women had been excluded from participation in the World Anti-Slavery Congress in London in 1840, he refused to take his seat as a delegate. On July 4, 1854, he burned a copy of the Constitution, which he declared was "a covenant with death and an agreement with Hell." Garrison was attacked by mobs, jailed, and vilified in both the northern and southern press. Georgia maintained an offer of $5,000 for his capture. Even members of the abolitionist movement were deeply divided in their responses. Many thought his uncompromising tone would drive away potential allies. Others, including Frederick Douglass, felt that non-resistance was a powerless strategy in the face of the massive expansion and entrenchment of slavery as a fully developed social order. Despite these controversies, and even though the *Liberator* never generated circulation above 3,000, Garrison was the most influential white abolitionist propagandist of the thirty years preceding Emancipation.

To the Public

In the month of August, I issued proposals for publishing "THE LIBERATOR" in Washington City; but the enterprise, though hailed in different sections of the country, was palsied by public indifference. Since that time, the removal of the *Genius of Universal Emancipation* to the Seat of Government has rendered less imperious the establishment of a similar periodical in that quarter.

During my recent tour for the purpose of exciting the minds of the people by a series of discourses on the subject of slavery, every place that I visited gave fresh evidence of the fact, that a greater revolution in public sentiment was to be effected in the free States—*and particularly in New-England*—than at the South. I found contempt more bitter, opposition more active, detraction more relentless, prejudice more stubborn, and apathy more frozen, than among slave-owners themselves. Of course, there were individual exceptions to the contrary. This state of things afflicted, but did not dishearten me. I determined, at every hazard, to lift up the standard of emancipation in the eyes of the nation, *within sight of Bunker Hill*[1] *and in the birthplace of liberty*. That standard is now unfurled; and long may it float, unhurt by the spoliations of time or the missiles of a desperate foe—yea, till every chain be broken, and every bondman set free! Let Southern oppressors tremble—let their secret abettors tremble—let their Northern apologists tremble—let all the enemies of the persecuted blacks tremble.

I deem the publication of my original Prospectus unnecessary, as it has obtained a wide circulation. The principles therein inculcated will be steadily pursued in this paper, excepting that I shall not array myself as the political partisan of any man. In defending the great cause of human rights, I wish to derive the assistance of all religions and of all parties.

Assenting to the "self-evident truth" maintained in the American Declaration of Independence, "that all men are created equal, and endowed by their Creator with certain inalienable rights—among which are life, liberty and the pursuit of happiness," I shall strenuously contend for the immediate enfranchisement of our slave population. In Park-Street Church, on the Fourth of July, 1829, in an address on slavery, I unreflectingly assented to the popular but pernicious doctrine of *gradual* abolition. I seize this opportunity to make a full and unequivocal recantation, and thus publicly to ask pardon of my God, of my country, and of my brethren the poor slaves, for having uttered a sentiment so full of timidity, injustice, and absurdity. A similar recantation, from my pen, was published in the *Genius of Universal Emancipation* at Baltimore, in September, 1829. My conscience is now satisfied.

I am aware that many object to the severity of my language; but is there not cause for severity? I *will be* as harsh as truth, and as uncompromising as justice. On this subject, I do not wish to think, or speak, or write, with moderation. No! no! Tell a man whose house is on fire to give a moderate alarm; tell him to moderately rescue his wife from the hands of the ravisher; tell the mother to gradually extricate her babe from the fire into which it has fallen;—but urge me not to use moderation in a cause like the present. I am in earnest—I will not equivocate—I will not excuse—I will not retreat a single inch—AND I WILL BE HEARD. The apathy of the people is enough to make every statue leap from its pedestal, and to hasten the resurrection of the dead.

It is pretended, that I am retarding the cause of emancipation by the coarseness of my invective and the precipitancy of my measures. *The charge is not true.* On this question my influence,—humble as it is,—is felt at this moment to a considerable extent, and shall be felt in coming years—not perniciously, but beneficially—not as a curse, but as a blessing; and posterity will bear testimony that I was right. I desire to thank God, that he enables me to disregard "the fear of man which bringeth a

---

1. Site in Boston of an important early battle in the American Revolution.

snare," and to speak his truth in its simplicity and power. And here I close with this fresh dedication:

"Oppression! I have seen thee, face to face,
And met thy cruel eye and cloudy brow;
But thy soul-withering glance I fear not now—
For dread to prouder feelings doth give place
Of deep abhorrence! Scorning the disgrace
Of slavish knees that at thy footstool bow,
I also kneel—but with far other vow
Do hail thee and thy herd of hirelings base:—
I swear, while life-blood warms my throbbing veins,
Still to oppose and thwart, with heart and hand,
Thy brutalising sway—till Afric's chains
Are burst, and Freedom rules the rescued land,—
Trampling Oppression and his iron rod:
Such is the vow I take—SO HELP ME GOD"

William Lloyd Garrison.
Boston, January 1, 1831.

—1831

Fanny Kemble
1809–1893

Frances Anne Kemble's parents, the actors Charles and Marie Kemble, operated the London theater Covent Garden but sent their daughter to school in France, hoping to prepare her for a different kind of life. Their ambitions for her ended when they ran deeply into debt and, to help save the theater, she took to the stage as Juliet in an 1829 production of William Shakespeare's *Romeo and Juliet*. The role made her reputation and launched her career as the "leading lady of the nineteenth-century stage." Three years later, Fanny and her father began a theatrical tour of the United States. In Boston, New York, and beyond, she was a sensation, followed from city to city by admirers, among them Pierce Butler, a Philadelphia socialite who was heir to two of the largest plantations in Georgia. In 1834, Kemble retired and married Butler, convinced that she could persuade him to emancipate his slaves. She could not. Moreover, she soon began to strain against the authority he tried to assume over her. In defiance of his wishes, she published her *Journal of a Residence in America* in 1835. The book, with its frank observations of American society, culture, and politics, set off an uproar of criticism, much of it sexist in nature. For instance, Edgar Allan Poe in *The Southern Literary Messenger* complained that "a female, and a young one too, cannot speak with the self-confidence which marks this book, without jarring somewhat upon American notions of the retiring delicacy of the female character."

When her husband took her to Georgia for the winter of 1838–1839, Kemble began to advocate for his slaves, especially the women, bringing their grievances before him. She kept a journal in which she recorded her thoughts on the cruelty and destructiveness of slavery. The manuscript was not published for twenty-five years, finally appearing in 1863 as *Journal of a*

Residence on a Georgian Plantation in 1838–1839. The war was not going well for the North, and the reviewer for *The Atlantic Monthly* welcomed the book's candid portrait of slavery, seeing it as a tonic for northern resolve: "it is the first ample, lucid, faithful, detailed account, from the actual head-quarters of a slave-plantation in this country, of the workings of the system,—its persistent, hopeless, helpless crushing of humanity in the slave, and the more fearful moral and mental dry-rot it generates in the master." Kemble's refusal to abandon her abolitionist principles during her residence in Georgia led eventually to her separation from her husband in 1844. She lived the rest of her long life as a single woman, crossing the Atlantic every year to summer in the Swiss Alps and touring England, Canada, and America to give dramatic readings from Shakespeare's plays.

from Journal of a Residence on a Georgian Plantation in 1838–1839

Dear E——,—I can not give way to the bitter impatience I feel at my present position, and come back to the North without leaving my babies; and though I suppose their stay will not in any case be much prolonged in these regions of swamp and slavery, I must, for their sakes, remain where they are, and learn this dreary lesson of human suffering to the end. The record, it seems to me, must be utterly wearisome to you, as the instances themselves, I suppose, in a given time (thanks to that dreadful reconciler to all that is evil—habit), would become to me.

This morning I had a visit from two of the women, Charlotte and Judy, who came to me for help and advice for a complaint, which it really seems to me every other woman on the estate is cursed with, and which is a direct result of the conditions of their existence; the practice of sending women to labor in the fields in the third week after their confinement is a specific for causing this infirmity, and I know no specific for curing it under these circumstances. As soon as these poor things had departed with such comfort as I could give them, and the bandages they especially begged for, three other sable graces introduced themselves, Edie, Louisa, and Diana; the former told me she had had a family of seven children, but had lost them all through "ill luck," as she denominated the ignorance and ill treatment which were answerable for the loss of these, as of so many other poor little creatures their fellows. Having dismissed her and Diana with the sugar and rice they came to beg, I detained Louisa, whom I had never seen but in the presence of her old grandmother, whose version of the poor child's escape to, and hiding in the woods, I had a desire to compare with the heroine's own story. She told it very simply, and it was most pathetic. She had not finished her task one day, when she said she felt ill, and unable to do so, and had been severely flogged by Driver Bran, in whose "gang" she then was. The next day, in spite of this encouragement to labor, she had again been unable to complete her appointed work; and Bran having told her that he'd tie her up and flog her if she did not get it done, she had left the field and run into the swamp. "Tie you up, Louisa!" said I; "what is that?" She then described to me that they were fastened up by their wrists to a beam or a branch of a tree, their feet barely touching the ground, so as to allow them no purchase for resistance or evasion of the lash, their clothes turned over their heads, and their backs scored with a leather thong, either by the driver himself, or, if he pleases to inflict their punishment by deputy, any of the men he may choose to summon to the office; it might be father, brother, husband, or lover, if the overseer so ordered it. I turned sick, and my blood curdled listening to these details from the slender young slip of a lassie, with her poor piteous face and murmuring, pleading voice. "Oh," said I, "Louisa; but the rattlesnakes—the dreadful rattlesnakes in the swamps; were you not afraid of those horrible creatures?" "Oh, missis," said the poor child, "me no tink of dem; me forget al 'bout dem for de fretting." "Why did you come home at last?" "Oh, missis, me starve with hunger, me most dead with hunger before me come back." "And were you flogged, Louisa?" said I, with a shudder at what the answer might be. "No, missis, me go to hospital; me almost dead and sick so long, 'spec Driver Bran him forgot 'bout de flogging." I am getting perfectly savage over all these doings, E——, and really think I should consider my own throat and those of my children well cut if some night the people were to take it into their heads to clear off scores in that fashion.

The Calibanish[1] wonderment of all my visitors at the exceedingly coarse and simple furniture and rustic means of comfort of my abode is very droll. I have never inhabited any apartment so perfectly devoid of what we should consider the common decencies of life; but to them, my rude chintz-covered sofa and common pine-wood table, with its green baize cloth, seem the adornings of a palace; and often in the evening, when my bairns[2] are asleep, and M—— up stairs keeping watch over them, and I sit writing this daily history for your edification, the door of the great barn-like room is opened stealthily, and one after another, men and women come trooping silently in, their naked feet falling all but inaudibly on the bare boards as they betake themselves to the hearth, where they squat down on their hams in a circle, the bright blaze from the huge pine logs, which is the only light of this half of the room, shining on their sooty limbs and faces, and making them look like a ring of ebony idols surrounding my domestic hearth. I have had as many as fourteen at a time squatting silently there for nearly half an hour, watching me writing at the other end of the room. The candles on my table give only light enough for my own occupation, the fire-light illuminates the rest of the apartment; and you can not imagine any thing stranger than the effect of all these glassy whites of eyes and grinning white teeth turned toward me, and shining in the flickering light. I very often take no notice of them at all, and they seem perfectly absorbed in contemplating me. My evening dress probably excites their wonder and admiration no less than my rapid and continuous writing, for which they have sometimes expressed compassion, as if they thought it must be more laborious than hoeing; sometimes at the end of my day's journal I look up and say suddenly, "Well, what do you want?" when each black figure springs up at once, as if moved by machinery; they all answer, "Me come say ha do (how d'ye do), missis;" and then they troop out as noiselessly as they entered, like a procession of sable dreams, and I go off in search, if possible, of whiter ones.

Two days ago I had a visit of great interest to me from several lads from twelve to sixteen years old, who had come to beg me to give them work. To make you understand this, you must know that, wishing very much to cut some walks and drives through the very picturesque patches of woodland not far from the house, I announced, through Jack, my desire to give employment in the woodcutting line to as many lads as chose, when their unpaid task was done, to come and do some work for me, for which I engaged to pay them. At the risk of producing a most dangerous process of reflection and calculation in their brains, I have persisted in paying what I

---

1. A character in Shakespeare's *The Tempest* described as "a savage and deformed slave."   2. Children.

considered wages to every slave that has been my servant; and these my laborers must, of course, be free to work or no, as they like, and if they work for me must be paid by me. The proposition met with unmingled approbation from my "gang;" but I think it might be considered dangerously suggestive of the rightful relation between work and wages; in short, very involuntarily no doubt, but, nevertheless, very effectually I am disseminating ideas among Mr. ———'s dependents, the like of which have certainly never before visited their wool-thatched brains. . . .

Before closing this letter, I have a mind to transcribe to you the entries for to-day recorded in a sort of day-book, where I put down very succinctly the number of people who visit me, their petitions and ailments, and also such special particulars concerning them as seem to me worth recording. You will see how miserable the physical condition of many of these poor creatures is; and their physical condition, it is insisted by those who uphold this evil system, is the only part of it which is prosperous, happy, and compares well with that of Northern laborers. Judge from the details I now send you; and never forget, while reading them, that the people on this plantation are well off, and consider themselves well off, in comparison with the slaves on some of the neighboring estates.

Fanny has had six children; all dead but one. She came to beg to have her work in the field lightened.

Nanny has had three children; two of them are dead. She came to implore that the rule of sending them into the field three weeks after their confinement might be altered.

Leah, Caesar's wife, has had six children; three are dead.

Sophy, Lewis's wife, came to beg for some old linen. She is suffering fearfully; has had ten children; five of them are dead. The principal favor she asked was a piece of meat, which I gave her.

Sally, Scipio's wife, has had two miscarriages and three children born, one of whom is dead. She came complaining of incessant pain and weakness in her back. This woman was a mulatto daughter of a slave called Sophy, by a white man of the name of Walker, who visited the plantation.

Charlotte, Renty's wife, had had two miscarriages, and was with child again. She was almost crippled with rheumatism, and showed me a pair of poor swollen knees that made my heart ache. I have promised her a pair of flannel trowsers, which I must forthwith set about making.

Sarah, Stephen's wife—this woman's case and history were alike deplorable. She had had four miscarriages, had brought seven children into the world, five of whom were dead, and was again with child. She complained of dreadful pains in the back, and an internal tumor which swells with the exertion of working in the fields; probably, I think, she is ruptured. She told me she had once been mad and had ran into the woods, where she contrived to elude discovery for some time, but was at last tracked and brought back, when she was tied up by the arms, and heavy logs fastened to her feet, and was severely flogged. After this she contrived to escape again, and lived for some time skulking in the woods, and she supposes mad, for when she was taken again she was entirely naked. She subsequently recovered from this derangement, and seems now just like all the other poor creatures who come to me for help and pity. I suppose her constant childbearing and hard labor in the fields at the same time may have produced the temporary insanity.

Sukey, Bush's wife, only came to pay her respects. She had had four miscarriages; had brought eleven children into the world, five of whom are dead.

Molly, Quambo's wife, also only came to see me. Hers was the best account I have yet received; she had had nine children, and six of them were still alive.

This is only the entry for to-day, in my diary, of the people's complaints and visits. Can you conceive a more wretched picture than that which it exhibits of the conditions under which these women live? Their cases are in no respect singular, and though they come with pitiful entreaties that I will help them with some alleviation of their pressing physical distresses, it seems to me marvelous with what desperate patience (I write it advisedly, patience of utter despair) they endure their sorrow-laden existence. Even the poor wretch who told that miserable story of insanity, and lonely hiding in the swamps, and scourging when she was found, and of her renewed madness and flight, did so in a sort of low, plaintive, monotonous murmur of misery, as if such sufferings were all "in the day's work."

I ask these questions about their children because I think the number they bear as compared with the number they rear a fair gauge of the effect of the system on their own health and that of their offspring. There was hardly one of these women, as you will see by the details I have noted of their ailments, who might not have been a candidate for a bed in a hospital, and they had come to me after working all day in the fields.

—1863

Benjamin Drew
1812–1903

Benjamin Drew was a member of a group of Boston abolitionists that included the publisher John P. Jewett. Jewett, who published Harriet Beecher Stowe's *Uncle Tom's Cabin* in 1852, assisted Drew in his efforts to arrange a tour of Upper Canada in the early 1850s. He also helped broker an introduction with the Canadian Anti-Slavery Society. With officers of that group, Drew interviewed more than 100 of the 30,000 African Americans living in Upper Canada—mostly escaped slaves from the United States. Published by Jewett in 1856, Drew's *A North Side View of Slavery* (1856) records "direct and unimpeachable testimony" in which the former slaves speak for themselves. These slave stories shed "a peculiar lustre on the Institution of the South [and] reveal the hideousness of the sin, which, while calling on the North to fall down and worship it, almost equals the tempter himself in the felicity of scriptural quotations." Arranged regionally, *A North Side View of Slavery* focuses on the major cities and towns that Drew visited and paints an unflinchingly harsh portrait of slavery—of the common and severe abuses that all slaves experienced. Yet, as the entries included in this anthology suggest, the volume offers a glimpse of the diverse range of individual experience that fueled Drew's desire to put a personal face on slavery.

One of Drew's more famous (although brief) interviews is with Harriet Tubman, who escaped slavery at age twenty-nine in 1849. Tubman went on to lead or organize more than a dozen dangerous escape attempts on the Underground Railroad that resulted in the liberation of more than one hundred slaves. The majority of people Drew interviewed traveled the Underground Railroad, and their repeated efforts to escape speak to the perilous nature of the informal route of roads, foot paths, river crossings, and safe houses that led to freedom in the North.

from A North Side View of Slavery; The Refugee, or, The Narratives of Fugitive Slaves in Canada

Harriet Tubman

I grew up like a neglected weed,—ignorant of liberty, having no experience of it. Then I was not happy or contented: every time I saw a white man I was afraid of being carried away. I had two sisters carried away in a chain-gang,—one of them left two children. We were always uneasy. Now I've been free, I know what a dreadful condition slavery is. I have seen hundreds of escaped slaves, but I never saw one who was willing to go back and be a slave. I have no opportunity to see my friends in my native land. We would rather stay in our native land, if we could be as free there as we are here. I think slavery is the next thing to hell. If a person would send another into bondage, he would, it appears to me, be bad enough to send him into hell, if he could.

William Grose

I was held as a slave at Harper's Ferry, Va. When I was twenty-five years old, my two brothers who were twelve miles out, were sent for to the ferry, so as to catch us all three together, which they did. We were then taken to Baltimore to be sold down south. The reason was, that I had a free wife in Virginia, and they were afraid we would get away through her means. My wife and two children were then keeping boarders; I was well used, and we were doing well. All at once, on Sunday morning, a man came to my house before I was up, and called me to go to his store to help put up some goods. My wife suspected it was a trap: but I started to go. When I came in sight of him, my heart failed me; I sent him word I could not come. On inquiry in a certain quarter, I was told that I was sold, and was advised to make my escape into Pennsylvania. I then went to my owner's, twelve miles, and remained there three days, they telling me I was not sold. The two brothers were all this time in jail, but I did not then know it. I was sent to the mill to get some offal,[1]—then two men came in, grabbed me and handcuffed me, and took me off. How I felt that day I cannot tell. I had never been more than twenty miles from home, and now I was taken away from my mother and wife and children. About four miles from the mill, I met my wife in the road coming to bring me some clean clothes. She met me as I was on horseback, handcuffed. She thought I was on the farm, and was surprised to see me. They let me get down to walk and talk with her until we came to the jail: then they put me in, and kept her outside. She had then eight miles to go on foot, to get clothes ready for me to take along. I was so crazy, I do n't know what my wife said. I was beside myself to think of going south. I was as afraid of traders as I would be of a bear. This was Tuesday.

The man who had bought us came early Wednesday morning, but the jailer would not let us out, he hoping to make a bargain with somebody else, and induce our owners to withdraw the bond from the man that had us. Upon this, the trader and jailer got into a quarrel, and the trader produced a pistol, which the jailer and his brother took away from him. After some time, the jailer let us out. We were handcuffed together: I was in the middle, a hand of each brother fastened to mine. We

---

1. Trimmings from animal hide.

walked thus to Harper's Ferry: there my wife met me with some clothes. She said but little; she was in grief and crying. The two men with us told her they would get us a good home. We went by the cars to Baltimore—remained fifteen days in jail. Then we were separated, myself and one brother going to New Orleans, and the other remained in B. Him I have not seen since, but have heard that he was taken to Georgia. There were about seventy of us, men, women, and children shipped to New Orleans. Nothing especial occurred except on one occasion, when, after some thick weather, the ship came near an English island: the captain then hurried us all below and closed the hatches. After passing the island, we had liberty to come up again.

We waited on our owners awhile in New Orleans, and after four months, my brother and I were sold together as house servants in the city, to an old widower, who would not have a white face about him. He had a colored woman for a wife—she being a slave. He had had several wives whom he had set free when he got tired of them. This woman came for us to the yard,—then we went before him. He sent for a woman, who came in, and said he to me, "That is your wife.["] I was scared half to death, for I had one wife whom I liked, and did n't want another,—but I said nothing. He assigned one to my brother in the same way. There was no ceremony about it—he said "Cynthia is your wife, and Ellen is John's." As we were not acclimated, he sent us into Alabama to a watering-place, where we remained three months till late in the fall—then we went back to him. I was hired out one month in a gambling saloon, where I had two meals a day and slept on a table; then for nine months to an American family, where I got along very well; then to a man who had been mate of a steamboat, and whom I could not please. After I had been in New Orleans a year, my wife came on and was employed in the same place, (in the American family).

One oppression there was, my wife did not dare let it be known she was from Virginia, through fear of being sold. When my master found out that I had a free-woman for a wife there, he was angry about it, and began to grumble. Then she went to a lawyer to get a certificate by which she could remain there. He would get one for a hundred dollars, which was more than she was able to pay: so she did not get the certificate, but promised to take one by and by. His hoping to get the money kept him from troubling her,—and before the time came for her taking it, she left for a distant place. He was mad about it, and told me that if she ever came there again, he'd put her to so much trouble that she would wish she had paid the hundred dollars and got the certificate. This did not disturb me, as I knew she would not come back any more.

After my wife was gone, I felt very uneasy. At length, I picked up spunk, and said I would start. All this time, I dreamed on nights that I was getting clear. This put the notion into my head to start—a dream that I had reached a free soil and was perfectly safe. Sometimes I felt as if I would get clear, and again as if I would not. I had many doubts. I said to myself—I recollect it well,—I can't die but once; if they catch me, they can but kill me: I'll defend myself as far as I can. I armed myself with an old razor, and made a start alone, telling no one, not even my brother. All the way along, I felt a dread—a heavy load on me all the way. I would look up at the telegraph wire, and dread that the news was going on ahead of me. At one time I was on a canal-boat— it did not seem to go fast enough for me, and I felt very much cast down about it; at last I came to a place where the telegraph wire was broken, and I felt as if the heavy load was rolled off me. I intended to stay in my native country,—but I saw so many mean-looking men, that I did not dare to stay. I found a friend who helped me on the way to Canada, which I reached in 1851.

I served twenty-five years in slavery, and about five I have been free. I feel now like a man, while before I felt more as though I were but a brute. When in the United States, if a white man spoke to me, I would feel frightened, whether I were in the right or wrong; but now it is quite a different thing,—if a white man speaks to me, I can look him right in the eyes—if he were to insult me, I could give him an answer. I have the rights and privileges of any other man. I am now living with my wife and children, and doing very well. When I lie down at night, I do not feel afraid of over-sleeping, so that my employer might jump on me if he pleased. I am a true British subject, and I have a vote every year as much as any other man. I often used to wonder in the United States, when I saw carriages going round for voters, why they never asked me to vote. But I have since found out the reason,—I know they were using my vote instead of my using it—now I use it myself. Now I feel like a man, and I wish to God that all my fellow-creatures could feel the same freedom that I feel. I am not prejudiced against all the white race in the United States,—it is only the portion that sustain the cursed laws of slavery.

Here's something I want to say to the colored people in the United States: You think you are free there, but you are very much mistaken: if you wish to be free men, I hope you will all come to Canada as soon as possible. There is plenty of land here, and schools to educate your children. I have no education myself, but I do n't intend to let my children come up as I did. I have but two, and instead of making servants out of them, I'll give them a good education, which I could not do in the southern portion of the United States. True, they were not slaves there, but I could not have given them any education.

I have been through both Upper and Lower Canada,[2] and I have found the colored people keeping stores, farming, etc., and doing well. I have made more money since I came here, than I made in the United States. I know several colored people who have become wealthy by industry—owning horses and carriages,—one who was a fellow-servant of mine, now owns two span of horses, and two as fine carriages as there are on the bank. As a general thing, the colored people are more sober and industrious than in the States: there they feel when they have money, that they cannot make what use they would like of it, they are so kept down, so looked down upon. Here they have something to do with their money, and put it to a good purpose.

I am employed in the Clifton House,[3] at the Falls.

Sophia Pooley

I was born in Fishkill, New York State, twelve miles from North River. My father's name was Oliver Burthen, my mother's Dinah. I am now more than ninety years old. I was stolen from my parents when I was seven years old, and brought to Canada; that was long before the American Revolution. There were hardly any white people in Canada then—nothing here but Indians and wild beasts. Many a deer I

2. The Constitutional Act of 1791 established Upper and Lower Canada—roughly the southern portions of the provinces Ontario and Quebec.   3. A renowned hotel at Niagara Falls, built in 1833.

have helped catch on the lakes in a canoe: one year we took ninety. I was a woman grown when the first governor of Canada came from England: that was Gov. Simcoe.[4]

My parents were slaves in New York State. My master's sons-in-law, Daniel Outwaters and Simon Knox, came into the garden where my sister and I were playing among the currant bushes, tied their handkerchiefs over our mouths, carried us to a vessel, put us in the hold, and sailed up the river. I know not how far nor how long—it was dark there all the time. Then we came by land. I remember when we came to Genesee,—there were Indian settlements there,—Onondagas, Senecas, and Oneidas. I guess I was the first colored girl brought into Canada. The white men sold us at Niagara to old Indian Brant,[5] the king. I lived with old Brant about twelve or thirteen years as nigh as I can tell. Brant lived part of the time at Mohawk, part at Ancaster, part at Preston, then called Lower Block: the Upper Block was at Snyder's Mills. While I lived with old Brant we caught the deer. It was at Dundas at the outlet. We would let the hounds loose, and when we heard them bark we would run for the canoe—Peggy, and Mary, and Katy, Brant's daughters and I. Brant's sons, Joseph and Jacob, would wait on the shore to kill the deer when we fetched him in. I had a tomahawk, and would hit the deer on the head—then the squaws would take it by the horns and paddle ashore. The boys would bleed and skin the deer and take the meat to the house. Sometimes white people in the neighborhood, John Chisholm and Bill Chisholm, would come and say 'twas their hounds, and they must have the meat. But we would not give it up.

Canada was then filling up with white people. And after Brant went to England, and kissed the queen's hand, he was made a colonel.[6] Then there began to be laws in Canada. Brant was only half Indian: his mother was a squaw—I saw her when I came to this country. She was an old body; her hair was quite white. Brant was a good looking man—quite portly. He was as big as Jim Douglass who lived here in the bush, and weighed two hundred pounds. He lived in an Indian village—white men came among them and they intermarried. They had an English schoolmaster, an English preacher, and an English blacksmith. When Brant went among the English, he wore the English dress—when he was among the Indians, he wore the Indian dress,—broadcloth leggings, blanket, moccasins, fur cap. He had his ears slit with a long loop at the edge, and in these he hung long silver ornaments. He wore a silver half-moon on his breast with the king's name on it, and broad silver bracelets on his arms. He never would paint, but his people painted a great deal. Brant was always for making peace among his people; that was the reason of his going about so much. I used to talk Indian better than I could English. I have forgotten some of it—there are none to talk it with now.

Brant's third wife, my mistress, was a barbarous creature. She could talk English, but she would not. She would tell me in Indian to do things, and then hit me with

4. A British soldier, John Graves Simcoe (1752–1806) was the first lieutenant governor of Upper Canada, serving 1791 to 1797. He helped found Toronto (then York) and, during the Revolutionary War, commanded a corps of Loyalists. Simcoe introduced an array of institutions (a British legal system), built major roads, and was a vocal opponent of slavery. He called for the abolition of slavery and became a primary architect of the Anti-Slavery Act of 1793—the first act to limit slavery in the British Empire. Its limitations eventually ended slavery in Canada by 1810: Slaves in the province would remain enslaved until death; new slaves could not be brought into Upper Canada; and children born to slaves would be freed at age twenty-five. 5. A Mohawk chief, Joseph Brant, named Thayendanegea in Mohawk (1742–1807), was an ally of the British. Educated at an Indian school at Lebanon, Connecticut, by Sir William Johnson, Brant was a member of the Church of England and for a spell was a missionary. He translated portions of the Book of Common Prayer and New Testament into the Mohawk language. 6. Brant traveled to England in 1785 to raise money for the construction of the first Episcopal church in Upper Canada.

any thing that came to hand, because I did not understand her. I have a scar on my head from a wound she gave me with a hatchet; and this long scar over my eye, is where she cut me with a knife. The skin dropped over my eye; a white woman bound it up.[7] Brant was very angry, when he came home, at what she had done, and punished her as if she had been a child. Said he, "you know I adopted her as one of the family, and now you are trying to put all the work on her."

I liked the Indians pretty well in their place; some of them were very savage,— some friendly. I have seen them have the war-dance—in a ring with only a cloth about them, and painted up. They did not look ridiculous—they looked savage,— enough to frighten anybody. One would take a bowl and rub the edge with a knotted stick: then they would raise their tomahawks and whoop. Brant had two colored men for slaves: one of them was the father of John Patten, who lives over yonder, the other called himself Simon Ganseville. There was but one other Indian that I knew, who owned a slave. I had no care to get my freedom.

At twelve years old, I was sold by Brant to an Englishman in Ancaster, for one hundred dollars,—his name was Samuel Hatt, and I lived with him seven years: then the white people said I was free, and put me up to running away. He did not stop me—he said he could not take the law into his own hands. Then I lived in what is now Waterloo.[8] I married Robert Pooley, a black man. He ran away with a white woman: he is dead.

Brant died two years before the second war with the United States. His wife survived him until the year the stars fell. She was a pretty squaw: her father was an English colonel. She hid a crock of gold before she died, and I never heard of its being found. Brant was a freemason.

I was seven miles from Stoney Creek at the time of the battle—the cannonade made every thing shake well.

I am now unable to work, and am entirely dependent on others for subsistence: but I find plenty of people in the bush to help me a good deal.

—1856

⌒ END OF TRANSATLANTIC EXCHANGES ⌒

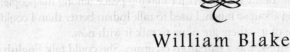

William Blake
1757–1827

In August 1803, William Blake was deemed an enemy of the state. While he was ejecting a drunken soldier from his property, Blake and the soldier scuffled. Each accused the other of violent and belligerent behavior, but the soldier's claim that Blake had condemned the King led to an indictment for sedition. Although Blake was acquitted, the charge hinged on the soldier's

---

7. Drew notes: "The scars spoken of were quite perceptible, but the writer saw many worse cicatrices of wounds not inflicted by *Indian* savages but by civilized men."   8. A town in southern Ontario, founded by Mennonites from Pennsylvania in 1804.

statement that he had "damned the King of England—his country and subjects—that his soldiers were all bound for slaves." What words, if any, Blake spoke are not known, but the incident captures the aversion to the ideologies and institutions of English society that shaped his creative energies.

Born in 1757 to James Blake, a London hosier (a merchant of stockings, gloves, and haberdashery), William was one of six children, two of whom died in infancy. By all accounts, the Blake household was a loving one. His parents were attentive and kind, and the long hours they labored in their shop saw the family move from a meager to a comfortable lifestyle by the late 1760s. James was part of an emerging entrepreneurial class that began to question the class strictures of English society and the Church of England. At some point in the mid-1760s, he became a dissenter, turning to the Baptist faith. His decision was not uncommon: A growing dissent movement during the second half of the eighteenth century was fueled by political and religious ire, and by a desire for greater individual legal rights and religious expression in a hierarchical society that oppressed the merchant and artisan classes. James's decision sheds light on Blake's intellectual and emotional makeup: that art, politics, and religion are inextricably linked.

As a child, Blake was temperamental and opinionated, leading his father to keep him out of school and to apprentice him at fifteen to the engraver James Basire. Although the reputation that Basire had earned in his youth as an eminent engraver had waned somewhat, Blake prospered under his tutelage, and, at age twenty-three, he enrolled in the Royal Academy. Its president, Sir Joshua Reynolds, shaped the Academy's training routines and artistic ideology, and neither the man nor his methods fit with Blake. Students learned through a highly mimetic method that required them to sketch still life and live models under specific conditions and according to strict rules. A celebrated portraitist, Reynolds commanded considerable sums for his work and advocated a style that was historically informed and classical in aesthetics. The rule-breaker in Blake, which as a child had kept him out of school and under foot in his parent's hosier shop, found it difficult to follow such rigid instruction. He sought a style that focused on the sublime not the aggrandizing (the style of many of Reynolds's portraits). Reynolds instructed Blake to "correct" his style and to "work with less extravagance and more simplicity."

Even though some of Blake's poems, such as the *Songs of Innocence and Experience* (1789–1794), appear undemanding and could be readily sung to children, there is nothing simple about his work, either in content, form, or physical construction. From his collections of illustrated songs, many of which are written in the diction and meter of children's verse, to his longer narrative poems, Blake constructs a mythology to capture his political and religious ideas. He also pioneered a new method of engraving for his highly graphical works.

His first collection of verse, *Poetical Sketches*, appeared in 1783, but it is the *Songs*, published six years later and praised by William Wordsworth and Samuel Taylor Coleridge, that revealed his calling as an artist. Blake's composition style, termed "illuminated printing," used a complex system of etching (in reverse) on copper plates with an acid-gum solution. He then immersed the plate in a strong acid bath, which would eat the plate area around where he had engraved the words of his poems and any illustrations. This plate, inked, was pressed on paper, and Blake (or his wife) would complete the page by adding watercolors. This revolutionary printing process was labor-intensive and time-consuming, yielding few volumes because each was individually made. They were also expensive—prohibitively so—and Blake never found popular or financial success, remaining poor throughout his life.

Blake's politics were as radical as his printing methods. In a series of longer poems, he attacked the rigid political, social, and religious codes of late eighteenth- and early nineteenth-century England. *There Is No Natural Religion* (1788), *The Marriage of Heaven and Hell* (1790–1793), *The French Revolution* (1791), *America: A Prophecy* (1793), *Visions of the Daughters of Albion* (1793), *The Book of Urizen* (1794), the *Songs of Experience* (1793–1794),

Europe: A Prophecy (1794), *The Book of Los* (1795), *The Four Zoas* (1795–1804), and *Jerusalem* (1804): Each of these increasingly complex and difficult poems encodes Blake's response to the rapid social and political transformation of his world. He was an enthusiastic supporter of the American and French Revolutions, but there is an apocalyptic belief that colors much of his view of the world, a sense that authoritarian political and religious institutions will overwhelm subversive forces: "I must create a system or be enslaved by another man; I will not reason and compare: my business is to create," as he writes in *Jerusalem*.

In *America* (1793), Blake explores political oppression and revolution through mythologized images of the events and people that shaped the American Revolution. George Washington and Thomas Paine share the same stage with Urizen (who symbolizes hobbled reason and thus is a source of political oppression) and Orc (who symbolizes the spirit of revolution and personifies the American and French Revolutions). Blake sees in the American Revolution the potential for other revolutions—political and spiritual—that will radically alter the world, and the struggle of Orc to free himself from Urizen mirrors America's fight to separate from England. The frontispiece to *America* captures the spirit of the work (see Figure 4). Many readers believe the massive figure is Orc, a symbol of revolt, sitting shackled, slumped over and weary. But the figure may also be Albion's Angel, one of King George III's minions, who embodies the power of the monarchy. These opposed readings, however, both speak to the piece's presentation of the horrors of war, as suggested by the cowering children who are clinging to the female figure.

The Ecchoing Green

The Sun does arise,
And make happy the skies.
The merry bells ring
To welcome the Spring.
The sky-lark and thrush,   5
The birds of the bush,
Sing louder around,
To the bells chearful sound
While our sports shall be seen
On the Ecchoing Green.   10

Old John with white hair
Does laugh away care,
Sitting under the oak,
Among the old folk,
They laugh at our play,   15
And soon they all say,
Such such were the joys
When we all girls & boys,
In our youth time were seen,
On the Ecchoing Green.   20

Till the little ones weary
No more can be merry
The sun does descend,

And our sports have an end:
Round the laps of their mothers   25
Many sisters and brothers,
Like birds in their nest,
Are ready for rest:
And sport no more seen,
On the darkening Green.   30

—1789

The Little Black Boy

My mother bore me in the southern wild,
And I am black, but O! my soul is white
White as an angel is the English child:
But I am black as if bereav'd of light.

My mother taught me underneath a tree   5
And sitting down before the heat of day,
She took me *on* her lap and kissed me,
And, pointing to the east, began to say.

Look on the rising sun: there God does live
And gives his light and gives his heat away.   10
And flowers and trees and beasts and men recieve
Comfort in morning joy in the noon day.

And we are put on earth a little space
That we may learn to bear the beams of love.
And these black bodies and this sun-burnt face   15
Is but a cloud, and like a shady grove.

For when our souls have learn'd the heat to bear
The cloud will vanish we shall hear his voice
Saying: come out from the grove, my love & care,
And round my golden tent like lambs rejoice.   20

Thus did my mother say, and kissed me.
And thus I say to little English boy.
When I from black and he from white cloud free,
And round the tent of God like lambs we joy:

Ill shade him from the heat till he can bear,   25
To lean in joy upon our fathers knee
And then Ill stand and stroke his silver hair,
And be like him and he will then love me.

—1789

The Sick Rose

O Rose thou art sick.
The invisible worm,
That flies in the night
In the howling storm:

Has found out thy bed   5
Of crimson joy:
And his dark secret love
Does thy life destroy.

—1789

The Lamb

Little Lamb who made thee
Dost thou know who made thee
Gave thee life & bid thee feed,
By the stream & o'er the mead;
Gave thee clothing of delight,   5
Softest clothing wooly bright;
Gave thee such a tender voice,
Making all the vales rejoice:
Little Lamb who made thee
Dost thou know who made thee   10

Little Lamb, I'll tell thee.
Little Lamb, I'll tell thee;
He is called by thy name
For he calls himself a Lamb:
He is meek & he is mild,   15
He became a little child:
I a child & thou a lamb,
We are called by his name.
Little Lamb God bless thee
Little Lamb God bless thee   20

—1789

The Tyger

Tyger Tyger, burning bright,
In the forests of the night;
What immortal hand or eye,
Could frame thy fearful symmetry?

In what distant deeps or skies,   5
Burnt the fire of thine eyes?

On what wings dare he aspire?
What the hand dare sieze the fire?

And what shoulder & what art,
Could twist the sinews of thy heart?   10
And when thy heart began to beat,
What dread hand? & what dread feet?

What the hammer? what the chain,
In what furnace was thy brain?
What the anvil? what dread grasp,   15
Dare its deadly terrors clasp!

When the stars threw down their spears
And water'd heaven with their tears:
Did he smile his work to see?
Did he who made the Lamb make thee?   20

Tyger Tyger burning bright,
In the forests of the night:
What immortal hand or eye,
Dare frame thy fearful symmetry?

—1789

The Chimney Sweeper[1]

When my mother died I was very young,
And my father sold me while yet my tongue
Could scarcely cry weep! weep! weep! weep!
So your chimneys I sweep & in soot I sleep.

There's little Tom Dacre, who cried when his head,   5
That curl'd like a lamb's back, was shav'd, so I said:
Hush, Tom never mind it, for when your head's bare
You know that the soot cannot spoil your white hair

And so he was quiet, & that very night,
As Tom was a-sleeping, he had such a sight,   10
That thousands of sweepers, Dick, Joe, Ned, & Jack
Were all of them lock'd up in coffins of black,

And by came an Angel who had a bright key,
And he open'd the coffins & set them all free.
Then down a green plain leaping, laughing, they run   15
And wash in a river, and shine in the Sun.

_____
1. From *Innocence*.

Then naked & white, all their bags left behind,
They rise upon clouds, and sport in the wind
And the Angel told Tom if he'd be a good boy,
He'd have God for his father & never want joy.   20

And so Tom awoke and we rose in the dark
And got with our bags & our brushes to work.
Tho' the morning was cold, Tom was happy & warm
So if all do their duty they need not fear harm.

—1789

The Chimney Sweeper[1]

A little black thing among the snow:
Crying weep, weep, in notes of woe!
Where are thy father & mother? say?
They are both gone up to the church to pray.

Because I was happy upon the heath   5
And smil'd among the winter's snow:
They clothed me in the clothes of death,
And taught me to sing the notes of woe.

And because I am happy & dance & sing,
They think they have done me no injury: 10
And are gone to praise God & his Priest & King,
Who make up a heaven of our misery.

—1789

London

I wander thro' each charter'd street,
Near where the charter'd Thames does flow
And mark in every face I meet
Marks of weakness, marks of woe.

In every cry of every Man,   5
In every Infants cry of fear,
In every voice; in every ban,
The mind-forg'd manacles I hear

How the Chimney-sweepers cry
Every blackning Church appalls.   10
And the hapless Soldiers sigh
Runs in blood down Palace walls

---

1. From *Experience*.

But most thro' midnight streets I hear
How the youthful Harlots curse
Blasts the new born Infant's tear   15
And blights with plagues the Marriage hearse.

—1789

America: A Prophecy

LAMBETH

Printed by William Blake in the year 1793.

PLATE 1

PRELUDIUM

The shadowy daughter of Urthona[1] stood before red Orc.[2]
When fourteen suns had faintly journey'd o'er his dark abode;
His food she brought in iron baskets, his drink in cups of iron;
Crown'd with a helmet & dark hair the nameless female stood;
A quiver with its burning stores, a bow like that of night,   5
When pestilence is shot from heaven; no other arms she need:
Invulnerable tho' naked, save where clouds roll round her loins,
Their awful folds in the dark air; silent she stood as night;
For never from her iron tongue could voice or sound arise;
But dumb till that dread day when Orc assay'd his fierce embrace.   10

Dark virgin; said the hairy youth. thy father stern abhorr'd;
Rivets my tenfold chains while still on high my spirit soars;
Sometimes an eagle screaming in the sky, sometimes a lion,
Stalking upon the mountains, & sometimes a whale I lash
The raging fathomless abyss, anon a serpent folding   15
Around the pillars of Urthona, and round thy dark limbs,
On the Canadian wilds I fold, feeble my spirit folds.
For chained beneath I rend these caverns; when thou bringest food
I howl my joy: and my red eyes seek to behold thy face
In vain! these clouds roll to & fro, & hide thee from my sight.   20

PLATE 2

Silent as despairing love, and strong as jealousy,
The hairy shoulders rend the links, free are the wrists of fire;
Round the terrific loins he siez'd the panting struggling womb;
It joy'd: she put aside her clouds & smiled her first-born smile;
As when a black cloud shews its light'nings to the silent deep   5

Soon as she saw the terrible boy then burst the virgin cry.

I know thee, I have found thee, & I will not let thee go;
Thou art the image of God who dwells in darkness of Africa;

---

1. "Earth owner": individual creative imagination.   2. Revolution.

And thou art fall'n to give me life in regions of dark death.
On my American plains I feel the struggling afflictions   10
Endur'd by roots that writhe their arms into the nether deep:
I see a serpent in Canada, who courts me to his love;
In Mexico an Eagle, and a Lion in Peru;
I see a Whale in the South-sea, drinking my soul away.
O what limb rending pains I feel. thy fire & my frost   15
Mingle in howling pains, in furrows by thy lightnings rent;
This is eternal death; and this the torment long foretold.

[The stern Bard ceas'd, asham'd of his own song; enrag'd he swung
His harp aloft sounding, then dash'd its shining frame against
A ruin'd pillar in glittring fragments; silent he turn'd away,   20
And wander'd down the vales of Kent in sick & drear lamentings.][3]

PLATE 3
A PROPHECY

The Guardian Prince of Albion[4] burns in his nightly tent,
Sullen fires across the Atlantic glow to America's shore:
Piercing the souls of warlike men, who rise in silent night,
Washington, Franklin, Paine & Warren, Gates, Hancock & Green[5];
Meet on the coast glowing with blood from Albions fiery Prince.   5

Washington spoke; Friends of America look over the Atlantic sea;
A bended bow is lifted in heaven, & a heavy iron chain
Descends link by link from Albions cliffs across the sea to bind
Brothers & sons of America, till our faces pale and yellow;
Heads deprest, voices weak, eyes downcast, hands work-bruis'd,   10
Feet bleeding on the sultry sands, and the furrows of the whip
Descend to generations that in future times forget.——

The strong voice ceas'd; for a terrible blast swept over the heaving sea;
The eastern cloud rent; on his cliffs stood Albions wrathful Prince
A dragon form clashing his scales at midnight he arose,   15
And flam'd red meteors round the land of Albion beneath
His voice, his locks, his awful shoulders, and his glowing eyes.

PLATE 4
Appear to the Americans upon the cloudy night.

Solemn heave the Atlantic waves between the gloomy nations,
Swelling, belching from its deeps red clouds & raging Fires;
Albion is sick. America faints! enrag'd the Zenith grew.
As human blood shooting its veins all round the orbed heaven   5
Red rose the clouds from the Atlantic in vast wheels of blood

---

3. This stanza was not printed in the first edition. 4. England. 5. Statesmen and political activists. See headnotes for Washington, Franklin, and Paine. Joseph Warren (1741–1775), Boston physician killed during the American Revolution; Horatio Gates (c. 1728–1806), American general; John Hancock (1737–1793), American statesman; and Nathaniel Green (1742–1786), American general.

And in the red clouds rose a Wonder o'er the Atlantic sea;
Intense! naked! a Human fire fierce glowing, as the wedge
Of iron heated in the furnace; his terrible limbs were fire
With myriads of cloudy terrors banners dark & towers   10
Surrounded; heat but not light went thro' the murky atmosphere

The King of England looking westward trembles at the vision

PLATE 5
Albions Angel stood beside the Stone of night, and saw
The terror like a comet, or more like the planet red
That once inclos'd the terrible wandering comets in its sphere.
Then Mars thou wast our center, & the planets three flew round
Thy crimsom disk; so e'er the Sun was rent from thy red sphere;   5
The Spectre glowd his horrid length staining the temple long
With beams of blood; & thus a voice came forth, and shook the temple

PLATE 6
The morning comes, the night decays, the watchmen leave their stations;
The grave is burst, the spices shed, the linen wrapped up;
The bones of death, the cov'ring clay, the sinews shrunk & dry'd.
Reviving shake. inspiring move, breathing! awakening!
Spring like redeemed captives when their bonds & bars are burst;   5
Let the slave grinding at the mill, run out into the field;
Let him look up into the heavens & laugh in the bright air;
Let the inchained soul shut up in darkness and in sighing,
Whose face has never seen a smile in thirty weary years;
Rise and look out, his chains are loose, his dungeon doors are open.   10
And let his wife and children return from the oppressors scourge;
They look behind at every step & believe it is a dream.
Singing. The Sun has left his blackness, & has found a fresher morning
And the fair Moon rejoices in the clear & cloudless night;
For Empire is no more, and now the Lion & Wolf shall cease.   15

PLATE 7
In thunders ends the voice. Then Albions Angel[6] wrathful burnt
Beside the Stone of Night; and like the Eternal Lions howl
In famine & war, reply'd. Art thou not Orc, who serpent-form'd
Stands at the gate of Enitharmon[7] to devour her children;
Blasphemous Demon, Antichrist, hater of Dignities;   5
Lover of wild rebellion, and transgresser of Gods Law;
Why dost thou come to Angels eyes in this terrific form?

PLATE 8
The terror answered: I am Orc, wreath'd round the accursed tree:
The times are ended; shadows pass the morning gins to break;

---

6. King George III.   7. Spiritual beauty.

The fiery joy, that Urizen[8] perverted to ten commands,
What night he led the starry hosts thro' the wide wilderness;
That stony law I stamp to dust: and scatter religion abroad   5
To the four winds as a torn book, & none shall gather the leaves;
But they shall rot on desart sands, & consume in bottomless deeps;
To make the desarts blossom, & the deeps shrink to their fountains,
And to renew the fiery joy, and burst the stony roof.
That pale religious letchery, seeking Virginity,   10
May find it in a harlot, and in coarse-clad honesty
The undefil'd tho' ravish'd in her cradle night and morn:
For every thing that lives is holy, life delights in life;
Because the soul of sweet delight can never be defil'd.
Fires inwrap the earthly globe, yet man is not consumd;   15
Amidst the lustful fires he walks: his feet become like brass,
His knees and thighs like silver, & his breast and head like gold.

PLATE 9
Sound! sound! my loud war-trumpets & alarm my Thirteen Angels![9]
Loud howls the eternal Wolf! the eternal Lion lashes his tail!
America is darkned; and my punishing Demons terrified
Crouch howling before their caverns deep like skins dry'd in the wind.
They cannot smite the wheat, nor quench the fatness of the earth,   5
They cannot smite with sorrows, nor subdue the plow and spade,
They cannot wall the city, nor moat round the castle of princes.
They cannot bring the stubbed oak to overgrow the hills.
For terrible men stand on the shores, & in their robes I see
Children take shelter from the lightnings, there stands Washington   10
And Paine and Warren with their foreheads reard toward the east
But clouds obscure my aged sight. A vision from afar!
Sound! sound! my loud war-trumpets & alarm my thirteen Angels:
Ah vision from afar! Ah rebel form that rent the ancient
Heavens! Eternal Viper self-renew'd, rolling in clouds   15
I see thee in thick clouds and darkness on America's shore.
Writhing in pangs of abhorred birth; red flames the crest rebellious
And eyes of death; the harlot womb oft opened in vain
Heaves in enormous circles, now the times are return'd upon thee,
Devourer of thy parent, now thy unutterable torment renews.   20
Sound! sound! my loud war trumpets & alarm my thirteen Angels!
Ah terrible birth! a young one bursting! where is the weeping mouth?
And where the mothers milk? instead those ever-hissing jaws
And parched lips drop with fresh gore; now roll thou in the clouds
Thy mother lays her length outstretch'd upon the shore beneath.   25
Sound! sound! my loud war-trumpets & alarm my thirteen Angels!
Loud howls the eternal Wolf: the eternal Lion lashes his tail!

---

8. Reason.   9. The thirteen United States.

PLATE 10
Thus wept the Angel voice & as he wept the terrible blasts
Of trumpets, blew a loud alarm across the Atlantic deep.
No trumpets answer; no reply of clarions or of fifes,
Silent the Colonies remain and refuse the loud alarm.

On those vast shady hills between America & Albions shore;   5
Now barr'd out by the Atlantic sea: call'd Atlantean hills:
Because from their bright summits you may pass to the Golden world.
An ancient palace, archetype of mighty Emperies,
Rears its immortal pinnacles, built in the forest of God
By Ariston the king of beauty for his stolen bride,   10

Here on their magic seats the thirteen Angels sat perturb'd
For clouds from the Atlantic hover o'er the solemn roof,

PLATE 11
Fiery the Angels rose, & as they rose deep thunder roll'd
Around their shores: indignant burning with the fires of Orc
And Bostons Angel cried aloud as they flew thro' the dark night.

He cried: Why trembles honesty and like a murderer,
Why seeks he refuge from the frowns of his immortal station,   5
Must the generous tremble & leave his joy, to the idle: to the pestilence!
That mock him? who commanded this? what God? what Angel!
To keep the gen'rous from experience till the ungenerous
Are unrestrained performers of the energies of nature;
Till pity is become a trade, and generosity a science,   10
That men get rich by, & the sandy desert is giv'n to the strong
What God is he, writes laws of peace, & clothes him in a tempest
What pitying Angel lusts for tears, and fans himself with sighs
What crawling villain preaches abstinence & wraps himself
In fat of lambs? no more I follow, no more obedience pay.   15

PLATE 12
So cried he, rending off his robe & throwing down his scepter.
In sight of Albions Guardian, and all the thirteen Angels
Rent off their robes to the hungry wind, & threw their golden scepters
Down on the land of America, indignant they descended
Headlong from out their heav'nly heights, descending swift as fires   5
Over the land; naked & flaming are their lineaments seen
In the deep gloom, by Washington & Paine & Warren they stood
And the flame folded roaring fierce within the pitchy night
Before the Demon red, who burnt towards America,
In black smoke thunders and loud winds rejoicing in its terror   10
Breaking in smoky wreaths from the wild deep, & gath'ring thick
In flames as of a furnace on the land from North to South

PLATE 13

What time the thirteen Governors that England sent convene
In Bernards[10] house; the flames coverd the land, they rouze they cry
Shaking their mental chains they rush in fury to the sea
To quench their anguish; at the feet of Washington down fall'n
They grovel on the sand and writhing lie, while all   5
The British soldiers thro' the thirteen states sent up a howl
Of anguish: threw their swords & muskets to the earth & ran
From their encampments and dark castles seeking where to hide
From the grim flames; and from the visions of Orc; in sight
Of Albions Angel; who enrag'd his secret clouds open'd   10
From north to south, and burnt outstretchd on wings of wrath cov'ring
The eastern sky, spreading his awful wings across the heavens;
Beneath him rolld his num'rous hosts, all Albions Angels camp'd
Darkend the Atlantic mountains & their trumpets shook the valleys
Arm'd with diseases of the earth to cast upon the Abyss,   15
Their numbers forty millions, must'ring in the eastern sky.

PLATE 14

In the flames stood & view'd the armies drawn out in the sky
Washington Franklin Paine & Warren Allen Gates & Lee[11]:
And heard the voice of Albions Angel give the thunderous command:
His plagues obedient to his voice flew forth out of their clouds
Falling upon America, as a storm to cut them off   5
As a blight cuts the tender corn when it begins to appear.
Dark is the heaven above, & cold & hard the earth beneath;
And as a plague wind fill'd with insects cuts off man & beast;
And as a sea o'erwhelms a land in the day of an earthquake;

Fury! rage! madness! in a wind swept through America   10
And the red flames of Orc that folded roaring fierce around
The angry shores, and the fierce rushing of th'inhabitants together:
The citizens of New-York close their books & lock their chests;
The mariners of Boston drop their anchors and unlade;
The scribe of Pensylvania casts his pen upon the earth;   15
The builder of Virginia throws his hammer down in fear.

Then had America been lost, o'erwhelm'd by the Atlantic,
And Earth had lost another portion of the infinite,
But all rush together in the night in wrath and raging fire
The red fires rag'd! the plagues recoil'd! then rolld they back with fury   20

PLATE 15

On Albions Angels: then the Pestilence began in streaks of red
Across the limbs of Albions Guardian, the spotted plague smote Bristols

---

10. Francis Bernard (1712–1774), governor of Massachusetts from 1760 to 1769.   11. Ethan Allen (1748–1789),
American revolutionary general; and Harry Lee (1756–1818), American revolutionary cavalry commander.

And the Leprosy Londons Spirit, sickening all their bands:
The millions sent up a howl of anguish and threw off their hammerd mail,
And cast their swords & spears to earth, & stood a naked multitude.   5
Albions Guardian writhed in torment on the eastern sky
Pale quivring toward the brain his glimmering eyes, teeth chattering
Howling & shuddering his legs quivering; convuls'd each muscle & sinew
Sick'ning lay Londons Guardian, and the ancient miter'd York
Their heads on snowy hills, their ensigns sick'ning in the sky   10

The plagues creep on the burning winds driven by flames of Orc,
And by the fierce Americans rushing together in the night
Driven o'er the Guardians of Ireland and Scotland and Wales
They spotted with plagues forsook the frontiers & their banners seard
With fires of hell, deform their ancient heavens with shame & woe.   15
Hid in his caves the Bard of Albion felt the enormous plagues.
And a cowl of flesh grew o'er his head & scales on his back & ribs;
And rough with black scales all his Angels fright their ancient heavens
The doors of marriage are open, and the Priests in rustling scales
Rush into reptile coverts, hiding from the fires of Orc,   20
That play around the golden roofs in wreaths of fierce desire,
Leaving the females naked and glowing with the lusts of youth

For the female spirits of the dead pining in bonds of religion;
Run from their fetters reddening, & in long drawn arches sitting:
They feel the nerves of youth renew, and desires of ancient times,   25
Over their pale limbs as a vine when the tender grape appears

PLATE 16
Over the hills, the vales, the cities, rage the red flames fierce;
The Heavens melted from north to south; and Urizen who sat
Above all heavens in thunders wrap'd, emerg'd his leprous head
From out his holy shrine, his tears in deluge piteous
Falling into the deep sublime! flag'd with grey-brow'd snows   5
And thunderous visages, his jealous wings wav'd over the deep;
Weeping in dismal howling woe he dark descended howling
Around the smitten bands, clothed in tears & trembling shudd'ring cold.
His stored snows he poured forth, and his icy magazines
He open'd on the deep, and on the Atlantic sea white shiv'ring.   10
Leprous his limbs, all over white, and hoary was his visage,
Weeping in dismal howlings before the stern Americans
Hiding the Demon red with clouds & cold mists from the earth;
Till Angels & weak men twelve years should govern o'er the strong:
And then their end should come, when France receiv'd the Demons light.   15

Stiff shudderings shook the heav'nly thrones! France Spain & Italy,
In terror view'd the bands of Albion, and the ancient Guardians
Fainting upon the elements, smitten with their own plagues
They slow advance to shut the five gates of their law-built heaven

Filled with blasting fancies and with mildews of despair   20
With fierce disease and lust, unable to stem the fires of Orc;
But the five gates were consum'd, & their bolts and hinges melted
And the fierce flames burnt round the heavens, & round the abodes of men

FINIS

—1793

Visions of the Daughters of Albion

The Eye sees more than the Heart knows.

Printed by Will:m Blake: 1793

The Argument
I loved Theotormon[1]
And I was not ashamed
I trembled in my virgin fears
And I hid in Leutha's[2] vale!

I plucked Leutha's flower,
And I rose up from the vale;
But the terrible thunders tore
My virgin mantle in twain.

[Plate 1]

Visions

ENSLAV'D, the Daughters of Albion weep: a trembling lamentation
Upon their mountains; in their valleys. sighs toward America.

For the soft soul of America, Oothoon[3] wanderd in woe,
Along the vales of Leutha seeking flowers to comfort her;
And thus she spoke to the bright Marygold of Leutha's vale   5

Art thou a flower! art thou a nymph! I see thee now a flower:
Now a nymph! I dare not pluck thee from thy dewey bed!

The Golden nymph replied; pluck thou my flower Oothoon the mild
Another flower shall spring, because the soul of sweet delight
Can never pass away. she ceas'd & closd her golden shrine.   10

Then Oothoon pluck'd the flower saying, I pluck thee from thy bed,
Sweet flower, and put thee here to glow between my breasts
And thus I turn my face to where my whole soul seeks.

Over the waves she went in wing'd exulting swift delight;
And over Theotormons reign, took her impetuous course.   15

_____

1. Desire and jealousy.   2. Sex under law, thus sinful and guilty.   3. Thwarted love.

Bromion rent her with his thunders. on his stormy bed
Lay the faint maid, and soon her woes appalld his thunders hoarse

Bromion spake. behold this harlot here on Bromions bed
And let the jealous dolphins sport around the lovely maid:
Thy soft American plains are mine, and mine thy north & south: 20
Stampt with my signet are the swarthy childen of the sun:
They are obedient, they resist not, they obey the scourge:
Their daughters worship terrors and obey the violent:

[Plate 2]

Now thou maist marry Bromions harlot, and protect the child
Of Bromions rage, that Oothoon shall put forth in nine moons time
Then storms rent Theotormons limbs; he rolled his waves around.
And folded his black jealous waters round the adulterate pair
Bound back to back in Bromions caves Terror & meekness dwell   5
At entrance Theotormon sits wearing the threshold hard
With secret tears; beneath him sound like waves on a desert shore
The voice of slaves beneath the sun, and children bought with money,
That shiver in religious caves beneath the burning fires
Of lust, that belch incessant from the summits of the earth   10

Oothoon weeps not: she cannot weep! her tears are locked up;
But she can howl incessant, writhing her soft snowy limbs.
And calling Theotormons Eagles to prey upon her flesh.

I call with holy voice! kings of the sounding air,
Rend away this defiled bosom that I may reflect.   15
The image of Theotormon on my pure transparent breast.

The Eagles at her call descend & rend their bleeding prey;
Theotormon severely smiles. her soul reflects the smile;
As the clear spring mudded with feet of beasts grows pure & smiles

The Daughters of Albion hear her woes, & eccho back her sighs.   20

Why does my Theotormon sit weeping upon the threshold;
And Oothoon hovers by his side, perswading him in vain:
I cry arise O Theotormon for the village dog
Barks at the breaking day, the nightingale has done lamenting,
The lark does rustle in the ripe corn, and the Eagle returns   25
From nightly prey, and lifts his golden beak to the pure east;
Shaking the dust from his immortal pinions to awake
The sun that sleeps too long. Arise my Theotormon I am pure.
Because the night is gone that clos'd me in its deadly black.
They told me that the night & day were all that I could see;   30
They told me that I had five senses to inclose me up.
And they inclos'd my infinite brain into a narrow circle.

And sunk my heart into the Abyss, a red round globe hot burning
Till all from life I was obliterated and erased.
Instead of morn arises a bright shadow, like an eye   35
In the eastern cloud; instead of night a sickly charnel house;
That Theotormon hears me not! to him the night and morn
Are both alike: a night of sighs, a morning of fresh tears;

[Plate 3]

And none but Bromion can hear my lamentations.

With what sense is it that the chicken shuns the ravenous hawk
With what sense does the tame pigeon measure out the expanse?
With what sense does the bee form cells? have not the mouse & frog
Eyes and ears and sense of touch? yet are their habitations,   5
And, their pursuits, as different as their forms and as their joys:
Ask the wild ass why he refuses burdens: and the meek camel
Why he loves man: is it because of eye ear mouth or skin
Or breathing nostrils? No, for these the wolf and tyger have.
Ask the blind worm the secrets of the grave, and why her spires   10
Love to curl round the bones of death! and ask the rav'nous snake
Where she gets poison: & the wing'd eagle why he loves the sun
And then tell me the thoughts of man, that have been hid of old.

Silent I hover all the night, and all day could be silent.
If Theotormon once would turn his loved eyes upon me;   15
How can I be defild when I reflect thy image pure?
Sweetest the fruit that the worm feeds on. & the soul prey'd on by woe
The new wash'd lamb ting'd with the village smoke & the bright swan
By the red earth of our immortal river: I bathe my wings.
And I am white and pure to hover round Theotormons breast.   20

Then Theotormon broke his silence. and he answered.

Tell me what is the night or day to one oerflowd with woe?
Tell me what is a thought? & of what substance is it made?
Tell me what is a joy? & in what gardens do joys grow?
And in what rivers swim the sorrows? and upon what mountains   25

[Plate 4]

Wave shadows of discontent? and in what houses dwell the wretched
Drunken with woe forgotten, and shut up from cold despair.

Tell me where dwell the thoughts forgotten till thou call them forth
Tell me where dwell the joys of old? & where the ancient loves?
And when will they renew again & the night of oblivion past?   5
That I might traverse times & spaces far remote and bring
Comforts into a present sorrow and a night of pain
Where goest thou O thought? to what remote land is thy flight?

If thou returnest to the present moment of affliction
Wilt thou bring comforts on thy wings. and dews and honey and balm;   10
Or poison From the desart wilds, from the eyes of the envier.

Then Bromion said: and shook the cavern with his lamentation

Thou knowest that the ancient trees seen by thine eyes have fruit;
But knowest thou that trees and fruits flourish upon the earth
To gratify senses unknown? trees beasts and birds unknown: 15
Unknown, not unpercievd, spread in the infinite microscope,
In places yet unvisited by the voyager, and in worlds
Over another kind of seas, and in atmospheres unknown?
Ah! are there other wars, beside the wars of sword and fire!
And are there other sorrows, beside the sorrows of poverty?
And are their other joys, besides the joys of riches and ease?   20
And is there not one law for both the lion and the ox?
And is there not eternal fire, and eternal chains?
To bind the phantoms of existence from eternal life?

Then Oothoon waited silent all the day, and all the night,   25

[Plate 5]

But when the morn arose, her lamentation renewd.
The Daughters of Albion hear her woes, & eccho back her sighs.

O Urizen! Creator of men! mistaken Demon of heaven:
Thy joys are tears! thy labour vain, to form men to thine image.
How can one joy absorb another? are not different joys   5
Holy, eternal, infinite! and each joy is a Love.

Does not the great mouth laugh at a gift? & the narrow eyelids mock
At the labour that is above payment, and wilt thou take the ape
For thy councellor? or the dog for a schoolmaster to thy children?
Does he who contemns poverty, and he who turns with abhorrence   10
From usury: feel the same passion or are they moved alike?
How can the giver of gifts experience the delights of the merchant?
How the industrious citizen the pains of the husbandman.
How different far the fat fed hireling with hollow drum;
Who buys whole corn fields into wastes, and sings upon the heath: 15
How different their eye and ear! how different the world to them!
What are his nets & gins & traps, & how does he surround him
With cold floods of abstraction, and with forests of solitude,
To build him castles and high spires, where kings & priests may dwell.
Till she who burns with youth and knows no fixed lot; is bound   20
In spells of law to one she loaths: and must she drag the chain
Of life, in weary lust! must chilling murderous thoughts, obscure
The clear heaven of her eternal spring! to bear the wintry rage
Of a harsh terror driv'n to madness, bound to hold a rod

Over her shrinking shoulders all the day; & all the night   25
To turn the wheel of false desire: and longings that wake her womb
To the abhorred birth of cherubs in the human form
That live a pestilence & die a meteor & are no more.
Till the child dwell with one he hates, and do the deed he loaths
And the impure scourge force his seed into its unripe birth   30
E'er yet his eyelids can behold the arrows of the day.
Does the whale worship at thy footsteps as the hungry dog?
Or does he scent the mountain prey, because his nostrils wide
Draw in the ocean? does his eye discern the flying cloud
As the ravens eye? or does he measure the expanse like the vulture?   35
Does the still spider view the cliffs where eagles hide their young?
Or does the fly rejoice, because the harvest is brought in?
Does not the eagle scorn the earth & despise the treasures beneath?
But the mole knoweth what is there, & the worm shall tell it thee.
Does not the worm erect a pillar in the mouldering church yard?   40

[Plate 6]

And a palace of eternity in the jaws of the hungry grave
Over his porch these words are written. Take thy bliss O Man!
And sweet shall be thy taste, & sweet thy infant joys renew!

Infancy, fearless, lustful, happy! nestling for delight
In laps of pleasure; Innocence! honest, open, seeking   5
The vigorous joys of morning light; open to virgin bliss.
Who taught thee modesty, subtil modesty! child of night & sleep
When thou awakest. wilt thou dissemble all thy secret joys
Or wert thou not awake when all this mystery was disclos'd!
Then comst thou forth a modest virgin knowing to dissemble   10
With nets found under thy night pillow, to catch virgin joy,
And brand it with the name of whore: & sell it in the night,
In silence, ev'n without a whisper, and in seeming sleep:
Religious dreams and holy vespers, light thy smoky fires;
Once were thy fires lighted by the eyes of honest morn   15
And does my Theotormon seek this hypocrite modesty!
This knowing, artful, secret, fearful, cautious, trembling hypocrite.
Then is Oothoon a whore indeed! and all the virgin joys
Of life are harlots: and Theotormon is a sick mans dream
And Oothoon is the crafty slave of selfish holiness.   20

But Oothoon is not so, a virgin fill'd with virgin fancies
Open to joy and to delight where ever beauty appears
If in the morning sun I find it: there my eyes are fix'd

[Plate 7]

In happy copulation; if in evening mild wearied with work,
Sit on a bank and draw the pleasures of this free born joy.

The moment of desire! the moment of desire! The virgin
That pines for man; shall awaken her womb to enormous joys
In the secret shadows of her chamber; the youth shut up from   5
The lustful joy, shall forget to generate. & create an amorous image
In the shadows of his curtains and in the folds of his silent pillow.
Are not these the places of religion? the rewards of continence?
The self enjoyings of self denial? Why dost thou seek religion?
Is it because acts are not lovely, that thou seekest solitude,   10
Where the horrible darkness is impressed with reflections of desire.

Father of Jealousy, be thou accursed from the earth!
Why hast thou taught my Theotormon this accursed thing?
Till beauty fades from off my shoulders, darken'd and cast out,
A solitary shadow wailing on the margin of non-entity.   15
I cry, Love! Love! Love! happy happy Love! free as the mountain wind!
Can that be Love, that drinks another as a sponge drinks water?
That clouds with jealousy his nights, with weepings all the day:
To spin a web of age around him, grey and hoary! dark!
Till his eyes sicken at the fruit that hangs before his sight.   20
Such is self-love that envies all! a creeping skeleton
With lamplike eyes watching around the frozen marriage bed.

But silken nets and traps of adamant will Oothoon spread,
And catch for thee girls of mild silver, or of furious gold:
I'll lie beside thee on a bank & view their wanton play   25
In lovely copulation bliss on bliss with Theotormon:
Red as the rosy morning, lustful as the first born beam,
Oothoon shall view his dear delight, nor e'er with jealous cloud
Come in the heaven of generous love; nor selfish blightings bring.

Does the sun walk in glorious raiment. on the secret floor   30

[Plate 8]

Where the cold miser spreads his gold? or does the bright cloud drop
On his stone threshold? does his eye behold the beam that brings
Expansion to the eye of pity? or will he bind himself
Beside the ox to thy hard furrow? does not that mild beam blot
The bat, the owl, the glowing tyger, and the king of night.   5
The sea fowl takes the wintry blast, for a cov'ring to her limbs:
And the wild snake, the pestilence to adorn him with gems & gold.
And trees & birds, & beasts, & men, behold their eternal joy.
Arise you little glancing wings. and sing your infant joy!
Arise and drink your bliss, for every thing that lives is holy!   10

Thus every morning wails Oothoon. but Theotormon sits
Upon the margind ocean conversing with shadows dire.

The Daughters of Albion hear her woes, & eccho back her sighs.

The End

                                                                      —1793

Robert Burns
1759–1796

Twenty-seven years old, penniless, and ready to leave Scotland for Jamaica, Robert Burns published *Poems, Chiefly in the Scottish Dialect* (1786) as a means of raising money for the trip. Burns hoped to be on the Atlantic, far away from the slings and arrows of outraged critics, by the time the book was reviewed: "I was pretty sure my Poems would meet with some applause, but at the worst, the roar of the Atlantic would deafen the voice of Censure," wrote Burns. *Poems* was far more successful than he expected. Indeed, it was so successful that he decided not only to stay in Scotland but also to go at once to Edinburgh "without a single acquaintance in town, or a single letter of introduction" in his pocket. While Burns was there, his poetry was praised by the *Edinburgh Magazine*, which made much of the persona of the poet as an unlettered, poor farmer, declaring him "a striking example of native genius bursting through the obscurity of poverty and the obstructions of a laborious life."

Although the image of Burns as an uneducated ploughman solely concerned with Scottish rural life was long lived, it was not wholly accurate, for Burns's considerable knowledge of national and international politics manifests itself in his poems, as does his familiarity with English and Scottish poetry and ballad traditions. The book's revolutionary overtones were among the many qualities that endeared it to American readers. It took only two years for the Americans, who had been buying imported editions, to produce their own: Three days after Independence Day in 1788, the Philadelphia edition appeared, and by December another edition was printed in New York.

Many of the topics and subjects treated in *Poems* reflect Burns's surroundings and life events leading up to publication. Indeed, his ploughman persona was not entirely fictional, as he had tried his hand as a farmer in Ayrshire. And this experience is clearly a source of inspiration for poems such as "To a Mouse," which is subtitled, "On Turning Her Up in Her Nest with the Plough, November, 1785." Even after the success of *Poems*, Burns returned to farming, using the profits of his poetry to subsidize his agricultural efforts. As before, his crops went awry, and he was unable to make his agricultural endeavors as profitable as his publishing ones. He did, however, succeed in marrying his longtime sweetheart, Jean Armour; the success of the book did, quite literally, afford him the opportunity to marry her, as Burns's poverty had been one of the reasons why they were not able to wed earlier.

Another feature of Burns's life reflected in his poems is the dialect, Lowland Scots, spoken in his native village of Mauchline. In the Highlands, Gaelic, the indigenous language of Scotland, was spoken. Lowland Scots is not Gaelic but is more closely related to northern English. It is rooted in a long tradition of spoken verse and in the writings of poets of the Middle Ages and early Renaissance, such as William Dunbar, Robert Henryson, and David Lyndsay. Burns's use of Lowland Scots helped preserve this language, which had been in decline since Scottish Reformers chose English as the official language of the Church and since English became more pervasive due to the Union of the Crowns in 1603 and the Union of Parliaments in 1707. The effect of English becoming the required language of Scotland was that Lowland Scots began to fragment into a variety of dialects. In the present it has only a vestigial presence. Burns attempted to preserve and perpetuate Scottish language and culture not only by using it in his original compositions but also by collecting traditional Scottish songs and contributing them to several late eighteenth-century musical anthologies, including *The Scots Musical Museum* (1787) and *Merry Muses of Caledonia* (1800).

Although the language of Burns's poems had, even in his day, a limited audience of people who could understand it, and although he died at a young age (from heart failure in his thirty-seventh year), the legacy of his poetry is evident from Scotland to "some place far abroad, / Where sailors gang to fish for Cod [Cape Cod, Massachusetts]." Burns's bid for posterity was secured during the years immediately following his death with several editions printed in London, Edinburgh, and Philadelphia. He won a working-class readership through several inexpensive chapbooks published in Britain and America, most notably chapbooks of *The Soldier's Return*, issued in Britain during the Napoleonic Wars and in Boston during the War of 1812. He influenced many British and American writers, from Sir Walter Scott to William Wordsworth to Walt Whitman. The latter wrote that "there are many things in Burns's poems and character that specially endear him to America." But Burns's nineteenth-century influence was not limited to Britain and the United States; as early as 1835, James Edward MacDonald was using a hand-bound copy of Burns's poems to teach them to schoolchildren in Whycocomagh, Nova Scotia.

Public celebrations of Burns's birthday are a longstanding tradition and one of the cornerstones of his poetic afterlife. These events celebrate Burns's life and works as well as Scotland and Scotland's diaspora. Called Burns Night in the United Kingdom or Burns Supper in the United States, these meals consist of haggis (a dish made with seasoned sheep or calf innards mixed with suet and oatmeal), tatties (potatoes), and neeps (turnips) and feature bagpipe music, toasts, and a reading of Burns's poem "To a Haggis." The toasts are spoken monuments to Burns and testify to the ways in which, as one Canadian toast notes, "throughout the old world and the new / Brave Rabbie's Star comes shining through." Written monuments to Burns abound and include works dedicated to him as well as allusions to him in literature, such as the title to J. D. Salinger's *Catcher in the Rye* (1951). And there are of course physical monuments to Burns in bronze and stone from Old Scotland to Nova Scotia, testaments to the staying power of one of the greatest poets of the age.

Poor Mailie's Elegy

Lament in rhyme, lament in prose,
Wi' *saut*[1] tears tricklin down your nose;
Our *Bardie's*[2] fate is at a close,
        Past a' *remead!*[3]
The last, sad *cape-stane*[4] o' his woes   5
        Poor *Mailie's* dead!

It's no the loss o' *warl's gear*,[5]
That could sae bitter draw the tear,
Or mak our bardie, *dowie*,[6] wear
        The mournin' weed: 10
He's lost a friend an' *neebor*[7] dear,
        In *Mailie* dead.

Thro' a' the town she trotted by him;
A lang half-mile she could descry him;
Wi' kindly bleat, when she did spy him,
        She ran wi' speed: 15
A friend mair faithfu' ne'er cam nigh him,
        Than *Mailie* dead.

---

1. Salt.   2. Poet's.   3. Cure.   4. Copingstone or capstone.   5. Worldly property.   6. Sad.   7. Neighbor.

I *wat*[8] she was a sheep o' sense,
An' could behave hersel wi' *mense*[9]:
I'll say't, she never brak a fence,
        Thro' thievish greed.
Our bardie, lanely, keeps the *spence*[10]
        Sin' *Mailie's* dead.

20

Or, if he wanders up the *howe*,[11]
Her livin image in her yowe
Comes bleatin till him, owre the *knowe*,[12]
        For bits o' bread;
An' down the briny pearls *rowe*[13]
        For *Mailie* dead.

25

30

She was nae *get*[14] o' moorlan tips,
Wi' *tauted ket*,[15] an' hairy hips;
For her *forbears*[16] were brought in ships,
        Frae 'yont the Tweed:
A bonier *fleesh*[17] ne'er cross'd the *clips*[18]
        Than *Mailie's*—dead.

35

Wae worth[19] that man wha first did shape
That vile, *wanchancie*[20] thing—a *raep!*[21]
It makes guid fellows *girn*[22] an' gape,
        Wi' chokin dread;
An' Robin's bonnet wave wi' crape
        For *Mailie* dead.

40

O, a' ye bards on bonie Doon!
An' wha on Ayr your *chanters*[23] tune!
Come, join the melancholious *croon*[24]
        O' Robin's reed!
His heart will never get aboon[25]—
        His *Mailie's* dead!

45

—1783

To a Mouse

On Turning Her Up in Her Nest with the Plough, November, 1785

Wee, sleekit,[1] corwin, tim'rous beastie,
O, what a panic's in thy breastie!
Thou need na start awa sae[2] hasty
        Wi' bickering brattle![3]
I wad be laith[4] to rin an' chase thee,
        Wi' murdering pattle![5]

5

---

8. Knew. 9. Discretion. 10. Inner room. 11. Valley. 12. Knoll. 13. Roll. 14. Offspring. 15. Matted fleece. 16. Ancestors.
17. Fleece. 18. Shears. 19. Woe to. 20. Unlucky. 21. Rope. 22. Grimace. 23. Bag-pipes. 24. Moan or chant. 25. Above.

1. Sleek. 2. So. 3. Scurry. 4. Loath. 5. Plow scraper.

I'm truly sorry man's dominion
Has broken nature's social union,
An' justifies that ill opinion
      Which makes thee startle   10
At me, thy poor, earth-born companion
      An' fellow mortal!

I doubt na, whyles,[6] but thou may thieve;
What then? poor beastie, thou maun[7] live!
A daimen icker in a thrave[8]   15
      'S a sma' request;
I'll get a blessin wi' the lave,[9]
      An' never miss 't!

Thy wee-bit housie, too, in ruin!
Its silly wa's[10] the win's are strewn!   20
An' naething, now, to big[11] a new ane,
      O' foggage[12] green!
An' bleak December's win's ensuin,
      Baith snell[13] an' keen!

Thou saw the fields laid bare an' waste,   25
An' weary *winter* comin fast,
An' cozie here, beneath the blast,
      Thou thought to dwell,
Till crash! the cruel coulter[14] past
      Out thro' thy cell.   30

That wee bit heap o' leaves an' stibble,[15]
Has cost thee monie a weary nibble!
Now thou's turned out, for a' thy trouble,
      But[16] house or hald,[17]
To thole[18] the winter's sleety dribble,   35
      An' cranreuch[19] cauld!

But Mousie, thou art no thy lane,[20]
In proving foresight may be vain:
The best-laid schemes o' mice an' men
      Gang aft agley,[21]
An' lea'e us nought but grief an' pain,   40
      For promis'd joy!

Still thou art blest, compared wi' me!
The present only toucheth thee:
But och! I backward cast my e'e,[22]   45

---

6. Sometimes. 7. Must. 8. Odd ear in 24 bundles. 9. Rest. 10. Weak walls. 11. Build. 12. Rank grass. 13. Bitter.
14. Plow-blade. 15. Stubble. 16. Without. 17. Goods. 18. Endure. 19. Frost. 20. Not alone. 21. Go oft awry. 22. Eye.

On prospects drear!
An' forward, tho' I canna see,
    I guess an' fear!

—1786

To a Louse

On Seeing one on a Lady's Bonnet at Church

Ha! Whare ye gaun,[1] ye crowlan[2] ferlie![3]
Your impudence protects you sairly[4]:
I canna say but ye strunt[5] rarely,
    Owre *gawze* and *lace;*
Tho' faith, I fear ye dine but sparely,   5
    On sic a place.

Ye ugly, creepan, blastet[6] wonner,
Detested, shunn'd, by saunt an' sinner,
How daur ye set your fit upon her,
    Sae fine a *Lady!*
Gae somewhere else and seek your dinner,   10
    On some poor body.

Swith,[7] in some beggar's haffet[8] squattle,[9]
There ye may creep, and sprawl,[10] and sprattle,[11]
Wi'ither kindred, jumping cattle,[12]   15
    In shoals and nations;
Whare *horn* nor *bane*[13] ne'er daur unsettle,
    Your thick plantations.

Now haud[14] you there, ye're out o' sight,
Below the fatt'rels,[15] snug, and tight,
Na faith ye[16] yet! Ye'll no be right,   20
    Till ye've got on it,
The vera tapmost, towrin height
    O' *Miss's* bonnet.

My sooth! Right bauld ye set your nose,   25
As plump an' gray as onie grozet[17]
O for some rank, mercurial rozet,[18]
    Or fell,[19] red smeddum,[20]
I'd gie you sic a hearty dose o't,
    Wad dress your droddum![21]   30

I wad na been surpriz'd to spy
You on an auld wife's *flainen toy*[22];

---

1. Going. 2. Crawling. 3. Wonder [contemptuous]. 4. Surely. 5. Strut. 6. Blasted, cursed. 7. Off. 8. Temple. 9. Squat.
10. Struggle. 11. Scramble. 12. Beasts. 13. Combs were made of horn or bone. 14. Stay. 15. Ribbon ends. 16. Confound
you. 17. Gooseberry. 18. Rosin soap. 19. Deadly. 20. Powder. 21. Beat your rear end. 22. Flannel cap.

Or aiblins[23] some bit duddle[24] boy,
    On's *wylecoat*[25];
But Miss's fine *Lunardi*,[26] fye!
    How daur ye do't?   35

O *Jenny* dinna toss your head,
An' set your beauties a' abroad![27]
Ye little ken what cursed speed
    The blastie's[28] makin!   40
Thae *winks* and *finger-ends*, I dread,
    Are notice takin!

O wad some Pow'r the giftie gie[29] us
To see oursels as others see us!
It wad frae monie a blunder free us   45
    An' foolish notion:
What airs in dress an' gait wad lea'e us,
    And ev'n Devotion!

                    —1786

Afton Water

Flow gently, sweet Afton, among thy green braes![1]
Flow gently, I'll sing thee a song in thy praise!
My Mary's asleep by thy murmuring stream—
Flow gently, sweet Afton, disturb not her dream!

Thou stock-dove whose echo resounds thro' the glen,   5
Ye wild whistling blackbirds in yon thorny den,
Thou green-crested lapwing, thy screaming forbear—
I charge you, disturb not my slumbering fair!

How lofty, sweet Afton, thy neighbouring hills,
Far mark'd with the courses of clear, winding rills![2]   10
There daily I wander, as noon rises high,
My flocks and my Mary's sweet cot[3] in my eye.

How pleasant thy banks and green vallies below,
Where wild in the woodlands the primroses blow;
There oft, as mild Ev'ning weeps over the lea,[4]   15
The sweet-scented birk[5] shades my Mary and me.

Thy crystal stream, Afton, how lovely it glides,
And winds by the cot where my Mary resides!
How wanton thy waters her snowy feet lave,[6]
As, gathering sweet flowerets, she stems thy clear wave.   20

---

23. Maybe. 24. Ragged. 25. Flannel vest. 26. Bonnet. 27. Abroad. 28. Dwarf. 29. Gift give.

1. Banks. 2. Brooks. 3. Cottage. 4. Meadow. 5. Birch. 6. Wash.

Flow gently, sweet Afton, among thy green braes!
Flow gently, sweet river, the theme of my lays!
My Mary's asleep by thy murmuring stream—
Flow gently, sweet Afton, disturb not her dream!

—1792

Comin' Thro' the Rye [1]

CHORUS

Comin thro' the rye, poor body,
   Comin thro' the rye,
She draigl't[1] a' her petticoatie,
   Comin thro' the rye!

O, Jenny's a' weet, poor body,   5
   Jenny's seldom dry:
She draigl't a' her petticoatie,
   Comin thro' the rye!

Gin[2] a body meet a body
   Comin thro' the rye,   10
Gin a body kiss a body,
   Need a body cry?

Gin a body meet a body
   Comin thro' the glen,
Gin a body kiss a body,   15
   Need the warld ken?[3]

CHORUS

—1796

Comin' Thro' the Rye [2]

CHORUS

Comin' thro' the rye, my jo,[1]
   An' comin' thro' the rye;
She fand a straun[2] o' staunin' graith,[3]
   Comin' thro' the rye.

O gin a body meet a body,   5
   Comin throu the rye;
Gin a body f—k a body,
   Need a body cry.

---

1. Bedraggled. 2. If. 3. Know.

1. Sweetheart. 2. Stand. 3. Tools.

Gin a body meet a body,
    Comin' thro' the glen;
Gin a body f—k a body,   10
    Need the warld ken.[4]

Gin a body meet a body,
    Comin' thro' the grain;
Gin a body f—k a body,   15
    C—t's a body's ain.[5]

Gin a body meet a body,
    By a body's sel,[6]
What na body f—s a body,
    Wad a body tell.   20

Mony a body meets a body,
    They dare na weel avow[7];
Mony a body f—s a body,
    Ye wadna think it true.

—1799

Scots, wha hae wi' Wallace bled

Scots, wha hae[1] wi' Wallace bled,
Scots, wham[2] Bruce has aften led,
Welcome to your gory bed
    Or to victorie!

Now's the day, and now's the hour: 5
See the front o' battle lour,[3]
See approach proud Edward's[4] power—
    Chains and slaverie!

Wha will be a traitor knave?
Wha can fill a coward's grave?   10
Wha sae base as be a slave?—
    Let him turn, and flee!

Wha for Scotland's King and Law
Freedom's sword will strongly draw,
Freeman stand or freeman fa',[5]   15
    Let him follow me!

---

4. Know. 5. Own. 6. Self. 7. Acknowledge.

1. Who have. 2. Whom. 3. Glare. 4. Edward II (1307–1327) was defeated by Scottish forces under Robert Bruce (1274–1329), ensuring Scotland's independence until 1707. 5. Fall.

By Oppression's woes and pains,
By your sons in servile chains,
We will drain our dearest veins
  But they shall be free!

Lay the proud usurpers low!
Tyrants fall in every foe!
Liberty's in every blow!
  Let us do, or die!

—1794

A Red, Red Rose

O, my luve is like a red, red rose,
  That's newly sprung in June.
O, my luve is like the melodie,
  That's sweetly play'd in tune.

As fair art thou, my bonie lass,
  So deep in luve am I,
And I will luve thee still, my dear,
  Till a' the seas gang¹ dry.

Till a' the seas gang dry, my dear,
  And the rocks melt wi' the sun!
And I will luve thee still, my dear,
  While the sands o' life shall run.

And fare thee weel, my only luve,
  And fare thee weel a while!
And I will come again, my luve,
  Tho' it were ten thousand mile!

—1796

Auld Lang Syne

Should auld acquaintance be forgot,
  And never brought to mind?
Should auld acquaintance be forgot,
  And auld lang syne!¹

---

1. Go.

1. Long ago times.

    For auld lang syne, my dear,   5
    For auld lang syne,
    We'll tak a cup o' kindness yet
    For auld lang syne!

And surely ye'll be[2] your pint-stowp,[3]
  And surely I'll be mine,   10
And we'll tak a cup o' kindness yet
  For auld lang syne!

CHORUS

We twa hae run about the braes,[4]
  And pou'd[5] the gowans[6] fine,
But we've wander'd monie a weary fit[7]   15
  Sin'[8] auld lang syne.

CHORUS

We twa hae paidl'd in the burn
  Frae morning sun till dine,[9]
But seas between us braid[10] hae roar'd
  Sin' auld lang syne.   20

CHORUS

And there's a hand, my trusty fiere,[11]
  And gie's a hand o' thine,
And we'll tak a right guid-willie waught[12]
  For auld lang syne!

CHORUS

    For auld lang syne, my dear,   25
    For auld lang syne,
    We'll tak a cup o' kindness yet
    For auld lang syne!

—1796

❈

CONTEMPORARY RESPONSE

Fitz-Greene Halleck
1790–1867

The son of a Loyalist during the American Revolution, Fitz-Greene Halleck's poetics and politics reflected his British sympathies. Indeed, his poem "Burns" is a tip of the hat to Robert Burns, the Scottish poet whose use of common speech and simple meter strongly influenced

---

2. Buy.   3. Pint cup.   4. Slopes.   5. Pulled.   6. Daisies.   7. Foot.   8. Since.   9. Noon meal.   10. Broad.   11. Friend.
12. Good-will draft.

much early nineteenth-century American poetry. "Burns" was written during Halleck's 1822 tour of Europe and first appeared in the 1827 volume *Alnwick Castle, with Other Poems.* The poem was so well regarded in England and Scotland that for many years a copy hung on the wall in Burns's birthplace. Residing for most of his life in New York City, Halleck, along with Washington Irving, formed the Author's Club, a veritable receiving line for authors from across the Atlantic, numbering Charles Dickens and William Makepeace Thackeray among the writers they welcomed to Manhattan.

from Burns

To a Rose, Brought from Near Alloway Kirk,[1]
in Ayrshire,[2] in the Autumn of 1822

Wild Rose of Alloway! my thanks;
    Thou 'mindst me of that autumn noon
When first we met upon "the banks
    And braes o' bonny Doon."[3]

Like thine, beneath the thorn-tree's bough,   5
    My sunny hour was glad and brief,
We've crossed the winter sea, and thou
    Art withered—flower and leaf.

And will not thy death-doom be mine—
    The doom of all things wrought of clay—   10
And withered my life's leaf like thine,
    Wild rose of Alloway?

Not so his memory, for whose sake
    My bosom bore thee far and long,
His—who a humbler flower could make   15
    Immortal as his song,

The memory of Burns—a name
    That calls, when brimmed her festal cup,
A nation's glory and her shame,
    In silent sadness up.   20

A nation's glory—be the rest
    Forgot—she's canonized his mind;
And it is joy to speak the best
    We may of human kind.

I've stood beside the cottage-bed   25
    Where the Bard-peasant first drew breath;
A straw-thatched roof above his head,
    A straw-wrought couch beneath.

And I have stood beside the pile,
    His monument—that tells to Heaven   30

---

1. Church.   2. Robert Burns's village in Scotland.   3. Paraphrase of Robert Burns, "The Banks o' Doon" (1783).

The homage of earth's proudest isle
  To that Bard-peasant given!

Bid thy thoughts hover o'er that spot,
  Boy-minstrel, in thy dreaming hour;
And know, however low his lot,   35
  A Poet's pride and power:

The pride that lifted Burns from earth,
  The power that gave a child of song
Ascendency o'er rank and birth,
  The rich, the brave, the strong;   40

And if despondency weigh down
  Thy spirit's fluttering pinions[4] then,
Despair—thy name is written on
  The roll of common men.

There have been loftier themes than his,   45
  And longer scrolls, and louder lyres,[5]
And lays lit up with Poesy's
  Purer and holier fires:

Yet read the names that know not death;
  Few nobler ones than Burns are there;   50
And few have won a greener wreath
  Than that which binds his hair.

His is that language of the heart,
  In which the answering heart would speak,
Thought, word, that bids the warm tear start,   55
  Or the smile light the cheek;

And his that music, to whose tone
  The common pulse of man keeps time,
In cot or castle's mirth or moan,
  In cold or sunny clime. . . .   60

All ask the cottage of his birth,
  Gaze on the scenes he loved and sung,
And gather feelings not of earth
  His fields and streams among.

They linger by the Doon's low trees,   65
  And pastoral Nith, and wooded Ayr,
And round thy sepulchres, Dumfries![6]
  The poet's tomb is there.

---

4. Wings.   5. Stringed instrument associated with poetry.   6. Doon, Nith, Ayr, and Dumfries are places in Scotland associated with Burns.

But what to them the sculptor's art,
  His funeral columns, wreaths and urns?
Wear they not graven on the heart
  The name of Robert Burns?   70

                                                          —1827

Mary Wollstonecraft
1759–1797

One of the foremothers of feminism, Mary Wollstonecraft penned A *Vindication of the Rights of Woman* (1792), a radical call for equal rights and education for women. In this work, she focuses on, among many other subjects, the ways in which women are educated and forced to comply with artificial gender roles during their upbringing and adult lives. She witnessed much during her childhood that would shape her views on gender: On more than one occasion she had to protect her mother from her father's drunken anger over his business failures. Throughout her life, she witnessed firsthand the ways in which patriarchal tyranny can manifest in the domestic sphere and the political one as well. After her mother passed away, Wollstonecraft left her home and supported herself by teaching at a school in London. This experience led to her publishing *Thoughts on the Education of Daughters* (1786), the first of many publications on women and education.

Her next book on this topic was *The Female Reader* (1789), published by Joseph Johnson, a radical London publisher whose circle included Anna Laetitia Barbauld, Joel Barlow, William Blake, William Godwin, Thomas Paine, William Wordsworth, and others. Wollstonecraft was prolific during 1788–1789, also publishing *Mary* and *Original Stories from Real Life*. The Johnson Circle provided a forge for Wollstonecraft's radical ideas. As one of the only women who was a part of the group, she proved herself as integral to the development of its members' thoughts as her transatlantic counterpart Margaret Fuller was, decades later, to Ralph Waldo Emerson and his Transcendentalists. In addition to catalyzing each others' radical views, the Johnson Circle was inspired by the American Revolution's focus on equality as well as that of the French Revolution, which was erupting across the Channel. Edmund Burke, who was quite liberal with regard to American and Irish efforts to attain freedom from British rule, emerged as the foremost conservative critic of the French Revolution's attempts to level class distinctions. However, his *Reflections on the Revolution in France* (1790) did not go long unanswered. Wollstonecraft replied during the same year with A *Vindication of the Rights of Men*. This work earned her success and fame, and it spurred her on to publish, two years later, A *Vindication of the Rights of Woman*.

One of the initiatives of the French Revolution was equal rights for women, a notion that Wollstonecraft gave one of its first and most powerful articulations in English. The draw to Revolutionary France proved powerful, and Wollstonecraft relocated there in late 1792. While there, she met several other expatriates with similar views, including Helen Maria Williams, who had written *Letters from France, 1790*. Williams's book detailed the abuses of authority of the French aristocracy by focusing on the story of a young nobleman whose father so opposed his son's wish to marry a woman of the lower class that he had his son imprisoned to prevent the marriage. Wollstonecraft also met the American expatriate Gilbert Imlay, who had fought in the American Revolution and had traveled to France to sell Parisians fraudulent land claims to made-up towns in Kentucky. He was to prove equally dishonest in his relationship with Wollstonecraft, who registered herself as his wife at the American Embassy in order to obtain legal protection from the French Revolution, which was turning increasingly bloody and anti-English. Like Williams, Wollstonecraft published her own firsthand account of events in France—*Historical and Moral View of the Progress of the French Revolution* (1794).

Shortly after Wollstonecraft gave birth to a daughter, Fanny, fathered by Imlay, he left them and traveled to London, where he took up with an actress. In order to put more distance between himself and his family and to have them locate some stolen pieces of artwork, Imlay sent Wollstonecraft and Fanny on a tour of Scandinavia, which resulted in *Letters Written during a Short Residence in Sweden, Norway, and Denmark* (1796). This book, comprised of her letters to Imlay, contains not only her sentiments toward him and his actions but also views of the cultures of Scandinavia from an English perspective, and some of the most well-written and poetic landscape descriptions and musings in Romantic prose. By the time she returned to him in autumn 1795, he was living with someone else, with whom he would move to Paris. The circumstances drove Wollstonecraft to a suicide attempt: Placing stones in her pockets, she jumped from a bridge into the Thames but was rescued by witnesses. By the next summer, she had renewed her acquaintance with William Godwin of the Johnson Circle. Like Wollstonecraft, Godwin was also a famous author. His *Political Justice* (1793) delineated a progression toward enlightenment, reason, equality, and the demise of aristocratic government. Each other's intellectual equal, the two became very close and fell in love. Although both were opposed to marriage as a societal institution in which the wife became the property of the husband, the two wed; true to their principles, they kept separate living quarters and remained active writers. Ten days after giving birth to their daughter, Mary, Wollstonecraft died from complications of the birth.

Wollstonecraft was vilified by many of the thinkers of the mid-late nineteenth century, who judged her life according to Victorian notions of gender and propriety. Her work did, however, inspire many who wrote on behalf of women's rights, including her daughter Mary Shelley, George Eliot, Margaret Fuller, and Elizabeth Cady Stanton. During her thirty-seven years, Wollstonecraft penned works whose full implications regarding women, education, language, and society were worked out by writers of the centuries that followed and have still to be realized in a world where gender inequity persists.

from A Vindication of the Rights of Men

in a Letter to the Right Honourable Edmund Burke; Occasioned by his Reflections on the Revolution in France

Mr. Burke's Reflections on the French Revolution first engaged my attention as the transient topic of the day. . . . My indignation was roused by the sophistical arguments, that every moment crossed me, in the questionable shape of natural feelings and common sense. . . . I have confined my strictures, in a great measure, to the grand principles at which he has levelled many ingenious arguments in a very specious garb.

[ON THE "CULT OF SENSIBILITY"]

Sensibility is the *manie*[1] of the day, and compassion the virtue which is to cover a multitude of vices, whilst justice is left to mourn in sullen silence, and balance truth in vain.

In life, an honest man with a confined understanding is frequently the slave of his habits and the dupe of his feelings, whilst the man with a clearer head and colder heart makes the passions of others bend to his interest; but truly sublime is the char-

---

1. Cultural craze or fad.

acter that acts from principle. . . . All your pretty flights arise from your pampered sensibility; and that, vain of this fancied pre-eminence of organs, you foster every emotion till the fumes, mounting to your brain, dispel the sober suggestions of reason. It is not in this view surprising, that when you should argue you become impassioned, and that reflection inflames your imagination, instead of enlightening your understanding.

Quitting now the flowers of rhetoric, let us, Sir, reason together.[2] . . .

The birthright of man, to give you, Sir, a short definition of this disputed right, is such a degree of liberty, civil and religious, as is compatible with the liberty of every other individual with whom he is united in a social compact, and the continued existence of that compact.[3]

Liberty, in this simple, unsophisticated sense, I acknowledge, is a fair idea that has never yet received a form in the various governments that have been established on our bounteous globe; the demon of property has ever been at hand to encroach on the sacred rights of men, and to fence round with awful pomp laws that war with justice. . . . If there is any thing like argument, or first principles, in your wild declamation, behold the result:—that we are to reverence the rust of antiquity, and term the unnatural customs, which ignorance and mistaken self-interest have consolidated, the sage fruit of experience: nay, that, if we do discover some errors, our *feelings* should lead us to excuse, with blind love, or unprincipled filial affection, the venerable vestiges of ancient days. These are gothic notions of beauty—the ivy is beautiful, but, when it insidiously destroys the trunk from which it receives support, who would not grub it up? . . .

The civilization which has taken place in Europe has been very partial, and, like every custom that an arbitrary point of honour has established, refines the manners at the expence of morals, by making sentiments and opinions current in conversation that have no root in the heart, or weight in the cooler resolves of the mind.—And what has stopped its progress?—hereditary property—hereditary honours. The man has been changed into an artificial monster by the station in which he was born, and the consequent homage that benumbed his faculties like the torpedo's touch[4];—or a being, with a capacity of reasoning, would not have failed to discover, as his faculties unfolded, that true happiness arose from the friendship and intimacy which can only be enjoyed by equals; and that charity is not a condescending distribution of alms, but an intercourse of good offices and mutual benefits, founded on respect for justice and humanity.

[DIVINE RIGHTS AND HUMAN EQUALITY]

Are we to seek for the rights of men in the ages when a few marks were the only penalty imposed for the life of a man, and death for death when the property of the rich was touched? when—I blush to discover the depravity of our nature—when a deer was killed![5] Are these the laws that it is natural to love, and sacrilegious to invade?—Were the rights of men understood when the law authorized or tolerated murder?—or is power and right the same in your creed? . . .

It is necessary emphatically to repeat, that there are rights which men inherit at their birth, as rational creatures, who were raised above the brute creation by their improvable faculties; and that, in receiving these, not from their forefathers but, from God, prescription can never undermine natural rights.

2. Isaiah 1.18.   3. Alludes to John Locke (1632–1704), *Two Treatises of Government* (1690), and Jean-Jacques Rousseau (1712–1778), *The Social Contract* (1762).   4. A stingray's sting.   5. Killing a deer on a nobleman's property was forbidden by English law.

A father may dissipate his property without his child having any right to complain;—but should he attempt to sell him for a slave, or fetter him with laws contrary to reason; nature, in enabling him to discern good from evil, teaches him to break the ignoble chain, and not to believe that bread becomes flesh, and wine blood, because his parents swallowed the Eucharist with this blind persuasion.[6]

There is no end to this implicit submission to authority—some where it must stop, or we return to barbarism; and the capacity of improvement, which gives us a natural sceptre on earth, is a cheat, an ignis-fatuus,[7] that leads us from inviting meadows into bogs and dunghills. And if it be allowed that many of the precautions, with which any alteration was made, in our government, were prudent, it rather proves its weakness that substantiates an opinion of the soundness of the stamina, or the excellence of the constitution.

But on what principle Mr. Burke could defend American independence, I cannot conceive; for the whole tenor of his plausible arguments settles slavery on an everlasting foundation. Allowing his servile reverence for antiquity, and prudent attention to self-interest, to have the force which he insists on, the slave trade ought never to be abolished; and, because our ignorant forefathers, not understanding the native dignity of man, sanctioned a traffic that outrages every suggestion of reason and religion, we are to submit to the inhuman custom, and term an atrocious insult to humanity the love of our country, and a proper submission to the laws by which our property is secured.—Security of property! Behold, in a few words, the definition of English liberty. And to this selfish principle every nobler one is sacrificed.—The Briton takes place of the man, and the image of God is lost in the citizen! But it is not that enthusiastic flame which in Greece and Rome consumed every sordid passion: no, self is the focus; and the disparting rays rise not above our foggy atmosphere. But softly—it is only the property of the rich that is secure; the man who lives by the sweat of his brow has no asylum from oppression. . . . It is a farce to pretend that a man fights *for his country, his hearth, or his altars,* when he has neither liberty nor property.—His property is in his nervous arms—and they are compelled to pull a strange rope at the surly command of a tyrannic boy, who probably obtained his rank on account of his family connections, or the prostituted vote of his father, whose interest in a borough, or voice as a senator, was acceptable to the minister. . . .

Misery, to reach your heart, I perceive, must have its cap and bells[8]; your tears are reserved, very *naturally* considering your character, for the declamation of the theatre, or for the downfall of queens, whose rank alters the nature of folly, and throws a graceful veil over vices that degrade humanity; whilst the distress of many industrious mothers, whose *helpmates* have been torn from them, and the hungry cry of helpless babes, were vulgar sorrows that could not move your commiseration, though they might extort an alms. . . .

A brutal attachment to children has appeared most conspicuous in parents who have treated them like slaves, and demanded due homage for all the property they transferred to them, during their lives. It has led them to force their children to break the most sacred ties; to do violence to a natural impulse, and run into legal prostitution to increase wealth or shun poverty. . . . It appears to be a natural suggestion of reason, that a man should be freed from implicit obedience to parents and private

6. The Catholic doctrine of transubstantiation holds that the communion wafer and wine are the body and blood of Jesus Christ.   7. A false light or spirit, a will o' the wisp.   8. Jester's hat.

punishments, when he is of an age to be subject to the jurisdiction of the laws of his country; and that the barbarous cruelty of allowing parents to imprison their children, to prevent their contaminating their noble blood by following the dictates of nature when they chose to marry, or for any misdemeanor that does not come under the cognizance of public justice, is one of the most arbitrary violations of liberty.[9]

Who can recount all the unnatural crimes which the *laudable*, *interesting* desire of perpetuating a name has produced? The younger children have been sacrificed to the eldest son; sent into exile, or confined in convents, that they might not encroach on what was called, with shameful falsehood, the *family* estate.[10] Will Mr Burke call this parental affection reasonable or virtuous?—No; it is the spurious offspring of over-weening, mistaken pride—and not that first source of civilization, natural parental affection, that makes no difference between child and child, but what reason justifies by pointing out superior merit.

Another pernicious consequence which unavoidably arises from this artificial affection is, the insuperable bar which it puts in the way of early marriages. It would be difficult to determine whether the minds or bodies of our youth are most injured by this impediment. Our young men become selfish coxcombs. . . .

The same system has an equally pernicious effect on female morals.—Girls are sacrificed to family convenience, or else marry to settle themselves in a superior rank, and coquet, without restraint, with the fine gentleman whom I have already described.

[WOMEN, PROPERTY, AND VIRTUE]

Property, I do not scruple to aver it, should be fluctuating, which would be the case, if it were more equally divided amongst all the children of a family; else it is an everlasting rampart, in consequence of a barbarous feudal institution, that enables the elder son to overpower talents and depress virtue.

Besides, an unmanly servility, most inimical to true dignity of character is, by this means, fostered in society. Men of some abilities play on the follies of the rich, and mounting to fortune as they degrade themselves, they stand in the way of men of superior talents, who cannot advance in such crooked paths, or wade through the filth which *parasites* never boggle at. Pursuing their way straight forward, their spirit is either bent or broken by the rich man's contumelies[11] or the difficulties they have to encounter.

The only security of property that nature authorizes and reason sanctions is, the right a man has to enjoy the acquisitions which his talents and industry have acquired; and to bequeath them to whom he chooses. . . . Overreaching, adultery, and coquetry, are venial offences, though they reduce virtue to an empty name, and make wisdom consist in saving appearances.

"On this scheme of things a king *is* but a man; a queen *is* but a woman; a woman *is* but an animal, and an animal not of the highest order."[12]—All true, Sir; if she is not more attentive to the duties of humanity than queens and fashionable ladies in general are. I will still further accede to the opinion you have so justly conceived of the spirit which begins to animate this age.—"All homage paid to the sex in general, as such, and without distinct views, is to be regarded as *romance* and folly." Undoubtedly; because such homage vitiates them, prevents their endeavouring to obtain solid

---

9. A "lettre de cachet" allowed French nobility to imprison anyone they pleased.   10. The French Revolution abolished primogeniture, the practice of protecting an estate by transferring it whole to the eldest son.   11. Abusive insults.   12. Edmund Burke (1729–1797), *Reflections on the Revolution in France* (1790), quoted throughout paragraph.

personal merit; and, in short, makes those beings vain inconsiderate dolls, who ought to be prudent mothers and useful members of society. "Regicide and sacrilege are but fictions of superstition corrupting jurisprudence, by destroying its simplicity. The murder of a king, or a queen, or a bishop, are only common homicide."—Again I agree with you; but you perceive, Sir, that by leaving out the word *father*, I think the whole extent of the comparison invidious. . . .

[THE RIGHTS OF THE POOR]

The rich and weak, a numerous train, will certainly applaud your system, and loudly celebrate your pious reverence for authority and establishments—they find it pleasanter to enjoy than to think; to justify oppression than correct abuses.—*The rights of men* are grating sounds that set their teeth on edge; the impertinent enquiry of philosophic meddling innovation. If the poor are in distress, they will make some *benevolent* exertions to assist them; they will confer obligations, but not do justice. Benevolence is a very amiable specious quality; yet the aversion which men feel to accept a right as a favour, should rather be extolled as a vestige of native dignity, than stigmatized as the odious offspring of ingratitude. The poor consider the rich as their lawful prey; but we ought not too severely to animadvert on[13] their ingratitude. When they receive an alms they are commonly grateful at the moment; but old habits quickly return, and cunning has ever been a substitute for force. . . .

Among all your plausible arguments, and witty illustrations, your contempt for the poor always appears conspicuous, and rouses my indignation. The following paragraph in particular struck me, as breathing the most tyrannic spirit, and displaying the most factitious feelings. "Good order is the foundation of all good things. To be enabled to acquire, the people, without being servile, must be tractable and obedient. The magistrate must have his reverence, the laws their authority. The body of the people must not find the principles of natural subordination by art rooted out of their minds. They must respect that property of which they *cannot* partake. *They must labour to obtain what by labour can be obtained; and when they find, as they commonly do, the success disproportioned to the endeavour, they must be taught their consolation in the final proportions of eternal justice.* Of this consolation, whoever deprives them, deadens their industry, and strikes at the root of all acquisition as of all conservation. He that does this, is the cruel oppressor, the merciless enemy, of the poor and wretched; at the same time that, by his wicked speculations, he exposes the fruits of successful industry, and the accumulations of fortune, (ah! there's the rub)[14] to the plunder of the negligent, the disappointed, and the unprosperous."

This is contemptible hard-hearted sophistry, in the specious form of humility, and submission to the will of Heaven.—It is, Sir, *possible* to render the poor happier in this world, without depriving them of the consolation which you gratuitously grant them in the next. They have a right to more comfort than they at present enjoy; and more comfort might be afforded them, without encroaching on the pleasures of the rich: not now waiting to enquire whether the rich have any right to exclusive pleasures. What do I say?—encroaching! No; if an intercourse were established between them, it would impart the only true pleasure that can be snatched in this land of shadows, this hard school of moral discipline.

I know, indeed, that there is often something disgusting in the distresses of poverty, at which the imagination revolts, and starts back to exercise itself in the more attractive

---

13. Censure, condemn.   14. William Shakespeare (1564–1616), *Hamlet*, 3.1.65.

Arcadia of fiction. The rich man builds a house, art and taste give it the highest finish. His gardens are planted, and the trees grow to recreate the fancy of the planter, though the temperature of the climate may rather force him to avoid the dangerous damps they exhale, than seek the umbrageous retreat. Every thing on the estate is cherished but man;—yet, to contribute to the happiness of man, is the most sublime of all enjoyments. But if, instead of sweeping pleasure-grounds, obelisks, temples, and elegant cottages, as *objects* for the eye, the heart was allowed to beat true to nature, decent farms would be scattered over the estate, and plenty smile around. Instead of the poor being subject to the griping hand of an avaricious steward, they would be watched over with fatherly solicitude, by the man whose duty and pleasure it was to guard their happiness, and shield from rapacity the beings who, by the sweat of their brow, exalted him above his fellows.

I could almost imagine I see a man thus gathering blessings as he mounted the hill of life; or consolation, in those days when the spirits lag, and the tired heart finds no pleasure in them. It is not by squandering alms that the poor can be relieved, or improved—it is the fostering sun of kindness, the wisdom that finds them employments calculated to give them habits of virtue, that meliorates their condition. . . .

Why cannot large estates be divided into small farms? these dwellings would indeed grace our land. Why are huge forests still allowed to stretch out with idle pomp and all the indolence of Eastern [Asian] grandeur? Why does the brown waste meet the traveller's view, when men want work? But commons cannot be enclosed without *acts of parliament* to increase the property of the rich![15] Why might not the industrious peasant be allowed to steal a farm from the heath? This sight I have seen;—the cow that supported the children grazed near the hut, and the cheerful poultry were fed by the chubby babes, who breathed a bracing air, far from the diseases and the vices of cities. Domination blasts all these prospects; virtue can only flourish amongst equals, and the man who submits to a fellow-creature, because it promotes his worldly interest, and he who relieves only because it is his duty to lay up a treasure in heaven,[16] are much on a par, for both are radically degraded by the habits of their life.

In this great city, that proudly rears its head, and boasts of its population and commerce, how much misery lurks in pestilential corners, whilst idle mendicants assail, on every side, the man who hates to encourage impostors, or repress, with angry frown, the plaints of the poor! How many mechanics, by a flux of trade or fashion, lose their employment; whom misfortunes, not to be warded off, lead to the idleness that vitiates their character and renders them afterwards averse to honest labour! Where is the eye that marks these evils, more gigantic than any of the infringements of property, which you piously deprecate? Are these remediless evils? And is the humane heart satisfied with turning the poor over to *another* world, to receive the blessings this could afford? . . .

What were the outrages of a day to these continual miseries?[17] Let those sorrows hide their diminished head[18] before the tremendous mountain of woe that thus defaces our globe! Man preys on man; and you mourn . . . for the empty pageant of a name, when slavery flaps her wing, and the sick heart retires to die in lonely wilds, far from the abodes of men. Did the pangs you felt for insulted nobility, the anguish that rent your heart when the gorgeous robes were torn off the idol human weakness had set up [Queen Marie Antoinette], deserve to be compared with the long-drawn sigh of melan-

---

15. Eighteenth-century acts of enclosure seized publicly shared pastures, making them the private property of the rich. 16. Matthew 6.20. 17. Compares constant suffering of poor to the Queen's imprisonment. 18. John Milton (1608–1674), *Paradise Lost* (1667), 4.35.

choly reflection, when misery and vice are thus seen to haunt our steps, and swim on the top of every cheering prospect? Why is our fancy to be appalled by terrific perspective of a hell beyond the grave?—Hell stalks abroad;—the lash resounds on the slave's naked sides; and the sick wretch, who can no longer earn the sour bread of unremitting labour, steals to a ditch to bid the world a long good night—or, neglected in some ostentatious hospital, breathes his last amidst the laugh of mercenary attendants.

Such misery demands more than tears—I pause to recollect myself; and smother the contempt I feel rising for your rhetorical flourishes and infantine sensibility.

—1790

from A Vindication of the Rights of Woman

from To M. Talleyrand-Périgord, Late Bishop of Autun[1]

Contending for the rights of woman, my main argument is built on this simple principle, that if she be not prepared by education to become the companion of man, she will stop the progress of knowledge and virtue; for truth must be common to all, or it will be inefficacious with respect to its influence on general practice. . . .

In this work I have produced many arguments, which to me were conclusive, to prove that the prevailing notion respecting a sexual character was subversive of morality, and I have contended, that to render the human body and mind more perfect, chastity must more universally prevail, and that chastity will never be respected in the male world till the person of a woman is not, as it were, idolized, when little virtue or sense embellish it with the grand traces of mental beauty, or the interesting simplicity of affection.

Consider, Sir, dispassionately, these observations—for a glimpse of this truth seemed to open before you when you observed, "that to see one half of the human race excluded by the other from all participation of government, was a political phænomenon that, according to abstract principles, it was impossible to explain."[2] If so, on what does your constitution rest? If the abstract rights of man will bear discussion and explanation, those of woman, by a parity of reasoning, will not shrink from the same test: though a different opinion prevails in this country, built on the very arguments which you use to justify the oppression of woman—prescription.

Consider, I address you as a legislator, whether, when men contend for their freedom, and to be allowed to judge for themselves respecting their own happiness, it be not inconsistent and unjust to subjugate women, even though you firmly believe that you are acting in the manner best calculated to promote their happiness? Who made man the exclusive judge, if woman partake with him the gift of reason?

In this style, argue tyrants of every denomination, from the weak king to the weak father of a family; they are all eager to crush reason; yet always assert that they usurp its throne only to be useful. Do you not act a similar part, when you *force* all women, by denying them civil and political rights, to remain immured in their families groping in the dark? for surely, Sir, you will not assert, that a duty can be binding which is not founded on reason? If indeed this be their destination, arguments may be drawn from reason: and thus augustly supported, the more understanding women acquire, the more they will be attached to their duty—comprehending it—for unless they comprehend it, unless

---

1. Charles Maurice de Talleyrand (1754–1838), French diplomat, advocated educating girls to be subservient to men.
2. Talleyrand, *Report on Public Instruction* (1790). Universal suffrage was not achieved in France until 1944.

their morals be fixed on the same immutable principle as those of man, no authority can make them discharge it in a virtuous manner. They may be convenient slaves, but slavery will have its constant effect, degrading the master and the abject dependent.

But, if women are to be excluded, without having a voice, from a participation of the natural rights of mankind, prove first, to ward off the charge of injustice and inconsistency, that they want reason—else this flaw in your NEW CONSTITUTION will ever shew that man must, in some shape, act like a tyrant, and tyranny, in whatever part of society it rears its brazen front, will ever undermine morality.

I have repeatedly asserted, and produced what appeared to me irrefragable arguments drawn from matters of fact, to prove my assertion, that women cannot, by force, be confined to domestic concerns; for they will, however ignorant, intermeddle with more weighty affairs, neglecting private duties only to disturb, by cunning tricks, the orderly plans of reason which rise above their comprehension.

Besides, whilst they are only made to acquire personal accomplishments, men will seek for pleasure in variety, and faithless husbands will make faithless wives; such ignorant beings, indeed, will be very excusable when, not taught to respect public good, nor allowed any civil rights, they attempt to do themselves justice by retaliation.

The box of mischief thus opened in society, what is to preserve private virtue, the only security of public freedom and universal happiness?

Let there be then no coercion *established* in society, and the common law of gravity prevailing, the sexes will fall into their proper places. And, now that more equitable laws are forming your citizens, marriage may become more sacred: your young men may choose wives from motives of affection, and your maidens allow love to root out vanity.

The father of a family will not then weaken his constitution and debase his sentiments, by visiting the harlot, nor forget, in obeying the call of appetite, the purpose for which it was implanted. And, the mother will not neglect her children to practise the arts of coquetry, when sense and modesty secure her the friendship of her husband.

But, till men become attentive to the duty of a father, it is vain to expect women to spend that time in their nursery which they, "wise in their generation,"[3] choose to spend at their glass; for this exertion of cunning is only an instinct of nature to enable them to obtain indirectly a little of that power of which they are unjustly denied a share: for, if women are not permitted to enjoy legitimate rights, they will render both men and themselves vicious, to obtain illicit privileges.

I wish, Sir, to set some investigations of this kind afloat in France; and should they lead to a confirmation of my principles, when your constitution is revised the Rights of Woman may be respected, if it be fully proved that reason calls for this respect, and loudly demands Justice for one half of the human race.

I am, SIR,

Your's respectfully,

M. W.

Introduction

After considering the historic page, and viewing the living world with anxious solicitude, the most melancholy emotions of sorrowful indignation have depressed my spirits, and I have sighed when obliged to confess, that either nature has made a great dif-

---

3. Luke 16.8.

ference between man and man, or that the civilization which has hitherto taken place in the world has been very partial. I have turned over various books written on the subject of education, and patiently observed the conduct of parents and the management of schools; but what has been the result?—a profound conviction that the neglected education of my fellow-creatures is the grand source of the misery I deplore; and that women, in particular, are rendered weak and wretched by a variety of concurring causes, originating from one hasty conclusion. The conduct and manners of women, in fact, evidently prove that their minds are not in a healthy state; for, like the flowers which are planted in too rich a soil, strength and usefulness are sacrificed to beauty; and the flaunting leaves, after having pleased a fastidious eye, fade, disregarded on the stalk, long before the season when they ought to have arrived at maturity.—One cause of this barren blooming I attribute to a false system of education, gathered from the books written on this subject by men who, considering females rather as women than human creatures, have been more anxious to make them alluring mistresses than affectionate wives and rational mothers; and the understanding of the sex has been so bubbled by this specious homage, that the civilized women of the present century, with a few exceptions, are only anxious to inspire love, when they ought to cherish a nobler ambition, and by their abilities and virtues exact respect.

In a treatise, therefore, on female rights and manners, the works which have been particularly written for their improvement must not be overlooked; especially when it is asserted, in direct terms, that the minds of women are enfeebled by false refinement; that the books of instruction, written by men of genius, have had the same tendency as more frivolous productions; and that, in the true style of Mahometanism,[4] they are treated as a kind of subordinate beings, and not as a part of the human species, when improveable reason is allowed to be the dignified distinction which raises men above the brute creation, and puts a natural sceptre in a feeble hand.

Yet, because I am a woman, I would not lead my readers to suppose that I mean violently to agitate the contested question respecting the equality or inferiority of the sex; but as the subject lies in my way, and I cannot pass it over without subjecting the main tendency of my reasoning to misconstruction, I shall stop a moment to deliver, in a few words, my opinion.—In the government of the physical world it is observable that the female in point of strength is, in general, inferior to the male. This is the law of nature; and it does not appear to be suspended or abrogated in favour of woman. A degree of physical superiority cannot, therefore, be denied—and it is a noble prerogative! But not content with this natural pre-eminence, men endeavour to sink us still lower, merely to render us alluring objects for a moment; and women, intoxicated by the adoration which men, under the influence of their senses, pay them, do not seek to obtain a durable interest in their hearts, or to become the friends of the fellow creatures who find amusement in their society.

I am aware of an obvious inference:—from every quarter have I heard exclamations against masculine women; but where are they to be found? If by this appellation men mean to inveigh against their ardour in hunting, shooting, and gaming, I shall most cordially join in the cry; but if it be against the imitation of manly virtues, or, more properly speaking, the attainment of those talents and virtues, the exercise of which ennobles the human character, and which raise females in the scale of animal

---

4. Refers to the mistaken belief that the *Koran* denies women souls.

being, when they are comprehensively termed mankind;—all those who view them with a philosophic eye must, I should think, wish with me, that they may every day grow more and more masculine.

This discussion naturally divides the subject. I shall first consider women in the grand light of human creatures, who, in common with men, are placed on this earth to unfold their faculties; and afterwards I shall more particularly point out their peculiar designation.

I wish also to steer clear of an error which many respectable writers have fallen into; for the instruction which has hitherto been addressed to women, has rather been applicable to *ladies*, if the little indirect advice, that is scattered through Sandford and Merton,[5] be excepted; but, addressing my sex in a firmer tone, I pay particular attention to those in the middle class, because they appear to be in the most natural state. Perhaps the seeds of false-refinement, immorality, and vanity, have ever been shed by the great. Weak, artificial beings, raised above the common wants and affections of their race, in a premature unnatural manner, undermine the very foundation of virtue, and spread corruption through the whole mass of society! As a class of mankind they have the strongest claim to pity; the education of the rich tends to render them vain and helpless, and the unfolding mind is not strengthened by the practice of those duties which dignify the human character.—They only live to amuse themselves, and by the same law which in nature invariably produces certain effects, they soon only afford barren amusement.

But as I purpose taking a separate view of the different ranks of society, and of the moral character of women, in each, this hint is, for the present, sufficient; and I have only alluded to the subject, because it appears to me to be the very essence of an introduction to give a cursory account of the contents of the work it introduces.

My own sex, I hope, will excuse me, if I treat them like rational creatures, instead of flattering their *fascinating* graces, and viewing them as if they were in a state of perpetual childhood, unable to stand alone. I earnestly wish to point out in what true dignity and human happiness consists—I wish to persuade women to endeavour to acquire strength, both of mind and body, and to convince them that the soft phrases, susceptibility of heart, delicacy of sentiment, and refinement of taste, are almost synonymous with epithets of weakness, and that those beings who are only the objects of pity and that kind of love, which has been termed its sister, will soon become objects of contempt.

Dismissing then those pretty feminine phrases, which the men condescendingly use to soften our slavish dependence, and despising that weak elegancy of mind, exquisite sensibility, and sweet docility of manners, supposed to be the sexual characteristics of the weaker vessel, I wish to shew that elegance is inferior to virtue, that the first object of laudable ambition is to obtain a character as a human being, regardless of the distinction of sex; and that secondary views should be brought to this simple touchstone.

This is a rough sketch of my plan; and should I express my conviction with the energetic emotions that I feel whenever I think of the subject, the dictates of experience and reflection will be felt by some of my readers. Animated by this important object, I shall disdain to cull my phrases or polish my style;—I aim at being useful, and sincerity will render me unaffected; for, wishing rather to persuade by the force of my arguments, than dazzle by the elegance of my language, I shall not waste my time in rounding periods, or in fabricating the turgid bombast of artificial feelings, which,

---

5. Thomas Day (1748–1789), *The History of Sandford and Merton* (1783), a morality tale for children.

coming from the head, never reach the heart.—I shall be employed about things, not words!—and, anxious to render my sex more respectable members of society, I shall try to avoid that flowery diction which has slided from essays into novels, and from novels into familiar letters and conversation.

These pretty superlatives, dropping glibly from the tongue, vitiate the taste, and create a kind of sickly delicacy that turns away from simple unadorned truth; and a deluge of false sentiments and over-stretched feelings, stifling the natural emotions of the heart, render the domestic pleasures insipid, that ought to sweeten the exercise of those severe duties, which educate a rational and immortal being for a nobler field of action.

The education of women has, of late, been more attended to than formerly; yet they are still reckoned a frivolous sex, and ridiculed or pitied by the writers who endeavour by satire or instruction to improve them. It is acknowledged that they spend many of the first years of their lives in acquiring a smattering of accomplishments; meanwhile strength of body and mind are sacrificed to libertine notions of beauty, to the desire of establishing themselves,—the only way women can rise in the world,—by marriage. And this desire making mere animals of them, when they marry they act as such children may be expected to act:—they dress; they paint, and nickname God's creatures.[6]—Surely these weak beings are only fit for a seraglio![7]—Can they be expected to govern a family with judgment, or take care of the poor babes whom they bring into the world?

If then it can be fairly deduced from the present conduct of the sex, from the prevalent fondness for pleasure which takes place of ambition and those nobler passions that open and enlarge the soul; that the instruction which women have hitherto received has only tended, with the constitution of civil society, to render them insignificant objects of desire—mere propagators of fools!—if it can be proved that in aiming to accomplish them, without cultivating their understandings, they are taken out of their sphere of duties, and made ridiculous and useless when the short-lived bloom of beauty is over, I presume that *rational* men will excuse me for endeavouring to persuade them to become more masculine and respectable.

Indeed the word masculine is only a bugbear: there is little reason to fear that women will acquire too much courage or fortitude; for their apparent inferiority with respect to bodily strength, must render them, in some degree, dependent on men in the various relations of life; but why should it be increased by prejudices that give a sex to virtue,[8] and confound simple truths with sensual reveries?

Women are, in fact, so much degraded by mistaken notions of female excellence, that I do not mean to add a paradox when I assert, that this artificial weakness produces a propensity to tyrannize, and gives birth to cunning, the natural opponent of strength, which leads them to play off those contemptible infantine airs that undermine esteem even whilst they excite desire. Let men become more chaste and modest, and if women do not grow wiser in the same ratio, it will be clear that they have weaker understandings. It seems scarcely necessary to say, that I now speak of the sex in general. Many individuals have more sense than their male relatives; and, as nothing preponderates where there is a constant struggle for an equilibrium, without it has naturally more gravity, some women govern their husbands without degrading themselves, because intellect will always govern.

---

6. William Shakespeare (1564–1616), *Hamlet*, 3.1.145–148.   7. Harem.   8. "Virtue" contains the Latin word for "man," *vir*.

from Chapter 1. The Rights and Involved Duties of Mankind Considered

In the present state of society it appears necessary to go back to first principles in search of the most simple truths, and to dispute with some prevailing prejudice every inch of ground. To clear my way, I must be allowed to ask some plain questions, and the answers will probably appear as unequivocal as the axioms on which reasoning is built; though, when entangled with various motives of action, they are formally contradicted, either by the words or conduct of men.

In what does man's pre-eminence over the brute creation consist? The answer is as clear as that a half is less than the whole; in Reason.

What acquirement exalts one being above another? Virtue; we spontaneously reply.

For what purpose were the passions implanted? That man by struggling with them might attain a degree of knowledge denied to the brutes; whispers Experience.

Consequently the perfection of our nature and capability of happiness, must be estimated by the degree of reason, virtue, and knowledge, that distinguish the individual, and direct the laws which bind society: and that from the exercise of reason, knowledge and virtue naturally flow, is equally undeniable, if mankind be viewed collectively.

The rights and duties of man thus simplified, it seems almost impertinent to attempt to illustrate truths that appear so incontrovertible; yet such deeply rooted prejudices have clouded reason, and such spurious qualities have assumed the name of virtues, that it is necessary to pursue the course of reason as it has been perplexed and involved in error, by various adventitious circumstances, comparing the simple axiom with casual deviations.

Men, in general, seem to employ their reason to justify prejudices, which they have imbibed, they can scarcely trace how, rather than to root them out. The mind must be strong that resolutely forms its own principles; for a kind of intellectual cowardice prevails which makes many men shrink from the task, or only do it by halves. Yet the imperfect conclusions thus drawn, are frequently very plausible, because they are built on partial experience, on just, though narrow, views. . . .

The civilization of the bulk of the people of Europe is very partial; nay, it may be made a question, whether they have acquired any virtues in exchange for innocence, equivalent to the misery produced by the vices that have been plastered over unsightly ignorance, and the freedom which has been bartered for splendid slavery. The desire of dazzling by riches, the most certain pre-eminence that man can obtain, the pleasure of commanding flattering sycophants, and many other complicated low calculations of doting self-love, have all contributed to overwhelm the mass of mankind, and make liberty a convenient handle for mock patriotism. For whilst rank and titles are held of the utmost importance, before which Genius "must hide its diminished head,"[9] it is, with a few exceptions, very unfortunate for a nation when a man of abilities, without rank or property, pushes himself forward to notice.—Alas! what unheard of misery have thousands suffered to purchase a cardinal's hat for an intriguing obscure adventurer, who longed to be ranked with princes, or lord it over them by seizing the triple crown![10] . . .

Nothing can set the regal character in a more contemptible point of view, than the various crimes that have elevated men to the supreme dignity.—Vile intrigues, unnatural crimes, and every vice that degrades our nature, have been the steps to this distinguished eminence; yet millions of men have supinely

---

9. John Milton (1608–1674), *Paradise Lost* (1667), 4.35.   10. Worn by the Pope.

allowed the nerveless limbs of the posterity of such rapacious prowlers to rest quietly on their ensanguined[11] thrones.

What but a pestilential vapour can hover over society when its chief director is only instructed in the invention of crimes, or the stupid routine of childish ceremonies? Will men never be wise?—will they never cease to expect corn from tares, and figs from thistles?[12]

It is impossible for any man, when the most favourable circumstances concur, to acquire sufficient knowledge and strength of mind to discharge the duties of a king, entrusted with uncontrouled power; how then must they be violated when his very elevation is an insuperable bar to the attainment of either wisdom or virtue; when all the feelings of a man are stifled by flattery, and reflection shut out by pleasure! Surely it is madness to make the fate of thousands depend on the caprice of a weak fellow creature, whose very station sinks him *necessarily* below the meanest of his subjects! But one power should not be thrown down to exalt another—for all power inebriates weak man; and its abuse proves that the more equality there is established among men, the more virtue and happiness will reign in society. But this and any similar maxim deduced from simple reason, raises an outcry—the church or the state is in danger, if faith in the wisdom of antiquity is not implicit; and they who, roused by the sight of human calamity, dare to attack human authority, are reviled as despisers of God, and enemies of man. These are bitter calumnies, yet they reached one of the best of men, whose ashes still preach peace,[13] and whose memory demands a respectful pause, when subjects are discussed that lay so near his heart.—

After attacking the sacred majesty of Kings, I shall scarcely excite surprise by adding my firm persuasion that every profession, in which great subordination of rank constitutes its power, is highly injurious to morality.

A standing army, for instance, is incompatible with freedom; because subordination and rigour are the very sinews of military discipline; and despotism is necessary to give vigour to enterprizes that one will directs. A spirit inspired by romantic notions of honour, a kind of morality founded on the fashion of the age, can only be felt by a few officers, whilst the main body must be moved by command, like the waves of the sea; for the strong wind of authority pushes the crowd of subalterns forward, they scarcely know or care why, with headlong fury.

Besides, nothing can be so prejudicial to the morals of the inhabitants of country towns as the occasional residence of a set of idle superficial young men, whose only occupation is gallantry, and whose polished manners render vice more dangerous, by concealing its deformity under gay ornamental drapery. An air of fashion, which is but a badge of slavery, and proves that the soul has not a strong individual character, awes simple country people into an imitation of the vices, when they cannot catch the slippery graces, of politeness. Every corps is a chain of despots, who, submitting and tyrannizing without exercising their reason, become dead weights of vice and folly on the community. A man of rank or fortune, sure of rising by interest, has nothing to do but to pursue some extravagant freak; whilst the needy *gentleman*, who is to rise, as the phrase turns, by his merit, becomes a servile parasite or vile pander.

---

11. Bloody, and inherited by blood.   12. Matthew 7.16.   13. Richard Price (1723–1791), who angered Edmund Burke by advocating the rights of the people over the "divine right" of kings.

Sailors, the naval gentlemen, come under the same description, only their vices assume a different and a grosser cast. They are more positively indolent, when not discharging the ceremonials of their station; whilst the insignificant fluttering of soldiers may be termed active idleness. More confined to the society of men, the former acquire a fondness for humour and mischievous tricks; whilst the latter, mixing frequently with well-bred women, catch a sentimental cant.—But mind is equally out of the question, whether they indulge the horse-laugh, or polite simper.

May I be allowed to extend the comparison to a profession where more mind is certainly to be found; for the clergy have superior opportunities of improvement, though subordination almost equally cramps their faculties? The blind submission imposed at college to forms of belief[14] serves as a novitiate to the curate, who must obsequiously respect the opinion of his rector or patron, if he mean to rise in his profession. Perhaps there cannot be a more forcible contrast than between the servile dependent gait of a poor curate and the courtly mien of a bishop. And the respect and contempt they inspire render the discharge of their separate functions equally useless.

It is of great importance to observe that the character of every man is, in some degree, formed by his profession. A man of sense may only have a cast of countenance that wears off as you trace his individuality, whilst the weak, common man has scarcely ever any character, but what belongs to the body; at least, all his opinions have been so steeped in the vat consecrated by authority, that the faint spirit which the grape of his own vine yields cannot be distinguished.

Society, therefore, as it becomes more enlightened, should be very careful not to establish bodies of men who must necessarily be made foolish or vicious by the very constitution of their profession.

from Chapter 2. The Prevailing Opinion of a Sexual Character Discussed

To account for, and excuse the tyranny of man, many ingenious arguments have been brought forward to prove, that the two sexes, in the acquirement of virtue, ought to aim at attaining a very different character: or, to speak explicitly, women are not allowed to have sufficient strength of mind to acquire what really deserves the name of virtue. Yet it should seem, allowing them to have souls, that there is but one way appointed by Providence to lead *mankind* to either virtue or happiness.

If then women are not a swarm of ephemeron[15] triflers, why should they be kept in ignorance under the specious name of innocence? Men complain, and with reason, of the follies and caprices of our sex, when they do not keenly satirize our headstrong passions and groveling vices.—Behold, I should answer, the natural effect of ignorance! The mind will ever be unstable that has only prejudices to rest on, and the current will run with destructive fury when there are no barriers to break its force. Women are told from their infancy, and taught by the example of their mothers, that a little knowledge of human weakness, justly termed cunning, softness of temper, *outward* obedience, and a scrupulous attention to a puerile kind of propriety, will obtain for them the protection of man; and should they be beautiful, every thing else is needless, for, at least, twenty years of their lives.

---

14. Oxford and Cambridge Universities required sworn allegiance to the thirty-nine articles of the Church of England and made chapel attendance compulsory.   15. Short-lived, insignificant.

Thus Milton describes our first frail mother[16]; though when he tells us that women are formed for softness and sweet attractive grace, I cannot comprehend his meaning, unless, in the true Mahometan strain, he meant to deprive us of souls, and insinuate that we were beings only designed by sweet attractive grace, and docile blind obedience, to gratify the senses of man when he can no longer soar on the wing of contemplation.

How grossly do they insult us who thus advise us only to render ourselves gentle, domestic brutes! For instance, the winning softness so warmly, and frequently, recommended, that governs by obeying. What childish expressions, and how insignificant is the being—can it be an immortal one? who will condescend to govern by such sinister methods! "Certainly," says Lord Bacon, "man is of kin to the beasts by his body; and if he be not of kin to God by his spirit, he is a base and ignoble creature!"[17] Men, indeed, appear to me to act in a very unphilosophical manner when they try to secure the good conduct of women by attempting to keep them always in a state of childhood. Rousseau was more consistent when he wished to stop the progress of reason in both sexes, for if men eat of the tree of knowledge, women will come in for a taste; but, from the imperfect cultivation which their understandings now receive, they only attain a knowledge of evil.[18]

Children, I grant, should be innocent; but when the epithet is applied to men, or women, it is but a civil term for weakness. For if it be allowed that women were destined by Providence to acquire human virtues, and by the exercise of their understandings, that stability of character which is the firmest ground to rest our future hopes upon, they must be permitted to turn to the fountain of light, and not forced to shape their course by the twinkling of a mere satellite. Milton, I grant, was of a very different opinion; for he only bends to the indefeasible right of beauty, though it would be difficult to render two passages which I now mean to contrast, consistent. But into similar inconsistencies are great men often led by their senses.

> To whom thus Eve with *perfect beauty* adorn'd.
> "My Author and Disposer, what thou bidst
> *Unargued* I obey; So God ordains;
> God is *thy law, thou mine:* to know no more
> Is Woman's *happiest* knowledge and her *praise*."[19]

These are exactly the arguments that I have used to children; but I have added, your reason is now gaining strength, and, till it arrives at some degree of maturity, you must look up to me for advice—then you ought to *think*, and only rely on God.

Yet in the following lines Milton seems to coincide with me; when he makes Adam thus expostulate with his Maker.

> Hast thou not made me here thy substitute,
> And these inferior far beneath me set?
> Among *unequals* what society
> Can sort, what harmony or true delight?
> Which must be mutual, in proportion due
> Giv'n and receiv'd; but in *disparity*

16. John Milton (1608–1674), *Paradise Lost* (1667), 4.296–299.   17. Francis Bacon (1561–1626), *Essays* (1625).   18. Jean-Jacques Rousseau (1712–1778), *Emile, or Education* (1762).   19. *Paradise Lost*, 4.634–638.

> The one intense, the other still remiss
> Cannot well suit with either, but soon prove
> Tedious alike: of *fellowship* I speak
> Such as I seek, fit to participate
> All rational delight—[20]

In treating, therefore, of the manners of women, let us, disregarding sensual arguments, trace what we should endeavour to make them in order to co-operate, if the expression be not too bold, with the supreme Being.

By individual education, I mean, for the sense of the word is not precisely defined, such an attention to a child as will slowly sharpen the senses, form the temper, regulate the passions as they begin to ferment, and set the understanding to work before the body arrives at maturity; so that the man may only have to proceed, not to begin, the important task of learning to think and reason. . . .

In fact, it is a farce to call any being virtuous whose virtues do not result from the exercise of its own reason. This was Rousseau's opinion respecting men: I extend it to women, and confidently assert that they have been drawn out of their sphere by false refinement, and not by an endeavour to acquire masculine qualities. Still the regal homage which they receive is so intoxicating, that till the manners of the times are changed, and formed on more reasonable principles, it may be impossible to convince them that the illegitimate power, which they obtain, by degrading themselves, is a curse, and that they must return to nature and equality, if they wish to secure the placid satisfaction that unsophisticated affections impart. But for this epoch we must wait—wait, perhaps, till kings and nobles, enlightened by reason, and, preferring the real dignity of man to childish state, throw off their gaudy hereditary trappings: and if then women do not resign the arbitrary power of beauty—they will prove that they have *less* mind than man.

I may be accused of arrogance; still I must declare what I firmly believe, that all the writers who have written on the subject of female education and manners from Rousseau to Dr. Gregory,[21] have contributed to render women more artificial, weak characters, than they would otherwise have been; and, consequently, more useless members of society. . . . My objection extends to the whole purport of those books, which tend, in my opinion, to degrade one half of the human species, and render women pleasing at the expense of every solid virtue.

Though, to reason on Rousseau's ground, if man did attain a degree of perfection of mind when his body arrived at maturity, it might be proper, in order to make a man and his wife *one*, that she should rely entirely on his understanding; and the graceful ivy, clasping the oak that supported it, would form a whole in which strength and beauty would be equally conspicuous. But, alas! husbands, as well as their helpmates, are often only overgrown children; nay, thanks to early debauchery, scarcely men in their outward form—and if the blind lead the blind, one need not come from heaven to tell us the consequence.[22]

Many are the causes that, in the present corrupt state of society, contribute to enslave women by cramping their understandings and sharpening their senses. One, perhaps, that silently does more mischief than all the rest, is their disregard of order.

---

20. *Paradise Lost*, 8.381–391.   21. John Gregory (1724–1773), *A Father's Legacy to His Daughters* (1774).
22. Matthew 15.14.

To do every thing in an orderly manner, is a most important precept, which women, who, generally speaking, receive only a disorderly kind of education, seldom attend to with that degree of exactness that men, who from their infancy are broken into method, observe. This negligent kind of guess-work, for what other epithet can be used to point out the random exertions of a sort of instinctive common sense, never brought to the test of reason? prevents their generalizing matters of fact—so they do to-day, what they did yesterday, merely because they did it yesterday.

This contempt of the understanding in early life has more baneful consequences than is commonly supposed; for the little knowledge which women of strong minds attain, is, from various circumstances, of a more desultory kind than the knowledge of men, and it is acquired more by sheer observations on real life, than from comparing what has been individually observed with the results of experience generalized by speculation. Led by their dependent situation and domestic employments more into society, what they learn is rather by snatches; and as learning is with them, in general, only a secondary thing, they do not pursue any one branch with that persevering ardour necessary to give vigour to the faculties, and clearness to the judgment. In the present state of society, a little learning is required to support the character of a gentleman; and boys are obliged to submit to a few years of discipline. But in the education of women, the cultivation of the understanding is always subordinate to the acquirement of some corporeal accomplishment; even while enervated by confinement and false notions of modesty, the body is prevented from attaining that grace and beauty which relaxed half-formed limbs never exhibit. Besides, in youth their faculties are not brought forward by emulation; and having no serious scientific study, if they have natural sagacity it is turned too soon on life and manners. They dwell on effects, and modifications, without tracing them back to causes; and complicated rules to adjust behaviour are a weak substitute for simple principles.

As a proof that education gives this appearance of weakness to females, we may instance the example of military men, who are, like them, sent into the world before their minds have been stored with knowledge or fortified by principles. The consequences are similar; soldiers acquire a little superficial knowledge, snatched from the muddy current of conversation, and, from continually mixing with society, they gain, what is termed a knowledge of the world; and this acquaintance with manners and customs has frequently been confounded with a knowledge of the human heart. But can the crude fruit of casual observation, never brought to the test of judgment, formed by comparing speculation and experience, deserve such a distinction? Soldiers, as well as women, practice the minor virtues with punctilious politeness. Where is then the sexual difference, when the education has been the same? All the difference that I can discern, arises from the superior advantage of liberty, which enables the former to see more of life.

It is wandering from my present subject, perhaps, to make a political remark; but, as it was produced naturally by the train of my reflections, I shall not pass it silently over.

Standing armies can never consist of resolute, robust men; they may be well disciplined machines, but they will seldom contain men under the influence of strong passions, or with very vigorous faculties. And as for any depth of understanding, I will venture to affirm, that it is as rarely to be found in the army as amongst women; and the cause, I maintain, is the same. It may be further observed, that officers are also particularly attentive to their persons, fond of dancing, crowded rooms, adventures, and ridicule. Like the *fair* sex, the business of their lives is gallantry.—They were taught to please, and they only live to please. Yet they do not lose their rank in the distinction of sexes, for they are still reckoned superior to women, though in what their superiority consists, beyond what I have just mentioned, it is difficult to discover.

The great misfortune is this, that they both acquire manners before morals, and a knowledge of life before they have, from reflection, any acquaintance with the grand ideal outline of human nature. The consequence is natural; satisfied with common nature, they become a prey to prejudices, and taking all their opinions on credit, they blindly submit to authority. So that, if they have any sense, it is a kind of instinctive glance, that catches proportions, and decides with respect to manners; but fails when arguments are to be pursued below the surface, or opinions analyzed.

May not the same remark be applied to women? Nay, the argument may be carried still further, for they are both thrown out of a useful station by the unnatural distinctions established in civilized life. Riches and hereditary honours have made cyphers of women to give consequence to the numerical figure; and idleness has produced a mixture of gallantry and despotism into society, which leads the very men who are the slaves of their mistresses to tyrannize over their sisters, wives, and daughters. This is only keeping them in rank and file, it is true. Strengthen the female mind by enlarging it, and there will be an end to blind obedience; but, as blind obedience is ever sought for by power, tyrants and sensualists are in the right when they endeavour to keep women in the dark, because the former only want slaves, and the latter a play-thing. The sensualist, indeed, has been the most dangerous of tyrants, and women have been duped by their lovers, as princes by their ministers, whilst dreaming that they reigned over them.

I now principally allude to Rousseau, for his character of Sophia[23] is, undoubtedly, a captivating one, though it appears to me grossly unnatural; however it is not the superstructure, but the foundation of her character, the principles on which her education was built, that I mean to attack; nay, warmly as I admire the genius of that able writer, whose opinions I shall often have occasion to cite, indignation always takes place of admiration, and the rigid frown of insulted virtue effaces the smile of complacency, which his eloquent periods[24] are wont to raise, when I read his voluptuous reveries. Is this the man, who, in his ardour for virtue, would banish all the soft arts of peace, and almost carry us back to Spartan discipline? Is this the man who delights to paint the useful struggles of passion, the triumphs of good dispositions, and the heroic flights which carry the glowing soul out of itself?—How are these mighty sentiments lowered when he describes the pretty foot and enticing airs of his little favourite! But, for the present, I waive the subject, and, instead of severely reprehending the transient effusions of overweening sensibility, I shall only observe, that whoever has cast a benevolent eye on society, must often have been gratified by the sight of a humble mutual love, not dignified by sentiment, or strengthened by a union in intellectual pursuits. The domestic trifles of the day have afforded matters for cheerful converse, and innocent caresses have softened toils which did not require great exercise of mind or stretch of thought: yet, has not the sight of this moderate felicity excited more tenderness than respect? An emotion similar to what we feel when children are playing, or animals sporting, whilst the contemplation of the noble struggles of suffering merit has raised admiration, and carried our thoughts to that world where sensation will give place to reason.

Women are, therefore, to be considered either as moral beings, or so weak that they must be entirely subjected to the superior faculties of men. . . .

---

23. Jean-Jacques Rousseau (1712–1778), *Emile, or Education* (1762).   24. Sentences.

Probably the prevailing opinion, that woman was created for man, may have taken its rise from Moses's poetical story[25]; yet, as very few, it is presumed, who have bestowed any serious thought on the subject, ever supposed that Eve was, literally speaking, one of Adam's ribs, the deduction must be allowed to fall to the ground; or, only be so far admitted as it proves that man, from the remotest antiquity, found it convenient to exert his strength to subjugate his companion, and his invention to shew that she ought to have her neck bent under the yoke, because the whole creation was only created for his convenience or pleasure.

Let it not be concluded that I wish to invert the order of things; I have already granted, that, from the constitution of their bodies, men seem to be designed by Providence to attain a greater degree of virtue. I speak collectively of the whole sex; but I see not the shadow of a reason to conclude that their virtues should differ in respect to their nature. In fact, how can they, if virtue has only one eternal standard? I must therefore, if I reason consequentially, as strenuously maintain that they have the same simple direction, as that there is a God.

It follows then that cunning should not be opposed to wisdom, little cares to great exertions, or insipid softness, varnished over with the name of gentleness, to that fortitude which grand views alone can inspire.

I shall be told that woman would then lose many of her peculiar graces, and the opinion of a well known poet might be quoted to refute my unqualified assertion. For Pope has said, in the name of the whole male sex,

> Yet ne'er so sure our passion to create,
> As when she touch'd the brink of all we hate.[26]

In what light this sally places men and women, I shall leave to the judicious to determine; meanwhile I shall content myself with observing, that I cannot discover why, unless they are mortal, females should always be degraded by being made subservient to love or lust.

To speak disrespectfully of love is, I know, high treason against sentiment and fine feelings; but I wish to speak the simple language of truth, and rather to address the head than the heart. To endeavour to reason love out of the world, would be to out Quixote Cervantes,[27] and equally offend against common sense; but an endeavour to restrain this tumultuous passion, and to prove that it should not be allowed to dethrone superior powers, or to usurp the sceptre which the understanding should ever coolly wield, appears less wild.

Youth is the season for love in both sexes; but in those days of thoughtless enjoyment provision should be made for the more important years of life, when reflection takes place of sensation. But Rousseau, and most of the male writers who have followed his steps, have warmly inculcated that the whole tendency of female education ought to be directed to one point:—to render them pleasing.

Let me reason with the supporters of this opinion who have any knowledge of human nature, do they imagine that marriage can eradicate the habitude of life? The woman who has only been taught to please will soon find that her charms are oblique sunbeams, and that they cannot have much effect on her husband's heart when they

---

25. Genesis 2.21–23, believed to have been written by Moses. 26. Alexander Pope (1688–1744), "Epistle II" (1735), 51–52. 27. Miguel de Cervantes y Saavedra (1547–1616), *Don Quixote de la Mancha* (1605).

are seen every day, when the summer is passed and gone. Will she then have sufficient native energy to look into herself for comfort, and cultivate her dormant faculties? or, is it not more rational to expect that she will try to please other men; and, in the emotions raised by the expectation of new conquests, endeavour to forget the mortification her love or pride has received? When the husband ceases to be a lover—and the time will inevitably come, her desire of pleasing will then grow languid, or become a spring of bitterness; and love, perhaps, the most evanescent of all passions, gives place to jealousy or vanity.

I now speak of women who are restrained by principle or prejudice; such women, though they would shrink from an intrigue with real abhorrence, yet, nevertheless, wish to be convinced by the homage of gallantry that they are cruelly neglected by their husbands; or, days and weeks are spent in dreaming of the happiness enjoyed by congenial souls till their health is undermined and their spirits broken by discontent. How then can the great art of pleasing be such a necessary study? it is only useful to a mistress; the chaste wife, and serious mother, should only consider her power to please as the polish of her virtues, and the affection of her husband as one of the comforts that render her task less difficult and her life happier.—But, whether she be loved or neglected, her first wish should be to make herself respectable, and not to rely for all her happiness on a being subject to like infirmities with herself.

The worthy Dr. Gregory fell into a similar error. I respect his heart; but entirely disapprove of his celebrated Legacy to his Daughters.

He advises them to cultivate a fondness for dress, because a fondness for dress, he asserts, is natural to them. I am unable to comprehend what either he or Rousseau mean, when they frequently use this indefinite term. If they told us that in a pre-existent state the soul was fond of dress, and brought this inclination with it into a new body, I should listen to them with a half smile, as I often do when I hear a rant about innate elegance.—But if he only meant to say that the exercise of the faculties will produce this fondness—I deny it.—It is not natural; but arises, like false ambition in men, from a love of power.

Dr. Gregory goes much further; he actually recommends dissimulation, and advises an innocent girl to give the lie to her feelings, and not dance with spirit, when gaiety of heart would make her feel eloquent without making her gestures immodest. In the name of truth and common sense, why should not one woman acknowledge that she can take more exercise than another? or, in other words, that she has a sound constitution; and why, to damp innocent vivacity, is she darkly to be told that men will draw conclusions which she little thinks of?—Let the libertine draw what inference he pleases; but, I hope, that no sensible mother will restrain the natural frankness of youth by instilling such indecent cautions. Out of the abundance of the heart the mouth speaketh; and a wiser than Solomon[28] hath said, that the heart should be made clean, and not trivial ceremonies observed, which it is not very difficult to fulfill with scrupulous exactness when vice reigns in the heart.

Women ought to endeavour to purify their heart[29]; but can they do so when their uncultivated understandings make them entirely dependent on their senses for employment and amusement, when no noble pursuit sets them above the little vanities of the day, or enables them to curb the wild emotions that agitate a reed over

---

28. Luke 11.31.   29. Matthew 5.8.

which every passing breeze has power? To gain the affections of a virtuous man is affectation necessary? Nature has given woman a weaker frame than man; but, to ensure her husband's affections, must a wife, who by the exercise of her mind and body whilst she was discharging the duties of a daughter, wife, and mother, has allowed her constitution to retain its natural strength, and her nerves a healthy tone, is she, I say, to condescend to use art and feign a sickly delicacy in order to secure her husband's affection? Weakness may excite tenderness, and gratify the arrogant pride of man; but the lordly caresses of a protector will not gratify a noble mind that pants for, and deserves to be respected. Fondness is a poor substitute for friendship!

In a seraglio, I grant, that all these arts are necessary; the epicure must have his palate tickled, or he will sink into apathy; but have women so little ambition as to be satisfied with such a condition? Can they supinely dream life away in the lap of pleasure, or the languor of weariness, rather than assert their claim to pursue reasonable pleasures and render themselves conspicuous by practising the virtues which dignify mankind? Surely she has not an immortal soul who can loiter life away merely employed to adorn her person, that she may amuse the languid hours, and soften the cares of a fellow-creature who is willing to be enlivened by her smiles and tricks, when the serious business of life is over.

Besides, the woman who strengthens her body and exercises her mind will, by managing her family and practising various virtues, become the friend, and not the humble dependent of her husband; and if she, by possessing such substantial qualities, merit his regard, she will not find it necessary to conceal her affection, nor to pretend to an unnatural coldness of constitution to excite her husband's passions. In fact, if we revert to history, we shall find that the women who have distinguished themselves have neither been the most beautiful nor the most gentle of their sex.

Nature, or, to speak with strict propriety, God, has made all things right; but man has sought him out many inventions to mar the work. I now allude to that part of Dr. Gregory's treatise, where he advises a wife never to let her husband know the extent of her sensibility or affection. Voluptuous precaution, and as ineffectual as absurd.— Love, from its very nature, must be transitory. To seek for a secret that would render it constant, would be as wild a search as for the philosopher's stone,[30] or the grand panacea: and the discovery would be equally useless, or rather pernicious to mankind. The most holy band of society is friendship. It has been well said, by a shrewd satirist, "that rare as true love is, true friendship is still rarer."[31] . . .

This is an obvious truth, and the cause not lying deep, will not elude a slight glance of inquiry.

Love, the common passion, in which chance and sensation take place of choice and reason, is, in some degree, felt by the mass of mankind; for it is not necessary to speak, at present, of the emotions that rise above or sink below love. This passion, naturally increased by suspense and difficulties, draws the mind out of its accustomed state, and exalts the affections; but the security of marriage, allowing the fever of love to subside, a healthy temperature is thought insipid, only by those who have not sufficient intellect to substitute the calm tenderness of friendship, the confidence of respect, instead of blind admiration, and the sensual emotions of fondness.

This is, must be, the course of nature.—Friendship or indifference inevitably succeeds love.—And this constitution seems perfectly to harmonize with the system

---

30. Mythical stone that turns lead to gold.   31. François Duc de la Rochefoucauld (1613–1680), *Reflections* (1665).

of government which prevails in the normal world. Passions are spurs to action, and open the mind; but they sink into mere appetites, become a personal and momentary gratification, when the object is gained, and the satisfied mind rests in enjoyment. The man who had some virtue whilst he was struggling for a crown, often becomes a voluptuous tyrant when it graces his brow; and, when the lover is not lost in the husband, the dotard, a prey of childish caprices, and fond jealousies, neglects the serious duties of life, and the caresses which should excite confidence in his children are lavished on the overgrown child, his wife.

In order to fulfil the duties of life, and to be able to pursue with vigour the various employments which form the moral character, a master and mistress of a family ought not to continue to love each other with passion. I mean to say, that they ought not to indulge those emotions which disturb the order of society, and engross the thoughts that should be otherwise employed. The mind that has never been engrossed by one object wants vigour—if it can long be so, it is weak.

A mistaken education, a narrow, uncultivated mind, and many sexual prejudices, tend to make women more constant than men; but, for the present, I shall not touch on this branch of the subject. I will go still further, and advance, without dreaming of a paradox, that an unhappy marriage is often very advantageous to a family, and that the neglected wife is, in general, the best mother. . . .

I do not mean to allude to the romantic passion, which is the concomitant of genius.—Who can clip its wing? But that grand passion not proportioned to the puny enjoyments of life, is only true to the sentiment, and feeds on itself. The passions which have been celebrated for their durability have always been unfortunate. They have acquired strength by absence and constitutional melancholy.—The fancy has hovered round a form of beauty dimly seen—but familiarity might have turned admiration into disgust; or, at least, into indifference, and allowed the imagination leisure to start fresh game. With perfect propriety, according to this view of things, does Rousseau make the mistress of his soul, Eloisa, love St. Preux, when life was fading before her[32]; but this is no proof of the immortality of the passion.

Of the same complexion is Dr. Gregory's advice respecting delicacy of sentiment, which he advises a woman not to acquire, if she have determined to marry. This determination, however, perfectly consistent with his former advice, he calls *indelicate*, and earnestly persuades his daughters to conceal it, though it may govern their conduct;—as if it were indelicate to have the common appetites of human nature.

Noble morality! and consistent with the cautious prudence of a little soul that cannot extend its views beyond the present minute division of existence. If all the faculties of woman's mind are only to be cultivated as they respect her dependence on man; if, when a husband be obtained, she have arrived at her goal, and meanly proud rests satisfied with such a paltry crown, let her grovel contentedly, scarcely raised by her employments above the animal kingdom; but, if, struggling for the prize of her high calling, she look beyond the present scene, let her cultivate her understanding without stopping to consider what character the husband may have whom she is destined to marry. Let her only determine, without being too anxious about present happiness, to acquire the qualities that ennoble a rational being, and a rough inelegant husband may shock her taste without destroying her peace of mind. She

---

32. Jean-Jacques Rousseau (1712–1778), *Julie, or the New Heloise* (1761).

will not model her soul to suit the frailties of her companion, but to bear with them: his character may be a trial, but not an impediment to virtue.

If Dr. Gregory confined his remark to romantic expectations of constant love and congenial feelings, he should have recollected that experience will banish what advice can never make us cease to wish for, when the imagination is kept alive at the expence of reason.

I own it frequently happens that women who have fostered a romantic unnatural delicacy of feeling, waste their lives in *imagining* how happy they should have been with a husband who could love them with a fervid increasing affection every day, and all day. But they might as well pine married as single—and would not be a jot more unhappy with a bad husband than longing for a good one. That a proper education; or, to speak with more precision, a well stored mind, would enable a woman to support a single life with dignity, I grant; but that she should avoid cultivating her taste, lest her husband should occasionally shock it, is quitting a substance for a shadow. To say the truth, I do not know of what use is an improved taste, if the individual be not rendered more independent of the casualties of life; if new sources of enjoyment, only dependent on the solitary operations of the mind, are not opened. People of taste, married or single, without distinction, will ever be disgusted by various things that touch not less observing minds. On this conclusion the argument must not be allowed to hinge; but in the whole sum of enjoyment is taste to be denominated a blessing?

The question is, whether it procures most pain or pleasure? The answer will decide the propriety of Dr. Gregory's advice, and shew how absurd and tyrannic it is thus to lay down a system of slavery; or to attempt to educate moral beings by any other rules than those deduced from pure reason, which apply to the whole species.

Gentleness of manners, forbearance and long-suffering, are such amiable God-like qualities, that in sublime poetic strains the Deity has been invested with them; and, perhaps, no representation of his goodness so strongly fastens on the human affections as those that represent him abundant in mercy and willing to pardon.[33] Gentleness, considered in this point of view, bears on its front all the characteristics of grandeur, combined with the winning graces of condescension; but what a different aspect it assumes when it is the submissive demeanour of dependence, the support of weakness that loves, because it wants protection; and is forbearing, because it must silently endure injuries; smiling under the lash at which it dare not snarl. Abject as this picture appears, it is the portrait of an accomplished woman, according to the received opinion of female excellence, separated by specious reasoners from human excellence. Or, they kindly restore the rib, and make one moral being of a man and woman; not forgetting to give her all the "submissive charms."[34]

How women are to exist in that state where there is to be neither marrying nor giving in marriage,[35] we are not told. For though moralists have agreed that the tenor of life seems to prove that *man* is prepared by various circumstances for a future state, they constantly concur in advising *woman* only to provide for the present. Gentleness, docility, and a spaniel-like affection are, on this ground, consistently recommended as the cardinal virtues of the sex; and, disregarding the arbitrary economy of nature, one writer has declared that it is masculine for a woman to be melancholy. She was created to be the toy of man, his rattle, and it must jingle in his ears whenever, dismissing reason, he chooses to be amused. . . .

---

33. Isaiah 55.7.   34. John Milton (1608–1674), *Paradise Lost* (1867), 4.497–499.   35. Matthew 22.30.

As a philosopher, I read with indignation the plausible epithets which men use to soften their insults; and, as a moralist, I ask what is meant by such heterogeneous associations, as fair defects,[36] amiable weaknesses, &c.? If there be but one criterion of morals, but one archetype for man, women appear to be suspended by destiny, according to the vulgar tale of Mahomet's coffin[37]; they have neither the unerring instinct of brutes, nor are allowed to fix the eye of reason on a perfect model. They were made to be loved, and must not aim at respect, lest they should be hunted out of society as masculine.

But to view the subject in another point of view. Do passive indolent women make the best wives? Confining our discussion to the present moment of existence, let us see how such weak creatures perform their part? Do the women who, by the attainment of a few superficial accomplishments, have strengthened the prevailing prejudice, merely contribute to the happiness of their husbands? Do they display their charms merely to amuse them? And have women, who have early imbibed notions of passive obedience, sufficient character to manage a family or educate children? So far from it, that, after surveying the history of woman, I cannot help, agreeing with the severest satirist, considering the sex as the weakest as well as the most oppressed half of the species. What does history disclose but marks of inferiority, and how few women have emancipated themselves from the galling yoke of sovereign man?—So few, that the exceptions remind me of an ingenious conjecture respecting Newton: that he was probably a being of a superior order, accidentally caged in a human body. Following the same train of thinking, I have been led to imagine that the few extraordinary women who have rushed in eccentrical directions out of the orbit prescribed to their sex, were *male* spirits, confined by mistake in female frames. But if it be not philosophical to think of sex when the soul is mentioned, the inferiority must depend on the organs; or the heavenly fire, which is to ferment the clay, is not given in equal portions. . . .

Surely there can be but one rule of right, if morality has an eternal foundation, and whoever sacrifices virtue, strictly so called, to present convenience, or whose *duty* it is to act in such a manner, lives only for the passing day, and cannot be an accountable creature.

The poet then should have dropped his sneer when he says,

> If weak women go astray,
> The stars are more in fault than they.[38]

For that they are bound by the adamantine chain of destiny is most certain, if it be proved that they are never to exercise their own reason, never to be independent, never to rise above opinion, or to feel the dignity of a rational will that only bows to God, and often forgets that the universe contains any being but itself and the model of perfection to which its ardent gaze is turned, to adore attributes that, softened into virtues, may be imitated in kind, though the degree overwhelms the enraptured mind.

If, I say, for I would not impress by declamation when Reason offers her sober light, if they be really capable of acting like rational creatures, let them not be treated like slaves; or, like the brutes who are dependent on the reason of man, when they associate with him; but cultivate their minds, give them the salutary, sublime curb of

---

36. *Paradise Lost*, 10.891–892.   37. The prophet of the Muslims, whose coffin was said to be suspended in mid-air in the tomb.   38. Matthew Prior (1664–1721), "Hans Carvel" (1701), 11–12.

principle, and let them attain conscious dignity by feeling themselves only depend-ent on God. Teach them, in common with man, to submit to necessity, instead of giving, to render them more pleasing, a sex to morals.

Further, should experience prove that they cannot attain the same degree of strength of mind, perseverance, and fortitude, let their virtues be the same in kind, though they may vainly struggle for the same degree; and the superiority of man will be equally clear, if not clearer; and truth, as it is a simple principle, which admits of no modification, would be common to both. Nay, the order of society as it is at present regulated would not be inverted, for woman would then only have the rank that reason assigned her, and arts could not be practised to bring the balance even, much less to turn it.

These may be termed Utopian dreams.—Thanks to that Being who impressed them on my soul, and gave me sufficient strength of mind to dare to exert my own reason, till, becoming dependent only on him for the support of my virtue, I view, with indignation, the mistaken notions that enslave my sex.

I love man as my fellow; but his scepter, real, or usurped, extends not to me, unless the reason of an individual demands my homage; and even then the submis-sion is to reason, and not to man. In fact, the conduct of an accountable being must be regulated by the operations of its own reason; or on what foundation rests the throne of God? . . .

from Chapter 3. The Same Subject Continued

If it be granted that woman was not created merely to gratify the appetite of man, or to be the upper servant, who provides his meals and takes care of his linen, it must fol-low, that the first care of those mothers or fathers, who really attend to the education of females, should be, if not to strengthen the body, at least, not to destroy the consti-tution by mistaken notions of beauty and female excellence; nor should girls ever be allowed to imbibe the pernicious notion that a defect can, by any chemical process of reasoning, become an excellence. In this respect, I am happy to find, that the author of one of the most instructive books, that our country has produced for children,[39] coincides with me in opinion; I shall quote his pertinent remarks to give the force of his respectable authority to reason.

But should it be proved that woman is naturally weaker than man, whence does it follow that it is natural for her to labour to become still weaker than nature intend-ed her to be? Arguments of this cast are an insult to common sense, and savour of passion. The *divine right* of husbands, like the divine right of kings, may, it is to be hoped, in this enlightened age, be contested without danger, and, though conviction may not silence many boisterous disputants, yet, when any prevailing prejudice is attacked, the wise will consider, and leave the narrow-minded to rail with thought-less vehemence at innovation.

The mother, who wishes to give true dignity of character to her daughter, must, regardless of the sneers of ignorance, proceed on a plan diametrically opposite to that which Rousseau has recommended with all the deluding charms of eloquence and philosophical sophistry: for his eloquence renders absurdities plausible, and his dogmat-ic conclusions puzzle, without convincing, those who have not ability to refute them.

---

39. Thomas Day (1748–1789), *Sandford and Merton* (1783).

Throughout the whole animal kingdom every young creature requires almost continual exercise, and the infancy of children, conformable to this intimation, should be passed in harmless gambols, that exercise the feet and hands, without requiring very minute direction from the head, or the constant attention of a nurse. In fact, the care necessary for self-preservation is the first natural exercise of the understanding, as little inventions to amuse the present moment unfold the imagination. But these wise designs of nature are counteracted by mistaken fondness or blind zeal. The child is not left a moment to its own direction, particularly a girl, and thus rendered dependent—dependence is called natural.

To preserve personal beauty, woman's glory! the limbs and faculties are cramped with worse than Chinese bands,[40] and the sedentary life which they are condemned to live, whilst boys frolic in the open air, weakens the muscles and relaxes the nerves.— As for Rousseau's remarks, which have since been echoed by several writers, that they have naturally, that is from their birth, independent of education, a fondness for dolls, dressing, and talking—they are so puerile as not to merit a serious refutation. That a girl, condemned to sit for hours together listening to the idle chat of weak nurses, or to attend at her mother's toilet,[41] will endeavour to join the conversation, is, indeed, very natural; and that she will imitate her mother or aunts, and amuse herself by adorning her lifeless doll, as they do in dressing her, poor innocent babe! is undoubtedly a most natural consequence. For men of the greatest abilities have seldom had sufficient strength to rise above the surrounding atmosphere; and, if the page of genius have always been blurred by the prejudices of the age, some allowance should be made for a sex, who, like kings, always see things through a false medium.

Pursuing these reflections, the fondness for dress, conspicuous in women, may be easily accounted for, without supposing it the result of a desire to please the sex on which they are dependent. The absurdity, in short, of supposing that a girl is naturally a coquette, and that a desire connected with the impulse of nature to propagate the species, should appear even before an improper education has, by heating the imagination, called it forth prematurely, is so unphilosophical, that such a sagacious observer as Rousseau would not have adopted it, if he had not been accustomed to make reason give way to his desire of singularity, and truth to a favorite paradox. . . .

I have, probably, had an opportunity of observing more girls in their infancy than J. J. Rousseau—I can recollect my own feelings, and I have looked steadily around me; yet, so far from coinciding with him in opinion respecting the first dawn of the female character, I will venture to affirm, that a girl, whose spirits have not been damped by inactivity, or innocence tainted by false shame, will always be a romp, and the doll will never excite attention unless confinement allows her no alternative. Girls and boys, in short, would play harmlessly together, if the distinction of sex was not inculcated long before nature makes any difference.—I will go further, and affirm, as an indisputable fact, that most of the women, in the circle of my observation, who have acted like rational creatures, or shewn any vigour of intellect, have accidentally been allowed to run wild—as some of the elegant formers of the fair sex would insinuate.

The baneful consequences which flow from inattention to health during infancy, and youth, extend further than is supposed—dependence of body naturally produces

---

40. Alludes to the practice of binding girls' feet to keep them from growing to full size.   41. Help dress and groom her mother.

dependence of mind; and how can she be a good wife or mother, the greater part of whose time is employed to guard against or endure sickness? Nor can it be expected that a woman will resolutely endeavour to strengthen her constitution and abstain from enervating indulgencies, if artificial notions of beauty, and false descriptions of sensibility, have been early entangled with her motives of action. Most men are sometimes obliged to bear with bodily inconveniencies, and to endure, occasionally, the inclemency of the elements; but genteel women are, literally speaking, slaves to their bodies, and glory in their subjection.

I once knew a weak woman of fashion, who was more than commonly proud of her delicacy and sensibility. She thought a distinguishing taste and puny appetite the height of all human perfection, and acted accordingly.—I have seen this weak sophisticated being neglect all the duties of life, yet recline with self-complacency on a sofa, and boast of her want of appetite as a proof of delicacy that extended to, or, perhaps, arose from, her exquisite sensibility: for it is difficult to render intelligible such ridiculous jargon.—Yet, at the moment, I have seen her insult a worthy old gentlewoman, whom unexpected misfortunes had made dependent on her ostentatious bounty, and who, in better days, had claims on her gratitude. Is it possible that a human creature could have become such a weak and depraved being, if, like the Sybarites,[42] dissolved in luxury, every thing like virtue had not been worn away, or never impressed by precept, a poor substitute, it is true, for cultivation of mind, though it serves as a fence against vice?

Such a woman is not a more irrational monster than some of the Roman emperors, who were depraved by lawless power. Yet, since kings have been more under the restraint of law, and the curb, however weak, of honour, the records of history are not filled with such unnatural instances of folly and cruelty, nor does the despotism that kills virtue and genius in the bud, hover over Europe with that destructive blast which desolates Turkey, and renders the men, as well as the soil, unfruitful. . . .

It is time to effect a revolution in female manners—time to restore to them their lost dignity—and make them, as a part of the human species, labour by reforming themselves to reform the world. It is time to separate unchangeable morals from local manners.—If men be demi-gods—why let us serve them! And if the dignity of the female soul be as disputable as that of animals—if their reason does not afford sufficient light to direct their conduct whilst unerring instinct is denied—they are surely of all creatures the most miserable! and, bent beneath the iron hand of destiny, must submit to be a *fair defect* in creation. But to justify the ways of Providence respecting them, by pointing out some irrefragable reason for thus making such a large portion of mankind accountable and not accountable, would puzzle the subtilest casuist.[43] . . .

If women be educated for dependence; that is, to act according to the will of another fallible being, and submit, right or wrong, to power, where are we to stop? Are they to be considered as viceregents allowed to reign over a small domain, and answerable for their conduct to a higher tribunal, liable to error?

It will not be difficult to prove that such delegates will act like men subjected by fear, and make their children and servants endure their tyrannical oppression. As they submit without reason, they will, having no fixed rules to square their conduct by, be kind, or cruel, just as the whim of the moment directs; and we ought not to

---

42. Inhabitants of Sybarus, known for pursuit of pleasure.   43. Theologian.

wonder if sometimes, galled by their heavy yoke, they take a malignant pleasure in resting it on weaker shoulders.

But, supposing a woman, trained up to obedience, be married to a sensible man, who directs her judgment without making her feel the servility of her subjection, to act with as much propriety by this reflected light as can be expected when reason is taken at second hand, yet she cannot ensure the life of her protector; he may die and leave her with a large family.

A double duty devolves on her; to educate them in the character of both father and mother; to form their principles and secure their property. But, alas! she has never thought, much less acted for herself. She has only learned to please men, to depend gracefully on them; yet, encumbered with children, how is she to obtain another protector—a husband to supply the place of reason? A rational man, for we are not treading on romantic ground, though he may think her a pleasing docile creature, will not choose to marry a *family* for love, when the world contains many more pretty creatures. What is then to become of her? She either falls an easy prey to some mean fortune-hunter, who defrauds her children of their paternal inheritance, and renders her miserable; or becomes the victim of discontent and blind indulgence. Unable to educate her sons, or impress them with respect; for it is not a play on words to assert, that people are never respected, though filling an important station, who are not respectable; she pines under the anguish of unavailing impotent regret. The serpent's tooth enters into her very soul, and the vices of licentious youth bring her with sorrow, if not with poverty also, to the grave.

This is not an overcharged picture; on the contrary, it is a very possible case, and something similar must have fallen under every attentive eye.

I have, however, taken it for granted, that she was well-disposed, though experience shews, that the blind may as easily be led into a ditch as along the beaten road.[44] But supposing, no very improbable conjecture, that a being only taught to please must still find her happiness in pleasing;—what an example of folly, not to say vice, will she be to her innocent daughters! The mother will be lost in the coquette, and, instead of making friends of her daughters, view them with eyes askance, for they are rivals— rivals more cruel than any other, because they invite a comparison, and drive her from the throne of beauty, who has never thought of a seat on the bench of reason.

It does not require a lively pencil, or the discriminating outline of a caricature, to sketch the domestic miseries and petty vices which such a mistress of a family diffuses. Still she only acts as a woman ought to act, brought up according to Rousseau's system. She can never be reproached for being masculine, or turning out of her sphere; nay, she may observe another of his grand rules, and, cautiously preserving her reputation free from spot, be reckoned a good kind of woman. Yet in what respect can she be termed good? She abstains, it is true, without any great struggle, from committing gross crimes; but how does she fulfil her duties? Duties!—in truth she has enough to think of to adorn her body and nurse a weak constitution.

With respect to religion, she never presumed to judge for herself; but conformed, as a dependent creature should, to the ceremonies of the church which she was brought up in, piously believing that wiser heads than her own have settled that business:—and not to doubt is her point of perfection. She therefore pays her tythe of

---

44. Matthew 15.14.

mint and cummin[45]—and thanks her God that she is not as other women are. These are the blessed effects of a good education! These the virtues of man's help-mate!

I must relieve myself by drawing a different picture.

Let fancy now present a woman with a tolerable understanding, for I do not wish to leave the line of mediocrity, whose constitution, strengthened by exercise, has allowed her body to acquire its full vigour; her mind, at the same time, gradually expanding itself to comprehend the moral duties of life, and in what human virtue and dignity consist.

Formed thus by the discharge of the relative duties of her station, she marries from affection, without losing sight of prudence, and looking beyond matrimonial felicity, she secures her husband's respect before it is necessary to exert mean arts to please him and feed a dying flame, which nature doomed to expire when the object became familiar, when friendship and forbearance take place of a more ardent affection.—This is the natural death of love, and domestic peace is not destroyed by struggles to prevent its extinction. I also suppose the husband to be virtuous; or she is still more in want of independent principles.

Fate, however, breaks this tie.—She is left a widow, perhaps, without a sufficient provision; but she is not desolate! The pang of nature is felt; but after time has softened sorrow into melancholy resignation, her heart turns to her children with redoubled fondness, and anxious to provide for them, affection gives a sacred heroic cast to her maternal duties. She thinks that not only the eye sees her virtuous efforts from whom all her comfort now must flow, and whose approbation is life; but her imagination, a little abstracted and exalted by grief, dwells on the fond hope that the eyes which her trembling hand closed, may still see how she subdues every wayward passion to fulfil the double duty of being the father as well as the mother of her children. Raised to heroism by misfortunes, she represses the first faint dawning of a natural inclination, before it ripens into love, and in the bloom of life forgets her sex—forgets the pleasure of an awakening passion, which might again have been inspired and returned. She no longer thinks of pleasing, and conscious dignity prevents her from priding herself on account of the praise which her conduct demands. Her children have her love, and her brightest hopes are beyond the grave, where her imagination often strays.

I think I see her surrounded by her children, reaping the reward of her care. The intelligent eye meets hers, whilst health and innocence smile on their chubby cheeks, and as they grow up the cares of life are lessened by their grateful attention. She lives to see the virtues which she endeavoured to plant on principles, fixed into habits, to see her children attain a strength of character sufficient to enable them to endure adversity without forgetting their mother's example.

The task of life thus fulfilled, she calmly waits for the sleep of death, and rising from the grave, may say—Behold, thou gavest me a talent—and here are five talents.[46]

I wish to sum up what I have said in a few words, for I here throw down my gauntlet, and deny the existence of sexual virtues, not excepting modesty. For man and woman, truth, if I understand the meaning of the word, must be the same; yet the fanciful female character, so prettily drawn by poets and novelists, demanding the sacrifice of truth and sincerity, virtue becomes a relative idea, having no other foundation than utility, and of that utility men pretend arbitrarily to judge, shaping it to their own convenience.

---

45. Matthew 33.23.   46. Matthew 25.15–28.

Women, I allow, may have different duties to fulfil; but they are *human* duties, and the principles that should regulate the discharge of them, I sturdily maintain, must be the same.

To become respectable, the exercise of their understanding is necessary, there is no other foundation for independence of character; I mean explicitly to say that they must only bow to the authority of reason, instead of being the *modest* slaves of opinion.

In the superior ranks of life how seldom do we meet with a man of superior abilities, or even common acquirements? The reason appears to me clear, the state they are born in was an unnatural one. The human character has ever been formed by the employments the individual, or class, pursues; and if the faculties are not sharpened by necessity, they must remain obtuse. The argument may fairly be extended to women; for, seldom occupied by serious business, the pursuit of pleasure gives that insignificancy to their character which renders the society of the *great* so insipid. The same want of firmness, produced by a similar cause, forces them both to fly from themselves to noisy pleasures, and artificial passions, till vanity takes place of every social affection, and the characteristics of humanity can scarcely be discerned. Such are the blessings of civil governments, as they are at present organized, that wealth and female softness equally tend to debase mankind, and are produced by the same cause; but allowing women to be rational creatures, they should be incited to acquire virtues which they may call their own, for how can a rational being be ennobled by any thing that is not obtained by its *own* exertions?

from Chapter 13. Some Instances of the Folly Which the Ignorance of Women Generates; with Concluding Reflections on the Moral Improvement That a Revolution in Female Manners Might Naturally Be Expected to Produce

[CONCLUSION]

That women at present are by ignorance rendered foolish or vicious, is, I think, not to be disputed; and, that the most salutary effects tending to improve mankind might be expected from a REVOLUTION in female manners, appears, at least, with a face of probability, to rise out of the observation. For as marriage has been termed the parent of those endearing charities which draw man from the brutal herd, the corrupting intercourse that wealth, idleness, and folly, produce between the sexes, is more universally injurious to morality than all the other vices of mankind collectively considered. To adulterous lust the most sacred duties are sacrificed, because before marriage, men, by a promiscuous intimacy with women, learned to consider love as a selfish gratification—learned to separate it not only from esteem, but from the affection merely built on habit, which mixes a little humanity with it. Justice and friendship are also set at defiance, and that purity of taste is vitiated which would naturally lead a man to relish an artless display of affection rather than affected airs. But that noble simplicity of affection, which dares to appear unadorned, has few attractions for the libertine, though it be the charm, which by cementing the matrimonial tie, secures to the pledges of a warmer passion the necessary parental attention; for children will never be properly educated till friendship subsists between parents. Virtue flies from a house divided against itself—and a whole legion of devils take up their residence there.[47]

---

47. Mark 3.25.

The affection of husbands and wives cannot be pure when they have so few sentiments in common, and when so little confidence is established at home, as must be the case when their pursuits are so different. That intimacy from which tenderness should flow, will not, cannot subsist between the vicious.

Contending, therefore, that the sexual distinction which men have so warmly insisted upon, is arbitrary, I have dwelt on an observation, that several sensible men, with whom I have conversed on the subject, allowed to be well founded; and it is simply this, that the little chastity to be found amongst men, and consequent disregard of modesty, tend to degrade both sexes; and further, that the modesty of women, characterized as such, will often be only the artful veil of wantonness instead of being the natural reflection of purity, till modesty be universally respected.

From the tyranny of man, I firmly believe, the greater number of female follies proceed; and the cunning, which I allow makes at present a part of their character, I likewise have repeatedly endeavoured to prove, is produced by oppression.

Were not dissenters, for instance, a class of people, with strict truth, characterized as cunning? And may I not lay some stress on this fact to prove, that when any power but reason curbs the free spirit of man, dissimulation is practised, and the various shifts of art are naturally called forth? Great attention to decorum, which was carried to a degree of scrupulosity, and all that puerile bustle about trifles and consequential solemnity, which Butler's caricature of a dissenter,[48] brings before the imagination, shaped their persons as well as their minds in the mould of prim littleness. I speak collectively, for I know how many ornaments to human nature have been enrolled amongst sectaries; yet, I assert, that the same narrow prejudice for their sect, which women have for their families, prevailed in the dissenting part of the community, however worthy in other respects; and also that the same timid prudence, or headstrong efforts, often disgraced the exertions of both. Oppression thus formed many of the features of their character perfectly to coincide with that of the oppressed half of mankind; or is it not notorious that dissenters were, like women, fond of deliberating together, and asking advice of each other, till by a complication of little contrivances, some little end was brought about? A similar attention to preserve their reputation was conspicuous in the dissenting and female world, and was produced by a similar cause.

Asserting the rights which women in common with men ought to contend for, I have not attempted to extenuate their faults; but to prove them to be the natural consequence of their education and station in society. If so, it is reasonable to suppose that they will change their character, and correct their vices and follies, when they are allowed to be free in a physical, moral, and civil sense.

Let woman share the rights and she will emulate the virtues of man; for she must grow more perfect when emancipated, or justify the authority that chains such a weak being to her duty.—If the latter, it will be expedient to open a fresh trade with Russia for whips; a present which a father should always make to his son-in-law on his wedding day, that a husband may keep his whole family in order by the same means; and without any violation of justice reign, wielding this sceptre, sole master of his house, because he is the only being in it who has reason:—the divine, indefeasible earthly sovereignty breathed into man by the Master of the universe. Allowing

---

48. Samuel Butler (1612–1680), *Hudibras* (1662–1678).

this position, women have not any inherent rights to claim; and, by the same rule, their duties vanish, for rights and duties are inseparable.

Be just then, O ye men of understanding! and mark not more severely what women do amiss, than the vicious tricks of the horse or the ass for whom ye provide provender—and allow her the privileges of ignorance, to whom ye deny the rights of reason, or ye will be worse than Egyptian task-masters, expecting virtue where nature has not given understanding!

—1792

On Poetry and Our Relish for the Beauties of Nature[1]

A taste for rural scenes, in the present state of society, appears to be very often an arti-ficial sentiment, rather inspired by poetry and romances, than a real perception of the beauties of nature. But, as it is reckoned a proof of refined taste to praise the calm pleasures which the country affords, the theme is never exhausted. Yet it may be made a question, whether this romantic kind of declamation, has much effect on the conduct of those, who leave, for a season, the crowded cities in which they were bred.

I have been led to these reflections, by observing, when I have resided for any length of time in the country, how few people seem to contemplate nature with their own eyes. I have "brushed the dew away" in the morning; but, pacing over the printless grass, I have wondered that, in such delightful situation, the sun was allowed to rise in solitary majesty, whilst my eyes alone hailed its beautifying beams. The webs of the evening have still been spread across the hedged path, unless some labouring man, trudging to work, disturbed the fairy structure; yet, in spite of this supineness, when I joined the social circle, every tongue rang changes on the pleas-ures of the country.

Having frequently had occasion to make the same observation, I was led to endeav-our, in one of my solitary rambles, to trace the cause, and likewise to enquire why the poetry written in the infancy of society, is most natural: which, strictly speaking (for *nat-ural* is a very indefinite expression) is merely to say, that it is the transcript of immediate sensations, in all their native wildness and simplicity, when fancy, awakened by the sight of interesting objects, was most actively at work. At such moments, sensibility quickly furnishes similes, and the sublimated spirits combine images, which rising spontaneously, it is not necessary coldly to ransack the understanding or memory, till the laborious efforts of judgment exclude present sensations, and damp the fire of enthusiasm.

The effusions of a vigorous mind, will ever tell us how far the understanding has been enlarged by thought, and stored with knowledge. The richness of the soil even appears on the surface; and the result of profound thinking, often mixing, with play-ful grace, in the reveries of the poet, smoothly incorporates with the ebullitions of animal spirits, when the finely fashioned nerve vibrates acutely with rapture, or when, relaxed by soft melancholy, a pleasing languor prompts the long-drawn sigh, and feeds the slowly falling tear.

The poet, the man of strong feelings, gives us only an image of his mind, when he was actually alone, conversing with himself, and marking the impression which

---

1. Published in the *Monthly Magazine* III (April 1797), 279–282.

nature had made on his own heart.—If, at this sacred moment, the idea of some departed friend, some tender recollection when the soul was most alive to tenderness, intruded unawares into his thoughts, the sorrow which it produced is artlessly, yet poetically expressed—and who can avoid sympathizing?

Love to man leads to devotion—grand and sublime images strike the imagination—God is seen in every floating cloud, and comes from the misty mountain to receive the noblest homage of an intelligent creature—praise. How solemn is the moment, when all affections and remembrances fade before the sublime admiration which the wisdom and goodness of God inspires, when he is worshipped in a *temple not made with hands*, and the world seems to contain only the mind that formed, and the mind that contemplates it! These are not the weak responses of ceremonial devotion; nor, to express them, would the poet need another poet's aid: his heart burns within him, and he speaks the language of truth and nature with resistless energy.

Inequalities, of course, are observable in his effusions; and a less vigorous fancy, with more taste, would have produced more elegance and uniformity; but, as passages are softened or expunged during the cooler moments of reflection, the understanding is gratified at the expence of those involuntary sensations, which, like the beauteous tints of an evening sky, are so evanescent, that they melt into new forms before they can be analyzed. For however eloquently we may boast of our reason, man must often be delighted he cannot tell why, or his blunt feelings are not made to relish the beauties which nature, poetry, or any of the imitative arts, afford.

The imagery of the ancients seems naturally to have been borrowed from surrounding objects and their mythology. When a hero is to be transported from one place to another, across pathless wastes, is any vehicle so natural, as one of the fleecy clouds on which the poet has often gazed, scarcely conscious that he wished to make it his chariot? Again, when nature seems to present obstacles to his progress at almost every step, when the tangled forest and steep mountain stand as barriers, to pass over which the mind longs for supernatural aid; an interposing deity, who walks on the waves, and rules the storm, severely felt in the first attempts to cultivate a country, will receive from the impassioned fancy "a local habitation and a name."[2]

It would be a philosophical enquiry, and throw some light on the history of the human mind, to trace, as far as our information will allow us to trace, the spontaneous feelings and ideas which have produced the images that now frequently appear unnatural, because they are remote; and disgusting, because they have been servilely copied by poets, whose habits of thinking, and views of nature must have been different; for, though the understanding seldom disturbs the current of our present feelings, without dissipating the gay clouds which fancy has been embracing, yet it silently gives the colour to the whole tenour of them, and the dream is over, when truth is grossly violated, or images introduced, selected from books, and not from local manners or popular prejudices.

In a more advanced state of civilization, a poet is rather the creature of art, than of nature. The books that he reads in his youth, become a hot-bed in which artificial fruits are produced, beautiful to the common eye, though they want the true hue and flavour. His images do not arise from sensations; they are copies; and, like the works of the painters who copy ancient statues when they draw men and

---

2. William Shakespeare (1564–1616), *A Midsummer Night's Dream* (1600), 5.1.15–17.

women of their own times, we acknowledge that the features are fine, and the proportions just; yet they are men of stone; insipid figures, that never convey to the mind the idea of a portrait taken from life, where the soul gives spirit and homogeneity to the whole. The silken wings of fancy are shrivelled by rules; and a desire of attaining elegance of diction, occasions an attention to words, incompatible with sublime, impassioned thoughts.

A boy of abilities, who has been taught the structure of verse at school, and been roused by emulation to compose rhymes whilst he was reading works of genius, may, by practice, produce pretty verses, and even become what is often termed an elegant poet: yet his readers, without knowing what to find fault with, do not find themselves warmly interested. In the works of the poets who fasten on their affections, they see grosser faults, and the very images which shock their taste in the modern; still they do not appear as puerile or extrinsic in one as the other.—Why?—because they did not appear so to the author.

It may sound paradoxical, after observing that those productions want vigour, that are merely the work of imitation, in which the understanding has violently directed, if not extinguished, the blaze of fancy, to assert, that, though genius be only another word for exquisite sensibility, the first observers of nature, the true poets, exercised their understanding much more than their imitators. But they exercised it to discriminate things, whilst their followers were busy to borrow sentiments and arrange words.

Boys who have received a classical education, load their memory with words, and the correspondent ideas are perhaps never distinctly comprehended. As a proof of this assertion, I must observe, that I have known many young people who could write tolerably smooth verses, and string epithets prettily together, when their prose themes showed the barrenness of their minds, and how superficial the cultivation must have been, which their understanding had received.

Dr. Johnson, I know, has given a definition of genius,[3] which would overturn my reasoning, if I were to admit it.—He imagines, that a *strong mind, accidentally led to some particular study* in which it excels, is a genius.—Not to stop to investigate the causes which produced this happy *strength* of mind, experience seems to prove, that those minds have appeared most vigorous, that have pursued a study, after nature had discovered a bent; for it would be absurd to suppose, that a slight impression made on the weak faculties of a boy, is the fiat of fate, and not to be effaced by any succeeding impression, or unexpected difficulty. Dr. Johnson in fact, appears sometimes to be of the same opinion (how consistently I shall not now enquire), especially when he observes, "that Thomson looked on nature with the eye which she only gives to a poet."[4]

But, though it should be allowed that books may produce some poets, I fear they will never be the poets who charm our cares to sleep, or extort admiration. They may diffuse taste, and polish the language; but I am inclined to conclude that they will seldom rouse the passions, or amend the heart.

And, to return to the first subject of discussion, the reason why most people are more interested by a scene described by a poet, than by a view of nature, probably arises from the want of a lively imagination. The poet contracts the prospect, and, selecting the most picturesque part in his *camera*,[5] the judgment is directed, and the whole force

---

3. Samuel Johnson (1709–1784), *Lives of the English Poets* (1779).   4. *Lives of the English Poets* (1779).   5. *Camera obscura*, a box into which images were projected.

of the languid faculty turned towards the objects which excited the most forcible emotions in the poet's heart; the reader consequently feels the enlivened description, though he was not able to receive a first impression from the operations of his own mind.

Besides, it may be further observed, that gross minds are only to be moved by forcible representations. To rouse the thoughtless, objects must be presented, calculated to produce tumultuous emotions; the unsubstantial, picturesque forms which a contemplative man gazes on, and often follows with ardour till he is mocked by a glimpse of unattainable excellence, appear to them the light vapours of a dreaming enthusiast, who gives up the substance for the shadow. It is not within that they seek amusement; their eyes are seldom turned on themselves; consequently their emotions, though sometimes fervid, are always transient, and the nicer perceptions which distinguish the man of genuine taste, are not felt, or make such a slight impression as scarcely to excite any pleasurable sensations. Is it surprising then that they are often overlooked, even by those who are delighted by the same images concentrated by the poet?

But even this numerous class is exceeded, by witlings, who, anxious to appear to have wit and taste, do not allow their understandings or feelings any liberty; for, instead of cultivating their faculties and reflecting on their operations, they are busy collecting prejudices; and are predetermined to admire what the suffrage of time announces as excellent, not to store up a fund of amusement for themselves, but to enable them to talk.

These hints will assist the reader to trace some of the causes why the beauties of nature are not forcibly felt, when civilization, or rather luxury, has made considerable advances—those calm sensations are not sufficiently lively to serve as a relaxation to the voluptuary, or even to the moderate pursuer of artificial pleasures. In the present state of society, the understanding must bring back the feelings to nature, or the sensibility must have such native strength, as rather to be whetted than destroyed by the strong exercises of passion.

That the most valuable things are liable to the greatest perversion, is however as trite as true:—for the same sensibility, or quickness of senses, which makes a man relish the tranquil scenes of nature, when sensation, rather than reason, imparts delight, frequently makes a libertine of him, by leading him to prefer the sensual tumult of love a little refined by sentiment, to the calm pleasures of affectionate friendship, in whose sober satisfactions, reason, mixing her tranquillizing convictions, whispers, that content, not happiness, is the reward of virtue in this world.

—1797

Susanna Rowson
1762–1824

Twice before she was twenty-one, Susanna Rowson made the perilous Atlantic crossing. She was born in Portsmouth, England, to William Haswell, a naval officer, and his wife, Susanna, who died soon after. Haswell moved to the United States and worked as a tax collector, bringing his daughter after him when she reached the age of five. During the American Revolution, their home was confiscated and they were deported to England, where Susanna took on the responsibility of supporting her now destitute father. She married a poor actor, William Rowson, whose drinking barred success. She soon began writing to supplement her husband's meager income and then took to the stage in 1792. Within a year, the couple had emigrated to the United States, working in theater companies, first in Philadelphia and then in Boston, where they settled permanently in 1796. Rowson soon opened The Young Girls' Academy, which she operated until her death, earning notoriety by teaching geography, history, and republican political theory to female students.

The subtitle of one of her ten sentimental novels, *Mentoria; or, The Young Lady's Friend* (1791), captures Rowson's sense of what unified her life's varied work. Like her school, her writings were meant to help young women understand the sexist world around them and achieve a measure of rational self-possession within it. One of the first people to successfully make a living by writing for the transatlantic literary market, Rowson was versatile by necessity. In addition to novels, she wrote plays, poems, songs, textbooks, essays, and conduct books that provided advice to young women on how to behave and marry well.

Rowson's second novel, *Charlotte: A Tale of Truth* was published first in London in 1791, gaining only moderate success. Upon republication in Philadelphia in 1794, it became the best-selling American novel of the first half of the nineteenth century, going through more than two hundred editions. The novel's bitter tale of a schoolgirl's seduction by a dashing officer was based on the scandalous elopement of Rowson's cousin, John Montresor, with young Charlotte Stanley. Rowson's worldly and maternal narrator repeatedly addresses the reader directly to enforce didactic conclusions and control the story's implied prurience. This combination of vicarious sexual adventure and practical morality broke the longstanding American prohibition against reading novels. Not just a bestseller, *Charlotte* established a market for novels that would last into the present. It even inspired a literary cult. For decades, readers left flowers at a tombstone said to mark the grave of the actual Charlotte, in Trinity Churchyard in New York.

For much of the twentieth century, *Charlotte* was dismissed as mawkish and even "subliterate." But recognition of its staggering popularity and influence has forced a reappraisal. Debate continues over the novel's sexual politics. The narrator seems to encourage her young readers to negotiate gender hierarchies rather than attempt to overturn them, and the book's portraits of women as either dependent or conniving strike some critics as damagingly stereotypical. On the other hand, many see the narrator's construction of the novel as a space for female solidarity, along with her advice for survival in a sexist world, as the best kind of hard-nosed feminist pragmatism.

from Charlotte: A Tale of Truth

Preface

For the perusal of the young and thoughtless of the fair sex, this Tale of Truth is designed; and I could wish my fair readers to consider it as not merely the effusion of Fancy, but as a reality. The circumstances on which I have founded this novel were related to me some little time since by an old lady who had personally known Charlotte, though she concealed the real names of the characters, and likewise the place where the unfortunate scenes were acted: yet as it was impossible to offer a relation to the public in such an imperfect state, I have thrown over the whole a slight veil of fiction, and substituted names and places according to my own fancy. The principal characters in this little tale are now consigned to the silent tomb: it can therefore hurt the feelings of no one; and may, I flatter myself, be of service to some who are so unfortunate as to have neither friends to advise, or understanding to direct them, through the various and unexpected evils that attend a young and unprotected woman in her first entrance into life.

While the tear of compassion still trembled in my eye for the fate of the unhappy Charlotte, I may have children of my own, said I, to whom this recital may be of use, and if to your own children, said Benevolence, why not to the many daughters of Misfortune who, deprived of natural friends, or spoilt by a mistaken education, are thrown on an unfeeling world without the least power to defend themselves from the snares not only of the other sex, but from the more dangerous arts of the profligate of their own.

Sensible as I am that a novel writer, at a time when such a variety of works are ushered into the world under that name, stands but a poor chance for fame in the annals of literature, but conscious that I wrote with a mind anxious for the happiness of that sex whose morals and conduct have so powerful an influence on mankind in general; and convinced that I have not wrote a line that conveys a wrong idea to the head or a corrupt wish to the heart, I shall rest satisfied in the purity of my own intentions, and if I merit not applause, I feel that I dread not censure.

If the following tale should save one hapless fair one from the errors which ruined poor Charlotte, or rescue from impending misery the heart of one anxious parent, I shall feel a much higher gratification in reflecting on this trifling performance, than could possibly result from the applause which might attend the most elegant finished piece of literature whose tendency might deprave the heart or mislead the understanding.

Chapter I
A Boarding School

"Are you for a walk," said Montraville to his companion, as they arose from table; "are you for a walk? or shall we order the chaise and proceed to Portsmouth?"[1] Belcour preferred the former; and they sauntered out to view the town, and to make remarks on the inhabitants, as they returned from church.

Montraville was a Lieutenant in the army: Belcour was his brother officer: they had been to take leave of their friends previous to their departure for America, and were now returning to Portsmouth, where the troops waited orders for embarkation. They had stopped at Chichester to dine; and knowing they had sufficient time to reach the place of destination before dark, and yet allow them a walk, had resolved, it being Sunday afternoon, to take a survey of the Chichester ladies as they returned from their devotions.

They had gratified their curiosity, and were preparing to return to the inn without honouring any of the belles with particular notice, when Madame Du Pont, at the head of her school, descended from the church. Such an assemblage of youth and innocence naturally attracted the young soldiers: they stopped; and, as the little cavalcade passed, almost involuntarily pulled off their hats. A tall, elegant girl looked at Montraville and blushed: he instantly recollected the features of Charlotte Temple, whom he had once seen and danced with at a ball at Portsmouth. At that time he thought on her only as a very lovely child, she being then only thirteen; but the improvement two years had made in her person, and the blush of recollection which suffused her cheeks as she passed, awakened in his bosom new and pleasing ideas. Vanity led him to think that pleasure at again beholding him might have occasioned the emotion he had witnessed, and the same vanity led him to wish to see her again.

"She is the sweetest girl in the world," said he, as he entered the inn. Belcour stared. "Did you not notice her?" continued Montraville, "she had on a blue bonnet,

---

1. A port city in southern England.

and with a pair of lovely eyes of the same colour, has contrived to make me feel dev-ilish odd about the heart."

"Pho," said Belcour, "a musket ball from our friends, the Americans, may in less than two months make you feel worse."

"I never think of the future," replied Montraville, "but am determined to make the most of the present, and would willingly compound with any kind Familiar[2] who would inform me who the girl is, and how I might be likely to obtain an interview."

But no kind Familiar at that time appearing, and the chaise which they had ordered, driving up to the door, Montraville and his companion were obliged to take leave of Chichester and its fair inhabitant, and proceed on their journey.

But Charlotte had made too great an impression on his mind to be easily eradicated: having therefore spent three whole days in thinking on her and in endeavouring to form some plan for seeing her, he determined to set off for Chichester, and trust to chance either to favour or frustrate his designs. Arriving at the verge of the town, he dis-mounted, and sending the servant forward with the horses, proceeded toward the place, where, in the midst of an extensive pleasure ground, stood the mansion which contained the lovely Charlotte Temple. Montraville leaned on a broken gate, and looked earnestly at the house. The wall which surrounded it was high, and perhaps the Argus's[3] who guarded the Hesperian fruit within, were more watchful than those famed of old.[4]

"'Tis a romantic attempt," said he; "and should I even succeed in seeing and con-versing with her, it can be productive of no good: I must of necessity leave England in a few days, and probably may never return; why then should I endeavour to engage the affections of this lovely girl, only to leave her a prey to a thousand inquietudes, of which at present she has no idea? I will return to Portsmouth and think no more about her."

The evening now was closed; a serene stillness reigned; and the chaste Queen of Night with her silver crescent faintly illuminated the hemisphere. The mind of Montraville was hushed into composure by the serenity of the surrounding objects. "I will think on her no more," said he, and turned with an intention to leave the place; but as he turned, he saw the gate which led to the pleasure grounds open, and two women come out, who walked arm-in-arm across the field.

"I will at least see who these are," said he. He overtook them, and giving them the compliments of the evening, begged leave to see them into the more frequented parts of the town: but how was he delighted, when, waiting for an answer, he discov-ered, under the concealment of a large bonnet, the face of Charlotte Temple.

He soon found means to ingratiate himself with her companion, who was a French teacher at the school, and, at parting, slipped a letter he had purposely writ-ten, into Charlotte's hand, and five guineas into that of Mademoiselle, who promised she would endeavour to bring her young charge into the field again the next evening.

Chapter VI
An Intriguing Teacher

Madame Du Pont was a woman every way calculated to take the care of young ladies, had that care entirely devolved on herself; but it was impossible to attend the education of a numerous school without proper assistants; and those assistants were not always the

---

2. Magical assistant.   3. A hundred-eyed giant in Greek mythology.   4. One of Hercules' labors was to steal golden apples guarded by three young women, the Hesperides.

kind of people whose conversation and morals were exactly such as parents of delicacy and refinement would wish a daughter to copy. Among the teachers at Madam Du Pont's school, was Mademoiselle La Rue, who added to a pleasing person and insinuating address, a liberal education and the manners of a gentlewoman. She was recommended to the school by a lady whose humanity overstepped the bounds of discretion: for though she knew Miss La Rue had eloped from a convent with a young officer, and, on coming to England, had lived with several different men in open defiance of all moral and religious duties; yet, finding her reduced to the most abject want, and believing the penitence which she professed to be sincere, she took her into her own family, and from thence recommended her to Madame Du Pont, as thinking the situation more suitable for a woman of her abilities. But Mademoiselle possessed too much of the spirit of intrigue to remain long without adventures. At church, where she constantly appeared, her person attracted the attention of a young man who was upon a visit at a gentleman's seat in the neighbourhood: she had met him several times clandestinely; and being invited to come out that evening, and eat some fruit and pastry in a summer-house belonging to the gentleman he was visiting, and requested to bring some of the ladies with her, Charlotte being her favourite, was fixed on to accompany her.

The mind of youth eagerly catches at promised pleasure: pure and innocent by nature, it thinks not of the dangers lurking beneath those pleasures, till too late to avoid them: when Mademoiselle asked Charlotte to go with her, she mentioned the gentleman as a relation, and spoke in such high terms of the elegance of his gardens, the sprightliness of his conversation, and the liberality with which he ever entertained his guests, that Charlotte thought only of the pleasure she should enjoy in the visit,— not on the imprudence of going without her governess's knowledge, or of the danger to which she exposed herself in visiting the house of a gay young man of fashion.

Madame Du Pont was gone out for the evening, and the rest of the ladies retired to rest, when Charlotte and the teacher stole out at the back gate, and in crossing the field, were accosted by Montraville, as mentioned in the first chapter.

Charlotte was disappointed in the pleasure she had promised herself from this visit. The levity of the gentlemen and the freedom of their conversation disgusted her. She was astonished at the liberties Mademoiselle permitted them to take; grew thoughtful and uneasy, and heartily wished herself at home again in her own chamber.

Perhaps one cause of that wish might be, an earnest desire to see the contents of the letter which had been put into her hand by Montraville.

Any reader who has the least knowledge of the world, will easily imagine the letter was made up of encomiums on her beauty, and vows of everlasting love and constancy; nor will he be surprised that a heart open to every gentle, generous sentiment, should feel itself warmed by gratitude for a man who professed to feel so much for her; nor is it improbable but her mind might revert to the agreeable person and martial appearance of Montraville.

In affairs of love, a young heart is never in more danger than when attempted by a handsome young soldier. A man of an indifferent appearance, will, when arrayed in a military habit, shew to advantage; but when beauty of person, elegance of manner, and an easy method of paying compliments, are united to the scarlet coat, smart cockade, and military sash, ah! well-a-day for the poor girl who gazes on him: she is in imminent danger; but if she listens to him with pleasure, 'tis all over with her, and from that moment she has neither eyes nor ears for any other object.

Now, my dear sober matron, (if a sober matron should deign to turn over these pages, before she trusts them to the eye of a darling daughter,) let me intreat you not to put on a grave face, and throw down the book in a passion and declare 'tis enough to turn the heads of half the girls in England; I do solemnly protest, my dear madam, I mean no more by what I have here advanced, than to ridicule those romantic girls, who foolishly imagine a red coat and silver epaulet constitute the fine gentleman; and should that fine gentleman make half a dozen fine speeches to them, they will imagine themselves so much in love as to fancy it a meritorious action to jump out of a two pair of stairs window, abandon their friends, and trust entirely to the honour of a man, who perhaps hardly knows the meaning of the word, and if he does, will be too much the modern man of refinement, to practise it in their favour.

Gracious heaven! when I think on the miseries that must rend the heart of a doating parent, when he sees the darling of his age at first seduced from his protection, and afterwards abandoned, by the very wretch whose promises of love decoyed her from the paternal roof—when he sees her poor and wretched, her bosom torn between remorse for her crime and love for her vile betrayer—when fancy paints to me the good old man stooping to raise the weeping penitent, while every tear from her eye is numbered by drops from his bleeding heart, my bosom glows with honest indignation, and I wish for power to extirpate those monsters of seduction from the earth.

Oh my dear girls—for to such only am I writing—listen not to the voice of love, unless sanctioned by paternal approbation: be assured, it is now past the days of romance: no woman can be run away with contrary to her own inclination: then kneel down each morning, and request kind heaven to keep you free from temptation, or, should it please to suffer you to be tried, pray for fortitude to resist the impulse of inclination when it runs counter to the precepts of religion and virtue.

Chapter VII
Natural Sense of Propriety Inherent in the Female Bosom

"I cannot think we have done exactly right in going out this evening, Mademoiselle," said Charlotte, seating herself when she entered her apartment: "nay, I am sure it was not right; for I expected to be very happy, but was sadly disappointed."

"It was your own fault, then," replied Mademoiselle: "for I am sure my cousin omitted nothing that could serve to render the evening agreeable."

"True," said Charlotte: "but I thought the gentlemen were very free in their manner: I wonder you would suffer them to behave as they did."

"Prithee, don't be such a foolish little prude," said the artful woman, affecting anger: "I invited you to go in hopes it would divert you, and be an agreeable change of scene; however, if your delicacy was hurt by the behaviour of the gentlemen, you need not go again; so there let it rest."

"I do not intend to go again," said Charlotte, gravely taking off her bonnet, and beginning to prepare for bed: "I am sure, if Madame Du Pont knew we had been out to-night, she would be very angry; and it is ten to one but she hears of it by some means or other."

"Nay, Miss," said La Rue, "perhaps your mighty sense of propriety may lead you to tell her yourself: and in order to avoid the censure you would incur, should she hear of it by accident, throw the blame on me: but I confess I deserve it: it will be a very kind return for that partiality which led me to prefer you before any of the rest of the ladies; but perhaps it will give you pleasure," continued she, letting fall some hypocritical tears, "to see me deprived of bread, and for an action which by the most rigid could only be esteemed an inadvertency, lose my place and character, and be driven again into the world, where I have already suffered all the evils attendant on poverty."

This was touching Charlotte in the most vulnerable part: she rose from her seat, and taking Mademoiselle's hand—"You know, my dear La Rue," said she, "I love you too well, to do any thing that would injure you in my governess's opinion: I am only sorry we went out this evening."

"I don't believe it, Charlotte," said she, assuming a little vivacity; "for if you had not gone out, you would not have seen the gentleman who met us crossing the field; and I rather think you were pleased with his conversation."

"I had seen him once before," replied Charlotte, "and thought him an agreeable man; and you know one is always pleased to see a person with whom one has passed several chearful hours. But," said she pausing, and drawing the letter from her pocket, while a gentle suffusion of vermillion tinged her neck and face, "he gave me this letter; what shall I do with it?

"Read it, to be sure," returned Mademoiselle.

"I am afraid I ought not," said Charlotte: "my mother has often told me, I should never read a letter given me by a young man, without first giving it to her."

"Lord bless you, my dear girl," cried the teacher smiling, "have you a mind to be in leading strings all your life time. Prithee open the letter, read it, and judge for yourself; if you show it your mother, the consequence will be, you will be taken from school, and a strict guard kept over you; so you will stand no chance of ever seeing the smart young officer again."

"I should not like to leave school yet," replied Charlotte, "till I have attained a greater proficiency in my Italian and music. But you can, if you please, Mademoiselle, take the letter back to Montraville, and tell him I wish him well, but cannot, with any propriety, enter into a clandestine correspondence with him." She laid the letter on the table, and began to undress herself.

"Well," said La Rue, "I vow you are an unaccountable girl: have you no curiosity to see the inside now? for my part I could no more let a letter addressed to me lie unopened so long, than I could work miracles: he writes a good hand," continued she, turning the letter, to look at the superscription.

"'Tis well enough," said Charlotte, drawing it towards her.

"He is a genteel young fellow," said La Rue carelessly, folding up her apron at the same time; "but I think he is marked with the small pox."

"Oh you are greatly mistaken," said Charlotte eagerly; "he has a remarkable clear skin and fine complexion."

"His eyes, if I could judge by what I saw," said La Rue, "are grey and want expression."

"By no means," replied Charlotte; "they are the most expressive eyes I ever saw."

"Well, child, whether they are grey or black is of no consequence: you have determined not to read his letter; so it is likely you will never either see or hear from him again."

Charlotte took up the letter, and Mademoiselle continued—

"He is most probably going to America; and if ever you should hear any account of him, it may possibly be that he is killed; and though he loved you ever so fervently, though his last breath should be spent in a prayer for your happiness, it can be nothing to you: you can feel nothing for the fate of the man, whose letters you will not open, and whose sufferings you will not alleviate, by permitting him to think you would remember him when absent, and pray for his safety."

Charlotte still held the letter in her hand: her heart swelled at the conclusion of Mademoiselle's speech, and a tear dropped upon the wafer that closed it.

"The wafer is not dry yet," said she, "and sure there can be no great harm——" She hesitated. La Rue was silent. "I may read it, Mademoiselle, and return it afterwards."

"Certainly," replied Mademoiselle.

"At any rate I am determined not to answer it," continued Charlotte, as she opened the letter.

Here let me stop to make one remark, and trust me my very heart aches while I write it; but certain I am, that when once a woman has stifled the sense of shame in her own bosom, when once she has lost sight of the basis on which reputation, honour, every thing that should be dear to the female heart, rests, she grows hardened in guilt, and will spare no pains to bring down innocence and beauty to the shocking level with herself: and this proceeds from that diabolical spirit of envy, which repines at seeing another in the full possession of that respect and esteem which she can no longer hope to enjoy.

Mademoiselle eyed the unsuspecting Charlotte, as she perused the letter, with a malignant pleasure. She saw, that the contents had awakened new emotions in her youthful bosom: she encouraged her hopes, calmed her fears, and before they parted for the night, it was determined that she should meet Montraville the ensuing evening.

Chapter XII

Nature's last, best gift:
Creature in whom excell'd, whatever could
To sight or thought be nam'd!
Holy, divine! good, amiable, and sweet!
How thou art fall'n!——

When Charlotte left her restless bed, her languid eye and pale cheek discovered to Madame Du Pont the little repose she had tasted.

"My dear child," said the affectionate governess, "what is the cause of the languor so apparent in your frame? Are you not well?"

"Yes, my dear Madam, very well," replied Charlotte, attempting to smile, "but I know not how it was; I could not sleep last night, and my spirits are depressed this morning."

"Come chear up, my love," said the governess; "I believe I have brought a cordial to revive them. I have just received a letter from your good mama, and here is one for yourself."

Charlotte hastily took the letter: it contained these words—

"As to-morrow is the anniversary of the happy day that gave my beloved girl to the anxious wishes of a maternal heart, I have requested your governess to let you come home and spend it with us; and as I know you to be a good affectionate child, and make it your study to improve in those branches of education which you know will give most pleasure to your delighted parents, as a reward for your diligence and attention I have prepared an agreeable surprise for your reception. Your grand-father, eager to embrace the darling of his aged heart, will come in the chaise for you; so hold yourself in readiness to attend him by nine o'clock. Your dear father joins in every tender wish for your health and future felicity, which warms the heart of my dear Charlotte's affectionate mother,   L. TEMPLE."

"Gracious heaven!" cried Charlotte, forgetting where she was, and raising her streaming eyes, as in earnest supplication.

Madame Du Pont was surprised. "Why these tears, my love?" said she. "Why this seeming agitation? I thought the letter would have rejoiced, instead of distressing you."

"It does rejoice me," replied Charlotte, endeavouring at composure, "but I was praying for merit to deserve the unremitted attentions of the best of parents."

"You do right," said Madame Du Pont, "to ask the assistance of heaven that you may continue to deserve their love. Continue, my dear Charlotte, in the course you have ever pursued, and you will insure at once their happiness and your own."

"Oh!" cried Charlotte, as her governess left her, "I have forfeited both for ever! Yet let me reflect:—the irrevocable step is not yet taken: it is not too late to recede from the brink of a precipice, from which I can only behold the dark abyss of ruin, shame, and remorse!"[5]

She arose from her seat, and flew to the apartment of La Rue. "Oh Mademoiselle!" said she, "I am snatched by a miracle from destruction! This letter has saved me: it has opened my eyes to the folly I was so near committing. I will not go, Mademoiselle; I will not wound the hearts of those dear parents who make my happiness the whole study of their lives."

"Well," said Mademoiselle, "do as you please, Miss; but pray understand that my resolution is taken, and it is not in your power to alter it. I shall meet the gentlemen at the appointed hour, and shall not be surprised at any outrage which Montraville may commit, when he finds himself disappointed. Indeed I should not be astonished, was he to come immediately here, and reproach you for your instability in the hearing of the whole school: and what will be the consequence? you will bear the odium of having formed the resolution of eloping, and every girl of spirit will laugh at your want of fortitude to put it in execution, while prudes and fools will load you with reproach and contempt. You will have lost the confidence of your parents, incurred their anger, and the scoffs of the world; and what fruit do you expect to reap from this piece of heroism, (for such no doubt you think it is?) you will have the pleasure to reflect, that you have deceived the man who adores you, and whom in your heart you prefer to all other men, and that you are separated from him for ever."

This eloquent harangue was given with such volubility, that Charlotte could not find an opportunity to interrupt her, or to offer a single word till the whole was finished, and then found her ideas so confused, that she knew not what to say.

At length she determined that she would go with Mademoiselle to the place of assignation, convince Montraville of the necessity of adhering to the resolution of remaining behind; assure him of her affection, and bid him adieu.

---

5. After meeting Montraville every evening for a week, Charlotte has consented to elope with him to America, together with La Rue and Belcour.

Charlotte formed this plan in her mind, and exulted in the certainty of its success. "How shall I rejoice," said she, "in this triumph of reason over inclination, and, when in the arms of my affectionate parents, lift up my soul in gratitude to heaven as I look back on the dangers I have escaped!"

The hour of assignation arrived: Mademoiselle put what money and valuables she possessed in her pocket, and advised Charlotte to do the same; but she refused; "my resolution is fixed," said she; "I will sacrifice love to duty."

Mademoiselle smiled internally; and they proceeded softly down the back stairs and out of the garden gate. Montraville and Belcour were ready to receive them.

"Now," said Montraville, taking Charlotte in his arms, "you are mine for ever."

"No," said she, withdrawing from his embrace, "I am come to take an everlasting farewel."

It would be useless to repeat the conversation that here ensued; suffice it to say, that Montraville used every argument that had formerly been successful, Charlotte's resolution began to waver, and he drew her almost imperceptibly towards the chaise.

"I cannot go," said she: "cease, dear Montraville, to persuade. I must not: religion, duty, forbid."

"Cruel Charlotte," said he, "if you disappoint my ardent hopes, by all that is sacred, this hand shall put a period to my existence. I cannot—will not live without you."

"Alas! my torn heart!" said Charlotte, "how shall I act?"

"Let me direct you," said Montraville, lifting her into the chaise.

"Oh! my dear forsaken parents!" cried Charlotte.

The chaise drove off. She shrieked, and fainted into the arms of her betrayer.

Chapter XXXIII
Which People Void of Feeling Need Not Read

When Mrs. Beauchamp entered the apartment of the poor sufferer, she started back with horror.[6] On a wretched bed, without hangings and but poorly supplied with covering, lay the emaciated figure of what still retained the resemblance of a lovely woman, though sickness had so altered her features that Mrs. Beauchamp had not the least recollection of her person. In one corner of the room stood a woman washing, and, shivering over a small fire, two healthy but half naked children; the infant was asleep beside its mother, and, on a chair by the bed side, stood a porrenger and wooden spoon, containing a little gruel, and a tea-cup with about two spoonfulls of wine in it. Mrs. Beauchamp had never before beheld such a scene of poverty; she shuddered involuntarily, and exclaiming—"heaven preserve us!" leaned on the back of a chair ready to sink to the earth. The doctor repented having so precipitately brought her into this affecting scene; but there was no time for apologies: Charlotte caught the sound of her voice, and starting almost out of bed, exclaimed—"Angel of peace and mercy, art thou come to deliver me? Oh, I know you are, for whenever you was near me I felt eased of half my sorrows; but you don't know me, nor can I, with all the recollection I am mistress of, remember your name just now, but I know that benevolent countenance, and the softness of that voice which has so often comforted the wretched Charlotte."

---

6. Charlotte has been abandoned in America by Montraville, has given birth to a child, and now lies gravely ill in the house of a kind poor couple who have taken her in and brought Mrs. Beauchamp, a wealthy woman, to see her.

Mrs. Beauchamp had, during the time Charlotte was speaking, seated herself on the bed and taken one of her hands; she looked at her attentively, and at the name of Charlotte she perfectly conceived the whole shocking affair. A faint sickness came over her. "Gracious heaven," said she, "is this possible?" and bursting into tears, she reclined the burning head of Charlotte on her own bosom; and folding her arms about her, wept over her in silence. "Oh," said Charlotte, "you are very good to weep thus for me: it is a long time since I shed a tear for myself: my head and heart are both on fire, but these tears of your's seem to cool and refresh it. Oh now I remember you said you would send a letter to my poor father: do you think he ever received it? or perhaps you have brought me an answer: why don't you speak, Madam? Does he say I may go home? Well he is very good; I shall soon be ready."

She then made an effort to get out of bed; but being prevented, her frenzy again returned, and she raved with the greatest wildness and incoherence. Mrs. Beauchamp, finding it was impossible for her to be removed, contented herself with ordering the apartment to be made more comfortable, and procuring a proper nurse for both mother and child; and having learnt the particulars of Charlotte's fruitless application to Mrs. Crayton from honest John, she amply rewarded him for his benevolence, and returned home with a heart oppressed with many painful sensations, but yet rendered easy by the reflexion that she had performed her duty towards a distressed fellow-creature.

Early the next morning she again visited Charlotte, and found her tolerably composed; she called her by name, thanked her for her goodness, and when her child was brought to her, pressed it in her arms, wept over it, and called it the offspring of disobedience. Mrs. Beauchamp was delighted to see her so much amended, and began to hope she might recover, and, spite of her former errors, become an useful and respectable member of society; but the arrival of the doctor put an end to these delusive hopes: he said nature was making her last effort, and a few hours would most probably consign the unhappy girl to her kindred dust.

Being asked how she found herself, she replied—"Why better, much better, doctor. I hope now I have but little more to suffer. I had last night a few hours sleep, and when I awoke recovered the full power of recollection. I am quite sensible of my weakness; I feel I have but little longer to combat with the shafts of affliction. I have an humble confidence in the mercy of him who died to save the world, and trust that my sufferings in this state of mortality, joined to my unfeigned repentance, through his mercy, have blotted my offences from the sight of my offended maker. I have but one care—my poor infant! Father of mercy," continued she, raising her eyes, "of thy infinite goodness, grant that the sins of the parent be not visited on the unoffending child. May those who taught me to despise thy laws be forgiven; lay not my offences to their charge, I beseech thee; and oh! shower the choicest of thy blessings on those whose pity has soothed the afflicted heart, and made easy even the bed of pain and sickness."

She was exhausted by this fervent address to the throne of mercy, and though her lips still moved her voice became inarticulate: she lay for some time as it were in a dose, and then recovering, faintly pressed Mrs. Beauchamp's hand, and requested that a clergyman might be sent for.

On his arrival she joined fervently in the pious office, frequently mentioning her ingratitude to her parents as what lay most heavy at her heart. When she had performed the last solemn duty, and was preparing to lie down, a little bustle on the outside door occasioned Mrs. Beauchamp to open it, and enquire the cause. A man in appearance about forty, presented himself, and asked for Mrs. Beauchamp.

"That is my name, Sir," said she.

"Oh then, my dear Madam," cried he, "tell me where I may find my poor, ruined, but repentant child."

Mrs. Beauchamp was surprised and affected; she knew not what to say; she foresaw the agony this interview would occasion Mr. Temple, who had just arrived in search of his Charlotte, and yet was sensible that the pardon and blessing of her father would soften even the agonies of death to the daughter.

She hesitated. "Tell me, Madam," cried he wildly, "tell me, I beseech thee, does she live? Shall I see my darling once again? Perhaps she is in this house. Lead, lead me to her, that I may bless her, and then lie down and die."

The ardent manner in which he uttered these words occasioned him to raise his voice. It caught the ear of Charlotte: she knew the beloved sound: and uttering a loud shriek, she sprang forward as Mr. Temple entered the room. "My adored father." "My long lost child." Nature could support no more, and they both sunk lifeless into the arms of the attendants.

Charlotte was again put into bed, and a few moments restored Mr. Temple: but to describe the agony of his sufferings is past the power of any one, who, though they may readily conceive, cannot delineate the dreadful scene. Every eye gave testimony of what each heart felt—but all were silent.

When Charlotte recovered, she found herself supported in her father's arms. She cast on him a most expressive look, but was unable to speak. A reviving cordial was administered. She then asked, in a low voice, for her child: it was brought to her: she put it in her father's arms. "Protect her," said she, "and bless your dying————"

Unable to finish the sentence, she sunk back on her pillow: her countenance was serenely composed; she regarded her father as he pressed the infant to his breast with a steadfast look; a sudden beam of joy passed across her languid features, she raised her eyes to heaven—and then closed them for ever.

—1791

Joanna Baillie
1762–1851

A Series of Plays: in which it is attempted to delineate the stronger passions of the mind—each passion being the subject of a tragedy and a comedy is long on title, but short on authorship. The series garnered wide critical and popular attention, and its anonymous appearance in 1798 led to sustained speculation about who penned what came to be known as the *Plays on the Passions*. The plays were a sensation both for the emotionally charged and audience-engaging plots and for the theoretical introduction on the aesthetics of drama. Guessing at their authorship became a common parlor game in London literary circles, and even Baillie's close friends were unaware she had written the volume until 1800, when her authorship was revealed with the appearance of a third edition. As a result, the Scottish Baillie came to be viewed as one of the leading playwrights of the period.

Baillie was the well-educated daughter of an Anglican minister. In 1784, she moved to London, where she became a prominent literary and somewhat less prominent social figure, counting Anna Barbauld and Maria Edgeworth among her friends. She first turned her pen to poetry and in 1790 produced *Poems Wherein It Is Attempted to Describe Certain Views of Nature and Rustic Manners*. Published anonymously in 1790 and revised in 1840, these poems reveal a playful and technically skilled poet who was interested in nature and domesticity and had a strong musical sensibility.

Baillie's reputation, however, rests on her work as a playwright: She composed twenty-eight plays during her long career. The "Introductory Discourse" attached to *Plays on the Passions* makes an intelligent and impassioned plea for a revolution in drama. She believed plays should address emotional and personal situations that everyone can relate to, and that they should be written in everyday language. (Consider the echoes of Wordsworth's argument in the preface to *Lyrical Ballads*.) At the same time, they should avoid the conventionalism of the sentimental and comic plays of the day that pandered to audience taste. One consequence of Baillie's reaction against popular drama is that her plays were more readerly than theatrical and can be viewed as "closet drama"—plays (like Shelley's *Prometheus Unbound*) designed more for quiet reading that dramatic performance. For instance, the most popular work in *Plays on the Passions*, the tragedy *De Monfort*, was well received but had a short run in the theater; the script offers an intense psychological portrait of hatred that provides meaty roles for the cast and makes it an engrossing tale to read, but that also makes the play very difficult to stage effectively for a wide audience.

from Plays on the Passions

from *Introductory Discourse*

If man is an object of so much attention to man, engaged in the ordinary occurrences of life, how much more does he excite his curiosity and interest when placed in extraordinary situations of difficulty and distress? It cannot be any pleasure we receive from the sufferings of a fellow-creature which attracts such multitudes of people to a public execution, though it is the horror we conceive for such a spectacle that keeps so many more away. To see a human being bearing himself up under such circumstances, or struggling with the terrible apprehensions which such a situation impresses, must be the powerful incentive that makes us press forward to behold what we shrink from, and wait with trembling expectation for what we dread. For though few at such a spectacle can get near enough to distinguish the expression of face, or the minuter parts of a criminal's behaviour, yet from a considerable distance will they eagerly mark whether he steps firmly; whether the motions of his body denote agitation or calmness; and if the wind does but ruffle his garment, they will, even from that change upon the outline of his distant figure, read some expression connected with his dreadful situation. Though there is a greater proportion of people in whom this strong curiosity will be overcome by other dispositions and motives; though there are many more who will stay away from such a sight than will go to it; yet there are very few who will not be eager to converse with a person who has beheld it; and to learn, very minutely, every circumstance connected with it, except the very act itself of inflicting death. To lift up the roof of his dungeon, like the *Diable boiteux*,[1] and look upon a criminal the night before he suffers, in his still hours of privacy, when all that disguise is removed which is imposed by respect for the opinion of others, the strong

1. Novel by Alain René Le Sage (1668–1747).

motive by which even the lowest and wickedest of men still continue to be actuated, would present an object to the mind of every person, not withheld from it by great timidity of character, more powerfully attractive than almost any other.

Revenge, no doubt, first began among the savages of America that dreadful custom of sacrificing their prisoners of war. But the perpetration of such hideous cruelty could never have become a permanent national custom, but for this universal desire in the human mind to behold man in every situation, putting forth his strength against the current of adversity, scorning all bodily anguish, or struggling with those feelings of nature which, like a beating stream, will ofttimes burst through the artificial barriers of pride. Before they begin those terrible rites they treat their prisoners kindly; and it cannot be supposed that men, alternately enemies and friends to so many neighbouring tribes, in manners and appearance like themselves, should so strongly be actuated by a spirit of public revenge. This custom, therefore, must be considered as a grand and terrible game, which every tribe plays against another; where they try not the strength of the arm, the swiftness of the feet, nor the acuteness of the eye, but the fortitude of the soul. Considered in this light, the excess of cruelty exercised upon their miserable victim, in which every hand is described as ready to inflict its portion of pain, and every head ingenious in the contrivance of it, is no longer to be wondered at. To put into his measure of misery one agony less, would be, in some degree, betraying the honour of their nation, would be doing a species of injustice to every hero of their own tribe who had already sustained it, and to those who might be called upon to do so; among whom each of these savage tormenters has his chance of being one, and has prepared himself for it from his childhood. Nay, it would be a species of injustice to the haughty victim himself, who would scorn to purchase his place among the heroes of his nation at an easier price than his undaunted predecessors.

Amongst the many trials to which the human mind is subjected, that of holding intercourse,[2] real or imaginary, with the world of spirits: of finding itself alone with a being terrific and awful, whose nature and power are unknown, has been justly considered as one of the most severe. The workings of nature in this situation, we all know, have ever been the object of our most eager inquiry. No man wishes to see the Ghost himself, which would certainly procure him the best information on the subject, but every man wishes to see one who believes that he sees it, in all the agitation and wildness of that species of terror. To gratify this curiosity how many people have dressed up hideous apparitions to frighten the timid and superstitious! and have done it at the risk of destroying their happiness or understanding for ever. For the instances of intellect being destroyed by this kind of trial are more numerous, perhaps, in proportion to the few who have undergone it, than by any other.

How sensible are we of this strong propensity within us, when we behold any person under the pressure of great and uncommon calamity! Delicacy and respect for the afflicted will, indeed, make us turn ourselves aside from observing him, and cast down our eyes in his presence; but the first glance we direct to him will involuntarily be one of the keenest observation, how hastily soever it may be checked; and often will a returning look of inquiry mix itself by stealth with our sympathy and reserve.

But it is not in situations of difficulty and distress alone, that man becomes the object of this sympathetic curiosity: he is no less so when the evil he contends with arises

---

2. Dialogue or interaction.

in his own breast, and no outward circumstance connected with him either awakens our attention or our pity. What human creature is there, who can behold a being like himself under the violent agitation of those passions which all have, in some degree, experienced, without feeling himself most powerfully excited by the sight? I say, all have experienced: for the bravest man on earth knows what fear is as well as the coward; and will not refuse to be interested for one under the dominion of this passion, provided there be nothing in the circumstances attending it to create contempt. Anger is a passion that attracts less sympathy than any other, yet the unpleasing and distorted features of an angry man will be more eagerly gazed upon by those who are no wise concerned with his fury, or the objects of it, than the most amiable placid countenance in the world. Every eye is directed to him; every voice hushed to silence in his presence: even children will leave off their gambols as he passes, and gaze after him more eagerly than the gaudiest equipage. The wild tossings of despair; the gnashing of hatred and revenge; the yearnings of affection, and the softened mien of love; all the language of the agitated soul, which every age and nation understand, is never addressed to the dull or inattentive.

It is not merely under the violent agitations of passion, that man so rouses and interests us; even the smallest indications of an unquiet mind, the restless eye, the muttering lip, the half-checked exclamation and the hasty start, will set our attention as anxiously upon the watch, as the first distant flashes of a gathering storm. When some great explosion of passion bursts forth, and some consequent catastrophe happens, if we are at all acquainted with the unhappy perpetrator, how minutely shall we endeavour to remember every circumstance of his past behaviour! and with what avidity shall we seize upon every recollected word or gesture, that is in the smallest degree indicative of the supposed state of his mind, at the time when they took place. If we are not acquainted with him, how eagerly shall we listen to similar recollections from another! Let us understand, from observation or report, that any person harbours in his breast, concealed from the world's eye, some powerful rankling passion of what kind soever it may be, we shall observe every word, every motion, every look, even the distant gait of such a man, with a constancy and attention bestowed upon no other. Nay, should we meet him unexpectedly on our way, a feeling will pass across our minds as though we found ourselves in the neighbourhood of some secret and fearful thing. If invisible, would we not follow him into his lonely haunts, into his closet, into the midnight silence of his chamber? There is, perhaps, no employment which the human mind will with so much avidity pursue, as the discovery of concealed passion, as the tracing the varieties and progress of a perturbed soul. . . .

The highest pleasures we receive from poetry, as well as from the real objects which surround us in the world, are derived from the sympathetic interest we all take in beings like ourselves; and I will even venture to say, that were the grandest scenes which can enter into the imagination of man, presented to our view, and all reference to man completely shut out from our thoughts, the objects that composed it would convey to our minds little better than dry ideas of magnitude, colour, and form; and the remembrance of them would rest upon our minds like the measurement and distances of the planets. . . .

[T]he last part of the task which I have mentioned as peculiarly belonging to Tragedy,—unveiling the human mind under the dominion of those strong and fixed passions, which, seemingly unprovoked by outward circumstances, will from small beginnings brood within the breast, till all the better dispositions, all the fair gifts of nature, are borne down before them,—her poets in general have entirely neglected, and even her first and greatest have but imperfectly attempted. They have made use of the passions to mark their several characters, and animate their scenes, rather than to open to our view the nature and portraitures of those great disturbers of the human breast, with whom we are all, more or less, called upon to contend. . . . To trace them in their rise and progress in the heart, seems but rarely to have been the object of any dramatist. We commonly find the characters of a tragedy affected by the passions in a transient, loose, unconnected manner; or if they are represented as under the permanent influence of the more powerful ones, they are generally introduced to our notice in the very height of their fury, when all that timidity, irresolution, distrust, and a thousand delicate traits, which make the infancy of every great passion more interesting, perhaps, than its full-blown strength, are fled. The impassioned character is generally brought into view under those irresistible attacks of their power, which it is impossible to repel; whilst those gradual steps that lead him into this state, in some of which a stand might have been made against the foe, are left entirely in the shade. Those passions that may be suddenly excited, and are of short duration, as anger, fear, and oftentimes jealousy, may in this manner be fully represented; but those great masters of the soul, ambition, hatred, love, every passion that is permanent in its nature, and varied in progress, if represented to us but in one stage of its course, is represented imperfectly. It is a characteristic of the more powerful passions, that they will increase and nourish themselves on very slender aliment; it is from within that they are chiefly supplied with what they feed on; and it is in contending with opposite passions and affections of the mind that we best discover their strength, not with events. But in Tragedy it is events, more frequently than opposite affections, which are opposed to them; and those often of such force and magnitude, that the passions themselves are almost obscured by the splendour and importance of the transactions to which they are attached. . . .

From this general view, which I have endeavoured to communicate to my reader of Tragedy, and those principles in the human mind upon which the success of her efforts depends, I have been led to believe, that an attempt to write a series of tragedies, of simpler construction, less embellished with poetical decorations, less constrained by that lofty seriousness which has so generally been considered as necessary for the support of tragic dignity, and in which the chief object should be to delineate the progress of the higher passions in the human breast, each play exhibiting a particular passion, might not be unacceptable to the public. . . .

It may, perhaps, be supposed, from my publishing these plays, that I have written them for the closet rather than the stage.[3] If, upon perusing them with attention, the reader is disposed to think they are better calculated for the first than the last, let him impute it to want of skill in the author, and not to any previous design. A play but of small poetical merit, that is suited to strike and interest the spectator, to catch the attention of him who will not, and of him who cannot read, is a more valuable and useful production than one whose elegant and harmonious pages are admired in the libraries of the tasteful and refined. To have received approbation from an audience of my countrymen, would have been more pleasing to me than any other praise. A few tears from the simple and young would have been, in my eyes, pearls of great price; and the spontaneous, untutored plaudits of the rude and uncultivated would have come to my heart as offer-

---

3. A closet play is intended for private reading, not public performance.

ings of no mean value. I should, therefore, have been better pleased to have introduced them to the world from the stage than from the press. I possess, however, no likely channel to the former mode of public introduction: and, upon further reflection, it appeared to me, that by publishing them in this way, I have an opportunity afforded me of explaining the design of my work, and enabling the public to judge, not only of each play by itself, but as making a part likewise of the whole; an advantage which, perhaps, does more than over-balance the splendour and effect of theatrical representation. . . .

Before I close this discourse, let me crave the forbearance of my reader, if he has discovered in the course of it any unacknowledged use of the thoughts of other authors, which he thinks ought to have been noticed; and let me beg the same favour, if in reading the following plays, any similar neglect seems to occur. There are few writers who have sufficient originality of thought to strike out for themselves new ideas upon every occasion. When a thought presents itself to me, as suited to the purpose I am aiming at, I would neither be thought proud enough to reject it, on finding that another has used it before me, nor mean enough to make use of it without acknowledging the obligation, when I can at all guess to whom such acknowledgments are due. But I am situated where I have no library to consult; my reading through the whole of my life has been of a loose, scattered, unmethodical kind, with no determined direction, and I have not been blessed by nature with the advantages of a retentive or accurate memory. . . . If this volume should appear, to any candid and liberal critic, to merit that he should take the trouble of pointing out to me in what parts of it I seem to have made that use of other authors' writings, which, according to the fair laws of literature, ought to have been acknowledged, I shall think myself obliged to him. I shall examine the sources he points out as having supplied my own lack of ideas; and if this book should have the good fortune to go through a second edition, I shall not fail to own my obligations to him, and the authors from whom I may have borrowed.

How little credit soever, upon perusing these plays, the reader may think me entitled to in regard to the execution of the work, he will not, I flatter myself, deny me some credit in regard to the plan. I know of no series of plays, in any language, expressly descriptive of the different passions. . . . However, if I perform it ill, I am still confident that this (pardon me if I call it so) noble design will not be suffered to fall to the ground: some one will arise after me who will do it justice; and there is no poet possessing genius for such a work, who will not at the same time possess that spirit of justice and of candour, which will lead him to remember me with respect.

—1798

London

It is a goodly sight through the clear air,
From Hampstead's heathy height to see at once
England's vast capital in fair expanse,
Towers, belfries, lengthen'd streets, and structures fair.
St. Paul's high dome amidst the vassal bands   5
Of neighb'ring spires, a regal chieftain stands,
And over fields of ridgy roofs appear,
With distance softly tinted, side by side,
In kindred grace, like twain of sisters dear,

The Towers of Westminster, her Abbey's pride;   10
While, far beyond, the hills of Surrey shine
Through thin soft haze, and show their wavy line.
View'd thus, a goodly sight! but when survey'd
Through denser air when moisten'd winds prevail,
In her grand panoply of smoke array'd,   15
While clouds aloft in heavy volumes sail,
She is sublime.—She seems a curtain'd gloom
Connecting heaven and earth,—a threat'ning sign of doom.
With more than natural height, rear'd in the sky
'Tis then St. Paul's arrests the wondering eye;   20
The lower parts in swathing mist conceal'd,
The higher through some half spent shower reveal'd,
So far from earth removed, that well, I trow,
Did not its form man's artful structure show,
It might some lofty alpine peak be deem'd,   25
The eagle's haunt, with cave and crevice seam'd.
Stretch'd wide on either hand, a rugged screen,
In lurid dimness, nearer streets are seen
Like shoreward billows of a troubled main,[1]
Arrested in their rage. Through drizzly rain,   30
Cataracts of tawny sheen pour from the skies,
Of furnace smoke black curling columns rise,
And many tinted vapours, slowly pass
O'er the wide draping of that pictured mass.

   So shows by day this grand imperial town,   35
And, when o'er all the night's black stole is thrown,
The distant traveller doth with wonder mark
Her luminous canopy athwart the dark,
Cast up, from myriads of lamps that shine
Along her streets in many a starry line:—   40
He wondering looks from his yet distant road,
And thinks the northern streamers[2] are abroad.
"What hollow sound is that?" approaching near,
The roar of many wheels breaks on his ear.
It is the flood of human life in motion!   45
It is the voice of a tempestuous ocean!
With sad but pleasing awe his soul is fill'd,
Scarce heaves his breast, and all within is still'd,
As many thoughts and feelings cross his mind,—
Thoughts, mingled, melancholy, undefined,   50
Of restless, reckless man, and years gone by,
And Time fast wending to Eternity.

                                                    —1790

─────────────────────
1. The open sea.   2. The northern lights.

A Mother to Her Waking Infant

Now in thy dazzling half-oped eye,
Thy curled nose, and lip awry,
Thy up-hoist arms, and noddling head,
And little chin with crystal spread,
Poor helpless thing! what do I see,
    That I should sing of thee? 5

From thy poor tongue no accents come,
Which can but rub thy toothless gum:
Small understanding boasts thy face,
Thy shapeless limbs nor step, nor grace: 10
A few short words thy feats may tell,
    And yet I love thee well.

When sudden wakes the bitter shriek,
And redder swells thy little cheek; 15
When rattled keys thy woes beguile,
And thro' the wet eye gleams the smile,
Still for thy weakly self is spent
    Thy little silly plaint.

But when thy friends are in distress,
Thou'lt laugh and chuckle ne'er the less; 20
Nor e'en with sympathy be smitten,
Tho' all are sad but thee and kitten;
Yet puny varlet that thou art,
    Thou twitchest at the heart.

Thy rosy round cheek so soft and warm; 25
Thy pinky hand, and dimpled arm;
Thy silken locks that scantly peep,
With gold-tip'd ends, where circle deep
Around thy neck in harmless grace
So soft and sleekly hold their place, 30
Might harder hearts with kindness fill,
    And gain our right good will.

Each passing clown bestows his blessing,
Thy mouth is worn with old wives' kissing;
E'en lighter looks the gloomy eye 35
Of surly sense, when thou art by;
And yet I think whoe'er they be,
    They love thee not like me.

Perhaps when time shall add a few
Short years to thee, thou'lt love me too. 40
Then wilt thou, thro' life's weary way

Become my sure and cheering stay:
Wilt care for me, and be my hold,
    When I am weak and old.

Thou'lt listen to my lengthen'd tale,   45
And pity me when I am frail—
But see, the sweepy spinning fly
Upon the window takes thine eye.
Go to thy little senseless play—
    Thou dost not heed my lay.   50

—1790

A Child to His Sick Grandfather

Grand-dad, they say you're old and frail,
Your stocked legs begin to fail:
Your knobbed stick (that was my horse)
Can scarce support your bended corse
While back to wall, you lean so sad,   5
    I'm vex'd to see you, dad.

You us'd to smile, and stroke my head,
And tell me how good children did;
But now I wot not how it be,
You take me seldom on your knee;   10
Yet ne'ertheless I am right glad
    To sit beside you, dad.

How lank and thin your beard hangs down!
Scant are the white hairs on your crown:
How wan and hollow are your cheeks!   15
Your brow is rough with crossing streaks
But yet, for all his strength be fled,
    I love my own old dad.

The housewives round their potions brew,
And gossips come to ask for you;   20
And for your weal each neighbour cares,
And good men kneel, and say their prayers:
And ev'ry body looks so sad,
    When you are ailing, dad.

You will not die, and leave us, then?   25
Rouse up and be our dad again.
When your are quiet and laid in bed,
We'll doff our shoes and softly tread;

And when you wake we'll aye be near,
    To fill old dad his cheer.   30

When thro' the house you shift your stand,
I'll lead you kindly by the hand:
When dinner's set, I'll with you bide,
And aye be serving by your side:
And when the weary fire burns blue,   35
    I'll sit and talk with you.

I have a tale both long and good,
About a partlet and her brood;
And cunning greedy fox, that stole,
By dead of midnight thro' a hole,   40
Which slily to the hen-roost led,—
    You love a story, dad?

And then I have a wondrous tale
Of men all clad in coats of mail,
With glitt'ring swords—you nod,—I think?   45
Your fixed eyes begin to wink:
Down on your bosom sinks your head:
    You do not hear me, dad.

                            —1790

Thunder

Spirit of strength! to whom in wrath 'tis given,
To mar the earth and shake its vasty dome,
Behold the sombre robes whose gathering folds,
Thy secret majesty conceal. Their skirts
Spread on mid air move slow and silently,   5
O'er noon-day's beam thy sultry shroud is cast,
Advancing clouds from every point of heaven,
Like hosts of gathering foes in pitchy volumes,
Grandly dilated, clothe the fields of air,
And brood aloft o'er the empurpled earth.   10
Spirit of strength! it is thy awful hour;
The wind of every hill is laid to rest,
And far o'er sea and land deep silence reigns.

    Wild creatures of the forest homeward hie,
And in their dens with fear unwonted cower;   15
Pride in the lordly palace is put down,
While in his humble cot the poor man sits
With all his family round him hush'd and still,

In awful expectation. On his way
The traveller stands aghast and looks to heaven.   20
On the horizon's verge thy lightning gleams,
And the first utterance of thy deep voice
Is heard in reverence and holy fear.

    From nearer clouds bright burst more vivid gleams,
As instantly in closing darkness lost;   25
Pale sheeted flashes cross the wide expanse
While over boggy moor or swampy plain,
A streaming cataract of flame appears,
To meet a nether fire from earth cast up,
Commingling terribly; appalling gloom   30
Succeeds, and lo! the rifted centre pours
A general blaze, and from the war of clouds,
Red, writhing falls the embodied bolt of heaven.
Then swells the rolling peal, full, deep'ning, grand,
And in its strength lifts the tremendous roar,   35
With mingled discord, rattling, hissing, growling;
Crashing like rocky fragments downward hurl'd,
Like the upbreaking of a ruined world,
In awful majesty the explosion bursts
Wide and astounding o'er the trembling land.   40
Mountain, and cliff, repeat the dread turmoil,
And all, to man's distinctive senses known,
Is lost in the immensity of sound.
Peal after peal succeeds with waning strength,
And hush'd and deep each solemn pause between.   45

    Upon the lofty mountain's side
The kindled forest blazes wide;
Huge fragments of the rugged steep
Are tumbled to the lashing deep;
Firm rooted in his cloven rock,   50
Crashing falls the stubborn oak.
The lightning keen in wasteful ire
Darts fiercely on the pointed spire,
Rending in twain the iron-knit stone,
And stately towers to earth are thrown.   55
No human strength may brave the storm,
Nor shelter screen the shrinking form,
Nor castle wall its fury stay,
Nor massy gate impede its way:
It visits those of low estate,   60
It shakes the dwellings of the great,
It looks athwart the vaulted tomb,
And glares upon the prison's gloom.
Then dungeons black in unknown light,

Flash hideous on the wretches' sight,   65
And strangely groans the downward cell,
Where silence deep is wont to dwell.

    Now eyes, to heaven up-cast, adore,
Knees bend that never bent before,
The stoutest hearts begin to fail,   70
And many a manly face is pale;
Benumbing fear awhile up-binds,
The palsied action of their minds,
Till waked to dreadful sense they lift their eyes,
And round the stricken corse shrill shrieks of horror rise.   75

    Now rattling hailstones, bounding as they fall
To earth, spread motly winter o'er the plain;
Receding peals sound fainter on the ear,
And roll their distant grumbling far away:
The lightning doth in paler flashes gleam,   80
And through the rent cloud, silvered with his rays,
The sun on all this wild affray looks down,
As, high enthroned above all mortal ken,
A higher Power beholds the strife of men.

                              —1790

Song: Woo'd and Married and A'
(Version taken from an old song of that name)

The bride she is winsome and bonny,
    Her hair it is snooded[1] sae sleek,
And faithfu' and kind is her Johnny,
    Yet fast fa' the tears on her cheek.
New pearlins[2] are cause of her sorrow,   5
    New pearlins and plenishing too,
The bride that has a' to borrow,
    Has e'en right mickle ado,
        Woo'd and married and a'![3]
        Woo'd and married and a'!
    Is na' she very weel aff   10
        To be woo'd and married at a'?

Her mither then hastily spak,
    "The lassie is glaikit[4] wi' pride;
In my pouch I had never a plack[5]   15
    On the day when I was a bride.
E'en tak' to your wheel and be clever,
    And draw out your thread in the sun;

---

1. Bound. 2. Lace, silk. 3. All. 4. Foolish. 5. Coin.

The gear that is gifted it never
  Will last like the gear that is won.   20
    Woo'd and married and a'!
    Wi' havins and tocher[6] sae sma'!
I think ye are very weel aff,
  To be woo'd and married at a'!"

"Toot, toot!" quo' her grey-headed faither,   25
  "She's less o' a bride than a bairn,[7]
She's ta'en like a cout frae the heather,
  Wi' sense and discretion to learn.
Half husband, I trow, and half daddy,
  As humour inconstantly leans,   30
The chiel maun[8] be patient and steady,
  That yokes wi' a mate in her teens.
    A kerchief sae douce and sae neat,
    O'er her locks that the winds used to blaw!
  I'm baith like to laugh and to greet,[9]   35
    When I think o' her married at a'!"

Then out spak' the wily bridegroom,
  Weel waled[10] were his wordies, I ween,
"I'm rich, though my coffer be toom,
  Wi' the blinks o' your bonny blue een.   40
I'm prouder o' thee by my side,
  Though thy ruffles or ribbons be few,
Than if Kate o' the Croft were my bride,
  Wi' purfles[11] and pearlins enow.
    Dear and dearest of ony!   45
    Ye're woo'd and buikit[12] and a'!
  And do ye think scorn o' your Johnny,
    And grieve to be married at a'?"

She turn'd, and she blush'd, and she smiled,
  And she looket sae bashfully down;   50
The pride o' her heart was beguiled,
  And she played wi' the sleeves o' her gown;
She twirled the tag o' her lace,
  And she nippet her boddice sae blue,
Syne blinket sae sweet in his face,
  And aff like a maukin[13] she flew.   55
    Woo'd and married and a'!
    Wi' Johnny to roose[14] her and a'!
  She thinks hersel very weel aff,
  To be woo'd and married at a'!   60

—1822

---

6. Possessions and dowry. 7. Child. 8. Fellow must. 9. Weep. 10. Well chosen. 11. Embroidery.
12. Registered.   13. Rabbit.   14. Praise.

∼TRANSATLANTIC EXCHANGES ∼

Women's Rights

> It would be an endless task to trace the variety of meannesses, cares, and sorrows, into which women are plunged by the prevailing opinion, that they were created rather to feel than reason, and that all the power they obtain must be obtained by their charms and weakness.
> —Mary Wollstonecraft, *A Vindication of the Rights of Woman* (1792)

> She rose to His Requirement—dropt
> The Playthings of her Life
> To take the honorable Work
> Of Woman and of Wife—
> —Emily Dickinson, #732 (c. 1863)

Writing some seventy years apart and on different continents, the British Wollstonecraft and the American Dickinson offer parallel responses—one angry, the other ironic—to the rigid oppressiveness of patriarchal society. Similarly, the American Transcendentalist Sophia Ripley writes wryly in the periodical *The Dial* in 1841 that "even the clergy have frequently flattered 'the feebler sex,' by proclaiming to them from the pulpit what lovely beings they may become, if they will only be good, quiet, and gentle, attend exclusively to their domestic duties, and the cultivation of religious feelings, which the other sex very kindly relinquish to them as their inheritance" (p. 366). The powerful notion of "sensibility," against which Wollstonecraft, Dickinson, and Ripley were reacting, shaped Romantic expectations of female conduct. Sensibility is about feeling—the ability to feel, and to feel well and deeply (as though this were a skill to be cultivated). Women are presented as embodiments of sensibility, who are nurturing by nature, with maternal instincts. The literature of sensibility focused on strong emotions represented as typically feminine: compassion, pity, and sympathy. Thus the literature of sensibility reinforced the ideology of separate spheres that defined masculine and feminine employments and environments according to a series of binary oppositions. Men think and work outside of the house, while women feel and run the home. Men are rational; women, emotional. Men are scientific; women, spiritual. Men are political; women, poetical. Men are carnal; women, pure.

In response to the dominance of the sexist ideologies of sensibility and separate spheres, women called for educational, legal, and religious reforms during the transatlantic Romantic century. In *A Vindication of the Rights of Woman*, Wollstonecraft responded to Jean-Jacques Rousseau's novel *Emile* (1762), in which he proposed a model of female education aimed at making girls useful to men. Wollstonecraft, one of the earliest and most vocal champions of women's rights in England, attempts to subvert sensibility in favor of reason, so that each woman can break free of the societal role in which "gentleness, docility, and a spaniel-like affection are . . . the cardinal virtues of the sex." Wollstonecraft aimed her withering irony at the belief that woman "was created to be the toy of man, his rattle, and it must jingle in his ears whenever, dismissing reason, he chooses to be amused." Nevertheless, "I do not wish [women] to have power over men," Wollstonecraft writes elsewhere in *Vindication*, "but over themselves." Wollstonecraft extends to women the demand for individual human rights that was at the center of the revolutionary era—for the radicals of the period, each individual, male or female, black or white, rich or poor, should have ultimate power over his or her own self.

This was a truly bold stance, for during the transatlantic Romantic century, believers in women's rights confronted a patriarchal society that sharply restricted the autonomy of the female body and mind. Women were bound by law and custom to abandon their individual interests, even their selves, in order to serve their husbands. In English common law, women were held to a different legal standard, being viewed as a legal extension (or dependent) of their husbands. In his 1765 *Commentaries on the Laws of England*, William Blackstone wrote that "by marriage, the husband and wife are one person in law . . . the very being or legal existence of the woman is suspended during the marriage, or at least is incorporated and consolidated into that of the husband; under whose wing, protection, and *cover*, she performs every thing." Since women had little or no legal identity outside of the marriage, they faced hard limits to their ability to own property, execute contracts, or engage in business ventures. And though the Reform Acts of 1832, 1867, and 1884 extended voting rights to previously disenfranchised English subjects (the working class), women were not granted voting rights until the Representation of the People Act was passed in 1918 (even then suffrage was restricted to women over thirty). Laws governing marriage and divorce were equally slow to change. Under the 1839 Custody of Infants Act, only women "of unblemished character" were given access to their children in the event of separation or divorce. The Matrimonial Causes Act of 1857 somewhat improved female access to divorce and partially extended the rights women had to property ownership, but women were not allowed full rights to ownership until 1870, with the passage of the Married Women's Property Act.

Just as they were denied opportunities to participate legally in the public world, women also faced serious restrictions on their intellectual development. The viewpoint forwarded by Rousseau in *Emile*, that women should be trained to serve men, resulted in women being consistently denied access to institutions of higher learning. Many women turned instead to writing and self-education as means to both improve themselves as individuals and to participate in the outside world. Writing, in other words, allowed women to voice their concerns and to detail their experience in public, in spite of the legal measures that restricted their lives.

In order to do so, though, they had to challenge deeply ingrained prejudices about writing itself. During the seventeenth and eighteenth centuries, many saw writing as an unserious and even trivial occupation, and thus as an acceptable pastime for women. As Joseph Addison suggested dismissively, women "have more spare time on their hands, and lead a more sedentary life," and thus were well suited to the unmasculine pursuit of writing. A similar whiff of disdain surrounds much nineteenth-century male commentary on female writing.

Men not only saw writing as fundamentally unserious, they also expected women writers to produce stereotypically feminine writing—writing suited to the gender role defined for them by the ideology of sensibility. For instance, in an essay on the poet Felicia Hemans in *Tait's Edinburgh Magazine* in 1847, George Gilfillan writes:

> You could not . . . open a page of her writings without feeling this is written by a lady. . . . Her works are a versified *journal* of a quiet, ideal, and beautiful life—the life at once of a woman and a poetess, with just enough, and no more, of romance to cast around it a mellow autumnal colouring. . . . You are saved the ludicrous image of a double-dyed Blue . . . sweating at some stupendous treatise or tragedy from morn to noon, and from noon to dewy eve—you see a graceful and gifted woman, passing from the cares of her family, and the enjoyments of her family, to inscribe on her tablets some fine thought or feeling.

There is a condescending tone here that suggests writing is an inconsequential mental activity that is therefore fit for women. And implicit in Gilfillan's seemingly positive review of Hemans's poetry is the ideology of separate spheres. Hemans's poetry is the product of home life, the domain of the private (the "*journal* of a quiet, ideal, and beautiful life"). Because her poetry falls within expected conventions (the pastoral, for instance, with its "mellow autumnal colouring"), she is "graceful and gifted." The poems, while pleasing, are quaint, the effusions of a gentle mind on gentle topics. Most importantly for Gilfillan, Hemans's poetry does not have the polemical charge of, say, Mary Wollstonecraft or a "double-dyed Blue."

The Bluestockings to whom Gilfillan refers were a group of pioneering literary women who, like Wollstonecraft, saw writing as a potentially powerful and important tool for their own liberation. An informal collective of artistic and intellectual women, they met in one another's London homes for intellectual conversation. James Boswell records in his *Life of Samuel Johnson* (1791) that the term derived from the clothing of impoverished writer and naturalist Benjamin Stillingfleet, who attended the gatherings wearing the blue-gray socks typical of a laborer or tradesman, not the evening socks of black silk worn by a gentleman. The term derides the aspirations of these women to counter the social customs of the day—they refused to dress, act, or socialize according to the conventions of polite London society. The group thrived from 1770 to 1785; its changing membership included the likes of Elisabeth Vesey, who initiated the meetings in the 1750s; novelist Elizabeth Montagu; poet and educator Hannah More; translator Elizabeth Carter; and novelist Frances Burney. The women debated moral and political matters and discussed literature and philosophy, believing that conversation was a valuable educational tool. They taught themselves classical languages, and translating became a key activity of many members. The ideas and educational philosophy cultivated in these meetings surfaced in the many published works of the members, including More's influential *Strictures on the Modern System of Female Education* (1799):

> But, though a well-bred young lady may lawfully learn most of the fashionable arts; yet, let me ask,—Does it seem to be the true end of education to make of women fashion dancers, singers, players, painters, actresses, sculptors, gilders, varnishers, engravers, and embroiderers?

More challenges the educational double standard that sees women as irrational beings and thus concentrates their attention on trivial, "decorative pursuits." Far from calling for absolute educational equality, though, she limited herself to suggesting that women should be more effectively prepared for their roles as wives and mothers.

While educational reform was a central goal of progressive women in the United States and Canada, the North American women's rights movement also became strongly intertwined with the cause of another disenfranchised group: slaves. For instance, the abolition of slavery and women's liberation were influentially linked by transatlantic reformer Fanny Wright. Following a visit to the United States in 1818, Wright had published a celebrated study of American democracy in which she called for parliamentary reform in England, *Views of Society and Manners in America* (1821). Wright returned to America in 1825, purchased two thousand acres in Tennessee, and started "Nashoba"—a community in which she offered land to slaves whose freedom she purchased from neighboring farmers. Her *Course of Popular Lectures*, published four years later, centered on the connections between those disenfranchised by gender and race. Wright argued for the abolition of slavery, better national education, increased use and distribution of birth control, and the vote for women. The connection between race and gender also led Wright to make a courageous call for miscegenation, marriage between races, which she saw as an important method for breaking down the racial barriers in America.

By mid-century, abolition and women's rights were inextricably connected for many political reformers in the United States. Abolitionists Lucretia Mott and Elizabeth Cady Stanton attended the Anti-Slavery Society convention in London in 1840, where both hoped to speak but were denied the opportunity and required to sit behind a curtain. The two Quakers pledged to hold their own convention, and in 1848 they convened a meeting at Seneca Falls in New York, which was attended by the freed slave and popular abolitionist Frederick Douglass and 240 other delegates. There, Stanton delivered her *Declaration of Sentiments*, modeled after the *Declaration of Independence* (1776), in which she made the bold statement that "The history of mankind is a history of repeated injuries and usurpations on the part of man toward woman, having in direct object the establishment of an absolute tyranny over her." She argued that women's rights were human rights: "all men and women are created equal; that they are endowed by their Creator with certain inalienable rights." Similarly, the escaped slave Sojourner Truth connected abolition and feminism in her address *Ain't I A Woman?* to the Women's Convention in Akron, Ohio, in 1851:

That man over there says that women need to be helped into carriages, and lifted over ditches, and to have the best place everywhere. Nobody ever helps me into carriages, or over mud-puddles, or gives me any best place! And ain't I a woman? Look at me! Look at my arm! I have ploughed and planted, and gathered into barns, and no man could head me! And ain't I a woman? I could work as much and eat as much as a man—when I could get it—and bear the lash as well! And ain't I a woman? I have borne thirteen children, and seen most all sold off to slavery, and when I cried out with my mother's grief, none but Jesus heard me! And ain't I a woman?

The Seneca Falls convention and the multiracial feminist movement sparked significant changes, beginning with New York's Married Women's Property Act of 1848, which protected the individual rights of married women, allowed them to maintain custody of children in cases of divorce, and granted them the right to own property. (Other states soon passed similar legislation.) Building on this momentum, Cady Stanton formed the National Woman Suffrage Association in 1869 to begin a comprehensive campaign for women's political enfranchisement. In the same year, when the territory of Wyoming was formed, legislators permitted women to vote in that state. Other states would follow suit, but the Nineteenth Amendment, granting women over thirty the right to vote, was not passed until 1920.

Judith Sargent Murray
1751–1820

Judith Sargent Murray was able to share her brother's tutor and thus received the type of thorough education that sexism denied to almost all women of her day. She began writing verses at an early age, and her second husband, Reverend John Murray, the Universalist minister of her native Gloucester, Massachusetts, encouraged her writing. Her poetry was first published in the *Massachusetts Magazine*, which also printed a series of her essays called "The Gleaner" (a title shared by the 1798 three-volume collection of her works). Murray also wrote plays (*The Medium, or Virtue Triumphant* and *The Traveller Returned*) for Boston theaters, but these did not equal the achievement of her essays and verse. She outlived her husband, who died in 1815, and she passed away five years later at the Mississippi home of her daughter, Julia Maria Murray. "On the Equality of the Sexes" (1792), the first American feminist manifesto, makes a confidently rationalist plea for women's right to education. The essay unequivocally demonstrates its author's rationality and humanity through the use of rigorously logical argumentation, then delves into a sharply sarcastic parody of the Adam and Eve tale.

On the Equality of the Sexes

That minds are not alike, full well I know,
This truth each day's experience will show;
To heights surprising some great spirits soar,
With inborn strength mysterious depths explore;
Their eager gaze surveys the path of light,   5
Confest it stood to Newton's[1] piercing sight.
    Deep science, like a bashful maid retires,

---

1. Sir Isaac Newton (1642–1727), English scientist and philosopher.

And but the *ardent* breast her worth inspires;
By perseverance the coy fair is won.
And Genius, led by Study, wears the crown.   10
    But some there are who wish not to improve,
Who never can the path of knowledge love,
Whose souls almost with the dull body one,
With anxious care each mental pleasure shun;
Weak is the level'd, enervated mind,   15
And but while here to vegetate design'd.
The torpid spirit mingling with its clod,
Can scarcely boast its origin from God;
Stupidly dull—they move progressing on—
They eat, and drink, and all their work is done.   20
While others, emulous of sweet applause,
Industrious seek for each event a cause,
Tracing the hidden springs whence knowledge flows,
Which nature all in beauteous order shows.
    Yet cannot I their sentiments imbibe,   25
Who this distinction to the sex ascribe,
As if a woman's form must needs enrol,
A weak, servile, an inferior soul;
And that the guise of man must still proclaim,
Greatness of mind, and him, to be the same: 30
Yet as the hours revolve fair proofs arise,
Which the bright wreath of growing fame supplies;
And in past times some men have *sunk so low*,
That female records nothing *less* can show.
But imbecility is still confin'd,   35
And by the lordly sex to us consign'd;
They rob us of the power t' improve,
And then declare we only trifles love;
Yet haste the era, when the world shall know,
That such distinctions only dwell below;   40
The soul unfetter'd, to no sex confin'd,
Was for the abodes of cloudless day design'd.
    Mean time we emulate their manly fires,
Though erudition all their thoughts inspires,
Yet nature with *equality* imparts,   45
And *noble passions*, swell e'en *female hearts*.

Is it upon mature consideration we adopt the idea, that nature is thus partial in her
distributions? Is it indeed a fact, that she hath yielded to one half of the human
species so unquestionable a mental superiority? I know that to both sexes elevated
understandings, and the reverse, are common. But, suffer me to ask, in what the
minds of females are so notoriously deficient, or unequal. May not the intellectual
powers be ranged under these four heads—imagination, reason, memory and judg-

ment. The province of imagination hath long since been surrendered up to us, and we have been crowned undoubted sovereigns of the regions of fancy. Invention is perhaps the most arduous effort of the mind; this branch of imagination hath been particularly ceded to us, and we have been time out of mind invested with that creative faculty. Observe the variety of fashions (here I bar the contemptuous smile) which distinguish and adorn the female world; how continually are they changing, insomuch that they almost render the wise man's assertion problematical, and we are ready to say, *there is something new under the sun*.[2] Now what a playfulness, what an exuberance of fancy, what strength of inventive imagination, doth this continual variation discover? Again, it hath been observed, that if the turpitude of the conduct of our sex, hath been ever so enormous, so extremely ready are we, that the very first thought presents us with an apology, so plausible, as to produce our actions even in an amiable light. Another instance of our creative powers, is our talent for slander; how ingenious are we at inventive scandal? what a formidable story can we in a moment fabricate merely from the force of a prolifick imagination? how many reputations, in the fertile brain of a female, have been utterly despoiled? how industrious are we at improving a hint? suspicion how easily do we convert into conviction, and conviction, embellished by the power of eloquence, stalks abroad to the surprise and confusion of unsuspecting innocence. Perhaps it will be asked if I furnish these facts as instances of excellency in our sex. Certainly not; but as proofs of a creative faculty, of a lively imagination. Assuredly great activity of mind is thereby discovered, and was this activity properly directed, what beneficial effects would follow. Is the needle and kitchen sufficient to employ the operations of a soul thus organized? I should conceive not. Nay, it is a truth that those very departments leave the intelligent principle vacant, and at liberty for speculation. Are we deficient in reason? we can only reason from what we know, and if an opportunity of acquiring knowledge hath been denied us, the inferiority of our sex cannot fairly be deduced from thence. Memory, I believe, will be allowed us in common, since every one's experience must testify, that a loquacious old woman is as frequently met with, as a communicative old man; their subjects are alike drawn from the fund of other times, and the transactions of their youth, or of maturer life, entertain, or perhaps fatigue you, in the evening of their lives. "But our judgment is not so strong—we do not distinguish so well."— Yet it may be questioned, from what doth this superiority, in this determining faculty of the soul proceed. May we not trace its source in the difference of education, and continued advantages? Will it be said that the judgment of a male of two years old, is more sage than that of a female's of the same age? I believe the reverse is generally observed to be true. But from that period what partiality! how is the one exalted, and the other depressed, by the contrary modes of education which are adopted! the one is taught to aspire, and the other is early confined and limited. As their years increase, the sister must be wholly domesticated, while the brother is led by the hand through all the flowery paths of science. Grant that their minds are by nature equal, yet who shall wonder at the *apparent* superiority, if indeed custom becomes *second nature*; nay if it taketh place of nature, and that it doth the experience of each day will evince. At length arrived at womanhood, the uncultivated

---

2. Paraphrases Ecclesiastes 1.8.

fair one feels a void, which the employments allotted her are by no means capable of filling. What can she do? to books she may not apply; or if she doth, *to those only of the novel kind*, lest she merit the appellation of a *learned lady*; and what ideas have been affixed to this term, the observation of many can testify. Fashion, scandal, and sometimes what is still more reprehensible, are then called in to her relief; and who can say to what lengths the liberties she takes may proceed. Meantime she herself is most unhappy; she feels the want of a cultivated mind. Is she single, she in vain seeks to fill up time from sexual employments or amusements. Is she united to a person whose soul nature made equal to her own, education hath set him so far above her, that in those entertainments which are productive of such rational felicity, she is not qualified to accompany him. She experiences a mortifying consciousness of inferiority, which embitters every enjoyment. Doth the person to whom her adverse fate hath consigned her, possess a mind incapable of improvement, she is equally wretched, in being so closely connected with an individual whom she cannot but despise. Now, was she permitted the same instructors as her brother, (with an eye however to their particular departments) for the employment of a rational mind an ample field would be opened. In astronomy she might catch a glimpse of the immensity of the Deity, and thence she would form amazing conceptions of the august and supreme Intelligence. In geography she would admire Jehovah in the midst of his benevolence; thus adapting this globe to the various wants and amusements of its inhabitants. In natural philosophy she would adore the infinite majesty of heaven, clothed in condescension; and as she traversed the reptile world, she would hail the goodness of a creating God. A mind, thus filled, would have little room for the trifles with which our sex are, with too much justice, accused of amusing themselves, and they would thus be rendered fit companions for those, who should one day wear them as their crown. Fashions, in their variety, would then give place to conjectures, which might perhaps conduce to the improvement of the literary world; and there would be no leisure for slander or detraction. Reputation would not then be blasted, but serious speculations would occupy the lively imaginations of the sex. Unnecessary visits would be precluded, and that custom would only be indulged by way of relaxation, or to answer the demands of consanguinity and friendship. Females would become discreet, their judgments would be invigorated, and their partners for life being circumspectly chosen, an unhappy Hymen[3] would then be as rare, as is now the reverse.

Will it be urged that those acquirements would supersede our domestick duties. I answer that every requisite in female economy[4] is easily attained; and, with truth I can add, that when once attained, they require no further *mental attention*. Nay, while we are pursuing the needle, or the superintendency of the family, I repeat, that our minds are at full liberty for reflection; that imagination may exert itself in full vigor; and that if a just foundation is early laid, our ideas will then be worthy of rational beings. If we were industrious we might easily find time to arrange them upon paper, or should avocations press too hard for such an indulgence, the hours allotted for conversation would at least become more refined and rational. Should it still be vociferated, "Your domestick employments are sufficient"—I would calmly ask, is it reasonable, that a candidate for immortality, for the joys of heaven, an intelligent being, who is to spend an eternity in

---

3. Greek god of marriage.   4. Housekeeping.

contemplating the works of Deity, should at present be so degraded, as to be allowed no other ideas, than those which are suggested by the mechanism of a pudding, or the sewing the seams of a garment? Pity that all such censures of female improvement do not go one step further, and deny their future existence; to be consistent they surely ought.

Yes, ye lordly, ye haughty sex, our souls are by nature *equal* to yours; the same breath of God animates, enlivens, and invigorates us; and that we are not fallen lower than yourselves, let those witness who have greatly towered above the various discouragements by which they have been so heavily oppressed; and though I am unacquainted with the list of celebrated characters on either side, yet from the observations I have made in the contracted circle in which I have moved, I dare confidently believe, that from the commencement of time to the present day, there hath been as many females, as males, who, by the *mere force of natural powers*, have merited the crown of applause; who, *thus unassisted*, have seized the wreath of fame. I know there are who assert, that as the animal powers of the one sex are superiour, of course their mental faculties also must be stronger; thus attributing strength of mind to the transient organization of this earth born tenement. But if this reasoning is just, man must be content to yield the palm to many of the brute creation, since by not a few of his brethren of the field, he is far surpassed in bodily strength. Moreover, was this argument admitted, it would prove too much, for occular demonstration evinceth, that there are many robust masculine ladies, and effeminate gentlemen. Yet I fancy that Mr. Pope,[5] though clogged with an enervated body, and distinguished by a diminutive stature, could nevertheless lay claim to greatness of soul; and perhaps there are many other instances which might be adduced to combat so unphilosophical an opinion. Do we not often see, that when the clay built tabernacle[6] is well nigh dissolved, when it is just ready to mingle with the parent soil, the immortal inhabitant aspires to, and even attaineth heights the most sublime, and which were before wholly unexplored. Besides, were we to grant that animal strength proved any thing, taking into consideration the accustomed impartiality of nature, we should be induced to imagine, that she had invested the female mind with superiour strength as an equivalent for the bodily powers of man. But waving this however palpable advantage, for *equality only*, we wish to contend.

I am aware that there are many passages in the sacred oracles which seem to give the advantage to the other sex; but I consider all these as wholly metaphorical. Thus David was a man after God's own heart, yet see him enervated by his licentious passions! behold him following Uriah[7] to the death, and shew me wherein could consist the immaculate Being's complacency. Listen to the curses which Job bestoweth upon the day of his nativity,[8] and tell me where is his perfection, where his patience—*literally* it existed not. David and Job were types of him who was to come[9]; and the superiority of man, as exhibited in scripture, being also emblematical, all arguments deduced from thence, of course fall to the ground. The exquisite delicacy of the female mind proclaimeth the exactness of its texture, while its nice sense of honour announceth its innate, its native grandeur. And indeed, in one respect, the preeminence seems to be tacitly allowed us, for after an education which limits and confines, and employments and recreations which naturally tend to enervate the body, and debilitate the mind; after we have from early youth been adorned with ribbons, and

5. Alexander Pope (1688–1744), English poet.   6. The body.   7. 2 Samuel 11.3–27. Uriah was sent to death by his wife's lover.   8. Job 3.1–12.   9. King David and Job foreshadowed the sufferings of Jesus.

other gewgaws, dressed out like the ancient victims previous to a sacrifice, being taught by the care of our parents in collecting the most showy materials that the ornamenting our exteriour ought to be the principal object of our attention; after, I say, fifteen years thus spent, we are introduced into the world, amid the united adulation of every beholder. Praise is sweet to the soul; we are immediately intoxicated by large draughts of flattery, which being plentifully administered, is to the pride of our hearts the most acceptable incense. It is expected that with the other sex we should commence immediate war, and that we should triumph over the machinations of the most artful. We must be constantly upon our guard; prudence and discretion must be our characteristicks; and we must rise superiour to, and obtain a complete victory over those who have been long adding to the native strength of their minds, by an unremitted study of men and books, and who have, moreover, conceived from the loose characters which they have been portrayed in the extensive variety of their reading, a most contemptible opinion of the sex. Thus unequal, we are, notwithstanding, forced to the combat, and the infamy which is consequent upon the smallest deviation in our conduct, proclaims the high idea which was formed of our native strength; and thus, indirectly at least, is the preference acknowledged to be our due. And if we are allowed an equality of acquirement, let serious studies equally employ our minds, and we will bid our souls arise to equal strength. We will meet upon even ground, the despot man; we will rush with alacrity to the combat, and, crowned by success, we shall then answer the exalted expectations which are formed. Though sensibility, soft compassion, and gentle commiseration, are inmates in the female bosom, yet against every deep laid art, altogether fearless of the event, we will set them in array; for assuredly the wreath of victory will encircle the spotless brow. If we meet an equal, a sensible friend, we will reward him with the hand of amity, and through life we will be assiduous to promote his happiness; but from every deep laid scheme for our ruin, retiring into ourselves, amid the flowery paths of science, we will indulge in all the refined and sentimental pleasures of contemplation. And should it still be urged, that the studies thus insisted upon would interfere with our more peculiar department,[10] I must further reply, that *early hours*, and close application, will do wonders; and to her who is from the first dawn of reason taught to fill up time rationally, both the requisites will be easy. I grant that niggard[11] fortune is too generally unfriendly to the mind; and that much of that valuable treasure, time, is necessarily expended upon the wants of the body; but it should be remembered, that in embarrassed circumstances our companions have as little leisure for literary improvement, as is afforded to us; for most certainly their provident care is at least as requisite as our exertions. Nay, we have even more leisure for sedentary pleasures, as our avocations are more retired, much less laborious, and, as hath been observed, by no means require that avidity of attention which is proper to the employments of the other sex. In high life, or, in other words, where the parties are in possession of affluence, the objection respecting time is wholly obviated, and of course falls to the ground; and it may also be repeated, that many of those hours which are at present swallowed up in fashion and scandal, might be redeemed, were we habituated to useful reflections. But in one respect, O ye arbiters of our fate! we confess that the superiority is undubitably yours; you are by nature formed for our protectors; we pretend not to vie with you in

10. Duties as women.   11. Stingy.

bodily strength; upon this point we will never contend for victory. Shield us then, we beseech you, from external evils, and in return we will transact *your* domestick affairs. Yes, *your*, for are you not equally interested in those matters with ourselves? Is not the elegancy of neatness as agreeable to your sight as to ours; is not the well favoured viand equally delightful to your taste; and doth not your sense of hearing suffer as much, from the discordant sounds prevalent in an ill regulated family, produced by the voices of children and many *et ceteras*?

CONSTANTIA.[12]

By way of supplement to the foregoing pages, I subjoin the following extract from a letter, wrote to a friend in the December of 1780.

And now assist me, O thou genius of my sex, while I undertake the arduous task of endeavouring to combat that vulgar, that almost universal errour, which hath, it seems, enlisted even Mr. P— under its banners. The superiority of your sex hath, I grant, been time out of mind esteemed a truth incontrovertible; in consequence of which persuasion, every plan of education hath been calculated to establish this favourite tent. Not long since; weak and presuming as I was, I amused myself with selecting some arguments from nature, reason, and experience, against this so generally received idea. I confess that to sacred testimonies[13] I had not recourse. I held them to be merely metaphorical, and thus regarding them, I could not persuade myself that there was any propriety in bringing them to decide in this *very important debate*. However, as you, sir, confine yourself entirely to the sacred oracles, I mean to bend the whole of my artillery against those supposed proofs, which you have from thence provided, and from which you have formed an intrenchment *apparently* so invulnerable. And first, to begin with our great progenitors[14]; but here, suffer me to premise, that it is for mental strength I mean to contend, for with respect to animal powers, I yield them undisputed to that sex, which enjoys them in common with the lion, the tyger, and many other beasts of prey; therefore your observations respecting the *rib under the arm, at a distance from the head, &c. &c.* in no sort militate against my view.[15] Well, but the woman was first in the transgression. Strange how blind *self love* renders you men; were you not wholly absorbed in a partial admiration of your own abilities, you would long since have acknowledged the force of what I am now going to urge. It is true some ignoramuses have absurdly enough informed us, that the beauteous fair of paradise, was seduced from her obedience, by a malignant demon, *in the guise of a baleful serpent*; but we, who are better informed, know that the fallen spirit presented himself to her view, *a shining angel still*; for thus, saith the cricks in the Hebrew tongue, ought the word to be rendered.[16] Let us examine her motive—Hark! the seraph declares that she shall attain a perfection of knowledge; for is there aught which is not comprehended under one or other of the terms *good* and *evil*. It doth not appear that she was governed by any one sensual appetite; but merely by a desire of adorning her mind; a laudable ambition fired her soul, and a thirst for knowledge impelled the predilection so fatal in its consequences. Adam could not plead the same deception;

---

12. Murray's pseudonym.   13. Scripture.   14. Ancestors.   15. See Genesis 2.22.   16. Isaiah 14.12 refers to Satan as "Lucifer," Latin for "light carrier."

assuredly he was not deceived; nor ought we to admire his superiour strength, or wonder at his sagacity, when we so often confess that example is much more infuential than precept. His gentle partner stood before him, a melancholy instance of the direful effects of disobedience; he saw her not possessed of that wisdom which she had fondly hoped to obtain, but he beheld the once blooming female, disrobed of that innocence, which had heretofore rendered her so lovely. To him then deception became impossible, as he had proof positive of the fallacy of the argument, which the deceiver had suggested. What then could be his inducement to burst the barriers, and to fly directly in the face of that command, which *immediately* from the mouth of deity *he* had received, since, I say, he could not plead that fascinating stimulous, the accumulation of knowledge, as indisputable conviction was so visibly portrayed before him. What mighty cause impelled him to sacrifice myriads of beings yet unborn, and by one impious act, which *he saw* would be productive of such fatal effects, entail undistinguished ruin upon a race of beings, which he was yet to produce. Blush, ye vaunters of fortitude; ye boasters of resolution; ye haughty lords of the creation; blush when ye remember, that he was influenced by no other motive than a bare pusillanimous attachment to a woman! by sentiments so exquisitely soft, that all his sons have, from that period, when they have designed to degrade them, described as highly feminine. Thus it should seem, that all the arts of the grand deceiver (since means adequate to the purpose are, I conceive, invariably pursued) were requisite to mislead our general mother, while the father of mankind forfeited his own, and relinquished the happiness of posterity, merely in compliance with the blandishments of a female. The subsequent subjection the apostle Paul explains as a figure; after enlarging upon the subject, he adds, "*This is a great mystery; but I speak concerning Christ and the church.*"[17] Now we know with what consummate wisdom the unerring father of eternity hath formed his plans; all the types which he hath displayed, he hath permitted *materially* to fail, in the very virtue for which *they* were famed. The reason for this is obvious, we might otherwise mistake his economy, and render that honour to the creature, which is due only to the creator. I know that Adam was a figure of him[18] who was to come. The grace contained in his figure, is the reason of my rejoicing, and while I am very far from prostrating before the shadow, I yield joyfully in all things the preeminence to the Second Federal Head.[19] Confiding faith is prefigured by Abraham, yet he exhibits a contrast to affiance, when he says of his fair companion, she is my sister.[20] Gentleness was the characterstick of Moses,[21] yet he hesitated not to reply to Jehovah himself, with unsaintlike tongue he murmured at the waters of strife, and with rash hands he break the Tables,[22] which were inscribed by the finger of divinity. David, dignified with the title of the man after God's own heart, and yet how stained was his life. Solomon was celebrated for wisdom,[23] but folly is wrote in legible characters upon his almost every action. Lastly, let us turn our eyes to man in the aggregate. He is manifested as the figure of strength, but that we may not regard him as any thing more than a figure, his soul is formed in no sort superior, but every way equal to the mind of her, who is the emblem of weakness, and whom he hails the gentle companion of his better days.

—1790

---

17. Ephesians 5.32.   18. Adam foreshadows Jesus.   19. Jesus oversees God's second covenant with his people.   20. Genesis 12.13, "affiance": marriage.   21. Numbers 12.3.   22. Tablets on which the Ten Commandments were written. Exodus 32.19.   23. 1 Kings 11.1–10.

Charlotte Dacre
1772–1825

Charlotte King's literary identity was an enticing mystery. The daughter of John King, a notorious London moneylender, occasional blackmailer, and radical writer, she published under the pseudonyms Rosa Mathilda, Rosa, and Charlotte Dacre. Charlotte and her sister, Sophia, first came to the public's attention with the 1798 publication of a volume of gothic verse, *Trifles of Helicon*. Many of the poems were republished in *Hours of Solitude* in 1805, under the name Charlotte Dacre, although by this date Charlotte had published verse in the *Morning Post* and *Morning Herald* as Rosa Mathilda (which the title page of *Hours of Solitude* notes as the author's other *nom du plume*). The frontispiece of *Hours of Solitude* is a portrait of a dark-haired, dark-eyed, fair-skinned "Rosa Mathilda"—the very image of the gothic heroine that populates the gothic novels of the late eighteenth and early nineteenth centuries.

In name and in the image attached to *Hours of Solitude*, Charlotte Dacre played cannily with public expectations of genre and literary celebrity, suggesting a more exotic pedigree than "King." Indeed, "Dacre" and "Rosa Mathilda" appeal to the gothic genre in which Dacre wrote extensively: She emphasizes sentiment and extreme sensibility in the verse of *Hours* and her gothic novels, *The Confessions of the Nun of St. Omer* (1805). The popular *Zofloya, or, The Moor* (1806) echoes the style of gothic novelist Mathew Lewis as Dacre accentuates the horrifying and the erotic. Dacre's use of "Mathilda" even echoes the name of the heroine of Lewis's successful and scandalous gothic novel *The Monk* (1796). Her work participates in the aesthetics of the Della Cruscans, a group of late eighteenth-century writers working in a similar style of emotionally charged verse, often viewed as excessive and pretentious by contemporaries.

The Female Philosopher

You tell me, fair one, that you ne'er can love,
   And seem with scorn to mock the dangerous fire;
But why, then, trait'ress, do you seek to move
   In others what *your* breast can ne'er inspire?

You tell me, you my *friend* alone will be,   5
   Yet speak of friendship in a voice so sweet,
That, while I struggle to be coldly free,
   I feel my heart with wildest throbbings beat.

Vainly indiff'rence would you bid us feel,
   While so much languor in those eyes appear;   10
Vainly the stoic's happiness reveal,
   While soft emotion all your features wear.

O, form'd for love! O, wherefore should you fly
   From the seducing charm it spreads around?
O why enshrine your soul with apathy?   15
   Or wish in frozen fetters to be bound?

Life is a darksome and a dreary day,
   The solitary wretch no pleasure knows;
Love is the star that lights him on his way,
   And guides him on to pleasure and repose.   20

But oft, forgetful of thy plan severe,
   I've seen thee fondly gaze—I've heard thee sigh;
I've mark'd thy strain of converse, sadly dear,
   While softest rapture lighten'd from thine eye.

Then have I thought some wayward youth employ'd   25
   Thy secret soul, but left thee to despair,
And oft with pleasing sorrow have enjoy'd
   The task of chasing thy corrosive care.

Yet pride must save me from a dastard love,
   A grov'ling love, that cannot hope return: 30
A soul like mine was never form'd to prove
   Those viler passions with which some can burn.

Then fear not me; for since it is thy will,
   Adhere with stubborn coolness to thy vow;
Grant me thy philosophic friendship still—   35
   I'll grant thee *mine* with all the powers I know.

—1805

Sojourner Truth
1797–1883

Sojourner Truth was one of the most forceful abolitionist and feminist speakers of the nineteenth century. For the first three decades of her life, as Isabella Baumfree, she was a slave, sold from master to master in New York. When she was emancipated along with the rest of the state's slaves in 1827, she settled in New York City, where she worked as a domestic and joined a Christian religious community led by a charismatic figure who called himself Matthias. During the depression of 1837 to 1844, a wave of intense revivalism swept the Northeast. Baumfree felt called by God to adopt the name Sojourner Truth and go on the road as a Methodist preacher. Her rhetorical power grew as she addressed huge crowds at evangelical camp meetings across the region. During a long stay at a utopian socialist community, the Northampton Association, Truth met many supporters of women's rights and learned of the abolition movement led by William Lloyd Garrison. While living at the Association, she recorded her life story, and she constructed her subsequent public identity, in *The Narrative of Sojourner Truth* (1850), with help from abolitionist Olive Gilbert, whom she met at Northampton. Truth published the book at her own expense and sold copies personally at public political gatherings and revival meetings. For the rest of her life, the proceeds from the book's sale would be a mainstay of her livelihood. In 1851, she returned to public speaking, this time as a lecturer for the abolitionist cause, touring with George Thompson, the celebrated English Parliamentary radical.

The first of her speeches for which there is a record was delivered at a women's rights convention in Akron, Ohio, in May 1851. The speech was transcribed by Francis Dana Gage, who attempted to render Truth's idiomatic speech typographically. Gage's spelling captures the way that many in Truth's audiences focused on what they saw as her authenticity rather than on the self-consciousness of her performances. It is strikingly appropriate that this first speech begins by explicitly making the political connection for which Truth has since remained the central symbol: "Wall, chilern, whar dar is so much racket dar must be somethin' out o' kilter. I tink dat 'twixt de niggers of the Souf and de womin at de Norf, all talkin' 'bout rights, de white men will be in a fix pretty soon." Truth would continue to sound this note for the rest of her long life. In 1867, following Emancipation, she attended the meeting of the American Equal Rights Association in New York City. There she argued, against the objections of former slave and abolitionist Frederick Douglass and many others, that now more than ever was the time to institute women's suffrage, for otherwise black women would simply trade one master for another.

Speech at the American Equal Rights Association, May 9–10, 1867

Mrs. Mott then introduced the venerable Sojourner Truth, who was greeted with loud cheers, after which she said:

My friends, I am rejoiced that you are glad, but I dont' know how you will feel when I get through. I come from another field—the country of the slave. They have got their liberty—so much good luck to have slavery partly destroyed; not entirely. I want it root and branch destroyed. Then we will all be free indeed. I feel that if I have to answer for the deeds done in my body just as much as a man, I have a right to have just as much as a man. There is a great stir about colored men getting their rights, but not a word about the colored women; and if colored men get their rights, and not colored women theirs, you see the colored men will be masters over the women, and it will be just as bad as it was before. So I am for keeping the thing going while things are stirring; because if we wait till it is still, it will take a great while to get it going again. White women are a great deal smarter, and know more than colored women, while colored women do not know scarcely anything. They go out washing, which is about as high as a colored woman gets, and their men go about idle, strutting up and down; and when the women come home, they ask for their money and take it all, and then scold because there is no food. I want you to consider on that, chil'n. I call you chil'n; you are somebody's chil'n, and I am old enough to be mother of all that is here. I want women to have their rights. In the Courts women have no right, no voice; nobody speaks for them. I wish woman to have her voice there among the pettifoggers. If it is not a fit place for women it is unfit for men to be there. I am above eighty years old; it is about time for me to be going. I have been forty years a slave and forty years free and would be here forty years more to have equal rights for all. I suppose I am kept here because something remains for me to do; I suppose I am yet to help to break the chain. I have done a great deal of work; as much as a man, but did not get so much pay. I used to work in the field and bind grain, keeping up with the cradler; but men doing no more, got twice as much pay; so with the German women. They work in the field and do as much work, but do not get the pay. We do as much, we eat as much, we want as much. I suppose I am about the only colored woman that goes about to speak for the rights of the colored. What we want is a little money. You men know that you get as much again as women when you write, or for what you do. When we get our rights we shall not have to come to you for money, for then we shall have money enough in our own pockets; and may be you will ask us for money. But help us now until we get it. It is a good consolation to know that when we have got this battle once fought we shall not be coming to you any more. You have been having our right so long, that you think, like a slaveholder, that you own us. I know that it is hard for one who has held the reins for so long to give up; it cuts like a knife. It will feel all the better when it closes up again. I have been in Washington about three years, seeing about these colored people. Now colored men have the right to vote; and what I want is to have colored women have the right to vote. There ought to be equal rights now more than ever, since colored people have got their freedom. I am going to talk several times while I am here; so now I will do a little singing. I have not heard any singing since I came here.

Accordingly, suiting the action to the word, Sojourner sang, "We are going home." There, children, said she, after singing, we shall rest from all our labors; first do all we have to do here. There I am determined to go, not to stop short of that beautiful place, and I do not mean to stop till I get there, and meet you there too.

—1867

Sophia Ripley
1803–1861

The forward-looking daughter of an elite Boston family, Sophia Ripley attended Margaret Fuller's celebrated conversations for women at Elizabeth Peabody's bookstore on West Street. There Ripley participated in an ethos of intense feminist inquiry into religious and philosophical traditions and social institutions. Her essay, "Woman," appeared in Fuller's Transcendentalist magazine, *The Dial*. Ripley gently ridicules the idealized image of woman as an "etherial being" (p. 366) and asks why she is expected to marry a husband and then spend "life in conforming to him, instead of moulding herself to her own ideal" (p. 367). She calls for women to be granted the full scope of human education, experience, and activity.

Ripley herself went on to become an active and central participant in the utopian socialist movement that swept New England in the 1840s. Together with her husband, George, she signed the Articles of Association for the Brook Farm Institute of Agriculture and Education, and on April 1, 1841, the Ripleys began living communally with about twenty others on a milk farm in West Roxbury. This community was designed to relieve women's domestic labor in the home by taking advantage of economies of scale in cleaning, food preparation, and childcare. The resulting free time would then be devoted to the kind of education that would allow them to achieve their full potential. When Brook Farm went bankrupt in 1846, the Ripleys moved to New York City. Sophia continued on her course of religious and intellectual experimentation by converting to Catholicism at a time when that faith was associated with working-class Irish immigrants and regarded with deep suspicion by Protestant New Englanders.

Woman

There have been no topics, for the two last years, more generally talked of than woman, and "the sphere of woman." In society, everywhere, we hear the same oft-repeated things said upon them by those who have little perception of the difficulties of the subject; and even the clergy have frequently flattered "the feebler sex," by proclaiming to them from the pulpit what lovely beings they may become, if they will only be good, quiet, and gentle, attend exclusively to their domestic duties, and the cultivation of religious feelings, which the other sex very kindly relinquish to them as their inheritance. Such preaching is very popular!

Blessed indeed would that man be, who could penetrate the difficulties of this subject, and tell the world faithfully and beautifully what new thing he has discovered about it, or what old truth he has brought to light. The poet's lovely vision of an etherial being, hovering half seen above him, in his hour of occupation, and gliding gently into his retirement, sometimes a guardian angel, sometimes an unobtrusive companion, wrapt in a silvery veil of mildest radiance, his idealized Eve or Ophelia,[1] is an exquisite picture for the eye; the sweet verse in which he tells us of her, most witching music to the ear; but she is not woman, she is only the spiritualized image of that tender class of women he loves the best,—one whom no true woman could or would become; and if the poet could ever be unkind, we should deem him most so when he reproves the sex, planted as it is, in the midst of wearing cares and perplexities, for its departure from this high, beautified ideal of his, to which he loves to give the name of woman. Woman may be soothed by his sweet numbers, but she cannot be helped by his counsels, for he knows her not as she is and must be. All adjusting of the whole sex to a sphere is vain, for no two persons naturally have the same. Character, intellect creates the sphere of each. What is individual and peculiar to each determines it. We hear a great deal everywhere of the religious duties of women. That heaven has placed man and woman in different positions, given them different starting points, (for what is the whole of life, with its varied temporal relations, but a starting point,) there can be no doubt; but religion belongs to them as beings, not as male and female. The true teacher addresses the same language to both. Christ did so, and this separation is ruinous to the highest improvement of both. Difference of position surely does not imply different qualities of head and heart, for the same qualities, as we see every day, are demanded in a variety of positions, the variety merely giving them a different direction.

As we hear a great deal in society, and from the pulpit, of the religious duties of women, so do we hear a great deal of the contemplative life they lead, or ought to lead. It seems an unknown, or at least an unacknowledged fact, that, in the spot where man throws aside his heavy responsibilities, his couch of rest is often prepared by his faithful wife, at the sacrifice of all her quiet contemplation and leisure. She is pursued into her most retired sanctuaries by petty anxieties, haunting her loneliest hours, by temptations taking her by surprise, by cares so harassing, that the most powerful talents and the most abundant intellectual and moral resources are scarce sufficient to give her strength to ward them off. If there is a

---

1. Eve: the first woman according to Christian tradition; Ophelia: a character in William Shakespeare's *Hamlet* who commits suicide when she feels ignored by the title character.

being exposed to turmoil and indurating care, it is woman, in the retirement of her own home: and if she makes peace and warmth there, it is not by her sweet religious sensibility, her gentle benevolence, her balmy tenderness, but by a strength and energy as great and untiring as leads man to battle, or supports him in the strife of the political arena, though these sturdier qualities unfold often, both in man and woman, in an atmosphere of exquisite refinement and sensibility. The gentle breeze of summer pauses to rest its wing upon the broad oak-leaf, as upon the violet's drooping flower. If woman's position did not bring out all the faculties of the soul, we might demand a higher for her; but she does not need one higher or wider than nature has given her. Very few of her sex suspect even how noble and beautiful is that which they legitimately occupy, for they are early deprived of the privilege of seeing things as they are.

In our present state of society woman possesses not; she is under possession. A dependant, except in extreme hours of peril or moral conflict, when each is left to the mercy of the unfriendly elements alone, for in every mental or physical crisis of life the Infinite has willed each soul to be alone, nothing interposing between it and himself. At times, when most a being needs protection, none but the highest can protect. Man may soothe, but he cannot shelter from, or avert the storm, however solemnly he may promise it to himself or others in the bright hours. When most needed he is most impotent.

Woman is educated with the tacit understanding, that she is only half a being, and an appendage. First, she is so to her parents, whose opinions, perhaps prejudices, are engrafted into her before she knows what an opinion is. Thus provided she enters life, and society seizes her; her faculties of observation are sharpened, often become fearfully acute, though in some sort discriminating, and are ever after so occupied with observing that she never penetrates. In the common course of events she is selected as the life-companion of some one of the other sex; because selected, she fixes her affections upon him, and hardly ventures to exercise upon him even her powers of observation. Then he creates for her a home, which should be constructed by their mutual taste and efforts. She finds him not what she expected; she is disappointed and becomes captious, complaining of woman's lot, or discouraged and crushed by it. She thinks him perfect, adopts his prejudices, adds them to her early stock, and ever defends them with his arguments; where she differs from him in taste and habits, she believes herself in the wrong and him in the right, and spends life in conforming to him, instead of moulding herself to her own ideal. Thus she loses her individuality, and never gains his respect. Her life is usually bustle and hurry, or barren order, dreary decorum and method, without vitality. Her children perhaps love her, but she is only the upper nurse; the father, the oracle. His wish is law, hers only the unavailing sigh uttered in secret. She looks out into life, finds nothing there but confusion, and congratulates herself that it is man's business, not hers, to look through it all, and find stern principle seated tranquilly at the centre of things. Is this woman's destiny? Is she to be the only adventurer, who pursues her course through life aimless, tossed upon the waves of circumstance, intoxicated by joy, panic-struck by misfortune, or stupidly receptive of it? Is she neither to soar to heaven like the lark, nor bend her way, led by an unerring guide, to climes congenial to her nature? Is she always to flutter and flutter, and at last drop into the wave? Man would not have it so, for he reveres the gently firm. Man does not ridicule nor expose to suffering the woman who aspires, he wishes not for blind reverence, but intelligent affection; not for supremacy, but to be understood; not for obedience, but companionship; it is the weak and ignorant of her own sex who brand her, but the enigma still remains unsolved, why are so many of the sex allowed to remain weak and frivolous?

The minor cares of life thronging the path of woman, demand as much reflection and clear-sightedness, and involve as much responsibility, as those of man. Why is she not encouraged to think and penetrate through externals to principles? She should be seen, after the first dreamlike years of unconscious childhood are passed, meekly and reverently questioning and encouraged to question the opinions of others, calmly contemplating beauty in all its forms, studying the harmony of life, as well as of outward nature, deciding nothing, learning all things, gradually forming her own ideal, which, like that represented in the sculptured figures of the old Persian sovereigns, should cheeringly and protectingly hover over her. Society would attract her, and then gracefully mingling in it, she should still be herself, and there find her relaxation, not her home. She should feel that our highest hours are always our lonely ones, and that nothing is good that does not prepare us for these. Beautiful and graceful forms should come before her as revelations of divine beauty, but no charm of outward grace should tempt her to recede one hair's breadth from her uncompromising demand for the noblest nature in her chosen companion, guided in her demands by what she finds within herself, seeking an answering note to her own inner melody, but not sweetly lulling herself into the belief that she has found in him the full-toned harmony of the celestial choirs. If her demand is satisfied, let her not lean, but attend on him as a watchful friend. Her own individuality should be as precious to her as his love. Let her see that the best our most sympathising friend can do for us is, to throw a genial atmosphere around us, and strew our path with golden opportunities; but our path can never be another's, and we must always walk alone. Let no drudgery degrade her high vocation of creator of a happy home. Household order must prevail, but let her ennoble it by detecting its relation to that law which keeps the planets in their course. Every new relation and every new scene should be a new page in the book of the mysteries of life, reverently and lovingly perused, but if folded down, never to be read again, it must be regarded as only the introduction to a brighter one. The faults of those she loves should never be veiled by her affection, but placed in their true relation to character by the deep insight with which she penetrates beneath them. With high heroic courage, she should measure the strength of suffering before it comes, that she may not meet it unprepared. Her life-plan should be stern, but not unyielding. Her hours, precious treasures lent to her, carefully to be protected from vulgar intrusion, but which women are constantly scattering around them, like small coin, to be picked up by every needy wayfarer. Thought should be her atmosphere; books her food; friends her occasional solace. Prosperity will not dazzle her, for her own spirit is always brighter than its sunshine, and if the deepest sorrow visits her, it will only come to lift her to a higher region, where, with all of life far beneath her, she may sit regally apart till the end.

Is this the ideal of a perfect woman, and if so, how does it differ from a perfect man?

—1841

Elizabeth Cady Stanton
1815–1902

Elizabeth Cady Stanton was one of the only girls to attend the Johnstown Academy in upstate New York, where she studied the classical languages and won second prize in Greek. Visiting her father's legal practice, she was infuriated when she heard women being told that common law not only recognized the legitimacy of social, economic, and political discrimination on the basis of sex but also provided no redress for even the most basic injustices within a marriage. Her anger was compounded when she was unable to follow her brother to Union College because of her sex. Instead, she attended Emma Willard's female seminary, one of the first women's schools to offer a full curriculum. When she married abolitionist Henry Brewster Stanton, the word "obey" was omitted from the vows, and the couple spent their honeymoon at the 1840 World Anti-Slavery Convention in London. The convention at first refused to recognize female delegates and then forced them to sit behind a curtain. In response, Stanton vowed, with Lucretia Mott, to organize a women's rights convention in the United States. That meeting finally occurred in 1848 (a year marked by revolutionary uprisings of another kind all across Europe) in Seneca Falls, New York. Stanton opened the convention by reading her "Declaration of Sentiments" to the nearly three hundred delegates (including about forty men), wryly appropriating the language and form of the Declaration of Independence in order to enumerate the specifics of women's oppression. In attendance was the great abolitionist Frederick Douglass, whose speech "The Meaning of the Fourth of July to the Negro" similarly appropriates republican rhetorical traditions. The convention adopted eleven resolutions drafted by Stanton. All carried unanimously, except a call for women's suffrage, which Douglass's eloquent support helped to pass narrowly.

Stanton spent the next half century as a writer, editor, orator, and activist, working in support of women's rights and the abolition of slavery. During the Civil War, she founded the American Equal Rights Association, which called for the enfranchisement of freedmen and all women. In 1868, she co-founded the feminist weekly *Revolution*. In 1895, she published one of her most radical and widely read works, *The Woman's Bible*, a feminist reinterpretation of scripture designed to refute biblical arguments for women's oppression. Despite the abuse to which she and the delegates to the Seneca Falls convention were subjected in the popular press, the movement for full equality they launched continues into the present.

Declaration of Sentiments

When, in the course of human events, it becomes necessary for one portion of the family of man to assume among the people of the earth a position different from that which they have hitherto occupied, but one to which the laws of nature and of nature's God entitle them, a decent respect to the opinions of mankind requires that they should declare the causes that impel them to such a course.

We hold these truths to be self-evident: that all men and women are created equal; that they are endowed by their Creator with certain inalienable rights, that among these are life, liberty, and the pursuit of happiness; that to secure these rights governments are instituted, deriving their just powers from the consent of the governed. Whenever any form of government becomes destructive of these ends, it is the right of those who suffer from it to refuse allegiance to it, and to insist upon the institution of a new government, laying its foundation on such principles, and organizing its powers in such form as to them shall seem most likely to effect their safety and happiness. Prudence, indeed, will dictate that governments long established should not be changed for light and transient causes; and accordingly, all experience hath shown that mankind are more disposed to suffer, while evils are sufferable, than to right themselves by abolishing the forms to which they were accustomed. But when a long train of abuses and usurpations, pursuing invariably the same object evinces a design to reduce them under absolute despotism, it is their duty to throw off such government, and to provide new guards for their future security. Such has been the patient sufferance of the women under this government, and such is now the necessity which constrains them to demand the equal station to which they are entitled.

The history of mankind is a history of repeated injuries and usurpations on the part of man toward woman, having in direct object the establishment of an absolute tyranny over her. To prove this, let facts be submitted to a candid world.

He has never permitted her to exercise her inalienable right to the elective franchise.

He has compelled her to submit to laws, in the formation of which she had no voice.

He has withheld from her rights which are given to the most ignorant and degraded men—both natives and foreigners.

Having deprived her of this first right of a citizen, the elective franchise, thereby leaving her without representation in the halls of legislation, he has oppressed her on all sides.

He has made her, if married, in the eye of the law, civilly dead.

He has taken from her all right in property, even to the wages she earns.

He has made her, morally, an irresponsible being, as she can commit many crimes with impunity, provided they be done in the presence of her husband. In the covenant of marriage, she is compelled to promise obedience to her husband, he becoming, to all intents and purposes, her master—the law giving him power to deprive her of her liberty, and to administer chastisement.

He has so framed the laws of divorce, as to what shall be the proper causes of divorce; in case of separation, to whom the guardianship of the children shall be given; as to be wholly regardless of the happiness of women—the law, in all cases, going upon a false supposition of the supremacy of man, and giving all power into his hands.

After depriving her of all rights as a married woman, if single and the owner of property, he has taxed her to support a government which recognizes her only when her property can be made profitable to it.

He has monopolized nearly all the profitable employments, and from those she is permitted to follow, she receives but a scanty remuneration.

He closes against her all the avenues to wealth and distinction, which he considers most honorable to himself. As a teacher of theology, medicine, or law, she is not known.

He has denied her the facilities for obtaining a thorough education—all colleges being closed against her.

He allows her in Church, as well as State, but a subordinate position, claiming Apostolic authority for her exclusion from the ministry, and, with some exceptions, from any public participation in the affairs of the Church.

He has created a false public sentiment, by giving to the world a different code of morals for men and women, by which moral delinquencies which exclude women from society, are not only tolerated but deemed of little account in man.

He has usurped the prerogative of Jehovah[1] himself, claiming it as his right to assign for her a sphere of action, when that belongs to her conscience and to her God.

---

1. A name for God.

He has endeavored, in every way that he could, to destroy her confidence in her own powers, to lessen her self-respect, and to make her willing to lead a dependent and abject life.

Now, in view of this entire disfranchisement of one-half the people of this country, their social and religious degradation,—in view of the unjust laws above mentioned, and because women do feel themselves aggrieved, oppressed, and fraudulently deprived of their most sacred rights, we insist that they have immediate admission to all the rights and privileges which belong to them as citizens of the United States.

In entering upon the great work before us, we anticipate no small amount of misconception, misrepresentation, and ridicule; but we shall use every instrumentality within our power to effect our object. We shall employ agents, circulate tracts, petition the state and national legislatures, and endeavor to enlist the pulpit and the press in our behalf. We hope this Convention will be followed by a series of Conventions, embracing every part of the country.

Firmly relying upon the final triumph of the Right and the True, we do this day affix our signatures to this declaration.

—1848

Resolutions

Whereas the great precept of nature is conceded to be, "that man shall pursue his own true and substantial happiness." Blackstone, in his Commentaries,[1] remarks, that this law of Nature being coeval with mankind, and dictated by God himself, is of course superior in obligation to any other. It is binding over all the globe, in all countries, and at all times; no human laws are of any validity if contrary to this, and such of them as are valid, derive all their force, and all their validity, and all their authority, mediately and immediately, from this original; therefore,

Resolved, That such laws as conflict, in any way, with the true and substantial happiness of woman, are contrary to the great precept of nature, and of no validity; for this is "superior in obligation to any other."

Resolved, That all laws which prevent woman from occupying such a station in society as her conscience shall dictate, or which place her in a position inferior to that of man, are contrary to the great precept of nature, and therefore of no force or authority.

Resolved, That woman is man's equal—was intended to be so by the Creator, and the highest good of the race demands that she should be recognized as such.

Resolved, That the women of this country ought to be enlightened in regard to the laws under which they live, that they may no longer publish their degradation, by declaring themselves satisfied with their present position, nor their ignorance, by asserting that they have all the rights they want.

Resolved, That inasmuch as man, while claiming for himself intellectual superiority, does not accord to woman moral superiority, it is pre-eminently his duty to encourage her to speak, and teach, as she has an opportunity, in all religious assemblies.

Resolved, That the same amount of virtue, delicacy, and refinement of behavior, that is required of woman in the social state, should also be required of man, and the same transgressions should be visited with equal severity on both man and woman.

---

1. William Blackstone (1723–1780), English jurist, author of *Commentaries on the Laws of England* (1765–1769).

Resolved, That the objection of indelicacy and impropriety, which is so often brought against woman when she addresses a public audience, comes with a very ill-grace from those who encourage, by their attendance, her appearance on the stage, in the concert, or in the feats of the circus.

Resolved, That woman has too long rested satisfied in the circumscribed limits which corrupt customs and a perverted application of the Scriptures have marked out for her, and that it is time she should move in the enlarged sphere which her great Creator has assigned her.

Resolved, That it is the duty of the women of this country to secure to themselves their sacred right to the elective franchise.

Resolved, That the equality of human rights results necessarily from the fact of the identity of the race in capabilities and responsibilities.

Resolved, therefore, That, being invested by the Creator with the same capabilities, and the same consciousness of responsibility for their exercise, it is demonstrably the right and duty of woman, equally with man, to promote every righteous cause, by every righteous means; and especially in regard to the great subjects of morale and religion, it is self-evidently her right to participate with her brother in teaching them, both in private and in public, by writing and by speaking, by any instrumentalities proper to be used, and in any assemblies proper to be held; and this being a self-evident truth, growing out of the divinely implanted principles of human nature, any custom or authority adverse to it, whether modern or wearing the hoary sanction of antiquity, is to be regarded as a self-evident falsehood, and at war with mankind.

—1848

END OF TRANSATLANTIC EXCHANGES

Mary Robinson
1758–1800

When Mary Darby was nine years old, her father left Bristol, England, for Labrador (with his mistress) to establish a whale fishery. The business folded within ten years, and he served in the Russian navy until his death in 1786. His infrequent support of Mrs. Darby during this period made life difficult for the family, and they eventually relocated to London. The change was significant, since Mary had to withdraw from a girl's school run by Hannah More and her sisters in Bristol. The subsequent events of Mary's personal and professional life in London rival the spectacular life of Lord Byron.

At age fifteen, Mary wed Thomas Robinson, a legal clerk, partly under pressure from her mother, who saw the match as a way to establish financial security for the whole family. Instead, Thomas's gambling addiction ruined them, and the couple spent more than a year in debtor's prison with their infant daughter. Mary began writing verse there, and her first collection of poetry, *Poems*, appeared in 1775.

The following year, Robinson's life took a dramatic turn. Renowned for her beauty, the sixteen-year-old accepted the invitation of David Garrick, one of the leading actors of the day and manager of the successful Drury Lane Theatre, to act. She had auditioned for Garrick in

1774, before the stint in prison, and, in December 1776, she debuted as Juliet in Shakespeare's *Romeo and Juliet*. In four highly successful seasons, she performed in thirty-six plays, one of which, a Royal performance, brought her to the attention of the Prince of Wales (later crowned as George IV) in 1779. He was smitten. The Prince and Robinson began a yearlong affair that ended in scandal: Tongues wagged and Robinson, the subject of much gossip, fled to France for six months. The Prince's pledge of £20,000 if she engaged in the affair was first retracted, then reduced to a £500 annual allowance. Robinson resumed her acting career upon her return to England, but a miscarriage in 1783 left her legs temporarily paralyzed, a condition from which she never fully recovered.

Robinson was equally prolific and flamboyant in her career as a poet. She steadily produced volumes of verse while acting. Two more volumes of *Poems* appeared in 1791 and 1794, and a sequence of highly erotic love sonnets, *Sappho and Phaon*, in 1796. Her style during this period was influenced by her correspondence with Robert Merry, the founder of the Society Della Crusca Florence in 1790. The poetry-filled epistles they exchanged were characteristic of the Della Cruscan style: highly artificial works (poetry for poetry's sake) that were rich in image and metaphor, often witty and erotic. The 1800 volume *Lyrical Tales* saw Robinson's range of interests expanded significantly, moving in tone and subject matter from the sometimes frivolous (a comedic poem about a cat) to the truly serious (the slavery of "The Negro Girl"). Her *Poetical Works*, published posthumously in 1806, includes "To the Poet Coleridge," which offers a rare intertextual glimpse of Coleridge's "Kubla Khan," a poem that stood in manuscript from 1798 to 1816, though he read it frequently to friends, including Robinson.

from Sappho and Phaon: In a Series of Legitimate Sonnets

Sappho, whom the ancients distinguished by the title of the TENTH MUSE, was born at Mytilene in the island of Lesbos,[1] six hundred years before the Christian era. As no particulars have been transmitted to posterity, respecting the origin of her family, it is most likely she derived but little consequence from birth or connections. At an early period of her life she was wedded to Cercolus, a native of the isle of Andros; he was possessed of considerable wealth, and though the Lesbian Muse is said to have been sparingly gifted with beauty, he became enamoured of her, more perhaps on account of mental, than personal charms. By this union she is said to have given birth to a daughter; but Cercolus leaving her, while young, in a state of widowhood, she never after could be prevailed on to marry.

The Fame which her genius spread even to the remotest parts of the earth, excited the envy of some writers who endeavoured to throw over her private character, a shade, which shrunk before the brilliancy of her poetical talents. Her soul was replete with harmony; that harmony which neither art nor study can acquire; she felt the intuitive superiority, and to the Muses she paid unbounded adoration.

The Mytilenians held her poetry in such high veneration, and were so sensible of the honour conferred on the country which gave her birth, that they coined money with the impression of her head; and at the time of her death, paid tribute to her memory, such as was offered to sovereigns only.

The story of Antiochus[2] has been related as an unequivocal proof of Sappho's skill in discovering, and powers of describing the passions of the human mind. That prince is said to have entertained a fatal affection for his mother-in-law Stratonice; which, though he endeavoured to subdue it's influence, preyed upon his frame, and

---

1. A Greek island.   2. King of Syria (d. 163 BC).

after many ineffectual struggles, at length reduced him to extreme danger. His physicians marked the symptoms attending his malady, and found them so exactly correspond with Sappho's delineation of the tender passion, that they did not hesitate to form a decisive opinion on the cause, which had produced so perilous an effect.

That Sappho was not insensible to the feelings she so well described, is evident in her writings: but it was scarcely possible, that a mind so exquisitely tender, so sublimely gifted, should escape those fascinations which even apathy itself has been awakened to acknowledge.

The scarce specimens now extant, from the pen of the Grecian Muse, have by the most competent judges been esteemed as the standard for the pathetic, the glowing, and the amatory. The ode, which has been so highly estimated, is written in a measure distinguished by the title of the Sapphic.[3] POPE made it his model in his juvenile production, beginning—

Happy the man—whose wish and care—[4]

Addison was of opinion, that the writings of Sappho were replete with such fascinating beauties, and adorned with such a vivid glow of sensibility, that, probably, had they been preserved entire, it would have been dangerous to have perused them. They possessed none of the artificial decorations of a feigned passion; they were the genuine effusions of a supremely enlightened soul, labouring to subdue a fatal enchantment; and vainly opposing the conscious pride of illustrious fame, against the warm susceptibility of a generous bosom.

Though few stanzas from the pen of the Lesbian poetess have darted through the shades of oblivion: yet, those that remain are so exquisitely touching and beautiful, that they prove beyond dispute the taste, feeling, and inspiration of the mind which produced them. In examining the curiosities of antiquity, we look to the perfections, and not the magnitude of those reliques, which have been preserved amidst the wrecks of time: as the smallest gem that bears the fine touches of a master, surpasses the loftiest fabric reared by the labours of false taste, so the precious fragments of the immortal Sappho, will be admired, when the voluminous productions of inferior poets are mouldered into dust.

When it is considered, that the few specimens we have of the poems of the Grecian Muse, have passed through three and twenty centuries, and consequently through the hands of innumerable translators: and when it is known that Envy frequently delights in the base occupation of depreciating merit which it cannot aspire to emulate; it may be conjectured, that some passages are erroneously given to posterity, either by ignorance or design. Sappho, whose fame beamed round her with the superior effulgence which her works had created, knew that she was writing for future ages: it is not therefore natural that she should produce any composition which might tend to tarnish her reputation, or to lessen that celebrity which it was the labour of her life to consecrate. The delicacy of her sentiments cannot find a more eloquent advocate than in her own effusions; she is said to have commended in the most animated panegyric, the virtues of her brother Lanychus; and with the most pointed and severe censure, to have contemned the passion which her brother Charaxus enter-

---

3. Sapphic verse is written in quatrains in which the first three lines have eleven syllables and the fourth line has five.
4. Alexander Pope (1688–1744), "Ode to Solitude" (1817).

tained for the beautiful Rhodope.[5] If her writings were, in some instances, too glowing for the fastidious refinement of modern times; let it be her excuse, and the honour of her country, that the liberal education of the Greeks was such, as inspired them with an unprejudiced enthusiasm for the works of genius: and that when they paid adoration to Sappho, they idolized the MUSE, and not the WOMAN.

I shall conclude this account with an extract from the works of the learned and enlightened ABBE BARTHELEMI; at once the vindication and eulogy of the Grecian Poetess.

SAPPHO undertook to inspire the Lesbian women with a taste for literature; many of them received instructions from her, and foreign women increased the number of her disciples. She loved them to excess, because it was impossible for her to love otherwise; and she expressed her tenderness in all the violence of passion: your surprize at this will cease, when you are acquainted with the extreme sensibility of the Greeks; and discover, that amongst them the most innocent connections often borrow the impassioned language of love.

A certain facility of manners, she possessed; and the warmth of her expressions were but too well calculated to expose her to the hatred of some women of distinction, humbled by her superiority; and the jealousy of some of her disciples, who happened not to be the objects of her preference. To this hatred she replied by truths and irony, which completely exasperated her enemies. She repaired to Sicily, where a statue was erected to her; it was sculptured by SILANION, one of the most celebrated staturists of his time. The sensibility of SAPPHO was extreme! she loved PHAON, who forsook her; after various efforts to bring him back, she took the leap of Leucata, and perished in the waves!

Death has not obliterated the stain imprinted on her character; for ENVY, which fastens on ILLUSTRIOUS NAMES, does not expire; but bequeaths her aspersions to that calumny which NEVER DIES.

Several Grecian women have cultivated POETRY, with success, but none have hitherto attained to the excellence of SAPPHO. And among other poets, there are few, indeed, who have surpassed her.

Sonnet IV

Why, when I gaze on Phaon's beauteous eyes,
　　Why does each thought in wild disorder stray?
　　Why does each fainting faculty decay,
And my chill'd breast in throbbing tumults rise?
Mute, on the ground my lyre neglected lies,　　　　　　　　　　　　5
　　The Muse forgot, and lost the melting lay;
　　My down-cast looks, my faultering lips betray,
That stung by hopeless passion,—Sappho dies!
　　Now, on a bank of cypress let me rest;
Come, tuneful maids, ye pupils of my care,　　　　　　　　　　　　10
　　Come with your dulcet numbers soothe my breast;
And, as the soft vibrations float on air,
　　Let pity waft my spirit to the blest,
To mock the barb'rous triumphs of despair!

---

5. Lanychus was renowned for his physical beauty. Charaxus bought the slave, Rhodopis, his lover, angering Sappho.

Sonnet XIV

Come, soft Aeolian harp,[6] while zephyr plays
  Along the meek vibration of thy strings,
  As twilight's hand her modest mantle brings,
Blending with sober grey, the western blaze!
O! prompt my Phaon's dreams with tend'rest lays,   5
  Ere night o'ershade thee with its humid wings,
  While the lorn Philomel[7] his sorrow sings
In leafy cradle, red with parting rays!
  Slow let thy dulcet tones on ether glide,
So steals the murmur of the am'rous dove;   10
  The mazy legions swarm on ev'ry side,
To lulling sounds the sunny people move!
  Let not the wise their little world deride,
The smallest sting can wound the breast of Love.

Sonnet XXVII

Oh! ye bright Stars! that on the Ebon fields
  Of Heav'n's vast empire, trembling seem to stand;
  'Till rosy morn unlocks her portal bland,
Where the proud Sun his fiery banner wields!
To flames, less fierce than mine, your lustre yields,   5
  And pow'rs more strong my countless tears command;
  Love strikes the feeling heart with ruthless hand,
And only spares the breast which dullness shields.
  Since, then, capricious nature but bestows
The fine affections of the soul, to prove   10
  A keener sense of desolating woes,
Far, far from me the empty boast remove;
  If bliss from coldness, pain from passion flows,
Ah! who would wish to feel, or learn to love?

Sonnet XXX

O'er the tall cliff that bounds the billowy main
  Shad'wing the surge that sweeps the lonely strand,
  While the thin vapours break along the sand,
Day's harbinger unfolds the liquid plain.
The rude Sea murmurs, mournful as the strain   5
  That love-lorn mistrels strike with trembling hand,
  While from their green beds rise the Syren[8] band
With tongues aërial to repeat my pain!
  The vessel rocks beside the pebbly shore,
The foamy curls its gaudy trappings lave;   10
  Oh! Bark propitious! bear me gently o'er,

---

6. A stringed instrument stirred by breezes.   7. A nightingale.   8. Mythical sea nymphs who lured ships to peril by singing.

Breathe soft, ye winds; rise slow, O! swelling wave!
   Lesbos; these eyes shall meet thy sands no more:
I fly, to seek my Lover, or my Grave!

Sonnet XXXIII

I WAKE! delusive phantoms hence, away!
   Tempt not the weakness of a lover's breast;
   The softest breeze can shake the halcyon's[9] nest,
And lightest clouds o'er cast the dawning ray!
'Twas but a vision! Now, the star of day   5
   Peers, like a gem on Aetna's[10] burning crest!
   Welcome, ye Hills, with golden vintage drest;
Sicilian forests brown, and vallies gay!
   A mournful stranger, from the Lesbian Isle,
Not strange, in loftiest eulogy of Song!   10
   She, who could teach the Stoic's cheek to smile,
Thaw the cold heart, and chain the wond'ring throng,
   Can find no balm, love's sorrows to beguile;
Ah! Sorrows known too soon! and felt too long!

                          —1796

The Negro Girl

I

Dark was the dawn, and o'er the deep
   The boist'rous whirlwinds blew;
The Sea-bird wheel'd its circling sweep,
   And all was drear to view—
When on the beach that binds the western shore   5
The love-lorn ZELMA stood, list'ning the tempest's roar.

II

Her eager Eyes beheld the main,
   While on her DRACO dear
She madly call'd, but call'd in vain,
   No sound could DRACO hear,   10
Save the shrill yelling of the fateful blast,
While ev'ry Seaman's heart, quick shudder'd as it past.

III

White were the billows, wide display'd
   The clouds were black and low;
The Bittern shriek'd, a gliding shade   15
   Seem'd o'er the waves to go!

---

9. A bird of prey.   10. An active volcano in Italy.

The livid flash illum'd the clam'rous main,
While ZELMA pour'd, unmark'd, her melancholy strain.

IV

"Be still!" she cried, "loud tempest cease!
  O! spare the gallant souls: 20
The thunder rolls—the winds increase—
  The Sea, like mountains, rolls!
While, from the deck, the storm-worn victims leap,
And o'er their struggling limbs, the furious billows sweep.

V

O! barb'rous Pow'r! relentless Fate!   25
  Does Heav'n's high will decree
That some should sleep on beds of state,—
  Some, in the roaring Sea?
Some, nurs'd in splendour, deal Oppression's blow,
While worth and DRACO pine—in Slavery and woe!   30

VI

Yon Vessel oft has plough'd the main
  With human traffic fraught;
Its cargo,—our dark Sons of pain—
  For worldly treasure bought!
What had they done?—O Nature tell me why—   35
Is taunting scorn the lot, of thy dark progeny?

VII

Thou gav'st, in thy caprice, the Soul
  Peculiarly enshrin'd:
Nor from the ebon Casket stole
  The Jewel of the mind!   40
Then wherefore let the suff'ring Negro's breast
Bow to his fellow, MAN, in brighter colours drest.

VIII

Is it the dim and glossy hue
  That marks him for despair?—
While men with blood their hands embrue,   45
  And mock the wretch's pray'r?
Shall guiltless Slaves the Scourge of tyrants feel,
And, e'en before their GOD! unheard, unpitied kneel.

IX

Could the proud rulers of the land
  Our Sable race behold;   50

Some bow'd by torture's Giant hand
   And others, basely sold!
Then would they pity Slaves, and cry, with shame,
Whate'er their TINTS may be, their SOULS are still the same!

X

Why seek to mock the Ethiop's face?
   Why goad our hapless kind?
Can features alienate the race—
   Is there no kindred mind?
Does not the cheek which vaunts the roseate hue
Oft blush for crimes, that Ethiops never knew?

XI

Behold! the angry waves conspire
   To check the barb'rous toil!
While wounded Nature's vengeful ire—
   Roars, round this trembling Isle!
And hark! her voice re-echoes in the wind—
Man was not form'd by Heav'n, to trample on his kind!

XII

Torn from my Mother's aching breast,
   My Tyrant sought my love—
But, in the Grave shall ZELMA rest,
   E'er she will faithless prove—
No DRACO!—Thy companion I will be
To that celestial realm, where Negroes shall be free!

XIII

The Tyrant WHITE MAN taught my mind—
   The letter'd page to trace;—
He taught me in the Soul to find
   No tint, as in the face:
He bade my Reason, blossom like the tree—
But fond affection gave, the ripen'd fruits to thee.

XIV

With jealous rage he mark'd my love;
   He sent thee far away;—
And prison'd in the plantain grove—
   Poor ZELMA pass'd the day—
But ere the moon rose high above the main,
ZELMA, and Love contriv'd, to break the Tyrant's chain.

55

60

65

70

75

80

XV

Swift, o'er the plain of burning Sand   85
   My course I bent to thee;
And soon I reach'd the billowy strand
   Which bounds the stormy Sea.—
DRACO! my Love! Oh yet, thy ZELMA's soul
Springs ardently to thee,—impatient of controul.   90

XVI

Again the lightning flashes white—
   The rattling cords among!
Now, by the transient vivid light,
   I mark the frantic throng!
Now up the tatter'd shrouds my DRACO flies—   95
While o'er the plunging prow, the curling billows rise.

XVII

The topmast falls—three shackled slaves—
   Cling to the Vessel's side!
Now lost amid the madd'ning waves—
   Now on the mast they ride—   100
See! on the forecastle my DRACO stands
And now he waves his chain, now clasps his bleeding hands.

XVIII

Why, cruel WHITE-MAN! when away
   My sable Love was torn,
Why did you let poor ZELMA stay,   105
   On Afric's sands to mourn?
No! ZELMA is not left, for she will prove
In the deep troubled main, her fond—her faithful LOVE."

XIX

The lab'ring Ship was now a wreck,
   The Shrouds were flutt'ring wide!
The rudder gone, the lofty deck   110
   Was rock'd from side to side—
Poor ZELMA's eyes now dropp'd their last big tear,
While, from her tawny cheek, the blood recoil'd with fear.

XX

Now frantic, on the sands she roam'd,   115
   Now shrieking stop'd to view
Where high the liquid mountains foam'd,
   Around the exhausted crew—

'Till, from the deck, her DRACO's well known form
Sprung mid the yawning waves, and buffetted the Storm.   120

XXI

Long, on the swelling surge sustain'd
   Brave DRACO sought the shore,
Watch'd the dark Maid, but ne'er complain'd,
   Then sunk, to gaze no more!
Poor ZELMA saw him buried by the wave—   125
And, with her heart's true Love, plung'd in a wat'ry grave.

—1800

To the Poet Coleridge

RAPT in the visionary theme!
   SPIRIT DIVINE! with THEE I'll wander,
Where the blue, wavy, lucid stream,
   'Mid forest glooms, shall slow meander!
With THEE I'll trace the circling bounds   5
   Of thy NEW PARADISE extended;
And listen to the varying sounds
   Of winds, and foamy torrents blended.

Now by the source which lab'ring heaves
   The mystic fountain, bubbling, panting,   10
While Gossamer its net-work weaves,
   Adown the blue lawn slanting!
I'll mark thy *sunny dome*, and view
Thy *Caves of Ice*, thy fields of dew!
Thy ever-blooming mead, whose flow'r   15
Waves to the cold breath of the moonlight hour!
Or when the day-star, peering bright
On the grey wing of parting night;
While more than vegetating pow'r
Throbs grateful to the burning hour,   20
As summer's whisper'd sighs unfold
Her million, million buds of gold;
Then will I climb the breezy bounds,
   Of thy NEW PARADISE extended,
And listen to the distant sounds   25
   Of winds, and foamy torrents blended!

SPIRIT DIVINE! with THEE I'll trace
Imagination's boundless space!
With thee, beneath thy *sunny dome*,
   I'll listen to the minstrel's lay,
   Hymning the gradual close of day;   30

In *Caves of Ice* enchanted roam,
Where on the glitt'ring entrance plays
The moon's-beam with its silv'ry rays;
   Or, when glassy stream, 35
     That thro' the deep dell flows,
   Flashes the noon's hot beam;
     The noon's hot beam, that midway shows
Thy flaming Temple, studded o'er
With all PERUVIA's lustrous store![1] 40
There will I trace the circling bounds
   Of thy NEW PARADISE extended!
And listen to the awful sounds,
   Of winds, and foamy torrents blended!

And now I'll pause to catch the moan 45
   Of distant breezes, cavern-pent;
Now, ere the twilight tints are flown,
Purpling the landscape, far and wide,
On the dark promontory's side
   I'll gather wild flow'rs, dew besprent, 50
And weave a crown for THEE,
GENIUS OF HEAV'N-TAUGHT POESY!
While, op'ning to my wond'ring eyes,
Thou bidst a new creation rise,
I'll raptur'd trace the circling bounds 55
   Of thy RICH PARADISE extended,
And listen to the varying sounds
   Of winds, and foaming torrents blended.

And now, with lofty tones inviting,
Thy NYMPH, her dulcimer swift smiting, 60
Shall wake me in ecstatic measures!
Far, far remov'd from mortal pleasures!
   In cadence rich, in cadence strong,
Proving the wondrous witcheries of song!
   I hear her voice! thy *sunny dome*, 65
   Thy *caves of ice*, loud repeat,
   Vibrations, madd'ning sweet,
     Calling the visionary wand'rer home.
She sings of THEE, O favour'd child
Of *Minstrelsy*, SUBLIMELY WILD! 70
Of thee, whose soul can feel the tone
Which gives to airy dreams *a magic* ALL THY OWN!

—1806

---

1. Jewels from Peru.

The Poor, Singing Dame

BENEATH an old wall, that went round an old Castle,
   For many a year, with brown ivy o'erspread;
A neat little Hovel, its lowly roof raising,
   Defied the wild winds that howl'd over its shed:
The turrets, that frown'd on the poor simple dwelling,   5
   Were rock'd to and fro, when the Tempest would roar,
And the river, that down the rich valley was swelling,
   Flow'd swiftly beside the green step of its door.

The Summer Sun, gilded the rushy-roof slanting,
   The bright dews bespangled its ivy-bound hedge   10
And above, on the ramparts, the sweet Birds were chanting,
   And wild buds thick dappled the clear river's edge.
When the Castle's rich chambers were haunted, and dreary,
   The poor little Hovel was still, and secure;
And no robber e'er enter'd, nor goblin nor fairy,   15
   For the splendours of pride had no charms to allure.

The Lord of the Castle, a proud, surly ruler,
   Oft heard the low dwelling with sweet music ring:
For the old Dame that liv'd in the little Hut chearly,
   Would sit at her wheel, and would merrily sing: 20
When with revels the Castle's great Hall was resounding,
   The Old Dame was sleeping, not dreaming of fear;
And when over the mountains the Huntsmen were bounding
   She would open her wicket,[1] their clamours to hear.

To the merry-ton'd horn, she would dance on the threshold,   25
   And louder, and louder, repeat her old Song:
And when Winter its mantle of Frost was displaying
   She caroll'd, undaunted, the bare woods among:
She would gather dry Fern, ever happy and singing,
   With her cake of brown bread, and her jug of brown beer,   30
And would smile when she heard the great Castle-bell ringing,
   Inviting the Proud—to their prodigal chear.

Thus she liv'd, ever patient and ever contented,
   Till Envy the Lord of the Castle possess'd,
For he hated that Poverty should be so chearful,   35
   While care could the fav'rites of Fortune molest;
He sent his bold yeoman with threats to prevent her,
   And still would she carol her sweet roundelay;

---

1. Door.

At last, an old Steward, relentless he sent her—
  Who bore her, all trembling, to Prison away!   40

Three weeks did she languish, then died, broken-hearted,
  Poor Dame! how the death-bell did mournfully sound!
And along the green path six young Bachelors bore her,
  And laid her, for ever, beneath the cold ground!
And the primroses pale, 'mid the long grass were growing,   45
  The bright dews of twilight bespangled her grave
And morn heard the breezes of summer soft blowing
  To bid the fresh flow'rets in sympathy wave.

The Lord of the Castle, from that fatal moment
  When poor Singing MARY was laid in her grave,   50
Each night was surrounded by Screech-owls appalling,
  Which o'er the black turrets their pinions would wave!
On the ramparts that frown'd on the river, swift flowing,
  They hover'd, still hooting a terrible song,
When his windows would rattle, the Winter blast blowing,   55
  They would shriek like a ghost, the dark alleys among!

Whenever he wander'd they followed him crying,
  At dawnlight, at Eve, still they haunted his way!
When the Moon shone across the wide common, they hooted,
  Nor quitted his path, till the blazing of day.   60
His bones began wasting, his flesh was decaying,
  And he hung his proud head, and he perish'd with shame;
And the tomb of rich marble, no soft tear displaying,
  O'ershadows the grave, of THE POOR SINGING DAME!

                                       —1800

William Wordsworth
1770–1850

Born and raised in England's Lake District, William Wordsworth was, in a sense, brought up by the region's beautiful and sublime nature. "I grew up fostered alike by beauty and by fear," the poet tells us, reflecting on his childhood among the mountains and lakes. Wordsworth's mother died when he was only eight years old. After her death, John Wordsworth sent his son William, along with two brothers, to board at Hawkshead Grammar School, separating them from their sister, Dorothy. There, without parental guidance, young Wordsworth was at liberty to roam the fells (mountainsides) and the nearby lake, Esthwaite Water. As recorded in *The Prelude* (1850), he roamed alone by day and by night, often getting into considerable mischief and sometimes witnessing shocking or sublime sights. These early experiences fostered Wordsworth's poetic sensibilities: His "beloved vale" was brought to life by his imaginative attempt to process his feelings of loss and reconcile his sense of nature's beauty with his experience of its destructive power.

This struggle to make sense of the sorrows and joys of internal and external nature was exacerbated by John Wordsworth's death during the boys' 1783 winter vacation. Returning to school, Wordsworth received a thorough education in Latin and Greek verse from his schoolmaster, William Taylor. Taylor also encouraged Wordsworth to compose his own verses, embarking him on a poetic career that spanned the rest of his eighty years. His first verse and his first published books, *An Evening Walk* (1793) and *Descriptive Sketches* (1793), typified the neoclassical style of the eighteenth century. During his time at Hawkshead, he became well versed in the tradition of pastoral poetry about rural landscapes and the lives of idealized shepherds. In models such as Milton's "Lycidas" (1638) and James Thomson's *The Seasons* (1844), Wordsworth saw how the pastoral mode could be used to register political and religious dissent in poetry nominally concerned only with nature. One of his earlier poems, "The Vail of Esthwaite," was an elegy for his father in which his own emotions were fused with descriptions of nature. This loco-descriptive and autobiographical verse tinged with elegiac sentiment was one of the earliest manifestations of elements that were to become the hallmark of many of Wordsworth's later poems.

Wordsworth earned a spot at St. John's College, Cambridge, but he later came to feel that his imagination had slept at university, that he was "neither for that time, nor for that place." In *The Prelude* he remarks that he squandered his college career reading "lazily in lazy books" and talking "unprofitable talk in the morning hours." Despite his ambivalence about Cambridge, the time between his matriculation and the award of his BA was as formative for his poetry as was his time at Hawkshead. Just as his rambles during his Hawkshead years were formative for his poetry's emotional perception of nature, his far more extensive college rambles fostered his poetry's political and spiritual perception of the natural world. When he should have been hitting the books, Wordsworth hit the road. During the summer before his final examinations, he and his friend Robert Jones took a walking tour of the Alps. Their walking tour of 1790 landed them in France at an important time: the anniversary of the fall of the Bastille, the event that began the French Revolution. It is no surprise, then, that the poetic memoirs of this trip in *Descriptive Sketches* and *The Prelude* contain politicized descriptions of nature.

After receiving his degree, Wordsworth went to London and there "ranged at large" through the metropolis, "free as a colt at pasture on the hills." *Ranging* is an apt word to describe the months Wordsworth spent walking around London and feeding on its culture, particularly its culture of dissent, which fed his revolutionary hopes and joys. "Proud and exulting, like an untired horse, / That cares not for its home," Wordsworth ranged farther and wider in political pastures, returning to France, where he stayed from 1791 to 1792. There, he met Michel Beaupuy (a captain of republican forces), who steeled Wordsworth's commitment to liberty, equality, and philanthropy. In France, he also met and soon fell in love with Annette Vallon, who gave birth to their child, Anne-Caroline Wordsworth, in 1792. Just as fate separated Wordsworth from his mother and father, it also distanced him from Annette and Anne-Caroline: England's declaration of war on France forced him back to his native land. On his way back through Paris, he walked through streets where a month earlier the bodies of those killed in the Revolution's September Massacres had been stacked. As Maximilien Robespierre's Reign of Terror took hold of France, Wordsworth's hopes for the Revolution's aims collapsed, one of the most devastating events of his emotional life.

A couple of years after his return to England, Wordsworth met Samuel Taylor Coleridge, and the two quickly became best friends, kindred spirits, and the single most profound influence on each other's poetry. The poets took to walking among the Quantock Hills and planning a book of poems that would embody their revolutionary ideals. Another powerful presence in Wordsworth's personal and poetic life of the time was his sister, Dorothy, with whom he was reunited after years of separation. The product of the time spent in the company of Coleridge and Dorothy was the *Lyrical Ballads* (1798). The book was not as successful as the authors hoped; although the poems did receive some praise, on the whole they were censured by critics, who

were against the politics and poetics of poems that championed society's outcasts and laborers
and were written in the common tongue. Not to be deterred, Wordsworth returned to the nature
of his childhood, settling with Dorothy in the Lake District village of Grasmere. They soon
attracted a community of writers to the region, including Coleridge, Robert Southey, and eventually Thomas De Quincey. Dubbed "The Lake School" or "The Lakers," Wordsworth,
Coleridge, and Southey were bitterly attacked by critics. Enough acclaim was earned by the
Ballads, though, for Wordsworth to bring out three more editions, in 1800, 1802, and 1805.

The years these editions spanned were a mixture of happiness and sadness for Wordsworth
as his circle welcomed new members but experienced a devastating loss. In 1802, Wordsworth
married Mary Hutchinson, his childhood friend, and in 1805, Wordsworth's seafaring brother,
John, drowned in a shipwreck. The loss of John devastated Wordsworth so much that for a spell
he ceased composing poetry. Eventually, though, he began to write to appease his disconsolate-
ness, and he experienced again the therapeutic effects of poetic composition. In *The Prelude*,
he noted how the most tragic moments in life eventually become

> Spots of time that with distinct pre-eminence retain
> A renovating virtue, whence, depressed,
> By false opinion and contentious thought,
> Or aught of heavier or more deadly weight . . .
> Our minds are nourished and invisibly repaired.

His poetry both created the radical republic that embodied his revolutionary hopes and raised
living monuments to those he had lost.

As he entered middle age, much of Wordsworth's earlier circumstances were reversed. He
was surrounded by a loving family, he began to move slowly and inexorably toward alignment
with the Anglican Church and the Crown, and his poetry began to achieve international fame.
His poetry saw more critical acclaim slowly but surely: Although *Poems in Two Volumes* (1807)
and *The Excursion* (1814) still met with censure, they met with much praise as well. He
remained an active poet through all his years. Twentieth- and twenty-first-century readers of
Wordsworth generally value his pre-1807 work the most, but the opposite was true of the
majority of his nineteenth-century readers, who praised his sonnets, including *Ecclesiastical
Sonnets* (1822), *The Excursion* (1814), *Guide to the Lakes* (1835), and collections now rarely
read, such as *Yarrow Revisited* (1836). His later life was not without its trials, though, most especially the death of Coleridge in 1834 (twenty years after their friendship was irrevocably damaged over misunderstandings), the failing mental health of Dorothy, and the death of his
daughter Dora in 1847. By the time of Wordsworth's death in 1850, he was England's Poet
Laureate and was lionized by many visitors from home—including poet Alfred Lord Tennyson
and critic Matthew Arnold—as well as those from abroad, among them the New England
Transcendentalists Margaret Fuller and Ralph Waldo Emerson.

Goody Blake and Harry Gill

A True Story.[1]

OH! what's the matter? what's the matter?
What is't that ails young Harry Gill?
That evermore his teeth they chatter,
Chatter, chatter, chatter still!
Of waistcoats Harry has no lack,   5
Good duffle gray, and flannel fine;

---

1. Based on an episode recounted in Erasmus Darwin (1731–1802), *Zoönomia* (1794–1796), a scientific text.

He has a blanket on his back,
And coats enough to smother nine.

In March, December, and in July
'Tis all the same with Harry Gill; 10
The neighbors tell, and tell you truly,
His teeth they chatter, chatter still.
At night, at morning, and at noon,
'Tis all the same with Harry Gill;
Beneath the sun, beneath the moon, 15
His teeth they chatter, chatter still!

Young Harry was a lusty drover,
And who so stout of limb as he?
His cheeks were red as ruddy clover;
His voice was like the voice of three, 20
Old Goody Blake was old and poor;
Ill fed she was, and thinly clad;
And any man who passed her door
Might see how poor a hut she had.

All day she spun in her poor dwelling; 25
And then her three hours' work at night,—
Alas! 'twas hardly worth the telling,
It would not pay for candle-light.
Remote from sheltering village green,
On a hill's northern side she dwelt, 30
Where from sea-blasts the hawthorns lean,
And hoary dews are slow to melt.

By the same fire to boil their pottage,
Two poor old Dames, as I have known,
Will often live in one small cottage; 35
But she, poor Woman! housed alone.
'Twas well enough when summer came,
The long, warm, lightsome summer-day;
Then at her door the *canty*² Dame
Would sit, as any linnet³ gay. 40

But when the ice our streams did fetter,
Oh! then how her old bones would shake!
You would have said, if you had met her,
'Twas a hard time for Goody Blake.
Her evenings then were dull and dead; 45
Sad case it was, as you may think,

2. Lively.   3. A songbird.

For very cold to go to bed;
And then for cold not sleep a wink!

O joy for her! whene'er in winter
The winds at night had made a rout;
And scattered many a lusty splinter
And many a rotten bough about.
Yet never had she, well or sick,
As every man who knew her says,
A pile beforehand, turf or stick,
Enough to warm her for three days.

Now, when the frost was past enduring,
And made her poor old bones to ache,
Could any thing be more alluring
Than an old hedge to Goody Blake?
And, now and then, it must be said,
When her old bones were cold and chill,
She left her fire, or left her bed,
To seek the hedge of Harry Gill.

Now Harry he had long suspected
This trespass of old Goody Blake;
And vowed that she should be detected,
And he on her would vengeance take.
And oft from his warm fire he'd go,
And to the fields his road would take;
And there, at night, in frost and snow,
He watched to seize old Goody Blake.

And once, behind a rick of barley,
Thus looking out did Harry stand:
The moon was full and shining clearly,
And crisp with frost the stubble land.
—He hears a noise—he's all awake—
Again!—on tip-toe down the hill
He softly creeps—'Tis Goody Blake,
She's at the hedge of Harry Gill!

Right glad was he when he beheld her:
Stick after stick did Goody pull:
He stood behind a bush of elder,
Till she had filled her apron full
When with her load she turned about,
The by-way back again to take;
He started forward with a shout,
And sprang upon poor Goody Blake.

And fiercely by the arm he took her,
And by the arm he held her fast,
And fiercely by the arm he shook her,
And cried, "I've caught you then at last!"   90
Then Goody, who had nothing said,
Her bundle from her lap let fall;
And, kneeling on the sticks, she prayed,
To God that is the judge of all.   95

She prayed, her withered hand uprearing,
While Harry held her by the arm—
"God! who art never out of hearing,
O may he never more be warm!"   100
The cold, cold moon above her head,
Thus on her knees did Goody pray;
Young Harry heard what she had said,
And icy cold he turned away.

He went complaining all the morrow   105
That he was cold and very chill;
His face was gloom, his heart was sorrow—
Alas! that day for Harry Gill!
That day he wore a riding-coat,
But not a whit the warmer he;   110
Another was on Thursday brought,
And ere the Sabbath he had three!

'Twas all in vain, a useless matter,
And blankets were about him pinned;
Yet still his jaws and teeth they clatter   115
Like a loose casement in the wind.
And Harry's flesh it fell away;
And all who see him say, 'tis plain,
That, live as long as live he may,
He never will be warm again.   120

No word to any man he utters,
A-bed or up, to young or old;
But ever to himself he mutters,
"Poor Harry Gill is very cold."
A-bed or up, by night or day,   125
His teeth they chatter, chatter still.
Now think, ye farmers all, I pray,
Of Goody Blake and Harry Gill!

—1798

The Complaint of a Forsaken Indian Woman

Written at Alfoxden, where I read Hearne's Journey with deep interest. It was composed for the volume of Lyrical Ballads.

When a Northern Indian, from sickness, is unable to continue his journey with his companions, he is left behind, covered over with deer-skins, and is supplied with water, food, and fuel, if the situation of the place will afford it. He is informed of the track which his companions intend to pursue, and if he be unable to follow, or overtake them, he perishes alone in the desert; unless he should have the good fortune to fall in with some other tribes of Indians. The females are equally, or still more, exposed to the same fate. See that very interesting work HEARNE'S *Journey from Hudson's Bay to the Northern Ocean.*[1] In the high northern latitudes, as the same writer informs us, when the northern lights vary their position in the air, they make a rustling and a crackling noise, as alluded to in the following poem.

Before I see another day,
Oh let my body die away!
In sleep I heard the northern gleams;
The stars, they were among my dreams;
In rustling conflict through the skies,   5
I heard, I saw the flashes drive,[2]
And yet they are upon my eyes,
And yet I am alive;
Before I see another day,
Oh let my body die away!   10

My fire is dead: it knew no pain;
Yet is it dead, and I remain:
All stiff with ice the ashes lie;
And they are dead, and I will die.
When I was well, I wished to live,   15
For clothes, for warmth, for food, and fire;
But they to me no joy can give,
No pleasure now, and no desire.
Then here contented will I lie!
Alone, I cannot fear to die.   20

Alas! ye might have dragged me on
Another day, a single one!
Too soon I yielded to despair;
Why did ye listen to my prayer?
When ye were gone my limbs were stronger;   25
And oh, how grievously I rue,
That, afterwards, a little longer,
My friends, I did not follow you!

---

1. Samuel Hearne (1745–1792), *Journey from Prince of Wales's Fort in Hudson's Bay, to the Northern Ocean* (1795).   2. The northern lights.

For strong and without pain I lay,
Dear friends, when ye were gone away.   30

My Child! they gave thee to another,
A woman who was not thy mother.
When from my arms my Babe they took,
On me how strangely did he look!
Through his whole body something ran,   35
A most strange working did I see;
—As if he strove to be a man,
That he might pull the sledge for me:
And then he stretched his arms, how wild!
Oh mercy! like a helpless child.   40

My little joy! my little pride!
In two days more I must have died.
Then do not weep and grieve for me;
I feel I must have died with thee.
O wind, that o'er my head art flying   45
The way my friends their course did bend,
I should not feel the pain of dying,
Could I with thee a message send;
Too soon, my friends, ye went away;
For I had many things to say.   50

I'll follow you across the snow;
Ye travel heavily and slow;
In spite of all my weary pain
I'll look upon your tents again.
—My fire is dead, and snowy white   55
The water which beside it stood:
The wolf has come to me to-night,
And he has stolen away my food.
For ever left alone am I;
Then wherefore should I fear to die?   60

Young as I am, my course is run,
I shall not see another sun;
I cannot lift my limbs to know
If they have any life or no.
My poor forsaken Child, if I   65
For once could have thee close to me,
With happy heart I then would die,
And my last thought would happy be;
But thou, dear Babe, art far away,
Nor shall I see another day.   70

—1798

Lines Written in Early Spring

I heard a thousand blended notes,
While in a grove I sate reclined,
In that sweet mood when pleasant thoughts
Bring sad thoughts to the mind.

To her fair works did nature link   5
The human soul that through me ran;
And much it griev'd my heart to think
What man has made of man.

Through primrose-tufts, in that sweet bower,
The periwinkle trail'd its wreathes;
And 'tis my faith that every flower   10
Enjoys the air it breathes.

The birds around me hopp'd and play'd:
Their thoughts I cannot measure,
But the least motion which they made,
It seem'd a thrill of pleasure.

The budding twigs spread out their fan,
To catch the breezy air;
And I must think, do all I can,
That there was pleasure there.

If I these thoughts may not prevent,
If such be of my creed the plan,
Have I not reason to lament
What man has made of man?

—1798

The Thorn

I

There is a thorn[1]; it looks so old,
In truth you'd find it hard to say,
How it could ever have been young,
It looks so old and grey.
Not higher than a two-years' child,   5
It stands erect this aged thorn;
No leaves it has, no thorny points;
It is a mass of knotted joints,
A wretched thing forlorn.

---

1. A thorn-bush.

It stands erect, and like a stone
With lichens it is overgrown.

II

Like rock or stone, it is o'ergrown
With lichens to the very top,
And hung with heavy tufts of moss,
A melancholy crop:
Up from the earth these mosses creep,
And this poor thorn they clasp it round
So close, you'd say that they were bent
With plain and manifest intent,
To drag it to the ground;
And all had joined in one endeavour
To bury this poor thorn for ever.

III

High on a mountain's highest ridge,
Where oft the stormy winter gale
Cuts like a scythe, while through the clouds
It sweeps from vale to vale;
Not five yards from the mountain-path,
This thorn you on your left espy;
And to the left, three yards beyond,
You see a little muddy pond
Of water, never dry;
I've measured it from side to side:
'Tis three feet long, and two feet wide.

IV

And close beside this aged thorn,
There is a fresh and lovely sight,
A beauteous heap, a hill of moss,
Just half a foot in height.
All lovely colours there you see,
All colours that were ever seen,
And mossy network too is there,
As if by hand of lady fair
The work had woven been,
And cups, the darlings of the eye,
So deep is their vermilion dye.

V

Ah me! what lovely tints are there!
Of olive-green and scarlet bright,

In spikes, in branches, and in stars,
Green, red, and pearly white.
This heap of earth o'ergrown with moss,
Which close beside the thorn you see,   50
So fresh in all its beauteous dyes,
Is like an infant's grave in size
As like as like can be:
But never, never any where,
An infant's grave was half so fair.   55

VI

Now would you see this aged thorn,
This pond and beauteous hill of moss,
You must take care and chuse your time
The mountain when to cross.
For oft there sits, between the heap   60
That's like an infant's grave in size,
And that same pond of which I spoke,
A woman in a scarlet cloak,
And to herself she cries,
"Oh misery! oh misery!   65
Oh woe is me! oh misery!"

VII

At all times of the day and night
This wretched woman thither goes,
And she is known to every star,
And every wind that blows;   70
And there beside the thorn she sits
When the blue day-light's in the skies,
And when the whirlwind's on the hill,
Or frosty air is keen and still,
And to herself she cries,   75
"Oh misery! oh misery!
Oh woe is me! oh misery!"

VIII

"Now wherefore thus, by day and night,
In rain, in tempest, and in snow,
Thus to the dreary mountain-top   80
Does this poor woman go?
And why sits she beside the thorn
When the blue day-light's in the sky,
Or when the whirlwind's on the hill,
Or frosty air is keen and still,   85
And wherefore does she cry?

Oh wherefore? wherefore? tell me why
Does she repeat that doleful cry?"

IX

I cannot tell; I wish I could;
For the true reason no one knows,
But if you'd gladly view the spot,
The spot to which she goes;
The heap that's like an infant's grave,
The pond—and thorn, so old and grey,
Pass by her door—'tis seldom shut—
And if you see her in her hut,
Then to the spot away!—
I never heard of such as dare
Approach the spot when she is there.

X

"But wherefore to the mountain-top
Can this unhappy woman go,
Whatever star is in the skies,
Whatever wind may blow?"
Nay rack your brain—'tis all in vain,
I'll tell you every thing I know;
But to the thorn, and to the pond
Which is a little step beyond,
I wish that you would go:
Perhaps when you are at the place
You something of her tale may trace.

XI

I'll give you the best help I can:
Before you up the mountain go,
Up to the dreary mountain-top,
I'll tell you all I know.
'Tis now some two and twenty years,
Since she (her name is Martha Ray)
Gave with a maiden's true good will
Her company to Stephen Hill;
And she was blithe and gay,
And she was happy, happy still
Whene'er she thought of Stephen Hill.

XII

And they had fix'd the wedding-day,
The morning that must wed them both;

90

95

100

105

110

115

120

But Stephen to another maid
Had sworn another oath;
And with this other maid to church
Unthinking Stephen went—
Poor Martha! on that woful day
A cruel, cruel fire, they say,
Into her bones was sent:
It dried her body like a cinder,
And almost turn'd her brain to tinder.

XIII

They say, full six months after this,
While yet the summer-leaves were green,
She to the mountain-top would go,
And there was often seen.
'Tis said, a child was in her womb,
As now to any eye was plain;
She was with child, and she was mad,
Yet often she was sober sad
From her exceeding pain.
Oh me! ten thousand times I'd rather
That he had died, that cruel father!

XIV

Sad case for such a brain to hold
Communion with a stirring child!
Sad case, as you may think, for one
Who had a brain so wild!
Last Christmas when we talked of this,
Old Farmer Simpson did maintain,
That in her womb the infant wrought
About its mother's heart, and brought
Her senses back again:
And when at last her time drew near,
Her looks were calm, her senses clear.

XV

No more I know, I wish I did,
And I would tell it all to you;
For what became of this poor child
There's none that ever knew:
And if a child was born or no,
There's no one that could ever tell;
And if 'twas born alive or dead,
There's no one knows, as I have said,
But some remember well,

That Martha Ray about this time
Would up the mountain often climb.

XVI

And all that winter, when at night
The wind blew from the mountain-peak,
'Twas worth your while, though in the dark,
The church-yard path to seek:
For many a time and oft were heard
Cries coming from the mountain-head,
Some plainly living voices were,
And others, I've heard many swear,
Were voices of the dead:
I cannot think, whate'er they say,
They had to do with Martha Ray.

XVII

But that she goes to this old thorn,
The thorn which I've described to you,
And there sits in a scarlet cloak,
I will be sworn is true.
For one day with my telescope,
To view the ocean wide and bright,
When to this country first I came,
Ere I had heard of Martha's name,
I climbed the mountain's height:
A storm came on, and I could see
No object higher than my knee.

XVIII

'Twas mist and rain, and storm and rain,
No screen, no fence could I discover,
And then the wind! in faith, it was
A wind full ten times over.
I looked around, I thought I saw
A jutting crag, and off I ran,
Head-foremost, through the driving rain,
The shelter of the crag to gain,
And, as I am a man,
Instead of jutting crag, I found
A woman seated on the ground.

XIX

I did not speak—I saw her face,
Her face it was enough for me;

I turned about and heard her cry,
"O misery! O misery!"
And there she sits, until the moon
Through half the clear blue sky will go,
And when the little breezes make   205
The waters of the pond to shake,
As all the country know,
She shudders and you hear her cry,
"Oh misery! oh misery!"

XX

"But what's the thorn? and what's the pond?   210
And what's the hill of moss to her?
And what's the creeping breeze that comes
The little pond to stir?"
I cannot tell; but some will say
She hanged her baby on the tree,   215
Some say she drowned it in the pond,
Which is a little step beyond,
But all and each agree,
The little babe was buried there,
Beneath that hill of moss so fair.   220

XXI

I've heard the scarlet moss is red
With drops of that poor infant's blood;
But kill a new-born infant thus!
I do not think she could.
Some say, if to the pond you go,   225
And fix on it a steady view,
The shadow of a babe you trace,
A baby and a baby's face,
And that it looks at you;
Whene'er you look on it, 'tis plain   230
The baby looks at you again.

XXII

And some had sworn an oath that she
Should be to public justice brought;
And for the little infant's bones
With spades they would have sought.   235
But then the beauteous hill of moss
Before their eyes began to stir;
And for full fifty yards around,
The grass it shook upon the ground;
But all do still aver   240

The little babe is buried there,
Beneath that hill of moss so fair.

XXIII

I cannot tell how this may be,
But plain it is, the thorn is bound
With heavy tufts of moss, that strive   245
To drag it to the ground.
And this I know, full many a time,
When she was on the mountain high,
By day, and in the silent night,
When all the stars shone clear and bright,   250
That I have heard her cry,
"Oh misery! oh misery!
O woe is me! oh misery!"

—1798

Note to *The Thorn*

This Poem ought to have been preceded by an introductory Poem, which I have been
prevented from writing by never having felt myself in a mood when it was probable
that I should write it well.—The character which I have here introduced speaking is
sufficiently common. The Reader will perhaps have a general notion of it, if he has
ever known a man, a Captain of a small trading vessel for example, who being past
the middle age of life, had retired upon an annuity or small independent income to
some village or country town of which he was not a native, or in which he had not
been accustomed to live. Such men having little to do become credulous and talkative from indolence; and from the same cause, and other predisposing causes by which
it is probable that such men may have been affected, they are prone to superstition.
On which account it appeared to me proper to select a character like this to exhibit
some of the general laws by which superstition acts upon the mind. Superstitious men
are almost always men of slow faculties and deep feelings; their minds are not loose,
but adhesive; they have a reasonable share of imagination, by which word I mean the
faculty which produces impressive effects out of simple elements; but they are utterly
destitute of fancy, the power by which pleasure and surprise are excited by sudden
varieties of situation and by accumulated imagery.

   It was my wish in this poem to show the manner in which such men cleave to the
same ideas; and to follow the turns of passion, always different, yet not palpably different, by which their conversation is swayed. I had two objects to attain; first, to represent a picture, which should not be unimpressive yet consistent with the character
that should describe it, secondly, while I adhered to the style in which such persons
describe, to take care that words, which in their minds are impregnated with passion,
should likewise convey passion to Readers who are not accustomed to sympathize with
men feeling in that manner or using such language. It seemed to me that this might
be done by calling in the assistance of Lyrical and rapid Metre. It was necessary that
the Poem, to be natural, should in reality move slowly; yet I hoped, that, by the aid of
the metre, to those who should at all enter into the spirit of the Poem, it would appear

to move quickly. The Reader will have the kindness to excuse this note as I am sensible that an introductory Poem is necessary to give this Poem its full effect.

Upon this occasion I will request permission to add a few words closely connected with "The Thorn" and many other Poems in these volumes. There is a numerous class of readers who imagine that the same words cannot be repeated without tautology[1]: this is a great error: virtual tautology is much oftener produced by using different words when the meaning is exactly the same. Words, a Poet's words more particularly, ought to be weighed in the balance of feeling and not measured by the space which they occupy on paper. For the Reader cannot be too often reminded that Poetry is passion: it is the history or science of feelings; now every man must know that an attempt is rarely made to communicate impassioned feelings without something of an accompanying consciousness of the inadequateness of our own powers, or the deficiencies of language. During such efforts there will be a craving in the mind, and as long as it is unsatisfied the Speaker will cling to the same words, or words of the same character. There are also various other reasons why repetition and apparent tautology are frequently beauties of the highest kind. Among the chief of these reasons is the interest which the mind attaches to words, not only as symbols of the passion, but as *things*, active and efficient, which are of themselves part of the passion. And further, from a spirit of fondness, exultation, and gratitude, the mind luxuriates in the repetition of words which appear successfully to communicate the feelings. The truth of these remarks might be shown by innumerable passages from the Bible and from the impassioned poetry of every nation.

"Awake, awake Deborah: awake, awake, utter a song: arise Barak, and lead thy captivity captive, thou son of Abinoam.

At her feet he bowed, he fell, he lay down: at her feet he bowed, he fell; where he bowed, there he fell down dead. Why is his chariot so long in coming? Why tarry the wheels of his chariot?"—*Judges*, chap. 5th, Verses 12th, 27th, and part of 28th.— See also the whole of that tumultuous and wonderful Poem.

—1800

Lines Written a Few Miles above Tintern Abbey

On Revisiting the Banks of the Wye during a Tour, July 13, 1798

Five years have passed[1]; five summers, with the length
Of five long winters! and again I hear
These waters,[2] rolling from their mountain-springs
With a sweet inland murmur.—Once again
Do I behold these steep and lofty cliffs,   5
Which on a wild secluded scene impress
Thoughts of more deep seclusion; and connect
The landscape with the quiet of the sky.
The day is come when I again repose
Here, under this dark sycamore, and view   10
These plots of cottage-ground, these orchard-tufts,
Which, at this season, with their unripe fruits,
Among the woods and copses lose themselves,

---

1. Redundancy.

1. Wordsworth visited Tintern, Wales, in 1793.   2. The Wye River.

Nor, with their green and simple hue, disturb
The wild green landscape. Once again I see   15
These hedge-rows, hardly hedge-rows, little lines
Of sportive wood run wild; these pastoral farms
Green to the very door; and wreathes of smoke
Sent up, in silence, from among the trees,
With some uncertain notice, as might seem,   20
Of vagrant dwellers in the houseless woods,
Or of some hermit's cave, where by his fire
The hermit sits alone.

              Though absent long,
These forms of beauty have not been to me,
As is a landscape to a blind man's eye: 25
But oft, in lonely rooms, and mid the din
Of towns and cities, I have owed to them,
In hours of weariness, sensations sweet,
Felt in the blood, and felt along the heart,
And passing even into my purer mind   30
With tranquil restoration:—feelings too
Of unremembered pleasure; such, perhaps,
As may have had no trivial influence
On that best portion of a good man's life;
His little, nameless, unremembered acts   35
Of kindness and of love. Nor less, I trust,
To them I may have owed another gift,
Of aspect more sublime; that blessed mood,
In which the burthen of the mystery,
In which the heavy and the weary weight   40
Of all this unintelligible world
Is lighten'd:—that serene and blessed mood,
In which the affections gently lead us on,
Until, the breath of this corporeal frame,
And even the motion of our human blood   45
Almost suspended, we are laid asleep
In body, and become a living soul:
While with an eye made quiet by the power
Of harmony, and the deep power of joy,
We see into the life of things.   50

              If this
Be but a vain belief, yet, oh! how oft,
In darkness, and amid the many shapes
Of joyless day-light; when the fretful stir
Unprofitable, and the fever of the world,
Have hung upon the beatings of my heart,   55
How oft, in spirit, have I turned to thee

O sylvan Wye! Thou wanderer through the wood
How often has my spirit turned to thee!

And now, with gleams of half-extinguish'd thought.
With many recognitions dim and faint,   60
And somewhat of a sad perplexity,
The picture of the mind revives again:
While here I stand, not only with the sense
Of present pleasure, but with pleasing thoughts
That in this moment there is life and food   65
For future years. And so I dare to hope
Though changed, no doubt, from what I was, when first
I came among these hills; when like a roe
I bounded o'er the mountains, by the sides
Of the deep rivers, and the lonely streams,   70
Wherever nature led; more like a man
Flying from something that he dreads, than one
Who sought the thing he loved. For nature then
(The coarser pleasures of my boyish days,
And their glad animal movements all gone by,)   75
To me was all in all.—I cannot paint
What then I was. The sounding cataract
Haunted me like a passion: the tall rock,
The mountain, and the deep and gloomy wood,
Their colours and their forms, were then to me   80
An appetite: a feeling and a love,
That had no need of a remoter charm,
By thought supplied, or any interest
Unborrowed from the eye.—That time is past,
And all its aching joys are now no more,   85
And all its dizzy raptures. Not for this
Faint I, nor mourn nor murmur: other gifts
Have followed, for such loss, I would believe,
Abundant recompence. For I have learned
To look on nature, not as in the hour   90
Of thoughtless youth, but hearing oftentimes
The still, sad music of humanity,
Not harsh nor grating, though of ample power
To chasten and subdue. And I have felt
A presence that disturbs me with the joy   95
Of elevated thoughts; a sense sublime
Of something far more deeply interfused,
Whose dwelling is the light of setting suns,
And the round ocean, and the living air,
And the blue sky, and in the mind of man,   100
A motion and a spirit, that impels
All thinking things, all objects of all thought,

And rolls through all things. Therefore am I still
A lover of the meadows and the woods,
And mountains; and of all that we behold   105
From this green earth; of all the mighty world
Of eye and ear, both what they half-create,
And what perceive; well pleased to recognize
In nature and the language of the sense,
The anchor of my purest thoughts, the nurse,   110
The guide, the guardian of my heart, and soul
Of all my moral being.

           Nor, perchance,
If I were not thus taught, should I the more
Suffer my genial spirits to decay:
For thou art with me, here, upon the banks   115
Of this fair river; thou, my dearest Friend,[3]
My dear, dear Friend, and in thy voice I catch
The language of my former heart, and read
My former pleasures in the shooting lights
Of thy wild eyes. Oh! yet a little while   120
May I behold in thee what I was once,
My dear, dear Sister! And this prayer I make,
Knowing that Nature never did betray
The heart that loved her; 'tis her privilege,
Through all the years of this our life, to lead   125
From joy to joy: for she can so inform
The mind that is within us, so impress
With quietness and beauty, and so feed
With lofty thoughts, that neither evil tongues,
Rash judgments, nor the sneers of selfish men,   130
Nor greetings where no kindness is, nor all
The dreary intercourse of daily life,
Shall e'er prevail against us, or disturb
Our chearful faith that all which we behold
Is full of blessings. Therefore let the moon   135
Shine on thee in thy solitary walk;
And let the misty mountain winds be free
To blow against thee: and in after years,
When these wild ecstasies shall be matured
Into a sober pleasure, when thy mind   140
Shall be a mansion for all lovely forms,
Thy memory be as a dwelling-place
For all sweet sounds and harmonies; Oh! then,
If solitude, or fear, or pain, or grief,
Should be thy portion, with what healing thoughts   145

---

3. Wordsworth's sister, Dorothy.

Of tender joy wilt thou remember me,
And these my exhortations! Nor, perchance,
If I should be, where I no more can hear
Thy voice, nor catch from thy wild eyes these gleams
Of past existence, wilt thou then forget   150
That on the banks of this delightful stream
We stood together; and that I, so long
A worshipper of Nature, hither came,
Unwearied in that service: rather say
With warmer love, oh! with far deeper zeal   155
Of holier love. Nor wilt thou then forget,
That after many wanderings, many years
Of absence, these steep woods and lofty cliffs,
And this green pastoral landscape, were to me
More dear, both for themselves, and for thy sake.   160

—1798

from Preface to *Lyrical Ballads*

The first Volume of these Poems[1] has already been sumitted to general perusal. It was published, as an experiment which, I hoped, might be of some use to ascertain, how far, by fitting to metrical arrangement a selection of the real language of men in a state of vivid sensation, that sort of pleasure and that quantity of pleasure may be imparted, which a Poet may rationally endeavour to impart. . . .

It is supposed, that by the act of writing in verse an Author makes a formal engagement that he will gratify certain known habits of association; that he not only thus apprizes the Reader that certain classes of ideas and expressions will be found in his book, but that others will be carefully excluded. This exponent or symbol held forth by metrical language must in different eras of literature have excited very different expectations . . . I will not take upon me to determine the exact import of the promise which by the act of writing in verse an Author in the present day makes to his reader: but it will undoubtedly appear to many persons that I have not fulfilled the terms of an engagement thus voluntarily contracted. They who have been accustomed to the gaudiness and inane phraseology of many modern writers, if they persist in reading this book to its conclusion, will, no doubt, frequently have to struggle with feelings of strangeness and aukwardness: they will look round for poetry, and will be induced to inquire by what species of courtesy these attempts can be permitted to assume that title. . . . I hope therefore the Reader will not censure me, if I attempt to state what I have proposed to myself to perform.

[Incidents and Situations from Common Life]

The principal object, then, proposed in these Poems was to chuse incidents and situations from common life, and to relate or describe them, throughout, as far as was possible, in a selection of language really used by men, and, at the same time, to throw

---

1. The 1798 edition of *Lyrical Ballads*.

over them a certain colouring of imagination, whereby ordinary things should be presented to the mind in an unusual way; and further, and above all, to make these incidents and situations interesting by tracing in them, truly though not ostentatiously, the primary laws of our nature: chiefly, as far as regards the manner in which we associate ideas in a state of excitement. Low and rustic life was generally chosen, because in that condition, the essential passions of the heart find a better soil in which they can attain their maturity, are less under restraint, and speak a plainer and more emphatic language; because in that condition of life our elementary feelings co-exist in a state of greater simplicity, and, consequently, may be more accurately contemplated, and more forcibly communicated because the manners of rural life germinate from those elementary feelings; and, from the necessary character of rural occupations, are more easily comprehended and are more durable, and lastly, because in that condition the passions of men are incorporated with the beautiful and permanent forms of nature. The language, too, of these men is adopted (purified indeed from what appear to be its real defects, from all lasting and rational causes of dislike or disgust) because such men hourly communicate with the best objects from which the best part of language is originally derived; and because, from their rank in society and the sameness and narrow circle of their intercourse, being less under the influence of social vanity they convey their feelings and notions in simple and unelaborated expressions. Accordingly, such a language, arising out of repeated experience and regular feelings, is a more permanent, and a far more philosophical language, than that which is frequently substituted for it by Poets, who think that they are conferring honour upon themselves and their art, in proportion as they separate themselves from the sympathies of men, and indulge in arbitrary and capricious habits of expression, in order to furnish food for fickle tastes, and fickle appetites of their own creation.

[Poetry and Feeling]

[A]ll good poetry is the spontaneous overflow of powerful feelings: but though this be true, Poems to which any value can be attached, were never produced on any variety of subjects but by a man who, being possessed of more than usual organic sensibility, had also thought long and deeply. For our continued influxes of feeling are modified and directed by our thoughts, which are indeed the representatives of all our past feelings; and, as by contemplating the relation of these general representatives to each other we discover what is really important to men, so, by the repetition and continuance of this act, our feelings will be connected with important subjects, till at length, if we be originally possessed of much sensibility, such habits of mind will be produced, that, by obeying blindly and mechanically the impulses of those habits, we shall describe objects, and utter sentiments, of such a nature, and in such connection with each other, that the understanding of the being to whom we address ourselves must necessarily be in some degree enlightened, and his affections ameliorated.

I have said that each of these poems has a purpose. I have also informed my Reader what this purpose will be found principally to be: namely to illustrate the manner in which our feelings and ideas are associated in a state of excitement. But, speaking in language somewhat more appropriate, it is to follow the fluxes and refluxes of the mind when agitated by the great and simple affections of our nature. . . . I should mention one other circumstance which distinguishes these Poems from the popular Poetry of the day; it is this, that the feeling therein developed gives importance to the action and situation and not the action and situation to the feeling. . . . I will not suffer a sense of false modesty to prevent me from asserting, that I point my Reader's attention to this mark of distinction, far less for the sake of these particular Poems than from the general importance of the subject. The subject is indeed important! For the human mind is capable of being excited without the application of gross and violent stimulants; and he must have a very faint perception of its beauty and dignity who does not know this, and who does not further know, that one being is elevated above another in proportion as he possesses this capability. It has therefore appeared to me, that to endeavour to pro-duce or enlarge this capability is one of the best services in which, at any period, a Writer can be engaged; but this service, excellent at all times, is especially so at the present day. For a multitude of causes, unknown to former times, are now acting with a combined force to blunt the discriminating powers of the mind, and unfitting it for all voluntary exertion to reduce it to a state of almost savage torpor. The most effective of these causes are the great national events which are daily taking place, and the encreas-ing accumulation of men in cities, where the uniformity of their occupations produces a craving for extraordinary incident, which the rapid communication of intelligence hourly gratifies. To this tendency of life and manners the literature and theatrical exhi-bitions of the country have conformed themselves. The invaluable works of our elder writers, I had almost said the works of Shakespear and Milton, are driven into neglect by frantic novels, sickly and stupid German Tragedies,[2] and deluges of idle and extrav-agant stories in verse.—When I think upon this degrading thirst after outrageous stim-ulation, I am almost ashamed to have spoken of the feeble effort with which I have endeavoured to conteract it; and, reflecting upon the magnitude of the general evil, I should be oppressed with no dishonorable melancholy, had I not a deep impression of certain inherent and indestructible qualities of the human mind, and likewise of cer-tain powers in the great and permanent objects that act upon it which are equally inherent and indestructible; and did I not further add to this impression a belief, that the time is approaching when the evil will be systematically opposed, by men of greater powers, and with far more distinguished success.

[The Style of Poetry]

Having dwelt thus long on the subjects and aim of these Poems, I shall request the Reader's permission to apprize him of a few circumstances relating to their *style*, in order, among other reasons, that I may not be censured for not having performed what I never attempted. The reader will find that personifications of abstract ideas rarely occur in these volumes; and, I hope, are utterly rejected as an ordinary device to elevate the style, and raise it above prose. I have proposed to myself to imitate, and, as far as is possible, to adopt the very language of men; and assuredly such personifications do not make any natural or regular part of that language. They are, indeed, a figure of speech occasionally prompted by passion, and I have made use of them as such; but I have endeavoured utterly to reject them as a mechanical device of style, or as a family language which Writers in metre seem to lay claim to by prescription. I have wished to keep my Reader in the company of flesh and blood, persuaded that by so doing I shall interest him. I am, however, well aware that others who pursue a different track may interest him likewise; I do not interfere with their claim, I only wish to prefer a claim of my own. There will

2. Such as the works of August von Kotzebue (1761–1819), whose many novels and plays were popular in England.

also be found in these volumes little of what is usually called poetic diction; as much pains has been taken to avoid it as others ordinarily take to produce it; this I have done for the reason already alleged, to bring my language near to the language of men, and further, because the pleasure which I have proposed to myself to impart is of a kind very different from that which is supposed by many persons to be the proper object of poetry. I do not know how without being culpably particular I can give my Reader a more exact notion of the style in which I wished these poems to be written, than by informing him that I have at all times endeavoured to look steadily at my subject, consequently, I hope, that there is in these Poems little falsehood of description, and my ideas are expressed in language fitted to their respective importance. Something I must have gained by this practice, as it is friendly to one property of all good poetry, namely, good sense; but it has necessarily cut me off from a large portion of phrases and figures of speech which from father to son have long been regarded as the common inheritance of Poets. I have also thought it expedient to restrict myself still further, having abstained from the use of many expressions, in themselves proper and beautiful, but which have been foolishly repeated by bad Poets, till such feelings of disgust are connected with them as it is scarcely possible by any art of association to overpower.

If in a poem there should be found a series of lines, or even a single line, in which the language, though naturally arranged and according to the strict laws of metre, does not differ from that of prose, there is a numerous class of critics, who, when they stumble upon these prosaisms as they call them, imagine that they have made a notable discovery, and exult over the Poet as over a man ignorant of his own profession. Now these men would establish a canon of criticism which the Reader will conclude he must utterly reject, if he wishes to be pleased with these volumes. And it would be a most easy task to prove to him, that not only the language of a large portion of every good poem, even of the most elevated character, must necessarily, except with reference to the metre, in no respect differ from that of good prose, but likewise that some of the most interesting parts of the best poems will be found to be strictly the language of prose, when prose is well written. The truth of this assertion might be demonstrated by innumerable passages from almost all the poetical writings, even of Milton himself. . . . [T]o illustrate the subject in a general manner, I will here adduce a short composition of Gray, who was at the head of those who by their reasonings have attempted to widen the space of separation betwixt Prose and Metrical composition, and was more than any other man curiously elaborate in the structure of his own poetic diction.

> In vain to me the smiling mornings shine,
> And reddening Phoebus[3] lifts his golden fire:
> The birds in vain their amorous descant[4] join,
> Or chearful fields resume their green attire:
> These ears alas! for other notes repine;
> A *different object do these eyes require;*
> *My lonely anguish melts no heart but mine;*
> *And in my breast the imperfect joys expire;*
> Yet Morning smiles the busy race to cheer,
> And new-born pleasure brings to happier men;

---

3. Apollo, Greek god of the sun.   4. Melody.

The fields to all their wonted tribute bear;
To warm their little loves the birds complain.
I fruitless mourn to him that cannot hear
And weep the more because I weep in vain.[5]

It will easily be perceived that the only part of this Sonnet which is of any value is the lines printed in Italics: it is equally obvious, that, except in the rhyme, and in the use of the single word "fruitless" for fruitlessly, which is so far a defect, the language of these lines does in no respect differ from that of prose.

By the foregoing quotation I have shewn that the language of Prose may yet be well adapted to Poetry; and I have previously asserted that a large portion of the language of every good poem can in no respect differ from that of good Prose. I will go further. I do not doubt that it may be safely affirmed, that there neither is, nor can be, any essential difference between the language of prose and metrical composition. . . . They both speak by and to the same organs; the bodies in which both of them are clothed may be said to be of the same substance, their affections are kindred, and almost identical, not necessarily differing even in degree; Poetry sheds no tears "such as Angels weep,"[6] but natural and human tears; she can boast of no celestial ichor[7] that distinguishes her vital juices from those of prose; the same human blood circulates through the veins of them both. . . .

[Definition of a Poet]

What is a Poet? To whom does he address himself? And what language is to be expected from him? He is a man speaking to men: a man, it is true, endued with more lively sensibility, more enthusiasm and tenderness, who has a greater knowledge of human nature, and a more comprehensive soul, than are supposed to be common among mankind; a man pleased with his own passions and volitions, and who rejoices more than other men in the spirit of life that is in him; delighting to contemplate similar volitions and passions as manifested in the goings-on of the Universe, and habitually impelled to create them where he does not find them. To these qualities he has added a disposition to be affected more than other men by absent things as if they were present; an ability of conjuring up in himself passions, which are indeed far from being the same as those produced by real events, yet (especially in those parts of the general sympathy which are pleasing and delightful) do more nearly resemble the passions produced by real events, than any thing which, from the motions of their own minds merely, other men are accustomed to feel in themselves; whence, and from practice, he has acquired a greater readiness and power in expressing what he thinks and feels, and especially those thoughts and feelings which, by his own choice, or from the structure of his own mind, arise in him without immediate external excitement.

But, whatever portion of this faculty we may suppose even the greatest Poet to possess, there cannot be a doubt but that the language which it will suggest to him, must, in liveliness and truth, fall far short of that which is uttered by men in real life, under the actual pressure of those passions, certain shadows of which the Poet thus produces, or feels to be produced, in himself. However exalted a notion we would wish to cher-

---

5. Thomas Gray (1716–1771), "Sonnet on the Death of Richard West" (1775).   6. John Milton (1608–1674), *Paradise Lost* (1667), 1.620.   7. Blood.

ish of the character of a Poet, it is obvious, that, while he describes and imitates passions, his situation is altogether slavish and mechanical, compared with the freedom and power of real and substantial action and suffering. So that it will be the wish of the Poet to bring his feelings near to those of the persons whose feelings he describes, nay, for short spaces of time perhaps, to let himself slip into an entire delusion, and even confound and identify his own feelings with theirs; modifying only the language which is thus suggested to him, by a consideration that he describes for a particular purpose, that of giving pleasure. Here, then, he will apply the principle on which I have so much insisted, namely, that of selection; on this he will depend for removing what would otherwise be painful or disgusting in the passion; he will feel that there is no necessity to trick out or to elevate nature: and, the more industriously he applies this principle, the deeper will be his faith that no words which his fancy or imagination can suggest, will be to be compared with those which are the emanations of reality and truth. . . .

Aristotle,[8] I have been told, hath said, that Poetry is the most philosophic of all writing: it is so: its object is truth, not individual and local, but general, and operative; not standing upon external testimony, but carried alive into the heart by passion; truth which is its own testimony, which gives strength and divinity to the tribunal to which it appeals, and receives them from the same tribunal. Poetry is the image of man and nature. The obstacles which stand in the way of the fidelity of the Biographer and Historian, and of their consequent utility, are incalculably greater than those which are to be encountered by the Poet who has an adequate notion of the dignity of his art. The Poet writes under one restriction only, namely, the necessity of giving immediate pleasure to a human Being possessed of that information which may be expected from him, not as a lawyer, a physician, a mariner, an astronomer or a natural philosopher, but as a Man. . . .

Nor let this necessity of producing immediate pleasure be considered as a degradation of the Poet's art. It is far otherwise. It is . . . a homage paid to the native and naked dignity of man, to the grand elementary principle of pleasure, by which he knows, and feels, and lives, and moves. We have no sympathy but what is propagated by pleasure. . . . We have no knowledge, that is, no general principles drawn from the contemplation of particular facts, but what has been built up by pleasure, and exists in us by pleasure alone. The Man of Science, the Chemist and Mathematician, whatever difficulties and disgusts they may have had to struggle with, know and feel this. However painful may be the objects with which the Anatomist's knowledge is connected, he feels that his knowledge is pleasure; and where he has no pleasure he has no knowledge. What then does the Poet? He considers man and the objects that surround him as acting and reacting upon each other, so as to produce an infinite complexity of pain and pleasure. . . .

The knowledge both of the Poet and the Man of science is pleasure; but the knowledge of the one cleaves to us as a necessary part of our existence, our natural and unalienable inheritance; the other is a personal and individual acquisition, slow to come to us, and by no habitual and direct sympathy connecting us with our fellowbeings. The Man of Science seeks truth as a remote and unknown benefactor; he cherishes and loves it in his solitude: the Poet, singing a song in which all human beings join with him, rejoices in the presence of truth as our visible friend and hourly companion. Poetry is the breath and finer spirit of all knowledge; it is the impassioned

---

8. Aristotle (384–322 BC), Greek philosopher.

expression which is in the countenance of all Science. Emphatically may it be said of the Poet, as Shakespeare hath said of man, "that he looks before and after."[9] He is the rock of defence for human nature; an upholder and preserver, carrying every where with him relationship and love. In spite of difference of soil and climate, of language and manners, of laws and customs, in spite of things silently gone out of mind, and things violently destroyed, the Poet binds together by passion and knowledge the vast empire of human society, as it is spread over the whole earth, and over all time.

[Emotion Recollected in Tranquillity]

I have said that Poetry is the spontaneous overflow of powerful feelings: it takes its origin from emotion recollected in tranquillity: the emotion is contemplated till by a species of reaction the tranquillity gradually disappears, and an emotion, kindred to that which was before the subject of contemplation, is gradually produced, and does itself actually exist in the mind. In this mood successful composition generally begins, and in a mood similar to this it is carried on; but the emotion, of whatever kind and in whatever degree, from various causes is qualified by various pleasures, so that in describing any passions whatsoever, which are voluntarily described, the mind will upon the whole be in a state of enjoyment. Now, if Nature be thus cautious in preserving in a state of enjoyment a being thus employed, the Poet ought to profit by the lesson thus held forth to him, and ought especially to take care, that whatever passions he communicates to his Reader, those passions, if his Reader's mind be sound and vigorous, should always be accompanied with an overbalance of pleasure. Now the music of harmonious metrical language, the sense of difficulty overcome, and the blind association of pleasure which has been previously received from works of rhyme or metre of the same or similar construction, an indistinct perception perpetually renewed of language closely resembling that of real life, and yet, in the circumstance of metre, differing from it so widely[,] all these imperceptibly make up a complex feeling of delight, which is of the most important use in tempering the painful feeling which will always be found intermingled with powerful descriptions of the deeper passions.

—1800

There was a Boy[1]

There was a Boy; ye knew him well, ye Cliffs
And Islands of Winander![2] many a time,
At evening, when the earliest stars had just begun
To move along the edges of the hills,
Rising or setting, would he stand alone,   5
Beneath the trees, or by the glimmering lake,
And there, with fingers interwoven, both hands
Press'd closely palm to palm and to his mouth
Uplifted, he, as through an instrument,
Blew mimic hootings to the silent owls   10
That they might answer him. And they would shout

9. William Shakespeare (1564–1616), *Hamlet* (1603), 4.4.34.

1. Autobiographical poem written in Gosler, Germany, and stitched into *The Prelude* (1850).   2. Windermere, Lake District.

Across the wat'ry vale and shout again
Responsive to his call, with quivering peals,
And long halloos, and screams, and echoes loud
Redoubled and redoubled, a wild scene   15
Of mirth and jocund din! And, when it chanced
That pauses of deep silence mock'd his skill,
Then, sometimes, in that silence, while he hung
Listening, a gentle shock of mild surprize
Has carried far into his heart the voice   20
Of mountain-torrents; or the visible scene
Would enter unawares into his mind
With all its solemn imagery, its rocks,
Its woods, and that uncertain heaven receiv'd
Into the bosom of the steady lake.   25
  Fair are the woods, and beauteous is the spot,
The vale where he was born: the Church-yard hangs
Upon a slope above the village school[3];
And there along that bank where I have pass'd
At evening, I believe, that near his grave   30
A full half-hour together I have stood,
Mute—for he died when he was ten years old.

—1800

Ruth: Or the Influences of Nature

When Ruth was left half desolate,
Her Father took another Mate;
And Ruth, not seven years old,
A slighted Child, at her own will
Went wandering over dale and hill,   5
In thoughtless freedom bold.

And she had made a Pipe of straw,
And from that oaten Pipe could draw
All sounds of winds and floods;
Had built a bower upon the green,   10
As if she from her birth had been
An infant of the woods.

Beneath her Father's roof, alone
She seemed to live; her thoughts her own;
Herself her own delight;   15
Pleased with herself, nor sad, nor gay;
And, passing thus the live-long day,
She grew to Woman's height.

---

3. The Hawkshead School, Vale of Esthwaite, where Wordsworth was sent to school after his mother's death.

412   William Wordsworth

There came a Youth from Georgia's shore,
A military Casque he wore,   20
With splendid feathers drest;
He brought them from the Cherokees;
The feathers nodded in the breeze,
And made a gallant crest.

From Indian blood you deem him sprung: 25
Ah no! he spake the English tongue,
And bore a Soldier's name;
And, when America was free
From battle and from jeopardy,[1]
He 'cross the ocean came.   30

With hues of genius on his cheek
In finest tones the Youth could speak
—While he was yet a Boy,
The moon, the glory of the sun,
And streams that murmur as they run,   35
Had been his dearest joy.

He was a lovely Youth! I guess
The panther in the Wilderness
Was not so fair as he;
And, when he chose to sport and play,   40
No dolphin ever was so gay
Upon the tropic sea.

Among the Indians he had fought,
And with him many tales he brought
Of pleasure and of fear;
Such tales as told to any Maid   45
By such a Youth, in the green shade,
Were perilous to hear.

He told of Girls—a happy rout!
Who quit their fold with dance and shout
Their pleasant Indian Town,   50
To gather strawberries all day long;
Returning with a choral song
When daylight is gone down.

He spake of plants divine and strange
That every hour their blossoms change,   55
Ten thousand lovely hues!

---

1. After the Revolution ended in 1783.

With budding, fading, faded flowers
They stand the wonder of the bowers
From morn to evening dews.

He told of the Magnolia, spread
High as a cloud, high over head!
The Cypress and her spire;
—Of flowers that with one scarlet gleam
Cover a hundred leagues, and seem
To set the hills on fire.

The Youth of green savannahs spake,
And many an endless, endless lake,
With all its fairy crowds
Of islands, that together lie
As quietly as spots of sky
Among the evening clouds.

And then he said, "How sweet it were
A fisher or a hunter there,
A gardener in the shade,
Still wandering with an easy mind,
To build a household fire, and find
A home in every glade!

What days and what sweet years! Ah me:
Our life were life indeed, with thee
So passed in quiet bliss,
And all the while," said he, "to know
That we were in a world of woe,
On such an earth as this!"

And then he sometimes interwove
Fond thoughts about a Father's love:
"For there," said he, "are spun
Around the heart such tender ties,
That our own children to our eyes
Are dearer than the sun.

Sweet Ruth! and could you go with me
My helpmate in the woods to be,
Our shed at night to rear;
Or run, my own adopted Bride,
A sylvan Huntress at my side,
And drive the flying deer!

Beloved Ruth!"—No more he said.
The wakeful Ruth at midnight shed

A solitary tear:
She thought again—and did agree
With him to sail across the sea,
And drive the flying deer.

"And now, as fitting is and right,
We in the Church our faith will plight,
A Husband and a Wife."
Even so they did; and I may say
That to sweet Ruth that happy day
Was more than human life.

Through dream and vision did she sink,
Delighted all the while to think
That on those lonesome floods,
And green savannahs, she should share
His board with lawful joy, and bear
His name in the wild woods.

But, as you have before been told,
This Stripling, sportive, gay, and bold,
And with his dancing crest
So Beautiful, through savage lands
Had roamed about, with vagrant bands
Of Indians in the West.

The wind, the tempest roaring high,
The tumult of a tropic sky,
Might well be dangerous food
For him, a Youth to whom was given
So much of earth—so much of Heaven,
And such impetuous blood.

Whatever in those climes he found
Irregular in sight or sound
Did to his mind impart
A kindred impulse, seemed allied
To his own powers, and justified
The workings of his heart.

Nor less, to feed voluptuous thought,
The beauteous forms of nature wrought,
Fair trees and lovely flowers;
The breezes their own languor lent;
The stars had feelings, which they sent
Into those gorgeous bowers.

Yet, in his worst pursuits, I ween
That sometimes there did intervene

100

105

110

115

120

125

130

135

140

Pure hopes of high intent:
For passions linked to forms so fair
And stately, needs must have their share
Of noble sentiment.

But ill he lived, much evil saw,   145
With men to whom no better law
Nor better life was known;
Deliberately, and undeceived,
These wild men's vices he received
And gave them back his own.   150

His genius and his moral frame
Were thus impaired, and he became
The slave of low desires:
A Man who without self-control
Would seek what the degraded soul   155
Unworthily admires.

And yet he with no feigned delight
Had wooed the Maiden, day and night
Had loved her, night and morn:
What could he less than love a Maid   160
Whose heart with so much nature played?
So kind and so forlorn!

Sometimes, most earnestly, he said,
"O Ruth! I have been worse than dead;
False thoughts, thoughts bold and vain,   165
Encompassed me on every side
When first, in confidence and pride,
I crossed the Atlantic Main.[2]

It was a fresh and glorious world,
A banner bright that was unfurled   170
Before me suddenly:
I looked upon those hills and plains,
And seemed as if let loose from chains,
To live at liberty.

But wherefore speak of this? for now,   175
Sweet Ruth! with thee, I know not how,
I feel my spirit burn—
Even as the east when day comes forth:
And, to the west, and south, and north,
The morning doth return."   180

---

2. Ocean.

Full soon that purer mind was gone;
No hope, no wish remained, not one,—
They stirred him now no more:
New objects did new pleasure give,
And once again he wished to live   185
As lawless as before.

Meanwhile, as thus with him it fared,
They for the voyage were prepared,
And went to the sea-shore;
But, when they thither came, the Youth
Deserted his poor Bride, and Ruth   190
Could never find him more.

"God help thee, Ruth!"—Such pains she had
That she in half a year was mad,
And in a prison housed;   195
And there she sang tumultuous songs,
By recollection of her wrongs
To fearful passion roused.

Yet sometimes milder hours she knew,
Nor wanted sun, nor rain, nor dew,   200
Nor pastimes of the May.
—They all were with her in her cell,
And a wild brook with cheerful kneel
Did o'er the pebbles play.

When Ruth three seasons thus had lain,   205
There came a respite to her pain;
She from her prison fled;
But of the Vagrant none took thought;
And where it liked her best she sought
Her shelter and her bread.   210

Among the fields she breathed again:
The master-current of her brain
Ran permanent and free;
And, coming to the banks of Tone,[3]
There did she rest; and dwelt alone   215
Under the greenwood tree.

The engines of her pain, the tools
That shaped her sorrow, rocks and pools,
And airs that gently stir

---

3. A river in Somerset, England.

The vernal leaves, she loved them still,   220
Nor ever taxed them with the ill
Which had been done to her.

A Barn her *winter* bed supplies;
But, till the warmth of summer skies
And summer days is gone,   225
(And in this tale we all agree)
She sleeps beneath the greenwood tree,
And other home hath none.

An innocent life, yet far astray!
And Ruth will, long before her day,   230
Be broken down and old:
Sore aches she needs must have! but less
Of mind, than body's wretchedness,
From damp, and rain, and cold.

If she is press'd by want of food,   235
She from her dwelling in the wood
Repairs to a road side;
And there she begs at one steep place
Where up and down with easy pace
The horsemen-travellers ride.   240

That oaten Pipe of hers is mute,
Or thrown away; but with a flute
Her loneliness she cheers:
This flute, made of a hemlock stalk,
At evening in his homeward walk   245
The Quantock Woodman hears.

I, too, have passed her on the hills,
Setting her little water-mills
By spouts and fountains wild—
Such small machinery as she turned   250
Ere she had wept, ere she had mourned,
A young and happy Child!

Farewell! and when thy days are told,
Ill-fated Ruth! in hallowed mould
Thy corpse shall buried be;   255
For thee a funeral bell shall ring,
And all the congregation sing
A Christian psalm for thee.

—1800

Nutting[1]

It seems a day
(I speak of one from many singled out)
One of those heavenly days that cannot die;
When forth I walked from our cottage-door,
And with a wallet[2] o'er my shoulder slung,   5
A nutting-crook in hand; and turn'd my steps
Towards the distant wood, a Figure quaint,
Trick'd out in proud disguise of Beggar's weeds[3]
Put on for the occasion, by advice
And exhortation of my frugal Dame.[4]   10
Motley acccoutrement! of power to smile
At thorns, and brakes, and brambles, and, in truth,
More ragged than need was. Among the woods,
And o'er the pathless rocks, I forc'd my way
Until, at length, I came to one dear nook   15
Unvisited, where not a broken bough
Droop'd with its wither'd leaves, ungracious sign
Of devastation, but the hazels rose
Tall and erect, with milk-white clusters hung,
A virgin scene!—A little while I stood,   20
Breathing with such suppression of the heart
As joy delights in; and with wise restraint
Voluptuous, fearless of a rival, eyed
The banquet; or beneath the trees I sate
Among the flowers, and with the flowers I play'd;   25
A temper known to those, who, after long
And weary expectation, have been bless'd
With sudden happiness beyond all hope.—
—Perhaps it was a bower beneath whose leaves
The violets of five seasons re-appear   30
And fade, unseen by any human eye,
Where fairy water-breaks[5] do murmur on
For ever, and I saw the sparkling foam,
And with my cheek on one of those green stones
That, fleec'd with moss, beneath the shady trees,   35
Lay round me, scatter'd like a flock of sheep,
I heard the murmur and the murmuring sound,
In that sweet mood when pleasure loves to pay
Tribute to ease, and, of its joy secure
The heart luxuriates with indifferent things,   40
Wasting its kindliness on stocks and stones,
And on the vacant air. Then up I rose,
And dragg'd to earth both branch and bough, with crash

---

1. Intended for *The Prelude* (1850).   2. Knapsack.   3. Clothes.   4. Ann Tyson, Wordsworth's guardian after the death of his mother.   5. Small rapids.

And merciless ravage: and the shady nook
Of hazels, and the green and mossy bower   45
Deform'd and sullied, patiently gave up
Their quiet being: and unless I now
Confound my present feelings with the past,
Even then, when from the bower I turn'd away,
Exulting, rich beyond the wealth of kings   50
I felt a sense of pain when I beheld
The silent trees, and saw the intruding sky.—

Then, dearest Maiden![6] move along these shades
In gentleness of heart; with gentle hand
Touch,—for there is a Spirit in the woods.   55

—1800

Michael

A Pastoral Poem

If from the public way you turn your steps
Up the tumultuous brook of Green-head Gill,[1]
You will suppose that with an upright path
Your feet must struggle; in such bold ascent
The pastoral Mountains front you, face to face.   5
But, courage! for around that boisterous Brook
The mountains have all open'd out themselves,
And made a hidden valley of their own.
No habitation can be seen; but such
As journey thither find themselves alone   10
With a few sheep, with rocks and stones, and kites[2]
That overhead are sailing in the sky.

It is in truth an utter solitude;
Nor should I have made mention of this Dell
But for one object which you might pass by,   15
Might see and notice not. Beside the brook
There is a straggling heap of unhewn stones!
And to that place a story appertains,
Which, though it be ungarnish'd with events,
Is not unfit, I deem, for the fire-side,   20
Or for the summer shade. It was the first,
The earliest of those tales that spake to me
Of Shepherds, dwellers in the valleys, men
Whom I already lov'd; not verily
For their own sakes, but for the fields and hills   25

6. Lucy, the fictitious subject of many of Wordsworth's poems.
1. A ravine in Grasmere.   2. A bird of prey.

Where was their occupation and abode.
And hence this Tale, while I was yet a boy
Careless of books, yet having felt the power
Of Nature, by the gentle agency
Of natural objects, led me on to feel   30
For passions that were not my own, and think
At random and imperfectly indeed
On man; the heart of man, and human life.
Therefore, although it be a history
Homely and rude, I will relate the same   35
For the delight of a few natural hearts,
And with yet fonder feeling, for the sake
Of youthful Poets, who among these Hills
Will be my second self when I am gone.

Upon the Forest-side in Grasmere Vale   40
There dwelt a Shepherd, Michael was his name,
An old man, stout of heart, and strong of limb.
His bodily frame had been from youth to age
Of an unusual strength; his mind was keen
Intense and frugal, apt for all affairs,   45
And in his Shepherd's calling he was prompt
And watchful more than ordinary men.
Hence had he learn'd the meaning of all winds,
Of blasts of every tone, and often-times,
When others heeded not, he heard the South   50
Make subterraneous music, like the noise
Of Bagpipers on distant Highland hills;
The Shepherd, at such warning, of his flock
Bethought him, and he to himself would say
The winds are now devising work for me!   55
And truly at all times the storm, that drives
The Traveller to a shelter, summon'd him
Up to the mountains: he had been alone
Amid the heart of many thousand mists
That came to him, and left him, on the heights.   60
So liv'd he till his eightieth year was pass'd.

And grossly that man errs, who should suppose
That the green Valleys, and the Streams and Rocks
Were things indifferent to the Shepherd's thoughts.
Fields, where with chearful spirits he had breath'd   65
The common air; the hills, which he so oft
Had climb'd, with vigorous steps; which had impress'd
So many incidents upon his mind
Of hardship, skill or courage, joy or fear;
Which, like a book, preserv'd the memory   70

Of the dumb animals, whom he had sav'd,
Had fed or shelter'd, linking to such acts,
So grateful in themselves, the certainty
Of honourable gains; these fields, these hills
Which were his living Being, even more   75
Than his own Blood—what could they less? had laid
Strong hold on his affections, were to him
A pleasurable feeling of blind love,
The pleasure which there is in life itself.

He had not passed his days in singleness.   80
He had a Wife, a comely Matron, old
Though younger than himself full twenty years.
She was a woman of a stirring life
Whose heart was in her house: two wheels she had
Of antique form; this large, for spinning wool,   85
That small for flax; and if one wheel had rest,
It was because the other was at work.
The Pair had but one Inmate[3] in their house,
An only Child, who had been born to them
When Michael telling o'er his years began   90
To deem that he was old, in Shepherd's phrase,
With one foot in the grave. This only son,
With two brave sheep dogs tried in many a storm,
The one of an inestimable worth,
Made all their Household. I may truly say,   95
That they were as a proverb in the vale
For endless industry. When day was gone,
And from their occupations out of doors
The Son and Father were come home, even then
Their labour did not cease, unless when all   100
Turn'd to the cleanly supper-board, and there
Each with a mess of pottage and skimm'd milk,
Sate round the basket pil'd with oaten cakes,
And their plain home-made cheese. Yet when their meal
Was ended, LUKE (for so the Son was nam'd)   105
And his old Father, both betook themselves
To such convenient work as might employ
Their hands by the fire-side; perhaps to card
Wool for the House-wife's spindle, or repair
Some injury done to sickle, flail, or scythe,   110
Or other implement of house or field.

Down from the ceiling, by the chimney's edge,
That in our ancient uncouth country style

---

3. Fellow inhabitant.

Did with a huge projection overbrow
Large space beneath, as duly as the light   115
Of day grew dim, the House-wife hung a lamp;
An aged utensil, which had perform'd
Service beyond all others of its kind.
Early at evening did it burn and late,
Surviving Comrade of uncounted Hours   120
Which going by from year to year had found
And left the Couple neither gay perhaps
Nor chearful, yet with objects and with hopes
Living a life of eager industry.
And now, when LUKE was in his eighteenth year,   125
There by the light of this old lamp they sate,
Father and Son, while late into the night
The House-wife plied her own peculiar work,
Making the cottage thro' the silent hours
Murmur as with the sound of summer flies.   130
Not with a waste of words, but for the sake
Of pleasure, which I know that I shall give
To many living now, I of this Lamp
Speak thus minutely: for there are no few
Whose memories will bear witness to my tale.   135
This Light was famous in its neighbourhood,
And was a public Symbol of the life,
That thrifty Pair had liv'd. For, as it chanc'd,
Their Cottage on a plot of rising ground
Stood single, with large prospect North and South,   140
High into Easedale, up to Dunmal-Raise,
And Westward to the village near the Lake;
And from this constant light so regular
And so far seen, the House itself by all
Who dwelt within the limits of the vale,   145
Both old and young, was nam'd The Evening Star.

Thus living on through such a length of years,
The Shepherd, if he lov'd himself, must needs
Have lov'd his Help-mate; but to Michael's heart
This Son of his old age was yet more dear—   150
Effect which might perhaps have been produc'd
By that instinctive tenderness, the same
Blind Spirit, which is in the blood of all,
Or that a child, more than all other gifts,
Brings hope with it, and forward-looking thoughts,   155
And stirrings of inquietude, when they
By tendency of nature needs must fail.
From such, and other causes, to the thoughts
Of the old Man his only Son was now
The dearest object that he knew on earth.   160

Exceeding was the love he bare to him,
His Heart and his Heart's joy! for oftentimes
Old Michael, while he was a babe in arms,
Had done him female service, not alone
For dalliance and delight, as is the use   165
Of Fathers, but with patient mind enforc'd
To acts of tenderness; and he had rock'd
His cradle, as with a woman's gentle hand.

And in a later time, ere yet the Boy
Had put on Boy's attire, did Michael love,   170
Albeit of a stern unbending mind,
To have the young one in his sight, when he
Had work by his own door, or when he sate
With sheep before him on his Shepherd's stool,
Beneath that large old Oak, which near their door   175
Stood, and from its enormous breadth of shade
Chosen for the Shearer's covert from the sun,
Thence in our rustic dialect was call'd
The CLIPPING TREE, a name which yet it bears.
There, while they two were sitting in the shade,   180
With others round them, earnest all and blithe,
Would Michael exercise his heart with looks
Of fond correction and reproof bestow'd
Upon the child, if he disturb'd the sheep
By catching at their legs, or with his shouts   185
Scar'd them, while they lay still beneath the shears.

And when by Heaven's good grace the Boy grew up
A healthy Lad, and carried in his cheek
Two steady roses that were five years old,
Then Michael from a winter coppice[4] cut   190
With his own hand a sapling, which he hoop'd
With iron, making it throughout in all
Due requisites a perfect Shepherd's Staff,
And gave it to the Boy; wherewith equipp'd
He as a Watchman oftentimes was plac'd   195
At gate or gap, to stem or turn the flock,
And to his office prematurely call'd
There stood the urchin, as you will divine,
Something between a hindrance and a help,
And for this cause not always, I believe,   200
Receiving from his Father hire of praise.
Though nought was left undone which staff or voice,
Or looks, or threatening gestures, could perform.
But soon as Luke, full ten years old, could stand

---

4. Grove of trees.

Against the mountain blasts, and to the heights,   205
Not fearing toil, nor length of weary ways,
He with his Father daily went, and they
Were as companions, why should I relate
That objects which the Shepherd loved before
Were dearer now? that from the Boy there came   210
Feelings and emanations, things which were
Light to the sun and music to the wind;
And that the Old Man's heart seemed born again.
Thus in his Father's sight the Boy grew up:
And now, when he had reached his eighteenth year,   215
He was his comfort and his daily hope.

While this good household thus were living on
From day to day, to Michael's ear there came
Distressful tidings. Long before the time
Of which I speak, the Shepherd had been bound   220
In surety⁵ for his Brother's Son, a man
Of an industrious life, and ample means;
But unforeseen misfortunes suddenly
Had press'd upon him, and old Michael now
Was summon'd to discharge the forfeiture,   225
A grievous penalty, but little less
Than half his substance. This un-look'd for claim,
At the first hearing, for a moment took
More hope out of his life than he supposed
That any old man ever could have lost.   230
As soon as he had gather'd so much strength
That he could look his trouble in the face,
It seem'd that his sole refuge was to sell
A portion of his patrimonial fields.⁶
Such was his first resolve; he thought again,   235
And his heart fail'd him. "Isabel," said he,
Two evenings after he had heard the news,
"I have been toiling more than seventy years,
And in the open sun-shine of God's love
Have we all liv'd; yet if these fields of ours   240
Should pass into a Stranger's hand, I think
That I could not lie quiet in my grave.
Our lot is a hard lot; the Sun itself
Has scarcely been more diligent than I,
And I have liv'd to be a fool at last   245
To my own family. An evil Man
That was, and made an evil choice, if he
Were false to us; and if he were not false,
There are ten thousand to whom loss like this

---

5. Made financially responsible by law.   6. Fields inherited from his father by primogeniture.

Had been no sorrow. I forgive him—but   250
'Twere better to be dumb than to talk thus.
When I began, my purpose was to speak
Of remedies and of a chearful hope.
Our Luke shall leave us, Isabel; the land
Shall not go from us, and it shall be free;   255
He shall possess it, free as is the wind
That passes over it. We have, thou knowest,
Another Kinsman, he will be our friend
In this distress. He is a prosperous man,
Thriving in trade, and Luke to him shall go,   260
And with his Kinsman's help and his own thrift,
He quickly will repair this loss, and then
May come again to us. If here he stay,
What can be done? Where every one is poor
What can be gained?" At this the old Man paus'd,   265
And Isabel sate silent, for her mind
Was busy, looking back into past times.
There's Richard Bateman, thought she to herself,
He was a parish-boy at the church-door
They made a gathering for him, shillings, pence,   270
And halfpennies, wherewith the Neighbours bought
A Basket, which they fill'd with Pedlar's wares,
And with this Basket on his arm, the Lad
Went up to London, found a Master there,
Who out of many chose the trusty Boy   275
To go and overlook his merchandise
Beyond the seas, where he grew wond'rous rich,
And left estates and monies to the poor,
And at his birth-place, built a Chapel, floor'd
With Marble, which he sent from foreign lands.   280
These thoughts, and many others of like sort,
Pass'd quickly thro' the mind of Isabel,
And her face brighten'd. The old Man was glad,
And thus resum'd. "Well! Isabel, this scheme
These two days, has been meat and drink to me.   285
Far more than we have lost is left us yet.
—We have enough—I wish indeed that I
Were younger, but this hope is a good hope.
—Make ready Luke's best garments, of the best
Buy for him more, and let us send him forth   290
To-morrow, or the next day, or to-night:
—If he could go, the Boy should go to-night."

Here Michael ceas'd, and to the fields went forth
With a light heart. The House-wife for five days
Was restless morn and night, and all day long   295

Wrought on with her best fingers to prepare
Things needful for the journey of her Son.
But Isabel was glad when Sunday came
To stop her in her work; for, when she lay
By Michael's side, she through the last two nights   300
Heard him, how he was troubled in his sleep:
And when they rose at morning she could see
That all his hopes were gone. That day at noon
She said to Luke, while they two by themselves
Were sitting at the door, "Thou must not go,   305
We have no other Child but thee to lose,
None to remember—do not go away,
For if thou leave thy Father he will die."
The Lad made answer with a jocund voice,
And Isabel, when she had told her fears,   310
Recover'd heart. That evening her best fare
Did she bring forth, and all together sate
Like happy people round a Christmas fire.

Next morning Isabel resum'd her work,
And all the ensuing week the house appear'd   315
As chearful as a grove in Spring: at length
The expected letter from their Kinsman came,
With kind assurances that he would do
His utmost for the welfare of the Boy,
To which requests were added, that forthwith   320
He might be sent to him. Ten times or more
The letter was read over; Isabel
Went forth to shew it to the neighbours round:
Nor was there at that time on English Land
A prouder heart than Luke's. When Isabel   325
Had to her house return'd, the Old Man said,
"He shall depart to-morrow." To this word
The House-wife answered, talking much of things
Which, if at such short notice he should go,
Would surely be forgotten. But at length   330
She gave consent, and Michael was at ease.

Near the tumultuous brook of Green-head Gill,
In that deep Valley, Michael had design'd
To build a Sheep-fold; and, before he heard
The tidings of his melancholy loss,   335
For this same purpose he had gathered up
A heap of stones, which close to the brook side
Lay thrown together, ready for the work.
With Luke that evening thitherward he walk'd;
And soon as they had reach'd the place he stopp'd,   340

And thus the Old Man spake to him. "My Son,
To-morrow thou wilt leave me; with full heart
I look upon thee, for thou art the same
That wert a promise to me ere thy birth,
And all thy life hast been my daily joy.   345
I will relate to thee some little part
Of our two histories; 'twill do thee good
When thou art from me, even if I should speak
On things thou canst not know of.—After thou
First cam'st into the world—as oft befalls   350
To new-born infants, thou didst sleep away
Two days, and blessings from thy Father's tongue
Then fell upon thee. Day by day pass'd on,
And still I lov'd thee with encreasing love.
Never to living ear came sweeter sounds   355
Than when I heard thee by our own fire-side
First uttering without words a natural tune,
While thou, a feeding babe, didst in thy joy
Sing at thy Mother's breast. Month followed month,
And in the open fields my life was pass'd   360
And on the mountains, else I think that thou
Hadst been brought up upon thy father's knees.
—But we were playmates, Luke; among these hills,
As well thou know'st, in us the old and young
Have play'd together, nor with me didst thou   365
Lack any pleasure which a boy can know."

Luke had a manly heart; but at these words
He sobb'd aloud. The Old Man grasp'd his hand,
And said, "Nay do not take it so—I see
That these are things of which I need not speak.   370
—Even to the utmost I have been to thee
A kind and a good Father: and herein
I but repay a gift which I myself
Receiv'd at others' hands, for, though now old
Beyond the common life of man, I still   375
Remember them who lov'd me in my youth.
Both of them sleep together: here they liv'd,
As all their Forefathers had done, and when
At length their time was come, they were not loth
To give their bodies to the family mold.   380
I wish'd that thou should'st live the life they liv'd.
But 'tis a long time to look back, my Son,
And see so little gain from sixty years.
These fields were burthen'd when they came to me;
'Till I was forty years of age, not more   385
Than half of my inheritance was mine.

I toil'd and toil'd; God bless'd me in my work,
And 'till these three weeks past the land was free.
—It looks as if it never could endure
Another Master. Heaven forgive me, Luke,   390
If I judge ill for thee, but it seems good
That thou should'st go." At this the Old Man paus'd;
Then, pointing to the Stones near which they stood,
Thus, after a short silence, he resum'd:
"This was a work for us, and now, my Son,   395
It is a work for me. But, lay one Stone—
Here, lay it for me, Luke, with thine own hands.
I for the purpose brought thee to this place.
Nay, Boy, be of good hope:—we both may live
To see a better day. At eighty-four   400
I still am strong and stout;—do thou thy part;
I will do mine—I will begin again
With many tasks that were resign'd to thee;
Up to the heights, and in among the storms,
Will I without thee go again, and do   405
All works which I was wont to do alone,
Before I knew thy face.—Heaven bless thee, Boy!
Thy heart these two weeks has been beating fast
With many hopes—it shoud be so—yes—yes—
I knew that thou could'st never have a wish   410
To leave me, Luke, thou hast been bound to me
Only by links of love, when thou art gone
What will be left to us!—But, I forget
My purposes. Lay now the corner-stone,
As I requested, and hereafter, Luke,   415
When thou art gone away, should evil men
Be thy companions, let this sheep-fold be
Thy anchor and thy shield; amid all fear
And all temptation, let it be to thee
An emblem of the life thy Fathers liv'd,   420
Who, being innocent, did for that cause
Bestir them in good deeds. Now, fare thee well—
When thou return'st, thou in this place wilt see
A work which is not here, a covenant
'Twill be between us—but, whatever fate   425
Befall thee, I shall love thee to the last,
And bear thy memory with me to the grave."

The Shepherd ended here; and Luke stoop'd down,
And as his Father had requested, laid
The first stone of the Sheep-fold; at the sight   430
The Old Man's grief broke from him, to his heart
He press'd his Son, he kissed him and wept;
And to the House together they return'd.

Next morning, as had been resolv'd, the Boy
Began his journey, and when he had reach'd   435
The public Way, he put on a bold face;
And all the Neighbours, as he pass'd their doors
Came forth with wishes and with farewell pray'rs,
That follow'd him 'till he was out of sight.

A good report did from their Kinsman come,   440
Of Luke and his well-doing; and the Boy
Wrote loving letters, full of wond'rous news,
Which, as the House-wife phrased it, were throughout
The prettiest letters that were ever seen.
Both parents read them with rejoicing hearts.   445
So, many months pass'd on: and once again
The Shepherd went about his daily work
With confident and chearful thoughts; and now
Sometimes when he could find a leisure hour
He to that valley took his way, and there   450
Wrought at the Sheep-fold. Meantime Luke began
To slacken in his duty; and, at length
He in the dissolute city gave himself
To evil courses: ignominy and shame
Fell on him, so that he was driven at last   455
To seek a hiding-place beyond the seas.

There is a comfort in the strength of love;
'Twill make a thing endurable, which else
Would break the heart:—Old Michael found it so.
I have convers'd with more than one who well   460
Remember the Old Man, and what he was
Years after he had heard this heavy news.
His bodily frame had been from youth to age
Of an unusual strength. Among the rocks
He went, and still look'd up upon the sun,   465
And listen'd to the wind; and as before
Perform'd all kinds of labour for his Sheep,
And for the land, his small inheritance.
And to that hollow Dell from time to time
Did he repair, to build the Fold of which   470
His flock had need. 'Tis not forgotten yet
The pity which was then in every heart
For the Old Man—and 'tis believed by all
That many and many a day he thither went,
And never lifted up a single stone.   475

There, by the Sheep-fold, sometimes was he seen
Sitting alone, with that his faithful Dog,
Then old, beside him, lying at his feet.
The length of full seven years from time to time

He at the building of this Sheep-fold wrought,   480
And left the work unfinished when he died.

Three years, or little more, did Isabel,
Survive her Husband: at her death the estate
Was sold, and went into a Stranger's hand.
The Cottage which was nam'd The Evening Star   485
Is gone, the ploughshare has been through the ground
On which it stood; great changes have been wrought
In all the neighbourhood, yet the Oak is left
That grew beside their Door; and the remains
Of the unfinished Sheep-fold may be seen   490
Beside the boisterous brook of Green-head Gill.

—1800

To Toussaint L'Ouverture[1]

Toussaint, the most unhappy man of men!
Whether the whistling Rustic tend his plough
Within thy hearing, or thy head be now
Pillowed in some deep dungeon's earless den;—
O miserable Chieftain! where and when   5
Wilt thou find patience? Yet die not; do thou
Wear rather in thy bonds a cheerful brow:
Though fallen thyself, never to rise again,
Live, and take comfort. Thou hast left behind
Powers that will work for thee; air, earth, and skies;   10
There's not a breathing of the common wind
That will forget thee; thou hast great allies;
Thy friends are exultations, agonies,
And love, and man's unconquerable mind.

—1807

To Thomas Clarkson[1]

On the Final Passing of the Bill for the
Abolition of the Slave Trade, March, 1807

Clarkson! it was an obstinate Hill to climb;
How toilsome—nay, how dire—it was, by Thee
Is known,—by none, perhaps, so feelingly:
But Thou, who, starting in thy fervent prime,
Didst first lead forth this pilgrimage sublime,   5
Hast heard the constant Voice its charge repeat,
Which, out of thy young heart's oracular seat,

1. (1743–1803) Liberator of Haiti from slavery, imprisoned and killed by Napoleon.
1. (1760–1846) Abolitionist and friend of Wordsworth.

First roused thee.—O true yoke-fellow of Time,
With unabating effort, see, the palm
Is won, and by all Nations shall be worn!   10
The bloody Writing is forever torn;
And Thou henceforth shalt have a good Man's calm,
A great Man's happiness; thy zeal shall find
Repose at length, firm Friend of human kind!

—1807

The world is too much with us

The world is too much with us; late and soon,
Getting and spending, we lay waste our powers:
Little we see in nature that is ours;
We have given our hearts away, a sordid boon!
The Sea that bares her bosom to the moon;   5
The Winds that will be howling at all hours
And are up-gathered now like sleeping flowers;
For this, for everything, we are out of tune;
It moves us not. Great God! I'd rather be
A Pagan suckled in a creed outworn;   10
So might I, standing on this pleasant lea,[1]
Have glimpses that would make me less forlorn;
Have sight of Proteus[2] rising from the sea;
Or hear old Triton[3] blow his wreathed horn.

—1807

Composed upon Westminster Bridge, Sept. 3, 1802

Earth has not anything to shew more fair:
Dull would he be of soul who could pass by
A sight so touching in its majesty:
This City[1] now doth like a garment wear
The beauty of the morning; silent, bare,   5
Ships, towers, domes, theatres, and temples lie
Open unto the fields, and to the sky;
All bright and glittering in the smokeless air.
Never did sun more beautifully steep
In his first splendour, valley, rock, or hill;   10
Ne'er saw I, never felt, a calm so deep!
The river glideth at his own sweet will:
Dear God! the very houses seem asleep;
And all that mighty heat is lying still!

—1807

---

1. Lawn.   2. Shape-changer who guards the seals of Poseidon, god of the sea.   3. Son of Poseidon, often shown blowing a conch shell.

1. London.

I griev'd for Buonaparte[1]

I griev'd for Buonaparte, with a vain
And an unthinking grief! the vital blood
Of that Man's mind what can it be? What food
Fed his first hopes? What knowledge could *He* gain?
'Tis not in battles that from youth we train   5
The Governor who must be wise and good,
And temper with the sternness of the brain
Thoughts motherly, and meek as womanhood.
Wisdom doth live with children round her knees:
Books, leisure, perfect freedom, and the talk   10
Man holds with week-day man in the hourly walk
Of the mind's business: these are the degrees
By which true Sway doth mount; this is the stalk
True Power doth grow on; and her rights are these.

—1802

She was a Phantom of Delight[1]

She was a Phantom of delight
When first she gleamed upon my sight;
A lovely Apparition, sent
To be a moment's ornament;
Her eyes as stars of Twilight fair;   5
Like Twilight's, too, her dusky hair;
But all things else about her drawn
From May-time and the cheerful Dawn;
A dancing Shape, an Image gay,
To haunt, to startle, and waylay.   10

I saw her upon nearer view,
A Spirit, yet a Woman too!
Her household motions light and free,
And steps of virgin liberty;
A countenance in which did meet   15
Sweet records, promises as sweet;
A Creature, not too bright or good
For human nature's daily food;
For transient sorrows, simple wiles,
Praise, blame, love, kisses, tears, and smiles.   20

And now I see with eye serene
The very pulse of the machine;

---

1. Napoleon Bonaparte (1769–1821), who in 1802 declared himself First Consul of France for life and invaded Switzerland.
1. Written for Wordsworth's wife, Mary.

A Being breathing thoughtful breath,
A Traveller between life and death;
The reasons firm, the temperate will,   25
Endurance, foresight, strength, and skill;
A perfect Woman, nobly planned,
To warn, to comfort, and command;
And yet a Spirit still, and bright
With something of an angel light.   30

—1807

I wandered lonely as a cloud

I wandered lonely as a cloud
That floats on high o'er vales and hills,
When all at once I saw a crowd,
A host, of golden daffodils;
Beside the lake, beneath the trees,   5
Fluttering and dancing in the breeze.

Continuous as the stars that shine
And twinkle on the milky way,
They stretched in never-ending line
Along the margin of a bay: 10
Ten thousand saw I at a glance,
Tossing their heads in sprightly dance.

The waves beside them danced; but they
Outdid the sparkling waves in glee:—
A Poet could not but be gay,   15
In such a jocund company:
I gazed—and gazed—but little thought
What wealth the show to me had brought:

For oft when on my couch I lie
In vacant or in pensive mood,   20
They flash upon that inward eye
Which is the bliss of solitude;
And then my heart with pleasure fills,
And dances with the daffodils.

—1807

My heart leaps up

My heart leaps up when I behold
  A Rainbow in the sky:
So was it when my life began;
So is it now I am a Man;

So be it when I shall grow old,   5
   Or let me die!
The Child is Father of the Man;
And I could wish my days to be
Bound each to each by natural piety.

—1807

Ode:

Intimations of Immortality from Recollections of Early Childhood

> The Child is Father of the Man;
> And I could wish my days to be
> Bound each to each by natural piety.

1

There was a time when meadow, grove, and stream,
The earth, and every common sight,
   To me did seem
   Apparelled in celestial light,
The glory and the freshness of a dream.
It is not now as it hath been of yore;—
   Turn wheresoe'er I may,
    By night or day,
The things which I have seen I now can see no more.

2

   The Rainbow comes and goes,   10
   And lovely is the Rose,
   The Moon doth with delight
Look round her when the heavens are bare,
   Waters on a starry night
   Are beautiful and fair;   15
   The sunshine is a glorious birth;
   But yet I know, where'er I go,
That there hath past away a glory from the earth.

3

Now, while the birds thus sing a joyous song,
   And while the young lambs bound   20
   As to the tabor's[1] sound,
To me alone there came a thought of grief:
A timely utterance gave that thought relief,
   And I again am strong:

---

1. Drum.

The cataracts blow their trumpets from the steep;   25
No more shall grief of mine the season wrong;
I hear the Echoes through the mountains throng,
The Winds come to me from the fields of sleep,
     And all the earth is gay;
       Land and sea   30
   Give themselves up to jollity,
     And with the heart of May
   Doth every Beast keep holiday;—
     Thou Child of Joy,
Shout round me, let me hear thy shouts, thou happy Shepherd-boy!   35

4

Ye blessèd Creatures, I have heard the call
   Ye to each other make; I see
The heavens laugh with you in your jubilee;
   My heart is at your festival,
   My head hath its coronal,[2]
The fulness of your bliss, I feel—I feel it all.   40
   Oh evil day! if I were sullen
   While Earth herself is adorning,
     This sweet May-morning,
   And the Children are culling[3]
     On every side,   45
   In a thousand valleys far and wide,
Fresh flowers; while the sun shines warm,
And the Babe leaps up on his Mother's arm:—
   I hear, I hear, with joy I hear!
   —But there's a Tree, of many, one,   50
A single Field which I have looked upon,
Both of them speak of something that is gone:
   The Pansy at my feet
   Doth the same tale repeat:
Whither is fled the visionary gleam?   55
Where is it now, the glory and the dream?

5

Our birth is but a sleep and a forgetting:
The Soul that rises with us, our life's Star,
   Hath had elsewhere its setting,
     And cometh from afar: 60
   Not in entire forgetfulness,
   And not in utter nakedness,
But trailing clouds of glory do we come
   From God, who is our home: 65

---

2. Crown.   3. Picking.

Heaven lies about us in our infancy!
Shades of the prison-house begin to close
   Upon the growing Boy,
But He beholds the light, and whence it flows,
   He sees it in his joy;
The Youth, who daily farther from the east
   Must travel, still is Nature's Priest,
    And by the vision splendid
    Is on his way attended;
At length the Man perceives it die away,   75
And fade into the light of common day.

6

Earth fills her lap with pleasures of her own;
Yearnings she hath in her own natural kind,
And, even with something of a Mother's mind,
    And no unworthy aim,
    The homely Nurse doth all she can
To make her Foster-child, her Inmate Man,
    Forget the glories he hath known,
And that imperial palace whence he came.

7

Behold the Child among his new-born blisses,   85
A six years' Darling of a pigmy size!
See, where 'mid work of his own hand he lies,
Fretted by sallies of his mother's kisses,
With light upon him from his father's eyes!
See, at his feet, some little plan or chart,   90
Some fragment from his dream of human life,
Shaped by himself with newly-learned art;
    A wedding or a festival,
    A mourning or a funeral;
     And this hath now his heart,   95
    And unto this he frames his song;
     Then will he fit his tongue
To dialogues of business, love, or strife;
    But it will not be long
    Ere this be thrown aside,   100
    And with new joy and pride
The little Actor cons another part;
Filling from time to time his "humorous stage"[4]
With all the Persons, down to palsied Age,
That Life brings with her in her equipage;   105

---

4. Samuel Daniel (1562–1619), "Sonnet."

As if his whole vocation
Were endless imitation.

8

Thou, whose exterior semblance doth belie
  Thy Soul's immensity;
Thou best Philosopher, who yet dost keep
Thy heritage, thou Eye among the blind,
That, deaf and silent, read'st the eternal deep,
Haunted for ever by the eternal mind,—
  Mighty Prophet! Seer blest!
  On whom those truths do rest,
Which we are toiling all our lives to find,
In darkness lost, the darkness of the grave;
Thou, over whom thy Immortality
Broods like the Day, a Master o'er a Slave,
A Presence which is not to be put by;
Thou little Child, yet glorious in the might
Of heaven-born freedom on thy being's height,
Why with such earnest pains dost thou provoke
The years to bring the inevitable yoke,
Thus blindly with thy blessedness at strife?
Full soon thy Soul shall have her earthly freight,
And custom lie upon thee with a weight,
Heavy as frost, and deep almost as life!

110

115

120

125

9

O joy! that in our embers
Is something that doth live,
That Nature yet remembers
What was so fugitive!
The thought of our past years in me doth breed
Perpetual benediction: not indeed
For that which is most worthy to be blest—
Delight and liberty, the simple creed
Of Childhood, whether busy or at rest,
With new-fledged hope still fluttering in his breast:—
  Not for these I raise
  The song of thanks and praise;
  But for those obstinate questionings
  Of sense and outward things,
  Fallings from us, vanishings;
  Blank misgivings of a Creature
Moving about in worlds not realised,
High instincts before which our mortal nature
Did tremble like a guilty Thing surprised:

130

135

140

145

But for those first affections,
　　Those shadowy recollections,
　　Which, be they what they may,   150
Are yet the fountain light of all our day,
Are yet a master light of all our seeing;
　　Uphold us, cherish, and have power to make
Our noisy years seem moments in the being
Of the eternal Silence: truths that wake,   155
　　To perish never;
Which neither listlessness, nor mad endeavour,
　　Nor Man nor Boy,
Nor all that is at enmity with joy,
Can utterly abolish or destroy!   160
　　Hence in a season of calm weather
　　Though inland far we be,
Our Souls have sight of that immortal sea
　　Which brought us hither,
　　Can in a moment travel thither,   165
And see the Children sport upon the shore,
And hear the mighty waters rolling evermore.

10

Then sing, ye Birds, sing, sing a joyous song!
　　And let the young Lambs bound
　　As to the tabor's sound!   170
We in thought will join your throng,
　　Ye that pipe and ye that play,
　　Ye that through your hearts to-day
　　Feel the gladness of the May!
What though the radiance which was once so bright   175
Be now for ever taken from my sight,
　　Though nothing can bring back the hour
Of splendour in the grass, of glory in the flower;
　　We will grieve not, rather find
　　Strength in what remains behind;   180
　　In the primal sympathy
　　Which having been must ever be;
　　In the soothing thoughts that spring
　　Out of human suffering;
　　In the faith that looks through death,   185
In years that bring the philosophic mind.

11

And O, ye Fountains, Meadows, Hills, and Groves,
Forebode not any severing of our loves!
Yet in my heart of hearts I feel your might;

I only have relinquished one delight 190
To live beneath your more habitual sway.
I love the Brooks which down their channels fret,
Even more than when I tripped lightly as they;
The innocent brightness of a new-born Day
    Is lovely yet; 195
The Clouds that gather round the setting sun
Do take a sober colouring from an eye
That hath kept watch o'er man's mortality;
Another race hath been, and other palms[5] are won.
Thanks to the human heart by which we live, 200
Thanks to its tenderness, its joys, and fears,
To me the meanest flower that blows can give
Thoughts that do often lie too deep for tears.

—1807

The Solitary Reaper

Behold her, single in the field,
Yon solitary Highland Lass![1]
Reaping and singing by herself;
Stop here, or gently pass!
Alone she cuts, and binds the grain, 5
And sings a melancholy strain;
O listen! for the Vale profound
Is overflowing with the sound.

No Nightingale did ever chaunt
More welcome notes to weary bands 10
Of Travellers in some shady haunt,
Among Arabian Sands:
No sweeter voice was ever heard
In spring-time from the Cuckoo-bird,
Breaking the silence of the seas 15
Among the farthest Hebrides.[2]

Will no one tell me what she sings?—
Perhaps the plaintive numbers flow
For old, unhappy, far-off things,
And battles long ago: 20
Or is it some more humble lay,
Familiar matter of today?

---

5. Trophies.

1. Girl of northern Scotland.   2. Islands in northern Scotland.

Some natural sorrow, loss, or pain,
That has been, and may be again!

Whate'er the theme, the Maiden sang   25
As if her song could have no ending;
I saw her singing at her work,
And o'er the sickle bending;—
I listen'd till I had my fill.
And, as I mounted up the hill,   30
The music in my heart I bore,
Long after it was heard no more.

—1807

Gold and Silver Fishes, in a Vase

The soaring Lark is blest as proud
    When at Heaven's gate she sings;
The roving Bee proclaims aloud
    Her flight by vocal wings;
While Ye, in lasting durance pent,   5
    Your silent lives employ
For something "more than dull content
    Though haply less than joy."

Yet might your glassy prison seem
    A place where joy is known,   10
Where golden flash and silver gleam
    Have meanings of their own;
While, high and low, and all about,
    Your motions, glittering Elves!
Ye weave—no danger from without,   15
    And peace among yourselves.

Type of a sunny human breast
    Is your transparent Cell;
Where Fear is but a transient Guest,
    No sullen Humours dwell;   20
Where, sensitive of every ray
    That smites this tiny sea,
Your scaly panoplies[1] repay
    The loan with usury.[2]

How beautiful! Yet none knows why   25
    This ever-graceful change,

---

1. Armor. 2. Interest.

Renewed—renewed incessantly—
  Within your quiet range.
Is it that ye with conscious skill
  For mutual pleasure glide;
And sometimes, not without your will,   30
  Are dwarfed, or magnified?

Fays—Genii[3] of gigantic size—
  And now, in twilight dim,
Clustering like constelled Eyes
  In wings of Cherubim,[4]   35
When they abate their fiery glare:
  Whate'er your forms express,
Whate'er ye seem, whate'er ye are,
  All leads to gentleness.   40

Cold though your nature be, 'tis pure;
  Your birthright is a fence
From all that haughtier kinds endure
  Through tyranny of sense.
Ah! not alone by colours bright   45
  Are Ye to Heaven allied,
When, like essential Forms of light,
  Ye mingle, or divide.

For day-dreams soft as e'er beguiled
  Day-thoughts while limbs repose;   50
For moonlight fascinations mild
  Your gift, ere shutters close;
Accept, mute Captives! thanks and praise;
  And may this tribute prove
That gentle admirations raise   55
  Delight resembling love.

                                        —1836

Liberty

(Sequel to the above.)

[Addressed to a Friend; the Gold and Silver Fishes having
been removed to a pool in the pleasure-ground of Rydal Mount.[1]]

"The liberty of a people consists in being governed by laws which they
have made for themselves, under whatever form it be of government. The

---

3. Elves and genies.   4. Angels.

1. Wordsworth's home in the Lake District.

liberty of a private man, in being master of his own time and actions, as far
as may consist with the laws of God and of his country. Of this latter we
are here to discourse."

—COWLEY

Those breathing Tokens of your kind regard,
(Suspect not, Anna, that their fate is hard;
Not soon does aught to which mild fancies cling,
In lonely spots, become a slighted thing;)
Those silent Inmates now no longer share,   5
Nor do they need, our hospitable care,
Removed in kindness from their glassy Cell
To the fresh waters of a living Well;
That spreads into an elfin pool opaque
Of which close boughs a glimmering mirror make,   10
On whose smooth breast with dimples light and small
The fly may settle, leaf or blossom fall.
—There swims, of blazing sun and beating shower
Fearless (but how obscured!) the golden Power,
That from his bauble prison used to cast   15
Gleams by the richest jewel unsurpast;
And near him, darkling like a sullen Gnome,
The silver Tenant of the crystal dome;
Dissevered both from all the mysteries
Of hue and altering shape that charmed all eyes.   20
They pined, perhaps, they languished while they shone;
And, if not so, what matters beauty gone
And admiration lost, by change of place
That brings to the inward Creature no disgrace?
But if the change restore his birthright, then,   25
Whate'er the difference, boundless is the gain.
Who can divine what impulses from God
Reach the caged Lark, within a town-abode,
From his poor inch or two of daisied sod?
O yield him back his privilege! No sea   30
Swells like the bosom of a man set free;
A wilderness is rich with liberty.
Roll on, ye spouting Whales, who die or keep
Your independence in the fathomless Deep!
Spread, tiny Nautilus,[2] the living sail;   35
Dive, at thy choice, or brave the freshening gale!
If unreproved the ambitious Eagle mount
Sunward to seek the daylight in its fount,
Bays, gulfs, and Ocean's Indian width, shall be,
Till the world perishes, a field for thee!   40

---

2. Coiled shellfish.

While musing here I sit in shadow cool,
And watch these mute Companions, in the pool,
Among reflected boughs of leafy trees,
By glimpses caught—disporting at their ease—
Enlivened, braced, by hardy luxuries,   45
I ask what warrant fixed them (like a spell
Of witchcraft fixed them) in the crystal Cell;
To wheel with languid motion round and round,
Beautiful, yet in a mournful durance bound.
Their peace, perhaps, our lightest footfall marred;   50
On their quick sense our sweetest music jarred;
And wither could they dart, if seized with fear?
No sheltering stone, no tangled root was near.
When fire or taper ceased to cheer the room,
They wore away the night in starless gloom;   55
And, when the sun first dawned upon the streams,
How faint their portion of his vital beams!
Thus, and unable to complain, they fared,
While not one joy of ours by them was shared.

Is there a cherished Bird (I venture now   60
To snatch a sprig from Chaucer's reverend brow[3])—
Is there a brilliant Fondling of the cage,[4]
Though sure of plaudits on his costly stage,
Though fed with dainties from the snow-white hand
Of a kind Mistress, fairest of the land,   65
But gladly would escape; and, if need were,
Scatter the colours from the plumes that bear
The emancipated captive through blithe air
Into strange woods, where he at large may live
On best or worst which they and Nature give?   70
The Beetle loves his unpretending track,
The Snail the house he carries on his back:
The far-fetched Worm with pleasure would disown
The bed we give him, though of softest down;
A noble instinct; in all Kinds the same,   75
All Ranks! What Sovereign, worthy of the name,
If doomed to breathe against his lawful will
An element that flatters him—to kill,
But would rejoice to barter outward show
For the least boon that freedom can bestow?   80

But most the Bard is true to inborn right,
Lark of the dawn, and Philomel[5] of night,

---

3. Geoffrey Chaucer (c. 1343–1400) is depicted wearing a laurel wreath in honor of his poetic achievements.   4. Alludes to Chaucer's "Squire's Tale" in *The Canterbury Tales* (1386–1400).   5. Philomela of Ovid (43 BC–17 AD), *Metamorphosis* (1 AD).

Exults in freedom, can with rapture vouch
For the dear blessings of a lowly couch,
A natural meal—days, months, from Nature's hand;   85
Time, place, and business, all at his command!
Who bends to happier duties, who more wise
Than the industrious Poet, taught to prize,
Above all grandeur, a pure life uncrossed
By cares in which simplicity is lost?   90
That life—the flowery path which winds by stealth,
Which Horace[6] needed for his spirit's health;
Sighed for, in heart and genius, overcome
By noise, and strife, and questions wearisome,
And the vain splendours of Imperial Rome?   95
Let easy mirth his social hours inspire,
And fiction animate his portive lyre,
Attuned to verse that crowning light Distress
With garlands cheats her into happiness;
Give me the humblest note of those sad strains   100
Drawn forth by pressure of his gilded chains,
As a chance sunbeam from his memory fell
Upon the Sabine Farm[7] he loved so well;
Or when the prattle of Bandusia's spring[8]
Haunted his ear—he only listening—   105
He proud to please, above all rivals, fit
To win the palm of gaiety and wit;
He, doubt not, with involuntary dread,
Shrinking from each new favour to be shed,
By the World's Ruler, on his honoured head!   110

     In a deep vision's intellectual scene,
Such earnest longings and regrets as keen
Depressed the melancholy Cowley,[9] laid
Under a fancied yew-tree's luckless shade;
A doleful bower for penitential song,   115
Where Man and Muse complained of mutual wrong;
While Cam's[10] ideal current glided by,
And antique Towers nodded their foreheads high,
Citadels dear to studious privacy.
But Fortune, who had long been used to sport   120
With this tried Servant of a thankless Court,
Relenting met his wishes; and to You
The remnant of his days at least was true;
You, whom, though long deserted, he loved best;

---

6. (65–8 BC), Roman poet and general.   7. In 34 BC, Mæcenas awarded Horace the Sabine Farm as a writing retreat.   8. A nearby spring that Horace celebrated in verse.   9. Abraham Cowley (1618–1667), British poet.   10. River that flows through Cambridge, England.

You, Muses, Books, Fields, Liberty, and Rest!   125
But happier they who, fixing hope and aim
On the humanities of peaceful fame,
Enter *betimes* with more than martial fire
The generous course, aspire, and still aspire;
Upheld by warnings heeded not too late   130
Stifle the contradictions of their fate,
And to one purpose cleave, their Being's godlike mate!

    Thus, gifted Friend, but with the placid brow
That Woman ne'er should forfeit, keep *thy* vow;
With modest scorn reject whate'er would blind   135
The ethereal eyesight, cramp the winged mind!
Then, with a blessing granted from above
To every act, word, thought, and look of love,
Life's book for Thee may lie unclosed, till age
Shall with a thankful tear bedrop its latest page.[11]   140

—1836

TRANSATLANTIC EXCHANGES

Wordsworth in Britain and America

First published in 1798, *Lyrical Ballads* broke radically with the conventions of eighteenth-century neoclassical poetry. This collection was the result of the collaboration of William Wordsworth and Samuel Taylor Coleridge, the fruit of a friendship that grew during long walks punctuated with animated discussions and critiques of the reigning poetics. According to the preface to *Lyrical Ballads* (first published in the 1800 edition and expanded in the 1802 edition), it was high time that poetry dispensed with its use of high-flown language. According to the conventions of eighteenth-century versification, a poet might refer to the sky, for instance, as "Yon azure, empyrean firmament"; however, for Wordsworth and Coleridge, this description would best be rendered as "the blue, heavenly sky." Also, neoclassical poets often personified nature as a god, goddess, deity, or other mythological being, describing the sea as "the realm of Poseidon." Wordsworth and Coleridge sought to disabuse poets of using references to classical mythology to mediate their experiences and descriptions of nature. Describe the natural world as you see it, and invest it with your own spirituality, emotion, and imagination—these are some of the commandments the two young poets sought to convey to their readers and fellow poets. The *Ballads'* critique of existing poetical practices also included a redefinition of the hero of neoclassical verse. Whereas poetry traditionally

---

11. [Wordsworth's note] There is now, alas! no possibility of the anticipation, with which the above Epistle concludes, being realised: nor were the verses ever seen by the Individual for whom they were intended. She accompanied her husband, the Rev. Wm. Fletcher, to India, and died of cholera, at the age of thirty-two or thirty-three years, on her way from Shalapore to Bombay, deeply lamented by all who knew her.

    Her enthusiasm was ardent, her piety steadfast; and her great talents would have enabled her to be eminently useful in the difficult path of life to which she had been called. The opinion she entertained of her own performances, given to the world under her maiden name, Jewsbury, was modest and humble, and, indeed, far below their merits; as is often the case with those who are making trial of their powers with a hope to discover what they are best fitted for. In one quality, viz., quickness in the motions of her mind, she was in the author's estimation unequalled.

focused on kings, queens, and demigod warriors and adventurers, the *Ballads* sang of the common man and woman, of rural laborers and the homeless.

As would be expected, these poems ruffled more than a few critical feathers, but Wordsworth persisted in bringing them before the public again and again. Published initially as one volume in 1798, the collection was expanded; two-volume versions of the *Ballads* were published in 1800, 1802, and 1805. One of the most acrid responses to the "Lake Poets" (Wordsworth, Coleridge, and Robert Southey) was penned by Francis Jeffrey, who used a review of Southey's *Thalaba* to lash out at all "Lakers":

> [T]here is a class of persons (we are afraid they cannot be called *readers*), to whom the representation of vulgar manners, in vulgar language, will afford much entertainment. We are afraid, however, that the ingenious writers who supply the hawkers and ballad-singers, have very nearly monopolized that department, and are probably better qualified to hit the taste of their customers, than Mr. Southey, or any of his brethren, can yet pretend to be.

Additionally and equally as cruel, the *Critical Review* of 1801 did not hesitate to pronounce that Wordsworth and Coleridge's "'experiment' . . . has failed, not because the language of conversation is little adapted to 'the purposes of poetic pleasure', but because it has been tried upon uninteresting subjects."

American reviewers were much more sanguine and receptive to Wordsworth's poetics and politics. Wordsworth's poetry was first reprinted in America in New Hampshire's *Farmer's Journal* of 1799. In 1800, the editor, Joseph Dennie, moved to Philadelphia and there started the *Port Folio* under the pen name Oliver Oldschool. This newspaper rapidly achieved a wide circulation and enjoyed considerable popularity. Oldschool used his paper to create an American taste for Wordsworth's poetry, reprinting so many selections from *Lyrical Ballads* that Philadelphia demanded its own edition of the book by 1802, a demand readily met by the printers James Humphreys and Joseph Groff, who published the contents of the 1798 and 1800 volumes in one compact edition. *Relf's Philadelphia Gazette* asked readers to not let "the name of Ballads give rise to prejudices in the minds of those who have never seen this work; for it is as much Superior to those things commonly known by that name, as happiness is preferable to misery." The 1802 American edition sold for only a day's wages, placing it within the grasp of working-class readers, who could not afford the British edition, priced at a week's wages.

Given the radical politics of *Lyrical Ballads*, which was more sympathetic to American democracy than British monarchy, it is no surprise that the poems were well received in America. Wordsworth's *Preface* makes clear that he views poetical and political revolutions as inextricably linked attempts to make outwardly manifest the inherent qualities with which the Divine Creator has endowed human minds. The *Preface* is the declaration of equality for the citizens of the *Ballads*: the idiot boy, the forsaken Indian woman, the old huntsman, and many others. The *Ballads* themselves are the voices of these characters, the representation of the under-represented. Wordsworth's call to pens is forward-pointing, and it is easy to see how early Americans would have been inspired by it. Wordsworth himself, in a letter to Henry Reed, his American editor, makes it clear that he considers his U.S. audience to be among the ideal readers of the *Preface*:

> It is gratifying to one whose aim as an author has been to reach the hearts of his fellow-creatures of all ranks and in all stations to find that he has succeeded in any quarter; and still more must he be gratified to learn that he has pleased in a distant country men of simple habits and cultivated taste, who are at the same time widely acquainted with literature.

Leigh Hunt
1784–1859

Born in 1784, the seventh of eight children, Hunt was the first child of Isaac and Mary Shewell Hunt born in England. Hunt's mother was the daughter of a prominent Philadelphia merchant, but the Hunts fled the city at the start of the Revolutionary War for fear that Isaac's Loyalist leanings would endanger the family. Hunt's father's connections to America played a role in his first publication: A warmly noticed volume of juvenile verse in 1801, it sold well in large part because of a number of English and American subscribers Isaac Hunt helped generate.

In England, Isaac Hunt, a lawyer by training, became a renowned preacher. Because of financial mismanagement, he served time in debtor's prison while Leigh was a young child. Hunt was educated as a charity boy at Christ's Church, also attended by Samuel Taylor Coleridge and Charles Lamb. The school's broad education shaped his imagination: Indeed, his own critical and poetic efforts bear signs of the school's focus on classical literature and familiarity with a range of humanities topics. Such a breadth of reading shows in his poetry and criticism. He wrote in every form of poetry and translated from French, Greek, and Italian. He was a strong reader of poetry as well, and a critical thinker who helped define the aesthetics of Romanticism for mid-nineteenth-century readers. His editorial activities—he founded, edited, or wrote for *The Examiner* (1808–1822), *The Reflector* (1810–1812), *The Indicator* (1819), and *The Companion* (1828)—gave him a platform from which to opine on the state of the arts and the country. The platform, however, attracted much attention. In 1817, Hunt was the center of John Gibson Lockhart's vilification of the "Cockney School" in the influential periodical *Blackwood's Edinburgh Magazine*, but the circumference of the target included John Keats and even William Wordsworth. Part of Lockhart's ire was fueled by Hunt's radical politics, but it was also shaped by the anonymous review practice of the day. Reviews lashed out under the aegis of anonymity, with the hope of generating debate and journal sales. While Hunt was wounded by Lockhart's derision, he suffered a worse reprimand in 1813, when he and his brother were found guilty of libeling the Prince Regent (calling him in print a liar, hypocrite, and obese "Adonis") and were sentenced to two years in prison and a fine of £500.

Hunt's pen, however, was not always this sharp, and his satire of contemporary writers in "The Feast of the Poets" in the March 1812 issue of *The Reflector* was more playful than spiteful. In the poem, Apollo joins the leading poets of the day at the feast table. He is dismissive of the vast majority of them, including Byron, Coleridge, and Wordsworth. Revised editions of the poem, however, reversed Apollo's estimations, and Hunt was criticized for the change of heart. Editions in 1815, 1832, and 1844 followed suit and document Hunt's evolving opinions. Hunt's reputation as a critic increased until the 1850s, and many prominent writers came calling—including Nathaniel Hawthorne and Ralph Waldo Emerson from America. Hunt's *Autobiography* (1850) is an exemplary model of the genre and fascinating for his portraits of a large number of writers from the first half of the nineteenth century.

from The Feast of the Poets

For Coleridge had vexed him[1] long since, I suppose,
By his idling, and gabbling, and muddling in prose;

---

1. Apollo.

And Wordsworth, one day, made his very hairs bristle,
By going and changing his harp for a whistle.
The bards, for a moment, stood making a pause,   5
And looked rather awkward, and lax round the jaws,
When one began spouting the cream of orations
In praise of bombarding one's friends and relations;
And t'other some lines he had made on a straw,
Showing how he had found it, and what it was for,   10
And how, when 'twas balanced, it stood like a spell!—
And how, when 'twas balanced no longer, it fell!—
A wild thing of scorn he described it to be,
But he said it was patient to heaven's decree:—
Then he gazed upon nothing, and looking forlorn,   15
Dropt a *natural* tear for *that wild thing of scorn!*
Apollo half laughed betwixt anger and mirth,
And cried, 'Was there ever such trifling on earth?
What! think ye a bard's a mere gossip, who tells
Of the ev'ry-day feelings of every one else,   20
And that poetry lies, not in something select,
But in gath'ring the refuse that others reject?
Must a ballad doled out by a spectacled nurse
About Two-Shoes or Thumb, be your model of verse;
And your writings, instead of sound fancy and style,   25
Look more like the morbid abstractions of bile?
There is one of you here, who, instead of these fits,
And becoming a joke to half-thinkers and wits,
Should have brought back our fine old pre-eminent way,
And been the first man at my table to-day: 30
But resolved as I am to maintain the partitions
'Twixt wit and mere wildness, he knows the conditions;
And if he retains but a spark of my fire,
Will show it this instant,—and blush,—and retire.'
He spoke; and poor Wordsworth, his cheeks in a glow,   35
(For he felt the God in him) made symptoms to go,
When Apollo, in pity, to screen him from sight,
Threw round him a cloud that was purple and white,
The same that of old used to wrap his own shoulders,
When coming from heaven, he'd spare the beholders: 40
'Twas culled from the east, at the dawning of day,
In a bright show'ry season 'twixt April and May.
Yet the bard was no sooner obeying his king,
And gliding away like a shadow of spring,
Than the latter, who felt himself touched more and more   45
Tow'rds a writer whose faults were as one to five score,
And who found that he shouldn't well know what to say,
If he sent, after all, his best poet away,
Said, 'Come, my dear Will,—imperfections apart,—

Let us have a true taste of our exquisite art;   50
You know very well you've the key to my heart.'
   At this the glad cloud, with a soft heaving motion,
Stopped short, like a sail in a nook of the ocean;
And out of its bosom there trembled and came
A voice, that grew upwards, and gathered like flame: 55
Of nature it told, and of simple delights
On days of green sunshine, and eye-lifting nights;
Of summer-sweet isles and their noon-shaded bowers,
Of mountains, and valleys, trees, waters, and flowers,
Of hearts, young and happy, and all that they show   60
For the home that we came from and wither we go;
Of wisdom in age by this feeling renewed,
Of hopes that stand smiling o'er passions subdued,
Of the springs of sweet waters in evil that lie;—
Of all, which, in short, meets the soul's better eye   65
When we go to meek nature our hearts to restore,
And bring down the Gods to walk with us once more.

—1814

Robert Hutchinson Rose
1776–1842

In "A Humble Imitation of Some Stanzas, written by W. Wordsworth, in Germany, on One of the Coldest Days of the Century" (1804), Robert Hutchinson Rose sets his sights on critiquing the ambiguity in the final stanzas of many of the poems in *Lyrical Ballads*. The final stanza of Rose's parody alludes to the morally opaque ending of Wordsworth's "Strange Fits of Passion I Have Known," in which the speaker dwells upon the death of his lover:

> What fond and wayward thoughts will slide
> Into a Lover's head–
> "O mercy!" to myself I cried,
> "If Lucy should be dead!"

Wordsworth's intention is to represent the speaker's love for Lucy. For Rose the expression does not convey this insofar as the speaker's thought of Lucy's death is described as "wayward," which can also denote a perverse or wrong notion. Similarly, Rose's parodic final stanza lends itself first to a moral reading, as an affirmation that the speaker's marital fidelity to Molly will last beyond the grave. Yet the verse's ambiguity also allows it to be read as an oath that he will never again suffer through the torment of matrimonial domesticity.

   The parody is quoted here in its entirety (on the left-hand side of the page) with a parallel text of the original Wordsworth poem. The typography of the two poems has been slightly altered to create the parallel text.

A Humble Imitation of Some Stanzas, written by W. Wordsworth, in Germany, on One of the Coldest Days of the Century

R. Shallow [Robert H. Rose]

My Molly and I we sat down by the fire,
And she was preparing the vittle;
And as I was hungry, I had a
    desire
To ask her a question, and so I
    drew nigher,
And ask'd, had she put on the kettle.
The table was set, and the cups
    they were laid,
But Molly mov'd slower and slower;
At breakfast her speech was cut-
    ting and rough,
At dinner, Heaven knows, it was
    crabbed enough,
But *now* it is fifty times more.

So, I thought I might hasten the
    supper perhaps,
If the fire a little I'd move;
For, said I, if I wait for this treach-
    erous heat,
I fear 'twill be long ere my supper I
    eat,
So I put some more wood in the stove.

Alas! for the man that has married
    a shrew!
What perils his safety environ!
I scarcely had put on the stick,
    before Moll
Raps me over the head with the
    tongs—to the wall
I reel'd; for the tongs were of iron.

Stock-still then I stood, like a trav-
    eller bemaz'd,
The weight of her hand I'd oft tried,
But never the tongs: could I have
    got forth,

Written in Germany, on One of the Coldest Days of the Century

W. Wordsworth

A fig for your languages, German and Norse,
Let me have the song of the Kettle,
And the tongs and the poker, instead of that
    horse
That gallops away with such fury and
    force
On this dreary dull plate of black metal.[1]
Our earth is no doubt made of excellent
    stuff,
But her pulses beat slower and slower,
The weather in Forty was cutting and
    rough,
And then, as Heaven knows, the glass[2]
    stood low enough,
And *now* it is four degrees lower.

Here's a Fly, a disconsolate creature,
    perhaps
A child of the field, or the grove,
And sorrow for him! This dull treacherous
    heat
Has seduc'd the poor fool from his winter
    retreat,
And he creeps to the edge of my stove.

Alas! how he fumbles about the
    domains
Which this comfortless oven environ,
He cannot find out in what track he must
    crawl,
Now back to the tiles, and now back to the
    wall,
And now on the brink of the iron.

Stock-still there he stands like a traveller
    bemaz'd,
The best of his skill he has tried;
His feelers methinks I can see him put
    forth

1. An ornamental plate on a woodstove.   2. Thermometer.

To the east and the west, and the south and the North
I'd have fled, without guide-post or guide.

See! my spindles sink under me, foot, leg and thigh,
My eyesight and hearing are lost;
Between life and death my blood freezes and thaws,
I thought I was dead; or at least, by the laws,
I thought I should give up the ghost.

No table or chair was there near me, but I
At length just got hold of a *poker*,
And then to escape did I boldly presume,
I brandish'd my poker, and out of the room
I flew, for my Moll was no joker.

Yet, Heaven be my witness, if Molly should die,
How firmly her loss I'd sustain;
Though women their favours should offer in crowds,
As well might they spend all their breath on the clouds,
I ne'er would be wedded again.

—1804

To the East and the West, and the South and the North,
But he finds neither guide-post nor guide.

See! His spindles sink under him, foot, leg and thigh,
His eyesight and hearing are lost,
Between life and death his blood freezes and thaws,
And his two pretty pinions[3] of blue dusky gauze
Are glued to his sides by the frost.

No Brother, no Friend has he near him, while I
Can draw warmth from the cheek of my Love,
As best and as glad in this desolate gloom,
As if green summer grass were the floor of my room,
And woodbines were hanging above.

Yet, God is my witness, thou small helpless Thing,
Thy life I would gladly sustain
Til summer comes up from the South, and with crowds
Of thy brethren a march thou should'st sound through the clouds,
And back to the forests again.

—1800

Elizabeth Palmer Peabody
1804–1894

On December 9, 1825, the twenty-two-year-old Elizabeth Palmer Peabody, who would later operate a Boston bookstore that was a central meeting place for Transcendentalists and other reformers, wrote her first letter to William Wordsworth. She did not have the courage to send it until a year later. She wrote to ask if he would compose poetry especially for children, as she believed his words were capable of educating them to connect the heart and the intellect and of awakening their souls. In the Massachusetts Temple School for children, she and Amos Bronson Alcott had been teaching Wordsworth's "Ode: Intimations of Immortality from Recollections of Early Childhood," a poem that shows how spiritual perception of nature can

---

3. Wings.

lift the weight of earthly cares that threatens to crush the heavenly freedom that is humankind's divine birthright. Peabody interpreted this poem as speaking to the birth and development of children, as well as of America.

In a later letter to Wordsworth, she notes that if poetry could be made to shape America's people, "we might see *grand souls* indeed, which would do in the republic of letters, in the temple of lofty sciences, what they did fifty years since in politics. And it is necessary that this more interior revolution should take place, to give life to, or even perpetuate those forms of freedom which Washington and his friends left to us." For Peabody, this internal revolution was inseparable from a poetical revolution, and together these would complete America's political revolution.

Because she felt sure that Wordsworth's influence would be invaluable, she wrote again to let him know he had developed a substantial American audience: "You can never know what a deep and even wide enthusiasm your poetry has awakened here." "Enthusiasm" is the operative word here. She is using the word in its Greek sense to imply that Wordsworth was awakening a sense of God within Americans, or awakening the divine spirit within individuals. Works of art in their own right, Peabody's letters to Wordsworth contain theology, philosophy, some of the first literary criticism on transatlantic Romanticism, and, with regard to America's literary revolution, a declaration of gratitude as well as independence.

Letter to Wordsworth
Boston September 7th 1835

Mr. Wordsworth— / Dear Sir—

Perhaps you have not forgotten one of your disciples, an American girl, to whom you were kind enough once to write. A private opportunity of sending to England by a respectable bookseller of our city, prompts me to take the opportunity of expressing to you the *heart-blessing* experienced from perusing, in the solitude of the country, your "Yarrow Revisited"[1] and its charming accompaniments—which I have been dreaming over—dreaming of Heaven, and the kingdom of Heaven-on-Earth.—I have taken courage also to send you a book of my own writing which will make known to you something of a very interesting mind engaged in bringing the children of the English language under the fostering influences of the true English literature. You will be pleased to find yourself made fosterfather to young spirit;—how I should like to know what you would say to the commentary of that young child on "Our birth is but a sleep and a forgetting!"[2] How I wish you could have seen how like the breeze of Spring the first stanzas of that one passed over these opening blossoms of Life—the very sound of wakening nature seemed to breathe from their lit-up faces, as their whole natures responded to the "thronging echoes," the "trumpet cataract," the "Shouting Shepherd boy."—[3]. . .

But what shall I say of these last songs that have waked up anew the hearts of all your *foster children*. Let me thank you in the first place for all you have sung of *women* (in the name of my sex)—from the "Phantom of delight" opening out into the "Woman breathing thoughtful breath"[4]—even unto the "Statue of the Soul"[5] sculptured by Faith out of Frailty's Self. You have done all that Milton left undone. Over what has been beautifully called "the terrible purity of Comus' lady"[6] you have poured the holy tenderness of the Virgin Mother of Christianity—and attracted *the very soul*—into a confidential communion with the awful chastity it adores.—Every

---

1. Wordsworth, *Yarrow Revisited and Other Poems* (1835). 2. See p. 435. 3. See p. 435. 4. See pp. 432–433. 5. Wordsworth, "The Russian Fugitive" (1835), 2.176. 6. William Ellery Channing (1780–1842), "Review of John Milton," *Christian Examiner* III (1826).

music-distilled word that your muse has dropt on this subject, inspired a "holy envy" of her lot whose portrait we have beheld

"Even though the Atlantic Ocean roll between—"[7]

for is not its original the poet's daughter?[8] What blessedness must be theirs who not only dwell in Nature's Delphos,[9] but who have the divine voice interpreted without being obliged to witness any Sybil[10] contortions,—who read the First Precept of Wisdom—without any weary pilgrimage from the artificial abodes of this world—but in the preparation of infancy—amid "intimations of immortality" yet untouched by the *froth of custom*,—who were born—indeed—(may I not say it without irreverence?) where the Power of the Most High hath overshadowed, and the Song of Goodwill to men & Glory to God[11] hath welcomed them upon the shores of being—

> "Blest the Starry promises—
> And the firmament benign
> Hallowed be it—where they shine."[12]

A worthier voice than mine will doubtless soon speak to all English & American ears a fitting gratitude for this blessed little volume—concerning which I have said nothing though I began—to thank you for it.—

If thus—like "the lark who sweetest sings when nearest heaven" & the swan whose music grows more heart-thrilling as he approaches the vision of his inspiring god, your voice reverses the common law of nature, and seems fresher, younger, & more birdlike as earth recedes & time changes into Eternity, what blessed proof is it—that this mortal putteth on immortality, & how truly may your disciples put in your claim as the Columbus of Poetry on whom a New World has opened with its mines & solitudes.—I would even say more—as the Messiah of the reign of the Saints—a true Christian prophet—

With deepest respect

Elizabeth P. Peabody

—1835

Robert Browning
1812–1889

Just as the poet Percy Bysshe Shelley was influenced by his predecessor William Wordsworth, Shelley also became an important influence for many who wrote in the years following his death, including the young Robert Browning, whose first poem "Pauline: A Fragment of a Confession" (1833) was imitative of Shelley's style. And Browning of course was influential upon other poets, most notably Robert Lowell and Ezra Pound in the twentieth century, who noted that Browning wrote "Words that were winged." Born in a suburb of London, Browning spent most of his first thirty-four years there, studying foreign languages, reading literature, and riding horses. He shared Shelley's liberalism, religious skepticism, and condemnation of

---

7. Wordsworth, "Lines Suggested by a Portrait from the Pencil of F. Stone" (1835).   8. Dora Wordsworth (1804–1849).   9. Greek island said to be the residence of Oracle, a prophet.   10. An ancient Greek prophet or oracle.   11. Luke 1.35, 2.14.   12. "Like a Shipwrecked Sailor Tost" (1835).

Wordsworth's apostasy. Browning's "The Lost Leader" (1845) is, in some senses, an extension of Shelley's "To Wordsworth" (1816). Browning outlived Shelley by many years and thus witnessed Wordsworth's abandonment of his early radicalism and his later commitment to Queen Victoria and the Church of England. Browning's poem depicts a Judas-like Wordsworth, who has betrayed his fellow disciples and principles for "a handful of silver" when he accepts a salaried sinecure as Comptroller of Stamps for his native Westmorland.

Browning himself would venture away from the radicalism of Shelley and the early Wordsworth. But he would never align himself with the Church, Crown, and country of England, which he left to elope with poet Elizabeth Barrett. While living in Italy, both husband and wife perfected their poetic craft and wrote and published their best work. After the death of his wife in 1861, Browning returned to England, where he was lionized in London and where he eventually died. He was buried in Westminster Abbey and eulogized by Henry James, his friend and fellow writer. Like his wife, Browning is a Victorian writer, and yet the use of emotion in his writing speaks to his immersion in Romantic writing and sensibility. He reworks the "closet drama" of the period (drama never meant to be staged, only read, such as Shelley's *Prometheus Unbound* [1820]) into his own Victorian/Romantic form of versification—the dramatic monologue.

The Lost Leader

I

Just for a handful of silver[1] he left us,
    Just for a riband[2] to stick in his coat—
Found the one gift of which fortune bereft us,
    Lost all the others she lets us devote;
They, with the gold to give, doled him out silver,   5
    So much was theirs who so little allowed:
How all our copper had gone for his service!
    Rags—were they purple, his heart had been proud!
We that had loved him so, followed him, honored him,
    Lived in his mild and magnificent eye,   10
Learned his great language, caught his clear accents,
    Made him our pattern to live and to die!
Shakespeare was of us, Milton was for us,
    Burns, Shelley, were with us,—they watch from their graves!
He alone breaks from the van[3] and the freemen,   15
    —He alone sinks to the rear and the slaves!

II

We shall march prospering,—not thro' his presence;
    Songs may inspirit us,—not from his lyre[4];
Deeds will be done,—while he boasts his quiescence,
    Still bidding crouch whom the rest bade aspire: 20
Blot out his name, then, record one lost soul more,
    One task more declined, one more footpath untrod,
One more devils'-triumph and sorrow for angels,
    One wrong more to man, one more insult to God!

---

1. What Judas was paid for betraying Jesus.   2. Symbol of the Poet Laureateship.   3. Vanguard.   4. Harp associated with poetry.

Life's night begins: let him never come back to us! 25
    There would be doubt, hesitation and pain,
Forced praise on our part—the glimmer of twilight,
    Never glad confident morning again!
Best fight on well, for we taught him—strike gallantly,
    Menace our heart ere we master his own; 30
Then let him receive the new knowledge and wait us,
    Pardoned in heaven, the first by the throne!

—1845

William Parsons Atkinson
1820–1890

According to Ralph Waldo Emerson, William Wordsworth "alone treated the human mind well." Emerson's Wordsworth had unveiled the divinity of *all* human minds and souls, and in so doing he became part and parcel of the Transcendentalists' growing support for the abolition of slavery. In Emerson's account of his visit to the poet, he notes Wordsworth's prescient prediction of an American civil war precipitated by slavery. American lawyer and editor George Ticknor also spoke with Wordsworth for hours on the topic. Additionally, the poet received an appeal for help from William P. Atkinson, who, in a May 25, 1845, letter to Wordsworth, explained his reasons for his faith in the cause and in Wordsworth's approbation of it. Atkinson requested an unpublished poem for an abolitionist anthology he was editing. Wordsworth sent a poem ("To My Grandchildren") for the anthology, although many years earlier he had declined a similar request for an English abolitionist collection. Wordsworth's support of the American abolitionists indicates that the radicalism of his earliest anti-slavery statements, including "To Thomas Clarkson" (p. 430) and "To Toussaint L'Ouverture" (p. 430), was being rekindled by American correspondents and visitors. Throughout the war, many northerners continued to read Wordsworth, while many southerners, following the example of their leader, Jefferson Davis, creased the spines of their copies of Lord Byron. Wordsworth's appearance in other anthologies alongside abolitionist writers such as Harriet Beecher Stowe, author of *Uncle Tom's Cabin* (1852), only strengthened his association with the cause.

Letter to Wordsworth

Dear Sir,

    I am one of the few in this country who are actively engaged in behalf of the slave: one of those called Abolitionists. . . . I am now,—and it is this which leads me to write you,—preparing for the press a selection of poetry, the proceeds of the sale of which will be given to the support of lectures and papers devoted to the cause of Emancipation. . . . I have collected many fugitive pieces, and marked many that are well known. For the latter, I have been many times to your published writings. I am now bold enough to ask of you an unpublished contributio[n.] I should not ask it for myself, but I trust your interest in a great question of philanthropy. . . . Such a contribution from you would be of the greatest value to my undertaking.

    Accept herewith the renewed acknowledgement of my obligation to you. In times of peculiar spiritual loneliness, when my mind was but half developed, my principles half formed, your words were more to me than anything save the Gospel. It is the confidence this knowledge gives me, that leads me to write you now.

—1845

Henry Reed
1808–1854

One of the first professors of English literature, Henry Reed left the legal profession to assume this role at the University of Pennsylvania, where he remained his whole career, attaining the rank of provost. Early in his professorship, Reed began to correspond with his favorite poet, William Wordsworth, and the two exchanged letters up until Wordsworth's death, after which he continued warm correspondence with Wordsworth's wife, Mary, and his brother, Christopher. Sadly, Wordsworth and Reed never met, for Reed was not able to lure the poet to America. Reed himself did not cross the Atlantic until 1854. After spending the summer in England, he booked passage on the *Arctic* bound for America. The ship left Liverpool on September 27, 1854, but never reached its port across the Atlantic. One of the last letters he wrote was to Mary Wordsworth thanking her for her hospitality during his visit.

Reed almost single-handedly spread Wordsworth's poetry to every city and town in America. His 1837 edition of *The Complete Poetical Works of William Wordsworth* sold so well that it was reprinted in countless editions over the next twenty years, guaranteeing that Wordsworth's verse would always be on American booksellers' shelves. Reed's tome included the complete works of the poet, and it sold for a cheaper price than English editions because of its large, double-columned pages, which fit in one volume the works of the seven-volume English edition. When Americans visited Wordsworth, he would praise the Reed edition, taking it down from his bookcase and noting that England had never produced one as good. In an interesting instance of transatlantic typographical double-cross, Edward Moxon, Wordsworth's London publisher, produced his own version of the Reed edition by issuing Wordsworth's complete works in a single, double-columned volume nearly identical to Reed's. This hardly seemed unjust given that Reed had pirated the text of his American edition from Moxon's and had not paid the publisher or the poet any royalties.

After Reed printed his edition in 1837, he wrote an article on Wordsworth for the *New York Review* (1839) that wrested the poet and his poetry from the personas created by Massachusetts communities of interpreters, such as the Unitarians of Cambridge and the Transcendentalists of Concord. Reed's Wordsworth was not the young, radical Wordsworth championed by the Massachusetts reformers but the orthodox, conservative Anglican poet of simple piety. Reed worked hard to create and safeguard this image of the poet: He solicited and reprinted sonnets from Wordsworth that acknowledged the Episcopal Church as a legitimate branch of the Anglican Church, and he refused to hand over to the Massachusetts abolitionists a poem that Wordsworth sent him for inclusion in an anti-slavery anthology. Reed's essay "The British Poets," excerpted below, buttresses this persona of the poet by distancing the religion of his poetry from charges of pantheism and from the "immorality" and atheism of his fellow poets, Lord Byron and Percy Bysshe Shelley.

from Lectures on the British Poets

There has been expended a great deal of comparative criticism between the poetry of Wordsworth and Byron. During this whole course I have refrained from entering upon comparisons between the poets, because it is a mode of criticism as unsatisfactory as it is easy. There would not be the least difficulty in placing them in comparison and in contrast, and in describing the true relation between the minds and the aspirations of these two poets; but it would be an uncalled-for deviation from the habit of my lectures. To any who are disposed to measure their worth by comparisons rather than independently, let me only suggest for reflection one significant forewarning of the abiding judgment of posterity,—the final award of fame:—the fact, indisputable by any one, that every succeeding year has worn away some crumbling portion of Lord Byron's splendid popularity, while the majestic splendour of Wordsworth's poetry has steadily been rising to a loftier stature amid the permanent edifices of the great poets of the English language. . . .

There is a beautiful expression of Wordsworth's meditative fancy inspired by musing over some gold and silver fishes in a vase, which I allude to, however, rather because of a higher inspiration prompted by the slight hint,—the restoration of them to freedom. It tells his deep sympathy with the liberty of all the mere animal creation:—

"Who can divine what impulses from God
Reach the caged lark, within a town-abode,
From his poor inch or two of daisied sod?
Oh, yield him back his privilege! No sea
Swells like the bosom of a man set free;
A wilderness is rich with liberty.
Roll on, ye spouting whales, who die or keep
Your independence in the fathomless deep!
Spread, tiny nautilus, the living sail;
Dive at thy choice, or brave the freshening gale.
If unreproved the ambitious eagle mount
Sunward to seek the daylight in its fount,
Bays, gulfs, and oceans, Indian width, shall be,
Till the world perishes, a field for thee."[1]

But the noblest dedication of Wordsworth's genius has been in his communion with his fellow-men,—a sympathy as expanded as ever filled the human heart, comprehensive of the highest and the lowliest of the race, and shedding a glory on all conditions of humanity:—

"'Tis nature's law
That none, the meanest of created things,
Of forms created the most vile and brute,
The dullest or most noxious, should exist
Divorced from good,—a spirit and pulse of good,—
A life and soul to every mode of being
Inseparably linked. Then be assured
That least of all can aught that ever owned
The heaven-regarding eye and front sublime
Which man is born to, sink, howe'er depressed,
So low as to be scorned without a sin,
Without offence to God, cast out of view,
Like the dry remnant of a garden-flower

1. See p. 442.

Whose seeds are shed, or as an implement
Worn out and useless.   15
No! man is dear to man; the poorest poor
Long for some moments in a weary life
When they can know and feel that they have been
Themselves the fathers and the dealers out
Of some small blessings, have been kind to such   20
As needed kindness, for this single cause:—
That we have all of us one human heart."

In Wordsworth's highly-cultivated affection for human nature, of course, is comprehended that reverence of womanly nature which we have observed as an element in
the genius of all the great English poets. It is part of his comprehensive scheme for elevating and purifying humanity, to throw the light of his imagination upon the meek
majesty of the female heart, its faithfulness, its fortitude, its heroism. What can be
more touchingly beautiful than the account of a woman's slowly-wasting spirit, in the
story of the "Deserted Cottage," in the first book of the "Excursion"? The sanity of
Wordsworth's genius admits of no romantic exaggeration or vapid sentimentality on
this subject. While it is his delight to show how divine a thing a woman may be made,
he regards her moving in the orbit of domestic life, not as enshrined by a superstitious
chivalry, but the being that God gave because it was not good for man to be alone. It
is a worthy and no light effort of poetic genius to take from the extravagances of
romance all that is attractive, and to blend it with the daily household worth of
woman, and, thus preserving its beauty, to reveal the spiritual and the practical which
in their harmony make up the perfection of female loveliness.

I had it much at heart to treat of Wordsworth's political poems, and to show how
valuable a use they might subserve in elevating and chastening public sentiment. But
the subject is too fine a one to be injured by such hurried discussion as I would now
be compelled to give it. Let me only, in evidence of his large-hearted sympathy with
our institutions, repeat an unpublished sonnet, composed on reading an account of
what he charitably calls some misdoings in our land:—

"Men of the Western World! in Fate's dark book
Whence this opprobrious leaf of dire portent?
Think ye your British ancestors forsook
Their narrow isle, for outrage provident?
Think ye they fled restraint they ill could brook,   5
To give in their descendants freer vent
And wider range to passions turbulent,
To mutual tyranny a deadlier look?
'Nay,' said a voice more soft than zephyr's breath;
'Dive through the stormy surface of the flood   10
To the great current flowing underneath;
Think on the countless springs of silent good;
So shall the truth be known and understood,
And thy grieved spirit brighten strong in faith.'"

—1859

∽ END OF TRANSATLANTIC EXCHANGES ∽

Sir Walter Scott
1771–1832

A native of Edinburgh, Sir Walter Scott wrote works that concerned themselves with Scotland's history and its affiliation with England, for which he advocated much to the chagrin of Scottish nationalists. After an education that included study of the classical Roman poets Horace and Virgil, he clerked for lawyers and eventually (in 1788) enrolled in classes on civil law. During this course of study at Edinburgh University, he befriended William Clerk, with whom he spent many nights studying to be admitted to the bar as well as some evenings *at* the bar (in the modern sense), which sometimes ended with Scott's being the "first to begin a row and last to end it." He also joined several societies, indulging his interest in Scottish oral tradition as well as German literature. His initial publishing endeavors were unsuccessful; he began by publishing translations of the German poet Bürger's "Lenoré" (1796), a poem that would influence William Wordsworth's "The Thorn" (1798) and George Eliot's *Adam Bede* (1859) but at the time was a "dead loss" to the publishers. He also compiled *Minstrelsy of the Scottish Border* (1802–1803), a multivolume collection of ballads indigenous to the frontier between England and Scotland. These volumes met with success and inspired Scott to publish more of his own verse that imitated these early ballads.

The Lay of the Last Minstrel (1805) was influenced by the poems of Ossian (James Macpherson) as well as the ballads Scott collected for the third volume of *Minstrelsy*. Scott set out to write a "Romance of Border chivalry and Enchantment" that would illustrate the "customs and manners that anciently prevailed on the Borders of England and Scotland." He also wished to record local history, as did Wordsworth and Samuel Taylor Coleridge in their *Lyrical Ballads* (1798), so he based the poem on the oral history of Gilpin Horner—a sixteenth-century Scotsman who defended his lands from English-allied rival clans and raided in return, thus becoming the subject of many legends. The success of *The Lay of the Last Minstrel* allowed him to devote less of his time to the law and more to writing, a career with which he could now help support himself and his family (he called it his "staff, but not his crutch").

In later years, Scott befriended the Lake Poets (Wordsworth, Coleridge, and Robert Southey), especially Wordsworth, with whom he embarked upon walking tours of Scotland. He visited Wordsworth, too, staying at Dove Cottage in Grasmere, where the poet and his sister lived such a spartan existence that Scott would often sneak out in the mornings to enjoy a full breakfast at the local pub. Nevertheless, the plenteous food for thought nourished their friendship and kept Scott there for long periods of time. Although influenced by the Lake Poets, Scott's poetry and prose exerted a reciprocal influence as well, especially (for instance) on Wordsworth's *White Doe of Rylstone* (1815). His most profound influence, though, was on the writers and readers of the United States. In the American South, towns were named after places associated with Scott and his novels, and the writer Mark Twain (Samuel Clemens) drew upon Scott's novels in his *Connecticut Yankee in King Arthur's Court* (1889). Before Twain, James Fenimore Cooper's *Leatherstocking* novels (1823–1841), which were inspired by Scott's *Waverley* novels (1814–1819), began to approach the staggering success of their models. Scott's brother Thomas, who immigrated to Canada, could speak to their popularity in all of North America: Many there believed Thomas to be the author of the novels, a rumor that began with Walter himself. Further testimony to the readership Scott enjoyed on both sides of the Atlantic is offered by the long list of distinguished writers who visited him at Abbotsford, his vast lands and home in his Scottish Border country, among them two Americans, Washington Irving and George Ticknor.

Lochinvar[1]

Oh! young Lochinvar is come out of the west,
Through all the wide Border his steed was the best;
And save his good broadsword he weapons had none.
He rode all unarmed and he rode all alone.
So faithful in love and so dauntless in war,   5
There never was knight like the young Lochinvar.

He stayed not for brake[2] and he stopped not for stone,
He swam the Eske river[3] where ford there was none,
But ere he alighted at Netherby gate
The bride had consented, the gallant came late: 10
For a laggard in love and a dastard in war
Was to wed the fair Ellen of brave Lochinvar.

So boldly he entered the Netherby Hall,
Among bridesmen, and kinsmen, and brothers, and all:
Then spoke the bride's father, his hand on his sword,—   15
For the poor craven bridegroom said never a word,—
'Oh! come ye in peace here, or come ye in war,
Or to dance at our bridal, young Lord Lochinvar?'—

'I long wooed your daughter, my suit you denied;
Love swells like the Solway,[4] but ebbs like its tide—   20
And now am I come, with this lost love of mine,
To lead but one measure, drink one cup of wine.
There are maidens in Scotland more lovely by far,
That would gladly be bride to the young Lochinvar.'

The bride kissed the goblet; the knight took it up,   25
He quaffed off the wine, and he threw down the cup,
She looked down to blush, and she looked up to sigh,
With a smile on her lips and a tear in her eye.
He took her soft hand ere her mother could bar,—
'Now tread we a measure!' said young Lochinvar.   30

So stately his form, and so lovely her face,
That never a hall such a galliard[5] did grace;
While her mother did fret, and her father did fume,
And the bridegroom stood dangling his bonnet and plume;
And the bride-maidens whispered, ''Twere better by far   35
To have matched our fair cousin with young Lochinvar.'

One touch to her hand and one word in her ear,
When they reached the hall-door, and the charger stood near;

---

1. From *Marmion* (1808).   2. Thicket.   3. In Edinburgh.   4. Solway Firth, southwest Scotland.   5. A dance.

So light to the croupe[6] the fair lady he swung,
So light to the saddle before her he sprung!   40
'She is won! we are gone, over bank, bush, and scaur[7];
They'll have fleet steeds that follow,' quoth young Lochinvar.

There was mounting 'mong Graemes of the Netherby clan;
Fosters, Fenwicks, and Musgraves, they rode and they ran:
There was racing and chasing on Cannobie Lee,   45
But the lost bride of Netherby ne'er did they see.
So daring in love and so dauntless in war,
Have ye e'er heard of gallant like young Lochinvar?

                                                          —1808

Jock of Hazeldean

"Why weep ye by the tide, ladie?
   Why weep ye by the tide?
I'll wed ye to my youngest son,
   And ye sall[1] be his bride:
And ye sall be his bride, ladie,
   Sae comely to be seen"—
But aye she loot the tears down fa'[2]
   For Jock of Hazeldean.

"Now let this wilfu' grief be done,
   And dry that cheek so pale;
Young Frank is chief of Errington,
   And lord of Langley-dale;
His step is first in peaceful ha',
   His sword in battle keen"—
But aye she loot the tears down fa'   15
   For Jock of Hazeldean.

"A chain of gold ye sall not lack,
   Nor braid to bind your hair;
Nor mettled hound, nor managed hawk,
   Nor palfrey[3] fresh and fair;
And you, the foremost o' them a',   20
   Shall ride our forest queen"—
But aye she loot the tears down fa'
   For Jock of Hazeldean.

The kirk[4] was deck'd at morning-tide,
   The tapers glimmer'd fair;   25
The priest and bridegroom wait the bride,
   And dame and knight are there.

---

6. Rump of a horse.   7. Rocky crag.

1. Shall.   2. Loot: let; fa': fall.   3. Saddle horse.   4. Church.

They sought her baith by bower and ha';
   The ladie was not seen!   30
She's o'er the Border and awa'
   Wi' Jock of Hazeldean.

—1816

The Dreary Change

The sun upon the Weirdlaw Hill,
   In Ettrick's[1] vale, is sinking sweet;
The westland wind is hush and still,
   The lake lies sleeping at my feet.
Yet not the landscape to mine eye   5
   Bears those bright hues that once it bore;
Though evening, with her richest dye,
   Flames o'er the hills of Ettrick's shore.

With listless look along the plain,
   I see Tweed's silver current glide,   10
And coldly mark the holy fane
   Of Melrose rise in ruin'd pride.
The quiet lake, the balmy air,
   The hill, the stream, the tower, the tree,—
Are they still such as once they were?   15
   Or is the dreary change in me?

Alas, the warp'd and broken board,
   How can it bear the painter's dye!
The harp of strain'd and tuneless chord,
   How to the minstrel's skill reply!   20
To aching eyes each landscape lowers,
   To feverish pulse each gale blows chill;
And Araby's or Eden's bowers
   Were barren as this moorland hill.

—1817

Proud Maisie

Proud Maisie is in the wood,
   Walking so early;
Sweet Robin sits on the bush,
   Singing so rarely.

"Tell me, thou bonny bird,
   When shall I marry me?"   5

---

1. Scottish village.

"When six braw[1] gentlemen
    Kirkward shall carry ye."

"Who makes the bridal bed,
    Birdie, say truly?"   10
"The gray-headed sexton[2]
    That delves the grave duly.

The glow-worm o'er grave and stone
    Shall light thee steady;
The owl from the steeple sing,   15
    'Welcome, proud lady.'"

—1818

Lucy Ashton's Song[1]

Look not thou on beauty's charming;
Sit thou still when kings are arming;
Taste not when the wine-cup glistens;
Speak not when the people listens;
Stop thine ear against the singer;   5
From the red gold keep thy finger;
Vacant heart and hand and eye,
Easy live and quiet die.

—1819

Samuel Taylor Coleridge
1772–1834

In 1794, Samuel Taylor Coleridge met and befriended Robert Southey, Britain's future Poet Laureate (1813), at Oxford. With similar radical politics, the soon fast friends hatched a plan to abscond from England for what they saw as the more favorable political climate of America. On the banks of the Susquehanna River in Pennsylvania, they hoped to establish Pantisocracy—a utopian community, primarily agrarian, where property and labor would be divided among all residents. A community of twelve couples would labor for only two to three hours daily, spending the rest of their time discussing philosophy. There would be no masters and servants, no social hierarchy and no aristocracy. Coleridge wrote of the plan in The Friend (1809) that the community would combine "the innocence of the patriarchal Age with the knowledge and genuine refinements of European culture." Pantisocracy grew out of the environment of the mid-1790s, a time of political distress for radicals, as England waged war on revolutionary France and repressed dissent at home. America seemed to offer greater potential for social and political

---

1. Fine.   2. Church-keeper.
1. From Tales of My Landlord (1819).

reform than England. But the plan collapsed in 1796, with Southey losing interest and Coleridge losing faith in democracy. As he wrote to Southey: "Americans love freedom because their ledgers furnish irrefragable arguments in favour of it."

Coleridge was born on October 21, 1772, the youngest child of John Coleridge, a parish vicar and schoolteacher, who died when his son was nine. At the time, Coleridge was enrolled in the boarding school Christ's Hospital, where he met his lifelong friend, poet and essayist Charles Lamb. He distinguished himself early, excelling in Latin and Greek and earning a scholarship to Cambridge. He left university without a degree in 1794, when he met Southey at Oxford and began to establish himself as a Unitarian preacher and to write poetry in earnest. In Bristol in 1795, Coleridge developed his skill (and reputation) as a captivating speaker, and in October of this year he married Sara Fricker; the two would have three sons. Bristol was a major slaving port, and he lectured on the evils of the slave trade, on religion and politics, and on the war in France. In 1796 and 1797, Coleridge published two volumes of verse, including "Religious Musings," in which he called the American statesman Benjamin Franklin "the Patriot Sage" who "called the red lightnings from the o'er-rushing cloud / And dashed the beauteous terrors on the earth / Smiling majestic." At this time, Coleridge also began the short-lived *The Watchman*, a liberal-minded newspaper edited and largely written by himself. In order to drum up subscription interest in the newspaper, he undertook a speaking tour, drawing on his network of Unitarian associates to gather audiences.

It was also during 1797 that Coleridge would make one of the most important friendships of his life. Introduced to William Wordsworth in 1795, the men began an intense friendship in July 1797, when the Wordsworths took up lodging near the Coleridge family. The two men walked and talked, producing *Lyrical Ballads* in 1798, which would include nineteen of Wordsworth's poems and four of Coleridge's: "Rime of the Ancyent Marinere," "The Foster-Mother's Tale," "The Nightingale: A Conversational Poem," and "The Dungeon." William, his sister Dorothy, and Coleridge soon set off on a tour of Germany, where over the course of a year Coleridge threw himself into the study of German literature, philosophy, and theology. From 1798 to 1800, Coleridge wrote the gothic, dream-infused poems "Christabel" and "Kubla Khan," and a second volume of *Lyrical Ballads* was issued with Wordsworth's preface and a less antiquated-looking "Ancient Mariner."

As his marital troubles and opium addiction deepened, Coleridge's poetic production tapered off significantly. In April 1802, he wrote an early version of "Dejection: An Ode" in a letter to Sara Hutchinson (with whom he later fell in love). The poem, which he revised and published in *The Morning Post* in October of the same year, laments the dimming of his imagination and seems to acknowledge the onset of a period of lessened ambition.

For the next fifteen years, Coleridge wrote widely on politics and philosophy and pursued a variety of careers, never settling on one. In 1804, he took up a minor government post in Malta for a period of two years—a time during which his opium addiction worsened significantly. In 1806, Coleridge sat for a portrait by the American painter Washington Allston, who recalled Coleridge's enthusiasm for art, architecture, and Rome (where the two met): Coleridge "called Rome the *silent* city; but I never could think of it as such, while with him . . . the fountain of his mind was never dry . . . . its living stream seemed specially to flow for every classic ruin over which we wandered." Channeling this overflowing stream of thought, Coleridge delivered several series of lectures (1808–1818) on literary, political, and philosophical topics; started a second newspaper, *The Friend*, in 1809–1810; and staged a successful play of his writing, *Remorse*, in London. Then, after this long period of relative quiescence, 1816–1818 saw a flurry of publication. "Christabel" and "Kubla Khan," long known only in manuscript and in parlor recitations, appeared in May 1816 as *Christabel; Kubla Khan: A Vision; The Pains of Sleep* to the dismay of reviewers. A second volume of verse, *Sibylline Leaves*, followed in 1817 and included a radically different version of "Ancient Mariner" (the version included in this anthology), to which Coleridge had added explanatory marginal notes. In 1817, he also released a literary autobiography, *Biographia Literaria*, in which he offers a defense of his own writing and of Wordsworth's poetry and maps out his own ideas about the imagination. The *Lay Sermons* on social reform appeared in 1816–1817, continuing the project of *The Statesman's Manual* (1816). Coleridge also gathered material from *The Friend* into a three-volume collection of political and religious essays. At this time, in an attempt to control his addiction and protect his fragile health, Coleridge moved into the home of his physician in Highgate, London, where he would reside for the rest of his life. At Highgate he was able to devote himself to increasingly conservative theological and political writing (such as *Aids to Reflection* in 1825 and *On the Constitution of Church and State* in 1830).

Coleridge's influence in America was powerful and widespread. Although *Lyrical Ballads* and *Christabel; Kubla Khan: A Vision; The Pains of Sleep* were published in American editions within a few years of their appearance in London, most Americans came to know Coleridge through his political and philosophical writings and through his role as a public intellectual, the "Sage of Highgate." This nickname was given to him around the time he began to hold weekly lectures in 1822, which his nephew recorded as "Table Talk." American minister and scholar James Marsh's 1829 edition of *Aids to Reflection* included a lengthy critical introduction that established Coleridge's reputation as an important philosopher and theologian. Marsh's edition made a deep impression on Ralph Waldo Emerson and on the New England Transcendentalists as a group. Frederick Henry Hedge would later recall that "the writings of Coleridge, recently edited by Marsh . . . created a ferment in the minds of some of the younger clergy of the day. There was a promise in the air of a new era of intellectual life." Emerson visited Coleridge in the summer of 1833, recording in *English Traits* (1856) that Coleridge, who by then had abandoned liberal Christianity for the Church of England, "burst into a declamation on the folly and ignorance of Unitarianism." And in her *Papers on Literature and Art* (1846), the American Transcendentalist Margaret Fuller wrote: "Give Coleridge a canvass, and he will paint a single mood as if his colors were made of the mind's own atoms. . . . [H]e is all life; not impassioned, not vehement, but searching, intellectual life, which seems 'listening through the frame' to its own pulses."

The Rime of the Ancient Mariner

In Seven Parts

Facile credo, plures esse Naturas invisibiles quam visibiles in rerum universitate. Sed horum omnium familiam quis nobis enarrabit, et gradus et cognationes et discrimina et singulorum munera? Quid agunt? quae loca habitant? Harum rerum notitiam semper ambivit ingenium humanum, nunquam attigit. Juvat, interea, non diffiteor, quandoque in animo, tanquam in tabulâ, majoris et melioris mundi imaginem contemplari: ne mens assuefacta hodiernae vitae minutiis se contrahat nimis, et tota subsidat in pusillas cogitationes. Sed veritati interea invigilandum est, modusque servandus, ut certa ab incertis, diem a nocte, distinguamus.

T. Burnet. *Archaeol. Phil.* p. 68.

I can easily believe, that there are more invisible than visible Beings in the universe. But who shall describe for us their families and their ranks and relationships and distinguishing features and functions? What they do and where they live? The human mind has always desired knowledge of these things, never attaining it. I do not doubt, however, that it is sometimes beneficial to contemplate, in thought, as in a Picture, the image of a greater and better world; lest the intellect, habituated to the trivia of daily life, may contract itself too much, and wholly sink into trifles. But at the same time we must be vigilant for truth, and maintain proportion that we may distinguish certain from uncertain, day from night.

466   Samuel Taylor Coleridge

An ancient Mariner
meeteth three Gallants
bidden to a wedding-
feast, and detaineth
one.

It is an ancient Mariner,
And he stoppeth one of three.
"By thy long gray beard and glittering eye,
Now wherefore stopp'st thou me?

"The Bridegroom's doors are opened wide,   5
And I am next of kin;
The guests are met, the feast is set:
May'st hear the merry din."

He holds him with his skinny hand,
"There was a ship," quoth he.   10
"Hold off! unhand me, gray-beard loon!"
Eftsoons[1] his hand dropt he.

The wedding-guest is
spellbound by the eye
of the old sea-faring
man, and constrained
to hear his tale.

He holds him with his glittering eye—
The wedding-guest stood still,
And listens like a three years' child: 15
The Mariner hath his will.

The wedding-guest sat on a stone:
He can not choose but hear;
And thus spake on that ancient man,
The bright-eyed Mariner.   20

The ship was cheer'd, the harbour clear'd,
Merrily did we drop
Below the kirk,[2] below the hill,
Below the light-house top.

The Mariner tells how
the ship sailed
southward with a good
wind and fair weather,
till it reached the line.

The Sun came up upon the left,   25
Out of the sea came he;
And he shone bright, and on the right
Went down into the sea.

Higher and higher every day,
Till over the mast at noon[3]—   30
The Wedding-Guest here beat his breast,
For he heard the loud bassoon.

The wedding-guest
heareth the bridal
music; but the Mariner
continueth his tale.

The bride hath paced into the hall,
Red as a rose is she;
Nodding their heads before her goes   35
The merry minstrelsy.

The Wedding-Guest he beat his breast,
Yet he can not choose but hear;
And thus spake on that ancient man,
The bright-eyed Mariner.   40

---

1. Immediately.   2. Church.   3. The ship is at the equator.

The ship drawn by a storm toward the south pole.

And now the STORM-BLAST came, and he
Was tyrannous and strong:
He struck with his o'ertaking wings,
And chased us south along.

With sloping masts and dipping prow,   45
As who pursued with yell and blow
Still treads the shadow of his foe
And forward bends his head,
The ship drove fast, loud roared the blast,
And southward aye we fled.   50

And now there came both mist and snow,
And it grew wondrous cold:
And ice, mast-high, came floating by,
As green as emerald.

The land of ice, and of fearful sounds, where no living thing was to be seen.

And through the drifts the snowy clifts   55
Did send a dismal sheen:
Nor shapes of men nor beast we ken[4]—
The ice was all between.

The ice was here, the ice was there,
The ice was all around: 60
It cracked and growled, and roared and howled,
Like noises in a swound![5]

Till a great sea-bird called the Albatross, came through the snow-fog, and was received with great joy and hospitality.

At length did cross an Albatross,
Thorough the fog it came;
As if it had been a Christian soul,   65
We hailed it in God's name.

It ate the food it ne'er had eat,
And round and round it flew.
The ice did split with a thunder-fit;
The helmsman steered us through!   70

And lo! the Albatross proveth a bird of good omen, and followeth the ship as it returned northward through fog and floating ice.

And a good south wind sprung up behind;
The Albatross did follow,
And every day, for food or play,
Came to the mariner's hollo!

In mist or cloud, on mast or shroud,   75
It perched for vespers nine;
Whiles all the night, through fog-smoke white,
Glimmered the white moon-shine.

The ancient Mariner inhospitably killeth the pious bird of good omen.

"God save thee, ancient Mariner!
From the fiends, that plague thee thus!—   80

---

4. Knew.   5. Swoon.

Why look'st thou so?"—With my cross-bow
I shot the ALBATROSS.

Part the Second

The Sun now rose upon the right[6]:
Out of the sea came he,
Still hid in mist, and on the left   85
Went down into the sea.

And the good south wind still blew behind,
But no sweet bird did follow,
Nor any day for food or play
Came to the mariners' hollo!   90

His shipmates cry out against the ancient Mariner, for killing the bird of good luck.

And I had done a hellish thing,
And it would work 'em woe:
For all averred, I had killed the bird
That made the breeze to blow.
Ah wretch! said they, the bird to slay,   95
That made the breeze to blow!

But when the fog cleared off, they justify the same, and thus make themselves accomplices in the crime.

Nor dim nor red, like God's own head,
The glorious Sun uprist:
Then all averred, I had killed the bird
That brought the fog and mist.   100
'Twas right, said they, such birds to slay,
That bring the fog and mist.

The fair breeze continues; the ship enters the Pacific Ocean, and sails northward, even till it reaches the Line.

The fair breeze blew, the white foam flew,
The furrow followed free;
We were the first that ever burst   105
Into that silent sea.

The ship hath been suddenly becalmed.

Down dropt the breeze, the sails dropt down,
'Twas sad as sad could be;
And we did speak only to break
The silence of the sea!   110

All in a hot and copper sky,
The bloody Sun, at noon,
Right up above the mast did stand,
No bigger than the Moon.

Day after day, day after day,   115
We stuck, nor breath nor motion;
As idle as a painted ship
Upon a painted ocean.

6. The ship has rounded Cape Horn and is now sailing north.

And the Albatross
begins to be avenged.

Water, water, every where,
And all the boards did shrink;   120
Water, water, every where,
Nor any drop to drink.

A spirit had followed
them; one of the
invisible inhabitants of
this planet, neither
departed souls nor
angels; concerning
whom the learned Jew,
Josephus, and the
Platonic Constantino-
politan, Michael
Psellus, may be
consulted. They are
very numerous, and
there is no climate or
element without one
or more.

The very deep did rot: O Christ!
That ever this should be!
Yea, slimy things did crawl with legs   125
Upon the slimy sea.

About, about, in reel and rout
The death-fires[7] danced at night;
The water, like a witch's oils,
Burnt green, and blue and white.   130

And some in dreams assured were
Of the Spirit that plagued us so;
Nine fathom deep he had followed us
From the land of mist and snow.

And every tongue, through utter drought,   135
Was withered at the root;
We could not speak, no more than if
We had been choak'd with soot.

The shipmates, in
their sore distress,
would fain throw the
whole guilt on the
ancient Mariner; in
sign whereof they hang
the dead sea-bird
round his neck.

Ah! well a-day! what evil looks
Had I from old and young!   140
Instead of the cross, the Albatross
About my neck was hung.

Part the Third

There passed a weary time. Each throat
Was parched, and glazed each eye.
A weary time! a weary time!   145
How glazed each weary eye,

The ancient Mariner
beholdeth a sign in the
element afar off.

When looking westward, I beheld
A something in the sky.

At first it seemed a little speck,
And then it seemed a mist;   150
It moved and moved, and took at last
A certain shape, I wist.[8]

A speck, a mist, a shape, I wist!
And still it neared and neared:

---

7. Phosphorescent plankton or "St. Elmo's fire," ionized gas clinging to the mast.   8. Knew.

As if it dodged a water-sprite,   155
It plunged and tacked and veered.

At its nearer approach,
it seemeth him to be a
ship; and at a dear
ransom he freeth his
speech from the bonds
of thirst.

With throats unslaked, with black lips baked,
We could nor laugh nor wail;
Through utter drought all dumb we stood!
I bit my arm, I sucked the blood,   160
And cried, A sail! a sail!

With throats unslaked, with black lips baked,
Agape they heard me call:

A flash of joy.

Gramercy!⁹ they for joy did grin,
And all at once their breath drew in,   165
As they were drinking all.

And horror follows.
For can it be a *ship*
that comes onward
without wind or tide?

See! see! (I cried) she tacks no more!
Hither to work us weal;¹⁰
Without a breeze, without a tide,
She steadies with upright keel!   170

The western wave was all a-flame.
The day was well nigh done!
Almost upon the western wave
Rested the broad bright Sun;
When that strange shape drove suddenly   175
Betwixt us and the Sun.

It seemeth him but the
skeleton of a ship.

And straight the Sun was flecked with bars,
(Heaven's Mother send us grace!)
As if through a dungeon-grate he peer'd
With broad and burning face.   180

And its ribs are seen as
bars on the face of the
setting Sun.

Alas! (thought I, and my heart beat loud)
How fast she nears and nears!
Are those *her* sails that glance in the Sun,
Like restless gossameres?¹¹

The spectre-woman
and her death-mate,
and no other on board
the skeleton-ship.

Are those *her* ribs through which the Sun   185
Did peer, as through a grate?
And is that Woman all her crew?
Is that a DEATH? and are there two?
Is DEATH that woman's mate?

Like vessel, like crew!

Her lips were red, *her* looks were free,   190
Her locks were yellow as gold:
Her skin was as white as leprosy,
The Night-Mair LIFE-IN-DEATH was she,
Who thicks man's blood with cold.

---

9. Great thanks!   10. Good.   11. Cobwebs, sheer fabric.

DEATH, and LIFE-IN-DEATH have diced for the ship's crew, and she (the latter) winneth the ancient Mariner.

The naked hulk alongside came,   195
And the twain were casting dice;
"The game is done! I've, I've won!"
Quoth she, and whistles thrice.

No twilight within the courts of the Sun.

The Sun's rim dips; the stars rush out:
At one stride comes the dark;   200
With far-heard whisper, o'er the sea,
Off shot the spectre-bark.

At the rising of the Moon,

We listened and looked sideways up!
Fear at my heart, as at a cup,
My life-blood seemed to sip!   205
The stars were dim, and thick the night,
The steersman's face by his lamp gleamed white;

From the sails the dew did drip—
Till clomb[12] above the eastern bar
The horned Moon, with one bright star   210
Within the nether tip.[13]

One after another,

One after one, by the star-dogged Moon,
Too quick for groan or sigh,
Each turned his face with a ghastly pang,
And cursed me with his eye.   215

His ship-mates drop down dead;

Four times fifty living men
(And I heard nor sigh nor groan),
With heavy thump, a lifeless lump,
They dropped down one by one.

But LIFE-IN-DEATH begins her work on the ancient Mariner.

The souls did from their bodies fly,—   220
They fled to bliss or woe!
And every soul, it passed me by,
Like the whizz of my CROSS-BOW!

Part the Fourth

The wedding-guest feareth that a spirit is talking to him;

"I FEAR thee, ancient Mariner!
I fear thy skinny hand!   225
And thou art long, and lank, and brown,
As is the ribbed sea-sand.

But the ancient Mariner assureth him of his bodily life, and proceedeth to relate his horrible penance.

I fear thee and thy glittering eye,
And thy skinny hand, so brown."—
Fear not, fear not, thou Wedding-Guest!   230
This body dropt not down.

Alone, alone, all, all alone,
Alone on a wide wide sea!

---

12. Climbed.   13. Sailors saw a star dogging the moon as an omen of evil.

And never a saint took pity on
My soul in agony.   235

He despiseth the creatures of the calm,

The many men, so beautiful!
And they all dead did lie:
And a thousand thousand slimy things
Lived on; and so did I.

And envieth that they should live, and so many lie dead.

I looked upon the rotting sea,   240
And drew my eyes away;
I looked upon the rotting deck,
And there the dead men lay.

I looked to Heaven, and tried to pray;
But or ever a prayer had gusht,   245
A wicked whisper came, and made
My heart as dry as dust.

I closed my lids, and kept them close,
And the balls like pulses beat;
For the sky and the sea, and the sea and the sky   250
Lay, like a load, on my weary eye,
And the dead were at my feet.

But the curse liveth for him in the eye of the dead men.

The cold sweat melted from their limbs,
Not rot nor reek did they:
The look with which they looked on me   255
Had never passed away.

In his loneliness and fixedness he yearneth towards the journeying Moon, and the stars that still sojourn, yet still move onward; and every where the blue sky belongs to them, and is their appointed rest, and their native country, and their own natural homes, which they enter unannounced, as lords that are certainly expected, and yet there is a silent joy at their arrival.

An orphan's curse would drag to Hell
A spirit from on high;
But oh! more horrible than that
Is the curse in a dead man's eye!   260
Seven days, seven nights, I saw that curse,
And yet I could not die.

The moving Moon went up the sky,
And nowhere did abide:
Softly she was going up,   265
And a star or two beside—

Her beams bemocked the sultry main,
Like April hoar-frost spread;
But where the ship's huge shadow lay,
The charmed water burnt alway   270
A still and awful red.

By the light of the Moon he beholdeth God's creatures of the great calm.

Beyond the shadow of the ship,
I watched the water-snakes:
They moved in tracks of shining white,

And when they reared, the elfish light   275
Fell off in hoary flakes.

Within the shadow of the ship
I watched their rich attire:
Blue, glossy green, and velvet black,
They coiled and swam; and every track   280
Was a flash of golden fire.

Their beauty and their happiness.

O happy living things! no tongue
Their beauty might declare:
A spring of love gushed from my heart,

He blesseth them in his heart.

And I blessed them unaware!   285
Sure my kind saint took pity on me,
And I blessed them unaware.

The spell begins to break.

The self same moment I could pray;
And from my neck so free
The Albatross fell off, and sank   290
Like lead into the sea.

Part the Fifth

By grace of the holy Mother, the ancient Mariner is refreshed with rain.

Oh SLEEP! it is a gentle thing,
Belov'd from pole to pole!
To Mary Queen the praise be given!
She sent the gentle sleep from Heaven,   295
That slid into my soul.

The silly[14] buckets on the deck,
That had so long remained,
I dreamt that they were filled with dew;
And when I awoke, it rained.   300

My lips were wet, my throat was cold,
My garments all were dank;
Sure I had drunken in my dreams,
And still my body drank.

He heareth sounds and seeth strange sights and commotions in the sky and the element.

I moved, and could not feel my limbs: 305
I was so light—almost
I thought that I had died in sleep,
And was a blessed ghost.

And soon I heard a roaring wind:
It did not come anear;
But with its sound it shook the sails,   310
That were so thin and sere.

---

14 Helpless.

The upper air burst into life!
And a hundred fire-flags[15] sheen,
To and fro they were hurried about!   315
And to and fro, and in and out,
The wan stars danced between.

And the coming wind did roar more loud,
And the sails did sigh like sedge[16];
And the rain poured down from one black cloud;   320
The Moon was at its edge.

The thick black cloud was cleft, and still
The Moon was at its side:
Like waters shot from some high crag,
The lightning fell with never a jag,   325
A river steep and wide.

The bodies of the ship's crew are inspirited, and the ship moves on.

The loud wind never reached the ship,
Yet now the ship moved on!
Beneath the lightning and the Moon
The dead men gave a groan.   330

They groaned, they stirred, they all uprose,
Nor spake, nor moved their eyes;
It had been strange, even in a dream,
To have seen those dead men rise.

The helmsman steered, the ship moved on;   335
Yet never a breeze up blew;
The mariners all 'gan work the ropes,
Where they were wont to do;
They raised their limbs like lifeless tools—
We were a ghastly crew.   340

The body of my brother's son
Stood by me, knee to knee:
The body and I pulled at one rope,
But he said naught to me.

But not by the souls of the men, nor by daemons of earth or middle air, but by a blessed troop of angelic spirits, sent down by the invocation of the guardian saint.

"I fear thee, ancient Mariner!"   345
Be calm, thou Wedding-Guest!
'Twas not those souls that fled in pain,
Which to their corses[17] came again,
But a troop of spirits blest:

For when it dawned—they dropped their arms,   350
And clustered round the mast;

---

15. Meteors or lightning.   16. Marsh grass.   17. Corpses.

Sweet sounds rose slowly through their mouths,
And from their bodies passed.

Around, around, flew each sweet sound,
Then darted to the Sun;   355
Slowly the sounds came back again,
Now mixed, now one by one.

Sometimes a-dropping from the sky
I heard the sky-lark sing;
Sometimes all little birds that are,   360
How they seemed to fill the sea and air
With their sweet jargoning![18]

And now 'twas like all instruments,
Now like a lonely flute;
And now it is an angel's song,   365
That makes the heavens be mute.

It ceased; yet still the sails made on
A pleasant noise till noon,
A noise like of a hidden brook
In the leafy mouth of June,   370
That to the sleeping woods all night
Singeth a quiet tune.

Till noon we quietly sailed on,
Yet never a breeze did breathe:
Slowly and smoothly went the ship,   375
Moved onward from beneath.

The lonesome spirit from the south-pole carries on the ship as far as the line, in obedience to the angelic troop, but still requireth vengeance.

Under the keel nine fathom deep,
From the land of mist and snow,
The spirit slid: and it was he
That made the ship to go.   380
The sails at noon left off their tune,
And the ship stood still also.

The Sun, right up above the mast,
Had fixt her to the ocean;
But in a minute she 'gan stir,   385
With a short uneasy motion—
Backwards and forwards half her length,
With a short uneasy motion.

Then like a pawing horse let go,
She made a sudden bound: 390
It flung the blood into my head,
And I fell down in a swound.

18. Twittering.

The Polar Spirit's fellow-daemons, the invisible inhabitants of the element, take part in his wrong; and two of them relate, one to the other, that penance long and heavy for the ancient Mariner hath been accorded to the Polar Spirit, who returneth southward.

How long in that same fit I lay,
I have not to declare;
But ere my living life returned,   395
I heard and in my soul discerned
Two VOICES in the air.

"Is it he?" quoth one, "Is this the man?
By him who died on cross,
With his cruel bow he laid full low,   400
The harmless Albatross.

The spirit who bideth by himself
In the land of mist and snow,
He loved the bird that loved the man
Who shot him with his bow."   405

The other was a softer voice,
As soft as honey-dew.
Quoth he, "The man hath penance done,
And penance more will do."

Part the Sixth

FIRST VOICE.

"But tell me, tell me! speak again,   410
Thy soft response renewing—
What makes that ship drive on so fast?
What is the OCEAN doing?"

SECOND VOICE.

"Still as a slave before his lord,
The OCEAN hath no blast;   415
His great bright eye most silently
Up to the Moon is cast—

If he may know which way to go;
For she guides him smooth or grim.
See, brother, see! how graciously   420
She looketh down on him."

FIRST VOICE.

The Mariner hath been cast into a trance; for the angelic power causeth the vessel to drive northward, faster than human life could endure.

"But why drives on that ship so fast,
Without or wave or wind?"

SECOND VOICE.

"The air is cut away before,
And closes from behind.   425

Fly, brother, fly! more high, more high!
Or we shall be belated:
For slow and slow that ship will go,
When the Mariner's trance is abated."

The supernatural
motion is retarded; the
Mariner awakes, and
his penance begins
anew.

I woke, and we were sailing on   430
As in a gentle weather:
'Twas night, calm night, the moon was high;
The dead men stood together.

All stood together on the deck,
For a charnel-dungeon[19] fitter: 435
All fixed on me their stony eyes,
That in the Moon did glitter.

The pang, the curse, with which they died,
Had never passed away:
I could not draw my eyes from theirs,   440
Nor turn them up to pray.

The curse is finally
expiated.

And now this spell was snapt: once more
I viewed the ocean green,
And looked far forth, yet little saw
Of what had else been seen—   445

Like one, that on a lonesome road
Doth walk in fear and dread,
And having once turn'd round, walks on,
And turns no more his head;
Because he knows, a frightful fiend   450
Doth close behind him tread.

But soon there breathed a wind on me,
Nor sound nor motion made:
Its path was not upon the sea,
In ripple or in shade.   455

It raised my hair, it fanned my cheek
Like a meadow-gale of spring—
It mingled strangely with my fears,
Yet it felt like a welcoming.

Swiftly, swiftly flew the ship,   460
Yet she sailed softly too:
Sweetly, sweetly blew the breeze—
On me alone it blew.

And the ancient
Mariner beholdeth his
native country.

Oh! dream of joy! is this indeed
The light-house top I see?   465
Is this the hill? is this the kirk?
Is this mine own countree?

We drifted o'er the harbour-bar,
And I with sobs did pray—
O let me be awake, my God!   470
Or let me sleep alway.

---

19. A place where dead bodies are stored.

The harbour-bay was clear as glass,
So smoothly it was strewn!
And on the bay the moonlight lay,
And the shadow of the moon.   475

The rock shone bright, the kirk no less,
That stands above the rock:
The moonlight steeped in silentness
The steady weathercock.

And the bay was white with silent light,   480
Till rising from the same,

The angelic spirits
leave the dead bodies,
Full many shapes, that shadows were,
In crimson colours came.

And appear in their
own forms of light.
A little distance from the prow
Those crimson shadows were: 485
I turned my eyes upon the deck—
Oh, Christ! what saw I there!

Each corse lay flat, lifeless and flat,
And, by the holy rood![20]
A man all light, a seraph-man,[21]   490
On every corse there stood.

This seraph-band, each waved his hand:
It was a heavenly sight!
They stood as signals to the land,
Each one a lovely light;   495

This seraph-band, each waved his hand,
No voice did they impart—
No voice; but oh! the silence sank
Like music on my heart.

But soon I heard the dash of oars,   500
I heard the Pilot's cheer;
My head was turned perforce away
And I saw a boat appear.

The Pilot, and the Pilot's boy,
I heard them coming fast: 505
Dear Lord in Heaven! it was a joy
The dead men could not blast.

I saw a third—I heard his voice:
It is the Hermit good!
He singeth loud his godly hymns   510

---

20. Cross.   21. Seraph: the highest order of angels.

That he makes in the wood.
He'll shrieve[22] my soul, he'll wash away
The Albatross's blood.

Part the Seventh

The Hermit of the
Wood,

This Hermit good lives in that wood
Which slopes down to the sea.   515
How loudly his sweet voice he rears!
He loves to talk with marineres
That come from a far countree.

He kneels at morn, and noon, and eve—
He hath a cushion plump: 520
It is the moss that wholly hides
The rotted old oak-stump.

The Skiff-boat neared: I heard them talk,
"Why, this is strange, I trow!
Where are those lights so many and fair,   525
That signal made but now?"

Approacheth the ship
with wonder.

"Strange, by my faith!" the Hermit said—
"And they answered not our cheer!
The planks looked warped! and see those sails,
How thin they are and sere!   530
I never saw aught like to them,
Unless perchance it were

"Brown skeletons of leaves that lag
My forest-brook along;
When the ivy-tod[23] is heavy with snow,   535
And the owlet whoops to the wolf below,
That eats the she-wolf's young."

"Dear Lord! it hath a fiendish look—
(The Pilot made reply)
I am a-feared"—"Push on, push on!"   540
Said the Hermit cheerily.

The boat came closer to the ship,
But I nor spake nor stirred;
The boat came close beneath the ship,
And straight a sound was heard.   545

The ship suddenly
sinketh.

Under the water it rumbled on,
Still louder and more dread:
It reachd the ship, it split the bay;
The ship went down like lead.

---

22. Absolve.   23. Clump of ivy.

*The ancient Mariner is
saved in the Pilot's
boat.*

Stunned by that loud and dreadful sound,   550
Which sky and ocean smote,
Like one that hath been seven days drowned,
My body lay afloat;
But swift as dreams, myself I found
Within the Pilot's boat.   555

Upon the whirl, where sank the ship,
The boat spun round and round;
And all was still, save that the hill
Was telling of the sound.

I moved my lips—the Pilot shrieked   560
And fell down in a fit;
The holy Hermit raised his eyes,
And prayed where he did sit.

I took the oars: the Pilot's boy,
Who now doth crazy go,   565
Laughed loud and long, and all the while
His eyes went to and fro.
"Ha! ha!" quoth he, "full plain I see,
The Devil knows how to row."

And now, all in my own countree,   570
I stood on the firm land!
The Hermit stepped forth from the boat,
And scarcely he could stand.

*The ancient Mariner
earnestly entreateth
the Hermit to shrieve
him; and the penance
of life falls on him.*

"O shrieve me, shrieve me, holy man!"
The Hermit crossed his brow.   575
"Say quick," quoth he, "I bid thee say—
What manner of man art thou?"

Forthwith this frame of mine was wrenched
With a woeful agony,
Which forced me to begin my tale;   580
And then it left me free.

*And ever and anon
throughout his future
life an agony
constraineth him to
travel from land to
land,*

Since then, at an uncertain hour,
That agony returns:
And till my ghastly tale is told,
This heart within me burns.   585

I pass, like night, from land to land;
I have strange power of speech;
That moment that his face I see,
I know the man that must hear me:
To him my tale I teach.   590

What loud uproar bursts from that door!
The wedding-guests are there:
But in the garden-bower the bride
And bride-maids singing are;
And hark the little vesper bell,   595
Which biddeth me to prayer!

O Wedding-Guest! this soul hath been
Alone on a wide wide sea:
So lonely 'twas, that God himself
Scarce seemed there to be.   600

O sweeter than the marriage-feast,
'Tis sweeter far to me,
To walk together to the kirk
With a goodly company!—

To walk together to the kirk,   605
And all together pray,
While each to his great Father bends,
Old men, and babes, and loving friends,
And youths and maidens gay!

And to teach by his
own example, love and
reverence to all things
that God made and
loveth.

Farewell, farewell! but this I tell   610
To thee, thou Wedding-Guest!
He prayeth well, who loveth well
Both man and bird and beast.

He prayeth best, who loveth best
All things both great and small;   615
For the dear God who loveth us,
He made and loveth all."

The Mariner, whose eye is bright,
Whose beard with age is hoar,
Is gone: and now the Wedding-Guest   620
Turned from the bridegroom's door.

He went like one that hath been stunned,
And is of sense forlorn[24]:
A sadder and a wiser man,
He rose the morrow morn.   625

—1817

---

24. Forsaken.

This Lime-Tree Bower My Prison

In the June of 1797, some long-expected Friends[1] paid a visit to the author's cottage; and on the morning of their arrival, he met with an accident, which disabled him from walking during the whole time of their stay. One evening, when they had left him for a few hours, he composed the following lines in the garden-bower.

Well, they are gone, and here must I remain,
This lime-tree bower my prison! I have lost
Beauties and feelings, such as would have been
Most sweet to my remembrance even when age
Had dimmed mine eyes to blindness! They, meanwhile,   5
Friends, whom I never more may meet again,
On springy heath, along the hill-top edge,
Wander in gladness, and wind down, perchance,
To that still roaring dell, of which I told;
The roaring dell, o'erwooded, narrow, deep,   10
And only speckled by the mid-day sun;
Where its slim trunk the ash from rock to rock
Flings arching like a bridge;—that branchless ash,
Unsunned and damp, whose few poor yellow leaves
Ne'er tremble in the gale, yet tremble still,   15
Fanned by the waterfall! and there my friends
Behold the dark green file of long lank weeds,
That all at once (a most fantastic sight!)
Still nod and drip beneath the dripping edge
Of the blue clay-stone.   20

                    Now, my friends emerge
Beneath the wide wide Heaven—and view again
The many-steepled tract magnificent
Of hilly fields and meadows, and the sea,
With some fair bark,[2] perhaps, whose sails light up
The slip of smooth clear blue betwixt two Isles   25
Of purple shadow! Yes! they wander on
In gladness all; but thou, methinks, most glad,
My gentle-hearted Charles! for thou hast pined
And hungered after Nature, many a year,
In the great City pent, winning thy way   30
With sad yet patient soul, through evil and pain
And strange calamity![3] Ah! slowly sink
Behind the western ridge, thou glorious sun!
Shine in the slant beams of the sinking orb,
Ye purple heath-flowers! richlier burn, ye clouds!   35
Live in the yellow light, ye distant groves!
And kindle, thou blue ocean! So my Friend

---

1. Dorothy and William Wordsworth and Charles Lamb. 2. Boat. 3. Charles Lambs' sister, Mary, murdered their mother in a fit of insanity.

Struck with deep joy may stand, as I have stood,
Silent with swimming sense; yea, gazing round
On the wide landscape, gaze till all doth seem   40
Less gross than bodily; and of such hues
As veil the Almighty Spirit, when yet he makes
Spirits perceive his presence.

                A delight
Comes sudden on my heart, and I am glad
As I myself were there! Nor in this bower,   45
This little lime-tree bower, have I not marked
Much that has soothed me. Pale beneath the blaze
Hung the transparent foliage; and I watched
Some broad and sunny leaf, and loved to see
The shadow of the leaf and stem above   50
Dappling its sunshine! And that walnut-tree
Was richly tinged, and a deep radiance lay
Full on the ancient ivy, which usurps
Those fronting elms, and now, with blackest mass
Makes their dark branches gleam a lighter hue   55
Through the late twilight: and though now the bat
Wheels silent by, and not a swallow twitters,
Yet still the solitary humble bee
Sings in the bean-flower! Henceforth I shall know
That Nature ne'er deserts the wise and pure;   60
No plot so narrow, be but Nature there,
No waste so vacant, but may well employ
Each faculty of sense, and keep the heart
Awake to Love and Beauty! and sometimes
'Tis well to be bereft of promised good,   65
That we may lift the Soul, and contemplate
With lively joy the joys we can not share.
My gentle-hearted Charles! when the last rook
Beat its straight path along the dusky air
Homewards, I blest it! deeming, its black wing   70
(Now a dim speck, now vanishing in light)
Had crossed the mighty orb's dilated glory,
While thou stood'st gazing; or when all was still,
Flew creeking o'er thy head, and had a charm
For thee, my gentle-hearted Charles, to whom   75
No sound is dissonant which tells of Life.

                          —1800

The Dungeon[1]

And this place our forefathers made for man!
This is the process of our love and wisdom,

---

1. Originally part of Coleridge's play, *Osorio* (5.2.1–30), which was never performed.

To each poor brother who offends against us—
Most innocent, perhaps—and what if guilty?
Is this the only cure? Merciful God!   5
Each pore and natural outlet shrivell'd up
By Ignorance and parching Poverty,
His energies roll back upon his heart,
And stagnate and corrupt; till chang'd to poison,
They break out on him, like a loathsome plague-spot;   10
Then we call in our pamper'd mountebanks[2]—
And this is their best cure! uncomforted
And friendless solitude, groaning and tears,
And savage faces, at the clanking hour,
Seen through the steams and vapour of his dungeon,   15
By the lamp's dismal twilight! So he lies
Circled with evil, till his very soul
Unmoulds its essence, hopelessly deform'd
By sights of ever more deformity!

With other ministrations thou, O Nature!   20
Healest thy wandering and distemper'd child:
Thou pourest on him thy soft influences,
Thy sunny hues, fair forms, and breathing sweets,
Thy melodies of woods, and winds, and waters,
Till he relent, and can no more endure   25
To be a jarring and a dissonant thing,
Amid this general dance and minstrelsy;
But, bursting into tears, wins back his way,
His angry spirit heal'd and harmoniz'd
By the benignant touch of Love and Beauty.   30

—1797

Kubla Khan: or, A Vision in a Dream
Of the Fragment of Kubla Khan

The following fragment is here published at the request of a poet of great and deserved celebrity,[1] and, as far as the Author's own opinions are concerned, rather as a psychological curiosity, than on the ground of any supposed *poetic* merits.

In the summer of the year 1797, the Author, then in ill health, had retired to a lonely farm house between Porlock and Linton, on the Exmoor confines of Somerset and Devonshire. In consequence of a slight indisposition, an anodyne[2] had been prescribed, from the effects of which he fell asleep in his chair at the moment that he was reading the following sentence, or words of the same substance, in "Purchas's Pilgrimage": "Here the Khan Kubla commanded a palace to be built, and a stately garden thereunto: and thus ten miles of fertile ground were inclosed with a wall."[3] The Author continued for about

2. Charlatans, swindlers.

1. George Gordon, Lord Byron.   2. Painkiller; elsewhere, Coleridge notes he took two grams of opium.   3. Samuel
Purchase, *Purchas his Pilgrimage* (1613).

three hours in a profound sleep, at least of the external senses, during which time he has the most vivid confidence, that he could not have composed less than from two to three hundred lines; if that indeed can be called composition in which all the images rose up before him as *things*, with a parallel production of the correspondent expressions, without any sensation or consciousness of effort. On awaking he appeared to himself to have a distinct recollection of the whole, and taking his pen, ink, and paper, instantly and eagerly wrote down the lines that are here preserved. At this moment he was unfortunately called out by a person on business from Porlock, and detained by him above an hour, and on his return to his room, found, to his no small surprise and mortification, that though he still retained some vague and dim recollection of the general purpose of the vision, yet, with the exception of some eight or ten scattered lines and images, all the rest had passed away like the images on the surface of a stream into which a stone has been cast, but, alas! without the after restoration of the latter:

> Then all the charm
> Is broken—all that phantom-world so fair
> Vanishes, and a thousand circlets spread,
> And each mis-shape[s] the other. Stay awhile,
> Poor youth! who scarcely dar'st lift up thine eyes—
> The stream will soon renew its smoothness, soon
> The visions will return! And lo, he stays,
> And soon the fragments dim of lovely forms
> Come trembling back, unite, and now once more
> The pool becomes a mirror.
> [Coleridge, "The Picture," lines 91–100]

Yet from the still surviving recollections in his mind, the Author has frequently purposed to finish for himself what had been originally, as it were, given to him. Σαμερον αδιον ασω:[4] but the to-morrow is yet to come.

As a contrast to this vision, I have annexed a fragment of a very different character, describing with equal fidelity the dream of pain and disease.

—1816

Kubla Khan

In Xanadu did Kubla Khan
A stately pleasure-dome decree:
Where Alph, the sacred river, ran
Through caverns measureless to man
   Down to a sunless sea.   5
So twice five miles of fertile ground
With walls and towers were girdled round:
And here were gardens bright with sinuous rills,
Where blossomed many an incense-bearing tree;
And here were forests ancient as the hills,   10
And folding[5] sunny spots of greenery.

---

4. "Today I shall sing more sweetly."   5. "Enfolding" in later versions.

But oh! that deep romantic chasm which slanted
Down the green hill athwart a cedarn cover!
A savage place: as holy and inchanted
As e'er beneath a waning moon was haunted   15
By woman wailing for her demon-lover!
And from this chasm, with ceaseless turmoil seething,
As if this earth in fast thick pants were breathing,
A mighty fountain momently was forced:
Amid whose swift half-intermitted burst   20
Huge fragments vaulted like rebounding hail,
Or chaffy grain beneath the thresher's flail:
And mid these dancing rocks at once and ever
It flung up momently the sacred river.
Five miles meandering with a mazy motion   25
Through wood and dale the sacred river ran,
Then reached the caverns measureless to man,
And sank in tumult to a lifeless ocean:
And 'mid this tumult Kubla heard from far
Ancestral voices prophesying war!   30

      The shadow of the dome of pleasure
      Floated midway on the waves;
      Where was heard the mingled measure
      From the fountain and the caves.
It was a miracle of rare device,   35
A sunny pleasure-dome with caves of ice!

   A damsel with a dulcimer
      In a vision once I saw:
      It was an Abyssinian maid,
      And on her dulcimer she played,   40
      Singing of Mount Abora.
      Could I revive within me
      Her symphony and song,
      To such a deep delight 'twould win me,
That with music loud and long,   45
I would build that dome in air,
That sunny dome! those caves of ice!
And all who heard should see them there,
And all should cry, Beware! Beware!
His flashing eyes, his floating hair!   50
Weave a circle round him thrice,
And close your eyes with holy dread,
For he on honey-dew hath fed,
And drank the milk of Paradise.

—1816

The Eolian Harp[1]

Composed at Clevedon, Somersetshire

My pensive Sara! thy soft cheek reclined
Thus on mine arm, most soothing sweet it is
To sit beside our cot,[2] our cot o'ergrown
With white-flowered jasmin, and the broad-leaved myrtle,
(Meet emblems they of Innocence and Love!)   5
And watch the clouds, that late were rich with light,
Slow saddening round, and mark the star of eve
Serenely brilliant (such should wisdom be)
Shine opposite! How exquisite the scents
Snatched from yon bean-field! and the world so hushed! 10
The stilly murmur of the distant sea
Tells us of silence.

  And that simplest lute,
Placed length-ways in the clasping casement, hark!
How by the desultory breeze caressed,   15
Like some coy maid half yielding to her lover,
It pours such sweet upbraiding, as must needs
Tempt to repeat the wrong! And now, its strings
Boldlier swept, the long sequacious[3] notes
Over delicious surges sink and rise,   20
Such a soft floating witchery of sound
As twilight Elfins make, when they at eve
Voyage on gentle gales from Fairy-Land,
Where Melodies round honey-dropping flowers,
Footless and wild, like birds of Paradise,   25
Nor pause, nor perch, hovering on untamed wing!
O the one life within us and abroad,
Which meets all motion and becomes its soul,
A light in sound, a sound-like power in light
Rhythm in all thought, and joyance everywhere— 30
Methinks, it should have been impossible
Not to love all things in a world so filled;
Where the breeze warbles, and the mute still air
Is Music slumbering on her instrument.

  And thus, my love! as on the midway slope 35
Of yonder hill I stretch my limbs at noon,
Whilst through my half-closed eyelids I behold
The sunbeams dance, like diamonds, on the main,
And tranquil muse upon tranquillity;
Full many a thought uncalled and undetained, 40

---

1. An aeolian harp is a stringed instrument that sounds when breezes flow over it. 2. Cottage. 3. Flowing.

And many idle flitting phantasies,
Traverse my indolent and passive brain,
As wild and various as the random gales
That swell and flutter on this subject lute!

   And what if all of animated nature   45
Be but organic harps diversely framed,
That tremble into thought, as o'er them sweeps
Plastic and vast, one intellectual breeze,
At once the Soul of each, and God of All?
   But thy more serious eye a mild reproof   50
Darts, O beloved woman! nor such thoughts
Dim and unhallowed dost thou not reject,
And biddest me walk humbly with my God.
Meek daughter in the family of Christ!
Well hast thou said and holily dispraised
These shapings of the unregenerate mind;   55
Bubbles that glitter as they rise and break
On vain Philosophy's aye-babbling spring.
For never guiltless may I speak of him,
The Incomprehensible! save when with awe   60
I praise him, and with Faith that inly feels;
Who with his saving mercies healed me,
A sinful and most miserable man,
Wildered and dark, and gave me to possess
Peace, and this cot, and thee, heart-honoured Maid!   65

—1796

The Foster-Mother's Tale[1]
A Dramatic Fragment

   Foster-Mother. I never saw the man whom you describe.
   Maria. 'Tis strange! he spake of you familiarly
As mine and Albert's common Foster-mother.
   Foster-Mother. Now blessings on the man, whoe'er he be,
That joined your names with mine! O my sweet lady,   5
As often as I think of those dear times
When you two little ones would stand at eve
On each side of my chair, and make me learn
All you had learnt in the day; and how to talk
In gentle phrase, then bid me sing to you—   10
'Tis more like heaven to come than what *has* been!
   Maria. O my dear Mother! this strange man has left me
Troubled with wilder fancies, than the moon

---

1. Originally part of Coleridge's play, *Osorio* (4.2.3–83).

Breeds in the love-sick maid who gazes at it,
Till lost in inward vision, with wet eye   15
She gazes idly!—But that entrance,[2] Mother!
    Foster-Mother. Can no one hear? It is a perilous tale!
    Maria. No one.
    Foster-Mother.   My husband's father told it me,
Poor old Leoni! (Angels rest his soul!)
He was a woodman, and could fell and saw   20
With lusty[3] arm. You know that huge round beam
Which props the hanging wall of the old Chapel?—
Beneath that tree, while yet it was a tree,
He found a baby wrapt in mosses lined
With thistle-beards, and such small locks of wool   25
As hang on brambles. Well, he brought him home,
And reared him at the then Lord Velez' cost.
And so the babe grew up a pretty boy
A pretty boy, but most unteachable—
And never learnt a prayer, nor told a bead;   30
But knew the names of birds, and mocked their notes,
And whistled, as he were a bird himself!
And all the autumn 'twas his only play
To get the seeds of wild flowers, and to plant them
With earth and water, on the stumps of trees.   35
A Friar, who oft cull'd simples[4] in the wood,
A grey-haired man—he loved this little boy,
The boy loved him—and, when the Friar taught him,
He soon could write with the pen: and from that time,
Lived chiefly at the Convent or the Castle.   40
So he became a very learned youth.
But Oh! poor wretch!—he read, and read, and read,
Till his brain turned—and ere his twentieth year,
He had unlawful thoughts of many things:
And though he prayed, he never loved to pray   45
With holy men, nor in a holy place;—
But yet his speech, it was so soft and sweet,
The late Lord Velez ne'er was wearied with him:
And once, as by the north side of the chapel
They stood together, chained in deep discourse,   50
The earth heav'd under them with such a groan,
That the wall tottered, and had well-nigh fallen
Right on their heads. My Lord was sorely frightened;
A fever seized him, and he made confession
Of all the heretical and lawless talk   55
Which brought this judgment: so the youth was seized
And cast into that hole. My husband's father

---

2. Entrance to a dungeon.   3. Strong, virile.   4. Medicinal herbs.

Sobbed like a child—it almost broke his heart:
And once, as he was working in the cellar,
He heard a voice distinctly; 'twas the youth's,   60
Who sung a doleful song about green fields,
How sweet it were on lake or wild savannah,
To hunt for food, and be a naked man,
And wander up and down at liberty.
He always doted on the youth, and now   65
His love grew desperate; and defying death,
He made that cunning entrance I describ'd:
And the young man escaped.
    Maria.   'Tis a sweet tale:
Such as would lull a listening child to sleep,
His rosy face besoil'd with unwiped tears.—   70
And what became of him?
    Foster-Mother.   He went on shipboard
With those bold voyagers, who made discovery
Of golden lands.[5] Leoni's younger brother
Went likewise, and when he return'd to Spain,
He told Leoni, that the poor mad youth,   75
Soon after they arriv'd in that new world,
In spite of his dissuasion, seized a boat,
And all alone, set sail by silent moonlight
Up a great river, great as any sea,
And ne'er was heard of more: but 'tis supposed,   80
He lived and died among the savage men.

—1797

Dejection: An Ode[1]

Late, late yestreen I saw the new Moon,
    With the old Moon in her arms;
And I fear, I fear, my Master dear!
    We shall have a deadly storm.
        BALLAD OF SIR PATRICK SPENCE[2]

I

Well! If the Bard was weather-wise, who made
  The grand old ballad of Sir Patrick Spence,
  This night, so tranquil now, will not go hence
Unroused by winds, that ply a busier trade
Than those which mould yon cloud in lazy flakes,   5
Or the dull sobbing draft, that moans and rakes

5. South America.

1. Published October 4, 1802, Wordsworth's wedding day and Coleridge's seventh wedding anniversary.   2. From *Reliques of English Poetry* (1756), edited by Thomas Percy (1724–1811), a collection of traditional ballads.

Upon the strings of this Eolian lute,
    Which better far were mute.
  For lo! the New-moon winter-bright!
  And overspread with phantom light,   10
  (With swimming phantom light o'erspread
  But rimmed and circled by a silver thread)
I see the old Moon in her lap, foretelling
  The coming on of rain and squally blast.
And oh! that even now the gust were swelling,   15
  And the slant night-shower driving loud and fast!
Those sounds which oft have raised me, whilst they awed,
    And sent my soul abroad,
Might now, perhaps, their wonted impulse give,
Might startle this dull pain, and make it move and live!   20

II

A grief without a pang, void, dark, and drear,
  A stifled, drowsy, unimpassioned grief,
  Which finds no natural outlet, no relief,
    In word, or sigh, or tear—
O Lady! in this wan and heartless mood,   25
To other thoughts by yonder throstle[3] woo'd,
  All this long eve, so balmy and serene,
Have I been gazing on the western sky,
  And its peculiar tint of yellow green:
And still I gaze—and with how blank an eye!   30
And those thin clouds above, in flakes and bars,
That give away their motion to the stars;
Those stars, that glide behind them or between,
Now sparkling, now bedimmed, but always seen:
Yon crescent Moon, as fixed as if it grew   35
In its own cloudless, starless lake of blue;
I see them all so excellently fair,
I see, not feel how beautiful they are!

III

  My genial[4] spirits fail;
  And what can these avail   40
To lift the smothering weight from off my breast?
    It were a vain endeavor,
    Though I should gaze forever
On that green light that lingers in the west:
I may not hope from outward forms to win   45
The passion and the life, whose fountains are within.

---

3. Thrush.　4. Creative.

IV

O Lady! we receive but what we give,
And in our life alone does Nature live:
Ours is her wedding-garment, ours her shroud!
    And would we aught behold, of higher worth,   50
Than that inanimate[5] cold world allowed
To the poor loveless ever-anxious crowd,
    Ah! from the soul itself must issue forth,
A light, a glory, a fair luminous cloud
    Enveloping the Earth—   55
And from the soul itself must there be sent
    A sweet and potent voice, of its own birth,
Of all sweet sounds the life and element!

V

O pure of heart; thou need'st not ask of me
What this strong music in the soul may be!   60
What, and wherein it doth exist,
This light, this glory, this fair luminous mist,
This beautiful and beauty-making power.
    Joy, virtuous Lady! Joy that ne'er was given,
Save to the pure, and in their purest hour,   65
Life, and Life's effluence, cloud at once and shower
Joy, Lady! is the spirit and the power
Which wedding Nature to us gives in dower,[6]
    A new Earth and new Heaven,
Undreamt of by the sensual and the proud—   70
Joy is the sweet voice, Joy the luminous cloud—
    We in ourselves rejoice!
And thence flows all that charms or ear or sight,
    All melodies the echoes of that voice,
All colors a suffusion from that light.   75

VI

There was a time when, though my path was rough,
    This joy within me dallied with distress,
And all misfortunes were but as the stuff
    Whence Fancy made me dreams of happiness:
For hope grew round me, like the twining vine,
And fruits, and foliage, not my own, seemed mine.   80
But now afflictions bow me down to earth:
Nor care I that they rob me of my mirth,
    But oh! each visitation

---

5. Soulless.   6. As a wedding gift.

Suspends what nature gave me at my birth,   85
  My shaping spirit of Imagination.
For not to think of what I needs must feel,
  But to be still and patient, all I can;
And haply by abstruse research to steal
  From my own nature all the natural man—   90
  This was my sole resource, my only plan:
Till that which suits a part infects the whole,
And now is almost grown the habit of my soul.

VII

Hence, viper thoughts, that coil around my mind,
  Reality's dark dream!   95
I turn from you, and listen to the wind,
  Which long has raved unnoticed. What a scream
Of agony by torture lengthened out
That lute sent forth! Thou Wind, that ravest without,
Bare craig, or mountain-tairn,[7] or blasted tree,   100
Or pine-grove whither woodman never clomb,
Or lonely house, long held the witches' home,
  Methinks were fitter instruments for thee,
Mad Lutanist! who in this month of showers,
Of dark-brown gardens, and of peeping flowers,   105
Mak'st Devils' yule,[8] with worse than wintry song,
The blossoms, buds, and timorous leaves among.
  Thou Actor, perfect in all tragic sounds!
Thou mighty Poet, e'en to frenzy bold!
  What tell'st thou now about?   110
  'Tis of the rushing of a host[9] in rout,
  With groans of trampled men, with smarting wounds—
At once they groan with pain, and shudder with the cold!
But hush! there is a pause of deepest silence!
  And all that noise, as of a rushing crowd,   115
With groans and tremulous shudderings—all is over—
  It tells another tale, with sounds less deep and loud!
    A tale of less affright,
    And tempered with delight,
As Otway's[10] self had framed the tender lay   120
    'Tis of a little child,
    Upon a lonesome wild,
Not far from home, but she hath lost her way:
And now moans low in bitter grief and fear,
And now screams loud, and hopes to make her mother hear.   125

---

7. Small lake.   8. Christmas.   9. Army.   10. Thomas Otway (1652–1685), English playwright famous for tragedies full of pathos.

VIII

'Tis midnight, but small thoughts have I of sleep;
Full seldom may my friend such vigils keep!
Visit her, gentle Sleep! with wings of healing,
   And may this storm be but a mountain-birth,[11]
May all the stars hang bright above her dwelling,   130
   Silent as though they watched the sleeping Earth!
     With light heart may she rise,
     Gay fancy, cheerful eyes,
   Joy lift her spirit, joy attune her voice;
To her may all things live, from pole to pole,   135
Their life the eddying of her living soul!
   O simple spirit, guided from above,
Dear Lady! friend devoutest of my choice,
Thus mayest thou ever, evermore rejoice.

—1802

from Biographia Literaria
or, Biographical Sketches of My Literary Life and Opinions

from Chapter 4

[On Meeting Wordsworth]

I was in my twenty-fourth year, when I had the happiness of knowing Mr.
Wordsworth personally, and while memory lasts, I shall hardly forget the sudden
effect produced on my mind, by his recitation of a manuscript poem.[1] . . . There was
here, no mark of strained thought, or forced diction, no crowd or turbulence of
imagery, and, as the poet hath himself well described in his lines "on revisiting the
Wye," manly reflection, and human associations had given both variety, and an additional interest to natural objects, which in the passion and appetite of the first love
they had seemed to him neither to need or permit. The occasional obscurities, which
had risen from an imperfect controul over the resources of his native language, had
almost wholly disappeared, together with that worse defect of arbitrary and illogical
phrases, at once hackneyed, and fantastic, which hold so distinguished a place in the
technique of ordinary poetry, and will, more or less, alloy the earlier poems of the truest
genius, unless the attention has been specifically directed to their worthlessness and
incongruity. . . . It was not however the freedom from false taste, whether as to common defects, or to those more properly his own, which made so unusual an impression on my feelings immediately, and subsequently on my judgement. It was the
union of deep feeling with profound thought; the fine balance of truth in observing
with the imaginative faculty in modifying the objects observed; and above all the
original gift of spreading the tone, the *atmosphere*, and with it the depth and height
of the ideal world around forms, incidents, and situations, of which, for the common

---

11. Brief.
1. "Guilt and Sorrow."

view, custom had bedimmed all the lustre, had dried up the sparkle and the dew drops. To find no contradiction in the union of old and new; to contemplate the ANCIENT of days and all his works with feelings as fresh, as if all had then sprang forth at the first creative fiat[2]; characterizes the mind that feels the riddle of the world, and may help to unravel it. To carry on the feelings of childhood into the powers of manhood; to combine the child's sense of wonder and novelty with the appearances, which every day for perhaps forty years had rendered familiar;

> With sun and moon and stars throughout the year,
> And man and woman[3];

this is the character and privilege of genius, and one of the marks which distinguish genius from talents. And therefore is it the prime merit of genius and its most unequivocal mode of manifestation, so to represent familiar objects as to awaken in the minds of others a kindred feeling concerning them and that freshness of sensation which is the constant accompaniment of mental, no less than of bodily, convalescence. Who has not a thousand times seen snow fall on water? Who has not watched it with a new feeling, from the time that he has read Burns' comparison of sensual pleasure

> To snow that falls upon a river
> A moment white—then gone for ever![4]

from Chapter 11
[Literature as a Trade]

With no other privilege than that of sympathy and sincere good wishes, I would address an affectionate exhortation to the youthful literati, grounded on my own experience. It will be but short; for the beginning, middle, and end converge to one charge: NEVER PURSUE LITERATURE AS A TRADE. With the exception of one extraordinary man, I have never known an individual, least of all an individual of genius, healthy or happy without a *profession*, i.e., some regular employment, which does not depend on the will of the moment, and which can be carried on so far *mechanically* that an average quantum only of health, spirits, and intellectual exertion are requisite to its faithful discharge. Three hours of leisure, unannoyed by any alien anxiety, and looked forward to with delight as a change and recreation, will suffice to realize in literature a larger product of what is truly *genial*, than weeks of compulsion. Money, and immediate reputation form only an arbitrary and accidental end of literary labor. The *hope* of increasing them by any given exertion will often prove a stimulant to industry; but the *necessity* of acquiring them will in all works of genius convert the stimulant into a *narcotic*. Motives by excess reverse their very nature, and instead of exciting, stun and stupify the mind. For it is one contradistinction of genius from talent, that its predominant end is always comprized in the means; and this is one of the many points, which establish an analogy between genius and virtue. Now though talents may exist without genius, yet as genius cannot exist, certainly not manifest itself,

---

2. Divine command.   3. Adapted from John Milton (1608–1674), "To Mr. Cyriack Skinner Upon His Blindness" (1673).
4. Robert Burns (1759–1796), "Tam O'Shanter" (1791).

without talents, I would advise every scholar, who feels the genial power working within him, so far to make a division between the two, as that he should devote his *talents* to the acquirement of competence in some known trade or profession, and his genius to objects of his tranquil and unbiassed choice; while the consciousness of being actuated in both alike by the sincere desire to perform his duty, will alike ennoble both. My dear young friend (I would say) suppose yourself established in any honourable occupation. From the manufactory or counting-house, from the law-court, or from having visited your last patient, you return at evening,

> Dear tranquil time, when the sweet sense of home
> Is sweetest————[5]

to your family, prepared for its social enjoyments, with the very countenances of your wife and children brightened, and their voice of welcome made doubly welcome, by the knowledge that, as far as they are concerned, you have satisfied the demands of the day by the labor of the day. Then, when you retire into your study, in the books on your shelves you revisit so many venerable friends with whom you can converse. Your own spirit scarcely less free from personal anxieties than the great minds, that in those books are still living for you! Even your writing desk with its blank paper and all its other implements will appear as a chain of flowers, capable of linking your feelings as well as thoughts to events and characters past or to come; not a chain of iron which binds you down to think of the future and the remote by recalling the claims and feelings of the peremptory present. But why should I say *retire*? The habits of active life and daily intercourse with the stir of the world will tend to give you such self-command, that the presence of your family will be no interruption. Nay, the social silence, or undisturbing voices of a wife or sister will be like a restorative atmosphere, or soft music which moulds a dream without becoming its object. . . .

It would be a sort of irreligion, and scarcely less than a libel on human nature to believe, that there is any established and reputable profession or employment, in which a man may not continue to act with honesty and honor; and doubtless there is likewise none, which may not at times present temptations to the contrary. But woefully will that man find himself mistaken, who imagines that the profession of literature, or (to speak more plainly) the *trade* of authorship, besets its members with fewer or with less insidious temptations, than the church, the law, or the different branches of commerce. But I have treated sufficiently on this unpleasant subject in an early chapter of this volume. I will conclude the present therefore with a short extract from HERDER,[6] whose name I might have added to the illustrious list of those, who have combined the successful pursuit of the muses, not only with the faithful discharge, but with the highest honors and honorable emoluments, of an established profession: "With the greatest possible solicitude avoid authorship. Too early or immoderately employed, it makes the head *waste* and the heart empty; even were there no other worse consequences. A person, who reads only to print, in all probability reads amiss; and he, who sends away through the pen and the press every thought, the moment it occurs to him, will in a short time have sent all away, and will become a mere journeyman of the printing-office, a *compositor*."

---

5. Coleridge, "William Wordsworth" (1817), lines 92–93.   6. Johann Gottfried von Herder (1744–1803), German philosopher, author of *Letters on the Study of Theology*, the source of the following extract.

To which I may add from myself, that what medical physiologists affirm of certain secretions, applies equally to our thoughts; they too must be taken up again into the circulation, and be again and again re-secreted in order to ensure a healthful vigor, both to the mind and to its intellectual offspring.

from Chapter 13
[Imagination and Fancy]

Thus far had the work been transcribed for the press, when I received the following letter from a friend,[7] whose practical judgement I have had ample reason to estimate and revere, and whose taste and sensibility preclude all the excuses which my self-love might possibly have prompted me to set up in plea against the decision of advisers of equal good sense, but with less tact and feeling.

Dear C.

You ask my opinion concerning your Chapter on the Imagination, both as to the impressions it made on myself, and as to those which I think it will make on the PUBLIC, *i.e., that part of the public, who from the title of the work and from its forming a sort of introduction to a volume of poems, are likely to constitute the great majority of your readers.*

As to myself, and stating in the first place the effect on my understanding, your opinions and method of argument were not only so new to me, but so directly the reverse of all I had ever been accustomed to consider as truth, that even if I had comprehended your premises sufficiently to have admitted them, and had seen the necessity of your conclusions, I should still have been in that state of mind, . . . you have so ingeniously evolved, as the antithesis to that in which a man is, when he makes a bull. In your own words, I should have felt as if I had been standing on my head.

The effect on my feelings, on the other hand, I cannot better represent, than by supposing myself to have known only our light airy modern chapels of ease, and then for the first time to have been placed, and left alone, in one of our largest Gothic cathedrals in a gusty moonlight night of autumn. "Now in glimmer, and now in gloom;"[8] often in palpable darkness not without a chilly sensation of terror; then suddenly emerging into broad yet visionary lights with coloured shadows, of fantastic shapes yet all decked with holy insignia and mystic symbols; and ever and anon coming out full upon pictures and stone-work images of great men, with whose names I was familiar, but which looked upon me with countenances and an expression, the most dissimilar to all I had been in the habit of connecting with those names. Those whom I had been taught to venerate as almost super-human in magnitude of intellect, I found perched in little fret-work niches, as grotesque dwarfs; while the grotesques, in my hitherto belief, stood guarding the high altar with all the characters of Apotheosis.[9] In short, what I had supposed substances were thinned away into shadows, while every where shadows were deepened into substances:

> If substance may be call'd what shadow seem'd,
> For each seem'd either!   *Milton*[10]

---

7. Coleridge himself.   8. From Coleridge's "Christabel" (1816).   9. Divinity.   10. John Milton (1608–1674), *Paradise Lost*, 2.669–670.

Yet after all, I could not but repeat the lines which you had quoted from a MS. poem of your own in the FRIEND, *and applied to a work of Mr. Wordsworth's though with a few of the words altered:*

————————An orphic tale indeed,
A tale obscure of high and passionate thoughts
to a strange music chaunted![11]

Be assured, however, that I look forward anxiously to your great book on the CON-STRUCTIVE PHILOSOPHY, *which you have promised and announced: and that I will do my best to understand it. Only I will not promise to descend into the dark cave of Trophonius[12] with you, there to rub my own eyes, in order to make the sparks and figured flashes, which I am required to see.*

So much for myself. But as for the PUBLIC, *I do not hesitate a moment in advising and urging you to withdraw the Chapter from the present work, and to reserve it for your announced treatises on the Logos or communicative intellect in Man and Diety. First, because imperfectly as I understand the present Chapter, I see clearly that you have done too much, and yet not enough. You have been obliged to omit so many links, from the necessity of compression, that what remains, looks (if I may recur to my former illustration) like the fragments of the winding steps of an old ruined tower. Secondly, a still stronger argument (at least one that I am sure will be more forcible with you) is, that your readers will have both right and reason to complain of you. This Chapter, which cannot, when it is printed, amount to so little as an hundred pages, will of necessity greatly increase the expense of the work; and every reader who, like myself, is neither prepared or perhaps calculated for the study of so abstruse a subject so abstrusely treated, will, as I have before hinted, be almost entitled to accuse you of a sort of imposition on him. For who, he might truly observe, could from your title-page, viz. "My Literary Life and Opinions," published too as introductory to a volume of miscellaneous poems, have anticipated, or even conjectured, a long treatise on ideal Realism, which holds the same relation in abstruseness to Plotinus, as Plotinus does to Plato. It will be well, if already you have not too much of metaphysical disquisition in your work, though as the larger part of the disquisition is historical, it will doubtless be both interesting and instructive to many to whose* unprepared *minds your speculations on the esemplastic[13] power would be utterly unintelligible. . . .*

I could also add to these arguments one derived from pecuniary motives, and particularly from the probable effects on the sale of your present publication; but they would weigh little with you compared with the preceding. Besides, I have long observed, that arguments drawn from your own personal interests more often act on you as narcotics than as stimulants, and that in money concerns you have some small portion of pig nature in your moral idiosyncracy, and like these amiable creatures, must occasionally be pulled backward from the boat in order to make you enter it. All success attend you, for if hard thinking and hard reading are merits, you have deserved it.

Your affectionate, & c.

In consequence of this very judicious letter, which produced complete conviction on my mind, I shall content myself for the present with stating the main result of the

---

11. Coleridge, "William Wordsworth" (1817), lines 45–47.   12. Architect of the temple of Apollo at Delphi.   13. Coleridge's neologism for "molding into unity."

Chapter, which I have reserved for that future publication, a detailed prospectus of which the reader will find at the close of the second volume.

The IMAGINATION then I consider either as primary, or secondary. The primary IMAGINATION I hold to be the living Power and prime Agent of all human Perception, and as a repetition in the finite mind of the eternal act of creation in the infinite I AM. The secondary I consider as an echo of the former, co-existing with the conscious will, yet still as identical with the primary in the *kind* of its agency, and differing only in *degree*, and in the *mode* of its operation. It dissolves, diffuses, dissipates, in order to re-create; or where this process is rendered impossible, yet still at all events it struggles to idealize and to unify. It is essentially *vital*, even as all objects (*as* objects) are essentially fixed and dead.

FANCY, on the contrary, has no other counters to play with, but fixities and definites. The Fancy is indeed no other than a mode of Memory emancipated from the order of time and space; and blended with, and modified by that empirical phenomenon of the will, which we express by the word CHOICE. But equally with the ordinary memory it must receive all its materials ready made from the law of association.

Whatever more than this, I shall think it fit to declare concerning the powers and privileges of the imagination in the present work, will be found in the critical essay on the uses of the Supernatural in poetry and the principles that regulate its introduction: which the reader will find prefixed to the poem of *The Ancient Mariner.*[14]

from Chapter 14
[Controversy over *Lyrical Ballads*]

During the first year that Mr. Wordsworth and I were neighbours, our conversations turned frequently on the two cardinal points of poetry, the power of exciting the sympathy of the reader by a faithful adherence to the truth of nature, and the power of giving the interest of novelty by the modifying colours of imagination. The sudden charm, which accidents of light and shade, which moon-light or sun-set diffused over a known and familiar landscape, appeared to represent the practicability of combining both. These are the poetry of nature. The thought suggested itself (to which of us I do not recollect) that a series of poems might be composed of two sorts. In the one, the incidents and agents were to be, in part at least, supernatural; and the excellence aimed at was to consist in the interesting of the affections by the dramatic truth of such emotions, as would naturally accompany such situations, supposing them real. And real in *this* sense they have been to every human being who, from whatever source of delusion, has at any time believed himself under supernatural agency. For the second class, subjects were to be chosen from ordinary life; the characters and incidents were to be such, as will be found in every village and its vicinity, where there is a meditative and feeling mind to seek after them, or to notice them, when they present themselves.

In this idea originated the plan of the *Lyrical Ballads*; in which it was agreed, that my endeavours should be directed to persons and characters supernatural, or at least romantic; yet so as to transfer from our inward nature a human interest and a sem-

---

14. This essay was never written.

blance of truth sufficient to procure for these shadows of imagination that willing suspension of disbelief for the moment, which constitutes poetic faith. Mr. Wordsworth,
on the other hand, was to propose to himself as his object, to give the charm of novelty to things of every day, and to excite a feeling analogous to the supernatural, by
awakening the mind's attention from the lethargy of custom, and directing it to the
loveliness and the wonders of the world before us; an inexhaustible treasure, but for
which in consequence of the film of familiarity and selfish solicitude we have eyes,
yet see not, ears that hear not, and hearts that neither feel nor understand.

With this view I wrote the "Ancient Mariner," and was preparing among other
poems, the "Dark Ladie," and the "Christabel," in which I should have more nearly
realized my ideal, than I had done in my first attempt. But Mr. Wordsworth's industry had proved so much more successful, and the number of his poems so much
greater, that my compositions, instead of forming a balance, appeared rather an inter-
polation of heterogeneous matter. Mr. Wordsworth added two or three poems written
in his own character, in the impassioned, lofty, and sustained diction, which is characteristic of his genius. In this form the *Lyrical Ballads* were published; and were presented by him, as an *experiment*, whether subjects, which from their nature rejected
the usual ornaments and extra-colloquial style of poems in general, might not be so
managed in the language of ordinary life as to produce the pleasurable interest, which
it is the peculiar business of poetry to impart. To the second edition he added a preface of considerable length; in which notwithstanding some passages of apparently a
contrary import, he was understood to contend for the extension of this style to
poetry of all kinds, and to reject as vicious and indefensible all phrases and forms of
style that were not included in what he (unfortunately, I think, adopting an equivocal expression) called the language of *real life*.[15] From this preface, prefixed to poems
in which it was impossible to deny the presence of original genius, however mistaken
its direction might be deemed, arose the whole long continued controversy. For from
the conjunction of perceived power with supposed heresy I explain the inveteracy
and in some instances, I grieve to say, the acrimonious passions, with which the controversy has been conducted by the assailants.

Had Mr. Wordsworth's poems been the silly, the childish things, which they were
for a long time described as being; had they been really distinguished from the compositions of other poets merely by meanness of language and inanity of thought; had
they indeed contained nothing more than what is found in the parodies and pretended imitations of them; they must have sunk at once, a dead weight, into the
slough of oblivion, and have dragged the preface along with them. But year after year
increased the number of Mr. Wordsworth's admirers. They were found too not in the
lower classes of the reading public, but chiefly among young men of strong sensibility and meditative minds; and their admiration (inflamed perhaps in some degree by
opposition) was distinguished by its intensity, I might almost say, by its *religious* fervour. These facts, and the intellectual energy of the author, which was more or less
consciously felt, where it was outwardly and even boisterously denied, meeting with
sentiments of aversion to his opinions, and of alarm at their consequences, produced
an eddy of criticism, which would of itself have borne up the poems by the violence,

---

15. See p. 404.

with which it whirled them round and round. With many parts of this preface in the sense attributed to them and which the words undoubtedly seem to authorise, I never concurred; but on the contrary objected to them as erroneous in principle, and as contradictory (in appearance at least) both to other parts of the same preface, and to the author's own practice in the greater number of the poems themselves. Mr. Wordsworth in his recent collection has, I find, degraded this prefatory disquisition to the end of his second volume, to be read or not at the reader's choice. But he has not, as far as I can discover, announced any change in his poetic creed. [At] all events, considering it as the source of a controversy, in which I have been honored more, than I deserve, by the frequent conjunction of my name with his, I think it expedient to declare once for all, in what points I coincide with his opinions, and in what points I altogether differ. But in order to render myself intelligible I must previously, in as few words as possible, explain my ideas, first, of a POEM; and secondly, of POETRY itself, in *kind*, and in *essence*.

[What Is Poetry? What Is a Poet?]

A poem is that species of composition, which is opposed to works of science, by proposing for its *immediate* object pleasure, not truth; and from all other species (having *this* object in common with it) it is discriminated by proposing to itself such delight from the *whole*, as is compatible with a distinct gratification from each component *part*. . . .

But if this should be admitted as a satisfactory character of a poem, we have still to seek for a definition of poetry. The writings of PLATO, and Bishop TAYLOR,[16] and the *Theoria Sacra* of BURNET,[17] furnish undeniable proofs that poetry of the highest kind may exist without metre, and even without the contra-distinguishing objects of a poem. The first chapter of Isaiah (indeed a very large proportion of the whole book) is poetry in the most emphatic sense; yet it would be not less irrational than strange to assert, that pleasure, and not truth, was the immediate object of the prophet. In short, whatever *specific* import we attach to the word, poetry, there will be found involved in it, as a necessary consequence, that a poem of any length neither can be, or ought to be, all poetry. . . .

What is poetry? is so nearly the same question with, what is a poet? that the answer to the one is involved in the solution of the other. For it is a distinction resulting from the poetic genius itself, which sustains and modifies the images, thoughts, and emotions of the poet's own mind. The poet, described in ideal perfection, brings the whole soul of man into activity, with the subordination of its faculties to each other, according to their relative worth and dignity. He diffuses a tone, and spirit of unity, that blends, and (as it were) *fuses*, each into each, by that synthetic and magical power, to which we have exclusively appropriated the name of imagination. This power, first put in action by the will and understanding, and retained under their irremissive, though gentle and unnoticed, controul (*laxis effertur habenis* [led by slack reins]) reveals itself in the balance or reconciliation of opposite or discordant qualities: of sameness, with difference; of the general, with the concrete; the idea, with the image; the individual, with the representative; the sense of novelty and freshness,

---

16. Jeremy Taylor (1613–1667), English theologian.   17. Thomas Burnet (c. 1635–1715), English cleric and scientist.

with old and familiar objects; a more than usual state of emotion, with more than usual order; judgement ever awake and steady self-possession, with enthusiasm and feeling profound or vehement; and while it blends and harmonizes the natural and the artificial, still subordinates art to nature; the manner to the matter; and our admiration of the poet to our sympathy with the poetry. . . .

Finally, GOOD SENSE is the BODY of poetic genius, FANCY its DRAPERY, MOTION its LIFE, and IMAGINATION the SOUL that is every where, and in each; and forms all into one graceful and intelligent whole.

from Chapter 17

[Content and Language of Wordsworth's Poetry]

As far then as Mr. Wordsworth in his preface contended, and most ably contended, for a reformation in our poetic diction, as far as he has evinced the truth of passion, and the *dramatic* propriety of those figures and metaphors in the original poets, which stript of their justifying reasons, and converted into mere artifices of connection or ornament, constitute the characteristic falsity in the poetic style of the moderns; and as far as he has, with equal acuteness and clearness, pointed out the process in which this change was effected, and the resemblances between that state into which the reader's mind is thrown by the pleasureable confusion of thought from an unaccustomed train of words and images; and that state which is induced by the natural language of empassioned feeling; he undertook a useful task, and deserves all praise, both for the attempt and for the execution. . . .

My own differences from certain supposed parts of Mr. Wordsworth's theory ground themselves on the assumption, that his words had been rightly interpreted, as purporting that the proper diction for poetry in general consists altogether in a language taken, with due exceptions, from the mouths of men in real life, a language which actually constitutes the natural conversation of men under the influence of natural feelings. . . . The poet informs his reader, that he had generally chosen *low and rustic life*; but not *as* low and rustic, or in order to repeat that pleasure of doubtful moral effect, which persons of elevated rank and of superior refinement oftentimes derive from a happy *imitation* of the rude unpolished manners and discourse of their inferiors. . . . He chose low and rustic life, "because in that condition the essential passions of the heart find a better soil, in which they can attain their maturity, are less under restraint, and speak a plainer and more emphatic language; because in that condition of life our elementary feelings coexist in a state of greater simplicity, and consequently may be more accurately contemplated, and more forcibly communicated; because the manners of rural life germinate from those elementary feelings; and from the necessary character of rural occupations are more easily comprehended, and are more durable; and lastly, because in that condition the passions of men are incorporated with the beautiful and permanent forms of nature."[18]

Now it is clear to me, that in the most interesting of the poems, in which the author is more or less dramatic, as the "Brothers," "Michael," "Ruth," the "Mad Mother," &c. the persons introduced are by no means taken *from low* or *rustic life* in the common acceptation of those words; and it is not less clear, that the sentiments

---

18. See p. 405.

and language, as far as they can be conceived to have been really transferred from the minds and conversation of such persons, are attributable to causes and circumstances not necessarily connected with "their occupations and abode." The thoughts, feelings, language, and manners of the shepherd-farmers in the vales of Cumberland and Westmoreland, as far as they are actually adopted in those poems, may be accounted for from causes, which will and do produce the same results in *every* state of life, whether in town or country. As the two principal I rank that INDEPENDENCE, which raises a man above servitude, or daily toil for the profit of others, yet not above the necessity of industry and a frugal simplicity of domestic life; and the accompanying unambitious, but solid and religious EDUCATION, which has rendered few books familiar, but the bible, and the liturgy or hymn book. . . .

I am convinced, that for the human soul to prosper in rustic life, a certain vantage-ground is pre-requisite. It is not every man, that is likely to be improved by a country life or by country labours. Education, or original sensibility, or both, must pre-exist, if the changes, forms, and incidents of nature are to prove a sufficient stimulant. And where these are not sufficient, the mind contracts and hardens by want of stimulants; and the man becomes selfish, sensual, gross, and hard-hearted. . . .

I adopt with full faith the principle of Aristotle, that poetry as poetry is essentially *ideal*, that it avoids and excludes all *accident*; that its apparent individualities of rank, character, or occupation must be *representative* of a class; and that the *persons* of poetry must be clothed with *generic* attributes, with the *common* attributes of the class; not with such as one gifted individual might *possibly* possess, but such as from his situation it is most probable before-hand, that he *would* possess. If my premises are right, and my deductions legitimate, it follows that there can be no *poetic* medium between the swains of Theocritus[19] and those of an imaginary golden age.

The characters of the vicar and the shepherd-mariner in the poem of the BROTHERS, those of the shepherd of Green-head Gill in the "MICHAEL,"[20] have all the verisimilitude and representative quality, that the purposes of poetry can require. They are persons of a known and abiding class, and their manners and sentiments the natural product of circumstances common to the class. . . .

On the other hand, in the poems which are pitched at a lower note, as the "Harry Gill,"[21] "Idiot Boy," &c. the *feelings* are those of human nature in general; though the poet has judiciously laid the *scene* in the country, in order to place *himself* in the vicinity of interesting images, without the necessity of ascribing a sentimental perception of their beauty to the persons of his drama. . . .

In the "Thorn,"[22] the poet himself acknowledges in a note the necessity of an introductory poem, in which he should have pourtrayed the character of the person from whom the words of the poem are supposed to proceed: a superstitious man moderately imaginative, of slow faculties and deep feelings, "a captain of a small trading vessel, for example, who being past the middle age of life, had retired upon an annuity, or small independent income, to some village or country town of which he was not a native, or in which he had not been accustomed to live. Such men having nothing to do become credulous and talkative from indolence." But in a poem, still more in a lyric poem (and the NURSE in Shakespeare's Romeo and Juliet alone prevents me from extending the remark even to dramatic *poetry*, if indeed the Nurse

---

19. Greek poet of third century BC.   20. See p. 419.   21. See p. 386.   22. See p. 392.

itself can be deemed altogether a case in point) it is not possible to imitate truly a dull and garrulous discourser, without repeating the effects of dulness and garrulity. . . .

Still more must I hesitate in my assent to the sentence which immediately follows the former citation[:] . . . "The language too of these men is adopted (purified indeed from what appears to be its real defects, from all lasting and rational causes of dislike or disgust) because such men hourly communicate with the best objects from which the best part of language is originally derived; and because, from their rank in society, and the sameness and narrow circle of their intercourse, being less under the action of social vanity, they convey their feelings and notions in simple and unelaborated expressions." To this I reply; that a rustic's language, purified from all provincialism and grossness, and so far re-constructed as to be made consistent with the rules of grammar (which are in essence no other than the laws of universal logic, applied to Psychological materials) will not differ from the language of any other man of common-sense, however learned or refined he may be, except as far as the notions, which the rustic has to convey, are fewer and more indiscriminate. This will become still clearer, if we add the consideration (equally important though less obvious) that the rustic, from the more imperfect development of his faculties, and from the lower state of their cultivation, aims almost solely to convey *insulated facts*, either those of his scanty experience or his traditional belief; while the educated man chiefly seeks to discover and express those *connections* of things, or those relative *bearings* of fact to fact, from which some more or less general law is deducible. For *facts* are valuable to a wise man, chiefly as they lead to the discovery of the in-dwelling *law*, which is the true *being* of things, the sole solution of their modes of existence, and in the knowledge of which consists our dignity and our power.

As little can I agree with the assertion, that from the objects with which the rustic hourly communicates, the best part of language is formed. For first, if to communicate with an object implies such an acquaintance with it, as renders it capable of being discriminately reflected on; the distinct knowledge of an uneducated rustic would furnish a very scanty vocabulary. The few things, and modes of action, requisite for his bodily conveniences, would alone be individualized; while all the rest of nature would be expressed by a small number of confused, general terms. Secondly, I deny that the words and combinations of words derived from the objects, with which the rustic is familiar, whether with distinct or confused knowledge, can be justly said to form the best part of language. It is more than probable, that many classes of the brute creation possess discriminating sounds, by which they can convey to each other notices of such objects as concern their food, shelter, or safety. Yet we hesitate to call the aggregate of such sounds a language, otherwise than metaphorically. The best part of human language, properly so called, is derived from reflection on the acts of the mind itself. It is formed by a voluntary appropriation of fixed symbols to internal acts, to processes and results of imagination, the greater part of which have no place in the consciousness of uneducated man; though in civilized society, by imitation and passive remembrance of what they hear from their religious instructors and other superiors, the most uneducated share in the harvest which they neither sowed or reaped. . . .

The positions, which I controvert, are contained in the sentences—"*a selection of the* REAL *language of men;*"—"*the language of these men* (i.e., men in low and rustic life) *I propose to myself to imitate, and as far as possible, to adopt the very language of men.*" "*Between the language of prose and that of metrical composition, there neither is, nor can be any essential difference.*" It is against these exclusively, that my opposition is directed.

I object, in the very first instance, to an equivocation in the use of the word "real." Every man's language varies, according to the extent of his knowledge, the activity of his faculties, and the depth or quickness of his feelings. Every man's language has, first, its *individualities*; secondly, the common properties of the *class* to which he belongs; and thirdly, words and phrases of *universal* use. The language of Hooker, Bacon, Bishop Taylor, and Burke, differ from the common language of the learned class only by the superior number and novelty of the thoughts and relations which they had to convey. The language of Algernon Sidney differs not at all from that, which every well educated gentleman would wish to write, and (with due allowances for the undeliberateness, and less connected train, of thinking natural and proper to conversation) such as he would wish to talk. Neither one or the other differ half as much from the general language of cultivated society, as the language of Mr. Wordsworth's homeliest composition differs from that of a common peasant. For "real" therefore, we must substitute *ordinary*, or *lingua communis* [common language]. And this, we have proved, is no more to be found in the phraseology of low and rustic life, than in that of any other class. Omit the peculiarities of each, and the result of course must be common to all. . . .

Neither is the case rendered at all more tenable by the addition of the words, "*in a state of excitement.*" For the nature of a man's words, when he is strongly affected by joy, grief, or anger, must necessarily depend on the number and quality of the general truths, conceptions and images, and of the words expressing them, with which his mind had been previously stored. For the property of passion is not to *create*; but to set in increased activity. At least, whatever new connections of thoughts or images, or (which is equally, if not more than equally, the appropriate effect of strong excitement) whatever generalizations of truth or experience, the heat of passion may produce; yet the terms of their conveyance must have pre-existed in his former conversations, and are only collected and crowded together by the unusual stimulation. It is indeed very possible to adopt in a poem the unmeaning repetitions, habitual phrases, and other blank counters, which an unfurnished or confused understanding interposes at short intervals, in order to keep hold of his subject which is still slipping from him, and to give him time for recollection; or in mere aid of vacancy, as in the scanty companies of a country stage the same player pops backwards and forwards, in order to prevent the appearance of empty spaces, in the procession of Macbeth, or Henry VIIIth. But what assistance to the poet, or ornament to the poem, these can supply, I am at a loss to conjecture. Nothing assuredly can differ either in origin or in mode more widely from the *apparent* tautologies of intense and turbulent feeling, in which the passion is greater and of longer endurance, than to be exhausted or satisfied by a single representation of the image or incident exciting it. Such repetitions I admit to be a beauty of the highest kind; as illustrated by Mr. Wordsworth himself from the song of Deborah [Judges 5.27]. "*At her feet he bowed, he fell, he lay down; at her feet he bowed, he fell; where he bowed, there he fell down dead.*"[23]

—1817

23. See p. 400.

⸻∞∞∞⸻

CONTEMPORARY RESPONSE

Frederic Henry Hedge

1805–1890

Like many of his fellow Transcendentalists, Frederic Henry Hedge received his schooling at Harvard, where his father, Levi Hedge, was professor of logic. Like Ralph Waldo Emerson, he attended the College for his undergraduate degree and then read theology at the Divinity School. Following in his father's footsteps, Hedge eventually became a professor at his alma mater, returning to the Divinity School from 1852 to 1872 as professor of ecclesiastical history and serving as professor of German literature in the College from 1872 on. His interest in German metaphysics (made famous by philosophers like Immanuel Kant, Friedrich Schelling, and Johann Gottlieb Fichte) quickened his interest in Samuel Taylor Coleridge, whom he considered a joint laborer in the task of introducing German Idealism to the English-speaking world. It is no coincidence that both men had traveled to Germany to study its philosophy and literature. Coleridge went with William and Dorothy Wordsworth in 1798, just after the *Lyrical Ballads* was published; Hedge, at his father's behest, traveled there twenty years later with George Bancroft, who was soon to establish himself as one of America's most famous historians.

After Coleridge introduced German Transcendentalism to Britain and America, his writings were buttressed in New England by the likes of Hedge, Emerson, Rhoda Newcomb, Margaret Fuller, and James Marsh. As a result, philosophy, literature, and theology in these places underwent a transformation as controversial as it was inexorable. British and American Romanticism and Transcendentalism were the results, in part, of this influence. Indeed, Emerson referred to the community of Transcendentalists that met at his house in Concord as the "Hedge Club." When asked about the role he played in the Transcendental movement, Hedge brought up his article on Coleridge, noting that it "was the *first word* . . . which any American had uttered in respectful recognition of the claims of Transcendentalism." For Emerson, the article confirmed that the word made flesh (in Greek, the *Logos*, as John's Gospel describes Jesus) was alive and kicking, for he referred to the essay as "a living, leaping Logos."

from Coleridge

Nature, it would seem, had endowed Mr. Coleridge with a singularly fertile and creative mind,—a mind which, if left to itself with no other training than opportunity might supply, would have enriched the world with manifold and pleasing productions. The marks of this creative tendency are still visible in some of his poetical productions; we would mention in particular the "Ancient Mariner," and the tragedies.

But at an early period of his education, our author's mind acquired a bias which proved injurious to its productive faculty, and which, by changing the tendency of his intellect from the creative to the reflective, in process of time seduced him from the open highway of literary fame, into more devious and darksome paths. We refer to the discipline which he received at the grammar school at Christ's-Hospital,[1] as described in his life.[2] Such a discipline, though admirably adapted to invigorate the understanding, and to strengthen the judgment, was ill-suited to unfold a poet's talent, or to nourish creative genius of any kind. It was precisely the training to make a critic; and although we are unwilling to ascribe any irresistible influence to education alone, we cannot help believing that the strong tendency to criticism which has ever marked Mr.

---

1. The London school Coleridge attended after his father's death.   2. [Hedge's note] See *Biographia Literaria*, Chapter 1.

Coleridge's literary pursuits, is in part the effect of early discipline. We do not mean that Mr. Coleridge has at any period of his life been a writer of critiques, as that business is generally understood, but that he has ever inclined to comment upon the sayings and doings of others, rather than to say and do himself. This propensity, however, has not been exercised on literary subjects alone; it has found a wider scope and a freer field in deep and comprehensive speculations on topics of national and universal interest, particularly those which agitated Europe at the commencement of the present century. It has been employed on knotty questions in politics, philosophy, and religion, it has canvassed the rights and duties of civil government, criticized the movements of nations, and passed judgment on the tendencies and characteristics of the age. The results of these speculations were first given to the world in "The Morning Post," and afterwards in "The Friend,"[3] a collection of original essays, which for depth of thought, clearness of judgment, sound reasoning, and forcible expression, have few rivals in the English language. For the American edition of this work, as also for the republication of the "Aids to Reflection," and "The Statesman's Manual,"[4] we take this opportunity of expressing our obligations to President Marsh.[5] Next to the writer of a good book, he most deserves our gratitude, who in any way helps to increase its circulation. This praise is due, in an eminent degree, to Mr. Marsh; nor does this comprise the whole of his claims to our regard and good wishes; in the valuable dissertation which accompanies the "Aids to Reflection," he has done much to illustrate Mr. Coleridge's philosophical opinions, and has evinced a philosophical talent of his own, which we cannot but hope will some day be employed in more extensive undertakings. . . .

In a review of Mr. Coleridge's literary life, we must not omit to notice that marked fondness for metaphysics, and particularly for German metaphysics, which has exercised so decisive an influence over all his writings. Had it been given to him to interpret German metaphysics to his countrymen, as Mr. Cousin[6] has interpreted them to the French nation, or had it been possible for him to have constructed a system of his own, we should not have regretted his indulgence of a passion which we must now condemn as a source of morbid dissatisfaction with received opinions, unjustified by any serious attempt to introduce others and better. From his vigorous understanding, his acute dialectic powers, his complete knowledge of the subject, his historical research, and power of expression, something more might have been expected than the meagre sketch contained in his autobiography. That Mr. Coleridge has done so little in the way of original production in this department, we ascribe to the same mental defect which has already been remarked upon, namely, the preponderance of the reflective over the creative faculty, and the consequent inability to collect, and embody in systematic forms, the results of his inquiries. But though so ill-qualified for the work of production, one would think the translator of Wallenstein[7] might have interpreted for us all that is most valuable in the speculations of Kant[8] and his followers. It has been said that these works are untranslatable, but without sufficient grounds. That they are not translatable by one who has not an intimate acquaintance with the transcendental philosophy, is abundantly evident from the recent attempt which has been made in England to translate Tenneman.[9] But in this respect, and indeed in every

---

3. The Morning Post was a London newspaper. The Friend, a literary and political magazine edited by Coleridge.   4. Aids to Reflection (1825); The Statesman's Manual (1816).   5. James Marsh (1794–1842), professor of philosophy at the University of Vermont.   6. Victor Cousin (1792–1867), French philosopher.   7. Coleridge translated Friedrich Schiller's three Wallenstein plays into English.   8. Immanuel Kant (1724–1804), German philosopher.   9. Wilhelm Gottlieb Tenneman (1761–1819), German philosopher.

respect, Mr. Coleridge is eminently fitted for such a task; and it is the more to be regretted that he has not undertaken it, as the number of those who are thus fitted is exceedingly small, while the demand for information on this subject is constantly increasing. We are well aware that a mere translation, however perfect, would be inadequate to convey a definite notion of transcendentalism to one who has not the metaphysical talent necessary to conceive and reproduce in himself a system whose only value to us must depend upon our power to construct it for ourselves from the materials of our own consciousness, and which in fact exists to us only on this condition.

While we are on this ground, we beg leave to offer a few explanatory remarks respecting German metaphysics,[10] which seem to us to be called for by the present state of feeling among literary men in relation to this subject. We believe it impossible to understand fully the design of Kant and his followers, without being endowed to a certain extent with the same powers of abstraction and synthetic generalization which they possess in so eminent a degree. In order to become fully master of their meaning, one must be able to find it in himself. Not all are born to be philosophers, or are capable of becoming philosophers, any more than all are capable of becoming poets or musicians. The works of the transcendental philosophers may be translated word for word, but still it will be impossible to get a clear idea of their philosophy, unless we raise ourselves at once to a transcendental point of view. Unless we take our station with the philosopher and proceed from his ground as our starting-point, the whole system will appear to us an inextricable puzzle. As in astronomy the motions of the heavenly bodies seem confused to the geocentric observer, and are intelligible only when referred to their heliocentric place, so there is only one point from which we can clearly understand and decide upon the speculations of Kant and his followers; that point is the interior consciousness, distinguished from the common consciousness, by its being an active and not a passive state. In the language of the school, it is a free intuition, and can only be attained by a vigorous effort of the will. It is from an ignorance of this primary condition, that the writings of these men have been denounced as vague and mystical. Viewing them from the distance we do, their discussions seem to us like objects half enveloped in mist; the little we can distinguish seems most portentously magnified and distorted by the unnatural refraction through which we behold it, and the point where they touch the earth is altogether lost. The effect of such writing upon the uninitiated, is like being in the company of one who has inhaled an exhilarating gas. We witness the inspiration, and are astounded at the effects, but we can form no conception of the feeling until we ourselves have experienced it. To those who are without the veil, then, any *exposé*[11] of transcendental views must needs be unsatisfactory. Now if any one chooses to deny the point which these writers assume, if any one chooses to call in question the metaphysical existence of this interior consciousness, and to pronounce the whole system a mere fabrication, or a gross self-delusion,—to such a one the disciples of this school have nothing further to say; for him their system was not conceived. Let him content himself, if he can, with "that compendious philosophy which talking of mind, but thinking of brick and mortar, or other images equally abstracted from body, contrives a theory of spirit, by nicknaming matter, and in a few hours can qualify the dullest of its disciples to explain the *omne scibile* by reducing all things to impressions,

---

10. [Hedge's note] When we speak of *German* metaphysics we wish to be understood as referring to the systems of intellectual philosophy which have prevailed in Germany since Kant. Our remarks do not apply to Leibnitz, Wolf, or any of Kant's predecessors.   11. Statement.

ideas, and sensations."[12] The disciples of Kant wrote for minds of quite another stamp, they wrote for minds that seek with faith and hope a solution of questions which that philosophy meddles not with,—questions which relate to spirit and form, substance and life, free will and fate, God and eternity. Let those who feel no interest in these questions, or who believe not in the possibility of our approaching any nearer to a solution of them, abstain for ever from a department of inquiry for which they have neither talent nor call. There are certain periods in the history of society, when, passing from a state of spontaneous production to a state of reflection, mankind are particularly disposed to inquire concerning themselves and their destination, the nature of their being, the evidence of their knowledge, and the grounds of their faith. Such a tendency is one of the characteristics of the present age, and the German philosophy is the strongest expression of that tendency; it is a striving after information on subjects which have been usually considered as beyond the reach of human intelligence, an attempt to penetrate into the most hidden mysteries of our being. In every philosophy there are three things to be considered, the object, the method, and the result. In the transcendental system, the *object* is to discover in every form of finite existence, an infinite and unconditioned as the ground of its existence, or rather as the ground of our knowledge of its existence, to refer all phenomena to certain *noumena* or laws of cognition. It is not a *ratio essendi*, but a *ratio cognoscendi*[13]; it seeks not to explain the existence of God and creation, objectively considered, but to explain our knowledge of their existence. It is not a skeptical philosophy; it seeks not to overthrow, but to build up; it wars not with the common opinions and general experience of mankind, but aims to place these on a scientific basis, and to verify them by scientific demonstrations.

The method is synthetical, proceeding from a given point, the lowest that can be found in our consciousness, and deducing from that point "the whole world of intelligences, with the whole system of their representations."[14] The correctness or philosophical propriety of the construction which is to be based upon this given point, this absolute thesis, must be assumed for a while, until proved by the successful completion of the system which it is designed to establish. The test by which we are to know that the system is complete, and the method correct, is the same as that by which we judge of the correct construction of the material arch,—continuity and self-dependence. The last step in the process, the keystone of the fabric, is the deduction of time, space, and variety, or, in other words, (as time, space, and variety include the elements of all empiric knowledge) the establishing of a coincidence between the facts of ordinary experience and those which we have discovered within ourselves, and scientifically derived from our first fundamental position. When this step is accomplished, the system is complete, the hypothetical frame-work may then fall, and the structure will support itself.[15] . . .

If now it be asked, as probably it will be asked, whether any definite and substantial good has resulted from the labors of Kant and his followers, we answer, Much. More than metaphysics ever before accomplished, these men have done for the advancement of the human intellect. It is true the immediate, and if we may so speak, the calculable results of their speculations are not so numerous nor so evident as might have been expected: these are chiefly comprised under the head of method. Yet even here we have enough to make us rejoice that such men have been, and that they have lived and spoken in our

12. Samuel Taylor Coleridge, *Biographia Literaria* (1817).   13. "Reason for being" and "reason for knowing," philosophical terms used on Kant's *Critique of Practical Reason* (1788).   14. *Biographia Literaria*.   15. [Hedge's note] We give the *ideal* of the method proposed; we are by no means prepared to say that this idea has been realized, or that it can be realized.

day. We need mention only the sharp and rightly dividing lines that have been drawn within and around the kingdom of human knowledge; the strongly marked distinctions of subject and object, reason and understanding, phenomena and noumena;—the categories established by Kant; the moral liberty proclaimed by him as it had never been proclaimed by any before; the authority and evidence of law and duty set forth by Fichte[16]; the universal harmony illustrated by Schelling.[17] But in mentioning these things, which are the direct results of the critical philosophy, we have by no means exhausted all that that philosophy has done for liberty and truth. The preeminence of Germany among the nations of our day in respect of intellectual culture, is universally acknowledged; and we do fully believe that whatever excellence that nation has attained in science, in history, or poetry is mainly owing to the influence of her philosophy, to the faculty which that philosophy has imparted of seizing on the spirit of every question, and determining at once the point of view from which each subject should be regarded,—in one word, to the transcendental method. In theology this influence has been most conspicuous. We are indebted to it for that dauntless spirit of inquiry which has investigated, and that amazing erudition which has illustrated, every corner of biblical lore. Twice it has saved the religion of Germany—once from the extreme of fanatic extravagance, and again from the verge of speculative infidelity. But, though most conspicuous in theology, this influence has been visible in every department of intellectual exertion to which the Germans have applied themselves for the last thirty years. It has characterized each science and each art, and all bear witness to its quickening power. A philosophy which has given such an impulse to mental culture and scientific research, which has done so much to establish and to extend the spiritual in man, and the ideal in nature, needs no apology; it commends itself by its fruits, it lives in its fruits, and must ever live, though the name of its founder be forgotten, and not one of its doctrines survive.

—1833

Robert Southey
1774–1843

The Poet Laureate of England for thirty years, Robert Southey was one of the most important public intellectuals of his day. He was the son of a Bristol cloth-maker but was raised by a domineering aunt who drove him to take refuge in poetry and drama. Sent to Oxford to prepare for the ministry, he read political tracts by Thomas Paine, William Godwin, and other republican radicals. Like his close friends and fellow Lake Poets, William Wordsworth and Samuel Taylor Coleridge, Southey became an enthusiastic supporter of the French Revolution. His first epic poem, *Joan of Arc* (1796), allegorized events in revolutionary France, making Joan into an egalitarian hero. With Coleridge, he planned to found a utopian socialist community, a Pantisocracy, in Pennsylvania. But when the project collapsed and England declared war on revolutionary France, Southey reversed political course. He gradually transformed himself into a passionate Tory conservative, using his position as Poet Laureate to urge the government to crush working-class reform movements like Chartism. The Chartists derive their name from the "People's Charter" drafted by William Lovett

16. Johann Gottlieb Fichte (1762–1814), German philosopher.   17. Friedrich Schelling (1775–1854), German philosopher.

in 1838, who sought to resolve the inequalities of the Reform Act of 1832. The Charter's demands included the vote for all men; annual general elections; redesigned electoral districts; and the removal of property ownership as a stipulation for holding a seat in Parliament.

During the course of his transition from radical to conservative, Southey wrote *Madoc* (1805), a two-volume epic poem about the conquest of America by a twelfth-century Welsh prince. After discovering a land of plenty, Madoc recruits a force of settlers, and together they leave behind the stultifying hierarchies of Druidic Wales to found a society of equals in the New World. These adventurers arrive in Aztlan (now Mexico) where, like the Spanish conquistador, Hernán Cortés, they form an alliance with a subject tribe, the Hoamen, and go on to overthrow the Aztec king. The Hoamen are described as a proud and generous people held in subjection by cruel and superstitious Aztec priests. Thus Southey's tale trades in both dominant Romantic ways of thinking about Native Americans: noble savagism and primitivism. Both are theories of racial inferiority, though, for throughout Southey's long poem the European Madoc is represented as bringing the light of truth to a benighted continent.

from Madoc

VI.

ERILLYAB.

"At morning, their high priest, Ayayaca,
Came with our guide[1]: the venerable man
With reverential awe accosted us,
For we, he weened,[2] were children of a race
Mightier than they, and wiser, and by Heaven   5
Beloved and favoured more: he came to give
Fit welcome, and he led us to the queen.
The fate of war had reft her of her realm;
Yet with affection and habitual awe,
And old remembrances, which gave their love   10
A deeper and religious character,
Fallen as she was, and humbled as they were,
Her faithful people still, in all they could,
Obeyed Erillyab.[3] She, too, in her mind
Those recollections cherished, and such thoughts   15
As, though no hope tempered their bitterness,
Gave to her eye a spirit, and a strength
And pride to features, which perchance had borne,
Had they been fashioned to a happier fate,
Meaning more gently and more womanly,   20
Yet not more worthy of esteem and love.
She sate upon the threshold of her hut;
For in the palace where her sires had reigned
The conqueror dwelt. Her son was at her side,
A boy now near to manhood; by the door,   25
Bare of its bark, the head and branches shorn,

---

1. Madoc, leader of the adventurers, is speaking, describing his travels to the King of Wales. 2. Believed. 3. Queen of the Hoamen, who have been conquered by the Aztecs.

Stood a young tree, with many a weapon hung,
Her husband's war-pole, and his monument.
There had his quiver mouldered, his stone-axe
Had there grown green with moss, his bow-string there   30
Sung as it cut the wind. She welcomed us
With a proud sorrow in her mien; fresh fruits
Were spread before us, and her gestures said
That when he lived, whose hand was wont to wield
Those weapons,—that in better days,—that ere   35
She let the tresses of her widowhood
Grow wild, she could have given to guests like us,
A worthier welcome. Soon a man approached,
Hooded with sable, his half-naked limbs
Smeared black; the people, at his sight, drew round,   40
The women wailed and wept, the children turned,
And hid their faces on their mothers' knees.
He to the Queen addrest his speech, then looked
Around the children, and laid hands on two,
Of different sexes, but of age alike,   45
Some six years each: they at his touch shrieked out;
But then Lincoya[4] rose, and to my feet
Led them, and told me that the conquerors claimed
These innocents for tribute; that the Priest
Would lay them on the altar of his god,   50
Tear out their little hearts in sacrifice,
Yea, with more cursed wickedness, himself
Feast on their flesh!—I shuddered, and my hand
Instinctively unsheathed the holy sword.
He, with most passionate and eloquent signs,   55
Eye-speaking earnestness, and quivering lips,
Besought me to preserve himself, and those
Who now fell suppliant round me—youths and maids,
Gray-headed men and mothers with their babes.
I caught the little victims up, I kissed   60
Their innocent cheeks, I raised my eyes to heaven,
I called upon Almighty God, to hear
And bless the vow I made: in our own tongue
Was that sworn promise of protection vowed,—
Impetuous feeling made no pause for thought.   65
Heaven heard the vow; the suppliant multitude
Saw what was stirring in my breast; the Priest,
With eye inflamed, and rapid answer, raised
His menacing hand; the tone, the bitter smile,
Interpreting his threat.   70
                              "Meanwhile the Queen,
With watchful eye and steady countenance,

---

4. Madoc's native guide.

Had listened; now she rose, and to the Priest
Addressed her speech. Low was her voice and calm,
As one who spake with effort to subdue
Sorrow that struggled still; but as she spake,   75
Her features kindled to more majesty,
Her eye became more animate, her voice
Rose to the height of feeling; on her son
She called, and from her husband's monument
His battle-axe she took; and I could see,   80
That as she gave the boy his father's arms,
She called his father's spirit to look on,
And bless them to his vengeance.

                "Silently
The tribe stood listening as Erillyab spake;
The very Priest was awed: once he essayed   85
To answer; his tongue failed him, and his lip
Grew pale, and fell. He to his countrymen,
Of rage and shame and wonder full, returned,
Bearing no victims for their shrines accurst,
But tidings that the Hoamen had cast off   90
Their vassalage, roused to desperate revolt
By men, in hue and speech and garment strange,
Who, in their folly, dared defy the power
Of Aztlan.

          "When the king of Aztlan heard
The unlooked-for tale, ere yet he roused his strength,   95
Or pitying our rash valour, or belike
Curious to see the man so bravely rash,
He sent to bid me to his court. Surprised,
I should have given to him no credulous faith,
But fearlessly Erillyab bade me trust   100
Her honourable foe. Unarmed I went,
Lincoya with me, to exchange our speech,
So as he could, of safety first assured;
For to their damned idols he had been
A victim doomed, and from the bloody rites,   105
Flying, been carried captive far away.

    "From early morning, till the midnoon hour,
We travelled in the mountains; then a plain
Opened below, and rose upon the sight,
Like boundless ocean from a hill-top seen.   110
A beautiful and populous plain it was;
Fair woods were there, and fertilising streams,
And pastures spreading wide, and villages
In fruitful groves embowered, and stately towns,
And many a single dwelling specking it,   115
As though, for many a year, the land had been

The land of peace. Below us, where the base
Of the great mountains to the level sloped,
A broad blue lake extended far and wide
Its waters dark beneath the light of noon.   120
There Aztlan stood upon the farther shore;
Amid the shade of trees its dwellings rose,
Their level roofs with turrets set around,
And battlements all burnished white, that shone
Like silver in the sun-shine. I beheld   125
The imperial city, her far-circling walls,
Her garden groves, and stately palaces,
Her temples mountain size, her thousand roofs;
And when I saw her might and majesty,
My mind misgave me then. We reached the shore: 130
A floating islet waited for me there,
The beautiful work of man. I set my foot
Upon green-growing herbs and flowers, and sate
Embowered in odorous shrubs: four long light boats
Yoked to the garden, with accordant song,   135
And dip and dash of oar in harmony,
Bore me across the lake. Then in a car,
Aloft by human bearers was I borne.
And through the city-gate, and through long lines
Of marshalled multitudes that thronged the way,   140
We reached the palace court. Four priests were there,
Each held a burning censer in his hand,
And strewed the precious gum⁵ as I drew nigh,
And held the steaming fragrance forth to me,
As I had been a god. They led me in,   145
Where, on his throne, the royal Azteca
Coanocotzin sate. 'Stranger,' said he,
'Welcome! and be this coming to thy weal!
A desperate warfare doth thy courage court;
But thou shalt see the people, and the power   150
Whom thy deluded zeal would call to arms;
So may the knowledge make thee timely wise.
The valiant love the valiant. Come with me!'
So saying, he arose; we went together forth
To the Great Temple. 'Twas a huge square hill   155
Or, rather, like a rock it seemed, hewn out
And squared by patient labour. Never yet
Did our forefathers, o'er beloved chief
Fallen in his glory, heap a monument
Of that prodigious bulk, though every shield   160
Was laden for his grave, and every hand

---

5. Incense.

Toiled unremitting, at the willing work,
From morn till eve, all the long summer-day.

    "The ascent was lengthened with provoking art,
By steps that led but to a wearying path   165
Round the whole structure; then another flight,
Another road around, and thus a third,
And yet a fourth, before we reached the height.
'Lo, now,' Coanocotzin cried, 'thou seest
The cities of this widely-peopled plain;   170
And, wert thou on yon farthest temple-top,
Yet as far onward wouldst thou see the land
Well husbanded, like this, and full of men.
They tell me that two floating palaces
Brought thee and all thy people;—when I sound   175
The tambour[6] of the god, ten cities hear
Its voice, and answers to the call, in arms.'

    "In truth, I felt my weakness, and the view
Had wakened no unreasonable fear,
But that a nearer sight had stirred my blood;   180
For on the summit where we stood, four towers
Were piled with human skulls, and all around
Long files of human heads were strung, to parch
And whiten in the sun. What then I felt
Was more than natural courage,—'twas a trust   185
In more than mortal strength,—a faith in God,—
Yea, inspiration from Him! I exclaimed,
'Not though ten cities ten times told obeyed
The king of Aztlan's bidding, should I fear
The power of man!'

                      'Art thou, then, more than man?'   190
He answered; and I saw his tawny cheek
Lose its life-colour, as the fear arose;
Nor did I undeceive him from that fear,
For, sooth, I knew not how to answer him,
And therefore let it work.

                 So not a word   195
Spake he, till we again had reached the court;
And I, too, went in silent thoughtfulness:
But then when, save Lincoya, there was none,
To hear our speech, again did he renew
The query,—'Stranger! art thou more than man,   200
That thou should'st set the power of man at nought?'

    "Then I replied, 'Two floating palaces
Bore me, and all my people, o'er the seas.

---

6. Drum.

When we departed from our mother-land,
The Moon was newly born; we saw her wax   205
And wane, and witnessed her new birth again;
And all that while, alike by day and night,
We travelled through the sea, and caught the winds,
And made them bear us forward. We must meet
In battle, if the Hoamen are not freed   210
From your accursed tribute,—thou and I,
My people, and thy countless multitudes.
Your arrows shall fall from us, as the hail
Leaps on a rock,—and when ye smite with swords,
Not blood, but fire, shall follow from the stroke.   215
Yet think not thou that we are more than men!
Our knowledge is our power, and God our strength.
God, whose almighty will created thee,
And me, and all that hath the breath of life.
He is our strength;—for in His name I speak,—   220
And when I tell thee that thou shalt not shed
The life of man in bloody sacrifice,
It is His holy bidding that I speak:
And if thou wilt not listen and obey,
When I shall meet thee in the battle field,   225
It is His holy cause for which I shall fight,
And I shall have His power to conquer thee!'

    "'And thinkest thou our gods are feeble? cried
The king of Aztlan! 'dost thou deem they lack
Power to defend their altars, and to keep   230
The kingdom that they gave us strength to win?
The gods of thirty nations have opposed
Their irresistible might, and they lie now
Conquered and caged and fettered at their feet.
That they who serve them are no coward race,   235
Let prove the ample realm they won in arms:
And I, their leader, am not of the sons
Of the feeble!' As he spake, he reached a mace,
The trunk and knotted root of some young tree,
Such as old Albion, and his monster-brood,   240
From the oak-forest for their weapons plucked,
When father Brute and Corineus[7] set foot
On the white island first. 'Lo, this,' quoth he,
'My club!' and he threw back his robe; 'and this
The arm that wields it!—'twas my father's once: 245

---

7. Brutus and Corineus, the legendary Trojan founders of Britain, battled the giant, Albion, for control of the southern part of England.

Erillyab's husband, King Tepollomi,
He felt its weight—did I not show thee him?
He lights me at my evening banquet.' There,
In the very deed, the dead Tepollomi
Stood up against the wall, by devilish art   250
Preserved; and from his black and shriveled hand
The steady lamp hung down.
      "My spirit rose
At that abomination; I exclaimed,
'Thou art of noble nature, and full fain
Would I in friendship plight my hand with thine;   255
But till that body in the grave be laid,
Till thy polluted altars be made pure,
There is no peace between us. May my God,
Who, though thou knowest Him not, is also thine,
And, after death, will be thy dreadful Judge,   260
May it please Him to visit thee, and shed
His mercy on thy soul!—But if thy heart
Be hardened to the proof, come when thou wilt!
I know thy power, and thou shalt then know mine."

          —1805

William Hazlitt
1778–1830

When William Hazlitt was five years old, his father, a Unitarian minister with republican politics, moved the family to America. The elder Hazlitt preached, lectured, and founded the first
Unitarian Church in Boston, returning to England after a period of four years. Hazlitt's father was
a radical who advocated from the pulpit for American independence and the French Revolution.
William inherited a radical political sensibility from his father and an obstinacy that made his
unwavering moral compass (and pugnacious personality) difficult for friends and associates to
understand during the politically turbulent and culturally vibrant Romantic period. Hazlitt, a dissenter like his father, valued liberty and equality, and he began to attack those whom he felt had
lost their revolutionary fire, especially William Wordsworth and Robert Southey.

 Between the ages of fifteen and eighteen, while a student at Hackney College in London,
Hazlitt began his career as an essayist. His periodical publications during this time cover an
extraordinary range of topics: boxing, painting, literature, economics, and politics. His interests
were well suited to the form of the miscellaneous essay, in which he gave voice to his strong
opinions on people and politics. Working variously as a parliamentary reporter, a dramatic
critic, and a lecturer on literary topics, he demonstrated a keen understanding of literary and
dramatic form. "On Gusto" and "On the Love of the Country" both first appeared in Leigh
Hunt's periodical *The Examiner* as entries in a regular column titled "The Round Table."

On Gusto

Gusto in art is power or passion defining any object. It is not so difficult to explain this term in what relates to expression (of which it may be said to be the highest degree) as in what relates to things without expression, to the natural appearances of objects, as mere colour or form. In one sense, however, there is hardly any object entirely devoid of expression, without some character of power belonging to it, some precise association with pleasure or pain: and it is in giving this truth of character from the truth of feeling, whether in the highest or the lowest degree, but always in the highest degree of which the subject is capable, that gusto consists.

There is a gusto in the colouring of Titian.[1] Not only do his heads seem to think—his bodies seem to feel. This is what the Italians mean by the *morbidezza*[2] of his flesh-colour. It seems sensitive and alive all over; not merely to have the look and texture of flesh, but the feeling in itself. For example, the limbs of his female figures have a luxurious softness and delicacy, which appears conscious of the pleasure of the beholder. As the objects themselves in nature would produce an impression on the sense, distinct from every other object, and having something divine in it, which the heart owns and the imagination consecrates, the objects in the picture preserve the same impression, absolute, unimpaired, stamped with all the truth of passion, the pride of the eye, and the charm of beauty. Rubens makes his flesh-colour like flowers; Albano's is like ivory; Titian's is like flesh, and like nothing else. It is as different from that of other painters, as the skin is from a piece of white or red drapery thrown over it. The blood circulates here and there, the blue veins just appear, the rest is distinguished throughout only by that sort of tingling sensation to the eye, which the body feels within itself. This is gusto. Vandyke's flesh-colour, though it has great truth and purity, wants gusto. It has not the internal character, the living principle in it. It is a smooth surface, not a warm, moving mass. It is painted without passion, with indifference. The hand only has been concerned. The impression slides off from the eye, and does not, like the tones of Titian's pencil, leave a sting behind it in the mind of the spectator! The eye does not acquire a taste or appetite for what it sees. In a word, gusto in painting is where the impression made on one sense excites by affinity those of another.

Michael Angelo's forms are full of gusto. They everywhere obtrude the sense of power upon the eye. His limbs convey an idea of muscular strength, of moral grandeur, and even of intellectual dignity: they are firm, commanding, broad, and massy, capable of executing with ease the determined purposes of the will. His faces have no other expression than his figures, conscious power and capacity. They appear only to think what they shall do, and to know that they can do it. This is what is meant by saying that his style is hard and masculine. It is the reverse of Correggio's, which is effeminate. That is, the gusto of Michael Angelo consists in expressing energy of will without proportionable sensibility, Correggio's in expressing exquisite sensibility without energy of will. In Correggio's faces as well as figures we see neither bones nor muscles, but then what a soul is there, full of sweetness and of grace—pure, playful, soft, angelical! There is sentiment enough in a hand painted by Correggio to set up a school of history painters. Whenever we look at the hands of Correggio's women or of Raphael's, we always wish to touch them.

---

1. Italian painter (1477–1576).   2. Delicacy.

Again, Titian's landscapes have a prodigious gusto, both in the colouring and forms. We shall never forget one that we saw many years ago in the Orleans Gallery of Acteon hunting. It had a brown, mellow, autumnal look. The sky was of the colour of stone. The winds seemed to sing through the rustling branches of the trees, and already you might hear the twanging of bows resound through the tangled mazes of the wood. Mr West,[2] we understand, has this landscape. He will know if this description of it is just. The land-scape back-ground of the St Peter Martyr is another well known instance of the power of this great painter to give a romantic interest and an appropriate character to the objects of his pencil, where every circumstance adds to the effect of the scene—the bold trunks of the tall forest trees, the trailing ground plants, with that tall convent spire rising in the distance, amidst the blue sapphire mountains and the golden sky.

Rubens has a great deal of gusto in his Fauns and Satyrs, and in all that expresses motion, but in nothing else. Rembrandt has it in everything; everything in his pic-tures has a tangible character. If he puts a diamond in the ear of a burgomaster's wife, it is of the first water; and his furs and stuffs are proof against a Russian winter. Raphael's gusto was only in expression; he had no idea of the character of anything but the human form. The dryness and poverty of his style in other respects is a phenomenon in the art. His trees are like sprigs of grass stuck in a book of botanical specimens. Was it that Raphael never had time to go beyond the walls of Rome? That he was always in the streets, at church, or in the bath? He was not one of the Society of Arcadians.[3]

Claude's landscapes, perfect as they are, want gusto. This is not easy to explain. They are perfect abstractions of the visible images of things; they speak the visible language of nature truly. They resemble a mirror or a microscope. To the eye only they are more perfect than any other landscapes that ever were or will be painted; they give more of nature, as cognisable by one sense alone; but they lay an equal stress on all visible impressions. They do not interpret one sense by another; they do not distin-guish the character of different objects as we are taught, and can only be taught, to distinguish them by their effect on the different senses. That is, his eye wanted imagi-nation: it did not strongly sympathise with his other faculties. He saw the atmosphere, but he did not feel it. He painted the trunk of a tree or a rock in the foreground as smooth—with as complete an abstraction of the gross, tangible impression, as any other part of the picture. His trees are perfectly beautiful, but quite immovable; they have a look of enchantment. In short, his landscapes are unequalled imitations of nature, released from its subjection to the elements, as if all objects were become a delightful fairy vision, and the eye had rarefied and refined away the other senses.

The gusto in the Greek statues is of a very singular kind. The sense of perfect form nearly occupies the whole mind, and hardly suffers it to dwell on any other feel-ing. It seems enough for them to be, without acting or suffering. Their forms are ideal, spiritual. Their beauty is power. By their beauty they are raised above the frailties of pain or passion; by their beauty they are deified.

The infinite quantity of dramatic invention in Shakspeare takes from his gusto. The power he delights to show is not intense, but discursive. He never insists on any-thing as much as he might, except a quibble. Milton has great gusto. He repeats his blows twice; grapples with and exhausts his subject. His imagination has a double rel-

---

2. Benjamin West (1738–1820), American painter who served as president of the Royal Academy of Art.   3. Nature enthusiasts.

ish of its objects, an inveterate attachment to the things he describes, and to the words describing them.

> ——Or where Chineses drive
> With sails and wind their *cany* waggons *light*.
>
>   . . .
>
> Wild above rule or art, *enormous* bliss.[4]

There is a gusto in Pope's compliments, in Dryden's satires, and Prior's tales; and among prose writers Boccacio and Rabelais had the most of it. We will only mention one other work which appears to us to be full of gusto, and that is the *Beggar's Opera*. If it is not, we are altogether mistaken in our notions on this delicate subject.

—1816

On the Love of the Country
To the Editor of the Round Table.

Sir,—I do not know that any one has ever explained satisfactorily the true source of our attachment to natural objects, or of that soothing emotion which the sight of the country hardly ever fails to infuse into the mind. Some persons have ascribed this feeling to the natural beauty of the objects themselves, others to the freedom from care, the silence and tranquillity which scenes of retirement afford—others to the healthy and innocent employments of a country life—others to the simplicity of country manners—and others to different causes; but none to the right one. All these causes may, I believe, have a share in producing this feeling; but there is another more general principle, which has been left untouched, and which I shall here explain, endeavouring to be as little sentimental as the subject will admit.

Rousseau, in his Confessions,[1] (the most valuable of all his works), relates, that when he took possession of his room at Annecy, at the house of his beloved mistress and friend, he found that he could see 'a little spot of green' from his window, which endeared his situation the more to him, because, he says, it was the first time he had had this object constantly before him since he left Boissy, the place where he was at school when a child.[2] Some such feeling as that here described will be found lurking at the bottom of all our attachments of this sort. Were it not for the recollections habitually associated with them, natural objects could not interest the mind in the manner they do. No doubt, the sky is beautiful; the clouds sail majestically along its bosom; the sun is cheering; there is something exquisitely graceful in the manner in which a plant or tree puts forth its branches; the motion with which they bend and tremble in the evening breeze is soft and lovely; there is music in the babbling of a brook; the view from the top of a mountain is full of grandeur; nor can we behold the ocean with indifference. Or, as the Minstrel sweetly sings—

> 'Oh how can'st thou renounce the boundless store
> Of charms which Nature to her votary yields!

---

4. John Milton (1608–1674), *Paradise Lost* (1667), 3.438–439, 5.291.

1. *Confessions of Jean-Jacques Rousseau* (1782).   2. [Hazlitt's note] Pope also declares that he had a particular regard for an old post which stood in the court-yard before the house where he was brought up.

The warbling woodland, the resounding shore,
The pomp of groves, and garniture of fields;
All that the genial ray of morning gilds,
And all that echoes to the song of even,
All that the mountain's sheltering bosom shields,
And all the dread magnificence of heaven,
Oh how can'st thou renounce, and hope to be forgiven!'³

It is not, however, the beautiful and magnificent alone that we admire in Nature; the most insignificant and rudest objects are often found connected with the strongest emotions; we become attached to the most common and familiar images as to the face of a friend whom we have long known, and from whom we have received many benefits. It is because natural objects have been associated with the sports of our childhood, with air and exercise, with our feelings in solitude, when the mind takes the strongest hold of things, and clings with the fondest interest to whatever strikes its attention; with change of place, the pursuit of new scenes, and thoughts of distant friends: it is because they have surrounded us in almost all situations, in joy and in sorrow, in pleasure and in pain; because they have been one chief source and nourishment of our feelings, and a part of our being, that we love them as we do ourselves.

There is, generally speaking, the same foundation for our love of Nature as for all our habitual attachments, namely, association of ideas. But this is not all. That which distinguishes this attachment from others is the transferable nature of our feelings with respect to physical objects; the associations connected with any one object extending to the whole class. My having been attached to any particular person does not make me feel the same attachment to the next person I may chance to meet; but, if I have once associated strong feelings of delight with the objects of natural scenery, the tie becomes indissoluble, and I shall ever after feel the same attachment to other objects of the same sort. I remember when I was abroad, the trees, and grass, and wet leaves, rustling in the walks of the Thuilleries,⁴ seemed to be as much English, to be as much the same trees and grass, that I had always been used to, as the sun shining over my head was the same sun which I saw in England; the faces only were foreign to me. Whence comes this difference? It arises from our always imperceptibly connecting the idea of the individual with man, and only the idea of the class with natural objects. In the one case, the external appearance or physical structure is the least thing to be attended to; in the other, it is every thing. The springs that move the human form, and make it friendly or adverse to me, lie hid within it. There is an infinity of motives, passions, and ideas contained in that narrow compass, of which I know nothing, and in which I have no share. Each individual is a world to himself, governed by a thousand contradictory and wayward impulses. I can, therefore, make no inference from one individual to another; nor can my habitual sentiments, with respect to any individual, extend beyond himself to others. But it is otherwise with respect to Nature. There is neither hypocrisy, caprice, nor mental reservation in her favours. Our intercourse with her is not liable to accident or change, interruption or disappointment. She smiles on us still the same. Thus, to give an obvious instance, if I have once enjoyed the cool shade of a tree, and been lulled into a deep repose by the sound of a brook running at its feet, I am sure that wherever I can find a tree and a brook, I can enjoy the same pleasure again. Hence, when I imagine

3. James Beattie (1735–1803), The Minstrel (1771), 1.73–81.   4. Tuileries, Paris palace destroyed by fire in 1871.

these objects, I can easily form a mystic personification of the friendly power that inhabits them, Dryad or Naiad,[5] offering its cool fountain or its tempting shade. Hence the origin of the Grecian mythology. All objects of the same kind being the same, not only in their appearance, but in their practical uses, we habitually confound them together under the same general idea; and, whatever fondness we may have conceived for one, is immediately placed to the common account. The most opposite kinds and remote trains of feeling gradually go to enrich the same sentiment; and in our love of Nature, there is all the force of individual attachment, combined with the most airy abstraction. It is this circumstance which gives that refinement, expansion, and wild interest to feelings of this sort, when strongly excited, which every one must have experienced who is a true lover of Nature. The sight of the setting sun does not affect me so much from the beauty of the object itself, from the glory kindled through the glowing skies, the rich broken columns of light, or the dying streaks of day, as that it indistinctly recalls to me numberless thoughts and feelings with which, through many a year and season, I have watched his bright descent in the warm summer evenings, or beheld him struggling to cast a 'farewel sweet' through the thick clouds of winter. I love to see the trees first covered with leaves in the spring, the primroses peeping out from some sheltered bank, and the innocent lambs running races on the soft green turf; because, at that birth-time of Nature, I have always felt sweet hopes and happy wishes—which have not been fulfilled! The dry reeds rustling on the side of a stream,—the woods swept by the loud blast,—the dark massy foliage of autumn,—the grey trunks and naked branches of the trees in winter,—the sequestered copse and wide extended heath,—the warm sunny showers, and December snows,—have all charms for me; there is no object, however trifling or rude, that has not, in some mood or other, found the way to my heart; and I might say, in the words of the poet,

'To me the meanest flower that blows can give
Thoughts that do often lie too deep for tears.'[6]

Thus Nature is a kind of universal home, and every object it presents to us an old acquaintance with unaltered looks.

——'Nature did ne'er betray
The heart that lov'd her, but through all the years
Of this our life, it is her privilege
To lead from joy to joy.'[7]

For there is that consent and mutual harmony among all her works, one undivided spirit pervading them throughout, that, if we have once knit ourselves in hearty fellowship to any of them, they will never afterwards appear as strangers to us, but, which ever way we turn, we shall find a secret power to have gone out before us, moulding them into such shapes as fancy loves, informing them with life and sympathy, bidding them put on their festive looks and gayest attire at our approach, and to pour all their sweets and choicest treasures at our feet. For him, then, who has well acquainted himself with Nature's works, she wears always one face, and speaks the same well-known language, striking on the heart, amidst unquiet thoughts and the tumult of the world, like the music of one's native tongue heard in some far-off country.

5. In Greek mythology, spirits of nature.   6. William Wordsworth, "Ode: Intimations of Immortality from Recollections of Early Childhood," see p. 434.   7. William Wordsworth, "Lines Written a Few Miles above Tintern Abbey," see p. 400.

We do not connect the same feelings with the works of art as with those of nature, because we refer them to man, and associate with them the separate interests and passions which we know belong to those who are the authors or possessors of them. Nevertheless, there are some such objects, as a cottage, or a village church, which excite in us the same sensations as the sight of nature, and which are, indeed, almost always included in descriptions of natural scenery.

> 'Or from the mountain's sides
> View wilds and swelling floods,
> And hamlets brown, and dim-discover'd spires,
> And hear their simple bell.'[8]

Which is in part, no doubt, because they are surrounded with natural objects, and, in a populous country, inseparable from them; and also because the human interest they excite relates to manners and feelings which are simple, common, such as all can enter into, and which, therefore, always produce a pleasing effect upon the mind.

—1814

Thomas Moore
1779–1852

The New World was a land of promise for Thomas Moore, as he writes in the preface to his 1806 *Epistles, Odes, and Other Poems*. Three years earlier, he had traveled to America with "illusive ideas" about the "purity of the government and the primitive happiness of the people." His view of the country came from his reading of many books that outlined a common theme:

> [D]iscontent at home enhances every distant temptation, and the western world has long been looked to as a retreat from real or imaginary oppression; as, in short, the elysian Atlantis, where persecuted patriots might find their visions realized, and be welcomed by kindred spirits to liberty and repose.

The reality of the wilds of North America, which Moore saw as teeming with crude people and hurly-burly politics, shocked him. He struggled with the democratic manners of the New World, especially with the atmosphere of Washington, DC, during Jefferson's presidency: "There certainly is a close approximation to savage life not only in the liberty which they enjoy, but in the violence of party spirit and of private animosity which results from it. . . ." Moore traveled to America and Canada for fourteen months during 1803–1804, and the poems presented in this anthology capture his more positive experience while visiting Canada—a country he found more to his liking because of its English echoes. Indeed, Moore was more pro-English than Irish Nationalist and found comfort in the familiar people and politics of Canada.

Born to Roman Catholic parents in 1779, Moore acted and wrote poetry and drama. He studied law but was not admitted to the bar. Perhaps one of the most prominent European writers to visit North America, he was offered the newly founded position of Poet Laureate of Ireland, which he declined. Soon after, he was appointed registrar of admiralty prize-court,

---

8. William Collins (1721–1759), "Ode to Evening" (1748).

Bermuda, and in November 1803 he sailed for Virginia. Appointing a deputy to cover his post after four unsatisfying months, Moore sailed for America in early 1804. His portraits of America and Canada are an amalgam of firsthand accounts and images from the texts that inspired him to take his trip abroad, such as Isaac Weld's *Travels through the States of North America, and the Provinces of Upper and Lower Canada, during the Years 1795, 1796, and 1797* (1799), a book which Moore brought with him on his trip. Moore's poetry about Canada was especially important to early Canadian writers, offering poetic models and inspiration to poets such as Adam Kidd and Alexander McLachlan. "A Canadian Boat Song" was an international (musical and poetical) success. Published in London in 1805, in a three-voice setting, the poem was quickly reprinted in Boston, Philadelphia, and New York, and was reprinted often on both sides of the Atlantic for forty years (in a variety of musical arrangements). "Boat Song" and the two other poems included in this anthology appeared in Moore's 1806 *Epistles, Odes and Other Poems*. The collection was highly critical of America, fueled by Moore's moral and social irritation with the country. Moore's attitude led the reviewer Francis Jeffrey to censure him as "the most licentious of modern versifiers." Deeply insulted, Moore challenged Jeffrey to a duel with pistols. At the appointed hour, the two faced off but fell into conversation, planting the seeds for a lifelong friendship. Soon after, police intervention revealed that both men's pistols were unloaded, leading the event to be famously dubbed the "leadless duel."

A Canadian Boat Song

Written on the River St. Lawrence.

et remigem cantus hortatur.
QUINTILIAN.[1]

Faintly as tolls the evening chime
Our voices keep tune and our oars keep time.
Soon as the woods on shore look dim,
We'll sing at St. Ann's our parting hymn.
Row, brothers, row, the stream runs fast,   5
The Rapids are near and the daylight's past.

  Why should we yet our sail unfurl?
There is not a breath the blue wave to curl.
But, when the wind blows off the shore,
Oh! sweetly we'll rest our weary oar.   10
Blow, breezes, blow, the stream runs fast,
The Rapids are near and the daylight's past.

  Utawas'[2] tide! this trembling moon
Shall see us float over thy surges soon.
Saint of this green isle! hear our prayers,   15
Oh, grant us cool heavens and favouring airs.
Blow, breezes, blow, the stream runs fast.
The Rapids are near and the daylight's past.

—1806

---

1. "And we urged our oars with song." Marcus Fabius Quintilianus (c. 35–95), Roman rhetorician.   2. Ottawa river.

A Ballad. The Lake of the Dismal Swamp.

Written at Norfolk, in Virginia.

"They tell of a young man, who lost his mind upon the death of a girl he loved, and who, suddenly disappearing from his friends, was never afterwards heard of. As he had frequently said, in his ravings, that the girl was not dead, but gone to the Dismal Swamp, it is supposed he had wandered into that dreary wilderness, and had died of hunger, or been lost in some of its dreadful morasses."   —ANON.

"La Poésie a ses monstres comme la nature."   —D'ALEMBERT.[1]

"They made her a grave, too cold and damp
    "For a soul so warm and true;
"And she's gone to the Lake of the Dismal Swamp,
"Where, all night long, by a firefly lamp,
    "She paddles her white canoe.   5

"And her firefly lamp I soon shall see,
    "And her paddle I soon shall hear;
Long and loving our life shall be,
"And I'll hide the maid in a cypress tree,
    "When the footstep of death is near."   10

Away to the Dismal Swamp he speeds—
    His path was rugged and sore,
Through tangled juniper, beds of reeds,
Through many a fen, where the serpent feeds,
    And man never trod before.   15

And, when on the earth he sunk to sleep,
    If slumber his eyelids knew,
He lay, where the deadly vine doth weep
Its venomous tear and nightly steep
    The flesh with blistering dew!   20

And near him the she wolf stirr'd the brake,
    And the copper snake breath'd in his ear,
Till he starting cried, from his dream awake,
"O, when shall I see the dusky Lake,
    "And the white canoe of my dear?"   25

He saw the Lake, and a meteor bright
    Quick over its surface play'd—
"Welcome," he said, "my dear one's light!"
And the dim shore echoed, for many a night,
    The name of the death-cold maid.   30

---

1. "Poetry has its monsters like nature." Jean Le Rond d'Alembert (1717–1783).

Till he hollow'd a boat of the birchen bark,
   Which carried him off from shore;
Far, far he follow'd the meteor spark,
The wind was high and the clouds were dark,
   And the boat return'd no more.   35

But oft, from the Indian hunter's camp
   This lover and maid so true
Are seen at the hour of midnight damp
To cross the Lake by a firefly lamp,
   And paddle their white canoe!   40

—1806

Ballad Stanzas

I knew by the smoke, that so gracefully curl'd
   Above the green elms, that a cottage was near,
And I said, "If there's peace to be found in the world,
   "A heart that was humble might hope for it here!"

It was noon, and on flowers that languish'd around   5
   In silence repos'd the voluptuous bee;
Every leaf was at rest, and I heard not a sound
   But the woodpecker tapping the hollow beech-tree.

And, "Here in this lone little wood," I exclaim'd,
   "With a maid who was lovely to soul and to eye,   10
"Who would blush when I prais'd her, and weep if I blam'd,
   "How blest could I live, and how calm could I die!

"By the shade of yon sumach,[1] whose red berry dips
   "In the gush of the fountain, how sweet to recline,
"And to know that I sigh'd upon innocent lips,   15
   "Which had never been sigh'd on by any but mine!"

—1806

William Ellery Channing
1780–1842

Born on April 7, 1780, in Newport, Rhode Island, William Ellery Channing shared his birthday
with one of his favorite poets, William Wordsworth, who was ten years his elder. After visiting the
poet in 1822, Channing became one of the first to apply his works to Unitarian theology. Channing

---

1. A large shrub.

visited Samuel Taylor Coleridge and Robert Southey as well, and the broad-minded ways in which he allowed their poetry to affect his understanding of God paved the way for the New England Transcendentalists, who always looked to Channing as a guiding light. The Romantics' obsession with a life that grows like a seed toward God and, like the rest of the natural world, becomes a type or symbol of God was compelling to Channing and his fellow American theologians and authors. Elizabeth Palmer Peabody and Ralph Waldo Emerson referred to him as "our bishop." Channing's transatlantic theological connections do not begin or end with the English Romantic poets, though, for he also had a strong link with Scottish-American Presbyterianism through his father's education at Princeton. Fusing this tradition with the liberal Unitarianism of Harvard—which was influenced by the Unitarian radical Joseph Priestley, who emigrated from London to Pennsylvania—he was able to construct a theology that counterbalanced Calvinist and Puritanical notions of humankind's innate wretchedness with the notion of Divine Providence (from the Latin word *to see for*), which guided souls toward salvation and perfection. In Channing's interpretation of the Bible, he did not find suitable passages to support the notion of the Trinity, the cornerstone of the Calvinist, Catholic, and Episcopal churches in America.

After his education at Harvard and after serving as an administrator there, Channing remained in Massachusetts, marrying his cousin Ruth Gibbs and becoming the minister of Boston's Federal Street Church, where he would remain until his death. From this pulpit, he became the leader of Unitarianism in its struggle with the Calvinists of the day as well as the leader of a number of philanthropic ministries to the poor. These pastoral roles helped him practice what he preached and preach what he practiced: a religion based upon adherence to scripture as applied to life through reason and conscience to bring about the betterment of self and others, an almost organic spiritual growth toward goodness. The same principles he pre-scribed for the growth of self, he also recommended for the growth of a nation. He believed that a country could commit murder through unjustified use of force and that it should safe-guard human rights and value education highly.

from Likeness to God

Discourse at the Ordination of the Rev. F. A. Farley.
Providence, R. I. 1828.

EPHESIANS V. 1: "Be ye therefore followers of God, as dear children."

To promote true religion is the purpose of the Christian ministry. For this it was ordained. On the present occasion, therefore, when a new teacher is to be given to the church, a discourse on the character of true religion will not be inappropriate. I do not mean, that I shall attempt, in the limits to which I am now confined, to set before you all its properties, signs, and operations; for in so doing I should burden your memories with divisions and vague generalities, as uninteresting as they would be unprofitable. My purpose is, to select one view of the subject, which seems to me of primary dignity and importance; and I select this, because it is greatly neglected, and because I attrib-ute to this neglect much of the inefficacy, and many of the corruptions, of religion.

The text calls us to follow or imitate God, to seek accordance with or likeness to him; and to do this, not fearfully and faintly, but with the spirit and hope of beloved children. The doctrine which I propose to illustrate, is derived immediately from these words, and is incorporated with the whole New Testament. I affirm, and would maintain, that true religion consists in proposing, as our great end, a growing likeness to the Supreme Being. Its noblest influence consists in making us more and more par-takers of the Divinity. For this it is to be preached. Religious instruction should aim chiefly to turn men's aspirations and efforts to that perfection of the soul, which constitutes it a bright image of God. Such is the topic now to be discussed; and I implore HIM, whose glory I seek, to aid me in unfolding and enforcing it with simplicity and clearness, with a calm and pure zeal, and with unfeigned charity.

I begin with observing, what all indeed will understand, that the likeness to God, of which I propose to speak, belongs to man's higher or spiritual nature. It has its foundation in the original and essential capacities of the mind. In proportion as these are unfolded by right and vigorous exertion, it is extended and brightened. In proportion as these lie dormant, it is obscured. In proportion as they are perverted and overpowered by the appetites and passions, it is blotted out. In truth, moral evil, if unresisted and habitual, may so blight and lay waste these capacities, that the image of God in man may seem to be wholly destroyed.

The importance of this assimilation to our Creator, is a topic which needs no labored discussion. All men, of whatever name, or sect, or opinion, will meet me on this ground. All, I presume, will allow, that no good in the compass of the universe, or within the gift of omnipotence, can be compared to a resemblance of God, or to a participation of his attributes. I fear no contradiction here. Likeness to God is the supreme gift. He can communicate nothing so precious, glorious, blessed, as himself. To hold intellectual and moral affinity with the Supreme Being, to partake his spirit, to be his children by derivations of kindred excellence, to bear a growing conformity to the perfection which we adore, this is a felicity which obscures and annihilates all other good.

It is only in proportion to this likeness, that we can enjoy either God or the universe. That God can be known and enjoyed only through sympathy or kindred attributes, is a doctrine which even Gentile philosophy discerned. That the pure in heart can alone see and commune with the pure Divinity, was the sublime instruction of ancient sages as well as of inspired prophets. It is indeed the lesson of daily experience. To understand a great and good being, we must have the seeds of the same excellence. How quickly, by what an instinct, do accordant minds recognise one another! No attraction is so powerful as that which subsists between the truly wise and good; whilst the brightest excellence is lost on those who have nothing congenial in their own breasts. God becomes a real being to us, in proportion as his own nature is unfolded within us. To a man who is growing in the likeness of God, faith begins even here to change into vision. He carries within himself a proof of a Deity, which can only be understood by experience. He more than believes, he feels the Divine presence; and gradually rises to an intercourse with his Maker, to which it is not irreverent to apply the name of friendship and intimacy. The Apostle John intended to express this truth, when he tells us, that he, in whom a principle of divine charity or benevolence has become a habit and life, "dwells in God and God in him."[1]

It is plain, too, that likeness to God is the true and only preparation for the enjoyment of the universe. In proportion as we approach and resemble the mind of God, we are brought into harmony with the creation; for, in that proportion, we possess the principles from which the universe sprung; we carry within ourselves the perfections, of which its beauty, magnificence, order, benevolent adaptations, and boundless purposes, are the results and manifestations. God unfolds himself in his

---

1. 1 John 4.

works to a kindred mind. It is possible, that the brevity of these hints may expose to the charge of mysticism, what seems to me the calmest and clearest truth. I think, however, that every reflecting man will feel, that likeness to God must be a principle of sympathy or accordance with his creation; for the creation is a birth and shining forth of the Divine Mind, a work through which his spirit breathes.[2] In proportion as we receive this spirit, we possess within ourselves the explanation of what we see. We discern more and more of God in every thing, from the frail flower to the everlasting stars. Even in evil, that dark cloud which hangs over the creation, we discern rays of light and hope, and gradually come to see, in suffering and temptation, proofs and instruments of the sublimest purposes of Wisdom and Love.[3]

I have offered these very imperfect views, that I may show the great importance of the doctrine which I am solicitous to enforce. I would teach, that likeness to God is a good so unutterably surpassing all other good, that whoever admits it as attainable, must acknowledge it to be the chief aim of life. I would show, that the highest and happiest office of religion is, to bring the mind into growing accordance with God; and that by the tendency of religious systems to this end, their truth and worth are to be chiefly tried.

I am aware that it may be said, that the Scriptures, in speaking of man as made in the image of God,[4] and in calling us to imitate him, use bold and figurative language. It may be said, that there is danger from too literal an interpretation; that God is an unapproachable being; that I am not warranted in ascribing to man a like nature to the Divine; that we and all things illustrate the Creator by contrast, not by resemblance; that religion manifests itself chiefly in convictions and acknowledgments of utter worthlessness; and that to talk of the greatness and divinity of the human soul, is to inflate that pride through which Satan fell, and through which man involves himself in that fallen spirit's ruin.

I answer, that, to me, Scripture and reason hold a different language. In Christianity particularly, I meet perpetual testimonies to the divinity of human nature. This whole religion expresses an infinite concern of God for the human soul, and teaches that he deems no methods too expensive for its recovery and exaltation. Christianity, with one voice, calls me to turn my regards and care to the spirit within me, as of more worth than the whole outward world. It calls us to "be perfect as our Father in heaven is perfect;"[5] and every where, in the sublimity of its precepts, it implies and recognises the sublime capacities of the being to whom they are addressed. It assures us that human virtue is "in the sight of God of great price,"[6] and speaks of the return of a human being to virtue as an event which increases the joy of heaven. In the New Testament, Jesus Christ, the Son of God, the brightness of his glory, the express and unsullied image of the Divinity, is seen mingling with men as a friend and brother, offering himself as their example, and promising to his true followers a share in all his splendors and joys. In the New Testament, God is said to communicate his own spirit, and all his fulness to the human soul. In the New Testament man is exhorted to aspire after "honor, glory, and immortality";[7] and Heaven, a word expressing the nearest approach to God, and a divine happiness, is everywhere proposed as the end of his being. In truth, the very essence of Christian faith is, that we trust in God's mercy, as revealed in Jesus Christ, for a state of celes-

---

2. Genesis 2.7.   3. Compare William Wordsworth, "Ode: Intimations of Immortality," p. 434.   4. Genesis 1.27.
5. Matthew 5.48.   6. 1 Peter 3.4.   7. Romans 2.7.

tial purity, in which we shall grow for ever in the likeness, and knowledge, and enjoyment of the Infinite Father. Lofty views of the nature of man are bound up and interwoven with the whole Christian system. Say not, that these are at war with humility; for who was ever humbler than Jesus, and yet who ever possessed such a consciousness of greatness and divinity? Say not that man's business is to think of his sin, and not of his dignity; for great sin implies a great capacity; it is the abuse of a noble nature; and no man can be deeply and rationally contrite, but he who feels, that in wrong-doing he has resisted a divine voice, and warred against a divine principle, in his own soul.—I need not, I trust, pursue the argument from revelation. There is an argument from nature and reason, which seems to me so convincing, and is at the same time so fitted to explain what I mean by man's possession of a like nature to God, that I shall pass at once to its exposition.

That man has a kindred nature with God, and may bear most important and ennobling relations to him, seems to me to be established by a striking proof. This proof you will understand, by considering, for a moment, how we obtain our ideas of God. Whence come the conceptions which we include under that august name? Whence do we derive our knowledge of the attributes and perfections which constitute the Supreme Being? I answer, we derive them from our own souls. The divine attributes are first developed in ourselves, and thence transferred to our Creator. The idea of God, sublime and awful as it is, is the idea of our own spiritual nature, purified and enlarged to infinity. In ourselves are the elements of the Divinity. God, then, does not sustain a figurative resemblance to man. It is the resemblance of a parent to a child, the likeness of a kindred nature.

We call God a Mind. He has revealed himself as a Spirit. But what do we know of mind, but through the unfolding of this principle in our own breasts? That unbounded spiritual energy which we call God, is conceived by us only through consciousness, through the knowledge of ourselves.—We ascribe thought or intelligence to the Deity, as one of his most glorious attributes. And what means this language? These terms we have framed to express operations or faculties of our own souls. The Infinite Light would be for ever hidden from us, did not kindred rays dawn and brighten within us. God is another name for human intelligence raised above all error and imperfection, and extended to all possible truth.

The same is true of God's goodness. How do we understand this, but by the principle of love implanted in the human breast? Whence is it, that this divine attribute is so faintly comprehended, but from the feeble development of it in the multitude of men? Who can understand the strength, purity, fulness, and extent of divine philanthropy, but he in whom selfishness has been swallowed up in love?

The same is true of all the moral perfections of the Deity. These are comprehended by us, only through our own moral nature. It is conscience within us, which, by its approving and condemning voice, interprets to us God's love of virtue and hatred of sin; and without conscience, these glorious conceptions would never have opened on the mind. It is the lawgiver in our own breasts, which gives us the idea of divine authority, and binds us to obey it. The soul, by its sense of right, or its perception of moral distinctions, is clothed with sovereignty over itself, and through this alone, it understands and recognises the Sovereign of the Universe. Men, as by a natural inspiration, have agreed to speak of conscience as the voice of God, as the Divinity within us. This principle, reverently obeyed, makes us more and more par-takers of the moral perfection of the Supreme Being, of that very excellence, which constitutes the rightfulness of his sceptre, and enthrones him over the universe. Without this inward law, we should be as incapable of receiving a law from Heaven, as the brute. Without this, the thunders of Sinai might startle the outward ear, but would have no meaning, no authority to the mind. I have expressed here a great truth. Nothing teaches so encouragingly our relation and resemblance to God; for the glory of the Supreme Being is eminently moral. We blind ourselves to his chief splendor, if we think only or mainly of his power, and overlook those attributes of rectitude and goodness, to which he subjects his omnipotence, and which are the foundations and very substance of his universal and immutable Law. And are these attributes revealed to us through the principles and convictions of our own souls? Do we understand through sympathy God's perception of the right, the good, the holy, the just? Then with what propriety is it said, that in his own image he made man!

I am aware, that it may be objected to these views, that we receive our idea of God from the universe, from his works, and not so exclusively from our own souls. The universe, I know, is full of God. The heavens and earth declare his glory. In other words, the effects and signs of power, wisdom, and goodness, are apparent through the whole creation. But apparent to what? Not to the outward eye; not to the acutest organs of sense; but to a kindred mind, which interprets the universe by itself. It is only through that energy of thought, by which we adapt various and complicated means to distant ends, and give harmony and a common bearing to multiplied exertions, that we understand the creative intelligence which has established the order, dependencies, and harmony of nature. We see God around us, because he dwells within us. It is by a kindred wisdom, that we discern his wisdom in his works. The brute, with an eye as piercing as ours, looks on the universe; and the page, which to us is radiant with characters of greatness and goodness, is to him a blank. In truth, the beauty and glory of God's works, are revealed to the mind by a light beaming from itself. We discern the impress of God's attributes in the universe, by accordance of nature, and enjoy them through sympathy.—I hardly need observe, that these remarks in relation to the universe apply with equal, if not greater force, to revelation.

I shall now be met by another objection, which to many may seem strong. It will be said, that these various attributes of which I have spoken, exist in God in Infinite Perfection, and that this destroys all affinity between the human and the Divine mind. To this I have two replies. In the first place, an attribute, by becoming perfect, does not part with its essence. Love, wisdom, power, and purity do not change their nature by enlargement. If they did, we should lose the Supreme Being through his very infinity. Our ideas of him would fade away into mere sounds. For example, if wisdom in God, because unbounded, have no affinity with that attribute in man, why apply to him that term? It must signify nothing. Let me ask what we mean, when we say that we discern the marks of intelligence in the universe? We mean, that we meet there the proofs of a mind like our own. We certainly discern proofs of no other; so that to deny this doctrine would be to deny the evidences of a God, and utterly to subvert the foundations of religious belief. What man can examine the structure of a plant or an animal, and see the adaptation of its parts to each other and to common ends, and not feel, that it is the work of an intelligence akin to his own, and that he traces these marks of design by the same spiritual energy in which they had their origin?

But I would offer another answer to this objection, that God's infinity places him beyond the resemblance and approach of man. I affirm, and trust that I do not speak too strongly, that there are traces of infinity in the human mind; and that, in this very respect, it bears a likeness to God. The very conception of infinity, is the mark of a nature to which no limit can be prescribed. This thought, indeed, comes to us, not so much from abroad, as from our own souls. We ascribe this attribute to God, because we possess capacities and wants, which only an unbounded being can fill, and because we are conscious of a tendency in spiritual faculties to unlimited expansion. We believe in the Divine infinity, through something congenial with it in our own breasts. I hope I speak clearly, and if not, I would ask those to whom I am obscure, to pause before they condemn. To me it seems, that the soul, in all its higher actions, in original thought, in the creations of genius, in the soarings of imagination, in its love of beauty and grandeur, in its aspirations after a pure and unknown joy, and especially in disinterestedness, in the spirit of self-sacrifice, and in enlightened devotion, has a character of infinity. There is often a depth in human love, which may be strictly called unfathomable. There is sometimes a lofty strength in moral principle, which all the power of the outward universe cannot overcome. There seems a might within, which can more than balance all might without. There is, too, a piety, which swells into a transport too vast for utterance, and into an immeasurable joy. I am speaking, indeed, of what is uncommon, but still of realities. We see, however, the tendency of the soul to the infinite, in more familiar and ordinary forms. Take, for example, the delight which we find in the vast scenes of nature, in prospects which spread around us without limits, in the immensity of the heavens and the ocean, and especially in the rush and roar of mighty winds, waves, and torrents, when, amidst our deep awe, a power within seems to respond to the omnipotence around us. The same principle is seen in the delight ministered to us by works of fiction or of imaginative art, in which our own nature is set before us in more than human beauty and power. In truth, the soul is always bursting its limits. It thirsts continually for wider knowledge. It rushes forward to untried happiness. It has deep wants, which nothing limited can appease. Its true element and end is an unbounded good. Thus, God's infinity has its image in the soul; and through the soul, much more than through the universe, we arrive at this conception of the Deity.

In these remarks I have spoken strongly. But I have no fear of expressing too strongly the connexion between the Divine and the human mind. My only fear is, that I shall dishonor the great subject. The danger to which we are most exposed, is that of severing the Creator from his creatures. The propensity of human sovereigns to cut off communication between themselves and their subjects, and to disclaim a common nature with their inferiors, has led the multitude of men, who think of God chiefly under the character of a king, to conceive of him as a being who places his glory in multiplying distinctions between himself and all other beings. The truth is, that the union between the Creator and the creature surpasses all other bonds in strength and intimacy. He penetrates all things, and delights to irradiate all with his glory. Nature, in all its lowest and inanimate forms, is pervaded by his power; and, when quickened by the mysterious property of life, how wonderfully does it show forth the perfections of its Author! How much of God may be seen in the structure of a single leaf, which, though so frail as to tremble in every wind, yet holds connexions and living communications with the earth, the air, the clouds, and the distant sun, and, through these sympathies with the universe, is itself a revelation of an omnipotent mind! God delights to diffuse himself everywhere. Through his energy, unconscious matter clothes itself with proportions, powers, and beauties, which reflect his wisdom and love. How much more must he delight to frame conscious and happy recipients of his perfections, in whom his wisdom and love may substantially dwell, with whom he may form spiritual ties, and to whom he may be an everlasting spring of moral energy and happiness! How far the Supreme Being may communicate his attributes to his intelligent offspring, I stop not to inquire. But that his almighty goodness will impart to them powers and glories, of which the material universe is but a faint emblem, I cannot doubt. That the soul, if true to itself and its Maker, will be filled with God, and will manifest him, more than the sun, I cannot doubt. Who can doubt it, that believes and understands the doctrine of human immortality? . . .

I conclude with saying, let the minister cherish a reverence for his own nature. Let him never despise it even in its most forbidding forms. Let him delight in its beautiful and lofty manifestations. Let him hold fast as one of the great qualifications for his office, a faith in the greatness of the human soul, that faith, which looks beneath the perishing body, beneath the sweat of the laborer, beneath the rags and ignorance of the poor, beneath the vices of the sensual and selfish, and discerns in the depths of the soul a divine principle, a ray of the Infinite Light, which may yet break forth and "shine as the sun"[8] in the kingdom of God. Let him strive to awaken in men a consciousness of the heavenly treasure within them, a consciousness of possessing what is of more worth than the outward universe. Let hope give life to all his labors. Let him speak to men, as to beings liberally gifted, and made for God. Let him always look round on a congregation with the encouraging trust, that he has hearers prepared to respond to the simple, unaffected utterance of great truths, and to the noblest workings of his own mind. Let him feel deeply for those, in whom the divine nature is overwhelmed by the passions. Let him sympathize tenderly with those, in whom it begins to struggle, to mourn for sin, to thirst for a new life. Let him guide and animate to higher and diviner virtue, those in whom it has gained strength. Let him strive to infuse courage, enterprise, devout trust, and an inflexible will, into men's labors for their own perfection. In one word, let him cherish an unfaltering and growing faith in God as the Father and quickener of the human mind, and in Christ as its triumphant and immortal friend. That by such preaching he is to work miracles, I do not say. That he will rival in sudden and outward effects what is wrought by the preachers of a low and terrifying theology, I do not expect or desire. That all will be made better, I am far from believing. His office is, to act on free beings, who, after all, must determine themselves; who have the power to withstand all foreign agency; who are to be saved, not by mere preaching, but by their own prayers and toil. Still I believe that such a minister will be a benefactor beyond all praise to the human soul. I believe, and know, that, on those who will admit his influence, he will work deeply, powerfully, gloriously. His function is the sublimest under heaven; and his reward will be, a growing power of spreading truth, virtue, moral strength, love, and happiness, without limit and without end.

—1828

---

8. Matthew 13.43.

from Self-Culture[1]

MY RESPECTED FRIENDS:

By the invitation of the committee of arrangements for the Franklin lectures, I now appear before you to offer some remarks introductory to this course. My principal inducement for so doing is my deep interest in those of my fellow citizens, for whom these lectures are principally designed. I understood that they were to be attended chiefly by those, who are occupied by manual labor; and, hearing this, I did not feel myself at liberty to decline the service, to which I had been invited. I wished by compliance to express my sympathy with this large portion of my race. I wished to express my sense of obligation to those, from whose industry and skill I derive almost all the comforts of life. I wished still more to express my joy in the efforts they are making for their own improvement, and my firm faith in their success. These motives will give a particular character and bearing to some of my remarks. I shall speak occasionally as among those who live by the labor of their hands. But I shall not speak as one separated from them. I belong rightfully to the great fraternity of working men. Happily in this community we all are bred and born to work; and this honorable mark, set on us all, should bind together the various portions of the community.

I have expressed my strong interest in the mass of the people; and this is founded not on their usefulness to the community so much as on what they are in themselves. Their condition is indeed obscure; but their importance is not on this account a whit the less. The multitude of men cannot from the nature of the case be distinguished; for the very idea of distinction is, that a man stands out from the multitude. They make little noise and draw little notice in their narrow spheres of action; but still they have their full proportion of personal worth and even of greatness. Indeed every man, in every condition, is great. It is only our own diseased sight which makes him little. A man is great as a man, be he where or what he may. The grandeur of his nature turns to insignificance all outward distinctions. His powers of intellect, of conscience, of love, of knowing God, of perceiving the beautiful, of acting on his own mind, on outward nature, and on his fellow creatures, these are glorious prerogatives. Through the vulgar error of undervaluing what is common, we are apt indeed to pass these by as of little worth. But as in the outward creation, so in the soul, the common is the most precious. Science and art may invent splendid modes of illuminating the apartments of the opulent; but these are all poor and worthless, compared with the common light which the sun sends into all our windows, which he pours freely, impartially over hill and valley, which kindles daily the eastern and western sky; and so the common lights of reason, and conscience, and love are of more worth and dignity than the rare endowments which give celebrity to a few. Let us not disparage that nature which is common to all men; for no thought can measure its grandeur. It is the image of God, the image even of his infinity, for no limits can be set to its unfolding. He who possesses the divine powers of the soul is a great being, be his place what it may. You may clothe him with rags, may immerse him in a dungeon, may chain him to slavish tasks. But he is still great. You may shut him out of your houses; but God opens to him heavenly mansions. He makes no show indeed in the streets of a splendid city; but a clear thought, a pure affection, a resolute act of a virtuous will have a dignity of quite another kind and far higher

---

1. An address delivered in Boston, September 1838.

than accumulations of brick and granite and plaster and stucco, however cunningly put together, or though stretching far beyond our sight. Nor is this all. If we pass over this grandeur of our common nature, and turn our thoughts to that comparative greatness, which draws chief attention, and which consists in the decided superiority of the individual to the general standard of power and character, we shall find this as free and frequent a growth among the obscure and unnoticed as in more conspicuous walks of life. The truly great are to be found every where, nor is it easy to say, in what condition they spring up most plentifully. Real greatness has nothing to do with a man's sphere. It does not lie in the magnitude of his outward agency, in the extent of the effects which he produces. The greatest men may do comparatively little abroad. Perhaps the greatest in our city at this moment are buried in obscurity. Grandeur of character lies wholly in force of soul, that is, in the force of thought, moral principle and love, and this may be found in the humblest condition of life. A man brought up to an obscure trade, and hemmed in by the wants of a growing family, may, in his narrow sphere, perceive more clearly, discriminate more keenly, weigh evidence more wisely, seize on the right means more decisively, and have more presence of mind in difficulty, than another who has accumulated vast stores of knowledge by laborious study; and he has more of intellectual greatness. Many a man, who has gone but a few miles from home, understands human nature better, detects motives and weighs character more sagaciously, than another, who has travelled over the known world, and made a name by his reports of different countries. It is force of thought which measures intellectual, and so it is force of principle which measures moral greatness, that highest of human endowments, that brightest manifestation of the Divinity. The greatest man is he who chooses the Right with invincible resolution, who resists the sorest temptations from within and without, who bears the heaviest burdens cheerfully, who is calmest in storms and most fearless under menace and frowns, whose reliance on truth, on virtue, on God is most unfaltering; and is this a greatness, which is apt to make a show, or which is most likely to abound in conspicuous station. The solemn conflicts of reason with passion; the victories of moral and religious principle over urgent and almost irresistible solicitations to self-indulgence; the hardest sacrifices of duty, those of deep-seated affection and of the heart's fondest hopes; the consolations, hopes, joys, and peace of disappointed, persecuted, scorned, deserted virtue; these are of course unseen; so that the true greatness of human life is almost wholly out of sight. Perhaps in our presence, the most heroic deed on earth is done in some silent spirit, the loftiest purpose cherished, the most generous sacrifice made, and we do not suspect it. I believe this greatness to be most common among the multitude, whose names are never heard. Among common people will be found more of hardship borne manfully, more of unvarnished truth, more of religious trust, more of that generosity which gives what the giver needs himself, and more of a wise estimate of life and death, than among the more prosperous.—And even in regard to influence over other beings, which is thought the peculiar prerogative of distinguished station, I believe, that the difference between the conspicuous and the obscure does not amount to much. Influence is to be measured, not by the extent of purpose it covers, but by its *kind*. A man may spread his mind, his feelings and opinions through a great extent; but if his mind be a low one, he manifests no greatness. A wretched artist may fill a city with daubs,[2] and by a false showy style achieve a reputation; but the man

---

2. Poorly made paintings.

of genius, who leaves behind him one grand picture, in which immortal beauty is embodied, and which is silently to spread a true taste in his art, exerts an incomparably higher influence. Now the noblest influence on earth is that exerted on character; and he, who puts forth this, does a great work, no matter how narrow or obscure his sphere. The father and mother of an unnoticed family who, in their seclusion, awaken the mind of one child to the idea and love of perfect goodness, who awaken in him a strength of will to repel all temptation, and who send him out prepared to profit by the conflicts of life, surpass in influence a Napoleon[3] breaking the world to his sway. And not only is their work higher in kind; who knows, but that they are doing a greater work even as to extent or surface than the conqueror? Who knows, but that the being, whom they inspire with holy and disinterested principles, may communicate himself to others; and that by a spreading agency, of which they were the silent origin, improvements may spread through a nation, through the world? In these remarks you will see why I feel and express a deep interest in the obscure, in the mass of men. The distinctions of society vanish before the light of these truths. I attach myself to the multitude, not because they are voters and have political power; but because they are men, and have within their reach the most glorious prizes of humanity.

In this country the mass of the people are distinguished by possessing means of improvement, of self-culture, possessed no where else. To incite them to the use of these, is to render them the best service they can receive. Accordingly I have chosen for the subject of this lecture, Self-culture, or the care which every man owes to himself, to the unfolding and perfecting of his nature. . . .

Before entering on the discussion, let me offer one remark. Self-culture is something possible. It is not a dream. It has foundations in our nature. Without this conviction, the speaker will but declaim, and the hearer listen without profit. There are two powers of the human soul which make self-culture possible, the self-searching and the self-forming power. We have first the faculty of turning the mind on itself; of recalling its past, and watching its present operations; of learning its various capacities and susceptibilities, what it can do and bear, what it can enjoy and suffer; and of thus learning in general what our nature is, and what it was made for. It is worthy of observation, that we are able to discern not only what we already are, but what we may become, to see in ourselves germs and promises of a growth to which no bounds can be set, to dart beyond what we have actually gained to the idea of Perfection as the end of our being. It is by this self-comprehending power that we are distinguished from the brutes, which give no signs of looking into themselves. Without this there would be no self-culture, for we should not know the work to be done; and one reason why self-culture is so little proposed is, that so few penetrate into their own nature. To most men, their own spirits are shadowy, unreal, compared with what is outward. When they happen to cast a glance inward, they see there only a dark, vague chaos. They distinguish perhaps some violent passion, which has driven them to injurious excess; but their highest powers hardly attract a thought; and thus multitudes live and die as truly strangers to themselves, as to countries, of which they have heard the name, but which human foot has never trodden.

But self-culture is possible, not only because we can enter into and search ourselves. We have a still nobler power, that of acting on, determining and forming our-

---

3. Napoleon Bonaparte (1769–1821), Emperor of post-Revolutionary France.

selves. This is a fearful as well as glorious endowment, for it is the ground of human responsibility. We have the power not only of tracing our powers, but of guiding and impelling them, not only of watching our passions, but of controlling them, not only of seeing our faculties grow, but of applying to them means and influences to aid their growth. We can stay or change the current of thought. We can concentrate the intellect on objects which we wish to comprehend. We can fix our eyes on perfection and make almost every thing speed us towards it. This is indeed a noble prerogative of our nature. Possessing this, it matters little what or where we are now, for we can conquer a better lot, and even be happier for starting from the lowest point. Of all the discoveries which men need to make, the most important at the present moment, is that of the self-forming power treasured up in themselves. They little suspect its extent, as little as the savage apprehends the energy which the mind is created to exert on the material world. It transcends in importance all our power over outward nature. There is more of divinity in it, than in the force which impels the outward universe; and yet how little we comprehend it! How it slumbers in most men unsuspected, unused! This makes self-culture possible, and binds it on us as a solemn duty.

I. I am first to unfold the idea of self-culture; and this, in its most general form, may easily be seized. To cultivate any thing, be it a plant, an animal, a mind, is to make grow. Growth, expansion is the end. Nothing admits culture, but that which has a principle of life, capable of being expanded. He, therefore, who does what he can to unfold all his powers and capacities, especially his nobler ones, so as to become a well proportioned, vigorous, excellent, happy being, practises self-culture.

This culture of course has various branches corresponding to the different capacities of human nature; but though various, they are intimately united and make progress together. The soul which our philosophy divides into various capacities, is still one essence, one life; and it exerts at the same moment, and blends in the same act its various energies of thought, feeling and volition. Accordingly in a wise self-culture all the principles of our nature grow at once by joining harmonious action, just as all parts of the plant are unfolded together. When therefore you hear of different branches of self-improvement, you will not think of them as distinct processes going on independently on each other, and requiring each its own separate means. Still a distinct consideration of these is needed to a full comprehension of the subject, and these I shall proceed to unfold.

First, self-culture is Moral, a branch of singular importance. When a man looks into himself he discovers two distant orders or kinds of principles, which it behooves him especially to comprehend. He discovers desires, appetites, passions which terminate in himself, which crave and seek his own interest, gratification, distinction; and he discovers another principle, an antagonist to these, which is Impartial, Disinterested, Universal, enjoining on him a regard to the rights and happiness of other beings, and laying on him obligations which *must* be discharged, cost what they may, or however they may clash with his particular pleasure or gain. No man, however narrowed to his own interest, however hardened by selfishness, can deny, that there springs up within him a great idea in opposition to interest, the idea of Duty, that an inward voice calls him more or less distinctly to revere and exercise Impartial Justice, and Universal Good-will. This disinterested principle in human nature we call sometimes reason, sometimes conscience, sometimes the moral sense or faculty.

But, be its name what it may, it is a real principle in each of us, and it is the supreme power within us, to be cultivated above all others, for on its culture the right development of all others depends. The passions indeed may be stronger than the conscience, may lift up a louder voice; but their clamour differs wholly from the tone of command in which the conscience speaks. They are not clothed with its authority, its binding power. In their very triumphs they are rebuked by the moral principle, and often cower before its still deep menacing voice. No part of self-knowledge is more important than to discern clearly these two great principles, the self-seeking and the disinterested; and the most important part of self-culture is to depress the former, and to exalt the latter, or to enthrone the sense of duty within us. There are no limits to the growth of this moral force in man, if he will cherish it faithfully. There have been men, whom no power in the universe could turn from the Right, to whom death in its most dreadful forms has been less dreaded, than transgression of the inward law of universal justice and love.

In the next place, self-culture is Religious. When we look into ourselves we discover powers, which link us with this outward, visible, finite, ever changing world. We have sight and other senses to discern, and limbs and various faculties to secure and appropriate the material creation. And we have too a power, which cannot stop at what we see and handle, at what exists within the bounds of space and time, which seeks for the Infinite, Uncreated cause, which cannot rest till it ascend to the Eternal, All-comprehending Mind. This we call the religious principle, and its grandeur cannot be exaggerated by human language; for it marks out a being destined for higher communion than with the visible universe. To develop this, is eminently to educate ourselves. The true idea of God, unfolded clearly and livingly within us, and moving us to adore and obey him, and to aspire after likeness to him, is the noblest growth in human, and I may add, in celestial natures. The religious principle, and the moral, are intimately connected, and grow together. The former is indeed the perfection and highest manifestation of the latter. They are both disinterested. It is the essence of true religion to recognize and adore in God the attributes of Impartial Justice and Universal Love, and to hear him commanding us in the conscience to become what we adore.

Again. Self-culture is Intellectual. We cannot look into ourselves without discovering the intellectual principle, the power which thinks, reasons, and judges, the power of seeking and acquiring truth. This indeed we are in no danger of overlooking. The intellect being the great instrument by which men compass their wishes, it draws more attention than any of our other powers. When we speak to men of improving themselves, the first thought which occurs to them is, that they must cultivate their understanding, and get knowledge and skill. By education, men mean almost exclusively intellectual training. For this, schools and colleges are instituted, and to this the moral and religious discipline of the young is sacrificed. Now I reverence, as much as any man, the intellect; but let us never exalt it above the moral principle. With this it is most intimately connected. In this its culture is founded, and to exalt this is its highest aim. Whoever desires that his intellect may grow up to soundness, to healthy vigour, must begin with moral discipline. Reading and study are not enough to perfect the power of thought. One thing above all is needful, and that is, the Disinterestedness which is the very soul of virtue. To gain truth, which is the great object of the understanding, I must seek it disinterestedly. Here is the first and grand condition of intellectual progress. I must choose to receive the truth, no matter how it bears on myself. I must follow it, no matter where it leads, what interests it opposes, to what persecution or loss it lays me open, from what party it severs me, or to what party it allies. Without this fairness of mind, which is only another phrase for disinterested love of truth, great native powers of understanding are perverted and lead astray; genius runs wild; "the light within us becomes darkness."[4] The subtlest reasoners, for want of this, cheat themselves as well as others, and become entangled in the web of their own sophistry. It is a fact well known in the history of science and philosophy, that men, gifted by nature with singular intelligence, have broached the grossest errors, and even sought to undermine the grand primitive truths on which human virtue, dignity and hope depend. And on the other hand, I have known instances of men of naturally moderate powers of mind, who by a disinterested love of truth and their fellow creatures, have gradually risen to no small force and enlargement of thought. Some of the most useful teachers in the pulpit and in schools, have owed their power of enlightening others, not so much to any natural superiority, as to the simplicity, impartiality and disinterestedness of their minds, to their readiness to live and die for the truth. A man, who rises above himself, looks from an eminence on nature and providence, on society and life. Thought expands as by a natural elasticity, when the pressure of selfishness is removed. The moral and religious principles of the soul, generously cultivated, fertilize the intellect. Duty, faithfully performed, opens the mind to Truth, both being of one family, alike immutable, universal and everlasting. . . .

II. I now proceed to enquire into the Means by which the self-culture, just described, may be promoted; and here I know not where to begin. The subject is so extensive, as well as important, that I feel myself unable to do any justice to it, especially in the limits to which I am confined. I beg you to consider me as presenting but hints, and such as have offered themselves with very little research to my own mind. . . .

One thing is essential to the strong purpose of self-culture now insisted on, namely, faith in the practicableness of this culture. A great object, to awaken resolute choice, must be seen to be within our reach. The truth, that progress is the very end of our being, must not be received as a tradition, but comprehended and felt as a reality. Our minds are apt to pine and starve, by being imprisoned within what we have already attained. A true faith, looking up to something better, catching glimpses of a distant perfection, prophesying to ourselves improvements proportioned to our conscientious labors, gives energy of purpose, gives wings to the soul; and this faith will continually grow, by acquainting ourselves with our own nature, and with the promises of divine help and immortal life which abound in revelation. . . .

The purpose of self-culture, this is the life and strength of all the methods we use for our own elevation. I reiterate this principle on account of its great importance; and I would add a remark to prevent its misapprehension. When I speak of the purpose of self-culture, I mean, that it should be sincere. In other words, we must make self-culture really and truly our end, or choose it for its own sake, and not merely as a means or instrument of something else. And here I touch a common and

---

4. Matthew 6.22–23.

very pernicious error. Not a few persons desire to improve themselves only to get property and to rise in the world; but such do not properly choose improvement, but something outward and foreign to themselves; and so low an impulse can produce only a stinted, partial, uncertain growth. A man, as I have said, is to cultivate himself because he is a man. He is to start with the conviction, that there is something greater within him than in the whole material creation, than in all the worlds which press on the eye and ear; and that inward improvements have a worth and dignity in themselves, quite distinct from the power they give over outward things. Undoubtedly a man is to labor to better his condition, but first to better himself. If he knows no higher use of his mind than to invent and drudge for his body, his case is desperate as far as culture is concerned.

In these remarks, I do not mean to recommend to the laborer indifference to his outward lot. I hold it important, that every man in every class should possess the means of comfort, of health, of neatness in food and apparel, and of occasional retirement and leisure. These are good in themselves, to be sought for their own sakes, and still more, they are important means of the self-culture for which I am pleading. A clean, comfortable dwelling, with wholesome meals, is no small aid to intellectual and moral progress. A man living in a damp cellar or a garret open to rain and snow, breathing the foul air of a filthy room, and striving without success to appease hunger on scanty or unsavoury food, is in danger of abandoning himself to a desperate, selfish recklessness. Improve then your lot. Multiply comforts, and still more get wealth if you can by honorable means, and if it do not cost too much. A true cultivation of the mind is fitted to forward you in your worldly concerns, and you ought to use it for this end. Only, beware, lest this end master you; lest your motives sink as your condition improves; lest you fall victims to the miserable passion of vying with those around you in show, luxury and expense. Cherish a true respect for yourselves. Feel that your nature is worth more than every thing which is foreign to you. He who has not caught a glimpse of his own rational and spiritual being, of something within himself superior to the world and allied to the divinity, wants the true spring of that purpose of self-culture, on which I have insisted as the first of all the means of improvement. . . .

I have time to consider but one more means of self-culture. We find it in our Free Government, in our Political relations and duties. It is a great benefit of free institutions, that they do much to awaken and keep in action a nation's mind. We are told, that the education of the multitude is necessary to the support of a republic; but it is equally true, that a republic is a powerful means of educating the multitude. It is the people's University. In a free state, solemn responsibilities are imposed on every citizen; great subjects are to be discussed; great interests to be decided. The individual is called to determine measures affecting the well-being of millions and the destinies of posterity. He must consider not only the internal relations of his native land, but its connexion with foreign states, and judge of a policy which touches the whole civilized world. He is called by his participation in the national sovereignty, to cherish public spirit, a regard to the general weal. A man who purposes to discharge faithfully these obligations, is carrying on a generous self-culture. The great public questions, which divide opinion around him and provoke earnest discussion, of necessity invigorate his intellect, and accustom him to look beyond himself. He grows up to a robustness, force, enlargement of mind, unknown under despotic rule. . . .

Among the best people, especially among the more religious, there are some, who, through disgust with the violence and frauds of parties, withdraw themselves from all political action. Such, I conceive, do wrong. God has placed them in the relations, and imposed on them the duties of citizens; and they are no more authorized to shrink from these duties than from those of sons, husbands, or fathers. They owe a great debt to their country, and must discharge it by giving support to what they deem the best men and the best measures. Nor let them say, that they can do nothing. Every good man, if faithful to his convictions, benefits his country. All parties are kept in check by the spirit of the better portion of people, whom they contain. Leaders are always compelled to ask what their party will bear, and to modify their measures, so as not to shock the men of principle within their ranks. A good man, not tamely subservient to the body with which he acts, but judging it impartially, criticising it freely, bearing testimony against its evils, and withholding his support from wrong, does good to those around him, and is cultivating generously his own mind. . . .

One important topic remains. That great means of self-improvement, Christianity, is yet untouched, and its greatness forbids me now to approach it. I will only say, that if you study Christianity in its original records and not in human creeds; if you consider its clear revelations of God, its life-giving promises of pardon and spiritual strength, its correspondence to man's reason, conscience and best affections, and its adaptation to his wants, sorrows, anxieties and fears; if you consider the strength of its proofs, the purity of its precepts, the divine greatness of the character of its author, and the immortality which it opens before us, you will feel yourselves bound to welcome it joyfully, gratefully, as affording aids and incitements to self-culture, which would vainly be sought in all other means.

I have thus presented a few of the means of self-culture. The topics, now discussed, will I hope suggest others to those who have honored me with their attention, and create an interest which will extend beyond the present hour. I owe it however to truth to make one remark. I wish to raise no unreasonable hopes. I must say then, that the means, now recommended to you, though they will richly reward every man of every age who will faithfully use them, will yet not produce their full and happiest effect, except in cases where early education has prepared the mind for future improvement. They, whose childhood has been neglected, though they may make progress in future life, can hardly repair the loss of their first years; and I say this, that we may all be excited to save our children from this loss, that we may prepare them, to the extent of our power, for an effectual use of all the means of self-culture, which adult age may bring with it. With these views, I ask you to look with favor on the recent exertions of our legislature and of private citizens, in behalf of our public schools, the chief hope of our country. The legislature has of late appointed a board of education, with a secretary, who is to devote his whole time to the improvement of public schools. An individual more fitted to this responsible office, than the gentleman who now fills it,[5] cannot, I believe, be found in our community; and if his labors shall be crowned with success, he will earn a title to the gratitude of the good people of this State, unsurpassed by that of any other living citizen. Let me also recall to your minds a munificent individual,[6] who, by a generous donation, has encouraged

---

5. Horace Mann (1796–1859), educational reformer.   6. Edmund Dwight (1789–1841), Boston philanthropist.

the legislature to resolve on the establishment of one or more institutions called Normal Schools, the object of which is, to prepare accomplished teachers of youth, a work, on which the progress of education depends more than on any other measure. The efficient friends of education are the true benefactors of their country, and their names deserve to be handed down to that posterity, for whose highest wants they are generously providing.

There is another mode of advancing education in our whole country, to which I ask your particular attention. You are aware of the vast extent and value of the public lands of the Union. By annual sales of these, large amounts of money are brought into the national treasury, which are applied to the current expenses of the Government. For this application there is no need. In truth, the country has received detriment from the excess of its revenues. Now, I ask, why shall not the public lands be consecrated, (in whole or in part, as the case may require,) to the education of the people? This measure would secure at once what the country most needs, that is, able, accomplished, quickening teachers of the whole rising generation. The present poor remuneration of instructers is a dark omen, and the only real obstacle which the cause of education has to contend with. We need for our schools gifted men and women, worthy, by their intelligence and their moral power, to be entrusted with a nation's youth; and to gain these we must pay them liberally, as well as afford other proofs of the consideration in which we hold them. In the present state of the country, when so many paths of wealth and promotion are opened, superior men cannot be won to an office so responsible and laborious as that of teaching, without stronger inducements than are now offered, except in some of our large cities. The office of instructer ought to rank and be recompensed as one of the most honorable in society; and I see not how this is to be done, at least in our day, without appropriating to it the public domain. This is the people's property, and the only part of their property which is likely to be soon devoted to the support of a high order of institutions for public education. This object, interesting to all classes of society, has peculiar claims on those whose means of improvement are restricted by narrow circumstances. The mass of the people should devote themselves to it as one man, should toil for it with one soul. Mechanics, Farmers, Laborers! Let the country echo with your united cry, "The Public Lands for Education." Send to the public councils men who will plead this cause with power. No party triumphs, no trades-unions, no associations, can so contribute to elevate you as the measure now proposed. Nothing but a higher education can raise you in influence and true dignity. . . .

But some will say, "Be it granted that the working classes may find some leisure; should they not be allowed to spend it in relaxation? Is it not cruel, to summon them from toils of the hand to toils of the mind? They have earned pleasure by the day's toil and ought to partake it." Yes, let them have pleasure. Far be it from me to dry up the fountains, to blight the spots of verdure,[7] where they refresh themselves after life's labors. But I maintain, that self-culture multiplies and increases their pleasures, that it creates new capacities of enjoyment, that it saves their leisure from being, what it too often is, dull and wearisome, that it saves them from rushing for excitement to indulgences destructive to body and soul. It is one of the great benefits of self-improvement, that it raises a people above the gratifications of the brute, and gives

---

7. Greenery.

them pleasures worthy of men. In consequence of the present intellectual culture of our country, imperfect as it is, a vast amount of enjoyment is communicated to men, women and children, of all conditions, by books, an enjoyment unknown to ruder times. At this moment, a number of gifted writers are employed in multiplying entertaining works. Walter Scott,[8] a name conspicuous among the brightest of his day, poured out his inexhaustible mind in fictions, at once so sportive and thrilling, that they have taken their place among the delights of all civilized nations. How many millions have been chained to his pages! How many melancholy spirits has he steeped in forgetfulness of their cares and sorrows! What multitudes, wearied by their day's work, have owed some bright evening hours and balmier sleep to his magical creations! And not only do fictions give pleasure. In proportion as the mind is cultivated, it takes delight in history and biography, in descriptions of nature, in travels, in poetry, and even graver works. Is the laborer then defrauded of pleasure by improvement? There is another class of gratifications to which self-culture introduces the mass of the people. I refer to lectures, discussions, meetings of associations for benevolent and literary purposes, and to other like methods of passing the evening, which every year is multiplying among us. A popular address from an enlightened man, who has the tact to reach the minds of the people, is a high gratification, as well as a source of knowledge. . . .

* * *

I conclude with recalling to you the happiest feature of our age, and that is, the progress of the mass of the people in intelligence, self-respect, and all the comforts of life. What a contrast does the present form with past times! Not many ages ago, the nation was the property of one man, and all its interests were staked in perpetual games of war, for no end but to build up his family, or to bring new territories under his yoke. Society was divided into two classes, the highborn and the vulgar, separated from one another by a great gulph, as impassable as that between the saved and the lost. The people had no significance as individuals, but formed a mass, a machine, to be wielded at pleasure by their lords. In war, which was the great sport of the times, those brave knights, of whose prowess we hear, cased themselves and their horses in armour, so as to be almost invulnerable, whilst the common people on foot were left, without protection, to be hewn in pieces or trampled down by their betters. Who, that compares the condition of Europe a few ages ago, with the present state of the world, but must bless God for the change. The grand distinction of modern times is, the emerging of the people from brutal degradation, the gradual recognition of their rights, the gradual diffusion among them of the means of improvement and happiness, the creation of a new power in the state, the power of the people. And it is worthy remark, that this revolution is due in a great degree to religion, which, in the hands of the crafty and aspiring, had bowed the multitude to the dust, but which, in the fullness of time, began to fulfil its mission of freedom. It was religion, which, by teaching men their near relation to God, awakened in them the consciousness of their importance as individuals. It was the struggle for religious rights, which opened men's eyes to all their rights. It was resistance to religious usurpation, which led men to withstand political oppression. It was religious discussion, which roused the minds of all classes to free and vigorous thought. It was

---

8. Sir Walter Scott (1771–1832), Scottish novelist and poet.

religion, which armed the martyr and patriot in England against arbitrary power, which braced the spirits of our fathers against the perils of the ocean and wilderness, and sent them to found here the freest and most equal state on earth.

Let us thank God for what has been gained. But let us not think every thing gained. Let the people feel that they have only started in the race. How much remains to be done! What a vast amount of ignorance, intemperance, coarseness, sensuality, may still be found in our community! What a vast amount of mind is palsied and lost! When we think that every house might be cheered by intelligence, disinterestedness and refinement, and then remember, in how many houses the higher powers and affections of human nature are buried as in tombs, what a darkness gathers over society. And how few of us are moved by this moral desolation? How few understand, that to raise the depressed, by a wise culture, to the dignity of men, is the highest end of the social state? Shame on us, that the worth of a fellow creature is so little felt.

I would, that I could speak with an awakening voice to the people, of their wants, their privileges, their responsibilities. I would say to them, You cannot, without guilt and disgrace, stop where you are. The past and the present call on you to advance. Let what you have gained be an impulse to something higher. Your nature is too great to be crushed. You were not created what you are, merely to toil, eat, drink and sleep, like the inferior animals. If you will, you can rise. No power in society, no hardship in your condition can depress you, keep you down, in knowledge, power, virtue, influence, but by your own consent. Do not be lulled to sleep by the flatteries which you hear, as if your participation in the national sovereignty made you equal to the noblest of your race. You have many and great deficiencies to be remedied; and the remedy lies, not in the ballot box, not in the exercise of your political powers, but in the faithful education of yourselves and your children. These truths you have often heard and slept over. Awake! Resolve earnestly on Self-culture. Make yourselves worthy of your free institutions, and strengthen and perpetuate them by your intelligence and your virtues.

—1838

⸻ TRANSATLANTIC EXCHANGES ⸻
Religion and Revivalism

The Puritans who set sail from Plymouth, England, and settled in Plymouth, Massachusetts, brought their religion with them. Geographical space in America came to represent religious freedom for colonists who had come to the country's shores to escape persecution in their native countries. However, the Puritans formed a theocracy (government by religion) in America that proved to be just as intolerant of those betraying its religious edicts as the government of their former country had been of them. America was perceived as the New Eden, and the Puritans thought of themselves as the elect who were meant to erect a "city on a hill" that was to be an example to all nations. This was not the first time nor would it be the last that religion would become a force of oppression and domination of those not deemed among the elect.

Puritanism was not the only sect of Christianity to cross the Atlantic and take root in America. Quakers, who believed that each individual was guided by an inner light, settled in vast numbers in Philadelphia, Pennsylvania, and elsewhere, voicing early and consistently their opposition to slavery. John Wesley and George Whitefield challenged Puritanism. The Anglican ministers came to America and preached a message of the powerful awakening of spirituality in each individual through a personal relationship with Jesus, which was aptly termed the Great Awakening. Borrowing preaching techniques from Welsh revivalists, these men gave emotionally charged sermons to crowds so large that the churches overflowed, forcing the congregations to gather in open fields. The Great Awakening, with its emphasis on the intrinsic worth of every soul, was an important influence on the notion of individual rights that underpinned the Declaration of Independence.

The message of Wesley and Whitefield hit home in the African American community. Several prominent abolitionists and writers, such as Phillis Wheatley and Olaudah Equiano, explained the role that Whitefield played in their conversions. The writings of the earliest Africans, Afro-Caribbeans, Afro-British, Afro-Canadians, and Afro-Americans constitute a major yet comparatively unsung contribution to the theology of the period. Writers such as Quobna Ottobah Cugoano, Equiano, Ukawsaw Gronniosaw, John Marrant, and Wheatley settled in various places on the Atlantic Rim, evincing a cultural as well as religious hybridity. The Christianity of these writers is fused with the various beliefs held by their ancestral tribes in Africa. Many people mixed Protestant and tribal beliefs and others; for example, communities in Louisiana and Catholic colonies in the Caribbean mixed Catholicism and practices of "conjure magic." Central to all of these new forms of Christianity was the development of a theology of liberation. Exodus in the Torah and the Passion of the New Testament had a special significance for those who were seeking to bring about liberation from systematic oppression by the laws, governments, economics, and cultures of nations whose Christianity buttressed racial supremacy. This radical element took the Enlightenment notion of human rights many steps further, rejecting Whitefield's acceptance of slavery and insisting on the force of his belief that African Americans had souls, spiritual agency, and membership among the saved.

There were many transatlantic connections in these movements; for instance, John Marrant was born in America but traveled to England, where Elizabeth Countess of Huntingdon encouraged his ordination and his preaching throughout Nova Scotia to large Christian communities of escaped slaves. Marrant also preached in Boston. There he met the minister Boston King and the congregations of free black Christians who had formed their own Masonic Lodge, whose members traced their roots back to ancient Egypt and the builders of the pyramids. Much work remains to be done on this second Great Awakening and revival of religion into a more radical liberation theology that played, and is still playing, an important role in upholding civil liberties for the marginalized in America. Similar to African American and "Black Atlantic" subversions of the Christianity of European Americans, Native American writers, such as Samson Occom and William Apess, also pointed out the great contradiction between genocide and colonization, on the one hand, and a gospel of love, on the other.

Religion played an important role in the American Revolution as well. Loyalists in the colonies refused to rebel against King George III because according to the Church of England the king was one of God's representatives on earth. But revolutionaries argued that God had endowed each individual with inalienable rights. Of course, they contradictorily extended these rights to only property-owning European American men. Thomas Paine used a geographical argument to dismiss the belief that God had granted England control over America; he asked why God would have placed America such a long distance from England if the colony were meant to be under its dominion. This question hints at Deist beliefs, which Paine at one time entertained. Deists saw the universe as one giant machine that God had set in motion: a clock, so to speak, that would run for eternity without further intervention by the clockmaker. Thus the independence of America could be justified as one of many revolutions, one of many wheels turning in divine and inexorable motion. The ties of the King to the Church were such that the liturgy of Anglican masses had to be rewritten to remove references to him in post-1776 American worship: "God save the State" took the place of "God save the King" in the evensong "Preces and Responses." The opposition to any who refused to make these liturgical changes was fierce. For instance, when the Reverend Charles Inglis refused to omit the prayers for King George III during mass, the revolutionaries burned his church. Loyalists like Isaac Hunt argued that England and America were part of one divinely ordained political family, which would be damaged irrevocably by violence. Many Loyalists fled America to Canada and back to England, but the Church of England remained in America, becoming the Episcopal Church.

In England, the religious rhetoric of dissent against the crown flourished in the wake of the American Revolution. Clergy and believers whose views differed from those promulgated by the Church of England referred to themselves as dissenters. Many dissenting academies were set up to teach alternative theology and politics. These academies were necessary for the education of those who refused to swear allegiance to the Thirty-Nine Articles of the Church of England, required in order to attend Oxford, Cambridge, and other schools and colleges where pluralism was not tolerated. In the time surrounding the French Revolution, dissenting religion would play an important role in London and even seep its way into Oxford and Cambridge. The poet Samuel Taylor Coleridge studied at Jesus College, Cambridge, under the radical William Frend, who was later put on trial for his religious and political beliefs. Years later, the poet Percy Bysshe Shelley would be "sent down" (i.e., expelled) from University College, Oxford, for co-writing a pamphlet on atheism. London was one of the strongholds of revolutionary religious dissent. As opposed to the French Revolution's replacement of churches with temples devoted to the human faculty of reason, Anglo-American religious reform was centered, for the most part, on undermining the divine authority of the crown. One common element, though, is that English, French, and American radicals saw the established church as upholding royal authority. The radical theology of William Blake sang the divinity of the individual and placed London as the New Jerusalem. Blake's millenarian theology was not uncommon for the time, for many saw the revolutions in America and France as hailing Christ's return to earth for a golden age of a thousand years, as foretold in the Bible's Book of Revelation. In London, Richard Price preached a "Discourse on the Love of Our Country" that advocated for the divine right of British citizens to elect and impeach their leader. The American Elhanan Winchester also preached in London, telling his listeners that the events of the American and French Revolutions corresponded precisely to St. John's description of the end of the Old World and creation of the New in the Book of Revelation. Joseph Priestley's pro-Revolutionary sermonizing roused the ire of an angry mob that torched his library and laboratory.

Priestley emigrated to America, settling in Pennsylvania and bringing to America his dissenting religion, Unitarianism, which would take firmest root in New England. Unitarians rejected belief in the Trinity (the Father, Son, and Holy Spirit), and they believed that humans were perfectible through reason and Divine Providence. Harvard College became a Unitarian stronghold in 1805 when Henry Ware was placed at the helm of the Divinity School. William Ellery Channing was Ralph Waldo Emerson's mentor there, but Emerson rejected his teachers' belief in the veracity of miracles and the divinity of Christ, announcing his even more radical Transcendentalist views in an address to the 1838 class of the Divinity School.

Taking their name from the German Transcendental philosophers (Immanuel Kant, Johann Gottlieb Fichte, Freidrich Schelling, and others), the New England Transcendentalists believed in the world of the mind as the realm of the infinite, the presence of God in nature as a material manifestation and illustration of the spiritual and ideal, the divinity of the self, and the religious sovereignty of conscience. This religion drew from sources across the Atlantic and Pacific: Its sense of oneness with nature owed much to Eastern religions, and its sense of revelation in nature and the natural world as sacred owed much to Native American religions as well as the influence of Swedenborgianism. Emanuel Swedenborg advocated a "New Church" founded on his writings, which were based in the following doctrines: that evil originates in man and should be shunned; that good acts are to be performed as a form of divinity; that there is one God, Jesus Christ, who embodies the Holy Trinity; and that man should live a life of charity. In 1787 and 1817, churches was founded on his writings in England and America, respectively. Swedenborg was a primary source for the central Transcendentalist doctrines: the empowerment of the individual through revelation, communion with the "oversoul" (a divine and pervasive spirit in nature), and the trust in the individual's conscience did away with the need for Unitarian ministers as arbiters of God's teachings and will. Transcendentalism also inherited the Unitarian legacy of reform, as Channing and others had labored on behalf of the poor, embracing the rights of the working class (albeit from a privileged position). The Transcendentalists carried on this mission as well as other reforms. They sought to protect nature from the axes and saws of industry, designating it as intrinsically valuable. The women associated with the Transcendentalists, such as Margaret Fuller and Elizabeth Palmer Peabody, promoted women's rights and access to education. As the tensions that led to the Civil War mounted, the Transcendentalists grew ever more active in the abolitionist movement. Unitarianism did not thrive, however, in England. By the 1830s many of the radicals who had embraced the belief now distanced themselves from it. When Emerson and Channing visited London to see Coleridge, whose Unitarian beliefs had inspired their own, he upbraided them for clinging to what he saw as an obsolescent theology. By this time both William Wordsworth and Coleridge were securely in the fold of the Church of England.

In the time leading up to the Civil War, religion was a central part of the ongoing transatlantic debate over the rights of people whose ancestry could be traced back to Africa. Sojourner Truth combined the struggle for women's rights and African American civil liberties in her life, words, and ministry. On the other hand, supporters of slavery in the American South and the Caribbean colonies argued that dark skin was the mark of Cain, overlooking the Middle Eastern roots of Christianity and the peoples who first practiced it. Pro-slavery notions of white supremacy hinged upon another fallacious biblical interpretation: that Africans were descended from Ham, who had been cursed by his father, Noah. Abolitionists countered with two theological points: the monogenist belief that all races are descended from Adam (and are thus equal) as well as the belief that all souls pre-exist with God before taking corporeal form as humans, so material appearance with regard to race and gender does not constitute a legitimate criterion for the establishment of hierarchy. Slaveholders also attempted to demonstrate that slavery was justified in the Bible by wrongfully equating the vastly different notions of slavery in ancient Israel with the torture, rape, and racial supremacy that characterized plantation slavery in the Caribbean and the southern states. Many used the Bible to argue against interracial marriage, despite the fact that the main people who feared miscegenation were the white masters who had fathered many of their slaves through rape. Abolitionists pointed out that Moses's wife was Ethiopian, and the activism of biracial abolitionists such as Frederick Douglass proved the absurdity of notions of racial inferiority. The geographical location of churches also determined to some degree their stances on the issue of slavery: The Church of England was, by the time of the Civil War in America, entirely against slavery; however, the American branch (the Episcopal Church) contained many advocates for gradual emancipation, a clearly less radical stance than that of immediate liberation. Also, for instance, many southern supporters of the Church of Scotland donated vast sums of money to support it, but after Frederick Douglass preached in Scotland, the city of Edinburgh resounded with chants of "Send back the money!" Harriet Beecher Stowe's Uncle Tom's Cabin (1852) portrays its main character, a slave, as a Christ figure, and Stowe stated that God directed her to write the book, which sold in record high numbers on both sides of the Atlantic.

John Wesley
1703–1791

Leader and founder of the Methodist church John Wesley was saved from a fire that almost killed him in his early youth, and this incident informed his understanding of the role Divine Providence plays in the lives of Christians. He was educated, ordained, and received his first teaching and preaching appointments at Oxford University. As a member of the "Holy Club," established with his brother Charles, he ministered to Oxford's poor and marginalized, once interceding on behalf of a man imprisoned solely because he was gay. During his voyage to America in the winter of 1735–1736, he encountered Moravians (an offshoot of a Protestant sect forced from Moravia and Bohemia by seventeenth-century religious wars) and was heartened by the placid piety with which they weathered the rough conditions of the Atlantic crossing. After a failed missionary experience in Georgia, Wesley returned to England and joined a London-based group of German Moravians founded by Nicholas Ludwig Von Zinzendorf.

In 1738, Wesley developed a personal aspect of his faith and relationship with his savior, which became the crux of his message in the more than 40,000 sermons he would go on to preach in parishes and fields across Britain, Ireland, and the European Continent. He also retained his commitment to bettering the lives of the working class by encouraging education and a more equal distribution of wealth. It was Wesley's encouragement to others to develop a personal relationship with Christ as well as his passionate preaching that helped religion undergo the Great Awakening. His influence redefined the sermon by following the example of Welsh revivalists and taking it out of the church and into nature, and by making preaching not a calm reading of theological minutiae but the impassioned intonation of the spirit within. Despite opposition from many other Christian sects, Wesleyan Methodists survived by forming communities and training lay preachers to proselytize on their behalf. The opposition from the Anglican Church became so fierce that many Methodists considered severing ties with the Church, to which Wesley always remained loyal. After Wesley's death in 1791, the Methodists separated from the Church of England and its American branch, the Episcopal Church.

The Almost Christian[1]

Almost thou persuadest me to be a Christian. ACTS 26:28

And many there are who go thus far: ever since the Christian religion was in the world there have been many in every age and nation who were "almost persuaded to be Christians."[2] But seeing it avails nothing before God to go only thus far, it highly imports us to consider: first, what is implied in being almost; secondly, what, in being altogether a Christian.

Now, in the being almost a Christian is implied first, heathen honesty. No one, I suppose, will make any question of this; especially, since by heathen honesty here I mean not that which is recommended in the writings of their philosophers only, but such as the common heathens expected one of another, and many of them actually practiced. By the rules of this they were taught that they ought not to be unjust; not to take away their neighbor's goods either by robbery or theft; not to oppress the poor, neither to use extortion towards any; not to cheat or overreach either the poor or rich in whatsoever commerce they had with them; to defraud no man of his right; and, if it were possible, to owe no man any thing.

Again, the common heathens allowed that some regard was to be paid to truth as well as to justice. Yet again there was a sort of love and assistance which they expected one from another. They expected whatever assistance any one could give another without prejudice to himself.

A second thing implied in the being almost a Christian is the having a form of godliness, of that godliness which is prescribed in the gospel of Christ; the having the

---

1. Preached at St. Mary's, the University Church of Oxford.   2. Acts. 26:28.

outside of a real Christian. Accordingly the almost Christian does nothing which the gospel forbids. He taketh not the name of God in vain: he blesseth and curseth not: he sweareth not at all, but his communication is yea, yea; nay, nay. He profanes not the day of the Lord, nor suffers it to be profaned even by the stranger that is within his gates. He not only avoids all actual adultery, fornication, and uncleanness, but every word or look that either directly or indirectly tends thereto.

He does not willingly wrong, hurt, or grieve any man; but in all things acts and speaks by that plain rule, "Whatsoever thou wouldest not he should do unto thee, that do not thou to another."[3] And in doing good he does not confine himself to cheap and easy offices of kindness, but labors and suffers for the profit of many, that by all means he may help some.

He that hath the form of godliness uses also the means of grace; yea, all of them, and at all opportunities. He constantly frequents the house of God. More especially when he approaches the table of the Lord it is not with a light or careless behaviour, but with an air, gesture, and deportment which speak nothing else but "God be merciful to me a sinner."

To this, if we add the constant use of family prayer by those who are masters of families, and the setting times apart for private addresses to God, with a daily seriousness of behaviour; he who uniformly practices this outward religion has the form of godliness. There needs but one thing more in order to his being almost a Christian, and that is sincerity.

By sincerity I mean a real, inward principle of religion from whence these outward actions flow. And, indeed, if we have not this, we have not heathen honesty. If any man to avoid punishment, to avoid the loss of his friends, or his gain, or his reputation, should not only abstain from doing evil, but also do ever so much good, yea, and use all the means of grace, yet we could not with any propriety say, This man is even almost a Christian. If he has no better principle in his heart, he is only a hypocrite altogether. Sincerity, therefore, is necessarily implied in the being almost a Christian. This is the moving principle, both in his doing good, his abstaining from evil, and his using the ordinances of God.

But here it will probably be inquired, Is it possible, that any man living should go so far as this and nevertheless be only almost a Christian? What more than this can be implied in the being a Christian altogether? I answer, first, that it is possible to go thus far and yet be but almost a Christian, I learn not only from the oracles of God, but also from the sure testimony of experience.

Brethren, great is "my boldness towards you in this behalf." And "forgive me this wrong,"[4] if I declare my own folly upon the housetop, for yours and the gospel's sake. Suffer me then to speak freely of myself even as of another man.

I did go thus far for many years, as many of this place can testify; using diligence to eschew all evil, and to have a conscience void of offence; redeeming the time; buying up every opportunity of doing all good to all men; constantly and carefully using all the public and all the private means of grace; endeavoring after a steady seriousness of behaviour, at all times, and in all places; and, God is my record, before whom I stand, doing all this in sincerity; having a real design to serve God; a hearty desire to do his will in all things; to please him, who had called me to "fight the good fight"

---

3. Matthew 7.12.   4. 2 Corinthians 7.4, 12.13.

and to "lay hold on eternal life."[5] Yet my own conscience beareth me witness in the Holy Ghost that all this time I was but almost a Christian.

If it be inquired, What more than this is implied in the being altogether a Christian? I answer, first, the love of God. For thus saith his word, "Thou shalt love the Lord thy God with all thy heart, and with all thy soul, and with all thy mind, and with all thy strength."[6] Such a love of God is this, as engrosses the whole heart, as takes up all the affections, as fills the entire capacity of the soul, and employs the utmost extent of all it faculties. He that thus loves the Lord his God, his spirit continually "rejoiceth in God his Saviour."[7] His delight is in the Lord, his Lord and his All, to whom "in every thing he giveth thanks." "All his desire is unto God and to the remembrance of his name."[8] His heart is ever crying out, "Whom have I in heaven but thee, and there is none upon earth that I desire beside thee."[9] Indeed, what can he desire beside God? Not the world, or the things of the world, For he is "crucified to the world, and the world crucified to him."[10]

The second thing implied in the being altogether a Christian is the love of our neighbor. For thus said our Lord in the following words, "Thou shalt love thy neighbor as thyself."[11] If any man ask, Who is my neighbor? we reply, every man in the world; every child of his, who is the Father of the spirits of all flesh. Nor may we in any wise except our enemies, or the enemies of God and their own souls. But every Christian loveth these also as himself, yea, "as Christ loved us."[12]

There is yet one thing more that may be separately considered, though it cannot actually be separate from the preceding, which is implied in the being altogether a Christian, and that is the ground of all, even faith. Very excellent things are spoken of this throughout the oracles of God. "Every one," saith the beloved disciple, "That believeth is born of God."[13] "To as many as received him, gave he power to become the sons of God, even to them that believe in his name."[14] And "this is the victory that overcometh the world, even our faith." Yea, our Lord himself declares, "He that believeth in the Son hath everlasting life; and cometh not into condemnation, but is passed from death unto life."[15]

But here let no man deceive his own soul. It is diligently to be noted, the faith which bringeth not forth repentance and love and all good works is not that right living faith which is here spoken of, but a dead and devilish one. For, even the devils believe, and yet, for all this faith they be but devils.

"The right and true Christian faith is," to go on in the words of our own church, "not only to believe that Holy Scripture and the articles of our faith are true, but also to have a sure trust and confidence to be saved from everlasting damnation by Christ. It is a sure trust and confidence which a man hath in God, that by the merits of Christ his sins are forgiven, and he reconciled to the favor of God; whereof doth follow a loving heart to obey his commandments."[16]

Now whosoever has this faith which purifies the heart (by the power of God, who dwelleth therein) from pride, anger, desire, from all unrighteousness, from "all filthiness of flesh and spirit"[17]; which fills it with love stronger than death, both to God and to all mankind; love that doth the works of God, glorying to spend and to

---

5. 1 Timothy 6.12.   6. The first of the Ten Commandments.   7. From the Magnificat, the prayer of Mary after the Annunciation.   8. Romans 14.   9. Psalm 73.25.   10. Galatians 6.14.   11. Matthew 5.43.   12. Ephesians 5.2.   13. 1 John 5.1.   14. 1 John 1.12.   15. 1. John 5.10.   16. Anglican Book of Common Prayer.   17. 2. Corinthians 7.1.

be spent for all men, and that endureth with joy not only the reproach of Christ, the being mocked, despised, and hated of all men, but whatsoever the wisdom of God permits the malice of men or devils to inflict; whosoever has this faith, thus working by love, is not almost only, but altogether a Christian.

But who are the living witnesses of these things? I beseech you, brethren, as in the presence of that God, before whom "hell and destruction are without a covering,"[18] that each of you would ask his own heart, "Am I of that number? Do I so far practice justice, mercy, and truth, as even the rules of heathen honesty require? If so, have I the very outside of a Christian? Do I seriously use all the ordinances of God at all opportunities? And is all this done with a sincere design and desire to please God in all things?"

Are not many of you conscious that you never came thus far; that you have not been even almost a Christian; that you have not come up to the standard of heathen honesty; at least, not to the form of Christian godliness?—much less hath God seen sincerity in you, a real design of pleasing him in all things. You never so much as intended to devote all your words and works, your business, studies, diversions, to his glory. You never even designed or desired that whatsoever you did should be done "in the name of the Lord Jesus," and as such should be a "spiritual sacrifice, acceptable to God through Christ."[19]

But supposing you had, do good designs and good desires make a Christian? By no means, unless they are brought to good effect. "Hell is paved," saith one, "with good intentions."[20] The great question of all, then, still remains. Is the love of God shed abroad in your heart? Can you cry out, "My God and my All?"[21] Do you desire nothing but him? Are you happy in God? Is he your glory, your delight, your crown of rejoicing? And is this commandment written in your heart, That he who loveth God love his brother also? Do you then love your neighbor as yourself? Do you love every man, even your enemies, even the enemies of God, as your own soul? As Christ loved you? Yea, dost thou believe that Christ loved thee, and gave himself for thee? Hast thou faith in his blood? Believest thou the Lamb of God hath taken away thy sins and cast them as a stone into the depth of the sea? That he hath blotted out the handwriting that was against thee, taking it out of the way, nailing it to his cross? Hast thou indeed redemption through his blood, even the remission of thy sins? And doth his Spirit bear witness with thy spirit that thou art a child of God?

The God and Father of our Lord Jesus Christ, who now standeth in the midst of us, knoweth that if any man die without this faith and this love, good it were for him that he had never been born. "Awake, then, thou that sleepest, and call upon thy God: call in the day when he may be found. Let him not rest till he make his goodness to pass before thee,"[22] till he proclaim unto thee the name of the Lord; "the Lord, the Lord God, merciful and gracious, long suffering, and abundant in goodness and truth, keeping mercy for thousands, forgiving iniquity, and transgression, and sin."[23] Let no man persuade thee by vain words to rest short of this prize of thy high calling. But cry unto him day and night, who, "while we were without strength, died for the ungodly,"[24] until thou knowest in whom thou hast

---

18. Job 26.6.   19. Romans 12.1.   20. St. Bernard of Clairvaux (1091–1153).   21. John 20.28.   22. Ephesians 5.14.
23. Exodus 34.7.   24. Romans 5.6.

believed and canst say, "My Lord, and my God!"[25] Remember "always to pray, and not to faint,"[26] till thou also canst lift up thy hand unto heaven and declare to him that liveth for ever and ever, "Lord, thou knowest all things, thou knowest that I love thee."[27]

May we all thus experience what it is to be not almost only, but altogether Christians; being justified freely by his grace through the redemption that is in Jesus; knowing we have peace with God through Jesus Christ; rejoicing in hope of the glory of God; and having the love of God shed abroad in our hearts by the Holy Ghost given unto us!

—1741

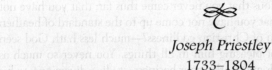

Joseph Priestley
1733–1804

Born near Leeds to a family of English dissenters, Priestley's adherence to non-Anglican faith kept him out of English universities, which required students to subscribe to the Thirty-Nine Articles of the Church of England. During his studies at the Dissenting Academy at Daventry, a non-conformist school for clergy, he did, however, receive a broad base of knowledge as well as preparatory training to become a minister. Leaving the academy in 1755, he became assistant minister at Suffolk, where he remained for three years, and then at Cheshire, which was much more accepting of his latitudinarianism, that is, his liberal and rationalist approach to theology. His *Rudiments of English Grammar* (1761) secured him a reputation and a teaching position at Warrington Academy. Here, he published yet another book, *The Theory of Language and Universal Grammar* (1762) and married his lifelong partner, Mary Wilkinson. In 1767, he returned to Leeds to take a position as minister. While at Leeds he began to dissent not only theologically but also politically from the Church and King by outwardly supporting religious toleration and the American Revolution, especially in his *Address to Protestant Dissenters of All Denominations, on the Approaching Election of Members of Parliament, with Respect to the State of Public Liberty in General and of American Affairs in Particular* (London and Boston, 1773; Philadelphia, 1774). During his six years tutoring the Earl of Shelburne, he was hardly able to mute his radicalism, which he took up with renewed vigor during his time as a minister at Birmingham. Not only did he argue for the right to dissent from the Anglican Church, but also, in *An History of the Corruptions of Christianity* (1782), he claimed that the Unitarian Church, which did not subscribe to the doctrine of the Trinity, was the true character and successor of the early church. Priestley so vociferously supported the French Revolution that on July 14, 1791, the second anniversary of the storming of the Bastille in Paris, he became the target of a violent British reaction to the Revolution. His laboratory, house, and library were burned, and he and his family fled to London and eventually across the Atlantic to America. His move to Pennsylvania ignited intellectual fires in America, most notably American Unitarianism, which burned most brightly at Harvard and was the crucible in which Ralph Waldo Emerson's and other Transcendentalists' views were formed. Priestley became somewhat of a Promethean figure for English Romantic radicals. He inspired Samuel Taylor Coleridge's and Robert Southey's Pantisocracy—a plan to build an ideal community on the banks of the Susquehanna (near Priestley) in a utopia of communal property, plain living, and high thinking. A true Romantic-era Renaissance man, Priestley contributed

---

25. John 20.28.   26. Luke 18.1.   27. John 16.30.

widely to theology (religious freedom and toleration), philosophy (academic freedom, utilitarianism, doctrine of necessity), and chemistry (isolation of oxygen, nitrous oxide, hydrogen chloride, ammonia, and other elements).

from An Address to Protestant Dissenters

Part I.

My Fellow-Citizens,

The present very critical situation of things in this country, in which you have so much at stake, and in which it cannot be denied that you have considerable weight, is a sufficient apology for an address to you with respect to it. The approaching election for members of parliament calls for *all*, and perhaps for the *last*, efforts of the friends of liberty in this country; and every real friend of this great cause among us, who is acquainted with the history of your ancestors, will naturally look to you for the most active concurrence and support.

Religious liberty, indeed, is the immediate ground on which you stand, but this cannot be maintained except upon the basis of *civil liberty*; and therefore the old *Puritans* and *Nonconformists* were always equally distinguished for their noble and strenuous exertions in favour of them both. Their zeal in this cause, and the valuable effects of it, are so well known, that even Mr. Hume[1] (an historian of the most unsuspected impartiality in this case) acknowledges, that whatever civil liberty we now enjoy is to be ascribed to them. In fact, all our princes, who have ever entertained designs upon the liberties of their subjects, have been jealous of your principles and influence, and have accordingly used their first and utmost efforts to crush you. . . .

The measures that are now carrying on against the *North American* colonies are alone a sufficient indication of the disposition of the court towards you. The *pretence* for such outrageous proceedings, conducted with such indecent and unjust precipitation, is much too slight to account for them. The *true cause* of such violent animosity must have existed much earlier and deeper.[2] In short, it can be nothing but the Americans (particularly those of *New England*) being chiefly *Dissenters and Whigs*. For the whole conduct of the present ministry demonstrates, that what was *merit* in the two late reigns, is *demerit* in this. And can you suppose that those who are so violently hostile to the *offspring* of the English Dissenters, should be friendly to the remains of the *parent stock*? I trust that both you and they will make it appear, that you have not degenerated from the principles and spirit of your illustrious ancestors, and that you are no more to be outwitted or overawed than they were.

It is said, that a great part of the resentment of the court against the Dissenters has arisen from a notion that they were the chief abettors of Mr. *Wilkes*[3]; and I believe that, in general, they were the friends of his *cause*, because it was the cause of liberty and of the constitution. But they took no part in this business more than the other friends of this country; except that Dissenters, having more depending upon public liberty, are more interested to keep a watchful eye upon every thing that relates to it. So that if your conduct in this affair has given *peculiar* offence, it must have been

---

1. David Hume (1711–1776), Scottish philosopher.   2. The events surrounding the American Revolution.   3. John Wilkes (1727–1797), English radical newspaper editor.

because the same conduct appears more offensive in you than in any others; which implies a prejudice against you as *Dissenters*, of which you ought to be apprised, that you may act accordingly.

Do not imagine, however, that what I have hitherto said is a preamble to a declaration of war, or that I wish you to take arms in defence of your liberties, as your brethren in America will probably be compelled to do. That were equally ineffectual and improper. But it is most earnestly to be wished, that you would exert yourselves in doing what the constitution of your country both permits and *requires* of all good citizens. Carefully avoid all undue influence on the approaching election, and strenuously exert yourselves to procure a return of men who are known to be friends to civil and religious liberty.

Attend particularly to the characters of the several candidates for whom your votes are requested. Regard none of their *professions* of zeal for the public service, but look to their past *conduct*; and if, in any case, they have promoted the corrupt measures of the court, and have concurred in passing any of the late laws that are unfavourable to your liberties, be not accessary to their *future crimes*, by giving them another opportunity of betraying you, and acting the same part over again. More especially avoid, as you would the pestilence, every man who voted against the repeal of the oppressive laws to which you are exposed, and take every proper method of expressing your just sense of their enmity towards you. Consider them as the declared enemies of liberty, justice, and humanity.

The conduct of the *Quakers*[4] is said to be peculiarly chaste and exemplary with respect to elections. They join as a body to discountenance all undue influence, and admit not the smallest favour, or hardly a civility, from those for whom they give their votes. And certainly you cannot too carefully avoid all suspicion of corruption in a business of so much importance, and where freedom and independence of mind are so much concerned.

The popular cry against members of parliament is, that they are *corrupt*, subservient to all the measures of the court; and that, in fact, they *sell* their constituents. But is it really any wonder that a man should *sell* what he is known to have bought and paid for? Instead of making the office a matter of favour, honour, and trust, is it not made exceedingly burdensome and expensive to them? And is this an age in which a man can be expected to be at very great expenses, without endeavouring to reimburse himself? There *are* characters so truly disinterested and great. I could name several such; but, certainly, it were absurd to expect they should be found every where.

If, then, you would have it in your power, with any face and decency, to call your constituents to account, or even upbraid them for sacrificing your liberties in the House, do not oblige them to sacrifice their fortunes in order to get thither. Have no demands upon them *before* they enter upon their office, that you may have the more *afterwards*.

An eminent foreigner has foretold, that "England will lose its liberty whenever the legislative part of the constitution should be more corrupt than the executive."[5] But he had no occasion to have said so much. Our liberties must necessarily be gone whenever the power of the House of Commons shall be united to that of the crown,

---

4. A radical religious sect.   5. William Blackstone (1723–1780), *Commentaries on the Laws of England* (1765–1769).

whether the court be corrupt or not. For how can there be any *equilibrium*, when every weight is thrown into one scale? But he might have said farther, and more to my present purpose, that the House of Commons will lose its liberty and independence, whenever the *electors* shall be more corrupt than the *elected*.

If, therefore, you wish that your representatives be uncorrupt and independent, first shew them the example of being so yourselves. This step is certainly necessary in order to gain your point, though it will not absolutely insure it. The disease may perhaps be too desperate for any power of medicine: acquit yourselves, however, of all just blame, by applying all such as are of approved efficacy. This conduct will at least mitigate the evil, and make you the objects of compassion in your sufferings.

The diseases of our constitution are too many to yield to any remedy, while the court has so much to give, and so many lucrative places to dispose of; so that it is to be feared, that though your members be sent to parliament in the most uncorrupt and honourable manner, they will not long continue uncorrupt. It is too much to be expected of human nature, especially in this luxurious and expensive age. . . .

The hope of mankind (who have been so long debased and trampled upon by forms of unequal government) is that, in time, this horrible evil may find its own antidote and cure. *Kings* being always worse educated than other man, the race of them may be expected to degenerate, till they be little better than idiots, as is the case already with several of them, needless to be named, and it is said will be the case with others, when the present reigning princes shall be no more; while those that are not the objects of *contempt*, will be the objects of *hatred* and *execration*.

In this situation, the temptation to men to assert their natural rights, and seize the invaluable blessings of freedom, will be very great. And it may be hoped that, enlightened as the world now is with respect to the theory of government, and taught by the experience of so many past ages, they will no more suffer themselves to be transferred, like the live stock of a farm, from one worn-out royal line to another, but establish every where forms of free and equal government; by which, at infinitely less expense than they are now at to be *oppressed* and *abused*, every man may be secured in the enjoyment of as much of his natural rights as is consistent with the good of the whole community. If this should ever be the case, even the past usurpations of the *Pope* will not excite more astonishment and indignation, than the present disgraceful subjection of the *many* to the *few* in civil respects.

Part II.

My Fellow-Citizens,

As your late representatives have acted as if they were the representatives of all *North America*, and in that assumed capacity have engaged in measures which threaten nothing less than the ruin of the whole British empire, it were greatly to be wished that their successors might learn by their example to know themselves better, and keep within their proper province. This is a business of so much consequence, that I cannot help subjoining a few plain considerations relating to it. It is true that I can advance nothing *new* upon the subject, but I shall endeavour to comprise the merits of the case in a very small compass, which may give it a chance of being better understood; and some advantage may arise from the same things being said in a different manner, and upon a different occasion.

The minds of many, indeed, are so obstinately shut against conviction, and they are so blindly bent on pushing the vindictive schemes of the present ministry, without regard to reason or consequences, that I despair of making any impression upon them. But I wish to address myself to those who have not yet taken their part, or who, though they may have been deceived by the false lights in which this affair has been represented, are cool enough to attend to what may be said on the other side. On such I should think that some impression might be made by *three considerations*; one drawn from the nature and history of our constitution, another from the nature of things and the principles of liberty in general, and the third from the effects which the oppression of America may have on the liberties of this country.

It has ever been a fundamental maxim in our government, that the representatives of the people should have a voice in enacting all the laws by which they are governed, and that they should have the sole power of giving their own money. Without these privileges there can be no true British liberty. These maxims were so well understood, and were held so inviolable in all former times, that though all the kings of this country, since the conquest, have had several *realms*, principalities, subject to them, each has always had its separate legislative body, its separate laws, and its separate system of taxation: and no one of them ever thought of laying a tax upon another.

When the Kings of England were likewise Dukes of *Normandy*, and held other principalities in France, the English parliament never thought of making laws for the Normans, or the Normans for the English; and still less did either of them presume to tax the other. *Scotland*, though united under one head with England, had its own system of laws and taxation, altogether independent of the English, till the union of the parliaments of both the nations. *Wales* also, and several *Counties Palatine*,[6] taxed themselves, without any controul from the parliament of England; and so does *Ireland* to this day. So independent were all these governments of one another, though the same king had a negative upon the resolutions of them all, that when a man fled from any one of the realms, and took refuge in another, he was as effectually exempted from the jurisdiction of the country he had left, as if he had gone into the dominions of another prince; so that no process at law commenced in the former could affect him.

Agreeably to these ideas, it could not but have been understood, that when many of our ancestors, the old *Puritans*, quitted the realm of England, they freed themselves from the laws of England. Indeed they could have had no other motive for leaving this country; and how could they have expected any relief from taking refuge in America, if they had found in that country, or carried with them the same laws and the same administration by which they were aggrieved in this? But going into a country which was *out of the realm of England*, and not occupied, they found themselves at first without any laws whatever. But they enacted laws for themselves, voluntarily choosing, from their regard to the country from which they came, to have the same common head and centre of concord, the King of Great Britain; and therefore submitted to his negative upon all their proceedings. They adopted as many of the laws of *England* as they chose, but no more; and if they had preferred the laws of *Scotland*, those of Ireland, or those of any foreign country, they were at liberty to have done it.

These *Colonists* also provided for the expenses of their own separate governments, granting the king aids for that purpose, according to their own judgment and

---

6. Areas ruled by an earl, count, or prince-bishop with autonomy from the Crown.

ability, without the interference of the English parliament, till the fatal period of the *stamp act*,[7] which was absolutely an innovation in our constitution, confounding the first and fundamental ideas belonging to the system of *different realms subject to the same king*, and even introduced *a language quite new to us*; viz, that of *America being subject to England*. For America was never thought to be within the realm of England, any more than Scotland or Ireland. If there have been any *exceptions* to this system of legislation, or taxation, with respect to America, it has been the exercise of *tyranny*, and it has not been the less so for having been *disguised*, or having passed *without suspicion*.

According to the language that was universally in use till of late years, to say that *America was subject to England*, would have been considered as equally absurd, with saying that it was subject to Ireland or to Hanover, that is, the subject of subjects; all being equally subject to one king, who is himself subject to the laws, and who is no longer our *legal and rightful king*, than he is so. In this great principle the very essence of our liberty, and the independent liberty of each part of the *common empire*, consists.

Secondly, with respect to the principles of *liberty in general*, I would observe, that if any realm or country be taxed by another, the people so taxed have no proper liberty left, but are in a state of as *absolute despotism* as any of which we read in history, or of which we can form an idea; since the same *foreign power* that can take *one penny* from them without their consent, may take *the last penny* that they have; so that, in fact, they have no property at all of their own, every thing they have being at the mercy of others. This would be the case with *England*, if we were taxed at the pleasure of the king, or by the parliament of *Ireland*, or by the houses of representatives of *America*: it would be the case of the Irish if they were taxed by the English; and therefore it will be the case of the Americans, if they be taxed by us.

It is said that Leeds, Manchester, and other large towns in England, send no representatives to parliament, and yet are taxed by it. But there is this very essential and obvious difference between their case and that of the Americans; viz. that those who tax Leeds, Manchester, &c. always tax themselves at the same time, and in the same proportion; and while this is the case, those towns have no reason to be apprehensive of partiality or oppression. To make the cases parallel, let the parliament lay a separate tax on the towns that send no representatives, and exempt from such tax those that do send members. In this case I doubt not but that the unrepresented towns would complain as loudly as the Americans do now, who see that we assume a power of loading them, and easing ourselves; and that we are endeavouring to establish a *principle*, which will at once give us all the property they have. If there be in nature a justifiable case of resistance to government, it is this; and if the Americans have any thing of the spirit of Englishmen, they will risk every thing, rather than submit to such a claim. They are willing to be our *fellow-subjects* having the same common head; but are not willing to be our *slaves*.

It is alleged, that we have *protected* the Americans, and that they ought to pay for that protection; but have we not also protected Ireland, and the electorate of Hanover, without pretending either to make laws for them, or to tax them? What we may do, or *attempt* to do, when this new doctrine shall have been established in the case of the Americans, is as yet unknown. Any favour that we do the Americans, certainly gives

---

7. The 1765 act imposing taxes on many trade goods.

us a claim upon their *gratitude*, but it does not make them our slaves. Besides, they have, in many respects, made abundant requital, and we were actually reaping a rich harvest for the little we have sowed in that fruitful soil. But our present ministry resemble the man, who would kill the hen that laid the golden eggs, in order that he might come at all the treasure at once; and the event will equally disappoint them both. Or rather, they resemble the dog, who, by catching at the shadow, lost the substance.

Many persons of this country are so grossly ignorant as to imagine, that while we are heavily taxed for the welfare of the common empire, and have even incurred a prodigious debt on that account, the Americans pay nothing at all. But have not the Americans their own separate governments to support, as well as we have ours, and do they not tax themselves for that purpose, and do we help them to bear any part of those taxes? If they incur debts, as they sometimes do, do they not discharge them as well as they can? And should we not laugh at them, if they should pretend to have any demand upon us for the payment of them? Should we not also treat the Irish with the same contempt in the same case?

In a *common cause* the Americans have always been ready to exert themselves with as much zeal as we have shewn; nay, by our own acknowledgment, they have done more. For at the close of the last war, we voluntarily voted them large sums of money, because we were sensible that they had exerted themselves even beyond their ability. But their exertions were *voluntary*, as was our acknowledgment.

As to the conduct of the present ministry with respect to America, it is no part of my present argument; but I cannot help observing, that it must give pain to every reasonable man to see an English parliament so readily giving their sanction to measures so exceedingly absurd and ruinous. Admitting that the East India Company has been injured by some of the inhabitants of Boston,[8] reasonable people would have contented themselves with demanding *satisfaction*, and would not have punished the innocent with the guilty, by *blocking up their port*.

An offence of this nature could not in reason or equity draw upon them the *abolition of their charter*; which demonstrates, that none of the colonies have the least security for so much as the *form* of a free constitution, all being at the mercy of a foreign power.

An offence of this kind did not require that a fleet of eleven ships of war, and eight regiments should be sent thither, with a power to commit all crimes and murders with impunity, and that the wretched inhabitants should be compelled, upon every accusation, to leave their friends, and submit to a trial, and consequently an iniquitous trial, in a foreign country; an instance of oppression which, of itself, is absolutely intolerable, and which it cannot be conceived, that any person who has arms in his hands, and the spirit of a man within him, can possibly submit to.

What man, finding that the government of his country provided him no satisfaction for the murder of a near relation or friend (which will necessarily be the case, when a trial cannot be had upon the spot, or without crossing the Atlantic ocean, whither he cannot carry his witnesses, and still less his *feelings*), will not think himself not only excusable, but even bound in conscience to take his own satisfaction, and engage his private friends to assist him in procuring *blood for blood*?

---

8. Boston Tea Party (1773): Patriots disguised as Mohawks boarded three East India Company ships and dumped their cargoes of tea into Boston Harbor.

I need not ask any *Englishman,* how the *Americans* (whom prelatical tyranny[9] drove from this country, and who are grown numerous, strong, and high-spirited under a very different treatment) must feel in these circumstances; especially when, at the same time, they see the boundaries of *Canada* extended, and made a perfect arbitrary government, as a model, no doubt, for their own in due time, and a check upon them till that time. It is what he himself would feel in the same circumstances.

Lastly, do you imagine, my fellow-citizens, that we can sit still, and be the idle spectators of the chains which are forging for our brethren in America, *with safety to ourselves?* Let us suppose *America* to be completely enslaved, in consequence of which the English court can command all the *money,* and all the *force* of that country; will they like to be so arbitrary *abroad,* and have their power confined *at home;* especially as troops in abundance can be transported in a few weeks from America to England; where, with the present standing army, they may instantly reduce us to what they please? And can it be supposed that the Americans, being slaves themselves, and having been enslaved *by us,* willl not, in return, willingly contribute their aid to bring us into the same condition?

—1773

John Marrant
1755–1791

Seeking to disrupt a packed church where George Whitefield was preaching, John Marrant experienced a conversion to Christianity, which embarked him on a physical and spiritual journey to spread God's word along the Atlantic Rim. His voyages began when, rejected by his family, he set off walking through the woods of Charleston, South Carolina. In a journey that mirrored Jesus's forty days and nights in the desert and the Jews' exodus, Marrant wandered through the woods, relying upon God and faith for spiritual and physical nourishment. He dwelt among the Cherokee, Creek, Choctaw, and Chickasaw tribes, proselytizing as he went. After being pressed to fight for the British Navy during the American Revolution, Marrant eventually ended up in Britain, where he was ordained in a chapel of the Countess of Huntingdon (the Methodist convert who would later befriend Phillis Wheatley) and where he, along with William Aldridge, published *A Narrative of the Lord's Wonderful Dealings with John Marrant, a Black (Now Going to Preach the Gospel in Nova Scotia) Born in New York, in North America* (London, 1785). As the title to his book indicates, he sailed for Nova Scotia that very same year accompanied by a fellow black Huntingdonian, William Furmage. Near Shelburne, he preached to the settlements of the 3,500 black Loyalists who had been transported there after the American Revolution. After enduring the treachery of white and black ministers who were not happy to lose their parishioners to Marrant, he left for Boston, arriving in 1788. There, he met Prince Hall and became a member of the first African American Masonic Lodge, which Hall had founded in 1784. Along with Hall and other black preachers, such as Boston King, Moses Wilkinson, and John Ball, Marrant helped create black Christian churches dedicated to liberty and education.

It was to the brethren of the African Masonic Lodge that he preached the sermon included in this anthology. It was delivered on June 24, 1789, in Boston's South School in celebration of

---

9. The Prelacy (Anglican Bishops) placed restrictions on the religious practices of Puritans, prompting their move to Massachusetts in the 1630s.

the Festival of St. John the Baptist. It is believed that Marrant and Hall collaborated on the sermon, which gives a biblical history of the Masons. It reconfigures a Christianity that had become
synonymous with whiteness and the exclusion of blacks, and instead forms a community based on
harmony and commonalities rather than discord and differences. This message is clear in his commentary on the various Freemasons who helped create Solomon's Temple: "although they were of
different nations and different colors, yet were they in perfect harmony among themselves." After
spreading his message in Boston, he returned to England in 1790 and died there a year later.

from A Narrative of the Lord's Wonderful Dealings with John Marrant, a Black, (Now Going to Preach the Gospel in Nova Scotia) Born in New York, in North America

I remained with my relations till the commencement of the American troubles.[1] . . .
In those troublesome times, I was pressed on board the Scorpion sloop of war, as their
musician, as they were told I could play on music.—I continued in his majesty's service six years and eleven months; and with shame confess, that a lamentable stupor
crept over all my spiritual vivacity, life, and vigour; I got cold and dead. . . . My gracious God, my dear Father in his dear Son, roused me every now and then by dangers
and deliverances.—I was at the siege of Charles-Town,[2] and passed through many
dangers. When the town was taken, my old royal benefactor and convert, the king of
the Cherokee Indians, riding into the town with general Clinton,[3] saw me, and knew
me. He alighted off his horse, and came to me; said he was glad to see me; that his
daughter was very happy, and sometimes longed to get out of the body.

Some time after this I was cruising about in the American seas, and cannot help
mentioning a singular deliverance I had from the most imminent danger, and the use
the Lord made of it to me. We were overtaken by a violent storm; I was washed overboard, and thrown on again; dashed into the sea a second time, and tossed upon deck
again. I now fastened a rope round my middle as a security against being thrown into
the sea again; but, alas! forgot to fasten it to any part of the ship; being carried away
the third time by the fury of the waves, when in the sea, I found the rope both useless and an incumbrance. I was in the sea the third time about eight minutes, and the
sharks came round me in great numbers; one of an enormous size, that could easily
have taken me into his throat at once, passed and rubbed against my side. I then cried
more earnestly to the Lord than I had done for some time; and he who heard Jonah's
prayer,[4] did not shut out mine, for I was thrown aboard again; these were the means
the Lord used to revive me, and I began now to set out afresh.

I was in the engagement with the Dutch off the Dogger Bank,[5] on board the
Princess Amelia of 84 guns. We had a great number killed and wounded: the deck was
running with blood, six men were killed, and three wounded, stationed at the same
gun with me; my head and face were covered with the blood and brains of the slain:
I was wounded, but did not fall, till a quarter of an hour before the engagement ended,
and was happy during the whole of it.[6] After being in the hospital three months and

---

1. The American Revolution.   2. The 1780 defeat of American revolutionaries. Marrant's sloop, *The Scorpion*, was stationed
near Charleston, South Carolina.   3. Henry Clinton (c. 1738–1795), Commander of British forces.   4. Jonah 2.   5. In
the North Sea between England and Denmark.   6. In 1781, assigned escort duty for British merchant ships, Marrant's
ship responded to a Dutch attack.

16 days, I was sent to the West-Indies on board a ship of war, and after cruising in those seas, we returned home as a convoy. Being taken ill of my old wounds, I was put into the hospital at Plymouth, and had not been there long, when the physician gave it as his opinion, that I should not be capable of serving the king again; I was therefore discharged, and came to London, where I lived with a respectable and pious merchant three years, who was unwilling to part with me. During this time I saw my call to the ministry fuller and clearer; had a feeling concern for the salvation of my countrymen: I carried them constantly in the arms of prayer and faith to the throne of grace, and had continual sorrow in my heart for my brethren, for my kinsmen, according to the flesh.[7]—I wrote a letter to my brother, who returned me an answer, in which he prayed some ministers would come and preach to them, and desired me to shew it to the minister whom I attended. I used to exercise my gifts on a Monday evening in prayer and exhortation, and was approved of, and sent down to Bath, where I was ordained, in Lady Huntingdon's chapel. Her Ladyship[8] having seen the letter from my brother in Nova-Scotia, thought Providence called me there: To which place I am now bound, and expect to sail in a few days.

I have now only to entreat the earnest prayer of all my kind Christian friends, that I may be carried safe there; kept humble, made useful and successful; that strangers may hear, obey and turn to Christ; that Indian tribes may stretch out their hands to God; that the black nations may be made white in the blood of the Lamb; that vast multitudes of hard tongues, and of a strange speech, may learn the language of Canaan, and sing the song of Moses, and of the Lamb; and, anticipating the glorious prospect, may we all with fervent hearts, and willing tongues, sing hallelujah; the kingdoms of the world are become the kingdoms of our God, and of his Christ. Amen and Amen.[9]

—1785

Frances Trollope
1780–1863

Author of *Domestic Manners of the Americans* (1832), Frances Trollope was born in England but lived in America from 1827 to 1831. Her original purpose for coming to America was to accompany her husband, Thomas Anthony Trollope, whose idea of selling high-priced British goods in Cincinnati failed miserably, as did his other business ventures. In part to rescue the family from financial dire straits, she penned *Domestic Manners of the Americans*, which proved to be highly profitable. It piqued the interest of the British, Spanish, and French (the latter two countries published translations) and the ire of the Americans, who published responses in pamphlet form. To many Americans, the work perpetuated a stereotype of the country as a cultural caricature of British manners and mores and fueled the anxieties of those in the New World seeking to step out of the shadow of the Old. Trollope's depiction of American religion was equally unflattering in its humorous portrayal of zeal and ritual. She laid bare the blatant hypocrisy of a country that saw itself as the Christian nation of the elect, had declared itself independent from Britain for the purpose of establishing a broader conception of individual rights, but was supported economically by slavery.

---

7. Romans 9.2–3.   8. Selina Shirley Hastings, Countess of Huntingdon (1707–1791).   9. Revelation 7–17.

Although she would write further travel books about Belgium and France, Trollope turned her attention to novel writing, weaving her travel experiences into the fiction. Her further thoughts on American slavery are expressed in the book *Jonathan Jefferson Whitlaw* (1836). In the twenty-eight other novels she wrote, America was often a topic of the characters' conversations and narrators' observations, especially in *The Barnabys in America* (1843).

from Domestic Manners of the Americans

Religion

I had often heard it observed, before I visited America, that one of the great blessings of its constitution was the absence of a national religion, the country being thus exonerated from all obligation of supporting the clergy; those only contributing to do so whose principles led them to it. My residence in the country has shown me that a religious tyranny may be exerted very effectually without the aid of the government, in a way much more oppressive than the paying of tithe, and without obtaining any of the salutary decorum, which I presume no one will deny is the result of an established mode of worship.

As it was impossible to remain many weeks in the country without being struck with the strange anomalies produced by its religious system, my early notes contain many observations on the subject; but as nearly the same scenes recurred in every part of the country, I state them here, not as belonging to the West alone, but to the whole Union, the same cause producing the same effect everywhere.

The whole people appear to be divided into an almost endless variety of religious factions, and I was told, that to be well received in society, it was necessary to declare yourself as belonging to some one of these. Let your acknowledged belief be what it may, you are said to be *not a Christian*, unless you attach yourself to a particular congregation. Besides the broad and well-known distinctions of Episcopalian, Roman Catholic, Presbyterian, Calvinist, Baptist, Quaker, Swedenborgian, Universalist, Dunker,[1] etc., etc., etc., there are innumerable others springing out of these, each of which assumes a church government of its own; of this, the most intriguing and factious individual is invariably the head; and in order, as it should seem, to show a reason for this separation, each congregation invests itself with some queer variety of external observance that has the melancholy effect of exposing *all* religious ceremonies to contempt.

It is impossible, in witnessing all these unseemly vagaries, not to recognise the advantages of an established church as a sort of head-quarters for quiet unpresuming Christians, who are contented to serve faithfully, without insisting upon having each a little separate banner, embroidered with a device of his own imagining.

The Roman Catholics alone appear exempt from the fury of division and subdivision that has seized every other persuasion. Having the Pope for their common head, regulates, I presume, their movements, and prevents the outrageous display of individual whim, which every other sect is permitted.

I had the pleasure of being introduced to the Roman Catholic bishop of Cincinnati, and have never known in any country a priest of a character and bearing more truly apostolic. He was an American, but I should never have discovered it from his pronunciation or manner. He received his education partly in England, and partly

---

1. Baptist sect that believed in full immersion during baptism.

in France. His manners were highly polished; his piety active and sincere, and infinitely more mild and tolerant than that of the factious sectarians who form the great majority of the American priesthood.

I believe I am sufficiently tolerant; but this does not prevent my seeing that the object of all religious observances is better obtained, when the government of the church is confined to the wisdom and experience of the most venerated among the people, than when it is placed in the hands of every tinker and tailor who chooses to claim a share in it. Nor is this the only evil attending the want of a national religion, supported by the state. As there is no legal and fixed provision for the clergy, it is hardly surprising that their services are confined to those who can pay them. The vehement expressions of insane or hypocritical zeal, such as were exhibited during "the revival",[2] can but ill atone for the want of village worship, any more than the eternal talk of the admirable and unequalled government can atone for the continual contempt of social order. Church and state hobble along, side by side, notwithstanding their boasted independence. Almost every man you meet will tell you, that he is occupied in labours most abundant for the good of his country; and almost every woman will tell you, that besides those things that are within (her house), she has coming upon her daily the care of all the churches. Yet spite of this universal attention to the government, its laws are half asleep; and spite of the old women and their Dorcas societies,[3] atheism is awake and thriving.

In the smaller cities and towns, prayer-meetings take the place of almost all other amusements; but as the thinly scattered population of most villages can give no parties, and pay no priests, they contrive to marry, christen, and bury, without them. A stranger taking up his residence in any city of America, must think the natives the most religious people upon earth; but if chance lead him among her western villages, he will rarely find either churches or chapels, prayer or preacher; except, indeed, at that most terrific saturnalia,[4] "a camp-meeting". I was much struck with the answer of a poor woman, whom I saw ironing on a Sunday. "Do you make no difference in your occupations on a Sunday?" I said. "I beant a Christian, ma'am; we have got no opportunity" was the reply. It occurred to me, that in a country where "all men are equal", the government would be guilty of no great crime, did it so far interfere as to give them all *an opportunity* of becoming Christians if they wished it. But should the federal government dare to propose building a church, and endowing it, in some village that has never heard "the bringing home of bell and burial",[5] it is perfectly certain that not only the sovereign state where such an abomination was proposed, would rush into the Congress to resent the odious interference, but that all the other states would join the clamour, and such an intermeddling administration would run great risk of impeachment and degradation.

Where there is a church government so constituted as to deserve human respect, I believe it will always be found to receive it, even from those who may not assent to the dogma of its creed; and where such respect exists, it produces a decorum in manners and language often found wanting where it does not. Sectarians will not venture to rhapsodise, nor infidels to scoff, in the common intercourse of society. Both are injurious to the cause of rational religion, and to check both must be advantageous.

It is certainly possible that some of the fanciful variations upon the ancient creeds of the Christian Church, with which transatlantic religionists amuse themselves, might

---

2. The Great Awakening, see pp. 544.   3. Inspired by the ministry of Dorcas (Acts 9), these societies of women organized relief for the poor.   4. Bawdy Roman celebration of winter solstice and the god Saturn.   5. William Shakespeare (1564–1616), *Hamlet* (1603), 5.1.256–257.

inspire morbid imaginations in Europe as well as in America; but before they can disturb the solemn harmony *here*, they must prelude by a defiance, not only to commonsense, but what is infinitely more appalling, to common usage. They must at once rank themselves with the low and the illiterate, for only such prefer the eloquence of the tub to that of the pulpit. The aristocracy must ever, as a body, belong to the established church, and it is but a small proportion of the influential classes, who would be willing to allow that they do not belong to the aristocracy. That such feelings influence the professions of men, it were ignorance or hypocrisy to deny; and that nation is wise who knows how to turn even such feelings into a wholesome stream of popular influence.

As a specimen of the tone in which religion is mixed in the ordinary intercourse of society, I will transcribe the notes I took of a conversation, at which I was present, at Cincinnati; I wrote them immediately after the conversation took place.

Dr A.: "I wish, Mrs M., that you would explain to me what a revival is. I hear it talked of all over the city, and I know it means something about Jesus Christ and religion; but that is all I know; will you instruct me farther?"

Mrs M.: "I expect, Dr A., that you want to laugh at me. But that makes no difference; I am firm in my principles, and I fear no one's laughter."

Dr A.: "Well, but what is a revival?"

Mrs M.: "It is difficult, very difficult, to make those see who have no light; to make those understand whose souls are darkened. A revival means just an elegant kindling of the spirit; it is brought about to the Lord's people by the hands of his saints, and it means salvation in the highest."

Dr A.: "But what is it the people mean by talking of feeling the revival? and waiting in spirit for the revival? and the ecstasy of the revival?"

Mrs M.: "O Doctor! I am afraid that you are too far gone astray to understand all that. It is a glorious assurance, a whispering of the everlasting covenant, it is the bleating of the lamb, it is the welcome of the shepherd, it is the essence of love, it is the fulness of glory,[6] it is being in Jesus, it is Jesus being in us, it is taking the Holy Ghost into our bosoms, it is sitting ourselves down by God, it is being called to the high places, it is eating and drinking and sleeping in the Lord, it is becoming a lion in the faith, it is being lowly and meek, and kissing the hand that smites, it is being mighty and powerful, and scorning reproof, it is——"

Dr A.: "Thank you, Mrs M., I feel quite satisfied; and I think I understand a revival now almost as well as you do yourself."

Mrs A.: "My! Where can you have learnt all that stuff, Mrs M.?"

Mrs M.: "How benighted you are! From the Holy Book, from the Word of the Lord, from the Holy Ghost and Jesus Christ themselves."

Mrs A.: "It does seem so droll to me, to hear you talk of 'the Word of the Lord'. Why, I have been brought up to look upon the Bible as nothing better than an old newspaper."

Mrs O.: "Surely, you only say this for the sake of hearing what Mrs M. will say in return—you do not mean it?"

Mrs A.: "La, yes! to be sure I do."

Dr A.: "I profess that I by no means wish my wife to read all she might find there. What says the Colonel, Mrs M.?"

---

6. All biblical figurations of Jesus.

Mrs M.: "As to that, I never stop to ask him. I tell him every day that I believe in Father, Son, and Holy Ghost, and that it is his duty to believe in them too; and then my conscience is clear, and I don't care what he believes. Really, I have no notion of one's husband interfering in such matters."

Dr A.: "You are quite right. I am sure I give my wife leave to believe just what she likes: but she is a good woman, and does not abuse the liberty; for she believes nothing."

It was not once, nor twice, nor thrice, but many many times, during my residence in America, that I was present when subjects which custom as well as principle had taught me to consider as fitter for the closet than the tea-table, were thus lightly discussed. I hardly know whether I was more startled at first hearing, in little dainty namby-pamby tones, a profession of atheism over a tea-cup, or at having my attention called from a Johnny cake to a rhapsody on election and the second birth.[7]

But, notwithstanding this revolting licence, persecution exists to a degree unknown, I believe, in our well-ordered land since the days of Cromwell.[8] I had the following anecdote from a gentleman perfectly well acquainted with the circumstances: A tailor sold a suit of clothes to a sailor a few moments before he sailed, which was on a Sunday morning. The corporation of New York prosecuted the tailor, and he was convicted, and sentenced to a fine greatly beyond his means to pay. Mr F., a lawyer of New York, defended him with much eloquence, but in vain. His powerful speech, however, was not without effect; for it raised him such a host of Presbyterian enemies as sufficed to destroy his practice. Nor was this all: his nephew was at the time preparing for the bar, and soon after the above circumstance occurred, his certificates were presented, and refused, with this declaration, that "no man of the name and family of F. should be admitted." I have met this young man in society; he is a person of very considerable talent; and being thus cruelly robbed of his profession, has become the editor of a newspaper.

—1832

Andrews Norton
1786–1853

A friend, correspondent, and visitor of Joanna Baillie, Anna Laetitia Barbauld, William Wordsworth, and Samuel Taylor Coleridge, Andrews Norton was instrumental in bringing British Romanticism to America. As the librarian at Harvard, he bought and edited the works of these writers, making sure they were available on the library shelves to be read by the likes of Ralph Waldo Emerson, Henry David Thoreau, Theodore Parker, and other students at the College and Divinity School. Unfortunately for Norton, these students read into this literature a critique of the Unitarian theology Norton thought it buttressed. Referred to by his adversaries as the "hard-headed Unitarian Pope," Norton was Dexter Professor of Sacred Literature at the Harvard Divinity School and helped to make the institution a stronghold of Unitarian theology. Thus, when the liberal Emerson delivered his radical address to the 1838 graduating class, telling them they could attain the heights Christ reached, Norton was displeased. Emerson was forthwith banned from speaking there for over twenty years. The *Divinity School*

---

7. When "born again," Christians number themselves among the saved or the elect.   8. Oliver Cromwell (1599–1658) ruled England after dethroning Charles I; Catholics were persecuted during his rule.

Address was published and reviewed in several newspapers, where Norton attacked it, referring to the *Address* as "nonsense and impiety." Moreover, Norton published his *Discourse on the Latest Form of Infidelity* (1839), which defended the miracles of Christ against all claims to the contrary by Transcendentalists at home and abroad. The Emerson–Norton controversy, which became a point of departure of the radical Transcendentalists from the conservative Unitarians of the Divinity School, demonstrates how divergent interpretations of the Romantic writers were at the heart of one of the most famous debates in American theology.

from Discourse on the Latest Form of Infidelity

I address you, Gentlemen, and our friends who are assembled with us, on an occasion of more than common interest; as it is your first meeting since joining together in a society as former pupils of the Theological School in this place. Many of you may look back over a considerable portion of time that has elapsed since your residence here. . . .

I see among you many, who, I know, will recall our former connexion with the same interest as I do, and whom I am privileged to regard as friends. As for those of you, Gentlemen, to whom I have not stood in the relation of an instructer, we also have an intimate connexion with each other. Your office is to defend, explain, and enforce the truths of Christianity; and with the importance of those truths no one can be more deeply impressed than myself. So far as you are faithful to your duty, the strong sympathy of all good men is with you.

But we meet in a revolutionary and uncertain state of religious opinion, existing throughout what is called the Christian world. Our religion is very imperfectly understood, and received by comparatively a small number with intelligent faith. In proportion as our view is more extended, and we are better acquainted with what is and what has been, we shall become more sensible of the great changes that have long been in preparation, but which of late have been rapidly developed. The present state of things imposes new responsibilities upon all, who know the value of our faith and have ability to maintain it. Let us then employ this occasion in considering some of the characteristics of the times and some of those opinions now prevalent, which are at war with a belief in Christianity.

By a belief in Christianity, we mean the belief that Christianity is a revelation by God of the truths of religion; and that the divine authority of him[1] whom God commissioned to speak to us in his name was attested, in the only mode in which it could be, by miraculous displays of his power. Religious truths are those truths, and those alone, which concern the relations of man to God and eternity. It is only as an immortal being and a creature of God, that man is capable of religion. Now those truths which concern our higher nature, and all that can with reason deeply interest us in our existence, we Christians receive, as we trust, on the testimony of God. He who rejects Christianity must admit them, if he admit them at all, upon some other evidence.

But the fundamental truths of religion taught by Christianity became very early connected with human speculations, to which the same importance was gradually attached, and for the proof of which the same divine authority was claimed. These speculations spread out and consolidated into systems of theology, presenting aspects equally hostile to reason and to our faith; so hostile, that, for many centuries, a true Christian in belief and heart, earnest to communicate to others the blessings of his faith, would have

---

1. Jesus.

experienced, anywhere in Christendom, a fate similar to that which his Master suffered among the Jews. It would be taking a different subject from what I have proposed, to attempt to explain and trace the causes of this monstrous phenomenon. The false representations of Christianity, that have come down to us from less enlightened times, have ceased to retain their power over far the larger portion of those individuals who form, for good or evil, the character of the age in which they live. But the reaction of the human intellect and heart against their imposition has as yet had but little tendency to procure the reception of more correct notions of Christianity. On the contrary, the inveterate and enormous errors, that have prevailed, have so perverted men's conceptions, have so obscured and perplexed the whole subject, have so stood in the way of all correct knowledge of facts, and all just reasoning; there are so few works in Christian theology not at least colored and tainted by them; and they still present such obstacles at every step to a rational investigation of the truth; that the degree of learning, reflection, judgment, freedom from worldly influences, and independence of thought, necessary to ascertain for one's self the true character of Christianity, is to be expected from but few. The greater number, consequently, confound the systems that have been substituted for it with Christianity itself, and receive them in its stead, or, in rejecting them, reject our faith. The tendency of the age is to the latter result.

This tendency is strengthened by the political action of the times, especially in the Old World.[2] Ancient institutions and traditionary power are there struggling to maintain themselves against the vast amount of new energy that has been brought into action. Long-existing forms of society are giving way. The old prejudices by which they were propped up are decaying. Wise men look with awe at the spectacle; as if they saw in some vast tower, hanging over a populous city, rents opening, and its sides crumbling and inclining. But in the contest between the new and the old, which has spread over Europe, erroneous representations of Christianity are in alliance with established power. They have long been so. The institutions connected with them have long been principal sources of rank and emolument. What passes for Christianity is thus placed in opposition to the demands of the mass of men, and is regarded by them as inimical to their rights; while, on the other hand, those, to whom false Christianity affords aid, repel all examination into the genuineness of its claims.

The commotion of men's minds in the rest of the civilized world, produces a sympathetic action in our own country. We have indeed but little to guard us against the influence of the depraving literature and noxious speculations which flow in among us from Europe. We have not yet any considerable body of intellectual men, devoted to the higher departments of thought, and capable of informing and guiding others in attaining the truth. There is no controlling power of intellect among us.

Christianity, then, has been grossly misrepresented, is very imperfectly understood, and powerful causes are in operation to obstruct all correct knowledge of it, and to withdraw men's thoughts and affections from it. But at the present day there is little of that avowed and zealous infidelity, the infidelity of highly popular authors, acknowledged enemies of our faith, which characterized the latter half of the last century. Their writings, often disfigured by gross immoralities, are now falling into disrepute. But the effects of those writings, and of the deeply seated causes by which they were produced, are still widely diffused. There is now no bitter warfare against

---

2. The French Revolution and other democratic movements.

Christianity, because such men as then waged it would now consider our religion as but a name, a pretence, the obsolete religion of the state, the superstition of the vulgar. But infidelity has but assumed another form, and in Europe, and especially in Germany, has made its way among a very large portion of nominally Christian theologians. Among them are now to be found those whose writings are most hostile to all that characterizes our faith. Christianity is undermined by them with the pretence of settling its foundations anew. Phantoms are substituted for the realities of revelation.

It is asserted, apparently on good authority, that the celebrated atheist Spinoza composed the work in which his opinions are most fully unfolded, in the Dutch language, and committed it to his friend, the physician Mayer, to translate into Latin; that, where the name *God* now appears, Spinoza had written *Nature*; but that Mayer induced him to substitute the former word for the latter, in order partially to screen himself from the odium to which he might be exposed.[3] Whether this anecdote be true or not, a similar abuse of language appears in many of the works to which I refer. The holiest names are there; a superficial or ignorant reader may be imposed upon by their occurrence; but they are there as words of show, devoid of their essential meaning, and perverted to express some formless and powerless conception. In Germany the theology of which I speak has allied itself with atheism, with pantheism, and with the other irreligious speculations, that have appeared in those metaphysical systems from which the God of Christianity is excluded.

There is no subject of historical inquiry of more interest than the history of opinions; there is none of more immediate concern than the state of opinions; for opinions govern the world. Except in cases of strong temptation, men's evil passions must coincide with or must pervert their opinions, before they can obtain the mastery. It is, therefore, not a light question, what men think of Christianity. It is a question on which, in the judgment of an intelligent believer, the condition of the civilized world depends. With these views we will consider the aspect that infidelity has taken in our times.

The latest form of infidelity is distinguished by assuming the Christian name, while it strikes directly at the root of faith in Christianity, and indirectly of all religion, by denying the miracles attesting the divine mission of Christ. The first writer, so far as I know, who maintained the impossibility of a miracle was Spinoza, whose argument, disengaged from the use of language foreign from his opinions, is simply this, that the laws of nature are the laws by which God is bound, Nature and God being the same, and therefore laws from which Nature or God can never depart. The argument is founded on atheism. The denial of the possibility of miracles must involve the denial of the existence of God; since, if there be a God, in the proper sense of the word, there can be no room for doubt, that he may act in a manner different from that in which he displays his power in the ordinary operations of nature. It deserves notice, however, that in Spinoza's discussion of this subject we find that affectation of religious language, and of religious reverence and concern, which is so striking a characteristic of many of the irreligious speculations of our day, and of which he, perhaps, furnished the prototype; for he has been regarded as a profound teacher, a patriarch of truth, by some of the most noted among the infidel philosophers and theologians of Germany. "I will show from Scripture," he says, "that the decrees and commands of God, and consequently his providence, are nothing but the

---

3. Benedict Spinoza (1632–1677), Dutch philosopher whose works were published with Ludwig Mayer's editorial assistance.

order of nature."—"If any thing should take place in nature which does not follow from its laws, *that* would necessarily be repugnant to the order which God has established in nature by its universal laws, and, therefore, contrary to nature and its laws; and consequently the belief of such an event would cause universal doubt and lead to atheism."[4] So strong a hold has religion upon the inmost nature of man, that even its enemies, in order to delude their followers, thus assume its aspect and mock its tones.

What has been stated is the great argument of Spinoza, to which every thing in his discussion of the subject refers; but this discussion may appear like the text-book of much that has been written in modern times concerning it. There is one, however, among the writings against the miracles of Christianity, of a different kind, the famous Essay of Hume.[5] None has drawn more attention, or has more served as a groundwork for infidelity. Yet, considering the sagacity of the author, and the celebrity of his work, it is remarkable, that, in his main argument, the whole point to be proved is broadly assumed in the premises. "It is a miracle," he says, "that a dead man should come to life; because that has never been observed, in any age or country. There must, therefore, be a uniform experience against every miraculous event; otherwise the event would not merit that appellation." The conclusion, if conclusion it may be called, is easily made. If a miracle has never been observed in any age or country, if uniform experience shows that no miracle ever occurred, then it follows that all accounts of past miracles are undeserving of credit. But if there be an attempt to stretch this easy conclusion, and to represent it as involving the intrinsic incredibility of a miracle, the argument immediately gives way. "Experience," says Hume, "is our only guide in reasoning concerning matters of fact." Experience is the foundation of such reasoning, but we may draw inferences from our experience. We may conclude from it the existence of a power capable of works which we have never known it to perform; and no one, it may be presumed, who believes that there is a God, will say, that he is convinced by his experience, that God can manifest his power only in conformity to the laws which he has imposed upon nature.

Hume cannot be charged with affecting religion; but in the conclusion of his Essay, he says, in mockery; "I am the better pleased with the method of reasoning here delivered, as I think it may serve to confound those dangerous friends, or disguised enemies, to the Christian religion, who have undertaken to defend it by the principles of human reason. Our most holy religion is founded on *faith*, not on reason; and it is a sure method of exposing it, to put it to such a trial as it is by no means fitted to endure." What Hume said in derision has been virtually repeated, apparently in earnest, by some of the modern disbelievers of miracles, who still choose to profess a belief in Christianity.

To deny that a miracle is capable of proof, or to deny that it may be proved by evidence of the same nature as establishes the truth of other events, is, in effect, as I have said, to deny the existence of God. A miracle can be incapable of proof, only because it is physically or morally impossible; since what is possible may be proved. To deny that the truth of a miracle may be established, involves the denial of creation; for there can be no greater miracle than creation. It equally implies, that no species of being that propagates its kind ever had a commencement; for if there was a first plant that grew without seed, or a first man without parents, of if of any series of events there was a first without such antecedents as the laws of nature require, then there was a miracle. . . .

---

4. *A Theologico-Political Treatise* (1670). 5. David Hume (1711–1776), Scottish philosopher, author of *A Treatise on Human Nature* (1739).

Of the facts on which religion is founded, we can pretend to no assurance, except that derived from the testimony of God, from the Christian revelation. He who has received this testimony is a Christian; and we may ask now, as was asked by an apostle; "Who is he that overcomes the world, but he who believes that Jesus was the Son of God."[6] Christian faith alone affords such consolation and support as the heart needs amid the deprivations and sufferings of life; it alone gives action and strength to all that is noblest in our nature; it alone furnishes a permanent and effectual motive for growing virtue; it alone enables man to act conformably to his nature and destiny. This is always true. But we may have a deeper sense of the value of our faith, if we look abroad on the present state of the world, and see, all around, the waves heaving and the tempest rising. Everywhere is instability and uncertainty. But from the blind conflict between men exasperated and degraded by injustice and suffering, and men corrupted and hardened by the abuse of power, from the mutual outrages of angry political parties, in which the most unprincipled and violent become the leaders, from the fierce collision of mere earthly passions and cravings, whatever changes may result, no good is to be hoped. . . .

Gentlemen, I have addressed your understandings, not your feelings. But the subject of Christianity is one which cannot be rightly apprehended without the strongest feeling; not the transient excitement existing for an hour, and then forgotten, but a feeling possessing the whole heart, and governing our lives. Of the form of infidelity, which we have been considering, there can be but one opinion among honest men. Great moral offences in individuals are, indeed, commonly connected with the peculiar character of their age, and with a prevailing want of moral sentiment in regard to such offences, in the community in which they are committed. This may be pleaded in excuse for the individual; but the essential nature of the offence remains. It is a truth, which few among us will question, that, for any one to pretend to be a Christian teacher, who disbelieves the divine origin and authority of Christianity, and would undermine the belief of others, is treachery towards God and man. If I were to address such a one, I would implore him by all his remaining self-respect, by his sense of common honesty, by his regard to the well-being of his fellow-men, by his fear of God, if he believe that there is a God, and by the awful realities of the future world, to stop short in his course; and, if he cannot become a Christian, to cease to be a pretended Christian teacher, and to assume his proper character.

If we have taken a correct view of the state of opinion throughout the world, you will perceive, that it is a subject of very serious consideration, and of individual action, to all of us who have faith in Christianity, and especially to you, Gentlemen, who have devoted yourselves to the Christian ministry. Every motive, that addresses the better part of our nature, urges you to be faithful in your office. A sincere moral purpose will strengthen your judgment and ability; for he who has no other object but to do right, will not find it difficult to ascertain his duty, and the means of performing it. He who earnestly desires to serve his fellow-men is so strongly drawn toward the truth, as the essential means of human happiness, that he is not likely to be turned aside by any dangerous error. Our Saviour referred to no supernatural illumination when he said; *If any one will do the will of him who sent me, he shall know concerning my doctrine, whether it be*

---

6. 1 John 5.5.

from God, or whether I speak from myself.[7] What you believe and feel, it is the business of your lives, and this is a great privilege, to make others believe and feel. In the view of the worldly, the sphere of your duties may often appear humble; but you will not on that account break through it to seek for notoriety beyond. Deep and permanent feeling is very quiet and persevering. It cannot fail in its purposes. It cannot but communicate itself in some degree to others, and it is secure of the approbation of God.

—1839

Amos Bronson Alcott
1799–1888

If Theodore Parker and Ralph Waldo Emerson found in the British Romantics and German Transcendentalists a ladder from earth to the heavens, Amos Bronson Alcott wished to pull the ladder up after him and never descend the rungs. After reading William Wordsworth's "Ode. Intimations of Immortality," which held that souls pre-exist with God before they are born on earth, Alcott took these words as Gospel. Although Percy Bysshe Shelley once responded to the "Ode" by stopping a mother and child to ask her what her baby could tell him of life in heaven, Alcott took Shelley's response to a new level by interviewing many Massachusetts children about the divine prenatal care they had received. His discussions at the Temple School with pupils about their notions of heaven were recorded by his fellow teacher Elizabeth Palmer Peabody in *Record of a School* (1835). *Record of Conversations on the Gospels Held in Mr. Alcott's School, Unfolding the Doctrine and Discipline of Human Culture* (1836) was Alcott's sequel to Peabody's book. Here he gave transcripts of interpretations of scripture developed through Socratic dialogue with children. Although his Temple School ended up closing and being condemned by many contemporary Americans, in England a school called Alcott House was founded on his educational principles. Ultimately, his principles and Peabody's were to have a lasting effect on education in America, particularly on the Kindergarten Movement. Some of the practices they helped to bring about include the encouragement of imagination and creativity in children (often by getting them out of the classroom and into the outdoors), more widespread use of the Socratic method as opposed to lecture, the abolition of physical punishment, and the inclusion of organized recreation, otherwise known as recess.

from Record of Conversation on the Gospels
Held in Mr. Alcott's School
CONVERSATION II.
Testimony of Nature and Scripture to Spirit.
Nature and Scripture.
Idea of Spirit.
II. Analogical Evidence.

1. Physiological Facts.—Reproduction and growth; light and shade; incubation and birth; budding and efflorescence; fountain and stream.
2. Psychological Facts.—Birth and death; renovation and decay; sense of imperfection; standard of perfection in conscience; idea of absolute and derivative being.

---

7. John 14.23.

3. Historical Facts.—Record of spirit, or Scripture; General Preface to the Gospels from the Sacred Text; credibility of witnesses; authenticity of the Gospel Record; sum of results.

MR. ALCOTT.   What was the conclusion to which we came, after the conversation of Wednesday last?

Idea of Spirit.

SEVERAL.   That there was a Spirit.

MR. ALCOTT.   Did each of you conclude and feel it proved *in your own heart*, that there is a Spirit?

(*All held up hands.*)

MR. ALCOTT.   What do you understand by an *inward proof of* Spirit?

CHARLES.   What one feels, and thinks.

MR. ALCOTT.   Are there *outward evidences* of Spirit?

Analogical Evidence.

CHARLES.   Actions, any actions, outward actions, an earthquake, the creeping of a worm.

Physiological Facts.

GEORGE K.   Moving, the creeping of a baby.

LEMUEL.   The moving of a leaf, lightning.

ANDREW.   A waterfall, a rose.

FRANK.   Walking.

SAMUEL R.   A tree.

EDWARD C.   A star.

SUSAN.   The sun.

GEORGE B.   A steam engine.

MR. ALCOTT.   Where does the spirit work in that?

GEORGE B.   In the men that work it.

CHARLES.   No; in the steam.

EDWARD J.   In the machinery, and the steam, and the men, and all.

MR. ALCOTT.   You perceive then what I mean by outward evidence of spirit?

CHARLES.   Things, external nature.

MR. ALCOTT.   And this will be our subject in part to-day.

Reproduction and Growth.

MR. ALCOTT.   Do smaller things prove greater things, or greater things smaller things? How many do not understand me?

(*Several held up their hands.*)

Does an acorn prove there has been an oak, or an oak prove there has been an acorn?

(*Some said one and some the other, as they did also to the next question.*)

MR. ALCOTT.   Which was first in time, an acorn or an oak?

GEORGE K.   Sometimes one is first and sometimes the other. In the woods, oaks grow up wild; and you can plant acorns and have oaks.

SAMUEL R.   I think God made oaks first, and all the other oaks there have ever been, came from the acorns of those first oaks.

Light and Shade.

MR. ALCOTT.   Does light prove darkness, or darkness light?

SEVERAL.   Each proves the other.

MR. ALCOTT.   Can nothing prove something?

ALL.   No.

MR. ALCOTT.   But darkness is mere absence of light. Is darkness any thing to your spirit?

SEVERAL.   No.

CHARLES.   I think darkness is something.

MR. ALCOTT.   Is darkness any thing to your senses?

ANDREW.   No; it only seems so.

MR. ALCOTT.   What does it seem to be?

ANDREW.   It is the shadow of light.

Incubation and Birth.

MR. ALCOTT.   Does the egg foretel the chick, or the chick the egg? (*They first said one, and then the other, and then both, and some referred to God who could make either.*)

Budding and Efflorescence.

MR. ALCOTT.   Which has most meaning, a bud or a flower?

SEVERAL.   A flower.

SUSAN.   A bud, because it is going to be a flower, and makes you think of it.

EDWARD J.   Perhaps the bud will be picked.

MR. ALCOTT.   Accidents are always excepted.

(*He then asked like questions about many things, among the rest a brook and the ocean, the cradle and the grave, and similar answers were returned. He remarked that their answers showed which minds were historical and which were analytic. He then went on:*)

Psychological Facts.

Which is the superior, spirit or body?

ALL.   Spirit.

MR. ALCOTT.   Lemuel, will you give me a reason?

Renovation and Decay.

LEMUEL.   Because the body decays, and the spirit cannot decay; and the spirit is not seen; and when the spirit is gone the body cannot do any thing.

MR. ALCOTT.   Is it the invisibleness and the undecaying nature of the spirit, which makes it superior, then? Have you ever seen any perfect visible thing?

GEORGE B.   Yes; a rose.

MR. ALCOTT.   Did it remain perfect?

GEORGE B.   No.

MR. ALCOTT.   What thing is perfect and remains perfect?

GEORGE K.   Jesus' body was perfect, for it ascended into heaven.

MR. ALCOTT.   Is there proof that his body ascended?

GEORGE K.   The Bible says so.

CHARLES.   The Bible says the disciples saw him ascend.

MR. ALCOTT.   Yes, they saw him ascend; yet not perhaps his body;— and besides, Jesus' body suffered pain; and was it perfect, while it was suffering pain?

(*No answer.*)

Can you say that your bodily senses are perfect, that they have never deceived you?

(*None held up hands.*)

When you look round the world, and see no perfect, visible thing, what do you feel?

(*No answer.*)

Sense of Imperfection.

Is there not something within you which measures all imperfection?

CHARLES.   Yes, the thought of Perfection.

MR. ALCOTT.   By what do you measure your thought of Perfection?

CHARLES.   By God.

MR. ALCOTT.   Is the imperfection in the outward world a proof of something perfect within?

(*No answer.*)

For instance, you tell me that you have seen a person do something wrong: now, what do you make the standard? How do you know it is wrong?

CHARLES.   By Reason.

LEMUEL.   No; Judgment judges.

EDWARD J.   We measure by the spirit.

MR. ALCOTT.   What is in the spirit; a sense of—what?

LEMUEL.   A Sense of Good—of Perfection.

MR. ALCOTT.   Where is all proof, then?

LEMUEL.   In Conscience and in God.

Standard of Perfection in Conscience.

MR. ALCOTT.   And when Jesus utters the divine injunction, "Be ye Perfect, even as your Father in Heaven is Perfect,"[1] he does but reannounce the sentiment of Duty in every conscience, which ever utters the same words.

Now, do perfect things prove imperfect things, or imperfect things prove perfect things?

GEORGE K.   They prove each other.

MR. ALCOTT.   Does your spirit prove there is a God, or because there is a God, must your spirit be?

CHARLES.   Each proves the other.

Idea of Absolute and Derivative Being.

MR. ALCOTT.   All proof then is in God, spirit being its own proof, because there is more of God in it, than in any thing outward. As an acorn reminds you of an oak, so does the spirit within remind you of God. Your spirits, like the acorns, (if you choose to carry on the figure,) drop off from God, to plant themselves in Time. Once they were within the oak, but they come out individual differing acorns, the seeds of new oaks. The other things mentioned are proofs of the same kind. Spirits are born out of the Supreme Spirit, and by their power of reproducing spirit, constantly prove their own existence from his existence, and his existence from their own.—That there is a spirit in us all you have proofs, as you have shown.

---

1. Matthew 5.48.

Historical Facts.

There are yet other proofs of spirit, especially the Life of Jesus Christ, which we are going to study. He took a body and came into the world almost two thousand years before we did. He was seen, and those who saw and knew him,—his friends,—wrote down what he said and did; and their words make what are called the GOSPELS. Luke was one of these friends. He began an account of Jesus,—the Gospel of his life, that is, the Good News of his life,—in these words: Mr. Alcott read

The General Preface to the Gospels.

Mark i. 1.

Luke i. 1–4.

A. D. 44. Probably written at Jerusalem.

Record of Gospels or Scripture.

1 The beginning of the Gospel of Jesus Christ, the Son of God.

A. D. 64. Written in Achaia.

1 Forasmuch as many have taken in hand to set forth in order a declaration of those things which are most surely believed among us,

2 Even as they delivered them unto us, which from the beginning were eyewitnesses, and ministers of the word;

3 It seemed good to me also, having had perfect understanding of all things from the very first, to write unto thee in order, most excellent Theophilus,

4 That thou mightest know the certainty of those things, wherein thou hast been instructed.

You perceive that Luke wrote this Gospel—this good news of Jesus Christ—for a particular friend. He had himself learned most of the facts from others, for he was not an eyewitness from the beginning.

Credibility of Witnesses.

Now I suppose that you can place entire confidence in these words, which are called the Gospels. You doubtless believe that they have a meaning, all of them, worth finding out; and you feel sure that they are all true.

GEORGE K.   There are some things I think *truer*. I believe those words, but I am more sure of some things.

MR. ALCOTT.   Of what?

GEORGE K.   Why—that the Stove is in the room.

CHARLES.   I do not believe that those words are the same as Luke wrote down.

Authenticity of the Gospel Record.

MR. ALCOTT.   Luke wrote in Greek; and these words are translated. But the Greek words are yet preserved, and those are the very words of Luke, as can be satisfactorily proved; for great care was taken of so valuable a writing, by the earliest Christians.

(Some more conversation ensued on this subject, in which Charles was told that there had been a great deal of dispute concerning these writings in the early ages; and that it was now an undisputed fact,—except by an individ-

ual here and there,—that these writings all belonged to the persons by whom they were said to be written. And that this was a subject he might examine for himself, when he was older.)

Subject.   You may now tell me what has been the subject of to-day's conversation.
            LEMUEL.   Outward Evidences of Spirit.
            CHARLES.   In Nature.
            OTHERS.   And in the Gospel.
            MR. ALCOTT.   And the Evidence for the Gospel Record.

—1836

Charles King Newcomb
1820–1894

A prolific Transcendentalist writer, Charles King Newcomb's thirty-eight volumes of unpublished journals and commonplace books detail his daily activities, his health, and his moral, political, and literary opinions. Among the volumes, one on Samuel Taylor Coleridge, William Wordsworth, and Ralph Waldo Emerson stands out, revealing Newcomb as an enthusiastic yet highly moralistic reader. Indeed, after reading Newcomb's journals, Emerson professed that his friend was "the subtlest observer & diviner of character I ever met." Emerson's journals and writings attest to Newcomb's strong presence, as do the writings of Henry David Thoreau, Nathaniel Hawthorne, and Margaret Fuller, to name a few. The small amount of scholarship on Newcomb treats him as a minor figure, a friend and confidante of Emerson and Fuller. Newcomb is seldom anthologized, and the one monograph devoted to him—a selection of journal entries—provides a glimpse of the more complete picture that has yet to be recovered from his unpublished writings. Newcomb was an important conduit of British Romantic thought for Emerson and other Transcendentalists. His understanding of these poets was developed during his time as an undergraduate at Brown University.

It is no coincidence that Newcomb received his first lessons at Brown in latitudinarianism—an attitude of intellectual resistance to the Church's insistence on prescribed practices such as church order and liturgy for greater freedom of opinion in religious belief. Although nominally Baptist, Brown was a sanctuary for those seeking an alternative to the orthodox Unitarianism of the Harvard Divinity School. Not surprisingly, when Newcomb graduated, he was unable to enter the priesthood because he resisted sectarianism. At Brown, Newcomb joined the United Brothers Society, which grew to include a number of philosophers instrumental in the introduction of British and Continental Romanticism to America: Frederic Henry Hedge, Orestes Brownson, and Emerson. The society was so secretive—and, at times, playfully gothic—that its first meeting was held at midnight in a dark room with guards posted at the door. Indeed, the organization's existence was revealed only when packages of books addressed to them began to arrive at Brown. The packages contained more British Romantic literature than this anthology. Professor Robinson Potter Dunn was also an integral part of Newcomb's education in the British authors of the day, and before the existence of the United Brothers, he had acquired several editions of contemporary English authors for Brown's library. Dunn was appointed to one of the earliest professorships of English literature in either the Old or New World. Officially his lectures were listed as courses in rhetoric, but they were most assuredly on English literature, as his lecture notes and those of his students make clear. The lending lists of the Brown library suggest that Dunn and his students were in a constant struggle to borrow editions of Wordsworth, Coleridge, Scott, Southey, and others. Brown students rivaled those at Harvard in their borrowing of and from the texts of Coleridge. The Transcendentalist James Freeman Clarke noted of his time at Harvard that his "real professors of rhetoric were Charles Lamb and Coleridge, Walter Scott and Wordsworth." Newcomb could have penned these very words: During his student years at Brown, he filled his journals and commonplace books with quotations from and commentary on Coleridge, Emerson, and Wordsworth.

The influence of these authors is manifest in Newcomb's story "The Two Dolons," published in the July 1842 issue of *The Dial* at the behest of Fuller and Emerson. The story centers on the young boy Dolon's spiritual communion with nature. This story was certainly an homage to, and perhaps a parody of, notions of nature's spirituality evident in American Transcendentalism and British Romanticism. If the story meant to maintain an ironic distance from the Transcendentalists, it was certainly not interpreted this way by the group's leader. After Emerson read the story, he remarked of Newcomb that

> Charles is a Religious Intellect. Let it be to his praise that when I carried his MS[1] story to the woods, & read it in the armchair of the upturned root of a pinetree, I felt . . . some efficient faith again in the repairs of the Universe, some independency of natural relations whilst spiritual affinities can be so perfect & compensating.

The Two Dolons

From the MS Symphony of Dolon.

The First Dolon.

Dolon, wont to be much in the air, in the fields and woods, beneath the sky, the clouds, the branches and leaves, and in the mists, those clouds of earth, almost lived in nature, like a sea-fairy in the ocean, everywhere in which it is at home, and has a place where it may be as if it sought it by roaming,—the gurgle-reserved silent meadows of high green waving grass, the atmosphere and air-like water, the rocks over which the waves oscillated reflected sunniness, like shadows on the country landscape of clouds passing overhead, the rocks ivied over with seaweed and vines and grass, like ruins of the sea-ages, the woods and caves of tree-coral, as if petrified forests of an ancient race of human fishes, and the coral edifice-like places with interwoven open intricate roofs, like the pine-woods, and near the surface, which was like the high heaven of the sea-earth, where seemed to be sky and clouds, which were outwardly only reflected to the sight of men, though to men it seems as if the light in the ocean must be air-like, or grave moon-light, for even the sunlit noon surface is like a bright day moonlight. Dolon had always been in Nature, unspecially and really as if in his proper place. Nature is not primarily a sentiment to children; sentiment may be a feeling in it, but it is place and not sentiment which leads them to it. A child will act from the fulness of its affections and feelings as if from consciousness, but these are the spirit which thus affect him, and he acts from them as facts which buoy him up and float him; not as sentiment which is need of the fact, and makes him a seeker, as men, who away from their home, or outwardly related to their sphere, feel that which develops in them sentiment and aspiration, but does not put them in the natural position of the sentiment, and the sentiment thus acts, out of its place, from depths which the surface in its hurried action, is as if dissevered from. Children do all in the fact, as a mermaid may joy and frolic in the water

---

1. Abbreviation for "manuscript."

which it is always in, and as one who is out in the night may see shooting stars; the direct act is as if extra, while the regular course goes on, an exuberance of the real from the real. A child's whole person, as well as nature, (of which Dolon was an ideal-like though most natural exemplification, for the most natural is the most ideal and common,) shows that its proper sphere is Nature; out of Nature it is more of an individuality, like a king in un-state relations, than of an individual thing in life which individualizes by giving all things a place in it, and leaving them to their life in their own places like passengers in a vessel; a flower in the house is a flower in form, but in nature the form is the flower, the flower in life, and the flower is by its life rather than by that which is a form called self which Life has taken, as a boat is not a boat till it is launched. Life is the unpersonalizer of persons, the unifier of individuals, as playing is of a stage-company; the relation of things to things, and a rotatory circle like the earth, which, by moving on its axis, faces all parts of the infinite space around it. Dolon, restrained in the house, would seek nature like a caged bird the air. Those deep, heaven-like eyes required the broad and high beautiful realities of nature, if only for freedom, and space, and color,—which is somewhat of a good substitute for nature in houses, especially if of forms, as in carpets. The individual things of nature are related to man, as well as man is to man; and man must be with stars, and trees, and grasses, as he must with man, to be at ease. Life lives in her forms, and is evolved from them, like rays of light from the sun, and we truly live only in her atmosphere; individualities are thus universalized, as if in the whole they neutralized each, and kept each other in active relation to her, like spans of horses; for, left to itself, the vital becomes a centred isolation in the individual, like water in anything whose pores are closed; as if individuality was only a form which Life, like Genius, had taken, and which has no life in itself, but by being in life; and out of it, it ceases to be, like rays of light separated from the sun. All things in nature are centred to face each other, and the relation, represented to men by influence, is sure, however they may be as persons; the sea and the sky face, and the mutual relation goes on, though the sea tosses about, and the sky is covered with clouds; men receive influence from Nature, though they never look at her or think of her, and are busy in some mechanical labor, if only they be in her. There is as it were a quiet inward depth and gentle positiveness-like reserve, in men who live in the air; they have not the prominence and selfness of those who live in the house, and Nature is around them mighty and absolute as a Monarch, and gentle, quiet, and familiar-like, like a great family dog lying by the doorsteps in the yard, where the children are playing and the men are working. Children are troublesome or noisy, and often restless, within the house and in their present mode of life; for they are shut out from their life-place; the life which would be developed as unobviously and quietly as fruit grows, gives them an excitement or uneasiness of which activity is the effect. Nature is their play-ground and place, and their activity is modified from its original spirit of gentleness and unity, by its being without the Nature which acts on them, as the moon on the tides, and in which they are Beings in Life, and not, as in the house, beings who, the only Being, (like Noblemen from the city-Court alone in the country places,) are not only free, but at needs to be Persons, for they are living things, and life is not around them to meet life, and they create a life for themselves out of their own life, like sailors at sea forming their cabin into a homelike room out of such materials as they have,—or like parrots who encaged and taken from their native clime and woods, talk with the men instead of singing with their mates. Children in the house are as if obtrusive, and men interfere with men; that which in the air and great natural house would be harmony, is a noise in the small artificial house, as even music makes a noise if confined; in Nature all sounds harmonize and blend; and children are more sociable with man by not being given to themselves in Nature, in which fact they recognise the greatness of man, as if next representative to Nature and theirself. A child is not so inquisitive and talkative in Nature; life answers there for itself, and all else, all outwardly seen, is Mystery, and inspires no questions, but a quiet, subdued wonder, like an under-current of comprehension in the mind's state of worship; and a child's looking is unoutward, as if the child saw by its personal power of motion, as if it could fly around like a bird up among stars, but the Being abode fast, and as the child-person remained there, took its own time, and the child instinctively acknowledges its reality by making no subject-personal of aught, and only gratifying his impulses. He talks and prates as he goes along in the horseman's arms, as if he were the horseman; but even the horseman will have no cause to find fault with him, for any want of a deep down practical quiet realizing of his dependence and happiness-expressed gratitude. The infinite senses of man which are adapted to this infinite-like finite, great Nature, are disused and closed by his present life, and his nature becomes estranged from it, and he is as if a stranger in it, and when in it, its beauty comes to him rather through sight and feeling than unity. Deep and great is the soul's long denied appetite; it is as if faint to loss of consciousness, and slow is the reformation of the soul's form. Man in Nature is in an infinity; though there seems a limit, the difference is real between the effect as a reality and appearance; the horizon-enclosed lake will not answer for the ocean, though to the sight it is as large; there is a depth below the earth as well as above it, and the ground is as a solid-floored tree-top, like those which the birds alight on, though merely as tops the shrubs would answer as well. Men have made substitutes for the great Natural Building which is God's theatre and concert room, and though we can see and hear them wherever they are, neither they nor the music are as if they were on his stage, where living is the acting, and where voices rise in infinite fading cadences, like ripples disappearing as they go over the surface of the water like a sail. Men hear their own voices now like finished echoes, and they can seldom get beyond themselves; for they carry their own limit about with them, from which they rebound, like waves in an enclosed place upon themselves; and all life radiates, and returns nor lingers. The purest holy incense rising from the altar will form a cloud in the roof of the greatest Cathedral, and smoke the pictures of Raphael and Guido[2] on the walls.

When a little boy, Dolon loved to hear fairy stories, though he heard them as one hears music which is an atmosphere to the ear as air is to the lungs, and does not require listening, the sounds creating feelings which are in their kind and place what the blood is in its kind and place; and he sat much on the ground in the woods, as if a fairy land, and fairies were all around him, and he felt and seemed as if he saw them. He was a beautiful boy, with long auburn-brown hair, a fair and delicate complexion, light blue eyes, and eyelids which at the side-view lay gently-heavily folded over his eyes, as if the eyes were homes, like heaven air, for two little heavenly fairies, like a spring-fountain in the fresh meadows for little fishes, and the lids were curtains which opened them to the world and covered them from mortal sight, like a cave opening into a forest, and the eyes seemed inlets into the boy's being, and one could find him

---

2. Raffaelo Sanzio (1483–1520) and Guido Reni (1575–1642) or Guido Cagnacci (1601–1681), Italian painters.

there as Dolon found fairies, and men find God, in the air, which was so like his eyes, only they were like a soul which had taken the eye for a form. We do not see the expression in eyes, when we look at them for it a second time; for when we first look, the spiritual in the eye suggests a form to us, and then we look as on a form for the type of the form that is created within us, and spirit is not to be bodily seen.

At length, his father said he must go to a regular school, and that it would not do for Dolon to be growing up so visionary and romantic. He did not see that the so-called visionary was as real to the inner sense, as the so-called real is to the outward sense; that Poetry is a fertility of humanity, and the real life of the deep and substantial part of man, in which also great experience goes on, even like that which a life in the world would give, only it is deeper and more individual within the man; and that the outward is not for the individual as an outward person, but as an inward related soul, whose human feelings and life are expressed by poetry. Men's relations to Nature are closed by their coming between the realities of soul and Nature; their life is erected into a sense, and is not diffused around, like the ocean with its great proportionate surface. Human nature, if left to itself, will be full of life, like the great western forests and standing water, and Poetry is the physical inworld of the spiritual nature, with its life developed in forms; forms are not mere *forms continent of* life, but forms which are *formed life*. Dolon's living relation to things answered at school for activity and readiness in the usual course of systematic learning; for life is ready and willing to meet all that comes before it, and his teacher saw he learned in this spirit of life, by the natural way of the correspondence of means to ends, and that if lessons were given him he so earnestly, singly, and simply, and unconsciously made his own use of them, that he allowed him to learn after his own natural manner, and felt towards him as what he was and not as what, canon-judged, he outwardly did; and his mother liked to have him free, and sent him to school only half of the day, so that he had all the rest for the air and fields and woods. His father wanted him to learn more decidedly, but always saw that Dolon had better be left to himself, at least for the present, and he had a quiet unconscious pride in his son, and felt he did not know how to manage such a being, who was so positive by being himself, though so gentle, and whose only resistance to formal elementary study was an indifference, an unrealizing, as of objects by a blind man, as one placed in a relation by a master of ceremonies, but for what depended upon something to be developed or completed, like children who are being collected in a room and position by elder sisters of their child-host, who smile in their silent designs which are not to be told till all is ready to begin, as if in the humor of mystery. Life is life's teacher, and children deal only with life; all that they make is an imitation of life, and knowledge, as imparted by the present old method, is the only positive thing to them in all nature; all things are to them by being towards them; they do not know and use means, but go along enjoying all, like one on a beautiful road on his way to a place which he does not keep in mind; nature carries them and leaves them free to look and feel as they please, like an infant unconsciously borne in the nurse's arms to a family friend.

At school, Dolon loved to hear about the classic Mythology, (of which the teacher talked and read to him,) as before he had about the fairies. The sky and earth were full of undefined God-Beings, at the same time that there was a history in the theogony,[3] and much which gave local significances and associations, and humanized natural

---

3. The story of the origin of the Greek gods.

objects, the stars, the pine trees, the reeds, the laurel, and so forth; and the Gods being more human and heroic, and more spiritually expressive, answered his advance in life. There is less intellectualness in the relations of youth than of men to the imaginary, for it is more as to the real, and they experience as if from the real; the beautiful is not music and sympathy to them, but has its natural, physical-like effect; the thing which is beautiful acts as a thing upon the child, and Being answers Being rather than looks at each other, and each feels the other as what they internally are. Genius is matured youth living with life within it, which before was out of it or with it. It is as if nature was continented within it, and lived through its own life, as before it lived in the general life. All forms are facts to youth, and recognised by them as beings, not as persons; the sunshine reflects itself in their eyes, and all things are true to them by the realizing of their natures; the cause is known and believed through its effect.

Dolon loved to go and sit on a large rock within a wood which bordered on an old potatoe moss-hilled field, separated from the house by a large hay-field. The woods sloped down from the rock toward the western and southern sky, and Dolon came and sat here, almost regularly, every pleasant late afternoon and early evening. Underneath a part of the rock which was separated from the part on which he sat by an imperfect ravine, was a small cave within a cleft.

Dolon has often heard sounds like footsteps on the dry leaves among the bushes around the rock, as of a person moving stationarily about, but he never saw any one, and thought the sound was of some animal. One afternoon, sitting in the sunset upon the rock, he rose and raised his eyes up to a pine tree which overhung one end of the rock; seated on branches near the top, in an opening of branches which had been broken off, or interlashed aside, was a man earnestly and inwardly, as if in contemplation, looking down on Dolon. It was as if Dolon had been moved to rise by something, which was himself without any thought or consciousness of his; their souls faced by their faces; each involuntarily started at first, but the man continued to look as unconsciously as if he thought he was invisible, and Dolon's combined surprise and wonder was lost in the innocence and simplicity of the reality. The man was dressed in a crimson tunic over a white dress, with a fillet[4] on his head, and the golden light of the setting sun shone on a strong profile, and heightened the effect of his dress in the dark tree, and the pale shade of the other half of his face gave a mysterious effect to his whole form. Just at this time, Dolon's attention was diverted by the voices of his father and mother approaching the rock with some company, and on immediately looking up to the man again, he saw he was hastily descending and in an instant disappeared behind the edge of the rock; Dolon hastened to the edge to see him, but it was sloping and slippery with dead pine-leaves, and when he got there, the man was with self-possessed eagerness hastening into the bushes. The people had reached the rock, and Dolon asked if they had seen the man, and when they inquired about him, told them what he had seen. The women affrightedly exclaimed, "oh that must be the man"; and proposed to instantly return home. Dolon, gently amazed, asked if they knew who he was, and his mother said, there was a crazy man about, who believed in all the Greek and Roman Gods and Goddesses, and that it was thought he carried out the whole worship and made sacrifices, for sheep and calves had been found killed, bedecked with flowers before stone-piled altars; and said, that she was afraid to have Dolon go

---

4. A narrow band to bind hair, often an adornment of sacrificial victims.

about so alone in the woods. 'Oh how beautiful,' said Dolon, 'I wish I could see him and talk with him.' One of the company said, that he had been a great scholar, and living so in the old Greek literature had turned his head, and that he was of a most respectable family, and had been a remarkably pure and earnest character, and did not seem crazy, except in this belief of his, yet was decidedly so, and all his family thought so, he was so sincere and earnest in his belief, but they never thought he would so carry it out, or they would have confined him before he left home.

Dolon was in a retired state, as if thinking or lost, but a youth's reflection is the person in a passive relation to his nature, as if the personality had aerially vanished, unseen, like the raising of an eyelid, and the Being had incarnated itself in human form, like the soul of man in Jesus, and had become the person. Men in absence of mind are somewhat youthlike, though their Being-Nature is less free and full and formed than in youth, and they are as if their personality were folded aside, and they were quietly getting at their Being, while a youth is freshly individual, and his Being comes out as if his nature, and personality disappears, as a soul from the body at death. The youth instinctively, unconsciously, waits before his Being for his nature to act through it, and the Being not merely assists him, but comes beside him and spiritually over him, like one who answers the call or want of a child by going to it and doing all for it.

Dolon went home with the others, and was serious all the evening. Youth's seriousness is a state of himself, and not as a man's, himself in a state; his nature is affected as is the temperature of water by the condition of the sky, but its form remains a form, and its relations continue in all its parts, though all are modified yet in equal proportion, and it recedes together and in order, like a highly disciplined army. The youth neither introverts or extraverts, but is as he is affected.

Dolon continued in this state, and was all the three next days in Nature, and toward the sunset, sat as usual upon the rock, and they were the nights of the new moon. Something had met him which required the conformation of his nature to meet, and which in men would have given need of a high consciousness, as the sleeper in the dark, awaked by something which has touched him, or is near him, cannot sleep again till he ascertains it, and he looks about in the dark with eyes which, though open, cannot see till they are used to the darkness. The crazy man as a fact, combined with Dolon's condition from the general experience of his humanity, of which this event was crisis-like, had made this impression on him as if his nature was related to them as to things which, as inner principles, acted upon it; and this was the first intellectual development of a youth who had lived in Nature, and been a Being of Nature, but whose relations also comprehended men as they are, as, his parents, the school, and this crazy man, and whose nature partook of this modified humanity, though it so naturalized it by being a form of it, such as it was, as if a primitive condition, like air and water, which remain elements, though their essences are in different proportions from those of the optimum, and a lake enclosing hills, rocks, and cataracts; whereas men are forms of the original humanity which has become incomplete and disharmonized by the disproportionate development of parts, like a full-formed tree whose sap ceases to equally circulate. It was a relation of his nature, not of his intellect, which looks out of one's nature as from an observatory; its consciousness was in the relation of his Being to the Nature which thus was around him, as a blind man's sense is in his feelings. As a person, Dolon had a kind of instinctive quiet consciousness, as if God had put into his soul a celestial flower-plant on which were heavenly little fairies, and the consciousness was a feeling of an experience, like natural effects, going on within him; the life lives within him, and he neither sees, orders, or interferes with it. He did not think, though it was as if thoughts were taking forms within him, and taking their place as forms in the fresh spiritual inworld of his humanity. He was quiet and passive, and himself, as though there was an opening in the state of his humanity, and the forms there were shone upon by the sky, but the opening was of his own nature, like the cleft in a rock, and though the forms rose near the surface, did not rise beyond a level with himself, like stars brightly appearing in heaven. He was in Nature, and at unity with it, though he was if there was something instinctively engaging him, like a child keeping by its mother's side, with its hand in hers, while it has a certain care of doing or seeing something, it has not defined to itself what.

The experience going on within him was as if Poetry which he heard, and was quietly and really related to, as to a tale which a child realizes, (so far as it does realize, the effect upon him taking care of itself;) and what in men would be thought and consciousness, was in Dolon the Poet, whose effect, however, was deeper by being within him, and being him. Thought and consciousness may be conditions of the Being in a certain state, to which the Person is passive, having a life towards the life which thus outwardly comes to him. His being was, unconsciously, before the Great Mystery of Nature, the Universe, Truth, Man, God. It was acting below an instinctive sense of his childhood's relation to nature in his fairy faith, and his life,— (and for the first time he felt his fairy relation had gone;) of the Mythologies which had been faiths to men somewhat like his fairy faith, and of their bearing on Nature; of this Nature with its self-derived-like life, and its invisible, unformed, in effect unreal God or Gods; of the crazy man's belief in that which had been ages before a belief, and of the difference between his outward and inward relation to it, in which Dolon acknowledged the sanity and insanity of the man, at the same time; of the difference between this man's and his own relation to the Mythology; of belief and its subjects, and of faith.

While all this experience was taking place, Dolon had the self-possession and patience and repose, the being of Life. Even a child's plaintiveness is sometimes tragically serene and possessed.

As Dolon sat on the rock in the bright soft moonlight, on the evening of the third day, his face as it were transfigured, he thought he heard a sound, like the voice of a man engaged in low prayer and invocation; but as he listened, it stopped, and the trees were murmuring in the gentle night-breeze, and he did not know that the crazy man, who had been fasting all day as before a great sacrifice, was performing an antesacrificial service in the cave below. Presently he heard a rustling on the dry-leaved ground, and there was a bowing of the trees as of an audience gathered to welcome. There was a sound behind him of something ascending the rock, and looking, he saw just rising from the rock, in the face of the moon, the man, whom he instantly recognised as if he knew, dressed in a surplice-like robe, gathered in at the waist by a white tasseled girdle, and a wreath of laurel and wild lilies of the valley on his left arm. A repose was on his spiritual expressive face, but there was a character in it which showed it was not primitive, soul's repose. Their faces faced, but he did not look at

Dolon as before, though the same expression was in reserve in his face, but as one who was earnestly, reverently, and composedly, to do something. He took the wreath from his arm, and approaching, laid his hand on Dolon's head, on which he put the wreath, looking earnestly up to the heaven, and taking a sacrificial knife from his girdle, plunged it in Dolon's breast. For a moment, as looking from an absent sense, he bent over the body, which had fallen backwards on the rock and lay facing heaven, and then with his hands clasped on his breast, slowly and solemnly descended, and threw himself prostrate before the rock as before an altar.

—1842

⟶ END OF TRANSATLANTIC EXCHANGES ⟵

Washington Irving
1783–1859

Washington Irving was born in New York City when it had a population of little more than twenty thousand, and he spent his youth wandering the woods that grew where Greenwich Village now stands. The well-educated youngest son of a wealthy New York merchant, Irving developed a sharp eye for the business of authorship, especially after the publisher of his first book, *Salmagundi* (1807–1808), kept the copyright and the profits from its sale. He went on to become an internationally respected author and, as one of the most cosmopolitan and well-traveled figures of the early national period in the United States, he was appointed ambassador to Spain.

During an 1817 visit to Abbotsford, Sir Walter Scott encouraged the financially troubled Irving to turn to writing to support himself. In response to Scott's prompting, Irving sat down to produce an accessible, lighthearted, and saleable manuscript. The result, *The Sketch Book of Geoffrey Crayon, Gent.* (1819–1820), is a miscellany, a loose collection of legends and tales, topical essays, and humorous caricatures of English and American "types." Irving's Federalist heritage and his roots in the post-Revolutionary urban elite show clearly in his breezy neoclassical style, as well as in the gentlemanly confidence of his essay on the "literary animosity daily growing up between England and America" (p. 596). In "Rip Van Winkle," he adapts a traditional German folktale to show the distance between the rapidly modernizing post-Revolutionary North and the backwardness of the colonial era. The conservative Irving's final feelings about the real significance of the Revolution show most clearly in the way a prominent pub sign is merely painted over, replacing King George III's face with that of George Washington.

In New York, where the market for literature was still in its infancy, *The Sketch Book* was published as a series of pamphlets, in essence a small magazine modeled after Joseph Addison and Richard Steele's *Tatler* and *Spectator*. In London, though, the book was issued in two handsomely bound volumes. Both editions sold very well, and Irving became the first American writer to earn critical and popular acclaim on both sides of the Atlantic and to live successfully on the income from his writing. Summing up the significance of Irving's international success, the poet William Cullen Bryant wrote that *The Sketch Book* "showed the possibility of an American acquiring a fame bounded only by the limits of his own language."

Rip Van Winkle

A Posthumous Writing of Diedrich Knickerbocker

By Woden, God of Saxons,
From whence comes Wensday, that is Wodensday,
Truth is a thing that ever I will keep
Unto thylke day in which I creep into
My sepulchre——

CARTWRIGHT[1]

Whoever has made a voyage up the Hudson must remember the Kaatskill mountains.[2] They are a dismembered branch of the great Appalachian family, and are seen away to the west of the river, swelling up to a noble height, and lording it over the surrounding country. Every change of season, every change of weather, indeed, every hour of the day, produces some change in the magical hues and shapes of these mountains, and they are regarded by all the good wives, far and near, as perfect barometers. When the weather is fair and settled, they are clothed in blue and purple, and print their bold outlines on the clear evening sky, but, sometimes, when the rest of the landscape is cloudless, they will gather a hood of gray vapors about their summits, which, in the last rays of the setting sun, will glow and light up like a crown of glory.

At the foot of these fairy mountains, the voyager may have descried the light smoke curling up from a village, whose shingle-roofs gleam among the trees, just where the blue tints of the upland melt away into the fresh green of the nearer landscape. It is a little village of great antiquity, having been founded by some of the Dutch colonists, in the early times of the province, just about the beginning of the government of the good Peter Stuyvesant,[3] (may he rest in peace!) and there were some of the houses of the original settlers standing within a few years, built of small yellow bricks brought from Holland, having latticed windows and gable fronts, surmounted with weather-cocks.

In that same village, and in one of these very houses (which, to tell the precise truth, was sadly time-worn and weather-beaten), there lived many years since, while the country was yet a province of Great Britain, a simple good-natured fellow of the name of Rip Van Winkle. He was a descendant of the Van Winkles who figured so gallantly in the chivalrous days of Peter Stuyvesant, and accompanied him to the siege of Fort Christina.[4] He inherited, however, but little of the martial character of his ancestors. I have observed that he was a simple good-natured man; he was, moreover, a kind neighbor, and an obedient hen-pecked husband. Indeed, to the latter circumstance might be owing that meekness of spirit which gained him such universal popularity; for those men are most apt to be obsequious and conciliating abroad, who are under the discipline of shrews at home. Their tempers, doubtless, are rendered pliant and malleable in the fiery furnace of domestic tribulation; and a curtain lecture is worth all the sermons in the world for teaching the virtues of patience and long-suffering. A termagant wife may, therefore, in some respects, be considered a tolerable blessing; and if so, Rip Van Winkle was thrice blessed.

---

1. William Cartwright (1611–1643), "The Ordinary" (1635). Sir Walter Scott (1771–1832) also uses these lines as an epigraph in his novel *The Antiquary* (1816).   2. The Hudson River flows through New York's Catskill mountains.   3. Peter Stuyvesant (1592–1672), Dutch governor of New Netherlands.   4. A Swedish settlement near what is now Wilmington, Delaware.

Certain it is, that he was a great favorite among all the good wives of the village, who, as usual, with the amiable sex, took his part in all family squabbles; and never failed, whenever they talked those matters over in their evening gossipings, to lay all the blame on Dame Van Winkle. The children of the village, too, would shout with joy whenever he approached. He assisted at their sports, made their playthings, taught them to fly kites and shoot marbles, and told them long stories of ghosts, witches, and Indians. Whenever he went dodging about the village, he was surrounded by a troop of them, hanging on his skirts, clambering on his back, and playing a thousand tricks on him with impunity; and not a dog would bark at him throughout the neighborhood.

The great error in Rip's composition was an insuperable aversion to all kinds of profitable labor. It could not be from the want of assiduity or perseverance; for he would sit on a wet rock, with a rod as long and heavy as a Tartar's lance,[5] and fish all day without a murmur, even though he should not be encouraged by a single nibble. He would carry a fowling-piece on his shoulder for hours together, trudging through woods and swamps, and up hill and down dale, to shoot a few squirrels or wild pigeons. He would never refuse to assist a neighbor even in the roughest toil, and was a foremost man at all country frolics for husking Indian corn, or building stone-fences; the women of the village, too, used to employ him to run their errands, and to do such little odd jobs as their less obliging husbands would not do for them. In a word Rip was ready to attend to anybody's business but his own; but as to doing family duty, and keeping his farm in order, he found it impossible.

In fact, he declared it was of no use to work on his farm; it was the most pestilent little piece of ground in the whole country; every thing about it went wrong, and would go wrong, in spite of him. His fences were continually falling to pieces; his cow would either go astray, or get among the cabbages; weeds were sure to grow quicker in his fields than anywhere else; the rain always made a point of setting in just as he had some out-door work to do; so that though his patrimonial estate had dwindled away under his management, acre by acre, until there was little more left than a mere patch of Indian corn and potatoes, yet it was the worst conditioned farm in the neighborhood.

His children, too, were as ragged and wild as if they belonged to nobody. His son Rip, an urchin begotten in his own likeness, promised to inherit the habits, with the old clothes of his father. He was generally seen trooping like a colt at his mother's heels, equipped in a pair of his father's cast-off galligaskins,[6] which he had much ado to hold up with one hand, as a fine lady does her train in bad weather.

Rip Van Winkle, however, was one of those happy mortals, of foolish, well-oiled dispositions, who take the world easy, eat white bread or brown, whichever can be got with least thought or trouble, and would rather starve on a penny than work for a pound. If left to himself, he would have whistled life away in perfect contentment; but his wife kept continually dinning in his ears about his idleness, his carelessness, and the ruin he was bringing on his family. Morning, noon, and night, her tongue was incessantly going, and everything he said or did was sure to produce a torrent of household eloquence. Rip had but one way of replying to all lectures of the kind, and that, by frequent use, had grown into a habit. He shrugged his shoulders, shook his head, cast up his eyes, but said nothing. This, however, always provoked a fresh volley

5. The Tartars were a twelfth-century Mongolian tribe.   6. Loose breeches worn in the seventeenth century.

from his wife; so that he was fain to draw off his forces, and take to the outside of the house—the only side which, in truth, belongs to a hen-pecked husband.

Rip's sole domestic adherent was his dog Wolf, who was as much hen-pecked as his master; for Dame Van Winkle regarded them as companions in idleness, and even looked upon Wolf with an evil eye, as the cause of his master's going so often astray. True it is, in all points of spirit befitting an honorable dog, he was as courageous an animal as ever scoured the woods—but what courage can withstand the ever-during and all-besetting terrors of a woman's tongue? The moment Wolf entered the house his crest fell, his tail drooped to the ground, or curled between his legs, he sneaked about with a gallows air, casting many a sidelong glance at Dame Van Winkle, and at the least flourish of a broom-stick or ladle, he would fly to the door with yelping precipitation.

Times grew worse and worse with Rip Van Winkle as years of matrimony rolled on; a tart temper never mellows with age, and a sharp tongue is the only edged tool that grows keener with constant use. For a long while he used to console himself, when driven from home, by frequenting a kind of perpetual club of the sages, philosophers, and other idle personages of the village; which held its sessions on a bench before a small inn, designated by a rubicund portrait of His Majesty George the Third. Here they used to sit in the shade through a long lazy summer's day, talking listlessly over village gossip, or telling endless sleepy stories about nothing. But it would have been worth any statesman's money to have heard the profound discussions that sometimes took place, when by chance an old newspaper fell into their hands from some passing traveller. How solemnly they would listen to the contents, as drawled out by Derrick Van Bummel, the schoolmaster, a dapper learned little man, who was not to be daunted by the most gigantic word in the dictionary; and how sagely they would deliberate upon public events some months after they had taken place.

The opinions of this junto were completely controlled by Nicholas Vedder, a patriarch of the village, and landlord of the inn, at the door of which he took his seat from morning till night, just moving sufficiently to avoid the sun and keep in the shade of a large tree; so that the neighbors could tell the hour by his movements as accurately as by a sundial. It is true he was rarely heard to speak, but smoked his pipe incessantly. His adherents, however (for every great man has his adherents), perfectly understood him, and knew how to gather his opinions. When anything that was read or related displeased him, he was observed to smoke his pipe vehemently, and to send forth short, frequent and angry puffs; but when pleased, he would inhale the smoke slowly and tranquilly, and emit it in light and placid clouds; and sometimes, taking the pipe from his mouth, and letting the fragrant vapor curl about his nose, would gravely nod his head in token of perfect approbation.

From even this stronghold the unlucky Rip was at length routed by his termagant wife, who would suddenly break in upon the tranquillity of the assemblage and call the members all to naught; nor was that august personage, Nicholas Vedder himself, sacred from the daring tongue of this terrible virago, who charged him outright with encouraging her husband in habits of idleness.

Poor Rip was at last reduced almost to despair; and his only alternative, to escape from the labor of the farm and clamor of his wife, was to take gun in hand and stroll away into the woods. Here he would sometimes seat himself at the foot of a tree, and share the contents of his wallet with Wolf, with whom he sympathized as a fellow-sufferer in persecution. "Poor Wolf," he would say, "thy mistress leads thee a dog's life of it; but never mind, my lad, whilst I live thou shalt never want a friend to stand by thee!" Wolf would wag his tail, look wistfully in his master's face, and if dogs can feel pity I verily believe he reciprocated the sentiment with all his heart.

In a long ramble of the kind on a fine autumnal day, Rip had unconsciously scrambled to one of the highest parts of the Kaatskill mountains. He was after his favorite sport of squirrel shooting, and the still solitudes had echoed and re-echoed with the reports of his gun. Panting and fatigued, he threw himself, late in the afternoon, on a green knoll, covered with mountain herbage, that crowned the brow of a precipice. From an opening between the trees he could overlook all the lower country for many a mile of rich woodland. He saw at a distance the lordly Hudson, far, far below him, moving on its silent but majestic course, with the reflection of a purple cloud, or the sail of a lagging bark, here and there sleeping on its glassy bosom, and at last losing itself in the blue highlands.

On the other side he looked down into a deep mountain glen, wild, lonely, and shagged, the bottom filled with fragments from the impending cliffs, and scarcely lighted by the reflected rays of the setting sun. For some time Rip lay musing on this scene; evening was gradually advancing; the mountains began to throw their long blue shadows over the valleys; he saw that it would be dark long before he could reach the village, and he heaved a heavy sigh when he thought of encountering the terrors of Dame Van Winkle.

As he was about to descend, he heard a voice from a distance, hallooing, "Rip Van Winkle! Rip Van Winkle!" He looked round, but could see nothing but a crow winging its solitary flight across the mountain. He thought his fancy must have deceived him, and turned again to descend, when he heard the same cry ring through the still evening air: "Rip Van Winkle! Rip Van Winkle!"—at the same time Wolf bristled up his back, and giving a low growl, skulked to his master's side, looking fearfully down into the glen. Rip now felt a vague apprehension stealing over him; he looked anxiously in the same direction, and perceived a strange figure slowly toiling up the rocks, and bending under the weight of something he carried on his back. He was surprised to see any human being in this lonely and unfrequented place, but supposing it to be some one of the neighborhood in need of his assistance, he hastened down to yield it.

On nearer approach he was still more surprised at the singularity of the stranger's appearance. He was a short square-built old fellow, with thick bushy hair, and a grizzled beard. His dress was of the antique Dutch fashion—a cloth jerkin[7] strapped round the waist—several pair of breeches, the outer one of ample volume, decorated with rows of buttons down the sides, and bunches at the knees. He bore on his shoulder a stout keg, that seemed full of liquor, and made signs for Rip to approach and assist him with the load. Though rather shy and distrustful of this new acquaintance, Rip complied with his usual alacrity; and mutually relieving one another, they clambered up a narrow gully, apparently the dry bed of a mountain torrent. As they ascended, Rip every now and then heard long rolling peals, like distant thunder, that seemed to issue out of a deep ravine, or rather cleft, between lofty rocks, toward which their rugged path conducted. He paused for an instant, but supposing it to be the muttering of one of those transient thunder-showers which often take place in mountain heights, he proceeded. Passing through the ravine, they came to a hollow, like a small amphithe-

---

7. A close-fitting jacket.

atre, surrounded by perpendicular precipices, over the brinks of which impending trees shot their branches, so that you only caught glimpses of the azure sky and the bright evening cloud. During the whole time Rip and his companion had labored on in silence; for though the former marvelled greatly what could be the object of carrying a keg of liquor up this wild mountain, yet there was something strange and incomprehensible about the unknown, that inspired awe and checked familiarity.

On entering the amphitheatre, new objects of wonder presented themselves. On a level spot in the centre was a company of odd-looking personages playing at nine-pins.[8] They were dressed in a quaint outlandish fashion; some wore short doublets,[9] others jerkins, with long knives in their belts, and most of them had enormous breeches, of similar style with that of the guide's. Their visages, too, were peculiar: one had a large beard, broad face, and small piggish eyes: the face of another seemed to consist entirely of nose, and was surmounted by a white sugar-loaf hat set off with a little red cock's tail. They all had beards, of various shapes and colors. There was one who seemed to be the commander. He was a stout old gentleman, with a weather-beaten countenance; he wore a laced doublet, broad belt and hanger, high-crowned hat and feather, red stockings, and high-heeled shoes, with roses in them. The whole group reminded Rip of the figures in an old Flemish painting, in the parlor of Dominie Van Shaick, the village parson, and which had been brought over from Holland at the time of the settlement.

What seemed particularly odd to Rip was, that though these folks were evidently amusing themselves, yet they maintained the gravest faces, the most mysterious silence, and were, withal, the most melancholy party of pleasure he had ever witnessed. Nothing interrupted the stillness of the scene but the noise of the balls, which, whenever they were rolled, echoed along the mountains like rumbling peals of thunder.

As Rip and his companion approached them, they suddenly desisted from their play, and stared at him with such fixed statue-like gaze, and such strange, uncouth, lack-lustre countenances, that his heart turned within him, and his knees smote together. His companion now emptied the contents of the keg into large flagons,[10] and made signs to him to wait upon the company. He obeyed with fear and trembling; they quaffed the liquor in profound silence, and then returned to their game.

By degrees Rip's awe and apprehension subsided. He even ventured, when no eye was fixed upon him, to taste the beverage, which he found had much of the flavor of excellent Hollands. He was naturally a thirsty soul, and was soon tempted to repeat the draught. One taste provoked another; and he reiterated his visits to the flagon so often that at length his senses were overpowered, his eyes swam in his head, his head gradually declined, and he fell into a deep sleep.

On waking, he found himself on the green knoll whence he had first seen the old man of the glen. He rubbed his eyes—it was a bright sunny morning. The birds were hopping and twittering among the bushes, and the eagle was wheeling aloft, and breasting the pure mountain breeze. "Surely," thought Rip, "I have not slept here all night." He recalled the occurrences before he fell asleep. The strange man with a keg of liquor—the mountain ravine—the wild retreat among the rocks—the woe-begone party at ninepins—the flagon—"Oh! that flagon! that wicked flagon!" thought Rip—"what excuse shall I make to Dame Van Winkle!"

---

8. A form of bowling.   9. A close-fitting body-suit, often worn with hose.   10. Large bottles.

He looked round for his gun, but in place of the clean well-oiled fowling-piece, he found an old firelock lying by him, the barrel incrusted with rust, the lock falling off, and the stock worm-eaten. He now suspected that the grave roysters of the mountain had put a trick upon him, and having dosed him with liquor, had robbed him of his gun. Wolf, too, had disappeared, but he might have strayed away after a squirrel or partridge. He whistled after him and shouted his name, but all in vain; the echoes repeated his whistle and shout, but no dog was to be seen.

He determined to revisit the scene of the last evening's gambol, and if he met with any of the party, to demand his dog and gun. As he rose to walk, he found himself stiff in the joints, and wanting in his usual activity. "These mountain beds do not agree with me," thought Rip; "and if this frolic should lay me up with a fit of the rheumatism, I shall have a blessed time with Dame Van Winkle." With some difficulty he got down into the glen: he found the gully up which he and his companion had ascended the preceding evening; but to his astonishment a mountain stream was now foaming down it, leaping from rock to rock, and filling the glen with babbling murmurs. He, however, made shift to scramble up its sides, working his toilsome way through thickets of birch, sassafras, and witch-hazel, and sometimes tripped up or entangled by the wild grapevines that twisted their coils or tendrils from tree to tree, and spread a kind of network in his path.

At length he reached to where the ravine had opened through the cliffs to the amphitheatre; but no traces of such opening remained. The rocks presented a high impenetrable wall over which the torrent came tumbling in a sheet of feathery foam, and fell into a broad deep basin, black from the shadows of the surrounding forest. Here, then, poor Rip was brought to a stand. He again called and whistled after his dog; he was only answered by the cawing of a flock of idle crows, sporting high in air about a dry tree that overhung a sunny precipice; and who, secure in their elevation, seemed to look down and scoff at the poor man's perplexities. What was to be done? the morning was passing away, and Rip felt famished for want of his breakfast. He grieved to give up his dog and gun; he dreaded to meet his wife; but it would not do to starve among the mountains. He shook his head, shouldered the rusty firelock, and, with a heart full of trouble and anxiety, turned his steps homeward.

As he approached the village he met a number of people, but none whom he knew, which somewhat surprised him, for he had thought himself acquainted with every one in the country round. Their dress, too, was of a different fashion from that to which he was accustomed. They all stared at him with equal marks of surprise, and whenever they cast their eyes upon him, invariably stroked their chins. The constant recurrence of this gesture induced Rip, involuntarily, to do the same, when to his astonishment, he found his beard had grown a foot long!

He had now entered the skirts of the village. A troop of strange children ran at his heels, hooting after him, and pointing at his gray beard. The dogs, too, not one of which he recognized for an old acquaintance, barked at him as he passed. The very village was altered; it was larger and more populous. There were rows of houses which he had never seen before, and those which had been his familiar haunts had disappeared. Strange names were over the doors—strange faces at the windows—every thing was strange. His mind now misgave him; he began to doubt whether both he and the world around him were not bewitched. Surely this was his native village, which he had left but the day before. There stood the Kaatskill mountains—there ran the silver Hudson at a distance—there was every hill and dale precisely as it had always been—Rip was sorely perplexed—"That flagon last night," thought he, "has addled my poor head sadly!"

It was with some difficulty that he found the way to his own house, which he approached with silent awe, expecting every moment to hear the shrill voice of Dame Van Winkle. He found the house gone to decay—the roof fallen in, the windows shattered, and the doors off the hinges. A half-starved dog that looked like Wolf was skulking about it. Rip called him by name, but the cur snarled, showed his teeth, and passed on. This was an unkind cut indeed—"My very dog," sighed poor Rip, "has forgotten me!"

He entered the house, which, to tell the truth, Dame Van Winkle had always kept in neat order. It was empty, forlorn, and apparently abandoned. This desolateness overcame all his connubial fears—he called loudly for his wife and children—the lonely chambers rang for a moment with his voice, and then all again was silence.

He now hurried forth, and hastened to his old resort, the village inn—but it too was gone. A large rickety wooden building stood in its place, with great gaping windows, some of them broken and mended with old hats and petticoats, and over the door was painted, "the Union Hotel, by Jonathan Doolittle." Instead of the great tree that used to shelter the quiet little Dutch inn of yore, there now was reared a tall naked pole, with something on the top that looked like a red night-cap, and from it was fluttering a flag, on which was a singular assemblage of stars and stripes—all this was strange and incomprehensible. He recognized on the sign, however, the ruby face of King George, under which he had smoked so many a peaceful pipe; but even this was singularly metamorphosed. The red coat was changed for one of blue and buff, a sword was held in the hand instead of a sceptre, the head was decorated with a cocked hat, and underneath was painted in large characters, GENERAL WASHINGTON.

There was, as usual, a crowd of folk about the door, but none that Rip recollected. The very character of the people seemed changed. There was a busy, bustling, disputatious tone about it, instead of the accustomed phlegm and drowsy tranquillity. He looked in vain for the sage Nicholas Vedder, with his broad face, double chin, and fair long pipe, uttering clouds of tobacco-smoke instead of idle speeches; or Van Bummel, the schoolmaster, doling forth the contents of an ancient newspaper. In place of these, a lean, bilious-looking fellow, with his pockets full of handbills, was haranguing vehemently about rights of citizens—elections—members of congress— liberty—Bunker's Hill—heroes of seventy-six—and other words, which were a perfect Babylonish jargon to the bewildered Van Winkle.

The appearance of Rip, with his long grizzled beard, his rusty fowling-piece, his uncouth dress, and an army of women and children at his heels, soon attracted the attention of the tavern politicians. They crowded round him, eyeing him from head to foot with great curiosity. The orator bustled up to him, and, drawing him partly aside, inquired "on which side he voted?" Rip stared in vacant stupidity. Another short but busy little fellow pulled him by the arm, and, rising on tiptoe, inquired in his ear, "Whether he was Federal or Democrat?" Rip was equally at a loss to comprehend the question; when a knowing, self-important old gentleman, in a sharp cocked hat, made his way through the crowd, putting them to the right and left with his elbows as he passed, and planting himself before Van Winkle, with one arm akimbo, the other resting on his cane, his keen eyes and sharp hat penetrating, as it were, into his very soul, demanded in an austere tone, "what brought him to the election with a gun on his shoulder, and a mob at his heels, and whether he meant to breed a riot in the village?"—"Alas! gentlemen," cried Rip, somewhat dismayed, "I am a poor quiet man, a native of the place, and a loyal subject of the king, God bless him!"

Here a general shout burst from the by-standers—"A tory! a tory! a spy! a refugee! hustle him! away with him!" It was with great difficulty that the self-important man in the cocked hat restored order; and, having assumed a tenfold austerity of brow, demanded again of the unknown culprit, what he came there for, and whom he was seeking? The poor man humbly assured him that he meant no harm, but merely came there in search of some of his neighbors, who used to keep about the tavern.

"Well—who are they?—name them."

Rip bethought himself a moment, and inquired, "Where's Nicholas Vedder?"

There was a silence for a little while, when an old man replied, in a thin piping voice, "Nicholas Vedder! why, he is dead and gone these eighteen years! There was a wooden tombstone in the church-yard that used to tell all about him, but that's rotten and gone too."

"Where's Brom Dutcher?"

"Oh, he went off to the army in the beginning of the war; some say he was killed at the storming of Stony Point[11]—others say he was drowned in a squall at the foot of Antony's Nose. I don't know—he never came back again."

"Where's Van Bummel, the schoolmaster?"

"He went off to the wars too, was a great militia general, and is now in congress."

Rip's heart died away at hearing of these sad changes in his home and friends, and finding himself thus alone in the world. Every answer puzzled him too, by treating of such enormous lapses of time, and of matters which he could not understand: war—congress—Stony Point;—he had no courage to ask after any more friends, but cried out in despair, "Does nobody here know Rip Van Winkle?"

"Oh, Rip Van Winkle!" exclaimed two or three, "Oh, to be sure! that's Rip Van Winkle yonder, leaning against the tree."

Rip looked, and beheld a precise counterpart of himself, as he went up the mountain: apparently as lazy, and certainly as ragged. The poor fellow was now completely confounded. He doubted his own identity, and whether he was himself or another man. In the midst of his bewilderment, the man in the cocked hat demanded who he was, and what was his name?

"God knows," exclaimed he, at his wit's end; "I'm not myself—I'm somebody else—that's me yonder—no—that's somebody else got into my shoes—I was myself last night, but I fell asleep on the mountain, and they've changed my gun, and every thing's changed, and I'm changed, and I can't tell what's my name, or who I am!"

The by-standers began now to look at each other, nod, wink significantly, and tap their fingers against their foreheads. There was a whisper also, about securing the gun, and keeping the old fellow from doing mischief, at the very suggestion of which the self-important man in the cocked hat retired with some precipitation. At this critical moment a fresh comely woman pressed through the throng to get a peep at the gray-bearded man. She had a chubby child in her arms, which, frightened at his looks, began to cry. "Hush, Rip," cried she, "hush, you little fool; the old man won't

---

11. Site of a midnight battle during the American Revolution.

hurt you." The name of the child, the air of the mother, the tone of her voice, all awakened a train of recollections in his mind. "What is your name, my good woman?" asked he.

"Judith Gardenier."

"And your father's name?"

"Ah, poor man, Rip Van Winkle was his name, but it's twenty years since he went away from home with his gun, and never has been heard of since—his dog came home without him; but whether he shot himself, or was carried away by the Indians, nobody can tell. I was then but a little girl."

Rip had but one question more to ask; but he put it with a faltering voice:

"Where's your mother?"

"Oh, she too had died but a short time since; she broke a blood-vessel in a fit of passion at a New-England peddler."

There was a drop of comfort, at least, in this intelligence. The honest man could contain himself no longer. He caught his daughter and her child in his arms. "I am your father!" cried he—"Young Rip Van Winkle once—old Rip Van Winkle now!—Does nobody know poor Rip Van Winkle?"

All stood amazed, until an old woman, tottering out from among the crowd, put her hand to her brow, and peering under it in his face for a moment, exclaimed, "Sure enough! it is Rip Van Winkle—it is himself! Welcome home again, old neighbor—Why, where have you been these twenty long years?"

Rip's story was soon told, for the whole twenty years had been to him but as one night. The neighbors stared when they heard it; some were seen to wink at each other, and put their tongues in their cheeks: and the self-important man in the cocked hat, who, when the alarm was over, had returned to the field, screwed down the corners of his mouth, and shook his head—upon which there was a general shaking of the head throughout the assemblage.

It was determined, however, to take the opinion of old Peter Vanderdonk, who was seen slowly advancing up the road. He was a descendant of the historian of that name, who wrote one of the earliest accounts of the province. Peter was the most ancient inhabitant of the village, and well versed in all the wonderful events and traditions of the neighborhood. He recollected Rip at once, and corroborated his story in the most satisfactory manner. He assured the company that it was a fact, handed down from his ancestor the historian, that the Kaatskill mountains had always been haunted by strange beings. That it was affirmed that the great Hendrick Hudson,[12] the first discoverer of the river and country, kept a kind of vigil there every twenty years, with his crew of the Half-moon; being permitted in this way to revisit the scenes of his enterprise, and keep a guardian eye upon the river, and the great city called by his name. That his father had once seen them in their old Dutch dresses playing at nine-pins in a hollow of the mountain; and that he himself had heard, one summer afternoon, the sound of their balls, like distant peals of thunder.

To make a long story short, the company broke up, and returned to the more important concerns of the election. Rip's daughter took him home to live with her; she had a snug, well-furnished house, and a stout cheery farmer for a husband, whom Rip recollected for one of the urchins that used to climb upon his back. As to Rip's

---

12. Henry Hudson (c. 1570–c. 1611), English explorer employed by the Dutch East India Company.

son and heir, who was the ditto of himself, seen leaning against the tree, he was employed to work on the farm; but evinced an hereditary disposition to attend to anything else but his business.

Rip now resumed his old walks and habits; he soon found many of his former cronies, though all rather the worse for the wear and tear of time; and preferred making friends among the rising generation, with whom he soon grew into great favor.

Having nothing to do at home, and being arrived at that happy age when a man can be idle with impunity, he took his place once more on the bench at the inn door, and was reverenced as one of the patriarchs of the village, and a chronicle of the old times "before the war." It was some time before he could get into the regular track of gossip, or could be made to comprehend the strange events that had taken place during his torpor. How that there had been a revolutionary war—that the country had thrown off the yoke of old England—and that, instead of being a subject of his Majesty George the Third, he was now a free citizen of the United States. Rip, in fact, was no politician; the changes of states and empires made but little impression on him; but there was one species of despotism under which he had long groaned, and that was—petticoat government. Happily that was at an end; he had got his neck out of the yoke of matrimony, and could go in and out whenever he pleased, without dreading the tyranny of Dame Van Winkle. Whenever her name was mentioned, however, he shook his head, shrugged his shoulders, and cast up his eyes; which might pass either for an expression of resignation to his fate, or joy at his deliverance.

He used to tell his story to every stranger that arrived at Mr. Doolittle's hotel. He was observed, at first, to vary on some points every time he told it, which was, doubtless, owing to his having so recently awaked. It at last settled down precisely to the tale I have related, and not a man, woman, or child in the neighborhood, but knew it by heart. Some always pretended to doubt the reality of it, and insisted that Rip had been out of his head, and that this was one point on which he always remained flighty. The old Dutch inhabitants, however, almost universally gave it full credit. Even to this day they never hear a thunderstorm of a summer afternoon about the Kaatskill, but they say Hendrick Hudson and his crew are at their game of nine-pins; and it is a common wish of all hen-pecked husbands in the neighborhood, when life hangs heavy on their hands, that they might have a quieting draught out of Rip Van Winkle's flagon.

NOTE.

The foregoing Tale, one would suspect, had been suggested to Mr. Knickerbocker by a little German superstition about the Emperor Frederick *der Rothbart*, and the Kypphaüser mountain: the subjoined note, however, which he had appended to the tale, shows that it is an absolute fact, narrated with his usual fidelity:

"The story of Rip Van Winkle may seem incredible to many, but nevertheless I give it my full belief, for I know the vicinity of our old Dutch settlements to have been very subject to marvellous events and appearances. Indeed, I have heard many stranger stories than this, in the villages along the Hudson; all of which were too well authenticated to admit of a doubt. I have even talked with Rip Van Winkle myself, who, when last I saw him, was a very venerable old man, and so perfectly rational and consistent on every other point, that I think no conscientious person could refuse to take this into the bargain; nay, I have seen a certificate on the subject taken before a country justice, and signed with a cross, in the justice's own handwriting. The story, therefore, is beyond the possibility of doubt.

D. K."

POSTSCRIPT.

The following are travelling notes from a memorandum-book of Mr. Knickerbocker:

The Kaatsberg, or Catskill Mountains, have always been a region full of fable. The Indians considered them the abode of spirits, who influenced the weather, spreading sunshine or clouds over the landscape, and sending good or bad hunting seasons. They were ruled by an old squaw spirit, said to be their mother. She dwelt on the highest peak of the Catskills, and had charge of the doors of day and night to open and shut them at the proper hour. She hung up the new moons in the skies, and cut up the old ones into stars. In times of drought, if properly propitiated, she would spin light summer clouds out of cobwebs and morning dew, and send them off from the crest of the mountain, flake after flake, like flakes of carded cotton, to float in the air; until, dissolved by the heat of the sun, they would fall in gentle showers, causing the grass to spring, the fruits to ripen, and the corn to grow an inch an hour. If displeased, however, she would brew up clouds black as ink, sitting in the midst of them like a bottle-bellied spider in the midst of its web; and when these clouds broke, woe betide the valleys!

In old times, say the Indian traditions, there was a kind of Manitou or Spirit, who kept about the wildest recesses of the Catskill Mountains, and took a mischievous pleasure in wreaking all kinds of evils and vexations upon the red men. Sometimes he would assume the form of a bear, a panther, or a deer, lead the bewildered hunter a weary chase through tangled forests and among ragged rocks; and then spring off with a loud ho! ho! leaving him aghast on the brink of a beetling precipice or raging torrent.

The favorite abode of this Manitou is still shown. It is a great rock or cliff on the loneliest part of the mountains, and, from the flowering vines which clamber about it, and the wild flowers which abound in its neighborhood, is known by the name of the Garden Rock. Near the foot of it is a small lake, the haunt of the solitary bittern, with water-snakes basking in the sun on the leaves of the pond-lilies which lie on the surface. This place was held in great awe by the Indians, insomuch that the boldest hunter would not pursue his game within its precincts. Once upon a time, however, a hunter who had lost his way, penetrated to the garden rock, where he beheld a number of gourds placed in the crotches of trees. One of these he seized and made off with it, but in the hurry of his retreat he let it fall among the rocks, when a great stream gushed forth, which washed him away and swept him down precipices, where he was dashed to pieces, and the stream made its way to the Hudson, and continues to flow to the present day; being the identical stream known by the name of the Kaaters-kill.

—1819

English Writers on America

"Methinks I see in my mind a noble and puissant nation, rousing herself like
a strong man after sleep, and shaking her invincible locks; methinks I see her
as an eagle, mewing her mighty youth, and kindling her endazzled eyes at the
full mid-day beam."

—MILTON ON THE LIBERTY OF THE PRESS.[1]

It is with feelings of deep regret that I observe the literary animosity daily growing up
between England and America. Great curiosity has been awakened of late with
respect to the United States, and the London press has teemed with volumes of travels through the Republic; but they seem intended to diffuse error rather than knowledge; and so successful have they been, that, notwithstanding the constant intercourse between the nations, there is no people concerning whom the great mass of the
British public have less pure information, or entertain more numerous prejudices.

English travellers are the best and the worst in the world. Where no motives of
pride or interest intervene, none can equal them for profound and philosophical views
of society, or faithful and graphical description of external objects; but when either
the interest or reputation of their own country comes in collision with that of another, they go to the opposite extreme, and forget their usual probity and candor, in the
indulgence of splenetic remark, and an illiberal spirit of ridicule.

Hence, their travels are more honest and accurate, the more remote the country
described. I would place implicit confidence in an Englishman's description of the
regions beyond the cataracts of the Nile; of unknown islands in the Yellow Sea[2]; of the
interior of India; or of any other tract which other travellers might be apt to picture out
with the illusions of their fancies. But I would cautiously receive his account of his immediate neighbors, and of those nations with which he is in habits of most frequent intercourse. However I might be disposed to trust his probity, I dare not trust his prejudices.

It has also been the peculiar lot of our country to be visited by the worst kind of
English travellers. While men of philosophical spirit and cultivated minds have been
sent from England to ransack the poles, to penetrate the deserts, and to study the
manners and customs of barbarous nations, with which she can have no permanent
intercourse of profit or pleasure; it has been left to the broken-down tradesman, the
scheming adventurer, the wandering mechanic, the Manchester and Birmingham
agent, to be her oracles respecting America. From such sources she is content to
receive her information respecting a country in a singular state of moral and physical
development; a country in which one of the greatest political experiments in the history of the world is now performing; and which presents the most profound and
momentous studies to the statesman and the philosopher.

That such men should give prejudicial accounts of America, is not a matter of
surprise. The themes it offers for contemplation, are too vast and elevated for their
capacities. The national character is yet in a state of fermentation: it may have its
frothiness and sediment, but its ingredients are sound and wholesome; it has already
given proofs of powerful and generous qualities; and the whole promises to settle
down into something substantially excellent. But the causes which are operating to
strengthen and ennoble it, and its daily indications of admirable properties, are all lost

---

1. John Milton (1608–1674), *Areopagitica* (1644).   2. An arm of the Pacific Ocean between China and the Koreas.

upon these purblind observers; who are only affected by the little asperities incident to its present situation. They are capable of judging only of the surface of things; of those matters which come in contact with their private interests and personal gratifications. They miss some of the snug conveniences and petty comforts which belong to an old, highly-finished, and over-populous state of society; where the ranks of useful labor are crowded, and many earn a painful and servile subsistence, by studying the very caprices of appetite and self-indulgence. These minor comforts, however, are all-important in the estimation of narrow minds; which either do not perceive, or will not acknowledge, that they are more than counterbalanced among us, by great and generally diffused blessings.

They may, perhaps, have been disappointed in some unreasonable expectation of sudden gain. They may have pictured America to themselves an El Dorado,[3] where gold and silver abounded, and the natives were lacking in sagacity, and where they were to become strangely and suddenly rich, in some unforeseen but easy manner. The same weakness of mind that indulges absurd expectations, produces petulance in disappointment. Such persons become embittered against the country on finding that there, as everywhere else, a man must sow before he can reap; must win wealth by industry and talent; and must contend with the common difficulties of nature, and the shrewdness of an intelligent and enterprising people.

Perhaps, through mistaken or ill-directed hospitality, or from the prompt disposition to cheer and countenance the stranger, prevalent among my countrymen, they may have been treated with unwonted respect in America; and, having been accustomed all their lives to consider themselves below the surface of good society, and brought up in a servile feeling of inferiority, they become arrogant, on the common boon of civility; they attribute to the lowliness of others their own elevation; and underrate a society where there are no artificial distinctions, and where, by any chance, such individuals as themselves can rise to consequence.

One would suppose, however, that information coming from such sources, on a subject where the truth is so desirable, would be received with caution by the censors of the press; that the motives of these men, their veracity, their opportunities of inquiry and observation, and their capacities for judging correctly, would be rigorously scrutinized, before their evidence was admitted, in such sweeping extent, against a kindred nation. The very reverse, however, is the case, and it furnishes a striking instance of human inconsistency. Nothing can surpass the vigilance with which English critics will examine the credibility of the traveller who publishes an account of some distant and comparatively unimportant country. How warily will they compare the measurements of a pyramid, or the description of a ruin; and how sternly will they censure any inaccuracy in these contributions of merely curious knowledge, while they will receive, with eagerness and unhesitating faith, the gross misrepresentations of coarse and obscure writers, concerning a country with which their own is placed in the most important and delicate relations. Nay, they will even make these apocryphal volumes text-books, on which to enlarge, with a zeal and an ability worthy of a more generous cause.

I shall not, however, dwell on this irksome and hackneyed topic; nor should I have adverted to it, but for the undue interest apparently taken in it by my countrymen, and certain injurious effects which I apprehend it might produce upon the

---

3. A mythical golden city.

national feeling. We attach too much consequence to these attacks. They cannot do us any essential injury. The tissue of misrepresentations attempted to be woven round us, are like cobwebs woven round the limbs of an infant giant. Our country continually outgrows them. One falsehood after another falls off of itself. We have but to live on, and every day we live a whole volume of refutation.

All the writers of England united, if we could for a moment suppose their great minds stooping to so unworthy a combination, could not conceal our rapidly growing importance and matchless prosperity. They could not conceal that these are owing, not merely to physical and local, but also to moral causes—to the political liberty, the general diffusion of knowledge, the prevalence of sound, moral, and religious principles, which give force and sustained energy to the character of a people, and which in fact, have been the acknowledged and wonderful supporters of their own national power and glory.

But why are we so exquisitely alive to the aspersions of England? Why do we suffer ourselves to be so affected by the contumely she has endeavored to cast upon us? It is not in the opinion of England alone that honor lives, and reputation has its being. The world at large is the arbiter of a nation's fame: with its thousand eyes it witnesses a nation's deeds, and from their collective testimony is national glory or national disgrace established.

For ourselves, therefore, it is comparatively of but little importance whether England does us justice or not; it is, perhaps, of far more importance to herself. She is instilling anger and resentment into the bosom of a youthful nation, to grow with its growth, and strengthen with its strength. If in America, as some of her writers are laboring to convince her, she is hereafter to find an invidious rival, and a gigantic foe, she may thank those very writers for having provoked rivalship, and irritated hostility. Every one knows the all-pervading influence of literature at the present day, and how much the opinions and passions of mankind are under its control. The mere contests of the sword are temporary; their wounds are but in the flesh, and it is the pride of the generous to forgive and forget them; but the slanders of the pen pierce to the heart; they rankle longest in the noblest spirits; they dwell ever present in the mind, and render it morbidly sensitive to the most trifling collision. It is but seldom that any one overt act produces hostilities between two nations; there exists, most commonly, a previous jealousy and ill-will, a predisposition to take offence. Trace these to their cause, and how often will they be found to originate in the mischievous effusions of mercenary writers, who, secure in their closets, and for ignominious bread, concoct and circulate the venom that is to inflame the generous and the brave.

I am not laying too much stress upon this point; for it applies most emphatically to our particular case. Over no nation does the press hold a more absolute control than over the people of America; for the universal education of the poorest classes makes every individual a reader. There is nothing published in England on the subject of our country, that does not circulate through every part of it. There is not a calumny dropped from an English pen, nor an unworthy sarcasm uttered by an English statesman, that does not go to blight good-will, and add to the mass of latent resentment. Possessing, then, as England does, the fountain-head whence the literature of the language flows, how completely is it in her power, and how truly is it her duty, to make it the medium of amiable and magnanimous feeling—a stream where the two nations might meet together and drink in peace and kindness. Should she, however, persist in turning it to waters of bitterness, the time may come when she may repent her folly. The present friendship of America may be of but little moment to her; but the future destinies of that country do not admit of a doubt; over those of England, there lower some shadows of uncertainty. Should, then, a day of gloom arrive—should those reverses overtake her, from which the proudest empires have not been exempt—she may look back with regret at her infatuation, in repulsing from her side a nation she might have grappled to her bosom, and thus destroying her only chance for real friendship beyond the boundaries of her own dominions.

There is a general impression in England, that the people of the United States are inimical to the parent country. It is one of the errors which have been diligently propagated by designing writers. There is, doubtless, considerable political hostility, and a general soreness at the illiberality of the English press; but, collectively speaking, the prepossessions of the people are strongly in favor of England. Indeed, at one time they amounted, in many parts of the Union, to an absurd degree of bigotry. The bare name of Englishman was a passport to the confidence and hospitality of every family, and too often gave a transient currency to the worthless and the ungrateful. Throughout the country, there was something of enthusiasm connected with the idea of England. We looked to it with a hallowed feeling of tenderness and veneration, as the land of our forefathers—the august repository of the monuments and antiquities of our race—the birthplace and mausoleum of the sages and heroes of our paternal history. After our own country, there was none in whose glory we more delighted—none whose good opinion we were more anxious to possess—none toward which our hearts yearned with such throbbings of warm consanguinity. Even during the late war, whenever there was the least opportunity for kind feelings to spring forth, it was the delight of the generous spirits of our country to show that, in the midst of hostilities, they still kept alive the sparks of future friendship.

Is all this to be at an end? Is this golden band of kindred sympathies, so rare between nations, to be broken forever?—Perhaps it is for the best—it may dispel an illusion which might have kept us in mental vassalage; which might have interfered occasionally with our true interests, and prevented the growth of proper national pride. But it is hard to give up the kindred tie! and there are feelings dearer than interest—closer to the heart than pride—that will still make us cast back a look of regret as we wander farther and farther from the paternal roof, and lament the waywardness of the parent that would repel the affections of the child.

Short-sighted and injudicious, however, as the conduct of England may be in this system of aspersion, recrimination on our part would be equally ill-judged. I speak not of a prompt and spirited vindication of our country, or the keenest castigation of her slanderers—but I allude to a disposition to retaliate in kind, to retort sarcasm and inspire prejudice, which seems to be spreading widely among our writers. Let us guard particularly against such a temper; for it would double the evil, instead of redressing the wrong. Nothing is so easy and inviting as the retort of abuse and sarcasm; but it is a paltry and an unprofitable contest. It is the alternative of a morbid mind, fretted into petulance, rather than warmed into indignation. If England is willing to permit the mean jealousies of trade, or the rancorous animosities of politics, to deprave the integrity of her press, and poison the fountain of public opinion, let us beware of her example. She may deem it her interest to diffuse error, and engender antipathy, for the purpose of checking emigration: we have no purpose of the kind to serve. Neither have we any spirit of national jealousy to gratify; for as yet, in all our rivalships with England, we are the rising and the gaining party. There can be no end to answer, therefore, but the gratification of resentment—a mere spirit of retaliation—and even that is impotent. Our retorts are never republished in England; they fall short, therefore, of their aim; but they foster a querulous and peevish temper among our writers; they sour the sweet flow of our early literature, and sow thorns and brambles among its blossoms. What is still worse, they circulate through our own country, and, as far as they have effect, excite virulent national prejudices. This last is the evil most especially to be deprecated. Governed, as we are, entirely by public opinion, the utmost care should be taken to preserve the purity of the public mind. Knowledge is power, and truth is knowledge; whoever, therefore, knowingly propagates a prejudice, willfully saps the foundation of his country's strength.

The members of a republic, above all other men, should be candid and dispassionate. They are, individually, portions of the sovereign mind and sovereign will, and should be enabled to come to all questions of national concern with calm and unbiased judgments. From the peculiar nature of our relations with England, we must have more frequent questions of a difficult and delicate character with her, than with any other nation,—questions that affect the most acute and excitable feelings: and as, in the adjustment of these, our national measures must ultimately be determined by popular sentiment, we cannot be too anxiously attentive to purify it from all latent passion or prepossession.

Opening, too, as we do, an asylum for strangers from every portion of the earth, we should receive all with impartiality. It should be our pride to exhibit an example of one nation, at least, destitute of national antipathies, and exercising, not merely the overt acts of hospitality, but those more rare and noble courtesies which spring from liberality of opinion.

What have we to do with national prejudices? They are the inveterate diseases of old countries, contracted in rude and ignorant ages, when nations knew but little of each other, and looked beyond their own boundaries with distrust and hostility. We, on the contrary, have sprung into national existence in an enlightened and philosophic age, when the different parts of the habitable world, and the various branches of the human family, have been indefatigably studied and made known to each other; and we forego the advantages of our birth, if we do not shake off the national prejudices, as we would the local superstitions, of the old world.

But above all let us not be influenced by any angry feelings, so far as to shut our eyes to the perception of what is really excellent and amiable in the English character. We are a young people, necessarily an imitative one, and must take our examples and models, in a great degree, from the existing nations of Europe. There is no country more worthy of our study than England. The spirit of her constitution is most analogous to ours. The manners of her people—their intellectual activity—their freedom of opinion—their habits of thinking on those subjects which concern the dearest interests and most sacred charities of private life, are all congenial to the American character; and, in fact, are all intrinsically excellent: for it is in the moral feeling of the people that the deep foundations of British prosperity are laid; and however the superstructure may be timeworn, or overrun by abuses, there must be something solid in the basis, admirable in the materials, and stable in the structure of an edifice that so long has towered unshaken amidst the tempests of the world.

Let it be the pride of our writers, therefore, discarding all feelings of irritation, and disdaining to retaliate the illiberality of British authors, to speak of the English nation without prejudice, and with determined candor. While they rebuke the indiscriminating bigotry with which some of our countrymen admire and imitate every thing English, merely because it is English, let them frankly point out what is really worthy of approbation. We may thus place England before us as a perpetual volume of reference, wherein are recorded sound deductions from ages of experience; and while we avoid the errors and absurdities which may have crept into the page, we may draw thence golden maxims of practical wisdom, wherewith to strengthen and to embellish our national character.

—1819

George Gordon, Lord Byron
1788–1824

Lord Byron is now most famous for creating the Byronic hero—a brooding, sexualized figure who is above but condemned by the reigning morality and who is driven inexorably to doom by a tragic "flaw" and guilt. In his lifetime, Lord Byron was famous *as* the Byronic hero. He once said that he awoke one morning and found himself famous. And though his London fame did come quite suddenly, his verses and eccentric behavior had drawn attention earlier in Edinburgh and Cambridge. While a student at Trinity College, Cambridge, he kept a bear in his room, which must have raised a few eyebrows, especially after he argued that it should be allowed to teach at the College. Although his first book of poems, *Fugitive Pieces* (1806), was privately printed, he sought a wider audience with the revised edition, *Hours of Idleness* (1809). But this book did not gain him fame, merely a small bit of infamy, as it was reviewed unfavorably in the *Edinburgh Review*. Spurred to satire, Byron lashed back with the scathing *English Bards and Scotch Reviewers* (1809), a parody of the *Edinburgh Review*'s contributors and the up-and-coming poets of the day. This book earned him recognition and the scorn of many a lampooned writer. It was his next major publication, *Childe Harold's Pilgrimage* (1812), a mock epic largely based on his travels in Spain and Greece, that gained him an elite English readership, which was then bolstered by *Tales* (1812–1814), *Manfred* (1816), and the unfinished *Don Juan* (1819–1823). It was not the ornate English printings but the pirated editions of his poems that gained him international fame. The London editions printed by his publisher, John Murray, were too expensive to garner readers from outside the ruling class. However, unauthorized Continental reprints by the Parisian printing firm A. and W. Galignani sold well in Europe, Britain, and America, where several printers followed suit. American editions of Byron sold through twenty thousand copies in Philadelphia and New York in one year alone, a staggering number when one considers that a decent London print run was five hundred copies.

Byron's public and private personas continued to garner as much attention as his verse. In fact, he suffered a great deal of persecution: Relentless teasing as a child over his deformed foot and the review of *Hours* were only preludes to the notoriety and calumny that brought about his exile from England. Amid rumors of an affair with his half-sister Augusta, which destroyed his marriage with Anne Isabelle Milbanke, Lady Byron, he left his native island. The controversy over their split and Byron's departure for Europe was so divisive and enduring that the American author Harriet Beecher Stowe entered the fray some fifty years later with her book *Lady Byron Vindicated* (1876). Despite condemnations of his personal and poetic "immorality" by religiously affiliated, propriety-bound newspapers and magazines in New and Old England, the number of his readers rose with every censure. Byron's sexuality continued to be obsessed over by his "polite" audiences, who were put off by rumors of his homosexuality as well as his voracious heterosexual appetite. On April 25, 1816, Byron was ostracized by London society and eventually removed to Geneva, where he was joined by Percy and Mary Shelley as well as her stepsister Claire Clairmont, with whom Byron had a child in early 1817. By autumn of this same year, he was in Venice, where by his own calculations, he was involved with over two hundred women.

In 1819, he entered into a more permanent relationship with Teresa Guiccioli, who involved him in the Carbonari plot against Austrian control over Italy and brought him to Pisa, where he was once again in the company of the Shelleys. This would not be the last time he would take up the cause of a nation whose sovereignty was being threatened: He later aided the Greeks in their war for independence from the Turks. Although he died from a fever while training his troops for combat, he is still honored by the Greeks as a hero for his commitment to the cause. So lasting was the Byronic hero, partially created from the heroes of his poems and the persona of the poet, that it not only inspired several writers and thinkers—Goethe, Nietzsche, Balzac, Stendhal, Pushkin, Dostoevsky, Shelley, Arnold, Poe, Emerson, Melville, and others— but also inspired Americans to go and fight by his side. A typical example is Samuel Gridley Howe, who left his studies at Brown University to sail for Greece to aid Byron. When he arrived and found Byron already dead, he absconded back to America with his hero's helmet, which was eventually returned. Byron's example of a hero who was unjustly persecuted, pensive, and above the morality of his peers inspired the young escaped slave Harriet Jacobs; her *Incidents in the Life of a Slave Girl* (1861), one of the most important contributions to early American autobiography, contains multiple allusions to Byron. On the opposite end of the political spectrum, Byron was appropriated by those who fought on behalf of oppressors: He was Jefferson Davis's favorite poet and the twentieth-century Italian dictator Benito Mussolini's as well.

She Walks in Beauty

She[1] walks in beauty, like the night
  Of cloudless climes and starry skies;
And all that's best of dark and bright
  Meet in her aspect and her eyes:
Thus mellow'd to that tender light   5
  Which heaven to gaudy day denies.

One shade the more, one ray the less,
  Had half impair'd the nameless grace
Which waves in every raven tress,
  Or softly lightens o'er her face;   10
Where thoughts serenely sweet express
  How pure, how dear their dwelling-place.

And on that cheek, and o'er that brow,
  So soft, so calm, yet eloquent,
The smiles that win, the tints that glow,   15
  But tell of days in goodness spent,

---

1. Lady Wilmot Horton, Byron's cousin, whom he had seen at a ball in a black mourning dress decorated with spangles.

A mind at peace with all below,
   A heart whose love is innocent!

              —1814

Darkness

I had a dream, which was not all a dream.
The bright sun was extinguish'd, and the stars
Did wander darkling[1] in the eternal space,
Rayless, and pathless, and the icy earth
Swung blind and blackening in the moonless air;   5
Morn came and went—and came, and brought no day,[2]
And men forgot their passions in the dread
Of this their desolation; and all hearts
Were chill'd into a selfish prayer for light:
And they did live by watchfires—and the thrones,   10
The palaces of crowned kings—the huts,
The habitations of all things which dwell,
Were burnt for beacons; cities were consumed,
And men were gather'd round their blazing homes
To look once more into each other's face;   15
Happy were those who dwelt within the eye
Of the volcanos, and their mountain-torch:
A fearful hope was all the world contain'd;
Forests were set on fire—but hour by hour
They fell and faded—and the crackling trunks   20
Extinguish'd with a crash—and all was black.
The brows of men by the despairing light
Wore an unearthly aspect, as by fits
The flashes fell upon them; some lay down
And hid their eyes and wept; and some did rest   25
Their chins upon their clenched hands, and smiled;
And others hurried to and fro, and fed
Their funeral piles with fuel, and look'd up
With mad disquietude on the dull sky,
The pall of a past world; and then again   30
With curses cast them down upon the dust,
And gnash'd their teeth and howl'd: the wild birds shriek'd,
And, terrified, did flutter on the ground,
And flap their useless wings; the wildest brutes
Came tame and tremulous; and vipers crawl'd   35
And twined themselves among the multitude,
Hissing, but stingless—they were slain for food:
And War, which for a moment was no more,

---

1. In darkness.   2. A reversal of Genesis 1.

Did glut himself again;—a meal was bought
With blood, and each sate sullenly apart   40
Gorging himself in gloom: no love was left;
All earth was but one thought—and that was death,
Immediate and inglorious; and the pang
Of famine fed upon all entrails—men
Died, and their bones were tombless as their flesh;   45
The meagre by the meagre were devour'd,
Even dogs assail'd their masters, all save one,
And he was faithful to a corse,[3] and kept
The birds and beasts and famish'd men at bay,
Till hunger clung them, or the dropping dead   50
Lured their lank jaws; himself sought out no food,
But with a piteous and perpetual moan,
And a quick desolate cry, licking the hand
Which answer'd not with a caress—he died.
The crowd was famish'd by degrees; but two   55
Of an enormous city did survive,
And they were enemies: they met beside
The dying embers of an altar-place
Where had been heap'd a mass of holy things
For an unholy usage; they raked up,   60
And shivering scraped with their cold skeleton hands
The feeble ashes, and their feeble breath
Blew for a little life, and made a flame
Which was a mockery; then they lifted up
Their eyes as it grew lighter, and beheld   65
Each other's aspects—saw, and shriek'd, and died—
Even of their mutual hideousness they died,
Unknowing who he was upon whose brow
Famine had written Fiend. The world was void,
The populous and the powerful was a lump,   70
Seasonless, herbless, treeless, manless, lifeless—
A lump of death—a chaos of hard clay.
The rivers, lakes, and ocean all stood still,
And nothing stirr'd within their silent depths;
Ships sailorless lay rotting on the sea,   75
And their masts fell down piecemeal; as they dropp'd
They slept on the abyss without a surge—
The waves were dead; the tides were in their grave,
The Moon, their mistress, had expired before;
The winds were wither'd in the stagnant air,   80
And the clouds perish'd; Darkness had no need
Of aid from them—She was the Universe.

                                                            —1816

---

3. Corpse.

from English Bards and Scotch Reviewers

Next comes the dull disciple of thy school,
That mild apostate from poetic rule,   230
The simple WORDSWORTH, framer of a lay,
As soft as evening in his favourite May,
Who warns his friend "to shake off toil and trouble,
And quit his books for fear of growing double;"[1]
Who, both by precept and example, shows   235
That prose is verse, and verse is merely prose,[2]
Convincing all, by demonstration plain,
Poetic souls delight in prose insane;
And Christmas stories tortured into rhyme
Contain the essence of the true sublime: 240
Thus, when he tells the tale of Betty Foy,
The idiot mother of "an idiot boy;"[3]
A moon-struck silly lad who lost his way,
And, like his bard, confounded night with day;
So close on each pathetic part he dwells,   245
And each adventure so sublimely tells,
That all who view the "idiot in his glory,"
Conceive the Bard the hero of the story. . . .

Yet let them not to vulgar WORDSWORTH stoop,
The meanest object of the lowly group,
Whose verse of all but childish prattle void,   885
Seems blessed harmony to LAMBE and LLOYD[4]:
Let them—but hold my Muse, nor dare to teach
A strain, far, far beyond thy humble reach;
The native genius with their feeling given
Will point the path, and peal their notes to heaven.   890
And thou, too, SCOTT! resign to minstrels rude,
The wilder Slogan of a Border feud:
Let others spin their meagre lines for hire:
Enough for Genius if itself inspire!
Let SOUTHEY sing, altho' his teeming muse,   895
Prolific every spring, be too profuse;
Let simple WORDSWORTH chime his childish verse,
And brother COLERIDGE lull the babe at nurse.[5] . . .

—1809

---

1. William Wordsworth (1770–1850), "The Tables Turned" (1798), lines 2–4.   2. Preface to *Lyrical Ballads* (1800), pp.
404–410.   3. "The Idiot Boy" (1798).   4. Charles Lamb (1775–1834), English essayist, and Charles Lloyd (1775–1839),
English poet, both friends of Wordsworth.   5. Sir Walter Scott (1771–1832), Robert Southey (1774–1843), and Samuel
Taylor Coleridge (1772–1834), authors and friends of Wordsworth.

from Childe Harold's Pilgrimage

Canto the Third

Afin que cette application vous forçât de penser à autre chose: il n'y
a en vérité de remède que celui-là et le temps.
                              —*Lettre du Roi de Prusse à D'Alembert*, Sept. 7, 1776.[1]

I

Is thy face like thy mother's, my fair child,
ADA, sole daughter of my house and heart?[2]
When last I saw thy young blue eyes they smiled,
And then we parted,—not as now we part,
But with a hope.—
                              Awaking with a start,   5
The waters heave around me, and on high
The winds lift up their voices: I depart,
Whither I know not; but the hour's gone by,
When Albion's[3] lessening shores could grieve or glad mine eye.

II

Once more upon the waters, yet once more!   10
And the waves bound beneath me as a steed
That knows his rider. Welcome to their roar!
Swift be their guidance wheresoe'er it lead!
Though the strain'd mast should quiver as a reed,
And the rent canvass fluttering strew the gale,   15
Still must I on; for I am as a weed,
Flung from the rock on Ocean's foam to sail
Where'er the surge may sweep, the tempest's breath prevail.

III

In my youth's summer I did sing of One,
The wandering outlaw of his own dark mind[4];   20
Again I seize the theme, then but begun,
And bear it with me, as the rushing wind
Bears the cloud onwards: in that Tale I find
The furrows of long thought, and dried-up tears,

---

1. "So that this hard work will force you to think of other things: there is in truth no remedy but that, and time." Letter from Frederick II of Prussia (1712–1786) to Jean le Rond d'Alembert (1717–1783), French mathematician.   2. Augusta Ada (1815–1852), Byron's daughter, from whom he parted in 1816 and never saw again.   3. England's.   4. Byron wrote the semi-autobiographical first canto of *Childe Harold's Pilgrimage* at the age of twenty-one, seven years before writing the third canto.

Which, ebbing, leave a sterile track behind,   25
  O'er which all heavily the journeying years
Plod the last sands of life,—where not a flower appears.

IV

Since my young days of passion—joy, or pain,
  Perchance my heart and harp have lost a string,
And both may jar; it may be that in vain   30
  I would essay as I have sung to sing.
  Yet, though a dreary strain, to this I cling,
So that it wean me from the weary dream
  Of selfish grief or gladness—so it fling
Forgetfulness around me—it shall seem   35
To me, though to none else, a not ungrateful theme.

V

He, who grown aged in this world of woe,
  In deeds, not years, piercing the depths of life,
So that no wonder waits him; nor below
  Can love, or sorrow, fame, ambition, strife,   40
  Cut to his heart again with the keen knife
Of silent, sharp endurance: he can tell
  Why thought seeks refuge in lone caves, yet rife
With airy images, and shapes which dwell
Still unimpair'd, though old, in the soul's haunted cell.   45

VI

'T is to create, and in creating live
  A being more intense, that we endow
With form our fancy, gaining as we give
  The life we image, even as I do now.
  What am I? Nothing: but not so art thou,   50
Soul of my thought! with whom I traverse earth,
  Invisible but gazing, as I glow
Mix'd with thy spirit, blended with thy birth,
And feeling still with thee in my crush'd feelings' dearth.

VII

Yet must I think less wildly:—I *have* thought   55
  Too long and darkly, till my brain became,
In its own eddy boiling and o'erwrought,
  A whirling gulf of phantasy and flame:
  And thus, untaught in youth my heart to tame,
My springs of life were poison'd. 'T is too late!   60
  Yet am I changed; though still enough the same

In strength to bear what time can not abate,
And feed on bitter fruits without accusing Fate.

VIII

Something too much of this[5]: but now 't is past,
And the spell closes with its silent seal.   65
Long absent HAROLD re-appears at last,—
He of the breast which fain no more would feel,
Wrung with the wounds which kill not but ne'er heal;
Yet Time, who changes all, had alter'd him
In soul and aspect as in age: years steal   70
Fire from the mind as vigour from the limb,
And life's enchanted cup but sparkles near the brim.

IX

His had been quaff'd too quickly, and he found
The dregs were wormwood; but he fill'd again,
And from a purer fount, on holier ground,   75
And deem'd its spring perpetual—but in vain!
Still round him clung invisibly a chain
Which gall'd for ever, fettering though unseen,
And heavy though it clank'd not; worn with pain,
Which pined although it spoke not, and grew keen,   80
Entering with every step he took through many a scene.

X

Secure in guarded coldness, he had mix'd
Again in fancied safety with his kind,
And deem'd his spirit now so firmly fix'd
And sheathed with an invulnerable mind,   85
That, if no joy, no sorrow lurk'd behind;
And he, as one, might 'midst the many stand
Unheeded, searching through the crowd to find
Fit speculation, such as in strange land
He found in wonder-works of God and Nature's hand.   90

XI

But who can view the ripen'd rose nor seek
To wear it? who can curiously behold
The smoothness and the sheen of beauty's cheek,
Nor feel the heart can never all grow old?
Who can contemplate Fame through clouds unfold   95
The star which rises o'er her steep, nor climb?

---

5. William Shakespeare (1564–1616), *Hamlet* (1603), 3.2.160.

Harold, once more within the vortex, roll'd
On with the giddy circle, chasing Time,
Yet with a nobler aim than in his youth's fond prime.

XII

But soon he knew himself the most unfit   100
Of men to herd with Man, with whom he held
Little in common;—untaught to submit
His thoughts to others, though his soul was quell'd
In youth by his own thoughts; still uncompell'd,
He would not yield dominion of his mind   105
To spirits against whom his own rebell'd;
Proud though in desolation; which could find
A life within itself, to breathe without mankind.

XIII

Where rose the mountains, there to him were friends;
Where roll'd the ocean, thereon was his home;   110
Where a blue sky, and glowing clime, extends,
He had the passion and the power to roam;
The desert, forest, cavern, breaker's foam,
Were unto him companionship; they spake
A mutual language, clearer than the tome   115
Of his land's tongue, which he would oft forsake
For Nature's pages glass'd by sunbeams on the lake.

XIV

Like the Chaldean[6] he could watch the stars,
Till he had peopled them with beings bright
As their own beams; and earth, and earth-born jars,   120
And human frailties, were forgotten quite.
Could he have kept his spirit to that flight
He had been happy; but this clay will sink
Its spark immortal, envying it the light
To which it mounts, as if to break the link   125
That keeps us from yon heaven which woos us to its brink.

XV

But in Man's dwellings he became a thing
Restless and worn, and stern and wearisome,
Droop'd as a wild-born falcon with clipt wing,
To whom the boundless air alone were home.   130
Then came his fit again, which to o'ercome,

---

6. Ancient Babylonians, known for their expertise in astronomy.

As eagerly the barr'd-up bird will beat
His breast and beak against his wiry dome
Till the blood tinge his plumage, so the heat
Of his impeded soul would through his bosom eat.   135

XVI

Self-exiled Harold wanders forth again,
With nought of hope left, but with less of gloom;
The very knowledge that he lived in vain,
That all was over on this side the tomb,
Had made Despair a smilingness assume,   140
Which, though 't were wild,—as on the plunder'd wreck
When mariners would madly meet their doom
With draughts intemperate on the sinking deck,—
Did yet inspire a cheer which he forbore to check.

XVII

Stop!—for thy tread is on an Empire's dust!   145
An Earthquake's spoil is sepulchred[7] below!
Is the spot mark'd with no colossal bust,
Nor column trophied for triumphal show?
None; but the moral's truth tells simpler so,
As the ground was before, thus let it be;—   150
How that red rain hath made the harvest grow!
And is this all the world has gained by thee,
Thou first and last of fields, king-making Victory?

XVIII

And Harold stands upon this place of skulls,
The grave of France, the deadly Waterloo![8]   155
How in an hour the power which gave annuls
Its gifts, transferring fame as fleeting too!
In 'pride of place'[9] here last the eagle[10] flew,
Then tore with bloody talon the rent plain,
Pierced by the shaft of banded nations through;   160
Ambition's life and labours all were vain;
He wears the shatter'd links of the world's broken chain.

XIX

Fit retribution! Gaul[11] may champ the bit
And foam in fetters;—but is Earth more free?
Did nations combat to make *One* submit;   165

---

7. Entombed.   8. The site of Napoleon's defeat in 1815.   9. William Shakespeare (1564–1616), *Macbeth* (1603), 2.4.12.
10. Napoleon's standard.   11. France.

Or league to teach all kings true sovereignty?
What! shall reviving Thraldom[12] again be
The patch'd-up idol of enlighten'd days?
Shall we, who struck the Lion down, shall we
Pay the Wolf homage? proffering lowly gaze   170
And servile knees to thrones? No; *prove*[13] before ye praise!

XX

If not, o'er one fallen despot boast no more!
In vain fair cheeks were furrow'd with hot tears
For Europe's flowers long rooted up before
The trampler of her vineyards; in vain years   175
Of death, depopulation, bondage, fears,
Have all been borne, and broken by the accord
Of roused-up millions: all that most endears
Glory, is when the myrtle wreathes a sword
Such as Harmodius drew on Athens' tyrant lord.[14]   180

XXI

There was a sound of revelry by night,[15]
And Belgium's capital had gather'd then
Her Beauty and her Chivalry, and bright
The lamps shone o'er fair women and brave men;
A thousand hearts beat happily; and when   185
Music arose with its voluptuous swell,
Soft eyes look'd love to eyes which spake again,
And all went merry as a marriage-bell;—
But hush! hark! a deep sound strikes like a rising knell!

XXII

Did ye not hear it?—No; 'twas but the wind,   190
Or the car rattling o'er the stony street;
On with the dance! let joy be unconfined;
No sleep till morn, when Youth and Pleasure meet
To chase the glowing Hours with flying feet—
But hark!—that heavy sound breaks in once more   195
As if the clouds its echo would repeat;
And nearer, clearer, deadlier than before!
Arm! Arm! it is—it is—the cannon's opening roar!

---

12. Despotism.   13. Test.   14. Athenian heroes, Harmodius and Aristogeiton hid their swords in myrtle, a symbol of love and peace, in order to surprise and kill Hipparchus.   15. Duchess of Richmond's ball on the night before combat at Waterloo.

XXIII

Within a window'd niche of that high hall
Sate Brunswick's fated chieftain[16]; he did hear   200
That sound the first amidst the festival,
And caught its tone with Death's prophetic ear;
And when they smiled because he deem'd it near,
His heart more truly knew that peal too well
Which stretch'd his father on a bloody bier,   205
And roused the vengeance blood alone could quell:
He rush'd into the field, and, foremost fighting, fell.

XXIV

Ah! then and there was hurrying to and fro,
And gathering tears, and tremblings of distress,
And cheeks all pale, which but an hour ago   210
Blush'd at the praise of their own loveliness;
And there were sudden partings, such as press
The life from out young hearts, and choking sighs
Which ne'er might be repeated; who could guess
If ever more should meet those mutual eyes,   215
Since upon night so sweet such awful morn could rise!

XXV

And there was mounting in hot haste: the steed,
The mustering squadron, and the clattering car,
Went pouring forward with impetuous speed,
And swiftly forming in the ranks of war;   220
And the deep thunder peal on peal afar;
And near, the beat of the alarming drum
Roused up the soldier ere the morning star;
While throng'd the citizens with terror dumb,
Or whispering, with white lips—'The foe! They come! they come!'   225

XXVI

And wild and high the 'Cameron's gathering' rose!
The war-note of Lochiel,[17] which Albyn's[18] hills
Have heard, and heard too have her Saxon foes:—
How in the noon of night that pibroch[19] thrills,
Savage and shrill! But with the breath which fills   230
Their mountain-pipe, so fill the mountaineers
With the fierce native daring which instills

---

16. Frederick William, Duke of Brunswick (1771–1815), killed at Waterloo.   17. Chief of the Camerons, Scottish clan.
"Gathering": a clan song.   18. Scotland's.   19. Bagpipe.

The stirring memory of a thousand years,
And Evan's, Donald's[20] fame rings in each clansman's ears!

XXVII

And Ardennes[21] waves above them her green leaves,   235
Dewy with nature's tear-drops, as they pass,
Grieving, if aught inanimate e'er grieves,
Over the unreturning brave,—alas!
Ere evening to be trodden like the grass
Which now beneath them, but above shall grow   240
In its next verdure, when this fiery mass
Of living valour, rolling on the foe
And burning with high hope, shall moulder cold and low.

XXVIII

Last noon beheld them full of lusty life,
Last eve in Beauty's circle proudly gay,   245
The midnight brought the signal-sound of strife,
The morn the marshalling in arms,—the day
Battle's magnificently-stern array!
The thunder-clouds close o'er it, which when rent
The earth is cover'd thick with other clay,   250
Which her own clay shall cover, heap'd and pent,
Rider and horse,—friend, foe,—in one red burial blent!

XXIX

Their praise is hymn'd by loftier harps than mine;
Yet one I would select from that proud throng,
Partly because they blend me with his line,   255
And partly that I did his sire some wrong,
And partly that bright names will hallow song;
And his was of the bravest, and when shower'd
The death-bolts deadliest the thinn'd files along,
Even where the thickest of war's tempest lower'd,   260
They reach'd no nobler breast than thine, young, gallant Howard![22]

XXX

There have been tears and breaking hearts for thee,
And mine were nothing, had I such to give;
But when I stood beneath the fresh green tree,
Which living waves where thou didst cease to live,   265
And saw around me the wide field revive

---

20. Evan and Donald Cameron, famous Scottish warriors.   21. Forest in Belgium, France, and Luxembourg.   22. Major Frederick Howard (1785–1815), Byron's relative.

With fruits and fertile promise, and the Spring
Come forth her work of gladness to contrive,
With all her reckless birds upon the wing,
I turn'd from all she brought to those she could not bring.   270

XXXI

I turn'd to thee, to thousands, of whom each
And one as all a ghastly gap did make
In his own kind and kindred, whom to teach
Forgetfulness were mercy for their sake;
The Archangel's trump, not Glory's, must awake   275
Those whom they thirst for; though the sound of Fame
May for a moment soothe, it cannot slake
The fever of vain longing, and the name
So honour'd but assumes a stronger, bitterer claim.

XXXII

They mourn, but smile at length; and, smiling, mourn: 280
The tree will wither long before it fall;
The hull drives on, though mast and sail be torn;
The roof-tree sinks, but moulders on the hall
In massy hoariness; the ruin'd wall
Stands when its wind-worn battlements are gone;   285
The bars survive the captive they enthral;
The day drags through though storms keep out the sun;
And thus the heart will break, yet brokenly live on:

XXXIII

Even as a broken mirror, which the glass
In every fragment multiplies; and makes   290
A thousand images of one that was,
The same, and still the more, the more it breaks;
And thus the heart will do which not forsakes,
Living in shatter'd guise, and still, and cold,
And bloodless, with its sleepless sorrow aches,   295
Yet withers on till all without is old,
Showing no visible sign, for such things are untold.

XXXIV

There is a very life in our despair,
Vitality of poison, a quick root
Which feeds these deadly branches: for it were   300
As nothing did we die; but Life will suit
Itself to Sorrow's most detested fruit,
Like to the apples on the Dead Sea's shore,

All ashes to the taste. Did man compute
Existence by enjoyment, and count o'er   305
Such hours 'gainst years of life,—say, would he name threescore?

XXXV

The Psalmist number'd out the years of man:
They are enough, and if thy tale be *true*,
Thou, who didst grudge him even that fleeting span,
More than enough, thou fatal Waterloo!   310
Millions of tongues record thee, and anew
Their children's lips shall echo them, and say—
'Here, where the sword united nations drew,
Our countrymen were warring on that day!'
And this is much, and all which will not pass away.   315

XXXVI

There sunk the greatest, nor the worst of men,[23]
Whose spirit antithetically mixt
One moment of the mightiest, and again
On little objects with like firmness fixt,
Extreme in all things! hadst thou been betwixt,   320
Thy throne had still been thine, or never been;
For daring made thy rise as fall: thou seek'st
Even now to re-assume the imperial mien,
And shake again the world, the Thunderer of the scene!

XXXVII

Conqueror and captive of the earth art thou!   325
She trembles at thee still, and thy wild name
Was ne'er more bruited in men's minds than now
That thou art nothing, save the jest of Fame,
Who woo'd thee once, thy vassal, and became
The flatterer of thy fierceness, till thou wert   330
A god unto thyself; nor less the same
To the astounded kingdoms all inert,
Who deem'd thee for a time whate'er thou didst assert.

XXXVIII

Oh, more or less than man—in high or low,
Battling with nations, flying from the field;   335
Now making monarchs' necks thy footstool, now
More than thy meanest soldier taught to yield:
An empire thou couldst crush, command, rebuild,

---

23. Napoleon.

But govern not thy pettiest passion, nor,
However deeply in men's spirits skill'd,   340
Look through thine own, nor curb the lust of war,
Nor learn that tempted Fate will leave the loftiest star.

XXXIX

Yet well thy soul hath brook'd the turning tide
With that untaught innate philosophy,
Which, be it wisdom, coldness, or deep pride,   345
Is gall and wormwood to an enemy.
When the whole host of hatred stood hard by,
To watch and mock thee shrinking, thou hast smiled
With a sedate and all-enduring eye;
When Fortune fled her spoil'd and favourite child,   350
He stood unbow'd beneath the ills upon him piled.

XL

Sager than in thy fortunes; for in them
Ambition steel'd thee on too far to show
That just habitual scorn, which could contemn
Men and their thoughts; 't was wise to feel, not so   355
To wear it ever on thy lip and brow,
And spurn the instruments thou wert to use
Till they were turn'd unto thine overthrow:
'T is but a worthless world to win or lose,
So hath it proved to thee and all such lot who choose.   360

XLI

If, like a tower upon a headlong rock,
Thou hadst been made to stand or fall alone,
Such scorn of man had help'd to brave the shock;
But men's thoughts were the steps which paved thy throne,
Their admiration thy best weapon shone;   365
The part of Philip's[24] son was thine, not then
(Unless aside thy purple had been thrown)
Like stern Diogenes[25] to mock at men;
For sceptred cynics[26] earth were far too wide a den.

XLII

But quiet to quick bosoms is a hell,   370
And *there* hath been thy bane; there is a fire

---

24. Philip of Macedonia (382–336 BC), father of Alexander the Great (356–323 BC), military commander. 25. Diogenes (412–323 BC), Greek philosopher and cynic. 26. Alexander is reported to have said, "If I were not Alexander, I should wish to be Diogenes."

And motion of the soul which will not dwell
In its own narrow being, but aspire
Beyond the fitting medium of desire;
And, but once kindled, quenchless evermore,   375
Preys upon high adventure, nor can tire
Of aught but rest; a fever at the core,
Fatal to him who bears, to all who ever bore.

XLIII

This makes the madmen who have made men mad
By their contagion,—Conquerors and Kings,   380
Founders of sects and systems, to whom add
Sophists, Bards, Statesmen, all unquiet things
Which stir too strongly the soul's secret springs,
And are themselves the fools to those they fool;
Envied, yet how unenviable! what stings   385
Are theirs! One breast laid open were a school
Which would unteach mankind the lust to shine or rule.

XLIV

Their breath is agitation, and their life
A storm whereon they ride, to sink at last;
And yet so nursed and bigoted to strife,   390
That should their days, surviving perils past,
Melt to calm twilight, they feel overcast
With sorrow and supineness, and so die;
Even as a flame unfed which runs to waste
With its own flickering, or a sword laid by,   395
Which eats into itself and rusts ingloriously.

XLV

He who ascends to mountain-tops, shall find
The loftiest peaks most wrapt in clouds and snow;
He who surpasses or subdues mankind,
Must look down on the hate of those below.   400
Though high *above* the sun of glory glow,
And far *beneath* the earth and ocean spread,
Round him are icy rocks, and loudly blow
Contending tempests on his naked head,
And thus reward the toils which to those summits led.   405

XLVI

Away with these! true Wisdom's world will be
Within its own creation, or in thine,
Maternal Nature! for who teems like thee,

Thus on the banks of thy majestic Rhine?[27]
There Harold gazes on a work divine,   410
A blending of all beauties,—streams and dells,
Fruit, foliage, crag, wood, cornfield, mountain, vine,
And chiefless castles breathing stern farewells
From gray but leafy walls, where Ruin greenly dwells.

XLVII

And there they stand, as stands a lofty mind,   415
Worn, but unstooping to the baser crowd,
All tenantless, save to the crannying wind,
Or holding dark communion with the cloud.
There was a day when they were young and proud,
Banners on high, and battles pass'd below;   420
But they who fought are in a bloody shroud,
And those which waved are shredless dust ere now,
And the bleak battlements shall bear no future blow.

XLVIII

Beneath these battlements, within those walls,
Power dwelt amidst her passions; in proud state   425
Each robber chief upheld his armèd halls,
Doing his evil will, nor less elate
Than mightier heroes of a longer date.
What want these outlaws conquerors should have,
But History's purchased page to call them great?   430
A wider space, an ornamented grave?
Their hopes were not less warm, their souls were full as brave.

XLIX

In their baronial feuds and single fields,
What deeds of prowess unrecorded died!
And Love, which lent a blazon to their shields   435
With emblems well devised by amorous pride,
Through all the mail[28] of iron hearts would glide:
But still their flame was fierceness, and drew on
Keen contest and destruction near allied;
And many a tower for some fair mischief won,   440
Saw the discolour'd Rhine beneath its ruin run.

L

But Thou, exulting and abounding river!
Making thy waves a blessing as they flow

---

27. German river.   28. Armor.

Through banks whose beauty would endure for ever,
Could man but leave thy bright creation so,   445
Nor its fair promise from the surface mow
With the sharp scythe of conflict,—then to see
Thy valley of sweet waters, were to know
Earth paved like Heaven; and to seem such to me,
Even now what wants thy stream?—that it should Lethe[29] be.   450

LI

A thousand battles have assail'd thy banks,
But these and half their fame have pass'd away,
And Slaughter heap'd on high his weltering ranks;
Their very graves are gone, and what are they?
Thy tide wash'd down the blood of yesterday,   455
And all was stainless, and on thy clear stream
Glass'd with its dancing light the sunny ray;
But o'er the blacken'd memory's blighting dream
Thy waves would vainly roll, all sweeping as they seem.

LII

Thus Harold inly said, and pass'd along,   460
Yet not insensibly to all which here
Awoke the jocund birds to early song
In glens which might have made even exile dear.
Though on his brow were graven lines austere,
And tranquil sternness which had ta'en the place   465
Of feelings fierier far but less severe,
Joy was not always absent from his face,
But o'er it in such scenes would steal with transient trace.

LIII

Nor was all love shut from him, though his days
Of passion had consumed themselves to dust.   470
It is in vain that we would coldly gaze
On such as smile upon us; the heart must
Leap kindly back to kindness, though disgust
Hath wean'd it from all wordlings: thus he felt,
For there was soft remembrance, and sweet trust   475
In one fond breast[30] to which his own would melt,
And in its tenderer hour on that his bosom dwelt.

---

29. River of forgetfulness that flows through Hades, the Greek underworld.   30. Byron's half-sister, Augusta Leigh (1783–1851).

LIV

And he had learn'd to love (I know not why,
For this in such as him seems strange of mood)
The helpless looks of blooming infancy,   480
Even in its earliest nurture; what subdued,
To change like this, a mind so far imbued
With scorn of man, it little boots to know;
But thus it was; and though in solitude
Small power the nipp'd affections have to grow,   485
In him this glow'd when all beside had ceased to glow.

LV

And there was one soft breast, as hath been said,
Which unto his was bound by stronger ties
Than the church links withal; and, though unwed,
That love was pure, and, far above disguise,   490
Had stood the test of mortal enmities
Still undivided, and cemented more
By peril, dreaded most in female eyes;
But this was firm, and from a foreign shore
Well to that heart might his these absent greetings pour!   495

1

The castled crag of Drachenfels[31]
Frowns o'er the wide and winding Rhine,
Whose breast of waters broadly swells
Between the banks which bear the vine;
And hills all rich with blossom'd trees,   500
And fields which promise corn and wine,
And scatter'd cities crowning these,
Whose far white walls along them shine,
Have strew'd a scene, which I should see
With double joy wert *thou* with me.   505

2

And peasant girls, with deep blue eyes
And hands which offer early flowers,
Walk smiling o'er this paradise;
Above, the frequent feudal towers
Through green leaves lift their walls of gray;   510
And many a rock which steeply lowers,
And noble arch in proud decay,
Look o'er this vale of vintage-bowers;
But one thing want these banks of Rhine,—
Thy gentle hand to clasp in mine!   515

---

31. German castle in the Filter mountains.

3

I send the lilies given to me;
Though long before thy hand they touch,
I know that they must wither'd be,
But yet reject them not as such;
For I have cherish'd them as dear,   520
Because they yet may meet thine eye,
And guide thy soul to mine even here,
When thou behold'st them, drooping nigh,
And know'st them gather'd by the Rhine,
And offer'd from my heart to thine!   525

4

The river nobly foams and flows,
The charm of this enchanted ground,
And all its thousand turns disclose
Some fresher beauty varying round:
The haughtiest breast its wish might bound   530
Through life to dwell delighted here;
Nor could on earth a spot be found
To nature and to me so dear,
Could thy dear eyes in following mine
Still sweeten more these banks of Rhine!   535

LVI

By Coblentz,[32] on a rise of gentle ground,
There is a small and simple pyramid,
Crowning the summit of the verdant mound;
Beneath its base are heroes' ashes hid,
Our enemy's,—but let not that forbid   540
Honour to Marceau![33] o'er whose early tomb
Tears, big tears, gush'd from the rough soldier's lid,
Lamenting and yet envying such a doom,
Falling for France whose rights he battled to resume.

LVII

Brief, brave, and glorious was his young career,—   545
His mourners were two hosts, his friends and foes;
And fitly may the stranger lingering here
Pray for his gallant spirit's bright repose;
For he was Freedom's champion, one of those,
The few in number, who had not o'er-stept   550
The charter to chastise which she bestows
On such as wield her weapons; he had kept
The whiteness of his soul, and thus men o'er him wept.

---

32. German town on the Rhine river.   33. François Marceau (1769–1796), French general killed near Coblenz.

LVIII

Here Ehrenbreitstein,[34] with her shatter'd wall
Black with the miner's blast, upon her height   555
Yet shows of what she was, when shell and ball
Rebounding idly on her strength did light,—
A tower of victory! from whence the flight
Of baffled foes was watch'd along the plain:
But Peace destroy'd what War could never blight,   560
And laid those proud roofs bare to Summer's rain,
On which the iron shower for years had pour'd in vain.

LIX

Adieu to thee, fair Rhine! How long delighted
The stranger fain would linger on his way!
Thine is a scene alike where souls united   565
Or lonely Contemplation thus might stray;
And could the ceaseless vultures cease to prey
On self-condemning bosoms, it were here,
Where Nature, nor too sombre nor too gay,
Wild but not rude, awful yet not austere,   570
Is to the mellow Earth as Autumn to the year.

LX

Adieu to thee again! a vain adieu!
There can be no farewell to scene like thine;
The mind is colour'd by thy every hue;
And if reluctantly the eyes resign   575
Their cherish'd gaze upon thee, lovely Rhine,
'T is with the thankful glance of parting praise;
More mighty spots may rise, more glaring shine,
But none unite in one attaching maze
The brilliant, fair, and soft,—the glories of old days,   580

LXI

The negligently grand, the fruitful bloom
Of coming ripeness, the white city's sheen,
The rolling stream, the precipice's gloom,
The forest's growth, and Gothic walls between,
The wild rocks shaped as they had turrets been   585
In mockery of man's art; and these withal
A race of faces happy as the scene,
Whose fertile bounties here extend to all,
Still springing o'er thy banks, though Empires near them fall.

---

34. Fortress in Coblenz on a cliff over the Rhine.

LXII

But these recede. Above me are the Alps,   590
The palaces of Nature, whose vast walls
Have pinnacled in clouds their snowy scalps,
And throned Eternity in icy halls
Of cold sublimity, where forms and falls
The avalanche—the thunderbolt of snow!   595
All that expands the spirit, yet appals,
Gather around these summits, as to show
How Earth may pierce to Heaven, yet leave vain man below.

LXIII

But ere these matchless heights I dare to scan,
There is a spot should not be pass'd in vain,—   600
Morat! the proud, the patriot field! where man
May gaze on ghastly trophies of the slain,
Nor blush for those who conquer'd on that plain;
Here Burgundy bequeath'd his tombless host,[35]
A bony heap, through ages to remain,   605
Themselves their monument;—the Stygian[36] coast
Unsepulchred they roam'd, and shriek'd each wandering ghost.

LXIV

While Waterloo with Cannæ's[37] carnage vies,
Morat and Marathon[38] twin names shall stand;
They were true Glory's stainless victories,   610
Won by the unambitious heart and hand
Of a proud, brotherly, and civic band,
All unbought champions in no princely cause
Of vice-entail'd Corruption; they no land
Doom'd to bewail the blasphemy of laws   615
Making kings' rights divine, by some Draconic clause.

LXV

By a lone wall a lonelier column rears
A gray and grief-worn aspect of old days;
'T is the last remnant of the wreck of years,
And looks as with the wild-bewildered gaze   620
Of one to stone converted by amaze,
Yet still with consciousness; and there it stands
Making a marvel that it not decays,

---

35. Morat, Switzerland, where the Swiss Confederation defeated the French House of Burgundy in 1476.   36. Pertaining to the river Styx in the Greek underworld.   37. Battle of Cannae, 216 BC.   38. Battle of Marathon, 490 BC.

When the coeval pride of human hands,
Levell'd Aventicum,[39] hath strew'd her subject lands.   625

LXVI

And there—oh! sweet and sacred be the name!—
Julia,[40] the daughter, the devoted, gave
Her youth to Heaven; her heart, beneath a claim
Nearest to Heaven's, broke o'er a father's grave.
Justice is sworn 'gainst tears, and hers would crave   630
The life she lived in; but the judge was just,
And then she died on him she could not save.
Their tomb was simple, and without a bust,
And held within their urn one mind, one heart, one dust.

LXVII

But these are deeds which should not pass away,   635
And names that must not wither, though the earth
Forgets her empires with a just decay,
The enslavers and the enslaved, their death and birth;
The high, the mountain-majesty of worth
Should be, and shall, survivor of its woe,   640
And from its immortality look forth
In the sun's face, like yonder Alpine snow,
Imperishably pure beyond all things below.

LXVIII

Lake Leman[41] woos me with its crystal face,
The mirror where the stars and mountains view   645
The stillness of their aspect in each trace
Its clear depth yields of their far height and hue.
There is too much of man here, to look through
With a fit mind the might which I behold;
But soon in me shall Loneliness renew   650
Thoughts hid, but not less cherish'd than of old,
Ere mingling with the herd had penn'd me in their fold.

LXIX

To fly from, need not be to hate, mankind:
All are not fit with them to stir and toil,
Nor is it discontent to keep the mind   655
Deep in its fountain, lest it overboil
In the hot throng, where we become the spoil

---

39. Ruins of a Roman town near Geneva.   40. Main character of *Julie or the New Heloise* (1761) by Jean-Jacques Rousseau (1712–1778).   41. Lake Geneva.

Of our infection, till too late and long
We may deplore and struggle with the coil,[42]
In wretched interchange of wrong for wrong   660
Midst a contentious world, striving where none are strong.

LXX

There, in a moment, we may plunge our years
In fatal penitence, and in the blight
Of our own soul turn all our blood to tears,
And colour things to come with hues of Night;   665
The race of life becomes a hopeless flight
To those that walk in darkness: on the sea,
The boldest steer but where their ports invite,
But there are wanderers o'er Eternity
Whose bark drives on and on, and anchor'd ne'er shall be.   670

LXXI

Is it not better, then, to be alone,
And love Earth only for its earthly sake?
By the blue rushing of the arrowy Rhone,
Or the plure bosom of its nursing lake,
Which feeds it as a mother who doth make   675
A fair but froward infant her own care,
Kissing its cries away as these awake;—
Is it not better thus our lives to wear,
Than join the crushing crowd, doom'd to inflict or bear?

LXXII

I live not in myself, but I become   680
Portion of that around me; and to me
High mountains are a feeling, but the hum
Of human cities torture: I can see
Nothing to loathe in nature, save to be
A link reluctant in a fleshly chain,   685
Class'd among creatures, when the soul can flee,
And with the sky, the peak, the heaving plain
Of ocean, or the stars, mingle, and not in vain.[43]

LXXIII

And thus I am absorb'd, and this is life:
I look upon the peopled desert past,   690
As on a place of agony and strife,

---

42. Tumult, confusion.   43. Compare William Wordsworth (1770–1850), "Lines Written a Few Miles above Tintern Abbey," p. 400.

Where, for some sin, to sorrow I was cast,
To act and suffer, but remount at last
With a fresh pinion[44]; which I feel to spring,
Though young, yet waxing vigorous, as the blast   695
Which it would cope with, on delighted wing,
Spurning the clay-cold bonds[45] which round our being cling.

LXXIV

And when at length the mind shall be all free
From what it hates in this degraded form,
Reft of its carnal life, save what shall be   700
Existent happier in the fly and worm,—
When elements to elements conform,
And dust is as it should be,[46] shall I not
Feel all I see, less dazzling, but more warm?
The bodiless thought? the Spirit of each spot?   705
Of which, even now, I share at times the immortal lot?

LXXV

Are not the mountains, waves, and skies, a part
Of me and of my soul, as I of them?
Is not the love of these deep in my heart
With a pure passion? should I not contemn   710
All objects, if compared with these? and stem
A tide of suffering, rather than forego
Such feelings for the hard and worldly phlegm
Of those whose eyes are only turn'd below,
Gazing upon the ground, with thoughts which dare not glow?   715

LXXVI

But this is not my theme; and I return
To that which is immediate, and require
Those who find contemplation in the urn,[47]
To look on One whose dust was once all fire,
A native of the land where I respire   720
The clear air for a while (a passing guest,
Where he became a being) whose desire
Was to be glorious;—'t was a foolish quest,
The which to gain and keep he sacrificed all rest.

---

44. Wing.   45. The body.   46. *The Book of Common Prayer's* memento mori or remembrance of death: "Ashes to ashes, dust to dust."   47. Container for ashes of the dead.

LXXVII

Here the self-torturing sophist, wild Rousseau,[48]   725
The apostle of affliction, he who threw
Enchantment over passion, and from woe
Wrung overwhelming eloquence, first drew
The breath which made him wretched; yet he knew
How to make madness beautiful, and cast   730
O'er erring deeds and thoughts a heavenly hue
Of words, like sunbeams, dazzling as they past
The eyes, which o'er them shed tears feelingly and fast.

LXXVIII

His love was passion's essence—as a tree
On fire by lightning; with ethereal flame   735
Kindled he was, and blasted; for to be
Thus, and enamour'd, were in him the same.
But his was not the love of living dame,
Nor of the dead who rise upon our dreams,
But of ideal beauty, which became   740
In him existence, and o'erflowing teems
Along his burning page, distemper'd though it seems.

LXXIX

This breathed itself to life in Julie, *this*
Invested her with all that's wild and sweet;
This hallow'd, too, the memorable kiss[49]   745
Which every morn his fever'd lip would greet,
From hers who but with friendship his would meet;
But to that gentle touch, through brain and breast
Flash'd the thrill'd spirit's love-devouring heat;
In that absorbing sigh perchance more blest   750
Than vulgar minds may be with all they seek possest.

LXXX

His life was one long war with self-sought foes,
Or friends by him self-banish'd; for his mind
Had grown Suspicion's sanctuary, and chose,
For its own cruel sacrifice, the kind   755
'Gainst whom he raged with fury strange and blind.
But he was phrensied,—wherefore, who may know?
Since cause might be which skill could never find;
But he was phrensied by disease or woe
To that worst pitch of all, which wears a reasoning show.   760

---

48. Jean-Jacques Rousseau (1712–1778), French philosopher.   49. *Confessions* (1782), Book 9.

LXXXI

For then he was inspired, and from him came,
As from the Pythian's mystic cave of yore,[50]
Those oracles which set the world in flame,
Nor ceased to burn till kingdoms were no more:
Did he not this for France, which lay before   765
Bow'd to the inborn tyranny of years?
Broken and trembling to the yoke she bore,
Till by the voice of him and his compeers
Roused up to too much wrath, which follows o'ergrown fears?

LXXXII

They made themselves a fearful monument!   770
The wreck of old opinions, things which grew,
Breathed from the birth of time: the veil they rent,
And what behind it lay, all earth shall view.
But good with ill they also overthrew,
Leaving but ruins, wherewith to rebuild   775
Upon the same foundation, and renew
Dungeons and thrones, which the same hour re-fill'd
As heretofore because ambition was self-will'd.

LXXXIII

But this will not endure, nor be endured;
Mankind have felt their strength, and made it felt!   780
They might have used it better, but, allured
By their new vigour, sternly have they dealt
On one another; pity ceased to melt
With her once natural charities. But they,
Who in oppression's darkness caved had dwelt,   785
They were not eagles, nourish'd with the day;
What marvel then, at times, if they mistook their prey?

LXXXIV

What deep wounds ever closed without a scar?
The heart's bleed longest, and but heal to wear
That which disfigures it; and they who war   790
With their own hopes and have been vanquish'd, bear
Silence, but not submission. In his lair
Fix'd Passion holds his breath, until the hour
Which shall atone for years; none need despair:
It came, it cometh, and will come,—the power   795
To punish or forgive—in *one* we shall be slower.

---

50. Location of the oracle at Delphi, Greece.

LXXXV

Clear, placid Leman! thy contrasted lake,
With the wild world I dwelt in, is a thing
Which warns me with its stillness to forsake
Earth's troubled waters for a purer spring.   800
This quiet sail is as a noiseless wing
To waft me from distraction; once I loved
Torn ocean's roar, but thy soft murmuring
Sounds sweet as if a Sister's voice reproved,
That I with stern delights should e'er have been so moved.   805

LXXXVI

It is the hush of night, and all between
Thy margin and the mountains, dusk, yet clear,
Mellow'd and mingling, yet distinctly seen,
Save darken'd Jura,[51] whose capt heights appear
Precipitously steep; and drawing near,   810
There breathes a living fragrance from the shore,
Of flowers yet fresh with childhood; on the ear
Drops the light drip of the suspended oar,
Or chirps the grasshopper one good-night carol more;—

LXXXVII

He is an evening reveller, who makes   815
His life an infancy, and sings his fill;—
At intervals, some bird from out the brakes[52]
Starts into voice a moment, then is still.
There seems a floating whisper on the hill,
But that is fancy, for the starlight dews   820
All silently their tears of love instil,
Weeping themselves away, till they infuse
Deep into Nature's breast the spirit of her hues.

LXXXVIII

Ye stars, which are the poetry of heaven!
If in your bright leaves[53] we would read the fate   825
Of men and empires,—'t is to be forgiven,
That in our aspirations to be great,
Our destinies o'erleap their mortal state,
And claim a kindred with you; for ye are
A beauty and a mystery, and create   830
In us such love and reverence from afar
That fortune, fame, power, life, have named themselves a star.

---

51. Mountain range in the Alps, visible from Geneva.   52. Thickets.   53. Leaves of a tree and pages of a book.

LXXXIX

All heaven and earth are still—though not in sleep,
But breathless, as we grow when feeling most;
And silent, as we stand in thoughts too deep:—   835
All heaven and earth are still. From the high host
Of stars to the lull'd lake and mountain-coast,
All is concentred in a life intense,
Where not a beam nor air nor leaf is lost,
But hath a part of being, and a sense   840
Of that which is of all Creator and defence.

XC

Then stirs the feeling infinite, so felt
In solitude where we are *least* alone;
A truth, which through our being then doth melt
And purifies from self: it is a tone,   845
The soul and source of music, which makes known
Eternal harmony, and sheds a charm,
Like to the fabled Cytherea's zone,[54]
Binding all things with beauty;—'t would disarm
The spectre Death, had he substantial power to harm.   850

XCI

Not vainly did the early Persian make
His altar the high places and the peak
Of earth-o'ergazing mountains, and thus take
A fit and unwall'd temple, there to seek
The Spirit, in whose honour shrines are weak   855
Uprear'd of human hands. Come, and compare
Columns and idol-dwellings, Goth or Greek,
With Nature's realms of worship, earth and air,
Nor fix on fond abodes to circumscribe thy pray'r!

XCII

The sky is changed!—and such a change! Oh night,   860
And storm, and darkness, ye are wondrous strong,
Yet lovely in your strength, as is the light
Of a dark eye in woman! Far along,
From peak to peak the rattling crags among,
Leaps the live thunder! Not from one lone cloud,   865
But every mountain now hath found a tongue,
And Jura answers, through her misty shroud,
Back to the joyous Alps who call to her aloud!

---

54. Venus's girdle gave its wearer the power to inspire love.

XCIII

And this is in the night:—Most glorious night!
Thou wert not sent for slumber! let me be   870
A sharer in thy fierce and far delight,
A portion of the tempest and of thee!
How the lit lake shines, a phosphoric sea,
And the big rain comes dancing to the earth!
And now again 't is black,—and now, the glee   875
Of the loud hills shakes with its mountain-mirth,
As if they did rejoice o'er a young earthquake's birth.

XCIV

Now, where the swift Rhone[55] cleaves his way between
Heights which appear as lovers who have parted
In hate, whose mining depths so intervene   880
That they can meet no more, though broken-hearted!
Though in their souls, which thus each other thwarted,
Love was the very root of the fond rage
Which blighted their life's bloom and then departed—
Itself expired, but leaving them an age   885
Of years all winters, war within themselves to wage:—

XCV

Now, where the quick Rhone thus hath cleft his way,
The mightiest of the storms hath ta'en his stand:
For here, not one, but many, make their play,
And fling their thunder-bolts from hand to hand,   890
Flashing and cast around. Of all the band,
The brightest through these parted hills hath fork'd
His lightnings, as if he did understand,
That in such gaps as desolation work'd,
There the hot shaft should blast whatever therein lurk'd.   895

XCVI

Sky, mountains, river, winds, lake, lightnings! ye,
With night, and clouds, and thunder, and a soul
To make these felt and feeling, well may be
Things that have made me watchful; the far roll
Of your departing voices, is the knoll[56]   900
Of what in me is sleepless,—if I rest.
But where of ye, oh tempests, is the goal?
Are ye like those within the human breast,
Or do ye find at length, like eagles, some high nest?

---

55. A river that flows into Lake Geneva, fed by an Alpine glacier. 56. Knell.

XCVII

Could I embody and unbosom now
That which is most within me,—could I wreak
My thoughts upon expression, and thus throw
Soul, heart, mind, passions, feelings, strong or weak,
All that I would have sought, and all I seek,
Bear, know, feel and yet breathe—into *one* word,
And that one word were Lightning, I would speak;
But as it is, I live and die unheard,
With a most voiceless thought, sheathing it as a sword.

905
910

XCVIII

The morn is up again, the dewy morn,
With breath all incense and with cheek all bloom,
Laughing the clouds away with playful scorn,
And living as if earth contain'd no tomb,—
And glowing into day. We may resume
The march of our existence; and thus I,
Still on thy shores, fair Leman! may find room
And food for meditation, nor pass by
Much that may give us pause if ponder'd fittingly.

915
920

XCIX

Clarens,[57] sweet Clarens, birthplace of deep Love!
Thine air is the young breath of passionate thought,
Thy trees take root in Love; the snows above,
The very Glaciers have his colours caught,
And sunset into rose-hues sees them wrought
By rays which sleep there lovingly: the rocks,
The permanent crags, tell here of Love, who sought
In them a refuge from the worldly shocks,
Which stir and sting the soul with hope that woos, then mocks.

925
930

C

Clarens! by heavenly feet thy paths are trod,—
Undying Love's, who here ascends a throne
To which the steps are mountains; where the god
Is a pervading life and light,—so shown
Not on those summits solely, nor alone
In the still cave and forest; o'er the flower
His eye is sparkling and his breath hath blown,
His soft and summer breath, whose tender power
Passes the strength of storms in their most desolate hour.

935
940

57. Village on Lake Geneva.

CI

All things are here of *him*; from the black pines
Which are his shade on high, and the loud roar
Of torrents where he listeneth, to the vines
Which slope his green path downward to the shore,
Where the bow'd waters meet him, and adore,   945
Kissing his feet with murmurs; and the wood,
The covert of old trees with trunks all hoar,
But light leaves, young as joy, stands where it stood,
Offering to him and his a populous solitude,—

CII

A populous solitude of bees and birds,   950
And fairy-form'd and many-colour'd things,
Who worship him with notes more sweet than words,
And innocently open their glad wings,
Fearless and full of life: the gush of springs,
And fall of lofty fountains, and the bend   955
Of stirring branches, and the bud which brings
The swiftest thought of beauty, here extend,
Mingling, and made by Love, unto one mighty end.

CIII

He who hath loved not, here would learn that lore,
And make his heart a spirit; he who knows   960
That tender mystery, will love the more,
For this is Love's recess, where vain men's woes
And the world's waste have driven him far from those,
For 't is his nature to advance or die;
He stands not still, but or decays or grows   965
Into a boundless blessing, which may vie
With the immortal lights in its eternity!

CIV

'T was not for fiction chose Rousseau this spot,
Peopling it with affections; but he found
It was the scene which passion must allot   970
To the mind's purified beings; 't was the ground
Where early Love his Psyche's zone unbound,
And hallow'd it with loveliness. 'T is lone,
And wonderful, and deep, and hath a sound,
And sense, and sight of sweetness; here the Rhone   975
Hath spread himself a couch, the Alps have rear'd a throne.

CV

Lausanne and Ferney,[58] ye have been the abodes
Of names which unto you bequeath'd a name;
Mortals, who sought and found, by dangerous roads,
A path to perpetuity of fame: 980
They were gigantic minds, and their steep aim
Was, Titan-like, on daring doubts to pile
Thoughts which should call down thunder and the flame
Of Heaven again assail'd, if Heaven the while
On man and man's research could deign do more than smile.   985

CVI

The one[59] was fire and fickleness, a child,
Most mutable in wishes, but in mind
A wit as various,—gay, grave, sage, or wild,—
Historian, bard, philosopher, combined.
He multiplied himself among mankind,   990
The Proteus of their talents; but his own
Breathed most in ridicule,—which, as the wind,
Blew where it listed, laying all things prone,—
Now to o'erthrow a fool, and now to shake a throne.

CVII

The other,[60] deep and slow, exhausting thought,   995
And hiving wisdom with each studious year,
In meditation dwelt, with learning wrought,
And shaped his weapon with an edge severe,
Sapping a solemn creed with solemn sneer;
The lord of irony,—that master-spell,   1000
Which stung his foes to wrath which grew from fear,
And doom'd him to the zealot's ready Hell,
Which answers to all doubts so eloquently well.

CVIII

Yet, peace be with their ashes for by them,
If merited, the penalty is paid;   1005
It is not ours to judge, far less condemn;
The hour must come when such things shall be made
Known unto all,—or hope and dread allay'd
By slumber, on one pillow,—in the dust,
Which, thus much we are sure, must lie decay'd;   1010

---

58. Lausanne, Switzerland, where Edward Gibbon (1737–1794) wrote *Decline and Fall of the Roman Empire* (1776–1788). Ferney, Switzerland, where Voltaire (1694–1778) lived out his final years.   59. Voltaire.   60. Gibbon.

And when it shall revive, as is our trust,
'T will be to be forgiven, or suffer what is just.

CIX

But let me quit man's works again to read
His Maker's, spread around me, and suspend
This page, which from my reveries I feed   1015
Until it seems prolonging without end.
The clouds above me to the white Alps tend,
And I must pierce them, and survey whate'er
May be permitted, as my steps I bend
To their most great and growing region, where   1020
The earth to her embrace compels the powers of air.

CX

Italia![61] too, Italia! looking on thee,
Full flashes on the soul the light of ages,
Since the fierce Carthaginian[62] almost won thee,
To the last halo of the chiefs and sages   1025
Who glorify thy consecrated pages;
Thou wert the throne and grave of empires; still
The fount, at which the panting mind assuages
Her thirst of knowledge, quaffing there her fill,
Flows from the eternal source of Rome's imperial hill.   1030

CXI

Thus far have I proceeded in a theme
Renew'd with no kind auspices:—to feel
We are not what we have been, and to deem
We are not what we should be, and to steel
The heart against itself; and to conceal,   1035
With a proud caution, love, or hate, or aught,—
Passion or feeling, purpose, grief, or zeal,—
Which is the tyrant spirit of our thought,
Is a stern task of soul;—no matter—it is taught.

CXII

And for these words, thus woven into song,   1040
It may be that they are a harmless wile,—
The colouring of the scenes which fleet along,
Which I would seize, in passing, to beguile
My breast, or that of others, for a while.
Fame is the thirst of youth,—but I am not   1045

---

61. Italy.   62. Hannibal (247–182 BC), military leader of Carthage.

So young as to regard men's frown or smile
As loss or guerdon[63] of a glorious lot;
I stood and stand alone,—remember'd or forgot.

CXIII

I have not loved the world, nor the world me;
I have not flatter'd its rank breath, nor bow'd   1050
To its idolatries a patient knee,
Nor coin'd my cheek to smiles, nor cried aloud
In worship of an echo; in the crowd
They could not deem me one of such: I stood
Among them, but not of them; in a shroud   1055
Of thoughts which were not their thoughts, and still could,
Had I not filed[64] my mind, which thus itself subdued.

CXIV

I have not loved the world, nor the world me,—
But let us part fair foes; I do believe,
Though I have found them not, that there may be   1060
Words which are things, hopes which will not deceive,
And virtues which are merciful nor weave
Snares for the failing: I would also deem
O'er others' griefs that some sincerely grieve;
That two, or one, are almost what they seem,   1065
That goodness is no name and happiness no dream.

CXV

My daughter![65] with thy name this song begun—
My daughter! with thy name thus much shall end—
I see thee not, I hear thee not, but none
Can be so wrapt in thee; thou art the friend   1070
To whom the shadows of far years extend:
Albeit my brow thou never shouldst behold,
My voice shall with thy future visions blend,
And reach into thy heart,—when mine is cold,—
A token and a tone even from thy father's mould.   1075

CXVI

To aid thy mind's development, to watch
Thy dawn of little joys, to sit and see
Almost thy very growth, to view thee catch
Knowledge of objects, wonders yet to thee!

---

63. Reward. 64. Defiled. William Shakespeare (1564–1616), *Macbeth* (1603), 3.1.66. 65. Augusta Ada.

To hold thee lightly on a gentle knee,   1080
And print on thy soft cheek a parent's kiss,—
This, it should seem, was not reserved for me;
Yet this was in my nature:—as it is,
I know not what is there, yet something like to this.

CXVII

Yet, though dull Hate as duty should be taught,   1085
I know that thou wilt love me; though my name
Should be shut from thee, as a spell still fraught
With desolation, and a broken claim;
Though the grave closed between us,—'t were the same,
I know that thou wilt love me; though to drain   1090
My blood from out thy being were an aim
And an attainment, all would be in vain,—
Still thou wouldst love me, still that more than life retain.

CXVIII

The child of love, though born in bitterness
And nurtured in convulsion,—of thy sire   1095
These were the elements, and thine no less.
As yet such are around thee, but thy fire
Shall be more temper'd and thy hope far higher.
Sweet be thy cradled slumbers! O'er the sea,
And from the mountains where I now respire,   1100
Fain would I waft such blessing upon thee,
As, with a sigh, I deem thou mightst have been to me!

—1816

CONTEMPORARY RESPONSE

Fitz-Greene Halleck
1790–1867

Both as a child and an adult, Byron experienced both same-sex and opposite-sex attractions; however, the most common persona of him that has persisted, until recently, is of a hyper-masculine heterosexual male. Perhaps because of discomfort with the ambiguity of his sexuality, he has been retroactively made to correspond to societal images of heterosexuality. There is, however, evidence of a tradition of a "queer" Byron, who can be placed on a transatlantic continuum with those his works inspired: Fitz-Greene Halleck, the "American Byron"; Walt Whitman; Oscar Wilde; and others. Before editing Byron's poetry and prose for American readers in 1834, Halleck contributed to the American taste for Byron by imitating the parodist's poetics in his own satires, which met with success among American readers. Halleck's "Fanny" is an imitation and parody of as well as an homage to Byron's *Beppo* (1818).

from Fanny

"A fairy vision
Of some gay creatures of the element,
That in the colors of the rainbow live,
And play in the plighted clouds."

MILTON.[1]

I.

Fanny was younger once than she is now,
    And prettier of course: I do not mean
To say that there are wrinkles on her brow;
    Yet, to be candid, she is past eighteen—
Perhaps past twenty—but the girl is shy   5
About her age, and Heaven forbid that I

II.

Should get myself in trouble by revealing
    A secret of this sort; I have too long
Loved pretty women with a poet's feeling,
    And when a boy, in day-dream and in song,   10
Have knelt me down and worshipped them: alas!
They never thanked me for't—but let that pass.

III.

I've felt full many a heartache in my day,
    At the mere rustling of a muslin gown,
And caught some dreadful colds, I blush to say,   15
    While shivering in the shade of beauty's frown.
They say her smiles are sunbeams—it may be—
But never a sunbeam would she throw on me.

IV.

But Fanny's is an eye that you may gaze on
    For half an hour, without the slightest harm;   20
E'en when she wore her smiling summer face on
    There was but little danger, and the charm
That youth and wealth once gave, has bade farewell.
Hers is a sad, sad tale—'tis mine its woes to tell.

V.

Her father kept, some fifteen years ago,   25
    A retail drygood shop in Chatham street,
And nursed his little earnings, sure though slow,
    Till, having mustered wherewithal to meet

---

1. John Milton (1608–1674), *Comus* (1637), lines 298–301.

The gaze of the great world, he breathed the air
Of Pearl street—and "set up" in Hanover square.   30

VI.

Money is power, 'tis said—I never tried;
    I'm but a poet—and bank-notes to me
Are curiosities, and closely eyed,
    Whene'er I get them, as a stone would be,
Tossed from the moon on Doctor Mitchill's[1] table,   35
Or classic brickbat from the tower of Babel.[2]

VII.

But he I sing of well has known and felt
    That money hath a power and a dominion;
For when in Chatham street the good man dwelt,
    No one would give a *sous*[3] for his opinion.   40
And though his neighbors were extremely civil,
Yet, on the whole, they thought him—a poor devil,

VIII.

A decent kind of person; one whose head
    Was not of brains particularly full;
It was not known that he had ever said   45
    Anything worth repeating—'twas a dull
Good, honest man—what Paulding's[4] muse would call
A "cabbage head"—but he excelled them all

IX.

In that most noble of the sciences,
    The art of making money; and he found   50
The zeal for quizzing him grew less and less,
    As he grew richer; till upon the ground
Of Pearl street, treading proudly in the might
And majesty of wealth, a sudden light

X.

Flashed like the midnight lightning on the eyes   55
    Of all who knew him; brilliant traits of mind,
And genius, clear, and countless as the dies
    Upon the peacock's plumage; taste refined,

---

1. Samuel Mitchill (1764–1831), American mineralogist. 2. Genesis 11.1–9. Brickbat: obscure writings. 3. French coin worth very little. 4. James Kirke Paulding (1779–1860), American author.

Wisdom and wit, were his—perhaps much more.
'Twas strange they had not found it out before. . . .   60

XVI.

Nor were these all the advantages derived
    From change of scene; for near his domicil[5]
He of the pair of polished lamps then lived,
    And in my hero's promenades, at will,
Could he behold them burning—and their flame   95
Kindled within his breast the love of fame,

XVII.

And politics, and country; the pure glow
    Of patriot ardor, and the consciousness
That talents such as his might well bestow
    A lustre on the city; she would bless   100
His name; and that some service should be done her,
He pledged "life, fortune, and his sacred honor."[6]

XVIII.

And when the sounds of music and of mirth,
    Bursting from Fashion's groups assembled there,
Were heard, as round their lone plebian hearth   105
    Fanny and he were seated—he would dare
To whisper fondly that the time might come
When he and his could give as brilliant routs[7] at home.

XIX.

And oft would Fanny near that mansion linger,
    When the cold winter moon was high in heaven,   110
And trace out, by the aid of Fancy's finger,
    Cards for some future party, to be given
When she, in turn, should be a *belle*,[8] and they
Had lived their little hour, and passed away. . . . .

CXXVI.

"There was a sound of revelry by night;"[9]
    Broadway was thronged with coaches, and within
A mansion of the best of brick, the bright
    And eloquent eyes of beauty bade begin
The dance; and music's tones swelled wild and high,   755
And hearts and heels kept tune in tremulous ecstacy.

---

5. Home.   6. Attributed to Thomas Nelson, Jr. (1738–1789), American revolutionary hero.   7. Parties.   8. A beautiful socialite.   9. See p. 611.

CXXVII.

For many a week, the note of preparation
    Had sounded through all circles far and near;
And some five hundred cards of invitation
    Bade beau and belle in full costume appear;   760
There was a most magnificent variety,
All quite select, and of the first society.

CXXVIII.

That is to say—the rich and the well-bred,
    The arbiters of fashion and gentility,
In different grades of splendor, from the head   765
    Down to the very toe of our nobility:
Ladies, remarkable for handsome eyes
Or handsome fortunes—learned men, and wise . . .

CXXXII.

The love of fun, fine faces, and good eating,
    Brought many who were tired of self and home;
And some were there in the high hope of meeting
    The lady of their bosom's love—and some   790
To study that deep science, how to please,
And manners in high life, and high-souled courtesies.

CXXXIII.

And he, the hero of the night was there,
    In breeches of light drab, and coat of blue.
Taste was conspicuous in his powdered hair,   795
    And in his frequent *jeux de mots*,[10] that drew
Peals of applauses from the listeners round
Who were delighted—as in duty bound.

CXXXIV.

'Twas Fanny's father—Fanny near him stood,
    Her power, resistless—and her wish, command;
And Hope's young promises were all made good;   800
    "She reigned a fairy queen in fairy land;"
Her dream of infancy a dream no more,
And then how beautiful the dress she wore!

---

10. Puns.

CXXXV.

Ambition with the sire had kept her word.   805
    He had the rose, no matter for its thorn,
And he seemed happy as a summer bird,
    Careering on wet wing to meet the morn.
Some said there was a cloud upon his brow;
It might be—but we'll not discuss that now.   810

CXXXVI.

I left him making rhymes while crossing o'er
    The broad and perilous wave of the North River.
He bade adieu, when safely on the shore,
    To poetry—and, as he thought, for ever.
That night his dream (if after deeds make known   815
Our plans in sleep) was an enchanting one.

CXXXVII.

He woke, in strength, like Samson from his slumber,[11]
    And walked Broadway, enraptured the next day;
Purchased a house there—I've forgot the number—
    And signed a mortgage and a bond, for pay.   820
Gave, in the slang phrase, Pearl-street the go-by,
And cut, for several months, St. Tammany.

CXXXVIII.

Bond, mortgage, title-deeds, and all completed,
    He bought a coach and half a dozen horses
(The bill's at Lawrence's—not yet receipted—   825
    You'll find the amount upon his list of losses),
Then filled his rooms with servants, and whatever
Is necessary for a "genteel liver."

CXXXIX.

This last removal fixed him: every stain
    Was blotted from his "household coat," and he   830
Now "showed the world he was a gentleman,"
    And, what is better, could afford to be;
His step was loftier than it was of old,
His laugh less frequent, and his manner told

CXL.

What lovers call "unutterable things"—   835
    That sort of dignity was in his mien

---

11. Judges 16.19.

Which awes the gazer into ice, and brings
    To recollection some great man we've seen,
The Governor, perchance, whose eye and frown,
'Twas shrewdly guessed, would knock Judge Skinner[12] down.   840

CXLI.

And for "Resources," both of purse and head,
    He was a subject worthy Bristed's[13] pen;
Believed devoutly all his flatterers said,
    And deemed himself a Crœsus[14] among men;
Spread to the liberal air his silken sails,   845
And lavished guineas like a Prince of Wales.[15]

CXLII.

He mingled now with those within whose veins
    The blood ran pure—the magnates of the land—
Hailed them as his companions and his friends,
    And lent them money and his note of hand.   850
In every institution, whose proud aim
Is public good alone, he soon became

CXLIII.

A man of consequence and notoriety;
    His name, with the addition of esquire,
Stood high upon the list of each society,   855
    Whose zeal and watchfulness the sacred fire
Of science, agriculture, art, and learning,
Keep on our country's altars bright and burning. . . .

CXLVI.

He was a trustee of a Savings Bank,
    And lectured soundly every evil doer,
Gave dinners daily to wealth, power, and rank,
    And sixpence every Sunday to the poor;
He was a wit, in the pun making line—   875
Past fifty years of age, and five feet nine.

CXLVII.

But as he trod to grandeur's pinnacle,
    With eagle eye and step that never faltered,
The busy tongue of scandal dared to tell

---

12. Judge Richard Skinner (1778–1833).   13. John Bristed (1778–1855), American author of works on bankruptcy.   14. King Crœsus of Lydia, legendary for his great wealth.   15. George IV (1762–1830), famous for his lavish lifestyle.

That cash was scarce with him, and credit altered;   880
And while he stood the envy of beholders,
The Bank Directors grinned, and shrugged their shoulders.

CXLVIII.

And when these, the Lord Burleighs[16] of the minute,
  Shake their sage heads, and look demure and holy,
Depend upon it there is something in it;   885
  For whether born of wisdom or of folly,
Suspicion is a being whose fell power
Blights every thing it touches, fruit and flower.

CXLIX.

Some friends (they were his creditors) once hinted
  About retrenchment and a day of doom;   890
He thanked them, as no doubt they kindly meant it,
  And made this speech when they had left the room:
"Of all the curses upon mortals sent,
One's creditors are the most impudent;

CL.

"Now I am one who knows what he is doing,   895
  And suits exactly to his means his ends;
How can a man be in the path to ruin,
  When all the brokers are his bosom friends?
Yet, on my hopes, and those of my dear daughter,
These rascals throw a bucket of cold water!   900

CLI.

"They'd wrinkle with deep cares the prettiest face,
  Pour gall and wormwood in the sweetest cup,
Poison the very wells of life—and place,
  Whitechapel needles, with their sharp points up
Even in the softest feather bed that e'er   905
Was manufactured by upholsterer."

CLII.

This said—he journeyed "at his own sweet will,"[17]
  Like one of Wordsworth's rivers, calmly on;
But yet, at times, Reflection, "in her still
  Small voice," would whisper, something must be done;   910

---

16. William Cecil, Lord Burghley (1521–1598), Queen Elizabeth's chief advisor.   17. William Wordsworth (1770–1850), "Composed upon Westminster Bridge, September 3, 1802" (1807), line 12.

He asked advice of Fanny, and the maid
Promptly and duteously lent her aid.

CLIII.

She told him, with that readiness of mind
    And quickness of perception which belong
Exclusively to gentle womankind,   915
    That to submit to slanderers was wrong,
And the best plan to silence and admonish them,
Would be to give "a party"—and astonish them.

CLIV.

The hint was taken—and the party given;
    And Fanny, as I said some pages since,   920
Was there in power and loveliness that even,
    And he, her sire, demeaned him like a prince,
And all was joy—it looked a festival,
Where pain might smooth his brow, and grief her smiles recall.

CLV.

But Fortune, like some others of her sex,   925
    Delights in tantalizing and tormenting;
One day we feed upon their smiles—the next
    Is spent in swearing, sorrowing, and repenting.
(If in the last four lines the author lies,
He's always ready to apologize.)   930

CLVI.

Eve never walked in Paradise more pure.
    Than on that morn when Satan played the devil
With her and all her race. A love-sick wooer
    Ne'er asked a kinder maiden, or more civil,
Than Cleopatra was to Antony   935
The day she left him on the Ionian sea.[18]

CLVII.

The serpent—loveliest in his coiled ring,
    With eye that charms, and beauty that out-vies
The tints of the rainbow—bears upon his sting
    The deadliest venom. Ere the dolphin dies   940
Its hues are brightest. Like an infant's breath
Are tropic winds before the voice of death

---

18. William Shakespeare (1564–1616), *Antony and Cleopatra* (1623), 2.1.

CLVIII.

Is heard upon the waters, summoning
    The midnight earthquake from its sleep of years
To do its task of wo. The clouds that fling   945
    The lightning, brighten ere the bolt appears;
The pantings of the warrior's heart are proud
Upon that battle morn whose night-dews wet his shroud;

CLIX.

The sun is loveliest as he sinks to rest;
    The leaves of autumn smile when fading fast;   950
The swan's last song is sweetest—and the best
    Of Meigs'[19] speeches, doubtless, was his last.
And thus the happiest scene, in these my rhymes,
Closed with a crash, and ushered in—hard times.

CLX.

St. Paul's tolled one[20]—and fifteen minutes after   955
    Down came, by accident, a chandelier;
The mansion tottered from the floor to rafter!
    Up rose the cry of agony and fear!
And there was shrieking, screaming, bustling, fluttering,
Beyond the power of writing or of uttering.   960

CLXI.

The company departed, and neglected
    To say good-by—the father stormed and swore—
The fiddlers grinned—the daughter looked dejected—
    The flowers had vanished from the polished floor,
And both betook them to their sleepless beds,   965
With hearts and prospects broken, but no heads.

CLXII.

The desolate relief of free complaining
    Came with the morn, and with it came bad weather;
The wind was east-northeast, and it was raining
    Throughout that day, which, take it altogether,   970
Was one whose memory clings to us through life,
Just like a suit in Chancery,[21] or a wife.

CLXIII.

That evening, with a most important face
    And dreadful knock, and tidings still more dreadful,

---

19. Return J. Meigs (1764–1825), American politician.   20. St. Paul's Chapel, New York City.   21. Second highest court
in England.

A notary came—sad things had taken place;   975
    My hero had forgot to "do the needful;"
A note (amount not stated), with his name on't,
Was left unpaid—in short, he had "stopped payment." . . .

CLXVI.

For two whole days they were the common talk;
    The party, and the failure, and all that,
The theme of loungers in their morning walk,
    Porter-house reasoning, and tea-table chat.
The third, some newer wonder came to blot them,   995
And on the fourth, the "meddling world" forgot them.

CLXVII.

Anxious, however, something to discover,
    I passed their house—the shutters were all closed;
The song of knocker and of bell was over;
    Upon the steps two chimney sweeps reposed;   1000
And on the door my dazzled eyebeam met
These cabalistic[22] words—"this house to let."

CLXVIII.

They live now, like chameleons, upon air[23]
    And hope, and such cold, unsubstantial dishes;
That they removed, is clear, but when or where   1005
    None knew. The curious reader, if he wishes,
May ask them, but in vain. Where grandeur dwells,
The marble dome—the popular rumor tells;

CLXIX.

But of the dwelling of the proud and poor,
    From their own lips the world will never know.   1010
When better days are gone—it is secure
    Beyond all other mysteries here below,
Except, perhaps, a maiden lady's age,
When past the noonday of life's pilgrimage.

CLXX.

Fanny! 'twas with her name my song began[24];   1015
    'Tis proper and polite her name should end it;
If in my story of her woes, or plan
    Or moral can be traced, 'twas not intended;
And if I've wronged her, I can only tell her
I'm sorry for it—so is my bookseller.   1020

---

22. Secret, mystical.   23. "Chameleons feed on light and air," is the first line of Percy Bysshe Shelley (1792–1827), "An Exhortation" (1820).   24. See p. 636, line 1067.

CLXXI.

I met her yesterday—her eyes were wet—
    She faintly smiled, and said she had been reading
The Treasurer's Report in the Gazette,
    McIntyre's speech, and Campbell's "Love lies bleeding;"[25]
She had a shawl on, 'twas not a Cashmere one,   1025
And if it cost five dollars, 'twas a dear one.

CLXXII.

Her father sent to Albany[26] a prayer
    For office, told how fortune had abused him,
And modestly requested to be Mayor—
    The Council very civilly refused him;   1030
Because, however much they might desire it,
The "public good," it seems, did not require it.

CLXXIII.

Some evenings since, he took a lonely stroll
    Along Broadway, scene of past joys and evils;
He felt that withering bitterness of soul,   1035
    Quaintly denominated the "blue devils;"[27]
And thought of Bonaparte and Belisarius,
Pompey, and Colonel Burr, and Caius Marius,[28]

CLXXIV.

And envying the loud playfulness and mirth
    Of those who passed him, gay in youth and hope,   1040
He took at Jupiter a shilling's worth
    Of gazing, through the showman's telescope;
Sounds as of far-off bells came on his ears,
He fancied 'twas the music of the spheres.

CLXXV.

He was mistaken, it was no such thing,   1045
    'Twas Yankee Doodle played by Scudder's band[29];
He muttered, as he lingered listening,
    Something of freedom and our happy land;
Then sketched, as to his home he hurried fast,
This sentimental song—his saddest, and his last.   1050

                                                           —1821

---

25. Nineteenth-century newspapers often printed transcripts of political speeches; Thomas Campbell (1777–1844), Scottish poet.   26. Capital of New York.   27. Depression.   28. Napoleon Bonaparte (1769–1821), Flavius Belisarius (505–565), Pompey the Great (106–48 BC), Aaron Burr (1756–1836), and Gaius Marius (157–86 BC), all military leaders.   29. Band that played on Broadway to lure visitors into Scudder's museum.

James Fenimore Cooper
1789–1851

James Fenimore Cooper's childhood mixed gentlemanly training with wilderness adventure on his father's vast estate near the headwaters of the Susquehanna River at Lake Otsego in New York. The brash and somewhat arrogant Cooper attended Yale College but was dismissed in his third year for disciplinary breaches. He went to sea to train as a naval officer but abandoned his commission at twenty-one to marry Susan Augusta De Lancey and to take up the life of a gentleman farmer. Some years later, Susan called his bluff when he boasted that he could write a better novel than one they were reading together. The product was a tale of manners titled *Precaution* (1820), which launched a career during which Cooper would produce over thirty novels. His second book, *The Spy* (1821) earned $4,000 during its first year in print, a huge sum in that day. He wrote his third novel, *The Pilot* (1823), in order to prove that he could write a more genuine tale of the sea than Sir Walter Scott, whom he both admired and scoffed at as a landlubber. In the end, Cooper made his international reputation with *The Leatherstocking Tales* (1823–1841), a series of frontier romances modeled on Scott's *Waverley* novels (1814–1819). Their spectacular success allowed him to abandon farming, move to New York City, and become North America's first self-supporting writer. He spent the years from 1826 to 1833 traveling in England, France, Germany, Switzerland, and Italy, where he developed a deep respect for the achievements of continuous tradition. Many of his later novels reflect his worry about whether the cultural blankness of the American frontier would cause the young nation to degenerate into barbarism.

Nevertheless, Cooper's main cultural role was as an apologist for American national expansion. *The Pioneers* (1823), the first of *The Leatherstocking Tales*, works up his childhood memories into a triumphal narrative of colonial settlement. His central characters, the frontiersman, Natty Bumppo, and Chingachgook, the last of the Mohicans, are vehicles for novelistic theorizing on the relations between "civilization" and "savagery." Cooper represents Natty as a mediating figure, a "white Indian" who models the reinvigoration of an exhausted Euro-American culture by the absorption of Native American cultural vitality. Symbolic incorporation was a way of simultaneously mourning and excusing imperial expansion and Indian removal. As Cooper put it more bluntly in *Notions of the Americans* (1828), "As a rule, the red man disappears before the superior moral and physical influence of the white, just as I believe the black man will eventually do the same thing, unless he shall seek shelter in some other region." The figure of the noble savage disappearing into the West also allowed dissociation of the present from a mythical past, making it possible for Cooper to regard the actual natives he came into contact with as representatives of "a stunted, dirty, and degraded race."

from The Pioneers, or the Sources of the Susquehanna

Chapter I.

> See, Winter comes, to rule the varied year,
> Sullen and sad, with all his rising train;
> Vapours, and clouds, and storms—
>
> THOMSON.[1]

---

1. James Thomson (1700–1748), "The Seasons: Winter" (1726), lines 1–3.

Near the centre of the great State of New-York lies an extensive district of country, whose surface is a succession of hills and dales, or, to speak with greater deference to geographical definitions, of mountains and valleys. It is among these hills that the Delaware takes its rise; and flowing from the limpid lakes and thousand springs of this country, the numerous sources of the mighty Susquehanna meander through the valleys, until, uniting, they form one of the proudest streams of which the old United States could boast. The mountains are generally arable to the top, although instances are not wanting, where their sides are jutted with rocks, that aid greatly in giving that romantic character to the country, which it so eminently possesses. The vales are narrow, rich, and cultivated; with a stream uniformly winding through each, now gliding peacefully under the brow of one of the hills, and then suddenly shooting across the plain, to wash the feet of its opposite rival. Beautiful and thriving villages are found interspersed along the margins of the small lakes, or situated at those points of the streams which are favourable to manufacturing; and neat and comfortable farms, with every indication of wealth about them, are scattered profusely through the vales, and even to the mountain tops. Roads diverge in every direction, from the even and graceful bottoms of the valleys, to the most rugged and intricate passes of the hills. Academies, and minor edifices for the encouragement of learning, meet the eye of the stranger, at every few miles, as he winds his way through this uneven territory; and places for the public worship of God abound with that frequency which characterizes a moral and reflecting people, and with that variety of exterior and canonical government which flows from unfettered liberty of conscience. In short, the whole district is hourly exhibiting how much can be done, in even a rugged country, and with a severe climate, under the dominion of mild laws, and where every man feels a direct interest in the prosperity of a commonwealth, of which he knows himself to form a distinct and independent part. The expedients of the pioneers who first broke ground in the settlement of this country, are succeeded by the permanent improvements of the yeoman, who intends to leave his remains to moulder under the sod which he tills, or, perhaps, of the son, who, born in the land, piously wishes to linger around the grave of his father. Only forty years have passed since this whole territory was a wilderness.

Very soon after the establishment of the independence of the States by the peace of 1783, the enterprise of their citizens was directed to a development of the natural advantages of their widely extended dominions. Before the war of the revolution the inhabited parts of the colony of New-York were limited to less than a tenth of her possessions. A narrow belt of country, extending for a short distance on either side of the Hudson with a similar occupation of fifty miles on the banks of the Mohawk, together with the islands of Nassau and Staten, and a few insulated settlements on chosen land along the margins of streams, composed the country that was then inhabited by less than two hundred thousand souls. Within the short period we have mentioned, her population has spread itself over five degrees of latitude and seven of longitude, and has swelled to the powerful number of nearly a million and a half, who are maintained in abundance, and can look forward to ages before the evil day must arrive, when their possessions will become unequal to their wants.

Our tale begins in 1793, about seven years after the commencement of one of the earliest of those settlements, which have conduced to effect that magical change in the power and condition of the state, to which we have alluded.

It was near the setting of the sun, on a clear, cold day in December of that year, when a sleigh was moving slowly up one of the mountains in the district which we have described. The day had been fine for the season, and but two or three large clouds, whose colour seemed brightened by the light reflected from the mass of snow that covered the earth, floated in a sky of the purest blue. The road wound along the brow of a precipice, and on one side was upheld by a foundation of logs, piled for many feet, one upon the other, while a narrow excavation in the mountain, in the opposite direction, had made a passage of sufficient width for the ordinary travelling of that day. But logs, excavation, and every thing that did not reach for several feet above the earth, lay promiscuously buried under the snow. A single track, barely wide enough to receive the sleigh, denoted the route of the highway, and this was sunken near two feet below the surrounding surface. In the vale, which lay at a distance of several hundred feet beneath them, there was what in the language of the country was called a *clearing*, and all the usual improvements of a new settlement; these even extended up the hill to the point where the road turned short and ran across the level land, which lay on the summit of the mountain; but the summit itself yet remained a forest. There was a glittering in the atmosphere, as if it were filled with innumerable shining particles, and the noble bay horses that drew the sleigh were covered, in many parts, with a coat of frost. The vapour from their nostrils was seen to issue like smoke; and every object in the view, as well as every arrangement of the travellers, denoted the depth of a winter in the mountains. The harness, which was of a deep dull black, differing from the glossy varnishing of the present day, was ornamented with enormous plates and buckles of brass, that shone like gold in the transient beams of the sun, which found their way obliquely through the tops of the trees. Huge saddles, studded with nails of the same material, and fitted with cloth that admirably served as blankets to the shoulders of the animals, supported four high, square-topped turrets, through which the stout reins led from the mouths of the horses to the hands of the driver, who was a negro, of apparently twenty years of age. His face, which nature had coloured with a glistening black, was now mottled with the cold, and his large shining eyes were moistened with a liquid that flowed from the same cause; still there was a smiling expression of good humour in his happy countenance, that was created by the thoughts of his home, and a Christmas fire-side, with its Christmas frolics. The sleigh was one of those large, comfortable, old-fashioned conveyances, which would admit a whole family within its bosom, but which now contained only two passengers besides the driver. Its outside was a modest green, and its inside of a fiery red, that was intended to convey the idea of heat in that cold climate. Large buffalo skins, trimmed around the edges with red cloth, cut into festoons, covered the back of the sleigh, and were spread over its bottom, and drawn up around the feet of the travellers—one of whom was a man of middle age, and the other a female, just entering upon womanhood. The former was of a large stature; but the precautions he had taken to guard against the cold left but little of his person exposed to view. A great-coat, that was abundantly ornamented, if it were not made more comfortable, by a profusion of furs, enveloped the whole of his figure, excepting the head, which was covered with a cap of martin skins, lined with morocco,[2] the sides of which were made to fall, if necessary, and were now drawn close over the ears, and were fastened beneath his chin with a black riband; its top was surmounted with the tail of the animal whose skin had furnished the materials for the cap,

---

2. Soft leather.

which fell back, not ungracefully, a few inches behind the head. From beneath this masque were to be seen part of a fine manly face, and particularly a pair of expressive, large blue eyes, that promised extraordinary itellect, covert humour, and great benevolence. The form of his companion was literally hid beneath the multitude and variety of garments which she wore. There were furs and silks peeping from under a large camlet[3] cloak, with a thick flannel lining, that, by its cut and size, was evidently intended for a masculine wearer. A huge hood of black silk, that was quilted with down, concealed the whole of her head, except at a small opening in front for breath, through which occasionally sparkled a pair of animated eyes of the deepest black.

Both the father and daughter (for such was the connexion between the travellers) were too much occupied with their different reflections to break the stillness, that received little or no interruption from the easy gliding of the sleigh, by the sound of their voices. The former was thinking of the wife that had held this their only child fondly to her bosom, when, four years before, she had reluctantly consented to relinquish the society of her daughter, in order that the latter might enjoy the advantages which the city could afford to her education. A few months afterward death had deprived him of the remaining companion of his solitude; but still he had enough of real regard for his child, not to bring her into the comparative wilderness in which he dwelt, until the full period had expired, to which he had limited her juvenile labours. The reflections of the daughter were less melancholy, and mingled with a pleased astonishment at the novel scenery that she met at every turn in the road.

The mountain on which they were journeying was covered with pines, that rose without a branch seventy or eighty feet, and which frequently towered to an additional height, that more than equalled that elevation. Through the innumerable vistas that opened beneath the lofty trees the eye could penetrate, until it was met by a distant inequality in the ground, or was stopped by a view of the summit of the mountain which lay on the opposite side of the valley to which they were hastening. The dark trunks of the trees rose from the pure white of the snow, in regularly formed shafts until, at a great height, their branches shot forth their horizontal limbs, that were covered with the meager foliage of an evergreen, affording a melancholy contrast to the torpor of nature below. To the travellers there seemed to be no wind; but these pines waved majestically at their topmost boughs, sending forth a dull, sighing sound, that was quite in consonance with the scene.

The sleigh had glided for some distance along the even surface, and the gaze of the female was bent in inquisitive, and, perhaps, timid glances, into the recesses of the forest, which were lighted by the unsullied covering of the earth, when a loud and continued howling was heard, pealing under the long arches of the woods, like the cry of a numerous pack of hounds. The instant the sounds reached the ears of the gentleman, whatever might have been the subject of his meditations, he forgot it; for he cried aloud to the black—

"Hold up, Aggy; there is old Hector; I should know his bay among ten thousand. The Leather-stocking has put his hounds into the hills this clear day, and they have started their game, you hear. There is a deer-track a few rods ahead;—and now, Bess, if thou canst muster courage enough to stand fire, I will give thee a saddle[4] for thy Christmas dinner."

---

3. A cloth made of wool and silk.   4. A cut of meat.

The black drew up, with a cheerful grin upon his chilled features, and began thrashing his arms together, in order to restore the circulation to his fingers, while the speaker stood erect, and, throwing aside his outer covering, stept from the sleigh upon a bank of snow, which sustained his weight without yielding more than an inch or two. A storm of sleet had fallen and frozen upon the surface a few days before, and but a slight snow had occurred since to purify, without weakening its covering.

In a few moments the speaker succeeded in extricating a double-barrelled fowling-piece from among a multitude of trunks and bandboxes. After throwing aside the thick mittens which had encased his hands, that now appeared in a pair of leather gloves tipped with fur, he examined his priming, and was about to move forward, when the light bounding noise of an animal plunging through the woods was heard, and directly a fine buck darted into the path, a short distance ahead of him. The appearance of the animal was sudden, and his flight inconceivably rapid; but the traveller appeared to be too keen a sportsman to be disconcerted by either. As it came first into view he raised the fowling-piece to his shoulder, and, with a practised eye and steady hand, drew a trigger; but the deer dashed forward undaunted, and apparently unhurt. Without lowering his piece, the traveller turned its muzzle towards his intended victim, and fired again. Neither discharge, however, seemed to have taken effect.

The whole scene had passed with a rapidity that confused the female, who was unconsciously rejoicing in the escape of the buck, as he rather darted like a meteor, than ran across the road before her, when a sharp, quick sound struck her ear, quite different from the full, round reports of her father's gun, but still sufficiently distinct to be known as the concussion produced by fire-arms. At the same instant that she heard this unexpected report, the buck sprang from the snow, to a great height in the air, and directly a second discharge, similar in sound to the first, followed, when the animal came to the earth, falling headlong, and rolling over on the crust once or twice with its own velocity. A loud shout was given by the unseen marksman, as triumphing in his better aim; and a couple of men instantly appeared from behind the trunks of two of the pines, where they had evidently placed themselves in expectation of the passage of the deer.

"Ha! Natty, had I known you were in ambush, I would not have fired," cried the traveller, moving towards the spot where the deer lay—near to which he was followed by the delighted black, with the sleigh; "but the sound of old Hector was too exhilarating to let me be quiet; though I hardly think I struck him either."

"No—no—Judge," returned the hunter, with an inward chuckle, and with that look of exultation, that indicates a consciousness of superior skill; "you burnt your powder, only to warm your nose this cold evening. Did ye think to stop a full grown buck, with Hector and the slut[5] open upon him, within sound, with that robin popgun in your hand? There's plenty of pheasants among the swamps; and the snow birds are flying round your own door, where you may feed them with crumbs, and shoot enough for a pot-pie, any day; but if you're for a buck, or a little bear's meat, Judge, you'll have to take the long rifle, with a greased wadding, or you'll waste more powder than you'll fill stomachs, I'm thinking."

As the speaker concluded, he drew his bare hand across the bottom of his nose, and again opened his enormous mouth with a kind of inward laugh.

---

5. A female dog.

654 James Fenimore Cooper

"The gun scatters well, Natty, and has killed a deer before now," said the traveller, smiling good humouredly. "One barrel was charged with buck shot; but the other was loaded for birds only. Here are two hurts that he has received; one through his neck, and the other directly through his heart. It is by no means certain, Natty, but I gave him one of the two."

"Let who will kill him," said the hunter, rather surlily, "I suppose the cretur is to be eaten." So saying, he drew a large knife from a leathern sheath, which was stuck through his girdle or sash, and cut the throat of the animal. "If there is two balls through the deer, I want to know if there wasn't two rifles fired—besides, who ever saw such a ragged hole from a smooth-bore, as this is through the neck?—and you will own yourself, Judge, that the buck fell at the last shot, which was sent from a truer and a younger hand, than your'n or mine 'ither; but for my part, although I am a poor man, I can live without the venison, but I don't love to give up my lawful dues in a free country. Though, for the matter of that, might often makes right here, as well as in the old country, for what I can see."

An air of sullen dissatisfaction pervaded the manner of the hunter during the whole of this speech; yet he thought it prudent to utter the close of the sentence in such an under tone, as to leave nothing audible but the grumbling sounds of his voice.

"Nay, Natty," rejoined the traveller, with undisturbed good humour, "it is for the honour that I contend. A few dollars will pay for the venison; but what will requite me for the lost honour of a buck's tail in my cap? Think, Natty, how I should triumph over that quizzing dog, Dick Jones, who has failed seven times this season already, and has only brought in one wood-chuck and a few gray squirrels."

"Ah! the game is becoming hard to find, indeed, Judge, with your clearings and betterments," said the old hunter, with a kind of disdainful resignation. "The time has been, when I have shot thirteen deer, without counting the fa'ns, standing in the door of my own hut!—and for bear's meat, if one wanted a ham or so from the cretur, he had only to watch a-nights, and he could shoot one by moonlight, through the cracks of the logs; no fear of his over-sleeping himself, n'ither, for the howling of the wolves was sartin to keep his eyes open. There's old Hector,"—patting with affection a tall hound, of black and yellow spots, with white belly and legs, that just then came in on the scent, accompanied by the slut he had mentioned; "see where the wolves bit his throat, the night I druve them from the venison I was smoking on the chimbly top—that dog is more to be trusted nor many a Christian man; for he never forgets a friends, and loves the hand that gives him bread."

There was a peculiarity in the manner of the hunter, that struck the notice of the young female, who had been a close and interested observer of his appearance and equipments, from the moment he first came into view. He was tall, and so meagre as to make him seem above even the six feet that he actually stood in his stockings. On his head, which was thinly covered with lank, sandy hair, he wore a cap made of fox-skin, resembling in shape the one we have already described, although much inferior in finish and ornaments. His face was skinny, and thin almost to emaciation; but yet bore no signs of disease;—on the contrary, it had every indication of the most robust and enduring health. The cold and the exposure had, together, given it a colour of uniform red; his gray eyes were glancing under a pair of shaggy brows, that overhung them in long hairs of gray mingled with their natural hue; his scraggy neck was bare, and burnt to the same tint with his face; though a small part of a shirt collar, made of the country check, was to be seen above the over-dress he wore. A kind of coat, made of dressed deer-skin, with the hair on, was belted close to his lank body, by a girdle of coloured worsted. On his feet were deer-skin moccasins, ornamented with porcupines' quills, after the manner of the Indians, and his limbs were guarded with long leggings of the same material as the moccasins, which, gartering over the knees of his tarnished buck-skin breeches, had obtained for him, among the settlers, the nick-name of Leather-stocking, notwith-standing his legs were protected beneath, in winter, by thick garments of woollen, duly made of good blue yarn. Over his left shoulder was slung a belt of deer-skin, from which depended an enormous ox horn, so thinly scraped, as to discover the dark powder that it contained. The larger end was fitted ingeniously and securely with a wooden bottom, and the other was stopped tight by a little plug. A leathern pouch hung before him, from which, as he concluded his last speech, he took a small measure, and, filling it accurately with powder, he commenced reloading the rifle, which, as its butt rested on the snow before him, reached nearly to the top of his fox-skin cap.

The traveller had been closely examining the wounds during these movements, and now, without heeding the ill-humour of the hunter's manner, exclaimed—

"I would fain establish a right, Natty, to the honour of this capture; and surely if the hit in the neck be mine, it is enough; for the shot in the heart was unnecessary—what we call an act of supererogation, Leather-stocking."

"You may call it by what larned name you please, Judge," said the hunter, throwing his rifle across his left arm, and knocking up a brass lid in the breech, from which he took a small piece of greased leather, and wrapping a ball in it, forced them down by main strength on the powder, where he continued to pound them while speaking. "It's far easier to call names, than to shoot a buck on the spring; but the cretur come by his end from a younger hand than 'ither your'n or mine, as I said before."

"What say you, my friend," cried the traveller, turning pleasantly to Natty's companion; "shall we toss up this dollar for the honour, and you keep the silver if you lose; what say you, friend?"

"That I killed the deer," answered the young man, with a little haughtiness, as he leaned on another long rifle, similar to that of Natty's.

"Here are two to one, indeed," replied the Judge, with a smile; "I am outvoted—overruled, as we say on the bench. There is Aggy, he can't vote, being a slave; and Bess is a minor—so I must even make the best of it. But you'll sell me the venison; and the deuce is in it, but I make a good story about its death."

"The meat is none of mine to sell," said Leather-stocking, adopting a little of his companion's hauteur; "for my part, I have known animals travel days with shots in the neck, and I'm none of them who'll rob a man of his rightful dues."

"You are tenacious of your rights, this cold evening, Natty," returned the Judge, with unconquerable good nature; "but what say you, young man, will three dollars pay you for the buck?"

"First let us determine the question of right to the satisfaction of us both," said the youth, firmly but respectfully, and with a pronunciation and language vastly superior to his appearance; "with how many shot did you load your gun?"

"With five, sir," said the Judge, gravely, a little struck with the other's manner; "are they not enough to slay a buck like this?"

"One would do it; but," moving to the tree from behind which he had appeared, "you know, sir, you fired in this direction—here are four of the bullets in the tree."

The Judge examined the fresh marks in the rough bark of the pine, and shaking his head, said with a laugh—

"You are making out the case against yourself, my young advocate—where is the fifth?"

"Here," said the youth, throwing aside the rough over-coat that he wore, and exhibiting a hole in his under garment, through which large drops of blood were oozing.

"Good God!" exclaimed the Judge, with horror; "have I been trifling here about an empty distinction, and a fellow-creature suffering from my hands without a murmur? But hasten—quick—get into my sleigh—it is but a mile to the village, where surgical aid can be obtained;—all shall be done at my expense, and thou shalt live with me until thy wound is healed—ay, and for ever afterwards, too."

"I thank you, sir, for your good intention, but must decline your offer. I have a friend who would be uneasy were he to hear that I am hurt and away from him. The injury is but slight, and the bullet has missed the bones; but I believe, sir, you will now admit my title to the venison."

"Admit it!" repeated the agitated Judge; "I here give thee a right to shoot deer, or bears, or any thing thou pleasest in my woods, for ever. Leather-stocking is the only other man that I have granted the same privilege to; and the time is coming when it will be of value. But I buy your deer—here, this bill will pay thee, both for thy shot and my own."

The old hunter gathered his tall person up into an air of pride, during this dialogue, and now muttered in an under tone—

"There's them living who say, that Nathaniel Bumppo's right to shoot in these hills, is of older date than Marmaduke Temple's right to forbid him. But if there's a law about it at all, though who ever heard tell of a law that a man should'nt kill deer where he pleased!—but if there is a law at all, it should be to keep people from the use of them smooth-bores. A body never knows where his lead will fly, when he pulls the trigger of one of them fancified fire-arms."

Without attending to the soliloquy of Natty, the youth bowed his head silently to the offer of the bank note, and replied—

"Excuse me, sir, I have need of the venison."

"But this will buy you many deer," said the Judge; "take it, I entreat you," and lowering his voice to nearly a whisper, he added—"it is for a hundred dollars."

For an instant only, the youth seemed to hesitate, and then, blushing even through the high colour that the cold had given to his cheeks, as if with inward shame at his own weakness, he again proudly declined the offer.

During this scene the female arose, and, regardless of the cold air, she threw back the hood which concealed her features, and now spoke, with great earnestness—

"Surely, surely,—young man—sir—you would not pain my father so much, as to have him think that he leaves a fellow-creature in this wilderness, whom his own hand has injured. I entreat you will go with us and receive medical aid for your hurts."

Whether his wound became more painful, or, there was something irresistible in the voice and manner of the fair pleader for her father's feelings, we know not, but the haughty distance of the young man's manner was sensibly softened by this appeal, and he stood, in apparent doubt, as if reluctant to comply with, and yet unwilling to refuse her request. The judge, for such being his office, must in future be his title, watched, with no little interest, the display of this singular contention in the feelings of the youth, and advancing, kindly took his hand, and, as he pulled him gently towards the sleigh, urged him to enter it.

"There is no human aid nearer than Templeton," he said; "and the hut of Natty is full three miles from this;—come—come, my young friend, go with us, and let the new doctor look to this shoulder of thine. Here is Natty will take the tidings of thy welfare to thy friend; and should'st thou require it, thou shalt be returned to thy home in the morning."

The young man succeeded in extricating his hand from the warm grasp of the judge, but continued to gaze on the face of the female, who, regardless of the cold, was still standing with her fine features exposed, which expressed feelings that eloquently seconded the request of her father. Leather-stocking stood, in the mean time, leaning upon his long rifle, with his head turned a little to one side, as if engaged in deep and sagacious musing; when, having apparently satisfied his doubts, by revolving the subject in his mind, he broke silence—

"It may be best to go, lad, after all; for if the shot hangs under the skin, my hand is getting too old to be cutting into human flesh, as I once used to. Though some thirty years agone, in the old war, when I was out under Sir William, I traveled seventy miles alone in the howling wilderness, with a rifle bullet in my thigh, and then cut it out with my own jack-knife. Old Indian John knows the time well. I met him with a party of the Delawares, on the trail of the Iroquois, who had been down and taken five scalps on the Schoharie.[6] But I made a mark on the red-skin that I'll warrant he carried to his grave. I took him on his posteerum, saving the lady's presence, as he got up from the amboosh, and rattled three buck shot into his naked hide, so close, that you might have laid a broad joe upon them all—" here Natty stretched out his long neck, and straightened his body, as he opened his mouth, which exposed a single tusk of yellow bone, while his eyes, his face, even his whole frame, seemed to laugh, although no sound was emitted, except a kind of thick hissing, as he inhaled his breath in quavers. "I had lost my bullet mould in crossing the Oneida outlet, and so had to make shift with the buck shot; but the rifle was true, and did'nt scatter like your two-legged thing there, Judge, which don't do, I find, to hunt in company with."

Natty's apology to the delicacy of the young lady was unnecessary, for, while he was speaking, she was too much employed in helping her father to remove certain articles of their baggage to hear him. Unable to resist the kind urgency of the travellers any longer, the youth, though still with an unaccountable reluctance expressed in his manner, suffered himself to be persuaded to enter the sleigh. The black, with the aid of his master, threw the buck across the baggage, and entering the vehicle themselves, the judge invited the hunter to do so likewise.

"No—no—" said the old man, shaking his head; "I have work to do at home this Christmas eve—drive on with the boy, and let your doctor look to the shoulder; though if he will only cut out the shot, I have yarbs that will heal the wound

_____
6. A tributary of the Hudson River.

quicker nor all his foreign 'intments." He turned and was about to move off, when, suddenly recollecting himself, he again faced the party, and added—"If you see any thing of Indian John about the foot of the lake, you had better take him with you, and let him lend the doctor a hand; for old as he is, he is curious at cuts and bruises, and it's likelier than not he'll be in with brooms to sweep your Christmas ha'arths."

"Stop—stop," cried the youth, catching the arm of the black as he prepared to urge his horses forward, "Natty—you need say nothing of the shot, nor of where I am going—remember, Natty, as you love me."

"Trust old Leather-stocking," returned the hunter, significantly; "he has'nt lived forty years in the wilderness, and not larnt from the savages how to hold his tongue— trust to me, lad; and remember old Indian John."

"And, Natty," said the youth eagerly, still holding the black by the arm, "I will just get the shot extracted, and bring you up, to-night, a quarter of the buck, for the Christmas dinner."

He was interrupted by the hunter, who held up his finger with an expressive gesture for silence, and moved softly along the margin of the road, keeping his eyes steadfastly fixed on the branches of a pine near him. When he had obtained such a position as he wished, he stopped, and cocking his rifle, threw one leg far behind him, and stretching his left arm to its utmost extent along the barrel of his piece, he began slowly to raise its muzzle in a line with the straight trunk of the tree. The eyes of the group in the sleigh naturally preceded the movement of the rifle, and they soon discovered the object of Natty's aim. On a small dead branch of the pine, which, at the distance of seventy feet from the ground, shot out horizontally, immediately beneath the living members of the tree, sat a bird, that in the vulgar language of the country was indiscriminately called a pheasant or a partridge. In size, it was but little smaller than a common barn-yard fowl. The baying of the dogs, and the conversation that had passed near the root of the tree on which it was perched, had alarmed the bird, which was now drawn up near the body of the pine, with a head and neck erect, that formed nearly a straight line with its legs. So soon as the rifle bore on the victim, Natty drew his trigger, and the partridge fell from its height with a force that buried it in the snow.

"Lie down, you old villain," exclaimed Leather-stocking, shaking his ramrod at Hector as he bounded towards the foot of the tree, "lie down, I say." The dog obeyed, and Natty proceeded, with great rapidity, though with the nicest accuracy, to reload his piece. When this was ended, he took up his game, and showing it to the party without a head, he cried—"Here is a nice tit-bit for an old man's Christmas—never mind the venison, boy, and remember Indian John; his yarbs are better nor all the foreign 'intments. Here, Judge," holding up the bird again, "do you think a smooth-bore would pick game off their roost, and not ruffle a feather?" The old man gave another of his remarkable laughs, which partook so largely of exultation, mirth, and irony, and shaking his head, he turned, with his rifle at a trail, and moved into the forest with short and quick steps, that were between a walk and a trot. At each movement that he made his body lowered several inches, his knees yielding with an inclination inward; but as the sleigh turned at a bend in the road, the youth cast his eyes in quest of his old companion, and he saw that he

was already nearly concealed by the trunks of the trees, while his dogs were following quietly in his footsteps, occasionally scenting the deer track, that they seemed
to know instinctively was now of no further use to them. Another jerk was given
to the sleigh, and Leather-stocking was hidden from view.

—1823

Catharine Maria Sedgwick
1789–1867

In the business of producing American historical romances, New York Knickerbocker James
Fenimore Cooper faced stiff competition from the Boston Bluestocking Catharine Maria
Sedgwick. The child of a ruling-class Federalist family, Sedgwick felt that her rank in society brought with it obligations to instruct those who had not been given her advantages. The
tremendous international success of Sir Walter Scott's historical romances inspired her to
take a similar approach to the American past, harnessing the power of fiction to forge a
national identity based on narratives of shared heritage. In the process, she created some of
the most self-reliant women in American fiction. Sedgwick was the author of more than
twenty novels, collections of stories, books of letters, and children's books, along with more
than one hundred pieces for magazines, annuals, and gift books. Most of her novels were published on both sides of the Atlantic, appearing in London within a few months of publication in the United States.

Sedgwick's best-known book is her third novel, *Hope Leslie: or, Early Times in the
Massachusetts* (1827). The novel is set during the period of Puritan settlement of the eastern seaboard. When it appeared, the question of native land claims east of the Mississippi
was at the forefront of public debate. *Hope Leslie* retells the history of conquest and colonization in a way that makes the European displacement of New England's native population seem inevitable and just. At the same time, the novel anticipates Nathaniel
Hawthorne's *The Scarlet Letter* (1850) by centering on a conflict between an audacious
heroine and the sexist Puritan oligarchy. Thus, it engages with the equally urgent contemporary debate about the position of women in American society. Hope Leslie is the foster
daughter of the Fletchers, a prominent Puritan family. Also living with the Fletchers is
Hope's soul mate, Magawisca, the captured daughter of a Pequod warrior. Together the two
explore the wilderness outside the bounds of the Puritan community. Both trust the
promptings of the heart above the dictates of convention and authority, and their passionate independence in thought and action bring them into conflict with their elders. Their
friend, Esther Downing, is an overly pious Puritan girl who cultivates the silence, industry,
and submissiveness expected of her. All three are potential love-objects for the Fletchers'
son, Everell. As with the plots of almost all historical romances that offer a marriage choice
between races, the marriage represents a founding moment for the nation, in which the
future identity of its people is determined. Like Cooper's Natty Bumppo, Hope is an intermediate figure, one whose white body is racially acceptable but whose absorption of native
cultural traditions has fitted her for the rigors of life in the New World. The chapter
excerpted here focuses on the noble Magawisca, Hope's native sister and the symbolic
source of her American self-reliance.

from Hope Leslie: or, Early Times in the Massachusetts
Chapter VII.

> "But the scene
> Is lovely round; a beautiful river there
> Wanders amid the fresh and fertile meads,
> The paradise he made unto himself,
> Mining the soil for ages. On each side
> The fields swell upward to the hills; beyond,
> Above the hills, in the blue distance, rise
> The mighty columns with which earth props heaven.
> There is a tale about these gray old rocks,
> A sad tradition."
>
> BRYANT.[1]

It is not our purpose to describe, step by step, the progress of the Indian fugitives.[2] Their sagacity in traversing their native forests, their skill in following and eluding an enemy, and all their politic devices, have been so well described in a recent popular work, that their usages have become familiar as household words, and nothing remains but to shelter defects of skill and knowledge under the veil of silence, since we hold it to be an immutable maxim, that a thing had better not be done than be ill done.

Suffice it to say, then, that the savages, after crossing the track of their pursuers, threaded the forest with as little apparent uncertainty as to their path as is now felt by travellers who pass through the same still romantic country in a stagecoach and on a broad turnpike. As they receded from the Connecticut the pine levels disappeared, the country was broken into hills, and rose into high mountains.

They traversed the precipitous sides of a river that, swollen by the vernal rains, wound its way among the hills, foaming and raging like an angry monarch. The river, as they traced its course, dwindled to a mountain rill, but still retaining its impetuous character, leaping and tumbling for miles through a descending defile, between high mountains, whose stillness, grandeur, and immobility contrasted with the noisy, reckless little stream as stern manhood with infancy. In one place, which the Indians called the throat of the mountain, they were obliged to betake themselves to the channel of the brook, there not being room on its margin for a footpath. The branches of the trees that grew from the rocky and precipitous declivities on each side met and interlaced, forming a sylvan canopy over the imprisoned stream. To Magawisca, whose imagination breathed a living spirit into all the objects of Nature, it seemed as if the spirits of the wood had stooped to listen to its sweet music.

After tracing this little sociable rill to its source, they again plunged into the silent forest, waded through marshy ravines, and mounted to the summits of steril hills, till at length, at the close of the third day, after having gradually descended for several miles, the hills on one side receded, and left a little interval of meadow, through which they wound into the lower valley of the Housatonic.

This continued and difficult march had been sustained by Everell with a spirit and fortitude that evidently won the favour of the savages, who always render hom-

---

1. William Cullen Bryant (1794–1878), "Monument Mountain" (1824), lines 41–50.   2. Mononotto, a Pequod chief, has freed his daughter Magawisca and son Oneco. Seeking revenge, he has captured their foster brother, Everell Fletcher, and foster sister, Faith.

age to superiority over physical evil. There was something more than this common feeling in the joy with which Mononotto noted the boy's silent endurance, and even contempt of pain. One noble victim seemed to him better than a "human hecatomb."[3] In proportion to his exultation in possessing an object worthy to avenge his son, was his fear that his victim would escape from him. During the march, Everell had twice, aided by Magawisca, nearly achieved his liberty. These detected conspiracies, though defeated, rendered the chief impatient to execute his vengeance, and he secretly resolved that it should not be delayed longer than the morrow.

As the fugitives emerged from the narrow defile, a new scene opened upon them; a scene of valley and hill, river and meadow, surrounded by mountains, whose encircling embrace expressed protection and love to the gentle spirits of the valley. A light summer shower had just fallen, and the clouds, "in thousand liveries dight," had risen from the western horizon, and hung their rich draperies about the clear sun. The horizontal rays passed over the valley, and flushed the upper branches of the trees, the summits of the hills, and the mountains with a flood of light, while the low grounds, reposing in deep shadow, presented one of those striking and accidental contrasts in nature that a painter would have selected to give effect to his art.

The gentle Housatonic wound through the depths of the valley, in some parts contracted to a narrow channel, and murmuring over the rocks that rippled its surface, and in others spreading wide its clear mirror, and lingering like a lover amid the vines, trees, and flowers that fringed its banks. Thus it flows now; but not, as then, in the sylvan freedom of Nature, when no clattering mills and bustling factories threw their prosaic shadows over the silver waters; when not even a bridge spanned their bosom; when not a trace of man's art was seen, save the little bark canoe that glided over them, or lay idly moored along the shore. The savage was rather the vassal than the master of nature, obeying her laws, but never usurping her dominion. He only used the land she prepared, and cast in his corn but where she seemed to invite him by mellowing and upheaving the rich mould. He did not presume to hew down her trees, the proud crest of her uplands, and convert them into "russet lawns and fallows gray." The axeman's stroke, that music to the *settler's* ear, never then violated the peace of Nature, or made discord in her music.

Imagination may be indulged in lingering for a moment in those dusky regions of the past, but it is not permitted to reasonable, instructed man to admire or regret tribes of human beings who lived and died, leaving scarcely a more enduring memorial than the forsaken nest that vanishes before one winter's storms.

But to return to our wanderers. They had entered the expanded vale by following the windings of the Housatonic around a hill, conical and easy of ascent, excepting on that side which overlooked the river, where, half way from the base to the summit, rose a perpendicular rock, bearing on its beetling front the age of centuries. On every other side the hill was garlanded with laurels, now in full and profuse bloom, here and there surmounted by an intervening pine, spruce, or hemlock, whose seared winter foliage was fringed with the bright, tender sprouts of spring. We believe there is a chord even in the heart of savage man that responds to the voice of Nature. Certain it is, the party paused, as it appeared, from a common instinct, at a little grassy nook, formed by the curve of the hill, to gaze on this singularly beautiful spot.

---

3. A sacrifice of many victims.

Everell looked on the smoke that curled from the huts of the village, imbosomed in pine-trees on the adjacent plain. The scene to him breathed peace and happiness, and gushing thoughts of home filled his eyes with tears. Oneco plucked clusters of laurels, and decked his little favourite, and the old chief fixed his melancholy eye on a solitary pine, scathed and blasted by tempests, that, rooted in the ground where he stood, lifted its topmost branches to the bare rock, where they seemed, in their wild desolation, to brave the elemental fury that had stripped them of beauty and life.

The leafless tree was truly, as it appeared to the eye of Mononotto, a fit emblem of the chieftain of a ruined tribe. "See you, child," he said, addressing Magawisca, "those unearthed roots? the tree must fall: hear you the death-song that wails through those blasted branches?"

"Nay, father, listen not to the sad strain; it is but the spirit of the tree mourning over its decay; rather turn thine ear to the glad song of this bright stream, image of the good. She nourishes the aged trees, and cherishes the tender flowerets, and her song is ever of happiness till she reaches the great sea, image of our eternity."

"Speak not to me of happiness, Magawisca; it has vanished with the smoke of our homes. I tell ye, the spirits of our race are gathered about this blasted tree. Samoset[4] points to that rock—that sacrifice-rock." His keen glance turned from the rock to Everell.

Magawisca understood its portentous meaning, and she clasped her hands in mute and agonizing supplication. He answered to the silent entreaty. "It is in vain; my purpose is fixed, and here it shall be accomplished. Why hast thou linked thy heart, foolish girl, to this English boy? I have sworn, kneeling on the ashes of our hut, that I would never spare a son of our enemy's race. The lights of heaven witnessed my vow, and think you that, now this boy is given into my hands to avenge thy brother, I will spare him? no, not to *thy* prayer, Magawisca. No; though thou lookest on me with thy mother's eye, and speakest with her voice, I will not break my vow."

Mononotto had indeed taken a final and fatal resolution; and prompted, as he fancied, by supernatural intimations, and perhaps dreading the relentings of his own heart, he determined on its immediate execution. He announced his decision to the Mohawks. A brief and animated consultation followed, during which they brandished their tomahawks, and cast wild and threatening glances at Everell, who at once comprehended the meaning of these menacing looks and gestures. He turned an appealing glance to Magawisca. She did not speak. "Am I to die now?" he asked; she turned, shuddering, from him.

Everell had expected death from his savage captors, but while it was comparatively distant he thought he was indifferent to it, or, rather, he believed he should welcome it as a release from the horrible recollection of the massacre at Bethel,[5] which haunted him day and night. But, now that his fate seemed inevitable, nature was appalled, and shrunk from it, and the impassive spirit for a moment endured a pang that there cannot be in any "corp'ral sufferance." The avenues of sense were closed, and past and future were present to the mind, as if it were already invested with the attributes of its eternity. From this agonizing excitement Everell was roused by a command from the savages to move onward. "It is then deferred," thought Magawisca; and heaving a deep sigh, as if for a moment relieved from a pressure on her overburdened heart, she looked to her father for an explanation; he said nothing, but proceeded in silence towards the village.

---

4. The first Algonquin to make contact with the settlers at Plymouth.   5. Everell's mother and sisters were killed in the raid during which he was captured.

The lower valley of the Housatonic, at the period to which our history refers, was inhabited by a peaceful, and, as far as that epithet could ever be applied to our savages, an agricultural tribe, whose territory, situate midway between the Hudson and the Connecticut, was bounded and defended on each side by mountains then deemed impraticable to a foe. These inland people had heard from the hunters of distant tribes, who occasionally visited them, of the aggressions and hostility of the English strangers; but, regarding it as no concern of theirs, they listened much as we listen to news of the Burmese war—Captain Symmes' theory—or lectures on phrenology.[6] One of their hunters, it is true, had penetrated to Springfield, and another had passed over the hills to the Dutch fort at Albany, and returned with the report that the strangers' skin was the colour of cowardice; that they served their women, and spoke an unintelligible language. There was little in this account to interest those who were so ignorant as to be scarcely susceptible of curiosity, and they hardly thought of the dangerous strangers at all, or only thought of them as a people from whom they had nothing to hope or fear, when the appearance of the ruined Pequod chief with his English captives roused them from their apathy.

The village was on a level, sandy plain, extending for about half a mile, and raised by a natural and almost perpendicular bank fifty feet above the level of the meadows. At one extremity of the plain was the hill we have described; the other was terminated by a broad green, appropriated to sports and councils.

The huts of the savages were irregularly scattered over the plain: some on cleared ground, and others just peeping out of copses of pine trees; some on the very verge of the plain, overlooking the meadows, and others under the shelter of a high hill that formed the northern boundary of the valley, and seemed stationed there to defend the inhabitants from their natural enemies, cold and wind.

The huts were the simplest of human art; but, as in no natural condition of society a perfect equality obtains, some were more spacious and commodious than others. All were made with flexible poles, firmly set in the ground, and drawn and attached together at the top. Those of the more indolent or least skilful were filled in with branches of trees and hung over with coarse mats, while those of the better order were neatly covered with bark, prepared with art and considerable labour for the purpose. Little garden patches adjoined a few of the dwellings, and were planted with beans, pumpkins, and squashes; the seeds of these vegetables, according to an Indian tradition (in which we may perceive the usual admixture of fable and truth), having been sent to them in the bill of a bird from the southwest by the Great Spirit.

The Pequod chief and his retinue passed just at twilight over the plain, by one of the many footpaths that indented it. Many of the women were still at work with their stone-pointed hoes in their gardens. Some of the men and children were at their sports on the green. Here a straggler was coming from the river with a string of fine trout; another fortunate sportsman appeared from the hillside with wild turkeys and partridges; while two emerged from the forest with still more noble game, a fat antlered buck.

This village, as we have described it, and perhaps from the affection its natural beauty inspired, remained the residence of the savages long after they had vanished from the surrounding country. Within the memory of the present generation the remnant of the tribe migrated to the West; and even now some of their families make a

---

6. Burma (now Myanmar) fought British colonial troops from 1823 to 1826. John C. Symmes (1780–1829) argued that Earth is hollow. Phrenology was the study of the shape of the head in order to establish character traits.

summer pilgrimage to this their Jerusalem,[7] and are regarded with a melancholy interest by the present occupants of the soil.

Mononotto directed his steps to the wigwam of the Housatonic chief, which stood on one side of the green. The chief advanced from his hut to receive him, and by the most animated gestures expressed to Mononotto his pleasure in the success of his incursion, from which it seemed that Mononotto had communicated with him on his way to the Connecticut.

A brief and secret consultation succeeded, which appeared to consist of propositions from the Pequod, and assent on the part of the Housatonic chief, and was immediately followed by a motion to separate the travellers. Mononotto and Everell were to remain with the chief, and the rest of the party to be conducted to the hut of his sister.

Magawisca's prophetic spirit too truly interpreted this arrangement; and thinking or hoping there might be some saving power in her presence, since her father tacitly acknowledged it by the pains he took to remove her, she refused to leave him. He insisted vehemently; but, finding her unyielding, he commanded the Mohawks to force her away.

Resistance was vain, but resistance she would still have made but for the interposition of Everell. "Go with them, Magawisca," he said, "and leave me to my fate. We shall meet again."

"Never!" she shrieked; "your fate is death."

"And after death we shall meet again," replied Everell, with a calmness that evinced his mind was already in a great degree resigned to the event that now appeared inevitable. "Do not fear for me, Magawisca. Better thoughts have put down my fears. When it is over, think of me."

"And what am I to do with this scorching fire till then?" she asked, pressing both her hands on her head. "Oh, my father, has your heart become stone?"

Her father turned from her appeal, and motioned to Everell to enter the hut. Everell obeyed; and when the mat dropped over the entrance and separated him from the generous creature whose heart had kept true time with his through all his griefs, who he knew would have redeemed his life with her own, he yielded to a burst of natural and not unmanly tears.

If this could be deemed a weakness, it was his last. Alone with his God, he realized the sufficiency of His presence and favour. He appealed to that mercy which is never refused, nor given in stinted measure to the humble suppliant. Every expression of pious confidence and resignation which he had heard with the heedless ear of childhood, now flashed like an illumination upon his mind.

His mother's counsels and instructions, to which he had often lent a wearied attention; the passages from the Sacred Book he had been compelled to commit to memory when his truant thoughts were ranging forest and field, now returned upon him as if a celestial spirit breathed them into his soul. Stillness and peace stole over him. He was amazed at his own tranquillity. "It may be," he thought, "that my mother is permitted to minister to me."

He might have been agitated by the admission of the least ray of hope; but hope was utterly excluded, and it was only when he thought of his bereft father that his courage failed him.

---

7. Middle eastern city, destination of pilgrimages.

But we must leave him to his solitude and silence, only interrupted by the distant hootings of the owl and the heavy tread of the Pequod chief, who spent the night in slowly pacing before the door of the hut.

Magawisca and her companions were conducted to a wigwam standing on that part of the plain on which they had first entered. It was completely enclosed on three sides by dwarf oaks. In front there was a little plantation of the edible luxuries of the savages. On entering the hut they perceived it had but one occupant, a sick, emaciated old woman, who was stretched on her mat, covered with skins. She raised her head as the strangers entered, and at the sight of Faith Leslie uttered a faint exclamation, deeming the fair creature a messenger from the spirit-land; but, being informed who they were and whence they came, she made every sign and expression of courtesy to them that her feeble strength permitted.

Her hut contained all that was essential to savage hospitality. A few brands were burning on a hearth-stone in the middle of the apartment. The smoke that found egress passed out by a hole in the centre of the roof, over which a mat was skilfully adjusted, and turned to the windward side by a cord that hung within. The old woman, in her long pilgrimage, had accumulated stores of Indian riches: piles of sleeping-mats lay in one corner; nicely-dressed skins garnished the walls; baskets of all shapes and sizes, gayly decorated with rude images of birds and flowers, contained dried fruits, medicinal herbs, Indian corn, nuts, and game. A covered pail, made of folds of birch bark, was filled with a kind of beer—a decoction of various roots and aromatic shrubs. Neatly-turned wooden spoons and bowls, and culinary utensils of clay, supplied all the demands of the inartificial housewifery of savage life.

The travellers, directed by their old hostess, prepared their evening repast—a short and simple process to an Indian; and, having satisfied the cravings of hunger, they were all, with the exception of Magawisca and one of the Mohawks, in a very short time stretched on their mats and fast asleep.

Magawisca seated herself at the feet of the old woman, and had neither spoken nor moved since she entered the hut. She watched anxiously and impatiently the movements of the Indian, whose appointed duty it appeared to be to guard her. He placed a wooden bench against the mat which served for a door, and stuffing his pipe with tobacco from a pouch slung over his shoulder, and then filling a gourd with the liquor in the pail, and placing it beside him, he quietly sat himself down to his night-watch.

The old woman became restless, and her loud and repeated groans at last withdrew Magawisca from her own miserable thoughts. She inquired if she could do aught to allay her pain; the sufferer pointed to a jar that stood on the embers, in which a medicinal preparation was simmering. She motioned to Magawisca to give her a spoonful of the liquor; she did so; and as she took it, "It is made," she said, "of all the plants on which the spirit of sleep has breathed;" and so it seemed to be, for she had scarcely swallowed it when she fell asleep.

Once or twice she waked and murmured something, and once Magawisca heard her say, "Hark to the wekolis![8] he is perched on the old oak by the sacrifice-rock, and his cry is neither musical nor merry: a bad sign in a bird."

But all signs and portents were alike to Magawisca; every sound rung a death-peal to her ear, and the hissing silence had in it the mystery and fearfulness of death. The

---

8. Whippoorwill, a nocturnal songbird.

night wore slowly and painfully away, as if, as in the fairy tale, the moments were counted by drops of heart's blood. But the most wearisome nights will end; the morning approached; the familiar notes of the birds of earliest dawn were heard, and the twilight peeped through the crevices of the hut, when a new sound fell on Magawisca's startled ear. It was the slow, measured tread of many feet. The poor girl now broke silence, and vehemently entreated the Mohawk to let her pass the door, or at least to raise the mat.

He shook his head with a look of unconcern, as if it were the petulant demand of a child, when the old woman, awakened by the noise, cried out that she was dying; that she must have light and air; and the Mohawk started up, impulsively, to raise the mat. It was held between two poles that formed the door-posts; and, while he was disengaging it, Magawisca, as if inspired, and quick as thought, poured the liquor from the jar on the fire into the hollow of her hand, and dashed it into the gourd which the Mohawk had just replenished. The narcotic was boiling hot, but she did not cringe; she did not even feel it; and she could scarcely repress a cry of joy when the savage turned round and swallowed, at one draught, the contents of the cup.

Magawisca looked eagerly through the aperture, but, though the sound of the footsteps had approached nearer, she saw no one. She saw nothing but a gentle declivity that sloped to the plain, a few yards from the hut, and was covered with a grove of trees; beyond and peering above them were the hill and the sacrifice-rock; the morning star, its rays not yet dimmed in the light of day, shed a soft trembling beam on its summit. This beautiful star, alone in the heavens when all other lights were quenched, spoke to the superstitious, or, rather, the imaginative spirit of Magawisca. "Star of promise," she thought, "thou dost still linger with us when day is vanished, and now thou art there alone to proclaim the coming sun; thou dost send in upon my soul a ray of hope; and though it be but as the spider's' slender pathway, it shall sustain my courage." She had scarcely formed this resolution when she needed all its efficacy, for the train whose footsteps she had heard appeared in full view.

First came her father, with the Housatonic chief; next, alone, and walking with a firm, undaunted step, was Everell, his arms folded over his breast, and his head a little inclined upward, so that Magawisca fancied she saw his full eye turned heavenward; after him walked all the men of the tribe, ranged according to their age, and the rank assigned to each by his own exploits.

They were neither painted nor ornamented according to the common usage at festivals and sacrifices, but everything had the air of hasty preparation. Magawisca gazed in speechless despair. The procession entered the wood, and for a few moments disappeared from her sight; again they were visible, mounting the acclivity of the hill by a winding, narrow footpath, shaded on either side by laurels. They now walked singly and slowly, but to Magawisca their progress seemed rapid as a falling avalanche. She felt that, if she were to remain pent in that prison-house, her heart would burst, and she sprang towards the doorway in the hope of clearing her passage; but the Mohawk caught her arm in his iron grasp, and putting her back, calmly retained his station. She threw herself on her knees to him; she entreated, she wept, but in vain: he looked on her with unmoved apathy. Already she saw the foremost of the party had reached the rock, and were forming a semicircle around it: again she appealed to her determined keeper, and again he denied her petition, but with a faltering tongue and a drooping eye.

Magawisca, in the urgency of a necessity that could brook no delay, had forgotten, or regarded as useless, the sleeping potion she had infused into the Mohawk's draught; she now saw the powerful agent was at work for her, and with that quickness of apprehension that made the operations of her mind as rapid as the impulses of instinct, she perceived that every emotion she excited but hindered the effect of the potion. Suddenly seeming to relinquish all purpose and hope of escape, she threw herself on a mat, and hid her face, burning with agonizing impatience, in her mantle. There we must leave her, and join that fearful company who were gathered together to witness what they believed to be the execution of exact and necessary justice.

Seated around their sacrifice-rock—their holy of holies—they listened to the sad story of the Pequod chief with dejected countenances and downcast eyes, save when an involuntary glance turned on Everell, who stood awaiting his fate, cruelly aggravated by every moment's delay, with a quiet dignity and calm resignation that would have become a hero or a saint. Surrounded by this dark cloud of savages, his fair countenance kindled by holy inspiration, he looked scarcely like a creature of earth.

There might have been among the spectators some who felt the silent appeal of the helpless, courageous boy; some whose hearts moved them to interpose to save the selected victim; but they were restrained by their interpretation of natural justice, as controlling to them as our artificial codes of laws to us.

Others, of a more cruel or more irritable disposition, when the Pequod described his wrongs and depicted his sufferings, brandished their tomahawks, and would have hurled them at the boy; but the chief said, "Nay, brothers, the work is mine; he dies by my hand—for my first-born—life for life; he dies by a single stroke, for thus was my boy cut off. The blood of sachems is in his veins. He has the skin, but not the soul of that mixed race, whose gratitude is like that vanishing mist," and he pointed to the vapour that was melting from the mountain tops into the transparent ether; "and their promises like this," and he snapped a dead branch from the pine beside which he stood, and broke it into fragments. "Boy as he is, he fought for his mother as the eagle fights for its young. I watched him in the mountain-path, when the blood gushed from his torn feet; not a word from his smooth lip betrayed his pain."

Mononotto embellished his victim with praises, as the ancients wreathed theirs with flowers. He brandished his hatchet over Everell's head, and cried exultingly, "See, he flinches not. Thus stood my boy when they flashed their sabres before his eyes and bade him betray his father. Brothers: My people have told me I bore a woman's heart towards the enemy. Ye shall see. I will pour out this English boy's blood to the last drop, and give his flesh and bones to the dogs and wolves."

He then motioned to Everell to prostrate himself on the rock, his face downward. In this position the boy would not see the descending stroke. Even at this moment of dire vengeance the instincts of a merciful nature asserted their rights.

Everell sunk calmly on his knees, not to supplicate life, but to commend his soul to God. He clasped his hands together. He did not—he could not speak; his soul was

> "Rapt in still communion, that transcends
> The imperfect offices of prayer."[9]

At this moment a sunbeam penetrated the trees that enclosed the area, and fell athwart his brow and hair, kindling it with an almost supernatural brightness. To the savages, this was a token that the victim was accepted, and they sent forth a shout

---

9. William Wordsworth (1770–1850), "The Excursion" (1814), lines 215–216.

that rent the air. Everell bent forward and pressed his forehead to the rock. The chief raised the deadly weapon, when Magawisca, springing from the precipitous side of the rock, screamed "Forbear!" and interposed her arm. It was too late. The blow was levelled—force and direction given; the stroke, aimed at Everell's neck, severed his defender's arm, and left him unharmed. The lopped, quivering member dropped over the precipice. Mononotto staggered and fell senseless, and all the savages, uttering horrible yells, rushed towards the fatal spot.

"Stand back!" cried Magawisca. "I have bought his life with my own. Fly, Everell—nay, speak not, but fly—thither—to the east!" she cried, more vehemently.

Everell's faculties were paralyzed by a rapid succession of violent emotions. He was conscious only of a feeling of mingled gratitude and admiration for his preserver. He stood motionless, gazing on her. "I die in vain, then," she cried, in an accent of such despair that he was roused. He threw his arms around her, and pressed her to his heart as he would a sister that had redeemed his life with her own, and then, tearing himself from her, he disappeared. No one offered to follow him. The voice of nature rose from every heart, and, responding to the justice of Magawisca's claim, bade him "God speed!" To all it seemed that his deliverance had been achieved by miraculous aid. All—the dullest and coldest—paid involuntary homage to the heroic girl, as if she were a superior being, guided and upheld by supernatural power.

Everything short of miracle she had achieved. The moment the opiate dulled the senses of her keeper, she escaped from the hut; and aware that, if she attempted to penetrate to her father through the semicircular line of spectators that enclosed him, she should be repulsed, and probably borne off the ground, she had taken the desperate resolution of mounting the rock where only her approach would be unperceived. She did not stop to ask herself if it were possible; but, impelled by a determined spirit, or rather, we would believe, by that inspiration that teaches the bird its unknown path, and leads the goat, with its young, safely over the mountain crags, she ascended the rock. There were crevices in it, but they seemed scarcely sufficient to support the eagle with his grappling talon; and twigs issuing from the fissures, but so slender that they waved like a blade of grass under the weight of the young birds that made a rest on them; and yet, such is the power of love, stronger than death, that with these inadequate helps Magawisca scaled the rock and achieved her generous purpose.

—1827

Lydia Howard Huntley Sigourney
1791–1865

Known on both sides of the Atlantic as the "American Hemans," Lydia Howard Huntley Sigourney achieved more fame during her lifetime than Nathaniel Hawthorne, Edgar Allan Poe, Henry David Thoreau, and other American authors—just as her inspiration, Felicia Dorothea Hemans, was more widely read than her British contemporaries, William Wordsworth, Samuel Taylor Coleridge, and Robert Southey. Born in Norwich, Connecticut, to Zerviah Wentworth Huntley and Ezekiel Huntley, a first-generation Scottish-American, she was already a prolific poet by age seven. Sigourney lived out her life in her home state, save the brief time she lived in

England and traveled Europe. Educated in Norwich and Hartford, she in turn served as an educator in both places, teaching in a school in the former and founding a girls' school in the latter. It was not long until her teaching of youth led to her writing for this same audience, her first publication being aptly titled *Moral Pieces in Prose and Verse* (1815). Other similar books followed and achieved a transatlantic readership, particularly works addressed to (young) women: *Letters to Young Ladies* (New York, 1833; London, 1834 and 1841; Glasgow, 1835); *The Way to Be Happy: Addressed to the Young* (London, 1835); *Letters to Mothers: On Their Various Important Duties and Privileges* (New York, 1838; London, 1839); *The Girl's Own Book* (London, 1852); *Mary Rice: and Other Tales* (London, 1859); and *Great and Good Women: Biographies for Girls* (Edinburgh, 1871). Her prolific publication record was due both to her brilliance as well as financial need. She left teaching to marry Charles Sigourney, whose hardware store in Hartford did not adequately provide for them, their son, and his three children from a previous marriage.

Sigourney's publishing was not confined to the realm of conduct books; also among her works were two thousand contributions in prose or poetry to three hundred or so journals as well as volumes of her own verse and an edition of Hemans. Among her most successful books were *Traits of the Aborigines of America* (Hartford and Cambridge, 1822); *Bell of St. Regis* (1834); *Lays from the West* (London, 1834); *The American Indians* (London, 1838); *Scenes in My Native Land* (Boston, 1844; London, 1845); *The Poetical Works* (Philadelphia, 1848; London, 1850), and many others; she published sixty-seven in all. Although she was popular in America, some critics such as Poe thought her work too derivative of English models. Among the British, though, her work was widely praised and read. During her residence in England in early 1841, she saw two volumes of her poetry through the press: *Pocahontas: and Other Poems* and *Poems, Religious and Elegiac*. During this time she made the acquaintance of several distinguished English authors, among them Samuel Rogers, Thomas Carlyle, and William Wordsworth, with whom she maintained a correspondence. America's voracious appetite for information on British authors (almost rivaling the present-day penchant for gossip about celebrities) was glutted by many prose and epistolary accounts of Americans touring in England, including Sigourney's *Pleasant Memories of Pleasant Lands: Being Poetical Records of a Visit to the Classic Spots and Most Eminent Persons in England, Scotland, and France* (London, 1843, 1845, and 1850). In addition to being read widely throughout Britain, her works were also appreciated by many in Europe; when she left England to spend two months in France, she was fêted by many upper-class admirers.

After her return from abroad and increasingly during her final years, Sigourney became a poet to whom many traveled to pay their respects. Her last years, like her earlier ones, were lived out in Connecticut and devoted to writing and also to improving the treatment of those with mental disabilities as well as deafness, muteness, and blindness. She also ministered to the poor. Another focus of her philanthropy was the abolition of slavery. Her labors in this cause did not cease until the end of her life; she passed away during the same year that the Civil War ended—1865.

The Indian's Welcome to the Pilgrim Fathers

"On Friday, March 16th, 1622, while the colonists were busied in their usual labors, they were much surprised to see a savage walk boldly towards them, and salute them with, 'much welcome, English, much welcome, Englishmen.'"

Above them spread a stranger sky
   Around, the sterile plain,
The rock-bound coast rose frowning nigh,
   Beyond,—the wrathful main:
Chill remnants of the wintry snow
   Still chok'd the encumber'd soil,

Yet forth these Pilgrim Fathers go,
  To mark their future toil.

'Mid yonder vale their corn must rise
  In Summer's ripening pride,
And there the church-spire woo the skies   10
  Its sister-school beside.
Perchance 'mid England's velvet green
  Some tender thought repos'd,—
Though nought upon their stoic mien[1]   15
  Such soft regret disclos'd.

When sudden from the forest wide
  A red-brow'd chieftain came,
With towering form, and haughty stride,
  And eye like kindling flame: 20
No wrath he breath'd, no conflict sought,
  To no dark ambush drew,
But simply *to the Old World brought*,
  The welcome of the New.

That *welcome* was a blast and ban   25
  Upon thy race unborn.
Was there no seer, thou fated Man!
  Thy lavish zeal to warn?
Thou in thy fearless faith didst hail
  A weak, invading band,   30
But who shall heed thy children's wail,
  Swept from their native land?

Thou gav'st the riches of thy streams,
  The lordship o'er thy waves,
The region of thine infant dreams,   35
  And of thy fathers' graves,
But who to yon proud mansions pil'd
  With wealth of earth and sea,
Poor outcast from thy forest wild,
  Say, who shall welcome thee?   40

—1835

Science and Religion

"What gives the mind this globe of earth to scan,
And chains brute instinct at the feet of man?
Bids the red comet on its car of flame
Reveal its periods and declare its name?
With deathless radiance gilds the historic page,   5

---

1. Appearance, expression.

And reaps the laurels of a buried age?"
  Majestic Science, from his cloister'd shrine,
Heard and replied, "This glorious power is mine."
  "But say, canst thou the erring spirit lead,
That feels its weakness and deplores its need?   10
Canst thou the prison of despair illume?
Find sin a pardon, or disarm the tomb?"
  With silent scorn the suppliant voice he spurn'd,
And to his ponderous tomes indignant turn'd.
Then from the cell, where long she dwelt apart,   15
Her humble mansion in the contrite heart,
Religion came; and where proud Science fail'd,
She bent her knee to earth, and with her Sire prevail'd.

—1841

Felicia Hemans
May, 1835.

Nature doth mourn for thee.
                There is no need
For Man to strike his plaintive lyre and fail,
As fail he must, if he attempt thy praise.
The little plant that never sang before,
Save one sad requiem, when its blossoms fell,   5
Sighs deeply through its drooping leaves for thee,
As for a florist fallen. The ivy wreath'd
Round the grey turrets of a buried race,
And the tall palm that like a prince doth rear
Its diadem 'neath Asia's burning sky,   10
With their dim legends blend thy hallow'd name.
Thy music, like baptismal dew, did make
Whate'er it touch'd most holy. The pure shell,
Laying its pearly lip on Ocean's floor,
The cloister'd chambers, where the sea-gods sleep,   15
And the unfathom'd melancholy main,
Lament for thee, through all the sounding deeps.
Hark! from the snow-breasted Himmaleh,[1] to where
Snowdon[2] doth weave his coronet of cloud,
From the scath'd pine tree, near the red man's hut,   20
To where the everlasting banian[3] builds
Its vast columnac temple, comes a moan
For thee, whose ritual made each rocky height
An altar, and each cottage-home, the haunt
Of Poesy.
          Yea, thou didst find the link   25

---

1. Himalaya, a mountain range in Asia. 2. Highest mountain in Wales. 3. Very large tree with aerial roots that form columns.

That joins mute Nature to ethereal mind,
And make that link a melody.
                    The couch
Of thy last sleep, was in the native clime
Of song and eloquence and ardent soul,
Spot fitly chosen for thee. Perchance, that isle   30
So lov'd of favoring skies, yet bann'd by fate,
Might shadow forth thine own unspoken lot.
For at thy heart, the ever-pointed thorn
Did gird itself, until the life-stream ooz'd
In gushes of such deep and thrilling song,   35
That angels poising on some silver cloud
Might linger 'mid the errands of the skies,
And listen, all unblam'd.
                    How tenderly
Doth Nature draw her curtain round thy rest,
And like a nurse, with finger on her lip,   40
Watch lest some step disturb thee, striving still
From other touch, thy sacred harp to guard.
Waits she thy waking, as the Mother waits
For some pale babe, whose spirit sleep hath stolen
And laid it dreaming on the lap of Heaven?   45
We say not thou art dead. We dare not. No.
For every mountain stream and shadowy dell
Where thy rich harpings linger, would hurl back
The falsehood on our souls. Thou spak'st alike
The simple language of the freckled flower,   50
And of the glorious stars. God taught it thee.
And from thy living intercourse with man
Thou shalt not pass away, until this earth
Drops her last gem into the doom's-day flame.
Thou hast but taken thy seat with that blest choir,   55
Whose hymns thy tuneful spirit learn'd so well
From this sublunar terrace, and so long
Interpreted.
                    Therefore, we will not say
Farewell to thee; for every unborn age
Shall mix thee with its household charities.   60
The sage shall greet thee with his benison,[4]
And Woman shrine thee as a vestal-flame
In all the temples of her sanctity,
And the young child shall take thee by the hand
And travel with a surer step to Heaven.   65

                                        —1841

---

4. Blessing.

Grassmere and Rydal Water[1]

O vale of Grassmere! tranquil, and shut out
From all the strife that shakes a jarring world,
How quietly thy village roofs are bower'd
In the cool verdure,[2] while thy graceful spire
Guardeth the ashes of the noble dead,   5
And, like a fix'd and solemn sentinel,
Holm-Crag[3] looks down on all.
              And thy pure lake,
Spreading its waveless breast of crystal out
'Tween thee and us, pencil, nor lip of man
May fitly show its loveliness. The soul   10
Doth hoard it as a gem, and, fancy-led,
Explore its curving shores, its lonely isle,
That like an emerald clasp'd in crystal, sleeps.

Ho, stern Helvellyn![4] with thy savage cliffs
And dark ravines, where the rash traveller's feet   15
Too oft have wander'd far and ne'er return'd,
Why dost thou press so close yon margin green,
Like border-chieftain seeking for his bride
Some cottage-maiden? Prince amid the hills,
That each upon his feudal seat maintains   20
Strict sovereignty, hast thou a tale of love
For gentle Grassmere, that thou thus dost droop
Thy plumed helmet o'er her, and peruse
With such a searching gaze her mirror'd brow?
She listeneth coyly, and her guileless depths   25
Are troubled at a tender thought from thee.
And yet methinks some speech of love should dwell
In scenes so beautiful. For not in vain,
Nor with a feeble voice, doth He who spread
Such glorious charms bespeak man's kindliness   30
For all whom He hath made, bidding the heart
Grasp every creature, with a warm embrace
Of brotherhood.
           Lo! what fantastic forms,
In sudden change, are traced upon the sky.
The sun doth subdivide himself, and shine   35
On either side of an elongate cloud,
Which, like an alligator huge and thin,
Pierceth his disk. And then an ostrich seem'd
Strangely to perch upon a wreath of foam,
And gaze disdainful on the kingly orb,   40

---

1. Small lakes in northern England.   2. Green vegetation.   3. Holm Crag, a rocky hill near Grasmere.   4. Mountain in Lake District.

That lay o'erspent and weary. But he roused
Up as a giant, and the welkin⁵ glow'd
With rushing splendour, while his puny foes
Vanish'd in air. Old England's oaks outstretch'd
Their mighty arms, and took that cloudless glance   45
Into their bosoms, as a precious thing
To be remember'd long.
                            And so we turn'd,
And through romantic glades pursued our way,
Where Rydal Water spends its thundering force,
And through the dark gorge makes a double plunge   50
Abruptly beautiful. Thicket, and rock,
And ancient summer-house, and sheeted foam
All exquisitely blent, while deafening sound
Of torrents battling with their ruffian foes
Fill'd the admiring gaze with awe, and wrought   55
A dim forgetfulness of all beside.
        Thee, too, I found within thy sylvan home,
Whose music thrill'd my heart when life was new,
Wordsworth! with wild enchantment circled round,
In love with Nature's self, and she with thee.   60
Thy ready hand, that from the landscape cull'd
Its long familiar charms, rock, tree, and spire,
With kindness half paternal leading on
My stranger footsteps through the garden walk,
Mid shrubs and flowers that from thy planting grew;   65
The group of dear ones gathering round thy board—
She, the first friend, still as in youth beloved—
The daughter, sweet companion—sons mature,
And favourite grandchild, with his treasured phrase—
The evening lamp, that o'er thy silver locks   70
And ample brow fell fitfully, and touch'd
Thy lifted eye with earnestness of thought,
Are with me as a picture, ne'er to fade
Till death shall darken all material things.

                                        —1841

Niagara

Flow on forever, in thy glorious robe
Of terror and of beauty. Yea, flow on
Unfathom'd and resistless. God hath set
His rainbow on thy forehead: and the cloud
Mantled around thy feet. And he doth give   5

---

5. Sky.

Thy voice of thunder, power to speak of Him
Eternally—bidding the lip of man
Keep silence—and upon thine altar pour
Incense of awe-struck praise.

                Earth fears to lift
The insect-trump that tells her trifling joys   10
Or fleeting triumphs, mid the peal sublime
Of thy tremendous hymn. Proud Ocean shrinks
Back from thy brotherhood, and all his waves
Retire abash'd. For he hath need to sleep,
Sometimes, like a spent laborer, calling home   15
His boisterous billows, from their vexing play,
To a long, dreary calm: but thy strong tide
Faints not, nor e'er with failing heart, forgets
Its everlasting lesson, night nor day.
The morning stars, that hail'd creation's birth,   20
Heard thy hoarse anthem, mixing with their song
Jehovah's[1] name; and the dissolving fires,
That wait the mandate of the day of doom
To wreck the earth, shall find it deep inscribed
Upon thy rocky scroll.

                The lofty trees   25
That list thy teachings, scorn the lighter lore
Of the too fitful winds; while their young leaves
Gather fresh greenness from thy living spray,
Yet tremble at the baptism. Lo! yon birds,
How bold they venture near, dipping their wing   30
In all thy mist and foam. Perchance 'tis meet
For them to touch thy garment's hem, or stir
Thy diamond wreath, who sport upon the cloud,
Unblam'd, or warble at the gate of heaven
Without reproof. But, as for us, it seems   35
Scarce lawful, with our erring lips to talk
Familiarly of thee. Methinks, to trace
Thine awful features, with our pencil's point,
Were but to press on Sinai.[2]

                Thou dost speak
Alone of God, who pour'd thee as a drop   40
From his right-hand,—bidding the soul that looks
Upon thy fearful majesty, be still,
Be humbly wrapp'd in its own nothingness,
And lose itself in Him.

                                   —1849

---

1. Old Testament name for God.   2. Desert peninsula in Egypt where Moses received the Ten Commandments.

Percy Bysshe Shelley
1792–1822

In March 1811, eighteen-year-old Percy Bysshe Shelley was expelled from Oxford University for his radical religious views. Six short months later, he ran away with and married sixteen-year-old Harriet Westbrook. His parents were not amused. Indeed, Shelley's father, Timothy Shelley, a member of Parliament, temporarily cut off his son's monthly allowance, the primary source of Shelley's livelihood. These two episodes capture key political and personal traits of Shelley's character above all, his critical attitude toward authority and power. Tyranny—in a word—was the target of much of Shelley's political and social attention. At Eton, a premiere school for boys, and Oxford University, Shelley scrutinized the rigid class structure that led students and faculty to lord their authority over others. He was often the target of bullies at Eton, where his idealism gained him the nickname "Mad Shelley," and such abuse as well as his general impressions of the class system led him to devote considerable energy to fighting against the most treacherous tendency among any governing body.

Shelley felt restricted by the ideology of Oxford University. He rebelled against what he saw as a narrow-mindedness rooted in the institution's Anglican tradition. Along with Thomas Jefferson Hogg, Shelley published *The Necessity of Atheism* (1811), a pamphlet that, following the skepticism of John Locke and David Hume, attacked the religious intolerance of Oxford's Anglican allegiance by arguing the impossibility of proving God's existence from nature and the material world. He distributed his call for free inquiry into religion widely to the university administrators, bishops, and College heads, and in response he was "sent down" (i.e., expelled). Shortly after that, he met and married Westbrook to rescue her from her tyrannical father and poverty, and with her he traveled to Ireland to pass out his *Address to the Irish People* (1812), a document sympathetic with the Irish-Catholic stirrings for freedom from the rule of the King and the Church of England.

Shelley saw in America the hope for salvation from the social and political ills—especially the aristocracy and monarchy—of England. "To the Republicans of North America" (composed in 1812 but not published until the latter half of the nineteenth century), for instance, opens with an impassioned address to his transatlantic counterparts:

> Brothers! between you and me
>   Whirlwinds sweep and billows roar:
> Yet in spirit oft I see
>   On thy wild and winding shore
> Freedom's bloodless banners wave,—
> Feel the pulses of the brave
> Unextinguished in the grave,—
>   See them drenched in sacred gore,—
> Catch the warrior's gasping breath
> Murmuring 'Liberty or death!'

Shelley's revolutionary politics, as articulated here, are indebted to one of his heroes, the radical political philosopher William Godwin, with whom he engaged in energetic correspondence between 1811 and 1813. Godwin, author of *Political Justice* (London, 1793; Philadelphia, 1796), sympathized with the French Revolution, declaring faith in human reason as the path to the elimination of kings and the beginning of self-governance. Around this time, Shelley joined Godwin's circle of friends. He met and fell in love with his daughter, Mary Wollstonecraft Godwin, who would go on to write *Frankenstein* (1818). Shelley also began work in the summer of 1811 on *Queen Mab*, his first long narrative poem that envisioned a fairy-tale vision of a utopian society through the lens of his radical religious, economic, and social ideas. In the poem, he meditates on free love, atheism, and vegetarianism, as he proposes key values for a more egalitarian society. Shelley had high hopes for the poem, desiring it to change the upper classes, even asking the printer to produce it "on fine paper & so as to catch the sight of the aristocrats," although in the same letter he admits that "they will not read it, but their sons & daughters may." The poem was popular—even though some booksellers were prosecuted by the Society for the Suppression of Vice for its content—and by the 1830s it was being read in the Americas and in Europe in one of many pirated editions. One notable edition is *The Poetical Works of Coleridge, Shelley and Keats*, published in Paris in 1829 by A. and W. Galignani with the aid of Mary Shelley, which introduced many American and Continental readers to Shelley's revolutionary writing.

In 1816, Shelley left England and his wife Harriet (who committed suicide later that year) to travel to Europe with Mary, her half-sister Claire Clairmont, and Lord Byron. The longer they remained abroad, the more radical Shelley became, advocating and practicing some of the ideals of *Queen Mab*: freedom of religion, free love, and vegetarianism. The Shelleys remained abroad from 1816. Shelley was highly productive in exile, and 1819 was an especially prolific year: In *Prometheus Unbound* he voiced his growing sense of the political tyranny imposed by the Crown, he attacked the political and personal corruption of aristocracies in *The Cenci*, and he composed *The Mask of Anarchy* to expose an infamous episode of brutal political violence, the Peterloo Massacre. In 1821, he published *Adonais*, an elegy to the recently deceased John Keats. Keats had a profound impact on Shelley; indeed, a copy of Keats's poems was found on Shelley's body after he drowned while sailing in 1822. He was eventually laid to rest near Keats in the Protestant Cemetery at Rome.

Shelley also elegized the imagined death of William Wordsworth's early political ideals, which had shaped Shelley's poetics and radical politics (the latter of which were also shaped by the political philosophers Thomas Paine and Jean Jacques Rousseau). His early adulation of Wordsworth makes sense, especially considering the early radicalism of Wordsworth when he sympathized with Godwin and the French Revolution. In the *Lyrical Ballads* (1798) and other pre-1807 poems, there emerges a Wordsworth deeply concerned with the plight of the poor and with the sanctity of liberty. This early Wordsworth contrasted starkly with the later writer: The poet who once protested against the aristocracy was now their Poet Laureate, and the poet who eschewed established religion for a quasi-pantheism was now Anglican. Wordsworth's apostasy, made evident by his move from Godwin back to the fold of England's Church and Crown, deeply troubled Shelley. In "To Wordsworth" (1816), Shelley responds to Wordsworth's "Ode. Intimations of Immortality" by showing how the years have distanced the poet from his early glory and ideals. Shelley's poem also elegizes the death of Wordsworth's radical beliefs by alluding to Wordsworth's own elegy to a poetic predecessor, his sonnet "Milton, Thou Should'st Be Living at This Hour."

Shelley's revolutionary enthusiasm to combat political and social tyranny informs a democratic view of the world that attracted many followers. The Chartists, working-class radicals who sought broader political representation, turned to *Queen Mab* in their efforts to collapse the hierarchical structure of British society. Shelley's view of democracy would shape Walt Whitman's political ideas and the poetics of Bliss Carman, Archibald Lampman, and, in the twentieth century, Allen Ginsberg. Shelley believed passionately in the political and social power of literature, arguing in his *Defence of Poetry* (1821) that "Poets are the unacknowledged legislators of the world" (p. 704).

Mont Blanc[1]

Lines Written in the Vale of Chamouni

1

The everlasting universe of things
Flows through the mind, and rolls its rapid waves,
Now dark—now glittering—now reflecting gloom—
Now lending splendour, where from secret springs
The source of human thought its tribute brings   5
Of waters,—with a sound but half its own,
Such as a feeble brook will oft assume
In the wild woods, among the mountains lone,
Where waterfalls around it leap for ever,
Where woods and winds contend, and a vast river   10
Over its rocks ceaselessly bursts and raves.

2

Thus thou, Ravine of Arve—dark, deep Ravine—
Thou many-coloured, many-voiced vale,
Over whose pines and crags and caverns sail
Fast cloud-shadows and sunbeams: awful[2] scene,   15
Where Power in likeness of the Arve comes down
From the ice gulphs that gird his secret throne,
Bursting thro' these dark mountains like the flame
Of lightning through the tempest;—thou dost lie,—
Thy giant brood of pines around thee clinging,   20
Children of elder time, in whose devotion
The chainless winds still come and ever came
To drink their odours, and their mighty swinging
To hear, an old and solemn harmony;
Thine earthly rainbows stretched across the sweep   25
Of the ethereal waterfall, whose veil
Robes some unsculptured image; the strange sleep
Which, when the voices of the desart fail,
Wraps all in its own deep eternity;—
Thy caverns echoing to the Arve's commotion,   30
A loud, lone sound no other sound can tame;
Thou art pervaded with that ceaseless motion
Thou art the path of that unresting sound—
Dizzy Ravine! and when I gaze on thee
I seem as in a trance sublime and strange   35
To muse on my own separate phantasy,
My own, my human mind, which passively
Now renders and receives fast influencings,

---

1. The highest mountain in the Alps, on the border between France and Italy.   2. Awesome, awe-inspiring.

Holding an unremitting interchange
With the clear universe of things around; 40
One legion of wild thoughts, whose wandering wings
Now float above thy darkness, and now rest
Where that or thou art no unbidden guest,
In the still cave of the witch Poesy,
Seeking among the shadows that pass by, 45
Ghosts of all things that are, some shade of thee,
Some phantom, some faint image; till the breast
From which they fled recalls them, thou art there!

3

Some say that gleams of a remoter world
Visit the soul in sleep,—that death is slumber, 50
And that its shapes the busy thoughts outnumber
Of those who wake and live.—I look on high;
Has some unknown omnipotence unfurled
The veil of life and death? or do I lie
In dream, and does the mightier world of sleep 55
Spread far around and inaccessibly
Its circles? For the very spirit fails,
Driven like a homeless cloud from steep to steep
That vanishes among the viewless gales!
Far, far above, piercing the infinite sky, 60
Mont Blanc appears,—still, snowy, and serene—
Its subject mountains their unearthly forms
Pile around it, ice and rock; broad vales between
Of frozen floods, unfathomable deeps,
Blue as the overhanging heaven, that spread 65
And wind among the accumulated steeps;
A desert peopled by the storms alone,
Save when the eagle brings some hunter's bone,
And the wolf tracts her there—how hideously
Its shapes are heaped around! rude, bare, and high, 70
Ghastly, and scarred, and riven.[3]—Is this the scene
Where the old Earthquake-dæmon[4] taught her young
Ruin? Were these their toys? or did a sea
Of fire, envelope once this silent snow?
None can reply—all seems eternal now. 75
The wilderness has a mysterious tongue
Which teaches awful doubt, or faith so mild,
So solemn, so serene, that man may be
But for such faith, with nature reconciled.
Thou hast a voice, great Mountain, to repeal 80
Large codes of fraud and woe; not understood

---

3. Split.   4. Dæmon: a powerful supernatural being.

By all, but which the wise and great and good
Interpret, or make felt, or deeply feel.

4

The fields, the lakes, the forests, and the streams,
Ocean, and all the living things that dwell   85
Within the daedal[5] earth, lightning, and rain,
Earthquake, and fiery flood, and hurricane,
The torpor of the year when feeble dreams
Visit the hidden buds, or dreamless sleep
Holds every future leaf and flower;—the bound   90
With which from that detested trance they leap;
The works and ways of man, their death and birth,
And that of him, and all that his may be;
All things that move and breathe with toil and sound
Are born and die; revolve, subside, and swell.   95
Power dwells apart in its tranquillity
Remote, serene, and inaccessible:
And *this*, the naked countenance of earth,
On which I gaze, even these primaeval mountains
Teach the adverting mind. The glaciers creep   100
Like snakes that watch their prey, from their far fountains,
Slow rolling on; there, many a precipice,
Frost and the Sun in scorn of mortal power
Have piled: dome, pyramid, and pinnacle,
A city of death, distinct with many a tower   105
And wall impregnable of beaming ice.
Yet not a city, but a flood of ruin
Is there, that from the boundary of the sky
Rolls its perpetual stream; vast pines are strewing
Its destined path, or in the mangled soil   110
Branchless and shattered stand: the rocks, drawn down
From yon remotest waste, have overthrown
The limits of the dead and living world,
Never to be reclaimed. The dwelling-place
Of insects, beasts, and birds, becomes its spoil;   115
Their food and their retreat for ever gone,
So much of life and joy is lost. The race
Of man, flies far in dread; his work and dwelling
Vanish, like smoke before the tempest's stream,
And their place is not known. Below, vast caves   120
Shine in the rushing torrent's restless gleam,
Which from those secret chasms in tumult welling
Meet in the vale, and one majestic River,
The breath and blood of distant lands, for ever

---

5. Daedalus was the designer of a complex labyrinth in Crete.

Rolls its loud waters to the ocean waves,   125
Breathes its swift vapours to the circling air.

5

Mont Blanc yet gleams on high:—the power is there,
The still and solemn power, of many sights,
And many sounds, and much of life and death.
In the calm darkness of the moonless nights,   130
In the lone glare of day, the snows descend
Upon that Mountain; none beholds them there,
Nor when the flakes burn in the sinking sun,
Or the star-beams dart through them:—Winds contend
Silently there, and heap the snow with breath   135
Rapid and strong, but silently! Its home
The voiceless lightning in these solitudes
Keeps innocently, and like vapour broods
Over the snow. The secret strength of things
Which governs thought, and to the infinite dome   140
Of heaven is as a law, inhabits thee!
And what were thou, and earth, and stars, and sea,
If to the human mind's imaginings
Silence and solitude were vacancy?

—1817

Hymn to Intellectual Beauty

1

The awful shadow of some unseen Power
  Floats, though unseen, amongst us, visiting
  This various world with as inconstant wing
As summer winds that creep from flower to flower.—
Like moonbeams that behind some piny mountain shower,   5
    It visits with inconstant glance
    Each human heart and countenance;
Like hues and harmonies of evening,—
    Like clouds in starlight widely spread,—
    Like memory of music fled,—   10
    Like aught that for its grace may be
Dear, and yet dearer for its mystery.

2

Spirit of BEAUTY, that dost consecrate
  With thine own hues all thou dost shine upon
  Of human thought or form,—where art thou gone?   15

Why dost thou pass away, and leave our state,
This dim vast vale of tears, vacant and desolate?—
    Ask why the sunlight not for ever
    Weaves rainbows o'er yon mountain river;
Why aught should fail and fade that once is shown;   20
    Why fear and dream and death and birth
    Cast on the daylight of this earth
    Such gloom,—why man has such a scope
For love and hate, despondency and hope?

3

No voice from some sublimer world hath ever   25
  To sage or poet these responses given—
    Therefore the names of God and ghost and Heaven,
Remain the records of their vain endeavour,
Frail spells—whose uttered charm might not avail to sever
    From all we hear and all we see,   30
    Doubt, chance, and mutability.
Thy light alone like mist o'er mountains driven,
    Or music by the night wind sent
    Through strings of some still instrument,
    Or moonlight on a midnight stream,   35
Gives grace and truth to life's unquiet dream.

4

Love, Hope, and Self-esteem, like clouds depart
  And come, for some uncertain moments lent.
  Man were immortal, and omnipotent,
Didst thou, unknown and awful as thou art,   40
Keep with thy glorious train firm state within his heart.
    Thou messenger of sympathies
    That wax and wane in lovers' eyes—
Thou, that to human thought art nourishment,
    Like darkness to a dying flame!   45
    Depart not—as thy shadow came:
    Depart not, lest the grave should be,
Like life and fear, a dark reality!

5

While yet a boy, I sought for ghosts, and sped
  Through many a listening chamber, cave and ruin,   50
  And starlight wood, with fearful steps pursuing
Hopes of high talk with the departed dead.
I called on poisonous names with which our youth is fed.
    I was not heard—I saw them not—

When musing deeply on the lot   55
Of life at that sweet time when winds are wooing
   All vital things that wake to bring
   News of birds and blossoming,—
   Sudden, thy shadow fell on me;
I shrieked, and clasped my hands in exstasy!   60

6

I vowed that I would dedicate my powers
  To thee and thine—have I not kept the vow?
  With beating heart and streaming eyes, even now
I call the phantoms of a thousand hours
Each from his voiceless grave: they have in visioned bowers   65
   Of studious zeal or love's delight
   Outwatched with me the envious night—
They know that never joy illumed my brow
   Unlinked with hope that thou wouldst free
   This world from its dark slavery,   70
   That thou, O awful LOVELINESS,
Wouldst give whate'er these words cannot express.

7

The day becomes more solemn and serene
  When noon is past—there is a harmony
  In autumn, and a lustre in its sky,   75
Which through the summer is not heard or seen,
As if it could not be, as if it had not been!
   Thus let thy power, which like the truth
   Of Nature on my passive youth
Descended, to my onward life supply   80
   Its calm—to one who worships thee,
   And every form containing thee,
   Whom, SPIRIT fair, thy spells did bind
To fear[1] himself, and love all humankind.

—1817

Ozymandias[1]

I met a traveller from an antique land
Who said: "Two vast and trunkless legs of stone
Stand in the desert. . . . Near them on the sand,
Half sunk, a shattered visage lies, whose frown,
And wrinkled lip, and sneer of cold command,   5

---

1. Revere.

1. The Egyptian ruler Ramses II, thirteenth century BC.

Tell that its sculptor well those passions read
Which yet survive, stamped on these lifeless things,
The hand that mocked them, and the heart that fed.
And on the pedestal, these words appear:
"My name is Ozymandias, King of Kings: 10
Look on my works, ye Mighty, and despair!"
Nothing beside remains. Round the decay
Of that colossal Wreck, boundless and bare,
The lone and level sands stretch far away."

—1817

Sonnet: England in 1819

An old, mad, blind, despised, and dying King,[1]—
Princes, the dregs of their dull race, who flow
Through public scorn,—mud from a muddy spring,—
Rulers who neither see nor feel nor know,
But leechlike to their fainting country cling,   5
Till they drop, blind in blood, without a blow,—
A people starved and stabbed in the untilled field,[2]—
An army, which liberticide and prey
Make as a two-edged sword to all who wield;—
Golden and sanguine laws which tempt and slay;   10
Religion Christless, Godless, a book sealed;
A Senate,—Time's worst statute unrepealed,[3]—
Are graves from which a glorious Phantom may
Burst, to illumine our tempestuous day.

—1819

The Mask of Anarchy

Written on the Occasion of the Massacre at Manchester[1]

As I lay asleep in Italy
There came a voice from over the Sea
And with great power it forth led me
To walk in the visions of Poesy.

I met Murder on the way—   5
He had a mask like Castlereagh[2]—
Very smooth he looked, yet grim;
Seven bloodhounds followed him.

All were fat; and well they might
Be in admirable plight,   10

---

1. King George III, deemed insane in 1811.   2. The "Peterloo Massacre" of 1819. See footnote 1 below.   3. Laws restricting civil rights of Catholics, dissenters, and women.

1. On August 16, 1819, English police violently dispersed 100,000 peaceful protesters, killing at least 12. The events were dubbed the "Peterloo Massacre."   2. Robert Stewart, Lord Castlereagh (1769–1822), British foreign secretary.

For one by one, and two by two,
He tossed them human hearts to chew
Which from his wide cloak he drew.

Next came Fraud, and he had on,
Like Eldon,[3] an ermined gown;   15
His big tears, for he wept well,
Turned to mill-stones as they fell:

And the little children, who
Round his feet played to and fro,
Thinking every tear a gem,   20
Had their brains knocked out by them.

Clothed with the Bible, as with light,
And the shadows of the night,
Like Sidmouth,[4] next, Hypocrisy
On a crocodile rode by.   25

And many more Destructions played
In this ghastly masquerade,
All disguised, even to the eyes,
Like Bishops, lawyers, peers, or spies.

Last came Anarchy: he rode   30
On a white horse splashed with blood;
He was pale even to the lips,
Like Death in the Apocalypse.

And he wore a kingly crown,
And in his grasp a sceptre shone;   35
On his brow this mark I saw—
"I AM GOD, AND KING, AND LAW!"

With a pace stately and fast
Over English land he passed,
Trampling to a mire of blood   40
The adoring multitude.

And a mighty troop around
With their trampling shook the ground,
Waving each a bloody sword,
For the service of their Lord.   45

And with glorious triumph, they
Rode through England proud and gay
Drunk as with intoxication
Of the wine of desolation.

---

3. John Scott, Lord Eldon (1751–1838), conservative politician known for public crying.   4. Henry Addington, Viscount Sidmouth (1757–1844), British home secretary who crushed dissent.

O'er fields and towns, from sea to sea,   50
Passed the Pageant swift and free,
Tearing up and trampling down,
Till they came to London town.

And each dweller, panic-stricken,
Felt his heart with terror sicken,   55
Hearing the tempestuous cry
Of the triumph of Anarchy.

For with pomp to meet him came,
Clothed in arms like blood and flame,
The hired Murderers who did sing   60
"Thou art God, and Law, and King!

We have waited, weak and lone,
For thy coming, Mighty One!
Our purses are empty, our swords are cold,
Give us glory, and blood, and gold."   65

Lawyers and priests, a motley crowd,
To the earth their pale brows bowed;
Like a bad prayer not over loud,
Whispering—"Thou art Law and God!"

Then all cried with one accord,   70
"Thou art King, and God, and Lord;
Anarchy, to Thee we bow,
Be thy name made holy now!"

And Anarchy the Skeleton
Bowed and grinned to every one,   75
As well as if his education
Had cost ten millions to the Nation.

For he knew the Palaces
Of our Kings were rightly his;
His the sceptre, crown, and globe,
And the gold-inwoven robe.   80

So he sent his slaves before
To seize upon the Bank and Tower,[5]
And was proceeding with intent
To meet his pensioned Parliament,   85

When one fled past, a maniac maid,
And her name was Hope, she said,
But she looked more like Despair,
And she cried out in the air:

---

5. Bank of England and Tower of London.

"My father Time is weak and grey   90
With waiting for a better day;
See how idiot-like he stands,
Fumbling with his palsied hands![6]

He has had child after child
And the dust of death is piled   95
Over every one but me—
Misery! oh Misery!"

Then she lay down in the street,
Right before the horses' feet,
Expecting, with a patient eye,   100
Murder, Fraud, and Anarchy—

When between her and her foes
A mist, a light, an image rose,
Small at first, and weak, and frail
Like the vapour of a vale: 105

Till as clouds grow on the blast,
Like tower-crowned giants striding fast,
And glare with lightnings as they fly,
And speak in thunder to the sky,

It grew—a Shape arrayed in mail[7]   110
Brighter than the Viper's scale,
And upborne on wings whose grain[8]
Was as the light of sunny rain.

On its helm, seen far away,
A planet, like the Morning's,[9] lay;   115
And those plumes its light rained through,
Like a shower of crimson dew.

With step as soft as wind it passed
O'er the heads of men—so fast
That they knew the presence there,   120
And looked,—but all was empty air.

As flowers beneath May's footstep waken
As stars from Night's loose hair are shaken
As waves arise when loud winds call
Thoughts sprung where'er that step did fall.   125

And the prostrate multitude
Looked—and ankle-deep in blood,
Hope, that maiden most serene,
Was walking with a quiet mien;

---

6. King George III, deemed insane in 1811.   7. Armor.   8. Color.   9. Venus, the morning star.

And Anarchy, the ghastly birth,
Lay dead earth upon the earth
The Horse of Death tameless as wind
Fled, and with his hoofs did grind
To dust the murderers thronged behind.   130

A rushing light of clouds and splendour,
A sense awakening and yet tender,
Was heard and felt—and at its close   135
These words of joy and fear arose

As if their Own indignant Earth,
Which gave the sons of England birth,
Had felt their blood upon her brow,   140
And shuddering with a mother's throe

Had turned every drop of blood
By which her face had been bedewed
To an accent unwithstood,—
As if her heart had cried aloud: 145

"Men of England, heirs of Glory,
Heroes of unwritten story,
Nurslings of one mighty Mother,
Hopes of her and one another!   150

Rise, like Lions after slumber
In unvanquishable number!
Shake your chains to Earth, like dew
Which in sleep had fallen on you—
Ye are many, they are few.   155

What is Freedom? ye can tell
That which Slavery is, too well—
For its very name has grown
To an echo of your own.

'Tis to work and have such pay   160
As just keeps life from day to day
In your limbs, as in a cell
For the tyrants' use to dwell:

So that ye for them are made
Loom and plough and sword and spade;   165
With or without your own will, bent
To their defence and nourishment.

'Tis to see your children weak
With their mothers pine and peak[10]

---

10. Grow weak and thin.

When the winter winds are bleak,—
They are dying whilst I speak.

'Tis to hunger for such diet
As the rich man in his riot
Casts to the fat dogs that lie
Surfeiting beneath his eye.

'Tis to let the Ghost of Gold[11]
Take from Toil a thousand fold
More than e'er its substance could
In the tyrannies of old.

Paper coin—that forgery
Of the title deeds which ye
Hold to something of the worth
Of the inheritance of Earth.

'Tis to be a slave in soul,
And to hold no strong control
Over your own wills, but be
All that others make of ye.

And, at length when ye complain
With a murmur weak and vain,
'Tis to see the Tyrant's crew
Ride over your wives and you—
Blood is on the grass like dew!

Then it is to feel revenge,
Fiercely thirsting to exchange
Blood for blood—and wrong for wrong—
Do not thus when ye are strong!

Birds find rest in narrow nest,
When weary of their winged quest;
Beasts find fare in woody lair
When storm and snow are in the air;

Horses, oxen, have a home
When from daily toil they come;
Household dogs, when the wind roars,
Find a home within warm doors;

Asses, swine, have litter spread,
And with fitting food are fed;
All things have a home but one—
Thou, O Englishman, hast none!

---

11. Paper money used to pay workers, who mistrusted it.

This is Slavery!—savage men,
Or wild beasts within a den,
Would endure not as ye do—
But such ills they never knew.

What art thou, Freedom? O! could slaves
Answer from their living graves
This demand, tyrants would flee
Like a dream's dim imagery;

Thou art not, as impostors say,
A shadow soon to pass away,
A superstition, and a name
Echoing from the cave of Fame.[12]

For the labourer, thou art bread
And a comely table spread,
From his daily labour come
To a neat and happy home.

Thou art clothes, and fire, and food
For the trampled multitude—
No—in countries that are free
Such starvation cannot be
As in England now we see!

To the rich thou art a check;
When his foot is on the neck
Of his victim, thou dost make
That he treads upon a snake.[13]

Thou art Justice—ne'er for gold
May thy righteous laws be sold
As laws are in England—thou
Shield'st alike the high and low.

Thou art Wisdom: Freemen never
Dream that God will damn for ever
All who think those things untrue
Of which Priests make such ado.

Thou art Peace—never by thee
Would blood and treasure wasted be
As tyrants wasted them, when all
Leagued to quench thy flame in Gaul.[14]

What if English toil and blood
Was poured forth, even as a flood?
It availed, Oh, Liberty!
To dim but not extinguish thee.

210

215

220

225

230

235

240

245

---

12. Rumor or gossip.   13. Alludes to the American revolutionary motto, "Don't tread on me."   14. France.

Thou art Love—the rich have kissed   250
Thy feet, and, like him following Christ,
Give their substance to the free
And through the rough world follow thee,

Or turn their wealth to arms, and make
War for thy beloved sake   255
On wealth and war and fraud—whence they
Drew the power which is their prey.

Science, Poetry, and Thought,
Are thy lamps; they make the lot
Of the dwellers in a cot[15]   260
So serene, they curse it not.

Spirit, Patience, gentleness,
All that can adorn and bless
Art thou—let deeds, not words, express
Thine exceeding loveliness.   265

Let a great Assembly be
Of the fearless and the free
On some spot of English ground
Where the plains stretch wide around.

Let the blue sky overhead,   270
The green earth on which ye tread,
All that must eternal be,
Witness the solemnity.

From the corners uttermost
Of the bounds of English coast,   275
From every hut, village, and town
Where those who live and suffer moan
For others' misery or their own;

From the workhouse and the prison
Where, pale as corpses newly risen,   280
Women, children, young and old,
Groan for pain, and weep for cold—

From the haunts of daily life
Where is waged the daily strife
With common wants and common cares   285
Which sows the human heart with tares

Lastly, from the palaces
Where the murmur of distress
Echoes, like the distant sound
Of a wind alive around   290

---

15. Cottage.

Those prison halls of wealth and fashion,
Where some few feel such compassion
For those who groan and toil and wail
As must make their brethren pale—

Ye who suffer woes untold
Or to feel, or to behold
Your lost country bought and sold
With a price of blood and gold—

Let a vast assembly be,
And with great solemnity
Declare with measured words that ye
Are, as God has made ye, free!

Be your strong and simple words
Keen to wound as sharpened swords,
And wide as targes[16] let them be,
With their shade to cover ye.

Let the tyrants pour around
With a quick and startling sound,
Like the loosening of a sea
Troops of armed emblazonry.

Let the charged artillery drive
Till the dead air seems alive
With the clash of clanging wheels,
And the tramp of horses' heels.

Let the fixed bayonet
Gleam with sharp desire to wet
Its bright point in English blood,
Looking keen as one for food.

Let the horsemen's scimitars[17]
Wheel and flash, like sphereless stars
Thirsting to eclipse their burning
In a sea of death and mourning.

Stand ye calm and resolute,
Like a forest close and mute,
With folded arms, and looks which are
Weapons of an unvanquished war,

And let Panic, who outspeeds
The career of armed steeds
Pass, a disregarded shade
Through your phalanx[18] undismayed.

---

16. Shields.   17. Swords.   18. Troops in formation.

Let the Laws of your own land,
Good or ill, between ye stand,
Hand to hand, and foot to foot,
Arbiters of the dispute,

The old laws of England—they   335
Whose reverend heads with age are grey,
Children of a wiser day;
And whose solemn voice must be
Thine own echo—Liberty!

On those who first should violate   340
Such sacred heralds in their state
Rest the blood that must ensue,
And it will not rest on you.

And, if then the tyrants dare,
Let them ride among you there,   345
Slash and stab and maim and hew,—
What they like, that let them do.

With folded arms and steady eyes,
And little fear and less surprise,
Look upon them as they slay   350
Till their rage has died away.

Then they will return with shame
To the place from which they came,
And the blood thus shed will speak
In hot blushes on their cheek.   355

Every woman in the land
Will point at them as they stand—
They will hardly dare to greet
Their acquaintance in the street.

And the bold, true warriors   360
Who have hugged Danger in wars
Will turn to those who would be free,
Ashamed of such base company.

And that slaughter to the Nation
Shall steam up like inspiration,   365
Eloquent, oracular,
A volcano heard afar;

And these words shall then become
Like Oppression's thundered doom
Ringing through each heart and brain   370
Heard again—again—again!

Rise like lions after slumber,
In unvanquishable number!
Shake your chains to earth like dew
Which in sleep had fallen on you—   375
Ye are many—they are few."

—1832

Ode to the West Wind

1

O wild West Wind, thou breath of Autumn's being,
Thou from whose unseen presence the leaves dead
Are driven like ghosts from an enchanter fleeing,

Yellow, and black, and pale, and hectic red,
Pestilence-stricken multitudes! O Thou   5
Who chariotest to their dark wintry bed

The winged seeds, where they lie cold and low,
Each like a corpse within its grave, until
Thine azure sister of the Spring shall blow

Her clarion[1] o'er the dreaming earth, and fill   10
(Driving sweet buds like flocks to feed in air)
With living hues and odours plain and hill:

Wild Spirit, which art moving everywhere;
Destroyer and Preserver; hear, O hear!

2

Thou on whose stream, mid the steep sky's commotion,   15
Loose clouds like earth's decaying leaves are shed,
Shook from the tangled boughs of heaven and ocean,

Angels of rain and lightning! there are spread
On the blue surface of thine airy surge,
Like the bright hair uplifted from the head   20

Of some fierce Maenad,[2] even from the dim verge
Of the horizon to the zenith's height,
The locks of the approaching storm. Thou dirge

Of the dying year, to which this closing night
Will be the dome of a vast sepulchre,   25
Vaulted with all thy congregated might

Of vapours, from whose solid atmosphere
Black rain, and fire, and hail, will burst: Oh hear!

---

1. Shrill trumpet.   2. Female votary of Bacchus, the Greek god of wine.

3

Thou who didst waken from his summer dreams
The blue Mediterranean, where he lay,
Lulled by the coil of his crystalline streams,   30

Beside a pumice isle in Baiae's bay,
And saw in sleep old palaces and towers
Quivering within the wave's intenser day,

All overgrown with azure moss, and flowers   35
So sweet, the sense faints picturing them! Thou
For whose path the Atlantic's level powers

Cleave themselves into chasms, while far below
The sea-blooms and the oozy woods which wear
The sapless foliage of the ocean, know   40

Thy voice, and suddenly grow grey with fear,
And tremble and despoil themselves: O hear!

4

If I were a dead leaf thou mightest bear;
If I were a swift cloud to fly with thee;
A wave to pant beneath thy power, and share   45

The impulse of thy strength, only less free
Than thou, O uncontrollable! if even
I were as in my boyhood, and could be

The comrade of thy wanderings over heaven,
As then, when to outstrip thy skiey speed   50
Scarce seemed a vision,—I would ne'er have striven

As thus with thee in prayer in my sore need.
Oh lift me as a wave, a leaf, a cloud!
I fall upon the thorns of life! I bleed!

A heavy weight of hours has chained and bowed   55
One too like thee—tameless, and swift, and proud.

5

Make me thy lyre, even as the forest is:
What if my leaves are falling like its own?
The tumult of thy mighty harmonies

Will take from both a deep autumnal tone,   60
Sweet though in sadness. Be thou, Spirit fierce,
My spirit! Be thou me, impetuous one!

Drive my dead thoughts over the universe,
Like withered leaves, to quicken a new birth;
And, by the incantation of this verse,   65

Scatter, as from an unextinguished hearth
Ashes and sparks, my words among mankind!
Be through my lips to unawakened earth

The trumpet of a prophecy! O Wind,
If Winter comes, can Spring be far behind?   70

—1820

To Wordsworth

Poet of Nature, thou hast wept to know
That things depart which never may return:
Childhood and youth, friendship, and love's first glow,
Have fled like sweet dreams, leaving thee to mourn.
These common woes I feel. One loss is mine,   5
Which thou too feel'st, yet I alone deplore.
Thou wert as a lone star whose light did shine
On some frail bark in winter's midnight roar:
Thou hast like to a rock-built refuge stood
Above the blind and battling multitude: 10
In honoured poverty thy voice did weave
Songs consecrate to truth and liberty.
Deserting these, thou leavest me to grieve,
Thus having been, that thou shouldst cease to be.

—1816

from A Defence of Poetry

or Remarks Suggested by an Essay Entitled "The Four Ages of Poetry"[1]

According to one mode of regarding those two classes of mental action which are called reason and imagination, the former may be considered as mind contemplating the relations borne by one thought to another, however produced; and the latter as mind acting upon those thoughts so as to color them with its own light, and composing from them, as from elements, other thoughts, each containing within itself the principle of its own integrity. The one is the τὸ ποιεῖν,[2] or the principle of synthesis, and has for its object those forms which are common to universal nature and existence itself; the other is the τὸ λογίζειν,[3] or principle of analysis, and its action regards the relations of things simply as relations; considering thoughts not in their integral unity, but as the algebraical representations which conduct to certain general results. Reason is the enumeration of quantities already known; imagination is the perception of the value of those quantities, both separately and as a whole. Reason respects the differences, and imagination the similitudes of things. Reason is to imagination as the instrument to the agent, as the body to the spirit, as the shadow to the substance.

Poetry, in a general sense, may be defined to be "the expression of the imagination"; and poetry is connate with the origin of man. Man is an instrument over

---

1. Thomas Love Peacock (1785–1866), "The Four Ages of Poetry" (1820).   2. Making.   3. Reasoning.

which a series of external and internal impressions are driven, like the alternations of an ever-changing wind over an Aeolian lyre,[4] which move it by their motion to ever-changing melody. But there is a principle within the human being (and perhaps within all sentient beings) which acts otherwise than in the lyre, and produces not melody alone, but harmony, by an internal adjustment of the sounds and motions thus excited to the impressions which excite them. It is as if the lyre could accommodate its chords to the motions of that which strikes them, in a determined proportion of sound—even as the musician can accommodate his voice to the sound of the lyre. A child at play by itself will express its delight by its voice and motions, and every inflection of tone and every gesture will bear exact relation to a corresponding antitype in the pleasurable impressions which awakened it. It will be the reflected image of that impression; and as the lyre trembles and sounds after the wind has died away, so the child seeks, by prolonging in its voice and motions the duration of the effect, to prolong also a consciousness of the cause. In relation to the objects which delight a child, these expressions are what poetry is to higher objects.

The savage (for the savage is to ages what the child is to years) expresses the emotions produced in him by surrounding objects in a similar manner; and language and gesture, together with plastic or pictorial imitation, become the image of the combined effect of those objects and his apprehension of them. Man in society, with all his passions and his pleasures, next becomes the object of the passions and pleasures of man; an additional class of emotions produces an augmented treasure of expression; and language, gesture, and the imitative arts become at once the representation and the medium, the pencil and the picture, the chisel and the statue, the chord and the harmony. The social sympathies, or those laws from which, as from its elements, society results, begin to develop themselves from the moment that two human beings coexist; the future is contained within the present as the plant within the seed; and equality, diversity, unity, contrast, mutual dependence, become the principles alone capable of affording the motives according to which the will of a social being is determined to action (inasmuch as he is social), and constitute pleasure in sensation, virtue in sentiment, beauty in art, truth in reasoning, and love in the intercourse of kind. Hence men, even in the infancy of society, observe a certain order in their words and actions distinct from that of the objects and the impressions represented by them, all expression being subject to the laws of that from which it proceeds.

But let us dismiss those more general considerations which might involve an inquiry into the principles of society itself, and restrict our view to the manner in which the imagination is expressed upon its forms.

In the youth of the world, men dance and sing and imitate natural objects, observing in these actions (as in all others) a certain rhythm or order. And, although all men observe a similar, they observe not the same order in the motions of the dance, in the melody of the song, in the combinations of language, in the series of their imitations of natural objects. For there is a certain order or rhythm belonging to each of these classes of mimetic representation, from which the hearer and the spectator receive an intenser and purer pleasure than from any other. The sense of an approximation to this order has been called taste by modern writers. Every man in the infancy of art observes an order which approximates more or less closely to that from which this highest delight results. But the diversity is not sufficiently marked as that its gradations should be sensible,

---

4. Wind harp.

except in those instances where the predominance of this faculty of approximation to the beautiful (for so we may be permitted to name the relation between this highest pleasure and its cause) is very great. Those in whom it exists to excess are poets, in the most universal sense of the word; and the pleasure resulting from the manner in which they express the influence of society or nature upon their own minds, communicates itself to others, and gathers a sort of reduplication from the community. Their language is vitally metaphorical; that is, it marks the before unapprehended relations of things, and perpetuates their apprehension, until words which represent them, become through time signs for portions or classes of thought instead of pictures of integral thoughts; and then, if no new poets should arise to create afresh the associations which have been thus disorganized, language will be dead to all the nobler purposes of human intercourse.

These similitudes or relations are finely said by Lord Bacon to be "the same footsteps of nature impressed upon the various subjects of the world"[5]—and he considers the faculty which perceives them as the storehouse of axioms common to all knowledge. In the infancy of society every author is necessarily a poet, because language itself is poetry; and to be a poet is to apprehend the true and the beautiful, in a word, the good which exists in the relation subsisting, first between existence and perception, and secondly between perception and expression. Every original language near to its source is in itself the chaos of a cyclic poem: the copiousness of lexicography and the distinctions of grammar are the works of a later age, and are merely the catalogue and the form of the creations of poetry.

But Poets, or those who imagine and express this indestructible order, are not only the authors of language and of music, of the dance and architecture and statuary and painting; they are the institutors of laws, and the founders of civil society, and the inventors of the arts of life, and the teachers who draw into a certain propinquity with the beautiful and the true that partial apprehension of the agencies of the invisible world which is called religion. Hence all original religions are allegorical, or susceptible of allegory, and like Janus have a double face of false and true. Poets, according to the circumstances of the age and nation in which they appeared, were called in the earlier epochs of the world, legislators or prophets. A poet essentially comprises and unites both these characters. For he not only beholds intensely the present as it is, and discovers those laws according to which present things ought to be ordered, but he beholds the future in the present, and his thoughts are the germs of the flower and the fruit of latest time. Not that I assert poets to be prophets in the gross sense of the word, or that they can foretell the form as surely as they foreknow the spirit of events; such is the pretence of superstition, which would make poetry an attribute of prophecy, rather than prophecy an attribute of poetry.

A Poet participates in the eternal, the infinite, and the one; as far as relates to his conceptions, time and place and number are not. The grammatical forms which express the moods of time, and the difference of persons and the distinction of place are convertible with respect to the highest poetry without injuring it as poetry and the choruses of Aeschylus,[6] and the Book of Job, and Dante's Paradise[7] would afford, more than any other writings, examples of this fact, if the limits of this essay did not forbid citation. The creations of sculpture, painting, and music, are illustrations still more decisive.

---

5. Francis Bacon (1561–1626), *De Augmentis Scientarium* (1623), 1.3.   6. Aeschylus (525–456 BC), Greek dramatist.
7. Dante Alighieri (1265–1321), Italian poet. *Paradise* is a section of the *Divine Comedy*.

Language, colour, form, and religious and civil habits of action are all the instruments and materials of poetry; they may be called poetry by that figure of speech which considers the effect as a synonym of the cause. But poetry in a more restricted sense expresses those arrangements of language, and especially metrical language, which are created by that imperial faculty whose throne is curtained within the invisible nature of man. And this springs from the nature itself of language, which is a more direct representation of the actions and passions of our internal being, and is susceptible of more various and delicate combinations, than colour, form, or motion, and is more plastic and obedient to the control of that faculty of which it is the creation. For language is arbitrarily produced by the imagination, and has relation to thoughts alone; but all other materials, instruments and conditions of art have relations among each other which limit and interpose between conception and expression. The former is as a mirror which reflects, the latter as a cloud which enfeebles, the light of which both are mediums of communication. Hence the fame of sculptors, painters and musicians (although the intrinsic powers of the great masters of these arts may yield in no degree to that of those who have employed language as the hieroglyphic of their thoughts) has never equalled that of poets in the restricted sense of the term, as two performers of equal skill will produce unequal effects from a guitar and a harp. The fame of legislators and founders of religions (so long as their institutions last) alone seems to exceed that of poets in the restricted sense; but it can scarcely be a question whether, if we deduct the celebrity which their flattery of the gross opinions of the vulgar usually conciliates, together with that which belonged to them in their higher character of poets, any excess will remain. . . .

Poetry is ever accompanied with pleasure: all spirits on which it falls open themselves to receive the wisdom which is mingled with its delight. In the infancy of the world, neither poets themselves nor their auditors are fully aware of the excellence of poetry: for it acts in a divine and unapprehended manner, beyond and above consciousness; and it is reserved for future generations to contemplate and measure the mighty cause and effect in all the strength and splendor of their union. Even in modern times, no living poet ever arrived at the fulness of his fame; the jury which sits in judgment upon a poet, belonging as he does to all time, must be composed of his peers: it must be impanelled by Time from the selectest of the wise of many generations. A poet is a nightingale, who sits in darkness and sings to cheer its own solitude with sweet sounds; his auditors are as men entranced by the melody of an unseen musician, who feel that they are moved and softened, yet know not whence or why. . . . [A] poet considers the vices of his contemporaries as the temporary dress in which his creations must be arrayed, and which cover without concealing the eternal proportions of their beauty. An epic or dramatic personage is understood to wear them around his soul, as he may the [ancient] armor or the modern uniform around his body; whilst it is easy to conceive a dress more graceful than either. The beauty of the internal nature cannot be so far concealed by its accidental vesture, but that the spirit of its form shall communicate itself to the very disguise, and indicate the shape it hides from the manner in which it is worn. A majestic form and graceful motions will express themselves through the most barbarous and tasteless costume. Few poets of the highest class have chosen to exhibit the beauty of their conceptions in its naked truth and splendor; and it is doubtful whether the alloy of costume, habit, etc., be not necessary to temper this planetary music for mortal ears.

The whole objection however of the immorality of poetry rests upon a misconception of the manner in which poetry acts to produce the moral improvement of man. Ethical science arranges the elements which poetry has created, and propounds schemes and proposes examples of civil and domestic life. Nor is it for want of admirable doctrines that men hate, and despise, and censure, and deceive, and subjugate one another. But poetry acts in another and diviner manner. It awakens and enlarges the mind itself by rendering it the receptacle of a thousand unapprehended combinations of thought. Poetry lifts the veil from the hidden beauty of the world, and makes familiar objects be as if they were not familiar; it re-produces all that it represents, and the impersonations clothed in its Elysian[8] light stand thenceforward in the minds of those who have once contemplated them as memorials of that gentle and exalted content which extends itself over all thoughts and actions with which it co-exists. The great secret of morals is love, or a going out of our own nature, and an identification of ourselves with the beautiful which exists in thought, action, or person, not our own. A man, to be greatly good, must imagine intensely and comprehensively; he must put himself in the place of another and of many others; the pains and pleasures of his species must become his own. The great instrument of moral good is the imagination; and poetry administers to the effect by acting upon the cause.

Poetry enlarges the circumference of the imagination by replenishing it with thoughts of ever new delight, which have the power of attracting and assimilating to their own nature all other thoughts, and which form new intervals and interstices whose void forever craves fresh food. Poetry strengthens the faculty which is the organ of the moral nature of man, in the same manner as exercise strengthens a limb. A poet therefore would do ill to embody his own conceptions of right and wrong (which are usually those of his place and time) in his poetical creations (which participate in neither). By this assumption of the inferior office of interpreting the effect, in which perhaps after all he might acquit himself but imperfectly, he would resign a glory in the participation of the cause. There was little danger that Homer, or any of the eternal poets, should have so far misunderstood themselves as to have abdicated this throne of their widest dominion. Those in whom the poetical faculty, though great, is less intense (as Euripides, Lucan, Tasso, Spenser)[9] have frequently affected a moral aim, and the effect of their poetry is diminished in exact proportion to the degree in which they compel us to advert to this purpose. . . .

We have more moral, political and historical wisdom than we know how to reduce into practice; we have more scientific and economical knowledge than can be accommodated to the just distribution of the produce which it multiplies. The poetry in these systems of thought is concealed by the accumulation of facts and calculating processes. There is no want of knowledge respecting what is wisest and best in morals, government, and political economy, or at least what is wiser and better than what men now practise and endure. But we let "I dare not wait upon I would, like the poor cat i' the adage."[10] We want the creative faculty to imagine that which we know; we want the generous impulse to act that which we imagine; we want the poetry of life: our calculations have outrun conception; we have eaten more than we can digest. The cultivation of those sciences which have enlarged the limits of the empire of man over the external world, has, for want of the poetical faculty, proportionally circumscribed those of the internal world; and man, having enslaved the elements,

---

8. Elysium, mythical home of the blessed after death.   9. Euripides (480–406 BC), Greek playwright; Marcus Annaeus Lucanus (39–65), Roman poet; Torquato Tasso (1544–1595), Italian poet; Edmund Spenser (1552–1599), English poet.
10. William Shakespeare, *Macbeth*, 1.7.44–45.

remains himself a slave. To what but a cultivation of the mechanical arts in a degree disproportioned to the presence of the creative faculty (which is the basis of all knowledge) is to be attributed the abuse of all invention for abridging and combining labour, to the exasperation of the inequality of mankind? From what other cause has it arisen that these inventions, which should have lightened, have added a weight to the curse imposed on Adam? Poetry, and the principle of Self (of which money is the visible incarnation) are the God and Mammon[11] of the world.

The functions of the poetical faculty are twofold: by one it creates new materials of knowledge and power and pleasure; by the other it engenders in the mind a desire to reproduce and arrange them according to a certain rhythm and order which may be called the beautiful and the good. The cultivation of poetry is never more to be desired than in periods when, from an excess of the selfish and calculating principle, the accumulation of the materials of external life exceed the quantity of the power of assimilating them to the internal laws of human nature. The body has then become too unwieldy for that which animates it.

Poetry is indeed something divine. It is at once the centre and circumference of knowledge; it is that which comprehends all science, and that to which all science must be referred. It is at the same time the root and blossom of all other systems of thought. It is that from which all spring, and that which adorns all; and that which, if blighted, denies the fruit and the seed, and withholds from the barren world the nourishment and the succession of the scions of the tree of life. It is the perfect and consummate surface and bloom of all things; it is as the odour and the colour of the rose to the texture of the elements which compose it, as the form and splendour of unfaded beauty to the secrets of anatomy and corruption. What were Virtue, Love, Patriotism, Friendship, etc.,—what were the scenery of this beautiful Universe which we inhabit; what were our consolations on this side of the grave,—and what were our aspirations beyond it,—if Poetry did not ascend to bring light and fire from those eternal regions where the owl-winged faculty of calculation dare not ever soar? Poetry is not like reasoning, a power to be exerted according to the determination of the will. A man cannot say, "I will compose poetry." The greatest poet even cannot say it: for the mind in creation is as a fading coal which some invisible influence, like an inconstant wind, awakens to transitory brightness. This power arises from within, like the colour of a flower which fades and changes as it is developed, and the conscious portions of our natures are unprophetic either of its approach or its departure. Could this influence be durable in its original purity and force, it is impossible to predict the greatness of the results; but when composition begins, inspiration is already on the decline, and the most glorious poetry that has ever been communicated to the world is probably a feeble shadow of the original conceptions of the poet. I appeal to the greatest poets of the present day whether it is not an error to assert that the finest passages of poetry are produced by labour and study. The toil and the delay recommended by critics can be justly interpreted to mean no more than a careful observation of the inspired moments, and an artificial connection of the spaces between their suggestions by the intertexture of conventional expressions—a necessity only imposed by a limitedness of the poetical faculty itself. For Milton conceived the Paradise Lost as a whole before he executed it in portions. We have his own authority also for the muse having "dictated" to him the "unpremeditated song."[12] And let this be an answer to

---

11. A false idol of money.   12. John Milton (1608–1674), *Paradise Lost* (1667), 9.21–24.

those who would allege the fifty-six various readings of the first line of the Orlando Furioso. Compositions so produced are to poetry what mosaic is to painting. The instinct and intuition of the poetical faculty is still more observable in the plastic and pictorial arts: a great statue or picture grows under the power of the artist as a child in the mother's womb, and the very mind which directs the hands in formation is incapable of accounting to itself for the origin, the gradations, or the media of the process.

Poetry is the record of the best and happiest moments of the happiest and best minds. We are aware of evanescent visitations of thought and feeling sometimes associated with place or person, sometimes regarding our own mind alone, and always arising unforeseen and departing unbidden, but elevating and delightful beyond all expression; so that even in the desire and the regret they leave, there cannot but be pleasure, participating as it does in the nature of its object. It is, as it were, the interpenetration of a diviner nature through our own, but its footsteps are like those of a wind over a sea, which the morning calm erases, and whose traces remain only as on the wrinkled sand which paves it. These and corresponding conditions of being are experienced principally by those of the most delicate sensibility and the most enlarged imagination; and the state of mind produced by them is at war with every base desire. The enthusiasm of virtue, love, patriotism, and friendship is essentially linked with emotions; and whilst they last, self appears as what it is, an atom to a Universe. Poets are not only subject to these experiences as spirits of the most refined organization, but they can colour all that they combine with the evanescent hues of this etherial world; a word or a trait in the representation of a scene or a passion will touch the enchanted chord, and reanimate, in those who have ever experienced these emotions, the sleeping, the cold, the buried image of the past. Poetry thus makes immortal all that is best and most beautiful in the world; it arrests the vanishing apparitions which haunt the interlunations of life, and veiling them, or in language or in form, sends them forth among mankind, bearing sweet news of kindred joy to those with whom their sisters abide—abide, because there is no portal of expression from the caverns of the spirit which they inhabit into the universe of things. Poetry redeems from decay the visitations of the divinity in man.

Poetry turns all things to loveliness: it exalts the beauty of that which is most beautiful, and it adds beauty to that which is most deformed; it marries exultation and horror, grief and pleasure, eternity and change; it subdues to union under its light yoke all irreconcilable things. It transmutes all that it touches, and every form moving within the radiance of its presence is changed by wondrous sympathy to an incarnation of the spirit which it breathes; its secret alchemy turns to potable gold the poisonous waters which flow from death through life; it strips the veil of familiarity from the world, and lays bare the naked and sleeping beauty which is the spirit of its forms.

All things exist as they are perceived: at least in relation to the percipient. "The mind is its own place, and of itself can make a heaven of hell, a hell of heaven."[13] But poetry defeats the curse which binds us to be subjected to the accident of surrounding impressions. And whether it spreads its own figured curtain or withdraws life's dark veil from before the scene of things, it equally creates for us a being within our being. It makes us the inhabitant of a world to which the familiar world is a chaos. It reproduces the common universe of which we are portions and percipients, and it purges from our inward sight the film of familiarity which obscures from us the wonder of our

---

13. *Paradise Lost*, 1.254–255.

being. It compels us to feel that which we perceive, and to imagine that which we know. It creates anew the universe after it has been annihilated in our minds by the recurrence of impressions blunted by reiteration. It justifies that bold and true word of Tasso: *Non merita nome di creatore, se non Iddio ed il Poeta.*[14]

A Poet, as he is the author to others of the highest wisdom, pleasure, virtue, and glory, so he ought personally to be the happiest, the best, the wisest, and the most illustrious of men. As to his glory, let time be challenged to declare whether the fame of any other institutor of human life be comparable to that of a poet. That he is the wisest, the happiest, and the best, inasmuch as he is a poet, is equally incontrovertible: the greatest poets have been men of the most spotless virtue, of the most consummate prudence, and (if we would look into the interior of their lives) the most fortunate of men. And the exceptions, as they regard those who possessed the poetic faculty in a high yet inferior degree, will be found on consideration to confirm rather than destroy the rule. Let us for a moment stoop to the arbitration of popular breath, and usurping and uniting in our own persons the incompatible characters of accuser, witness, judge and executioner, let us decide without trial, testimony, or form, that certain motives of those who are "there sitting where we dare not soar," are reprehensible. Let us assume that Homer was a drunkard, that Virgil was a flatterer, that Horace was a coward, that Tasso was a madman, that Lord Bacon was a peculator, that Raphael was a libertine, that Spenser was a Poet Laureate. It is inconsistent with this division of our subject to cite living poets, but posterity has done ample justice to the great names now referred to. Their errors have been weighed and found to have been dust in the balance; if their sins "were as scarlet, they are now white as snow"[15]; they have been washed in the blood of the mediator and redeemer, Time. Observe in what a ludicrous chaos the imputations of real or fictitious crime have been confused in the contemporary calumnies against poetry and poets; consider how little is as it appears—or appears as it is; look to your own motives, and judge not, lest ye be judged.

Poetry, as has been said, differs in this respect from logic: that it is not subject to the controul of the active power of the mind, and that its birth and recurrence has no necessary connection with the consciousness or will. It is presumptuous to determine that these are the necessary conditions of all mental causation, when mental effects are experienced insusceptible of being referred to them. The frequent recurrence of the poetical power, it is obvious to suppose, may produce in the mind a habit of order and harmony correlative with its own nature and with its effects upon other minds. But in the intervals of inspiration (and they may be frequent without being durable) a poet becomes a man, and is abandoned to the sudden reflux of the influences under which others habitually live. But as he is more delicately organized than other men, and sensible to pain and pleasure (both his own and that of others), in a degree unknown to them, he will avoid the one and pursue the other with an ardor proportioned to this difference. And he renders himself obnoxious to calumny, when he neglects to observe the circumstances under which these objects of universal pursuit and flight have disguised themselves in one another's garments.

But there is nothing necessarily evil in this error, and thus cruelty, envy, revenge, avarice, and the passions purely evil, have never formed any portion of the popular imputations on the lives of poets.

---

14. "No one merits the name of Creator except God and the Poet."   15. Isaiah 1.18.

I have thought it most favourable to the cause of truth to set down these remarks according to the order in which they were suggested to my mind by a consideration of the subject itself, instead of following that of the treatise that excited me to make them public. Thus although devoid of the formality of a polemical reply, if the views which they contain be just, they will be found to involve a refutation of the doctrines of "The Four Ages of Poetry" so far at least as regards the first division of the subject. I can readily conjecture what should have moved the gall of the learned and intelligent author of that paper. . . .

The first part of these remarks has related to poetry in its elements and principles; and it has been shown, as well as the narrow limits assigned them would permit, that what is called poetry in a restricted sense has a common source with all other forms of order and of beauty according to which the materials of human life are susceptible of being arranged, and which is poetry in a universal sense.

The second part will have for its object an application of these principles to the present state of the cultivation of poetry, and a defense of the attempt to idealize the modern forms of manners and opinions, and compel them into a subordination to the imaginative and creative faculty. For the literature of England, an energetic development of which has ever preceded or accompanied a great and free development of the national will, has arisen, as it were, from a new birth. In spite of the low-thoughted envy which would undervalue contemporary merit, our own will be a memorable age in intellectual achievements, and we live among such philosophers and poets as surpass beyond comparison any who have appeared since the last national struggle for civil and religious liberty. The most unfailing herald, companion, and follower of the awakening of a great people to work a beneficial change in opinion or institution, is poetry. At such periods there is an accumulation of the power of communicating and receiving intense and impassioned conceptions respecting man and nature. The persons in whom this power resides may often (as far as regards many portions of their nature) have little apparent correspondence with that spirit of good of which they are the ministers. But even whilst they deny and abjure, they are yet compelled to serve the power which is seated on the throne of their own soul. It is impossible to read the compositions of the most celebrated writers of the present day without being startled with the electric life which burns within their words. They measure the circumference and sound the depths of human nature with a comprehensive and all-penetrating spirit, and they are themselves perhaps the most sincerely astonished at its manifestations, for it is less their spirit than the spirit of the age. Poets are the hierophants of an unapprehended inspiration, the mirrors of the gigantic shadows which futurity casts upon the present, the words which express what they understand not; the trumpets which sing to battle, and feel not what they inspire; the influence which is moved not, but moves. Poets are the unacknowledged legislators of the world.

—1840

Contemporary Response
Christopher Pearse Cranch
1813–1892

Christopher Pearse Cranch's elegy in the Transcendentalist magazine *The Dial* consoles Percy Bysshe Shelley's readers by noting that the harvest of his lines of poetry is eternal. Cranch not only bestows immortality on Shelley's verse but also intimates the possibility of a heavenly resting place for the poet's spirit by envisioning the flames from his funeral pyre rising to heaven. Although it is euphemistically phrased, the poem is quite radical and bold: It hints that the poet deemed a heretic and atheist could be among the elect. Like Shelley, Cranch had studied the poetry of Greece and aspired to Shelley's success and mastery of poetic forms. Cranch was, like Ralph Waldo Emerson, a student of Harvard Divinity School who resigned his position as a clergyman. He wrote for the *Western Messenger* for years before returning to Boston to focus on painting, music, and poetry. After publishing verses in the *Messenger* and *The Dial*, he published a book of them, *The Bird and the Bell with Other Poems*, in 1875.

The Death of Shelley[1]

Fair was the morn,—a little bark bent
Like a gull o'er the waters blue,
And the mariners sang in their merriment,
For Shelley the faithful and true,
  Shelley was bound on his voyage o'er the sea,   5
  And wherever he sailed the heart beat free.

And a dark cloud flew, and the white waves hurled
The crests in their wrath, at the angry wind,
The little bark with its sails unfurled,
While the dreadful tempest gathered behind,—   10
  With the book of Plato pressed to his heart,
  Came to the beach Shelley's mortal part,

Then a pyre they kindled by ocean side,
Poets were they who Shelley did burn,
The beautiful flame to Heaven applied,   15
The ashes were pressed in the marble urn,
  In Rome shall those ashes long remain,
  And from Shelley's verse spring golden grain.

—1844

Felicia Dorothea Hemans
1793–1835

Felicia Dorothea Browne was born in Liverpool, England, and raised in Wales. She was a precocious child, learning Latin and modern languages at a young age, reading Shakespeare avidly by her sixth year, and memorizing the works of many poets after reading them only once. It was not long before she was writing as well, mainly to help with finances after her father left the family and emigrated to Quebec. By her fourteenth year, she had already published *Poems*

---

1. Percy Bysshe Shelley drowned when his schooner, *Ariel*, sank off Italy on July 8, 1822.

(1808), the subscribers to the book supplying her family with much-needed income. The book gained the attention of Percy Bysshe Shelley, who attempted to initiate a correspondence with her, but his interest was not reciprocated. Among the other readers was Anna Laetitia Barbauld, who praised the book in the *Monthly Review*, noting, however, that "if the youthful author were to content herself for some years with reading instead of writing, we should open any future work from her pen with an expectation of pleasure." Instead of waiting to publish again, a second book also came out in 1808: *England and Spain; or, Valour and Patriotism.* In 1812, Browne published *The Domestic Affections and Other Poems* before marrying Captain Alfred Hemans. Sadly, the title of this work was not descriptive of her married life; citing domestic "incompatibility," the Captain sailed to Italy in 1819 and never returned to his wife and their five children. Perhaps he was unable to understand and support his wife's refusal to be bound by discriminatory gender roles and to let her domestic "duties" halt her literary productions and aspirations. Among comments about the marriage attributed to Captain Hemans is that "it was the curse of having a literary wife that he could never get a pair of stockings mended." Gendered expectations also affected the reception of her poetry. Some critics saw her as a poet of domesticity, while others read a more radical message in her many poems of male abandonment and female resolve and courage. Many male critics of the day failed to pick up on her critiques of husbands' gender roles and the ways in which they can be destructive to family happiness.

Her own resolution to pursue her literary dreams remained firm throughout her marriage. During the years they lived together and in the years immediately following, she wrote and published four more volumes of poetry, securing an income for herself and her five sons and plotting an inexorable course toward the international fame she would later enjoy. By 1825, the first edition of her poems was printed in the United States, where her poems were widely read and set to music, her popularity and sales far exceeding any of her British or American contemporaries. Indeed one of the most popular American poets of the day, Lydia Huntley Sigourney, was honored to be referred to as "the American Hemans." At the height of her American fame, Hemans was offered $1,500 a year merely to be listed as an editor of a magazine, without being required to fulfill any editorial duties. Among the many works she published to achieve eminence at home and abroad were countless articles and essays as well as the following books: *Tales and Historic Scenes in Verse* (1819), *Stanzas to the Memory of the Late King* (1820), *Welsh Melodies* (1822), *The Forest Sanctuary* (1826), *Records of Woman* (1828), *Lays of Many Lands* (1830), and *Songs of the Affections* (1830). Toward the end of this prolific period, she was dealt a tragic blow. In 1827, her mother passed away, and the emotional trauma of this event is believed to have contributed to Hemans's own failing health. Still publishing, she struggled to fight the tuberculosis that took her life in only her forty-first year.

England's Dead

Son of the Ocean Isle!
Where sleep your mighty dead?
Show me what high and stately pile
    Is reared o'er Glory's bed.

Go, stranger! track the deep—   5
Free, free the white sail spread!
Wave may not foam, nor wild wind sweep,
    Where rest not England's dead.

On Egypt's burning plains,
    By the pyramid o'erswayed,   10
With fearful power the noonday reigns,
    And the palm trees yield no shade;—

But let the angry sun
From heaven look fiercely red,
Unfelt by those whose task is done!—
   There slumber England's dead.

The hurricane hath might
Along the Indian shore,
And far by Ganges'[1] banks at night
   Is heard the tiger's roar;—

But let the sound roll on!
It hath no tone of dread
For those that from their toils are gone,—
   There slumber England's dead.

Loud rush the torrent floods
The Western wilds among,
And free, in green Columbia's woods,
   The hunter's bow is strung;—

But let the floods rush on!
Let the arrow's flight be sped!
Why should *they* reck whose task is done?—
   There slumber England's dead.

The mountain storms rise high
In the snowy Pyrenees,[2]
And toss the pine boughs through the sky
   Like rose leaves on the breeze;—

But let the storm rage on!
Let the fresh wreaths be shed!
For the Roncesvalles'[3] field is won,—
   There slumber England's dead.

On the frozen deep's repose
'Tis a dark and dreadful hour,
When round the ship the ice fields close,
   And the northern night clouds lower;—

But let the ice drift on!
Let the cold blue desert spread!
Their course with mast and flag is done,—
   Even there sleep England's dead.

The warlike of the isles,
The men of field and wave!
Are not the rocks their funeral piles,
   The seas and shores their grave?

15

20

25

30

35

40

45

50

---

1. Holy river in India.   2. Mountains on the border between France and Spain.   3. A pass in the Pyrenees.

Go, stranger! track the deep—
Free, free the white sail spread!
Wave may not foam, nor wild wind sweep,   55
    Where rest not England's dead.

—1822

Song of Emigration

There was heard a song on the chiming sea,
A mingled breathing of grief and glee;
Man's voice, unbroken by sighs, was there,
Filling with triumph the sunny air;
Of fresh, green lands, and of pastures new,   5
It sang, while the bark through the surges flew.

    But ever and anon
      A murmur of farewell
    Told, by its plaintive tone,
      That from woman's lip it fell.   10

"Away, away o'er the foaming main!"
This was the free and the joyous strain,
"There are clearer skies than ours, afar,
We will shape our course by a brighter star;
There are plains whose verdure[1] no foot hath pressed,   15
And whose wealth is all for the first brave guest."

    "But, alas! that we should go,"
      Sang the farewell voices then,
    "From the homesteads, warm and low,
      By the brook and in the glen!"   20

"We will rear new homes under trees that glow
As if gems were the fruitage of every bough;
O'er our white walls we will train the vine,
And sit in its shadow at day's decline;
And watch our herds, as they range at will   25
Through the green savannas, all bright and still.

    "But woe for that sweet shade
      Of the flowering orchard trees,
    Where first our children played
      'Midst the birds and honey bees!   30

"All, all our own shall the forests be,
As to the bound of the roebuck free!
None shall say, 'Hither, no farther pass!'

---

1. Green vegetation.

We will track each step through the wavy grass,
We will chase the elk in his speed and might,   35
And bring proud spoils to the hearth at night."

   "But O, the gray church tower,
     And the sound of Sabbath bell,
   And the sheltered garden bower,
     We have bid them all farewell!   40

"We will give the names of our fearless race
To each bright river whose course we trace;
We will leave our memory with mounts and floods,
And the path of our daring in boundless woods;
And our works unto many a lake's green shore,   45
Where the Indians' graves lay, alone, before."

   "But who shall teach the flowers,
     Which our children loved, to dwell
   In a soil that is not ours?
     Home, home and friends, farewell!"   50

—1827

Burial of an Emigrant's Child in the Forests

SCENE.—*The banks of a solitary river in an American forest. A tent under pine trees in the foreground.* AGNES *sitting before the tent with a child in her arms apparently sleeping.*

  Agnes. Surely 'tis all a dream—a fever dream!
The desolation and the agony—
The strange, red sunrise, and the gloomy woods,
So terrible with their dark giant boughs,
And the broad, lonely river!—all a dream!   5
And my boy's voice will wake me, with its clear,
Wild singing tones, as they were wont to come
Through the wreathed sweetbrier at my lattice panes
In happy, happy England! Speak to me!
Speak to thy mother, bright one! she hath watch'd   10
All the dread night beside thee, till her brain
Is darken'd by swift waves of fantasies,
And her soul faint with longing for thy voice.
O, I *must* wake him with one gentle kiss
On his fair brow!   15
        (*Shudderingly.*)
The strange, damp, thrilling touch!
The marble chill! Now, now it rushes back—
Now I know all!—dead—*dead!*—a fearful word!
My boy hath left me in the wilderness,
To journey on without the blessèd light   20
In his deep, loving eyes. He's gone!—he's gone!

Her HUSBAND *enters.*

Husband. Agnes! my Agnes! hast thou look'd thy last
On our sweet slumberer's face? The hour is come—
The couch made ready for his last repose.

    Agnes. Not yet! thou canst not take him from me yet!   25
If he but left me for a few short days,
This were too brief a gazing time to draw
His angel image into my fond heart,
And fix its beauty there. And now—Oh! *now,*
Never again the laughter of his eye   30
Shall send its gladd'ning summer through my soul—
Never on earth again. Yet, yet delay!
Thou canst not take him from me.

    Husband. My beloved!
Is it not God hath taken him? the God   35
That took our first born, o'er whose early grave
Thou didst bow down thy saint-like head, and say,
"His will be done!"

    Agnes. Oh! that near household grave,
Under the turf of England, seemed not half—   40
Not half so much to part me from my child
As these dark woods. It lay beside our home,
And I could watch the sunshine, through all hours,
Loving and clinging to the grassy spot;
And I could dress its greensward with fresh flowers—   45
Familiar meadow flowers. O'er *thee,* my babe!
The primrose will not blossom! Oh! that now,
Together, by thy fair young sister's side,
We lay 'midst England's valleys!

    Husband. Dost thou grieve,   50
Agnes! that thou hast followed o'er the deep
An exile's fortunes? If it *thus* can be,
Then, after many a conflict cheerily met,
My spirit sinks at last.

    Agnes. Forgive! forgive!   55
My Edmund, pardon me! Oh! grief is wild—
Forget its words, quick spraydrops from a fount
Of unknown bitterness! Thou art my home!
Mine only and my blessèd one! Where'er
Thy warm heart beats in its true nobleness,   60
There is my country! *there* my head shall rest,
And throb no more. Oh! still, by thy strong love,
Bear up the feeble reed!
     (Kneeling with the child in her arms.)
              And thou, my God!
Hear my soul's cry from this dread wilderness!

Oh! hear, and pardon me! If I have made   65
This treasure, sent from thee, too much the ark
Fraught with mine earthward-clinging happiness,
Forgetting Him who gave, and might resume,
Oh! pardon me!
            If nature hath rebell'd,
And from thy light turn'd wilfully away,   70
Making a midnight of her agony,
When the despairing passion of her clasp
Was from its idol stricken at one touch
Of thine almighty hand—Oh, pardon me!
By thy Son's anguish, pardon! In the soul   75
The tempests and the waves will know thy voice—
Father! say, "Peace, be still"
    (*Giving the child to her husband.*)
                    Farewell, my babe!
Go from my bosom now to other rest!
With this last kiss on thine unsullied brow,
And on thy pale, calm cheek these contrite tears,   80
I yield thee to thy Maker!
    Husband. Now, my wife!
Thine own meek holiness beams forth once more
A light upon my path. Now shall I bear,
From thy dear arms, the slumberer to repose—   85
With a calm, trustful heart.
    Agnes. My Edmund! where—
Where wilt thou lay him?
    Husband. See'st thou where the spire
Of yon dark cypress reddens in the sun   90
To burning gold?—there—o'er yon willow-tuft?
Under that native desert monument
Lies his lone bed. Our Hubert, since the dawn,
With the gray mosses of the wilderness
Hath lined it closely through; and there breathed forth,   95
E'en from the fulness of his own pure heart,
A wild, sad forest hymn—a song of tears,
Which thou wilt learn to love. I heard the boy
Chanting it o'er his solitary task,
As wails a wood bird to the thrilling leaves,   100
Perchance unconsciously.
    Agnes. My gentle son!
The affectionate, the gifted! With what joy—
Edmund, rememberest thou?—with what bright joy
His baby brother ever to his arms   105
Would spring from rosy sleep, and playfully
Hide the rich clusters of his gleaming hair
In that kind, useful breast! Oh! now no more!

But strengthen me, my God! and melt my heart,
Even to a well-spring of adoring tears,   110
For many a blessing left.
                    (*Bending over the child.*)
Once more, farewell!
Oh! the pale, piercing sweetness of that look!
How can it be sustained? Away, away!
          (*After a short pause.*)
Edmund! my woman's nature still is weak—   115
I cannot see thee render dust to dust!
Go thou, my husband! to thy solemn task;
I will rest here, and still my soul with prayer
Till thy return.
          Husband. Then strength be with thy prayer!   120
Peace on thy bosom! Faith and heavenly hope
Unto thy spirit! Fare thee well a while!
We must be pilgrims of the woods again,
After this mournful hour.

(*He goes out with the child.*—AGNES *kneels in prayer.—*
After a time, voices without are heard singing.)

                                                          —1833

The Indian with His Dead Child[1]

In the silence of the midnight
   I journey with my dead;
In the darkness of the forest boughs
   A lonely path I tread.

But my heart is high and fearless,   5
   As by mighty wings upborne;
The mountain eagle hath no plumes
   So strong as love and scorn.

I have raised thee from the grave-sod,
   By the white man's path defiled;   10
On to th' ancestral wilderness
   I bear thy dust, my child!

I have ask'd the ancient deserts
   To give my dead a place
Where the stately footsteps of the free   15
   Alone should leave a trace.

---

1. [Hemans' note] An Indian, who had established himself in a township of Maine, feeling indignantly the want of sympathy evinced towards him by the white inhabitants, particularly on the death of his only child, gave up his farm soon afterwards, dug up the body of his child, and carried it with him two hundred miles through the forests to join the Canadian Indians.—See *Tudor's Letters on the Eastern States of America.*

And the tossing pines made answer—
   "Go, bring us back thine own!"
And the streams from all the hunters' hills
   Rush'd with an echoing tone.   20

Thou shalt rest by sounding waters
   That yet untamed may roll;
The voices of that chainless host
   With joy shall fill thy soul.

In the silence of the midnight   25
   I journey with the dead,
Where the arrows of my father's bow
   Their falcon flight have sped.

I have left the spoiler's dwellings
   For evermore behind: 30
Unmingled with their household sounds
   For me shall sweep the wind.

Alone, amidst their hearth-fires,
   I watched my child's decay,
Uncheer'd I saw the spirit-light   35
   From his young eyes fade away.

When his head sank on my bosom,
   When the death-sleep o'er him fell,
Was there one to say, "A friend is near!"
   There was none!—pale race, farewell!   40

To the forests, to the cedars,
   To the warrior and his bow,
Back, back!—I bore thee laughing thence,
   I bear thee slumbering now!

I bear thee unto burial   45
   With the mighty hunters gone;
I shall hear thee in the forest breeze,
   Thou wilt speak of joy, my son!

In the silence of the midnight
   I journey with the dead;   50
But my heart is strong, my step is fleet,
   My fathers' path I tread.

—1829

The American Forest Girl

"A fearful gift upon thy heart is laid,
Woman!—A power to suffer and to love;
Therefore thou so canst pity."

Wildly and mournfully the Indian drum
  On the deep hush of moonlight forests broke—
"Sing us a death-song, for thine hour is come."—
  So the red warriors to their captive spoke.
Still, and amidst those dusky forms alone,   5
  A youth, a fair-hair'd youth of England stood,
Like a king's son; though from his cheek had flown
  The mantling crimson of the island blood,
And his press'd lips look'd marble. Fiercely bright
And high around him blazed the fires of night,   10
Rocking beneath the cedars to and fro,
As the wind pass'd, and with a fitful glow
Lighting the victim's face: but who could tell
Of what within his secret heart befell,
Known but to heaven that hour? Perchance a thought   15
Of his far home then so intensely wrought,
That its full image, pictured to his eye
On the dark ground of mortal agony,
Rose clear as day!—and he might *see* the band
Of his young sisters wandering hand in hand   20
Where the laburnums[1] drooped; or haply binding
The jasmine up the door's low pillars winding;
Or, as day closed upon their gentle mirth,
Gathering, with braided hair, around the hearth,
Where sat their mother; and that mother's face   25
Its grave sweet smile yet wearing in the place
Where so it ever smiled! Perchance the prayer
Learned at her knee came back on his despair;
The blessing from her voice, the very tone
Of her "*Good-night!*" might breathe from boyhood gone   30
—He started and look'd up: thick cypress boughs,
  Full of strange sound, waved o'er him, darkly red
In the broad stormy firelight; savage brows,
  With tall plumes crested and wild hues o'erspread,
Girt him like feverish phantoms; and pale stars   35
Look'd through the branches as through dungeon bars,
Shedding no hope. He knew, he felt his doom—
Oh! what a tale to shadow with its gloom
That happy hall in England! Idle fear!
Would the winds tell it? who might dream or hear   40

---

1. Small poisonous trees.

The secret of the forests?—to the stake
   They bound him; and that proud young soldier strove
His father's spirit in his breast to wake,
   Trusting to die in silence! He, the love
Of many hearts!—the fondly rear'd—the fair,   45
Gladdening all eyes to see! And fetter'd there
He stood beside his death-pyre, and the brand
Flamed up to light in the chieftain's hand.
He thought upon his God.—Hush! hark! a cry
Breaks on the stern and dread solemnity—   50
A step hath pierced the ring!—Who dares intrude
On the dark hunters in their vengeful mood?—
A girl—a young slight girl—a fawn-like child
Of green savannas and the leafy wild,
Springing unmark'd till then, as some lone flower,   55
Happy because the sunshine is its dower;
Yet, one that knew how early tears are shed,
For *hers* had mourn'd a playmate brother dead.

She had sat gazing on the victim long,
Until the pity of her soul grew strong;   60
And, by its passion's deepening fervor sway'd,
Even to the stake she rush'd, and gently laid
His bright head on her bosom, and around
His form her slender arms to shield it wound
Like close Liannes[2]; then raised her glittering eye,   65
And clear-toned voice, then said, "He shall not die!"
"He shall not die!"—the gloomy forest thrilled
   To that sweet sound. A sudden wonder fell
On the fierce throng; and heart and hand were still'd,
   Struck down as by the whisper of a spell.   70
They gazed—their dark souls bow'd before the maid,
She of the dancing step in wood and glade!
And, as her cheek flush'd through its olive hue,
As her black tresses to the night-wind flew,
Something o'ermaster'd them from that young mien—   75
Something of heaven in silence felt and seen;
And seeming, to their childlike faith, a token
That the Great Spirit by her voice had spoken.

They loosed the bonds that held their captive's breath;
From his pale lips they took the cup of death;   80
They quench'd the brand beneath the cypress tree:
"Away," they cried, "young stranger, thou art free!"

                              —1826

---

2. Woody vines.

William Cullen Bryant
1794–1878

Descended from Puritan settlers of Massachusetts, William Cullen Bryant was born in the western part of the state in 1794. His childhood was spent adventuring in the forests and streams of his native state, and this play would later develop into a deep appreciation of nature in his poetry. During the cold New England winters, he sought refuge in the library of his father, Dr. Peter Bryant. A physician by trade, it would seem that Dr. Bryant intended his son to follow in his footsteps: He named the boy after the famous Scottish physician William Cullen. But Dr. Bryant was a poet, too, and an avid reader and collector of eighteenth- and early nineteenth-century literature. This would be the lead his son would follow, availing himself of his father's seven hundred books and steeping himself in the verses of the neoclassical poet Alexander Pope. From his father and Pope, Bryant learned the art of political verse satire, and the boy's first published poem, an attack on Thomas Jefferson entitled *The Embargo* (1808), garnered enough readership to support a second printing in 1809. The spirituality and precise detail that would characterize his later verse are due to the influence of his mother, Sarah Snell Bryant, who kept a diary and instilled in her son an appreciation of letters, literally, by teaching him the alphabet when he was eighteen months old and by encouraging his literary and spiritual growth.

Bryant's next lesson in poetry would not come until after he had attended college at Williams and embarked upon a short-lived career as a lawyer; it would come from an English writer who, like him, had spent his childhood roaming through nature as well as reading and writing poetry. In the verses of William Wordsworth, Bryant found the spiritual, the natural, and the political blended thoroughly. Bryant first read Wordsworth in 1810, when his father purchased the 1802 Philadelphia edition of Wordsworth and Samuel Taylor Coleridge's *Lyrical Ballads* and brought it back from Boston. When the young Bryant was later serving as a clerk with an established lawyer, he received a firm upbraiding from the attorney, who had caught him "wasting his time" reading *Lyrical Ballads*. Richard Henry Dana, poet and newspaper editor, recorded Bryant's feelings on the subject:

> I shall never forget with what feeling my friend Bryant . . . described to me the effect produced upon him by . . . Wordsworth's Ballads. He lived . . . at a period, too, when Pope was still the great idol in the Temple of Art. He said, that upon opening Wordsworth, a thousand springs seemed to gush up at once in his heart, and the face of nature, of a sudden, to change into a strange freshness and life. He had felt the sympathetic touch from an according mind, and . . . instantly his powers and affections shot over the earth and through his kind.

Dana was instrumental to Bryant's success as a poet. Their lifelong friendship of critiquing and encouraging each other's poetry began when a manuscript version of "Thanatopsis" crossed Dana's desk at the *North American Review*. Upon reading the poem, Dana was sure its author was British: "No American could produce a poem of such transcendent merit." Soon thereafter, Bryant's poem appeared in the *Review* (1817), and the two men became acquainted with each other. The poem's blend of Wordsworth's spiritual and elegiac tone with the earlier poetry of Britain's school of "Graveyard Poets" (such as Thomas Gray) and the earlier models of Greek and Roman pastoral elegy proved popular to American as well as British readers of the periodical. However, early popularity would not reliably earn Bryant a living, as the first edition of his poems (1821) would prove. Although between the 1830s and the 1870s his collected poems sold through over twenty separate printings in Britain and more than twice as many in

America, this did little to help him through the financial crunch of the 1820s. Bryant, newly married to Frances Fairchild, a distant relative of Alexander Pope, needed to ensure solvency.

In order to make ends meet, in 1825 he took up a position with the *New York Review*, leaving it a year later for an assistant editorship at the New York *Evening Post*. Three years later he became editor-in-chief and occupied this position for the rest of his life, using the eminence it gave him in the world of letters to increase his reputation as a poet and advocate for American literature. He saw America as a "rich and varied field for literature," yet Americans were still bound to British opinion and "do not praise a thing until [they] see the seal of transatlantic approbation on it." The blending of poetics and politics that Bryant had practiced as a boy continued through his poetic career, especially during the presidency of Andrew Jackson. Under Bryant's editorship, the *Evening Post* became a Jacksonian mouthpiece, and Bryant's editorials and poems buttressed the president's politics, most problematically his policy of the removal of American Indians from their ancestral lands. Bryant's poem "The Prairies" (1832) addresses this topic, justifying "manifest destiny" with a false claim that the Native Americans had taken these lands from an earlier race of people. Bryant wrote the poem after traveling to Illinois, in 1832, to visit his brothers who had settled there and to purchase land for himself. During his Midwestern tour he had to change his course to avoid Chief Blackhawk, who had been removed from his lands and was returning to them to honor his ancestors, a fact that complicates the notions of rightful ownership of land expressed in "The Prairies."

Bryant's traveling became an inspiration for his writing, and he continued to do both throughout the remainder of his life, visiting Canada, Mexico, the Caribbean, Europe, England, Scotland, and Ireland. His writing about these locales was initially published in the *Evening Post*, and later in book form: *Letters from a Traveller* (1852), *Letters from Spain and Other Countries* (1859), and *Letters from the East* (1869). Despite his ambitious travels, he remained active in local politics and developments, helping to establish New York City's Central Park. His love of nature manifested in articles for the *Evening Post* that addressed the need for a natural space in which New Yorkers could take refuge from the business and industry of the city. It was in Central Park that he gave his last public address and appearance: On an oppressively hot May 29, 1878, he spoke at the dedication of a statue erected in honor of the Italian patriot Giuseppe Mazzini. Walking across the park after the ceremony, he reached the home of his good friend James Grant Wilson and there suffered a fall, striking his head on the stone steps of Wilson's home. He died on June 12, 1878, and throughout New York City on that day, the flags flew at half-mast and the shops were draped in black.

Thanatopsis[1]

To him who in the love of Nature holds
Communion with her visible forms, she speaks
A various language; for his gayer hours
She has a voice of gladness, and a smile
And eloquence of beauty, and she glides   5
Into his darker musings, with a mild
And healing sympathy, that steals away
Their sharpness, ere he is aware. When thoughts
Of the last bitter hour come like a blight
Over thy spirit, and sad images   10
Of the stern agony, and shroud, and pall,
And breathless darkness, and the narrow house,

---

1. A meditation on death [Greek].

Make thee to shudder, and grow sick at heart;—
Go forth, under the open sky, and list
To Nature's teachings, while from all around—   15
Earth and her waters, and the depths of air—
Comes a still voice.—Yet a few days, and thee
The all-beholding sun shall see no more
In all his course; nor yet in the cold ground,
Where thy pale form was laid, with many tears,   20
Nor in the embrace of ocean, shall exist
Thy image. Earth, that nourished thee, shall claim
Thy growth, to be resolved to earth again,
And, lost each human trace, surrendering up
Thine individual being, shalt thou go   25
To mix for ever with the elements,
To be a brother to the insensible rock
And to the sluggish clod, which the rude swain
Turns with his share, and treads upon. The oak
Shall send his roots abroad, and pierce thy mould.   30

     Yet not to thine eternal resting-place
Shalt thou retire alone, nor couldst thou wish
Couch more magnificent. Thou shalt lie down
With patriarchs of the infant world—with kings,
The powerful of the earth—the wise, the good,   35
Fair forms, and hoary seers of ages past,
All in one mighty sepulchre. The hills
Rock-ribbed and ancient as the sun,—the vales
Stretching in pensive quietness between;
The venerable woods—rivers that move   40
In majesty, and the complaining brooks
That make the meadows green; and, poured round all,
Old Ocean's gray and melancholy waste,—
Are but the solemn decorations all
Of the great tomb of man. The golden sun,   45
The planets, all the infinite host of heaven,
Are shining on the sad abodes of death,
Through the still lapse of ages. All that tread
The globe are but a handful to the tribes
That slumber in its bosom.—Take the wings   50
Of morning, pierce the Barcan wilderness,[1]
Or lose thyself in the continuous woods
Where rolls the Oregon,[2] and hears no sound,
Save his own dashings—yet the dead are there:
And millions in those solitudes, since first   55

---

1. Barca: region north of the Sahara desert in Africa.   2. Oregon: a native name for the Columbia river.

The flight of years began, have laid them down
In their last sleep—the dead reign there alone.
So shalt thou rest, and what if thou withdraw
In silence from the living, and no friend
Take note of thy departure? All that breathe   60
Will share thy destiny. The gay will laugh
When thou art gone, the solemn brood of care
Plod on, and each one as before will chase
His favorite phantom; yet all these shall leave
Their mirth and their employments, and shall come   65
And make their bed with thee. As the long train
Of ages glide away, the sons of men,
The youth in life's green spring, and he who goes
In the full strength of years, matron and maid,
The speechless babe, and the gray-headed man—   70
Shall one by one be gathered to thy side,
By those, who in their turn shall follow them.

　　So live, that when thy summons comes to join
The innumerable caravan, which moves
To that mysterious realm, where each shall take   75
His chamber in the silent halls of death,
Thou go not, like the quarry-slave at night,
Scourged to his dungeon, but, sustained and soothed
By an unfaltering trust, approach thy grave,
Like one who wraps the drapery of his couch   80
About him, and lies down to pleasant dreams.

　　　　　　　　　　　　　　　　　　　　　　　—1821

To a Waterfowl

　　Whither, midst falling dew,
While glow the heavens with the last steps of day,
Far, through their rosy depths, dost thou pursue
　　　Thy solitary way?

　　Vainly the fowler's eye   5
Might mark thy distant flight to do thee wrong,
As, darkly seen against the crimson sky,
　　　Thy figure floats along.

　　Seek'st thou the plashy brink
Of weedy lake, or marge of river wide,   10
Or where the rocking billows rise and sink
　　　On the chafed ocean-side?

There is a Power whose care
Teaches thy way along that pathless coast—
The desert and illimitable air—   15
  Lone wandering, but not lost.

All day thy wings have fanned,
At that far height, the cold, thin atmosphere,
Yet stoop not, weary, to the welcome land,
  Though the dark night is near.   20

And soon that toil shall end;
Soon shalt thou find a summer home, and rest,
And scream among thy fellows; reeds shall bend,
  Soon, o'er thy sheltered nest.

Thou'rt gone, the abyss of heaven   25
Hath swallowed up thy form; yet, on my heart
Deeply has sunk the lesson thou hast given,
  And shall not soon depart.

He who, from zone to zone,
Guides through the boundless sky thy certain flight,   30
In the long way that I must tread alone,
  Will lead my steps aright.

                                              —1821

A Forest Hymn

The groves were God's first temples. Ere man learned
To hew the shaft, and lay the architrave,[1]
And spread the roof above them—ere he framed
The lofty vault, to gather and roll back
The sound of anthems; in the darkling wood,   5
Amid the cool and silence, he knelt down,
And offered to the Mightiest solemn thanks
And supplication. For his simple heart
Might not resist the sacred influence
Which, from the stilly twilight of the place,   10
And from the gray old trunks that high in heaven
Mingled their mossy boughs, and from the sound
Of the invisible breath that swayed at once
All their green tops, stole over him, and bowed
His spirit with the thought of boundless power   15
And inaccessible majesty. Ah, why
Should we, in the world's riper years, neglect

---

1. A supporting beam.

God's ancient sanctuaries, and adore
Only among the crowd, and under roofs
That our frail hands have raised? Let me, at least,   20
Here, in the shadow of this aged wood,
Offer one hymn—thrice happy, if it find
Acceptance in His ear.

                     Father, thy hand
Hath reared these venerable columns, thou   25
Didst weave this verdant roof. Thou didst look down
Upon the naked earth, and, forthwith, rose
All these fair ranks of trees. They, in thy sun,
Budded, and shook their green leaves in thy breeze,
And shot toward heaven. The century-living crow   30
Whose birth was in their tops, grew old and died
Among their branches, till, at last, they stood,
As now they stand, massy, and tall, and dark,
Fit shrine for humble worshipper to hold
Communion with his Maker. These dim vaults,   35
These winding aisles, of human pomp or pride
Report not. No fantastic carvings show
The boast of our vain race to change the form
Of thy fair works. But thou art here—thou fill'st
The solitude. Thou art in the soft winds   40
That run along the summit of these trees
In music; thou art in the cooler breath
That from the inmost darkness of the place
Comes, scarcely felt; the barky trunks, the ground,
The fresh moist ground, are all instinct with thee.   45
Here is continual worship;—nature, here,
In the tranquillity that thou dost love,
Enjoys thy presence. Noiselessly, around,
From perch to perch, the solitary bird
Passes; and yon clear spring, that, midst its herbs,   50
Wells softly forth and wandering steeps the roots
Of half the mighty forest, tells no tale
Of all the good it does. Thou has not left
Thyself without a witness, in the shades,
Of thy perfections. Grandeur, strength, and grace   55
Are here to speak of thee. This mighty oak—
By whose immovable stem I stand and seem
Almost annihilated—not a prince,
In all that proud old world beyond the deep,
E'er wore his crown as loftily as he   60
Wears the green coronal of leaves with which
Thy hand has graced him. Nestled at his root
Is beauty, such as blooms not in the glare

Of the broad sun. That delicate forest flower,
With scented breath and look so like a smile,   65
Seems, as it issues from the shapeless mould,
An emanation of the indwelling Life,
A visible token of the upholding Love,
That are the soul of this great universe.

My heart is awed within me when I think   70
Of the great miracle that still goes on,
In silence, round me—the perpetual work
Of thy creation, finished, yet renewed
Forever. Written on thy works I read
The lesson of thy own eternity.   75
Lo! all grow old and die—but see again,
How on the faltering footsteps of decay
Youth presses—ever-gay and beautiful youth
In all its beautiful forms. These lofty trees
Wave not less proudly that their ancestors   80
Moulder beneath them. Oh, there is not lost
One of earth's charms: upon her bosom yet,
After the flight of untold centuries,
The freshness of her far beginning lies
And yet shall lie. Life mocks the idle hate   85
Of his arch-enemy Death—yea, seats himself
Upon the tyrant's throne—the sepulchre,
And of the triumphs of his ghastly foe
Makes his own nourishment. For he came forth
From thine own bosom, and shall have no end.   90

There have been holy men who hid themselves
Deep in the woody wilderness, and gave
Their lives to thought and prayer, till they outlived
The generation born with them, nor seemed
Less aged than the hoary trees and rocks   95
Around them;—and there have been holy men
Who deemed it were not well to pass life thus.
But let me often to these solitudes
Retire, and in thy presence reassure
My feeble virtue. Here its enemies,   100
The passions, at thy plainer footsteps shrink
And tremble and are still. O God! when thou
Dost scare the world with tempests, set on fire
The heavens with falling thunderbolts, or fill
With all the waters of the firmament,   105
The swift dark whirlwind that uproots the woods
And drowns the villages; when, at thy call,
Uprises the great deep and throws himself

Upon the continent, and overwhelms
Its cities—who forgets not, at the sight   110
Of these tremendous tokens of thy power,
His pride, and lays his strifes and follies by?
Oh, from these sterner aspects of thy face
Spare me and mine, nor let us need the wrath
Of the mad unchained elements to teach   115
Who rules them. Be it ours to meditate,
In these calm shades, thy milder majesty,
And to the beautiful order of thy works
Learn to conform the order of our lives.

                                                                      —1832

To Cole,[1] the Painter, Departing for Europe

Thine eyes shall see the light of distant skies;
     Yet, COLE! thy heart shall bear to Europe's strand
     A living image of our own bright land,
Such as upon thy glorious canvas lies;
Lone lakes—savannas where the bison roves—   5
     Rocks rich with summer garlands—solemn streams—
     Skies, where the desert eagle wheels and screams—
Spring bloom and autumn blaze of boundless groves.
Fair scenes shall greet thee where thou goest—fair,
     But different—everywhere the trace of men,   10
     Paths, homes, graves, ruins, from the lowest glen
To where life shrinks from the fierce Alpine air.—
     Gaze on them, till the tears shall dim thy sight,
     But keep that earlier, wilder image bright.

                                                                      —1832

The Prairies

These are the gardens of the Desert, these
The unshorn fields, boundless and beautiful,
For which the speech of England has no name—
The Prairies. I behold them for the first,
And my heart swells, while the dilated sight   5
Takes in the encircling vastness. Lo! they stretch,
In airy undulations, far away,
As if the Ocean, in his gentlest swell,
Stood still, with all his rounded billows fixed,
And motionless forever.—Motionless?—   10
No—they are all unchained again. The clouds

---

1. Thomas Cole (1801–1848), English-born American landscape painter.

Sweep over with their shadows, and, beneath,
The surface rolls and fluctuates to the eye;
Dark hollows seem to glide along and chase
The sunny ridges. Breezes of the South!   15
Who toss the golden and the flame-like flowers,
And pass the prairie-hawk that, poised on high,
Flaps his broad wings, yet moves not—ye have played
Among the palms of Mexico and vines
Of Texas, and have crisped the limpid brooks   20
That from the fountains of Sonora[1] glide
Into the calm Pacific—have ye fanned
A nobler or a lovelier scene than this?
Man hath no power in all this glorious work:
The hand that built the firmament hath heaved   25
And smoothed these verdant swells, and sown their slopes
With herbage, planted them with island-groves,
And hedged them round with forests. Fitting floor
For this magnificent temple of the sky—
With flowers whose glory and whose multitude   30
Rival the constellations! The great heavens
Seem to stoop down upon the scene in love,—
A nearer vault, and of a tendered blue,
Than that which bends above our Eastern hills.

        As o'er the verdant waste I guide my steed,   35
Among the high rank grass that sweeps his sides
The hollow beating of his footstep seems
A sacrilegious sound. I think of those
Upon whose rest he tramples. Are they here—
The dead of other days?—and did the dust   40
Of these fair solitudes once stir with life
And burn with passion? Let the mighty mounds
That overlook the rivers, or that rise
In the dim forest crowded with old oaks,
Answer. A race, that long has passed away,   45
Built them; a disciplined and populous race
Heaped, with long toil, the earth, while yet the Greek
Was hewing the Pentelicus[2] to forms
Of symmetry, and rearing on its rock
The glittering Parthenon.[3] These ample fields   50
Nourished their harvests, here their herds were fed,
When haply by their stalls the bison lowed,
And bowed his manèd shoulder to the yoke.
All day this desert murmured with their toils,

---

1. A region in northern Mexico.   2. Mountain in Greece where white marble was quarried.   3. Temple of Athena in Athens.

Till twilight blushed, and lovers walked, and wooed   55
In a forgotten language, and old tunes,
From instruments of unremembered form,
Gave the soft winds a voice. The red-man came—
The roaming hunter-tribes, warlike and fierce,
And the mound-builders vanished from the earth.   60
The solitude of centuries untold
Has settled where they dwelt. The prairie-wolf
Hunts in their meadows, and his fresh-dug den
Yawns by my path. The gopher mines the ground
Where stood their swarming cities. All is gone;   65
All—save the piles of earth that hold their bones,
The platforms where they worshipped unknown gods,
The barriers which they builded from the soil
To keep the foe at bay—till o'er the walls
The wild beleaguerers broke, and, one by one,   70
The strongholds of the plain were forced, and heaped
With corpses. The brown vultures of the wood
Flocked to those vast uncovered sepulchres,
And sat, unscared and silent, at their feast.
Haply some solitary fugitive,   75
Lurking in marsh and forest, till the sense
Of desolation and of fear became
Bitterer than death, yielded himself to die.
Man's better nature triumphed then. Kind words
Welcomed and soothed him; the rude conquerors   80
Seated the captive with their chiefs; he chose
A bride among their maidens, and at length
Seemed to forget—yet ne'er forgot—the wife
Of his first love, and her sweet little ones,
Butchered, amid their shrieks, with all his race.   85

     Thus change the forms of being. Thus arise
Races of living things, glorious in strength,
And perish, as the quickening breath of God
Fills them, or is withdrawn. The red-man, too,
Has left the blooming wilds he ranged so long,   90
And, nearer to the Rocky Mountains, sought
A wilder hunting-ground. The beaver builds
No longer by these streams, but far away,
On waters whose blue surface ne'er gave back
The white man's face—among Missouri's springs,   95
And pools whose issues swell the Oregon—
He rears his little Venice. In these plains
The bison feeds no more. Twice twenty leagues
Beyond remotest smoke of hunter's camp,
Roams the majestic brute, in herds that shake   100

The earth with thundering steps—yet here I meet
His ancient footprints stamped beside the pool.

  Still this great solitude is quick with life.
Myriads of insects, gaudy as the flowers
They flutter over, gentle quadrupeds,   105
And birds, that scarce have learned the fear of man,
Are here, and sliding reptiles of the ground,
Startlingly beautiful. The graceful deer
Bounds to the wood at my approach. The bee,
A more adventurous colonist than man,   110
With whom he came across the eastern deep,
Fills the savannas with his murmurings,
And hides his sweets, as in the golden age,
Within the hollow oak. I listen long
To his domestic hum, and think I hear   115
The sound of that advancing multitude
Which soon shall fill these deserts. From the ground
Comes up the laugh of children, the soft voice
Of maidens, and the sweet and solemn hymn
Of Sabbath worshippers. The low of herds   120
Blends with the rustling of the heavy grain
Over the dark brown furrows. All at once
A fresher wind sweeps by, and breaks my dream,
And I am in the wilderness alone.

                   —1832

Thomas Carlyle
1795–1881

Early in his long career, Thomas Carlyle established himself as a public intellectual by voicing a bitter critique of capitalism as it was developing in England. In his influential essay "Signs of the Times" (1829) he argued that the world had entered an Age of Machinery in which everything had become mechanical, especially people. He said that the society built by the bourgeoisie was spiritually empty and that it crushed individuality and initiative. Above all, it was morally bankrupt, since its spectacular wealth was made from the labor of its poorest and weakest members. His solution to this problem was a return to authoritarianism. He despised the idea of democracy, was repelled by what he called "the mob," and believed throughout his life that only benevolent great men, or heroes, could manage to impose order on human societies.

  Carlyle's parents, James and Margaret Aitken Carlyle, were farmers in the Scottish village of Ecclefechan and raised their children in a staunch Calvinism. They believed that hard work and intense discipline were needed as guards against the inherent depravity of human nature. In 1809, Carlyle was sent to university at Edinburgh, where he studied for the ministry for five years but left without taking a degree. He had rejected his parents' dour creed, as well as the

Enlightenment rationalism of the English elite. After a period of depression and doubt, he experienced a spiritual awakening to what he called "natural supernaturalism." This was an affirmative personal faith that had much in common with the pantheism later articulated by his friend and correspondent, Ralph Waldo Emerson.

Carlyle first achieved international notoriety with *Sartor Resartus* (London, 1833–1834; Boston, 1836), a bizarre fictional biography of an imaginary philosopher, Diogenes Teufelsdrockh (roughly translatable as "divinely created devil's excrement"). The book was written in a dense, enigmatic style that earned it almost universal condemnation from reviewers. But it also earned him a dedicated following of readers who appreciated his slashing attacks on the shallowness and utilitarianism of modernity. By the end of his career, Carlyle had become intensely cynical and bitter, sometimes even cranky and self-parodic. For instance, he lashed out at the abolitionist movement in 1853 with a screed titled, "An Occasional Discourse on the Nigger Question." American poet and editor James Russell Lowell described Carlyle's decline with precise mockery: "Since Mr. Carlyle has become possessed with the hallucination that he is head-master of this huge boys' school which we call the world, his pedagogic birch has grown to the taller proportions and more ominous aspect of a gallows."

Signs of the Times

Were we required to characterise this age of ours by any single epithet, we should be tempted to call it, not an Heroical, Devotional, Philosophical, or Moral Age, but, above all others, the Mechanical Age. It is the Age of Machinery, in every outward and inward sense of that word; the age which, with its whole undivided might, forwards, teaches, and practises the great art of adapting means to ends. Nothing is now done directly, or by hand; all is by rule and calculated contrivance. For the simplest operation, some helps and accompaniments, some cunning abbreviating process is in readiness. Our old modes of exertion are all discredited, and thrown aside. On every hand, the living artisan is driven from his workshop, to make room for a speedier, inanimate one. The shuttle drops from the fingers of the weaver, and falls into iron fingers that ply it faster. The sailor furls his sail, and lays down his oar; and bids a strong, unwearied servant, on vaporous wings, bear him through the waters. Men have crossed oceans by steam; the Birmingham Fire-king has visited the fabulous East; and the genius of the Cape were there any Camoens now to sing it, has again been alarmed, and with far stranger thunders than Gama's.[1] There is no end to machinery. Even the horse is stripped of his harness, and finds a fleet fire-horse invoked in his stead. Nay, we have an artist that hatches chickens by steam; the very brood-hen is to be superseded! For all earthly, and for some unearthly purposes, we have machines and mechanic furtherances; for mincing our cabbages; for casting us into magnetic sleep. We remove mountains, and make seas our smooth highways; nothing can resist us. We war with rude nature; and, by our resistless engines, come off always victorious, and loaded with spoils.

What wonderful accessions have thus been made, and are still making, to the physical power of mankind; how much better fed, clothed, lodged, and, in all outward respects, accommodated men now are, or might be, by a given quantity of labour, is a grateful reflection which forces itself on every one. What changes, too, this addition of power is introducing into the social system; how wealth has more and more increased, and at the same time gathered itself more and more into masses, strangely altering the

---

1. Birmingham Fire-king: a steamship. Luiz vaz Camoens (1524–1580), Portuguese poet. Vasco de Gama (1460–1524), Portuguese explorer who discovered a route to the East around Africa's Cape of Good Hope.

old relations, and increasing the distance between the rich and the poor, will be a question for Political Economists—and a much more complex and important one than any they have yet engaged with. But leaving these matters for the present, let us observe how the mechanical genius of our time has diffused itself into quite other provinces. Not the external and physical alone is now managed by machinery, but the internal and spiritual also. Here too nothing follows its spontaneous course, nothing is left to be accomplished by old, natural methods. Every thing has its cunningly devised implements, its pre-established apparatus; it is not done by hand, but by machinery. Thus we have machines for Education: Lancastrian machines; Hamiltonian machines[2]—Monitors, maps, and emblems. Instruction, that mysterious communing of Wisdom with Ignorance, is no longer an indefinable tentative process, requiring a study of individual aptitudes, and a perpetual variation of means and methods, to attain the same end; but a secure, universal, straightforward business, to be conducted in the gross, by proper mechanism, with such intellect as comes to hand. Then, we have Religious machines, of all imaginable varieties—the Bible Society,[3] professing a far higher and heavenly structure, is found, on inquiry, to be altogether an earthly contrivance: supported by collection of moneys, by fomenting of vanities, by puffing, intrigue and chicane—and yet, in effect, a very excellent machine for converting the Heathen. It is the same in all other departments. Has any man, or any society of men, a truth to speak, a piece of spiritual work to do; they can nowise proceed at once and with the mere natural organs, but must first call a public meeting, appoint committees, issue prospectuses, eat a public dinner; in a word, construct or borrow machinery, wherewith to speak it and do it. Without machinery, they were hopeless, helpless—a colony of Hindoo weavers squatting in the heart of Lancashire. Then every machine must have its moving power, in some of the great currents of society: every little sect among us, Unitarians, Utilitarians, Anabaptists, Phrenologists, must each have its periodical, its monthly or quarterly Magazine—hanging out, like its windmill, into the *popularis aura*,[4] to grind meal for the society. . . .

These things, which we state lightly enough here, are yet of deep import, and indicate a mighty change in our whole manner of existence. For the same habit regulates not our modes of action alone, but our modes of thought and feeling. Men are grown mechanical in head and in heart, as well as in hand. They have lost faith in individual endeavour, and in natural force, of any kind. Not for internal perfection, but for external combinations and arrangements, for institutions, constitutions—for Mechanism of one sort or other, do they hope and struggle. Their whole efforts, attachments, opinions, turn on mechanism, and are of a mechanical character.

We may trace this tendency, we think, very distinctly, in all the great manifestations of our time; in its intellectual aspect, the studies it most favours and its manner of conducting them; in its practical aspects, its politics, arts, religion, morals; in the whole sources, and throughout the whole currents, of its spiritual, no less than its material activity. . . .

Nowhere, for example, is the deep, almost exclusive faith we have in Mechanism more visible than in the Politics of this time. Civil government does by its nature include much that is mechanical, and must be treated accordingly. We term it indeed, in ordinary language, the Machine of Society, and talk of it as the grand working wheel from which all private machines must derive, or to which they must adapt,

2. Joseph Lancaster (1778–1838) and Sir William Hamilton (1788–1856), English educational reformers.   3. A British evangelical society founded in 1804.   4. Public opinion.

their movements. Considered merely as a metaphor, all this is well enough; but here, as in so many other cases, the "foam hardens itself into a shell," and the shadow we have wantonly evoked stands terrible before us and will not depart at our bidding. Government includes much also that is not mechanical, and cannot be treated mechanically; of which latter truth, as appears to us, the political speculations and exertions of our time are taking less and less cognisance.

Nay, in the very outset, we might note the mighty interest taken in *mere political arrangements*, as itself the sign of a mechanical age. The whole discontent of Europe takes this direction. The deep, strong cry of all civilised nations—a cry which, every one now sees, must and will be answered, is, Give us a reform of Government! A good structure of legislation, a proper check upon the executive—a wise arrangement of the judiciary, is all that is wanting for human happiness. The Philosopher of this age is not a Socrates, a Plato, a Hooker, or Taylor,[5] who inculcates on men the necessity and infinite worth of moral goodness, the great truth that our happiness depends on the mind which is within us, and not on the circumstances which are without us; but a Smith, a De Lolme, a Bentham,[6] who chiefly inculcates the reverse of this—that our happiness depends entirely on external circumstances; nay, that the strength and dignity of the mind within us is itself the creature and consequence of these. Were the laws, the government, in good order, all were well with us; the rest would care for itself! Dissentients from this opinion, expressed or implied, are now rarely to be met with; widely and angrily as men differ in its application, the principle is admitted by all.

Equally mechanical, and of equal simplicity, are the methods proposed by both parties for completing or securing this all-sufficient perfection of arrangement. It is no longer the moral, religious, spiritual condition of the people that is our concern, but their physical, practical, economical condition, as regulated by public laws. Thus is the Body-politic more than ever worshipped and tended; but the Soul-politic less than ever. Love of country, in any high or generous sense, in any other than an almost animal sense, or mere habit, has little importance attached to it in such reforms, or in the opposition shown them. Men are to be guided only by their self-interests. Good government is a good balancing of these; and, except a keen eye and appetite for self-interest, requires no virtue in any quarter. To both parties it is emphatically a machine: to the discontented, a "taxing-machine"; to the contented, a "machine for securing property." Its duties and its faults are not those of a father, but of an active parish constable.

Thus it is by the mere condition of the machine, by preserving it untouched, or else by reconstructing it, and oiling it anew, that man's salvation as a social being is to be ensured and indefinitely promoted. Contrive the fabric of law aright, and without farther effort on your part, that divine spirit of freedom, which all hearts venerate and long for, will of herself come to inhabit it; and under her healing wings every noxious influence will wither, every good and salutary one more and more expand. Nay, so devoted are we to this principle, and at the same time so curiously mechanical, that a new trade, specially grounded on it, has arisen among us, under the name of "Codification," or code-making in the abstract; whereby any people, for a reasonable consideration, may be accommodated with a patent code;—more easily than curious individuals with patent breeches, for the people does not need to be measured first.

---

5. Socrates (469–399 BC) and Plato (427–347 BC), Greek philosophers; Richard Hooker (1534–1600) and Jeremy Taylor (1613–1667), English theologians. 6. Adam Smith (1723–1790), John Louis De Lolme (1741–1806), and Jeremy Bentham (1748–1832), English political philosophers.

To us who live in the midst of all this, and see continually the faith, hope, and, practice of every one founded on Mechanism of one kind or other, it is apt to seem quite natural, and as if it could never have been otherwise. Nevertheless, if we recollect or reflect a little, we shall find both that it has been, and might again be otherwise. The domain of Mechanism, meaning thereby political, ecclesiastical, or other outward establishments,—was once considered as embracing, and we are persuaded can at any time embrace, but a limited portion of man's interests, and by no means the highest portion.

To speak a little pedantically, there is a science of *Dynamics* in man's fortunes and nature, as well as of *Mechanics*. There is a science which treats of, and practically addresses, the primary, unmodified forces and energies of man, the mysterious springs of Love, and Fear, and Wonder, of Enthusiasm, Poetry, Religion, all which have a truly vital and *infinite* character; as well as a science which practically addresses the finite, modified developments of these, when they take the shape of immediate "motives," as hope of reward, or as fear of punishment.

Now it is certain, that in former times the wise men, the enlightened lovers of their kind, who appeared generally as Moralists, Poets, or Priests, did, without neglecting the Mechanical province, deal chiefly with the Dynamical; applying themselves chiefly to regulate, increase, and purify the inward primary powers of man; and fancying that herein lay the main difficulty, and the best service they could undertake. But a wide difference is manifest in our age. For the wise men, who now appear as Political Philosophers, deal exclusively with the Mechanical province; and occupying themselves in counting up and estimating men's motives, strive by curious checking and balancing, and other adjustments of Profit and Loss, to guide them to their true advantage: while, unfortunately, those same "motives" are so innumerable, and so variable in every individual, that no really useful conclusion can ever be drawn from their enumeration. But though Mechanism, wisely contrived, has done much for man in a social and moral point of view, we cannot be persuaded that it has ever been the chief source of his worth or happiness. Consider the great elements of human enjoyment, the attainments and possessions that exalt man's life to its present height, and see what part of these he owes to institutions, to Mechanism of any kind; and what to the instinctive, unbounded force, which Nature herself lent him, and still continues to him. Shall we say, for example, that Science and Art are indebted principally to the founders of Schools and Universities? Did not Science originate rather, and gain advancement, in the obscure closets of the Roger Bacons, Keplers, Newtons; in the workshops of the Fausts and the Watts[7]—wherever, and in what guise soever Nature, from the first times downwards, had sent a gifted spirit upon the earth? Again, were Homer and Shakspeare members of any beneficed guild, or made Poets by means of it? Were Painting and Sculpture created by forethought, brought into the world by institutions for that end? No; Science and Art have, from first to last, been the free gift of Nature; an unsolicited, unexpected gift— often even a fatal one. These things rose up, as it were, by spontaneous growth, in the free soil and sunshine of Nature. They were not planted or grafted, nor even greatly multiplied or improved by the culture or manuring of institutions. Generally speaking, they have derived only partial help from these; often enough have suffered

---

7. Roger Bacon (1214–1294), English alchemist; Johannes Kepler (1571–1630), German astronomer; Sir Isaac Newton (1643–1727), English scientist and mathematician; Faust, a legendary German alchemist; and James Watt (1736–1819), Scottish inventor.

damage. They made constitutions for themselves. They originated in the Dynamical nature of man, not in his Mechanical nature.

Or, to take an infinitely higher instance, that of the Christian Religion, which, under every theory of it, in the believing or unbelieving mind, must ever be regarded as the crowning glory, or rather the life and soul, of our whole modern culture: How did Christianity arise and spread abroad among men? Was it by institutions, and establishments and well-arranged systems of mechanism? Not so; on the contrary, in all past and existing institutions for those ends, its divine spirit has invariably been found to languish and decay. It arose in the mystic deeps of man's soul; and was spread abroad by the "preaching of the word," by simple, altogether natural and individual efforts; and flew, like hallowed fire, from heart to heart, till all were purified and illuminated by it; and its heavenly light shone, as it still shines, and as sun or star will ever shine, through the whole dark destinies of man. Here again was no Mechanism; man's highest attainment was accomplished, Dynamically, not Mechanically. Nay, we will venture to say, that no high attainment, not even any far-extending movement among men, was ever accomplished otherwise. Strange as it may seem, if we read History with any degree of thoughtfulness, we shall find that checks and balances of Profit and Loss have never been the grand agents with men; that they have never been roused into deep, thorough, all-pervading efforts by any computable prospect of Profit and Loss, for any visible, finite object; but always for some invisible and infinite one. The Crusades[8] took their rise in Religion; their visible object was, commercially speaking, worth nothing. It was the boundless Invisible world that was laid bare in the imaginations of those men; and in its burning light, the visible shrunk as a scroll. Not mechanical, nor produced by mechanical means, was this vast movement. No dining at Freemasons' Tavern,[9] with the other long train of modern machinery; no cunning reconciliation of "vested interests," was required here: only the passionate voice of one man, the rapt soul looking through the eyes of one man; and rugged, steel-clad Europe trembled beneath his words, and followed him whither he listed. In later ages it was still the same. The Reformation had an invisible, mystic, and ideal aim; the result was indeed to be embodied in external things; but its spirit, its worth, was internal, invisible, infinite. Our English Revolution too originated in Religion. Men did battle, in those old days, not for Purse sake, but for Conscience sake. Nay, in our own days, it is no way different. The French Revolution itself had something higher in it than cheap bread and a Habeas-corpus[10] act. Here too was an Idea; a Dynamic, not a Mechanic force. It was a struggle, though a blind and at last an insane one, for the infinite, divine nature of Right, of Freedom, of Country.

Thus does man, in every age, vindicate, consciously or unconsciously, his celestial birthright. Thus does Nature hold on her wondrous, unquestionable course; and all our systems and theories are but so many froth-eddies or sandbanks, which from time to time she casts up, and washes away. When we can drain the Ocean into our mill-ponds, and bottle up the Force of Gravity, to be sold by retail, in gas-jars; then may we hope to comprehend the infinitudes of man's soul under formulas of Profit and Loss; and rule over this too, as over a patent engine, by checks, and valves, and balances.

—1829

---

8. European military invasions of the Middle East during the Middle Ages.   9. Freemasons: a longstanding secret society.
10. A legal principle guaranteeing the right to know the charges against one.

TRANSATLANTIC EXCHANGES

Utopianism and Socialism

Along with thousands of young British radicals in the early 1790s, Samuel Taylor Coleridge was deeply inspired by the French Revolution's ideals of liberty and equality. But the increasing intensity of revolutionary violence in France challenged his faith in the promise of rational social progress. In 1794, Coleridge met Robert Southey, and the two poets became fast friends, talking of their shared wish for a retreat from the "shame and anguish of the evil day," as Coleridge puts it in a sonnet he addressed to Southey in 1794. After reading William Godwin's treatise *An Enquiry Concerning Political Justice* (London, 1793; Philadelphia, 1796), they had made plans to establish a Pantisocracy, a small community in which property would be owned communally and all members would rule equally. Coleridge and Southey would marry Edith and Sara Fricker, respectively, and then emigrate with them and ten other couples to Pennsylvania, where the exiled radical minister Joseph Priestley owned a tract of land on the Susquehanna River. Coleridge responded to the idea of Pantisocracy with an almost religious enthusiasm:

> O'er the ocean swell
> Sublime of Hope, I seek the cottag'd dell
> Where Virtue calm with careless step may stray,
> And dancing to the moonlight roundelay,
> The wizard Passions weave an holy spell.

Despite the force of their commitment, the plan collapsed when wealthy patrons gave Coleridge and Southey annuities that allowed them to devote themselves wholly to their more immediate interest, poetry.

During the Romantic period, several factors combined to give new vitality to what had always been a persistent thread of radical political speculation in English culture. First, a series of agricultural enclosure acts, pushed through Parliament by powerful agricultural capitalists, fenced the rural poor out of the commons on which their livelihood had depended for centuries. As William Cobbett observes, hundreds of thousands saw two available alternatives: wage work in the intolerably filthy and oppressive new industrial cities, or emigration to a romanticized America. For centuries, the English countryside had seemed to offer an ideal retreat from the cruelty of the city, and now, just when that possibility had been definitely foreclosed, seemingly limitless tracts of free land in North America made pastoral retreat seem newly possible. Finally, while the republican revolutions of the eighteenth century had sought only to overthrow entrenched monarchies, they inspired radicals to ask whether more total social change could be achieved in the New World. So, what had been a trickle of utopianism became a flood during the early nineteenth century.

The most influential versions of utopianism centered on two symbolic locations: the factory and the farm. French intellectual Henri de Saint-Simon saw industrialization as a chaotic and destructive but potentially beneficial process. He believed that development should be rationalized under the direction of a technocratic, scientific elite who could use the powerful tools developed by capitalism to build a perfect future society. Industrialist Robert Owen developed Saint-Simon's ideas through practical experimentation in model factory towns in England and the United States, especially New Lanarck in Scotland and New Harmony in Indiana. Here workers would live collectively and work efficiently under the direction of scientific and benevolent overseers. Quite similar plans, but with a stronger emphasis on agricultural production, were developed by French socialist Charles Fourier, who envisioned large collective farms called phalanxes. Fourier felt that a well-designed community could take advantage of natural human impulses, including altruism and friendly competition, to make cooperative work attractive and efficient. Fourier's ideas inspired the international Associationist movement, whose hundreds of thousands of participants founded dozens of communally owned and operated farms. Perhaps the most famous was Brook Farm in West Roxbury, outside Boston, Massachusetts. Initially proposed by George Ripley, Brook Farm earned the sympathies and sometimes the ridicule of most of the New England Transcendentalists, including Ralph Waldo Emerson, Henry David Thoreau, Margaret Fuller, and Nathaniel Hawthorne. Some observers, such as radical Boston bookseller Elizabeth Palmer Peabody, even saw the Farm as a new manifestation of the early Christian church, with its emphasis on the congregation as a community of equals before God.

The participants in this broad movement were unified above all by a powerful negative critique of capitalism as a world system that both relied on and reinforced the worst aspects of human nature: selfishness, competition, greed, and avarice. To be sure, their responses to this insight were sometimes quite whimsical: Fourier, for instance, proposed that children should be offered the work of trash collection since they naturally loved to play in the dirt. Nevertheless, by proposing that a society based on ruthless competition must be replaced by one in which people cooperated to fulfill their common needs, the utopians laid the groundwork for the most powerful alternative political movement of the last two centuries: socialism. Most utopians were elite radicals who saw themselves as conducting social experiments that would benefit the oppressed indirectly by inspiring society's current rulers to make changes from on high. But Orestes Brownson, in a powerful essay about Thomas Carlyle's *Chartism* (1839) titled "The Laboring Classes" (1840), pointed out that the rapidly growing working class might well take history into its own hands and overthrow capitalism on its own behalf. In *The Communist Manifesto* (1848), Karl Marx and Frederick Engels extended this insight, applying their experience as participants in the European Revolutions of 1848. They argued that what was most utopian about prior socialist theories was the notion that a small experimental community could survive under the pressure exerted by the surrounding capitalist world. Marx and Engels insisted that the working class was the one revolutionary force in the modern world that could transform it altogether, creating not just an isolated ideal farm or town but an international human society in which, as in Coleridge's vision of Pantisocracy, property was communal and power was democratic.

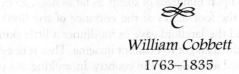

William Cobbett
1763–1835

William Cobbett began his public career as a brash Tory journalist and opponent of the American and French Revolutions. However, he eventually became a radical critic of the British government, an outspoken advocate of Parliamentary reform, and a well-known defender of the rights of the rural poor. Cobbett was born to a poor farm family in Farnham, Surrey, but was encouraged to read and write at a young age. As a young man, he first worked briefly as a copyist at the Inns of Court in London, then enlisted in the army, serving in Canada for almost seven years. The clerk of his regiment, he saw widespread corruption and profiteering by the officers, so he collected evidence and, upon returning to London in 1791, attempted to press charges. The case was squashed and Cobbett fled, first to revolutionary France, then to Philadelphia. Nevertheless, he remained a fierce Tory and Loyalist, catching the public's attention for the first time with a pamphlet in which he savaged Joseph Priestley and other supporters of the French Revolution. This began a period of several years during which Cobbett wrote

bitterly sarcastic conservative pamphlets under the pseudonym Peter Porcupine, with titles like
A Bone to Gnaw for the Democrats (1795) and *A Kick for a Bite* (1795). Cobbett returned to
London in 1800, where he began publishing the *Weekly Political Register*, a popular newspaper
that sold for two pennies. What he saw in his work as an investigative journalist moved him
steadily in the direction of radicalism. He spent two years in jail for sedition after condemning
the British army's use of German mercenaries to crush a protest in which a group of soldiers
demanded their back pay. This experience solidified his radical convictions, and he began to
much more aggressively harangue Parliament, which he had come to see as dominated, like the
military, by corrupt clubmen. He spent two more years in exile when the government suspended
habeas corpus, this time as a farmer on Long Island, and he carried Thomas Paine's bones in a
bag when he returned to London in 1819. For the next decade, he advocated extension of the
vote to the working class. In the last few years of his life, he spent much of his time touring the
countryside of England on horseback and writing his observations as articles for the *Political
Register*. These articles were later collected into the volume he is most widely remembered for
now, *Rural Rides* (1830). Cobbett was brought to trial one more time, for defending workers who
smashed harvesting equipment and burned haystacks to protect their livelihoods from mechanization. He successfully defended himself in court and was soon elected to Parliament from
Oldham, though he served only two years before dying in 1835 at his farm near Guilford.

from Rural Rides

It is time for me now, withdrawing myself from these objects visible to the eye, to
speak of the state of *the people*, and of the manner in which their affairs are affected
by the workings of the system. With regard to the labourers, they are, everywhere,
miserable. The wages for those who are employed on the land are, through all the
counties that I have come, twelve shillings a week for married men, and less for single ones; but a large part of them are not even at this season employed on the land.
The farmers, for want of means of profitable employment, suffer the men to fall upon
the parish[1]; and they are employed in digging and breaking stone for the roads; so that
the roads are nice and smooth for the sheep and cattle to walk on in their way to the
all-devouring jaws of the Jews[2] and other tax-eaters in London and its vicinity. None
of the best meat, except by mere accident, is consumed here. To-day (the 20th of
April), we have seen hundreds upon hundreds of sheep, as fat as hogs, go by this inn
door, their toes, like those of the foot marks at the entrance of the lion's den, all
pointing towards the Wen[3]; and the landlord gave us for dinner a little skinny, hard
leg of old ewe mutton! Where the man got it, I cannot imagine. Thus it is: every good
thing is literally driven or carried away out of the country. In walking out yesterday,
I saw three poor fellows digging stone for the roads, who told me that they never had
anything but bread to eat, and water to wash it down. One of them was a widower
with three children; and his pay was eighteenpence a day; that is to say, about three
pounds of bread a day each, for six days in the week; nothing for Sunday, and nothing for lodging, washing, clothing, candle-light, or fuel! Just such was the state of
things in France at the eve of the Revolution! Precisely such; and precisely the same
were the *causes*. Whether the effect will be the same, I do not take upon myself positively to determine. Just on the other side of the hedge, while I was talking to these
men, I saw about two hundred fat sheep in a rich pasture. I did not tell them what I

---

1. To apply for public assistance.   2. Cobbett shared the anti-Semitic idea that Jews were responsible for economic stagnation.   3. An excrescence. Cobbett derisively applies this term to London.

might have told them; but I explained to them why the farmers were unable to give them a sufficiency of wages. They listened with great attention; and said that they did believe that the farmers were in great distress themselves.

With regard to the farmers, it is said here that the far greater part, if sold up, would be found to be insolvent. The tradesmen in country towns are, and must be, in but little better state. They all tell you they do not sell half so many goods as they used to sell; and, of course, the manufacturers must suffer in the like degree. There is a diminution and deterioration, every one says, in the stocks upon the farms. *Sheep-washing* is a sort of business in this country; and I heard at Boston that the sheep-washers say that there is a gradual falling off in point of the numbers of sheep washed.

The farmers are all gradually sinking in point of property. The very rich ones do not feel that ruin is absolutely approaching; but they are all alarmed; and as to the poorer ones, they are fast falling into the rank of paupers. When I was at Ely a gentleman who appeared to be a great farmer told me in presence of fifty farmers, at the White Hart Inn, that he had seen that morning *three men* cracking stones on the road as paupers of the parish of Wilburton; and that all these men had been *overseers of the poor of that same parish within the last seven years*. Wheat keeps up in price to about an average of seven shillings a bushel; which is owing to our two successive bad harvests; but fat beef and pork are at a very low price, and mutton not much better. The beef was selling at Lynn[4] for five shillings the stone of fourteen pounds, and the pork at four and sixpence. The wool (one of the great articles of produce in these countries) selling for less than half of its former price.

And here let me stop to observe that I was well informed before I left London that merchants were exporting our long wool to France, where it paid *thirty per cent. duty*. Well, say the landowners, but we have to thank Huskisson[5] for this, at any rate; and that is true enough; for the law was most rigid against the export of wool; but what will the *manufacturers* say? Thus the collective[6] goes on, smashing one class and then another; and, resolved to adhere to the taxes, it knocks away, one after another, the props of the system itself. By every measure that it adopts for the sake of obtaining security, or of affording relief to the people, it does some act of crying injustice. To save itself from the natural effects of its own measures, it knocked down the country bankers, in direct violation of the law in 1822. It is now about to lay its heavy hand on the big brewers and the publicans, in order to pacify the call for a reduction of taxes, and with the hope of preventing such reduction in reality. It is making a trifling attempt to save the West Indians from total ruin, and the West India colonies from revolt; but by that same attempt it reflects injury on the British distillers, and on the growers of barley.[7] Thus it cannot do justice without doing injustice; it cannot do good without doing evil; and thus it must continue to do, until it take off, in reality, more than one half of the taxes.

One of the great signs of the poverty of people in the middle rank of life is the falling off of the audiences at the playhouses. There is a playhouse in almost every country town, where the players used to act occasionally; and in large towns almost always. In some places they have of late abandoned acting altogether. In others

---

4. Ely, Wilburton, and Lynn are parishes in Cambridgeshire.   5. William Huskisson (1770–1830), English politician who advocated duties on imported corn to protect farmers.   6. Government.   7. Cobbett lists several examples of misguided government interventions in the economy.

they have acted, very frequently, to not more than *ten or twelve persons*. At Norwich the playhouse had been shut up for a long time. I heard of one manager who has become a porter to a warehouse, and his company dispersed. In most places the insides of the buildings seem to be tumbling to pieces; and the curtains and scenes that they let down seem to be abandoned to the damp and the cobwebs. My appearance on the boards seemed to give new life to the drama. I was, until the birth of my third son, a constant haunter of the playhouse, in which I took great delight; but when *he* came into the world, I said, "Now, Nancy, it is time for us to leave off going to the play." It is really melancholy to look at things now, and to think of things then. I feel great sorrow on account of these poor players; for though they are made the tools of the government and the corporations and the parsons, it is not their fault, and they have uniformly, whenever I have come in contact with them, been very civil to me. I am not sorry that they are left out of the list of vagrants in the new act[8]; but in this case, as in so many others, the men have to be grateful to the *women*; for who believes that this merciful omission would have taken place if so many of the peers had not contracted matrimonial alliances with players; if so many playeresses had not become peeresses. We may thank God for disposing the hearts of our law-makers to be guilty of the same sins and foibles as ourselves; for when a lord had been sentenced to the pillory, the use of that ancient mode of punishing offences was abolished: when a lord (Castlereagh),[9] who was also a minister of state, had cut his own throat, the degrading punishment of burial in cross-roads was abolished; and now, when so many peers and great men have taken to wife play-actresses, which the law termed *vagrants*, that term, as applied to the children of Melpomene and Thalia,[10] is abolished! Laud we the gods that our rulers cannot, after all, divest themselves of flesh and blood! For the Lord have mercy on us, if their great souls were once to soar above that tenement!

Lord Stanhope[11] cautioned his brother peers, a little while ago, against the angry feeling which was *rising up in the poor against the rich*. His lordship is a wise and humane man, and this is evident from all his conduct. Nor is this angry feeling confined to the counties in the south, where the rage of the people, from the very nature of the local circumstances, is more formidable; woods and coppices and dingles and by-lanes and sticks and stones ever at hand, being resources unknown in counties like this. When I was at St. Ives, in Huntingdonshire, an open country, I sat with the farmers, and smoked a pipe by way of preparation for evening service, which I performed on a carpenter's bench in a wheelwright's shop; my friends, the players, never having gained any regular settlement in that grand mart for four-legged fat meat, coming from the Fens,[12] and bound to the Wen. While we were sitting, a hand-bill was handed round the table, advertising *farming stock* for sale; and amongst the implements of husbandry "an *excellent fire-engine, several steel traps, and spring guns!*" And that is the life, is it, of an English *farmer*? I walked on about six miles of the road from Holbeach to Boston. I have before observed upon the inexhaustible riches of this land. At the end of about five miles and three quarters I came to a public-house, and thought I would get some breakfast; but the poor woman, with a tribe of children

---

8. English law[s] punished "vagrancy" or homelessness with imprisonment.   9. Robert Stewart, Lord Castlereagh (1769–1822) committed suicide.   10. Two of the Greek muses, said to preside over the arts and sciences.   11. Philip Dormer Stanhope, Earl of Chesterfield (1674–1773), English politician.   12. Bogs.

about her, had not a morsel of either meat or bread! At a house called an inn, a little further on, the landlord had no meat except a little bit of chine of bacon; and though there were a good many houses near the spot, the landlord told me that the people were become so poor that the butchers had left off killing meat in the neighbourhood. Just the state of things that existed in France on the eve of the Revolution. On that very spot I looked round me and counted more than two thousand fat sheep in the pastures! How long, how long, good God! is this state of things to last? How long will these people starve in the midst of plenty? How long will fire-engines, steel traps, and spring guns be, in such a state of things, a protection to property? When I was at Beverley, a gentleman told me, it was Mr. Dawson of that place, that some time before a farmer had been sold up by his landlord; and that, in a few weeks afterwards, the farm-house was on fire, and that when the servants of the landlord arrived to put it out, they found the handle of the pump taken away and that the homestead was totally destroyed. This was told me in the presence of several gentlemen, who all spoke of it as a fact of perfect notoriety.

Another respect in which our situation so exactly resembles that of France on the eve of the Revolution is the *fleeing from the country* in every direction. When I was in Norfolk there were four hundred persons, generally young men, labourers, carpenters, wheelwrights, millwrights, smiths, and bricklayers; most of them with some money, and some farmers and others with good round sums. These people were going to Quebec, in timber-ships, and from Quebec by land into the United States. They had been told that they would not be suffered to land in the United States from on board of ship. The roguish villains had deceived them: but no matter; they will get into the United States; and going through Canada will do them good, for it will teach them to detest everything belonging to it. From Boston two great barge loads had just gone off by canal to Liverpool, most of them farmers; all carrying some money, and some as much as two thousand pounds each. From the North and West Riding of Yorkshire numerous waggons have gone, carrying people to the canals leading to Liverpool; and a gentleman whom I saw at Peterboro' told me that he saw some of them; and that the men all appeared to be respectable farmers. At Hull the scene would delight the eyes of the wise Burdett[13]; for here the emigration is going on in the "old Roman plan."[14] Ten large ships have gone this spring, laden with these fugitives from the fangs of taxation; some bound direct to the ports of the United States; others, like those at Yarmouth, for Quebec. Those that have most money go direct to the United States. The single men, who are taken for a mere trifle in the Canada ships, go that way, have nothing but their carcasses to carry over the rocks and swamps, and through the myriads of place-men and pensioners in that miserable region; there are about fifteen more ships going from this one port this spring. The ships are fitted up with berths as transports for the carrying of troops. I went on board one morning, and saw the people putting their things on board and stowing them away. Seeing a nice young woman, with a little baby in her arms, I told her that she was going to a country where she would be sure that her children would never want victuals; where she might make her own malt, soap, and candles, without being half put to death for it, and where the blaspheming Jews would not have a mortgage on the life's labour of her children.

---

13. Frances Burdett (1770–1844), English radical politician.   14. The method of sending entire colonies to settle conquered territories.

There is at Hull one farmer going who is seventy years of age, but who takes out five sons and fifteen hundred pounds! Brave and sensible old man! and good and affectionate father! He is performing a truly parental and sacred duty; and he will die with the blessing of his sons on his head, for having rescued them from this scene of slavery, misery, cruelty, and crime. Come, then, Wilmot Horton, with your sensible associates, Burdett and Poulett Thomson; come into Lincolnshire, Norfolk, and Yorkshire; come and bring Parson Malthus[15] along with you; regale your sight with this delightful "stream of emigration"; congratulate the "greatest captain of the age," and your brethren of the Collective: congratulate the "noblest assembly of free men," on these the happy effects of their measures. Oh! no, Wilmot! Oh! no, generous and sensible Burdett, it is not the aged, the infirm, the halt, the blind, and the idiots that go: it is the youth, the strength, the wealth, and the spirit that will no longer brook hunger and thirst, in order that the maws of tax-eaters and Jews may be crammed. You want the Irish to go, and so they will *at our expense*, and all the bad of them, to be kept at our expense on the rocks and swamps of Nova Scotia and Canada. You have no money to send them away with: the tax-eaters want it all; and thanks to the "improvements of the age," the steam-boats will continue to bring them in shoals in pursuit of the orts[16] of the food that their taskmasters have taken away from them.

After evening lecture, at Horncastle, a very decent farmer came to me and asked me about America, telling me that he was resolved to go, for that if he stayed much longer, he should not have a shilling to go with. I promised to send him a letter from Louth to a friend at New York, who might be useful to him there, and give him good advice. I forgot it at Louth; but I will do it before I go to bed. From the Thames, and from the several ports down the Channel, about two thousand have gone this spring. All the flower of the labourers of the east of Sussex and west of Kent will be culled out and sent off in a short time. From Glasgow the sensible Scotch are pouring out amain. Those that are poor and cannot pay their passages, or can rake together only a trifle, are going to a rascally heap of sand and rock and swamp, called Prince Edward's Island, in the horrible Gulf of St. Lawrence; but when the American vessels come over with Indian corn and flour and pork and beef and poultry and eggs and butter and cabbages and green pease and asparagus for the soldier-officers and other tax-eaters that we support upon that lump of worthlessness; for the lump itself bears nothing but potatoes; when these vessels come, which they are continually doing, winter and summer; towards the fall, with apples and pears and melons and cucumbers; and, in short, ever-lastingly coming and taking away the amount of taxes raised in England; when these vessels return, the sensible Scotch will go back in them for a dollar a head, till at last not a man of them will be left but the bed-ridden. Those villainous colonies are held for no earthly purpose but that of furnishing a pretence of giving money to the relations and dependents of the aristocracy; and they are the nicest channels in the world through which to send English taxes to enrich and strengthen the United States. Withdraw the English taxes, and, except in a small part in Canada, the whole of those horrible regions would be left to the bears and the savages in the course of a year.

This emigration is a famous blow given to the borough-mongers.[17] The way to New York is now as well known and as easy and as little expensive as from old York

---

15. Robert Wilmot Horton (1784–1841), Francis Burdett (1770–1844), Charles Poulett Thomson (1799–1841), and Thomas Malthus (1766–1834), English advocates of emigration as a solution to social and economic problems. 16. Scraps. 17. Corrupt politicians.

to London. First the Sussex parishes sent their paupers; they invited over others that were not paupers; they invited over people of some property; then persons of greater property; now substantial farmers are going; men of considerable fortune will follow. It is the letters written across the Atlantic that do the business. Men of fortune will soon discover that, to secure to their families their fortunes, and to take these out of the grasp of the inexorable tax-gatherer, they must get away. Every one that goes will take twenty after him; and thus it will go on. There can be no interruption but *war*: and war the Thing[18] dares not have. As to France or the Netherlands, or any part of that hell called Germany, Englishmen can never settle there. The United States form another England without its unbearable taxes, its insolent game laws, its intolerable dead-weight, and its treadmills.

—1830

Robert Owen
1771–1858

Utopian socialist Robert Owen was the author of dozens of polemical and philosophical tracts, pamphlets, lectures, addresses, manifestos, and treatises. The son of a Welsh saddle maker, he was apprenticed as a boy to a cloth manufacturer, then opened a small cotton spinning business in Manchester. By the time he was twenty, his success had brought him to the attention of the owners of the city's largest spinning factory, and they took him on first as manager and then part owner. On the first day of the nineteenth century, he moved to New Lanark, south of Glasgow, where he bought a number of spinning mills from the wealthy industrialist David Dale, whose daughter, Caroline, he married. Owen ran the New Lanark mills as a decades-long experiment in humane capitalism. He reduced the workday to twelve hours, raised the minimum working age to ten years, and subsidized clothing, food, and savings for his workers. Owen believed that individual character was formed by social environment and that poverty was not, as most of his contemporaries believed, the fault of the poor. So he built a progressive school system at New Lanark that emphasized cooperation, creativity, and nonviolent correction of children's behavior. He also became rich by raising worker productivity through what he felt were enlightened methods of oversight. For instance, he hung a "monitor cube" above each worker's head; colored sides represented their differing levels of performance for all to see.

Owen had grand ambitions for his ideas, and he campaigned for a wide spectrum of reforms, such as international labor unions, a national school system, child labor laws, and liberalization of marriage laws to allow women more control over their lives. His friendship with radical political philosopher William Godwin pushed him further and further from the mainstream of liberalism. He lost many supporters when he began to argue for the abolition of religion and the formation of workers into large, cooperative communities. Owen envisioned a socialist world in which human labor would be so productive that society's basic needs could be met with just a few hours of labor each week, and poverty and antagonism would be replaced by worldwide plenty and harmony. Beginning in the mid-1820s, Owen devoted his inexhaustible energy to planting model communities in Ireland, Scotland, England, and around the Atlantic Rim, hoping that a successful experiment would prove the value of his ideas to the world. In the United States, Owen founded the community of New Harmony, on the banks of

18. Government.

the Wabash River in Indiana. While his model communities did not succeed in transforming the broader capitalist society, they remain central to the longstanding communitarian tradition. And the vision of a just, cooperative, harmonious world that Owen articulated so clearly continues to inspire readers and visionaries around the world.

from The Revolution in the Mind and Practice of the Human Race

The extended and increasing misery of the human race, arising from the want of the requisite knowledge to trace its cause and provide a remedy, calls loudly for the simple and plain language of truth, in the spirit of charity and kindness, to declare both cause and remedy to the authorities of the world.

But more especially is that language, in that spirit, necessary to the government of Great Britain; because of its extended dominions, isolated situation, and peculiar position among the excited and contending nations of Europe, now having populations so deeply involved in anarchy and confusion.

The enormous power of the British empire for good or for evil, and its present peaceful and secure position, compared with other nations, call upon it to take a friendly direction to assist these nations out of the miserably entangled state into which they have fallen.

And fallen, because they know not how to construct a rational system for educating and governing any population.

To these nations a remedy for these evils can be alone made evident by a frank and straightforward avowal of important and vital truths, in language so plain as not to be misunderstood.

The British empire is now generally admitted to be the most advanced, and, next to the United States, the most secure, of any nation; yet all nations at this crisis, are subject to manifold casualties at home and abroad.

Great Britain is now, with the most ample means to create illimitable wealth, and to make its dominions an example of high prosperity and wisdom, involved, like other nations, in a complicated system of error in principle and practice, and which makes it a glaring example of poverty, crime, disease, and misery, among the majority of its population; while the few are deeply injured by an excess of wealth and luxury, and of injustice to the many.

Hitherto, all governments have acted, from necessity, as the circumstances in which they have been placed have compelled them to act; and so they must continue to do; therefore are they, rationally speaking, blameless, and require to be assisted out of their difficulties.

It is only by superior circumstances being brought to act upon governments, that their proceedings can be beneficially changed, and their condition permanently improved. It is therefore that I now wish to bring before the British government new associations of true and valuable ideas for practice, in order to create a new necessity, to induce it to feel, think, and act in future, rationally, for the permanent happiness of the population of every class.

Knowing, as I do, the overwhelming influence of circumstances over human nature, I naturally desire to create such superior new circumstances as will induce the British government to abandon this now worn-out system of falsehood and evil, and to adopt another in principle and practice, based on truth, and which, when wisely introduced, will produce illimitable goodness and happiness, not only to the population of the British dominions, but to the population of the world; for now, all nations look to the British government for wise advice and a rational example.

Your position[1] is, therefore, one of great power for good or evil; and I am now about to declare to you vital truths, in opposition to a mistaught public opinion, (believing that truth alone can now save the nations of Europe from domestic discontent, civil wars, and endless evils,) truths, which until now, could not have been spoken without endangering the life of the speaker.

The truth, then, is, "That the British government, advanced as it is beyond many other governments, is a government of evil, doing that which, for the happiness of all, it should not do, and leaving undone all that is requisite to produce permanent prosperity, goodness, and happiness to the population.

"That, by institutions emanating from laws based on ignorance of human nature, the mass of the people are kept in unnecessary degrading imbecility of mind, and in abject poverty.

"That, by these insane institutions and laws, many are kept in idleness, who desire to be employed, and who would willingly add to the wealth of the nation by producing more than they would consume; and that, instead of being compelled to be a dead-weight upon the most industrious, they would prefer to be industrious, and to assist to support others, which they might easily be arranged to do.

"That hitherto the British government has made no common-sense arrangements to educate the people in good habits and dispositions, to give them the most useful and valuable knowledge, and to train them to become rational beings, which should be the first and chief duty of all governments.

"That, instead of well-arranged measures to effect these results in the best manner, institutions have been formed and artificial laws have been adopted, to keep the people in brutal ignorance, and degrading poverty; to force them to acquire inferior and bad habits; and to lead them gradually to commit crime, and to advance from one crime to another, until they often become unbearable to society, and thus render necessary an artificial system of punishment.

"That the British Government, under this irrational conduct, continues to spare no expense, after it has, by most unwise and unjust measures, forced the people to acquire bad habits and commit crimes, to detect and punish those whose characters it has thus previously misformed; while, to give good habits and dispositions, sound and valuable knowledge, and to make the people rational beings, it is most sparing of expense; freely voting, with great unanimity, seventy thousand pounds to extend the stables of royalty, at the same period that it grudgingly voted thirty thousand pounds to most imperfectly educate the great mass of the untaught and illtaught within the British dominions.

"That the government sanctions, or permits, the most unhealthy and unwise arrangements to arise all over the country to create and nurse disease; and then, at an enormous expense, it adopts some little futile measures to attempt to stay aggravated disease and effect some partial cures, leaving the great causes which create the evil untouched and even unthought-of.

"That, while the government expresses a continual desire to give permanent prosperity to the people, it adopts the most efficient measures in practice to pre-

---

1. This introductory letter to Owen's manifesto is addressed to Queen Victoria.

vent the possible attainment of this object; and in which unfortunate result it succeeds to the astonishment of all who know the immense power which Great
Britain possesses to insure health, wealth, knowledge, goodness, and happiness, to
all, of every age.

"That the British Government, knowing (if it possesses any sound knowledge or
practical wisdom) that good and superior external circumstances will, of necessity,
form good and superior men and women, and that bad and inferior circumstances will
of necessity form bad and inferior men and women, yet, with the most ample means
to create universally the good and superior external circumstances, allows and
encourages the worst and most inferior to be created and daily increased; although to
create and maintain the good and superior would be far more economical, and more
easy to govern; while they would ensure happiness to all, without any of the repulsive
feelings, anxieties, and turmoil, which now prevent the possible existence of a
healthy state of society, or the adoption of measures, to make men and women feel,
think, and act, like rational beings."

In fact, *the British Government, in consequence of its members having been taught and
trained in error from their birth, and not knowing how to devise governmental arrangements
to create a superior character, and a superfluity of wealth for all, is, directly or indirectly,
the cause of all the ignorance, poverty, disease, disunion, crime, and their consequent miseries, now so prevalent throughout the British dominions.*

And, little as it may be suspected, owing to the same misinstruction and want of
knowledge, *the British Government is also, directly or indirectly, the cause of all the
unkindness and want of charity from man to man, and of all the inferior and injurious passions, which afflict the subjects of the empire.*

Were the British Government in possession of knowledge to enable it to devise
and carry into execution efficient practical measures to well form the character and
create a superfluity of wealth for all (both of which, with the means now at its control, could be easily accomplished), it would prevent the further creation of poverty,
disunion, and crime, and it would also rapidly diminish these evils, which have been
so unwisely allowed to exist to the detriment of all.

*You have now the most ample means and power, by adopting the most simple and plain
common sense measures, thus, to change all that is now wrong in society, and gradually and
peaceably to supersede it by all that is right and most beneficial for every one.*

For instance, you might commence these practical operations in every county in
Ireland, beginning where they are the most immediately required to stay famine and
misery, both of which are scarcely to be equalled in savage life, where the least means
are to be found.

And immediately afterwards similar measures might be introduced into every
county in Great Britain; and thus would the surplus of labour (which could exist only
under a wretchedly false system), be at once taken up, and most advantageously
employed, both for the old and the new system.

It can no longer be hidden from the people that you hold the power of adversity
and prosperity in your hands, and that, through want of knowledge, you have, so far,
given them ignorance and adversity, instead of knowledge and prosperity.

It is a momentous and awful crisis in which all governments and people are
placed. It is the breaking up of the old irrational system, by which alone the human
race has been governed in a state of ignorance and inexperience, and in which their

characters have been misformed from the beginning. It is the commencement of the greatest change the population of the world has yet experienced; a change from the most irrational system, producing repulsion and misery, more or less, to all—to the rational system, which will produce attraction and happiness to every one. It is a change from all manner of irrational and inferior circumstances, from which all evil proceeds, to a new combination of very superior circumstances, which will produce continually goodness and happiness only.

Will you now investigate this all important subject, and, if you find that I have declared that only which is true, good, and practical, will you adopt the principles and practices now recommended?

—1849

George Ripley
1802–1880

George Ripley was a wide-ranging and open-minded reader, thinker, and activist. He was the lead editor of the fifteen-volume collection *Specimens of Foreign Standard Literature* (1830–1842), which first introduced European Romantic literature and philosophy to American audiences. He was also a liberal Unitarian minister and led Boston's Purchase Street Church for thirteen years, publishing influential theological essays in the *Christian Examiner* and the *Christian Register*. Ripley was radicalized by the harsh poverty that developed in urban Boston when 1837's financial panic deepened into a nationwide depression. In 1840, he galvanized the city by resigning his pastorship to found a utopian socialist community, the Brook Farm Institute of Agriculture and Education, together with his wife, Sophia. They believed that the deepening class division in society resulted from prejudices about the relative value of headwork and handwork. So it was potentially revolutionary for people like himself, cultural leaders of the elite, to perform their own manual labor. By setting a visible example of productive cooperation, the Ripleys hoped to convince the rest of society to follow their lead. During the planning phases of their venture, Ripley wrote to his close friend and fellow ex-minister Ralph Waldo Emerson, inviting him to join. Emerson agreed with much of what Ripley had to say and admired the motives behind the project, but he declined the invitation. He felt that his own community, Concord, was its own kind of utopia, and a more authentic one since it had grown organically, rather than being a kind of mechanical invention. This exchange was a definitive juncture in the history of Transcendentalism, a fork in the road that separated its individualist and collectivist wings.

Initially, Brook Farm was little more than a scheme for cooperative living for members of Boston's intellectual elite. But its character evolved rapidly. Increasingly, it came to be seen as the flagship of a nationwide communitarian movement. A number of Brook Farm residents became successful traveling lecturers, speaking regularly on socialist ideas. Thousands of visitors came to the Farm every year, including a majority of the reform-minded intellectuals of the period. Orestes Brownson sent his son to be educated at the Brook Farm school. Ripley's newspaper, *The Harbinger*, was the most widely read antebellum socialist periodical. In its pages, he argued that the pressures of competition at the heart of American capitalism were responsible not only for poverty but also for slavery, the oppression of women, and the invasion of Mexico. After the collapse of Brook Farm, during the last quarter century of his life, Ripley became the most powerful and acute literary critic in the United States, writing for Horace Greeley's *New York Tribune*.

Letter to Ralph Waldo Emerson
Boston, November 9, 1840.

My dear Sir,—Our conversation in Concord was of such a general nature, that I do not feel as if you were in complete possession of the idea of the Association which I wish to see established. As we have now a prospect of carrying it into effect, at an early period, I wish to submit the plan more distinctly to your judgment, that you may decide whether it is one that can have the benefit of your aid and coöperation.

Our objects, as you know, are to insure a more natural union between intellectual and manual labor than now exists; to combine the thinker and the worker, as far as possible, in the same individual; to guarantee the highest mental freedom, by providing all with labor, adapted to their tastes and talents, and securing to them the fruits of their industry; to do away the necessity of menial services, by opening the benefits of education and the profits of labor to all; and thus to prepare a society of liberal, intelligent, and cultivated persons, whose relations with each other would permit a more simple and wholesome life, than can be led amidst the pressure of our competitive institutions.

To accomplish these objects, we propose to take a small tract of land, which, under skillful husbandry, uniting the garden and the farm, will be adequate to the subsistence of the families; and to connect with this a school or college, in which the most complete instruction shall be given, from the first rudiments to the highest culture. Our farm would be a place for improving the race of men that lived on it; thought would preside over the operations of labor, and labor would contribute to the expansion of thought; we should have industry without drudgery, and true equality without its vulgarity.

An offer has been made to us of a beautiful estate, on very reasonable terms, on the borders of Newton, West Roxbury, and Dedham.[1] I am very familiar with the premises, having resided on them a part of last summer, and we might search the country in vain for anything more eligible. Our proposal now is for three or four families to take possession on the first of April next, to attend to the cultivation of the farm and the erection of buildings, to prepare for the coming of as many more in the autumn, and thus to commence the institution in the simplest manner, and with the smallest number, with which it can go into operation at all. It would thus be not less than two or three years, before we should be joined by all who mean to be with us; we should not fall to pieces by our own weight; we should grow up slowly and strong; and the attractiveness of our experiment would win to us all whose society we should want.

The step now to be taken at once is the procuring of funds for the necessary capital. According to the present modification of our plan, a much less sum will be required than that spoken of in our discussions at Concord. We thought then $50,000 would be needed; I find now, after a careful estimate, that $30,000 will purchase the estate and buildings for ten families, and give the required surplus for carrying on the operations for one year.

We propose to raise this sum by a subscription to a joint stock company, among the friends of the institution, the payment of a fixed interest being guaranteed to the subscribers, and the subscription itself secured by the real estate. No man then will be in danger of losing; he will receive as fair an interest as he would from any invest-

---

1. Towns near Boston.

ment, while at the same time he is contributing towards an institution, in which while the true use of money is retained, its abuses are done away. The sum required cannot come from rich capitalists; their instinct would protest against such an application of their coins; it must be obtained from those who sympathize with our ideas, and who are willing to aid their realization with their money, if not by their personal coöperation. There are some of this description on whom I think we can rely; among ourselves we can produce perhaps $10,000; the remainder must be subscribed for by those who wish us well, whether they mean to unite with us or not.

I can imagine no plan which is suited to carry into effect so many divine ideas as this. If wisely executed, it will be a light over this country and this age. If not the sunrise, it will be the morning star. As a practical man, I see clearly that we must have some such arrangement, or all changes less radical will be nugatory. I believe in the divinity of labor; I wish to "harvest my flesh and blood from the land;" but to do this, I must either be insulated and work to disadvantage, or avail myself of the services of hirelings, who are not of my order, and whom I can scarce make friends; for I must have another to drive the plough, which I hold. I cannot empty a cask of lime[2] upon my grass alone. I wish to see a society of educated friends, working, thinking, and living together, with no strife, except that of each to contribute the most to the benefit of all.

Personally, my tastes and habits would lead me in another direction. I have a passion for being independent of the world, and of every man in it. This I could do easily on the estate which is now offered, and which I could rent at a rate, that with my other resources, would place me in a very agreeable condition, as far as my personal interests were involved. I should have a city of God, on a small scale of my own; and please God, I should hope one day to drive my own cart to market and sell greens. But I feel bound to sacrifice this private feeling, in the hope of a great social good. I shall be anxious to hear from you. Your decision will do much towards settling the question with me, whether the time has come for the fulfillment of a high hope, or whether the work belongs to a future generation. All omens now are favorable; a singular union of diverse talents is ready for the enterprise; everything indicates that we ought to arise and build; and if we let slip this occasion, the unsleeping Nemesis will deprive us of the boon we seek. For myself, I am sure that I can never give so much thought to it again; my mind must act on other objects, and I shall acquiesce in the course of fate, with grief that so fair a light is put out. A small pittance of the wealth which has been thrown away on ignoble objects, during this wild contest for political supremacy, would lay the cornerstone of a house, which would ere long become the desire of nations.

I almost forgot to say that our friends, the "Practical Christians,"[3] insist on making their "Standard,"—a written document,—a prescribed test. This cuts them off. Perhaps we are better without them. They are good men; they have salt, which we needed with our spice; but we might have proved too liberal, too comprehensive, too much attached to the graces of culture, to suit their ideas. Instead of them, we have the offer of ten or twelve "Practical Men," from Mr. S. G. May, who himself is deeply interested in the proposal, and would like one day to share in its concerns. Pray write me with as much frankness as I have used towards you, and believe me ever your friend and faithful servant,

GEORGE RIPLEY

---

2. Fertilizer.   3. Followers of Adin Ballou (1803–1890), Christian socialist.

P.S. I ought to add, that in the present stage of the enterprise no proposal is considered as binding. We wish only to know what can probably be relied on, provided always, that no pledge will be accepted until the articles of association are agreed on by all parties.

I recollect you said that if you were sure of compeers of the right stamp you might embark yourself in the adventure: as to this, let me suggest the inquiry, whether our Association should not be composed of various classes of men? If we have friends whom we love and who love us, I think we should be content to join with others, with whom our personal sympathy is not strong, but whose general ideas coincide with ours, and whose gifts and abilities would make their services important. For instance, I should like to have a good washerwoman in my parish admitted into the plot. She is certainly not a Minerva or a Venus[4]; but we might educate her two children to wisdom and varied accomplishments, who otherwise will be doomed to drudge through life. The same is true of some farmers and mechanics, whom we should like with us.

—1840

Orestes Brownson
1803–1876

Orestes Brownson was raised by strict Vermont Congregationalist foster parents after his father's early death. Throughout his life he applied an intensely logical mind to the problem of living morally in the modern world. At nineteen he converted to Presbyterianism and a few years later became a Universalist preacher. During the 1820s, he worked closely with English radicals, Robert Dale Owen (the son of Robert Owen) and Fanny Wright, helping them build the New York Workingmen's Party. Perhaps because of the frustrations of electoral politics, Brownson soon came to accept William Ellery Channing's argument that workers and the poor should concentrate on "self-culture" rather than seek direct political confrontation with the wealthy. In 1836, he gathered a congregation of Boston's unchurched workers, describing his goals in *New Views of Christianity, Society, and the Church* (1836). He hoped that by uniting workers and their employers in Christian fellowship, his "Church of the Future" could overcome class antagonism and improve working and living conditions for the poor.

Together with Ralph Waldo Emerson and others, Brownson was a founding member of the Transcendentalist Club. For a time he was regarded as the leading intellectual in New England. His *Boston Quarterly Review* (1838–1842), which he described as "*The Dial* with a beard," had at least one thousand subscribers. He helped domesticate German Romanticism, translating much of Immanuel Kant's *Critique of Pure Reason* (1781). And his 1839 review of Andrews Norton's *Evidences of the Genuineness of the Four Gospels* (1837) was one of the most uncompromising defenses of Transcendentalism against its conservative critics. At the same time that he engaged in such intellectual combat, Brownson also acted as a passionate advocate for his working-class parishioners, becoming increasingly urgent and radical as the Panic of 1837 threw hundreds of thousands into crushing poverty.

In 1840 he published a review of Thomas Carlyle's *Chartism* (1839) titled "The Laboring Classes." In this explosive essay, Brownson describes the pattern of recurring recessions that result from competition under capitalism and that periodically throw society as a whole into

---

4. Greek goddesses of wisdom and love.

crisis. He warns that unless the ruling class takes immediate steps to ensure a measure of social and economic equality, there will come a violent confrontation, a revolution in which workers will attempt to overthrow the capitalist order that keeps them in grueling poverty. Brownson was viciously attacked for his apparent radicalism, even though he saw himself as delivering a warning, not a revolutionary manifesto. This may partly account for his subsequent conversion to Catholicism in 1844, a decision that the *Dublin Review* found newsworthy enough to dedicate a full article to its analysis. Over the next thirty years, Brownson retreated into conservatism, and by the end of his life he had been written out of the history of the Transcendentalist movement he helped to found.

from The Laboring Classes

There is no country in Europe, in which the condition of the laboring classes seems to us so hopeless as in that of England. This is not owing to the fact, that the aristocracy is less enlightened, more powerful, or more oppressive in England than elsewhere. The English laborer does not find his worst enemy in the nobility, but in the middling class. The middle class is much more numerous and powerful in England than in any other European country, and is of a higher character. It has always been powerful; for by means of the Norman Conquest[1] it received large accessions from the old Saxon nobility. The Conquest established a new aristocracy, and degraded the old to the condition of Commoners. The superiority of the English Commons is, we suppose, chiefly owing to this fact.

The middle class is always a firm champion of equality, when it concerns humbling a class above it; but it is its inveterate foe, when it concerns elevating a class below it. Manfully have the British Commoners struggled against the old feudal aristocracy, and so successfully that they now constitute the dominant power in the state. To their struggles against the throne and the nobility is the English nation indebted for the liberty it so loudly boasts, and which, during the last half of the last century, so enraptured the friends of Humanity throughout Europe.

But this class has done nothing for the laboring population, the real *proletarii*.[2] It has humbled the aristocracy; it has raised itself to dominion, and it is now conservative,—conservative in fact, whether it call itself Whig or Radical. From its near relation to the workingmen, its kindred pursuits with them, it is altogether more hostile to them than the nobility ever were or ever can be. This was seen in the conduct of England towards the French Revolution. So long as that Revolution was in the hands of the middle class, and threatened merely to humble monarchy and nobility, the English nation applauded it; but as soon as it descended to the mass of the people, and promised to elevate the laboring classes, so soon as the starving workingman began to flatter himself, that there was to be a Revolution for him too as well as for his employer, the English nation armed itself and poured out its blood and treasure to suppress it. Everybody knows that Great Britain, boasting of her freedom and of her love of freedom, was the life and soul of the opposition to the French Revolution; and on her head almost alone should fall the curses of Humanity for the sad failure of that glorious uprising of the people in behalf of their imprescriptible, and inalienable rights. Yet it was not the English monarchy, nor the English nobility, that was alone in fault. Monarchy and nobility would have been powerless, had they not had with them the great body of the

---

1. Invasion of England by William the Conqueror in 1066.   2. The poorest class in ancient Rome.

English Commoners. England fought in the ranks, nay, at the head of the allies, not for monarchy, not for nobility, nor yet for religion; but for trade and manufactures, for her middle class, against the rights and well-being of the workingman; and her strength and efficiency consisted in the strength and efficiency of this class.

No one can observe the signs of the times with much care, without perceiving that a crisis as to the relation of wealth and labor is approaching. It is useless to shut our eyes to the fact, and like the ostrich fancy ourselves secure because we have so concealed our heads that we see not the danger. We or our children will have to meet this crisis. The old war between the King and the Barons is well nigh ended, and so is that between the Barons and the Merchants and Manufacturers,—landed capital and commercial capital. The business man has become the peer of my Lord. And now commences the new struggle between the operative and his employer, between wealth and labor. Every day does this struggle extend further and wax stronger and fiercer; what or when the end will be God only knows.

We pass through our manufacturing villages, most of them appear neat and flourishing. The operatives are well dressed, and we are told, well paid. They are said to be healthy, contented, and happy. This is the fair side of the picture; the side exhibited to distinguished visitors. There is a dark side, moral as well as physical. Of the common operatives, few, if any, by their wages, acquire a competence.[3] A few of what Carlyle[4] terms not inaptly the *body-servants* are well paid, and now and then an agent or an overseer rides in his coach. But the great mass wear out their health, spirits, and morals, without becoming one whit better off than when they commenced labor. The bills of mortality in these factory villages are not striking, we admit, for the poor girls when they can toil no longer go home to die. The average life, working life we mean, of the girls that come to Lowell, for instance, from Maine, New Hampshire, and Vermont, we have been assured, is only about three years. What becomes of them then? Few of them ever marry; fewer still ever return to their native places with reputations unimpaired. "She has worked in a Factory," is almost enough to damn to infamy the most worthy and virtuous girl. We know no sadder sight on earth than one of our factory villages presents, when the bell at break of day, or at the hour of breakfast, or dinner, calls out its hundreds or thousands of operatives. We stand and look at these hard working men and women hurrying in all directions, and ask ourselves, where go the proceeds of their labors? The man who employs them, and for whom they are toiling as so many slaves, is one of our city nabobs,[5] revelling in luxury; or he is a member of our legislature, enacting laws to put money in his own pocket; or he is a member of Congress, contending for a high Tariff to tax the poor for the benefit of the rich; or in these times he is shedding crocodile tears over the deplorable condition of the poor laborer, while he docks his wages twenty-five per cent.; building miniature log cabins, shouting Harrison[6] and "hard cider." And this man too would fain pass for a Christian and a republican. He shouts for liberty, stickles for equality, and is horrified at a Southern planter who keeps slaves.

One thing is certain; that of the amount actually produced by the operative,[7] he retains a less proportion than it costs the master to feed, clothe, and lodge his slave. Wages is a cunning device of the devil, for the benefit of tender consciences, who would retain all the advantages of the slave system, without the expense, trouble, and odium of being slave-holders.

---

3. Enough to survive.   4. Thomas Carlyle (1795–1881), English political philosopher.   5. Wealthy person.   6. William Henry Harrison (1773–1841), ninth president of the United States.   7. The worker.

Now the great work for this age and the coming, is to raise up the laborer, and to realize in our own social arrangements and in the actual condition of all men, that equality between man and man, which God has established between the rights of one and those of another. In other words, our business is to emancipate the proletaries, as the past has emancipated the slaves. This is our work. There must be no class of our fellow men doomed to toil through life as mere workmen at wages. If wages are tolerated it must be, in the case of the individual operative, only under such conditions that by the time he is of a proper age to settle in life, he shall have accumulated enough to be an independent laborer on his own capital,—on his own farm or in his own shop. Here is our work. How is it to be done?

Reformers in general answer this question, or what they deem its equivalent, in a manner which we cannot but regard as very unsatisfactory. They would have all men wise, good, and happy; but in order to make them so, they tell us that we want not external changes, but internal; and therefore instead of declaiming against society and seeking to disturb existing social arrangements, we should confine ourselves to the individual reason and conscience; seek merely to lead the individual to repentance, and to reformation of life; make the individual a practical, a truly religious man, and all evils will either disappear, or be sanctified to the spiritual growth of the soul.

This is doubtless a capital theory, and has the advantage that kings, hierarchies, nobilities,—in a word, all who fatten on the toil and blood of their fellows, will feel no difficulty in supporting it. Nicholas of Russia, the Grand Turk,[8] his Holiness the Pope, will hold us their especial friends for advocating a theory, which secures to them the odor of sanctity even while they are sustaining by their anathemas or their armed legions, a system of things of which the great mass are and must be the victims. If you will only allow me to keep thousands toiling for my pleasure or my profit, I will even aid you in your pious efforts to convert their souls. I am not cruel; I do not wish either to cause, or to see suffering; I am therefore disposed to encourage your labors for the souls of the workingman, providing you will secure to me the products of his bodily toil. So far as the salvation of his soul will not interfere with my income, I hold it worthy of being sought; and if a few thousand dollars will aid you, Mr. Priest, in reconciling him to God, and making fair weather for him hereafter, they are at your service. I shall not want him to work for me in the world to come, and I can indemnify myself for what your salary costs me, by paying him less wages. A capital theory this, which one may advocate without incurring the reproach of a disorganizer, a jacobin, a leveller, and without losing the friendship of the rankest aristocrat in the land.

This theory, however, is exposed to one slight objection, that of being condemned by something like six thousand years' experience. For six thousand years its beauty has been extolled, its praises sung, and its blessings sought, under every advantage which learning, fashion, wealth, and power can secure; and yet under its practical operations, we are assured, that mankind, though totally depraved at first, have been growing worse and worse ever since.

The truth is, the evil we have pointed out is not merely individual in its character. It is not, in the case of any single individual, of any one man's procuring, nor can the efforts of any one man, directed solely to his own moral and religious perfection, do aught to remove it. What is purely individual in its nature, efforts of individuals to

8. Nicholas I (1796–1855), Emperor of Russia; "Grand Turk" is a western term for the sovereign of the Ottoman dynasty.

perfect themselves, may remove. But the evil we speak of is inherent in all our social arrangements, and cannot be cured without a radical change of those arrangements. Could we convert all men to Christianity in both theory and practice, as held by the most enlightened sect of Christians among us, the evils of the social state would remain untouched. Continue our present system of trade, and all its present evil consequences will follow, whether it be carried on by your best men or your worst. Put your best men, your wisest, most moral, and most religious men, at the head of your paper money banks, and the evils of the present banking system will remain scarcely diminished. The only way to get rid of its evils is to change the system, not its managers. The evils of slavery do not result from the personal characters of slave masters. They are inseparable from the system, let who will be masters. Make all your rich men good Christians, and you have lessened not the evils of existing inequality in wealth. The mischievous effects of this inequality do not result from the personal characters of either rich or poor, but from itself, and they will continue, just so long as there are rich men and poor men in the same community. You must abolish the system or accept its consequences. No man can serve both God and Mammon.[9] If you will serve the devil, you must look to the devil for your wages; we know no other way.

According to the Christianity of Christ no man can enter the kingdom of God, who does not labor with all zeal and diligence to establish the kingdom of God on the earth; who does not labor to bring down the high, and bring up the low; to break the fetters of the bound and set the captive free; to destroy all oppression, establish the reign of justice, which is the reign of equality, between man and man; to introduce new heavens and a new earth, wherein dwelleth righteousness, wherein all shall be as brothers, loving one another, and no one possessing what another lacketh. No man can be a Christian who does not labor to reform society, to mould it according to the will of God and the nature of man; so that free scope shall be given to every man to unfold himself in all beauty and power, and to grow up into the stature of a perfect man in Christ Jesus. No man can be a Christian who does not refrain from all practices by which the rich grow richer and the poor poorer, and who does not do all in his power to elevate the laboring classes, so that one man shall not be doomed to toil while another enjoys the fruits; so that each man shall be free and independent, sitting under "his own vine and figtree with none to molest or to make afraid."[10] We grant the power of Christianity in working out the reform we demand; we agree that one of the most efficient means of elevating the workingman is to christianize the community. But you must christianize it. It is the Gospel of Jesus you must preach, and not the gospel of the priests. Preach the Gospel of Jesus, and that will turn every man's attention to the crying evil we have designated, and will arm every Christian with power to effect those changes in social arrangements, which shall secure to all men the equality of position and condition, which it is already acknowledged they possess in relation to their rights. But let it be the genuine Gospel that you preach, and not that pseudo-gospel, which lulls the conscience asleep, and permits men to feel that they may be servants of God while they are slaves to the world, the flesh, and the devil; and while they ride roughshod over the hearts of their prostrate brethren. We must preach no Gospel that permits men to feel that they are honorable men and good Christians, although rich and with eyes standing out with fatness, while the great mass of their brethren are suf-

---

9. A false god of riches.   10. Paraphrases George Washington (1732–1799), "Letter to Touro Synagogue" (1790).

fering from iniquitous laws, from mischievous social arrangements, and pining away for the want of the refinements and even the necessaries of life.

—1840

Elizabeth Palmer Peabody
1804–1894

It is no coincidence that Elizabeth Palmer Peabody had strong interests in education and British poetry: Her mother and namesake taught and ran a school and edited an American edition of Edmund Spenser's verse. Following in her mother's footsteps, Peabody ran the Temple School with Amos Bronson Alcott, pioneered the Kindergarten Movement, and was instrumental in raising American appreciation and understanding of the poetry of William Wordsworth, with whom she corresponded. She would remain close to Ralph Waldo Emerson and his fellow Transcendentalists throughout her life. Indeed, it was out of Peabody's Boston bookshop that the Transcendentalist journal *The Dial* was published, and it was thanks to her early promotion of the works of Emerson and Nathaniel Hawthorne, the latter of whom married her sister Sophia, that these two writers achieved such recognition in America and England. First exposed to the theology and metaphysics of Samuel Taylor Coleridge and the German Transcendentalists during her nine years as secretary to the New England theologian and proto-Transcendentalist William Ellery Channing, Peabody readily saw how the philosophy of this movement could revolutionize education and bring about a much more equal America. Peabody's bookshop became a classroom of sorts for the intellectuals of the day. Hawthorne's as well as Margaret Fuller's books were printed there, and the views of many British and European intellectuals were eagerly discussed at the shop and amply represented among her stock of foreign books. The works of European reformers, such as Charles Fourier's plans for utopian living, provided foreign inspiration for domestic reform. These ideas spurred the Brook Farm community, a Massachusetts-based attempt at communal living and thinking conceived in Peabody's bookstore and carried out by Transcendentalists. Peabody wrote two articles about Brook Farm, which was meant to embody on a microcosmic level the potential America could achieve on the macrocosmic level.

from A Glimpse of Christ's Idea of Society

No sooner is it surmised that the kingdom of heaven and the Christian Church are the same thing, and that this thing is not an association *ex parte*[1] society, but a reorganization of society itself, on those very principles of Love to God and Love to Man which Jesus Christ realized in his own daily life, than we perceive the Day of Judgment for society is come, and all the words of Christ are so many trumpets of doom. For before the judgment-seat of his sayings how do our governments, our trades, our etiquettes, even our benevolent institutions and churches, look? What Church in Christendom, that numbers among its members a pauper or a negro, may stand the thunder of that one word, "Inasmuch as ye have not done it unto the least of these little ones, ye have not done it unto ME;"[2] and yet the Church of Christ, the kingdom of heaven, shall not come upon earth, according to our daily prayer, unless not only every church, but every trade, every form of social intercourse, every institution political or other, can abide this test.

---

1. Outside, beyond.   2. Matthew 25.40.

We are not extravagant. We admit that to be human implies to be finite; that to be finite implies obstruction, difficulty, temptation, and struggle; but we think it evident that *Jesus* believed men could make it a principle to be perfect as the Father in heaven is perfect; that they could *begin* to love and assist each other; that these principles could and would prevail over the Earth at last; that he aimed in his social action at nothing partial; that he did not despair of society itself being organized in harmony with the two commandments in which he generalized the Law and the Prophets.[3] He surely did not believe these things from experience or observation of the world, but from the consciousness of Pure Reason.[4] His own eye, so clear and pure, and bent inward on a complete soul, saw the immensity of it in its relation to God. Here was his witness, the Father who taught him the all-sufficient force to be roused in the consciousness of every other man. When he bade every man, in order to this awakening, live on the principle and plan that he lived on, of unfolding and obeying the divine instinct, under the conscious protection of the Being of beings, considered as a father,—he saw that a kingdom of Heaven on Earth must necessarily follow; in other words, that the moral law would become supreme, and human nature, sanctified and redeemed, be unfolded in beauty and peace. Only at first, and because of the evil already organized in the world, would the manifestation of the Eternal Peace be a sword, and the introduction into the world of the Life be, to the individuals who should do it, suffering and death.

We are desirous to establish this point, because it is often taken for granted, since the period of the French Revolution, that all movements towards new organization[5] are unchristian. One would think, from the tone of conservatives, that Jesus accepted the society around him as an adequate framework for individual development into beauty and life, instead of calling his disciples "out of the world."[6] We maintain, on the other hand, that Christ desired to reorganize society, and went to a depth of principle and a magnificence of plan for this end, which has never been appreciated, except here and there, by an individual, still less been carried out. Men, calling themselves Christians, are apt to say that it is visionary to think of reorganizing society on better principles; that whatever different arrangements might be made, human nature would reduce them to the same level. But when we think of the effect that a few great and good men have had, what worlds of thought and power open on our minds! Leaving Jesus at the head, and ranging through such names as Moses, Confucius, Socrates, Paul, Luther, Fénelon, Washington,[7] and whatever other men have worshipped the spirit and believed it would remove mountains, are we not authorized to hope infinitely? These men have trusted the soul in its possible union with God, and in just such degree as they did have they become Saviours of men. If one of them is so prominent over the rest as to have borne away that title pre-eminently, it is because he alone is sublime in his faith; he alone fully realized by life, as well as thought and feeling, that the soul and its Father are one, and greatly prayed that all his disciples should be one with God also, without a doubt of the ultimate answer of this prayer. He alone went so deeply into human nature as to perceive that what he called himself was universal. He alone, therefore, among men, is entitled to the grateful homage of all men, for he alone has *respected*

---

3. "Thou shalt love the Lord thy God" and "Thou shalt love thy neighbor as thyself." Matthew 22.37–40.   4. Divinely inspired intuition.   5. Social organization. 6. John 17.6–17.   7. Moses, leader of Israelites in the Bible; Confucius (551–449 BC), Chinese philosopher; Socrates (470–399 BC), Greek philosopher; Paul of Tarsus (3–67), early Christian evangelist; Martin Luther (1483–1546), German theologian and church reformer; François Fénelon (1651–1715), French theologian; and George Washington (1732–1799), American president.

all men, even the lost and dead. When it came to that extreme of circumstance still he did not despair, but said, "I am the resurrection and the life."[8] Here, indeed, was the consciousness of immortality which is absolute. The finite may go no farther than this. And human nature has not been insensible to this great manifestation, but has worshipped Jesus as the absolutely divine. There was a truth in this worship, the noblest of all idolatries, though in its evil effects we are made aware that "the corruption of the best is the worst,"[9] and see the *rationale* of the old commandment, that we should make no image of the unimaginable God, even out of any thing in heaven. Both the Church and the mass of our society are fierce to defend the position that Jesus of Nazareth lived a divine life in the flesh. Not satisfied with the admission of the fact, they would establish the necessity of it *a priori*,[10] by denying him that human element which makes evil a possibility. When Jesus said *I*, they would have us believe he meant to say the absolute spirit. Let us gladly admit it. When Jesus said *I*, he referred to a divine being. Jesus is doubtless one transparent form of the *infinite* Goodness,—but he is only *one form*, and there can be but one of a form in an Infinite Creation. Here is the common mistake. Jesus Christ is made the model of form and not reverenced as a quickening spirit purely. Because other men could not realize his form, they have been supposed to be essentially different natures, while another Jesus would not have been natural in any event. Oneness with God does not require any particular form. Raphael and Michael Angelo[11] might have been one with God no less than was Jesus, but they would doubtless still have been painters and sculptors, and not preachers, nor moral reformers. The same method of life which made Jesus what he was would make every other soul different from him in outward action and place. We do infinite injustice to this noble being when we fancy that he intended to cut men to a pattern; when we say that any special mode of activity makes a member of his Church. A member of the Church of Christ is the most individual of men. He works miracles at no man's and no woman's bidding. He ever says words not expected. He does deeds no man can foretell. His utterances are prophecies, which the future only can make significant. His intimacy with the Father isolates him even among his nearest friends. Ever and anon, like the lark, he departs even from the sight of his beloved mates on earth, into a "privacy of glorious light," where, however, his music "thrills not the less the bosom of the plain."[12]

But if the world has always been right in seeing that Jesus lived a divine life on the earth, the question is, What was that life? What was the principle and method of it? How did he live? Did he model himself on any form? Did he study tradition as something above himself? Did he ask for any daysman[13] between himself and God? And did he, or did he not, teach that we should live as he did? Did he, or did he not, imply that that depth of soul to which he applied the word *I* was an universal inheritance when he said, "Inasmuch as ye have not done it unto the least of these little ones, ye have not done it unto me?" If this will not, what can teach that the divine element reverenced in himself exists also to be reverenced in all other men?

But if there is a divine principle in man, it has a right, and it is its duty, to unfold itself from itself. Justice requires that it should have liberty of men to do so. A social organization which does not admit of this, which does not favor, and cherish, and act with main reference to promoting it, is inadequate, false, devilish. To call a society

---

8. John 11.25.   9. Traditional aphorism.   10. On principle.   11. Raffaelo (1483–1520) and Michelangelo (1475–1564), Italian painters.   12. William Wordsworth (1770–1850), "To the Skylark" (1827).   13. Mediator.

Christendom, which is diametrically opposite in principle to Christ's idea, is an insult to the beautiful soul of Jesus. To crush the life he led wherever it appears in other men is taking the name of Jesus in vain. Yet does any man say his soul is his own, and, standing by Jesus' side, commune with God first hand, calling the greatest names on earth brethren of Jesus, he is excommunicated as irreverent by the very society which laughs to scorn, which would imprison as mad, if not as impious, whoever proposed to live out his individuality, or to organize society on the Christian principles of co-operation. Not less fiercely than the necessity, *a priori*, of Jesus' own perfection is contended for is also the necessity, *a priori*, of a society of competition contended for whose highest possible excellence may be the balance of material interests; while the divine life is to be for men as they rise but a hope, a dream, a vision to be realized beyond the grave!

There are men and women, however, who have dared to say to one another, Why not have our daily life organized on Christ's own idea? Why not begin to move the mountain of custom and convention? Perhaps Jesus' method of thought and life is the Saviour,—is Christianity! For each man to think and live on this method is perhaps the second coming of Christ,—to do unto the little ones as we would do unto *him* would be perhaps the reign of the Saints,[14]—the kingdom of heaven. We have hitherto heard of Christ by the hearing of the ear[15]; now let us see him, let us be him, and see what will come of that. Let us communicate with each other, and live.

Such a resolution has often been made under the light of the Christian Idea; but the light has shone amidst darkness, and the darkness comprehended it not.[16] Religious communities have ever but partially entered into the Idea of Christ. They have all been Churches, *ex parte* society, in some degree. They have been tied up and narrowed by creeds and tests. Yet the temporary success of the Hernhutters, the Moravians, the Shakers, even the Rappites,[17] have cleared away difficulties and solved problems of social science. It has been made plain that the material goods of life, "the life that now is,"[18] are not to be sacrificed (as by the anchorite[19]) in doing fuller justice to the social principle. It has been proved, that with the same degree of labor, there is no way to compare with that of working in a community, banded by some sufficient Idea to animate the will of the laborers. A greater quantity of wealth is procured with fewer hours of toil, and without any degradation of any laborer. All these communities have demonstrated what the practical Dr. Franklin[20] said, that if every one worked bodily three hours daily, there would be no necessity of any one's working more than three hours.

But one rock upon which communities have split is, that this very ease of procuring wealth has developed the desire of wealth, and so the hours redeemed by community of labor have been reapplied to sordid objects too much. This is especially the case with the Shakers, whose fanaticism is made quite subservient to the passion for wealth engendered by their triumphant success. The missionary objects of the Moravians have kept them purer.

The great evil of Community, however, has been a spiritual one. The sacredness of the family and personal individuality have been sacrificed. Each man became the slave of the organization of the whole. In becoming a Moravian, a Shaker, or whatever, men have ceased to be men in some degree. Now a man must be religious, or he is not a man. But neither is a *Religieux*[21] a *man*. That there are other principles in

---

14. Revelations 20.4–6.   15. Job 42.5.   16. John 1.5.   17. Religious communities.   18. 1 Timothy 4.8.   19. Hermit.
20. Benjamin Franklin (1706–1790), American statesman and printer.   21. Religious fanatic.

human nature to be cultivated besides the religious must be said; though we are in danger, by saying it, of being cried out upon, as of old, "Behold a gluttonous man and a wine-bibber, a friend of publicans and sinners."[22] The liberal principle always exposes a man to this outcry, no less than the religious principle, passionately acted out, has ever exposed the enthusiast to the charge, "He hath a Devil."[23] *Inanes voces!*[24]

But although Christianity is a main cause, it is not the only cause of the movements toward Reform which are perceived all around us. In Europe and America there are opposite impelling forces, which have brought the common-sense of men to the same vision which Jesus saw in religious ecstasy or moral reason.

In Europe it is the reaction of corrupt organization. Wherever in Europe the mass are not wholly overborne by political despotism, there is a struggle after some means of co-operation for social well-being. The French and English presses have teemed, during the last quarter of a century, with systems of socialism. Many, perhaps the majority of these, have been planned on inadequate or false views of the nature of man. Some have supposed the seeds of evil were so superficial that a change of outward circumstances would restore peace and innocence forthwith to the earth. Such persons little appreciate the harm that false organization has actually done to the race. They little appreciate the power of custom, of disobedience to the natural laws of body and mind. They take every thing into consideration but the man himself. Yet the most futile of these schemers can afford some good hints, and very sharply and truly criticise society as it is, and teach all who will listen without heat or personal pique.

But in England there are degrees of co-operation which do not amount to community. Neighborhoods of poor people with very small capitals, and some with no capital but the weekly produce of their own hands, have clubbed together, to make sufficient capital to buy necessaries of life at wholesale, and deal them out from a common depot at cost to one another. These clubs have been often connected with some plan for mental cultivation, and of growth in the principles of co-operation by contemplation and consideration of its moral character. We have lately seen a little paper published by one of these clubs for the mutual edification of their various members which was Christian in its profession and spirit, and most ably supported in all its articles. Benevolent individuals of all sects in England are looking towards such operations for relief of the present distress. We have lately seen a plan for a self-supporting institution of three hundred families of the destitute poor, which was drawn up by the author of "Hampden in the Nineteenth Century"[25] (who has become a Christian and Spiritualist since he wrote that book). This plan numbers among its patrons some of the most respectable ministers of the Established Church,[26] and William Wordsworth of Rydal Mount, which proves to what a pressing necessity it answers. Reaction in Europe is a signal source of a movement towards reorganization. And in America reaction, no doubt, does something, but not all. The light here has come mainly from a better source. The theory of the Constitution of the United States, which placed the rights of man to equal social privileges on a deeper foundation than ancient compact, was the greatest discovery in political science the world has ever made. It was the dawn of a new day, which is tending fast to noonday light. It is true American life has never come up to the theory of the Constitution as it is, and yet is that theory but a

---

22. Luke 7.34.   23. John 10.20.   24. "Foolish voices!"   25. John Minter Morgan (1782–1854), *Hampden in the Nineteenth Century or Colloquies on the Errors and Improvement of Society* (1834).   26. The Church of England.

dawning ray of the Sun. The light has touched the Image of Memnon and waked a music which does not cease to unfold new harmonies.[27] The end of society is seen by many to be the perfection of the Individual spiritually, still more than a fair balance and growth of material good. This idea clothes itself in various forms. The Abolitionists, the Non-resistants, those so earnest against the imprisonment for debt and capital punishment,—in short, every set of social reformers, come ever and anon to the great principles that there is an infinite worth and depth in the individual soul; that it has temporal interests as well as eternal interests; that it is not only desirable that it should be saved hereafter, but that it live purely and beautifully now; that this world is not only probation, and in a large degree retribution; but it is the kingdom of heaven also, to all who apprehend God and Nature truly.

There have been some plans and experiments of community attempted in this country, which, like those elsewhere, are interesting chiefly as indicating paths in which we should not go. Some have failed because their philosophy of human nature was inadequate, and their establishments did not regard man as he is, with all the elements of devil and angel within his actual constitution. Brisbane[28] has made a plan worthy of study in some of its features, but erring in the same manner. He does not go down into a sufficient spiritual depth to lay foundations which may support his superstructure. Our imagination before we reflect, no less than our reason after reflection, rebels against this attempt to circumvent moral Freedom, and imprison it in his Phalanx. Yet we would speak with no scorn of a work which seems to have sprung from a true benevolence, and has in it much valuable thought. As a criticism on our society it is unanswerable. It is in his chapters on the education and *uses* of children that we especially feel his inadequacy to his work. But he forestalls harsh criticism by throwing out what he says, as a *feeler* after something better. As such it has worth certainly.

The prospectus of a plan of a community has also been published in a religious paper, called the "Practical Christian," edited at Mendon, Mass., by Adin Ballou,[29] which is worthy of more attention. With a single exception, the articles of this confederation please us. It is a business paper of great ability, and the relations of the private and common property are admirably adjusted. The moral exposition of this paper, which follows it, shows a deep insight into the Christian Idea, and no man can read it without feeling strongly called upon to "come out from the world."[30] But the objection to this plan is, that admittance as a member is made dependent on the taking of the temperance, abolition, nonresistance pledges, the pledge not to vote, etc. The interpretation of this in their exposition is very liberal and gentle, it is true; and as they there speak of their test rather as a pledge of faithfulness to one another, and as a means of mutual understanding, than as an impawnment of their own moral will, it is difficult for one who is a temperance man, an abolitionist, a nonresistant, and who does not at any rate vote, to find fault. But after all is said for it that can be, they must admit that this test makes their community a church only, and not *the* church of Christ's Idea, world-embracing. *This* can be founded on nothing short of faith in the universal man, as he comes out of the hands of the Creator, with no law over his liberty but the Eternal Ideas that lie at the foundation of his Being. Are you a man? This is the only ques-

---

27. According to legend, a statue of Memnon, King of the Ethiopians, spoke when the sun first fell on it at dawn.   28. Albert Brisbane (1809–1890), American socialist.   29. Adin Ballou (1803–1890), American Christian socialist.   30. 2 Corinthians 6.17.

tion that is to be asked of a member of human society. And the enounced laws of that society should be an elastic medium of these Ideas; providing for their ever-lasting unfolding into new forms of influence, so that the man of Time should be the growth of Eternity, consciously and manifestly.

To form such a society as this is a great problem, whose perfect solution will take all the ages of time; but let the Spirit of God move freely over the great deep of social existence, and a creative light will come at his word, and after that long Evening in which we are living, the Morning of the first day shall dawn on a Christian society.

The final cause of human society is the unfolding of the individual man into every form of perfection, without let or hindrance, according to the inward nature of each. In strict correspondence to this, the ground Idea of the little communities, which are the embryo of the kingdom to come, must be Education. When we consider that each generation of men is thrown, helpless, and ignorant even of the light within itself, into the arms of a full-grown generation which has a power to do it harm, all but unlimited, we acknowledge that no object it can propose to itself is to be compared with that of educating its children truly. Yet every passion has its ideal having its temple in society, while the schools and universities in all Christendom struggle for existence, how much more than the banks, the East India companies,[31] and other institutions for the accumulation of a doubtful external good! how much more than even the gambling houses and other temples of acknowledged vice!

The difficulty on this subject lies very deep in the present constitution of things. As long as Education is made the object of an Institution in society, rather than is the generating Idea of society itself, it must be apart from life. It is really too general an interest to suffer being a particular one. Moral and Religious Education is the indispensable condition and foundation of a true development. But an apparatus for this of a mechanical character, in any degree, is in the nature of things an absurdity. Morals and Religion are not something induced upon the human being, but an opening out of the inner life. What is now called moral and religious education, in the best institutions, is only a part of the intellectual exercises, as likely to act against as for the end. Those laws, which should be lived before they are intellectually apprehended, are introduced to the mind in the form of propositions, and assented to by the Reason, in direct opposition to the life which the constitution of society makes irresistible. Hence is perpetually reproduced that internal disorganization of the human being which was described of old in the fable of man's eating of the tree of Knowledge to the blinding of his eyes to the tree of Life, the whole apparatus of education being the tempting Serpent.[32] Moral and religious life should be the atmosphere in which the human being unfolds, it being freely lived in the community in which the child is born. Thus only may he be permitted to freely act out what is within him; and have no temptations but necessary ones; and the intellectual apprehension follow, rather than precede, his virtue. This is not to take captive the will, but to educate it. If there were no wrong action in the world organized in institutions, children could be allowed a little more moral experimenting than is now convenient for others, or safe for themselves. As the case now is, our children receive as an inheritance the punishment and anguish due to the crimes that have gone before them, and the Paradise of youth is curtailed of its fair proportions cruelly and unjustly, and to the detriment of the future man.

---

31. Chartered corporations for the colonization of South Asia.   32. Genesis 3.

In the true society, then, Education is the ground Idea. The highest work of man is to call forth man in his fellow and child. This was the work of the Christ in Jesus, and in his Apostles; and not only in them, but in Poets and Philosophers of olden time; in all who have had immortal aims, in *all* time, whether manifested in act or word, builded in temples, painted on canvas, or chiselled in stone. All action addressed to the immortal nature of man in a self-forgetting spirit is of the same nature,—the divine life. The organization which shall give freedom to this loving creative spirit, glimpses of which were severally called the Law in Rome, the Ideal in Greece, Freedom and Manliness in Northern Europe, and Christ by the earnest disciples of Jesus of Nazareth, is at once the true human society, and the only university of Education worthy the name.

—1841

Karl Marx and Frederick Engels
1818–1883 / 1820–1895

In December 1847, two German radicals, Karl Marx and Frederick Engels, attended the London congress of an international revolutionary organization, the League of the Just. They were commissioned to draw up a political program for the League, and *The Communist Manifesto* was published just two months later. After being exiled from Germany, Marx and Engels had thrown themselves into the popular movements that culminated in the Revolutions of 1848, and the *Manifesto* captures the confident mood of revolutionaries around the Atlantic Rim during those hopeful days.

Building on the work of orthodox political economists and on the vibrant utopian socialist tradition, the *Manifesto* offered a startlingly nuanced assessment of capitalism. According to Marx and Engels, human history had been driven by the conflict between contending social classes. During the preceding two centuries, the bourgeoisie (private business owners) had been responsible for a historically unprecedented acceleration of human progress. In addition to overthrowing powerful and entrenched aristocracies, they had organized staggering developments in scientific and technological possibility, as well as in culture and ideas. But along with such progress, capitalism brought with it new and more intense forms of oppression and poverty. In place of the more settled relationship between lord and peasant, this new social order relied on the ruthless and impersonal exploitation of wageworkers by the owners of capital. And in place of the stable world of feudalism, capitalism created a society in which "all that is solid melts into air, all that is holy is profaned." Most importantly, capitalism had produced a historic contradiction: It had invented the concrete tools that could build a world in which all human needs were fulfilled, but it could not organize further progress toward that future because of the chaos of competition. Distinguishing themselves from previous utopian socialists, Marx and Engels insisted that further progress would come not from small groups of radical intellectuals but through the self-activity of the working class. Just as it had been necessary for the bourgeoisie to organize its own liberation from the oppressive power of the aristocracy, so workers must free themselves from their exploiters and take control of the society's powerful productive forces. *The Manifesto* announces this historic task of the proletariat in thunderous, richly imagistic prose. Soon after a first printing of one thousand copies, it was translated into all of the major European languages, and it has never fallen out of print since. It remains one of the most influential political tracts of the modern era, having been translated into almost every living language.

In 1852, Marx replaced Margaret Fuller as the main foreign correspondent for Horace Greeley's *New York Tribune*, a position he filled for the next decade. He closely followed the developing conflict in the United States between the northern bourgeoisie and the southern slavocracy, hailing the American Civil War as a new stage in the American Revolution. He lived the rest of his life with his family in London, suffering grueling poverty and disease but always writing and organizing. Engels used profits from his Manchester textile mills to subsidize Marx's economic research in London's British Library. It was there that Marx wrote *Capital* (1867), his commanding critique of the new social and economic order that had overtaken the transatlantic world during the Romantic century.

from The Communist Manifesto

A spectre is haunting Europe—the spectre of communism. All the powers of old Europe have entered into a holy alliance to exorcise this spectre: Pope and Tsar, Metternich and Guizot,[1] French Radicals and German police-spies.

Where is the party in opposition that has not been decried as communistic by its opponents in power? Where is the opposition that has not hurled back the branding reproach of communism, against the more advanced opposition parties, as well as against its reactionary adversaries?

Two things result from this fact:

I. Communism is already acknowledged by all European powers to be itself a power.

II. It is high time that Communists should openly, in the face of the whole world, publish their views, their aims, their tendencies, and meet this nursery tale of the Spectre of Communism with a manifesto of the party itself.

To this end, Communists of various nationalities have assembled in London and sketched the following manifesto, to be published in the English, French, German, Italian, Flemish and Danish languages.

The history of all hitherto existing society is the history of class struggles.

Freeman and slave, patrician and plebeian, lord and serf, guild-master and journeyman, in a word, oppressor and oppressed, stood in constant opposition to one another, carried on an uninterrupted, now hidden, now open fight, a fight that each time ended, either in a revolutionary reconstitution of society at large, or in the common ruin of the contending classes.

In the earlier epochs of history, we find almost everywhere a complicated arrangement of society into various orders, a manifold gradation of social rank. In ancient Rome we have patricians, knights, plebeians, slaves; in the Middle Ages, feudal lords, vassals, guild-masters, journeymen, apprentices, serfs; in almost all of these classes, again, subordinate gradations.

The modern bourgeois society that has sprouted from the ruins of feudal society has not done away with class antagonisms. It has but established new classes, new conditions of oppression, new forms of struggle in place of the old ones.

Our epoch, the epoch of the bourgeoisie, possesses, however, this distinct feature: it has simplified class antagonisms. Society as a whole is more and more splitting up into two great hostile camps, into two great classes directly facing each other— Bourgeoisie and Proletariat.

From the serfs of the Middle Ages sprang the chartered burghers of the earliest towns. From these burgesses the first elements of the bourgeoisie were developed.

The discovery of America, the rounding of the Cape,[2] opened up fresh ground for the rising bourgeoisie. The East-Indian and Chinese markets, the colonisation of

---

1. Klemens Wenzel von Metternich (1773–1858), Austrian diplomat; François Guizot (1787–1874), French politician.
2. The Cape of Good Hope at the southern tip of Africa.

America, trade with the colonies, the increase in the means of exchange and in commodities generally, gave to commerce, to navigation, to industry, an impulse never before known, and thereby, to the revolutionary element in the tottering feudal society, a rapid development.

The feudal system of industry, in which industrial production was monopolised by closed guilds, now no longer sufficed for the growing wants of the new markets. The manufacturing system took its place. The guild-masters were pushed on one side by the manufacturing middle class; division of labour between the different corporate guilds vanished in the face of division of labour in each single workshop.

Meantime the markets kept ever growing, the demand ever rising. Even manufacturer no longer sufficed. Thereupon, steam and machinery revolutionised industrial production. The place of manufacture was taken by the giant, Modern Industry; the place of the industrial middle class by industrial millionaires, the leaders of the whole industrial armies, the modern bourgeois.

Modern industry has established the world market, for which the discovery of America paved the way. This market has given an immense development to commerce, to navigation, to communication by land. This development has, in its turn, reacted on the extension of industry; and in proportion as industry, commerce, navigation, railways extended, in the same proportion the bourgeoisie developed, increased its capital, and pushed into the background every class handed down from the Middle Ages.

We see, therefore, how the modern bourgeoisie is itself the product of a long course of development, of a series of revolutions in the modes of production and of exchange.

Each step in the development of the bourgeoisie was accompanied by a corresponding political advance of that class. An oppressed class under the sway of the feudal nobility, an armed and self-governing association in the medieval commune: here independent urban republic (as in Italy and Germany); there taxable "third estate" of the monarchy (as in France); afterwards, in the period of manufacturing proper, serving either the semi-feudal or the absolute monarchy as a counterpoise against the nobility, and, in fact, cornerstone of the great monarchies in general, the bourgeoisie has at last, since the establishment of Modern Industry and of the world market, conquered for itself, in the modern representative State, exclusive political sway. The executive of the modern state is but a committee for managing the common affairs of the whole bourgeoisie.

The bourgeoisie, historically, has played a most revolutionary part.

The bourgeoisie, wherever it has got the upper hand, has put an end to all feudal, patriarchal, idyllic relations. It has pitilessly torn asunder the motley feudal ties that bound man to his "natural superiors", and has left remaining no other nexus between man and man than naked self-interest, than callous "cash payment". It has drowned the most heavenly ecstasies of religious fervour, of chivalrous enthusiasm, of philistine sentimentalism, in the icy water of egotistical calculation. It has resolved personal worth into exchange value, and in place of the numberless indefeasible chartered freedoms, has set up that single, unconscionable freedom—Free Trade. In one word, for exploitation, veiled by religious and political illusions, it has substituted naked, shameless, direct, brutal exploitation.

The bourgeoisie has stripped of its halo every occupation hitherto honoured and looked up to with reverent awe. It has converted the physician, the lawyer, the priest, the poet, the man of science, into its paid wage labourers.

The bourgeoisie has torn away from the family its sentimental veil, and has reduced the family relation to a mere money relation.

The bourgeoisie has disclosed how it came to pass that the brutal display of vigour in the Middle Ages, which reactionaries so much admire, found its fitting complement in the most slothful indolence. It has been the first to show what man's activity can bring about. It has accomplished wonders far surpassing Egyptian pyramids, Roman aqueducts, and Gothic cathedrals; it has conducted expeditions that put in the shade all former Exoduses of nations and crusades.

The bourgeoisie cannot exist without constantly revolutionising the instruments of production, and thereby the relations of production, and with them the whole relations of society. Conservation of the old modes of production in unaltered form, was, on the contrary, the first condition of existence for all earlier industrial classes. Constant revolutionising of production, uninterrupted disturbance of all social conditions, everlasting uncertainty and agitation distinguish the bourgeois epoch from all earlier ones. All fixed, fast-frozen relations, with their train of ancient and venerable prejudices and opinions, are swept away, all new-formed ones become antiquated before they can ossify. All that is solid melts into air, all that is holy is profaned, and man is at last compelled to face with sober senses his real conditions of life, and his relations with his kind.

The need of a constantly expanding market for its products chases the bourgeoisie over the entire surface of the globe. It must nestle everywhere, settle everywhere, establish connexions everywhere.

The bourgeoisie has through its exploitation of the world market given a cosmopolitan character to production and consumption in every country. To the great chagrin of Reactionists, it has drawn from under the feet of industry the national ground on which it stood. All old-established national industries have been destroyed or are daily being destroyed. They are dislodged by new industries, whose introduction becomes a life and death question for all civilised nations, by industries that no longer work up indigenous raw material, but raw material drawn from the remotest zones; industries whose products are consumed, not only at home, but in every quarter of the globe. In place of the old wants, satisfied by the production of the country, we find new wants, requiring for their satisfaction the products of distant lands and climes. In place of the old local and national seclusion and self-sufficiency, we have intercourse in every direction, universal inter-dependence of nations. And as in material, so also in intellectual production. The intellectual creations of individual nations become common property. National one-sidedness and narrow-mindedness become more and more impossible, and from the numerous national and local literatures, there arises a world literature.

The bourgeoisie, by the rapid improvement of all instruments of production, by the immensely facilitated means of communication, draws all, even the most barbarian, nations into civilisation. The cheap prices of commodities are the heavy artillery with which it batters down all Chinese walls, with which it forces the barbarians' intensely obstinate hatred of foreigners to capitulate. It compels all nations, on pain of extinction, to adopt the bourgeois mode of production; it compels them to introduce what it calls civilisation into their midst, i.e., to become bourgeois themselves. In one word, it creates a world after its own image.

The bourgeoisie has subjected the country to the rule of the towns. It has created enormous cities, has greatly increased the urban population as compared with the rural, and has thus rescued a considerable part of the population from the idiocy of rural life. Just as it has made the country dependent on the towns, so it has made barbarian and semi-barbarian countries dependent on the civilised ones, nations of peasants on nations of bourgeois, the East on the West.

The bourgeoisie keeps more and more doing away with the scattered state of the population, of the means of production, and of property. It has agglomerated population, centralised the means of production, and has concentrated property in a few hands. The necessary consequence of this was political centralisation. Independent, or but loosely connected provinces, with separate interests, laws, governments, and systems of taxation, became lumped together into one nation, with one government, one code of laws, one national class-interest, one frontier, and one customs-tariff.

The bourgeoisie, during its rule of scarce one hundred years, has created more massive and more colossal productive forces than have all preceding generations together. Subjection of Nature's forces to man, machinery, application of chemistry to industry and agriculture, steam-navigation, railways, electric telegraphs, clearing of whole continents for cultivation, canalisation of rivers, whole populations conjured out of the ground—what earlier century had even a presentiment that such productive forces slumbered in the lap of social labour?

We see then: the means of production and of exchange, on whose foundation the bourgeoisie built itself up, were generated in feudal society. At a certain stage in the development of these means of production and of exchange, the conditions under which feudal society produced and exchanged, the feudal organisation of agriculture and manufacturing industry, in one word, the feudal relations of property became no longer compatible with the already developed productive forces; they became so many fetters. They had to be burst asunder; they were burst asunder.

Into their place stepped free competition, accompanied by a social and political constitution adapted in it, and the economic and political sway of the bourgeois class.

A similar movement is going on before our own eyes. Modern bourgeois society, with its relations of production, of exchange and of property, a society that has conjured up such gigantic means of production and of exchange, is like the sorcerer who is no longer able to control the powers of the nether world whom he has called up by his spells. For many a decade past the history of industry and commerce is but the history of the revolt of modern productive forces against modern conditions of production, against the property relations that are the conditions for the existence of the bourgeois and of its rule. It is enough to mention the commercial crises that by their periodical return put the existence of the entire bourgeois society on its trial, each time more threateningly. In these crises, a great part not only of the existing products, but also of the previously created productive forces, are periodically destroyed. In these crises, there breaks out an epidemic that, in all earlier epochs, would have seemed an absurdity—the epidemic of over-production. Society suddenly finds itself put back into a state of momentary barbarism; it appears as if a famine, a universal war of devastation, had cut off the supply of every means of subsistence; industry and commerce seem to be destroyed; and why? Because there is too much civilisation, too much means of subsistence, too much industry, too much commerce. The productive forces at the disposal of society no longer tend to further the development of the conditions of bourgeois property; on the contrary, they have become too powerful for these conditions, by which they are fettered, and so soon as they overcome these fetters, they bring disorder into the whole of bourgeois society, endanger the existence of bourgeois property. The conditions of bourgeois society are too narrow to comprise the wealth created by them. And how does the bourgeoisie get over these crises? On the one hand by enforced destruction of a mass of productive forces; on the other, by the conquest of new markets, and by the more thorough exploitation of the old ones. That is to say, by paving the way for more extensive and more destructive crises, and by diminishing the means whereby crises are prevented.

The weapons with which the bourgeoisie felled feudalism to the ground are now turned against the bourgeoisie itself.

But not only has the bourgeoisie forged the weapons that bring death to itself; it has also called into existence the men who are to wield those weapons—the modern working class—the proletarians.

In proportion as the bourgeoisie, i.e., capital, is developed, in the same proportion is the proletariat, the modern working class, developed—a class of labourers, who live only so long as they find work, and who find work only so long as their labour increases capital. These labourers, who must sell themselves piecemeal, are a commodity, like every other article of commerce, and are consequently exposed to all the vicissitudes of competition, to all the fluctuations of the market.

Owing to the extensive use of machinery, and to the division of labour, the work of the proletarians has lost all individual character, and, consequently, all charm for the workman. He becomes an appendage of the machine, and it is only the most simple, most monotonous, and most easily acquired knack, that is required of him. Hence, the cost of production of a workman is restricted, almost entirely, to the means of subsistence that he requires for maintenance, and for the propagation of his race. But the price of a commodity, and therefore also of labour, is equal to its cost of production. In proportion, therefore, as the repulsiveness of the work increases, the wage decreases. Nay more, in proportion as the use of machinery and division of labour increases, in the same proportion the burden of toil also increases, whether by prolongation of the working hours, by the increase of the work exacted in a given time or by increased speed of machinery, etc.

Modern Industry has converted the little workshop of the patriarchal master into the great factory of the industrial capitalist. Masses of labourers, crowded into the factory, are organised like soldiers. As privates of the industrial army they are placed under the command of a perfect hierarchy of officers and sergeants. Not only are they slaves of the bourgeois class, and of the bourgeois State; they are daily and hourly enslaved by the machine, by the overlooker, and, above all, by the individual bourgeois manufacturer himself. The more openly this despotism proclaims gain to be its end and aim, the more petty, the more hateful and the more embittering it is.

The less the skill and exertion of strength implied in manual labour, in other words, the more modern industry becomes developed, the more is the labour of men superseded by that of women. Differences of age and sex have no longer any distinctive social validity for the working class. All are instruments of labour, more or less expensive to use, according to their age and sex.

No sooner is the exploitation of the labourer by the manufacturer, so far, at an end, that he receives his wages in cash, than he is set upon by the other portions of the bourgeoisie, the landlord, the shopkeeper, the pawnbroker, etc.

The lower strata of the middle class—the small tradespeople, shopkeepers, and retired tradesmen generally, the handicraftsmen and peasants—all these sink gradually into the proletariat, partly because their diminutive capital does not suffice for the scale on which Modern Industry is carried on, and is swamped in the competition with the large capitalists, partly because their specialised skill is rendered worthless by new methods of production. Thus the proletariat is recruited from all classes of the population.

The proletariat goes through various stages of development. With its birth begins its struggle with the bourgeoisie. At first the contest is carried on by individual labourers, then by the workpeople of a factory, then by the operative of one trade, in one locality, against the individual bourgeois who directly exploits them. They direct their attacks not against the bourgeois conditions of production, but against the instruments of production themselves; they destroy imported wares that compete with their labour, they smash to pieces machinery, they set factories ablaze, they seek to restore by force the vanished status of the workman of the Middle Ages.

At this stage, the labourers still form an incoherent mass scattered over the whole country, and broken up by their mutual competition. If anywhere they unite to form more compact bodies, this is not yet the consequence of their own active union, but of the union of the bourgeoisie, which class, in order to attain its own political ends, is compelled to set the whole proletariat in motion, and is moreover yet, for a time, able to do so. At this stage, therefore, the proletarians do not fight their enemies, but the enemies of their enemies, the remnants of absolute monarchy, the landowners, the non-industrial bourgeois, the petty bourgeois. Thus, the whole historical movement is concentrated in the hands of the bourgeoisie; every victory so obtained is a victory for the bourgeoisie.

But with the development of industry, the proletariat not only increases in number; it becomes concentrated in greater masses, its strength grows, and it feels that strength more. The various interests and conditions of life within the ranks of the proletariat are more and more equalised, in proportion as machinery obliterates all distinctions of labour, and nearly everywhere reduces wages to the same low level. The growing competition among the bourgeois, and the resulting commercial crises, make the wages of the workers ever more fluctuating. The increasing improvement of machinery, ever more rapidly developing, makes their livelihood more and more precarious; the collisions between individual workmen and individual bourgeois take more and more the character of collisions between two classes. Thereupon, the workers begin to form combinations (Trades' Unions) against the bourgeois; they club together in order to keep up the rate of wages; they found permanent associations in order to make provision beforehand for these occasional revolts. Here and there, the contest breaks out into riots.

Now and then the workers are victorious, but only for a time. The real fruit of their battles lies, not in the immediate result, but in the ever expanding union of the workers. This union is helped on by the improved means of communication that are created by modern industry, and that place the workers of different localities in contact with one another. It was just this contact that was needed to centralise the numerous local struggles, all of the same character, into one national struggle between classes. But every class struggle is a political struggle. And that union, to attain which the burghers of the Middle Ages, with their miserable highways, required centuries, the modern proletarian, thanks to railways, achieve in a few years.

This organisation of the proletarians into a class, and, consequently into a political party, is continually being upset again by the competition between the workers themselves. But it ever rises up again, stronger, firmer, mightier. It compels legislative recognition of particular interests of the workers, by taking advantage of the divisions among the bourgeoisie itself. Thus, the ten-hours' bill[3] in England was carried.

Altogether collisions between the classes of the old society further, in many ways, the course of development of the proletariat. The bourgeoisie finds itself involved in a constant battle. At first with the aristocracy; later on, with those portions of the bourgeoisie itself, whose interests have become antagonistic to the progress of industry; at all times with the bourgeoisie of foreign countries. In all these battles, it sees itself compelled to appeal to the proletariat, to ask for help, and thus, to drag it into the political arena. The bourgeoisie itself, therefore, supplies the proletariat with its own elements of political and general education, in other words, it furnishes the proletariat with weapons for fighting the bourgeoisie.

Further, as we have already seen, entire sections of the ruling class are, by the advance of industry, precipitated into the proletariat, or are at least threatened in their conditions of existence. These also supply the proletariat with fresh elements of enlightenment and progress.

Finally, in times when the class struggle nears the decisive hour, the progress of dissolution going on within the ruling class, in fact within the whole range of old society, assumes such a violent, glaring character, that a small section of the ruling class cuts itself adrift, and joins the revolutionary class, the class that holds the future in its hands. Just as, therefore, at an earlier period, a section of the nobility went over to the bourgeoisie, so now a portion of the bourgeoisie goes over to the proletariat, and in particular, a portion of the bourgeois ideologists, who have raised themselves to the level of comprehending theoretically the historical movement as a whole.

Of all the classes that stand face to face with the bourgeoisie today, the proletariat alone is a really revolutionary class. The other classes decay and finally disappear in the face of Modern Industry; the proletariat is its special and essential product.

The lower middle class, the small manufacturer, the shopkeeper, the artisan, the peasant, all these fight against the bourgeoisie, to save from extinction their existence as fractions of the middle class. They are therefore not revolutionary, but conservative. Nay more, they are reactionary, for they try to roll back the wheel of history. If by chance, they are revolutionary, they are only so in view of their impending transfer into the proletariat; they thus defend not their present, but their future interests, they desert their own standpoint to place themselves at that of the proletariat.

The "dangerous class", the social scum, that passively rotting mass thrown off by the lowest layers of the old society, may, here and there, be swept into the movement by a proletarian revolution; its conditions of life, however, prepare it far more for the part of a bribed tool of reactionary intrigue.

In the condition of the proletariat, those of old society at large are already virtually swamped. The proletarian is without property; his relation to his wife and children has no longer anything in common with the bourgeois family relations; modern industry labour, modern subjection to capital, the same in England as in France, in America as in Germany, has stripped him of every trace of national character. Law, morality, religion, are to him so many bourgeois prejudices, behind which lurk in ambush just as many bourgeois interests.

---

3. A law limiting the workday to ten hours.

All the preceding classes that got the upper hand sought to fortify their already acquired status by subjecting society at large to their conditions of appropriation. The proletarians cannot become masters of the productive forces of society, except by abolishing their own previous mode of appropriation, and thereby also every other previous mode of appropriation. They have nothing of their own to secure and to fortify; their mission is to destroy all previous securities for, and insurances of, individual property.

All previous historical movements were movements of minorities, or in the interest of minorities. The proletarian movement is the self-conscious, independent movement of the immense majority, in the interest of the immense majority. The proletariat, the lowest stratum of our present society, cannot stir, cannot raise itself up, without the whole superincumbent strata of official society being sprung into the air.

Though not in substance, yet in form, the struggle of the proletariat with the bourgeoisie is at first a national struggle. The proletariat of each country must, of course, first of all settle matters with its own bourgeoisie.

In depicting the most general phases of the development of the proletariat, we traced the more or less veiled civil war, raging within existing society, up to the point where that war breaks out into open revolution, and where the violent overthrow of the bourgeoisie lays the foundation for the sway of the proletariat.

Hitherto, every form of society has been based, as we have already seen, on the antagonism of oppressing and oppressed classes. But in order to oppress a class, certain conditions must be assured to it under which it can, at least, continue its slavish existence. The serf, in the period of serfdom, raised himself to membership in the commune, just as the petty bourgeois, under the yoke of the feudal absolutism, managed to develop into a bourgeois. The modern labourer, on the contrary, instead of rising with the process of industry, sinks deeper and deeper below the conditions of existence of his own class. He becomes a pauper, and pauperism develops more rapidly than population and wealth. And here it becomes evident, that the bourgeoisie is unfit any longer to be the ruling class in society, and to impose its conditions of existence upon society as an over-riding law. It is unfit to rule because it is incompetent to assure an existence to its slave within his slavery, because it cannot help letting him sink into such a state, that it has to feed him, instead of being fed by him. Society can no longer live under this bourgeoisie, in other words, its existence is no longer compatible with society.

The essential conditions for the existence and for the sway of the bourgeois class is the formation and augmentation of capital; the condition for capital is wage-labour. Wage-labour rests exclusively on competition between the labourers. The advance of industry, whose involuntary promoter is the bourgeoisie, replaces the isolation of the labourers, due to competition, by the revolutionary combination, due to association. The development of Modern Industry, therefore, cuts from under its feet the very foundation on which the bourgeoisie produces and appropriates products. What the bourgeoisie therefore produces, above all, are its own grave-diggers. Its fall and the victory of the proletariat are equally inevitable.

—1848

John Keats
1795–1821

"I cannot be deceived in that colour; that drop of blood is my death warrant. I must die"—so wrote John Keats in February 1820, after watching his health decline and experiencing the first of a series of lung hemorrhages. Keats's prediction is not simply prescient; his medical training (which he abandoned to pursue poetry) equipped him to gauge his health. He suffered several more attacks before succumbing to tuberculosis one year later in February 1821 at the age of twenty-five. Keats's mother had died from tuberculosis when he was fourteen, and the disease had taken his brother Tom in December 1819. The Keats brothers were extremely close, and John nursed Tom, fully aware of the risk to his own health.

Keats's father ran a London livery stable, owned by his wife's family. He eventually inherited the business, which provided his family with a comfortable living. Keats attended a private school in Enfield, run by Reverend John Clarke. By all accounts, he was an active child, boisterous and athletic, and it was not until striking up a friendship with Clarke's son, Charles, that Keats took a serious interest in literature. Clarke introduced him to the works of the poet, translator, and dramatist George Chapman, who influenced Keats's first major poetic effort, "On First Looking into Chapman's Homer" (1816). Clarke also introduced Keats to Leigh Hunt, both the man and his writing. Through Hunt, Keats would eventually establish a network of acquaintances that included the painter Benjamin Robert Haydon, the writer Percy Bysshe Shelley, the essayist Charles Lamb, and the poet William Wordsworth.

Keats left school in 1811 to apprentice as a surgeon. Although he passed his exams and worked for a time as an apothecary (a general physician), he left medicine in 1817 to turn his attention to poetry, which he had been reading widely and writing while studying. Keats's first book, *Poems* (1817), generated little attention, with the exception of a warm review by Hunt, to whom Keats had dedicated the volume. His next production, the four-thousand-line *Endymion* (1818), was savaged by the reviewers, who rejected the mythological meditation on love as "calm, settled, drivelling imperturbable idiocy," in the words of John Gibson Lockhart in the August 1818 issue of the Tory periodical *Blackwood's Edinburgh Magazine*. Keats was not unscathed by the attack and by the reviewers grouping him with the "Cockney School" (poets with radical politics like Shelley and Hunt), but he recognized that the reviews were colored by editorial and political agendas and did not present honest and fair estimates of literary merit.

In Keats's short life, 1819 was his most productive year. This was the year of the great odes, although Keats wrote on an extraordinary range of subjects in numerous forms. He wrote the gothic "The Eve of St. Agnes," "Ode on a Grecian Urn," "Ode to a Nightingale," "To Autumn," and a sonnet, "'Bright star! would I were steadfast as thou art" to Fanny Brawne, to whom he became engaged. Many of the poems from this period appeared in *Lamia, Isabella, The Eve of St. Agnes, and Other Poems* (1820).

On the heels of this highly successful publication, Keats traveled to Italy in 1820, in the hope of finding relief from the symptoms of tuberculosis. He departed in mid-September 1820, and the following months saw his symptoms deepen, until he succumbed in February 1821. In addition to writing a sizable body of poetry in his short life, Keats left a substantial corpus of correspondence. His letters are valuable for the glimpses they provide into the life of a working poet. He maps the progress he is making on individual texts but also sketches out his large ideas about poetic ideas and styles. Indeed, his letters—including letters sent to his brother George, who had moved to America—can be said to constitute his theory of poetry, parallel to Shelley's "Defence of Poetry" (1840) or Wordsworth's "Preface" to the *Lyrical Ballads* (1798).

On First Looking into Chapman's Homer[1]

Much have I travell'd in the realms of gold,
   And many goodly states and kingdoms seen;
   Round many western islands have I been
Which bards in fealty to Apollo[2] hold.
Oft of one wide expanse had I been told   5
   That deep-brow'd Homer ruled as his demesne[3];
   Yet did I never breathe its pure serene
Till I heard Chapman speak out loud and bold:
Then felt I like some watcher of the skies
   When a new planet[4] swims into his ken;   10
Or like stout Cortez when with eagle eyes
   He star'd at the Pacific—and all his men
Look'd at each other with a wild surmise—
   Silent, upon a peak in Darien.[5]

—1816

To Autumn

1

Season of mists and mellow fruitfulness,
   Close bosom-friend of the maturing sun;
Conspiring with him how to load and bless
   With fruit the vines that round the thatch-eaves run;
To bend with apples the moss'd cottage-trees,   5
   And fill all fruit with ripeness to the core;
      To swell the gourd, and plump the hazel shells
With a sweet kernel; to set budding more,
   And still more, later flowers for the bees,
   Until they think warm days will never cease,   10
      For Summer has o'er-brimm'd their clammy cells.

2

Who hath not seen thee oft amid thy store?
   Sometimes whoever seeks abroad may find
Thee sitting careless on a granary floor,
   Thy hair soft-lifted by the winnowing wind;   15
Or on a half-reap'd furrow sound asleep,
   Drows'd with the fume of poppies, while thy hook[1]
      Spares the next swath and all its twined flowers:
And sometimes like a gleaner[2] thou dost keep

---

1. George Chapman (1559–1634), *The Whole Work of Homer* (1614). 2. Greek god of poetry. 3. Realm. 4. Uranus, discovered in 1781. 5. Mountain in Panama from which Hernán Cortés (1485–1547), the Spanish conquistador, first named the Pacific Ocean.

1. Scythe. 2. Harvester.

Steady thy laden head across a brook;   20
Or by a cyder-press, with patient look,
   Thou watchest the last oozings hours by hours.

3

Where are the songs of Spring? Ay, where are they?
   Think not of them, thou hast thy music too,—
While barred clouds bloom the soft-dying day,   25
   And touch the stubble-plains with rosy hue;
Then in a wailful choir the small gnats mourn
   Among the river sallows,[3] borne aloft
     Or sinking as the light wind lives or dies;
And full-grown lambs loud bleat from hilly bourn[4];   30
   Hedge-crickets sing; and now with treble soft
   The red-breast whistles from a garden-croft[5];
     And gathering swallows twitter in the skies.

—1820

The Eve of St. Agnes[1]

1

St. Agnes' Eve—Ah, bitter chill it was!
The owl, for all his feathers, was a-cold;
The hare limp'd trembling through the frozen grass,
And silent was the flock in woolly fold:
Numb were the Beadsman's fingers, while he told   5
His rosary, and while his frosted breath,
Like pious incense from a censer old,
Seem'd taking flight for heaven, without a death,
Past the sweet Virgin's picture, while his prayer he saith.

2

His prayer he saith, this patient, holy man;   10
Then takes his lamp, and riseth from his knees,
And back returneth, meagre, barefoot, wan,
Along the chapel aisle by slow degrees:
The sculptur'd dead, on each side, seem to freeze,
Emprison'd in black, purgatorial rails: 15
Knights, ladies, praying in dumb orat'ries,[2]
He passeth by; and his weak spirit fails
To think how they may ache in icy hoods and mails.

---

3. Willow trees.   4. Boundary.   5. Plot of farmland.

1. St. Agnes, the patron saint of virgins, was condemned to a night of rape before her execution but was saved by a storm.   2. Chapels.

3

Northward he turneth through a little door,
And scarce three steps, ere Music's golden tongue   20
Flatter'd to tears this aged man and poor;
But no—already had his deathbell rung;
The joys of all his life were said and sung:
His was harsh penance on St. Agnes' Eve:
Another way he went, and soon among   25
Rough ashes sat he for his soul's reprieve,
And all night kept awake, for sinners' sake to grieve.

4

That ancient Beadsman heard the prelude soft;
And so it chanc'd, for many a door was wide,
From hurry to and fro. Soon, up aloft,   30
The silver, snarling trumpets 'gan to chide:
The level chambers, ready with their pride,
Were glowing to receive a thousand guests:
The carved angels, ever eager-eyed,
Star'd, where upon their heads the cornice rests,   35
With hair blown back, and wings put cross-wise on their breasts.

5

At length burst in the argent[3] revelry,
With plume, tiara, and all rich array,
Numerous as shadows haunting fairily
The brain, new-stuff'd, in youth with triumphs gay   40
Of old romance. These let us wish away,
And turn, sole-thoughted, to one Lady there,
Whose heart had brooded, all that wintry day,
On love, and wing'd St. Agnes' saintly care,
As she had heard old dames full many times declare.   45

6

They told her how, upon St. Agnes' Eve,
Young virgins might have visions of delight,
And soft adorings from their loves receive
Upon the honey'd middle of the night,
If ceremonies due they did aright;   50
As, supperless to bed they must retire,
And couch supine their beauties, lily white;
Nor look behind, nor sideways, but require
Of Heaven with upward eyes for all that they desire.

---

3. Silver.

7

Full of this whim was thoughtful Madeline: 55
The music, yearning like a God in pain,
She scarcely heard: her maiden eyes divine,
Fix'd on the floor, saw many a sweeping train
Pass by—she heeded not at all: in vain
Came many a tiptoe, amorous cavalier,   60
And back retir'd; not cool'd by high disdain,
But she saw not: her heart was otherwhere:
She sigh'd for Agnes' dreams, the sweetest of the year.

8

She danc'd along with vague, regardless eyes,
Anxious her lips, her breathing quick and short: 65
The hallow'd hour was near at hand: she sighs
Amid the timbrels, and the throng'd resort
Of whisperers in anger, or in sport;
'Mid looks of love, defiance, hate, and scorn,
Hoodwink'd with faery fancy; all amort,   70
Save to St. Agnes and her lambs unshorn,
And all the bliss to be before to-morrow morn.

9

So, purposing each moment to retire,
She linger'd still. Meantime, across the moors,
Had come young Porphyro, with heart on fire   75
For Madeline. Beside the portal doors,
Buttress'd from moonlight, stands he, and implores
All saints to give him sight of Madeline,
But for one moment in the tedious hours,
That he might gaze and worship all unseen;   80
Perchance speak, kneel, touch, kiss—in sooth such things have been.

10

He ventures in: let no buzz'd whisper tell:
All eyes be muffled, or a hundred swords
Will storm his heart, Love's fev'rous citadel:
For him, those chambers held barbarian hordes,   85
Hyena foemen, and hot-blooded lords,
Whose very dogs would execrations howl
Against his lineage: not one breast affords
Him any mercy, in that mansion foul,
Save one old beldame,[4] weak in body and in soul.   90

---

4. Nurse.

11

Ah, happy chance! the aged creature came,
Shuffling along with ivory-headed wand,
To where he stood, hid from the torch's flame,
Behind a broad hall-pillar, far beyond
The sound of merriment and chorus bland: 95
He startled her; but soon she knew his face,
And grasp'd his fingers in her palsied hand,
Saying, "Mercy, Porphyro! hie thee from this place;
They are all here to-night, the whole blood-thirsty race!

12

"Get hence! get hence! there's dwarfish Hildebrand;   100
He had a fever late, and in the fit
He cursed thee and thine, both house and land:
Then there's that old Lord Maurice, not a whit
More tame for his grey hairs—Alas me! flit!
Flit like a ghost away."—"Ah, Gossip dear,   105
We're safe enough; here in this arm-chair sit,
And tell me how"—"Good Saints! not here, not here;
Follow me, child, or else these stones will be thy bier."[5]

13

He follow'd through a lowly arched way,
Brushing the cobwebs with his lofty plume,   110
And as she mutter'd "Well-a—well-a-day!"
He found him in a little moonlight room,
Pale, lattic'd, chill, and silent as a tomb.
"Now tell me where is Madeline," said he,
"O tell me, Angela, by the holy loom   115
Which none but secret sisterhood may see,
When they St. Agnes' wool are weaving piously."

14

"St. Agnes! Ah! it is St. Agnes' Eve—
Yet men will murder upon holy days:
Thou must hold water in a witch's sieve,   120
And be liege-lord of all the Elves and Fays,[6]
To venture so: it fills me with amaze
To see thee, Porphyro!—St. Agnes' Eve!
God's help! my lady fair the conjuror plays
This very night: good angels her deceive!   125
But let me laugh awhile, I've mickle[7] time to grieve."

---

5. Platform for holding a dead body.   6. Fairies.   7. Much.

15

Feebly she laugheth in the languid moon,
While Porphyro upon her face doth look,
Like puzzled urchin on an aged crone
Who keepeth clos'd a wond'rous riddle-book,   130
As spectacled she sits in chimney nook.
But soon his eyes grew brilliant, when she told
His lady's purpose; and he scarce could brook
Tears, at the thought of those enchantments cold
And Madeline asleep in lap of legends old.   135

16

Sudden a thought came like a full-blown rose,
Flushing his brow, and in his pained heart
Made purple riot: then doth he propose
A stratagem, that makes the beldame start:
"A cruel man and impious thou art: 140
Sweet lady, let her pray, and sleep, and dream
Alone with her good angels, far apart
From wicked men like thee. Go, go!—I deem
Thou canst not surely be the same that thou didst seem."

17

"I will not harm her, by all saints I swear,"   145
Quoth Porphyro: "O may I ne'er find grace
When my weak voice shall whisper its last prayer,
If one of her soft ringlets I displace.
Or look with ruffian passion in her face:
Good Angela, believe me by these tears;   150
Or I will, even in a moment's space,
Awake, with horrid shout, my foemen's ears,
And beard them, though they be more fang'd than wolves and bears."

18

"Ah! why wilt thou affright a feeble soul?
A poor, weak, palsy-stricken, churchyard thing,   155
Whose passing-bell may ere the midnight toll;
Whose prayers for thee, each morn and evening,
Were never miss'd."—Thus plaining,[8] doth she bring
A gentler speech from burning Porphyro;
So woeful, and of such deep sorrowing,   160
That Angela gives promise she will do
Whatever he shall wish, betide her weal or woe.

---

8. Complaining.

19

Which was, to lead him, in close secrecy,
Even to Madeline's chamber, and there hide
Him in a closet, of such privacy   165
That he might see her beauty unespied,
And win perhaps that night a peerless bride,
While legion'd fairies pac'd the coverlet,
And pale enchantment held her sleepy-eyed.
Never on such a night have lovers met,   170
Since Merlin⁹ paid his Demon all the monstrous debt.

20

"It shall be as thou wishest," said the Dame:
"All cates and dainties shall be stored there
Quickly on this feast-night: by the tambour¹⁰ frame
Her own lute thou wilt see: no time to spare,   175
For I am slow and feeble, and scarce dare
On such a catering trust my dizzy head.
Wait here, my child, with patience; kneel in prayer
The while: Ah! thou must needs the lady wed,
Or may I never leave my grave among the dead."   180

21

So saying, she hobbled off with busy fear.
The lover's endless minutes slowly pass'd;
The dame return'd, and whisper'd in his ear
To follow her; with aged eyes aghast
From fright of dim espial. Safe at last   185
Through many a dusky gallery, they gain
The maiden's chamber, silken, hush'd, and chaste;
Where Porphyro took covert, pleas'd amain.
His poor guide hurried back with agues in her brain.

22

Her falt'ring hand upon the balustrade,   190
Old Angela was feeling for the stair,
When Madeline, St. Agnes' charmed maid,
Rose, like a mission'd spirit, unaware:
With silver taper's light, and pious care,
She turn'd, and down the aged gossip led   195
To a safe level matting. Now prepare,
Young Porphyro, for gazing on that bed;
She comes, she comes again, like ring-dove fray'd¹¹ and fled.

---

9. Merlin the Magician of Arthurian legend.   10. Drum.   11. Afraid.

23

Out went the taper as she hurried in;
　Its little smoke, in pallid moonshine, died:
She clos'd the door, she panted, all akin
　To spirits of the air, and visions wide:
No utter'd syllable, or, woe betide!
　But to her heart, her heart was voluble,
　Paining with eloquence her balmy side;
As though a tongueless nightingale[12] should swell
Her throat in vain, and die, heart-stifled, in her dell.

24

A casement high and triple-arch'd there was,
　All garlanded with carven imag'ries
Of fruits, and flowers, and bunches of knot-grass,
　And diamonded with panes of quaint device,
Innumerable of stains and splendid dyes,
　As are the tiger-moth's deep-damask'd wings;
　And in the midst, 'mong thousand heraldries,
And twilight saints, and dim emblazonings,
A shielded scutcheon blush'd with blood of queens and kings.

25

Full on this casement shone the wintry moon,
　And threw warm gules[13] on Madeline's fair breast,
As down she knelt for heaven's grace and boon;
　Rose-bloom fell on her hands, together prest,
And on her silver cross soft amethyst,
　And on her hair a glory, like a saint:
　She seem'd a splendid angel, newly drest,
Save wings, for heaven:—Porphyro grew faint:
She knelt, so pure a thing, so free from mortal taint.

26

Anon his heart revives: her vespers done,
　Of all its wreathed pearls her hair she frees;
Unclasps her warmed jewels one by one;
　Loosens her fragrant bodice; by degrees
Her rich attire creeps rustling to her knees:
　Half-hidden, like a mermaid in sea-weed,
　Pensive awhile she dreams awake, and sees,
In fancy, fair St. Agnes in her bed,
But dares not look behind, or all the charm is fled.

---

12. Philomela, of Greek legend, whose tongue was cut out after she was raped by Tereus.　13. Red.

200

205

210

215

220

225

230

27

Soon, trembling in her soft and chilly nest,   235
In sort of wakeful swoon, perplex'd she lay,
Until the poppied[14] warmth of sleep oppress'd
Her soothed limbs, and soul fatigued away;
Flown, like a thought, until the morrow-day;
Blissfully haven'd both from joy and pain;   240
Clasp'd like a missal where swart Paynims[15] pray;
Blinded alike from sunshine and from rain,
As though a rose should shut, and be a bud again.

28

Stol'n to this paradise, and so entranced,
Porphyro gazed upon her empty dress,   245
And listen'd to her breathing, if it chanced
To wake into a slumberous tenderness;
Which when he heard, that minute did he bless,
And breath'd himself: then from the closet crept,
Noiseless as fear in a wide wilderness,   250
And over the hush'd carpet, silent, stept,
And 'tween the curtains peep'd, where, lo!—how fast she slept.

29

Then by the bed-side, where the faded moon
Made a dim, silver twilight, soft he set
A table, and, half anguish'd, threw thereon   255
A cloth of woven crimson, gold, and jet:—
O for some drowsy Morphean[16] amulet!
The boisterous, midnight, festive clarion,
The kettle-drum, and far-heard clarionet,
Affray his ears, though but in dying tone:—   260
The hall door shuts again, and all the noise is gone.

30

And still she slept an azure-lidded sleep,
In blanched linen, smooth, and lavender'd,
While he from forth the closet brought a heap
Of candied apple, quince, and plum, and gourd[17];   265
With jellies soother than the creamy curd,
And lucent syrops, tinct with cinnamon;
Manna and dates, in argosy[18] transferr'd
From Fez; and spiced dainties, every one,
From silken Samarcand[19] to cedar'd Lebanon.   270

---

14. Drugged. 15. A pagan. 16. Morpheus, god of sleep. 17. Melon. 18. Ship. 19. Fez, a city in Morocco; Samarcand, a city in southern Uzbekistan.

31

These delicates he heap'd with glowing hand
On golden dishes and in baskets bright
Of wreathed silver: sumptuous they stand
In the retired quiet of the night,
Filling the chilly room with perfume light.—   275
"And now, my love, my seraph[20] fair, awake!
Thou art my heaven, and I thine eremite:
Open thine eyes, for meek St. Agnes' sake,
Or I shall drowse beside thee, so my soul doth ache."

32

Thus whispering, his warm, unnerved arm   280
Sank in her pillow. Shaded was her dream
By the dusk curtains:—'twas a midnight charm
Impossible to melt as iced stream:
The lustrous salvers in the moonlight gleam:
Broad golden fringe upon the carpet lies: 285
It seem'd he never, never could redeem
From such a steadfast spell his lady's eyes;
So mus'd awhile, entoil'd in woofed[21] phantasies.

33

Awakening up, he took her hollow lute,—
Tumultuous,—and, in chords that tenderest be,   290
He play'd an ancient ditty, long since mute,
In Provence call'd, "La belle dame sans mercy"[22]:
Close to her ear touching the melody;—
Wherewith disturb'd, she utter'd a soft moan:
He ceased—she panted quick—and suddenly   295
Her blue affrayed eyes wide open shone:
Upon his knees he sank, pale as smooth-sculptured stone.

34

Her eyes were open, but she still beheld,
Now wide awake, the vision of her sleep:
There was a painful change, that nigh expell'd   300
The blisses of her dream so pure and deep
At which fair Madeline began to weep,
And moan forth witless words with many a sigh;
While still her gaze on Porphyro would keep;
Who knelt, with joined hands and piteous eye,   305
Fearing to move or speak, she look'd so dreamingly.

---

20. Angel.   21. Woven.   22. Alain Chartier (c. 1385–1433), French poet.

35

"Ah, Porphyro!" said she, "but even now
Thy voice was at sweet tremble in mine ear,
Made tuneable with every sweetest vow;
And those sad eyes were spiritual and clear: 310
How chang'd thou art! how pallid, chill, and drear!
Give me that voice again, my Porphyro,
Those looks immortal, those complainings dear!
Oh leave me not in this eternal woe,
For if thou diest, my Love, I know not where to go."   315

36

Beyond a mortal man impassion'd far
At these voluptuous accents, he arose,
Ethereal, flush'd, and like a throbbing star
Seen mid the sapphire heaven's deep repose;
Into her dream he melted, as the rose   320
Blendeth its odour with the violet,—
Solution sweet: meantime the frost-wind blows
Like Love's alarum, pattering the sharp sleet
Against the window-panes; St. Agnes' moon hath set.

37

'Tis dark: quick pattereth the flaw-blown[23] sleet: 325
"This is no dream, my bride, my Madeline!"
'Tis dark: the iced gusts still rave and beat:
"No dream, alas! alas! and woe is mine!
Porphyro will leave me here to fade and pine.—
Cruel! what traitor could thee hither bring?   330
I curse not, for my heart is lost in thine,
Though thou forsakest a deceived thing;—
A dove forlorn and lost with sick unpruned wing."

38

"My Madeline! sweet dreamer! lovely bride!
Say, may I be for aye thy vassal blest?   335
Thy beauty's shield, heart-shaped and vermeil[24] dyed?
Ah, silver shrine, here will I take my rest
After so many hours of toil and quest,
A famish'd pilgrim,—saved by miracle.
Though I have found, I will not rob thy nest   340
Saving of thy sweet self; if thou think'st well
To trust, fair Madeline, to no rude infidel.

---

23. Wind-blown.   24. Vermilion.

39

"Hark! 'tis an elfin-storm from faery land,
Of haggard[25] seeming, but a boon indeed:
Arise—arise! the morning is at hand;—   345
The bloated wassailers[26] will never heed:—
Let us away, my love, with happy speed;
There are no ears to hear, or eyes to see,—
Drown'd all in Rhenish[27] and the sleepy mead:
Awake! arise! my love, and fearless be,   350
For o'er the southern moors I have a home for thee."

40

She hurried at his words, beset with fears,
For there were sleeping dragons all around,
At glaring watch, perhaps, with ready spears—
Down the wide stairs a darkling way they found.—   355
In all the house was heard no human sound.
A chain-droop'd lamp was flickering by each door;
The arras,[28] rich with horseman, hawk, and hound,
Flutter'd in the besieging wind's uproar;
And the long carpets rose along the gusty floor.   360

41

They glide, like phantoms, into the wide hall;
Like phantoms to the iron porch they glide;
Where lay the Porter, in uneasy sprawl,
With a huge empty flagon by his side:
The wakeful bloodhound rose, and shook his hide,   365
But his sagacious eye an inmate owns:
By one, and one, the bolts fill easy slide:—
The chains lie silent on the footworn stones;—
The key turns, and the door upon its hinges groans.

42

And they are gone: ay, ages long ago   370
These lovers fled away into the storm.
That night the Baron dreamt of many a woe,
And all his warrior-guests, with shade and form
Of witch, and demon, and large coffin-worm,
Were long be-nightmar'd. Angela the old   375
Died palsy-twitch'd, with meagre face deform;
The Beadsman, after thousand aves told,
For aye unsought for slept among his ashes cold.

—1820

---

25. Wild.   26. Drunken carousers.   27. Wine from the Rhine Valley, Germany.   28. Tapestry.

Ode on a Grecian Urn

1

Thou still unravish'd bride of quietness,
    Thou foster-child of silence and slow time,
Sylvan[1] historian, who canst thus express
    A flowery tale more sweetly than our rhyme:
What leaf-fring'd legend haunts about thy shape   5
    Of deities or mortals, or of both,
        In Tempe or the dales of Arcady?[2]
    What men or gods are these? What maidens loth?
What mad pursuit? What struggle to escape?
    What pipes and timbrels?[3] What wild ecstasy?   10

2

Heard melodies are sweet, but those unheard
    Are sweeter; therefore, ye soft pipes, play on;
Not to the sensual ear, but, more endear'd,
    Pipe to the spirit ditties of no tone:
Fair youth, beneath the trees, thou canst not leave   15
    Thy song, nor ever can those trees be bare;
        Bold Lover, never, never canst thou kiss,
Though winning near the goal—yet, do not grieve;
    She cannot fade, though thou hast not thy bliss,
        For ever wilt thou love, and she be fair!   20

3

Ah, happy, happy boughs! that cannot shed
    Your leaves, nor ever bid the Spring adieu;
And, happy melodist, unwearied,
    For ever piping songs for ever new;
More happy love! more happy, happy love!   25
    For ever warm and still to be enjoy'd,
        For ever panting, and for ever young;
All breathing human passion far above,
    That leaves a heart high-sorrowful and cloy'd,
A burning forehead, and a parching tongue.   30

4

Who are these coming to the sacrifice?
    To what green altar, O mysterious priest,
Lead'st thou that heifer lowing at the skies,

---

1. Of forests or trees.   2. Beautiful regions of ancient Greece.   3. Tambourines.

And all her silken flanks with garlands drest?
What little town by river or sea shore,   35
  Or mountain-built with peaceful citadel,
    Is emptied of this folk, this pious morn?
And, little town, thy streets for evermore
  Will silent be; and not a soul to tell
    Why thou art desolate, can e'er return.   40

5

O Attic[4] shape! Fair attitude! with brede[5]
  Of marble men and maidens overwrought,
With forest branches and the trodden weed;
  Thou, silent form, dost tease us out of thought
As doth eternity: Cold Pastoral!   45
  When old age shall this generation waste,
    Thou shalt remain, in midst of other woe
Than ours, a friend to man, to whom thou say'st,
  Beauty is truth, truth beauty,—that is all
    Ye know on earth, and all ye need to know.   50

—1820

Ode to a Nightingale

1

My heart aches, and a drowsy numbness pains
  My sense, as though of hemlock[1] I had drunk,
Or emptied some dull opiate to the drains
  One minute past, and Lethe-wards[2] had sunk:
'Tis not through envy of thy happy lot,   5
  But being too happy in thine happiness,—
    That thou, light-winged Dryad[3] of the trees,
      In some melodious plot
Of beechen green, and shadows numberless,
  Singest of summer in full-throated ease.   10

2

O, for a draught of vintage![4] that hath been
  Cool'd a long age in the deep-delved earth,
Tasting of Flora and the country green,
  Dance, and Provençal song, and sunburnt mirth!

---

4. Grecian.   5. Braid.

1. Poisonous plant used as sedative.   2. Lethe: river of forgetfulness in Hades, the underworld of Greek mythology.   3. Wood-nymph.   4. Wine.

O for a beaker full of the warm South,   15
   Full of the true, the blushful Hippocrene,[5]
      With beaded bubbles winking at the brim,
        And purple-stained mouth;
   That I might drink, and leave the world unseen,
      And with thee fade away into the forest dim: 20

3

Fade far away, dissolve, and quite forget
   What thou among the leaves hast never known,
The weariness, the fever, and the fret
   Here, where men sit and hear each other groan;
Where palsy shakes a few, sad, last gray hairs,   25
   Where youth grows pale, and spectre-thin, and dies[6];
      Where but to think is to be full of sorrow
        And leaden-eyed despairs,
   Where Beauty cannot keep her lustrous eyes,
      Or new Love pine at them beyond to-morrow.   30

4

Away! away! for I will fly to thee,
   Not charioted by Bacchus and his pards,[7]
But on the viewless wings of Poesy,
   Though the dull brain perplexes and retards:
Already with thee! tender is the night,   35
   And haply the Queen-Moon is on her throne,
      Cluster'd around by all her starry Fays[8];
        But here there is no light,
Save what from heaven is with the breezes blown
      Through verdurous glooms and winding mossy ways.   40

5

I cannot see what flowers are at my feet,
   Nor what soft incense hangs upon the boughs,
But, in embalmed darkness, guess each sweet
   Wherewith the seasonable month endows
The grass, the thicket, and the fruit-tree wild;   45
   White hawthorn, and the pastoral eglantine[9];
      Fast fading violets cover'd up in leaves;
        And mid-May's eldest child,
The coming musk-rose, full of dewy wine,
      The murmurous haunt of flies on summer eves.   50

---

5. Water from the fountain of the Muses.   6. Tom Keats, the poet's brother, died of tuberculosis.   7. Bacchus, god of
wine, rode a chariot pulled by leopards.   8. Fairies.   9. Sweetbriar or honeysuckle.

6

Darkling I listen; and, for many a time
    I have been half in love with easeful Death,
Call'd him soft names in many a mused rhyme,
    To take into the air my quiet breath;
Now more than ever seems it rich to die,   55
    To cease upon the midnight with no pain,
        While thou art pouring forth thy soul abroad
            In such an ecstasy!
Still wouldst thou sing, and I have ears in vain—
    To thy high requiem become a sod.   60

7

Thou wast not born for death, immortal Bird!
    No hungry generations tread thee down;
The voice I hear this passing night was heard
    In ancient days by emperor and clown:
Perhaps the self-same song that found a path   65
    Through the sad heart of Ruth, when, sick for home,
        She stood in tears amid the alien corn;
            The same that oft-times hath
Charm'd magic casements, opening on the foam
    Of perilous seas, in faery lands forlorn.   70

8

Forlorn! the very word is like a bell
    To toll me back from thee to my sole self!
Adieu! the fancy cannot cheat so well
    As she is fam'd to do, deceiving elf.
Adieu! adieu! thy plaintive anthem fades   75
    Past the near meadows, over the still stream,
        Up the hill-side; and now 'tis buried deep
            In the next valley-glades:
Was it a vision, or a waking dream?
    Fled is that music:—Do I wake or sleep?   80

—1820

To George and Thomas Keats[1]

["Negative Capability"]

My dear Brothers

[21 Dec.] . . . —I spent Friday evening with Wells & went the next morning to see
Death on the Pale horse.[2] It is a wonderful picture, when West's age is considered; But
there is nothing to be intense upon; no women one feels mad to kiss; no face swelling

---

1. The poet's brothers.   2. A painting by Benjamin West (1738–1820).

into reality. the excellence of every Art is its intensity, capable of making all disagree-
ables evaporate, from their being in close relationship with Beauty & Truth—
Examine King Lear & you will find this examplified throughout; but in this picture
we have unpleasantness without any momentous depth of speculation excited, in
which to bury its repulsiveness. . . . [?27 Dec.] . . . I had not a dispute but a disquisition with Dilke,[3] on various subjects; several things dovetailed in my mind, & at once
it struck me, what quality went to form a Man of Achievement especially in
Literature & which Shakespeare posessed so enormously—I mean *Negative Capability*,
that is when man is capable of being in uncertainties, Mysteries, doubts, without any
irritable reaching after fact & reason—Coleridge, for instance, would let go by a fine
isolated verisimilitude caught from the Penetralium[4] of mystery, from being incapable
of remaining content with half knowledge. This pursued through Volumes would perhaps take us no further than this, that with a great poet the sense of Beauty overcomes every other consideration, or rather obliterates all consideration.

Shelley's poem[5] is out & there are words about its being objected too, as much as
Queen Mab was. Poor Shelley I think he has his Quota of good qualities, in sooth la!!
Write soon to your most sincere friend & affectionate Brother

John

—1817

To Richard Woodhouse[1]
[The "Egotistical Sublime"]

My dear Woodhouse,

Your Letter gave me a great satisfaction; more on account of its friendliness, than any
relish of that matter in it which is accounted so acceptable in the 'genus irritabile'.[2] The
best answer I can give you is in a clerklike manner to make some observations on two
principle points, which seem to point like indices into the midst of the whole pro and
con, about genius, and views and achievements and ambition and cœtera. 1st As to the
poetical Character itself, (I mean that sort of which, if I am any thing, I am a Member;
that sort distinguished from the wordsworthian or egotistical sublime; which is a thing
per se and stands alone) it is not itself—it has no self—it is every thing and nothing—
It has no character—it enjoys light and shade; it lives in gusto, be it foul or fair, high or
low, rich or poor, mean or elevated—It has as much delight in conceiving an Iago as an
Imogen.[3] What shocks the virtuous philosopher delights the camelion Poet. It does no
harm from its relish of the dark side of things any more than from its taste for the bright
one; because they both end in speculation. A Poet is the most unpoetical of any thing
in existence; because he has no Identity—he is continually in for[ming?]—and filling
some other Body—The Sun, the Moon, the Sea and Men and Women who are creatures of impulse are poetical and have about them an unchangeable attribute—the poet
has none; no identity—he is certainly the most unpoetical of all God's Creatures. If
then he has no self, and if I am a Poet, where is the Wonder that I should say I would

3. Charles Dilke (1789–1864), Keats's friend.   4. Secret part of a temple.   5. *Laon and Cyntha* (1817).

1. Lawyer for Keats's publisher.   2. Horace's term for poets: "irritable tribe."   3. Iago in William Shakespeare
(1564–1616), *Othello* (1622); Imogen in *Cymbeline* (1623).

write no more? Might I not at that very instant have been cogitating on the Characters of saturn and Ops?[4] It is a wretched thing to confess; but is a very fact that not one word I ever utter can be taken for granted as an opinion growing out of my identical nature— how can it, when I have no nature? When I am in a room with People if I ever am free from speculating on creations of my own brain, then not myself goes home to myself: but the identity of every one in the room begins to press upon me that, I am in a very little time annihilated—not only among Men; it would be the same in a Nursery of children: I know not whether I make myself wholly understood: I hope enough so to let you see that no dependence is to be placed on what I said that day.

In the second place I will speak of my views, and of the life I purpose to myself—I am ambitious of doing the world some good: if I should be spared that may be the work of maturer years—in the interval I will assay to reach to as high a summit in Poetry as the nerve bestowed upon me will suffer. The faint conceptions I have of Poems to come brings the blood frequently into my forehead—All I hope is that I may not lose all interest in human affairs—that the solitary indifference I feel for applause even from the finest Spirits, will not blunt any acuteness of vision I may have. I do not think it will—I feel assured I should write from the mere yearning and fondness I have for the Beautiful even if my night's labours should be burnt every morning and no eye ever shine upon them. But even now I am perhaps not speaking from myself; but from some character in whose soul I now live. I am sure however that this next sentence is from myself. I feel your anxiety, good opinion and friendliness in the highest degree, and am

Your's most sincerely

John Keats

—1818

To George and Georgiana Keats

[The "Vale of Soul-Making"]

My dear Brother & Sister—

[19 March] Yesterday I got a black eye—the first time I took a Cricket bat—Brown who is always one's friend in a disaster applied a leech to the eyelid, and there is no inflammation this morning though the ball hit me directly on the sight—'t was a white ball— I am glad it was not a clout—This is the second black eye I have had since leaving school—during all my school days I never had one at all—we must eat a peck before we die—This morning I am in a sort of temper indolent and supremely careless: I long after a stanza or two of Thompson's Castle of indolence[1]—My passions are all asleep from my having slumbered till nearly eleven and weakened the animal fibre all over me to a delightful sensation about three degrees on this side of faintness—if I had teeth of pearl and the breath of lillies I should call it langour—but as I am I must call it Laziness—In this state of effeminacy the fibres of the brain are relaxed in common with the rest of the body, and to such a happy degree that pleasure has no show of enticement and pain no unbearable frown. Neither Poetry, nor Ambition, nor Love have any alertness of coun-

---

4. Characters in Keats's *Hyperion*.

1. James Thomson (1700–1748), "The Castle of Indolence" (1748).

tenance as they pass by me: they seem rather like three figures on a greek vase—a Man and two women—whom no one but myself could distinguish in their disguisement. This is the only happiness; and is a rare instance of advantage in the body overpowering the Mind. I have this moment received a note from Haslam[2] in which he expects the death of his Father who has been for some time in a state of insensibility—his mother bears up he says very well—I shall go to town tommorrow to see him. This is the world—thus we cannot expect to give way many hours to pleasure—Circumstances are like Clouds continually gathering and bursting—While we are laughing the seed of some trouble is put into the wide arable land of events—while we are laughing it sprouts it grows and suddenly bears a poison fruit which we must pluck—Even so we have leisure to reason on the misfortunes of our friends; our own touch us too nearly for words. Very few men have ever arrived at a complete disinterestedness of Mind: very few have been influenced by a pure desire of the benefit of others—in the greater part of the Benefactors & to Humanity some meretricious motive has sullied their greatness—some melodramatic scenery has facinated them—From the manner in which I feel Haslam's misfortune I perceive how far I am from any humble standard of disinterestedness—Yet this feeling ought to be carried to its highest pitch, as there is no fear of its ever injuring society—which it would do I fear pushed to an extremity—For in wild nature the Hawk would loose his Breakfast of Robins and the Robin his of Worms The Lion must starve as well as the swallow—The greater part of Men make their way with the same instinctiveness, the same unwandering eye from their purposes, the same animal eagerness as the Hawk—The Hawk wants a Mate, so does the Man—look at them both they set about it and procure one in the same manner—They want both a nest and they both set about one in the same manner—they get their food in the same manner—The noble animal Man for his amusement smokes his pipe—the Hawk balances about the Clouds—that is the only difference of their leisures. This it is that makes the Amusement of Life—to a speculative Mind. I go among the Fields and catch a glimpse of a stoat or a fieldmouse peeping out of the withered grass—the creature hath a purpose and its eyes are bright with it—I go amongst the buildings of a city and I see a Man hurrying along—to what? The Creature has a purpose and his eyes are bright with it. But then as Wordsworth says, "we have all one human heart"[3]—there is an ellectric fire in human nature tending to purify—so that among these human creature[s] there is continually some birth of new heroism—The pity is that we must wonder at it: as we should at finding a pearl in rubbish—I have no doubt that thousands of people never heard of have had hearts completely disinterested: I can remember but two—Socrates and Jesus—their Histories evince it—What I heard a little time ago, Taylor observe with respect to Socrates, may be said of Jesus—That he was so great a man that though he transmitted no writing of his own to posterity, we have his Mind and his sayings and his greatness handed to us by others. It is to be lamented that the history of the latter was written and revised by Men interested in the pious frauds of Religion. Yet through all this I see his splendour. Even here though I myself am pursueing the same instinctive course as the veriest human animal you can think of—I am however young writing at random—straining at particles of light in the midst of a great darkness—without knowing the bearing of any one assertion of any one opinion. Yet may I not in this be free from sin? May there not be superior

2. William Haslam (c. 1795–1851), Keats's friend.   3. William Wordsworth (1770–1850), "The Old Cumberland Beggar" (1800), lines 152–153.

beings amused with any graceful, though instinctive attitude my mind may fall into, as I am entertained with the alertness of a Stoat or the anxiety of a Deer? Though a quarrel in the streets is a thing to be hated, the energies displayed in it are fine; the commonest Man shows a grace in his quarrel—By a superior being our reasoning may take the same tone—though erroneous they may be fine—This is the very thing in which consists poetry; and if so it is not so fine a thing as philosophy—For the same reason that an eagle is not so fine a thing as a truth—Give me this credit—Do you not think I strive—to know myself? Give me this credit—and you will not think that on my own account I repeat Milton's lines

> How charming is divine Philosophy
> Not harsh and crabbed as dull fools suppose
> But musical as is Apollo's lute—[4]

No—no for myself—feeling grateful as I do to have got into a state of mind to relish them properly—Nothing ever becomes real till it is experienced—Even a Proverb is no proverb to you till your Life has illustrated it— . . .

[21 April] I have been reading lately two very different books Robertson's America and Voltaire's Siecle De Louis XIV[5] It is like walking arm and arm between Pizzarro[6] and the great-little Monarch. In How lementable a case do we see the great body of the people in both instances: in the first, where Men might seem to inherit quiet of Mind from unsophisticated sense; from uncontamination of civilisation; and especially from their being as it were estranged from the mutual helps of Society and its mutual injuries—and thereby more immediately under the Protection of Providence—even there they had mortal pains to bear as bad; or even worse than Baliffs, Debts and Poverties of civilised Life—The whole appears to resolve into this—that Man is originally "a poor forked creature"[7] subject to the same mischances as the beasts of the forest, destined to hardships and disquietude of some kind or other. If he improves by degrees his bodily accomodations and comforts—at each stage, at each accent there are waiting for him a fresh set of annoyances—he is mortal and there is still a heaven with its Stars above his head. The most interesting question that can come before us is, How far by the persevering endeavours of a seldom appearing Socrates Mankind may be made happy—I can imagine such happiness carried to an extreme—but what must it end in?—Death—and who could in such a case bear with death—the whole troubles of life which are now frittered away in a series of years, would then be accumulated for the last days of a being who instead of hailing its approach, would leave this world as Eve left Paradise—But in truth I do not at all believe in this sort of perfectibility—the nature of the world will not admit of it— the inhabitants of the world will correspond to itself—Let the fish philosophise the ice away from the Rivers in winter time and they shall be at continual play in the tepid delight of summer. Look at the Poles and at the sands of Africa, Whirlpools and volcanoes—Let men exterminate them and I will say that they may arrive at earthly Happiness—The point at which Man may arrive is as far as the parallel state in inanimate nature and no further—For instance suppose a rose to have sensation, it blooms on a beautiful morning it enjoys itself—but there comes a cold wind, a hot sun—it can not escape it, it cannot destroy its annoyances—they are as native to the world as itself: no

---

4. John Milton (1608–1674), *Comus* (1637), lines 475–477.   5. William Robertson (1721–1793), *History of the Discovery and Settlement of America* (1777); Voltaire (1694–1778), *La Siecle de Louis XIV* (1751).   6. Pizzaro conquered the Incas in Peru.   7. William Shakespeare (1564–1616), *King Lear* (1608) 3.4.109–110.

more can man be happy in spite, the worldly elements will prey upon his nature—The common cognomen of this world among the misguided and superstitious is "a vale of tears"[8] from which we are to be redeemed by a certain arbitrary interposition of God and taken to Heaven—What a little circumscribed straightened notion! Call the world if you Please "The vale of Soul-making" Then you will find out the use of the world (I am speaking now in the highest terms for human nature admitting it to be immortal which I will here take for granted for the purpose of showing a thought which has struck me concerning it) I say "*Soul making*" Soul as distinguished from an Intelligence—There may be intelligences or sparks of the divinity in millions—but they are not Souls till they acquire identities, till each one is personally itself. Intelligences are atoms of perception—they know and they see and they are pure, in short they are God—how then are Souls to be made? How then are these sparks which are God to have identity given them—so as ever to possess a bliss peculiar to each ones individual existence? How, but by the medium of a world like this? This point I sincerely wish to consider because I think it a grander system of salvation than the chrystain religion—or rather it is a system of Spirit-creation—This is effected by three grand materials acting the one upon the other for a series of years—These three Materials are the *Intelligence*—the *human heart* (as distinguished from intelligence or Mind) and the *World* or *Elemental space* suited for the proper action of *Mind and Heart* on each other for the purpose of forming the *Soul* or *Intelligence destined to possess the sense of Identity.* I can scarcely express what I but dimly perceive—and yet I think I perceive it—that you may judge the more clearly I will put it in the most homely form possible—I will call the *world* a School instituted for the purpose of teaching little children to read—I will call the *human heart* the *horn Book*[9] used in that School—and I will call the *Child able to read, the Soul* made from that *school* and its *hornbook.* Do you not see how necessary a World of Pains and troubles is to school an Intelligence and make it a soul? A Place where the heart must feel and suffer in a thousand diverse ways! Not merely is the Heart a Hornbook, It is the Minds Bible, it is the Minds experience, it is the teat from which the Mind or intelligence sucks its identity— As various as the Lives of Men are—so various become their souls, and thus does God make individual beings, Souls, Identical Souls of the sparks of his own essence—This appears to me a faint sketch of a system of Salvation which does not affront our reason and humanity—I am convinced that many difficulties which christians labour under would vanish before it—There is one which even now Strikes me—the Salvation of Children—In them the Spark or intelligence returns to God without any identity—it having had no time to learn of, and be altered by, the heart—or seat of the human Passions—Through the medium of the Heart? And how is the heart to become this Medium but in a world of Circumstances?—There now I think what with Poetry and Theology you may thank your Stars that my pen is not very long winded—. . .

[T]his is the 3d of May & every thing is in delightful forwardness; the violets are not withered, before the peeping of the first rose; You must let me know every thing, how parcels go & come, what papers you have, & what Newspapers you want, & other things—God bless you my dear Brother & Sister

Your ever Affectionate Brother

John Keats

—1819

---

8. Psalm 83.7.   9. Textbook.

Thomas Chandler Haliburton
1796–1865

Lawyer, judge, politician, and humorist Thomas Chandler Haliburton was born in Windsor, Nova Scotia, in 1796. A third-generation Canadian, he felt—as did his family—a deep personal and political connection to the country. The strongly Tory family claimed to be descended from the Haliburtons of Scotland, the ancestors of Sir Walter Scott. Educated at a bastion of Anglican Toryism, King's Collegiate School, Haliburton's political sensibility remained that of a Loyalist. Revolutionary sentiments and events in America and France only strengthened loyalty to crown and King. During his highly successful legal career (culminating in a Supreme Court judgeship) and vocal political career, he supported British oversight of Nova Scotia's economy, yet fought for colonial control of public education. Such a position left him divided politically, open to charges of flip-flopping that were often silenced by Haliburton himself, who was famous for his eloquent yet sharp tongue. He was keenly aware of the struggles of the colony to assert its economic and cultural identity, and he increasingly became disenchanted with what he saw as self-interested politicians. In time, he became convinced that the colony was straying from Tory ideals and the sense of civil service he held dear. He moved to England in 1856, where he was elected to Parliament in 1858 and awarded an honorary doctorate from Oxford.

Haliburton's writing career earned him far more notoriety than his political and legal careers did. His first writings were nationalistic surveys of Nova Scotian history and culture: *A General Description of Nova Scotia* (1823) and *An Historical and Statistical Account of Nova Scotia in Two Volumes* (1829). His first book focused on events prior to British colonization, such as the expulsion of the Acadians, the descendants of early French settlers who were forced to relocate to Louisiana where they came to be known as Cajuns. *A General Description of Nova Scotia* provided Henry Wadsworth Longfellow with one of the main sources for his poem about the Acadians, *Evangeline* (1847). Haliburton's popularity, though, rests on his literary work. He gained international celebrity with his humorous *The Clockmaker; Or, the Sayings and Doings of Samuel Slick, of Slickville*, first published serially in the periodical the *Novascotian* in 1836 and in London in 1838. Following the travels of an American clockmaker, Sam Slick, as he wanders through Nova Scotia, Haliburton offers humorous sketches of American, British, and Nova Scotian political and cultural ideas. His main character is based on a court case Haliburton presided over, in which an American clockmaker was selling local farmers inoperable clocks. Little escapes Haliburton's scrutiny and ridicule as he both values and derides each country's defining characteristics: He extols the strength of British tradition, yet finds that it yokes progress; and he censures American ego yet admires the spirit of entrepreneurship that shapes the country. Nova Scotians—"Bluenoses"—are a combination of both. The popularity of Sam Slick led the American humorist Artemus Ward to call Haliburton the founder of the American school of humor, a movement that would later come to fruition in the work of Ward's protégé, Mark Twain.

from The Clockmaker

The Clockmaker

I had heard of Yankee clock pedlars, tin pedlars, and bible pedlars, especially of him who sold Polyglot[1] Bibles (*all in English*) to the amount of sixteen thousand pounds. The house of every substantial farmer had three substantial ornaments, a wooden

---

1. Mixed language.

clock, a tin reflector, and a Polyglot Bible. How is it that an American can sell his wares, at whatever price he pleases, where a Blue Nose[2] would fail to make a sale at all? I will enquire of the Clockmaker the secret of his success. What a pity it is, Mr. *Slick*, (for such was his name,) what a pity it is, said I, that you, who are so successful in teaching these people the value of *clocks*, could not also teach them the value of *time*. I guess, said he, they have got that ring to grow on their horns yet, which every four year old has in our country. We reckon hours and minutes to be dollars and cents. They do nothing in these parts, but eat, drink, smoke, sleep, ride about, lounge at taverns, make speeches at temperance meetings, and talk about "*House of Assembly*."[3] If a man don't hoe his corn, and he don't get a crop, he says it is all owing to the Bank; and if he runs into debt and is sued, why says the lawyers are a curse to the country. They are a most idle set of folks, I tell you. But how is it, said I, that you manage to sell such an immense number of clocks, (which certainly cannot be called necessary articles,) among a people with whom there seems to be so great a scarcity of money.

Mr. Slick paused, as if considering the propriety of answering the question, and looking me in the face, said, in a confidential tone, Why, I don't care if I do tell you, for the market is glutted, and I shall quit this circuit. It is done by a knowledge of *soft sawder*[4] and *human natur*. But here is Deacon Flint's, said he, I have but one clock left, and I guess I will sell it to him. At the gate of a most comfortable looking farm house stood Deacon Flint, a respectable old man, who had understood the value of time better than most of his neighbors, if one might judge from the appearance of every thing about him. After the usual salutation, an invitation to "alight" was accepted by Mr. Slick, who said, he wished to take leave of Mrs. Flint before he left Colchester. We had hardly entered the house, before the Clockmaker pointed to the view from the window, and addressing himself to me, said, if I was to tell them in Connecticut, there was such a farm as this away down east here in Nova Scotia, they would'nt believe me—why there aint such a location in all New England. The Deacon has a hundred acres of dyke—seventy, said the Deacon, only seventy. Well, seventy; but then there is your fine deep bottom, why I could run a ramrod[5] into it—Interval, we call it, said the Deacon, who, though evidently pleased at this eulogium,[6] seemed to wish the experiment of the ramrod to be tried in the right place—well interval if you please, (though Professor Eleazer Cumstick, in his work on Ohio, calls them bottoms,) is just as good as dyke. Then there is that water privilege, worth 3 or $4,000, twice as good as what Governor Cass paid $15,000 for. I wonder, Deacon, you don't put up a carding mill on it: the same works would carry a turning lathe, a shingle machine, a circular saw, grind bark, and————. Too old, said the Deacon, too old for all those speculations—old, repeated the Clockmaker, not you; why you are worth half a dozen of the young men we see, now-a-days, you are young enough to have—here he said something in a lower tone of voice, which I did not distinctly hear; but whatever it was, the Deacon was pleased, he smiled and said he did not think of such things now. But your beasts, dear me, your beasts must be put in and have a feed; saying which, he went out to order them to be taken to the stable. As the old gentleman closed the door after him, Mr. Slick drew near to me, and said in an under tone, that is what I call "*soft sawder*." An Englishman would pass that man as a sheep passes a hog in a pasture, without looking at him; or, said he, looking rather archly, if he was mounted

---

2. A conservative Nova Scotian.   3. Seat of government.   4. Haliburton coinage meaning flattery for the sake of persuasion.   5. Bottom: fertile bottomland; ramrod: a tool for cleaning rifles.   6. Eulogy.

on a pretty smart horse, I guess he'd trot away, *if he could.* Now I find—here his lecture on "*soft sawder*" was cut short by the entrance of Mrs. Flint. Jist come to say good bye, Mrs. Flint. What, have you sold all your clocks? yes, and very low, too, for money is scarce, and I wished to close the concarn[7]; no, I am wrong in saying all, for I have just one left. Neighbor Steel's wife asked to have the refusal of it, but I guess I won't sell it; I had but two of them, this one and the feller of it, that I sold Governor Lincoln. General Green, the Secretary of State for Maine, said he'd give me 50 dollars for this here one— it has composition wheels and patent axles, it is a beautiful article—a real first chop— no mistake, genuine superfine, but I guess I'll take it back; and beside, Squire Hawk might think kinder harder, that I did not give him the offer. Dear me, said Mrs. Flint, I should like to see it, where is it? It is in a chest of mine over the way, at Tom Tape's store, I guess he can ship it on to Eastport. That's a good man, said Mrs. Flint, jist let's look at it. Mr. Slick, willing to oblige, yielded to these entreaties, and soon produced the clock— a gawdy, highly varnished, trumpery looking affair. He placed it on the chimney-piece, where its beauties were pointed out and duly appreciated by Mrs. Flint, whose admiration was about ending in a proposal, when Mr. Flint returned from giving his directions about the care of the horses. The Deacon praised the clock, he too thought it a handsome one; but the Deacon was a prudent man, he had a watch, he was sorry, but he had no occasion for a clock. I guess you're in the wrong furrow this time, Deacon, it ant for sale, said Mr. Slick; and if it was, I reckon neighbor Steel's wife would have it, for she gives me no peace about it. Mrs. Flint said, that Mr. Steel had enough to do, poor man, to pay his interest, without buying clocks for his wife. It's no concarn of mine, said Mr. Slick, as long as he pays me, what he has to do, but I guess I don't want to sell it, and beside it comes too high; that clock can't be made at Rhode Island under 40 dollars. Why it ant possible, said the Clockmaker, in apparent surprise, looking at his watch, why as I'm alive it is 4 o'clock, and if I hav'nt been two hours here—how on airth shall I reach River Philip to-night? I'll tell you what, Mrs. Flint, I'll leave the clock in your care till I return on my way to the States—I'll set it a going and put it to the right time. As soon as this operation was performed, he delivered the key to the deacon with a sort of serio-comic injunction to wind up the clock every Saturday night, which Mrs. Flint said she would take care should be done, and promised to remind her husband of it, in case he should chance to forget it.

That, said the Clockmaker as soon as we were mounted, that I call 'human natur!' Now that clock is sold for 40 dollars—it cost me just 6 dollars and 50 cents. Mrs. Flint will never let Mrs. Steel have the refusal—nor will the deacon learn until I call for the clock, that having once indulged in the use of a superfluity, how difficult it is to give it up. We can do without any article of luxury we have never had, but when once obtained, it is not 'in human natur' to surrender it voluntarily. Of fifteen thousand sold by myself and partners in this Province, twelve thousand were left in this manner, and only ten clocks were ever returned—when we called for them they invariably bought them. We trust to 'soft sawder' to get them into the house, and to 'human natur' that they never come out of it.

The American Eagle

Jist look out of the door, said the Clockmaker, and see what a beautiful night it is, how calm, how still, how clear it is, beant it lovely?—I like to look up at them are

---

7. Concern.

stars, when I am away from home, they put me in mind of our national flag, and it is generally allowed to be the first flag in the univarse now. The British can whip all the world, and we can whip the British. Its near about the prettiest sight I know of, is one of our first class Frigates, manned with our free and enlightened citizens all ready for sea; it is like the great American Eagle, on its perch, balancing itself for a start on the broad expanse of blue sky, afeared of nothin of its kind, and president of all it surveys. It was a good emblem that we chose, warn't it? There was no evading so direct, and at the same time, so conceited an appeal as this. Certainly, said I, the emblem was well chosen. I was particularly struck with it on observing the device on your naval buttons during the last war—an eagle with an anchor in its claws. That was a natural idea, taken from an ordinary occurrence: a bird purloining the anchor of a frigate—an article so useful and necessary for the food of its young. It was well chosen, and exhibited great taste and judgment in the artist. The emblem is more appropriate than you are aware of—boasting of what you cannot perform—grasping at what you cannot attain—an emblem of arrogance and weakness—of ill-directed ambition and vulgar pretension. Its a common phrase, said he, (with great composure) among seamen, to say 'damn your buttons,' and I guess its natural for you to say so of the buttons of our navals; I guess you have a right to that are[8] oath. Its a sore subject, that, I reckon, and I believe I hadn't ought to have spoken of it to you at all. Brag is a good dog, but hold fast is a better one. He was evidently annoyed, and with his usual dexterity gave vent to his feelings, by a sally[9] upon the Blue Noses, who he says are a cross of English and Yankee, and therefore first cousins to us both. Perhaps, said he, that are Eagle might with more propriety have been taken off as perched on an anchor, instead of holding it in his claws, and I think it would have been more nateral; but I suppose it was some stupid foreign artist that made that are blunder, I never seed one yet that was equal to ourn.[10] If that Eagle is represented as trying what *he cant do*, its an honorable ambition arter all, but these Blue Noses wont try what *they can do*. They put me in mind of a great big hulk of a horse in a cart, that wont put his shoulder to the collar at all for all the lambastin in the world, but turns his head round and looks at you, as much as to say, 'what an everlastin heavy thing an empty cart is, isnt it?' *An Owl should be their emblem, and the motto, 'He sleeps all the days of his life.'* The whole country is like this night; beautiful to look at, but silent as the grave—still as death, asleep, becalmed. If the sea was always calm, said he, it would pyson the univarse; no soul could breathe the air, it would be so uncommon bad. Stagnant water is always onpleasant, but salt water when it gets tainted beats all natur; motion keeps it sweet and wholesome, and that our minister used to say is one of the 'wonders of the great deep.' This province is stagnant; it tante[11] deep like still water neither, for its shaller enough, gracious knows, but it is motionless, noiseless, lifeless. If you have ever been to sea, in a calm, you'd know what a plaguy tiresome thing it is for a man that's in a hurry. An everlastin flappin of the sails, and a creakin of the boombs, and an onsteady pitchin of the ship, and folks lyin about dozin away their time, and the sea a heavin a long heavy swell, like the breathin of the chist[12] of some great monster asleep. A passenger wonders the sailors are so plaguy easy about it, and he goes a lookin out east, and a spyin out west, to see if there's any change of a breeze, and says to himself, 'Well, if this aint dull music its a pity.' Then how

---

8. There.   9. Burst of verbal abuse.   10. Our own.   11. Ain't.   12. Chest.

streaked he feels when he sees a steamboat a clippin it by him like mad, and the folks on board pokin fun at him, and askin him if he has any word to send to home. Well, he says, if any soul ever catches me on board a sail vessel again, when I can go by steam, I'll give him leave to tell me of it, that's a fact. That's partly the case here. They are becalmed, and they see us going a head on them, till we are een[13] almost out of sight; yet they hant got a steamboat, and they hant got a rail road; indeed, I doubt if one half on em ever see'd or heerd tell of one or tother of them. I never see'd any folks like 'em except the Indians, and they wont even so much as look—they havn't the least morsel of curiosity in the world; from which one of our Unitarian preachers (they are dreadful hands at *doubtin* them. I dont *doubt* but some day or another, they will *doubt* whether every thing aint a *doubt*) in a very learned work, doubts whether they were ever descended from Eve at all. Old marm Eve's children, he says, are all lost, it is said, in consequence of *too much* curiosity, while these copper colored folks are lost from havin *too little*. How can they be the same? Thinks I, that may be logic, old Dubersome, but it ant sense, don't extremes meet? Now these Blue Noses have no motion in 'em, no enterprise, no spirit, and if any critter shows any symptoms of activity, they say he is a man of no judgment, he's speculative, he's a schemer, in short he's mad. They vegitate like a lettuce plant in sarse garden, they grow tall and spindlin, run to seed right off, grow as bitter as gaul and die.

A gall once came to our minister to hire as a house help; says she, minister, I suppose you dont want a young lady to do chamber business and breed worms do you? For I've half a mind to take a spell of livin out (she meant, said the Clock-maker, house work and rearing silk worms.) My pretty maiden, says he, a pattin her on the cheek, (for I've often observed old men always talk kinder pleasant to young women,) my pretty maiden where was you brought up? why, says she, I guess I warnt brought up at all, I growed up; under what platform, says he, (for he was very particular that all his house helps should go to his meetin,) under what Church platform? Church platform, says she, with a toss of her head, like a young colt that's got a check of the curb, I guess I warnt raised under a platform at all, but in as good a house as yourn, grand as you be— you said well said the old minister, quite shocked when you said you growd up, dear, for you have grown up in great ignorance. Then I guess you had better get a lady that knows more than me, says she, that's flat. I reckon I am every bit and grain as good as you be—If I dont understand a bum-byx (silk worm) both feedin, breedin, and rearin, then I want to know who does, that's all; church platform indeed, says she, I guess you were raised under a glass frame in March, and transplanted on Independence day, warnt you? And off she sot, lookin as scorney as a London lady, and leavin the poor minister standin starin like a stuck pig. Well, well, says he, a liftin up both hands, and turning up the whites of his eyes like a duck in thunder, if that dont bang the bush!! It fearly beats sheep shearin arter[14] the blackberry bushes have got the wool. It does, I vow; them are the tares them Unitarians sow in our grain fields at night; I guess they'll ruinate the crops yet, and make the grounds so everlastin foul; we'll have to pare the sod and burn it, to kill the roots. Our fathers sowed the right seed here in the wilderness, and watered it with their tears, and watched over it with fastin and prayer, and now its fairly run out, that's a fact, I snore. Its got choked up with all sorts of trash in natur, I declare. Dear, dear, I vow I never seed the beat o' that in all my born days.

---

13. Even.   14. After.

Now the Blue Noses are like that are gall; they have grown up, and grown up in ignorance of many things they hadnt ought not to know; and its as hard to teach grown up folks as it is to break a six year old horse; and they do ryle one's temper so—they act so ugly that it tempts one sometimes to break their confounded necks—its near about as much trouble as its worth. What remedy is there for all this supineness, said I; how can these people be awakened out of their ignorant slothfulness, into active exertion? The remedy, said Mr. Slick, is at hand—it is already workin its own cure. They must recede before our free and enlightened citizens like the Indians; our folks will buy them out, and they must give place to a more intelligent and ac-*tive* people. They must go to the lands of Labrador, or be located back of Canada; they can hold on there a few years, until the wave of civilization reaches them, and then they must move again, as the savages do. It is decreed; I hear the bugle of destiny a soundin of their retreat, as plain as any thing. Congress will give them a concession of land, if they petition, away to Alleghany backside territory, and grant them relief for a few years; for we are out of debt, and dont know what to do with our surplus revenue. The only way to shame them, that I know, would be to sarve them as Uncle Enoch sarved a neighbor of his in Varginy.

There was a lady that had a plantation near hand to hisn,[15] and there was only a small river atwixt the two houses, so that folks could hear each other talk across it. Well, she was a dreadful cross grained woman, a real catamount,[16] as savage as a she bear that has cubs, an old farrow critter, as ugly as sin, and one that both hooked and kicked too— a most particular onmarciful she devil, that's a fact. She used to have some of her niggers tied up every day, and flogged uncommon severe, and their screams and screeches were horrid—no soul could stand it; nothin was heerd all day, but *Oh Lord Missus! oh Lord Missus!* Enoch was fairly sick of the sound, for he was a tender hearted man, and says he to her one day, 'Now do marm find out some other place to give your cattle the cowskin, for it worries me to hear em take on so dreadful bad—I cant stand it, I vow; they are flesh and blood as well as we be, though the meat is a different color;' but it was no good— she jist up and told him to mind his own business, and she guessed she'd mind hern. He was determined to shame her out of it; so one mornin arter breakfast he goes into the cane field, and says he to Lavender, one of the black overseers, 'Muster up the whole gang of slaves, every soul, and bring 'em down to the whippin post, the whole stock of them, bulls, cows and calves. Well, away goes Lavender, and drives up all the niggers. Now you catch it, says he, you lazy villains; I tole you so many a time—I tole you Massa he lose all patience wid you, you good for nothin rascals. I grad, upon my soul, I werry grad; you mind now what old Lavender say anoder time. (The black overseers are always the most cruel, said the Clockmaker; they have no sort of feeling for their own people.)

Well, when they were gathered there according to orders, they looked streaked enough you may depend, thinkin they were going to get it all round, and the wenches they fell to a cryin, wringin their hands, and boo-hooing like mad. Lavender was there with his cowskin, grinnin like a chessy cat, and crackin it about, ready for business. Pick me out, says Enoch, four that have the loudest voices; hard matter dat, says Lavender, hard matter dat, Massa, dey all talk loud, dey all lub talk more better nor work—de idle villians; better gib 'em all a little tickle, jist to teach em larf[17] on tother side of de mouth; dat side bran new, they never use it yet. Do as I order you, Sir, said Uncle, or I'll have you triced up, you cruel old rascal you. When they were picked out

---

15. His own.   16. Mountain lion.   17. Laugh.

and sot by themselves, they hanged their heads, and looked like sheep going to the shambles. Now, says Uncle Enoch, my Pickininnies,[18] do you sing as loud as Niagara, at the very tip eend of your voice—

> Dont kill a nigger, pray,
> Let him lib anoder day.
>   *Oh Lord Missus—oh Lord Missus.*
> My back be very sore,
> No stand it any more,
>   *Oh Lord Missus—Oh Lord Missus.*

And all the rest of you join chorus, as loud as you can bawl, '*Oh Lord Missus.*' The black rascals understood the joke real well. They larfed ready to split their sides; they fairly lay down on the ground, and rolled over and over with lafter. Well, when they came to the chorus '*Oh Lord Missus,*' if they did'nt let go, its a pity. They made the river ring agin—they were heerd clean out to sea. All the folks ran out of the Lady's House, to see what on airth was the matter on Uncle Enoch's plantation—they thought there was actilly a rebellion there; but when they listened awhile, and heerd it over and over again, they took the hint, and returned a larfin in their sleeves. Says they, master Enoch Slick, he upsides with Missus this hitch any how. Uncle never heerd any thing more of '*oh Lord Missus*' arter that. Yes, they ought to be shamed out of it, those Blue Noses. When reason fails to convince, there is nothin left but ridicule. If they have no ambition, apply to their feelings, clap a blister on their pride, and it will do the business. Its like a puttin ginger under a horse's tail; it makes him carry up real hand*sum*, I tell you. When I was a boy, I was always late to school; well father's preachin I didn't mind much, but I never could bear to hear mother say, 'Why Sam, are you actilly up for all day? Well, I hope your airly risin wont hurt you, I declare. What on airth is agoin to happen now? Well, wonders will never cease. It raised my dander; at last says I, 'Now mother, dont say that are any more for gracious sake, for it makes me feel ugly, and I'll get up as airly as any on you'; and so I did, and I soon found what's worth knowin in this life, '*An airly start makes easy stages.*'

Mr. Slick's Opinion of the British

What success had you, said I, in the sale of your clocks among the Scotch in the eastern part of the Province? do you find them as gullible as the Blue Noses? Well, said he, you have heerd tell that a Yankee never answers one question, without axing another, havent you? Did you ever see an English Stage Driver make a bow? because if you hante obsarved it, I have, and a queer one it is, I swan.[19] He brings his right arm up, jist across his face, and passes on, with a knowin nod of his head, as much as to say, how do you do? but keep clear o' my wheels, or I'll fetch your horses a lick in the mouth as sure as youre born; jist as a bear puts up his paw to fend off the blow of a stick from his nose. Well, that's the way I pass them are bare breeched Scotchmen. Lord, if they were located down in these here Cumberland mashes, how the musquitoes would tickle them up, would'nt they? They'd set 'em scratching thereabouts, as an Irishman does his head, when he's in sarch of a lie. Them are fellers cut their eye teeth afore they ever sot

---

18. Belittling term for West Indian and African children.   19. Declare.

foot in this country, I expect. When they get a bawbee, they know what to do with it, that's a fact; they open their pouch and drop it in, and its got a spring like a fox trap—it holds fast to all it gets, like grim death to a dead nigger. They are proper skin flints,[20] you may depend. Oatmeal is no great shakes at best; it tante even as good for a horse as real yaller Varginy corn, but I guess I warnt long in finding out that the grits hardly pay for the riddlin. No, a Yankee has as little chance among them as a Jew has in New England; the sooner he clears out, the better. You can no more put a leake into them, than you can send a chisel into Teake wood—it turns the edge of the tool the first drive. If the Blue Noses knew the value of money as well as they do, they'd have more cash, and fewer clocks and tin reflectors, I reckon. Now, its different with the Irish; they never carry a puss,[21] for they never have a cent to put in it. They are always in love or in liquor, or else in a row; they are the merriest shavers[22] I ever seed. Judge Beeler, I dare say you have heerd tell of him—he's a funny feller—he put a notice over his factory gate at Lowell, 'no cigars or Irishmen admitted within these walls;' for, said he, the one will set a flame agoin among my cottons, and t'other among my galls. I wont have no such inflammable and dangerous things about me on no account. When the British wanted our folks to join in the treaty to chock the wheels of the slave trade, I recollect hearin old John Adams[23] say, we had ought to humor them; for, says he, they supply us with labor on easier terms, by shippin out the Irish. Says he, they work better, and they work cheaper, and they dont live so long. The blacks, when they are past work hang on for ever, and a proper bill of expence they be; but hot weather and new rum rub out the poor rates for tother ones. The English are the boys for tradin with; they shell out their cash like a sheaf of wheat in frosty weather—it flies all over the thrashin floor; but then they are a cross grained, ungainly, kicken breed of cattle, as I een a most ever see'd. Whoever gave them the name of John Bull,[24] knew what he was about, I tell you; for they are bull-necked, bull-headed folks, I vow; sulky, ugly tempered, vicious critters, a pawin and a roarin the whole time, and plaguy onsafe unless well watched. They are as headstrong as mules, and as conceited as peacocks.

The astonishment with which I heard this tirade against my countrymen, absorbed every feeling of resentment. I listened with amazement at the perfect composure with which he uttered it. He treated it as one of those self evident truths, that need neither proof nor apology, but as a thing well known and admitted by all mankind. There's no richer sight that I know of, said he, than to see one on 'em when he first lands in one of our great cities. He swells out as big as a balloon, his skin is ready to bust with wind—a regular walking bag of gas; and he prances over the pavement like a bear over hot iron—a great awkward hulk of a feller, (for they aint to be compared to the French in manners) a smirkin at you, as much as to say, 'look here, Jonathan, here's an Englishman; here's a boy that's got blood as pure as a Norman pirate, and lots of the blunt of both kinds, a pocket full of one, and a mouthful of tother; beant he lovely?' and then he looks as fierce as a tiger, as much as to say, 'say boo *to a goose*, if you dare.' No, I believe we may stump the Univarse; we improve on every thing, and we have improved on our own species. You'll sarch one while, I tell you, afore you'll find a man that, take him by and large, is equal to one of our free and enlightened citizens. He's the chap that has both speed, wind and bottom; he's clear grit—ginger to the back

20. Misers.   21. Purse.   22. Swindlers.   23. John Adams (1735–1826), second president of the United States. 24. Stereotypical Englishman.

bone, you may depend. Its generally allowed there aint the beat of them to be found any where. Spry as a fox, supple as an eel, and cute as a weasel. Though I say it that should'nt say it, they fairly take the shine off creation—they are actilly equal to cash.

He looked like a man who felt that he had expressed himself so aptly and so well, that any thing additional would only weaken its effect; he therefore changed the conversation immediately, by pointing to a tree at some little distance from the house, and remarking that it was the rock maple or sugar tree. Its a pretty tree, said he, and a profitable one too to raise. It will bear tapping for many years, tho' it gets exhausted at last. This Province is like that are tree, it is tapped till it begins to die at the top, and if they dont drive in a spile[25] and stop the everlastin flow of the sap, it will perish altogether. All the money that's made here, all the interest that's paid in it, and a pretty considerable portion of rent too, all goes abroad for investment, and the rest is sent to us to buy bread. Its drained like a bog, it has opened and covered trenches all through it, and then there's others to the foot of the upland to cut off the springs. Now you may make even a bog too dry; you may take the moisture out to that degree, that the very sile becomes dust and blows away. The English funds, and our banks, rail roads, and canals, are all absorbing your capital like a spunge, and will lick it up as fast as you can make it. That very Bridge we heerd of at Windsor, is owned in New Brunswick, and will pay tole to that province. The capitalists of Nova Scotia treat it like a hired house, they wont keep it in repair; they neither paint it to presarve the boards, nor stop a leak to keep the frame from rottin; but let it go to wrack sooner than drive a nail or put in a pane of glass. It will sarve our turn out they say. There's neither spirit, enterprise, nor patriotism here; but the whole country is as inactive as a bear in winter, that does nothin but scrouch up in his den, a thinkin to himself, "well if I ant an unfortunate divil, it's a pity; I have a most splendid warm cot as are a gentleman in these here woods, let him be who he will; but I got no socks to my feet, and have to sit for everlastingly a suckin of my paws to keep 'em warm; if it warn't for that, I guess, I'd make some o' them chaps that have hoofs to their feet and horns to their heads, look about them pretty sharp, I know." It's dismal now, aint it? If I had the framin of the Governor's message, if I would'nt shew 'em how to put timber together you may depend, I'd make them scratch their heads and stare, I know. I went down to Matanzas[26] in the Fulton Steam Boat once—well, it was the first of the kind they ever see'd, and proper scared they were to see a vessel, without sails or oars, goin right straight a head, nine knots an hour, in the very wind's eye, and a great streak of smoke arter her as long as the tail of a Comet. I believe they thought it was Old Nick[27] alive, a treatin himself to a swim. You could see the niggers a clippin it away from the shore, for dear life, and the soldiers a movin about as if they thought that we were a goin to take the whole country. Presently a little half starved orange-coloured looking Spanish officer, all dressed off in his livery, as fine as a fiddle, came off with two men in a boat to board us. Well, we yawed once or twice, and motioned to him to keep off for fear he should get hurt; but he came right on afore the wheel, and I hope I may be shot if the paddle didn't strike the bow of the boat with that force, it knocked up the starn like a plank tilt, when one of the boys playing on it is heavier than t'other; and chucked him right atop of the wheel house—you never see'd a feller in such a dunderment in your life. He had picked up a little English from

---

25. Small plug.   26. City in Cuba.   27. Satan.

seein our folks there so much, and when he got up, the first thing he said was, 'Damn all sheenery, I say, where's my boat?' and he looked round as if he thought it had jumped on board too. Your boat, said the Captain, why I expect it's gone to the bottom, and your men have gone down to look arter it, for we never see'd or heerd tell of one or t'other of them arter the boat was struck. Yes, I'd make 'em stare like that are Spanish officer, as if they had see'd out of their eyes for the first time. Governor Campbell[28] did'nt expect to see such a country as this, when he came here, I reckon; I know he did'nt. When I was a little boy, about knee high or so, and lived down Connecticut River, mother used to say, Sam, if you don't give over acting so like old Scratch,[29] I'll send you off to Nova Scotia as sure as you are born; I will, I vow. Well, Lord, how that are used to frighten me; it made my hair stand right up an eend, like a cat's back when she is wrathy; it made me drop it as quick as wink—like a tin night cap put on a dipt candle agoin to bed, it put the fun right out. Neighbor Dearborn's darter married a gentleman to Yarmouth, that speculates in the smugglin line; well, when she went on board to sail down to Nova Scotia, all her folks took on as if it was a funeral; they said she was goin to be buried alive like the nuns in Portengale that get a frolickin, break out of the pastur, and race off, and get catched and brought back agin. Says the old Colonel, her father, Deliverance, my dear, I would sooner foller you to your grave, for that would be an eend to your troubles, than to see you go off to that dismal country, that's nothin but an iceberg aground; and he howled as loud as an Irishman that tries to wake his wife when she is dead. Awful accounts we have of the country, that's a fact; but if the Province is not so bad as they make it out, the folks are a thousand times worse. You've seen a flock of partridges of a frosty mornin in the fall, a crowdin out of the shade to a sunny spot, and huddlin up there in the warmth—well, the Blue Noses have nothin else to do half the time but sun themselves. Whose fault is that? Why it's the fault of the legislature; *they don't encourage internal improvement, nor the investment of capital in the country; and the result is apathy, inaction and poverty.* They spend three months in Halifax, and what do they do? Father gave me a dollar once, to go to the fair at Hartford, and when I came back, says he, Sam, what have you got to show for it? Now I ax what have they to show for their three months' setting? They mislead folks; they make 'em believe all the use of the Assembly is to bark at Councillors, Judges, Bankers, and such cattle, to keep 'em from eatin up the crops; and it actilly costs more to feed them when they are watchin, than all the others could eat if they did break a fence and get in. Indeed some folks say they are the most breachy of the two, and ought to go to pound themselves. If their fences are good them hungry cattle could'nt break through; and if they aint, they ought to stake 'em up, and with them well; *but it's no use to make fences unless the land is cultivated.* If I see a farm all gone to wrack, I say here's bad husbandry and bad management; and if I see a Province like this, of great capacity, and great natural resources, poverty-stricken, I say there's bad legislation. No, said he, (with an air of more seriousness than I had yet observed,) *how much it is to be regretted, that, laying aside personal attacks and petty jealousies, they would not unite as one man, and with one mind and one heart apply themselves sedulously to the internal improvement and developement of this beautiful Province. Its value is utterly unknown, either to the general or local Government, and the only persons who duly appreciate it, are the Yankees.*

—1836

---

28. Lord William Campbell (c. 1730–1778), Governor of Nova Scotia (1766–1773) and South Carolina (1775).   29. Satan.

Mary Shelley
1797–1851

The daughter of famous radicals Mary Wollstonecraft and William Godwin, the wife of revolutionary poet Percy Bysshe Shelley, and the friend of the sensationally popular writer George Gordon, Lord Byron, Mary Shelley is arguably the most well known of this well-known set, due in large part to her novel *Frankenstein* (1818). This novel and its leading creature have inspired everything from films to breakfast cereals. The story took shape during Mary and Percy's stay with Byron in Lake Geneva, Switzerland. Byron proposed they all pen ghost stories. After suffering from writers' block, Mary eventually was haunted by the image of a creature looming over its creator, and so her writing commenced. *Frankenstein* was by no means the last time Shelley put pen to paper. Not as widely read, but equally excellent, Shelley's shorter fiction, such as "The Mortal Immortal" (1834) builds upon themes first laid out in her most famous novel. Death and abandonment, quite fittingly, occupy the works of an author whose mother died days after her birth; who outlived her father, daughters (Mary and Clara Everina), and son (William); and who lost her husband to a tragic drowning.

After her mother died, Mary was raised by her father and her stepmother, Mary Jane Clairmont, whom she resented. She got along better with one of her stepsisters, Jane "Claire" Clairmont. At the age of fourteen, Mary was sent to live in Dundee, Scotland, to help her parents, who were struggling financially. Not long after she returned to London in 1814, she met Percy Shelley—she was sixteen and he was twenty-one. By June they had become nearly inseparable, and two and a half years later they married. In the year the two met, they ventured abroad to the European Continent. In February 1815, Mary gave birth to a daughter, her namesake, who sadly passed away only ten days later; soon thereafter she was pregnant again and gave birth in October to William Godwin Shelley, named after Mary's father. The elder William, who had always been distant, initially did not approve wholeheartedly of Mary's and Percy's love. Despite the grandson who bore his name, and his friendship with and financial reliance upon Percy, he would not consent to their staying under his roof. Godwin's hostility in part spurred the trip that landed them on Lord Byron's doorstep in 1816. Claire Clairmont, who was pregnant with Byron's child (Allegra), accompanied them to Geneva. Two years later, *Frankenstein* was published in England. The reviewers of the time, assuming a novel containing such terrorizing scenes must be the work of a man, attributed the authorship to Percy, who had helped write the Preface. The dedication of the book to William Godwin was intended as an olive branch but may have been interpreted by him as bittersweet. On the one hand, the plot of the novel paid homage to Godwin's famous gothic novel *Caleb Williams* (1794), but on the other hand the themes of abandonment could be read as commentaries on the troubled relationship between father, daughter, and son-in-law. In the end, Godwin took the novel and Mary under his wing by writing an introduction to the second edition in 1823, but this reconciliation came after Percy's death.

After *Frankenstein*'s publication, the couple moved to Italy, where their lives were saddened by the deaths of Clara Everina (September 1818) and William (June 1819). The time was not devoid of happiness, though, for in November 1819 the couple had another child, Percy Florence. Settling in Pisa, they were befriended by fellow expatriates as well as Italian intellectuals, such as the academic Francesco Pachiani. After writing a novella, *Mathilda* (1819), based on a story begun by her mother, Mary Shelley also penned *Valperga* (1823), a gothic tale. In 1822, the Shelleys moved to the coast at Lerici. On July 8, 1822, Percy went sailing in the Gulf of Spezia and his boat capsized in a storm; on July 16, his body washed ashore, his face so disfigured that he was identifiable only by his clothes and the copy of Keats still lodged in his breast pocket. His body was burned in a funeral pyre on the shore. Byron, whose daughter Allegra had died that same year, was in attendance.

After spending the winter of 1822 with Byron, Leigh Hunt (a poet and newspaper editor), and Edward Trelawny (an author and swashbuckler who eventually moved to America), Mary returned to England in 1823 with Percy Florence and set about publishing *Valperga*, the second edition of *Frankenstein*, and the manuscript poems of her husband. By this time, Frankenstein had already reached such popularity that a Paris play was based on it, and it had acquired a sizable and growing American readership. Three years later she published another novel, *The Last Man* (1826), which depicts a plague that destroys all humankind but one man. Throughout the 1830s, she brought out editions of Percy's poetry and Godwin's writing, including a new printing of *Caleb Williams*, Trelawny's writing, and another edition of *Frankenstein* as well as two more novels: *Lodore* (1835), part of which is set in Illinois, and *Falkner* (1837). After Godwin's death in 1836, Mary brought out editions of his previously unpublished works accompanied by a memoir. In the 1840s, she toured the European Continent with her child Percy Florence, which resulted in *Rambles in Germany and Italy in 1840, 1842, and 1843* (1844). Throughout the 1840s she suffered from declining health, which her travel to warmer climes did not reverse. By 1851, she had developed a fatal brain tumor. She was buried in Bournemouth, England, near the home of her son.

The Mortal Immortal

A Tale

July 16, 1833.—This is a memorable anniversary for me; on it I complete my three hundred and twenty-third year!

The Wandering Jew?[1]—certainly not. More than eighteen centuries have passed over his head. In comparison with him, I am a very young Immortal.

Am I, then, immortal? This is a question which I have asked myself, by day and night, for now three hundred and three years, and yet cannot answer it. I detected a gray hair amidst my brown locks this very day—that surely signifies decay. Yet it may have remained concealed there for three hundred years—for some persons have become entirely white-headed before twenty years of age.

I will tell my story, and my reader shall judge for me. I will tell my story, and so contrive to pass some few hours of a long eternity, become so wearisome to me. For ever! Can it be? to live for ever! I have heard of enchantments, in which the victims were plunged into a deep sleep, to wake, after a hundred years, as fresh as ever: I have heard of the Seven Sleepers—thus to be immortal would not be so burthensome: but, oh! the weight of never-ending time—the tedious passage of the still-succeeding hours! How happy was the fabled Nourjahad![2]——But to my task.

All the world has heard of Cornelius Agrippa.[3] His memory is as immortal as his arts have made me. All the world has also heard of his scholar, who, unawares, raised the foul fiend during his master's absence, and was destroyed by him. The report, true or false, of this accident, was attended with many inconveniences to the renowned philosopher. All his scholars at once deserted him—his servants disappeared. He had no one near him to put coals on his ever-burning fires while he slept, or to attend to the changeful colours of his medicines while he studied. Experiment after experiment failed, because one pair of hands was insufficient to complete them: the dark spirits laughed at him for not being able to retain a single mortal in his service.

1. Offended Jesus en route to crucifixion and was condemned to walk the earth until it ends.   2. Main character of *The History of Nourjahad* (1767), by Frances Sheridan (1724–1766).   3. German occult writer (1486–1535).

I was then very young—very poor—and very much in love. I had been for about a year the pupil of Cornelius, though I was absent when this accident took place. On my return, my friends implored me not to return to the alchymist's abode. I trembled as I listened to the dire tale they told; I required no second warning; and when Cornelius came and offered me a purse of gold if I would remain under his roof, I felt as if Satan himself tempted me. My teeth chattered—my hair stood on end:—I ran off as fast as my trembling knees would permit.

My failing steps were directed whither for two years they had every evening been attracted,—a gently bubbling spring of pure living waters, beside which lingered a dark-haired girl, whose beaming eyes were fixed on the path I was accustomed each night to tread. I cannot remember the hour when I did not love Bertha; we had been neighbours and playmates from infancy—her parents, like mine, were of humble life, yet respectable—our attachment had been a source of pleasure to them. In an evil hour, a malignant fever carried off both her father and mother, and Bertha became an orphan. She would have found a home beneath my paternal roof, but, unfortunately, the old lady of the near castle, rich, childless, and solitary, declared her intention to adopt her. Henceforth Bertha was clad in silk—inhabited a marble palace—and was looked on as being highly favoured by fortune. But in her new situation among her new associates, Bertha remained true to the friend of her humbler days; she often visited the cottage of my father, and when forbidden to go thither, she would stray towards the neighbouring wood, and meet me beside its shady fountain.

She often declared that she owed no duty to her new protectress equal in sanctity to that which bound us. Yet still I was too poor to marry, and she grew weary of being tormented on my account. She had a haughty but an impatient spirit, and grew angry at the obstacles that prevented our union. We met now after an absence, and she had been sorely beset while I was away; she complained bitterly, and almost reproached me for being poor. I replied hastily,—

"I am honest, if I am poor!—were I not, I might soon become rich!"

This exclamation produced a thousand questions. I feared to shock her by owning the truth, but she drew it from me; and then, casting a look of disdain on me, she said—

"You pretend to love, and you fear to face the Devil for my sake!"

I protested that I had only dreaded to offend her;—while she dwelt on the magnitude of the reward that I should receive. Thus encouraged—shamed by her—led on by love and hope, laughing at my late fears, with quick steps and a light heart, I returned to accept the offers of the alchymist, and was instantly installed in my office.

A year passed away. I became possessed of no insignificant sum of money. Custom had banished my fears. In spite of the most painful vigilance, I had never detected the trace of a cloven foot; nor was the studious silence of our abode ever disturbed by demoniac howls. I still continued my stolen interviews with Bertha, and Hope dawned on me—Hope—but not perfect joy; for Bertha fancied that love and security were enemies, and her pleasure was to divide them in my bosom. Though true of heart, she was somewhat of a coquette in manner; and I was jealous as a Turk. She slighted me in a thousand ways, yet would never acknowledge herself to be in the wrong. She would drive me mad with anger, and then force me to beg her pardon. Sometimes she fancied that I was not sufficiently submissive, and then she had some story of a rival, favoured by her protectress. She was surrounded by silk-clad youths—the rich and gay—What chance had the sad-robed scholar of Cornelius compared with these?

On one occasion, the philosopher made such large demands upon my time, that I was unable to meet her as I was wont. He was engaged in some mighty work, and I was forced to remain, day and night, feeding his furnaces and watching his chemical preparations. Bertha waited for me in vain at the fountain. Her haughty spirit fired at this neglect; and when at last I stole out during the few short minutes allotted to me for slumber, and hoped to be consoled by her, she received me with disdain, dismissed me in scorn, and vowed that any man should possess her hand rather than he who could not be in two places at once for her sake. She would be revenged!—And truly she was. In my dingy retreat I heard that she had been hunting, attended by Albert Hoffer. Albert Hoffer was favoured by her protectress, and the three passed in cavalcade[4] before my smoky window. Methought that they mentioned my name—it was followed by a laugh of derision, as her dark eyes glanced contemptuously towards my abode.

Jealousy, with all its venom, and all its misery, entered my breast. Now I shed a torrent of tears, to think that I should never call her mine; and, anon, I imprecated a thousand curses on her inconstancy. Yet, still I must stir the fires of the alchymist, still attend on the changes of his unintelligible medicines.

Cornelius had watched for three days and nights, nor closed his eyes. The progress of his alembics[5] was slower than he expected: in spite of his anxiety, sleep weighed upon his eyelids. Again and again he threw off drowsiness with more than human energy; again and again it stole away his senses. He eyed his crucibles wistfully. "Not ready yet," he murmured; "will another night pass before the work is accomplished? Winzy, you are vigilant—you are faithful—you have slept, my boy—you slept last night. Look at that glass vessel. The liquid it contains is of a soft rose-colour: the moment it begins to change its hue, awaken me—till then I may close my eyes. First, it will turn white, and then emit golden flashes; but wait not till then; when the rose-colour fades, rouse me." I scarcely heard the last words, muttered, as they were, in sleep. Even then he did not quite yield to nature. "Winzy, my boy," he again said, "do not touch the vessel—do not put it to your lips; it is a philter[6]—a philter to cure love; you would not cease to love your Bertha—beware to drink!"

And he slept. His venerable head sunk on his breast, and I scarce heard his regular breathing. For a few minutes I watched the vessel—the rosy hue of the liquid remained unchanged. Then my thoughts wandered—they visited the fountain, and dwelt on a thousand charming scenes never to be renewed—never! Serpents and adders were in my heart as the word "Never!" half formed itself on my lips. False girl!—false and cruel! Never more would she smile on me as that evening she smiled on Albert. Worthless, detested woman! I would not remain unrevenged—she should see Albert expire at her feet—she should die beneath my vengeance. She had smiled in disdain and triumph—she knew my wretchedness and her power. Yet what power had she?—the power of exciting my hate—my utter scorn—my—oh, all but indifference! Could I attain that—could I regard her with careless eyes, transferring my rejected love to one fairer and more true, that were indeed a victory!

A bright flash darted before my eyes. I had forgotten the medicine of the adept; I gazed on it with wonder: flashes of admirable beauty, more bright than those which

---

4. Procession of carriages.   5. Distilling apparatus.   6. Potion, drug.

the diamond emits when the sun's rays are on it, glanced from the surface of the liquid; an odour the most fragrant and grateful stole over my sense; the vessel seemed one globe of living radiance, lovely to the eye, and most inviting to the taste. The first thought, instinctively inspired by the grosser sense, was, I will—I must drink. I raised the vessel to my lips. "It will cure me of love—of torture!" Already I had quaffed half of the most delicious liquor ever tasted by the palate of man, when the philosopher stirred. I started—I dropped the glass—the fluid flamed and glanced along the floor, while I felt Cornelius's gripe at my throat, as he shrieked aloud, "Wretch! you have destroyed the labour of my life!"

The philosopher was totally unaware that I had drunk any portion of his drug. His idea was, and I gave a tacit assent to it, that I had raised the vessel from curiosity, and that, frighted at its brightness, and the flashes of intense light it gave forth, I had let it fall. I never undeceived him. The fire of the medicine was quenched—the fragrance died away—he grew calm, as a philosopher should under the heaviest trials, and dismissed me to rest.

I will not attempt to describe the sleep of glory and bliss which bathed my soul in paradise during the remaining hours of that memorable night. Words would be faint and shallow types of my enjoyment, or of the gladness that possessed my bosom when I woke. I trod air—my thoughts were in heaven. Earth appeared heaven, and my inheritance upon it was to be one trance of delight. "This it is to be cured of love," I thought; "I will see Bertha this day, and she will find her lover cold and regardless; too happy to be disdainful, yet how utterly indifferent to her!"

The hours danced away. The philosopher, secure that he had once succeeded, and believing that he might again, began to concoct the same medicine once more. He was shut up with his books and drugs, and I had a holiday. I dressed myself with care; I looked in an old but polished shield, which served me for a mirror; methought my good looks had wonderfully improved. I hurried beyond the precincts of the town, joy in my soul, the beauty of heaven and earth around me. I turned my steps towards the castle—I could look on its lofty turrets with lightness of heart, for I was cured of love. My Bertha saw me afar off, as I came up the avenue. I know not what sudden impulse animated her bosom, but at the sight, she sprung with a light fawn-like bound down the marble steps, and was hastening towards me. But I had been perceived by another person. The old high-born hag, who called herself her protectress, and was her tyrant, had seen me, also; she hobbled, panting, up the terrace; a page as ugly as herself, held up her train, and fanned her as she hurried along, and stopped my fair girl with a "How, now, my bold mistress? whither so fast? Back to your cage—hawks are abroad!"

Bertha clasped her hands—her eyes were still bent on my approaching figure. I saw the contest. How I abhorred the old crone who checked the kind impulses of my Bertha's softening heart. Hitherto, respect for her rank had caused me to avoid the lady of the castle; now I disdained such trivial considerations. I was cured of love, and lifted above all human fears; I hastened forwards, and soon reached the terrace. How lovely Bertha looked! her eyes flashing fire, her cheeks glowing with impatience and anger, she was a thousand times more graceful and charming than ever—I no longer loved—Oh! no, I adored—worshipped—idolized her!

She had that morning been persecuted, with more than usual vehemence, to consent to an immediate marriage with my rival. She was reproached with the encouragement that she had shown him—she was threatened with being turned out of doors with disgrace and shame. Her proud spirit rose in arms at the threat; but when she remembered the scorn that she had heaped upon me, and how, perhaps, she had thus lost one whom she now regarded as her only friend, she wept with remorse and rage. At that moment I appeared. "O, Winzy!" she exclaimed, "take me to your mother's cot[7]; swiftly let me leave the detested luxuries and wretchedness of this noble dwelling—take me to poverty and happiness."

I clasped her in my arms with transport. The old lady was speechless with fury, and broke forth into invective only when we were far on our road to my natal cottage. My mother received the fair fugitive, escaped from a gilt cage to nature and liberty, with tenderness and joy; my father, who loved her, welcomed her heartily; it was a day of rejoicing, which did not need the addition of the celestial potion of the alchymist to steep me in delight.

Soon after this eventful day, I became the husband of Bertha. I ceased to be the scholar of Cornelius, but I continued his friend. I always felt grateful to him for having, unawares, procured me that delicious draught of a divine elixir, which, instead of curing me of love (sad cure! solitary and joyless remedy for evils which seem blessings to the memory), had inspired me with courage and resolution, thus winning for me an inestimable treasure in my Bertha.

I often called to mind that period of trance-like inebriation with wonder. The drink of Cornelius had not fulfilled the task for which he affirmed that it had been prepared, but its effects were more potent and blissful than words can express. They had faded by degrees, yet they lingered long—and painted life in hues of splendour. Bertha often wondered at my lightness of heart and unaccustomed gaiety; for, before, I had been rather serious, or even sad, in my disposition. She loved me the better for my cheerful temper, and our days were winged by joy.

Five years afterwards I was suddenly summoned to the bedside of the dying Cornelius. He had sent for me in haste, conjuring my instant presence. I found him stretched on his pallet, enfeebled even to death; all of life that yet remained animated his piercing eyes, and they were fixed on a glass vessel, full of a roseate liquid.

"Behold," he said, in a broken and inward voice, "the vanity of human wishes! a second time my hopes are about to be crowned, a second time they are destroyed. Look at that liquor—you remember five years ago I had prepared the same, with the same success;—then, as now, my thirsting lips expected to taste the immortal elixir— you dashed it from me! and at present it is too late."

He spoke with difficulty, and fell back on his pillow. I could not help saying,—

"How, revered master, can a cure for love restore you to life?"

A faint smile gleamed across his face as I listened earnestly to his scarcely intelligible answer.

"A cure for love and for all things—the Elixir of Immortality. Ah! if now I might drink, I should live for ever!"

As he spoke, a golden flash gleamed from the fluid; a well-remembered fragrance stole over the air; he raised himself, all weak as he was—strength seemed miraculously to re-enter his frame—he stretched forth his hand—a loud explosion startled me—a ray of fire shot up from the elixir, and the glass vessel which contained it was

---

7. Cottage.

shivered to atoms! I turned my eyes towards the philosopher; he had fallen back—his eyes were glassy—his features rigid—he was dead!

But I lived, and was to live for ever! So said the unfortunate alchymist, and for a few days I believed his words. I remembered the glorious drunkenness that had followed my stolen draught. I reflected on the change I had felt in my frame—in my soul. The bounding elasticity of the one—the buoyant lightness of the other. I surveyed myself in a mirror, and could perceive no change in my features during the space of the five years which had elapsed. I remembered the radiant hues and grateful scent of that delicious beverage—worthy the gift it was capable of bestowing——I was, then, IMMORTAL!

A few days after I laughed at my credulity. The old proverb, that "a prophet is least regarded in his own country," was true with respect to me and my defunct master. I loved him as a man—I respected him as a sage—but I derided the notion that he could command the powers of darkness, and laughed at the superstitious fears with which he was regarded by the vulgar. He was a wise philosopher, but had no acquaintance with any spirits but those clad in flesh and blood. His science was simply human; and human science, I soon persuaded myself, could never conquer nature's laws so far as to imprison the soul for ever within its carnal habitation. Cornelius had brewed a soul-refreshing drink—more inebriating than wine—sweeter and more fragrant than any fruit: it possessed probably strong medicinal powers, imparting gladness to the heart and vigor to the limbs; but its effects would wear out; already were they diminished in my frame. I was a lucky fellow to have quaffed health and joyous spirits, and perhaps long life, at my master's hands; but my good fortune ended there: longevity was far different from immortality.

I continued to entertain this belief for many years. Sometimes a thought stole across me—Was the alchymist indeed deceived? But my habitual credence was, that I should meet the fate of all the children of Adam at my appointed time—a little late, but still at a natural age. Yet it was certain that I retained a wonderfully youthful look. I was laughed at for my vanity in consulting the mirror so often, but I consulted it in vain—my brow was untrenched—my cheeks—my eyes—my whole person continued as untarnished as in my twentieth year.

I was troubled. I looked at the faded beauty of Bertha—I seemed more like her son. By degrees our neighbours began to make similar observations, and I found at last that I went by the name of the Scholar bewitched. Bertha herself grew uneasy. She became jealous and peevish, and at length she began to question me. We had no children; we were all in all to each other; and though, as she grew older, her vivacious spirit became a little allied to ill-temper, and her beauty sadly diminished, I cherished her in my heart as the mistress I had idolized, the wife I had sought and won with such perfect love.

At last our situation became intolerable: Bertha was fifty—I twenty years of age. I had, in very shame, in some measure adopted the habits of a more advanced age; I no longer mingled in the dance among the young and gay, but my heart bounded along with them while I restrained my feet; and a sorry figure I cut among the Nestors[8] of our village. But before the time I mention, things were altered—we were universally shunned; we were—at least, I was—reported to have kept up an iniqui-

8. Leaders.

tous acquaintance with some of my former master's supposed friends. Poor Bertha was pitied, but deserted. I was regarded with horror and detestation.

What was to be done? we sat by our winter fire—poverty had made itself felt, for none would buy the produce of my farm; and often I had been forced to journey twenty miles, to some place where I was not known, to dispose of our property. It is true we had saved something for an evil day—that day was come.

We sat by our lone fireside—the old-hearted youth and his antiquated wife. Again Bertha insisted on knowing the truth; she recapitulated all she had ever heard said about me, and added her own observations. She conjured me to cast off the spell; she described how much more comely gray hairs were than my chestnut locks; she descanted on the reverence and respect due to age—how preferable to the slight regard paid to mere children: could I imagine that the despicable gifts of youth and good looks outweighed disgrace, hatred, and scorn? Nay, in the end I should be burnt as a dealer in the black art, while she, to whom I had not deigned to communicate any portion of my good fortune, might be stoned as my accomplice. At length she insinuated that I must share my secret with her, and bestow on her like benefits to those I myself enjoyed, or she would denounce me—and then she burst into tears.

Thus beset, methought it was the best way to tell the truth. I revealed it as tenderly as I could, and spoke only of a very long life, not of immortality—which representation, indeed, coincided best with my own ideas. When I ended, I rose and said,

"And now, my Bertha, will you denounce the lover of your youth?—You will not, I know. But it is too hard, my poor wife, that you should suffer from my ill-luck and the accursed arts of Cornelius. I will leave you—you have wealth enough, and friends will return in my absence. I will go; young as I seem, and strong as I am, I can work and gain my bread among strangers, unsuspected and unknown. I loved you in youth; God is my witness that I would not desert you in age, but that your safety and happiness require it."

I took my cap and moved towards the door; in a moment Bertha's arms were round my neck, and her lips were pressed to mine. "No, my husband, my Winzy," she said, "you shall not go alone—take me with you; we will remove from this place, and, as you say, among strangers we shall be unsuspected and safe. I am not so very old as quite to shame you, my Winzy; and I dare say the charm will soon wear off, and, with the blessing of God, you will become more elderly-looking, as is fitting; you shall not leave me."

I returned the good soul's embrace heartily. "I will not, my Bertha; but for your sake I had not thought of such a thing. I will be your true, faithful husband while you are spared to me, and do my duty by you to the last."

The next day we prepared secretly for our emigration. We were obliged to make great pecuniary sacrifices—it could not be helped. We realised a sum sufficient, at least, to maintain us while Bertha lived; and, without saying adieu to any one, quitted our native country to take refuge in a remote part of western France.

It was a cruel thing to transport poor Bertha from her native village, and the friends of her youth, to a new country, new language, new customs. The strange secret of my destiny rendered this removal immaterial to me; but I compassionated her deeply, and was glad to perceive that she found compensation for her misfortunes in a variety of little ridiculous circumstances. Away from all tell-tale chroniclers, she sought to decrease the apparent disparity of our ages by a thousand feminine arts— rouge, youthful dress, and assumed juvenility of manner. I could not be angry—Did not I myself wear a mask? Why quarrel with hers, because it was less successful? I grieved deeply when I remembered that this was my Bertha, whom I had loved so fondly, and won with such transport—the dark-eyed, dark-haired girl, with smiles of enchanting archness and a step like a fawn—this mincing, simpering, jealous old woman. I should have revered her gray locks and withered cheeks; but thus!——It was my work, I knew; but I did not the less deplore this type of human weakness.

Her jealousy never slept. Her chief occupation was to discover that, in spite of outward appearances, I was myself growing old. I verily believe that the poor soul loved me truly in her heart, but never had woman so tormenting a mode of display- ing fondness. She would discern wrinkles in my face and decrepitude in my walk, while I bounded along in youthful vigour, the youngest looking of twenty youths. I never dared address another woman: on one occasion, fancying that the belle of the village regarded me with favouring eyes, she bought me a gray wig. Her constant dis- course among her acquaintances was, that though I looked so young, there was ruin at work within my frame; and she affirmed that the worst symptom about me was my apparent health. My youth was a disease, she said, and I ought at all times to prepare, if not for a sudden and awful death, at least to awake some morning white-headed, and bowed down with all the marks of advanced years. I let her talk—I often joined in her conjectures. Her warnings chimed in with my never-ceasing speculations con- cerning my state, and I took an earnest, though painful, interest in listening to all that her quick wit and excited imagination could say on the subject.

Why dwell on these minute circumstances? We lived on for many long years. Bertha became bed-rid and paralytic: I nursed her as a mother might a child. She grew peevish, and still harped upon one string—of how long I should survive her. It has ever been a source of consolation to me, that I performed my duty scrupulously towards her. She had been mine in youth, she was mine in age, and at last, when I heaped the sod over her corpse, I wept to feel that I had lost all that really bound me to humanity.

Since then how many have been my cares and woes, how few and empty my enjoyments! I pause here in my history—I will pursue it no further. A sailor without rudder or compass, tossed on a stormy sea—a traveller lost on a wide-spread heath, without landmark or star to guide him—such have I been: more lost, more hopeless than either. A nearing ship, a gleam from some far cot, may save them; but I have no beacon except the hope of death.

Death! mysterious, ill-visaged friend of weak humanity! Why alone of all mortals have you cast me from your sheltering fold? O, for the peace of the grave! the deep silence of the iron-bound tomb! that thought would cease to work in my brain, and my heart beat no more with emotions varied only by new forms of sadness!

Am I immortal? I return to my first question. In the first place, is it not more probable that the beverage of the alchymist was fraught rather with longevity than eternal life? Such is my hope. And then be it remembered, that I only drank half of the potion prepared by him. Was not the whole necessary to complete the charm? To have drained half the Elixir of Immortality is but to be half immortal—my For-ever is thus truncated and null.

But again, who shall number the years of the half of eternity? I often try to imag- ine by what rule the infinite may be divided. Sometimes I fancy age advancing upon me. One gray hair I have found. Fool! do I lament? Yes, the fear of age and death often creeps coldly into my heart; and the more I live, the more I dread death, even while I abhor life. Such an enigma is man—born to perish—when he wars, as I do, against the established laws of his nature.

But for this anomaly of feeling surely I might die: the medicine of the alchymist would not be proof against fire—sword—and the strangling waters. I have gazed upon the blue depths of many a placid lake, and the tumultuous rushing of many a mighty river, and have said, peace inhabits those waters; yet I have turned my steps away, to live yet another day. I have asked myself, whether suicide would be a crime in one to whom thus only the portals of the other world could be opened. I have done all, except present-ing myself as a soldier or duellist, an object of destruction to my—no, not my fellow-mortals, and therefore I have shrunk away. They are not my fellows. The inextinguishable power of life in my frame, and their ephemeral existence, place us wide as the poles asun-der. I could not raise a hand against the meanest or the most powerful among them.

Thus I have lived on for many a year—alone, and weary of myself—desirous of death, yet never dying—a mortal immortal. Neither ambition nor avarice can enter my mind, and the ardent love that gnaws at my heart, never to be returned—never to find an equal on which to expend itself—lives there only to torment me.

This very day I conceived a design by which I may end all—without self-slaughter, without making another man a Cain[9]—an expedition, which mortal frame can never survive, even endued with the youth and strength that inhabits mine. Thus I shall put my immortality to the test, and rest for ever—or return, the wonder and benefac-tor of the human species.

Before I go, a miserable vanity has caused me to pen these pages. I would not die, and leave no name behind. Three centuries have passed since I quaffed the fatal bev-erage: another year shall not elapse before, encountering gigantic dangers—warring with the powers of frost in their home—beset by famine, toil, and tempest—I yield this body, too tenacious a cage for a soul which thirsts for freedom, to the destructive elements of air and water—or, if I survive, my name shall be recorded as one of the most famous among the sons of men; and, my task achieved, I shall adopt more res-olute means, and, by scattering and annihilating the atoms that compose my frame, set at liberty the life imprisoned within, and so cruelly prevented from soaring from this dim earth to a sphere more congenial to its immortal essence.

—1834

William Apess
1798–1839

William Apess was the most productive and outspoken Native American writer of the nine-teenth century. His religious autobiography, *A Son of the Forest* (1829), describes a childhood of cruel deprivation on Massachusetts Pequot reservations scarred by depression, alcoholism, and poverty. He was raised by grandparents who abused him severely, once even breaking his arm, and he received almost no formal education. He left the reservation in his teens and

---

9. Genesis 4.1–13.

joined the U.S. Army, fighting in the Battle of Montreal during the War of 1812. After the war, Apess heard a call to Christian ministry while he was lost in a swamp one night. For almost a decade, he worked as an itinerant preacher, struggling all the while to feed his growing family. He was finally ordained in the Methodist Church in 1829.

Apess's second book, *The Experience of Five Christian Indians of the Pequot Tribe* (1833), describes the conversion experiences of five of his tribe members. His accounts of their epiphanies were designed to demonstrate the strength of Indian piety to an audience of white Christians who assumed this was an oxymoron. The first edition also included Apess's angry denunciation of Christian hypocrisy and racism, "An Indian's Looking-Glass for the White Man." The text is a paper sermon, replicating the rhythms, persona, and tone of a fiery preacher's attempt to break through his congregation's woodenness to a saving awareness of sin. Apess became a central leader of the Mashpee Revolt against the state of Massachusetts when it attempted to deny tribal sovereignty. He was jailed for thirty days for incitement to riot after forcibly unloading a white trespasser's cart of stolen firewood. His last published work, *Eulogy on King Philip* (1836), describes the seventeenth-century leader of the Wampanoags as a valiant defender of his homeland against aggressive Puritan invaders.

An Indian's Looking-Glass for the White Man

Having a desire to place a few things before my fellow creatures who are traveling with me to the grave, and to that God who is the maker and preserver both of the white man and the Indian, whose abilities are the same and who are to be judged by one God, who will show no favor to outward appearances but will judge righteousness. Now I ask if degradation has not been heaped long enough upon the Indians? And if so, can there not be a compromise? Is it right to hold and promote prejudices? If not, why not put them all away? I mean here, among those who are civilized. It may be that many are ignorant of the situation of many of my brethren within the limits of New England. Let me for a few moments turn your attention to the reservations in the different states of New England, and, with but few exceptions, we shall find them as follows: the most mean, abject, miserable race of beings in the world—a complete place of prodigality and prostitution.

Let a gentleman and lady of integrity and respectability visit these places, and they would be surprised; as they wandered from one hut to the other they would view, with the females who are left alone, children half-starved and some almost as naked as they came into the world. And it is a fact that I have seen them as much so—while the females are left without protection, and are seduced by white men, and are finally left to be common prostitutes for them and to be destroyed by that burning, fiery curse, that has swept millions, both of red and white men, into the grave with sorrow and disgrace—rum. One reason why they are left so is because their most sensible and active men are absent at sea. Another reason is because they are made to believe they are minors and have not the abilities given them from God to take care of themselves, without it is to see to a few little articles, such as baskets and brooms. Their land is in common stock, and they have nothing to make them enterprising.

Another reason is because those men who are Agents,[1] many of them are unfaithful and care not whether the Indians live or die; they are much imposed upon by their neighbors, who have no principle. They would think it no crime to go upon Indian lands and cut and carry off their most valuable timber, or anything else they chose;

---

1. State-appointed overseers of Indian affairs.

and I doubt not but they think it clear gain. Another reason is because they have no education to take care of themselves; if they had, I would risk them to take care of their own property.

Now I will ask if the Indians are not called the most ingenious people among us. And are they not said to be men of talents? And I would ask: Could there be a more efficient way to distress and murder them by inches than the way they have taken? And there is no people in the world but who may be destroyed in the same way. Now, if these people are what they are held up in our view to be, I would take the liberty to ask why they are not brought forward and pains taken to educate them, to give them all a common education, and those of the brightest and first-rate talents put forward and held up to office. Perhaps some unholy, unprincipled men would cry out, "The skin was not good enough"; but stop, friends—I am not talking about the skin but about principles. I would ask if there cannot be as good feelings and principles under a red skin as there can be under a white. And let me ask: Is it not on the account of a bad principle that we who are red children have had to suffer so much as we have? And let me ask: Did not this bad principle proceed from the whites or their forefathers? And I would ask: Is it worthwhile to nourish it any longer? If not, then let us have a change, although some men no doubt will spout their corrupt principles against it, that are in the halls of legislation and elsewhere. But I presume this kind of talk will seem surprising and horrible. I do not see why it should so long as they (the whites) say that they think as much of us as they do of themselves.

This I have heard repeatedly, from the most respectable gentlemen and ladies— and having heard so much precept, I should now wish to see the example. And I would ask who has a better right to look for these things than the naturalist[2] him- self—the candid man would say none.

I know that many say that they are willing, perhaps the majority of the people, that we should enjoy our rights and privileges as they do. If so, I would ask, Why are not we protected in our persons and property throughout the Union? Is it not because there reigns in the breast of many who are leaders a most unrighteous, unbecoming, and impure black principle, and as corrupt and unholy as it can be—while these very same unfeeling, self-esteemed characters pretend to take the skin as a pretext to keep us from our unalienable and lawful rights? I would ask you if you would like to be dis- franchised from all your rights, merely because your skin is white, and for no other crime. I'll venture to say, these very characters who hold the skin to be such a barrier in the way would be the first to cry out, "Injustice! awful injustice!"

But, reader, I acknowledge that this is a confused world, and I am not seeking for office, but merely placing before you the black inconsistency that you place before me—which is ten times blacker than any skin that you will find in the universe. And now let me exhort you to do away that principle, as it appears ten times worse in the sight of God and candid men than skins of color—more disgraceful than all the skins that Jehovah ever made. If black or red skins or any other skin of color is disgraceful to God, it appears that he has disgraced himself a great deal—for he has made fifteen colored people to one white and placed them here upon this earth.

Now let me ask you, white man, if it is a disgrace for to eat, drink, and sleep with the image of God, or sit, or walk and talk with them. Or have you the folly to think

---

2. Native American; Apess mocks the notion of the "natural man."

that the white man, being one in fifteen or sixteen, are the only beloved images of God? Assemble all nations together in your imagination, and then let the whites be seated among them, and then let us look for the whites, and I doubt not it would be hard finding them; for to the rest of the nations, they are still but a handful. Now suppose these skins were put together, and each skin had its national crimes written upon it—which skin do you think would have the greatest? I will ask one question more. Can you charge the Indians with robbing a nation almost of their whole continent, and murdering their women and children, and then depriving the remainder of their lawful rights, that nature and God require them to have? And to cap the climax, rob another nation[3] to till their grounds and welter out their days under the lash with hunger and fatigue under the scorching rays of a burning sun? I should look at all the skins, and I know that when I cast my eye upon that white skin, and if I saw those crimes written upon it, I should enter my protest against it immediately and cleave to that which is more honorable. And I can tell you that I am satisfied with the manner of my creation, fully—whether others are or not.

But we will strive to penetrate more fully into the conduct of those who profess to have pure principles and who tell us to follow Jesus Christ and imitate him and have his Spirit. Let us see if they come anywhere near him and his ancient disciples. The first thing we are to look at are his precepts, of which we will mention a few. "Thou shalt love the Lord thy God with all thy heart, with all thy soul, with all thy mind, and with all thy strength. The second is like unto it. Thou shalt love thy neighbor as thyself. On these two precepts hang all the law and the prophets" (Matt. 22:37,38,39,40). "By this shall all men know that they are my disciples, if ye have love one to another" (John 13:35). Our lord left this special command with his followers, that they should love one another.

Again, John in his Epistles says, "He who loveth God loveth his brother also" (I John 4:21). "Let us not love in word but in deed" (I John 3:18). "Let your love be without dissimulation. See that ye love one another with a pure heart fervently" (I Peter 1:22). "If any man say, I love God, and hateth his brother, he is a liar" (I John 4:20). "Whosoever hateth his brother is a murderer, and no murderer hath eternal life abiding in him" (I John 3:15). The first thing that takes our attention is the saying of Jesus, "Thou shalt love," etc. The first question I would ask my brethren in the ministry, as well as that of the membership: What is love, or its effects? Now, if they who teach are not essentially affected with pure love, the love of God, how can they teach as they ought? Again, the holy teachers of old said, "Now if any man have not the spirit of Christ, he is none of his" (Rom. 8:9). Now, my brethren in the ministry, let me ask you a few sincere questions. Did you ever hear or read of Christ teaching his disciples that they ought to despise one because his skin was different from theirs? Jesus Christ being a Jew, and those of his Apostles certainly were not whites—and did not he who completed the plan of salvation complete it for the whites as well as for the Jews, and others? And were not the whites the most degraded people on the earth at that time? And none were more so, for they sacrificed their children to dumb idols! And did not St. Paul labor more abundantly for building up a Christian nation among you than any of the Apostles? And you know as well as I that you are not indebted to a principle beneath a white skin for your religious services but to a colored one.

---

3. African peoples.

What then is the matter now? Is not religion the same now under a colored skin as it ever was? If so, I would ask, why is not a man of color respected? You may say, as many say, we have white men enough. But was this the spirit of Christ and his Apostles? If it had been, there would not have been one white preacher in the world—for Jesus Christ never would have imparted his grace or word to them, for he could forever have withheld it from them. But we find that Jesus Christ and his Apostles never looked at the outward appearances. Jesus in particular looked at the hearts, and his Apostles through him, being discerners of the spirit, looked at their fruit without any regard to the skin, color, or nation; as St. Paul himself speaks, "Where there is neither Greek nor Jew, circumcision nor uncircumcision, Barbarian nor Scythian, bond nor free—but Christ is all, and in all" [Col. 3:11]. If you can find a spirit like Jesus Christ and his Apostles prevailing now in any of the white congregations, I should like to know it. I ask: Is it not the case that everybody that is not white is treated with contempt and counted as barbarians? And I ask if the word of God justifies the white man in so doing. When the prophets prophesied, of whom did they speak? When they spoke of heathens, was it not the whites and others who were counted Gentiles? And I ask if all nations with the exception of the Jews were not counted heathens. And according to the writings of some, it could not mean the Indians, for they are counted Jews.[4] And now I would ask: Why is all this distinction made among these Christian societies? I would ask: What is all this ado about missionary societies, if it be not to Christianize those who are not Christians? And what is it for? To degrade them worse, to bring them into society where they must welter out their days in disgrace merely because their skin is of a different complexion. What folly it is to try to make the state of human society worse than it is. How astonished some may be at this—but let me ask: Is it not so? Let me refer you to the churches only. And, my brethren, is there any agreement? Do brethren and sisters love one another? Do they not rather hate one another? Outward forms and ceremonies, the lusts of the flesh, the lusts of the eye, and pride of life is of more value to many professors[5] than the love of God shed abroad in their hearts, or an attachment to his altar, to his ordinances, or to his children. But you may ask: Who are the children of God? Perhaps you may say, none but white. If so, the word of the Lord is not true.

I will refer you to St. Peter's precepts (Acts 10): "God is no respecter of persons," etc. Now if this is the case, my white brother, what better are you than God? And if no better, why do you, who profess his Gospel and to have his spirit, act so contrary to it? Let me ask why the men of a different skin are so despised. Why are not they educated and placed in your pulpits? I ask if his services well performed are not as good as if a white man performed them. I ask if a marriage or a funeral ceremony or the ordinance of the Lord's house would not be as acceptable in the sight of God as though he was white. And if so, why is it not to you? I ask again: Why is it not as acceptable to have men to exercise their office in one place as well as in another? Perhaps you will say that if we admit you to all of these privileges you will want more. I expect that I can guess what that is—Why, say you, there would be intermarriages. How that would be I am not able to say—and if it should be, it would be nothing strange or new to me; for I can assure you that I know a great many that have intermarried, both of the whites and the Indians—and many are their sons and daughters and people, too, of the first respectability. And I could point to some in the famous city of Boston and elsewhere.

---

4. Native Americans were thought by many to be descendants of the lost tribes of Israel.   5. Those who claim to be Christians.

You may look now at the disgraceful act in the statute law passed by the legislature of Massachusetts, and behold the fifty-pound fine levied upon any clergyman or justice of the peace that dare to encourage the laws of God and nature by a legitimate union in holy wedlock between the Indians and whites. I would ask how this looks to your lawmakers. I would ask if this corresponds with your sayings—that you think as much of the Indians as you do of the whites. I do not wonder that you blush, many of you, while you read; for many have broken the ill-fated laws made by man to hedge up the laws of God and nature. I would ask if they who have made the law have not broken it—but there is no other state in New England that has this law but Massachusetts; and I think, as many of you do not, that you have done yourselves no credit.

But as I am not looking for a wife, having one of the finest cast, as you no doubt would understand while you read her experience and travail of soul in the way to heaven, you will see that it is not my object. And if I had none, I should not want anyone to take my right from me and choose a wife for me; for I think that I or any of my brethren have a right to choose a wife for themselves as well as the whites—and as the whites have taken the liberty to choose my brethren, the Indians, hundreds and thousands of them, as partners in life, I believe the Indians have as much right to choose their partners among the whites if they wish. I would ask you if you can see anything inconsistent in your conduct and talk about the Indians. And if you do, I hope you will try to become more consistent. Now, if the Lord Jesus Christ, who is counted by all to be a Jew—and it is well known that the Jews are a colored people, especially those living in the East, where Christ was born—and if he should appear among us, would he not be shut out of doors by many, very quickly? And by those too who profess religion?

By what you read, you may learn how deep your principles are. I should say they were skin-deep. I should not wonder if some of the most selfish and ignorant would spout a charge of their principles now and then at me. But I would ask: How are you to love your neighbors as yourself? Is it to cheat them? Is it to wrong them in anything? Now, to cheat them out of any of their rights is robbery. And I ask: Can you deny that you are not robbing the Indians daily, and many others? But at last you may think I am what is called a hard and uncharitable man. But not so. I believe there are many who would not hesitate to advocate our cause; and those too who are men of fame and respectability— as well as ladies of honor and virtue. There is a Webster, an Everett, and a Wirt,[6] and many others who are distinguished characters—besides a host of my fellow citizens, who advocate our cause daily. And how I congratulate such noble spirits—how they are to be prized and valued; for they are well calculated to promote the happiness of mankind. They well know that man was made for society, and not for hissing-stocks and outcasts. And when such a principle as this lies within the hearts of men, how much it is like its God—and how it honors its Maker—and how it imitates the feelings of the Good Samaritan,[7] that had his wounds bound up, who had been among thieves and robbers.

Do not get tired, ye noble-hearted—only think how many poor Indians want their wounds done up daily; the Lord will reward you, and pray you stop not till this tree of distinction shall be leveled to the earth, and the mantle of prejudice torn from every American heart—then shall peace pervade the Union.

—1833

---

6. Daniel Webster (1782–1852), Edward Everett (1794–1865), and William Wirt (1772–1834), American politicians.
7. Luke 10.30–37.

Harriet Martineau

1802–1876

Born into a Unitarian family in Norwich, England, Harriet Martineau took an early and strong interest in religion and literature, nearly memorizing all of John Milton's *Paradise Lost* (1667) by age seven and devoting her late teens to acquiring a thorough knowledge of the Bible. It is not surprising, then, that her earliest writing was of a theological bent and published in the Unitarian *Monthly Repository* and that she was awarded prizes from the Central Unitarian Association for her essays. It was not long until she turned her attention to short stories, which won her fame and entrance to the London literary scene.

After a prolific period of writing short fiction and wrangling with the publishers over the quite substantial profits, Martineau was so exhausted that she took a vacation to America, setting sail in the summer of 1834. During her two years in America, she joined the abolitionists, and after her return to England built bridges between the anti-slavery advocates on both sides of the Atlantic. She distilled her experiences in America in two successful books: *Society in America* (1837) and *A Retrospect of Western Travel* (1838). She also celebrated those who had thrown off the yoke of slavery in other locations: Her book *The Hour and the Man* (1841) is about Toussaint L'Ouverture, who led the slave revolt in present-day Haiti and was taken out of power by the treachery of Napoleon. Her interest in philanthropy remained strong throughout her life. She spent her final years in the English Lake District, where (like her neighbor William Wordsworth) she advocated on behalf of the working class and the poor. Unlike Wordsworth, however, she distanced herself from the established religion that had such an early impact on her life.

from Society in America

Citizenship of People of Color

Before I entered New England, while I was ascending the Mississippi, I was told by a Boston gentleman that the people of color in the New England States were perfectly well-treated; that the children were educated in schools provided for them; and that their fathers freely exercised the franchise. This gentleman certainly believed he was telling me the truth. That he, a busy citizen of Boston, should know no better, is now as striking an exemplification of the state of the case to me as a correct representation of the facts would have been. There are two causes for his mistake. He was not aware that the schools for the colored children in New England are, unless they escape by their insignificance, shut up, or pulled down, or the schoolhouse wheeled away upon rollers over the frontier of a pious State, which will not endure that its colored citizens should be educated. He was not aware of a gentleman of color, and his family, being locked out of their own hired pew in a church, because their white brethren will not worship by their side. But I will not proceed with an enumeration of injuries, too familiar to Americans to excite any feeling but that of weariness; and too disgusting to all others to be endured. The other cause of this gentleman's mistake was, that he did not, from long custom, feel some things to be injuries, which he would call anything but good treatment, if he had to bear them himself. Would he think it good treatment to be forbidden to eat with fellow citizens; to be assigned to a particular gallery in his church; to be excluded from college, from municipal office, from professions, from scientific and literary associations? If he felt himself excluded from every department of society, but its humiliations and its drudgery, would he declare himself to be "perfectly well-treated in Boston?" Not a word more of statement is needed.

The colored race are citizens. They stand, as such, in the law, and in the acknowledgment of everyone who knows the law. They are citizens, yet their houses and schools are pulled down, and they can obtain no remedy at law. They are thrust out of offices, and excluded from the most honorable employments, and stripped of all the best benefits of society by fellow citizens who, once a year, solemnly lay their hands on their hearts, and declare that all men are born free and equal, and that rulers derive their just powers from the consent of the governed.

This system of injury is not wearing out. Lafayette,[1] on his last visit to the United States, expressed his astonishment at the increase of the prejudice against color. He remembered, he said, how the black soldiers used to mess[2] with the whites in the revolutionary war. It should ever be remembered that America is the country of the best friends the colored race has ever had. The more truth there is in the assertions of the oppressors of the blacks, the more heroism there is in their friends. The greater the excuse for the pharisees[3] of the community, the more divine is the equity of the redeemers of the colored race. If it be granted that the colored race are naturally inferior, naturally depraved, disgusting, cursed—it must be granted that it is a heavenly charity which descends among them to give such solace as it can to their incomprehensible existence. As long as the excuses of the one party go to enhance the merit of the other, the society is not to be despaired of, even with this poisonous anomaly at its heart.

Happily, however, the colored race is not cursed by God, as it is by some factions of his children. The less clear-sighted of them are pardonable for so believing. Circumstances, for which no living man is answerable, have generated an erroneous conviction in the feeble mind of man, which sees not beyond the actual and immediate. No remedy could ever have been applied, unless stronger minds than ordinary had been brought into the case. But it so happens, wherever there is an anomaly, giant minds rise up to overthrow it: minds gigantic, not in understanding, but in faith. While the mass of common men and women are despising, and disliking, and fearing, and keeping down the colored race, blinking the fact that they are citizens, the few of Nature's aristocracy are putting forth a strong hand to lift up this degraded race out of oppression, and their country from the reproach of it. If they were but one or two, trembling and toiling in solitary energy, the world afar would be confident of their success. But they number hundreds and thousands; and if ever they feel a passing doubt of their progress, it is only because they are pressed upon by the meaner multitude. Over the sea, no one doubts of their victory. It is as certain as that the risen sun will reach the meridian. Already have people of color crossed the thresholds of many whites, as guests, not as drudges or beggars. Already are they admitted to worship, and to exercise charity, among the whites.

The world has heard and seen enough of the reproach incurred by America, on account of her colored population. It is now time to look for the fairer side. Already is the world beyond the sea beginning to think of America, less as the country of the

---

1. Marquis de Lafayette (1757–1834), French nobleman who helped fund the American Revolution.   2. Eat.   3. Hypocrites.

double-faced pretender to the name of Liberty, than as the home of the single-hearted, clear-eyed Presence which, under the name of Abolitionism, is majestically passing through the land which is soon to be her throne.

Political Nonexistence of Women

One of the fundamental principles announced in the Declaration of Independence is, that governments derive their just powers from the consent of the governed. How can the political condition of women be reconciled with this?

Governments in the United States have power to tax women who hold property; to divorce them from their husbands; to fine, imprison, and execute them for certain offences. Whence do these governments derive their powers? They are not "just," as they are not derived from the consent of the women thus governed.

Governments in the United States have power to enslave certain women; and also to punish other women for inhuman treatment of such slaves. Neither of these powers are "just;" not being derived from the consent of the governed.

Governments decree to women in some States half their husbands' property; in others one-third. In some, a woman, on her marriage, is made to yield all her property to her husband; in others, to retain a portion, or the whole, in her own hands. Whence do governments derive the unjust power of thus disposing of property without the consent of the governed?

The democratic principle condemns all this as wrong; and requires the equal political representation of all rational beings. Children, idiots,[4] and criminals, during the season of sequestration, are the only fair exceptions.

The case is so plain that I might close it here; but it is interesting to inquire how so obvious a decision has been so evaded as to leave to women no political rights whatever. The question has been asked, from time to time, in more countries than one, how obedience to the laws can be required of women, when no woman has, either actually or virtually, given any assent to any law. No plausible answer has, as far as I can discover, been offered; for the good reason, that no plausible answer can be devised. The most principled democratic writers on government have on this subject sunk into fallacies, as disgraceful as any advocate of despotism has adduced. In fact, they have thus sunk from being, for the moment, advocates of despotism. Jefferson in America, and James Mill[5] at home, subside, for the occasion, to the level of the author of the Emperor of Russia's Catechism for the young Poles.

Jefferson says,

Were our State a pure democracy, in which all the inhabitants should meet together to transact all their business, there would yet be excluded from their deliberations,

1. Infants, until arrived at years of discretion;
2. Women, who, to prevent depravation of morals, and ambiguity of issue, could not mix promiscuously in the public meetings of men;
3. Slaves, from whom the unfortunate state of things with us takes away the rights of will and of property.[6]

---

4. People with mental disabilities, not used in derogatory sense.   5. Thomas Jefferson (1743–1826), American revolutionary and president; James Mill (1773–1836), Scottish philosopher and historian.   6. Letter to Samuel Kercheval, June 12, 1816.

If the slave disqualification, here assigned, were shifted up under the head of Women, their case would be nearer the truth than as it now stands. Woman's lack of will and of property, is more like the true cause of her exclusion from the representation, than that which is actually set down against her. As if there could be no means of conducting public affairs but by promiscuous meetings! As if there would be more danger in promiscuous meetings for political business than in such meetings for worship, for oratory, for music, for dramatic entertainments—for any of the thousand transactions of civilized life! The plea is not worth another word.

Mill says, with regard to representation, in his Essay on Government,[7] "One thing is pretty clear; that all those individuals, whose interests are involved in those of other individuals, may be struck off without inconvenience. . . . In this light, women may be regarded, the interest of almost all of whom is involved, either in that of their fathers or in that of their husbands."

The true democratic principle is, that no person's interests can be, or can be ascertained to be, identical with those of any other person. This allows the exclusion of none but incapables.

The interests of women who have fathers and husbands can never be identical with theirs, while there is a necessity for laws to protect women against their husbands and fathers. This statement is not worth another word.

Some who desire that there should be an equality of property between men and women, oppose representation, on the ground that political duties would be incompatible with the other duties which women have to discharge. The reply to this is, that women are the best judges here. God has given time and power for the discharge of all duties; and, if he had not, it would be for women to decide which they would take, and which they would leave. But their guardians follow the ancient fashion of deciding what is best for their wards. The Emperor of Russia discovers when a coat of arms and title do not agree with a subject prince. The King of France early perceives that the air of Paris does not agree with a free-thinking foreigner. The English Tories[8] feel the hardship that it would be to impose the franchise on every artisan, busy as he is in getting his bread. The Georgian planter perceives the hardship that freedom would be to his slaves. And the best friends of half the human race peremptorily decide for them as to their rights, their duties, their feelings, their powers. In all these cases, the persons thus cared for feel that the abstract decision rests with themselves; that, though they may be compelled to submit, they need not acquiesce.

I cannot enter upon the commonest order of pleas of all—those which relate to the virtual influence of woman; her swaying the judgment and will of man through the heart; and so forth. One might as well try to dissect the morning mist. I knew a gentleman in America who told me how much rather he had be a woman than the man he is—a professional man, a father, a citizen. He would give up all this for a woman's influence. I thought he was mated too soon. He should have married a lady, also of my acquaintance, who would not at all object to being a slave, if ever the blacks should have the upper hand; "it is so right that the one race should be subservient to the other!" Or rather—I thought it a pity that the one could not be a woman, and the other a slave; so that an injured individual of each class might be exalted into their places, to fulfill and enjoy the duties and privileges which they despise, and, in despising, disgrace.

---

7. Published in 1820.   8. British conservative party.

That woman has power to represent her own interests, no one can deny till she has
been tried. The modes need not be discussed here: they must vary with circumstances.
The fearful and absurd images which are perpetually called up to perplex the question—images of women on woolsacks in England, and under canopies in America,
have nothing to do with the matter. The principle being once established, the methods will follow, easily, naturally, and under a remarkable transmutation of the ludicrous into the sublime. The kings of Europe would have laughed mightily, two centuries ago, at the idea of a commoner, without robes, crown, or sceptre, stepping into
the throne of a strong nation. Yet who dared to laugh when Washington's superroyal
voice greeted the New World from the presidential chair, and the Old World stood
still to catch the echo?

The principle of the equal rights of both halves of the human race is all we have
to do with here. It is the true democratic principle which can never be seriously con-
troverted, and only for a short time evaded. Governments can derive their just powers only from the consent of the governed.

—1837

Ralph Waldo Emerson
1803–1882

In 1847, the American essayist Ralph Waldo Emerson made a speaking tour of Britain, where
he met Thomas De Quincey, William Makepeace Thackeray, and Alfred Lord Tennyson,
among many other members of the cultural elite. In London, he was elected to the Athenæum
Club (an exclusive club for white males engaged in pursuits in the arts and sciences), and his
course of public lectures was attended by all the most eminent Victorians. It can still seem surprising that the young Emerson, an obscure provincial preacher, would go on to achieve such
international fame. He was the product of an unbroken line of ministers stretching back nine
generations to the Reverend Peter Bulkeley, who emigrated from England in 1634. Emerson's
father died early, leaving the family to take in boarders to pay for necessities. Nevertheless, the
bookish young Waldo, as Emerson was called by his family, entered Harvard at fourteen, where
he supplemented his scholarships by working in the dining hall. He graduated only at the middle of his class.

After commencement, Emerson followed a path of little resistance, first teaching school
for some years, then returning to Harvard for a degree in divinity. He was made pastor of
Boston's Second Church, one of the city's oldest and most respectable congregations. His
position as a pillar of the establishment seemed secure when he was named chaplain of the
Massachusetts Legislature and elected to the Boston School Committee. Capping this success, he fell deeply in love with Ellen Tucker, and they were married in September 1829. Just
a year and a half later, she died of tuberculosis (a disease Emerson himself would suffer from
throughout his life). In his grief, he found that his rational Unitarian creed could offer only
a "corpse-cold" religious experience. Rather than healing emotion and inspiration, it emphasized what felt like petty reasoning about the historicity of miracles and the Trinitarian versus Unitarian nature of God. In little more than a year, he found a way to leave the church

behind, stating in a letter to his congregation that he could no longer in good conscience administer Communion.

Still seeking solace, Emerson left for a year of travel in Italy, Switzerland, and the British Isles, where he met, among many others, writers William Wordsworth and Samuel Taylor Coleridge. Their lives, as independent secular intellectuals, as members of what Coleridge called the "clerisy," seemed impressively fulfilling. Moreover, Coleridge's Romantic epistemological theories (freely adapted from the German philosopher Immanuel Kant) offered an escape from the impasse of rational religion. The mind had two ways of knowing, the reason and the understanding. The first comprehended the phenomena of this world, the material world of the senses, whereas the second allowed direct intuitive engagement with a higher, or transcendent, spiritual reality. Emerson also met Thomas Carlyle, a Scottish writer whose country life and cagey professionalism would shape Emerson's sense of how it was possible to live an idyllic life of the pen. The two would carry on a lifelong correspondence, and after Emerson oversaw the first American publication of Carlyle's *Sartor Resartus* in 1836, they operated as one another's transatlantic literary agents.

Back in New England, Emerson launched a new career as a speaker for the flourishing lyceum movement, in which local lecture series were founded across America with the intention of educating the public. Beginning with a series of lectures on natural history and moving on to a seemingly unlimited range of philosophical topics, he quickly established a reputation as an inspiring orator. Soon he was able to support himself on the proceeds of annual courses of public lectures in Boston and of lyceum speeches delivered in towns throughout New England and as far west as the Ohio Valley. His first short book, *Nature* (1836), articulates the new mode of spiritual experience to which he had turned after leaving his church. It discovers a divinity immanent in nature and announces that the higher reason, universal in all people, allows direct, intuitive access to it: "Standing on the bare ground . . . [t]he currents of the Universal Being circulate through me; I am part or particle of God" (p. 822). It was in this kind of ecstatic experience that Emerson found the emotional compensation he missed in orthodox Christianity. For "[t]he lover of nature . . . intercourse with heaven and earth, becomes part of his daily food. In the presence of nature, a wild delight runs through the man, in spite of real sorrows" (p. 821). Emerson catalogs the "uses" of nature, showing that it not only provides the material support, the "commodity," on which human life depends but also engenders our sense of beauty and morality, especially since the language of philosophy and spirituality is formed of metaphors from nature. The idea that language "corresponds" to nature drove Emerson's innovations as a writer of prose. In *Nature*, he makes his first somewhat tentative experiments with an accretive, sinuous, pithy style that he saw as organic; his essays grew like vines. *Nature* sold some five hundred copies in its first month, but it was more than a decade before another edition was needed. Nevertheless, it secured Emerson's position as one of the main voices of the "newness" of the 1830s.

A year after the publication of *Nature*, speaking before Harvard's Phi Beta Kappa society, Emerson delivered the address that would later be titled "The American Scholar." The poet Oliver Wendell Holmes characterized it as America's "intellectual Declaration of Independence." And indeed, no writer has come to be more firmly associated with American literary nationalism than Emerson. But he saw himself as a member of a transnational circle of sages, one that included figures like Johann Wolfgang von Goethe, Victor Cousin, Samuel Taylor Coleridge, and Thomas Carlyle. He does call on his audience to participate in the creation of a vibrant literary culture, but he is far less concerned with Americanness than with what it means to be a scholar, a "man thinking." The essay is an intellectual's credo, and its main emphasis is on the power and importance of critical, independent thought. Crucially, radical individualism is not shallow personalism or whimsical defiance of convention. Emerson believed not in any absolute independence of the self, but that the most reliable place to contact the divine, the transcendent, the transpersonal, was within: "To believe your own thought, to believe that what is true for you in your private heart is true for all men,—that is genius.

Speak your latent conviction, and it shall be the universal sense; for the inmost in due time becomes the outmost." More than just providing ideological leadership, Emerson also helped organize the flowering of American Romanticism, calling the first meeting of the Transcendental Club in 1836 and co-editing with Margaret Fuller the movement's most important magazine, *The Dial*.

Nature

"Nature is but an image or imitation of wisdom, the last thing of
the soul; nature being a thing which doth only do, but not know."
—PLOTINUS[1]

Introduction

Our age is retrospective. It builds the sepulchres of the fathers. It writes biographies, histories, and criticism. The foregoing generations beheld God and nature face to face; we, through their eyes. Why should not we also enjoy an original relation to the universe? Why should not we have a poetry and philosophy of insight and not of tradition, and a religion by revelation to us, and not the history of theirs? Embosomed for a season in nature, whose floods of life stream around and through us, and invite us by the powers they supply, to action proportioned to nature, why should we grope among the dry bones of the past, or put the living generation into masquerade out of its faded wardrobe? The sun shines to-day also. There is more wool and flax in the fields. There are new lands, new men, new thoughts. Let us demand our own works and laws and worship.

Undoubtedly we have no questions to ask which are unanswerable. We must trust the perfection of the creation so far, as to believe that whatever curiosity the order of things has awakened in our minds, the order of things can satisfy. Every man's condition is a solution in hieroglyphic to those inquiries he would put. He acts it as life, before he apprehends it as truth. In like manner, nature is already, in its forms and tendencies, describing its own design. Let us interrogate the great apparition, that shines so peacefully around us. Let us inquire, to what end is nature?

All science has one aim, namely, to find a theory of nature. We have theories of races and of functions, but scarcely yet a remote approach to an idea of creation. We are now so far from the road to truth, that religious teachers dispute and hate each other, and speculative men are esteemed unsound and frivolous. But to a sound judgment, the most abstract truth is the most practical. Whenever a true theory appears, it will be its own evidence. Its test is, that it will explain all phenomena. Now many are thought not only unexplained but inexplicable; as language, sleep, madness, dreams, beasts, sex.

Philosophically considered, the universe is composed of Nature and the Soul. Strictly speaking, therefore, all that is separate from us, all which Philosophy distinguishes as the NOT ME,[2] that is, both nature and art, all other men and my own body, must be ranked under this name, NATURE. In enumerating the values of nature and casting up their sum, I shall use the word in both senses;—in its common and in its philosophical import. In inquiries so general as our present one, the inaccuracy is not material; no confusion of thought will occur. Nature, in the common sense, refers to essences unchanged by man; space, the air, the river, the leaf. Art is applied to the mixture of his will with the same things, as in a house, a canal, a statue, a picture. But

---

1. Plotinus (c. 205–270), Roman philosopher.   2. Thomas Carlyle, *Sartor Resartus* (1834).

his operations taken together are so insignificant, a little chipping, baking, patching, and washing, that in an impression so grand as that of the world on the human mind, they do not vary the result.

Chapter I. Nature

To go into solitude, a man needs to retire as much from his chamber as from society. I am not solitary whilst I read and write, though nobody is with me. But if a man would be alone, let him look at the stars. The rays that come from those heavenly worlds, will separate between him and vulgar things. One might think the atmosphere was made transparent with this design, to give man, in the heavenly bodies, the perpetual presence of the sublime. Seen in the streets of cities, how great they are! If the stars should appear one night in a thousand years, how would men believe and adore; and preserve for many generations the remembrance of the city of God which had been shown! But every night come out these preachers of beauty, and light the universe with their admonishing smile.

The stars awaken a certain reverence, because though always present, they are always inaccessible; but all natural objects make a kindred impression, when the mind is open to their influence. Nature never wears a mean appearance. Neither does the wisest man extort all her secret, and lose his curiosity by finding out all her perfection. Nature never became a toy to a wise spirit. The flowers, the animals, the mountains, reflected all the wisdom of his best hour, as much as they had delighted the simplicity of his childhood.

When we speak of nature in this manner, we have a distinct but most poetical sense in the mind. We mean the integrity of impression made by manifold natural objects. It is this which distinguishes the stick of timber of the wood-cutter, from the tree of the poet. The charming landscape which I saw this morning, is indubitably made up of some twenty or thirty farms. Miller owns this field, Locke that, and Manning the woodland beyond. But none of them owns the landscape. There is a property in the horizon which no man has but he whose eye can integrate all the parts, that is, the poet. This is the best part of these men's farms, yet to this their land-deeds give them no title.

To speak truly, few adult persons can see nature. Most persons do not see the sun. At least they have a very superficial seeing. The sun illuminates only the eye of the man, but shines into the eye and the heart of the child. The lover of nature is he whose inward and outward senses are still truly adjusted to each other; who has retained the spirit of infancy even into the era of manhood. His intercourse with heaven and earth, becomes part of his daily food. In the presence of nature, a wild delight runs through the man, in spite of real sorrows. Nature says,—he is my creature, and maugre[3] all his impertinent griefs, he shall be glad with me. Not the sun or the summer alone, but every hour and season yields its tribute of delight; for every hour and change corresponds to and authorizes a different state of the mind, from breathless noon to grimmest midnight. Nature is a setting that fits equally well a comic or a mourning piece. In good health, the air is a cordial of incredible virtue. Crossing a bare common, in snow puddles, at twilight, under a clouded sky, without having in my thoughts any occurrence of special good fortune, I have enjoyed a perfect exhilaration. Almost I fear to think how glad I am. In the woods too, a man casts off his years, as the snake his slough, and at what period soever of life, is always a child. In the woods, is perpetual youth. Within

---

3. Despite.

these plantations of God, a decorum and sanctity reign, a perennial festival is dressed, and the guest sees not how he should tire of them in a thousand years. In the woods, we return to reason and faith. There I feel that nothing can befall me in life,—no disgrace, no calamity, (leaving me my eyes,) which nature cannot repair. Standing on the bare ground,—my head bathed by the blithe air, and uplifted into infinite space,—all mean egotism vanishes. I become a transparent eye-ball. I am nothing. I see all. The currents of the Universal Being circulate through me; I am part or particle of God. The name of the nearest friend sounds then foreign and accidental. To be brothers, to be acquaintances,—master or servant, is then a trifle and a disturbance. I am the lover of uncontained and immortal beauty. In the wilderness, I find something more dear and connate[4] than in streets or villages. In the tranquil landscape, and especially in the distant line of the horizon, man beholds somewhat as beautiful as his own nature.

The greatest delight which the fields and woods minister, is the suggestion of an occult relation between man and the vegetable. I am not alone and unacknowledged. They nod to me and I to them. The waving of the boughs in the storm, is new to me and old. It takes me by surprise, and yet is not unknown. Its effect is like that of a higher thought or a better emotion coming over me, when I deemed I was thinking justly or doing right.

Yet it is certain that the power to produce this delight, does not reside in nature, but in man, or in a harmony of both. It is necessary to use these pleasures with great temperance. For, nature is not always tricked in holiday attire, but the same scene which yesterday breathed perfume and glittered as for the frolic of the nymphs, is overspread with melancholy today. Nature always wears the colors of the spirit. To a man laboring under calamity, the heat of his own fire hath sadness in it. Then, there is a kind of contempt of the landscape felt by him who has just lost by death a dear friend. The sky is less grand as it shuts down over less worth in the population.

Chapter II. Commodity

Whoever considers the final cause of the world, will discern a multitude of uses that enter as parts into that result. They all admit of being thrown into one of the following classes: Commodity; Beauty; Language; and Discipline.

Under the general name of Commodity, I rank all those advantages which our senses owe to nature. This, of course, is a benefit which is temporary and mediate, not ultimate, like its service to the soul. Yet although low, it is perfect in its kind, and is the only use of nature which all men apprehend. The misery of man appears like childish petulance, when we explore the steady and prodigal provision that has been made for his support and delight on this green ball which floats him through the heavens. What angels invented these splendid ornaments, these rich conveniences, this ocean of air above, this ocean of water beneath, this firmament of earth between? this zodiac of lights, this tent of dropping clouds, this striped coat of climates, this fourfold year? Beasts, fire, water, stones, and corn serve him. The field is at once his floor, his work-yard, his play-ground, his garden, and his bed.

"More servants wait on man
  Than he'll take notice of."——[5]

---

4. Closely related.   5. George Herbert (1593–1633), "Man" (1633).

Nature, in its ministry to man, is not only the material, but is also the process and the result. All the parts incessantly work into each other's hands for the profit of man. The wind sows the seed; the sun evaporates the sea; the wind blows the vapor to the field; the ice, on the other side of the planet, condenses rain on this; the rain feeds the plant; the plant feeds the animal; and thus the endless circulations of the divine charity nourish man.

The useful arts are but reproductions or new combinations by the wit of man, of the same natural benefactors. He no longer waits for favoring gales, but by means of steam, he realizes the fable of Æolus's bag,[6] and carries the two and thirty winds in the boiler of his boat. To diminish friction, he paves the road with iron bars, and, mounting a coach with a ship-load of men, animals, and merchandise behind him, he darts through the country, from town to town, like an eagle or a swallow through the air. By the aggregate of these aids, how is the face of the world changed, from the era of Noah to that of Napoleon! The private poor man hath cities, ships, canals, bridges, built for him. He goes to the post-office, and the human race run on his errands; to the book-shop, and the human race read and write of all that happens, for him; to the court-house, and nations repair his wrongs. He sets his house upon the road, and the human race go forth every morning, and shovel out the snow, and cut a path for him.

But there is no need of specifying particulars in this class of uses. The catalogue is endless, and the examples so obvious, that I shall leave them to the reader's reflection, with the general remark, that this mercenary benefit is one which has respect to a farther good. A man is fed, not that he may be fed, but that he may work.

Chapter III. Beauty

A nobler want of man is served by nature, namely, the love of Beauty.

The ancient Greeks called the world κόσμος,[7] beauty. Such is the constitution of all things, or such the plastic power of the human eye, that the primary forms, as the sky, the mountain, the tree, the animal, give us a delight *in and for themselves*; a pleasure arising from outline, color, motion, and grouping. This seems partly owing to the eye itself. The eye is the best of artists. By the mutual action of its structure and of the laws of light, perspective is produced, which integrates every mass of objects, of what character soever, into a well colored and shaded globe, so that where the particular objects are mean and unaffecting, the landscape which they compose, is round and symmetrical. And as the eye is the best composer, so light is the first of painters. There is no object so foul that intense light will not make beautiful. And the stimulus it affords to the sense, and a sort of infinitude which it hath, like space and time, make all matter gay. Even the corpse hath its own beauty. But beside this general grace diffused over nature, almost all the individual forms are agreeable to the eye, as is proved by our endless imitations of some of them, as the acorn, the grape, the pine-cone, the wheat-ear, the egg, the wings and forms of most birds, the lion's claw, the serpent, the butterfly, sea-shells, flames, clouds, buds, leaves, and the forms of many trees, as the palm.

For better consideration, we may distribute the aspects of Beauty in a threefold manner.

---

6. In Homer's *Odyssey*, a bag full of wind.   7. Cosmos; order or harmony.

1. First, the simple perception of natural forms is a delight. The influence of the forms and actions in nature, is so needful to man, that, in its lowest functions, it seems to lie on the confines of commodity and beauty. To the body and mind which have been cramped by noxious work or company, nature is medicinal and restores their tone. The tradesman, the attorney comes out of the din and craft of the street, and sees the sky and the woods, and is a man again. In their eternal calm, he finds himself. The health of the eye seems to demand a horizon. We are never tired, so long as we can see far enough.

But in other hours, Nature satisfies the soul purely by its loveliness, and without any mixture of corporeal benefit. I have seen the spectacle of morning from the hill-top over against my house, from day-break to sun-rise, with emotions which an angel might share. The long slender bars of cloud float like fishes in the sea of crimson light. From the earth, as a shore, I look out into that silent sea. I seem to partake its rapid transformations: the active enchantment reaches my dust, and I dilate and conspire with the morning wind. How does Nature deify us with a few and cheap elements! Give me health and a day, and I will make the pomp of emperors ridiculous. The dawn is my Assyria[8]; the sun-set and moon-rise my Paphos,[9] and unimaginable realms of faerie, broad noon shall be my England of the senses and the understanding; the night shall be my Germany of mystic philosophy and dreams.

Not less excellent, except for our less susceptibility in the afternoon, was the charm, last evening, of a January sunset. The western clouds divided and subdivided themselves into pink flakes modulated with tints of unspeakable softness; and the air had so much life and sweetness, that it was a pain to come within doors. What was it that nature would say? Was there no meaning in the live repose of the valley behind the mill, and which Homer or Shakspeare could not re-form for me in words? The leafless trees become spires of flame in the sunset, with the blue east for their background, and the stars of the dead calices[10] of flowers, and every withered stem and stubble rimed with frost, contribute something to the mute music.

The inhabitants of cities suppose that the country landscape is pleasant only half the year. I please myself with observing the graces of the winter scenery, and believe that we are as much touched by it as by the genial influences of summer. To the attentive eye, each moment of the year has its own beauty, and in the same field, it beholds, every hour, a picture which was never seen before, and which shall never be seen again. The heavens change every moment, and reflect their glory or gloom on the plains beneath. The state of the crop in the surrounding farms alters the expression of the earth from week to week. The succession of native plants in the pastures and roadsides, which make the silent clock by which time tells the summer hours, will make even the divisions of the day sensible to a keen observer. The tribes of birds and insects, like the plants punctual to their time, follow each other, and the year has room for all. By water-courses, the variety is greater. In July, the blue pontederia or pickerel-weed blooms in large beds in the shallow parts of our pleasant river, and swarms with yellow butterflies in continual motion. Art cannot rival this pomp of purple and gold. Indeed the river is a perpetual gala, and boasts each month a new ornament.

---

8. A region on the upper Tigris river.   9. A town in Cyprus, fabled to be the birthplace of Aphrodite, the Greek goddess of love and beauty.   10. Funnel-shaped structures.

But this beauty of Nature which is seen and felt as beauty, is the least part. The shows of day, the dewy morning, the rainbow, mountains, orchards in blossom, stars, moonlight, shadows in still water, and the like, if too eagerly hunted, become shows merely, and mock us with their unreality. Go out of the house to see the moon, and 't is mere tinsel; it will not please as when its light shines upon your necessary journey. The beauty that shimmers in the yellow afternoons of October, who ever could clutch it? Go forth to find it, and it is gone: 't is only a mirage as you look from the windows of diligence.

2. The presence of a higher, namely, of the spiritual element is essential to its perfection. The high and divine beauty which can be loved without effeminacy, is that which is found in combination with the human will, and never separate. Beauty is the mark God sets upon virtue. Every natural action is graceful. Every heroic act is also decent, and causes the place and the bystanders to shine. We are taught by great actions that the universe is the property of every individual in it. Every rational creature has all nature for his dowry and estate. It is his, if he will. He may divest himself of it; he may creep into a corner, and abdicate his kingdom, as most men do, but he is entitled to the world by his constitution. In proportion to the energy of his thought and will, he takes up the world into himself. "All those things for which men plough, build, or sail, obey virtue"; said Sallust.[11] "The winds and waves," said Gibbon, "are always on the side of the ablest navigators."[12] So are the sun and moon and all the stars of heaven. When a noble act is done,—perchance in a scene of great natural beauty; when Leonidas and his three hundred martyrs consume one day in dying, and the sun and moon come each and look at them once in the steep defile of Thermopylæ[13]; when Arnold Winkelried,[14] in the high Alps, under the shadow of the avalanche, gathers in his side a sheaf of Austrian spears to break the line for his comrades; are not these heroes entitled to add the beauty of the scene to the beauty of the deed? When the bark of Columbus nears the shore of America;—before it, the beach lined with savages, fleeing out of all their huts of cane; the sea behind; and the purple mountains of the Indian Archipelago around, can we separate the man from the living picture? Does not the New World clothe his form with her palm-groves and savannahs as fit drapery? Ever does natural beauty steal in like air, and envelope great actions. When Sir Harry Vane[15] was dragged up the Tower-hill, sitting on a sled, to suffer death, as the champion of the English laws, one of the multitude cried out to him, "You never sate on so glorious a seat." Charles II, to intimidate the citizens of London, caused the patriot Lord Russell[16] to be drawn in an open coach, through the principal streets of the city, on his way to the scaffold. "But," to use the simple narrative of his biographer, "the multitude imagined they saw liberty and virtue sitting by his side." In private places, among sordid objects, an act of truth or heroism seems at once to draw to itself the sky as its temple, the sun as its candle. Nature stretcheth out her arms to embrace man, only let his thoughts be of equal greatness. Willingly does she follow his steps with the rose and the violet, and bend her lines of grandeur and grace to the decoration of her darling child. Only let his thoughts be of equal scope, and the frame will suit the picture. A virtuous man, is in unison with her

---

11. Sallust (86–34 BC), Roman historian.   12. Edward Gibbon (1737–1794), *The History of the Decline and Fall of the Roman Empire* (1776).   13. Leonidas, a Spartan king, was killed defending the pass of Thermopylæ against the Persian army of Xerxes.   14. Arnold Winkelried (d. 1386), Swiss military hero.   15. Sir Henry Vane (1613–1662), English Protestant dissenter.   16. William Russell (1639–1683), English politician.

works, and makes the central figure of the visible sphere. Homer, Pindar, Socrates, Phocion,[17] associate themselves fitly in our memory with the whole geography and climate of Greece. The visible heavens and earth sympathize with Jesus. And in common life, whosoever has seen a person of powerful character and happy genius, will have remarked how easily he took all things along with him,—the persons, the opinions, and the day, and nature became ancillary to a man.

3. There is still another aspect under which the beauty of the world may be viewed, namely, as it becomes an object of the intellect. Beside the relation of things to virtue, they have a relation to thought. The intellect searches out the absolute order of things as they stand in the mind of God, and without the colors of affection. The intellectual and the active powers seem to succeed each other in man, and the exclusive activity of the one, generates the exclusive activity of the other. There is something unfriendly in each to the other, but they are like the alternate periods of feeding and working in animals; each prepares and certainly will be followed by the other. Therefore does beauty, which, in relation to actions, as we have seen comes unsought, and comes because it is unsought, remain for the apprehension and pursuit of the intellect; and then again, in its turn, of the active power. Nothing divine dies. All good is eternally reproductive. The beauty of nature reforms itself in the mind, and not for barren contemplation, but for new creation.

All men are in some degree impressed by the face of the world. Some men even to delight. This love of beauty is Taste. Others have the same love in such excess, that, not content with admiring, they seek to embody it in new forms. The creation of beauty is Art.

The production of a work of art throws a light upon the mystery of humanity. A work of art is an abstract or epitome of the world. It is the result or expression of nature, in miniature. For although the works of nature are innumerable and all different, the result or the expression of them all is similar and single. Nature is a sea of forms radically alike and even unique. A leaf, a sun-beam, a landscape, the ocean, make an analogous impression on the mind. What is common to them all,—that perfectness and harmony, is beauty. Therefore the standard of beauty, is the entire circuit of natural forms,—the totality of nature; which the Italians expressed by defining beauty "il piu nell' uno."[18] Nothing is quite beautiful alone: nothing but is beautiful in the whole. A single object is only so far beautiful as it suggests this universal grace. The poet, the painter, the sculptor, the musician, the architect seek each to concentrate this radiance of the world on one point, and each in his several work to satisfy the love of beauty which stimulates him to produce. Thus is Art, a nature passed through the alembic[19] of man. Thus in art, does nature work through the will of a man filled with the beauty of her first works.

The world thus exists to the soul to satisfy the desire of beauty. Extend this element to the uttermost, and I call it an ultimate end. No reason can be asked or given why the soul seeks beauty. Beauty, in its largest and profoundest sense, is one expression for the universe. God is the all-fair. Truth, and goodness, and beauty, are but different faces of the same All. But beauty in nature is not ultimate. It is the herald of inward and eternal beauty, and is not alone a solid and satisfactory good. It must therefore stand as a part and not as yet the last or highest expression of the final cause of Nature.

---

17. Greek writers and politicians.   18. "The many in one."   19. A device for purifying by distillation.

Chapter IV. Language

A third use which Nature subserves to man is that of Language. Nature is the vehicle of thought, and in a simple, double, and threefold degree.

1. Words are signs of natural facts.
2. Particular natural facts are symbols of particular spiritual facts.
3. Nature is the symbol of spirit.

1. Words are signs of natural facts. The use of natural history is to give us aid in supernatural history. The use of the outer creation is to give us language for the beings and changes of the inward creation. Every word which is used to express a moral or intellectual fact, if traced to its root, is found to be borrowed from some material appearance. *Right* originally means *straight*; *wrong* means *twisted*. *Spirit* primarily means *wind*; *transgression*, the crossing of a *line*; *supercilious*, the *raising of the eye-brow*. We say the *heart* to express emotion, the *head* to denote thought; and *thought* and *emotion* are, in their turn, words borrowed from sensible things, and now appropriated to spiritual nature. Most of the process by which this transformation is made, is hidden from us in the remote time when language was framed; but the same tendency may be daily observed in children. Children and savages use only nouns or names of things, which they continually convert into verbs, and apply to analogous mental acts.

2. But this origin of all words that convey a spiritual import,—so conspicuous a fact in the history of language,—is our least debt to nature. It is not words only that are emblematic; it is things which are emblematic. Every natural fact is a symbol of some spiritual fact. Every appearance in nature corresponds to some state of the mind, and that state of the mind can only be described by presenting that natural appearance as its picture. An enraged man is a lion, a cunning man is a fox, a firm man is a rock, a learned man is a torch. A lamb is innocence; a snake is subtle spite; flowers express to us the delicate affections. Light and darkness are our familiar expression for knowledge and ignorance; and heat for love. Visible distance behind and before us, is respectively our image of memory and hope.

Who looks upon a river in a meditative hour, and is not reminded of the flux of all things? Throw a stone into the stream, and the circles that propagate themselves are the beautiful type of all influence. Man is conscious of a universal soul within or behind his individual life, wherein, as in a firmament, the natures of Justice, Truth, Love, Freedom, arise and shine. This universal soul, he calls Reason: it is not mine or thine or his, but we are its; we are its property and men. And the blue sky in which the private earth is buried, the sky with its eternal calm, and full of everlasting orbs, is the type of Reason. That which, intellectually considered, we call Reason, considered in relation to nature, we call Spirit. Spirit is the Creator. Spirit hath life in itself. And man in all ages and countries, embodies it in his language, as the FATHER.

It is easily seen that there is nothing lucky or capricious in these analogies, but that they are constant, and pervade nature. These are not the dreams of a few poets, here and there, but man is an analogist, and studies relations in all objects. He is placed in the centre of beings, and a ray of relation passes from every other being to him. And neither can man be understood without these objects, nor these objects without man. All the facts in natural history taken by themselves, have no value, but are barren like a single sex. But marry it to human history, and it is full of life. Whole

Floras, all Linnæus' and Buffon's[20] volumes, are but dry catalogues of facts; but the most trivial of these facts, the habit of a plant, the organs, or work, or noise of an insect, applied to the illustration of a fact in intellectual philosophy, or, in any way associated to human nature, affects us in the most lively and agreeable manner. The seed of a plant,—to what affecting analogies in the nature of man, is that little fruit made use of, in all discourse, up to the voice of Paul, who calls the human corpse a seed,—"It is sown a natural body; it is raised a spiritual body."[21] The motion of the earth round its axis, and round the sun, makes the day, and the year. These are certain amounts of brute light and heat. But is there no intent of an analogy between man's life and the seasons? And do the seasons gain no grandeur or pathos from that analogy? The instincts of the ant are very unimportant considered as the ant's; but the moment a ray of relation is seen to extend from it to man, and the little drudge is seen to be a monitor, a little body with a mighty heart, then all its habits, even that said to be recently observed, that it never sleeps, become sublime.

Because of this radical correspondence between visible things and human thoughts, savages, who have only what is necessary, converse in figures. As we go back in history, language becomes more picturesque, until its infancy, when it is all poetry; or, all spiritual facts are represented by natural symbols. The same symbols are found to make the original elements of all languages. It has moreover been observed, that the idioms of all languages approach each other in passages of the greatest eloquence and power. And as this is the first language, so is it the last. This immediate dependence of language upon nature, this conversion of an outward phenomenon into a type of somewhat in human life, never loses its power to affect us. It is this which gives that piquancy to the conversation of a strong-natured farmer or backwoodsman, which all men relish.

Thus is nature an interpreter, by whose means man converses with his fellow men. A man's power to connect his thought with its proper symbol, and so utter it, depends on the simplicity of his character, that is, upon his love of truth and his desire to communicate it without loss. The corruption of man is followed by the corruption of language. When simplicity of character and the sovereignty of ideas is broken up by the prevalence of secondary desires, the desire of riches, the desire of pleasure, the desire of power, the desire of praise,—and duplicity and falsehood take place of simplicity and truth, the power over nature as an interpreter of the will, is in a degree lost; new imagery ceases to be created, and old words are perverted to stand for things which are not; a paper currency is employed when there is no bullion in the vaults. In due time, the fraud is manifest, and words lose all power to stimulate the understanding or the affections. Hundreds of writers may be found in every long-civilized nation, who for a short time believe, and make others believe, that they see and utter truths, who do not of themselves clothe one thought in its natural garment, but who feed unconsciously upon the language created by the primary writers of the country, those, namely, who hold primarily on nature.

But wise men pierce this rotten diction and fasten words again to visible things; so that picturesque language is at once a commanding certificate that he who employs it, is a man in alliance with truth and God. The moment our discourse rises above the ground line of familiar facts, and is inflamed with passion or exalted by thought, it

---

20. Floras: books listing plant species. Carl Linnæus (1707–1778), Swedish botanist; Georges-Louis Leclerc, Comte de Buffon (1707–1788), French scientist.   21. 1 Corinthians 15:44.

clothes itself in images. A man conversing in earnest, if he watch his intellectual processes, will find that always a material image, more or less luminous, arises in his mind, contemporaneous with every thought, which furnishes the vestment of the thought. Hence, good writing and brilliant discourse are perpetual allegories. This imagery is spontaneous. It is the blending of experience with the present action of the mind. It is proper creation. It is the working of the Original Cause through the instruments he has already made.

These facts may suggest the advantage which the country-life possesses for a powerful mind, over the artificial and curtailed life of cities. We know more from nature than we can at will communicate. Its light flows into the mind evermore, and we forget its presence. The poet, the orator, bred in the woods, whose scenes have been nourished by their fair and appeasing changes, year after year, without design and without heed,—shall not lose their lesson altogether, in the roar of cities or the broil of politics. Long hereafter, amidst agitation and terror in national councils,—in the hour of revolution,—these solemn images shall reappear in their morning lustre, as fit symbols and words of the thoughts which the passing events shall awaken. At the call of a noble sentiment, again the woods wave, the pines murmur, the river rolls and shines, and the cattle low upon the mountains, as he saw and heard them in his infancy. And with these forms, the spells of persuasion, the keys of power are put into his hands.

3. We are thus assisted by natural objects in the expression of particular meanings. But how great a language to convey such pepper-corn informations! Did it need such noble races of creatures, this profusion of forms, this host of orbs in heaven, to furnish man with the dictionary and grammar of his municipal speech? Whilst we use this grand cipher to expedite the affairs of our pot and kettle, we feel that we have not yet put it to its use, neither are able. We are like travellers using the cinders of a volcano to roast their eggs. Whilst we see that it always stands ready to clothe what we would say, we cannot avoid the question, whether the characters are not significant of themselves. Have mountains, and waves, and skies, no significance but what we consciously give them, when we employ them as emblems of our thoughts? The world is emblematic. Parts of speech are metaphors because the whole of nature is a metaphor of the human mind. The laws of moral nature answer to those of matter as face to face in a glass. "The visible world and the relation of its parts, is the dial plate of the invisible."[22] The axioms of physics translate the laws of ethics. Thus, "the whole is greater than its part;" "reaction is equal to action;" "the smallest weight may be made to lift the greatest, the difference of weight being compensated by time;" and many the like propositions, which have an ethical as well as physical sense. These propositions have a much more extensive and universal sense when applied to human life, than when confined to technical use.

In like manner, the memorable words of history, and the proverbs of nations, consist usually of a natural fact, selected as a picture or parable of a moral truth. Thus; A rolling stone gathers no moss; A bird in the hand is worth two in the bush; A cripple in the right way, will beat a racer in the wrong; Make hay whilst the sun shines; 'T is hard to carry a full cup even; Vinegar is the son of wine; The last ounce broke the camel's back; Long-lived trees make roots first;—and the like. In their primary sense these are trivial facts, but we repeat them for the value of their analogical import. What is true of proverbs, is true of all fables, parables, and allegories.

---

22. Emanuel Swedenborg (1688–1772), Swedish mystic.

This relation between the mind and matter is not fancied by some poet, but stands in the will of God, and so is free to be known by all men. It appears to men, or it does not appear. When in fortunate hours we ponder this miracle, the wise man doubts, if, at all other times, he is not blind and deaf;

——"Can these things be,
    And overcome us like a summer's cloud,
    Without our special wonder?"[23]

for the universe becomes transparent, and the light of higher laws than its own, shines through it. It is the standing problem which has exercised the wonder and the study of every fine genius since the world began; from the era of the Egyptians and the Brahmins, to that of Pythagoras, of Plato, of Bacon, of Leibnitz, of Swedenborg.[24] There sits the Sphinx[25] at the road-side, and from age to age, as each prophet comes by, he tries his fortune at reading her riddle. There seems to be a necessity in spirit to manifest itself in material forms; and day and night, river and storm, beast and bird, acid and alkali, preëxist in necessary Ideas in the mind of God, and are what they are by virtue of preceding affections, in the world of spirit. A Fact is the end or last issue of spirit. The visible creation is the terminus or the circumference of the invisible world. "Material objects," said a French philosopher, "are necessarily kinds of *scoriæ* of the substantial thoughts of the Creator, which must always preserve an exact relation to their first origin; in other words, visible nature must have a spiritual and moral side."[26]

This doctrine is abstruse, and though the images of "garment," "scoriæ," "mirror," &c., may stimulate the fancy, we must summon the aid of subtler and more vital expositors to make it plain. "Every scripture is to be interpreted by the same spirit which gave it forth,"[27]—is the fundamental law of criticism. A life in harmony with nature, the love of truth and of virtue, will purge the eyes to understand her text. By degrees we may come to know the primitive sense of the permanent objects of nature, so that the world shall be to us an open book, and every form significant of its hidden life and final cause.

A new interest surprises us, whilst, under the view now suggested, we contemplate the fearful extent and multitude of objects; since "every object rightly seen, unlocks a new faculty of the soul."[28] That which was unconscious truth, becomes, when interpreted and defined in an object, a part of the domain of knowledge,—a new amount to the magazine of power.

Chapter V. Discipline

In view of this significance of nature, we arrive at once at a new fact, that nature is a discipline. This use of the world includes the preceding uses, as parts of itself.

Space, time, society, labor, climate, food, locomotion, the animals, the mechanical forces, give us sincerest lessons, day by day, whose meaning is unlimited. They educate both the Understanding and the Reason. Every property of matter is a school

---

23. William Shakespeare (1564–1616), *Macbeth* (1623), 3.4.110–112.   24. Brahmin: Hindu priest caste; Pythagoras (582–496 BC), Greek mathematician; Plato (427–347 BC), Greek philosopher; Francis Bacon (1561–1626), English scientist and philosopher; Gottfried Leibnitz (1646–1716), German scientist.   25. A legendary monster that guarded the Greek city of Thebes.   26. Guillaume Oegger (c. 1790–1853), "The True Messiah" (1829). *Scoriæ:* slag.   27. George Fox (1624–1691), English Quaker.   28. Samuel Taylor Coleridge (1772–1834), *Aids to Reflection* (1829).

for the understanding,—its solidity or resistance, its inertia, its extension, its figure, its divisibility. The understanding adds, divides, combines, measures, and finds everlasting nutriment and room for its activity in this worthy scene. Meantime, Reason transfers all these lessons into its own world of thought, by perceiving the analogy that marries Matter and Mind.

1. Nature is a discipline of the understanding in intellectual truths. Our dealing with sensible objects is a constant exercise in the necessary lessons of difference, of likeness, of order, of being and seeming, of progressive arrangement; of ascent from particular to general; of combination to one end of manifold forces. Proportioned to the importance of the organ to be formed, is the extreme care with which its tuition is provided,—a care pretermitted[29] in no single case. What tedious training, day after day, year after year, never ending, to form the common sense; what continual reproduction of annoyances, inconveniences, dilemmas; what rejoicing over us of little men; what disputing of prices, what reckonings of interest,—and all to form the Hand of the mind;—to instruct us that "good thoughts are no better than good dreams, unless they be executed!"[30]

The same good office is performed by Property and its filial systems of debt and credit. Debt, grinding debt, whose iron face the widow, the orphan, and the sons of genius fear and hate;—debt, which consumes so much time, which so cripples and disheartens a great spirit with cares that seem so base, is a preceptor whose lessons cannot be foregone, and is needed most by those who suffer from it most. Moreover, property, which has been well compared to snow,—"if it fall level to-day, it will be blown into drifts tomorrow,"—is merely the surface action of internal machinery, like the index on the face of a clock. Whilst now it is the gymnastics of the understanding, it is hiving in the foresight of the spirit, experience in profounder laws.

The whole character and fortune of the individual is affected by the least inequalities in the culture of the understanding; for example, in the perception of differences. Therefore is Space, and therefore Time, that man may know that things are not huddled and lumped, but sundered and individual. A bell and a plough have each their use, and neither can do the office of the other. Water is good to drink, coal to burn, wool to wear; but wool cannot be drunk, nor water spun, nor coal eaten. The wise man shows his wisdom in separation, in gradation, and his scale of creatures and of merits, is as wide as nature. The foolish have no range in their scale, but suppose every man is as every other man. What is not good they call the worst, and what is not hateful, they call the best.

In like manner, what good heed, nature forms in us! She pardons no mistakes. Her yea is yea, and her nay, nay.

The first steps in Agriculture, Astronomy, Zoölogy, (those first steps which the farmer, the hunter, and the sailor take,) teach that nature's dice are always loaded; that in her heaps and rubbish are concealed sure and useful results.

How calmly and genially the mind apprehends one after another the laws of physics! What noble emotions dilate the mortal as he enters into the counsels of the creation, and feels by knowledge the privilege to BE! His insight refines him. The beauty of nature shines in his own breast. Man is greater that he can see this, and the universe less, because Time and Space relations vanish as laws are known.

---

29. Ignored, neglected.   30. Paraphrased from Francis Bacon (1561–1626), "Of Great Place" (1597).

Here again we are impressed and even daunted by the immense Universe to be explored. 'What we know, is a point to what we do not know.' Open any recent journal of science, and weigh the problems suggested concerning Light, Heat, Electricity, Magnetism, Physiology, Geology, and judge whether the interest of natural science is likely to be soon exhausted.

Passing by many particulars of the discipline of nature we must not omit to specify two.

The exercise of the Will or the lesson of power is taught in every event. From the child's successive possession of his several senses up to the hour when he saith, "thy will be done!"[31] he is learning the secret, that he can reduce under his will, not only particular events, but great classes, nay the whole series of events, and so conform all facts to his character. Nature is thoroughly mediate. It is made to serve. It receives the dominion of man as meekly as the ass on which the Saviour rode.[32] It offers all its kingdoms to man as the raw material which he may mould into what is useful. Man is never weary of working it up. He forges the subtile and delicate air into wise and melodious words, and gives them wing as angels of persuasion and command. More and more, with every thought, does his kingdom stretch over things, until the world becomes, at last, only a realized will,—the double of the man.

2. Sensible objects conform to the premonitions of Reason and reflect the conscience. All things are moral; and in their boundless changes have an unceasing reference to spiritual nature. Therefore is nature glorious with form, color, and motion, that every globe in the remotest heaven; every chemical change from the rudest crystal up to the laws of life; every change of vegetation from the first principle of growth in the eye of a leaf, to the tropical forest and antediluvian coal-mine; every animal function from the sponge up to Hercules,[33] shall hint or thunder to man the laws of right and wrong, and echo the Ten Commandments. Therefore is nature always the ally of Religion: lends all her pomp and riches to the religious sentiment. Prophet and priest, David, Isaiah, Jesus, have drawn deeply from this source.

This ethical character so penetrates the bone and marrow of nature, as to seem the end for which it was made. Whatever private purpose is answered by any member or part, this is its public and universal function, and is never omitted. Nothing in nature is exhausted in its first use. When a thing has served an end to the uttermost, it is wholly new for an ulterior service. In God, every end is converted into a new means. Thus the use of Commodity, regarded by itself, is mean and squalid. But it is to the mind an education in the great doctrine of Use, namely, that a thing is good only so far as it serves; that a conspiring of parts and efforts to the production of an end, is essential to any being. The first and gross manifestation of this truth, is our inevitable and hated training in values and wants, in corn and meat.

It has already been illustrated, in treating of the significance of material things, that every natural process is but a version of a moral sentence. The moral law lies at the centre of nature and radiates to the circumference. It is the pith and marrow of every substance, every relation, and every process. All things with which we deal, preach to us. What is a farm but a mute gospel? The chaff and the wheat, weeds and plants, blight, rain, insects, sun,—it is a sacred emblem from the first furrow of spring to the last stack which the snow of winter overtakes in the fields. But the sailor, the shepherd, the

31. Matthew 6.10 and 26.42.   32. John 12.14.   33. Hero in Greek and Roman mythology. Antediluvian: before the Flood.

miner, the merchant, in their several resorts, have each an experience precisely parallel and leading to the same conclusions. Because all organizations are radically alike. Nor can it be doubted that this moral sentiment which thus scents the air, and grows in the grain, and impregnates the waters of the world, is caught by man and sinks into his soul. The moral influence of nature upon every individual is that amount of truth which it illustrates to him. Who can estimate this? Who can guess how much firmness the sea-beaten rock has taught the fisherman? how much tranquillity has been reflected to man from the azure sky, over whose unspotted deeps the winds forevermore drive flocks of stormy clouds, and leave no wrinkle or stain? how much industry and providence and affection we have caught from the pantomime of brutes? What a searching preacher of self-command is the varying phenomenon of Health!

Herein is especially apprehended the Unity of Nature,—the Unity in Variety,— which meets us everywhere. All the endless variety of things make a unique, an identical impression. Xenophanes[34] complained in his old age, that, look where he would, all things hastened back to Unity. He was weary of seeing the same entity in the tedious variety of forms. The fable of Proteus[35] has a cordial truth. Every particular in nature, a leaf, a drop, a crystal, a moment of time is related to the whole, and partakes of the perfection of the whole. Each particle is a microcosm, and faithfully renders the likeness of the world.

Not only resemblances exist in things whose analogy is obvious, as when we detect the type of the human hand in the flipper of the fossil saurus, but also in objects wherein there is great superficial unlikeness. Thus architecture is called 'frozen music,' by De Stael and Goethe. 'A Gothic church,' said Coleridge, 'is a petrified religion.' Michael Angelo maintained, that, to an architect, a knowledge of anatomy is essential. In Haydn's[36] oratorios, the notes present to the imagination not only motions, as, of the snake, the stag, and the elephant, but colors also; as the green grass. The granite is differenced in its laws only by the more or less of heat, from the river that wears it away. The river, as it flows, resembles the air that flows over it; the air resembles the light which traverses it with more subtile currents; the light resembles the heat which rides with it through Space. Each creature is only a modification of the other; the likeness in them is more than the difference, and their radical law is one and the same. Hence it is, that a rule of one art, or a law of one organization, holds true throughout nature. So intimate is this Unity, that, it is easily seen, it lies under the undermost garment of nature, and betrays its source in universal Spirit. For, it pervades Thought also. Every universal truth which we express in words, implies or supposes every other truth. *Omne verum vero consonat.*[37] It is like a great circle on a sphere, comprising all possible circles; which, however, may be drawn, and comprise it, in like manner. Every such truth is the absolute Ens[38] seen from one side. But it has innumerable sides.

The same central Unity is still more conspicuous in actions. Words are finite organs of the infinite mind. They cannot cover the dimensions of what is in truth. They break, chop, and impoverish it. An action is the perfection and publication of thought. A right action seems to fill the eye, and to be related to all nature. "The wise

---

34. Xenophanes of Colophon (570–480 BC), Greek philosopher.   35. Shape changer in Greek mythology.   36. Anne Louise Germaine de Stael (1766–1817), French author; Johann Wolfgang von Goethe (1749–1832), German author; Michelangelo (1475–1564), Italian painter; Franz Joseph Haydn (1732–1809), Austrian composer. Emerson uses single quotation marks to indicate paraphrases of other authors or common sayings, while he uses double quotes for word-for-word extracts.   37. Every truth agrees with every other.   38. Abstract being.

man, in doing one thing, does all; or, in the one thing he does rightly, he sees the likeness of all which is done rightly."

Words and actions are not the attributes of mute and brute nature. They introduce us to that singular form which predominates over all other forms. This is the human. All other organizations appear to be degradations of the human form. When this organization appears among so many that surround it, the spirit prefers it to all others. It says, 'From such as this, have I drawn joy and knowledge. In such as this, have I found and beheld myself. I will speak to it. It can speak again. It can yield me thought already formed and alive.' In fact, the eye,—the mind,—is always accompanied by these forms, male and female; and these are incomparably the richest informations of the power and order that lie at the heart of things. Unfortunately, every one of them bears the marks as of some injury; is marred and superficially defective. Nevertheless, far different from the deaf and dumb nature around them, these all rest like fountain-pipes on the unfathomed sea of thought and virtue whereto they alone, of all organizations, are the entrances.

It were a pleasant inquiry to follow into detail their ministry to our education, but where would it stop? We are associated in adolescent and adult life with some friends, who, like skies and waters, are coextensive with our idea; who, answering each to a certain affection of the soul, satisfy our desire on that side; whom we lack power to put at such focal distance from us, that we can mend or even analyze them. We cannot chuse but love them. When much intercourse with a friend has supplied us with a standard of excellence, and has increased our respect for the resources of God who thus sends a real person to outgo our ideal; when he has, moreover, become an object of thought, and, whilst his character retains all its unconscious effect, is converted in the mind into solid and sweet wisdom,—it is a sign to us that his office is closing, and he is commonly withdrawn from our sight in a short time.

Chapter VI. Idealism

Thus is the unspeakable but intelligible and practicable meaning of the world conveyed to man, the immortal pupil, in every object of sense. To this one end of Discipline, all parts of nature conspire.

A noble doubt perpetually suggests itself, whether this end be not the Final Cause of the Universe; and whether nature outwardly exists. It is a sufficient account of that Appearance we call the World, that God will teach a human mind, and so makes it the receiver of a certain number of congruent sensations, which we call sun and moon, man and woman, house and trade. In my utter impotence to test the authenticity of the report of my senses, to know whether the impressions they make on me correspond with outlying objects, what difference does it make, whether Orion[39] is up there in heaven, or some god paints the image in the firmament of the soul? The relations of parts and the end of the whole remaining the same, what is the difference, whether land and sea interact, and worlds revolve and intermingle without number or end,—deep yawning under deep,[40] and galaxy balancing galaxy, throughout absolute space, or, whether, without relations of time and space, the same appearances are inscribed in the constant faith of man. Whether nature enjoy a sub-

---

39. A constellation.   40. Psalm 42.7.

stantial existence without, or is only in the apocalypse of the mind, it is alike useful and alike venerable to me. Be it what it may, it is ideal to me, so long as I cannot try the accuracy of my senses.

The frivolous make themselves merry with the Ideal theory, as if its consequences were burlesque; as if it affected the stability of nature. It surely does not. God never jests with us, and will not compromise the end of nature, by permitting any inconsequence in its procession. Any distrust of the permanence of laws, would paralyze the faculties of man. Their permanence is sacredly respected, and his faith therein is perfect. The wheels and springs of man are all set to the hypothesis of the permanence of nature. We are not built like a ship to be tossed, but like a house to stand. It is a natural consequence of this structure, that, so long as the active powers predominate over the reflective, we resist with indignation any hint that nature is more short-lived or mutable than spirit. The broker, the wheelwright, the carpenter, the tollman, are much displeased at the intimation.

But whilst we acquiesce entirely in the permanence of natural laws, the question of the absolute existence of nature, still remains open. It is the uniform effect of culture on the human mind, not to shake our faith in the stability of particular phenomena, as of heat, water, azote[41]; but to lead us to regard nature as a phenomenon, not a substance; to attribute necessary existence to spirit; to esteem nature as an accident and an effect.

To the senses and the unrenewed understanding, belongs a sort of instinctive belief in the absolute existence of nature. In their view, man and nature are indissolubly joined. Things are ultimates, and they never look beyond their sphere. The presence of Reason mars this faith. The first effort of thought tends to relax this despotism of the senses, which binds us to nature as if we were a part of it, and shows us nature aloof, and, as it were, afloat. Until this higher agency intervened, the animal eye sees, with wonderful accuracy, sharp outlines and colored surfaces. When the eye of Reason opens, to outline and surface are at once added, grace and expression. These proceed from imagination and affection, and abate somewhat of the angular distinctness of objects. If the Reason be stimulated to more earnest vision, outlines and surfaces become transparent, and are no longer seen; causes and spirits are seen through them. The best, the happiest moments of life, are these delicious awakenings of the higher powers, and the reverential withdrawing of nature before its God.

Let us proceed to indicate the effects of culture.

1. Our first institution in the Ideal philosophy is a hint from nature herself. Nature is made to conspire with spirit to emancipate us. Certain mechanical changes, a small alteration in our local position apprizes us of a dualism. We are strangely affected by seeing the shore from a moving ship, from a balloon, or through the tints of an unusual sky. The least change in our point of view, gives the whole world a pictorial air. A man who seldom rides, needs only to get into a coach and traverse his own town, to turn the street into a puppet-show. The men, the women,—talking, running, bartering, fighting,—the earnest mechanic, the lounger, the beggar, the boys, the dogs, are unrealized at once, or, at least, wholly detached from all relation to the observer, and seen as apparent, not substantial beings. What new thoughts are suggested by seeing a face of country quite familiar, in the rapid movement of the rail-

---

41. Nitrogen.

road car! Nay, the most wonted objects, (make a very slight change in the point of vision,) please us most. In a camera obscura,[42] the butcher's cart, and the figure of one of our own family amuse us. So a portrait of a well-known face gratifies us. Turn the eyes upside down, by looking at the landscape through your legs, and how agreeable is the picture, though you have seen it any time these twenty years!

In these cases, by mechanical means, is suggested the difference between the observer and the spectacle,—between man and nature. Hence arises a pleasure mixed with awe; I may say, a low degree of the sublime is felt from the fact, proba-bly, that man is hereby apprized, that, whilst the world is a spectacle, something in himself is stable.

2. In a higher manner, the poet communicates the same pleasure. By a few strokes he delineates, as on air, the sun, the mountain, the camp, the city, the hero, the maiden, not different from what we know them, but only lifted from the ground and float before the eye. He unfixes the land and the sea, makes them revolve around the axis of his primary thought, and disposes them anew. Possessed himself by a heroic passion, he uses matter as symbols of it. The sensual man conforms thoughts to things; the poet conforms things to his thoughts. The one esteems nature as rooted and fast; the other, as fluid, and impresses his being thereon. To him, the refractory world is ductile and flexible; he invests dusts and stones with humanity and makes them the words of the Reason. The imagination may be defined to be, the use which the Reason makes of the material world. Shakespeare possesses the power of subordinating nature for the purposes of expression, beyond all poets. His imperial muse tosses the creation like a bauble from hand to hand, to embody any capricious shade of thought that is uppermost in his mind. The remotest spaces of nature are visited, and the farthest sundered things are brought together, by a subtile spiritual connexion. We are made aware that magnitude of material things is merely relative, and all objects shrink and expand to serve the passion of the poet. Thus, in his sonnets, the lays of birds, the scents and dyes of flowers, he finds to be the *shadow* of his beloved; time, which keeps her from him, is his *chest*; the suspicion she has awakened, is her *ornament*;

> The ornament of beauty is Suspect,
> A crow which flies in heaven's sweetest air.[43]

His passion is not the fruit of chance; it swells, as he speaks, to a city, or a state.

> No, it was builded far from accident;
> It suffers not in smiling pomp, nor falls
> Under the brow of thralling discontent;
> It fears not policy, that heretic,
> That works on leases of short numbered hours,
> But all alone stands hugely politic.[44]

In the strength of his constancy, the Pyramids seem to him recent and transitory. And the freshness of youth and love dazzles him with its resemblance to morning.

---

42. A box in which images are projected.   43. Sonnet 70.   44. Sonnet 124.

> Take those lips away
> Which so sweetly were forsworn;
> And those eyes,—the break of day,
> Lights that do mislead the morn.[45]

The wild beauty of this hyperbole, I may say, in passing, it would not be easy to match in literature.

This transfiguration which all material objects undergo through the passion of the poet,—this power which he exerts, at any moment, to magnify the small, to micrify the great,—might be illustrated by a thousand examples from his Plays. I have before me the Tempest, and will cite only these few lines.

> PROSPERO.   The strong based promontory
> Have I made shake, and by the spurs plucked up
> The pine and cedar.[46]

Prospero calls for music to sooth the frantic Alonzo, and his companions;

> A solemn air, and the best comforter
> To an unsettled fancy, cure thy brains
> Now useless, boiled within thy skull.[47]

Again;

> The charm dissolves space
> And, as the morning steals upon the night,
> Melting the darkness, so their rising senses
> Begin to chase the ignorant fumes that mantle
> Their clearer reason.
>
>   Their understanding
> Begins to swell: and the approaching tide
> Will shortly fill the reasonable shores
> That now lie foul and muddy.[48]

The perception of real affinities between events, (that is to say, of *ideal* affinities, for those only are real,) enables the poet thus to make free with the most imposing forms and phenomena of the world, and to assert the predominance of the soul.

3. Whilst thus the poet delights us by animating nature like a creator, with his own thoughts, he differs from the philosopher only herein, that the one proposes Beauty as his main end; the other Truth. But, the philosopher, not less than the poet, postpones the apparent order and relations of things to the empire of thought. "The problem of philosophy," according to Plato, "is, for all that exists conditionally, to find a ground unconditioned and absolute."[49] It proceeds on the faith that a law determines all phenomena, which being known, the phenomena can be predicted. That law, when in the mind, is an idea. Its beauty is infinite. The true philosopher and the true poet are one, and a beauty, which is truth, and a truth, which is beauty, is the aim of

---

45. *Measure for Measure* (1623), 4.1.1–4.   46. *The Tempest* (1623), 5.1.53–55. These lines belong in fact to Ariel.
47. 5.1.66–68.   48. 5.1.72–76, 87–90.   49. Samuel Taylor Coleridge (1772–1834), *The Friend* (1818).

both. Is not the charm of one of Plato's or Aristotle's definitions, strictly like that of the Antigone of Sophocles?[50] It is, in both cases, that a spiritual life has been imparted to nature; that the solid seeming block of matter has been pervaded and dissolved by a thought; that this feeble human being has penetrated the vast masses of nature with an informing soul, and recognised itself in their harmony, that is, seized their law. In physics, when this is attained, the memory disburthens itself of its cumbrous catalogues of particulars, and carries centuries of observation in a single formula.

Thus even in physics, the material is ever degraded before the spiritual. The astronomer, the geometer, rely on their irrefragable analysis, and disdain the results of observation. The sublime remark of Euler[51] on his law of arches, "This will be found contrary to all experience, yet it is true;" had already transferred nature into the mind, and left matter like an outcast corpse.

4. Intellectual science has been observed to beget invariably a doubt of the existence of matter. Turgot said, "He that has never doubted the existence of matter, may be assured he has no aptitude for metaphysical inquiries."[52] It fastens the attention upon immortal necessary uncreated natures, that is, upon Ideas; and in their beautiful and majestic presence, we feel that our outward being is a dream and a shade. Whilst we wait in this Olympus of gods, we think of nature as an appendix to the soul. We ascend into their region, and know that these are the thoughts of the Supreme Being. "These are they who were set up from everlasting, from the beginning, or ever the earth was. When he prepared the heavens, they were there; when he established the clouds above, when he strengthened the fountains of the deep. Then they were by him, as one brought up with him. Of them took he counsel."[53]

Their influence is proportionate. As objects of science, they are accessible to few men. Yet all men are capable of being raised by piety or by passion, into their region. And no man touches these divine natures, without becoming, in some degree, himself divine. Like a new soul, they renew the body. We become physically nimble and lightsome; we tread on air; life is no longer irksome, and we think it will never be so. No man fears age or misfortune or death, in their serene company, for he is transported out of the district of change. Whilst we behold unveiled the nature of Justice and Truth, we learn the difference between the absolute and the conditional or relative. We apprehend the absolute. As it were, for the first time, *we exist*. We become immortal, for we learn that time and space are relations of matter; that, with a perception of truth, or a virtuous will, they have no affinity.

5. Finally, religion and ethics, which may be fitly called,—the practice of ideas, or the introduction of ideas into life,—have an analogous effect with all lower culture, in degrading nature and suggesting its dependence on spirit. Ethics and religion differ herein; that the one is the system of human duties commencing from man; the other, from God. Religion includes the personality of God; Ethics does not. They are one to our present design. They both put nature under foot. The first and last lesson of religion is, "The things that are seen, are temporal; the things that are unseen are eternal."[54] It puts an affront upon nature. It does that for the unschooled, which philosophy does for Berkeley and Viasa.[55] The uniform language that may be heard in

---

50. Sophocles (d. 406 BC), *Antigone* (442 BC).   51. Leonhard Euler (1707–1783), Swiss mathematician.   52. Anne Robert Jacques Turgot (1727–1781), French economist.   53. Paraphrases Proverbs 8.23–30.   54. 2 Corinthians 4.18.   55. George Berkeley (1685–1753), Irish philosopher; Viasa: the legendary author of the Sanskrit scriptures, the Vedas.

the churches of the most ignorant sects, is,—'Contemn the unsubstantial shows of the world; they are vanities, dreams, shadows, unrealities; seek the realities of religion.' The devotee flouts nature. Some theosophists have arrived at a certain hostility and indignation towards matter, as the Manichean and Plotinus.[56] They distrusted in themselves any looking back to these flesh-pots of Egypt. Plotinus was ashamed of his body. In short, they might all better say of matter, what Michael Angelo said of external beauty, "it is the frail and weary weed, in which God dresses the soul, which he has called into time."[57]

It appears that motion, poetry, physical and intellectual science, and religion, all tend to affect our convictions of the reality of the external world. But I own there is something ungrateful in expanding too curiously the particulars of the general proposition, that all culture tends to imbue us with idealism. I have no hostility to nature, but a child's love to it. I expand and live in the warm day like corn and melons. Let us speak her fair. I do not wish to fling stones at my beautiful mother, nor soil my gentle nest. I only wish to indicate the true position of nature in regard to man, wherein to establish man, all right education tends; as the ground which to attain is the object of human life, that is, of man's connexion with nature. Culture inverts the vulgar views of nature, and brings the mind to call that apparent, which it uses to call real, and that real, which it uses to call visionary. Children, it is true, believe in the external world. The belief that it appears only, is an afterthought, but with culture, this faith will as surely arise on the mind as did the first.

The advantage of the ideal theory over the popular faith, is this, that it presents the world in precisely that view which is most desirable to the mind. It is, in fact, the view which Reason, both speculative and practical, that is, philosophy and virtue, take. For, seen in the light of thought, the world always is phenomenal[58]; and virtue subordinates it to the mind. Idealism sees the world in God. It beholds the whole circle of persons and things, of actions and events, of country and religion, not as painfully accumulated, atom after atom, act after act, in an aged creeping Past, but as one vast picture, which God paints on the instant eternity, for the contemplation of the soul. Therefore the soul holds itself off from a too trivial and microscopic study of the universal tablet. It respects the end too much, to immerse itself in the means. It sees something more important in Christianity, than the scandals of ecclesiastical history or the niceties of criticism; and, very incurious concerning persons or miracles, and not at all disturbed by chasms of historical evidence, it accepts from God the phenomenon, as it finds it, as the pure and awful form of religion in the world. It is not hot and passionate at the appearance of what it calls its own good or bad fortune, at the union or opposition of other persons. No man is its enemy. It accepts whatsoever befalls, as part of its lesson. It is a watcher more than a doer, and it is a doer, only that it may the better watch.

Chapter VII. Spirit

It is essential to a true theory of nature and of man, that it should contain somewhat progressive. Uses that are exhausted or that may be, and facts that end in the statement, cannot be all that is true of this brave lodging wherein man is harbored, and

---

56. Believers in direct intuitive communication with God. "The Manichean": Mani (c. 210–276), Persian prophet; Plotinus (c. 205–270), Greek philosopher.   57. Michelangelo (1475–1564), "Sonnet 51" (1623).   58. Mere appearance.

wherein all his faculties find appropriate and endless exercise. And all the uses of nature admit of being summed in one, which yields the activity of man an infinite scope. Through all its kingdoms, to the suburbs and outskirts of things, it is faithful to the cause whence it had its origin. It always speaks of Spirit. It suggests the absolute. It is a perpetual effect. It is a great shadow pointing always to the sun behind us.

The aspect of nature is devout. Like the figure of Jesus, she stands with bended head, and hands folded upon the breast. The happiest man is he who learns from nature the lesson of worship.

Of that ineffable essence which we call Spirit, he that thinks most, will say least. We can foresee God in the coarse and, as it were, distant phenomena of matter; but when we try to define and describe himself, both language and thought desert us, and we are as helpless as fools and savages. That essence refuses to be recorded in propositions, but when man has worshipped him intellectually, the noblest ministry of nature is to stand as the apparition of God. It is the great organ through which the universal spirit speaks to the individual, and strives to lead back the individual to it.

When we consider Spirit, we see that the views already presented do not include the whole circumference of man. We must add some related thoughts.

Three problems are put by nature to the mind: What is matter? Whence is it? and Whereto? The first of these questions only, the ideal theory answers. Idealism saith: matter is a phenomenon, not a substance. Idealism acquaints us with the total disparity between the evidence of our own being, and the evidence of the world's being. The one is perfect, the other, incapable of any assurance; the mind is a part of the nature of things; the world is a divine dream, from which we may presently awake to the glories and certainties of day. Idealism is a hypothesis to account for nature by other principles than those of carpentry and chemistry. Yet, if it only deny the existence of matter, it does not satisfy the demands of the spirit. It leaves God out of me. It leaves me in the splendid labyrinth of my perceptions, to wander without end. Then the heart resists it, because it baulks the affections in denying substantive being to men and women. Nature is so pervaded with human life, that there is something of humanity in all, and in every particular. But this theory makes nature foreign to me, and does not account for that consanguinity which we acknowledge to it.

Let it stand then, in the present state of our knowledge, merely as a useful introductory hypothesis, serving to apprize us of the eternal distinction between the soul and the world.

But when, following the invisible steps of thought, we come to inquire, Whence is matter? and Whereto? many truths arise to us out of the recesses of consciousness. We learn that the highest is present to the soul of man, that the dread universal essence, which is not wisdom, or love, or beauty, or power, but all in one, and each entirely, is that for which all things exist, and that by which they are; that spirit creates; that behind nature, throughout nature, spirit is present; that spirit is one and not compound; that spirit does not act upon us from without, that is, in space and time, but spiritually, or through ourselves. Therefore, that spirit, that is, the Supreme Being, does not build up nature around us, but puts it forth through us, as the life of the tree puts forth new branches and leaves through the pores of the old. As a plant upon the earth, so a man rests upon the bosom of God: he is nourished by unfailing fountains, and draws, at his need, inexhaustible power. Who can set bounds to the possibilities of man? Once inspire the infinite, by being admitted to behold the absolute natures of justice and truth, and we learn that man has access to the entire mind of the Creator, is himself the creator in the finite. This view, which admonishes me where the sources of wisdom and power lie, and points to virtue as to

> "The golden key
> Which opes the palace of eternity,"[59]

carries upon its face the highest certificate of truth, because it animates me to create my own world through the purification of my soul.

The world proceeds from the same spirit as the body of man. It is a remoter and inferior incarnation of God, a projection of God in the unconscious. But it differs from the body in one important respect. It is not, like that, now subjected to the human will. Its serene order is inviolable by us. It is therefore, to us, the present expositor of the divine mind. It is a fixed point whereby we may measure our departure. As we degenerate, the contrast between us and our house is more evident. We are as much strangers in nature, as we are aliens from God. We do not understand the notes of the birds. The fox and the deer run away from us; the bear and tiger rend us. We do not know the uses of more than a few plants, as corn and the apple, the potato and the vine. Is not the landscape, every glimpse of which hath a grandeur, a face of him? Yet this may show us what discord is between man and nature, for you cannot freely admire a noble landscape, if laborers are digging in the field hard by. The poet finds something ridiculous in his delight, until he is out of the sight of men.

Chapter VIII. Prospects

In inquiries respecting the laws of the world and the frame of things, the highest reason is always the truest. That which seems faintly possible—it is so refined, is often faint and dim because it is deepest seated in the mind among the eternal verities. Empirical science is apt to cloud the sight, and, by the very knowledge of functions and processes, to bereave the student of the manly contemplation of the whole. The savant[60] becomes unpoetic. But the best read naturalist who lends an entire and devout attention to truth, will see that there remains much to learn of his relation to the world, and that it is not to be learned by any addition or subtraction or other comparison of known quantities, but is arrived at by untaught sallies of the spirit, by a continual self-recovery, and by entire humility. He will perceive that there are far more excellent qualities in the student than preciseness and infallibility; that a guess is often more fruitful than an indisputable affirmation, and that a dream may let us deeper into the secret of nature than a hundred concerted experiments.

For, the problems to be solved are precisely those which the physiologist and the naturalist omit to state. It is not so pertinent to man to know all the individuals of the animal kingdom, as it is to know whence and whereto is this tyrannizing unity in his constitution, which evermore separates and classifies things, endeavouring to reduce the most diverse to one form. When I behold a rich landscape, it is less to my purpose to recite correctly the order and super-position of the strata, than to know why all thought of multitude is lost in a tranquil sense of unity. I cannot greatly honor minuteness in details, so long as there is no hint to explain the relation between

---

59. John Milton (1608–1674), *Comus* (1637), lines 13–14.   60. Learned person.

things and thoughts; no ray upon the *metaphysics* of conchology, of botany, of the arts, to show the relation of the forms of flowers, shells, animals, architecture, to the mind, and build science upon ideas. In a cabinet[61] of natural history, we become sensible of a certain occult recognition and sympathy in regard to the most bizarre forms of beast, fish, and insect. The American who has been confined, in his own country, to the sight of buildings designed after foreign models, is surprised on entering York Minster or St. Peter's at Rome, by the feeling that these structures are imitations also,—faint copies of an invisible archetype. Nor has science sufficient humanity, so long as the naturalist overlooks that wonderful congruity which subsists between man and the world; of which he is lord, not because he is the most subtile inhabitant, but because he is its head and heart, and finds something of himself in every great and small thing, in every mountain stratum, in every new law of color, fact of astronomy, or atmospheric influence which observation or analysis lay open. A perception of this mystery inspires the muse of George Herbert, the beautiful psalmist of the seventeenth century. The following lines are part of his little poem on Man.

> "Man is all symmetry,
> Full of proportions, one limb to another,
>   And to all the world besides.
> Each part may call the farthest, brother;
> For head with foot hath private amity,
>   And both with moons and tides.
>
> "Nothing hath got so far
> But man hath caught and kept it as his prey;
>   His eyes dismount the highest star;
>   He is in little all the sphere.
> Herbs gladly cure our flesh, because that they
>   Find their acquaintance there.
>
> "For us, the winds do blow.
> The earth doth rest, heaven move, and fountains flow;
>   Nothing we see, but means our good,
>   As our delight, or as our treasure;
> The whole is either our cupboard of food,
>   Or cabinet of pleasure.
>
> "The stars have us to bed;
> Night draws the curtain; which the sun withdraws.
>   Music and light attend our head.
>   All things unto our flesh are kind,
> In their descent and being; to our mind,
>   In their ascent and cause.
>
> "More servants wait on man
> Than he'll take notice of. In every path,
>   He treads down that which doth befriend him

---

61. Display case or museum.

> When sickness makes him pale and wan.
> Oh mighty love! Man is one world, and hath
> Another to attend him."[62]

The perception of this class of truths makes the eternal attraction which draws men to science, but the end is lost sight of in attention to the means. In view of this half-sight of science, we accept the sentence of Plato, that, "poetry comes nearer to vital truth than history."[63] Every surmise and vaticination[64] of the mind is entitled to a certain respect, and we learn to prefer imperfect theories, and sentences, which contain glimpses of truth, to digested systems which have no one valuable suggestion. A wise writer will feel that the ends of study and composition are best answered by announcing undiscovered regions of thought, and so communicating, through hope, new activity to the torpid spirit.

I shall therefore conclude this essay with some traditions of man and nature, which a certain poet[65] sang to me; and which, as they have always been in the world, and perhaps reappear to every bard, may be both history and prophecy.

'The foundations of man are not in matter, but in spirit. But the element of spirit is eternity. To it, therefore, the longest series of events, the oldest chronologies are young and recent. In the cycle of the universal man, from whom the known individuals proceed, centuries are points, and all history is but the epoch of one degradation.

'We distrust and deny inwardly our sympathy with nature. We own and disown our relation to it, by turns. We are, like Nebuchadnezzar, dethroned, bereft of reason, and eating grass like an ox.[66] But who can set limits to the remedial force of spirit?

'A man is a god in ruins. When men are innocent, life shall be longer, and shall pass into the immortal, as gently as we awake from dreams. Now, the world would be insane and rabid, if these disorganizations should last for hundreds of years. It is kept in check by death and infancy. Infancy is the perpetual Messiah, which comes into the arms of fallen men, and pleads with them to return to paradise.

'Man is the dwarf of himself. Once he was permeated and dissolved by spirit. He filled nature with his overflowing currents. Out from him sprang the sun and moon; from man, the sun; from woman, the moon. The laws of his mind, the periods of his actions externized themselves into day and night, into the year and the seasons. But, having made for himself this huge shell, his waters retired; he no longer fills the veins and veinlets; he is shrunk to a drop. He sees, that the structure still fits him, but fits him colossally. Say, rather, once it fitted him, now it corresponds to him from far and on high. He adores timidly his own work. Now is man the follower of the sun, and woman the follower of the moon. Yet sometimes he starts in his slumber, and wonders at himself and his house, and muses strangely at the resemblance betwixt him and it. He perceives that if his law is still paramount, if still he have elemental power, "if his word is sterling yet in nature," it is not conscious power, it is not inferior but superior to his will. It is Instinct.' Thus my Orphic poet sang.

At present, man applies to nature but half his force. He works on the world with his understanding alone. He lives in it, and masters it by a penny-wisdom; and he that works most in it, is but a half-man and whilst his arms are strong and his digestion good, his mind is imbruted and he is a selfish savage. His relation to nature, his power

---

62. George Herbert (1593–1633), "Man" (1633), stanzas 1–4, 6.   63. Aristotle (384–322 BC), *Poetics*.   64. Foretelling.
65. Emerson himself.   66. Daniel 4.31–33.

over it, is through the understanding; as by manure; the economic use of fire, wind, water, and the mariner's needle; steam, coal, chemical agriculture; the repairs of the human body by the dentist and the surgeon. This is such a resumption of power, as if a banished king should buy his territories inch by inch, instead of vaulting at once into his throne. Meantime, in the thick darkness, there are not wanting gleams of a better light,—occasional examples of the action of man upon nature with his entire force,— with reason as well as understanding. Such examples are; the traditions of miracles in the earliest antiquity of all nations; the history of Jesus Christ; the achievements of a principle, as in religious and political revolutions, and in the abolition of the Slave-trade; the miracles of enthusiasm,[67] as those reported of Swedenborg, Hohenlohe, and the Shakers[68]; many obscure and yet contested facts, now arranged under the name of Animal Magnetism; prayer; eloquence, self-healing; and the wisdom of children. These are examples of Reason's momentary grasp of the sceptre, the exertions of a power which exists not in time or space, but an instantaneous in-streaming causing power. The difference between the actual and the ideal force of man is happily figured by the schoolmen,[69] in saying, that the knowledge of man is an evening knowledge, *vespertina cognitio*, but that of God is a morning knowledge, *matutina cognitio*.

The problem of restoring to the world original and eternal beauty, is solved by the redemption of the soul. The ruin or the blank, that we see when we look at nature, is in our own eye. The axis of vision is not coincident with the axis of things, and so they appear not transparent but opake. The reason why the world lacks unity, and lies broken and in heaps, is, because man is disunited with himself. He cannot be a naturalist, until he satisfies all the demands of the spirit. Love is as much its demand, as perception. Indeed, neither can be perfect without the other. In the uttermost meaning of the words, thought is devout, and devotion is thought. Deep calls unto deep.[70] But in actual life, the marriage is not celebrated. There are innocent men who worship God after the tradition of their fathers, but their sense of duty has not yet extended to the use of all their faculties. And there are patient naturalists, but they freeze their subject under the wintry light of the understanding. Is not prayer also a study of truth,—a sally of the soul into the unfound infinite? No man ever prayed heartily, without learning something. But when a faithful thinker, resolute to detach every object from personal relations, and see it in the light of thought, shall, at the same time, kindle science with the fire of the holiest affections, then will God go forth anew into the creation.

It will not need, when the mind is prepared for study, to search for objects. The invariable mark of wisdom is to see the miraculous in the common. What is a day? What is a year? What is summer? What is woman? What is a child? What is sleep? To our blindness, these things seem unaffecting. We make fables to hide the baldness of the fact and conform it, as we say, to the higher law of the mind. But when the fact is seen under the light of an idea, the gaudy fable fades and shrivels. We behold the real higher law. To the wise, therefore, a fact is true poetry, and the most beautiful of fables. These wonders are brought to our own door. You also are a man. Man and woman, and their social life, poverty, labor, sleep, fear, fortune, are known to you. Learn that none of these things is superficial, but that each phenomenon hath its roots in the faculties and affections of the mind. Whilst the abstract question occu-

---

67. Possession by spirits.   68. Emanuel Swedenborg (1688–1772), Swedish mystic; Leopold Franz Hohenlohe (1794–1849), German bishop and healer; the Shakers were a radical religious sect.   69. Medieval philosophers.   70. Psalm 42.7.

pies your intellect, nature brings it in the concrete to be solved by your hands. It were a wise inquiry for the closet,[71] to compare, point by point, especially at remarkable crises in life, our daily history, with the rise and progress of ideas in the mind.

So shall we come to look at the world with new eyes. It shall answer the endless inquiry of the intellect,—What is truth? and of the affections,—What is good? by yielding itself passive to the educated Will. Then shall come to pass what my poet said; 'Nature is not fixed but fluid. Spirit alters, moulds, makes it. The immobility or bruteness of nature, is the absence of spirit; to pure spirit, it is fluid, it is volatile, it is obedient. Every spirit builds itself a house; and beyond its house, a world; and beyond its world, a heaven. Know then, that the world exists for you. For you is the phenomenon perfect. What we are, that only can we see. All that Adam had, all that Cæsar could, you have and can do. Adam called his house, heaven and earth; Cæsar called his house, Rome; you perhaps call yours, a cobler's trade; a hundred acres of ploughed land; or a scholar's garret. Yet line for line and point for point, your dominion is as great as theirs, though without fine names. Build, therefore your own world. As fast as you can conform your life to the pure idea in your mind, that will unfold its great proportions. A correspondent revolution in things will attend the influx of the spirit. So fast will disagreeable appearances, swine, spiders, snakes, pests, mad-houses, prisons, enemies, vanish; they are temporary and shall be no more seen. The sordor and filths of nature, the sun shall dry up, and the wind exhale. As when the summer comes from the south, the snow-banks melt, and the face of the earth becomes green before it, so shall the advancing spirit create its ornaments along its path, and carry with it the beauty it visits, and the song which enchants it; it shall draw beautiful faces, and warm hearts, and wise discourse, and heroic acts, around its way, until evil is no more seen. The kingdom of man over nature, which cometh not with observation,[72]—a dominion such as now is beyond his dream of God,—he shall enter without more wonder than the blind man feels who is gradually restored to perfect sight.'

—1836

The American Scholar

An Oration Delivered Before the Phi Beta Kappa Society, at Cambridge, August 31, 1837

Mr. President and Gentlemen,

I greet you on the re-commencement of our literary year. Our anniversary is one of hope, and, perhaps, not enough of labor. We do not meet for games of strength or skill, for the recitation of histories, tragedies, and odes, like the ancient Greeks; for parliaments of love and poesy, like the Troubadours[1]; nor for the advancement of science, like our cotemporaries in the British and European capitals. Thus far, our holiday has been simply a friendly sign of the survival of the love of letters amongst a people too busy to give to letters any more. As such, it is precious as the sign of an indestructible instinct. Perhaps the time is already come, when it ought to be, and will be, something else; when the sluggard intellect of this

---

71. A scholar's office.   72. Luke 17.20.

1. Court poets of medieval France.

continent will look from under its iron lids, and fill the postponed expectation of the world with something better than the exertions of mechanical skill. Our day of dependence, our long apprenticeship to the learning of other lands, draws to a close. The millions, that around us are rushing into life, cannot always be fed on the sere remains of foreign harvests. Events, actions arise, that must be sung, that will sing themselves. Who can doubt, that poetry will revive and lead in a new age, as the star in the constellation Harp, which now flames in our zenith, astronomers announce, shall one day be the pole-star for a thousand years?

In this hope, I accept the topic which not only usage, but the nature of our association, seem to prescribe to this day,—the AMERICAN SCHOLAR. Year by year, we come up hither to read one more chapter of his biography. Let us inquire what light new days and events have thrown on his character, and his hopes.

It is one of those fables, which, out of an unknown antiquity, convey an unlooked-for wisdom, that the gods, in the beginning, divided Man into men, that he might be more helpful to himself; just as the hand was divided into fingers, the better to answer its end.

The old fable covers a doctrine ever new and sublime; that there is One Man,— present to all particular men only partially, or through one faculty; and that you must take the whole society to find the whole man. Man is not a farmer, or a professor, or an engineer, but he is all. Man is priest, and scholar, and statesman, and producer, and soldier. In the *divided* or social state, these functions are parcelled out to individuals, each of whom aims to do his stint of the joint work, whilst each other performs his. The fable implies, that the individual, to possess himself, must sometimes return from his own labor to embrace all the other laborers. But unfortunately, this original unit, this fountain of power, has been so distributed to multitudes, has been so minutely subdivided and peddled out, that it is spilled into drops, and cannot be gathered. The state of society is one in which the members have suffered amputation from the trunk, and strut about so many walking monsters,—a good finger, a neck, a stomach, an elbow, but never a man.

Man is thus metamorphosed into a thing, into many things. The planter, who is Man sent out into the field to gather food, is seldom cheered by any idea of the true dignity of his ministry. He sees his bushel and his cart, and nothing beyond, and sinks into the farmer, instead of Man on the farm. The tradesman scarcely ever gives an ideal worth to his work, but is ridden by the routine of his craft, and the soul is subject to dollars. The priest becomes a form; the attorney, a statute-book; the mechanic, a machine; the sailor, a rope of a ship.

In this distribution of functions, the scholar is the delegated intellect. In the right state, he is, *Man Thinking*. In the degenerate state, when the victim of society, he tends to become a mere thinker, or, still worse, the parrot of other men's thinking.

In this view of him, as Man Thinking, the theory of his office is contained. Him nature solicits with all her placid, all her monitory pictures; him the past instructs; him the future invites. Is not, indeed, every man a student, and do not all things exist for the student's behoof? And, finally, is not the true scholar the only true master? But the old oracle[2] said, "All things have two handles: beware of the wrong one." In life, too often, the scholar errs with mankind and forfeits his privilege. Let us see him in his school, and consider him in reference to the main influences he receives.

---

2. Epictetus (c. 55–155), Greek philosopher.

I. The first in time and the first in importance of the influences upon the mind is that of nature. Every day, the sun; and, after sunset, night and her stars. Ever the winds blow; ever the grass grows. Every day, men and women, conversing, beholding and beholden. The scholar is he of all men whom this spectacle most engages. He must settle its value in his mind. What is nature to him? There is never a beginning, there is never an end, to the inexplicable continuity of this web of God, but always circular power returning into itself. Therein it resembles his own spirit, whose beginning, whose ending, he never can find,—so entire, so boundless. Far, too, as her splendors shine, system on system shooting like rays, upward, downward, without centre, without circumference,—in the mass and in the particle, nature hastens to render account of herself to the mind. Classification begins. To the young mind, every thing is individual, stands by itself. By and by, it finds how to join two things, and see in them one nature; then three, then three thousand; and so, tyrannized over by its own unifying instinct, it goes on tying things together, diminishing anomalies, discovering roots running under ground, whereby contrary and remote things cohere, and flower out from one stem. It presently learns, that, since the dawn of history, there has been a constant accumulation and classifying of facts. But what is classification but the perceiving that these objects are not chaotic, and are not foreign, but have a law which is also a law of the human mind? The astronomer discovers that geometry, a pure abstraction of the human mind, is the measure of planetary motion. The chemist finds proportions and intelligible method throughout matter; and science is nothing but the finding of analogy, identity, in the most remote parts. The ambitious soul sits down before each refractory fact; one after another, reduces all strange constitutions, all new powers, to their class and their law, and goes on for ever to animate the last fibre of organization, the outskirts of nature, by insight.

Thus to him, to this school-boy under the bending dome of day, is suggested, that he and it proceed from one root; one is leaf and one is flower; relation, sympathy, stirring in every vein. And what is that Root? Is not that the soul of his soul?—A thought too bold,—a dream too wild. Yet when this spiritual light shall have revealed the law of more earthly natures,—when he has learned to worship the soul, and to see that the natural philosophy that now is, is only the first gropings of its gigantic hand, he shall look forward to an ever expanding knowledge as to a becoming creator. He shall see, that nature is the opposite of the soul, answering to it part for part. One is seal, and one is print. Its beauty is the beauty of his own mind. Its laws are the laws of his own mind. Nature then becomes to him the measure of his attainments. So much of nature as he is ignorant of, so much of his own mind does he not yet possess. And, in fine, the ancient precept, "Know thyself," and the modern precept, "Study nature," become at last one maxim.

II. The next great influence into the spirit of the scholar, is, the mind of the Past,—in whatever form, whether of literature, of art, of institutions, that mind is inscribed. Books are the best type of the influence of the past, and perhaps we shall get at the truth,—learn the amount of this influence more conveniently,—by considering their value alone.

The theory of books is noble. The scholar of the first age received into him the world around; brooded thereon; gave it the new arrangement of his own mind, and uttered it again. It came into him, life; it went out from him, truth. It came to him, short-lived actions; it went out from him, immortal thoughts. It came to him, business; it went from him, poetry. It was dead fact; now, it is quick thought. It can stand, and it can go. It now endures, it now flies, it now inspires. Precisely in proportion to the depth of mind from which it issued, so high does it soar, so long does it sing.

Or, I might say, it depends on how far the process had gone, of transmuting life into truth. In proportion to the completeness of the distillation, so will the purity and imperishableness of the product be. But none is quite perfect. As no air-pump can by any means make a perfect vacuum, so neither can any artist entirely exclude the conventional, the local, the perishable from his book, or write a book of pure thought, that shall be as efficient, in all respects, to a remote posterity, as to cotemporaries, or rather to the second age. Each age, it is found, must write its own books; or rather, each generation for the next succeeding. The books of an older period will not fit this.

Yet hence arises a grave mischief. The sacredness which attaches to the act of creation,—the act of thought,—is transferred to the record. The poet chanting, was felt to be a divine man: henceforth the chant is divine also. The writer was a just and wise spirit: henceforward it is settled, the book is perfect; as love of the hero corrupts into worship of his statue. Instantly, the book becomes noxious: the guide is a tyrant. The sluggish and perverted mind of the multitude, slow to open to the incursions of Reason, having once so opened, having once received this book, stands upon it, and makes an outcry, if it is disparaged. Colleges are built on it. Books are written on it by thinkers, not by Man Thinking; by men of talent, that is, who start wrong, who set out from accepted dogmas, not from their own sight of principles. Meek young men grow up in libraries, believing it their duty to accept the views, which Cicero, which Locke, which Bacon,[3] have given, forgetful that Cicero, Locke, and Bacon were only young men in libraries, when they wrote these books.

Hence, instead of Man Thinking, we have the bookworm. Hence, the book-learned class, who value books, as such; not as related to nature and the human constitution, but as making a sort of Third Estate[4] with the world and the soul. Hence, the restorers of readings, the emendators, the bibliomaniacs of all degrees.

Books are the best of things, well used; abused, among the worst. What is the right use? What is the one end, which all means go to effect? They are for nothing but to inspire. I had better never see a book, than to be warped by its attraction clean out of my own orbit, and made a satellite instead of a system. The one thing in the world, of value, is the active soul. This every man is entitled to; this every man contains within him, although, in almost all men, obstructed, and as yet unborn. The soul active sees absolute truth; and utters truth, or creates. In this action, it is genius; not the privilege of here and there a favorite, but the sound estate of every man. In its essence, it is progressive. The book, the college, the school of art, the institution of any kind, stop with some past utterance of genius. This is good, say they,—let us hold by this. They pin me down. They look backward and not forward. But genius looks forward: the eyes of man are set in his forehead, not in his hindhead: man hopes: genius creates. Whatever talents may be, if the man create not, the pure efflux[5] of the Diety is not his;—cinders and smoke there may be, but not yet flame. There are creative manners, there are creative actions, and creative words; manners,

---

3. Marcus Tullius Cicero (106–43 BC), Roman orator; John Locke (1632–1704), English philosopher; Francis Bacon (1561–1626), English essayist.   4. French term for commoners, as opposed to the clergy and nobility.   5. Flowing forth.

actions, words, that is, indicative of no custom or authority, but springing spontaneous from the mind's own sense of good and fair.

On the other part, instead of being its own seer, let it receive from another mind
its truth, though it were in torrents of light, without periods of solitude, inquest, and
self-recovery, and a fatal disservice is done. Genius is always sufficiently the enemy of
genius by over influence. The literature of every nation bear me witness. The English
dramatic poets have Shakspearized now for two hundred years.

Undoubtedly there is a right way of reading, so it be sternly subordinated. Man
Thinking must not be subdued by his instruments. Books are for the scholar's idle
times. When he can read God directly, the hour is too precious to be wasted in other
men's transcripts of their readings. But when the intervals of darkness come, as come
they must,—when the sun is hid, and the stars withdraw their shining,—we repair to
the lamps which were kindled by their ray, to guide our steps to the East again, where
the dawn is. We hear, that we may speak. The Arabian proverb says, "A fig tree, looking on a fig tree, becometh fruitful."

It is remarkable, the character of the pleasure we derive from the best books. They
impress us with the conviction, that one nature wrote and the same reads. We read the
verses of one of the great English poets, of Chaucer, of Marvell, of Dryden, with the
most modern joy,—with a pleasure, I mean, which is in great part caused by the abstraction of all *time* from their verses. There is some awe mixed with the joy of our surprise,
when this poet, who lived in some past world, two or three hundred years ago, says that
which lies close to my own soul, that which I also had wellnigh thought and said. But
for the evidence thence afforded to the philosophical doctrine of the identity of all
minds, we should suppose some preëstablished harmony, some foresight of souls that
were to be, and some preparation of stores for their future wants, like the fact observed
in insects, who lay up food before death for the young grub they shall never see.

I would not be hurried by any love of system, by any exaggeration of instincts, to
underrate the Book. We all know, that, as the human body can be nourished on any food,
though it were boiled grass and the broth of shoes, so the human mind can be fed by any
knowledge. And great and heroic men have existed, who had almost no other information than by the printed page. I only would say, that it needs a strong head to bear that
diet. One must be an inventor to read well. As the proverb says, "He that would bring
home the wealth of the Indies, must carry out the wealth of the Indies." There is then creative reading as well as creative writing. When the mind is braced by labor and invention,
the page of whatever book we read becomes luminous with manifold allusion. Every sentence is doubly significant, and the sense of our author is as broad as the world. We then
see, what is always true, that, as the seer's hour of vision is short and rare among heavy
days and months, so is its record, perchance, the least part of his volume. The discerning
will read, in his Plato or Shakspeare, only that least part,—only the authentic utterances
of the oracle;—all the rest he rejects, were it never so many times Plato's and Shakspeare's.

Of course, there is a portion of reading quite indispensable to a wise man. History
and exact science he must learn by laborious reading. Colleges, in like manner, have
their indispensable office,—to teach elements. But they can only highly serve us, when
they aim not to drill, but to create; when they gather from far every ray of various genius
to their hospitable halls, and, by the concentrated fires, set the hearts of their youth on
flame. Thought and knowledge are natures in which apparatus and pretension avail
nothing. Gowns, and pecuniary foundations, though of towns of gold, can never coun-

tervail the least sentence or syllable of wit. Forget this, and our American colleges will recede in their public importance, whilst they grow richer every year.

III. There goes in the world a notion, that the scholar should be a recluse, a valetudinarian,—as unfit for any handiwork or public labor, as a penknife for an axe. The so-called 'practical men' sneer at speculative men, as if, because they speculate or *see*, they could do nothing. I have heard it said that the clergy,—who are always, more universally than any other class, the scholars of their day,—are addressed as women; that the rough, spontaneous conversation of men they do not hear, but only a mincing and diluted speech. They are often virtually disfranchised; and, indeed, there are advocates for their celibacy. As far as this is true of the studious classes, it is not just and wise. Action is with the scholar subordinate, but it is essential. Without it, he is not yet man. Without it, thought can never ripen into truth. Whilst the world hangs before the eye as a cloud of beauty, we cannot even see its beauty. Inaction is cowardice, but there can be no scholar without the heroic mind. The preamble of thought, the transition through which it passes from the unconscious to the conscious, is action. Only so much do I know, as I have lived. Instantly we know whose words are loaded with life, and whose not.

The world,—this shadow of the soul, or *other me*, lies wide around. Its attractions are the keys which unlock my thoughts and make me acquainted with myself. I run eagerly into this resounding tumult. I grasp the hands of those next me, and take my place in the ring to suffer and to work, taught by an instinct, that so shall the dumb abyss be vocal with speech. I pierce its order; I dissipate its fear; I dispose of it within the circuit of my expanding life. So much only of life as I know by experience, so much of the wilderness have I vanquished and planted, or so far have I extended my being, my dominion. I do not see how any man can afford, for the sake of his nerves and his nap, to spare any action in which he can partake. It is pearls and rubies to his discourse. Drudgery, calamity, exasperation, want, are instructors in eloquence and wisdom. The true scholar grudges every opportunity of action past by, as a loss of power.

It is the raw material out of which the intellect moulds her splendid products. A strange process too, this, by which experience is converted into thought, as a mulberry leaf is converted into satin. The manufacture goes forward at all hours.

The actions and events of our childhood and youth, are now matters of calmest observation. They lie like fair pictures in the air. Not so with our recent actions,—with the business which we now have in hand. On this we are quite unable to speculate. Our affections as yet circulate through it. We no more feel or know it, than we feel the feet, or the hand, or the brain of our body. The new deed is yet a part of life,—remains for a time immersed in our unconscious life. In some contemplative hour, it detaches itself from the life like a ripe fruit, to become a thought of the mind. Instantly, it is raised, transfigured; the corruptible has put on incorruption.[6] Henceforth it is an object of beauty, however base its origin and neighborhood. Observe, too, the impossibility of antedating this act. In its grub state, it cannot fly, it cannot shine, it is a dull grub. But suddenly, without observation, the selfsame thing unfurls beautiful wings, and is an angel of wisdom. So is there no fact, no event, in our private history, which shall not, sooner or later, lose its adhesive, inert form, and astonish us by soaring from our body into the empyrean. Cradle and infancy, school and playground, the fear of boys, and dogs, and ferules, the love of little maids and berries, and many another fact

---

6. 1 Corinthians 15.53.

that once filled the whole sky, are gone already; friend and relative, profession and party, town and country, nation and world, must also soar and sing.

Of course, he who has put forth his total strength in fit actions, has the richest return of wisdom. I will not shut myself out of this globe of action, and transplant an oak into a flower-pot, there to hunger and pine; nor trust the revenue of some single faculty, and exhaust one vein of thought, much like those Savoyards,[7] who, getting their livelihood by carving shepherds, shepherdesses, and smoking Dutchmen, for all Europe, went out one day to the mountain to find stock, and discovered that they had whittled up the last of their pine-trees. Authors we have, in numbers, who have written out their vein, and who, moved by a commendable prudence, sail for Greece or Palestine, follow the trapper into the prairie, or ramble round Algiers, to replenish their merchantable stock.

If it were only for a vocabulary, the scholar would be covetous of action. Life is our dictionary. Years are well spent in country labors; in town,—in the insight into trades and manufactures; in frank intercourse with many men and women; in science; in art; to the one end of mastering in all their facts a language by which to illustrate and embody our perceptions. I learn immediately from any speaker how much he has already lived, through the poverty or the splendor of his speech. Life lies behind us as the quarry from whence we get tiles and copestones for the masonry of to-day. This is the way to learn grammar. Colleges and books only copy the language which the field and the work-yard made.

But the final value of action, like that of books, and better than books, is, that it is a resource. That great principle of Undulation in nature, that shows itself in the inspiring and expiring of the breath; in desire and satiety; in the ebb and flow of the sea; in day and night; in heat and cold; and as yet more deeply ingrained in every atom and every fluid, is known to us under the name of Polarity,—these "fits of easy transmission and reflection," as Newton[8] called them, are the law of nature because they are the law of spirit.

The mind now thinks; now acts; and each fit reproduces the other. When the artist has exhausted his materials, when the fancy no longer paints, when thoughts are no longer apprehended, and books are a weariness,—he has always the resource to live. Character is higher than intellect. Thinking is the function. Living is the functionary. The stream retreats to its source. A great soul will be strong to live, as well as strong to think. Does he lack organ or medium to impart his truths? He can still fall back on this elemental force of living them. This is a total act. Thinking is a partial act. Let the grandeur of justice shine in his affairs. Let the beauty of affection cheer his lowly roof. Those 'far from fame,' who dwell and act with him, will feel the force of his constitution in the doings and passages of the day better than it can be measured by any public and designed display. Time shall teach him, that the scholar loses no hour which the man lives. Herein he unfolds the sacred germ of his instinct, screened from influence. What is lost in seemliness is gained in strength. Not out of those, on whom systems of education have exhausted their culture, comes the helpful giant to destroy the old or to build the new, but out of unhandselled[9] savage nature, out of terrible Druids and Berserkirs,[10] come at last Alfred[11] and Shakspeare.

---

7. Savoy is a region in the Alps.   8. Isaac Newton (1642–1727), *Optics* (1704).   9. Emerson's coinage for unpromising.   10. Celtic priests and Norse warriors.   11. Alfred the Great (c. 849–899), Anglo-Saxon king.

I hear therefore with joy whatever is beginning to be said of the dignity and necessity of labor to every citizen. There is virtue yet in the hoe and the spade, for learned as well as for unlearned hands. And labor is everywhere welcome; always we are invited to work; only be this limitation observed, that a man shall not for the sake of wider activity sacrifice any opinion to the popular judgments and modes of action.

I have now spoken of the education of the scholar by nature, by books, and by action. It remains to say somewhat of his duties.

They are such as become Man Thinking. They may all be comprised in self-trust. The office of the scholar is to cheer, to raise, and to guide men by showing them facts amidst appearances. He plies the slow, unhonored, and unpaid task of observation. Flamsteed and Herschel,[12] in their glazed observatories, may catalogue the stars with the praise of all men, and, the results being splendid and useful, honor is sure. But he, in his private observatory, cataloguing obscure and nebulous stars of the human mind, which as yet no man has thought of as such,—watching days and months, sometimes, for a few facts; correcting still his old records;—must relinquish display and immediate fame. In the long period of his preparation, he must betray often an ignorance and shiftlessness in popular arts, incurring the disdain of the able who shoulder him aside. Long he must stammer in his speech; often forego the living for the dead. Worse yet, he must accept,—how often! poverty and solitude. For the ease and pleasure of treading the old road, accepting the fashions, the education, the religion of society, he takes the cross of making his own, and, of course, the self-accusation, the faint heart, the frequent uncertainty and loss of time, which are the nettles and tangling vines in the way of the self-relying and self-directed; and the state of virtual hostility in which he seems to stand to society, and especially to educated society. For all this loss and scorn, what offset? He is to find consolation in exercising the highest functions of human nature. He is one, who raises himself from private considerations, and breathes and lives on public and illustrious thoughts. He is the world's eye. He is the world's heart. He is to resist the vulgar prosperity that retrogrades ever to barbarism, by preserving and communicating heroic sentiments, noble biographies, melodious verse, and the conclusions of history. Whatsoever oracles the human heart, in all emergencies, in all solemn hours, has uttered as its commentary on the world of actions,—these he shall receive and impart. And whatsoever new verdict Reason from her inviolable seat pronounces on the passing men and events of to-day,—this he shall hear and promulgate.

These being his functions, it becomes him to feel all confidence in himself, and to defer never to the popular cry. He and he only knows the world. The world of any moment is the merest appearance. Some great decorum, some fetish of a government, some ephemeral trade, or war, or man, is cried up by half mankind and cried down by the other half, as if all depended on this particular up or down. The odds are that the whole question is not worth the poorest thought which the scholar has lost in listening to the controversy. Let him not quit his belief that a popgun is a popgun, though the ancient and honorable of the earth affirm it to be the crack of doom. In silence, in steadiness, in severe abstraction, let him hold by himself; add observation to observation, patient of neglect, patient of reproach; and bide his own time,—happy enough, if he can satisfy himself alone, that this day he has seen something truly.

---

12. John Flamsteed (1646–1719) and William Herschel (1738–1822), English astronomers.

Success treads on every right step. For the instinct is sure, that prompts him to tell his brother what he thinks. He then learns, that in going down into the secrets of his own mind, he has descended into the secrets of all minds. He learns that he who has mastered any law in his private thoughts, is master to that extent of all men whose language he speaks, and of all into whose language his own can be translated. The poet, in utter solitude remembering his spontaneous thoughts and recording them, is found to have recorded that, which men in crowded cities find true for them also. The orator distrusts at first the fitness of his frank confessions,—his want of knowledge of the persons he addresses,—until he finds that he is the complement of his hearers;—that they drink his words because he fulfills for them their own nature; the deeper he dives into his privatest, secretest presentiment, to his wonder he finds, this is the most acceptable, most public, and universally true. The people delight in it; the better part of every man feels, This is my music; this is myself.

In self-trust, all the virtues are comprehended. Free should the scholar be,—free and brave. Free even to the definition of freedom, "without any hindrance that does not arise out of his own constitution." Brave; for fear is a thing, which a scholar by his very function puts behind him. Fear always springs from ignorance. It is a shame to him if his tranquility, amid dangerous times, arise from the presumption, that, like children and women, his is a protected class; or if he seek a temporary peace by the diversion of his thoughts from politics or vexed questions, hiding his head like an ostrich in the flowering bushes, peeping into microscopes, and turning rhymes, as a boy whistles to keep his courage up. So is the danger a danger still; so is the fear worse. Manlike let him turn and face it. Let him look into its eye and search its nature, inspect its origin,—see the whelping of this lion,—which lies no great way back; he will then find in himself a perfect comprehension of its nature and extent; he will have made his hands meet on the other side, and can henceforth defy it, and pass on superior. The world is his, who can see through its pretension. What deafness, what stone-blind custom, what overgrown error you behold, is there only by sufferance,— by your sufferance. See it to be a lie, and you have already dealt it its mortal blow.

Yes, we are the cowed,—we the trustless. It is a mischievous notion that we are come late into nature; that the world was finished a long time ago. As the world was plastic and fluid in the hands of God, so it is ever to so much of his attributes as we bring to it. To ignorance and sin, it is flint. They adapt themselves to it as they may; but in proportion as a man has any thing in him divine, the firmament flows before him and takes his signet[13] and form. Not he is great who can alter matter, but he who can alter my state of mind. They are the kings of the world who give the color of their present thought to all nature and all art, and persuade men by the cheerful serenity of their carrying the matter, that this thing which they do, is the apple which the ages have desired to pluck, now at last ripe, and inviting nations to the harvest. The great man makes the great thing. Wherever Macdonald sits, there is the head of the table. Linnæus makes botany the most alluring of studies, and wins it from the farmer and the herb-woman; Davy, chemistry; and Cuvier, fossils.[14] The day is always his, who works in it with serenity and great aims. The unstable estimates of men crowd to him whose mind is filled with a truth, as the heaped waves of the Atlantic follow the moon.

---

13. Seal.   14. Macdonald: type-name for a Scottish clan chief; Carl von Linné (1707–1778), Swedish botanist; Humphrey Davy (1778–1829), English chemist; George Cuvier (1769–1832), French naturalist.

For this self-trust, the reason is deeper than can be fathomed,—darker than can be enlightened. I might not carry with me the feeling of my audience in stating my own belief. But I have already shown the ground of my hope, in adverting to the doctrine that man is one. I believe man has been wronged; he has wronged himself. He has almost lost the light, that can lead him back to his prerogatives. Men are become of no account. Men in history, men in the world of to-day are bugs, are spawn, and are called "the mass" and "the herd." In a century, in a millennium, one or two men; that is to say,—one or two approximations to the right state of every man. All the rest behold in the hero or the poet their own green and crude being,—ripened; yes, and are content to be less, so *that* may attain to its full stature. What a testimony,—full of grandeur, full of pity, is borne to the demands of his own nature, by the poor clansman, the poor partisan, who rejoices in the glory of his chief. The poor and the low find some amends to their immense moral capacity, for their acquiescence in a political and social inferiority. They are content to be brushed like flies from the path of a great person, so that justice shall be done by him to that common nature which it is the dearest desire of all to see enlarged and glorified. They sun themselves in the great man's light, and feel it to be their own element. They cast the dignity of man from their downtrod selves upon the shoulders of a hero, and will perish to add one drop of blood to make that great heart beat, those giant sinews combat and conquer. He lives for us, and we live in him.

Men such as they are, very naturally seek money or power; and power because it is as good as money,—the "spoils," so called, "of office." And why not? for they aspire to the highest, and this, in their sleep-walking, they dream is highest. Wake them, and they shall quit the false good, and leap to the true, and leave governments to clerks and desks. This revolution is to be wrought by the gradual domestication of the idea of Culture. The main enterprise of the world for splendor, for extent, is the upbuilding of a man. Here are the materials strown along the ground. The private life of one man shall be a more illustrious monarchy,—more formidable to its enemy, more sweet and serene in its influence to its friend, than any kingdom in history. For a man, rightly viewed, comprehendeth the particular natures of all men. Each philosopher, each bard, each actor, has only done for me, as by a delegate, what one day I can do for myself. The books which once we valued more than the apple of the eye, we have quite exhausted. What is that but saying, that we have come up with the point of view which the universal mind took through the eyes of one scribe; we have been that man, and have passed on. First, one; then, another; we drain all cisterns, and, waxing greater by all these supplies, we crave a better and more abundant food. The man has never lived that can feed us ever. The human mind cannot be enshrined in a person, who shall set a barrier on any one side to this unbounded, unboundable empire. It is one central fire, which, flaming now out of the lips of Etna, lightens the capes of Sicily; and, now out of the throat of Vesuvius, illuminates the towers and vineyards of Naples.[15] It is one light which beams out of a thousand stars. It is one soul which animates all men.

But I have dwelt perhaps tediously upon this abstraction of the Scholar. I ought not to delay longer to add what I have to say, of nearer reference to the time and to this country.

---

15. Vesuvius and Etna are active volcanoes in Italy.

Historically, there is thought to be a difference in the ideas which predominate over successive epochs, and there are data for marking the genius of the Classic, of the Romantic, and now of the Reflective or Philosophical age. With the views I have intimated of the oneness or the identity of the mind through all individuals, I do not much dwell on these differences. In fact, I believe each individual passes through all three. The boy is a Greek; the youth, romantic; the adult, reflective. I deny not, however, that a revolution in the leading idea may be distinctly enough traced.

Our age is bewailed as the age of Introversion. Must that needs be evil? We, it seems, are critical; we are embarrassed with second thoughts; we cannot enjoy any thing for hankering to know whereof the pleasure consists; we are lined with eyes; we see with our feet; the time is infected with Hamlet's unhappiness,—

"Sicklied o'er with the pale cast of thought."[16]

Is it so bad then? Sight is the last thing to be pitied. Would we be blind? Do we fear lest we should outsee nature and God, and drink truth dry? I look upon the discontent of the literary class, as a mere announcement of the fact, that they find themselves not in the state of mind of their fathers, and regret the coming state as untried; as a boy dreads the water before he has learned that he can swim. If there is any period one would desire to be born in,—is it not the age of Revolution; when the old and the new stand side by side, and admit of being compared; when the energies of all men are searched by fear and by hope; when the historic glories of the old, can be compensated by the rich possibilities of the new era? This time, like all times, is a very good one, if we but know what to do with it.

I read with joy some of the auspicious signs of the coming days, as they glimmer already through poetry and art, through philosophy and science, through church and state.

One of these signs is the fact, that the same movement which effected the elevation of what was called the lowest class in the state, assumed in literature a very marked and as benign an aspect. Instead of the sublime and beautiful; the near, the low, the common, was explored and poetized. That, which had been negligently trodden under foot by those who were harnessing and provisioning themselves for long journeys into far countries, is suddenly found to be richer than all foreign parts. The literature of the poor, the feelings of the child, the philosophy of the street, the meaning of household life, are the topics of the time. It is a great stride. It is a sign,—is it not? of new vigor, when the extremities are made active, when currents of warm life run into the hands and the feet. I ask not for the great, the remote, the romantic; what is doing in Italy or Arabia; what is Greek art, or Provençal minstrelsy; I embrace the common, I explore and sit at the feet of the familiar, the low. Give me insight into to-day, and you may have the antique and future worlds. What would we really know the meaning of? The meal in the firkin[17]; the milk in the pan; the ballad in the street; the news of the boat; the glance of the eye; the form and the gait of the body;—show me the ultimate reason of these matters; show me the sublime presence of the highest spiritual cause lurking, as always it does lurk, in these suburbs and extremities of nature; let me see every trifle bristling with the polarity that ranges it instantly on an eternal law; and the shop, the plough, and the leger,[18] referred to the like cause by which light

---

16. William Shakespeare (1564–1616), *Hamlet* (1603), 3.1.85.   17. Bowl.   18. Ledger.

undulates and poets sing;—and the world lies no longer a dull miscellany and lumber-room, but has form and order; there is no trifle; there is no puzzle; but one design unites and animates the farthest pinnacle and the lowest trench.

This idea has inspired the genius of Goldsmith, Burns, Cowper, and, in a newer time, of Goethe, Wordsworth, and Carlyle. This idea they have differently followed and with various success. In contrast with their writing, the style of Pope, of Johnson, of Gibbon, looks cold and pedantic.[19] This writing is blood-warm. Man is surprised to find that things near are not less beautiful and wondrous than things remote. The near explains the far. The drop is a small ocean. A man is related to all nature. This perception of the worth of the vulgar is fruitful in discoveries. Goethe,[20] in this very thing the most modern of the moderns, has shown us, as none ever did, the genius of the ancients.

There is one man of genius, who has done much for this philosophy of life, whose literary value has never yet been rightly estimated;—I mean Emanuel Swedenborg.[21] The most imaginative of men, yet writing with the precision of a mathematician, he endeavored to engraft a purely philosophical Ethics on the popular Christianity of his time. Such an attempt, of course, must have difficulty, which no genius could surmount. But he saw and showed the connection between nature and the affections of the soul. He pierced the emblematic or spiritual character of the visible, audible, tangible world. Especially did his shade-loving muse hover over and interpret the lower parts of nature; he showed the mysterious bond that allies moral evil to the foul material forms, and has given in epical parables a theory of insanity, of beasts, of unclean and fearful things.

Another sign of our times, also marked by an analogous political movement, is, the new importance given to the single person. Every thing that tends to insulate the individual,—to surround him with barriers of natural respect, so that each man shall feel the world is his, and man shall treat with man as a sovereign state with a sovereign state;—tends to true union as well as greatness. "I learned," said the melancholy Pestalozzi,[22] "that no man in God's wide earth is either willing or able to help any other man." Help must come from the bosom alone. The scholar is that man who must take up into himself all the ability of the time, all the contributions of the past, all the hopes of the future. He must be an university of knowledges. If there be one lesson more than another, which should pierce his ear, it is, The world is nothing, the man is all; in yourself is the law of all nature, and you know not yet how a globule of sap ascends; in yourself slumbers the whole of Reason; it is for you to know all, it is for you to dare all. Mr. President and Gentlemen, this confidence in the unsearched might of man belongs, by all motives, by all prophecy, by all preparation, to the American Scholar. We have listened too long to the courtly muses of Europe. The spirit of the American freeman is already suspected to be timid, imitative, tame. Public and private avarice make the air we breathe thick and fat. The scholar is decent, indolent, complaisant. See already the tragic consequence. The mind of this country, taught to aim at low objects, eats upon itself. There is no work for any but the decorous and the complaisant. Young men of the fairest promise, who begin life upon our shores, inflated by the mountain winds, shined upon by all the stars of God, find the earth below not in unison with these,—but are hindered from action by the disgust which the principles on which business is managed inspire, and turn drudges,

19. Emerson contrasts "cold" neoclassical writers with "blood-warm" Romantics and their precursors.   20. Johann Wolfgang von Goethe (1749–1832), German writer.   21. Swedish mystic (1668–1772).   22. Johann Heinrich Pestalozzi (1746–1827), Swiss educator.

or die of disgust,—some of them suicides. What is the remedy? They did not yet see, and thousands of young men as hopeful now crowding to the barriers for the career, do not yet see, that, if the single man plant himself indomitably on his instincts, and there abide, the huge world will come round to him. Patience,—patience;—with the shades of all the good and great for company; and for solace, the perspective of your own infinite life; and for work, the study and the communication of principles, the making those instincts prevalent, the conversion of the world. Is it not the chief disgrace in the world, not to be an unit;—not to be reckoned one character;—not to yield that peculiar fruit which each man was created to bear, but to be reckoned in the gross, in the hundred, or the thousand, of the party, the section, to which we belong; and our opinion predicted geographically, as the north, or the south? Not so, brothers and friends,—please God, ours shall not be so. We will walk on our own feet; we will work with our own hands; we will speak our own minds. The study of letters shall be no longer a name for pity, for doubt, and for sensual indulgence. The dread of man and the love of man shall be a wall of defence and a wreath of joy around all. A nation of men will for the first time exist, because each believes himself inspired by the Divine Soul which also inspires all men.

—1837

<hr>

CONTEMPORARY RESPONSE
Sharpe's London Journal

At a time when American literary sensibilities were still in large part beholden to British aesthetics, the Englishman Sydney Smith's 1820 question, "In the four quarters of the American globe, who reads an American book?" burned hot in the faces of American authors. Sales of American books in England were generally poor but, ironically, American authors were not usually deemed successful at home until someone on the other side of the Atlantic had sung their praises. Ralph Waldo Emerson was among the first American writers who penned a declaration of literary independence from England. This background, compounded with the fact that Emerson's ideas were ridiculed and detested by many American writers and thinkers, such as Andrews Norton, makes his receiving praise in *Sharpe's London Journal* all the more complex. Emerson must have viewed this praise as a blessing, but a mixed one. The review proved that Old England was reading the works of New England; indeed, the reviewer remarks that the book being reviewed, Emerson's *Representative Men* (1850), has "more wisdom and practical downright sense in it than whole circulating libraries," which of course contained mainly British books. To add to the complexity, this praise is heaped on a book that holds up Napoleon, enemy of the British government, as an example of greatness that knows no national boundaries. Emerson's reviewer does not believe that *Representative Men*, or any of Emerson's other books, will achieve popularity, but the reviewer pays his writing a higher compliment, noting that Emerson's works contain truth, which is not national but universal: "Truth, knowledge, wisdom . . . these we should reverence and accept, wheresoever they may be found, permitting no prejudice, no vanity to defraud us of the possession."

Emerson's *Representative Men*

Of the multiplicity of books which the press in these years is continually sending forth, there is a small and comparatively neglected number deserving considerably more attention than the rest. These are the writings of a few recluse thinkers, who, holding themselves aloof from the allurements of a temporary popularity, have respect rather to that better and loftier distinction, which consists in giving shape and utterance to thoughts calculated to promote the spiritual elevation of humanity. These men aim, apparently, at that which is properly the end of all literature and philosophy—the discovery and publication of truth and wisdom. Being enlightened and inspired by these admirable realities, they seek to shed around them something of the grand effulgence which has illumined and exalted thir own souls. They would make their words a living and impressive testimony to whatsoever is highest, most beautiful, and excellent in man; and with splendid thoughts and images, would recall him to the contemplation of that potential worthiness, which is lodged as a germ within his soul, and which, by sedulous striving and endeavour, may be practically developed in his character and life.

Among the men thus earnestly devoted to this noblest work of literature, it is now almost becoming fashionable to reckon Emerson. His writings, though at first misapprehended and abused, both in America and England, have gradually won their way to the reverent admiration of many a thoughtful reader, and have gained, at length, a considerably wide celebrity; so that even the obtusest of gainsayers are beginning to perceive that it is no longer advisable to speak of him otherwise than respectfully. Two or three years ago, he was highly eulogised in "Blackwood," and Mr. Gilfillan,[1] more recently, has asserted (we suppose from personal knowledge) that "sincere spirits, in every part of the country, who have, many of them, no sympathy with Emerson's surmised opinions, delight, nevertheless, to do him honour, as an earnest, honest, and gifted man." When he was in England, in 1848, the intelligent classes of all opinions anxiously thronged to hear him lecture; even Exeter-hall was, for two evenings at least, quite handsomely occupied, and from time to time resounded with the applauses of the audience.

We are not prepared to say that everything Emerson has written ought to be received as worthy of implicit acceptation; but we nevertheless believe that he has written very little which is not fairly entitled to a candid consideration. The sayings of a man of genius are always worth examining. His very errors are instructive; and may often indirectly aid the cause of truth better than the most respectable array of commonplaces. To use a definition of his own, Emerson is a "man thinking." He does not expect you to receive his utterances without examination; he neither aspires nor desires to teach dogmatically; but seems to say to you, "Such and such a thought has arisen in my mind; see, friends what you can make of it." His originality of expression is very remarkable; and is indeed the occasion of much of that obscurity which has been attributed to his writings. It is not to be denied that these writings present considerable difficulties to unprepared readers. We have met with even intelligent persons who declared they could not apprehend his meaning. The frequent novelty of the thoughts, and the general uncommonness of the phraseology employed in uttering them, give to these productions a character of strangeness, which is not readily apprehensible to minds principally familiar with the easy clearness of the current literature. They require a sustained and vigilant attention, such, probably, as few ready and rapid readers may be inclined to give; their full and complete significance being nowise discernible at a glance, but to be gathered only by repeated and sedulous perusal. In short, Emerson is a writer whose works demand that almost obsolete kind of application which is expressed by the word *study*. He is, therefore, never likely to

---

1. George Gilfallan (1813–1878), Scottish author.

be popular, in the wide and ordinary sense of the expression. The greatest order of minds really never are so with the mass of their contemporaries. The popularity which Shakespeare enjoyed in his own age, is not the same kind of popularity which he enjoys at present with the poetical and philosophical class of minds that can best appreciate his excellences. The popularity of Cervantes was altogether secondary, and far inferior in extent to that of Lope de Vega,[2] who was the acknowledged prince of dramatists of his time, but whose works are now read only by critics and scholars out of motives of curiosity, while the illustrious Don Quixote is the delight of every household. For one earnest reader of Coleridge or William Wordsworth, there have probably been thousands who have derived a morbid and temporary gratification from the pages of Ainsworth or Eugene Sue.[3] The present popularity of a writer is no evidence or indication of the greatness of his genius, or of the ultimate influence which he will exercise upon society. A blaze of fireworks, or a burning tar-barrel, may very effectually illuminate a common street or market-place, and for a time exclude from observation more permanent and less ostentatious lights; but above, in the vast firmament, the stars send forth their lustres, gently and solemnly for ever, over boundless realms of space.

Ebenezer Elliott[4] has said, that through his habit of reading only the master-pieces of literature, he found their thoughts invariably suggested to him other thoughts, which, if not new in themselves, were at least new to him. This is precisely one of the merits of Emerson. He suggests as much as he teaches. If you have any capacity for reflection, he has the power to make you think. Accepting no hearsays, he strives to unravel the actual truth of things. He deals at first hand with the loftiest speculations, and, leading you through regions of difficult and abstruse thought, leaves you finally in possession of novel and commanding truths. Under the shifting appearances of existence, his genius has the power to detect the electric current which runs through them, and is the splendour and the mystery of life. Man and nature are his great themes, and the habitual objects of his reverence. He holds by a latent worthiness in man: not man as he finds him in commonplace and degenerate society; but man exalted to the height of his possibilities, through a wise and earnest culture. He exults in the beauty and magnificence of nature; but loves her not alone for the glories of her sensuous impressions, but rather in so far as she is the symbol of a ruling and predominating spirit. It is the divinity that is supreme, and pervades all the elements of creation; nor is man invested with any worth or greatness, save as he partakes of the Divine energy, and subordinates his aims to the constitution of the universe.

The leading lesson which Emerson inculcates, is, that all knowledge and inquiry should minister to the training and development of the individual man—to the unfolding and manifestation of whatsoever is most noble and enduring in his soul. He would have a man "to know his worth, and keep things under his feet." To promote the formation and culture of character, is the chief aim of all his writings. He insists that, under all circumstances, we should possess a cultivated self-reliance—or rather a reliance on the intuitions communicated by that remoter Power, whence every individuality derives its basis and its strength—that we should yield an habitual obedience to

2. Miguel de Cervantes (1547–1616), Author of *Don Quixote de la Mancha* (1604); Félix Lope de Vega (1562–1635), Spanish playwright.   3. Samuel Taylor Coleridge (1772–1834) and William Wordsworth (1770–1850), English Romantic poets; William Harrison Ainsworth (1805–1882), English novelist; Eugene Sue (1804–1857), French novelist.   4. Ebenezer Elliott (1781–1849), English poet.

the voice of moral sentiment, and strive to realize the aspirations that arise in us when we are most consciously in communion with exalted truths and feelings. He would have us, regardless of all customs and conventions, of all merely secular restraints, prescribed courtesies and compliances, to endeavour to attain to a nobleness and truthfulness of life and manners, which should exhibit a constant reference of every action to the highest known and revealed standards of right and purity, and give the impression of a mind in unison with the natural realities of things. Whatsoever aids are to be accepted as the means of successfully educing and elucidating the inborn character, must be restricted to their proper agency as means, that so the soul of man may grow in freedom, and be advanced to the very utmost, in its career of a spiritual development. Enlargement and elevation of soul and intellect, form the grand success of life. He only is turning his life to just account, who lives in conformity with the divine ordinances, and is rising progressively to higher stages of intellectual and moral energy and perfection.

To Emerson's mind, the workings of the universe are unfallible. God has ordained that truth and justice shall succeed, and that all falsehood in act or word, every lying and unjust pretension, shall finally and permanently fail. Hence, to him, the apparent success of cunning and injustice is a sheer delusion. He holds that, "In labour, as in life, there can be no cheating. The thief steals from himself; the swindler swindles himself. For the real price of labour is knowledge and virtue, whereof wealth and credit are signs. These signs, like paper money, may be counterfeited or stolen; but that which they represent—namely, knowledge and virtue—cannot be counterfeited or stolen. These ends of labour cannot be answered but by real exertions of the mind, and in obedience to pure motives. The cheat, the defaulter, the gambler, cannot extort the benefit, cannot extort the knowledge of material and moral nature, which his honest care and pains yield to the operative. The law of nature is, do the thing, and you shall have the power; but they who do not the thing, have not the power." In like manner, a lie is its own disgrace: there is so much abstracted from the man; he is the less a man to the extent of the enormity of the lie. Only in truth and rectitude is well-being possible: but he who pursues the true and good, has the furtherance of all nature to establish his endeavours, and his success is clenched by the enduring integrity of her laws.

—1850

Joseph Howe
1804–1873

In an 1838 poem "The Rhine" about the literary influence of the Rhine River, Joseph Howe writes of the infancy of Canadian literature:

> What though no ruins rise above
>   My Country's pleasant streams;
> Nor legends wild, of war or love,
>   Invoke the Poet's dreams.

No lawless power can there disturb
  The Peasant's tranquil sleep;
No towers, the free-born soul to curb,
  Frown o'er each lofty steep—
Then, German, keep your Drachenfels,
  Vine-clad and foaming Rhine,
The taint of bondage on them dwells,
  Far happier streams are mine.

The Drachenfels, as Howe notes, is "the Dragon Rock, celebrated in Byron's *Childe Harold*"—a jagged outcrop of rock that offers a stunning view of the Rhine and gives the river a gothic air. While the natural resources of Canada had not been featured in the landscape of the literary imagination, Howe prefers the freshness of the New World to the stifling political hierarchies of the Old, seeing himself as a shaper of Canadian literature and politics. Howe's political and literary activities reveal his deep conviction that Canada must forge its own identity.

Howe was born in Halifax, Nova Scotia. In his mid-teens, he apprenticed in the family printing firm run by his father, John, a Loyalist from Boston who held positions as the postmaster general and king's printer. At age twenty-eight, the younger Howe became an entrepreneur and acquired the *Novascotian*, a leading periodical of the nineteenth century. The journal was the province's cultural, literary, and political voice, and Howe demonstrated an awareness of the influence England and America had upon Canada. The periodical ran from 1824 to 1926, and its title offers a clear indication of Howe's—and the Howe family's—politics: Howe was a Nova Scotian who resisted that province's union with the Dominion of Canada in 1867, proposing that a North American union, or a closer political connection with England, would be more beneficial than confederation and independence. Howe eventually became premier of the province in 1860; a strong supporter of responsible government, he championed local literature, feeling that a country's political identity should be built upon a foundation of letters.

His long topographical poem "Acadia," composed during the 1820s and 1830s but first published posthumously in 1874, sketches an optimistic portrait of the future of Nova Scotia as he describes the expulsion of the Acadians and paints dehumanizing portraits of the savagery of Native Canadians and aggrandizing pictures of the industry and moral fiber of Nova Scotians. The poem was completed by the time of Howe's tour of England in 1836 with Thomas Chandler Haliburton (whose *The Clockmaker* had made him a literary celebrity). England held a great historical and cultural charm for Howe, as he writes in the *Novascotian* in 1830:

Though the blood of Britain flows in our veins—that would be of little consequence, if every thing else did not conspire to keep their spirit alive in our bosoms. The language which we speak, like a noble stream, has come rolling onwards, from the days of the Saxon Heptarchy, down to the present time—becoming in every age more pure and more expressive. . . . Of that stream we are taught to drink from our childhood upwards; and in every draught there is a magic influence. . . . Our souls are stirred by the impassioned eloquence of her Orators, and our feelings and taste refined by the high inspiration of her Poets.

Howe's patriotism is captured in images of water and poetry—as though the waters of Canada (which is a country of many rivers and lakes) connect all citizens across the country, and, in due course, across the Atlantic, to England and its literary traditions.

from Acadia

I

[Before the arrival of European settlers]

But see, where breaking through the leafy wood,   180
The Micmac bends beside the tranquil flood,
Launches his light canoe from off the strand,
And plies his paddle with a dexterous hand;
Or, as his bark along the water glides,
With slender spear his simple meal provides;   185
Or mark his agile figure, as he leaps
From crag to crag, and still his footing keeps,
For fast before him flies the desp'rate Deer,
For life is sweet, and death she knows is near.
No hound or horse assist him in the chase,   190
His hardy limbs are equal to the race,
For, since he left, unswathed, his mother's back
They've been familiar with each sylvan track;
They've borne him daily, as they bear him now,
Swift through the wood, and o'er the mountain's brow—   195
But mark—his bow is bent, his arrow flies,
And at his feet the bleeding victim dies.

While o'er the fallen tenant of the wild
A moment stands the forest's dusky child
From his dark brow his long and glossy hair   200
Is softly parted by the gentle air.
The glow of pride has flush'd his manly cheek,
And in his eye his kindled feelings speak.
For, as he casts his proud and fearless glance,
O'er each fair feature of the wide expanse,   205
The blushing flowers—the groves of stately pine—
The glassy lakes that in the sunbeams shine—
The swelling sea—the hills that heavenward soar—
The mountain stream, meandering to the shore—
Or hears the birds' blythe song, the woods' deep tone—   210
He feels, yes proudly feels, 'tis all his own.

Thus, as the am'rous Moor with joy survey'd
The budding beauties of Venetia's maid,
Drank in the beamings of her love lit eye,
Her bosom's swell, the music of her sigh   215
He felt, and who can tell that feeling's bliss,
Moor though he was, her beauties all were his.

With practised skill he soon divides his prey,
Then to his home pursues his devious way

Through many an Alder copse, and leafy shade,   220
And well known path by former ramble made,
To where a little cove, that strays between
Opposing hills, adds beauty to the scene
Which natures hand has negligently dressed
With charms well suited to the Indian's breast.   225

  The Camp extends along the pebbly shore,
A sylvan city, rude as those of yore,
By Patriarch hands within the desert built,
When fresh from Eden's joys and Eden's guilt.
Like those, 'tis man's abode where round him twine   230
Those ties that make a wilderness divine.
No architectural piles[1] salute the sky,
No marble column strikes the gazer's eye,
The solemn grandeur of the spacious hall,
The stuccoed ceiling and the pictured wall,   235
Art's skilful hand may sedulously rear,
The simple homes of Nature's sons are here.

  Some slender poles, with tops together bound,
And butts inserted firmly in the ground,
Form the rude frames—o'er which are closely laid   240
Birch bark and fir boughs, forming grateful shade,
And shelter from the storm, and sunny ray
Of summer noon, or winter's darker day.
A narrow opening, on the leeward side,
O'er which a skin is negligently tied,   245
Forms the rude entrance to the Indian's home—
Befitting portal for so proud a dome.
A fire is blazing brightly on the ground—
The motley inmates scatter'd careless round.
Some strip the maple, some the dye prepare,   250
Or weave the basket with assiduous care;
Others, around the box of bark entwine
Quills, pluck'd from off the "fretful porcupine,"[2]
And which may form, when curiously inlaid,
A bridal offering to some dark-eyed maid.   255
Some shape the bow, some form the feather'd dart,
Which soon may quiver in a foeman's heart.
The Squaws proceed, upon the coals to broil,
Steaks cut from off the newly furnished spoil,
And these with lobsters, roasted in the shell,   260
And eels, by Indian palates loved so well,

---

1. Buildings. 2. "Like quills upon the fretful porcupine," Shakespeare, *Hamlet*, 1.5.20.

Complete their frugal feast, for sweet content,
Which thrones have not, makes rich the Indian's tent.

    As to the West the glorious Sun retires,
The Micmacs kindle up their smouldering fires,   265
The aged Chiefs around the tents repose,
The dark Papoose[3] to laugh and gambol[4] goes;
While youths and maidens to the green advance,
And clustering round, prepare them for the dance.
Nor smile ye modern fair, who float along,   270
The dazzling spirits of the nightly throng,
Wafted by mingled music's softest tone,
With fashion's every grace around ye thrown,
Smile not at those, who, ere your sires were born,
Danced on the very spot you now adorn,   275
Kindling, with laughing eyes, love's hallow'd fire,
And swelling gallant hearts with fond desire.

    Crossing his legs upon a mossy seat,
With maple wand a youth begins to beat
On some dried bark, with measured time and slow,   280
A soft low tune—his voice's solemn flow
Mingling with every stroke. The dance begins,
Not such as now the modern fair one wins
To mazy evolutions, wild and free,
Where forms of radiant beauty seem to be   285
Like heavenly planets, whirling round at will,
Yet by fixed laws controll'd and govern'd still,
But slow and measured as the music's tone,
To which the dancers first beat time alone,
Murm'ring a low response. A broken shout,   290
To mark the changing time, at times rings out,
When all is soft, and faint, and slow again,
Till, by degrees, the music's swelling strain,
Sweeps through the Warriors' souls with rushing tide,
Rousing each thought of glory and of pride;   295
Then, while the deeds of other days return,
By music's power clothed in words that burn,
When ev'n the Dead, evoked by mem'ry's spell,
Burst into life, to fight where once they fell,
A savage joy the dancers' eyes bespeak,   300
A deeper tinge pervades each maiden's cheek,
The glossy clusters of their long dark hair
Are floating wildly on the ev'ning air,
As from the earth, with frantic bounds they spring,

---

3. Papoose: Native Canadian child.   4. Gambol: playfully dance.

And rock and grove with shouts of triumph ring. 305
Thus we may see the River steal along
Noiseless and slow, till growing deep and strong,
Its turbid waters foam, and curve, and leap,
Dashing with startling echo down the steep.

II

[The Micmac attack the European settlers]

Thus, while Acadia's charms my eye surveys,
My soul, unbidden, turns to other days,
When the stout-hearted rear'd amidst the wood,
Their sylvan Homes, and by their thresholds stood 30
With stern resolve the savage tribes to brave,
And win a peaceful dwelling, or a grave.
Gone are the Patriarchs—but we still may weep
Where "the forefathers of our Hamlets sleep."[5]
For us they freely pour'd life's crimson tide,— 35
For us they labor'd, and for us they died.
And though they rest in no time honor'd tomb,
Acadia's wild flowers o'er their ashes bloom.
Oh! could they now her smiling fields behold,
While in the breezes wave their crops of gold, 40
While on her thousand hills, her children stand,
And Peace and Plenty crown the happy land,
'Twould glad their Spirits, like some Seraph's strain
To know they had not toiled, and died in vain.

They felled the forest trees with sturdy stroke, 45
The virgin soil, with gentle culture broke,
Scatter'd the fruitful seeds the stumps between,
And Ceres[6] lured to many a sylvan scene.
Then rose the Log House by the water side,
Its seams by moss and sea weed well supplied, 50
Its roof with bark o'erspread—its humble door
Hung on a twisted withe[7]—the earth its floor,
With stones and harden'd clay its chimney form'd,
Its spacious hearth by hissing green wood warmed,
Round which, as night her deep'ning shadows throws, 55
The Hamlet's wearied inmates circling close.
The sturdy settler lays his axe aside,
Which all day long has quell'd the forest's pride.
The wooden cleats[8] that from the walls extend,
Receive his gun, his oft tried faithful friend, 60

---

5. Thomas Gray, "Elegy Written in a Country Churchyard" (lines 15–16).   6. Roman goddess of agriculture.   7. Slender branch.   8. Pegs, or supports.

Which crowns his frugal board with plenteous meals,
And guards his rest when sleep his eye-lids seals.

    As cautiously the miser locks his store,
The anxious parent barricades the door,
Then, having cleansed the balsam from his palm,   65
He bends him down, to where with cheek as calm
As summer ev'nings close, his Infant lies
Breathing as softly as a floweret sighs,
And while a father's transports swell his breast,
A kiss upon its coral lips is press'd.   70
A look of earnest rapture fondly given,
A prayer, in silent gladness, breathed to Heaven.
Meanwhile his wife, the mother of his child,
His dear companion in the dreary wild,
Spreads o'er his humble board their ev'ning fare,   75
And soothes his spirit with assiduous care,
Returns with grateful lips and fond embrace,
The kiss imprinted on her Babe's sweet face.
And while her eye betrays a mother's pride,
Points to her first-born, standing by her side,   80
Who waits the signal to his arms to spring,
And round his neck with filial transport cling. . . .

Then, half forgetful of their present lot,   105
They rove o'er scenes that ne'er can be forgot,
The joys and griefs of life—the light and shade
Of early thought, that ne'er from memory fade
Transport their spirits o'er the Atlantic's foam,
And bid them welcome to their island home.   110
As now their loved boy rests upon their knee,
They nestled once, as light of heart as he;
Anon they stand beside the narrow bed,
And hear cold earth on aged temples spread,
And mark the bursting sob and tearful eye,   115
That send to their lone hearts a sad reply. . . .

Why starts the mother from that soft repose?
What means the horror that her looks disclose?
Why are her children clasped with eager care,
While Hope seems wildly struggling with Despair?   160
Why has the father seized the axe and knife,
Like one resolved to combat Death for Life,
And yield no vantage that his arm can hold
Though hungry wolves assail his gentle fold?
Hark to that horrid and soul-piercing yell   165
That seems the war-cry of a fiend from Hell;

That starts the raven from the lofty pine
On which he closed his wing at day's decline,
And echoing back from the surrounding hills,
The beating hearts in that lone cottage chills;   170
For Hate, Revenge, and Murder's deepest tone,
Tell them the Micmac's toils are round them thrown.

    From the wild covert of the forest shade,
By stealthy march their slow approach was made;
Now, by the spreading foliage concealed,   175
Now, by some sudden op'ning half revealed,
As to the settler's dwelling they drew nigh,
And gazed upon it with malignant eye.
'Twas yet high noon when it appeared in sight,
But for his work the Indian loves the night.   180
In patient ambush scattered round they lay,
Content to linger ere they seized their prey.
They marked the settler at his weary moil,[9]
And smiled to think how they'd repay his toil;
Saw him partake the draught his boy would bring   185
To cheer his labor, from the crystal spring,
And vow'd, e'er morning's dawn, their souls should laugh,

    While the parch'd earth his blood should freely quaff;
And when he sought his home at eventide,
To taste the pleasures of his dear fireside,   190
With ears attentive—footsteps light and true,
And treacherous hearts, around the eaves they drew,
Listen'd the song the mother sung her child,
Heard the light converse that the hours beguiled,
And joyed to think the time would not be long   195
Ere midnight's cries would follow evening's song.

    When sleep had closed the weary cottar's eyes,
They sought to take the slumberers by surprise—
Essay'd the door, and then the window tried
With gentle pressure, studiously applied,   200
Nor knew how light a doting mother sleeps,
When near her babes its watch the spirit keeps.
The first faint whisper of alarm within,
Convinced them force, not fraud, their prey must win.
'Twas then their shout of fierce defiance rose,   205
While fast and vehement their heavy blows
On door and shutter diligently fell,

---

9. Hard work.

Each followed by a wild tumultuous yell;
Nor are the inmates idle—logs of wood,
Trunks, cribs, whate'er can make defences good,   210
Are piled against the bars that still are true,
Despite the efforts of the howling crew.
This done, the gun is seized—the Father fires,
Chance guides—a groan—one bleeding wretch expires.
Again he loads, again a savage dies—   215
Again the yells upon the welkin[10] rise,
Hope half persuades that till the dawn of day
The fierce besiegers may be kept at bay.
What scene so dark, what stroke of fate so rude,
That Hope cannot a moment's space intrude?   220
But soon he flies, for now an Indian flings
Himself upon the roof, which loudly rings
To every stroke the polished hatchet lends;
The bark which bears him, to the pressure bends,
It yields—it breaks—he falls upon the floor—   225
One blow—his fleeting term of life is o'er,
The settler's axe has dashed his reeking brain
Upon the hearth his soul had sworn to stain.
Fast through the breach two others downward leap,
But, ere they rise, a knife is planted deep   230
In one dark breast, by gentle Woman's hand,
Who, for her household, wields a household brand;
The axe has clove the other to the chin.
But now, *en masse*, the shrieking fiends leap in,
Till wounded, faint, o'erpowered, the Father falls   235
And hears the shout of triumph shake his walls.
The wretched Mother from her babe is torn,
Which on a red right hand aloft is borne,
Then dashed to earth before its Parent's eyes,
And, as its form, deform'd and quivering lies,   240
Life from its fragile tenement is trod,
And the bruised, senseless, and unsightly clod,
Is flung into the soft but bleeding breast
To which so late in smiling peace 'twas press'd.

Nor does the boy escape—the smouldering fire   245
Is stirred,—and, as its feeble flames aspire
In wanton cruelty they thrust his hands
Into the blaze, and on the reddening brands,
Like Montezuma[11] bid him seek repose
As though his couch were but a perfumed rose.   250
Sated with blood, at length the scalps they tear

---

10. Upper reaches of the sky.   11. Aztec emperor of Mexico (1466–1520), held hostage by Spaniards.

Ere life be yet extinct—for these, with care,
The Indian tribes, like precious coins, retain
To count their victories, and the victims slain.

Now plunder follows death—then one applies   255
Fire to the bed, from which the flames arise
Fiercely and fast, as anxious to efface
All record of so sad, so foul a place.
Around the cot the Indians form a ring,
And songs of joy and triumph wildly sing   260
With horrid gesture and demoniac strain,
Then plunge into the forest depths again.

Such are the scenes Acadia once display'd;
Such was the price our gallant Fathers paid
For this fair land, where now our footsteps rove   265
From lake to sea, from cliff to shady grove,
Uncheck'd by peril, unrestrained by fear
Of more unfriendly ambush lingering near
Than timid rabbits lurking in the fern
And peeping forth your worst intent to learn;   270
Or mottled squirrel, frisking round the pines
To seek the buds on which he lightly dines;
Or feather'd fav'rites, who, on ev'ry spray
Cheer and enchant with many a simple lay,
And though their plumage cannot boast the dyes   275
That deck the feather'd tribe 'neath milder skies,
Their ev'ning songs can sweeter strains impart
To charm the list'ning ear, or touch the heart.

—1874

Nathaniel Hawthorne
1804–1864

It seems no coincidence that Nathaniel Hawthorne was born on the fourth of July; through his
literary works, he sought not only to declare American independence from British literature
but also to preserve the autonomy of the people and state from the restrictions imposed by religion and its puritanical legacy of overly strict morality. He was certainly aware of the potential
dangers of a Puritan theocracy: He grew up in Salem and was descended from John Hathorne,
a judge in the Salem witchcraft trials. Hawthorne was haunted by his ancestral complicity in
the trials and the resulting persecution of innocent people believed to be witches, one of whom
pronounced a curse on the house of Hathorne before being put to death. Hawthorne's adding
the "w" to the spelling of his name may have been an attempt to distance himself from his

ancestors. His feelings about this episode in American history are expressed in *The Scarlet Letter* (1850), a commentary on the ways in which the mixture of church and state can prove oppressive, stunting the development of the souls it meant to save.

Ancestral predecessors were not the only ones to shape his fiction; literary ones did as well. In a sense, he was raised by books. The death of his father, also named Nathaniel Hawthorne, threw his mother, Elizabeth Clarke Manning, into a deep depression and solitude, which meant that young Hawthorne was left alone for vast intervals of time, punctuated by time spent with his two sisters, Louisa and Elizabeth. Not physically capable of sharing in youthful sports because of an injury, he spent his time alone reading the works of British writers—Edmund Spenser, William Shakespeare, John Milton, and others—in which he encountered powerfully dramatized struggles between good and evil. One of the few activities Hawthorne participated in, although not willingly, was attending church at the Salem Meeting House, during what he referred to as "the frozen purgatory of my childhood." One of his most memorable childhood years was spent on family property in the thick woods of Maine, to which he returned for his college years. From 1821 to 1825, he attended Bowdoin College, where he quit his reclusive ways and joined his fellow students in gambling, drinking, and studying, hopefully not in that order. While there he made two friends who later became famous: the future poet and Harvard professor Henry Wadsworth Longfellow and future American president Franklin Pierce. After graduation, however, Hawthorne once again returned to the comparative seclusion of his mother's house in Salem, devoting over a decade to success as a writer of fiction. After many setbacks, the years proved fruitful, yielding the publication of *Twice-Told Tales* in 1837. Although the book enjoyed moderate success, it did not generate enough to support Hawthorne, so he took a post in the Boston custom-house from 1839 to 1841. Finally breaking out of his solitary lifestyle, he joined the experiment in communal living, taking up residence with Transcendentalists at Brook Farm. His days there, however, were numbered. Required to shovel manure for up to sixteen hours a day, he later reflected, "I went to live in Arcady [paradise], and found myself up to my chin in a barnyard."

In 1842, *Twice-Told Tales* was reissued, and Hawthorne married Sophia Peabody, the sister of the feminist and educator Elizabeth Palmer Peabody. His sister-in-law was one of the first, along with Henry Wadsworth Longfellow, to bring Hawthorne's stories to the notice of the American public, reviewing them in a magazine of the day. She also introduced his work to British writers, sending it to William Wordsworth with a note about how it had been influenced by the poetry of the *Lyrical Ballads* (1798), which Wordsworth wrote with Samuel Taylor Coleridge. At home, Hawthorne was also gaining an audience among writers: Edgar Allan Poe penned a review in praise of Hawthorne's short stories. After taking up residence with Sophia in the "Old Manse," the Concord, Massachusetts, home where Ralph Waldo Emerson had been raised, Hawthorne received a request to write stories for publication in a magazine Poe was editing. Hawthorne was prolific during his years in the "Manse," setting up his desk in front of the window where Emerson's grandfather had watched the Revolutionary Battle of Lexington and Concord unfold in the field below. To this day, visitors to the house can gaze out this window, where Hawthorne's small desk still stands, and discern his signature scratched into one of the windowpanes. The house provided more than just inspiration for the stories; it also served as part of the title of his next book, *Mosses from an Old Manse* (1846), a collection of the stories he had published in the *Democratic National Review*.

Although *Mosses* did get the attention of writer Herman Melville, who praised it in a review, the work did not provide enough to support the Hawthorne family, which now included two children, Una and Julian, so Hawthorne took up a post in the Salem custom-house. Like the "Manse," the custom-house became the inspiration for and title of the introduction to *The Scarlet Letter* (1850). This work sold five thousand copies in two weeks alone in America and was reprinted and sold in several British editions as well. American reviewers immediately placed Hawthorne among the ranks of his British predecessors and peers, such as Sir Walter Scott, Charles Lamb, and Charles Dickens. Fortunately, sales of the book helped to support the family once his political appointment at the custom-house ended with the election of the rival party. Settling in Lenox, Massachusetts, Hawthorne made the acquaintance of Melville and entered into another prolific period, during which he wrote *The House of the Seven Gables* (1851), based on an actual house in Salem; *The Blithedale Romance* (1852), based on his experience living with the community on Brook Farm; and the *Life of Franklin Pierce* (1852), about his college friend from Bowdoin who was running for presidential office. In 1852, the Hawthornes returned to Concord, purchasing the former residence of writer Amos Bronson Alcott's family. Once Pierce was elected, Hawthorne was appointed United States consul to Liverpool, England, where the Hawthornes (who now numbered among their ranks another daughter, Rose) relocated for four years. After Hawthorne retired from this post in 1858, the family lived briefly in France, Switzerland, and Italy and spent time with the poets Robert and Elizabeth Barrett Browning. Hawthorne's time in England, to which he returned after touring Europe, was the inspiration for *Our Old Home* (1863), and *The Marble Faun* (1860, published simultaneously in Britain under the title of *Transformation*) was conceived during his visit to Rome.

By 1860, the family was back in its home in Concord, where the Civil War was in its nascent stages. Although a Unionist, Hawthorne did not sympathize with the radicalism of his Concord friends, such as Emerson, who actively disagreed with the pro-slavery politics of Pierce. Hawthorne's reflections on the Civil War were published in the *Atlantic Monthly* under the title "Chiefly About War-Matters" (July 1862). Throughout this time, Hawthorne's health was declining, and on a trip to New Hampshire with Pierce, he passed away during an evening stay in a hotel in Plymouth. He was buried back in Concord at the Sleepy Hollow Cemetery where, now, in death as in life, he is near Ralph Waldo Emerson, Henry David Thoreau, and Amos Bronson Alcott.

My Kinsman, Major Molineux

After the kings of Great Britain had assumed the right of appointing the colonial governors, the measures of the latter seldom met with the ready and general approbation, which had been paid to those of their predecessors, under the original charters. The people looked with most jealous scrutiny to the exercise of power, which did not emanate from themselves, and they usually rewarded the rulers with slender gratitude, for the compliances, by which, in softening their instructions from beyond the sea, they had incurred the reprehension of those who gave them. The annals of Massachusetts Bay will inform us, that of six governors, in the space of about forty years from the surrender of the old charter, under James II,[1] two were imprisoned by a popular insurrection; a third, as Hutchinson[2] inclines to believe, was driven from the province by the whizzing of a musket ball; a fourth, in the opinion of the same historian, was hastened to his grave by continual bickerings with the House of Representatives; and the remaining two, as well as their successors, till the Revolution, were favored with few and brief intervals of peaceful sway. The inferior members of the court party,[3] in times of high political excitement, led scarcely a more desirable life. These remarks may serve as preface to the following adventures, which chanced upon a summer night, not far from a hundred years ago. The reader, in order to avoid a long and dry detail of colonial affairs, is requested to dispense with an account of the train of circumstances, that had caused much temporary inflammation of the popular mind.

It was near nine o'clock of a moonlight evening, when a boat crossed the ferry with a single passenger, who had obtained his conveyance, at that unusual hour, by

---

1. The 1684 *Massachusetts Charter* stripped the colonies of self-government. James II (1633–1701) appointed the first royal governor in 1685.   2. Thomas Hutchinson (1711–1780), last royal governor.   3. Loyalists.

the promise of an extra fare. While he stood on the landing-place, searching in either pocket for the means of fulfilling his agreement, the ferryman lifted a lantern, by the aid of which, and the newly risen moon, he took a very accurate survey of the stranger's figure. He was a youth of barely eighteen years, evidently countrybred, and now, as it should seem, upon his first visit to town. He was clad in a coarse grey coat, well worn, but in excellent repair; his under garments were durably constructed of leather, and sat tight to a pair of serviceable and well-shaped limbs; his stockings of blue yarn, were the incontrovertible handiwork of a mother or a sister; and on his head was a three-cornered hat, which in its better days had perhaps sheltered the graver brow of the lad's father. Under his left arm was a heavy cudgel, formed of an oak sapling, and retaining a part of the hardened root; and his equipment was completed by a wallet,[4] not so abundantly stocked as to incommode the vigorous shoulders on which it hung. Brown, curly hair, well-shaped features, and bright, cheerful eyes, were nature's gifts, and worth all that art could have done for his adornment.

The youth, one of whose names was Robin, finally drew from his pocket the half of a little province-bill[5] of five shillings, which, in the depreciation of that sort of currency, did but satisfy the ferryman's demand, with the surplus of a sexangular piece of parchment valued at three pence.[6] He then walked forward into the town, with as light a step, as if his day's journey had not already exceeded thirty miles, and with as eager an eye, as if he were entering London city, instead of the little metropolis of a New England colony. Before Robin had proceeded far, however, it occurred to him, that he knew not whither to direct his steps; so he paused, and looked up and down the narrow street, scrutinizing the small and mean wooden buildings, that were scattered on either side.

"This low hovel cannot be my kinsman's dwelling," thought he, "nor yonder old house, where the moonlight enters at the broken casement; and truly I see none hereabouts that might be worthy of him. It would have been wise to inquire my way of the ferryman, and doubtless he would have gone with me, and earned a shilling from the Major for his pains. But the next man I meet will do as well."

He resumed his walk, and was glad to perceive that the street now became wider, and the houses more respectable in their appearance. He soon discerned a figure moving on moderately in advance, and hastened his steps to overtake it. As Robin drew nigh, he saw that the passenger was a man in years, with a full periwig of grey hair, a wide-skirted coat of dark cloth, and silk stockings rolled about his knees. He carried a long and polished cane, which he struck down perpendicularly before him, at every step; and at regular intervals he uttered two successive hems, of a peculiarly solemn and sepulchral intonation. Having made these observations, Robin laid hold of the skirt of the old man's coat, just when the light from the open door and windows of a barber's shop, fell upon both their figures.

"Good evening to you, honored Sir," said he, making a low bow, and still retaining his hold of the skirt. "I pray you to tell me whereabouts is the dwelling of my kinsman, Major Molineux?"

The youth's question was uttered very loudly; and one of the barbers, whose razor was descending on a well-soaped chin, and another who was dressing a Ramillies wig,[7] left their occupations, and came to the door. The citizen, in the meantime,

---

4. Knapsack.   5. Paper money.   6. Six-sided three-penny note, issued by Massachusetts in 1722.   7. Wig with a long braided tail and bows.

turned a long favored countenance upon Robin, and answered him in a tone of excessive anger and annoyance. His two sepulchral hems, however, broke into the very centre of his rebuke, with most singular effect, like a thought of the cold grave obtruding among wrathful passions.

"Let go my garment, fellow! I tell you, I know not the man you speak of. What! I have authority, I have—hem, hem—authority; and if this be the respect you show your betters, your feet shall be brought acquainted with the stocks, by daylight, tomorrow morning!"

Robin released the old man's skirt, and hastened away, pursued by an ill-mannered roar of laughter from the barber's shop. He was at first considerably surprised by the result of his question, but, being a shrewd youth, soon thought himself able to account for the mystery.

"This is some country representative," was his conclusion, "who has never seen the inside of my kinsman's door, and lacks the breeding to answer a stranger civilly. The man is old, or verily—I might be tempted to turn back and smite him on the nose. Ah, Robin, Robin! even the barber's boys laugh at you, for choosing such a guide! You will be wiser in time, friend Robin."

He now became entangled in a succession of crooked and narrow streets, which crossed each other, and meandered at no great distance from the water-side. The smell of tar was obvious to his nostrils, the masts of vessels pierced the moonlight above the tops of the buildings, and the numerous signs, which Robin paused to read, informed him that he was near the centre of business. But the streets were empty, the shops were closed, and lights were visible only in the second stories of a few dwelling-houses. At length, on the corner of a narrow lane, through which he was passing, he beheld the broad countenance of a British hero swinging before the door of an inn, whence proceeded the voices of many guests. The casement of one of the lower windows was thrown back, and a very thin curtain permitted Robin to distinguish a party at supper, round a well-furnished table. The fragrance of the good cheer steamed forth into the outer air, and the youth could not fail to recollect, that the last remnant of his travelling stock of provision had yielded to his morning appetite, and that noon had found, and left him, dinnerless.

"Oh, that a parchment three-penny might give me a right to sit down at yonder table," said Robin, with a sigh. "But the Major will make me welcome to the best of his victuals; so I will even step boldly in, and inquire my way to his dwelling."

He entered the tavern, and was guided by the murmur of voices, and fumes of tobacco, to the public room. It was a long and low apartment, with oaken walls, grown dark in the continual smoke, and a floor, which was thickly sanded, but of no immaculate purity. A number of persons, the larger part of whom appeared to be mariners, or in some way connected with the sea, occupied the wooden benches, or leather-bottomed chairs, conversing on various matters, and occasionally lending their attention to some topic of general interest. Three or four little groups were draining as many bowls of punch,[8] which the great West India trade had long since made a familiar drink in the colony. Others, who had the aspect of men who lived by regular and laborious handicraft, preferred the insulated bliss of an unshared potation,[9] and became more taciturn under its influence. Nearly all, in short, evinced a predilection for the Good Creature[10] in some of its various shapes, for this is a vice, to which, as the Fast-day sermons of a hun-

8. Rum drink.   9. Beverage.   10. Alcohol.

dred years ago will testify, we have a long hereditary claim. The only guests to whom Robin's sympathies inclined him, were two or three sheepish countrymen, who were using the inn somewhat after the fashion of a Turkish Caravansary[11]; they had gotten themselves into the darkest corner of the room, and, heedless of the Nicotian atmosphere,[12] were supping on the bread of their own ovens, and the bacon cured in their own chimney-smoke. But though Robin felt a sort of brotherhood with these strangers, his eyes were attracted from them, to a person who stood near the door, holding whispered conversation with a group of ill-dressed associates. His features were separately striking almost to grotesqueness, and the whole face left a deep impression in the memory. The forehead bulged out into a double prominence, with a vale between; the nose came boldly forth in an irregular curve, and its bridge was of more than a finger's breadth; the eyebrows were deep and shaggy, and the eyes glowed beneath them like fire in a cave.

While Robin deliberated of whom to inquire respecting his kinsman's dwelling, he was accosted by the innkeeper, a little man in a stained white apron, who had come to pay his professional welcome to the stranger. Being in the second generation from a French protestant, he seemed to have inherited the courtesy of his parent nation; but no variety of circumstance was ever known to change his voice from the one shrill note in which he now addressed Robin.

"From the country, I presume, sir?" said he, with a profound bow. "Beg to congratulate you on your arrival, and trust you intend a long stay with us. Fine town here, Sir, beautiful buildings, and much that may interest a stranger. May I hope for the honor of your commands in respect to supper?"

"The man sees a family likeness! the rogue has guessed that I am related to the Major!" thought Robin, who had hitherto experienced little superfluous civility.

All eyes were now turned on the country lad, standing at the door, in his worn three-cornered hat, grey coat, leather breeches, and blue yarn stockings, leaning on an oaken cudgel, and bearing a wallet on his back.

Robin replied to the courteous innkeeper, with such an assumption of consequence, as befitted the Major's relative.

"My honest friend," he said, "I shall make it a point to patronize your house on some occasion, when"—here he could not help lowering his voice—"I may have more than a parchment three-pence in my pocket. My present business," continued he, speaking with lofty confidence, "is merely to inquire the way to the dwelling of my kinsman, Major Molineux."

There was a sudden and general movement in the room, which Robin interpreted as expressing the eagerness of each individual to become his guide. But the innkeeper turned his eyes to a written paper on the wall, which he read, or seemed to read, with occasional recurrences to the young man's figure.

"What have we here?" said he, breaking his speech into little dry fragments. 'Left the house of the subscriber, bounden servant, Hezekiah Mudge—had on, when he went away, grey coat, leather breeches, master's third best hat. One pound currency reward to whoever shall lodge him in any jail in the province.'[13] Better trudge, boy, better trudge!"

Robin had begun to draw his hand towards the lighter end of the oak cudgel, but a strange hostility in every countenance, induced him to relinquish his purpose of breaking the courteous innkeeper's head. As he turned to leave the room, he encountered a

---

11. Inn for caravans of merchants.   12. Smoky air.   13. The innkeeper parodies common ads for escaped indentured servants.

sneering glance from the bold-featured personage whom he had before noticed; and no sooner was he beyond the door, than he heard a general laugh, in which the innkeeper's voice might be distinguished, like the dropping of small stones into a kettle.

"Now is it not strange," thought Robin, with his usual shrewdness, "is it not strange, that the confession of an empty pocket, should outweigh the name of my kinsman, Major Molineux? Oh, if I had one of these grinning rascals in the woods, where I and my oak sapling grew up together, I would teach him that my arm is heavy, though my purse be light!"

On turning the corner of the narrow lane, Robin found himself in a spacious street, with an unbroken line of lofty houses on each side, and a steepled building at the upper end, whence the ringing of a bell announced the hour of nine. The light of the moon, and the lamps from numerous shop windows, discovered people promenading on the pavement, and amongst them, Robin hoped to recognize his hitherto inscrutable relative. The result of his former inquiries made him unwilling to hazard another, in a scene of such publicity, and he determined to walk slowly and silently up the street, thrusting his face close to that of every elderly gentleman, in search of the Major's lineaments. In his progress, Robin encountered many gay and gallant figures. Embroidered garments, of showy colors, enormous periwigs, gold-laced hats, and silver hilted swords, glided past him and dazzled his optics. Travelled youths, imitators of the European fine gentlemen of the period, trod jauntily along, half-dancing to the fashionable tunes which they hummed, and making poor Robin ashamed of his quiet and natural gait. At length, after many pauses to examine the gorgeous display of goods in the shop windows, and after suffering some rebukes for the impertinence of his scrutiny into people's faces, the Major's kinsman found himself near the steepled building, still unsuccessful in his search. As yet, however, he had seen only one side of the thronged street; so Robin crossed, and continued the same sort of inquisition down the opposite pavement, with stronger hopes than the philosopher seeking an honest man,[14] but with no better fortune. He had arrived about midway towards the lower end, from which his course began, when he overheard the approach of some one, who struck down a cane on the flag-stones at every step, uttering, at regular intervals, two sepulchral hems.

"Mercy on us!" quoth Robin, recognizing the sound.

Turning a corner, which chanced to be close at his right hand, he hastened to pursue his researches, in some other part of the town. His patience was now wearing low, and he seemed to feel more fatigue from his rambles since he crossed the ferry, than from his journey of several days on the other side. Hunger also pleaded loudly within him, and Robin began to balance the propriety of demanding, violently and with lifted cudgel, the necessary guidance from the first solitary passenger, whom he should meet. While a resolution to this effect was gaining strength, he entered a street of mean appearance, on either side of which, a row of ill-built houses was straggling towards the harbor. The moonlight fell upon no passenger along the whole extent, but in the third domicile which Robin passed, there was a half-opened door, and his keen glance detected a woman's garment within.

"My luck may be better here," said he to himself.

Accordingly, he approached the door, and beheld it shut closer as he did so; yet an open space remained, sufficing for the fair occupant to observe the stranger, with-

14. Diogenes (c. 412–323 BC), Greek philosopher.

out a corresponding display on her part. All that Robin could discern was a strip of scarlet petticoat, and the occasional sparkle of an eye, as if the moonbeams were trembling on some bright thing.

"Pretty mistress,"—for I may call her so with a good conscience, thought the shrewd youth, since I know nothing to the contrary—"my sweet pretty mistress, will you be kind enough to tell me whereabouts I must seek the dwelling of my kinsman, Major Molineux?"

Robin's voice was plaintive and winning, and the female, seeing nothing to be shunned in the handsome country youth, thrust open the door, and came forth into the moonlight. She was a dainty little figure, with a white neck, round arms, and a slender waist, at the extremity of which her scarlet petticoat jutted out over a hoop, as if she were standing in a balloon. Moreover, her face was oval and pretty, her hair dark beneath the little cap, and her bright eyes possessed a sly freedom, which triumphed over those of Robin.

"Major Molineux dwells here," said this fair woman.

Now her voice was the sweetest Robin had heard that night, the airy counterpart of a stream of melted silver; yet he could not help doubting whether that sweet voice spoke Gospel truth. He looked up and down the mean street, and then surveyed the house before which they stood. It was a small, dark edifice of two stories, the second of which projected over the lower floor; and the front apartment had the aspect of a shop for petty commodities.

"Now truly I am in luck," replied Robin, cunningly, "and so indeed is my kinsman, the Major, in having so pretty a housekeeper. But I prithee[15] trouble him to step to the door; I will deliver him a message from his friends in the country, and then go back to my lodgings at the inn."

"Nay, the Major has been a-bed this hour or more," said the lady of the scarlet petticoat; "and it would be to little purpose to disturb him to-night, seeing his evening draught was of the strongest. But he is a kind-hearted man, and it would be as much as my life's worth, to let a kinsman of his turn away from the door. You are the good old gentleman's very picture, and I could swear that was his rainy-weather hat. Also, he has garments very much resembling those leather—But come in, I pray, for I bid you hearty welcome in his name."

So saying, the fair and hospitable dame took our hero by the hand; and though the touch was light, and the force was gentleness, and though Robin read in her eyes what he did not hear in her words, yet the slender waisted woman, in the scarlet petticoat, proved stronger than the athletic country youth. She had drawn his half-willing footsteps nearly to the threshold, when the opening of a door in the neighborhood, startled the Major's housekeeper, and, leaving the Major's kinsman, she vanished speedily into her own domicile. A heavy yawn preceded the appearance of a man, who, like the Moonshine of Pyramus and Thisbe,[16] carried a lantern, needlessly aiding his sister luminary in the heavens. As he walked sleepily up the street, he turned his broad, dull face on Robin, and displayed a long staff, spiked at the end.

"Home, vagabond, home!" said the watchman, in accents that seemed to fall asleep as soon as they were uttered. "Home, or we'll set you in the stocks by peep of day!"

---

15. Pray thee.   16. William Shakespeare (1564–1616), A Midsummer Night's Dream (1600), 3.1.

"This is the second hint of the kind," thought Robin. "I wish they would end my difficulties, by setting me there to-night."

Nevertheless, the youth felt an instinctive antipathy towards the guardian of midnight order, which at first prevented him from asking his usual question. But just when the man was about to vanish behind the corner, Robin resolved not to lose the opportunity, and shouted lustily after him—

"I say, friend! will you guide me to the house of my kinsman, Major Molineux?"

The watchman made no reply, but turned the corner and was gone; yet Robin seemed to hear the sound of drowsy laughter stealing along the solitary street. At that moment, also, a pleasant titter saluted him from the open window above his head; he looked up, and caught the sparkle of a saucy eye; a round arm beckoned to him, and next he heard light footsteps descending the staircase within. But Robin, being of the household of a New England clergyman, was a good youth, as well as a shrewd one; so he resisted temptation, and fled away.

He now roamed desperately, and at random, through the town, almost ready to believe that a spell was on him, like that, by which a wizard of his country, had once kept three pursuers wandering, a whole winter night, within twenty paces of the cottage which they sought. The streets lay before him, strange and desolate, and the lights were extinguished in almost every house. Twice, however, little parties of men, among whom Robin distinguished individuals in outlandish attire, came hurrying along, but though on both occasions they paused to address him, such intercourse did not at all enlighten his perplexity. They did but utter a few words in some language of which Robin knew nothing, and perceiving his inability to answer, bestowed a curse upon him in plain English, and hastened away. Finally, the lad determined to knock at the door of every mansion that might appear worthy to be occupied by his kinsman, trusting that perseverance would overcome the fatality which had hitherto thwarted him. Firm in this resolve, he was passing beneath the walls of a church, which formed the corner of two streets, when, as he turned into the shade of its steeple, he encountered a bulky stranger, muffled in a cloak. The man was proceeding with the speed of earnest business, but Robin planted himself full before him, holding the oak cudgel with both hands across his body, as a bar to further passage.

"Halt, honest man, and answer me a question," said he, very resolutely. "Tell me, this instant, whereabouts is the dwelling of my kinsman, Major Molineux?"

"Keep your tongue between your teeth, fool, and let me pass," said a deep, gruff voice, which Robin partly remembered. "Let me pass, I say, or I'll strike you to the earth!"

"No, no, neighbor!" cried Robin, flourishing his cudgel, and then thrusting its larger end close to the man's muffled face. "No, no, I'm not the fool you take me for, nor do you pass, till I have an answer to my question. Whereabouts is the dwelling of my kinsman, Major Molineux?"

The stranger, instead of attempting to force his passage, stepped back into the moonlight, unmuffled his own face and stared full into that of Robin.

"Watch here an hour, and Major Molineux will pass by," said he.

Robin gazed with dismay and astonishment, on the unprecedented physiognomy[17] of the speaker. The forehead with its double prominence, the broad-hooked nose, the shaggy eyebrows, and fiery eyes, were those which he had noticed at the inn, but the

---

17. Facial features viewed as indicators of moral character.

man's complexion had undergone a singular, or, more properly, a two-fold change. One side of the face blazed of an intense red, while the other was black as midnight, the division line being in the broad bridge of the nose; and a mouth, which seemed to extend from ear to ear, was black or red, in contrast to the color of the cheek. The effect was as if two individual devils, a fiend of fire and a fiend of darkness, had united themselves to form this infernal visage. The stranger grinned in Robin's face, muffled his parti-colored features, and was out of sight in a moment.

"Strange things we travellers see!" ejaculated Robin.

He seated himself, however, upon the steps of the church-door, resolving to wait the appointed time for his kinsman's appearance. A few moments were consumed in philosophical speculations, upon the species of the *genus homo*,[18] who had just left him, but having settled this point shrewdly, rationally, and satisfactorily, he was compelled to look elsewhere for amusement. And first he threw his eyes along the street; it was of more respectable appearance than most of those into which he had wandered, and the moon, "creating, like the imaginative power, a beautiful strangeness in familiar objects," gave something of romance to a scene, that might not have possessed it in the light of day. The irregular, and often quaint architecture of the houses, some of whose roofs were broken into numerous little peaks; while others ascended, steep and narrow, into a single point; and others again were square; the pure milk-white of some of their complexions, the aged darkness of others, and the thousand sparklings, reflected from bright substances in the plastered walls of many; these matters engaged Robin's attention for awhile, and then began to grow wearisome. Next he endeavored to define the forms of distant objects, starting away with almost ghostly indistinctness, just as his eye appeared to grasp them; and finally he took a minute survey of an edifice, which stood on the opposite side of the street, directly in front of the church-door, where he was stationed. It was a large square mansion, distinguished from its neighbors by a balcony, which rested on tall pillars, and by an elaborate Gothic window, communicating therewith.

"Perhaps this is the very house I have been seeking," thought Robin.

Then he strove to speed away the time, by listening to a murmur, which swept continually along the street, yet was scarcely audible, except to an unaccustomed ear like his; it was a low, dull, dreamy sound, compounded of many noises, each of which was at too great a distance to be separately heard. Robin marvelled at this snore of a sleeping town, and marvelled more, whenever its continuity was broken, by now and then a distant shout, apparently loud where it originated. But altogether it was a sleep-inspiring sound, and to shake off its drowsy influence, Robin arose, and climbed a window-frame, that he might view the interior of the church. There the moon-beams came trembling in, and fell down upon the deserted pews, and extended along the quiet aisles. A fainter, yet more awful radiance, was hovering round the pulpit, and one solitary ray had dared to rest upon the opened page of the great Bible. Had Nature, in that deep hour, become a worshipper in the house, which man had builded? Or was that heavenly light the visible sanctity of the place, visible because no earthly and impure feet were within the walls? The scene made Robin's heart shiver with a sensation of loneliness, stronger than he had ever felt in the remotest depths of his native woods; so he turned away, and sat down again before the door. There were graves around the church, and now an uneasy thought obtruded into

18. Human species.

Robin's breast. What if the object of his search, which had been so often and so strangely thwarted, were all the time mouldering in his shroud? What if his kinsman should glide through yonder gate, and nod and smile to him in passing dimly by?

"Oh, that any breathing thing were here with me!" said Robin.

Recalling his thoughts from this uncomfortable track, he sent them over forest, hill, and stream, and attempted to imagine how that evening of ambiguity and weariness, had been spent by his father's household. He pictured them assembled at the door, beneath the tree, the great old tree, which had been spared for its huge twisted trunk, and venerable shade, when a thousand leafy brethren fell. There, at the going down of the summer sun, it was his father's custom to perform domestic worship, that the neighbors might come and join with him like brothers of the family, and that the wayfaring man might pause to drink at that fountain, and keep his heart pure by freshening the memory of home. Robin distinguished the seat of every individual of the little audience; he saw the good man in the midst, holding the Scriptures in the golden light that shone from the western clouds; he beheld him close the book, and all rise up to pray. He heard the old thanksgivings for daily mercies, the old supplications for their continuance, to which he had so often listened in weariness, but which were now among his dear remembrances. He perceived the slight inequality of his father's voice when he came to speak of the Absent One; he noted how his mother turned her face to the broad and knotted trunk; how his elder brother scorned, because the beard was rough upon his upper lip, to permit his features to be moved; how his younger sister drew down a low hanging branch before her eyes; and how the little one of all, whose sports had hitherto broken the decorum of the scene, understood the prayer for her playmate, and burst into clamorous grief. Then he saw them go in at the door; and when Robin would have entered also, the latch tinkled into its place, and he was excluded from his home.

"Am I here, or there?" cried Robin, starting; for all at once, when his thoughts had become visible and audible in a dream, the long, wide, solitary street shone out before him.

He aroused himself, and endeavored to fix his attention steadily upon the large edifice which he had surveyed before. But still his mind kept vibrating between fancy and reality; by turns, the pillars of the balcony lengthened into the tall, bare stems of pines, dwindled down to human figures, settled again in their true shape and size, and then commenced a new succession of changes. For a single moment, when he deemed himself awake, he could have sworn that a visage, one which he seemed to remember, yet could not absolutely name as his kinsman's, was looking towards him from the Gothic window. A deeper sleep wrestled with, and nearly overcame him, but fled at the sound of footsteps along the opposite pavement. Robin rubbed his eyes, discerned a man passing at the foot of the balcony, and addressed him in a loud, peevish, and lamentable cry.

"Halloo, friend! must I wait here all night for my kinsman, Major Molineux?"

The sleeping echoes awoke, and answered the voice; and the passenger, barely able to discern a figure sitting in the oblique shade of the steeple, traversed the street to obtain a nearer view. He was himself a gentleman in his prime, of open, intelligent, cheerful, and altogether prepossessing countenance. Perceiving a country youth, apparently homeless and without friends, he accosted him in a tone of real kindness, which had become strange to Robin's ears.

"Well, my good lad, why are you sitting here?" inquired he. "Can I be of service to you in any way?"

"I am afraid not, Sir," replied Robin, despondingly; "yet I shall take it kindly, if you'll answer me a single question. I've been searching half the night for one Major Molineux; now, Sir, is there really such a person in these parts, or am I dreaming?"

"Major Molineux! The name is not altogether strange to me," said the gentleman, smiling. "Have you any objection to telling me the nature of your business with him?"

Then Robin briefly related that his father was a clergyman, settled on a small salary, at a long distance back in the country, and that he and Major Molineux were brothers' children. The Major, having inherited riches, and acquired civil and military rank, had visited his cousin in great pomp a year or two before; had manifested much interest in Robin and an elder brother, and, being childless himself, had thrown out hints respecting the future establishment of one of them in life. The elder brother was destined to succeed to the farm, which his father cultivated, in the interval of sacred duties; it was therefore determined that Robin should profit by his kinsman's generous intentions, especially as he had seemed to be rather the favorite, and was thought to possess other necessary endowments.

"For I have the name of being a shrewd youth," observed Robin, in this part of his story.

"I doubt not you deserve it," replied his new friend, good naturedly; "but pray proceed."

"Well, Sir, being nearly eighteen years old, and well-grown, as you see," continued Robin, raising himself to his full height, "I thought it high time to begin the world. So my mother and sister put me in handsome trim, and my father gave me half the remnant of his last year's salary, and five days ago I started for this place, to pay the Major a visit. But would you believe it, Sir? I crossed the ferry a little after dusk, and have yet found nobody that would show me the way to his dwelling; only an hour or two since, I was told to wait here, and Major Molineux would pass by."

"Can you describe the man who told you this?" inquired the gentleman.

"Oh, he was a very ill-favored fellow, Sir," replied Robin, "with two great bumps on his forehead, a hook nose, fiery eyes, and, what struck me as the strangest, his face was of two different colors. Do you happen to know such a man, Sir?"

"Not intimately," answered the stranger, "but I chanced to meet him a little time previous to your stopping me. I believe you may trust his word, and that the Major will very shortly pass through this street. In the mean time, as I have a singular curiosity to witness your meeting, I will sit down here upon the steps, and bear you company."

He seated himself accordingly, and soon engaged his companion in animated discourse. It was but of brief continuance, however, for a noise of shouting, which had long been remotely audible, drew so much nearer, that Robin inquired its cause.

"What may be the meaning of this uproar?" asked he. "Truly, if your town be always as noisy, I shall find little sleep, while I am an inhabitant."

"Why, indeed, friend Robin, there do appear to be three or four riotous fellows abroad to-night," replied the gentleman. "You must not expect all the stillness of your native woods, here in our streets. But the watch will shortly be at the heels of these lads, and—"

"Aye, and set them in the stocks by peep of day," interrupted Robin, recollecting his own encounter with the drowsy lantern-bearer. "But, dear Sir, if I may trust my ears, an army of watchmen would never make head against such a multitude of rioters. There were at least a thousand voices went to make up that one shout."

"May not one man have several voices, Robin, as well as two complexions?" said his friend.

"Perhaps a man may; but Heaven forbid that a woman should!" responded the shrewd youth, thinking of the seductive tones of the Major's housekeeper.

The sounds of a trumpet in some neighboring street now became so evident and continual, that Robin's curiosity was strongly excited. In addition to the shouts, he heard frequent bursts from many instruments of discord, and a wild and confused laughter filled up the intervals. Robin rose from the steps, and looked wistfully towards a point, whither several people seemed to be hastening.

"Surely some prodigious merrymaking is going on," exclaimed he. "I have laughed very little since I left home, Sir, and should be sorry to lose an opportunity. Shall we just step round the corner by that darkish house, and take our share of the fun?"

"Sit down again, sit down, good Robin," replied the gentleman, laying his hand on the skirt of the grey coat. "You forget that we must wait here for your kinsman; and there is reason to believe that he will pass by, in the course of a very few moments."

The near approach of the uproar had now disturbed the neighborhood; windows flew open on all sides; and many heads, in the attire of the pillow, and confused by sleep suddenly broken, were protruded to the gaze of whoever had leisure to observe them. Eager voices hailed each other from house to house, all demanding the explanation, which not a soul could give. Half-dressed men hurried towards the unknown commotion, stumbling as they went over the stone steps, that thrust themselves into the narrow foot-walk. The shouts, the laughter, and the tuneless bray, the antipodes[19] of music, came onward with increasing din, till scattered individuals, and then denser bodies, began to appear round a corner, at the distance of a hundred yards.

"Will you recognize your kinsman, Robin, if he passes in this crowd?" inquired the gentleman.

"Indeed, I can't warrant it, Sir; but I'll take my stand here, and keep a bright look out," answered Robin, descending to the outer edge of the pavement.

A mighty stream of people now emptied into the street, and came rolling slowly towards the church. A single horseman wheeled the corner in the midst of them, and close behind him came a band of fearful wind-instruments, sending forth a fresher discord, now that no intervening buildings kept it from the ear. Then a redder light disturbed the moonbeams, and a dense multitude of torches shone along the street, concealing by their glare whatever object they illuminated. The single horseman, clad in a military dress, and bearing a drawn sword, rode onward as the leader, and, by his fierce and variegated countenance, appeared like war personified; the red of one cheek was an emblem of fire and sword; the blackness of the other betokened the mourning which attends them. In his train, were wild figures in the Indian dress, and many fantastic shapes without a model, giving the whole march a visionary air, as if a dream had broken forth from some feverish brain, and were sweeping visibly through the midnight streets. A mass of people, inactive, except as applauding spectators, hemmed the procession in, and several women ran along the sidewalks, piercing the confusion of heavier sounds, with their shrill voices of mirth or terror.

---

19. Opposite extremes.

"The double-faced fellow has his eye upon me," muttered Robin, with an indefinite but uncomfortable idea, that he was himself to bear a part in the pageantry.

The leader turned himself in the saddle, and fixed his glance full upon the country youth, as the steed went slowly by. When Robin had freed his eyes from those fiery ones, the musicians were passing before him, and the torches were close at hand; but the unsteady brightness of the latter formed a veil which he could not penetrate. The rattling of wheels over the stones sometimes found its way to his ear, and confused traces of a human form appeared at intervals, and then melted into the vivid light. A moment more, and the leader thundered a command to halt; the trumpets vomited a horrid breath, and held their peace; the shouts and laughter of the people died away, and there remained only a universal hum, nearly allied to silence. Right before Robin's eyes was an uncovered cart. There the torches blazed the brightest, there the moon shone out like day, and there, in tar-and-feather dignity, sat his kinsman, Major Molineux!

He was an elderly man, of large and majestic person, and strong, square features, betokening a steady soul; but steady as it was, his enemies had found the means to shake it. His face was pale as death, and far more ghastly; the broad forehead was contracted in his agony, so that his eyebrows formed one grizzled line; his eyes were red and wild, and the foam hung white upon his quivering lip. His whole frame was agitated by a quick, and continual tremor, which his pride strove to quell, even in those circumstances of overwhelming humiliation. But perhaps the bitterest pang of all was when his eyes met those of Robin; for he evidently knew him on the instant, as the youth stood witnessing the foul disgrace of a head that had grown grey in honor. They stared at each other in silence, and Robin's knees shook, and his hair bristled, with a mixture of pity and terror. Soon, however, a bewildering excitement began to seize upon his mind; the preceding adventures of the night, the unexpected appearance of the crowd, the torches, the confused din, and the hush that followed, the spectre of his kinsman reviled by that great multitude, all this, and more than all, a perception of tremendous ridicule in the whole scene, affected him with a sort of mental inebriety.[20] At that moment a voice of sluggish merriment saluted Robin's ears; he turned instinctively, and just behind the corner of the church stood the lantern-bearer, rubbing his eyes, and drowsily enjoying the lad's amazement. Then he heard a peal of laughter like the ringing of silvery bells; a woman twitched his arm, a saucy eye met his, and he saw the lady of the scarlet petticoat. A sharp, dry cachinnation[21] appealed to his memory, and, standing on tiptoe in the crowd, with his white apron over his head, he beheld the courteous little innkeeper. And lastly, there sailed over the heads of the multitude a great, broad laugh, broken in the midst by two sepulchral hems; thus—

"Haw, haw, haw—hem, hem—haw, haw, haw, haw."

The sound proceeded from the balcony of the opposite edifice, and thither Robin turned his eyes. In front of the Gothic window stood the old citizen, wrapped in a wide gown, his grey periwig exchanged for a nightcap, which was thrust back from his forehead, and his silk stockings hanging down about his legs. He supported himself on his polished cane in a fit of convulsive merriment, which manifested itself on his solemn old features, like a funny inscription on a tombstone. Then Robin seemed to hear the voices of the barbers; of the guests of the inn; and of all who had made sport of him that night. The contagion was spreading among the multitude, when, all at

20. Drunkenness.   21. Laugh.

once, it seized upon Robin, and he sent forth a shout of laughter that echoed through the street; every man shook his sides, every man emptied his lungs, but Robin's shout was the loudest there. The cloud-spirits peeped from their silvery islands, as the congregated mirth went roaring up the sky! The Man in the Moon heard the far bellow; "Oho," quoth he, "the old Earth is frolicsome to-night!"

When there was a momentary calm in that tempestuous sea of sound, the leader gave the sign, the procession resumed its march. On they went, like fiends that throng in mockery round some dead potentate,[22] mighty no more, but majestic still in his agony. On they went, in counterfeited pomp, in senseless uproar, in frenzied merriment, trampling all on an old man's heart. On swept the tumult, and left a silent street behind.

"Well, Robin, are you dreaming?" inquired the gentleman, laying his hand on the youth's shoulder.

Robin started, and withdrew his arm from the stone post, to which he had instinctively clung, while the living stream rolled by him. His cheek was somewhat pale, and his eye not quite so lively as in the earlier part of the evening.

"Will you be kind enough to show me the way to the ferry?" said he, after a moment's pause.

"You have then adopted a new subject of inquiry?" observed his companion, with a smile.

"Why, yes, Sir," replied Robin, rather dryly. "Thanks to you, and to my other friends, I have at last met my kinsman, and he will scarce desire to see my face again. I begin to grow weary of a town life, Sir. Will you show me the way to the ferry?"

"No, my good friend Robin, not to-night, at least," said the gentleman. "Some few days hence, if you continue to wish it, I will speed you on your journey. Or, if you prefer to remain with us, perhaps, as you are a shrewd youth, you may rise in the world, without the help of your kinsman, Major Molineux."

—1832

The Birth-mark

In the latter part of the last century, there lived a man of science—an eminent proficient in every branch of natural philosophy—who, not long before our story opens, had made experience of a spiritual affinity, more attractive than any chemical one. He had left his laboratory to the care of an assistant, cleared his fine countenance from the furnace-smoke, washed the stain of acids from his fingers, and persuaded a beautiful woman to become his wife. In those days, when the comparatively recent discovery of electricity, and other kindred mysteries of nature, seemed to open paths into the region of miracle, it was not unusual for the love of science to rival the love of woman, in its depth and absorbing energy. The higher intellect, the imagination, the spirit, and even the heart, might all find their congenial aliment[1] in pursuits which, as some of their ardent votaries[2] believed, would ascend from one step of powerful intelligence to another, until the philosopher should lay his hand on the secret

---

22. Ruler, king.

1. Nourishment.   2. Devout followers.

of creative force, and perhaps make new worlds for himself. We know not whether Aylmer possessed this degree of faith in man's ultimate control over nature. He had devoted himself, however, too unreservedly to scientific studies, ever to be weaned from them by any second passion. His love for his young wife might prove the stronger of the two; but it could only be by intertwining itself with his love of science, and uniting the strength of the latter to its own.

Such a union accordingly took place, and was attended with truly remarkable consequences, and a deeply impressive moral. One day, very soon after their marriage, Aylmer sat gazing at his wife, with a trouble in his countenance that grew stronger, until he spoke.

"Georgiana," said he, "has it never occurred to you that the mark upon your cheek might be removed?"

"No, indeed," said she, smiling; but perceiving the seriousness of his manner, she blushed deeply. "To tell you the truth, it has been so often called a charm, that I was simple enough to imagine it might be so."

"Ah, upon another face, perhaps it might," replied her husband. "But never on yours! No, dearest Georgiana, you came so nearly perfect from the hand of Nature, that this slightest possible defect—which we hesitate whether to term a defect or a beauty—shocks me, as being the visible mark of earthly imperfection."

"Shocks you, my husband!" cried Georgiana, deeply hurt; at first reddening with momentary anger, but then bursting into tears. "Then why did you take me from my mother's side? You cannot love what shocks you!"

To explain this conversation, it must be mentioned, that, in the centre of Georgiana's left cheek, there was a singular mark, deeply interwoven, as it were, with the texture and substance of her face. In the usual state of her complexion,—a healthy, though delicate bloom,—the mark wore a tint of deeper crimson, which imperfectly defined its shape amid the surrounding rosiness. When she blushed, it gradually became more indistinct, and finally vanished amid the triumphant rush of blood, that bathed the whole cheek with its brilliant glow. But, if any shifting emotion caused her to turn pale, there was the mark again, a crimson stain upon the snow, in what Aylmer sometimes deemed an almost fearful distinctness. Its shape bore not a little similarity to the human hand, though of the smallest pigmy size. Georgiana's lovers were wont to say, that some fairy, at her birth-hour, had laid her tiny hand upon the infant's cheek, and left this impress there, in token of the magic endowments that were to give her such sway over all hearts. Many a desperate swain[3] would have risked life for the privilege of pressing his lips to the mysterious hand. It must not be concealed, however, that the impression wrought by this fairy sign-manual varied exceedingly, according to the difference of temperament in the beholders. Some fastidious persons—but they were exclusively of her own sex—affirmed that the Bloody Hand, as they chose to call it, quite destroyed the effect of Georgiana's beauty, and rendered her countenance even hideous. But it would be as reasonable to say, that one of those small blue stains, which sometimes occur in the purest statuary marble, would convert the Eve of Powers[4] to a monster. Masculine observers, if the birth-mark did not heighten their admiration, contented themselves with wishing it away, that the world might possess one living specimen of ideal loveliness, without

---

3. A young man of the country.   4. *Eve Before the Fall*, a statue by Hiram Powers (1805–1873), American sculptor.

the semblance of a flaw. After his marriage—for he thought little or nothing of the matter before—Aylmer discovered that this was the case with himself.

Had she been less beautiful—if Envy's self could have found aught else to sneer at—he might have felt his affection heightened by the prettiness of this mimic hand, now vaguely portrayed, now lost, now stealing forth again, and glimmering to-and-fro with every pulse of emotion that throbbed within her heart. But, seeing her otherwise so perfect, he found this one defect grow more and more intolerable, with every moment of their united lives. It was the fatal flaw of humanity, which Nature, in one shape or another, stamps ineffaceably on all her productions, either to imply that they are temporary and finite, or that their perfection must be wrought by toil and pain. The Crimson Hand expressed the ineludible gripe, in which mortality clutches the highest and purest of earthly mould, degrading them into kindred with the lowest, and even with the very brutes, like whom their visible frames return to dust. In this manner, selecting it as the symbol of his wife's liability to sin, sorrow, decay, and death, Aylmer's sombre imagination was not long in rendering the birth-mark a frightful object, causing him more trouble and horror than ever Georgiana's beauty, whether of soul or sense, had given him delight.

At all the seasons which should have been their happiest, he invariably, and without intending it—nay, in spite of a purpose to the contrary—reverted to this one disastrous topic. Trifling as it at first appeared, it so connected itself with innumerable trains of thought, and modes of feeling, that it became the central point of all. With the morning twilight, Aylmer opened his eyes upon his wife's face, and recognized the symbol of imperfection; and when they sat together at the evening hearth, his eyes wandered stealthily to her cheek, and beheld, flickering with the blaze of the wood fire, the spectral Hand that wrote mortality, where he would fain have[5] worshipped. Georgiana soon learned to shudder at his gaze. It needed but a glance, with the peculiar expression that his face often wore, to change the roses of her cheek into a deathlike paleness, amid which the Crimson Hand was brought strongly out, like a bas-relief[6] of ruby on the whitest marble.

Late, one night, when the lights were growing dim, so as hardly to betray the stain on the poor wife's cheek, she herself, for the first time, voluntarily took up the subject.

"Do you remember, my dear Aylmer," said she, with a feeble attempt at a smile—"have you any recollection of a dream, last night, about this odious Hand?"

"None!—none whatever!" replied Aylmer, starting; but then he added in a dry, cold tone, affected for the sake of concealing the real depth of his emotion:—"I might well dream of it; for before I fell asleep, it had taken a pretty firm hold of my fancy."

"And you did dream of it," continued Georgiana, hastily; for she dreaded lest a gush of tears should interrupt what she had to say—"A terrible dream! I wonder that you can forget it. Is it possible to forget this one expression?—'It is in her heart now—we must have it out!'—Reflect, my husband; for by all means I would have you recall that dream."

The mind is in a sad note, when Sleep, the all-involving, cannot confine her spectres within the dim region of her sway, but suffers them to break forth, affrighting this actual life with secrets that perchance belong to a deeper one. Aylmer now remembered his dream. He had fancied himself, with his servant Aminadab, attempting an opera-

---

5. Would have preferred to.   6. Raised sculpture carved on a flat surface.

tion for the removal of the birth-mark. But the deeper went the knife, the deeper sank the Hand, until at length its tiny grasp appeared to have caught hold of Georgiana's heart; whence, however, her husband was inexorably resolved to cut or wrench it away.

When the dream had shaped itself perfectly in his memory, Aylmer sat in his wife's presence with a guilty feeling. Truth often finds its way to the mind close-muffled in robes of sleep, and then speaks with uncompromising directness of matters in regard to which we practise an unconscious self-deception, during our waking moments. Until now, he had not been aware of the tyrannizing influence acquired by one idea over his mind, and of the lengths which he might find in his heart to go, for the sake of giving himself peace.

"Aylmer," resumed Georgiana, solemnly, "I know not what may be the cost to both of us, to rid me of this fatal birth-mark. Perhaps its removal may cause cureless deformity. Or, it may be, the stain goes as deep as life itself. Again, do we know that there is a possibility, on any terms, of unclasping the firm gripe of this little Hand, which was laid upon me before I came into the world?"

"Dearest Georgiana, I have spent much thought upon the subject," hastily interrupted Aylmer—"I am convinced of the perfect practicability of its removal."

"If there be the remotest possibility of it," continued Georgiana, "let the attempt be made, at whatever risk. Danger is nothing to me; for life—while this hateful mark makes me the object of your horror and disgust—life is a burthen which I would fling down with joy. Either remove this dreadful Hand, or take my wretched life! You have deep science! All the world bears witness of it. You have achieved great wonders! Cannot you remove this little, little mark, which I cover with the tips of two small fingers? Is this beyond your power, for the sake of your own peace, and to save your poor wife from madness?"

"Noblest—dearest—tenderest wife!" cried Aylmer, rapturously. "Doubt not my power. I have already given this matter the deepest thought—thought which might almost have enlightened me to create a being less perfect than yourself. Georgiana, you have led me deeper than ever into the heart of science. I feel myself fully competent to render this dear cheek as faultless as its fellow; and then, most beloved, what will be my triumph, when I shall have corrected what Nature left imperfect, in her fairest work! Even Pygmalion,[7] when his sculptured woman assumed life, felt not greater ecstasy than mine will be."

"It is resolved, then," said Georgiana, faintly smiling,—"And, Aylmer, spare me not, though you should find the birth-mark take refuge in my heart at last."

Her husband tenderly kissed her cheek—her right cheek—not that which bore the impress of the Crimson Hand.

The next day, Aylmer apprized his wife of a plan that he had formed, whereby he might have opportunity for the intense thought and constant watchfulness, which the proposed operation would require; while Georgiana, likewise, would enjoy the perfect repose essential to its success. They were to seclude themselves in the extensive apartments occupied by Aylmer as a laboratory, and where, during his toilsome youth, he had made discoveries in the elemental powers of nature, that had roused the admiration of all the learned societies in Europe. Seated calmly in this laboratory, the pale philosopher had investigated the secrets of the highest cloud-region, and of the profoundest

---

7. In Greek myth, Pygmalion sculpted a statue of a woman and then fell in love with it, prompting the goddess Athena to bring it to life.

mines; he had satisfied himself of the causes that kindled and kept alive the fires of the volcano; and had explained the mystery of fountains, and how it is that they gush forth, some so bright and pure, and others with such rich medicinal virtues, from the dark bosom of the earth. Here, too, at an earlier period, he had studied the wonders of the human frame, and attempted to fathom the very process by which Nature assimilates all her precious influences from earth and air, and from the spiritual world, to create and foster Man, her masterpiece. The latter pursuit, however, Aylmer had long laid aside, in unwilling recognition of the truth, against which all seekers sooner or later stumble, that our great creative Mother, while she amuses us with apparently working in the broadest sunshine, is yet severely careful to keep her own secrets, and, in spite of her pretended openness, shows us nothing but results. She permits us indeed, to mar, but seldom to mend, and, like a jealous patentee, on no account to make. Now, however, Aylmer resumed these half-forgotten investigations; not, of course, with such hopes or wishes as first suggested them; but because they involved much physiological truth, and lay in the path of his proposed scheme for the treatment of Georgiana.

As he led her over the threshold of the laboratory, Georgiana was cold and tremulous. Aylmer looked cheerfully into her face, with intent to reassure her, but was so startled with the intense glow of the birth-mark upon the whiteness of her cheek, that he could not restrain a strong convulsive shudder. His wife fainted.

"Aminadab! Aminadab!" shouted Aylmer, stamping violently on the floor.

Forthwith, there issued from an inner apartment a man of low stature, but bulky frame, with shaggy hair hanging about his visage, which was grimed with the vapors of the furnace. This personage had been Aylmer's under-worker during his whole scientific career, and was admirably fitted for that office by his great mechanical readiness, and the skill with which, while incapable of comprehending a single principle, he executed all the practical details of his master's experiments. With his vast strength, his shaggy hair, his smoky aspect, and the indescribable earthiness that incrusted him, he seemed to represent man's physical nature; while Aylmer's slender figure, and pale, intellectual face, were no less apt a type of the spiritual element.

"Throw open the door of the boudoir, Aminadab," said Aylmer, "and burn a pastille."[8]

"Yes, master," answered Aminadab, looking intently at the lifeless form of Georgiana; and then he muttered to himself:—"If she were my wife, I'd never part with that birth-mark."

When Georgiana recovered consciousness, she found herself breathing an atmosphere of penetrating fragrance, the gentle potency of which had recalled her from her deathlike faintness. The scene around her looked like enchantment. Aylmer had converted those smoky, dingy, sombre rooms, where he had spent his brightest years in recondite pursuits, into a series of beautiful apartments, not unfit to be the secluded abode of a lovely woman. The walls were hung with gorgeous curtains, which imparted the combination of grandeur and grace, that no other species of adornment can achieve; and as they fell from the ceiling to the floor, their rich and ponderous folds, concealing all angles and straight lines, appeared to shut in the scene from infinite space. For aught Georgiana knew, it might be a pavilion among the clouds. And

---

8. Incense.

Aylmer, excluding the sunshine, which would have interfered with his chemical processes, had supplied its place with perfumed lamps, emitting flames of various hue, but all uniting in a soft, empurpled radiance. He now knelt by his wife's side, watching her earnestly, but without alarm; for he was confident in his science, and felt that he could draw a magic circle round her, within which no evil might intrude.

"Where am I?—Ah, I remember!" said Georgiana, faintly; and she placed her hand over her cheek, to hide the terrible mark from her husband's eyes.

"Fear not, dearest!" exclaimed he. "Do not shrink from me! Believe me, Georgiana, I even rejoice in this single imperfection, since it will be such rapture to remove it."

"Oh, spare me!" sadly replied his wife—"Pray do not look at it again. I never can forget that convulsive shudder."

In order to soothe Georgiana, and, as it were, to release her mind from the burthen of actual things, Aylmer now put in practice some of the light and playful secrets, which science had taught him among its profounder lore. Airy figures, absolutely bodiless ideas, and forms of unsubstantial beauty, came and danced before her, imprinting their momentary footsteps on beams of light. Though she had some indistinct idea of the method of these optical phenomena, still the illusion was almost perfect enough to warrant the belief, that her husband possessed sway over the spiritual world. Then again, when she felt a wish to look forth from her seclusion, immediately, as if her thoughts were answered, the procession of external existence flitted across a screen. The scenery and the figures of actual life were perfectly represented, but with that bewitching, yet indescribable difference, which always makes a picture, an image, or a shadow, so much more attractive than the original. When wearied of this, Aylmer bade her cast her eyes upon a vessel, containing a quantity of earth. She did so, with little interest at first, but was soon startled, to perceive the germ of a plant, shooting upward from the soil. Then came the slender stalk—the leaves gradually unfolded themselves—and amid them was a perfect and lovely flower.

"It is magical!" cried Georgiana, "I dare not touch it."

"Nay, pluck it," answered Aylmer, "pluck it, and inhale its brief perfume while you may. The flower will wither in a few moments, and leave nothing save its brown seed-vessels—but thence may be perpetuated a race as ephemeral as itself."

But Georgiana had no sooner touched the flower than the whole plant suffered a blight, its leaves turning coal-black, as if by the agency of fire.

"There was too powerful a stimulus," said Aylmer thoughtfully.

To make up for this abortive experiment, he proposed to take her portrait by a scientific process of his own invention. It was to be effected by rays of light striking upon a polished plate of metal. Georgiana assented—but, on looking at the result, was affrighted to find the features of the portrait blurred and indefinable, while the minute figure of a hand appeared where the cheek should have been. Aylmer snatched the metallic plate, and threw it into a jar of corrosive acid.

Soon, however, he forgot these mortifying failures. In the intervals of study and chemical experiment, he came to her, flushed and exhausted, but seemed invigorated by her presence, and spoke in glowing language of the resources of his art. He gave a history of the long dynasty of the Alchemists, who spent so many ages in quest of the universal solvent, by which the Golden Principle[9] might be elicited from all things

---

9. Elixir of immortality.

vile and base. Aylmer appeared to believe, that, by the plainest scientific logic, it was altogether within the limits of possibility to discover this long-sought medium; but, he added, a philosopher who should go deep enough to acquire the power, would attain too lofty a wisdom to stoop to the exercise of it. Not less singular were his opinions in regard to the Elixir Vitæ. He more than intimated, that it was his option to concoct a liquid that should prolong life for years—perhaps interminably—but that it would produce a discord in nature, which all the world, and chiefly the quaffer of the immortal nostrum, would find cause to curse.

"Aylmer, are you in earnest?" asked Georgiana, looking at him with amazement and fear; "it is terrible to possess such power, or even to dream of possessing it!"

"Oh, do not tremble, my love!" said her husband, "I would not wrong either you or myself by working such inharmonious effects upon our lives. But I would have you consider how trifling, in comparison, is the skill requisite to remove this little Hand."

At the mention of the birth-mark, Georgiana, as usual, shrank, as if a red-hot iron had touched her cheek.

Again Aylmer applied himself to his labors. She could hear his voice in the distant furnace-room, giving directions to Aminadab, whose harsh, uncouth, misshapen tones were audible in response, more like the grunt or growl of a brute than human speech. After hours of absence, Aylmer reappeared, and proposed that she should now examine his cabinet of chemical products, and natural treasures of the earth. Among the former he showed her a small vial, in which, he remarked, was contained a gentle yet most powerful fragrance, capable of impregnating all the breezes that blow across a kingdom. They were of inestimable value, the contents of that little vial; and, as he said so, he threw some of the perfume into the air, and filled the room with piercing and invigorating delight.

"And what is this?" asked Georgiana, pointing to a small crystal globe, containing a gold-colored liquid. "It is so beautiful to the eye, that I could imagine it the Elixir of Life."

"In one sense it is," replied Aylmer, "or rather the Elixir of Immortality. It is the most precious poison that ever was concocted in this world. By its aid, I could apportion the lifetime of any mortal at whom you might point your finger. The strength of the dose would determine whether he were to linger out years, or drop dead in the midst of a breath. No king, on his guarded throne, could keep his life, if I, in my private station, should deem that the welfare of millions justified me in depriving him of it."

"Why do you keep such a terrific drug?" inquired Georgiana in horror.

"Do not mistrust me, dearest!" said her husband, smiling; "its virtuous potency is yet greater than its harmful one. But, see! here is a powerful cosmetic. With a few drops of this, in a vase of water, freckles may be washed away as easily as the hands are cleansed. A stronger infusion would take the blood out of the cheek, and leave the rosiest beauty a pale ghost."

"Is it with this lotion that you intend to bathe my cheek?" asked Georgiana anxiously.

"Oh, no!" hastily replied her husband—"this is merely superficial. Your case demands a remedy that shall go deeper."

In his interviews with Georgiana, Aylmer generally made minute inquiries as to her sensations, and whether the confinement of the rooms, and the temperature of the atmosphere, agreed with her. These questions had such a particular drift, that Georgiana began to conjecture that she was already subjected to certain physical influences, either breathed in with the fragrant air, or taken with her food. She fancied, likewise—but it might be altogether fancy—that there was a stirring up of her system,—a strange indefinite sensation creeping through her veins, and tingling, half painfully, half pleasurably, at her heart. Still, whenever she dared to look into the mirror, there she beheld herself, pale as a white rose, and with the crimson birth-mark stamped upon her cheek. Not even Aylmer now hated it so much as she.

To dispel the tedium of the hours which her husband found it necessary to devote to the processes of combination and analysis, Georgiana turned over the volumes of his scientific library. In many dark old tomes, she met with chapters full of romance and poetry. They were the works of the philosophers of the middle ages, such as Albertus Magnus, Cornelius Agrippa, Paracelsus, and the famous friar who created the prophetic Brazen Head.[10] All these antique naturalists stood in advance of their centuries, yet were imbued with some of their credulity, and therefore were believed, and perhaps imagined themselves, to have acquired from the investigation of nature a power above nature, and from physics a sway over the spiritual world. Hardly less curious and imaginative were the early volumes of the Transactions of the Royal Society,[11] in which the members, knowing little of the limits of natural possibility, were continually recording wonders, or proposing methods whereby wonders might be wrought.

But, to Georgiana, the most engrossing volume was a large folio from her husband's own hand, in which he had recorded every experiment of his scientific career, with its original aim, the methods adopted for its development, and its final success or failure, with the circumstances to which either event was attributable. The book, in truth, was both the history and emblem of his ardent, ambitious, imaginative, yet practical and laborious, life. He handled physical details, as if there were nothing beyond them; yet spiritualized them all, and redeemed himself from materialism, by his strong and eager aspiration towards the infinite. In his grasp, the veriest clod of earth assumed a soul. Georgiana, as she read, reverenced Aylmer, and loved him more profoundly than ever, but with a less entire dependence on his judgment than heretofore. Much as he had accomplished, she could not but observe that his most splendid successes were almost invariably failures, if compared with the ideal at which he aimed. His brightest diamonds were the merest pebbles, and felt to be so by himself, in comparison with the inestimable gems which lay hidden beyond his reach. The volume, rich with achievements that had won renown for its author, was yet as melancholy a record as ever mortal hand had penned. It was the sad confession, and continual exemplification, of the short-comings of the composite man—the spirit burthened with clay and working in matter—and of the despair that assails the higher nature, at finding itself so miserably thwarted by the earthly part. Perhaps every man of genius, in whatever sphere, might recognize the image of his own experience in Aylmer's journal.

So deeply did these reflections affect Georgiana, that she laid her face upon the open volume, and burst into tears. In this situation she was found by her husband.

---

10. Albertus Magnus (c. 1206–1280), German theologian and alchemist; Cornelius Agrippa (c. 1486–1534), German occultist; Paracelsus (1493–1541), Swiss alchemist; Roger Bacon (c. 1214–1294), English friar believed to have made a brass head speak.   11. British scientific society.

"It is dangerous to read in a sorcerer's books," said he, with a smile, though his countenance was uneasy and displeased. "Georgiana, there are pages in that volume, which I can scarcely glance over and keep my senses. Take heed lest it prove as detrimental to you!"

"It has made me worship you more than ever," said she.

"Ah! wait for this one success," rejoined he, "then worship me if you will. I shall deem myself hardly unworthy of it. But, come! I have sought you for the luxury of your voice. Sing to me, dearest!"

So she poured out the liquid music of her voice to quench the thirst of his spirit. He then took his leave, with a boyish exuberance of gaiety, assuring her that her seclusion would endure but a little longer, and that the result was already certain. Scarcely had he departed, when Georgiana felt irresistibly impelled to follow him. She had forgotten to inform Aylmer of a symptom, which, for two or three hours past, had begun to excite her attention. It was a sensation in the fatal birth-mark, not painful, but which induced a restlessness throughout her system. Hastening after her husband, she intruded, for the first time, into the laboratory.

The first thing that struck her eye was the furnace, that hot and feverish worker, with the intense glow of its fire, which, by the quantities of soot clustered above it, seemed to have been burning for ages. There was a distilling apparatus in full operation. Around the room were retorts,[12] tubes, cylinders, crucibles, and other apparatus of chemical research. An electrical machine stood ready for immediate use. The atmosphere felt oppressively close, and was tainted with gaseous odors, which had been tormented forth by the processes of science. The severe and homely simplicity of the apartment, with its naked walls and brick pavement, looked strange, accustomed as Georgiana had become to the fantastic elegance of her boudoir. But what chiefly, indeed almost solely, drew her attention, was the aspect of Aylmer himself.

He was pale as death, anxious, and absorbed, and hung over the furnace as if it depended upon his utmost watchfulness whether the liquid, which it was distilling, should be the draught of immortal happiness or misery. How different from the sanguine and joyous mien[13] that he had assumed for Georgiana's encouragement!

"Carefully now, Aminadab! Carefully, thou human machine! Carefully, thou man of clay!" muttered Aylmer, more to himself than his assistant. "Now, if there be a thought too much or too little, it is all over!"

"Hoh! hoh!" mumbled Aminadab—"look, master, look!"

Aylmer raised his eyes hastily, and at first reddened, then grew paler than ever, on beholding Georgiana. He rushed towards her, and seized her arm with a gripe that left the print of his fingers upon it.

"Why do you come hither? Have you no trust in your husband?" cried he impetuously. "Would you throw the blight of that fatal birth-mark over my labors? It is not well done. Go, prying woman, go!"

"Nay, Aylmer," said Georgiana, with the firmness of which she possessed no stinted endowment, "it is not you that have a right to complain. You mistrust your wife! You have concealed the anxiety with which you watch the development of this experiment. Think not so unworthily of me, my husband! Tell me all the risk we run; and fear not that I shall shrink, for my share in it is far less than your own!"

12. Beakers.   13. Appearance.

"No, no, Georgiana!" said Aylmer impatiently, "it must not be."

"I submit," replied she calmly. "And, Aylmer, I shall quaff whatever draught you bring me; but it will be on the same principle that would induce me to take a dose of poison, if offered by your hand."

"My noble wife," said Aylmer, deeply moved, "I knew not the height and depth of your nature, until now. Nothing shall be concealed. Know, then, that this Crimson Hand, superficial as it seems, has clutched its grasp into your being, with a strength of which I had no previous conception. I have already administered agents powerful enough to do aught except to change your entire physical system. Only one thing remains to be tried. If that fail us, we are ruined!"

"Why did you hesitate to tell me this?" asked she.

"Because, Georgiana," said Aylmer, in a low voice, "there is danger!"

"Danger? There is but one danger—that this horrible stigma shall be left upon my cheek!" cried Georgiana. "Remove it! remove it!—whatever be the cost—or we shall both go mad!"

"Heaven knows, your words are too true," said Aylmer, sadly. "And now, dearest, return to your boudoir. In a little while, all will be tested."

He conducted her back, and took leave of her with a solemn tenderness, which spoke far more than his words how much was now at stake. After his departure, Georgiana became wrapt in musings. She considered the character of Aylmer, and did it completer justice than at any previous moment. Her heart exulted, while it trembled, at his honorable love, so pure and lofty that it would accept nothing less than perfection, nor miserably make itself contented with an earthlier nature than he had dreamed of. She felt how much more precious was such a sentiment, than that meaner kind which would have borne with the imperfection for her sake, and have been guilty of treason to holy love, by degrading its perfect idea to the level of the actual. And, with her whole spirit, she prayed, that, for a single moment, she might satisfy his highest and deepest conception. Longer than one moment, she well knew, it could not be; for his spirit was ever on the march—ever ascending—and each instant required something that was beyond the scope of the instant before.

The sound of her husband's footsteps aroused her. He bore a crystal goblet, containing a liquor colorless as water, but bright enough to be the draught of immortality. Aylmer was pale; but it seemed rather the consequence of a highly wrought state of mind, and tension of spirit, than of fear or doubt.

"The concoction of the draught has been perfect," said he, in answer to Georgiana's look. "Unless all my science have deceived me, it cannot fail."

"Save on your account, my dearest Aylmer," observed his wife, "I might wish to put off this birth-mark of mortality by relinquishing mortality itself, in preference to any other mode. Life is but a sad possession to those who have attained precisely the degree of moral advancement at which I stand. Were I weaker and blinder, it might be happiness. Were I stronger, it might be endured hopefully. But, being what I find myself, methinks I am of all mortals the most fit to die."

"You are fit for heaven without tasting death!" replied her husband. "But why do we speak of dying? The draught cannot fail. Behold its effect upon this plant!"

On the window-seat there stood a geranium, diseased with yellow blotches, which had overspread all its leaves. Aylmer poured a small quantity of the liquid upon the soil in which it grew. In a little time, when the roots of the plant had taken up the moisture, the unsightly blotches began to be extinguished in a living verdure.

"There needed no proof," said Georgiana, quietly. "Give me the goblet. I joyfully stake all upon your word."

"Drink, then, thou lofty creature!" exclaimed Aylmer, with fervid admiration. "There is no taint of imperfection on thy spirit. Thy sensible frame, too, shall soon be all perfect!"

She quaffed the liquid, and returned the goblet to his hand.

"It is grateful," said she, with a placid smile. "Methinks it is like water from a heavenly fountain; for it contains I know not what of unobtrusive fragrance and deliciousness. It allays a feverish thirst, that had parched me for many days. Now, dearest, let me sleep. My earthly senses are closing over my spirit, like the leaves round the heart of a rose, at sunset."

She spoke the last words with a gentle reluctance, as if it required almost more energy than she could command to pronounce the faint and lingering syllables. Scarcely had they loitered through her lips, ere she was lost in slumber. Aylmer sat by her side, watching her aspect with the emotions proper to a man, the whole value of whose existence was involved in the process now to be tested. Mingled with this mood, however, was the philosophic investigation, characteristic of the man of science. Not the minutest symptom escaped him. A heightened flush of the cheek—a slight irregularity of breath—a quiver of the eyelid—a hardly perceptible tremor through the frame—such were the details which, as the moments passed, he wrote down in his folio volume. Intense thought had set its stamp upon every previous page of that volume; but the thoughts of years were all concentrated upon the last.

While thus employed, he failed not to gaze often at the fatal Hand, and not without a shudder. Yet once, by a strange and unaccountable impulse, he pressed it with his lips. His spirit recoiled, however, in the very act, and Georgiana, out of the midst of her deep sleep, moved uneasily and murmured, as if in remonstrance. Again, Aylmer resumed his watch. Nor was it without avail. The Crimson Hand, which at first had been strongly visible upon the marble paleness of Georgiana's cheek now grew more faintly outlined. She remained not less pale than ever; but the birth-mark, with every breath that came and went, lost somewhat of its former distinctness. Its presence had been awful; its departure was more awful still. Watch the stain of the rainbow fading out of the sky; and you will know how that mysterious symbol passed away.

"By Heaven, it is well nigh gone!" said Aylmer to himself, in almost irrepressible ecstasy. "I can scarcely trace it now. Success! Success! And now it is like the faintest rose-color. The slightest flush of blood across her cheek would overcome it. But she is so pale!"

He drew aside the window-curtain, and suffered the light of natural day to fall into the room, and rest upon her cheek. At the same time, he heard a gross, hoarse chuckle, which he had long known as his servant Aminadab's expression of delight.

"Ah, clod! Ah, earthly mass!" cried Aylmer, laughing in a sort of frenzy. "You have served me well! Matter and Spirit—Earth and Heaven—have both done their part in this! Laugh, thing of senses! You have earned the right to laugh."

These exclamations broke Georgiana's sleep. She slowly unclosed her eyes, and gazed into the mirror, which her husband had arranged for that purpose. A faint smile flitted over her lips, when she recognized how barely perceptible was now that Crimson Hand, which had once blazed forth with such disastrous brilliancy as to scare away all their happiness. But then her eyes sought Aylmer's face, with a trouble and anxiety that he could by no means account for.

"My poor Aylmer!" murmured she.

"Poor? Nay, richest! Happiest! Most favored!" exclaimed he. "My peerless bride, it is successful! You are perfect!"

"My poor Aylmer!" she repeated, with a more than human tenderness. "You have aimed loftily!—you have done nobly! Do not repent, that, with so high and pure a feeling, you have rejected the best that earth could offer. Aylmer—dearest Aylmer—I am dying!"

Alas, it was too true! The fatal Hand had grappled with the mystery of life, and was the bond by which an angelic spirit kept itself in union with a mortal frame. As the last crimson tint of the birth-mark—that sole token of human imperfection—faded from her cheek, the parting breath of the now perfect woman passed into the atmosphere, and her soul, lingering a moment near her husband, took its heavenward flight. Then a hoarse, chuckling laugh was heard again! Thus ever does the gross Fatality of Earth exult in its invariable triumph over the immortal essence, which, in this dim sphere of half-development, demands the completeness of a higher state. Yet, had Aylmer reached a profounder wisdom, he need not thus have flung away the happiness, which would have woven his mortal life of the self-same texture with the celestial. The momentary circumstance was too strong for him; he failed to look beyond the shadowy scope of Time, and living once for all in Eternity, to find the perfect Future in the present.

—1843

P's Correspondence

My unfortunate friend P. has lost the thread of his life by the interposition of long intervals of partially disordered reason. The past and present are jumbled together in his mind in a manner often productive of curious results, and which will be better understood after the perusal of the following letter than from any description that I could give. The poor fellow, without once stirring from the little whitewashed, iron-grated room to which he alludes in his first paragraph, is nevertheless a great traveller, and meets in his wanderings a variety of personages who have long ceased to be visible to any eye save his own. In my opinion, all this is not so much a delusion as a partly wilful and partly involuntary sport of the imagination, to which his disease has imparted such morbid energy that he beholds these spectral scenes and characters with no less distinctness than a play upon the stage, and with somewhat more of illusive credence. Many of his letters are in my possession, some based upon the same vagary as the present one, and others upon hypotheses not a whit short of it in absurdity. The whole form a series of correspondence, which, should fate seasonably remove my poor friend from what is to him a world of moonshine, I promise myself a pious pleasure in editing for the public eye. P. had always a hankering after literary reputation, and has made more than one unsuccessful effort to achieve it. It would not be a little odd, if, after missing his object while seeking it by the light of reason, he should prove to have stumbled upon it in his misty excursions beyond the limits of sanity.

LONDON, February 29, 1845.

MY DEAR FRIEND:

Old associations cling to the mind with astonishing tenacity. Daily custom grows up about us like a stone wall, and consolidates itself into almost as material an entity as mankind's strongest architecture. It is sometimes a serious question with me whether ideas be not really visible and tangible, and endowed with all the other qualities of matter. Sitting as I do at this moment in my hired apartment, writing beside the hearth, over which hangs a print of Queen Victoria,[1] listening to the muffled roar of the world's metropolis, and with a window at but five paces distant, through which, whenever I please, I can gaze out on actual London,—with all this positive certainty as to my whereabouts, what kind of notion, do you think, is just now perplexing my brain? Why,—would you believe it?—that all this time I am still an inhabitant of that wearisome little chamber,—that whitewashed little chamber,—that little chamber with its one small window, across which, from some inscrutable reason of taste or convenience, my landlord had placed a row of iron bars,—that same little chamber, in short, whither your kindness has so often brought you to visit me! Will no length of time or breadth of space enfranchise me from that unlovely abode? I travel; but it seems to be like the snail, with my house upon my head. Ah, well! I am verging, I suppose, on that period of life when present scenes and events make but feeble impressions in comparison with those of yore; so that I must reconcile myself to be more and more the prisoner of Memory, who merely lets me hop about a little with her chain around my leg.

My letters of introduction have been of the utmost service, enabling me to make the acquaintance of several distinguished characters who, until now, have seemed as remote from the sphere of my personal intercourse as the wits of Queen Anne's[2] time or Ben Jonson's compotators[3] at the Mermaid. One of the first of which I availed myself was the letter to Lord Byron.[4] I found his lordship looking much older than I had anticipated, although, considering his former irregularities of life and the various wear and tear of his constitution, not older than a man on the verge of sixty reasonably may look. But I had invested his earthly frame, in my imagination, with the poet's spiritual immortality. He wears a brown wig, very luxuriantly curled, and extending down over his forehead. The expression of his eyes is concealed by spectacles. His early tendency to obesity having increased, Lord Byron is now enormously fat,—so fat as to give the impression of a person quite overladen with his own flesh, and without sufficient vigor to diffuse his personal life through the great mass of corporeal substance which weighs upon him so cruelly. You gaze at the mortal heap; and, while it fills your eye with what purports to be Byron, you murmur within yourself, "For Heaven's sake, where is he?" Were I disposed to be caustic, I might consider this mass of earthly matter as the symbol, in a material shape, of those evil habits and carnal vices which unspiritualize man's nature and clog up his avenues of communication with the better life. But this would be too harsh; and, besides, Lord Byron's morals have been improving while his outward man has swollen to such unconscionable circumference. Would that he were leaner; for, though he did me the honor to present his hand, yet it was so puffed out with alien substance that I could not feel as if I had touched the hand that wrote Childe Harold.

---

1. Queen of England (1819–1901).   2. Reigned 1702–1714.   3. Drinking partners of Ben Jonson (1572–1637), English playwright.   4. George Gordon, Lord Byron (1788–1824), English poet.

On my entrance his lordship apologized for not rising to receive me, on the sufficient plea that the gout for several years past had taken up its constant residence in his right foot, which accordingly was swathed in many rolls of flannel and deposited upon a cushion. The other foot was hidden in the drapery of his chair. Do you recollect whether Byron's right or left foot was the deformed one?

The noble poet's reconciliation with Lady Byron is now, as you are aware, of ten years' standing; nor does it exhibit, I am assured, any symptom of breach or fracture. They are said to be, if not a happy, at least a contented, or at all events a quiet couple, descending the slope of life with that tolerable degree of mutual support which will enable them to come easily and comfortably to the bottom. It is pleasant to reflect how entirely the poet has redeemed his youthful errors in this particular. Her ladyship's influence, it rejoices me to add, has been productive of the happiest results upon Lord Byron in a religious point of view. He now combines the most rigid tenets of Methodism with the ultra doctrines of the Puseyites[5]; the former being perhaps due to the convictions wrought upon his mind by his noble consort, while the latter are the embroidery and picturesque illumination demanded by his imaginative character. Much of whatever expenditure his increasing habits of thrift continue to allow him is bestowed in the reparation or beautifying of places of worship; and this nobleman, whose name was once considered a synonyme of the foul fiend, is now all but canonized as a saint in many pulpits of the metropolis and elsewhere. In politics, Lord Byron is an uncompromising conservative, and loses no opportunity, whether in the House of Lords or in private circles, of denouncing and repudiating the mischievous and anarchical notions of his earlier day. Nor does he fail to visit similar sins in other people with the sincerest vengeance which his somewhat blunted pen is capable of inflicting. Southey[6] and he are on the most intimate terms. You are aware that, some little time before the death of Moore,[7] Byron caused that brilliant but reprehensible man to be evicted from his house. Moore took the insult so much to heart that, it is said to have been one great cause of the fit of illness which brought him to the grave. Others pretend that the lyrist died in a very happy state of mind, singing one of his own sacred melodies, and expressing his belief that it would be heard within the gate of paradise, and gain him instant and honorable admittance. I wish he may have found it so.

I failed not, as you may suppose, in the course of conversation with Lord Byron, to pay the weed of homage due to a mighty poet, by allusions to passages in Childe Harold, and Manfred, and Don Juan,[8] which have made so large a portion of the music of my life. My words, whether apt or otherwise, were at least warm with the enthusiasm of one worthy to discourse of immortal poesy. It was evident, however, that they did not go precisely to the right spot. I could perceive that there was some mistake or other, and was not a little angry with myself, and ashamed of my abortive attempt to throw back, from my own heart to the gifted author's ear, the echo of those strains that have resounded throughout the world. But by and by the secret peeped quietly out. Byron,—I have the information from his own lips, so that you need not hesitate to repeat it in literary circles,—Byron is preparing a new edition of his complete works, carefully corrected, expurgated, and amended, in accordance with his present creed of taste, morals, politics, and religion. It so happened that the very passages of highest inspiration to which I had

---

5. Followers of Edmund Pusey (1800–1882), Anglican reformer.   6. Robert Southey (1774–1843), English poet.   7. Thomas Moore (1779–1852), Irish poet.   8. Long poems by Byron: *Childe Harold's Pilgrimage* (1812–1818), *Manfred* (1817), and *Don Juan* (1818–1823).

alluded were among the condemned and rejected rubbish which it is his purpose to cast into the gulf of oblivion. To whisper you the truth, it appears to me that his passions having burned out, the extinction of their vivid and riotous flame has deprived Lord Byron of the illumination by which he not merely wrote, but was enabled to feel and comprehend what he had written. Positively he no longer understands his own poetry.

This became very apparent on his favoring me so far as to read a few specimens of Don Juan in the moralized version. Whatever is licentious, whatever disrespectful to the sacred mysteries of our faith, whatever morbidly melancholic or splenetically sportive, whatever assails settled constitutions of government or systems of society, whatever could wound the sensibility of any mortal, except a pagan, a republican, or a dissenter, has been unrelentingly blotted out, and its place supplied by unexceptionable verses in his lordship's later style. You may judge how much of the poem remains as hitherto published. The result is not so good as might be wished; in plain terms, it is a very sad affair indeed; for, though the torches kindled in Tophet have been extinguished, they leave an abominably ill odor, and are succeeded by no glimpses of hallowed fire. It is to be hoped, nevertheless, that this attempt on Lord Byron's part to atone for his youthful errors will at length induce the Dean of Westminster, or whatever churchman is concerned, to allow Thorwaldsen's statue of the poet its due niche in the grand old Abbey.[9] His bones, you know, when brought from Greece, were denied sepulture among those of his tuneful brethren there.

What a vile slip of the pen was that! How absurd in me to talk about burying the bones of Byron, who, I have just seen alive, and incased in a big, round bulk of flesh! But, to say the truth, a prodigiously fat man always impresses me as a kind of hobgoblin; in the very extravagance of his mortal system I find something akin to the immateriality of a ghost. And then that ridiculous old story darted into my mind, how that Byron died of fever at Missolonghi, above twenty years ago. More and more I recognize that we dwell in a world of shadows; and, for my part, I hold it hardly worth the trouble to attempt a distinction between shadows in the mind and shadows out of it. If there be any difference, the former are rather the more substantial.

Only think of my good fortune! The venerable Robert Burns[10]—now, if I mistake not, in his eighty-seventh year—happens to be making a visit to London, as if on purpose to afford me an opportunity of grasping him by the hand. For upwards of twenty years past he has hardly left his quiet cottage in Ayrshire[11] for a single night, and has only been drawn hither now by the irresistible persuasions of all the distinguished men in England. They wish to celebrate the patriarch's birthday by a festival. It will be the greatest literary triumph on record. Pray Heaven the little spirit of life within the aged bard's bosom may not be extinguished in the lustre of that hour! I have already had the honor of an introduction to him at the British Museum, where he was examining a collection of his own unpublished letters, interspersed with songs, which have escaped the notice of all his biographers.

Poh! Nonsense! What am I thinking of? How should Burns have been embalmed in biography when he is still a hearty old man?

The figure of the bard is tall and in the highest degree reverend, nor the less so that it is much bent by the burden of time. His white hair floats like a snowdrift around his

---

9. A sculpture of Byron by Bertel Thorwaldsen (1770–1844) was not allowed to be placed in Westminster Abbey's Poet's Corner because of Byron's alleged immorality.   10. Scottish poet (1759–1796).   11. Burns's native village.

face, in which are seen the furrows of intellect and passion, like the channels of head-long torrents that have foamed themselves away. The old gentleman is in excellent preservation, considering his time of life. He has that crickety sort of liveliness,—I mean the cricket's humor of chirping for any cause or none,—which is perhaps the most favorable mood that can befall extreme old age. Our pride forbids us to desire it for our-selves, although we perceive it to be a beneficence of nature in the case of others. I was surprised to find it in Burns. It seems as if his ardent heart and brilliant imagination had both burned down to the last embers, leaving only a little flickering flame in one cor-ner, which keeps dancing upward and laughing all by itself. He is no longer capable of pathos. At the request of Allan Cunningham,[12] he attempted to sing his own song to Mary in Heaven[13]; but it was evident that the feeling of those verses, so profoundly true and so simply expressed, was entirely beyond the scope of his present sensibilities; and, when a touch of it did partially awaken him, the tears immediately gushed into his eyes and his voice broke into a tremulous cackle. And yet he but indistinctly knew where-fore he was weeping. Ah, he must not think again of Mary in Heaven until he shake off the dull impediment of time and ascend to meet her there.

Burns then began to repeat Tam O'Shanter[14]; but was so tickled with its wit and humor—of which, however, I suspect he had but a traditionary sense—that he soon burst into a fit of chirruping laughter, succeeded by a cough, which brought this not very agreeable exhibition to a close. On the whole, I would rather not have witnessed it. It is a satisfactory idea, however, that the last forty years of the peasant poet's life have been passed in competence and perfect comfort. Having been cured of his bardic improvidence for many a day past, and grown as attentive to the main chance as a canny Scotsman should be, he is now considered to be quite well off as to pecu-niary circumstances. This, I suppose, is worth having lived so long for.

I took occasion to inquire of some of the countrymen of Burns in regard to the health of Sir Walter Scott. His condition, I am sorry to say, remains the same as for ten years past; it is that of a hopeless paralytic, palsied not more in body than in those nobler attributes of which the body is the instrument. And thus he vegetates from day to day and from year to year at that splendid fantasy of Abbotsford, which grew out of his brain, and became a symbol of the great romancer's tastes, feelings, studies, prej-udices, and modes of intellect. Whether in verse, prose, or architecture, he could achieve but one thing, although that one in infinite variety. There he reclines, on a couch in his library, and is said to spend whole hours of every day in dictating tales to an amanuensis,[15]—to an imaginary amanuensis; for it is not deemed worth any one's trouble now to take down what flows from that once brilliant fancy, every image of which was formerly worth gold and capable of being coined. Yet Cunningham, who has lately seen him, assures me that there is now and then a touch of the genius,—a striking combination of incident, or a picturesque trait of character, such as no other man alive could have bit off,—a glimmer from that ruined mind, as if the sun had suddenly flashed on a half-rusted helmet in the gloom of an ancient hall. But the plots of these romances become inextricably confused; the characters melt into one another; and the tale loses itself like the course of a stream flowing through muddy and marshy ground.

---

12. Allan Cunningham (1784–1842), English author.   13. "To Mary in Heaven" (1789).   14. Published in 1790.
15. Writing assistant.

For my part, I can hardly regret that Sir Walter Scott had lost his consciousness of outward things before his works went out of vogue. It was good that he should forget his fame rather than that fame should first have forgotten him. Were he still a writer, and as brilliant a one as ever, he could no longer maintain anything like the same position in literature. The world, nowadays, requires a more earnest purpose, a deeper moral, and a closer and homelier truth than he was qualified to supply it with. Yet who can be to the present generation even what Scott has been to the past? I had expectations from a young man,—one Dickens,[16]—who published a few magazine articles, very rich in humor, and not without symptoms of genuine pathos; but the poor fellow died shortly after commencing an odd series of sketches, entitled, I think, the Pickwick Papers.[17] Not impossibly the world has lost more than it dreams of by the untimley death of this Mr. Dickens.

Whom do you think I met in Pall Mall the other day? You would not hit it in ten guesses. Why, no less a man than Napoleon Bonaparte,[18] or all that is now left of him,—that is to say, the skin, bones, and corporeal substance, little cocked hat, green coat, white breeches, and small sword, which are still known by his redoubtable name. He was attended only by two policemen, who walked quietly behind the phantasm of the old ex-emperor, appearing to have no duty in regard to him except to see that none of the light-fingered gentry should possess themselves of his star of the Legion of Honor.[19] Nobody save myself so much as turned to look after him; nor, it grieves me to confess, could even I contrive to muster up any tolerable interest, even by all that the warlike spirit, formerly manifested within that now decrepit shape, had wrought upon our globe. There is no surer method of annihilating the magic influence of a great renown than by exhibiting the possessor of it in the decline, the overthrow, the utter degradation of his powers,—buried beneath his own mortality,—and lacking even the qualities of sense that enable the most ordinary men to bear themselves decently in the eye of the world. This is the state to which disease, aggravated by long endurance of a tropical climate, and assisted by old age,—for he is now above seventy,—has reduced Bonaparte. The British government has acted shrewdly in retransporting him from St. Helena[20] to England. They should now restore him to Paris, and there let him once again review the relics of his armies. His eye is dull and rheumy[21]; his nether lip hung down upon his chin. While I was observing him there chanced to be a little extra bustle in the street; and he, the brother of Caesar and Hannibal,[22]—the great captain who had veiled the world in battle-smoke and tracked it round with bloody footsteps,—was seized with a nervous trembling, and claimed the protection of the two policemen by a cracked and dolorous cry. The fellows winked at one another, laughed aside, and, patting Napoleon on the back, took each an arm and led him away.

Death and fury! Ha, villain, how came you hither? Avaunt! or I fling my inkstand at your head. Tush, tusk; it is all a mistake. Pray, my dear friend, pardon this little outbreak. The fact is, the mention of those two policemen, and their custody of Bonaparte, had called up the idea of that odious wretch—you remember him well—who was pleased to take such gratuitous and impertinent care of my person before I quitted New England. Forthwith up rose before my mind's eye that same little whitewashed room,

---

16. Charles Dickens (1812–1870), English novelist.   17. A novel by Dickens.   18. Emperor of France (1769–1821).
19. Award for valor in combat.   20. After being defeated by the British, Napoleon was exiled to the island of St. Helena.
21. Wet, mucousy.   22. Julius Caesar (c. 100–44 BC) and Hannibal (247–182 BC), both renowned military leaders.

with the iron-grated window,—strange that it should have been iron-grated!—where, in too easy compliance with the absurd wishes of my relatives, I have wasted several good years of my life. Positively it seemed to me that I was still sitting there, and that the keeper—not that he ever was my keeper neither, but only a kind of intrusive devil of a body-servant—had just peeped in at the door. The rascal! I owe him an old grudge, and will find a time to pay it yet. Fie! fie! The mere thought of him has exceedingly discomposed me. Even now that hateful chamber—the iron-grated window, which blasted the blessed sunshine as it fell through the dusty panes and made it poison to my soul—looks more distinct to my view than does this my comfortable apartment in the heart of London. The reality—that which I know to be such—hangs like remnants of tattered scenery over the intolerably prominent illusion. Let us think of it no more.

You will be anxious to hear of Shelley.[23] I need not say, what is known to all the world, that this celebrated poet has for many years past been reconciled to the Church of England. In his more recent works he has applied his fine powers to the vindication of the Christian faith, with an especial view to that particular development. Latterly, as you may not have heard, he has taken orders, and been inducted to a small country living in the gift of the Lord Chancellor. Just now, luckily for me, he has come to the metropolis to superintend the publication of a volume of discourses treating of the poetico-philosophical proofs of Christianity on the basis of the Thirty-nine Articles.[24] On my first introduction I felt no little embarrassment as to the manner of combining what I had to say to the author of Queen Mab, the Revolt of Islam, and Prometheus Unbound[25] with such acknowledgments as might be acceptable to a Christian minister and zealous upholder of the Established Church. But Shelley soon placed me at my ease. Standing where he now does, and reviewing all his successive productions from a higher point, he assures me that there is a harmony, an order, a regular procession, which enables him to lay his hand upon any one of the earlier poems and say, "This is my work," with precisely the same complacency of conscience wherewithal he contemplates the volume of discourses above mentioned. They are like the successive steps of a staircase, the lowest of which, in the depth of chaos, is as essential to the support of the whole as the highest and final one resting upon the threshold of the heavens. I felt half inclined to ask him what would have been his fate had he perished on the lower steps of his staircase, instead of building his way aloft into the celestial brightness.

How all this may be I neither pretend to understand nor greatly care, so long as Shelley has really climbed, as it seems he has, from a lower region to a loftier one. Without touching upon their religious merits, I consider the productions of his maturity superior, as poems, to those of his youth. They are warmer with human love, which has served as an interpreter between his mind and the multitude. The author has learned to dip his pen oftener into his heart, and has thereby avoided the faults into which a too exclusive use of fancy and intellect are wont to betray him. Formerly his page was often little other than a concrete arrangement of crystallizations, or even of icicles, as cold as they were brilliant. Now you take it to your heart, and are conscious of a heart-warmth responsive to your own. In his private character, Shelley can hardly have grown more gentle, kind, and affectionate than his friends always represented

---

23. Percy Bysshe Shelley (1792–1827), English poet.   24. Articles of the Church of England, to which all students at Oxford were required to swear allegiance. Shelley was expelled for writing a pamphlet, "The Necessity of Atheism."   25. *Queen Mab* (1813), *The Revolt of Islam* (1817), and *Prometheus Unbound* (1820).

him to be up to that disastrous night when he was drowned in the Mediterranean. Nonsense, again,—sheer nonsense! What am I babbling about? I was thinking of that old figment of his being lost in the Bay of Spezzia, and washed ashore near Via Reggio, and burned to ashes on a funeral pyre, with wine, and spices, and frankincense; while Byron stood on the beach and beheld a flame of marvellous beauty rise heavenward from the dead poet's heart, and that his fire-purified relics were finally buried near his child in Roman earth. If all this happened three-and-twenty years ago, how could I have met the drowned and burned and buried man here in London only yesterday?

Before quitting the subject, I may mention that Dr. Reginald Heber,[26] heretofore Bishop of Calcutta, but recently translated to a see in England, called on Shelley while I was with him. They appeared to be on terms of very cordial intimacy, and are said to have a joint poem in contemplation. What a strange, incongruous dream is the life of man!

Coleridge has at last finished his poem of Christabel.[27] It will be issued entire by old John Murray[28] in the course of the present publishing season. The poet, I hear, is visited with a troublesome affection of the tongue, which has put a period, or some lesser stop, to the life-long discourse that has hitherto been flowing from his lips. He will not survive it above a month, unless his accumulation of ideas be sluiced off in some other way. Wordsworth[29] died only a week or two ago. Heaven rest his soul, and grant that he may not have completed The Excursion! Methinks I am sick of everything he wrote, except his Laodamia. It is very sad, this inconstancy of the mind to the poets whom it once worshipped. Southey is as hale as ever, and writes with his usual diligence. Old Gifford[30] is still alive, in the extremity of age, and with most pitiable decay of what little sharp and narrow intellect the Devil had gifted him withal. One hates to allow such a man the privilege of growing old and infirm. It takes away our speculative license of kicking him.

Keats?[31] No; I have not seen him except across a crowded street, with coaches, drays, horsemen, cabs, omnibuses, foot-passengers, and divers other sensual obstructions intervening betwixt his small and slender figure and my eager glance. I would fain have met him on the sea-shore, or beneath a natural arch of forest trees, or the Gothic arch of an old cathedral, or among Grecian ruins, or at a glimmering fireside on the verge of evening, or at the twilight entrance of a cave, into the dreamy depths of which he would have led me by the hand; anywhere, in short, save at Temple Bar,[32] where his presence was blotted out by the porter-swollen bulks of these gross Englishmen. I stood and watched him fading away, fading away along the pavement, and could hardly tell whether he were an actual man or a thought that had slipped out of my mind and clothed itself in human form and habiliments merely to beguile me. At one moment he put his handkerchief to his lips, and withdrew it, I am almost certain, stained with blood. You never saw anything so fragile as his person. The truth is, Keats has all his life felt the effects of that terrible bleeding at the lungs caused by the article on his Endymion in the Quarterly Review,[33] and which so nearly brought him to the grave. Ever since he has glided about the world like a ghost, sighing a melancholy tone in the ear of here and there a friend, but never sending forth his

---

26. Churchman and composer of hymns (1783–1826). 27. Samuel Taylor Coleridge (1772–1834), "Christabel" (1816), a fragment. 28. Well-known London publisher. 29. William Wordsworth (1770–1850), author of The Excursion (1814) and "Laodamia" (1815). 30. William Gifford (1756–1826), English satirist. 31. John Keats (1795–1821), English poet. 32. One of London's gates, near the Temple Law Courts. 33. John Wilson Croker's 1818 review of Keats was believed to have caused his death.

voice to greet the multitude. I can hardly think him a great poet. The burden of a mighty genius would never have been imposed upon shoulders so physically frail and a spirit so infirmly sensitive. Great poets should have iron sinews.

Yet Keats, though for so many years he has given nothing to the world, is understood to have devoted himself to the composition of an epic poem. Some passages of it have been communicated to the inner circle of his admirers, and impressed them as the loftiest strains that have been audible on earth since Milton's[34] days. If I can obtain copies of these specimens, I will ask you to present them to James Russell Lowell,[35] who seems to be one of the poet's most fervent and worthiest worshippers. The information took me by surprise. I had supposed that all Keats's poetic incense, without being embodied in human language, floated up to heaven and mingled with the songs of the immortal choristers, who perhaps were conscious of an unknown voice among them, and thought their melody the sweeter for it. But it is not so; he has positively written a poem on the subject of Paradise Regained,[36] though in another sense than that which presented itself to the mind of Milton. In compliance, it may be imagined, with the dogma of those who pretend that all epic possibilities in the past history of the world are exhausted, Keats has thrown his poem forward into an indefinitely remote futurity. He pictures mankind amid the closing circumstances of the time-long warfare between good and evil. Our race is on the eve of its final triumph. Man is within the last stride of perfection; Woman, redeemed from the thraldom against which our sibyl[37] uplifts so powerful and so sad a remonstrance, stands equal by his side or communes for herself with angels; the Earth, sympathizing with her children's happier state, has clothed herself in such luxuriant and loving beauty as no eye ever witnessed since our first parents saw the sun rise over dewy Eden. Nor then indeed; for this is the fulfilment of what was then but a golden promise. But the picture has its shadows. There remains to mankind another peril,—a last encounter with the evil principle. Should the battle go against us, we sink back into the slime and misery of ages. If we triumph—But it demands a poet's eye to contemplate the splendor of such a consummation and not to be dazzled.

To this great work Keats is said to have brought so deep and tender a spirit of humanity that the poem has all the sweet and warm interest of a village tale no less than the grandeur which befits so high a theme. Such, at least, is the perhaps partial representation of his friends; for I have not read or heard even a single line of the performance in question. Keats, I am told, withholds it from the press, under an idea that the age has not enough of spiritual insight to receive it worthily. I do not like this distrust; it makes me distrust the poet. The universe is waiting to respond to the highest word that the best child of time and immortality can utter. If it refuse to listen, it is because he mumbles and stammers, or discourses things unseasonable and foreign to the purpose.

I visited the House of Lords the other day to hear Canning,[38] who, you know, is now a peer, with I forget what title. He disappointed me. Time blunts both point and edge, and does great mischief to men of his order of intellect. Then I stepped into the lower House and listened to a few words from Cobbett,[39] who looked as earthy as a real clodhopper, or rather as if he had lain a dozen years beneath the clods. The men whom I meet nowadays often impress me thus; probably because my spirits are not very good, and lead me to think much about graves, with the long grass upon them, and weather-

---

34. John Milton (1608–1674), English poet.   35. American critic (1819–1891).   36. Milton's 1671 poem.   37. Female prophet.   38. George Canning (1770–1827), British politician.   39. William Cobbett (1763–1835), British journalist.

worn epitaphs, and dry bones of people who made noise enough in their day, but now can only clatter, clatter, clatter, when the sexton's spade disturbs them. Were it only possible to find out who are alive and who dead, it would contribute infinitely to my peace of mind. Every day of my life somebody comes and stares me in the face whom I had quietly blotted out of the tablet of living men, and trusted nevermore to be pestered with the sight or sound of him. For instance, going to Drury Lane Theatre[40] a few evenings since, up rose before me, in the ghost of Hamlet's father, the bodily presence of the elder Kean, who did die, or ought to have died, in some drunken fit or other, so long ago that his fame is scarcely traditionary now. His powers are quite gone; he was rather the ghost of himself than the ghost of the Danish king.

In the stage-box sat several elderly and decrepit people, and among them a stately ruin of a woman on a very large scale, with a profile—for I did not see her front face—that stamped itself into my brain as a seal impresses hot wax. By the tragic gesture with which she took a pinch of snuff, I was sure it must be Mrs. Siddons.[41] Her brother, John Kemble,[42] sat behind,—a brokendown figure, but still with a kingly majesty about him. In lieu of all former achievements, Nature enables him to look the part of Lear far better than in the meridian of his genius. Charles Matthews[43] was likewise there; but a paralytic affection has distorted his once mobile countenance into a most disagreeable one-sidedness, from which he could no more wrench it into proper form than he could rearrange the face of the great globe itself. It looks as if, for the joke's sake, the poor man had twisted his features into an expression at once the most ludicrous and horrible that he could contrive, and at that very moment, as a judgment for making himself so hideous, an avenging Providence had seen fit to petrify him. Since it is out of his own power, I would gladly assist him to change countenance, for his ugly visage haunts me both at noontide and night-time. Some other players of the past generation were present, but none that greatly interested me. It behooves actors, more than all other men of publicity, to vanish from the scene betimes. Being at best but painted shadows flickering on the wall and empty sounds that echo another's thought, it is a sad disenchantment when the colors begin to fade and the voice to croak with age.

What is there new in the literary way on your side of the water? Nothing of the kind has come under any inspection, except a volume of poems published above a year ago by Dr. Channing.[44] I did not before know that this eminent writer is a poet; nor does the volume alluded to exhibit any of the characteristics of the author's mind as displayed in his prose works; although some of the poems have a richness that is not merely of the surface, but glows still the brighter the deeper and more faithfully you look into them. They seem carelessly wrought, however, like those rings and ornaments of the very purest gold, but of rude, native manufacture, which are found among the gold-dust from Africa. I doubt whether the American public will accept them; it looks less to the assay of metal than to the neat and cunning manufacture. How slowly our literature grows up! Most of our writers of promise have come to untimely ends. There was that wild fellow, John Neal,[45] who almost turned my boyish brain with his romances; he surely has long been dead, else he never could keep himself so quiet. Bryant has gone to his last sleep, with the Thanatopsis[46] gleaming

---

40. One of London's two theaters, where Edmund Kean was a famous Shakespearean actor.   41. Sarah Siddons (1775–1831), renowned tragedian.   42. English actor (1757–1823).   43. Manager of Covent Garden Theatre.   44. Confuses two William Ellery Channings, one a minister (1780–1842) and the other a poet (1818–1901), both Americans.   45. John Neal (1793–1876), American novelist.   46. Poem by William Cullen Bryant (1794–1878), see p. 717.

over him like a sculptured marble sepulchre by moonlight. Halleck, who used to write queer verses in the newspapers and published a Don Juanic poem called Fanny,[47] is defunct as a poet, though averred to be exemplifying the metempsychosis as a man of business. Somewhat later there was Whittier,[48] a fiery Quaker youth, to whom the muse had perversely assigned a battle-trumpet, and who got himself lynched, ten years agone, in South Carolina. I remember, too, a lad just from college, Longfellow[49] by name, who scattered some delicate verses to the winds, and went to Germany, and perished, I think, of intense application, at the University of Gottingen. Willis[50]— what a pity!—was lost, if I recollect rightly, in 1833, on his voyage to Europe, whither he was going to give us sketches of the world's sunny face. If these had lived, they might, one or all of them, have grown to be famous men.

And yet there is no telling: it may be as well that they have died. I was myself a young man of promise. O shattered brain, O broken spirit, where is the fulfilment of that promise? The sad truth is, that, when fate would gently disappoint the world, it takes away the hopefulest mortals in their youth; when it would laugh the world's hopes to scorn, it lets them live. Let me die upon this apothegm, for I shall never make a truer one.

What a strange substance is the human brain! Or rather,—for there is no need of generalizing the remark,—what an odd brain is mine! Would you believe it? Daily and nightly there come scraps of poetry humming in my intellectual ear—some as airy as birdnotes, and some as delicately neat as parlor-music, and a few as grand as organ-peals—that seem just such verses as those departed poets would have written had not an inexorable destiny snatched them from their inkstands. They visit me in spirit, perhaps desiring to engage my services as the amanuensis of their posthumous productions, and thus secure the endless renown that they have forfeited by going hence too early. But I have my own business to attend to; and besides, a medical gentleman, who interests himself in some little ailments of mine, advises me not to make too free use of pen and ink. There are clerks enough out of employment who would be glad of such a job.

Good bye! Are you alive or dead? and what are you about? Still scribbling for the Democratic?[51] And do those infernal compositors and proof-readers misprint your unfortunate productions as vilely as ever? It is too bad. Let every man manufacture his own nonsense, say I. Expect me home soon, and—to whisper you a secret—in company with the poet Campbell,[52] who purposes to visit Wyoming and enjoy the shadow of the laurels that he planted there. Campbell is now an old man. He calls himself well, better than ever in his life, but looks strangely pale, and so shadow-like that one might almost poke a finger through his densest material. I tell him, by way of joke, that he is as dim and forlorn as Memory, though as unsubstantial as Hope.

Your true friend, P.

P. S.—Pray present my most respectful regards to our venerable and revered friend Mr. Brockden Brown.[53] It gratifies me to learn that a complete edition of his works, in a double-columned octavo volume, is shortly to issue from the press at Philadelphia. Tell him that no American writer enjoys a more classic reputation on

47. Poem by Fitz-Greene Halleck (1790–1867), see p. 638.   48. John Greenleaf Whittier (1807–1892), American poet.   49. Henry Wadsworth Longfellow (1807–1882), American poet.   50. Nathaniel Parker Willis (1806–1867), American poet.   51. Hawthorne published several stories in the Democratic Review.   52. Thomas Campbell (1777–1874), Scottish poet.   53. Charles Brockden Brown (1771–1810), American novelist.

this side of the water. Is old Joel Barlow[54] yet alive? Unconscionable man! Why, he must have nearly fulfilled his century. And does he meditate an epic on the war between Mexico and Texas with machinery contrived on the principle of the steam-engine, as being the nearest to celestial agency that our epoch can boast? How can he expect ever to rise again, if, while just sinking into his grave, he persists in burdening himself with such a ponderosity of leaden verses?

—1854

Henry Wadsworth Longfellow
1807–1882

Henry Wadsworth Longfellow was born to a Portland, Maine, family that was descended on both sides from Massachusetts Pilgrims. His life was one of steady work and accomplishment, punctuated by personal tragedy. By its end he had become the transatlantic world's best-selling American poet and was celebrated as a public treasure. Longfellow's mother, Zilpah, introduced him early to literature, especially the poems of William Wordsworth and William Cullen Bryant. Longfellow attended Bowdoin College, where his father, the lawyer and Maine congressional representative Stephen Longfellow, was a trustee. One of his classmates was Nathaniel Hawthorne, but they were little more than acquaintances; he was probably repelled by the older Hawthorne's democratic radicalism and lackadaisical attitude toward classes. Longfellow was serious and ambitious, writing to his father, "I most eagerly aspire after future eminence in literature." Before long, he began to succeed in placing his poems in nationally circulated magazines, such as the *United States Literary Gazette* and the *Philadelphia Magazine*. After graduating in 1825, he lived for three years in France, Germany, Italy, and Spain, studying languages in preparation for a professorship that had been arranged for him at his alma mater. He taught at Bowdoin for five years, during which time he published six language textbooks, numerous essays and reviews of European literature, as well as *Outre-Mer; A Pilgrimage Beyond the Sea* (1835), an imitation of Washington Irving's witty sketches of European customs. In 1835, he was offered a position at Harvard College and to prepare for it went abroad for another year of study in Germany. His wife, Mary Storer Potter, died there of complications following a miscarriage. Longfellow was distraught but completed his studies and travels, paying calls on many of Europe's most eminent writers. After arriving in Cambridge, Massachusetts, he took solace in a routine of teaching, writing, and visiting and was soon recognized as the town's most cosmopolitan intellectual, unmistakable in his fine suits and manners.

In 1839, he published *Hyperion*, an autobiographical romance novel strongly influenced by German writer Johann Wolfgang von Goethe, as well as *Voices of the Night*, a collection that included his most famous poem, "A Psalm of Life." *Ballads and Other Poems* (1841) marked a conscious shift toward more historical materials and narrative forms. *Songs of Slavery* (1842), inspired by the slave revolt on the ship *Amistad*, recorded his lifelong opposition to what he regarded as an uncivilized practice. The next year he married Frances Appleton, the original of the heroine of *Hyperion*, and for two decades the couple lived a cultivated and full life. Longfellow published a steady stream of books, achieving the literary preeminence he had desired as a young man. *The Courtship of Myles Standish* (1858) sold ten thousand copies on the day it appeared in London.

---

54. American poet (1754–1812).

This long period of happiness ended in 1861. Frances died when her dress caught fire. Longfellow was severely burned attempting to put out the flames. He wrote to her sister several weeks later, "How I am alive after what my eyes have seen, I know not. I am at least patient, if not resigned; and thank God hourly . . . for the beautiful life we led together, and that I loved her more and more to the end." For the rest of his long life, he applied himself steadily to writing poems, many of them set distantly in the Old World. He produced the first American translation of Italian poet Dante Alighieri's *Divine Comedy* (1321). Longfellow's books were translated immediately after publication into most of the European languages.

Longfellow's poems are carefully crafted—often in forms adapted from the poetic practices of other cultures, including those of Italy, France, Germany, and Iceland—and treat historical, folkloric, and occasional subjects, again borrowing his materials from a broad range of national traditions. Usually, he treats serious topics in a straightforward manner and unabashedly directs the reader to proper moral conclusions. Poet Robert Frost once deplored the way that twentieth-century readers of Longfellow "laugh at his gentleness, at his lack of worldliness, at his detachment from the world and the meaning thereof. When and where has it been written that a poet must be a club-swinging warrior, a teller of barroom tales, a participant of unspeakable experiences?" Longfellow was certainly none of these. He was a professional poet who set out to please his audience with well-made, musical verses that would open their eyes to faraway places and cultures, or teach them to see useful truths in the ordinary and nearby.

A Psalm of Life

Tell me not, in mournful numbers,[1]
    Life is but an empty dream!—
For the soul is dead that slumbers,
    And things are not what they seem.

Life is real! Life is earnest!   5
    And the grave is not its goal;
Dust thou art, to dust returnest,[2]
    Was not spoken of the soul.

Not enjoyment, and not sorrow,
    Is our destined end or way;   10
But to act, that each to-morrow
    Find us farther than to-day.

Art is long, and Time is fleeting,[3]
    And our hearts, though stout and brave,
Still, like muffled drums, are beating   15
    Funeral marches to the grave.

In the world's broad field of battle,
    In the bivouac of Life,
Be not like dumb, driven cattle!
    Be a hero in the strife!   20

---

1. Meters.   2. Genesis 3.19.   3. Paraphrases Seneca (c. 4–65), *de Brevitatae Vitae*.

Trust no Future, howe'er pleasant!
  Let the dead Past bury its dead!
Act,—act in the living Present!
  Heart within, and God o'erhead!

Lives of great men all remind us
  We can make *our* lives sublime,
And, departing, leave behind us
  Footprints on the sands of time;   25

Footprints, that perhaps another,
  Sailing o'er life's solemn main,[4]
A forlorn and shipwrecked brother,
  Seeing, shall take heart again.   30

Let us, then, be up and doing,
  With a heart for any fate;
Still achieving, still pursuing,
  Learn to labor and to wait.   35

—1838

The Village Blacksmith

Under a spreading chestnut-tree
  The village smithy stands;
The smith, a mighty man is he,
  With large and sinewy hands;
And the muscles of his brawny arms   5
  Are strong as iron bands.

His hair is crisp, and black, and long,
  His face is like the tan;
His brow is wet with honest sweat,
  He earns whate'er he can,
And looks the whole world in the face,   10
  For he owes not any man.

Week in, week out, from morn till night,
  You can hear his bellows blow;
You can hear him swing his heavy sledge,
  With measured beat and slow,   15
Like a sexton ringing the village bell,
  When the evening sun is low.

---

4. Ocean.

And children coming home from school
   Look in at the open door;   20
They love to see the flaming forge,
   And hear the bellows roar,
And catch the burning sparks that fly
   Like chaff from a threshing-floor.

He goes on Sunday to the church,   25
   And sits among his boys;
He hears the parson pray and preach,
   He hears his daughter's voice,
Singing in the village choir,
   And it makes his heart rejoice.   30

It sounds to him like her mother's voice,
   Singing in Paradise!
He needs must think of her once more,
   How in the grave she lies;
And with his hard, rough hand he wipes   35
   A tear out of his eyes.

Toiling,—rejoicing,—sorrowing,
   Onward through life he goes;
Each morning sees some task begin,
   Each evening sees it close;   40
Something attempted, something done,
   Has earned a night's repose.

Thanks, thanks to thee, my worthy friend,
   For the lesson thou hast taught!
Thus at the flaming forge of life   45
   Our fortunes must be wrought;
Thus on its sounding anvil shaped
   Each burning deed and thought.

                             —1839

Burial of the Minnisink

On sunny slope and beechen swell,
The shadowed light of evening fell;
And, where the maple's leaf was brown,
With soft and silent lapse came down,
The glory, that the wood receives,   5
At sunset, in its golden leaves.

Far upward in the mellow light
Rose the blue hills. One cloud of white,
Around a far uplifted cone,

In the warm blush of evening shone;   10
An image of the silver lakes,
By which the Indian's soul awakes.

But soon a funeral hymn was heard
Where the soft breath of evening stirred
The tall, gray forest; and a band   15
Of stern in heart, and strong in hand,
Came winding down beside the wave,
To lay the red chief in his grave.

They sang, that by his native bowers
He stood, in the last moon of flowers,   20
And thirty snows had not yet shed
Their glory on the warrior's head;
But, as the summer fruit decays,
So died he in those naked days.

A dark cloak of the roebuck's skin   25
Covered the warrior, and within
Its heavy folds the weapons, made
For the hard toils of war, were laid;
The cuirass,[1] woven of plaited reeds,
And the broad belt of shells and beads.   30

Before, a dark-haired virgin train
Chanted the death dirge of the slain;
Behind, the long procession came
Of hoary men and chiefs of fame,
With heavy hearts, and eyes of grief,   35
Leading the war-horse of their chief.

Stripped of his proud and martial dress,
Uncurbed, unreined, and riderless,
With darting eye, and nostril spread,
And heavy and impatient tread,   40
He came; and oft that eye so proud
Asked for his rider in the crowd.

They buried the dark chief; they freed
Beside the grave his battle steed;
And swift an arrow cleaved its way   45
To his stern heart! One piercing neigh
Arose, and, on the dead man's plain,
The rider grasps his steed again.

—1839

---

1. Breastplate.

To the Driving Cloud

Gloomy and dark art thou, O chief of the mighty Omahas[1];
Gloomy and dark as the driving cloud, whose name thou hast taken!
Wrapped in thy scarlet blanket, I see thee stalk through the city's
Narrow and populous streets, as once by the margin of rivers
Stalked those birds unknown, that have left us only their footprints.   5
What, in a few short years, will remain of thy race but the footprints?

How canst thou walk these streets, who hast trod the green turf of the prairies?
How canst thou breathe this air, who hast breathed the sweet air of the mountains?
Ah! 't is in vain that with lordly looks of disdain thou dost challenge
Looks of disdain in return, and question these walls and these pavements,   10
Claiming the soil for thy hunting-grounds, while down-trodden millions
Starve in the garrets of Europe, and cry from its caverns that they, too,
Have been created heirs of the earth, and claim its division!

Back, then, back to thy woods in the regions west of the Wabash![2]
There as a monarch thou reignest. In autumn the leaves of the maple   15
Pave the floors of thy palace-halls with gold, and in summer
Pine-trees waft through its chambers the odorous breath of their branches.
There thou art strong and great, a hero, a tamer of horses!
There thou chasest the stately stag on the banks of the Elkhorn,
Or by the roar of the running-Water, or where the Omaha   20
Calls thee, and leaps through the wild ravine like a brave of the Blackfeet![3]

Hark! what murmurs arise from the heart of those mountainous deserts?
Is it the cry of the Foxes and Crows, or the mighty Behemoth,[4]
Who, unharmed, on his tusks once caught the bolts of the thunder,
And now lurks in his lair to destroy the race of the red man?   25
Far more fatal to thee and thy race than the Crows and the Foxes,
Far more fatal to thee and thy race than the tread of Behemoth,
Lo! the big thunder-canoe, that steadily breasts the Missouri's
Merciless current! and yonder, afar on the prairies, the camp-fires
Gleam through the night; and the cloud of dust in the gray of the daybreak   30
Marks not the buffalo's track, nor the Mandan's dexterous horse-race;
It is a caravan, whitening the desert where dwell the Camanches!
Ha! how the breath of these Saxons and Celts,[5] like the blast of the east-wind,
Drifts evermore to the west the scanty smokes of thy wigwams!

—1845

---

1. An agricultural tribe that lived along the Missouri River in present-day Nebraska.   2. A river in Indiana.   3. The Elkhorn and Omaha are rivers in Nebraska. The Blackfeet are a buffalo-hunting tribe of the northern plains, as are the Foxes and Crows.   4. Mammoth.   5. The Mandan and Comanches are horse-riding peoples of the western and southern plains. Longfellow uses "Saxons and Celts," the names of early inhabitants of England, to describe the settlers and soldiers who are displacing Native Americans.

The Slave's Dream

Beside the ungathered rice he lay,
    His sickle in his hand;
His breast was bare, his matted hair
    Was buried in the sand.
Again, in the mist and shadow of sleep,   5
    He saw his Native Land.

Wide through the landscape of his dreams
    The lordly Niger[1] flowed;
Beneath the palm-trees on the plain
    Once more a king he strode;
And heard the tinkling caravans   10
    Descend the mountain road.

He saw once more his dark-eyed queen
    Among her children stand;
They clasped his neck, they kissed his cheeks,   15
    They held him by the hand!—
A tear burst from the sleeper's lids
    And fell into the sand.

And then at furious speed he rode
    Along the Niger's bank:
His bridle-reins were golden chains,   20
    And, with a martial clank,
At each leap he could feel his scabbard of steel
    Smiting his stallion's flank.

Before him, like a blood-red flag,   25
    The bright flamingoes flew;
From morn till night he followed their flight,
    O'er plains where the tamarind grew,
Till he saw the roofs of Caffre[2] huts,
    And the ocean rose to view.   30

At night he heard the lion roar,
    And the hyena scream,
And the river-horse,[3] as he crushed the reeds
    Beside some hidden stream;
And it passed, like a glorious roll of drums,   35
    Through the triumph of his dream.

---

1. The largest river in West Africa.   2. Cafirs: southeast Africans; now often used as a term of abuse.   3. Hippopotamus.

The forests, with their myriad tongues,
  Shouted of liberty;
And the Blast of the Desert cried aloud,
  With a voice so wild and free,   40
That he started in his sleep and smiled
  At their tempestuous glee.

He did not feel the driver's whip,
  Nor the burning heat of day;
For Death had illumined the Land of Sleep,   45
  And his lifeless body lay
A worn-out fetter, that the soul
  Had broken and thrown away!

—1842

The Arsenal at Springfield[1]

This is the Arsenal. From floor to ceiling,
  Like a huge organ, rise the burnished arms;
But from their silent pipes no anthem pealing
  Startles the villages with strange alarms.

Ah! what a sound will rise, how wild and dreary,   5
  When the death-angel touches those swift keys!
What loud lament and dismal Miserere[2]
  Will mingle with their awful symphonies!

I hear even now the infinite fierce chorus,
  The cries of agony, the endless groan,   10
Which, through the ages that have gone before us,
  In long reverberations reach our own.

On helm and harness rings the Saxon hammer,
  Through Cimbric forest roars the Norseman's song,[3]
And loud, amid the universal clamor,   15
  O'er distant deserts sounds the Tartar gong.[4]

I hear the Florentine, who from his palace
  Wheels out his battle-bell with dreadful din,[5]
And Aztec priests upon their teocallis[6]
  Beat the wild war-drums made of serpent's skin;   20

The tumult of each sacked and burning village;
  The shout that every prayer for mercy drowns;

---

1. A large munitions factory and depot in southwestern Massachusetts.   2. A song of lament.   3. The Saxons and Cimbri were northern European tribes.   4. Tartars: a Mongolian tribe.   5. Attacking Siena in 1260, the army of Florence announced themselves with a bell.   6. Temples in ancient Mexico.

The soldiers' revels in the midst of pillage;
    The wail of famine in beleaguered towns;

The bursting shell, the gateway wrenched asunder,   25
    The rattling musketry, the clashing blade;
And ever and anon, in tones of thunder
    The diapason[7] of the cannonade.

Is it, O man, with such discordant noises,
    With such accursed instruments as these,   30
Thou drownest Nature's sweet and kindly voices,
    And jarrest the celestial harmonies?

Were half the power that fills the world with terror,
    Were half the wealth bestowed on camps and courts,
Given to redeem the human mind from error,   35
    There were no need of arsenals or forts:

The warrior's name would be a name abhorèd!
    And every nation, that should lift again
Its hand against a brother, on its forehead
    Would wear forevermore the curse of Cain![8]   40

Down the dark future, through long generations,
    The echoing sounds grow fainter and then cease;
And like a bell, with solemn, sweet vibrations,
    I hear once more the voice of Christ say, "Peace!"

Peace! and no longer from its brazen portals   45
    The blast of War's great organ shakes the skies!
But beautiful as songs of the immortals,
    The holy melodies of love arise.

—1845

Chaucer[1]

An old man in a lodge within a park;
    The chamber walls depicted all around
    With portraitures of huntsman, hawk, and hound,
    And the hurt deer. He listeneth to the lark,
Whose song comes with the sunshine through the dark   5
    Of painted glass in leaden lattice bound;
    He listeneth and he laugheth at the sound,
    Then writeth in a book like any clerk.

---

7. A burst of sound.   8. Genesis 4.4–13.

1. Geoffrey Chaucer (c. 1343–1400), English poet.

He is the poet of the dawn, who wrote
   The Canterbury Tales, and his old age   10
   Made beautiful with song; and as I read
I hear the crowing cock, I hear the note
   Of lark and linnet, and from every page
   Rise odors of ploughed field or flowery mead.

—1875

Shakespeare

A vision as of crowded city streets,
   With human life in endless overflow;
   Thunder of thoroughfares; trumpets that blow
   To battle; clamor, in obscure retreats,
Of sailors landed from their anchored fleets;   5
   Tolling of bells in turrets, and below
   Voices of children, and bright flowers that throw
   O'er garden-walls their intermingled sweets!
This vision comes to me when I unfold
   The volume of the Poet paramount,   10
   Whom all the Muses loved, not one alone;—
Into his hands they put the lyre of gold,
   And, crowned with sacred laurel at their fount,
   Placed him as Musagetes[1] on their throne.

—1875

Milton[1]

I pace the sounding sea-beach and behold
   How the voluminuous billows roll and run,
   Upheaving and subsiding, while the sun
   Shines through their sheeted emerald far unrolled,
And the ninth wave, slow gathering fold by fold   5
   All its loose-flowing garments into one,
   Plunges upon the shore, and floods the dun
   Pale reach of sands, and changes them to gold.
So in majestic cadence rise and fall
   The mighty undulations of thy song,   10
   O sightless bard, England's Mæonides![2]
And ever and anon, high over all
   Uplifted, a ninth wave superb and strong,
   Floods all the soul with its melodious seas.

—1875

---

1. Leader of the Muses.

1. John Milton (1608–1674), English poet.   2. Homer, early Greek poet.

Keats[1]

The young Endymion sleeps Endymion's sleep;
  The shepherd-boy whose tale was left half told!
  The solemn grove uplifts its shield of gold
  To the red rising moon, and loud and deep
The nightingale is singing from the steep;   5
  It is midsummer, but the air is cold;
  Can it be death? Alas, beside the fold
  A shepherd's pipe lies shattered near his sheep.
Lo! in the moonlight gleams a marble white,
  On which I read: "Here lieth one whose name   10
Was writ in water." And was this the meed[2]
Of his sweet singing? Rather let me write:
  "The smoking flax before it burst to flame
Was quenched by death, and broken the bruised reed."

                                —1875

John Greenleaf Whittier
1807–1892

Quaker poet John Greenleaf Whittier was once threatened with lynching by a pro-slavery mob and saw the offices of one of his newspapers burned by racist arsonists, but eventually he was accepted as New England's unofficial Poet Laureate. Whittier was born in a Massachusetts farmhouse built by his great-great-grandfather Thomas, who emigrated from England in 1638. There was no money for a formal education, and Whittier was a weak child, so he decided early in life to dedicate himself to writing, especially after reading the Scotch-dialect poetry of Robert Burns. When he was eighteen, his sister Mary sent one of his poems to William Lloyd Garrison's Newburyport *Free Press*, where it became Whittier's first publication. Garrison visited Whittier's parents and pushed them to enroll him in school. Whittier spent a year at Haverhill Academy and made an abortive attempt to become a schoolteacher. Garrison later placed him in the first of many professional editorial positions, at Boston's *American Manufacturer*, a weekly Whig newspaper. In 1833, Garrison convinced him to abandon plans to seek political office. Instead, Whittier joined the abolitionist cause and helped found the American Anti-Slavery Society. Looking back on his career, he recognized as its most significant turning point this moment when he made "his rustic reed of song / A weapon in the war with wrong. . . ."

    Whittier's poems are of two main kinds. First, there are polemical attacks on the oppression and exploitation of slaves, Native Americans, and wage workers, and then there are portraits of an idyllic New England past. These are two sides of the same coin, for his pastoral sketches of peaceful and egalitarian rural communities were meant to provide moral guidance to readers bewildered by the cruel and impersonal modern world that had grown up during his lifetime. His first collection, *Poems Written During the Progress of the Abolition Question in the United States*

---

1. John Keats (1795–1821), English poet, author of *Endymion* (1818).   2. Fitting reward.

(1837), was published by a group of Boston activists without his consent. In 1850, Whittier published *Songs of Labor, and Other Poems*, a groundbreaking series of portraits of craft and trade laborers, celebrating their sense of dignity and their pride in work well done. This book cemented his reputation as one of the leading American poets. During a long public career that lasted until well after the close of the Civil War, he worked tirelessly as a state representative, a newspaper editor, and a political organizer, playing a central role in the founding of the Republican Party that put Abraham Lincoln in office and rallied the North to defeat slavery at last.

Massachusetts to Virginia

Written on reading an account of the proceedings of the citizens of Norfolk, Va., in reference to George Latimer, the alleged fugitive slave, who was seized in Boston without warrant at the request of James B. Grey, of Norfolk, claiming to be his master. The case caused great excitement North and South, and led to the presentation of a petition to Congress, signed by more than fifty thousand citizens of Massachusetts, calling for such laws and proposed amendments to the Constitution as should relieve the Commonwealth from all further participation in the crime of oppression. George Latimer himself was finally given free papers for the sum of four hundred dollars.[1]

The blast from Freedom's Northern hills, upon its Southern way,
Bears greeting to Virginia from Massachusetts Bay:
No word of haughty challenging, nor battle bugle's peal,
Nor steady tread of marching files, nor clang of horsemen's steel.

No trains of deep-mouthed cannon along our highways go;   5
Around our silent arsenals untrodden lies the snow;
And to the land-breeze of our ports, upon their errands far,
A thousand sails of commerce swell, but none are spread for war.

We hear thy threats, Virginia! thy stormy words and high
Swell harshly on the Southern winds which melt along our sky;   10
Yet, not one brown, hard hand foregoes its honest labor here,
No hewer of our mountain oaks suspends his axe in fear.

Wild are the waves which lash the reefs along St. George's bank;
Cold on the shores of Labrador the fog lies white and dank;
Through storm, and wave, and blinding mist, stout are the hearts which man   15
The fishing-smacks of Marblehead, the seaboats of Cape Ann.[2]

The cold north light and wintry sun glare on their icy forms,
Bent grimly o'er their straining lines or wrestling with the storms;
Free as the winds they drive before, rough as the waves they roam,
They laugh to scorn the slaver's threat against their rocky home.   20

---

1. Latimer's escape, incarceration, and eventual manumission occurred in 1842.   2. This stanza mentions several areas along the Massachusetts coast.

What means the Old Dominion?[3] Hath she forgot the day
When o'er her conquered valleys swept the Briton's steel array?
How side by side, with sons of hers, the Massachusetts men
Encountered Tarleton's charge of fire, and stout Cornwallis, then?[4]

Forgets she how the Bay State,[5] in answer to the call   25
Of her old House of Burgesses, spoke out from Faneuil Hall?[6]
When, echoing back her Henry's[7] cry, came pulsing on each breath
Of Northern winds the thrilling sounds of "Liberty or Death!"

What asks the Old Dominion? If now her sons have proved
False to their fathers' memory, false to the faith they loved;   30
If she can scoff at Freedom, and its great charter[8] spurn,
Must we of Massachusetts from truth and duty turn?

We hunt your bondmen, flying from Slavery's hateful hell;
Our voices, at your bidding, take up the bloodhound's yell;
We gather, at your summons, above our fathers' graves,   35
From Freedom's holy altar-horns[9] to tear your wretched slaves!

Thank God! not yet so vilely can Massachusetts bow;
The spirit of her early time is with her even now;
Dream not because her Pilgrim blood moves slow and calm and cool,
She thus can stoop her chainless neck, a sister's slave and tool!   40

All that a sister State should do, all that a free State may,
Heart, hand, and purse we proffer, as in our early day;
But that one dark loathsome burden ye must stagger with alone,
And reap the bitter harvest which ye yourselves have sown!

Hold, while ye may, your struggling slaves, and burden God's free air   45
With woman's shriek beneath the lash, and manhood's wild despair;
Cling closer to the "cleaving curse" that writes upon your plains
The blasting of Almighty wrath against a land of chains.

Still shame your gallant ancestry, the cavaliers of old,
By watching round the shambles[10] where human flesh is sold;   50
Gloat o'er the new-born child, and count his market value, when
The maddened mother's cry of woe shall pierce the slaver's den!

Lower than plummet soundeth, sink the Virginia name;
Plant, if ye will, your fathers' graves with rankest weeds of shame;

---

3. Virginia.   4. Banastre Tarleton (1754–1833) and Charles Cornwallis (1738–1805), British military officers defeated during the American Revolution.   5. Massachusetts.   6. The House of Burgesses was the seat of Virginia's colonial legislature; Faneuil Hall is a meeting house in Boston.   7. Patrick Henry (1736–1799), Virginian Revolutionary leader.   8. The Declaration of Independence.   9. Sanctuary.   10. Slave market.

Be, if ye will, the scandal of God's fair universe;   55
We wash our hands forever of your sin and shame and curse.

A voice from lips whereon the coal from Freedom's shrine hath been,
Thrilled, as but yesterday, the hearts of Berkshire's mountain men[11]:
The echoes of that solemn voice are sadly lingering still
In all our sunny valleys, on every windswept hill.   60

And when the prowling man-thief came hunting for his prey
Beneath the very shadow of Bunker's shaft of gray,[12]
How, through the free lips of the son, the father's warning spoke;
How, from its bonds of trade and sect, the Pilgrim city broke!

A hundred thousand right arms were lifted up on high,   65
A hundred thousand voices sent back their loud reply;
Through the thronged towns of Essex[13] the startling summons rang,
And up from bench and loom and wheel her young mechanics[14] sprang!

The voice of free, broad Middlesex, of thousands as of one,
The shaft of Bunker calling to that of Lexington;   70
From Norfolk's ancient villages, from Plymouth's rocky bound
To where Nantucket feels the arms of ocean close her round;

From rich and rural Worcester, where through the calm repose
Of cultured vales and fringing woods the gentle Nashua flows,
To where Wachuset's wintry blasts the mountain larches stir,   75
Swelled up to Heaven the thrilling cry of "God save Latimer!"

And sandy Barnstable rose up, wet with the salt sea spray;
And Bristol sent her answering shout down Narragansett Bay!
Along the broad Connecticut old Hampden felt the thrill,
And the cheer of Hampshire's woodmen swept down from Holyoke Hill.[15]   80

The voice of Massachusetts! Of her free sons and daughters,
Deep calling unto deep aloud, the sound of many waters!
Against the burden of that voice what tyrant power shall stand?
No fetters in the Bay State! No slave upon her land!

Look to it well, Virginians! In calmness we have borne,   85
In answer to our faith and trust, your insult and your scorn;
You've spurned our kindest counsels; you've hunted for our lives;
And shaken round our hearths and homes your manacles and gyves![16]

---

11. Revolutionary militiamen from western Massachusetts.   12. Monument at Bunker Hill, site of a Revolutionary battle.   13. Whittier's home county.   14. Skilled laborers.   15. The previous three stanzas refer to several Massachusetts towns, counties, and landmarks.   16. Shackles.

We wage no war, we lift no arm, we fling no torch within
The fire-damps[17] of the quaking mine beneath your soil of sin;   90
We leave ye with your bondmen, to wrestle, while ye can,
With the strong upward tendencies and godlike soul of man!

But for us and for our children, the vow which we have given
For freedom and humanity is registered in heaven;
No slave-hunt in our borders,—no pirate on our strand!   95
No fetters in the Bay State,—no slave upon our land!

—1843

The Hunters of Men

These lines were written when the orators of the American Colonization Society were demanding that the free blacks should be sent to Africa, and opposing Emancipation unless expatriation followed.

Have ye heard of our hunting, o'er mountain and glen,
Through cane-brake[1] and forest,—the hunting of men?
The lords of our land to this hunting have gone,
As the fox-hunter follows the sound of the horn;
Hark! the cheer and the hallo! the crack of the whip,   5
And the yell of the hound as he fastens his grip!
All blithe are our hunters, and noble their match,
Though hundreds are caught, there are millions to catch.
So speed to their hunting, o'er mountain and glen,
Through cane-brake and forest,—the hunting of men!   10

Gay luck to our hunters! how nobly they ride
In the glow of their zeal, and the strength of their pride!
The priest with his cassock flung back on the wind,
Just screening the politic[2] statesman behind;
The saint and the sinner, with cursing and prayer,   15
The drunk and the sober, ride merrily there.
And woman, kind woman, wife, widow, and maid,
For the good of the hunted, is lending her aid:
Her foot's in the stirrup, her hand on the rein,
How blithely she rides to the hunting of men!   20

Oh, goodly and grand is our hunting to see,
In this "land of the brave and this home of the free."
Priest, warrior, and statesman, from Georgia to Maine,
All mounting the saddle, all grasping the rein;

---

17. Explosive gases in a mine.
1. Cane field.   2. Shrewd, sly.

Right merrily hunting the black man, whose sin   25
Is the curl of his hair and the hue of his skin!
Woe, now, to the hunted who turns him at bay!
Will our hunters be turned from their purpose and prey?
Will their hearts fail within them? their nerves tremble, when
All roughly they ride to the hunting of men?   30

Ho! alms for our hunters! all weary and faint,
Wax the curse of the sinner and prayer of the saint.
The horn is wound faintly, the echoes are still,
Over cane-brake and river, and forest and hill.
Haste, alms for our hunters! the hunted once more   35
Have turned from their flight with their backs to the shore:
What right have they here in the home of the white,
Shadowed o'er by our banner of Freedom and Right?
Ho! alms for the hunters! or never again
Will they ride in their pomp to the hunting of men!   40

Alms, alms for our hunters! why will ye delay,
When their pride and their glory are melting away?
The parson has turned; for, on charge of his own,
Who goeth a warfare, or hunting, alone?
The politic statesman looks back with a sigh,   45
There is doubt in his heart, there is fear in his eye.
Oh, haste, lest that doubting and fear shall prevail,
And the head of his steed take the place of the tail.
Oh, haste, ere he leave us! for who will ride then,
For pleasure or gain, to the hunting of men?   50

                                                                        —1835

The Fishermen

HURRAH! the seaward breezes
    Sweep down the bay amain;
Heave up, my lads, the anchor!
    Run up the sail again!
Leave to the lubber landsmen
    The rail-car and the steed;   5
The stars of heaven shall guide us,
    The breath of heaven shall speed.

From the hill-top looks the steeple,
    And the lighthouse from the sand;   10
And the scattered pines are waving
    Their farewell from the land.
One glance, my lads, behind us,
    For the homes we leave one sigh,

Ere we take the change and chances
    Of the ocean and the sky.   15

Now, brothers, for the icebergs
    Of frozen Labrador,[1]
Floating spectral in the moonshine,
    Along the low, black shore!   20
Where like snow the gannet's feathers
    On Brador's rocks are shed,
And the noisy murr[2] are flying,
    Like black scuds,[3] overhead;

Where in mist the rock is hiding,   25
    And the sharp reef lurks below,
And the white squall smites in summer,
    And the autumn tempests blow;
Where, through gray and rolling vapor,
    From evening unto morn,   30
A thousand boats are hailing,
    Horn answering unto horn.

Hurrah! for the Red Island,[4]
    With the white cross on its crown!
Hurrah! for Meccatina,[5]   35
    And its mountains bare and brown!
Where the Caribou's tall antlers
    O'er the dwarf-wood freely toss,
And the footstep of the Mickmack[6]
    Has no sound upon the moss.   40

There we'll drop our lines, and gather
    Old Ocean's treasures in,
Where'er the mottled mackerel
    Turns up a steel-dark fin.
The sea's our field of harvest,   45
    Its scaly tribes our grain;
We'll reap the teeming waters
    As at home they reap the plain!

Our wet hands spread the carpet,
    And light the hearth of home;   50
From our fish, as in the old time,
    The silver coin shall come.
As the demon fled the chamber
    Where the fish of Tobit[7] lay,

---

1. Newfoundland, Canada. 2. Murre, seabirds. 3. Clouds. 4. Prince Edward Island, Canada. 5. Gros Meccatina, island off Quebec. 6. Native Canadian tribe. 7. *The Book of Tobit* tells of a young man burning a fish to drive out a demon.

So ours from all our dwellings
    Shall frighten Want[8] away.   55

Though the mist upon our jackets
    In the bitter air congeals,
And our lines wind stiff and slowly
    From off the frozen reels;
Though the fog be dark around us,   60
    And the storm blow high and loud,
We will whistle down the wild wind,
    And laugh beneath the cloud!

In the darkness as in daylight,   65
    On the water as on land,
God's eye is looking on us,
    And beneath us is His hand!
Death will find us soon or later,
    On the deck or in the cot;   70
And we cannot meet him better
    Than in working out our lot.

Hurrah! hurrah! the west-wind
    Comes freshening down the bay,
The rising sails are filling;   75
    Give way, my lads, give way!
Leave the coward landsman clinging
    To the dull earth, like a weed;
The stars of heaven shall guide us,
    The breath of heaven shall speed!   80

                                                             —1850

The Lumbermen

Wildly round our woodland quarters
    Sad-voiced Autumn grieves;
Thickly down these swelling waters
    Float his fallen leaves.
Through the tall and naked timber,
    Column-like and old,   5
Gleam the sunsets of November,
    From their skies of gold.

O'er us, to the southland heading,
    Screams the gray wild-goose;
On the night-frost sounds the treading   10

---

8. Hunger.

Of the brindled moose.
Noiseless creeping, while we're sleeping,
    Frost his task-work plies;
Soon, his icy bridges heaping,
    Shall our log-piles rise.   15

When, with sounds of smothered thunder,
    On some night of rain,
Lake and river break asunder
    Winter's weakened chain,   20
Down the wild March flood shall bear them
    To the saw-mill's wheel,
Or where Steam, the slave, shall tear them
    With his teeth of steel.

Be it starlight, be it moonlight,   25
    In these vales below,
When the earliest beams of sunlight
    Streak the mountain's snow,
Crisps the hoar-frost, keen and early,
    To our hurrying feet,   30
And the forest echoes clearly
    All our blows repeat.

Where the crystal Ambijejis
    Stretches broad and clear,
And Millnoket's pine-black ridges   35
    Hide the browsing deer:
Where, through lakes and wide morasses,
    Or through rocky walls,
Swift and strong, Penobscot[1] passes
    White with foamy falls;   40

Where, through clouds, are glimpses given
    Of Katahdin's[2] sides,—
Rock and forest piled to heaven,
    Torn and ploughed by slides!
Far below, the Indian trapping,   45
    In the sunshine warm;
Far above, the snow-cloud wrapping
    Half the peak in storm!

Where are mossy carpets better
    Than the Persian weaves,   50
And than Eastern perfumes sweeter
    Seem the fading leaves;

---

1. The Penobscot river, and the lakes, Ambijejis and Millnoket, are all in central Maine.   2. Mount Ktaadn in Maine.

And a music wild and solemn,
    From the pine-tree's height,
Rolls its vast and sea-like volume 55
    On the wind of night;

Make we here our camp of winter;
    And, through sleet and snow,
Pitchy knot and beechen splinter
    On our hearth shall glow. 60
Here, with mirth to lighten duty,
    We shall lack alone
Woman's smile and girlhood's beauty,
    Childhood's lisping tone.

But their hearth is brighter burning 65
    For our toil to-day;
And the welcome of returning
    Shall our loss repay,
When, like seamen from the waters,
    From the woods we come, 70
Greeting sisters, wives, and daughters,
    Angels of our home!

Not for us the measured ringing
    From the village spire,
Not for us the Sabbath singing 75
    Of the sweet-voiced choir;
Ours the old, majestic temple,
    Where God's brightness shines
Down the dome so grand and ample,
    Propped by lofty pines! 80

Through each branch-enwoven skylight,
    Speaks He in the breeze,
As of old beneath the twilight
    Of lost Eden's[3] trees!
For His ear, the inward feeling 85
    Needs no outward tongue;
He can see the spirit kneeling
    While the axe is swung.

Heeding truth alone, and turning
    From the false and dim, 90
Lamp of toil or altar burning
    Are alike to Him.
Strike then, comrades! Trade is waiting

---

3. Genesis 2.8–25.

On our rugged toil;
Far ships waiting for the freighting   95
    Of our woodland spoil!

Ships whose traffic links these highlands,
    Bleak and cold, of ours,
With the citron-planted islands
    Of a clime of flowers;   100
To our frosts the tribute bringing
    Of eternal heats;
In our lap of winter flinging
    Tropic fruits and sweets.

Cheerly, on the axe of labor,   105
    Let the sunbeams dance,
Better than the flash of sabre
    Or the gleam of lance!
Strike! With every blow is given
    Freer sun and sky,   110
And the long-hid earth to heaven
    Looks, with wondering eye!

Loud behind us grow the murmurs
    Of the age to come;
Clang of smiths, and tread of farmers,   115
    Bearing harvest home!
Here her virgin lap with treasures
    Shall the green earth fill;
Waving wheat and golden maize-ears
    Crown each beechen hill.   120

Keep who will the city's alleys,
    Take the smooth-shorn plain;
Give to us the cedarn valleys,
    Rocks and hills of Maine!
In our North-land, wild and woody,   125
    Let us still have part:
Rugged nurse and mother sturdy,
    Hold us to thy heart!

Oh, our free hearts beat the warmer
    For thy breath of snow;   130
And our tread is all the firmer
    For thy rocks below.
Freedom, hand in hand with labor,
    Walketh strong and brave;
On the forehead of his neighbor   135
    No man writeth Slave!

Lo, the day breaks! old Katahdin's
    Pine-trees show its fires,
While from these dim forest gardens
    Rise their blackened spires.
Up, my comrades! up and doing!   140
    Manhood's rugged play
Still renewing, bravely hewing
    Through the world our way!

—1850

Edgar Allan Poe
1809–1849

Edgar Allan Poe was believed by most nineteenth-century readers to be a drunk, womanizing opium addict; he seemed to be an American combination of Samuel Taylor Coleridge's and Lord Byron's public personas. Poe admired both of these English authors. He borrowed Coleridge's philosophy and literary criticism in "Letter to B—" (1836), and he both satirizes and pays homage to Byron in "The Assignation" (1834). In this story, Poe presents Byron as Byronic hero, a noble man vexed by his excesses as a nobleman. Telltale signs linking the "stranger" in this story to Byron's persona abound: his prowess as a swimmer; his handsomeness, despondency, decadence, and untimely death; and his attachment to a married Italian noblewoman, the Marchesa di Mentoni (Teresa Guiccioli). Taken together these details paint a mental and physical portrait of Byron and raise a mirror to (and questions for) readers. Is Poe cashing in on or critiquing the public's prying curiosity about the personal lives of celebrities when he addresses the Byron figure with these questions: "Who then shall call thy conduct into question? who blame thee for thy visionary hours, or denounce those occupations as a wasting away of life which were but the overflowings of thine everlasting energies?"

As a child who had lost both parents to death, Poe felt some of his closest connections with the British authors he read among the books of John Allan, a merchant and family friend who took in the orphaned boy in 1811. As early as age fifteen, it seemed that Poe was consciously living his life to rival Byron's: He swam the James River in Richmond, Virginia, calling to mind among the spectators Byron's swimming from Sestos to Abydos. Poe would have been familiar with Byron from Allan's books as well as from the five years he lived in Britain (relocating there with the Allan family from 1815 to 1820, when Byron's notoriety and fame were growing rapidly). Poe desired Byronic literary fame, but this path was not among the ones Allan had laid out for him. Poe's stubborn pursuit of it opened a rift between him and his guardian. Allan wanted Poe to take over his merchant business and had sent the young man to the University of Virginia to groom him for such a life. However, Allan was shocked and dismayed when Poe asked him to pay the gambling debts accrued during many late-night games of cards with his classmates. Like his parents, both of whom were traveling actors, Poe felt drawn to the arts and to new places. At eighteen, he ventured to Boston, the city in which he was born, to secure the publication of his first book, *Tamerlane and Other Poems* (1827), which identified the author as "A Bostonian" and a Byronian. The book attracted little to no interest, so he sought to improve his finances and impress his guardian by enrolling in West

Point. Still acutely feeling the prodding of literary ambition, though, Poe decided to change course and sought Allan's permission to drop out, but was denied. He got himself dismissed through breaking rules and pleading guilty to charges against him. This and the death of Allan's wife, Frances Keeling Valentine, whose affection for and protection of Poe during her lifetime was unfailing, severed relations with Allan once and for all.

Poe had lost to death many of the women to whom he had become attached—from his mother Elizabeth Arnold Poe in 1811 to his foster mother Valentine in 1830. While he was in Britain he grew attached to the mother of his friend Rob Stanard, and when Mrs. Stanard passed away the young Poe would visit her grave at night. Dead and dying maternal presences were to haunt Poe's life and work; one of his earliest poems, "To Helen" (1831), is said to be about Mrs. Stanard. Sadly, Poe had not seen the last death of a woman to whom he was close. When he left West Point in 1830, he had already published another book, *Al Aaraaf, Tamerlane, and Minor Poems* (1829), and had received enough subscriptions from his classmates to publish another one, *Poems* (1830). He went to Baltimore to live with his Aunt Clemm and his cousin Virginia, whom he would later marry in 1836 and who would die in his arms in 1847. Much of Poe's work seemed prophetic of his future and mournful of his past. In 1838, he wrote "Ligeia" (published that September in the *American Museum* and featured in the 1840 two-volume collection *Tales of the Grotesque and Arabesque*), a story in which the narrator's wife Ligeia dies and haunts him, reappearing during the death of his second wife, Rowena. The narrator of "The Raven" (1845) wishes to communicate with his deceased wife, and "Annabel Lee" (1849), written after Virginia's death, is a lament by a man whose lover has died.

Like his parents, Poe spent his life traveling from place to place, hoping to make his artistic dreams profitable, but always struggling. After living and publishing stories in Baltimore, he returned to Richmond to edit the *Southern Literary Messenger* but soon found himself in Philadelphia and New York, where he published *Arthur Gordon Pym* in 1838 and penned a poem about "The Bells" of Fordham University. After Virginia's death, he visited Providence, where he courted the poet Sarah Helen Whitman in the graveyard that adjoined her house. He also revisited Richmond. His own death came only two years after Virginia's. In 1849 he was making his way to Philadelphia to take up an editorial position there. He made it only as far as Baltimore, where he was found lying in the street unconscious and where he was buried in an unmarked grave. After his death, his fellow writer Rufus Griswold collected, published, and introduced Poe's work, portraying him as a drunkard who possessed all the negative traits of a Byronic hero. Sarah Helen Whitman rushed to his defense, denouncing Griswold's scathing attack on his onetime friend. The effect of literary gossip about Poe was such that when a tombstone was finally placed on the site of his burial, the only writer who attended the ceremony was Walt Whitman.

Despite Americans' lack of appreciation for his works because of moral judgments of the author, Poe, like Walt Whitman, had a vast and appreciative readership overseas. Charles Baudelaire translated Poe, who was praised by other French writers, such as Paul Valéry and Stéphane Mallarmé, and credited with inaugurating the Symbolist movement in French poetry. The Irish gothic writer Bram Stoker, author of *Dracula* (1897), was also influenced by Poe's stories. By the twentieth century, Poe's reputation on both sides of the Atlantic was secure, his work inspiring many practitioners of the gothic genre, including Henry James, H.P. Lovecraft, Stephen King, Neil Gaiman, and Anne Rice.

Sonnet—to Science

Science! true daughter of Old Time thou art!
   Who alterest all things with thy peering eyes.
Why preyest thou thus upon the poet's heart,
   Vulture, whose wings are dull realities?

How should he love thee? or how deem thee wise.   5
   Who wouldst not leave him in his wandering
To seek for treasure in the jewelled skies.
   Albeit he soared with an undaunted wing?
Hast thou not dragged Diana[1] from her car?
   And driven the Hamadryad[2] from the wood   10
To seek a shelter in some happier star?
   Hast thou not torn the Naiad[3] from her flood,
The Elfin from the green grass, and from me
The summer dream beneath the tamarind tree?

                                —1829

The Raven

Once upon a midnight dreary, while I pondered, weak and weary,
Over many a quaint and curious volume of forgotten lore—
While I nodded, nearly napping, suddenly there came a tapping,
As of some one gently rapping, rapping at my chamber door—
"'Tis some visiter," I muttered, "tapping at my chamber door—   5
                 Only this and nothing more."

Ah, distinctly I remember it was in the bleak December;
And each separate dying ember wrought its ghost upon the floor.
Eagerly I wished the morrow;—vainly I had sought to borrow
From my books surcease of sorrow—sorrow for the lost Lenore—   10
For the rare and radiant maiden whom the angels name Lenore—
                 Nameless *here* for evermore.

And the silken, sad, uncertain rustling of each purple curtain
Thrilled me—filled me with fantastic terrors never felt before;
So that now, to still the beating of my heart, I stood repeating   15
"'Tis some visiter entreating entrance at my chamber door—
Some late visiter entreating entrance at my chamber door;—
                 This it is and nothing more."

Presently my soul grew stronger; hesitating then no longer,
"Sir," said I, "or Madam, truly your forgiveness I implore;   20
But the fact is I was napping, and so gently you came rapping,
And so faintly you came tapping, tapping at my chamber door,
That I scarce was sure I heard you"—here I opened wide the door;—
                 Darkness there and nothing more.

Deep into that darkness peering, long I stood there wondering, fearing,   25
Doubting, dreaming dreams no mortal ever dared to dream before;
But the silence was unbroken, and the stillness gave no token,

---

1. Roman goddess of nature, the moon, and fertility.　2. Tree nymph.　3. Water nymph.

And the only word there spoken was the whispered word, "Lenore?"
This I whispered, and an echo murmured back the word "Lenore!"
       Merely this and nothing more.   30

Back into the chamber turning, all my soul within me burning,
Soon again I heard a tapping somewhat louder than before.
"Surely," said I, "surely that is something at my window lattice;
Let me see, then, what thereat is, and this mystery explore—
Let my heart be still a moment and this mystery explore;—   35
      'Tis the wind and nothing more!

Open here I flung the shutter, when, with many a flirt and flutter
In there stepped a stately Raven of the saintly days of yore;
Not the least obeisance made he; not a minute stopped or stayed he;
But, with mien of lord or lady, perched above my chamber door—   40
Perched upon a bust of Pallas[1] just above my chamber door—
      Perched, and sat, and nothing more.

Then this ebony bird beguiling my sad fancy into smiling,
By the grave and stern decorum of the countenance it wore,
"Though thy crest be shorn and shaven, thou," I said, "art sure no craven,   45
Ghastly grim and ancient Raven wandering from the Nightly shore—
Tell me what thy lordly name is on the Night's Plutonian[2] shore!"
      Quoth the Raven, "Nevermore."

Much I marvelled this ungainly fowl to hear discourse so plainly,
Though its answer little meaning—little relevancy bore;   50
For we cannot help agreeing that no living human being
Ever yet was blessed with seeing bird above his chamber door—
Bird or beast upon the sculptured bust above his chamber door,
      With such name as "Nevermore."

But the Raven, sitting lonely on the placid bust, spoke only   55
That one word, as if his soul in that one word he did outpour.
Nothing farther then he uttered—not a feather then he fluttered—
Till I scarcely more than muttered "Other friends have flown before—
On the morrow *he* will leave me, as my hopes have flown before."
      Then the bird said "Nevermore."   60

Startled at the stillness broken by reply so aptly spoken,
"Doubtless," said I, "what it utters is its only stock and store
Caught from some unhappy master whom unmerciful Disaster
Followed fast and followed faster till his songs one burden bore—
Till the dirges of his Hope that melancholy burden bore   65
      Of 'Never—nevermore.'"

---

1. Pallas Athena, Greek goddess of wisdom. 2. Pluto: the Roman underworld.

But the Raven still beguiling all my fancy into smiling,
Straight I wheeled a cushioned seat in front of bird, and bust and door;
Then, upon the velvet sinking, I betook myself to linking
Fancy unto fancy, thinking what this ominous bird of yore—   70
What this grim, ungainly, ghastly, gaunt, and ominous bird of yore
     Meant in croaking "Nevermore."

This I sat engaged in guessing, but no syllable expressing
To the fowl whose fiery eyes now burned into my bosom's core;
This and more I sat divining, with my head at ease reclining   75
On the cushion's velvet lining that the lamp-light gloated o'er,
But whose velvet-violet lining with the lamp-light gloating o'er,
     She shall press, ah, nevermore!

Then, methought, the air grew denser, perfumed from an unseen censer[3]
Swung by Seraphim[4] whose foot-falls tinkled on the tufted floor.   80
"Wretch," I cried, "thy God hath lent thee—by these angels he hath sent thee
Respite—respite and nepenthe[5] from thy memories of Lenore;
Quaff, oh quaff this kind nepenthe and forget this lost Lenore!
     Quoth the Raven "Nevermore."

"Prophet!" said I, "thing of evil! prophet still, if bird or devil!—   85
Whether Tempter sent, or whether tempest tossed thee here ashore,
Desolate yet all undaunted, on this desert land enchanted—
On this home by Horror haunted—tell me truly, I implore—
Is there—*is* there balm in Gilead?[6]—tell me—tell me, I implore!"
     Quoth the Raven "Nevermore."   90

"Prophet!" said I, "thing of evil!—prophet still, if bird or devil!
By that Heaven that bends above us—by that God we both adore—
Tell this soul with sorrow laden if, within the distant Aidenn,[7]
It shall clasp a sainted maiden whom the angels name Lenore—
Clasp a rare and radiant maiden whom the angels name Lenore."   95
     Quoth the Raven "Nevermore."

"Be that word our sign of parting, bird or fiend!" I shrieked, upstarting—
"Get thee back into the tempest and the Night's Plutonian shore!
Leave no black plume as a token of that lie thy soul hath spoken!
Leave my loneliness unbroken!—quit the bust above my door!   100
Take thy beak from out my heart, and take thy form from off my door!"
     Quoth the Raven "Nevermore."

And the Raven, never flitting, still is sitting, *still* is sitting
On the pallid bust of Pallas just above my chamber door;

---

3. Vessel for burning incense.　4. An order of six-winged angels.　5. Magical drink that soothes sorrow.　6. Jeremiah
8.22.　7. Both Eden and Heaven.

And his eyes have all the seeming of a demon's that is dreaming,   105
And the lamp-light o'er him streaming throws his shadow on the floor;
And my soul from out that shadow that lies floating on the floor
        Shall be lifted—nevermore!

           —1845

Ulalume[1]—a Ballad

The skies they were ashen and sober;
    The leaves they were crispéd and sere—
    The leaves they were withering and sere:
It was night, in the lonesome October
    Of my most immemorial year;   5
It was hard by the dim lake of Auber,
    In the misty mid region of Weir:[2]—
It was down by the dank tarn[3] of Auber,
    In the ghoul-haunted woodland of Weir.

Here once, through an alley Titanic,   10
    Of cypress, I roamed with my Soul—
    Of cypress, with Psyche, my Soul.
These were days when my heart was volcanic
    As the scoriac[4] rivers that roll—
    As the lavas that restlessly roll   15
Their sulphurous currents down Yaanek,[5]
    In the ultimate climes of the Pole—
That groan as they roll down Mount Yaanek,
    In the realms of the Boreal Pole.

Our talk had been serious and sober.   20
    By our thoughts they were palsied and sere—
    Our memories were treacherous and sere;
For we knew not the month was October,
    And we marked not the night of the year—
    (Ah, night of all nights in the year!)   25
We noted not the dim lake of Auber,
    (Though once we had journeyed down here)
We remembered not the dank tarn of Auber,
    Nor the ghoul-haunted woodland of Weir.

And now, as the night was senescent,[6]   30
    And star-dials pointed to morn—
    As the star-dials hinted of morn—
At the end of our path a liquescent

---

1. *Ulalare:* to wail; *lumen:* light (Latin).   2. Daniel Auber (1782–1871), French composer; R. W. Weir (1803–1889), American landscape painter.   3. Small mountain lake.   4. Scoria: lava that has hardened on contact with air.   5. Volcano near the North Pole.   6. Waning.

And nebulous lustre was born,
Out of which a miraculous crescent   35
    Arose with a duplicate horn—
Astarte's bediamonded crescent,[7]
    Distinct with its duplicate horn.

And I said—"She is warmer than Dian[8];
    She rolls through an ether of sighs—   40
    She revels in a region of sighs.
She has seen that the tears are not dry on
    These cheeks where the worm never dies,
And has come past the stars of the Lion,
    To point us the path to the skies—   45
    To the Lethean[9] peace of the skies—
Come up, in despite of the Lion,
    To shine on us with her bright eyes—
Come up, through the lair of the Lion,
    With love in her luminous eyes."   50

But Psyche, uplifting her finger,
    Said—"Sadly this star I mistrust—
    Her pallor I strangely mistrust—
Ah, hasten!—ah, let us not linger!
    Ah, fly!—let us fly!—for we must."   55
In terror she spoke; letting sink her
    Wings till they trailed in the dust—
In agony sobbed; letting sink her
    Plumes till they trailed in the dust—
    Till they sorrowfully trailed in the dust.   60

I replied—"This is nothing but dreaming.
    Let us on, by this tremulous light!
    Let us bathe in this crystalline light!
Its Sibyllic[10] splendor is beaming
    With Hope and in Beauty to-night—   65
    See!—it flickers up the sky through the night!
Ah, we safely may trust to its gleaming
    And be sure it will lead us aright—
We surely may trust to a gleaming
    That cannot but guide us aright   70
Since it flickers up to Heaven through the night."

Thus I pacified Psyche and kissed her,
    And tempted her out of her gloom—
    And conquered her scruples and gloom;

---

7. Venus, the morning star.   8. The moon.   9. Lethe, river in the Greek underworld that induced forgetfulness.   10. Sybils, legendary Greek prophetesses.

And we passed to the end of the vista—   75
　　But were stopped by the door of a tomb—
　　By the door of a legended tomb:—
And I said—"What is written, sweet sister,
　　On the door of this legended[11] tomb?"
　　She replied—"Ulalume—Ulalume!—   80
　　'Tis the vault of thy lost Ulalume!"

Then my heart it grew ashen and sober
　　As the leaves that were crispéd and sere—
　　As the leaves that were withering and sere—
And I cried—"It was surely October,   85
　　On *this* very night of last year,
　　That I journeyed—I journeyed down here!—
　　That I brought a dread burden down here—
　　On this night, of all nights in the year,
　　Ah, what demon hath tempted me here?   90
Well I know, now, this dim lake of Auber—
　　This misty mid region of Weir:—
Well I know, now, this dank tarn of Auber—
　　This ghoul-haunted woodland of Weir."

Said we, then—the two, then—"Ah, can it   95
　　Have been that the woodlandish ghouls—
　　The pitiful, the merciful ghouls,
To bar up our way and to ban it
　　From the secret that lies in these wolds[12]—
　　From the thing that lies hidden in these wolds—   100
Have drawn up the spectre of a planet
　　From the limbo of lunary souls—

This sinfully scintillant planet
　　From the Hell of the planetary souls?"

　　　　　　　　　　　　　　　　　　　　—1847–1849

Annabel Lee

It was many and many a year ago,
　　In a kingdom by the sea,
That a maiden there lived whom you may know
　　By the name of Annabel Lee;—
And this maiden she lived with no other thought   5
　　Than to love and be loved by me.

I was a child and *she* was a child,
　　In this kingdom by the sea;

---

11. Inscribed with text.   12. Forests.

But we loved with a love that was more than love—
   I and my Annabel Lee—
With a love that the wingéd seraphs of heaven
   Coveted her and me.

And this was the reason that, long ago,
   In this kingdom by the sea,
A wind blew out of a cloud, chilling
   My beautiful Annabel Lee;
So that her high-born kinsmen came
   And bore her away from me,
To shut her up in a sepulchre,[1]
   In this kingdom by the sea.

The angels, not half so happy in Heaven,
   Went envying her and me—
Yes!—that was the reason (as all men know,
   In this kingdom by the sea)
That the wind came out of the cloud by night,
   Chilling and killing my Annabel Lee.

But our love it was stronger by far than the love
   Of those who were older than we—
   Of many far wiser than we—
And neither the angels in Heaven above,
   Nor the demons down under the sea,
Can ever dissever my soul from the soul
   Of the beautiful Annabel Lee:—

For the moon never beams, without bringing me dreams
   Of the beautiful Annabel Lee;
And the stars never rise, but I feel the bright eyes
   Of the beautiful Annabel Lee:—
And so, all the night-tide, I lie down by the side
Of my darling—my darling—my life and my bride,
   In the sepulchre there by the sea—
   In her tomb by the sounding sea.

—1849

Ligeia

And the will therein lieth, which dieth not. Who knoweth the mysteries of the will,
with its vigor? For God is but a great will pervading all things by nature of its
intentness. Man doth not yield himself to the angels, nor unto death utterly, save
only through the weakness of his feeble will.

—Joseph Glanvill[1]

---

1. Tomb.

1. Joseph Glanvill (1636–1680), English theologian. The quotation is a fabrication.

I cannot, for my soul, remember how, when, or even precisely where, I first became acquainted with the lady Ligeia. Long years have since elapsed, and my memory is feeble through much suffering. Or, perhaps, I cannot *now* bring these points to mind, because, in truth, the character of my beloved, her rare learning, her singular yet placid cast of beauty, and the thrilling and enthralling eloquence of her low musical language, made their way into my heart by paces so steadily and stealthily progressive that they have been unnoticed and unknown. Yet I believe that I met her first and most frequently in some large, old, decaying city near the Rhine.[2] Of her family—I have surely heard her speak. That it is of a remotely ancient date cannot be doubted. Ligeia! Ligeia! Buried in studies of a nature more than all else adapted to deaden impressions of the outward world, it is by that sweet word alone—by Ligeia—that I bring before mine eyes in fancy the image of her who is no more. And now, while I write, a recollection flashes upon me that I have *never known* the paternal name of her who was my friend and my betrothed, and who became the partner of my studies, and finally the wife of my bosom. Was it a playful charge on the part of my Ligeia? or was it a test of my strength of affection, that I should institute no inquiries upon this point? or was it rather a caprice of my own—a wildly romantic offering on the shrine of the most passionate devotion? I but indistinctly recall the fact itself—what wonder that I have utterly forgotten the circumstances which originated or attended it? And, indeed, if ever that spirit which is entitled *Romance*—if ever she, the wan and the misty-winged *Ashtophet*[3] of idolatrous Egypt, presided, as they tell, over marriages ill-omened, then most surely she presided over mine.

There is one dear topic, however, on which my memory fails me not. It is the *person* of Ligeia. In stature she was tall, somewhat slender, and, in her latter days, even emaciated. I would in vain attempt to portray the majesty, the quiet ease, of her demeanor, or the incomprehensible lightness and elasticity of her footfall. She came and departed as a shadow. I was never made aware of her entrance into my closed study save by the dear music of her low sweet voice, as she placed her marble hand upon my shoulder. In beauty of face no maiden ever equalled her. It was the radiance of an opium-dream[4]—an airy and spirit-lifting vision more wildly divine than the phantasies which hovered about the slumbering souls of the daughters of Delos.[5] Yet her features were not of that regular mould which we have been falsely taught to worship in the classical labors of the heathen. "There is no exquisite beauty," says Bacon, Lord Verulam, speaking truly of all the forms and *genera* of beauty, "without some *strangeness* in the proportion."[6] Yet, although I saw that the features of Ligeia were not of a classic regularity—although I perceived that her loveliness was indeed "exquisite," and felt that there was much of "strangeness" pervading it, yet I have tried in vain to detect the irregularity and to trace home my own perception of "the strange." I examined the contour of the lofty and pale forehead—it was faultless—how cold indeed that word when applied to a majesty so divine!—the skin rivalling the purest ivory, the commanding extent and repose, the gentle prominence of the regions above the temples; and then the raven-black, the glossy, the luxuriant and naturally-curling tresses, setting forth the full force of the Homeric epithet, "hyacinthine!"[7] I looked at the delicate outlines of the nose—and nowhere but in the graceful medallions of the Hebrews had I beheld a similar perfection. There were the same luxurious smoothness of surface, the same scarcely perceptible tendency to the

---

2. German river.   3. Ashtoreth: Phoenician goddess of fertility.   4. See Coleridge, "Christabel" (lines 484–486).   5. Greek isle.   6. Sir Francis Bacon (1561–1626), "Of Beauty" (1597).   7. *The Odyssey* describes Odysseus's hair as hyacinthine.

aquiline, the same harmoniously curved nostrils speaking the free spirit. I regarded the sweet mouth. Here was indeed the triumph of all things heavenly—the magnificent turn of the short upper lip—the soft, voluptuous slumber of the under—the dimples which sported, and the color which spoke—the teeth glancing back, with a brilliancy almost startling, every ray of the holy light which fell upon them in her serene and placid, yet most exultingly radiant of all smiles. I scrutinized the formation of the chin—and here, too, I found the gentleness of breadth, the softness and the majesty, the fullness and the spirituality, of the Greek—the contour which the god Apollo revealed but in a dream, to Cleomenes,[8] the son of the Athenian. And then I peered into the large eyes of Ligeia.

For eyes we have no models in the remotely antique. It might have been, too, that in these eyes of my beloved lay the secret to which Lord Verulam alludes. They were, I must believe, far larger than the ordinary eyes of our own race. They were even fuller than the fullest of the gazelle eyes of the tribe of the valley of Nourjahad.[9] Yet it was only at intervals—in moments of intense excitement—that this peculiarity became more than slightly noticeable in Ligeia. And at such moments was her beauty—in my heated fancy thus it appeared perhaps—the beauty of beings either above or apart from the earth—the beauty of the fabulous Houri[10] of the Turk. The hue of the orbs was the most brilliant of black, and, far over them, hung jetty lashes of great length. The brows, slightly irregular in outline, had the same tint. The "strangeness," however, which I found in the eyes, was of a nature distinct from the formation, or the color, or the brilliancy of the features, and must, after all, be referred to the *expression*. Ah, word of no meaning! behind whose vast latitude of mere sound we intrench our ignorance of so much of the spiritual. The expression of the eyes of Ligeia! How for long hours have I pondered upon it! How have I, through the whole of a midsummer night, struggled to fathom it! What was it—that something more profound than the well of Democritus[11]—which lay far within the pupils of my beloved? What *was* it? I was possessed with a passion to discover. Those eyes! those large, those shining, those divine orbs! they became to me twin stars of Leda,[12] and I to them devoutest of astrologers.

There is no point, among the many incomprehensible anomalies of the science of mind, more thrillingly exciting than the fact—never, I believe, noticed in the schools—that, in our endeavors to recall to memory something long forgotten, we often find ourselves *upon the very verge* of remembrance, without being able, in the end, to remember. And thus how frequently, in my intense scrutiny of Ligeia's eyes, have I felt approaching the full knowledge of their expression—felt it approaching—yet not quite be mine—and so at length entirely depart! And (strange, oh strangest mystery of all!) I found, in the commonest objects of the universe, a circle of analogies to that expression. I mean to say that, subsequently to the period when Ligeia's beauty passed into my spirit, there dwelling as in a shrine, I derived, from many existences in the material world, a sentiment such as I felt always aroused within me by her large and luminous orbs. Yet not the more could I define that sentiment, or analyze, or even steadily view it. I recognized it, let me repeat, sometimes in the survey of a rapidly-growing vine—in the contemplation of a moth, a butterfly, a chrysalis, a stream of running water. I have felt it in the ocean; in the falling of a meteor. I have felt it in the glances of unusually

8. Greek sculptor (d. 490 BC).   9. *The History of Nourjahad* (1767), a novel of the Middle East by Frances Sheridan (1724–1766).   10. Virgins awaiting the faithful in the afterlife.   11. Greek philosopher (460–370 BC) who wrote that "truth lies at the bottom of a well."   12. The constellation Gemini contains the stars Castor and Pollux, named for the mythical sons of Zeus and Leda, Queen of Sparta.

aged people. And there are one or two stars in heaven—(one especially, a star of the sixth magnitude, double and changeable, to be found near the large star in Lyra[13]) in a telescopic scrutiny of which I have been made aware of the feeling. I have been filled with it by certain sounds from stringed instruments, and not unfrequently by passages from books. Among innumerable other instances, I well remember something in a volume of Joseph Glanvill, which (perhaps merely from its quaintness—who shall say?) never failed to inspire me with the sentiment;—"And the will therein lieth, which dieth not. Who knoweth the mysteries of the will, with its vigor? For God is but a great will pervading all things by nature of its intentness. Man doth not yield him to the angels, nor unto death utterly, save only through the weakness of his feeble will."

Length of years, and subsequent reflection, have enabled me to trace, indeed, some remote connection between this passage in the English moralist and a portion of the character of Ligeia. An *intensity* in thought, action, or speech, was possibly, in her, a result, or at least an index, of that gigantic volition which, during our long intercourse, failed to give other and more immediate evidence of its existence. Of all the women whom I have ever known, she, the outwardly calm, the ever-placid Ligeia, was the most violently a prey to the tumultuous vultures of stern passion. And of such passion I could form no estimate, save by the miraculous expansion of those eyes which at once so delighted and appalled me—by the almost magical melody, modulation, distinctness and placidity of her very low voice—and by the fierce energy (rendered doubly effective by contrast with her manner of utterance) of the wild words which she habitually uttered.

I have spoken of the learning of Ligeia: it was immense—such as I have never known in woman. In the classical tongues was she deeply proficient, and as far as my own acquaintance extended in regard to the modern dialects of Europe, I have never known her at fault. Indeed upon any theme of the most admired, because simply the most abstruse of the boasted erudition of the academy, have I *ever* found Ligeia at fault? How singularly—how thrillingly, this one point in the nature of my wife has forced itself, at this late period only, upon my attention! I said her knowledge was such as I have never known in woman—but where breathes the man who has traversed, and successfully, *all* the wide areas of moral, physical, and mathematical science? I saw not then what I now clearly perceive, that the acquisitions of Ligeia were gigantic, were astounding; yet I was sufficiently aware of her infinite supremacy to resign myself, with a childlike confidence, to her guidance through the chaotic world of metaphysical investigation at which I was most busily occupied during the earlier years of our marriage. With how vast a triumph—with how vivid a delight—with how much of all that is ethereal in hope—did I *feel*, as she bent over me in studies but little sought—but less known—that delicious vista by slow degrees expanding before me, down whose long, gorgeous, and all untrodden path, I might at length pass onward to the goal of a wisdom too divinely precious not to be forbidden!

How poignant, then, must have been the grief with which, after some years, I beheld my well-grounded expectations take wings to themselves and fly away! Without Ligeia I was but as a child groping benighted. Her presence, her readings alone, rendered vividly luminous the many mysteries of the transcendentalism[14] in which we were immersed. Wanting the radiant lustre of her eyes, letters, lambent and

---

13. Vega or Alpha Lyrae.   14. The works of the German philosophers Immanuel Kant (1724–1804), Johann Gottlieb Fichte (1762–1814), Friedrich Schelling (1775–1854), and others.

golden, grew duller than Saturnian[15] lead. And now those eyes shone less and less frequently upon the pages over which I pored. Ligeia grew ill. The wild eyes blazed with a too—too glorious effulgence; the pale fingers became of the transparent waxen hue of the grave, and the blue veins upon the lofty forehead swelled and sank impetuously with the tides of the most gentle emotion. I saw that she must die—and I struggled desperately in spirit with the grim Azrael.[16] And the struggles of the passionate wife were, to my astonishment, even more energetic than my own. There had been much in her stern nature to impress me with the belief that, to her, death would have come without its terrors;—but not so. Words are impotent to convey any just idea of the fierceness of resistance with which she wrestled with the Shadow. I groaned in anguish at the pitiable spectacle. I would have soothed—I would have reasoned; but, in the intensity of her wild desire for life,—for life—*but* for life—solace and reason were alike the uttermost of folly. Yet not until the last instance, amid the most convulsive writhings of her fierce spirit, was shaken the external placidity of her demeanor. Her voice grew more gentle—grew more low—yet I would not wish to dwell upon the wild meaning of the quietly uttered words. My brain reeled as I hearkened entranced, to a melody more than mortal—to assumptions and aspirations which mortality had never before known.

That she loved me I should not have doubted; and I might have been easily aware that, in a bosom such as hers, love would have reigned no ordinary passion. But in death only, was I fully impressed with the strength of her affection. For long hours, detaining my hand, would she pour out before me the overflowing of a heart whose more than passionate devotion amounted to idolatry. How had I deserved to be so blessed by such confessions?—how had I deserved to be so cursed with the removal of my beloved in the hour of her making them? But upon this subject I cannot bear to dilate. Let me say only, that in Ligeia's more than womanly abandonment to a love, alas! all unmerited, all unworthily bestowed, I at length recognized the principle of her longing with so wildly earnest a desire for the life which was now fleeing so rapidly away. It is this wild longing—it is this eager vehemence of desire for life—*but* for life—that I have no power to portray—no utterance capable of expressing.

At high noon of the night in which she departed, beckoning me, peremptorily, to her side, she bade me repeat certain verses composed by herself not many days before. I obeyed her.—They were these:

Lo! 'tis a gala night
    Within the lonesome latter years!
An angel throng, bewinged, bedight[17]
    In veils, and drowned in tears,
Sit in a theatre, to see
    A play of hopes and fears,
While the orchestra breathes fitfully
    The music of the spheres.

Mimes, in the form of God on high,
    Mutter and mumble low,

---

15. Saturnus: alchemist's term for lead.   16. Angel of death.   17. Clothed.

And hither and thither fly
      Mere puppets they, who come and go
At bidding of vast formless things
      That shift the scenery to and fro,
Flapping from out their Condor wings
      Invisible Wo!

That motley drama!—oh, be sure
      It shall not be forgot!
With its Phantom chased forever more,
      By a crowd that seize it not,
Through a circle that ever returneth in
      To the self-same spot,
And much of Madness and more of Sin
      And Horror the soul of the plot.

But see, amid the mimic rout,
      A crawling shape intrude!
A blood-red thing that writhes from out
      The scenic solitude!
It writhes!—it writhes!—with mortal pangs
      The mimes become its food,
And the seraphs sob at vermin fangs
      In human gore imbued.

Out—out are the lights—out all!
      And over each quivering form,
The curtain, a funeral pall,
      Comes down with the rush of a storm,
And the angels, all pallid and wan,
      Uprising, unveiling, affirm
That the play is the tragedy, "Man,"
      And its hero the Conqueror Worm.

"O God!" half shrieked Ligeia, leaping to her feet and extending her arms aloft with a spasmodic movement, as I made an end of those lines—"O God! O Divine Father!—shall these things be undeviatingly so?—shall this Conqueror be not once conquered? Are we not part and parcel in Thee? Who—who knoweth the mysteries of the will with its vigor? Man doth not yield him to the angels, *nor unto death utterly,* save only through the weakness of his feeble will."

And now, as if exhausted with emotion, she suffered her white arms to fall, and returned solemnly to her bed of death. And as she breathed her last sighs, there came mingled with them a low murmur from her lips. I bent to them my ear and distinguished, again, the concluding words of the passage in Glanvill—"*Man doth not yield him to the angels, nor unto death utterly, save only through the weakness of his feeble will.*"

She died;—and I, crushed into the very dust with sorrow, could no longer endure the lonely desolation of my dwelling in the dim and decaying city by the Rhine. I had no lack of what the world calls wealth. Ligeia had brought me far more, very far more than ordinarily falls to the lot of mortals. After a few months, therefore, of weary and aimless wandering, I purchased, and put in some repair, an abbey, which I shall not name, in one of the wildest and least frequented portions of fair England. The gloomy and dreary grandeur of the building, the almost savage aspect of the domain, the many melancholy and time-honored memories connected with both, had much in unison with the feelings of utter abandonment which had driven me into that remote and unsocial region of the country. Yet although the external abbey, with its verdant decay hanging about it, suffered but little alteration, I gave way, with a child-like perversity, and perchance with a faint hope of alleviating my sorrows, to a display of more than regal magnificence within.—For such follies, even in childhood, I had imbibed a taste and now they came back to me as if in the dotage of grief. Alas, I feel how much even of incipient madness might have been discovered in the gorgeous and fantastic draperies, in the solemn carvings of Egypt, in the wild cornices and furniture, in the Bedlam[18] patterns of the carpets of tufted gold! I had become a bounden slave in the trammels of opium, and my labors and my orders had taken a coloring from my dreams. But these absurdities I must not pause to detail. Let me speak only of that one chamber, ever accursed, whither in a moment of mental alienation, I led from the altar as my bride—as the successor of the unforgotten Ligeia—the fair-haired and blue-eyed Lady Rowena Trevanion, of Tremaine.

There is no individual portion of the architecture and decoration of that bridal chamber which is not now visibly before me. Where were the souls of the haughty family of the bride, when, through thirst of gold, they permitted to pass the threshold of an apartment so bedecked, a maiden and a daughter so beloved? I have said that I minutely remember the details of the chamber—yet I am sadly forgetful on topics of deep moment—and here there was no system, no keeping, in the fantastic display, to take hold upon the memory. The room lay in a high turret of the castellated abbey, was pentagonal in shape, and of capacious size. Occupying the whole southern face of the pentagon was the sole window—an immense sheet of unbroken glass from Venice—a single pane, and tinted of a leaden hue, so that the rays of either the sun or moon, passing through it, fell with a ghastly lustre on the objects within. Over the upper portion of this huge window, extended the trellice-work of an aged vine, which clambered up the massy walls of the turret. The ceiling, of gloomy-looking oak, was excessively lofty, vaulted, and elaborately fretted with the wildest and most grotesque specimens of a semi-Gothic, semi-Druidical device. From out the most central recess of this melancholy vaulting, depended, by a single chain of gold with long links, a huge censer of the same metal, Saracenic[19] in pattern, and with many perforations so contrived that there writhed in and out of them, as if endued with a serpent vitality, a continual succession of parti-colored fires.

Some few ottomans and golden candelabra, of Eastern figure, were in various stations about—and there was the couch, too—the bridal couch—of an Indian model, and low, and sculptured of solid ebony, with a pall-like canopy above. In each of the angles of the chamber stood on end a gigantic sarcophagus of black granite, from the tombs of the kings over against Luxor,[20] with their aged lids full of immemorial sculpture. But in the draping of the apartment lay, alas! the chief phantasy of all. The lofty walls, gigantic in height—even unproportionably so—were hung from summit to foot, in vast folds, with a heavy and massive-looking tapestry—tapestry of a material which was found alike as a carpet on the floor, as a covering for the ottomans and the ebony

---

18. Asylum for the mentally ill in London, St. Mary's at Bethlehem.   19. Arabesque; Middle Eastern.   20. Egypt.

bed, as a canopy for the bed, and as the gorgeous volutes[21] of the curtains which partially shaded the window. The material was the richest cloth of gold. It was spotted all over, at irregular intervals, with arabesque figures, about a foot in diameter, and wrought upon the cloth in patterns of the most jetty black. But these figures partook of the true character of the arabesque only when regarded from a single point of view. By a contrivance now common, and indeed traceable to a very remote period of antiquity, they were made changeable in aspect. To one entering the room, they bore the appearance of simple monstrosities; but upon a farther advance, this appearance gradually departed; and step by step, as the visitor moved his station in the chamber, he saw himself surrounded by an endless succession of the ghastly forms which belong to the superstition of the Norman, or arise in the guilty slumbers of the monk. The phantasmagoric effect was vastly heightened by the artificial introduction of a strong continual current of wind behind the draperies—giving a hideous and uneasy animation to the whole.

In halls such as these—in a bridal chamber such as this—I passed, with the Lady of Tremaine, the unhallowed hours of the first month of our marriage—passed them with but little disquietude. That my wife dreaded the fierce moodiness of my temper—that she shunned me and loved me but little—I could not help perceiving; but it gave me rather pleasure than otherwise. I loathed her with a hatred belonging more to demon than to man. My memory flew back, (oh, with what intensity of regret!) to Ligeia, the beloved, the august, the beautiful, the entombed. I revelled in recollections of her purity, of her wisdom, of her lofty, her ethereal nature, of her passionate, her idolatrous love. Now, then, did my spirit fully and freely burn with more than all the fires of her own. In the excitement of my opium dreams (for I was habitually fettered in the shackles of the drug) I would call aloud upon her name, during the silence of the night, or among the sheltered recesses of the glens by day, as if, through the wild eagerness, the solemn passion, the consuming ardor of my longing for the departed, I could restore her to the pathway she had abandoned—ah, *could* it be forever?—upon the earth.

About the commencement of the second month of the marriage, the Lady Rowena was attacked with sudden illness, from which her recovery was slow. The fever which consumed her rendered her nights uneasy; and in her perturbed state of half-slumber, she spoke of sounds, and of motions, in and about the chamber of the turret, which I concluded had no origin save in the distemper of her fancy, or perhaps in the phantasmagoric influences of the chamber itself. She became at length convalescent—finally well. Yet but a brief period elapsed, ere a second more violent disorder again threw her upon a bed of suffering; and from this attack her frame, at all times feeble, never altogether recovered. Her illnesses were, after this epoch, of alarming character, and of more alarming recurrence, defying alike the knowledge and the great exertions of her physicians. With the increase of the chronic disease which had thus, apparently, taken too sure hold upon her constitution to be eradicated by human means, I could not fail to observe a similar increase in the nervous irritation of her temperament, and in her excitability by trivial causes of fear. She spoke again, and now more frequently and pertinaciously, of the sounds—of the slight sounds—and of the unusual motions among the tapestries, to which she had formerly alluded.

One night, near the closing in of September, she pressed this distressing subject with more than usual emphasis upon my attention. She had just awakened from an

---

21. Spiral or scroll-like ornaments.

unquiet slumber, and I had been watching, with feelings half of anxiety, half of vague terror, the workings of her emaciated countenance. I sat by the side of her ebony bed, upon one of the ottomans of India. She partly arose, and spoke, in an earnest low whisper, of sounds which she *then* heard, but which I could not hear—of motions which she *then* saw, but which I could not perceive. The wind was rushing hurriedly behind the tapestries, and I wished to show her (what, let me confess it, I could not *all* believe) that those almost inarticulate breathings, and those very gentle variations of the figures upon the wall, were but the natural effects of that customary rushing of the wind. But a deadly pallor, overspreading her face, had proved to me that my exertions to reassure her would be fruitless. She appeared to be fainting, and no attendants were within call. I remembered where was deposited a decanter of light wine which had been ordered by her physicians, and hastened across the chamber to procure it. But, as I stepped beneath the light of the censer, two circumstances of a startling nature attracted my attention. I had felt that some palpable although invisible object had passed lightly by my person; and I saw that there lay upon the golden carpet, in the very middle of the rich lustre thrown from the censer, a shadow—a faint, indefinite shadow of angelic aspect—such as might be fancied for the shadow of a shade. But I was wild with the excitement of an immoderate dose of opium, and heeded these things but little, nor spoke of them to Rowena. Having found the wine, I recrossed the chamber, and poured out a goblet-ful, which I held to the lips of the fainting lady. She had now partially recovered, however, and took the vessel herself, while I sank upon an ottoman near me, with my eyes fastened upon her person. It was then that I became distinctly aware of a gentle foot-fall upon the carpet, and near the couch; and in a second thereafter, as Rowena was in the act of raising the wine to her lips, I saw, or may have dreamed that I saw, fall within the goblet, as if from some invisible spring in the atmosphere of the room, three or four large drops of a brilliant and ruby colored fluid. If this I saw—not so Rowena. She swallowed the wine unhesitatingly, and I forbore to speak to her of a circumstance which must, after all, I considered, have been but the suggestion of a vivid imagination, rendered morbidly active by the terror of the lady, by the opium, and by the hour.

Yet I cannot conceal it from my own perception that, immediately subsequent to the fall of the ruby-drops, a rapid change for the worse took place in the disorder of my wife; so that, on the third subsequent night, the hands of her menials[22] prepared her for the tomb, and on the fourth, I sat alone, with her shrouded body, in that fantastic chamber which had received her as my bride.—Wild visions, opium-engendered, flitted, shadow-like, before me. I gazed with unquiet eye upon the sarcophagi in the angles of the room, upon the varying figures of the drapery, and upon the writhing of the parti-colored fires in the censer overhead. My eyes then fell, as I called to mind the circumstances of a former night, to the spot beneath the glare of the censer where I had seen the faint traces of the shadow. It was there, however, no longer; and breathing with greater freedom, I turned my glances to the pallid and rigid figure upon the bed. Then rushed upon me a thousand memories of Ligeia—and then came back upon my heart, with the turbulent violence of a flood, the whole of that unutterable wo with which I had regarded *her* thus enshrouded. The night waned; and still, with a bosom full of bitter thoughts of the one only and supremely beloved, I remained gazing upon the body of Rowena.

---

22. Servants.

It might have been midnight, or perhaps earlier, or later, for I had taken no note of time, when a sob, low, gentle, but very distinct, startled me from my revery.—I *felt* that it came from the bed of ebony—the bed of death. I listened in an agony of superstitious terror—but there was no repetition of the sound. I strained my vision to detect any motion in the corpse—but there was not the slightest perceptible. Yet I could not have been deceived. I *had* heard the noise, however faint, and my soul was awakened within me. I resolutely and perseveringly kept my attention riveted upon the body. Many minutes elapsed before any circumstance occurred tending to throw light upon the mystery. At length it became evident that a slight, a very feeble, and barely noticeable tinge of color had flushed up within the cheeks, and along the sunken small veins of the eyelids. Through a species of unutterable horror and awe, for which the language of mortality has no sufficiently energetic expression, I felt my heart cease to beat, my limbs grow rigid where I sat. Yet a sense of duty finally operated to restore my self-possession. I could no longer doubt that we had been precipitate in our preparations—that Rowena still lived. It was necessary that some immediate exertion be made; yet the turret was altogether apart from the portion of the abbey tenanted by the servants—there were none within call—I had no means of summoning them to my aid without leaving the room for many minutes—and this I could not venture to do. I therefore struggled alone in my endeavors to call back the spirit still hovering. In a short period it was certain, however, that a relapse had taken place; the color disappeared from both eyelid and cheek, leaving a wanness even more than that of marble; the lips became doubly shrivelled and pinched up in the ghastly expression of death; a repulsive clamminess and coldness overspread rapidly the surface of the body; and all the usual rigorous stiffness immediately supervened. I fell back with a shudder upon the couch from which I had been so startlingly aroused, and again gave myself up to passionate waking visions of Ligeia.

An hour thus elapsed when (could it be possible?) I was a second time aware of some vague sound issuing from the region of the bed. I listened—in extremity of horror. The sound came again—it was a sigh. Rushing to the corpse, I saw—distinctly saw—a tremor upon the lips. In a minute afterward they relaxed, disclosing a bright line of the pearly teeth. Amazement now struggled in my bosom with the profound awe which had hitherto reigned there alone. I felt that my vision grew dim, that my reason wandered; and it was only by a violent effort that I at length succeeded in nerving myself to the task which duty thus once more had pointed out. There was now a partial glow upon the forehead and upon the cheek and throat; a perceptible warmth pervaded the whole frame; there was even a slight pulsation at the heart. The lady *lived*; and with redoubled ardor I betook myself to the task of restoration. I chafed and bathed the temples and the hands, and used every exertion which experience, and no little medical reading, could suggest. But in vain. Suddenly, the color fled, the pulsation ceased, the lips resumed the expression of the dead, and, in an instant afterward, the whole body took upon itself the icy chilliness, the livid hue, the intense rigidity, the sunken outline, and all the loathsome peculiarities of that which has been, for many days, a tenant of the tomb.

And again I sunk into visions of Ligeia—and again, (what marvel that I shudder while I write?) *again* there reached my ears a low sob from the region of the ebony bed. But why shall I minutely detail the unspeakable horrors of that night? Why shall I pause to relate how, time after time, until near the period of the gray dawn, this hideous drama of revivification was repeated; how each terrific relapse was only into a sterner and apparently more irredeemable death; how each agony wore the aspect of a struggle with some invisible foe; and how each struggle was succeeded by I know not what of wild change in the personal appearance of the corpse? Let me hurry to a conclusion.

The greater part of the fearful night had worn away, and she who had been dead, once again stirred—and now more vigorously than hitherto, although arousing from a dissolution more appalling in its utter hopelessness than any. I had long ceased to struggle or to move, and remained sitting rigidly upon the ottoman, a helpless prey to a whirl of violent emotions, of which extreme awe was perhaps the least terrible, the least consuming. The corpse, I repeat, stirred, and now more vigorously than before. The hues of life flushed up with unwonted energy into the countenance—the limbs relaxed—and, save that the eyelids were yet pressed heavily together, and that the bandages and draperies of the grave still imparted their charnel character to the figure, I might have dreamed that Rowena had indeed shaken off, utterly, the fetters of Death. But if this idea was not, even then, altogether adopted, I could at least doubt no longer, when, arising from the bed, tottering, with feeble steps, with closed eyes, and with the manner of one bewildered in a dream, the thing that was enshrouded advanced bodily and palpably into the middle of the apartment.

I trembled not—I stirred not—for a crowd of unutterable fancies connected with the air, the stature, the demeanor of the figure, rushing hurriedly through my brain, had paralyzed—had chilled me into stone. I stirred not—but gazed upon the apparition. There was a mad disorder in my thoughts—a tumult unappeasable. Could it, indeed, be the *living* Rowena who confronted me? Could it indeed be Rowena *at all*—the fair-haired, the blue-eyed Lady Rowena Trevanion of Tremaine? Why, *why* should I doubt it? The bandage lay heavily about the mouth—but then might it not be the mouth of the breathing Lady of Tremaine? And the cheeks—there were the roses as in her noon of life—yes, these might indeed be the fair cheeks of the living Lady of Tremaine. And the chin, with its dimples, as in health, might it not be hers?—but *had she then grown taller since her malady*? What inexpressible madness seized me with that thought? One bound, and I had reached her feet! Shrinking from my touch, she let fall from her head, unloosened, the ghastly cerements[23] which had confined it, and there streamed forth, into the rushing atmosphere of the chamber, huge masses of long and dishevelled hair; *it was blacker than the raven wings of the midnight*! And now slowly opened *the eyes* of the figure which stood before me. "Here then, at least," I shrieked aloud, "can I never—can I never be mistaken—these are the full, and the black, and the wild eyes—of my lost love—of the lady—of the LADY LIGEIA."

—1838

The Fall of the House of Usher

Son coeur est un luth suspendu;
Sitôt qu'on le touche il résonne.

—DE BÉRANGER[1]

During the whole of a dull, dark, and soundless day in the autumn of the year, when the clouds hung oppressively low in the heavens, I had been passing alone, on horse-

---

23. Shrouds for the dead.

1. Pierre-Jean de Béranger (1780–1857), "Le Refus" (1831): "His heart is a lute tightly strung / As soon as one touches it, it sounds."

back, through a singularly dreary tract of country, and at length found myself, as the shades of the evening drew on, within view of the melancholy House of Usher. I know not how it was—but, with the first glimpse of the building, a sense of insufferable gloom pervaded my spirit. I say insufferable; for the feeling was unrelieved by any of that half-pleasurable, because poetic, sentiment, with which the mind usually receives even the sternest natural images of the desolate or terrible. I looked upon the scene before me—upon the mere house, and the simple landscape features of the domain—upon the bleak walls—upon the vacant eye-like windows—upon a few rank sedges[2]—and upon a few white trunks of decayed trees—with an utter depression of soul which I can compare to no earthly sensation more properly than to the after-dream of the reveller upon opium—the bitter lapse into every-day life—the hideous dropping off of the veil. There was an iciness, a sinking, a sickening of the heart—an unredeemed dreariness of thought which no goading of the imagination could torture into aught of the sublime. What was it—I paused to think—what was it that so unnerved me in the contemplation of the House of Usher? It was a mystery all insoluble; nor could I grapple with the shadowy fancies that crowded upon me as I pondered. I was forced to fall back upon the unsatisfactory conclusion, that while, beyond doubt, there *are* combinations of very simple natural objects which have the power of thus affecting us, still the analysis of this power lies among considerations beyond our depth. It was possible, I reflected, that a mere different arrangement of the particulars of the scene, of the details of the picture, would be sufficient to modify, or perhaps to annihilate its capacity for sorrowful impression; and, acting upon this idea, I reined my horse to the precipitous brink of a black and lurid tarn that lay in unruffled lustre by the dwelling, and gazed down—but with a shudder even more thrilling than before—upon the remodelled and inverted images of the gray sedge, and the ghastly tree-stems, and the vacant and eye-like windows.

Nevertheless, in this mansion of gloom I now proposed to myself a sojourn of some weeks. Its proprietor, Roderick Usher, had been one of my boon companions in boyhood; but many years had elapsed since our last meeting. A letter, however, had lately reached me in a distant part of the country—a letter from him—which, in its wildly importunate nature, had admitted of no other than a personal reply. The MS.[3] gave evidence of nervous agitation. The writer spoke of acute bodily illness—of a mental disorder which oppressed him—and of an earnest desire to see me, as his best, and indeed his only personal friend, with a view of attempting, by the cheerfulness of my society, some alleviation of his malady. It was the manner in which all this, and much more, was said—it was the apparent *heart* that went with his request—which allowed me no room for hesitation; and I accordingly obeyed forthwith what I still considered a very singular summons.

Although, as boys, we had been even intimate associates, yet I really knew little of my friend. His reserve had been always excessive and habitual. I was aware, however, that his very ancient family had been noted, time out of mind, for a peculiar sensibility of temperament, displaying itself, through long ages, in many works of exalted art, and manifested, of late, in repeated deeds of munificent yet unobtrusive charity, as well as in a passionate devotion to the intricacies, perhaps even more than to the orthodox and easily recognizable beauties, of musical science. I had learned, too, the

---

2. Grasses.   3. Abbreviation for manuscript, from Latin for "writing of the hand."

very remarkable fact, that the stem of the Usher race, all time-honoured as it was, had put forth, at no period, any enduring branch; in other words, that the entire family lay in the direct line of descent, and had always, with very trifling and very temporary variation, so lain. It was this deficiency, I considered, while running over in thought the perfect keeping of the character of the premises with the accredited character of the people, and while speculating upon the possible influence which the one, in the long lapse of centuries, might have exercised upon the other—it was this deficiency, perhaps of collateral issue, and the consequent undeviating transmission, from sire to son, of the patrimony with the name, which had, at length, so identified the two as to merge the original title of the estate in the quaint and equivocal appellation of the "House of Usher"—an appellation which seemed to include, in the minds of the peasantry who used it, both the family and the family mansion.

I have said that the sole effect of my somewhat childish experiment—that of looking down within the tarn—had been to deepen the first singular impression. There can be no doubt that the consciousness of the rapid increase of my superstition—for why should I not so term it?—served mainly to accelerate the increase itself. Such, I have long known, is the paradoxical law of all sentiments having terror as a basis. And it might have been for this reason only, that, when I again uplifted my eyes to the house itself, from its image in the pool, there grew in my mind a strange fancy—a fancy so ridiculous, indeed, that I but mention it to show the vivid force of the sensations which oppressed me. I had so worked upon my imagination as really to believe that about the whole mansion and domain there hung an atmosphere peculiar to themselves and their immediate vicinity—an atmosphere which had no affinity with the air of heaven, but which had reeked up from the decayed trees, and the gray wall, and the silent tarn—a pestilent and mystic vapour, dull, sluggish, faintly discernible, and leaden-hued.

Shaking off from my spirit what *must* have been a dream, I scanned more narrowly the real aspect of the building. Its principal feature seemed to be that of an excessive antiquity. The discoloration of ages had been great. Minute fungi overspread the whole exterior, hanging in a fine tangled web-work from the eaves. Yet all this was apart from an extraordinary dilapidation. No portion of the masonry had fallen; and there appeared to be a wild inconsistency between its still perfect adaptation of parts, and the crumbling condition of the individual stones. In this there was much that reminded me of the specious totality of old woodwork which has rotted for long years in some neglected vault, with no disturbance from the breath of the external air. Beyond this indication of extensive decay, however, the fabric gave little token of instability. Perhaps the eye of a scrutinizing observer might have discovered a barely perceptible fissure, which, extending from the roof of the building in front, made its way down the wall in a zigzag direction, until it became lost in the sullen waters of the tarn.

Noticing these things, I rode over a short causeway to the house. A servant in waiting took my horse, and I entered the Gothic archway of the hall. A valet, of stealthy step, thence conducted me, in silence, through many dark and intricate passages in my progress to the *studio* of his master. Much that I encountered on the way contributed, I know not how, to heighten the vague sentiments of which I have already spoken. While the objects around me—while the carvings of the ceilings, the sombre tapestries of the walls, the ebon blackness of the floors, and the phantasmagoric armorial trophies which rattled as I strode, were but matters to which, or to such as which, I had been accustomed from my infancy—while I hesitated not to acknowledge how familiar was all this—I still wondered to find how unfamiliar were the fancies which ordinary images were stirring up. On one of the staircases, I met the physician of the family. His countenance, I thought, wore a mingled expression of low cunning and perplexity. He accosted me with trepidation and passed on. The valet now threw open a door and ushered me into the presence of his master.

The room in which I found myself was very large and lofty. The windows were long, narrow, and pointed, and at so vast a distance from the black oaken floor as to be altogether inaccessible from within. Feeble gleams of encrimsoned light made their way through the trellissed panes, and served to render sufficiently distinct the more prominent objects around; the eye, however, struggled in vain to reach the remoter angles of the chamber, or the recesses of the vaulted and fretted ceiling. Dark draperies hung upon the walls. The general furniture was profuse, comfortless, antique, and tattered. Many books and musical instruments lay scattered about, but failed to give any vitality to the scene. I felt that I breathed an atmosphere of sorrow. An air of stern, deep, and irredeemable gloom hung over and pervaded all.

Upon my entrance, Usher arose from a sofa on which he had been lying at full length, and greeted me with a vivacious warmth which had much in it, I at first thought of an overdone cordiality—of the constrained effort of the *ennuyé*[4] man of the world. A glance, however, at his countenance convinced me of his perfect sincerity. We sat down; and for some moments, while he spoke not, I gazed upon him with a feeling half of pity, half of awe. Surely, man had never before so terribly altered, in so brief a period, as had Roderick Usher! It was with difficulty that I could bring myself to admit the identity of the wan being before me with the companion of my early boyhood. Yet the character of his face had been at all times remarkable. A cadaverousness of complexion; an eye large, liquid, and luminous beyond comparison; lips somewhat thin and very pallid, but of a surpassingly beautiful curve; a nose of a delicate Hebrew model, but with a breadth of nostril unusual in similar formations; a finely moulded chin, speaking, in its want of prominence, of a want of moral energy[5]; hair of a more than web-like softness and tenuity; these features, with an inordinate expansion above the regions of the temple, made up altogether a countenance not easily to be forgotten. And now in the mere exaggeration of the prevailing character of these features, and of the expression they were wont to convey, lay so much of change that I doubted to whom I spoke. The now ghastly pallor of the skin, and the now miraculous lustre of the eye, above all things startled and even awed me. The silken hair, too, had been suffered to grow all unheeded, and as, in its wild gossamer texture, it floated rather than fell about the face, I could not, even with effort, connect its Arabesque expression with any idea of simple humanity.

In the manner of my friend I was at once struck with an incoherence—an inconsistency; and I soon found this to arise from a series of feeble and futile struggles to overcome an habitual trepidancy—an excessive nervous agitation. For something of this nature I had indeed been prepared, no less by his letter, than by reminiscences of certain boyish traits, and by conclusions deducted from his peculiar physical conformation and temperament. His action was alternately vivacious and sullen. His voice varied rapidly from a tremulous indecision (when the animal spirits seemed utterly in

---

4. Bored (French).   5. Poe alludes to the pseudo-science of phrenology in which the shape of a person's head was used to predict character traits.

abeyance) to that species of energetic concision—that abrupt, weighty, unhurried, and hollow-sounding enunciation—that leaden, self-balanced, and perfectly modulated guttural utterance, which may be observed in the lost drunkard, or the irreclaimable eater of opium, during the periods of his most intense excitement.

It was thus that he spoke of the object of my visit, of his earnest desire to see me, and of the solace he expected me to afford him. He entered, at some length, into what he conceived to be the nature of his malady. It was, he said, a constitutional and a family evil, and one for which he despaired to find a remedy—a mere nervous affection, he immediately added, which would undoubtedly soon pass off. It displayed itself in a host of unnatural sensations. Some of these, as he detailed them, interested and bewildered me; although, perhaps, the terms and the general manner of their narration had their weight. He suffered much from a morbid acuteness of the senses; the most insipid food was alone endurable; he could wear only garments of certain texture; the odours of all flowers were oppressive; his eyes were tortured by even a faint light; and there were but peculiar sounds, and these from stringed instruments, which did not inspire him with horror.

To an anomalous species of terror I found him a bounden slave. "I shall perish," said he, "I *must* perish in this deplorable folly. Thus, thus, and not otherwise, shall I be lost. I dread the events of the future, not in themselves, but in their results. I shudder at the thought of any, even the most trivial, incident, which may operate upon this intolerable agitation of soul. I have, indeed, no abhorrence of danger, except in its absolute effect—in terror. In this unnerved—in this pitiable condition—I feel that the period will sooner or later arrive when I must abandon life and reason together, in some struggle with the grim phantasm, FEAR."

I learned, moreover, at intervals, and through broken and equivocal hints, another singular feature of his mental condition. He was enchained by certain superstitious impressions in regard to the dwelling which he tenanted, and whence, for many years, he had never ventured forth—in regard to an influence whose supposititious force was conveyed in terms too shadowy here to be re-stated—an influence which some peculiarities in the mere form and substance of his family mansion had, by dint of long sufferance, he said, obtained over his spirit—an effect which the *physique* of the gray wall and turrets, and of the dim tarn into which they all looked down, had, at length, brought about upon the *morale* of his existence.

He admitted, however, although with hesitation, that much of the peculiar gloom which thus afflicted him could be traced to a more natural and far more palpable origin—to the severe and long-continued illness—indeed to the evidently approaching dissolution—of a tenderly beloved sister, his sole companion for long years, his last and only relative on earth. "Her decease," he said, with a bitterness which I can never forget, "would leave him (him the hopeless and the frail) the last of the ancient race of the Ushers." While he spoke, the lady Madeline (for so was she called) passed slowly through a remote portion of the apartment, and, without having noticed my presence, disappeared. I regarded her with an utter astonishment not unmingled with dread—and yet I found it impossible to account for such feelings. A sensation of stupor oppressed me, as my eyes followed her retreating steps. When a door, at length, closed upon her, my glance sought instinctively and eagerly the countenance of the brother—but he had buried his face in his hands, and I could only perceive that a far more than ordinary wanness had overspread the emaciated fingers through which trickled many passionate tears.

The disease of the lady Madeline had long baffled the skill of her physicians. A settled apathy, a gradual wasting away of the person, and frequent although transient affections of a partially cataleptical character were the unusual diagnosis. Hitherto she had steadily borne up against the pressure of her malady, and had not betaken herself finally to bed; but on the closing in of the evening of my arrival at the house, she succumbed (as her brother told me at night with inexpressible agitation) to the prostrating power of the destroyer; and I learned that the glimpse I had obtained of her person would thus probably be the last I should obtain—that the lady, at least while living, would be seen by me no more.

For several days ensuing, her name was unmentioned by either Usher or myself: and during this period I was busied in earnest endeavours to alleviate the melancholy of my friend. We painted and read together, or I listened, as if in a dream, to the wild improvisations of his speaking guitar. And thus, as a closer and still closer intimacy admitted me more unreservedly into the recesses of his spirit, the more bitterly did I perceive the futility of all attempt at cheering a mind from which darkness, as if an inherent positive quality, poured forth upon all objects of the moral and physical universe in one unceasing radiation of gloom.

I shall ever bear about me a memory of the many solemn hours I thus spent alone with the master of the House of Usher. Yet I should fail in any attempt to convey an idea of the exact character of the studies, or of the occupations, in which he involved me, or led me the way. An excited and highly distempered ideality threw a sulphureous lustre over all. His long improvised dirges will ring forever in my ears. Among other things, I hold painfully in mind a certain singular perversion and amplification of the wild air of the last waltz of Von Weber.[6] From the paintings over which his elaborate fancy brooded, and which grew, touch by touch, into vagueness at which I shuddered the more thrillingly, because I shuddered knowing not why;—from these paintings (vivid as their images now are before me) I would in vain endeavour to educe more than a small portion which should lie within the compass of merely written words. By the utter simplicity, by the nakedness of his designs, he arrested and overawed attention. If ever mortal painted an idea, that mortal was Roderick Usher. For me at least—in the circumstances then surrounding me—there arose out of the pure abstractions which the hypochondriac contrived to throw upon his canvas, an intensity of intolerable awe, no shadow of which I felt ever yet in the contemplation of the certainly glowing yet too concrete reveries of Fuseli.[7]

One of the phantasmagoric conceptions of my friend, partaking not so rigidly of the spirit of abstraction, may be shadowed forth, although feebly, in words. A small picture presented the interior of an immensely long and rectangular vault or tunnel, with low walls, smooth, white, and without interruption or device. Certain accessory points of the design served well to convey the idea that this excavation lay at an exceeding depth below the surface of the earth. No outlet was observed in any portion of its vast extent, and no torch or other artificial source of light was discernible; yet a flood of intense rays rolled throughout, and bathed the whole in a ghastly and inappropriate splendour.

I have just spoken of that morbid condition of the auditory nerve which rendered all music intolerable to the sufferer, with the exception of certain effects of

6. Karl Maria Von Weber (1786–1826), German composer. Karl Gottlieb Reissinger (1798–1859) composed *The Last Waltz of Von Weber*.   7. Henry Fuseli (1741–1828), English painter.

stringed instruments. It was, perhaps, the narrow limits to which he thus confined himself upon the guitar, which gave birth, in great measure, to the fantastic character of his performances. But the fervid *facility* of his *impromptus* could not be so accounted for. They must have been, and were, in the notes, as well as in the words of his wild fantasias (for he not unfrequently accompanied himself with rhymed verbal improvisations), the result of that intense mental collectedness and concentration to which I have previously alluded as observable only in particular moments of the highest artificial excitement. The words of one of these rhapsodies I have easily remembered. I was, perhaps, the more forcibly impressed with it, as he gave it, because, in the under or mystic current of its meaning, I fancied that I perceived, and for the first time, a full consciousness on the part of Usher, of the tottering of his lofty reason upon her throne. The verses, which were entitled "The Haunted Palace," ran very nearly, if not accurately, thus:

I

In the greenest of our valleys,
    By good angels tenanted,
Once a fair and stately palace—
    Radiant palace—reared its head.
In the monarch Thought's dominion—
    It stood there!
Never seraph spread a pinion
    Over fabric half so fair.

II

Banners yellow, glorious, golden,
    On its roof did float and flow;
(This—all this—was in the olden
    Time long ago)
And every gentle air that dallied,
    In that sweet day,
Along the ramparts plumed and pallid,
    A winged odour went away.

III

Wanderers in that happy valley
    Through two luminous windows saw
Spirits moving musically
    To a lute's well-tunèd law,
Round about a throne, where sitting
    (Porphyrogene!)[8]
In state his glory well befitting,
    The ruler of the realm was seen.

---

8. Of royal birth.

IV

And all with pearl and ruby glowing
    Was the fair palace door,
Through which came flowing, flowing, flowing
    And sparkling evermore,
A troop of Echoes whose sweet duty
    Was but to sing,
In voices of surpassing beauty,
    The wit and wisdom of their king.

V

But evil things, in robes of sorrow,
    Assailed the monarch's high estate;
(Ah, let us mourn, for never morrow
    Shall dawn upon him, desolate!)
And, round about his home, the glory
    That blushed and bloomed
Is but a dim-remembered story
    Of the old time entombed.

VI

And travellers now within that valley,
    Through the red-litten windows see
Vast forms that move fantastically
    To a discordant melody;
While, like a rapid ghastly river,
    Through the pale door,
A hideous throng rush out forever,
    And laugh—but smile no more.

I well remember that suggestions arising from this ballad, led us into a train of thought, wherein there became manifest an opinion of Usher's which I mention not so much on account of its novelty, (for other men have thought thus,) as on account of the pertinacity with which he maintained it. This opinion, in its general form, was that of the sentience of all vegetable things. But, in his disordered fancy, the idea had assumed a more daring character, and trespassed, under certain conditions, upon the kingdom of inorganization. I lack words to express the full extent, or the earnest *abandon* of his persuasion. The belief, however, was connected (as I have previously hinted) with the gray stones of the home of his forefathers. The conditions of the sentience had been here, he imagined, fulfilled in the method of collocation of these stones—in the order of their arrangement, as well as in that of the many *fungi* which overspread them, and of the decayed trees which stood around—above all, in the long undisturbed endurance of this arrangement, and in its reduplication in the still waters of the tarn. Its evidence—the evidence of the sentience—was to be seen, he said (and I here started as he spoke), in the gradual yet certain condensation of an atmosphere of their own about the waters and the walls. The result was discoverable, he added, in that silent yet importunate and terrible influence which for centuries had moulded the destinies of his family, and which made *him* what I now saw him— what he was. Such opinions need no comment, and I will make none.

Our books—the books which, for years, had formed no small portion of the mental existence of the invalid—were, as might be supposed, in strict keeping with his character of phantasm. We pored together over such works as the Ververt et Chartreuse of Gresset; the Belphegor of Machiavelli; the Heaven and Hell of Swedenborg; the Subterranean Voyage of Nicholas Klimm of Holberg; the Chiromancy of Robert Flud, of Jean D'Indaginé, and of De la Chambre; the Journey into the Blue Distance of Tieck; and the City of the Sun of Campanella. One favourite volume was a small octavo edition of the *Directorium Inquisitorum*, by the Dominican Eymeric de Gironne; and there were passages in Pomponius Mela, about the old African Satyrs and Ægipans, over which Usher would sit dreaming for hours. His chief delight, however, was found in the perusal of an exceedingly rare and curious book in quarto Gothic—the manual of a forgotten church—the *Vigiliæ Mortuorum secundum Chorum Ecclesiæ Maguntinæ.*[9]

I could not help thinking of the wild ritual of this work, and of its probable influence upon the hypochondriac, when, one evening, having informed me abruptly that the lady Madeline was no more, he stated his intention of preserving her corpse for a fortnight, (previously to its final interment,) in one of the numerous vaults within the main walls of the building. The worldly reason, however, assigned for this singular proceeding, was one which I did not feel at liberty to dispute. The brother had been led to his resolution (so he told me) by consideration of the unusual character of the malady of the deceased, of certain obtrusive and eager inquiries on the part of her medical men, and of the remote and exposed situation of the burial-ground of the family. I will not deny that when I called to mind the sinister countenance of the person whom I met upon the staircase, on the day of my arrival at the house, I had no desire to oppose what I regarded as at best but a harmless, and by no means an unnatural, precaution.

At the request of Usher, I personally aided him in the arrangements for the temporary entombment. The body having been encoffined, we two alone bore it to its rest. The vault in which we placed it (and which had been so long unopened that our torches, half smothered in its oppressive atmosphere, gave us little opportunity for investigation) was small, damp, and entirely without means of admission for light; lying, at great depth, immediately beneath that portion of the building in which was my own sleeping apartment. It had been used, apparently, in remote feudal times, for the worst purposes of a donjon-keep, and, in later days, as a place of deposit for powder, or some other highly combustible substance, as a portion of its floor, and the whole interior of a long archway through which we reached it, were carefully sheathed with copper. The door, of massive iron, had been, also, similarly protected. Its immense weight caused an unusually sharp grating sound, as it moved upon its hinges.

Having deposited our mournful burden upon tressels within this region of horror, we partially turned aside the yet unscrewed lid of the coffin, and looked upon the face of the tenant. A striking similitude between the brother and sister now first arrested my attention; and Usher, divining, perhaps, my thoughts, murmured out some few words from which I learned that the deceased and himself had been twins, and that sympathies of a scarcely intelligible nature had always existed between them. Our

---

9. Poe catalogs books dealing with the occult, mysticism, and the persecution of heretics.

glances, however, rested not long upon the dead—for we could not regard her unawed. The disease which had thus entombed the lady in the maturity of youth, had left, as usual in all maladies of a strictly cataleptical character, the mockery of a faint blush upon the bosom and the face, and that suspiciously lingering smile upon the lip which is so terrible in death. We replaced and screwed down the lid, and, having secured the door of iron, made our way, with toil, into the scarcely less gloomy apartments of the upper portion of the house.

And now, some days of bitter grief having elapsed, an observable change came over the features of the mental disorder of my friend. His ordinary manner had vanished. His ordinary occupations were neglected or forgotten. He roamed from chamber to chamber with hurried, unequal, and objectless step. The pallor of his countenance had assumed, if possible, a more ghastly hue—but the luminousness of his eye had utterly gone out. The once occasional huskiness of his tone was heard no more; and a tremulous quaver, as if of extreme terror, habitually characterized his utterance. There were times, indeed, when I thought his unceasingly agitated mind was labouring with some oppressive secret, to divulge which he struggled for the necessary courage. At times, again, I was obliged to resolve all into the mere inexplicable vagaries of madness, for I beheld him gazing upon vacancy for long hours, in an attitude of the profoundest attention, as if listening to some imaginary sound. It was no wonder that his condition terrified—that it infected me. I felt creeping upon me, by slow yet certain degrees, the wild influences of his own fantastic yet impressive superstitions.

It was, especially, upon retiring to bed late in the night of the seventh or eighth day after the placing of the lady Madeline within the donjon, that I experienced the full power of such feelings. Sleep came not near my couch—while the hours waned and waned away. I struggled to reason off the nervousness which had dominion over me. I endeavoured to believe that much, if not all of what I felt, was due to the bewildering influence of the gloomy furniture of the room—of the dark and tattered draperies, which, tortured into motion by the breath of a rising tempest, swayed fitfully to and fro upon the walls, and rustled uneasily about the decorations of the bed. But my efforts were fruitless. An irrepressible tremour gradually pervaded my frame; and, at length, there sat upon my very heart an incubus[10] of utterly causeless alarm. Shaking this off with a gasp and a struggle, I uplifted myself upon the pillows, and, peering earnestly within the intense darkness of the chamber, hearkened—I know not why, except that an instinctive spirit prompted me—to certain low and indefinite sounds which came, through the pauses of the storm, at long intervals, I knew not whence. Overpowered by an intense sentiment of horror, unaccountable yet unendurable, I threw on my clothes with haste, (for I felt that I should sleep no more during the night) and endeavoured to arouse myself from the pitiable condition into which I had fallen, by pacing rapidly to and fro through the apartment.

I had taken but few turns in this manner, when a light step on an adjoining staircase arrested my attention. I presently recognised it as that of Usher. In an instant afterward he rapped, with a gentle touch, at my door, and entered, bearing a lamp. His countenance was, as usual, cadaverously wan—but, moreover, there was a species of mad hilarity in his eyes—an evidently restrained *hysteria* in his whole demeanour. His air appalled me—but anything was preferable to the solitude which I had so long endured, and I even welcomed his presence as a relief.

---

10. A spirit that drains the vitality of its sleeping victims.

"And you have not seen it?" he said abruptly, after having stared about him for some moments in silence—"you have not then seen it?—but, stay! you shall." Thus speaking, and having carefully shaded his lamp, he hurried to one of the casements, and threw it freely open to the storm.

The impetuous fury of the entering gust nearly lifted us from our feet. It was, indeed, a tempestuous yet sternly beautiful night, and one wildly singular in its terror and its beauty. A whirlwind had apparently collected its force in our vicinity; for there were frequent and violent alterations in the direction of the wind; and the exceeding density of the clouds (which hung so low as to press upon the turrets of the house) did not prevent our perceiving the life-like velocity with which they flew careering from all points against each other, without passing away into the distance. I say that even their exceeding density did not prevent our perceiving this—yet we had no glimpse of the moon or stars—nor was there any flashing forth of the lightning. But the under surfaces of the huge masses of agitated vapour, as well as all terrestrial objects immediately around us, were glowing in the unnatural light of a faintly luminous and distinctly visible gaseous exhalation which hung about and enshrouded the mansion.

"You must not—you shall not behold this!" said I, shudderingly, to Usher, as I led him, with a gentle violence, from the window to a seat. "These appearances, which bewilder you, are merely electrical phenomena not uncommon—or it may be that they have their ghastly origin in the rank miasma of the tarn. Let us close this casement;—the air is chilling and dangerous to your frame. Here is one of your favourite romances. I will read, and you shall listen;—and so we will pass away this terrible night together."

The antique volume which I had taken up was the "Mad Trist" of Sir Launcelot Canning,[11] but I had called it a favourite of Usher's more in sad jest than in earnest; for, in truth, there is little in its uncouth and unimaginative prolixity which could have had interest for the lofty and spiritual ideality of my friend. It was, however, the only book immediately at hand; and I indulged a vague hope that the excitement which now agitated the hypochondriac, might find relief (for the history of mental disorder is full of similar anomalies) even in the extremeness of the folly which I could read. Could I have judged, indeed, by the wild overstrained air of vivacity with which he hearkened, or apparently hearkened, to the words of the tale, I might well have congratulated myself upon the success of my design.

I had arrived at that well-known portion of the story where Ethelred, the hero of the Trist, having sought in vain for peaceable admission into the dwelling of the hermit, proceeds to make good an entrance by force. Here, it will be remembered, the words of the narrative run thus:

"And Ethelred, who was by nature of a doughty heart, and who was now mighty withal, on account of the powerfulness of the wine which he had drunken, waited no longer to hold parley with the hermit, who, in sooth, was of an obstinate and maliceful turn, but, feeling the rain upon his shoulders, and fearing the rising of the tempest, uplifted his mace outright, and, with blows, made quickly room in the plankings of the door for his gauntleted hand; and now pulling therewith sturdily, he so cracked, and ripped, and tore all asunder, that the noise of the dry and hollow-sounding wood alarmed and reverberated throughout the forest."

---

11. A title and author fabricated by Poe.

At the termination of this sentence I started and, for a moment, paused; for it appeared to me (although I at once concluded that my excited fancy had deceived me)— it appeared to me that, from some very remote portion of the mansion, there came, indistinctly, to my ears, what might have been, in its exact similarity of character, the echo (but a stifled and dull one certainly) of the very cracking and ripping sound which Sir Launcelot had so particularly described. It was, beyond doubt, the coincidence alone which had arrested my attention; for, amid the rattling of the sashes of the casements, and the ordinary commingled noises of the still increasing storm, the sound, in itself, had nothing, surely, which should have interested or disturbed me. I continued the story:

"But the good champion Ethelred, now entering within the door, was sore enraged and amazed to perceive no signal of the maliceful hermit; but, in the stead thereof, a dragon of a scaly and prodigious demeanour, and of a fiery tongue, which sate in guard before a palace of gold, with a floor of silver; and upon the wall there hung a shield of shining brass with this legend enwritten—

> Who entereth herein, a conqueror hath bin;
> Who slayeth the dragon, the shield he shall win.

And Ethelred uplifted his mace, and struck upon the head of the dragon, which fell before him, and gave up his pesty breath, with a shriek so horrid and harsh, and withal so piercing, that Ethelred had fain to close his ears with his hands against the dreadful noise of it, the like whereof was never before heard."

Here again I paused abruptly, and now with a feeling of wild amazement—for there could be no doubt whatever that, in this instance, I did actually hear (although from what direction it proceeded I found it impossible to say) a low and apparently distant, but harsh, protracted, and most unusual screaming or grating sound—the exact counterpart of what my fancy had already conjured up for the dragon's unnatural shriek as described by the romancer.

Oppressed, as I certainly was, upon the occurrence of the second and most extraordinary coincidence, by a thousand conflicting sensations, in which wonder and extreme terror were predominant, I still retained sufficient presence of mind to avoid exciting, by any observation, the sensitive nervousness of my companion. I was by no means certain that he had noticed the sounds in question; although, assuredly, a strange alteration had, during the last few minutes, taken place in his demeanour. From a position fronting my own, he had gradually brought round his chair, so as to sit with his face to the door of the chamber; and thus I could but partially perceive his features, although I saw that his lips trembled as if he were murmuring inaudibly. His head had dropped upon his breast—yet I knew that he was not asleep, from the wide and rigid opening of the eye as I caught a glance of it in profile. The motion of his body, too, was at variance with this idea—for he rocked from side to side with a gentle yet constant and uniform sway. Having rapidly taken notice of all this, I resumed the narrative of Sir Launcelot, which thus proceeded:

"And now, the champion, having escaped from the terrible fury of the dragon, bethinking himself of the brazen shield, and of the breaking up of the enchantment which was upon it, removed the carcass from out of the way before him, and approached valorously over the silver pavement of the castle to where the shield was upon the wall; which in sooth tarried not for his full coming, but fell down at his feet upon the silver floor, with a mighty great and terrible ringing sound."

No sooner had these syllables passed my lips, than—as if a shield of brass had indeed, at the moment, fallen heavily upon a floor of silver—I became aware of a distinct, hollow, metallic, and clangorous, yet apparently muffled reverberation. Completely unnerved, I leaped to my feet; but the measured rocking movement of Usher was undisturbed. I rushed to the chair in which he sat. His eyes were bent fixedly before him, and throughout his whole countenance there reigned a stony rigidity. But, as I placed my hand upon his shoulder, there came a strong shudder over his whole person; a sickly smile quivered about his lips; and I saw that he spoke in a low, hurried, and gibbering murmur, as if unconscious of my presence. Bending closely over him, I at length drank in the hideous import of his words.

"Not hear it?—yes, I hear it, and *have* heard it. Long—long—long—many minutes, many hours, many days, have I heard it—yet I dared not—oh, pity me, miserable wretch that I am!—I dared not—I *dared* not speak! We have put her living in the tomb! Said I not that my senses were acute? I *now* tell you that I heard her first feeble movements in the hollow coffin. I heard them—many, many days ago—yet I dared not—I *dared not speak*! And now—to-night—Ethelred—ha! ha!—the breaking of the hermit's door, and the death-cry of the dragon, and the clangour of the shield!—say, rather, the rending of her coffin, and the grating of the iron hinges of her prison, and her struggles within the coppered archway of the vault! Oh whither shall I fly? Will she not be here anon? Is she not hurrying to upbraid me for my haste? Have I not heard her footsteps on the stair? Do I not distinguish that heavy and horrible beating of her heart? MADMAN!"—here he sprang furiously to his feet, and shrieked out his syllables, as if in the effort he were giving up his soul—"MADMAN! I TELL YOU THAT SHE NOW STANDS WITHOUT THE DOOR!"

As if in the superhuman energy of his utterance there had been found the potency of a spell—the huge antique panels to which the speaker pointed threw slowly back, upon the instant, their ponderous and ebony jaws. It was the work of the rushing gust—but then without those doors there DID stand the lofty and enshrouded figure of the lady Madeline of Usher. There was blood upon her white robes, and the evidence of some bitter struggle upon every portion of her emaciated frame. For a moment she remained trembling and reeling to and fro upon the threshold, then, with a low moaning cry, fell heavily inward upon the person of her brother, and in her violent and now final death-agonies, bore him to the floor a corpse, and a victim to the terrors he had anticipated.

From that chamber, and from that mansion, I fled aghast. The storm was still abroad in all its wrath as I found myself crossing the old causeway. Suddenly there shot along the path a wild light, and I turned to see whence a gleam so unusual could have issued; for the vast house and its shadows were alone behind me. The radiance was that of the full, setting, and blood-red moon, which now shone vividly through that once barely discernible fissure, of which I have before spoken as extending from the roof of the building, in a zigzag direction, to the base. While I gazed, this fissure rapidly widened—there came a fierce breath of the whirlwind—the entire orb of the satellite burst at once upon my sight—my brain reeled as I saw the mighty walls rushing asunder—there was a long tumultuous shouting sound like the voice of a thousand waters—and the deep and dank tarn at my feet closed sullenly and silently over the fragments of the "HOUSE OF USHER."

—1839

The Man of the Crowd

Ce grand malheur, de ne pouvoir être seul.—LA BRUYÈRE[1]

It was well said of a certain German book that *"er lasst sich nicht lesen"*—it does not permit itself to be read. There are some secrets which do not permit themselves to be told. Men die nightly in their beds, wringing the hands of ghostly confessors, and looking them piteously in the eyes—die with despair of heart and convulsion of throat, on account of the hideousness of mysteries which will not *suffer themselves* to be revealed. Now and then, alas, the conscience of man takes up a burden so heavy in horror that it can be thrown down only into the grave. And thus the essence of all crime is undivulged.

Not long ago, about the closing in of an evening in autumn, I sat at the large bow-window of the D—— Coffee-House in London. For some months I had been ill in health, but was now convalescent, and, with returning strength, found myself in one of those happy moods which are so precisely the converse of *ennui*—moods of the keenest appetency, when the film from the mental vision departs—the αχλυς ἥ πριν επῆεν[2]—and the intellect, electrified, surpasses as greatly its every-day condition, as does the vivid yet candid reason of Leibnitz, the mad and flimsy rhetoric of Gorgias.[3] Merely to breathe was enjoyment; and I derived positive pleasure even from many of the legitimate sources of pain. I felt a calm but inquisitive interest in every thing. With a cigar in my mouth and a newspaper in my lap, I had been amusing myself for the greater part of the afternoon, now in poring over advertisements, now in observing the promiscuous company in the room, and now in peering through the smoky panes into the street.

This latter is one of the principal thoroughfares of the city, and had been very much crowded during the whole day. But, as the darkness came on, the throng momently increased; and, by the time the lamps were well lighted, two dense and continuous tides of population were rushing past the door. At this particular period of the evening I had never before been in a similar situation, and the tumultuous sea of human heads filled me, therefore, with a delicious novelty of emotion. I gave up, at length, all care of things within the hotel, and became absorbed in contemplation of the scene without.

At first my observations took an abstract and generalizing turn. I looked at the passengers in masses, and thought of them in their aggregate relations. Soon, however, I descended to details, and regarded with minute interest the innumerable varieties of figure, dress, air, gait, visage, and expression of countenance.

By far the greater number of those who went by had a satisfied, business-like demeanor, and seemed to be thinking only of making their way through the press. Their brows were knit, and their eyes rolled quickly; when pushed against by fellow-wayfarers they evinced no symptom of impatience, but adjusted their clothes and hurried on. Others, still a numerous class, were restless in their movements, had flushed faces, and talked and gesticulated to themselves, as if feeling in solitude on account of the very denseness of the company around. When impeded in their progress, these people suddenly ceased muttering, but redoubled their gesticulations, and awaited, with an absent and overdone smile upon the lips, the course of the persons impeding

1. "The great sorrow of the inability to be alone." Jean de la Bruyère (1645–1696), *Les Caractères* (1688).   2. "The mist that was previously upon it." Homer, *The Iliad*.   3. Baron Gottfried Wilhelm von Leibnitz (1646–1716), German philosopher; Gorgias (483–378 BC), Sicilian philosopher.

them. If jostled, they bowed profusely to the jostlers, and appeared overwhelmed with confusion.—There was nothing very distinctive about these two large classes beyond what I have noted. Their habiliments belonged to that order which is pointedly termed the decent. They were undoubtedly noblemen, merchants, attorneys, tradesmen, stock-jobbers—the Eupatrids[4] and the common-places of society—men of leisure and men actively engaged in affairs of their own—conducting business upon its own responsibility. They did not greatly excite my attention.

The tribe of clerks was an obvious one; and here I discerned two remarkable divisions. There were the junior clerks of flash houses—young gentlemen with tight coats, bright boots, well-oiled hair, and supercilious lips. Setting aside a certain dapperness of carriage, which may be termed *deskism* for want of a better word, the manner of these persons seemed to be an exact fac-simile of what had been the perfection of *bon ton*[5] about twelve or eighteen months before. They wore the cast-off graces of the gentry;—and this, I believe, involves the best definition of the class.

The division of the upper clerks of staunch firms, or of the "steady old fellows," it was not possible to mistake. These were known by their coats and pantaloons of black or brown, made to sit comfortably, with white cravats and waistcoats, broad solid-looking shoes, and thick hose or gaiters. They had all slightly bald heads, from which the right ears, long used to pen-holding, had an odd habit of standing off on end. I observed that they always removed or settled their hats with both hands, and wore watches, with short gold chains of a substantial and ancient pattern. Theirs was the affectation of respectability—if indeed there be an affectation so honorable.

There were many individuals of dashing appearance, whom I easily understood as belonging to the race of swell pick-pockets, with which all great cities are infested. I watched these gentry with much inquisitiveness, and found it difficult to imagine how they should ever be mistaken for gentlemen by gentlemen themselves. Their voluminousness of wristband, with an air of excessive frankness, should betray them at once.

The gamblers, of whom I descried not a few, were still more easily recognizable. They wore every variety of dress, from that of the desperate thimble-rig[6] bully, with velvet waistcoat, fancy neckerchief, gilt chains, and filigreed buttons, to that of the scrupulously inornate clergyman, than which nothing could be less liable to suspicion. Still all were distinguished by a certain sodden swarthiness of complexion, a filmy dimness of eye, and pallor and compression of lip. There were two other traits, moreover, by which I could always detect them: a guarded lowness of tone in conversation, and a more than ordinary extension of the thumb in a direction at right angles with the fingers. Very often, in company with these sharpers, I observed an order of men somewhat different in habits, but still birds of a kindred feather. They may be defined as the gentlemen who live by their wits. They seem to prey upon the public in two battalions—that of the dandies and that of the military men. Of the first grade the leading features are long locks and smiles; of the second, frogged coats and frowns.

Descending in the scale of what is termed gentility, I found darker and deeper themes for speculation. I saw Jew peddlers, with hawk eyes flashing from countenances whose every other feature wore only an expression of abject humility; sturdy professional street beggars scowling upon mendicants of a better stamp, whom despair alone had driven forth into the night for charity; feeble and ghastly invalids, upon

---

4. Wealthy people.   5. Trendy style.   6. A confidence game.

long, he rushed with an activity I could not have dreamed of seeing in one so aged, and which put me to much trouble in pursuit. A few minutes brought us to a large and busy bazaar, with the localities of which the stranger appeared well acquainted, and where his original demeanor again became apparent, as he forced his way to and fro, without aim, among the host of buyers and sellers.

During the hour and a half, or thereabouts, which we passed in this place, it required much caution on my part to keep him within reach without attracting his observation. Luckily I wore a pair of caoutchouc[11] overshoes, and could move about in perfect silence. At no moment did he see that I watched him. He entered shop after shop, priced nothing, spoke no word, and looked at all objects with a wild and vacant stare. I was now utterly amazed at his behavior, and firmly resolved that we should not part until I had satisfied myself in some measure respecting him.

A loud-toned clock struck eleven, and the company were fast deserting the bazaar. A shop-keeper, in putting up a shutter, jostled the old man, and at the instant I saw a strong shudder come over his frame. He hurried into the street, looked anxiously around him for an instant, and then ran with incredible swiftness through many crooked and peopleless lanes, until we emerged once more upon the great thoroughfare whence we had started—the street of the D—— Hotel. It no longer wore, however, the same aspect. It was still brilliant with gas; but the rain fell fiercely, and there were few persons to be seen. The stranger grew pale. He walked moodily some paces up the once populous avenue, then, with a heavy sigh, turned in the direction of the river, and, plunging through a great variety of devious ways, came out, at length, in view of one of the principal theatres. It was about being closed, and the audience were thronging from the doors. I saw the old man gasp as if for breath while he threw himself amid the crowd; but I thought that the intense agony of his countenance had, in some measure, abated. His head again fell upon his breast; he appeared as I had seen him at first. I observed that he now took the course in which had gone the greater number of the audience—but, upon the whole, I was at a loss to comprehend the waywardness of his actions.

As he proceeded, the company grew more scattered, and his old uneasiness and vacillation were resumed. For some time he followed closely a party of some ten or twelve roisterers; but from this number one by one dropped off, until three only remained together, in a narrow and gloomy lane, little frequented. The stranger paused, and, for a moment, seemed lost in thought; then, with every mark of agitation, pursued rapidly a route which brought us to the verge of the city, amid regions very different from those we had hitherto traversed. It was the most noisome quarter of London, where every thing wore the worst impress of the most deplorable poverty, and of the most desperate crime. By the dim light of an accidental lamp, tall, antique, worm-eaten, wooden tenements were seen tottering to their fall, in directions so many and capricious, that scarce the semblance of a passage was discernible between them. The paving -stones lay at random, displaced from their beds by the rankly-growing grass. Horrible filth festered in the dammed-up gutters. The whole atmosphere teemed with desolation. Yet, as we proceeded, the sounds of human life revived by sure degrees, and at length large bands of the most abandoned of a London populace were seen reeling to and fro. The spirits of the old man again flickered up, as a lamp which is near its death-hour. Once more

---

11. Rubber.

he strode onward with elastic tread. Suddenly a corner was turned, a blaze of light burst upon our sight, and we stood before one of the huge suburban temples of Intemperance—one of the palaces of the fiend, Gin.

It was now nearly daybreak; but a number of wretched inebriates still pressed in and out of the flaunting entrance. With a half shriek of joy the old man forced a passage within, resumed at once his original bearing, and stalked backward and forward, without apparent object, among the throng. He had not been thus long occupied, however, before a rush to the doors gave token that the host was closing them for the night. It was something even more intense than despair that I then observed upon the countenance of the singular being whom I had watched so pertinaciously. Yet he did not hesitate in his career, but, with a mad energy, retraced his steps at once, to the heart of the mighty London. Long and swiftly he fled, while I followed him in the wildest amazement, resolute not to abandon a scrutiny in which I now felt an interest all-absorbing. The sun arose while we proceeded, and, when we had once again reached that most thronged part of the populous town, the street of the D—— Hotel, it presented an appearance of human bustle and activity scarcely inferior to what I had seen on the evening before. And here, long, amid the momently increasing confusion, did I persist in my pursuit of the stranger. But, as usual, he walked to and fro, and during the day did not pass from out the turmoil of that street. And, as the shades of the second evening came on, I grew wearied unto death, and, stopping fully in front of the wanderer, gazed at him steadfastly in the face. He noticed me not, but resumed his solemn walk, while I, ceasing to follow, remained absorbed in contemplation. "This old man," I said at length, "is the type and the genius of deep crime. He refuses to be alone. *He is the man of the crowd*. It will be in vain to follow; for I shall learn no more of him, nor of his deeds. The worst heart of the world is a grosser book than the 'Hortulus Animæ,'[12] and perhaps it is but one of the great mercies of God that *'er lässt sich nicht lesen.'*"[13]

—1840

Margaret Fuller
1810–1850

Margaret Fuller was a pioneering investigative journalist, the first foreign correspondent for an American newspaper, the editor of one of the most important literary magazines of her day, and the author of the most influential feminist manifesto of the nineteenth century. Her father, a deeply serious lawyer and politician, wanted his first child to be a boy. Given a daughter instead, he decided to educate her as a son. She spent her days at age six reading Latin and soon progressed to French and German. She would later say that the effect of this intensive education "was a premature development of the brain, that made me a 'youthful prodigy' by day, and by

---

12. [Poe's note] *Hortulus Animæ cum Oratiunculis Aliquibus Superadditis'* of Grünninger.   13. "It does not allow itself to be read."

night a victim of spectral illusions, nightmare and somnambulism. . . ." Nevertheless, she would dedicate herself to the life of the mind. When her family moved to Cambridge, Massachusetts, she became part of the progressive intellectual movement there, Transcendentalism. Her knowledge of foreign literature impressed Ralph Waldo Emerson, Henry David Thoreau, George Ripley, Amos Bronson Alcott, and others, who uneasily welcomed her into their male-dominated circle. She deeply admired prominent European women writers, such as Madame de Stael and George Sand, and she began to write herself, starting by translating poems from the German writings of Johann Wolfgang von Goethe and Friedrich von Schiller. This work culminated in the publication of her first book, a translation of Johann Peter Eckermann's *Conversations with Goethe in the Last Years of His Life* (1836) which appeared as part of George Ripley's *Specimens of Foreign Standard Literature* (1838–1842), the series that first brought European Romantic literature and ideas to wide public attention in the United States.

After a period working as a schoolteacher in Providence, Fuller returned to Boston in 1838 and supported herself there by giving language lessons. These soon developed into a financially rewarding series of "conversations," evening classes for women in which she led Socratic dialogues on topics ranging from classical mythology to modern philosophy. Always her goal was to widen the horizons of women whose lives she felt had been limited by the narrow scope of their education. At the same time, she took on editing the new Transcendentalist quarterly, *The Dial*, with Emerson's cooperation and support. It was here that she published her essay "The Great Lawsuit. Man versus Men. Woman versus Women." (1843), in which she attacked sexist ideas of women's emotional and intellectual uniqueness, which always seemed to mean weakness. She argued that all humans contain a mixture of what are called masculine and feminine qualities, but that socially imposed gender roles stunted individual men and women, and therefore society as a whole. Still, women suffered the most seriously damaging effects of the gender hierarchy, and what they needed above all was to have arbitrary barriers to their growth removed so they could develop to the limits of their potential. Fuller's dense, highly allusive style demonstrated just how great that potential was, and the associative structure of the essay, with its multiple voices, attempted to replicate the lively interactivity of her famed conversations.

Horace Greeley, the editor of the *New-York Tribune*, offered her a job as a literary critic and published a book-length expansion of "The Great Lawsuit," retitled *Woman in the Nineteenth Century* (1846), which was quickly republished in London. After two years of hard work in New York and a disappointed romance, Fuller left in 1846 for England, a departure that realized a lifelong ambition. She met writers Thomas De Quincey, Thomas Carlyle, and William Wordsworth and made investigative visits to the great English industrial cities before moving on to a tour of western Europe, with extended stays in Paris and then Rome. She sent long letters home to the *Tribune*, which were avidly followed by readers fascinated by this brilliant woman's observations of European culture, as well as by the boundary-breaking spectacle of her solo travels. In Rome, she fell in love with Giovanni Ossoli, a young Italian nobleman with republican convictions, and together they threw themselves into the revolutionary movement of 1847–1849 led by Guiseppe Mazzini. Fuller retreated to the countryside for some months to give birth to a boy, Angelo, but soon returned to Rome, where she helped run a field hospital during the defense of the city against a French counter-revolutionary army. After the fall of Rome, Ossoli and Fuller, hounded by police, determined to return to the United States. Their ship ran aground near Fire Island, New York, on July 18, 1850. Fuller refused to leave her husband and child, and the three drowned the next day when the ship broke apart in a storm. Thoreau traveled to Fire Island to comb the beach for any remains that might have come ashore, especially the manuscript of her much anticipated history of the revolution. He found little more than a few letters and buttons. Despite this early end, Fuller's life had already posed an unavoidable challenge to the provincial American culture she so spectacularly left behind. Edgar Allan Poe responded to her challenge with his misogynist portrait of the unnaturally intelligent "Ligeia" (1838). Nathaniel Hawthorne satirized her as the overbearing Zenobia in his sarcastic memoir of Brook Farm, *The Blithedale Romance* (1852). On the other hand, Elizabeth Cady Stanton and others were inspired by her ideas and example to organize the first Women's Rights Convention at Seneca Falls, New York, in 1848.

The Great Lawsuit. Man versus Men. Woman versus Women.

This great suit has now been carried on through many ages, with various results. The decisions have been numerous, but always followed by appeals to still higher courts. How can it be otherwise, when the law itself is the subject of frequent elucidation, constant revision? Man has, now and then, enjoyed a clear, triumphant hour, when some irresistible conviction warmed and purified the atmosphere of his planet. But, presently, he sought repose after his labors, when the crowd of pigmy adversaries bound him in his sleep. Long years of inglorious imprisonment followed, while his enemies revelled in his spoils, and no counsel could be found to plead his cause, in the absence of that all-promising glance, which had, at times, kindled the poetic soul to revelation of his claims, of his rights.

Yet a foundation for the largest claim is now established. It is known that his inheritance consists in no partial sway, no exclusive possession, such as his adversaries desire. For they, not content that the universe is rich, would, each one for himself, appropriate treasure; but in vain! The many-colored garment, which clothed with honor an elected son,[1] when rent asunder for the many, is a worthless spoil. A band of robbers cannot live princely in the prince's castle; nor would he, like them, be content with less than all, though he would not, like them, seek it as fuel for riotous enjoyment, but as his principality, to administer and guard for the use of all living things therein. He cannot be satisfied with any one gift of the earth, any one department of knowledge, or telescopic peep at the heavens. He feels himself called to understand and aid nature, that she may, through his intelligence, be raised and interpreted; to be a student of, and servant to, the universe-spirit; and only king of his planet, that, as an angelic minister, he may bring it into conscious harmony with the law of that spirit.

Such is the inheritance of the orphan prince, and the illegitimate children of his family will not always be able to keep it from him, for, from the fields which they sow with dragon's teeth, and water with blood, rise monsters, which he alone has power to drive away.

But it is not the purpose now to sing the prophecy of his jubilee. We have said that, in clear triumphant moments, this has many, many times been made manifest, and those moments, though past in time, have been translated into eternity by thought. The bright signs they left hang in the heavens, as single stars or constellations, and, already, a thickly-sown radiance consoles the wanderer in the darkest night. Heroes have filled the zodiac of beneficent labors, and then given up their mortal part[2] to the fire without a murmur. Sages and lawgivers have bent their

---

1. Genesis 37.3–4.   2. [Fuller's note] Ovid, Apotheosis of Hercules, translated into clumsy English by Mr. Gay, as follows. Jove said, / Be all your fears forborne, / Th' Œtean fires do thou, great hero, scorn; / Who vanquished all things, shall subdue the flame; / The part alone of gross *maternal* frame, / Fire shall devour, while that from me he drew / Shall live immortal, and its force renew; / That, when he's dead, I'll raise to realms above, / May all the powers the righteous act approve. / If any God dissent, and judge too great / The sacred honors of the heavenly seat, / Even he shall own his deeds deserve the sky, / Even he, reluctant, shall at length comply. / Th' assembled powers assent.

whole nature to the search for truth, and thought themselves happy if they could buy, with the sacrifice of all temporal ease and pleasure, one seed for the future Eden. Poets and priests have strung the lyre with heart-strings, poured out their best blood upon the altar which, reared anew from age to age, shall at last sustain the flame which rises to highest heaven. What shall we say of those who, if not so directly, or so consciously, in connection with the central truth, yet, led and fashioned by a divine instinct, serve no less to develop and interpret the open secret of love passing into life, the divine energy creating for the purpose of happiness;—of the artist, whose hand, drawn by a preëxistent harmony to a certain medium, moulds it to expressions of life more highly and completely organized than are seen elsewhere, and, by carrying out the intention of nature, reveals her meaning to those who are not yet sufficiently matured to divine it; of the philosopher, who listens steadily for causes, and, from those obvious, infers those yet unknown; of the historian, who, in faith that all events must have their reason and their aim, records them, and lays up archives from which the youth of prophets may be fed. The man of science dissects the statement, verifies the facts, and demonstrates connection even where he cannot its purpose.

Lives, too, which bear none of these names, have yielded tones of no less significance. The candlestick, set in a low place, has given light as faithfully, where it was needed, as that upon the hill.[3] In close alleys, in dismal nooks, the Word has been read as distinctly, as when shown by angels to holy men in the dark prison. Those who till a spot of earth, scarcely larger than is wanted for a grave, have deserved that the sun should shine upon its sod till violets answer.

So great has been, from time to time, the promise, that, in all ages, men have said the Gods themselves came down to dwell with them; that the All-Creating wandered on the earth to taste in a limited nature the sweetness of virtue, that the All-Sustaining incarnated himself, to guard, in space and time, the destinies of his world; that heavenly genius dwelt among the shepherds, to sing to them and teach them how to sing. Indeed,

"Der stets den Hirten gnädig sich bewies."
"He has constantly shown himself favorable to shepherds."

And these dwellers in green pastures and natural students of the stars, were selected to hail, first of all, the holy child, whose life and death presented the type of excellence, which has sustained the heart of so large a portion of mankind in these later generations.

Such marks have been left by the footsteps of man, whenever he has made his way through the wilderness of men.[4] And whenever the pygmies stepped in one of these, they felt dilate within the breast somewhat that promised larger stature and purer blood. They were tempted to forsake their evil ways, to forsake the side of selfish personal existence, of decrepit skepticism, and covetousness of corruptible possessions. Conviction flowed in upon them. They, too, raised the cry; God is living, all is his, and all created beings are brothers, for they are his children. These were the triumphant moments; but as we have said, man slept and selfishness awoke.

Thus he is still kept out of his inheritance, still a pleader, still a pilgrim. But his reinstatement is sure. And now, no mere glimmering consciousness, but a certainty, is

---

3. Matthew 5.15–16.   4. This distinction between the ideal "man" and actually existing "men" also informs Fuller's title.

felt and spoken, that the highest ideal man can form of his own capabilities is that which he is destined to attain. Whatever the soul knows how to seek, it must attain. Knock, and it shall be opened; seek, and ye shall find. It is demonstrated, it is a maxim. He no longer paints his proper nature in some peculiar form and says, "Prometheus[5] had it," but "Man must have it." However disputed by many, however ignorantly used, or falsified, by those who do receive it, the fact of an universal, unceasing revelation, has been too clearly stated in words, to be lost sight of in thought, and sermons preached from the text, "Be ye perfect,"[6] are the only sermons of a pervasive and deep-searching influence.

But among those who meditate upon this text, there is great difference of view, as to the way in which perfection shall be sought.

Through the intellect, say some; Gather from every growth of life its seed of thought; look behind every symbol for its law. If thou canst *see* clearly, the rest will follow.

Through the life, say others; Do the best thou knowest to-day. Shrink not from incessant error, in this gradual, fragmentary state. Follow thy light for as much as it will show thee, be faithful as far as thou canst, in hope that faith presently will lead to sight. Help others, without blame that they need thy help. Love much, and be forgiven.

It needs not intellect, needs not experience, says a third. If you took the true way, these would be evolved in purity. You would not learn through them, but express through them a higher knowledge. In quietness, yield thy soul to the casual soul. Do not disturb its teachings by methods of thine own. Be still, seek not, but wait in obedience. Thy commission will be given.

Could we, indeed, say what we want, could we give a description of the child that is lost, he would be found. As soon as the soul can say clearly, that a certain demonstration is wanted, it is at hand. When the Jewish prophet described the Lamb, as the expression of what was required by the coming era, the time drew nigh.[7] But we say not, see not, as yet, clearly what we would. Those who call for a more triumphant expression of love, a love that cannot be crucified, show not a perfect sense of what has already been expressed. Love has already been expressed, that made all things new, that gave the worm its ministry as well as the eagle; a love, to which it was alike to descend into the depths of hell, or to sit at the right hand of the Father.[8]

Yet, no doubt, a new manifestation is at hand, a new hour in the day of man. We cannot expect to see him a completed being, when the mass of men lie so entangled in the sod, or use the freedom of their limbs only with wolfish energy. The tree cannot come to flower till its root be freed from the cankering worm, and its whole growth open to air and light. Yet something new shall presently be shown of the life of man, for hearts crave it now, if minds do not know how to ask it.

Among the strains of prophecy, the following; by an earnest mind of a foreign land, written some thirty years ago, is not yet outgrown; and it has the merit of being a positive appeal from the heart, instead of a critical declaration what man shall *not* do.

"The ministry of man implies, that he must be filled from the divine fountains which are being engendered through all eternity so that, at the mere name of his Master, he may be able to cast all his enemies into the abyss; that he may deliver all parts of nature from the barriers that imprison them; that he may purge the

---

5. In Greek myth, the bringer of fire to humankind.   6. Matthew 5.48.   7. Isaiah 7.14–25.   8. Mark 16.19.

terrestrial atmosphere from the poisons that infect it; that he may preserve the bodies of men from the corrupt influences that surround, and the maladies that afflict them; still more, that he may keep their souls pure from the malignant insinuations which pollute, and the gloomy images that obscure them; that we may restore its serenity to the Word, which false words of men till with mourning and sadness; that he may satisfy the desires of the angels, who await from him the development of the marvels of nature; that, in fine, his world may be filled with God, as eternity is."[9]

Another attempt we will give, by an obscure observer of our own day and country, to draw some lines of the desired image. It was suggested by seeing the design of Crawford's Orpheus,[10] and connecting with the circumstance of the American, in his garret at Rome, making choice of this subject, that of Americans here at home, showing such ambition to represent the character, by calling their prose and verse, Orphic sayings, Orphics.[11] Orpheus was a lawgiver by theocratic commission. He understood nature, and made all her forms move to his music. He told her secrets in the form of hymns, nature as seen in the mind of God. Then it is the prediction, that to learn and to do, all men must be lovers, and Orpheus was, in a high sense, a lover. His soul went forth towards all beings, yet could remain sternly faithful to a chosen type of excellence. Seeking what he loved, he feared not death nor hell, neither could any presence daunt his faith in the power of the celestial harmony that filled his soul.

It seemed significant of the state of things in this country, that the sculptor should have chosen the attitude of shading his eyes. When we have the statue here, it will give lessons in reverence.

> Each Orpheus must to the depths descend,
> For only thus the poet can be wise,
> Must make the sad Persephone[12] his friend,
> And buried love to second life arise;
> Again his love must lose through too much love,
> Must lose his life by living life too true,
> For what he sought below is passed above,
> Already done is all that he would do;
> Must tune all being with his single lyre,
> Must melt all rocks free from their primal pain,
> Must search all nature with his one soul's fire,
> Must bind anew all forms in heavenly chain.
> If he already sees what he must do,
> Well may he shade his eyes from the far-shining view.

Meanwhile, not a few believe, and men themselves have expressed the opinion, that the time is come when Euridice is to call for an Orpheus, rather than Orpheus for Euridice; that the idea of man, however imperfectly brought out, has been far more so

---

9. St. Martin [Fuller's note]. Louis Claude de Saint-Martin (1743–1803), *The Ministry of Man and Spirit* (1802).   10. Thomas Crawford (1814–1857), American sculptor. Orpheus: mythological Greek musician.   11. Fuller published several prose poems by Amos Bronson Alcott (1799–1888) in the *Dial* under the title "Orphic Sayings."   12. In Greek myth, the unwilling wife of Hades, the god of the underworld. She was almost rescued by Orpheus.

than that of woman, and that an improvement in the daughters will best aid the reformation of the sons of this age.

It is worthy of remark, that, as the principle of liberty is better understood and more nobly interpreted, a broader protest is made in behalf of woman. As men become aware that all men have not had their fair chance, they are inclined to say that no women have had a fair chance. The French revolution, that strangely disguised angel, bore witness in favor of woman, but interpreted her claims no less ignorantly than those of man. Its idea of happiness did not rise beyond outward enjoyment, unobstructed by the tyranny of others. The title it gave was Citoyen, Citoyenne,[13] and it is not unimportant to woman that even this species of equality was awarded her. Before, she could be condemned to perish on the scaffold for treason, but not as a citizen, but a subject. The right, with which this title then invested a human being, was that of bloodshed and license. The Goddess of Liberty was impure. Yet truth was prophesied in the ravings of that hideous fever induced by long ignorance and abuse. Europe is conning a valued lesson from the blood-stained page. The same tendencies, farther unfolded, will bear good fruit in this country.

Yet, in this country, as by the Jews, when Moses was leading them to the promised land,[14] everything has been done that inherited depravity could, to hinder the promise of heaven from its fulfilment. The cross, here as elsewhere, has been planted only to be blasphemed by cruelty and fraud. The name of the Prince of Peace has been profaned by all kinds of injustice towards the Gentile whom he said he came to save. But I need not speak of what has been done towards the red man, the black man. These deeds are the scoff of the world; and they have been accompanied by such pious words, that the gentlest would not dare to intercede with, "Father forgive them, for they know not what they do."[15]

Here, as elsewhere, the gain of creation consists always in the growth of individual minds, which live and aspire, as flowers bloom and birds sing, in the midst of morasses; and in the continual development of that thought, the thought of human destiny, which is given to eternity to fulfil, and which ages of failure only seemingly impede. Only seemingly, and whatever seems to the contrary, this country is as surely destined to elucidate a great moral law, as Europe was to promote the mental culture of man.

Though the national independence be blurred by the servility of individuals; though freedom and equality have been proclaimed only to leave room for a monstrous display of slave dealing and slave keeping; though the free American so often feels himself free, like the Roman, only to pamper his appetites and his indolence through the misery of his fellow beings, still it is not in vain, that the verbal statement has been made, "All men are born free and equal."[16] There it stands, a golden certainty, wherewith to encourage the good, to shame the bad. The new world may be called clearly to perceive that it incurs the utmost penalty, if it rejects the sorrowful brother. And if men are deaf, the angels hear. But men cannot be deaf. It is inevitable that an external freedom, such as has been achieved for the nation, should be so also for every member of it. That, which has once been clearly conceived in the intelligence, must be acted out. It has become a law, irrevocable as that of the Medes[17]

---

13. Masculine and feminine words for "citizen."   14. In Leviticus 12 and Numbers 30, Moses establishes women's subordination to father and husband.   15. Luke 23.34.   16. Paraphrases the Declaration of Independence.   17. Ancient inhabitants of present-day western Iran.

in their ancient dominion. Men will privately sin against it, but the law so clearly expressed by a leading mind of the age,

"Tutti fatti a sembianza d' un Solo;
Figli tutti d' un solo riscatto,
In qual ora, in qual parte del suolo
Trascorriamo quest' aura vital,
Siam fratelli, siam stretti ad un patte:
Maladetto colui che lo infrange,
Che s' innalza sul fiacco che piange,
Che contrista uno spirto immortal."[18]

"All made in the likeness of the One,
All children of one ransom,
In whatever hour, in whatever part of the soil
We draw this vital air,
We are brothers, we must be bound by one compact,
Accursed he who infringes it,
Who raises himself upon the weak who weep,
Who saddens an immortal spirit."

cannot fail of universal recognition.

We sicken no less at the pomp than at the strife of words. We feel that never were lungs so puffed with the wind of declamation, on moral and religious subjects, as now. We are tempted to implore these "word-heroes," these word-Catos, word-Christs,[19] to beware of cant above all things; to remember that hypocrisy is the most hopeless as well as the meanest of crimes, and that those must surely be polluted by it, who do not keep a little of all this morality and religion for private use.[20] We feel that the mind may "grow black and rancid in the smoke" even of altars. We start up from the harangue to go into our closet and shut the door. But, when it has been shut long enough, we remember that where there is so much smoke, there must be some fire; with so much talk about virtue and freedom must be mingled some desire for them; that it cannot be in vain that such have become the common topics of conversation among men; that the very newspapers should proclaim themselves Pilgrims, Puritans, Heralds of Holiness.[21] The king that maintains so costly a retinue cannot be a mere Count of Carabbas[22] fiction. We have waited here long in the dust; we are tired and hungry, but the triumphal procession must appear at last.

Of all its banners, none has been more steadily upheld, and under none has more valor and willingness for real sacrifices been shown, than that of the champions of the enslaved African. And this band it is, which, partly in consequence of a natural following out of principles, partly because many women have been prominent in that cause, makes, just now, the warmest appeal in behalf of woman!

---

18. Manzoni [Fuller's note]. Alessandro Manzoni (1785–1873), Italian poet.   19. Pompous reformers; imitators of Marcus Porcius Cato (234–149 BC), Roman moralist, or of Jesus.   20. Dr. Johnson's one piece of advice should be written on every door; "Clear your mind of cant." But Byron, to whom it was so acceptable, in clearing away the noxious vine, shook down the building too. Stirling's emendation is note-worthy, "Realize your cant, not cast it off" [Fuller's note].   21. Names of New England newspapers.   22. Ostentatiously wealthy character in the European folk-tale, "Puss in Boots."

Though there has been a growing liberality on this point, yet society at large is not so prepared for the demands of this party, but that they are, and will be for some time, coldly regarded as the Jacobins[23] of their day.

"Is it not enough," cries the sorrowful trader, "that you have done all you could to break up the national Union, and thus destroy the prosperity of our country, but now you must be trying to break up family union, to take my wife away from the cradle, and the kitchen hearth, to vote at polls, and preach from a pulpit! Of course, if she does such things, she cannot attend to those of her own sphere. She is happy enough as she is. She has more leisure than I have, every means of improvement, every indulgence."

"Have you asked her whether she was satisfied with these indulgences?"

"No, but I know she is. She is too amiable to wish what would make me unhappy, and too judicious to wish to step beyond the sphere of her sex. I will never consent to have our peace disturbed by any such discussions."

"'Consent'—you? it is not consent from you that is in question, it is assent from your wife."

"Am I not the head of my house?"

"You are not the head of your wife. God has given her a mind of her own."

"I am the head and she the heart."

"God grant you play true to one another then. If the head represses no natural pulse of the heart, there can be no question as to your giving your consent. Both will be of one accord, and there needs but to present any question to get a full and true answer. There is no need of precaution, of indulgence, or consent. But our doubt is whether the heart consents with the head, or only acquiesces in its decree; and it is to ascertain the truth on this point, that we propose some liberating measures."

Thus vaguely are these questions proposed and discussed at present. But their being proposed at all implies much thought, and suggests more. Many women are considering within themselves what they need that they have not, and what they can have, if they find they need it. Many men are considering whether women are capable of being and having more than they are and have, and whether, if they are, it will be best to consent to improvement in their condition.

The numerous party, whose opinions are already labelled and adjusted too much to their mind to admit of any new light, strive, by lectures on some model-woman of bridal-like beauty and gentleness, by writing or lending little treatises, to mark out with due precision the limits of woman's sphere, and woman's mission, and to prevent other than the rightful shepherd from climbing the wall, or the flock from using any chance gap to run astray.

Without enrolling ourselves at once on either side, let us look upon the subject from that point of view which to-day offers. No better, it is to be feared, than a high house-top. A high hill-top, or at least a cathedral spire, would be desirable.

It is not surprising that it should be the Anti-Slavery party that pleads for woman, when we consider merely that she does not hold property on equal terms with men; so that, if a husband dies without a will, the wife, instead of stepping at once into his place as head of the family, inherits only a part of his fortune, as if she were a child, or ward only, not an equal partner.

---

23. Radicals of the French Revolution.

We will not speak of the innumerable instances, in which profligate or idle men live upon the earnings of industrious wives; or if the wives leave them and take with them the children, to perform the double duty of mother and father, follow from place to place, and threaten to rob them of the children, if deprived of the rights of a husband, as they call them, planting themselves in their poor lodgings, frightening them into paying tribute by taking from them the children, running into debt at the expense of these otherwise so overtasked helots.[24] Though such instances abound, the public opinion of his own sex is against the man, and when cases of extreme tyranny are made known, there is private action in the wife's favor. But if woman be, indeed, the weaker party, she ought to have legal protection, which would make such oppression impossible.

And knowing that there exists, in the world of men, a tone of feeling towards women as towards slaves, such as is expressed in the common phrase, "Tell that to women and children;" that the infinite soul can only work through them in already ascertained limits; that the prerogative of reason, man's highest portion, is allotted to them in a much lower degree; that it is better for them to be engaged in active labor, which is to be furnished and directed by those better able to think, &c. &c.; we need not go further, for who can review the experience of last week, without recalling words which imply, whether in jest or earnest, these views, and views like these? Knowing this, can we wonder that many reformers think that measures are not likely to be taken in behalf of women, unless their wishes could be publicly represented by women?

That can never be necessary, cry the other side. All men are privately influenced by women; each has his wife, sister, or female friends, and is too much biassed by these relations to fail of representing their interests. And if this is not enough, let them propose and enforce their wishes with the pen. The beauty of home would be destroyed, the delicacy of the sex be violated, the dignity of halls of legislation destroyed, by an attempt to introduce them there. Such duties are inconsistent with those of a mother; and then we have ludicrous pictures of ladies in hysterics at the polls, and senate chambers filled with cradles.

But if, in reply, we admit as truth that woman seems destined by nature rather to the inner circle, we must add that the arrangements of civilized life have not been as yet such as to secure it to her. Her circle, if the duller, is not the quieter. If kept from excitement, she is not from drudgery. Not only the Indian carries the burdens of the camp, but the favorites of Louis the Fourteenth[25] accompany him in his journeys, and the washerwoman stands at her tub and carries home her work at all seasons, and in all states of health.

As to the use of the pen, there was quite as much opposition to woman's possessing herself of that help to free-agency as there is now to her seizing on the rostrum or the desk; and she is likely to draw, from a permission to plead her cause that way, opposite inferences to what might be wished by those who now grant it.

As to the possibility of her filling, with grace and dignity, any such position, we should think those who had seen the great actresses, and heard the Quaker preachers of modern times, would not doubt, that woman can express publicly the fulness of thought and emotion, without losing any of the peculiar beauty of her sex.

---

24. Slaves.   25. King of France (1638–1715).

As to her home, she is not likely to leave it more than she now does for balls, theatres, meetings for promoting missions, revival meetings, and others to which she flies, in hope of an animation for her existence, commensurate with what she sees enjoyed by men. Governors of Ladies' Fairs are no less engrossed by such a charge, than the Governor of the State by his; presidents of Washingtonian societies,[26] no less away from home than presidents of conventions. If men look straitly to it, they will find that, unless their own lives are domestic, those of the women will not be. The female Greek, of our day, is as much in the street as the male, to cry, What news! We doubt not it was the same in Athens of old. The women, shut out from the market-place, made up for it at the religious festivals. For human beings are not so constituted, that they can live without expansion; and if they do not get it one way, must another, or perish.

And, as to men's representing women fairly, at present, while we hear from men who owe to their wives not only all that is comfortable and graceful, but all that is wise in the arrangement of their lives, the frequent remark, "You cannot reason with a woman," when from those of delicacy, nobleness, and poetic culture, the contemptuous phrase, "Women and children," and that in no light sally of the hour, but in works intended to give a permanent statement of the best experiences, when not one man in the million, shall I say, no, not in the hundred million, can rise above the view that woman was made *for man*, when such traits as these are daily forced upon the attention, can we feel that man will always do justice to the interests of woman? Can we think that he takes a sufficiently discerning and religious view of her office and destiny, ever to do her justice, except when prompted by sentiment; accidentally or transiently, that is, for his sentiment will vary according to the relations in which he is placed. The lover, the poet, the artist, are likely to view her nobly. The father and the philosopher have some chance of liberality; the man of the world, the legislator for expediency, none.

Under these circumstances, without attaching importance in themselves to the changes demanded by the champions of woman, we hail them as signs of the times. We would have every arbitrary barrier thrown down. We would have every path laid open to woman as freely as to man. Were this done, and a slight temporary fermentation allowed to subside, we believe that the Divine would ascend into nature to a height unknown in the history of past ages, and nature, thus instructed, would regulate the spheres not only so as to avoid collision, but to bring forth ravishing harmony.

Yet then, and only then, will human beings be ripe for this, when inward and outward freedom for woman, as much as for man, shall be acknowledged as a right, not yielded as a concession. As the friend of the negro assumes that one man cannot, by right, hold another in bondage, should the friend of woman assume that man cannot, by right, lay even well-meant restrictions on woman. If the negro be a soul, if the woman be a soul, apparelled in flesh, to one master only are they accountable. There is but one law for all souls, and, if there is to be an interpreter of it, he comes not as man, or son of man, but as Son of God.

Were thought and feeling once so far elevated that man should esteem himself the brother and friend, but nowise the lord and tutor of woman, were he really bound with her in equal worship, arrangements as to function and employment would be of no consequence. What woman needs is not as a woman to act or rule, but as a nature

---

26. Women's patriotic societies.

to grow, as an intellect to discern, as a soul to live freely, and unimpeded to unfold such powers as were given her when we left our common home. If fewer talents were given her, yet, if allowed the free and full employment of these, so that she may render back to the giver his own with usury, she will not complain, nay, I dare to say she will bless and rejoice in her earthly birth-place, her earthly lot.

Let us consider what obstructions impede this good era, and what signs give reason to hope that it draws near.

I was talking on this subject with Miranda,[27] a woman, who, if any in the world, might speak without heat or bitterness of the position of her sex. Her father was a man who cherished no sentimental reverence for woman, but a firm belief in the equality of the sexes. She was his eldest child, and came to him at an age when he needed a companion. From the time she could speak and go alone, he addressed her not as a plaything, but as a living mind. Among the few verses he ever wrote were a copy addressed to this child, when the first locks were cut from her head, and the reverence expressed on this occasion for that cherished head he never belied. It was to him the temple of immortal intellect. He respected his child, however, too much to be an indulgent parent. He called on her for clear judgment, for courage, for honor and fidelity, in short for such virtues as he knew. In so far as he possessed the keys to the wonders of this universe, he allowed free use of them to her, and by the incentive of a high expectation he forbade, as far as possible, that she should let the privilege lie idle.

Thus this child was early led to feel herself a child of the spirit. She took her place easily, not only in the world of organized being, but in the world of mind. A dignified sense of self-dependence was given as all her portion, and she found it a sure anchor. Herself securely anchored, her relations with others were established with equal security. She was fortunate, in a total absence of those charms which might have drawn to her bewildering flatteries, and of a strong electric nature, which repelled those who did not belong to her, and attracted those who did. With men and women her relations were noble; affectionate without passion, intellectual without coldness. The world was free to her, and she lived freely in it. Outward adversity came, and inward conflict, but that faith and self-respect had early been awakened, which must always lead at last to an outward serenity, and an inward peace.

Of Miranda I had always thought as an example, that the restraints upon the sex were insuperable only to those who think them so, or who noisily strive to break them. She had taken a course of her own, and no man stood in her way. Many of her acts had been unusual, but excited no uproar. Few helped, but none checked her; and the many men, who knew her mind and her life, showed to her confidence as to a brother, gentleness as to a sister. And not only refined, but very coarse men approved one in whom they saw resolution and clearness of design. Her mind was often the leading one, always effective.

When I talked with her upon these matters, and had said very much what I have written, she smilingly replied, And yet we must admit that I have been fortunate, and this should not be. My good father's early trust gave the first bias, and the rest followed of course. It is true that I have had less outward aid, in after years, than most women, but that is of little consequence. Religion was early awakened in my soul, a sense that what the soul is capable to ask it must attain, and that, though I might be aided by others, I must depend on myself as the only constant friend. This self-dependence,

27. A fictional interlocutor who voices Fuller's own experience.

which was honored in me, is deprecated as a fault in most women. They are taught to learn their rule from without, not to unfold it from within.

This is the fault of man, who is still vain, and wishes to be more important to woman than by right he should be.

Men have not shown this disposition towards you, I said.

No, because the position I early was enabled to take, was one of self-reliance. And were all women as sure of their wants as I was, the result would be the same. The difficulty is to get them to the point where they shall naturally develop self-respect, the question how it is to be done.

Once I thought that men would help on this state of things more than I do now. I saw so many of them wretched in the connections they had formed in weakness and vanity. They seemed so glad to esteem women whenever they could!

But early I perceived that men never, in any extreme of despair, wished to be women. Where they admired any woman they were inclined to speak of her as above her sex. Silently I observed this, and feared it argued a rooted skepticism, which for ages had been fastening on the heart, and which only an age of miracles could eradicate.

Ever I have been treated with great sincerity; and I look upon it as a most signal instance of this, that an intimate friend of the other sex said in a fervent moment, that I deserved in some star to be a man. Another used as highest praise, in speaking of a character in literature, the words "a manly woman."

It is well known that of every strong woman they say she has a masculine mind.

This by no means argues a willing want of generosity towards woman. Man is as generous towards her, as he knows how to be.

Wherever she has herself arisen in national or private history, and nobly shone forth in any ideal of excellence, men have received her, not only willingly, but with triumph. Their encomiums indeed are always in some sense mortifying, they show too much surprise.

In every-day life the feelings of the many are stained with vanity. Each wishes to be lord in a little world, to be superior at least over one; and he does not feel strong enough to retain a life-long ascendant over a strong nature. Only a Brutus would rejoice in a Portia.[28] Only Theseus[29] could conquer before he wed the Amazonian Queen. Hercules wished rather to rest from his labors with Dejanira,[30] and received the poisoned robe, as a fit guerdon. The tale should be interpreted to all those who seek repose with the weak.

But not only is man vain and fond of power, but the same want of development, which thus affects him morally in the intellect, prevents his discerning the destiny of woman. The boy wants no woman, but only a girl to play ball with him, and mark his pocket handkerchief.

Thus in Schiller's Dignity of Woman,[31] beautiful as the poem is, there is no "grave and perfect man," but only a great boy to be softened and restrained by the influence of girls. Poets, the elder brothers of their race, have usually seen further; but what can you expect of every-day men, if Schiller was not more prophetic as to what women must be? Even with Richter[32] one foremost thought about a wife was that she would "cook him something good."

---

28. Plutarch (c. 46–120), *Lives*.   29. Theseus, legendary king of Athens, abducted the Amazon queen, Antiope.   30. Jealous lover of Hercules who poisoned him.   31. Friedrich von Schiller (1759–1805).   32. Jean Paul Richter (1763–1825), German novelist.

The sexes should not only correspond to and appreciate one another, but prophesy to one another. In individual instances this happens. Two persons love in one another the future good which they aid one another to unfold. This is very imperfectly done as yet in the general life. Man has gone but little way, now he is waiting to see whether woman can keep step with him, but instead of calling out like a good brother; You can do it if you only think so, or impersonally; Any one can do what he tries to do, he often discourages with school-boy brag; Girls can't do that, girls can't play ball. But let any one defy their taunts, break through, and be brave and secure, they rend the air with shouts.

No! man is not willingly ungenerous. He wants[33] faith and love, because he is not yet himself an elevated being. He cries with sneering skepticism; Give us a sign. But if the sign appears, his eyes glisten, and he offers not merely approval, but homage.

The severe nation[34] which taught that the happiness of the race was forfeited through the fault of a woman, and showed its thought of what sort of regard man owed her, by making him accuse her on the first question to his God, who gave her to the patriarch as a handmaid, and, by the Mosaical law, bound her to allegiance like a serf, even they greeted, with solemn rapture, all great and holy women as heroines, prophetesses, nay judges in Israel; and, if they made Eve listen to the serpent, gave Mary to the Holy Spirit. In other nations it has been the same down to our day. To the woman, who could conquer, a triumph was awarded. And not only those whose strength was recommended to the heart by association with goodness and beauty, but those who were bad, if they were steadfast and strong, had their claims allowed. In any age a Semiramis, an Elizabeth of England, a Catharine of Russia[35] makes her place good, whether in a large or small circle.

How has a little wit, a little genius, always been celebrated in a woman! What an intellectual triumph was that of the lonely Aspasia, and how heartily acknowledged! She, indeed, met a Pericles.[36] But what annalist, the rudest of men, the most plebeian of husbands, will spare from his page one of the few anecdotes of Roman women?—Sappho, Eloisa![37] The names are of thread-bare celebrity. The man habitually most narrow towards women will be flushed, as by the worst assault on Christianity, if you say it has made no improvement in her condition. Indeed, those most opposed to new acts in her favor are jealous of the reputation of those which have been done.

We will not speak of the enthusiasm excited by actresses, improvisatrici, female singers, for here mingles the charm of beauty and grace, but female authors, even learned women, if not insufferably ugly and slovenly, from the Italian professor's daughter, who taught behind the curtain, down to Mrs. Carter and Madame Dacier,[38] are sure of an admiring audience, if they can once get a platform on which to stand.

But how to get this platform, or how to make it of reasonably easy access is the difficulty. Plants of great vigor will almost always struggle into blossom, despite impediments. But there should be encouragement, and a free, genial atmosphere for those of more timid sort, fair play for each in its own kind. Some are like the little,

---

33. Lacks.   34. The Jews, whose scripture includes the story of Eve's fall.   35. Semiramis: legendary queen of Babylon; Elizabeth I (1558–1603), queen of England; Catharine (1762–1796), empress of Russia.   36. Aspasia (c. 470–410 BC), Greek philosopher and lover of Pericles (495–429 BC), a military leader.   37. Sappho (7th century BC), Greek poet. Eloisa (1101–1164), French abbess and lover of Abelard (1079–1142), a philosopher.   38. Elizabeth Carter (1717–1806), English poet; Anne LeFèvre Dacier (1654–1720), French translator of classics.

delicate flowers, which love to hide in the dripping mosses by the sides of mountain torrents, or in the shade of tall trees. But others require an open field, a rich and loosened soil, or they never show their proper hues.

It may be said man does not have his fair play either; his energies are repressed and distorted by the interposition of artificial obstacles. Aye, but he himself has put them there; they have grown out of his own imperfections. If there is a misfortune in woman's lot, it is in obstacles being interposed by men, which do not mark her state, and if they express her past ignorance, do not her present needs. As every man is of woman born, she has slow but sure means of redress, yet the sooner a general justness of thought makes smooth the path, the better.

Man is of woman born, and her face bends over him in infancy with an expression he can never quite forget. Eminent men have delighted to pay tribute to this image, and it is a hacknied observation, that most men of genius boast some remarkable development in the mother. The rudest tar brushes off a tear with his coat-sleeve at the hallowed name. The other day I met a decrepit old man of seventy, on a journey, who challenged the stage-company to guess where he was going. They guessed aright, "To see your mother." "Yes," said he, "she is ninety-two, but has good eye-sight still, they say. I've not seen her these forty years, and I thought I could not die in peace without." I should have liked his picture painted as a companion piece to that of a boisterous little boy, whom I saw attempt to declaim at a school exhibition.

> "O that those lips had language! Life has passed
> With me but roughly since I heard thee last."[39]

He got but very little way before sudden tears shamed him from the stage.

Some gleams of the same expression which shone down upon his infancy, angelically pure and benign, visit man again with hopes of pure love, of a holy marriage. Or, if not before, in the eyes of the mother of his child they again are seen, and dim fancies pass before his mind, that woman may not have been born for him alone, but have come from heaven, a commissioned soul, a messenger of truth and love.

In gleams, in dim fancies, this thought visits the mind of common men. It is soon obscured by the mists of sensuality, the dust of routine, and he thinks it was only some meteor or ignis fatuus that shone. But, as a Rosicrucian[40] lamp, it burns unwearied, though condemned to the solitude of tombs. And, to its permanent life, as to every truth, each age has, in some form, borne witness. For the truths, which visit the minds of careless men only in fitful gleams, shine with radiant clearness into those of the poet, the priest, and the artist.

Whatever may have been the domestic manners of the ancient nations, the idea of woman was nobly manifested in their mythologies and poems, where she appeared as Sita in the Ramayana,[41] a form of tender purity, in the Egyptian Isis,[42] of divine wisdom never yet surpassed. In Egypt, too, the Sphynx, walking the earth with lion tread, looked out upon its marvels in the calm, inscrutable beauty of a

---

39. William Cowper (1731–1800), "On the Receipt of My Mother's Picture" (1798).   40. The Rosicrucians were a ritual society purported to maintain an everlasting flame.   41. In the *Ramayana*, an epic poem of India, Sita is the lover of Rama.   42. Goddess of fertility.

virgin's face, and the Greek could only add wings to the great emblem. In Greece, Ceres and Proserpine,[43] significantly termed "the goddesses," were seen seated, side by side. They needed not to rise for any worshipper or any change; they were prepared for all things, as those initiated to their mysteries knew. More obvious is the meaning of those three forms, the Diana, Minerva, and Vesta.[44] Unlike in the expression of their beauty, but alike in this,—that each was self-sufficing. Other forms were only accessories and illustrations, none the complement to one like these. Another might indeed be the companion, and the Apollo[45] and Diana set off one another's beauty. Of the Vesta, it is to be observed, that not only deep-eyed deep-discerning Greece, but ruder Rome, who represents the only form of good man (the always busy warrior) that could be indifferent to woman, confided the permanence of its glory to a tutelary goddess, and her wisest legislator spoke of Meditation as a nymph.

In Sparta, thought, in this respect as all others, was expressed in the characters of real life, and the women of Sparta were as much Spartans as the men. The Citoyen, Citoyenne, of France, was here actualized. Was not the calm equality they enjoyed well worth the honors of chivalry? They intelligently shared the ideal life of their nation.

Generally, we are told of these nations, that women occupied there a very subordinate position in actual life. It is difficult to believe this, when we see such range and dignity of thought on the subject in the mythologies, and find the poets producing such ideals as Cassandra, Iphigenia, Antigone, Macaria,[46] (though it is not unlike our own day, that men should revere those heroines of their great princely houses at theatres from which their women were excluded,) where Sibylline priestesses[47] told the oracle of the highest god, and he could not be content to reign with a court of less than nine Muses. Even Victory wore a female form.[48]

But whatever were the facts of daily life, I cannot complain of the age and nation, which represents its thought by such a symbol as I see before me at this moment. It is a zodiac of the busts of gods and goddesses, arranged in pairs. The circle breathes the music of a heavenly order. Male and female heads are distinct in expression, but equal in beauty, strength, and calmness. Each male head is that of a brother and a king, each female of a sister and a queen. Could the thought, thus expressed, be lived out, there would be nothing more to be desired. There would be unison in variety, congeniality in difference.

Coming nearer our own time, we find religion and poetry no less true in their revelations. The rude man, but just disengaged from the sod, the Adam, accuses woman to his God, and records her disgrace to their posterity. He is not ashamed to write that he could be drawn from heaven by one beneath him. But in the same nation, educated by time, instructed by successive prophets, we find woman in as high a position as she has ever occupied. And no figure, that has ever arisen to greet our eyes, has been received with more fervent reverence than that of the Madonna. Heine calls her the Dame du Comptoir[49] of the Catholic Church, and this jeer well expresses a serious truth.

---

43. Goddesses of the harvest and the underworld.   44. Roman goddesses of the hunt, the arts, and the home.   45. God of the sun.   46. Powerful women of Greek myth.   47. Priestesses at Delphos.   48. Statues conventionally represented Victory as a woman.   49. Lady of the exchange, or bank. Heinrich Heine (1797–1856), German poet.

And not only this holy and significant image was worshipped by the pilgrim, and the favorite subject of the artist, but it exercised an immediate influence on the destiny of the sex. The empresses, who embraced the cross, converted sons and husbands. Whole calendars of female saints, heroic dames of chivalry, binding the emblem of faith on the heart of the best beloved, and wasting the bloom of youth in separation and loneliness, for the sake of duties they thought it religion to assume, with innumerable forms of poesy, trace their lineage to this one. Nor, however imperfect may be the action, in our day, of the faith thus expressed, and though we can scarcely think it nearer this ideal than that of India or Greece was near their ideal, is it in vain that the truth has been recognised, that woman is not only a part of man, bone of his bone and flesh of his flesh, born that men might not be lonely, but in themselves possessors of and possessed by immortal souls. This truth undoubtedly received a greater outward stability from the belief of the church, that the earthly parent of the Saviour of souls was a woman.

The Assumption of the Virgin,[50] as painted by sublime artists, Petrarch's Hymn to the Madonna,[51] cannot have spoken to the world wholly without result, yet oftentimes those who had ears heard not.

Thus, the Idea of woman has not failed to be often and forcibly represented. So many instances throng on the mind, that we must stop here, lest the catalogue be swelled beyond the reader's patience.

Neither can she complain that she has not had her share of power. This, in all ranks of society, except the lowest, has been hers to the extent that vanity could crave, far beyond what wisdom would accept. In the very lowest, where man, pressed by poverty, sees in woman only the partner of toils and cares, and cannot hope, scarcely has an idea of a comfortable home, he maltreats her, often, and is less influenced by her. In all ranks, those who are amiable and uncomplaining, suffer much. They suffer long, and are kind; verily they have their reward. But wherever man is sufficiently raised above extreme poverty, or brutal stupidity, to care for the comforts of the fireside, or the bloom and ornament of life, woman has always power enough, if she choose to exert it, and is usually disposed to do so in proportion to her ignorance and childish vanity. Unacquainted with the importance of life and its purposes, trained to a selfish coquetry and love of petty power, she does not look beyond the pleasure of making herself felt at the moment, and governments are shaken and commerce broken up to gratify the pique of a female favorite. The English shopkeeper's wife does not vote, but it is for her interest that the politician canvasses by the coarsest flattery. France suffers no woman on her throne, but her proud nobles kiss the dust at the feet of Pompadour and Dubarry,[52] for such are in the lighted foreground where a Roland would modestly aid in the closet.[53] Spain shuts up her women in the care of duennas, and allows them no book but the Breviary[54]; but the ruin follows only the more surely from the worthless favorite of a worthless queen.

It is not the transient breath of poetic incense, that women want; each can receive that from a lover. It is not life-long sway; it needs but to become a coquette, a shrew, or a good cook to be sure of that. It is not money, nor notoriety, nor the badges of authority, that men have appropriated to themselves. If demands made in their behalf lay stress on any of these particulars, those who make them have not searched deeply

---

50. Mary, the mother of Jesus, was said to have been taken physically to Heaven.   51. Francesco Petrarca (1304–1374), Italian poet.   52. Jeanne Antoinette Poisson, Marquise de Pompadour (1721–1764), and Marie Jeanne Bécu, Comtesse du Barry (1743–1793), mistresses of Louis XV, king of France.   53. Small room. Marie Jeanne Roland (1754–1793), French revolutionary.   54. Prayer-books.

into the need. It is for that which at once includes all these and precludes them; which would not be forbidden power, lest there be temptation to steal and misuse it; which would not have the mind perverted by flattery from a worthiness of esteem. It is for that which is the birthright of every being capable to receive it,—the freedom, the religious, the intelligent freedom of the universe, to use its means, to learn its secret as far as nature has enabled them, with God alone for their guide and their judge.

Ye cannot believe it, men; but the only reason why women ever assume what is more appropriate to you, is because you prevent them from finding out what is fit for themselves. Were they free, were they wise fully to develop the strength and beauty of woman, they would never wish to be men, or manlike. The well-instructed moon flies not from her orbit to seize on the glories of her partner. No; for she knows that one law rules, one heaven contains, one universe replies to them alike. It is with women as with the slave.

> "Vor dem Sklaven, wenn er die Kette bricht,
> Vor dem freien Menschen erzittert nicht."

Tremble not before the free man, but before the slave who has chains to break.

In slavery, acknowledged slavery, women are on a par with men. Each is a work-tool, an article of property—no more! In perfect freedom, such as is painted in Olympus, in Swedenborg's[55] angelic state, in rhe heaven where there is no marrying nor giving in marriage,[56] each is a purified intelligence, an enfranchised soul,—no less!

> Jene himmlissche Gestalten
> Sie fragen nicht nach Mann und Weib,
> Und keine Kleider, keine Falten
> Umgeben den verklrten Leib.[57]

The child who sang this was a prophetic form, expressive of the longing for a state of perfect freedom, pure love. She could not remain here, but was transplanted to another air. And it may be that the air of this earth will never be so tempered, that such can bear it long. But, while they stay, they must bear testimony to the truth they are constituted to demand.

That an era approaches which shall approximate nearer to such a temper than any has yet done, there are many tokens, indeed so many that only a few of the most prominent can here be enumerated.

The reigns of Elizabeth of England and Isabella of Castile foreboded this era. They expressed the beginning of the new state, while they forwarded its progress. These were strong characters, and in harmony with the wants of their time. One showed that this strength did not unfit a woman for the duties of a wife and mother; the other, that it could enable her to live and die alone. Elizabeth is certainly no pleasing example. In rising above the weakness, she did not lay aside the weaknesses ascribed to her sex; but her strength must be respected now, as it was in her own time.

We may accept it as an omen for ourselves, that it was Isabella who furnished Columbus with the means of coming hither. This land must back its debt to woman, without whose aid it would not have been brought into alliance with the civilized world.

---

55. Emanuel Swedenborg (1688–1772), *Heaven and Hell* (1758). 56. Matthew 22.30. 57. Johann Wolfgang von Goethe (1749–1832), *Wilhelm Meister* (1774). "Those heavenly forms / ask not if one is man or woman, / and no clothes, no folds / shroud the transfigured body."

The influence of Elizabeth on literature was real, though, by sympathy with its finer productions, she was no more entitled to give name to an era than Queen Anne.[58] It was simply that the fact of a female sovereign on the throne affected the course of a writer's thoughts. In this sense, the presence of a woman on the throne always makes its mark. Life is lived before the eyes of all men, and their imaginations are stimulated as to the possibilities of woman. "We will die for our King, Maria Theresa,"[59] cry the wild warriors, clashing their swords, and the sounds vibrate through the poems of that generation. The range of female character in Spenser alone might content us for one period. Britomart and Belphoebe have as much room in the canvass as Florimel; and where this is the case, the haughtiest Amazon will not murmur that Una should be felt to be the highest type.[60]

Unlike as was the English Queen to a fairy queen, we may yet conceive that it was the image of a queen before the poet's mind, that called up this splendid court of women.

Shakespeare's range is also great, but he has left out the heroic characters, such as the Macaria of Greece,[61] the Britomart of Spenser. Ford and Massinger[62] have, in this respect, shown a higher flight of feeling than he. It was the holy and heroic woman they most loved, and if they could not paint an Imogen, a Desdemona, a Rosalind, yet in those of a stronger mould, they showed a higher ideal, though with so much less poetic power to represent it, than we see in Portia or Isabella. The simple truth of Cordelia, indeed, is of this sort. The beauty of Cordelia is neither male nor female; it is the beauty of virtue.[63]

The ideal of love and marriage rose high in the mind of all the Christian nations who were capable of grave and deep feeling. We may take as examples of its English aspect, the lines,

> "I could not love thee, dear, so much,
> Loved I not honor more."[64]

The address of the Commonwealth's man to his wife as she looked out from the Tower window to see him for the last time on his way to execution. "He stood up in the cart, waved his hat, and cried, 'To Heaven, my love, to Heaven! and leave you in the storm!'"

Such was the love of faith and honor, a love which stopped, like Colonel Hutchinson's,[65] "on this side idolatry,"[66] because it was religious. The meeting of two such souls Donne describes as giving birth to an "abler soul."[67]

Lord Herbert wrote to his love,

> "Were not our souls immortal made,
> Our equal loves can make them such."[68]

In Spain the same thought is arrayed in a sublimity, which belongs to the sombre and passionate genius of the nation. Calderon's Justina resists all the temptation of

---

58. Queen of England (1665–1714).   59. Queen of Hungary and Bohemia (1717–1780).   60. Edmund Spenser (1552–1599), *The Faerie Queene* (1590).   61. Daughter of Hercules.   62. John Ford (1586–1640) and Philip Massinger (1583–1640), English playwrights.   63. The women named in these sentences are Shakespearean characters.   64. Richard Lovelace (1618–1657), "To Lucasta, Going to the War," (1649).   65. John Hutchinson (1615–1664), a "Commonwealth's man" during the English Civil War.   66. Ben Jonson (1572–1637), *Timber* (1640), of Shakespeare.   67. John Donne (1572–1631), "The Ecstacy" (1633), line 43.   68. Edward, Lord Herbert of Cherbury (1583–1648), "An Ode upon a Question Moved Whether Love Should Continue for Ever."

the Demon,[69] and raises her lover with her above the sweet lures of mere temporal happiness. Their marriage is vowed at the stake, their souls are liberated together by the martyr flame into "a purer state of sensation and existence."

In Italy, the great poets wove into their lives an ideal love which answered to the highest wants. It included those of the intellect and the affections, for it was a love of spirit for spirit. It was not ascetic and superhuman, but interpreting all things, gave their proper beauty to details of the common life, the common day; the poet spoke of his love not as a flower to place in his bosom, or hold carelessly in his hand, but as a light towards which he must find wings to fly, or "a stair to heaven." He delighted to speak of her not only as the bride of his heart, but the mother of his soul, for he saw that, in cases where the right direction has been taken, the greater delicacy of her frame, and stillness of her life, left her more open to spiritual influx than man is. So he did not look upon her as betwixt him and earth, to serve his temporal needs, but rather betwixt him and heaven, to purify his affections and lead him to wisdom through her pure love. He sought in her not so much the Eve as the Madonna.

In these minds the thought, which glitters in all the legends of chivalry, shines in broad intellectual effulgence, not to be misinterpreted. And their thought is reverenced by the world, though it lies so far from them as yet, so far, that it seems as though a gulf of Death lay between.

Even with such men the practice was often widely different from the mental faith. I say mental, for if the heart were thoroughly alive with it, the practice could not be dissonant. Lord Herbert's was a marriage of convention, made for him at fifteen; he was not discontented with it, but looked only to the advantages it brought of perpetuating his family on the basis of a great fortune. He paid, in act, what he considered a dutiful attention to the bond; his thoughts travelled elsewhere, and, while forming a high ideal of the companionship of minds in marriage, he seems never to have doubted that its realization must be postponed to some other stage of being. Dante,[70] almost immediately after the death of Beatrice,[71] married a lady chosen for him by his friends.

Centuries have passed since, but civilized Europe is still in a transition state about marriage, not only in practice, but in thought. A great majority of societies and individuals are still doubtful whether earthly marriage is to be a union of souls, or merely a contract of convenience and utility. Were woman established in the rights of an immortal being, this could not be. She would not in some countries be given away by her father, with scarcely more respect for her own feelings than is shown by the Indian chief, who sells his daughter for a horse, and beats her if she runs away from her new home. Nor, in societies where her choice is left free, would she be perverted, by the current of opinion that seizes her, into the belief that she must marry, if it be only to find a protector, and a home of her own.

Neither would man, if he thought that the connection was of permanent importance, enter upon it so lightly. He would not deem it a trifle, that he was to enter into the closest relations with another soul, which, if not eternal in themselves, must eternally affect his growth.

Neither, did he believe woman capable of friendship, would he, by rash haste, lose the chance of finding a friend in the person who might, probably, live half a century by

---

69. Pedro Calderón de la Barca (1600–1681), *El Magico Prodigioso* (1663).   70. Dante Alighieri (1265–1321), Italian poet.   71. Beatrice Portinari (1266–1290).

his side. Did love to his mind partake of infinity, he would not miss his chance of its revelations, that he might the sooner rest from his weariness by a bright fireside, and have a sweet and graceful attendant, "devoted to him alone." Were he a step higher, he would not carelessly enter into a relation, where he might not be able to do the duty of a friend, as well as a protector from external ill, to the other party, and have a being in his power pining for sympathy, intelligence, and aid, that he could not give.

Where the thought of equality has become pervasive, it shows itself in four kinds.

The household partnership. In our country the woman looks for a "smart but kind" husband, the man for a "capable, sweet-tempered" wife.

The man furnishes the house, the woman regulates it. Their relation is one of mutual esteem, mutual dependence. Their talk is of business, their affection shows itself by practical kindness. They know that life goes more smoothly and cheerfully to each for the other's aid; they are grateful and content. The wife praises her husband as a "good provider," the husband in return compliments her as a "capital housekeeper." This relation is good as far as it goes.

Next comes a closer tie which takes the two forms, either of intellectual companionship, or mutual idolatry. The last, we suppose, is to no one a pleasing subject of contemplation. The parties weaken and narrow one another; they lock the gate against all the glories of the universe that they may live in a cell together. To themselves they seem the only wise, to all others steeped in infatuation, the gods smile as they look forward to the crisis of cure, to men the woman seems an unlovely syren, to women the man an effeminate boy.

The other form, of intellectual companionship, has become more and more frequent. Men engaged in public life, literary men, and artists have often found in their wives companions and confidants in thought no less than in feeling. And, as in the course of things the intellectual development of woman has spread wider and risen higher, they have, not unfrequently, shared the same employment. As in the case of Roland[72] and his wife, who were friends in the household and the nation's councils, read together, regulated home affairs, or prepared public documents together indifferently."

It is very pleasant, in letters begun by Roland and finished by his wife, to see the harmony of mind and the difference of nature, one thought, but various ways of treating it.

This is one of the best instances of a marriage of friendship. It was only friendship, whose basis was esteem; probably neither party knew love, except by name.

Roland was a good man, worthy to esteem and be esteemed, his wife as deserving of admiration as able to do without it. Madame Roland is the fairest specimen we have yet of her class, as clear to discern her aim, as valiant to pursue it, as Spenser's Britomart, austerely set apart from all that did not belong to her, whether as woman or as mind. She is an antetype of a class to which the coming time will afford a field, the Spartan matron, brought by the culture of a book-furnishing age to intellectual consciousness and expansion.

Self-sufficing strength and clear-sightedness were in her combined with a power of deep and calm affection. The page of her life is one of unsullied dignity.

Her appeal to posterity is one against the injustice of those who committed such crimes in the name of liberty. She makes it in behalf of herself and her husband. I would put beside it on the shelf a little volume, containing a similar appeal from the

---

72. Jean Marie Roland (1734–1793), French revolutionary, husband of Marie Jeanne Roland (see note 53, p. 978).

verdict of contemporaries to that of mankind, that of Godwin in behalf of his wife, the celebrated, the by most men detested Mary Wolstonecraft.[73] In his view it was an appeal from the injustice of those who did such wrong in the name of virtue.

Were this little book interesting for no other cause, it would be so for the generous affection evinced under the peculiar circumstances. This man had courage to love and honor this woman in the face of the world's verdict, and of all that was repulsive in her own past history. He believed he saw of what soul she was, and that the thoughts she had struggled to act out were noble. He loved her and he defended her for the meaning and intensity of her inner life. It was a good fact.

Mary Wolstonecraft, like Madame Dudevant (commonly known as George Sand[74]) in our day, was a woman whose existence better proved the need of some new interpretation of woman's rights, than anything she wrote. Such women as these, rich in genius, of most tender sympathies, and capable of high virtue and a chastened harmony, ought not to find themselves by birth in a place so narrow, that in breaking bonds they become outlaws. Were there as much room in the world for such, as in Spenser's poem for Britomart, they would not run their heads so wildly against its laws. They find their way at last to purer air, but the world will not take off the brand it has set upon them. The champion of the rights of woman found in Godwin, one who pleads her own cause like a brother. George Sand smokes, wears male attire, wishes to be addressed as Mon frère[75]; perhaps, if she found those who were as brothers indeed, she would not care whether she were brother or sister.

We rejoice to see that she, who expresses such a painful contempt for men in most of her works, as shows she must have known great wrong from them, in La Roche Mauprat[76] depicting one raised, by the workings of love, from the depths of savage sensualism to a moral and intellectual life. It was love for a pure object, for a steadfast woman, one of those who, the Italian said, could make the stair to heaven.

Women like Sand will speak now, and cannot be silenced; their characters and their eloquence alike foretell an era when such as they shall easier learn to lead true lives. But though such forebode, not such shall be the parents of it. Those who would reform the world must show that they do not speak in the heat of wild impulse; their lives must be unstained by passionate error; they must be severe lawgivers to themselves. As to their transgressions and opinions, it may be observed, that the resolve of Eloisa to be only the mistress of Abelard, was that of one who saw the contract of marriage a seal of degradation. Wherever abuses of this sort are seen, the timid will suffer, the bold protest. But society is in the right to outlaw them till she has revised her law, and she must be taught to do so, by one who speaks with authority, not in anger and haste.

If Godwin's choice of the calumniated authoress of the "Rights of Woman," for his honored wife, be a sign of a new era, no less so is an article of great learning and eloquence, published several years since in an English review, where the writer, in doing full justice to Eloisa, shows his bitter regret that she lives not now to love him, who might have known better how to prize her love than did the egotistical Abelard.

These marriages, these characters, with all their imperfections, express an onward tendency. They speak of aspiration of soul, of energy of mind, seeking clearness and freedom. Of a like promise are the tracts now publishing by Goodwyn Barmby (the

73. Mary Wollstonecraft (1759–1797), English feminist philosopher whose husband, William Godwin (1756–1836), defended her in a memoir after her death.   74. Amandine Aurore Lucile Dudevant (1804–1876), French feminist novelist.   75. My brother.   76. Play by Georges Sand.

European Pariah as he calls himself) and his wife Catharine.[77] Whatever we may think of their measures, we see them in wedlock, the two minds are wed by the only contract that can permanently avail, of a common faith, and a common purpose.

We might mention instances, nearer home, of minds, partners in work and in life, sharing together, on equal terms, public and private interests, and which have not on any side that aspect of offence which characterizes the attitude of the last named; persons who steer straight onward, and in our freer life have not been obliged to run their heads against any wall. But the principles which guide them might, under petrified or oppressive institutions, have made them warlike, paradoxical, or, in some sense, Pariahs. The phenomenon is different, the law the same, in all these cases. Men and women have been obliged to build their house from the very foundation. If they found stone ready in the quarry, they took it peaceably, otherwise they alarmed the country by pulling down old towers to get materials.

These are all instances of marriage as intellectual companionship. The parties meet mind to mind, and a mutual trust is excited which can buckler them against a million. They work together for a common purpose, and, in all these instances, with the same implement, the pen.

A pleasing expression in this kind is afforded by the union in the names of the Howitts. William and Mary Howitt[78] we heard named together for years, supposing them to be brother and sister; the equality of labors and reputation, even so, was auspicious, more so, now we find them man and wife. In his late work on Germany, Howitt mentions his wife with pride, as one among the constellation of distinguished English women, and in a graceful, simple manner.

In naming these instances we do not mean to imply that community of employment is an essential to union of this sort, more than to the union of friendship. Harmony exists no less in difference than in likeness, if only the same key-note govern both parts. Woman the poem, man the poet; woman the heart, man the head; such divisions are only important when they are never to be transcended. If nature is never bound down, nor the voice of inspiration stifled, that is enough. We are pleased that women should write and speak, if they feel the need of it, from having something to tell; but silence for a hundred years would be as well, if that silence be from divine command, and not from man's tradition.

While Goetz von Berlichingen[79] rides to battle, his wife is busy in the kitchen; but difference of occupation does not prevent that community of life, that perfect esteem, with which he says,

"Whom God loves, to him gives he such a wife!"

Manzoni thus dedicates his Adelchi.[80]

"To his beloved and venerated wife, Enrichetta Luigia Blondel, who, with conjugal affections and maternal wisdom, has preserved a virgin mind, the author dedicates this Adelchi grieving that he could not, by a more splendid and more durable monument, honor the dear name and the memory of so many virtues."

---

77. Goodwyn and Catharine Barmby, English socialist publishers.   78. William Howitt (1792–1879) and Mary Howitt (1799–1888), English writers.   79. Play by Johann Wolfgang von Goethe (1749–1832).   80. Play by Alessandro Manzoni (1785–1873).

The relation could not be fairer, nor more equal, if she too had written poems. Yet the position of the parties might have been the reverse as well; the woman might have sung the deeds, given voice to the life of the man, and beauty would have been the result, as we see in pictures of Arcadia[81] the nymph singing to the shepherds, or the shepherd with his pipe allures the nymphs, either makes a good picture. The sounding lyre requires not muscular strength, but energy of soul to animate the hand which can control it. Nature seems to delight in varying her arrangements, as if to show that she will be fettered by no rule, and we must admit the same varieties that she admits.

I have not spoken of the higher grade of marriage union, the religious, which may be expressed as pilgrimage towards a common shrine. This includes the others; home sympathies, and household wisdom, for these pilgrims must know how to assist one another to carry their burdens along the dusty way; intellectual communion, for how sad it would be on such a journey to have a companion to whom you could not communicate thoughts and aspirations, as they sprang to life, who would have no feeling for the more and more glorious prospects that open as we advance, who would never see the flowers that may be gathered by the most industrious traveler. It must include all these. Such a fellow pilgrim Count Zinzendorf[82] seems to have found in his countess of whom he thus writes.

> "Twenty-five years' experience has shown me that just the help-mate whom I have is the only one that could suit my vocation. Who else could have so carried through my family affairs? Who lived so spotlessly before the world? Who so wisely aided me in my rejection of a dry morality? Who so clearly set aside the Pharisaism[83] which, as years passed, threatened to creep in among us? Who so deeply discerned as to the spirits of delusion which sought to bewilder us? Who would have governed my whole economy so wisely, richly, and hospitably when circumstances commanded? Who have taken indifferently the part of servant or mistress, without on the one side affecting an especial spirituality, on the other being sullied by any worldly pride? Who, in a community where all ranks are eager to be on a level, would, from wise and real causes, have known how to maintain inward and outward distinctions? Who, without a murmur, have seen her husband encounter such dangers by land and sea? Who undertaken with him and sustained such astonishing pilgrimages? Who amid such difficulties always held up her head, and supported me? Who found so many hundred thousands and acquitted them on her own credit? And, finally, who, of all human beings, would so well understand and interpret to others my inner and outer being as this one, of such nobleness in her way of thinking, such great intellectual capacity, and free from the theological perplexities that enveloped me?"

An observer[84] adds this testimony.

> "We may in many marriages regard it as the best arrangement, if the man has so much advantage over his wife that she can, without much thought of her own, be, by him, led and directed, as by a father. But it was not so with the Count and his consort. She was not made to be a copy; she was an original; and, while she

---

81. Conventional pastoral locale.   82. Nikolas Ludwig, Count von Zinzendorf (1700–1760), German leader of Moravian Church.   83. Hypocrisy. See Matthew 23.27.   84. Spangenberg [Fuller's note]. August Gotlieb Spangenberg (1704–1792), German Moravian.

loved and honored him, she thought for herself on all subjects with so much intelligence, that he could and did look on her as a sister and friend also."

Such a woman is the sister and friend of all beings, as the worthy man is their brother and helper.

Another sign of the time is furnished by the triumphs of female authorship. These have been great and constantly increasing. They have taken possession of so many provinces for which men had pronounced them unfit, that though these still declare there are some inaccessible to them, it is difficult to say just *where* they must stop.

The shining names of famous women have cast light upon the path of the sex, and many obstructions have been removed. When a Montague[85] could learn better than her brother, and use her lore to such purpose afterwards as an observer, it seemed amiss to hinder women from preparing themselves to see, or from seeing all they could when prepared. Since Somerville[86] has achieved so much, will any young girl be prevented from attaining a knowledge of the physical sciences, if she wishes it? De Stael's[87] name was not so clear of offence; she could not forget the woman in the thought; while she was instructing you as a mind, she wished to be admired as a woman. Sentimental tears often dimmed the eagle glance. Her intellect, too, with all its splendor, trained in a drawing room, fed on flattery, was tainted and flawed; yet its beams make the obscurest school house in New England warmer and lighter to the little rugged girls, who are gathered together on its wooden bench. They may never through life hear her name, but she is not the less their benefactress.

This influence has been such that the aim certainly is, how, in arranging school instruction for girls, to give them as fair a field as boys. These arrangements are made as yet with little judgment or intelligence, just as the tutors of Jane Grey,[88] and the other famous women of her time, taught them Latin and Greek, because they knew nothing else themselves, so now the improvement in the education of girls is made by giving them gentlemen as teachers, who only teach what has been taught themselves at college, while methods and topics need revision for those new cases, which could better be made by those who had experienced the same wants. Women are often at the head of these institutions, but they have as yet seldom been thinking women, capable to organize a new whole for the wants of the time, and choose persons to officiate in the departments. And when some portion of education is got of a good sort from the school, the tone of society, the much larger proportion received from the world, contradicts its purport. Yet books have not been furnished, and a little elementary instruction been given in vain. Women are better aware how large and rich the universe is, not so easily blinded by the narrowness and partial views of a home circle.

Whether much or little has or will be done, whether women will add to the talent of narration, the power of systematizing, whether they will carve marble as well as draw, is not important. But that it should be acknowledged that they have intellect which needs developing, that they should not be considered complete, if beings of affection and habit alone, is important.

Yet even this acknowledgment, rather obtained by woman than proffered by man, has been sullied by the usual selfishness. So much is said of women being better

---

85. Lady Mary Wortley Montagu (1689–1762), English writer.   86. Mary Somerville (1789–1872), English writer.
87. Madame de Stael (1766–1817), French writer.   88. Lady Jane Grey (1537–1554).

educated that they may be better companions and mothers *of men!* They should be fit for such companionship, and we have mentioned with satisfaction instances where it has been established. Earth knows no fairer, holier relation than that of a mother. But a being of infinite scope must not be treated with an exclusive view to any one relation. Give the soul free course, let the organization be freely developed, and the being will be fit for any and every relation to which it may be called. The intellect, no more than the sense of hearing, is to be cultivated, that she may be a more valuable companion to man, but because the Power who gave a power by its mere existence signifies that it must be brought out towards perfection.

In this regard, of self-dependence and a greater simplicity and fulness of being, we must hail as a preliminary the increase of the class contemptuously designated as old maids.

We cannot wonder at the aversion with which old bachelors and old maids have been regarded. Marriage is the natural means of forming a sphere, of taking root on the earth: it requires more strength to do this without such an opening, very many have failed of this, and their imperfections have been in every one's way. They have been more partial, more harsh, more officious and impertinent than others. Those, who have a complete experience of the human instincts, have a distrust as to whether they can be thoroughly human and humane, such as is hinted at in the saying, "Old maids' and bachelors' children are well cared for," which derides at once their ignorance and their presumption.

Yet the business of society has become so complex, that it could now scarcely be carried on without the presence of these despised auxiliaries, and detachments from the army of aunts and uncles are wanted to stop gaps in every hedge. They rove about, mental and moral Ishmaelites,[89] pitching their tents amid the fixed and ornamented habitations of men.

They thus gain a wider, if not so deep, experience. They are not so intimate with others, but thrown more upon themselves, and if they do not there find peace and incessant life, there is none to flatter them that they are not very poor and very mean.

A position, which so constantly admonishes, may be of inestimable benefit. The person may gain, undistracted by other relationships, a closer communion with the One. Such a use is made of it by saints and sibyls. Or she may be one of the lay sisters of charity, or more humbly only the useful drudge of all men, or the intellectual interpreter of the varied life she sees.

Or she may combine all these. Not "needing to care that she may please a husband," a frail and limited being, all her thoughts may turn to the centre, and by steadfast contemplation enter into the secret of truth and love, use it for the use of all men, instead of a chosen few, and interpret through it all the forms of life.

Saints and geniuses have often chosen a lonely position, in the faith that, if undisturbed by the pressure of near ties they could give themselves up to the inspiring spirit, it would enable them to understand and reproduce life better than actual experience could.

How many old maids take this high stand, we cannot say; it is an unhappy fact that too many of those who come before the eye are gossips rather, and not always good-natured gossips. But, if these abuse, and none make the best of their vocation,

---

89. Nomadic descendants of Ishmael, according to scriptural tradition. Genesis 25.16 and 37.25.

yet, it has nor failed to produce some good fruit. It has been seen by others, if not by themselves, that beings likely to be left alone need to be fortified and furnished within themselves, and education and thought have tended more and more to regard beings as related to absolute Being, as well as to other men. It has been seen that as the loss of no bond ought to destroy a human being, so ought the missing of none to hinder him from growing. And thus a circumstance of the time has helped to put woman on the true platform. Perhaps the next generation will look deeper into this matter, and find that contempt is put on old maids, or old women at all, merely because they do not use the elixir which will keep the soul always young. No one thinks of Michael Angelo's Persican Sibyl, or St. Theresa, or Tasso's Leonora, or the Greek Electra[90] as an old maid, though all had reached the period in life's course appointed to take that degree.

Even among the North American Indians, a race of men as completely engaged in mere instinctive life as almost any in the world, and where each chief, keeping many wives as useful servants, of course looks with no kind eye on celibacy in woman, it was excused in the following instance mentioned by Mrs. Jameson.[91] A woman dreamt in youth that she was betrothed to the sun. She built her a wigwam apart, filled it with emblems of her alliance and means of an independent life. There she passed her days, sustained by her own exertions, and true to her supposed engagement.

In any tribe, we believe, a woman, who lived as if she was betrothed to the sun, would be tolerated, and the rays which made her youth blossom sweetly would crown her with a halo in age.

There is on this subject a nobler view than heretofore, if not the noblest, and we greet improvement here, as much as on the subject of marriage. Both are fertile themes, but time permits not here to explore them.

If larger intellectual resources begin to be deemed necessary to woman, still more is a spiritual dignity in her, or even the mere assumption of it listened to with respect. Joanna Southcote, and Mother Ann Lee[92] are sure of a band of disciples; Ecstatica, Dolorosa, of enraptured believers who will visit them in their lowly huts, and wait for hours to revere them in their trances. The foreign noble traverses land and sea to hear a few words from the lips of the lowly peasant girl, whom he believes specially visited by the Most High. Very beautiful in this way was the influence of the invalid of St. Petersburg, as described by De Maistre.[93]

To this region, however misunderstood, and ill-developed, belong the phenomena of Magnetism, or Mesmerism,[94] as it is now often called, where the trance of the Ecstatica purports to be produced by the agency of one human being on another, instead of, as in her case, direct from the spirit.

The worldling has his sneer here as about the services of religion. "The churches can always be filled with women." "Show me a man in one of your magnetic states, and I will believe."

Women are indeed the easy victims of priestcraft, or self-delusion, but this might not be, if the intellect was developed in proportion to the other powers. They would then have a regulator and be in better equipoise, yet must retain the same nervous susceptibility, while their physical structure is such as it is.

---

90. A series of independent women.   91. Anna Brownell Jameson (1794–1860), English writer.   92. Joanna Southcote (1750–1814) and Ann Lee (1736–1784), English religious enthusiasts. Ecstatica and Dolorosa are fictional hermits. 93. Joseph de Maistre (1754–1821), French author.   94. Hypnotism.

It is with just that hope, that we welcome everything that tends to strengthen the fibre and develop the nature on more sides. When the intellect and affections are in harmony, when intellectual consciousness is calm and deep, inspiration will not be confounded with fancy.

The electrical, the magnetic element in woman has not been fairly developed at any period. Everything might be expected from it; she has far more of it than man. This is commonly expressed by saying that her intuitions are more rapid and more correct.

But I cannot enlarge upon this here, except to say that on this side is highest promise. Should I speak of it fully, my title should be Cassandra, my topic the Seeress of Prevorst,[95] the first, or the best observed subject of magnetism in our times, and who, like her ancestresses at Delphos,[96] was roused to ecstacy or phrenzy by the touch of the laurel.

In such cases worldlings sneer, but reverent men learn wondrous news, either from the person observed, or by the thoughts caused in themselves by the observation. Fenelon learns from Guyon,[97] Kerner from his Seeress what we fain would know. But to appreciate such disclosures one must be a child, and here the phrase, "women and children," may perhaps be interpreted aright, that only little child shall enter into the kingdom of heaven.[98]

All these motions of the time, tides that betoken a waxing moon, overflow upon our own land. The world at large is readier to let woman learn and manifest the capacities of her nature than it ever was before, and here is a less encumbered field, and freer air than anywhere else. And it ought to be so; we ought to pay for Isabella's jewels.[99]

The names of nations are feminine. Religion, Virtue, and Victory are feminine. To those who have a superstition as to outward signs it is not without significance that the name of the Queen of our mother-land should at this crisis be Victoria. Victoria the First. Perhaps to us it may be given to disclose the era there outwardly presaged.

Women here are much better situated than men. Good books are allowed with more time to read them. They are not so early forced into the bustle of life, nor so weighed down by demands for outward success. The perpetual changes, incident to our society, make the blood circulate freely through the body politic, and, if not favorable at present to the grace and bloom of life, they are so to activity, resource, and would be to reflection but for a low materialist tendency, from which the women are generally exempt.

They have time to think, and no traditions chain them, and few conventionalities compared with what must be met in other nations. There is no reason why the fact of a constant revelation should be hid from them, and when the mind once is awakened by that, it will not be restrained by the past, but fly to seek the seeds of a heavenly future.

Their employments are more favorable to the inward life than those of the men.

Woman is not addressed religiously here, more than elsewhere. She is told to be worthy to be the mother of a Washington, or the companion of some good man. But in many, many instances, she has already learnt that all bribes have the same flaw; that truth and good are to be sought for themselves alone. And already an ideal sweetness floats over many forms, shines in many eyes.

---

95. Subject of hypnotism in Justinus Kerner (1786–1862), *Seherin von Prevorst*.   96. The oracles at Delphi used laurel leaves in their rituals.   97. François Fénelon (1651–1715) learned mysticism from Jeanne Guyon (1648–1717).   98. Mark 10.14–15.   99. Isabella, Queen of Spain (1451–1504), funder of Columbus.

Already deep questions are put by young girls on the great theme, What shall I do to inherit eternal life?

Men are very courteous to them. They praise them often, check them seldom. There is some chivalry in the feelings towards "the ladies," which gives them the best seats in the stage-coach, frequent admission not only to lectures of all sorts, but to courts of justice, halls of legislature, reform conventions. The newspaper editor "would be better pleased that the Lady's Book[100] were filled up exclusively by ladies. It would, then, indeed, be a true gem, worthy to be presented by young men to the mistresses of their affections." Can gallantry go farther?

In this country is venerated, wherever seen, the character which Goethe spoke of as an Ideal. "The excellent woman is she, who, if the husband dies, can be a father to the children." And this, if rightly read, tells a great deal.

Women who speak in public, if they have a moral power, such as has been felt from Angelina Grimke and Abby Kelly,[101] that is, if they speak for conscience' sake, to serve a cause which they hold sacred, invariably subdue the prejudices of their hearers, and excite an interest proportionate to the aversion with which it had been the purpose to regard them.

A passage in a private letter so happily illustrates this, that I take the liberty to make use of it, though there is not opportunity to ask leave either of the writer or owner of the letter. I think they will pardon me when they see it in print; it is so good, that as many as possible should have the benefit of it.

Abby Kelly in the Town-House of ———

"The scene was not unheroic,—to see that woman, true to humanity and her own nature, a centre of rude eyes and tongues, even gentlemen feeling licensed to make part of a species of mob around a female out of her sphere. As she took her seat in the desk amid the great noise, and in the throng full, like a wave, of something to ensue, I saw her humanity in a gentleness and unpretension, tenderly open to the sphere around her, and, had she not been supported by the power of the will of genuineness and principle, she would have failed. It led her to prayer, which, in woman especially, is childlike; sensibility and will going to the side of God and looking up to him; and humanity was poured out in aspiration.

"She acted like a gentle hero, with her mild decision and womanly calmness. All heroism is mild and quiet and gentle, for it is life and possession, and combativeness and firmness show a want of actualness. She is as earnest, fresh, and simple as when she first entered the crusade. I think she did much good, more than the men in her place could do, for woman feels more as being and reproducing; this brings the subject more into home relations. Men speak through and mostly from intellect, and this addresses itself in others, which creates and is combative."

Not easily shall we find elsewhere, or before this time, any written observations on the same subject, so delicate and profound.

---

100. *Godey's Lady's Book*, popular magazine.   101. Angelina Grimke (1805–1879) and Abby Kelly (1811–1887), American abolitionists.

The late Dr. Channing,[102] whose enlarged and tender and religious nature shared every onward impulse of his time, though his thoughts followed his wishes with a deliberative caution, which belonged to his habits and temperament, was greatly interested in these expectations for women. His own treatment of them was absolutely and thoroughly religious. He regarded them as souls, each of which had a destiny of its own, incalculable to other minds, and whose leading it must follow, guided by the light of a private conscience. He had sentiment, delicacy, kindness, taste, but they were all pervaded and ruled by this one thought, that all beings had souls, and must vindicate their own inheritance. Thus all beings were treated by him with an equal, and sweet, though solemn courtesy. The young and unknown, the woman and the child, all felt themselves regarded with an infinite expectation, from which there was no reaction to vulgar prejudice. He demanded of all he met, to use his favorite phrase, "great truths."

His memory, every way dear and reverend, is by many especially cherished for this intercourse of unbroken respect.

At one time when the progress of Harriet Martineau[103] through this country, Angelina Grimke's appearance in public, and the visit of Mrs. Jameson had turned his thoughts to this subject, he expressed high hopes as to what the coming era would bring to woman. He had been much pleased with the dignified courage of Mrs. Jameson in taking up the defence of her sex, in a way from which women usually shrink, because, if they express themselves on such subjects with sufficient force and clearness to do any good, they are exposed to assaults whose vulgarity makes them painful. In intercourse with such a woman, he had shared her indignation at the base injustice, in many respects, and in many regions done to the sex; and been led to think of it far more than ever before. He seemed to think that he might some time write upon the subject. That his aid is withdrawn from the cause is a subject of great regret, for on this question, as on others, he would have known how to sum up the evidence and take, in the noblest spirit, middle ground. He always furnished a platform on which opposing parties could stand, and look at one another under the influence of his mildness and enlightened candor.

Two younger thinkers, men both, have uttered noble prophecies, auspicious for woman. Kinmont,[104] all whose thoughts tended towards the establishment of the reign of love and peace, thought that the inevitable means of this would be an increased predominance given to the idea of woman. Had he lived longer to see the growth of the peace party, the reforms in life and medical practice which seek to substitute water for wine and drugs, pulse for animal food, he would have been confirmed in his view of the way in which the desired changes are to be effected.

In this connection I must mention Shelley,[105] who, like all men of genius, shared the feminine development, and unlike many, knew it. His life was one of the first pulse-beats in the present reform-growth. He, too, abhorred blood and heat, and, by his system and his song, tended to reinstate a plant-like gentleness in the development of energy. In harmony with this his ideas of marriage were lofty, and of course no less so of woman, her nature, and destiny.

For woman, if by a sympathy as to outward condition, she is led to aid the enfranchisement of the slave, must no less so, by inward tendency, to favor measures

102. William Ellery Channing (1780–1842), American minister.   103. British author (1802–1876).   104. Charles Kinmont (1799–1838), Scottish philosopher.   105. Percy Bysshe Shelley (1792–1822), English poet.

which promise to bring the world more thoroughly and deeply into harmony with her nature. When the lamb takes place of the lion as the emblem of nations, both women and men will be as children of one spirit, perpetual learners of the word and doers thereof, not hearers only.

A writer in a late number of the New York Pathfinder, in two articles headed "Femality," has uttered a still more pregnant word than any we have named. He views woman truly from the soul, and not from society, and the depth and leading of his thoughts is proportionably remarkable. He views the feminine nature as a harmonizer of the vehement elements, and this has often been hinted elsewhere; but what he expresses most forcibly is the lyrical, the inspiring and inspired apprehensiveness of her being.

Had I room to dwell upon this topic, I could not say anything so precise, so near the heart of the matter, as may be found in that article; but, as it is, I can only indicate, not declare, my view.

There are two aspects of woman's nature, expressed by the ancients as Muse and Minerva.[106] It is the former to which the writer in the Pathfinder looks. It is the latter which Wordsworth has in mind, when he says,

> "With a placid brow,
> Which woman ne'er should forfeit, keep thy vow."[107]

The especial genius of woman I believe to be electrical in movement, intuitive in function, spiritual in tendency. She is great not so easily in classification, or re-creation, as in an instinctive seizure of causes, and a simple breathing out of what she receives that has the singleness of life, rather than the selecting or energizing of art.

More native to her is it to be the living model of the artist, than to set apart from herself any one form in objective reality; more native to inspire and receive the poem than to create it. In so far as soul is in her completely developed, all soul is the same; but as far as it is modified in her as woman, it flows, it breathes, it sings, rather than deposits soil, or finishes work, and that which is especially feminine flushes in blossom the face of earth, and pervades like air and water all this seeming solid globe, daily renewing and purifying its life. Such may be the especially feminine element, spoken of as Femality. But it is no more the order of nature that it should be incarnated pure in any form, than that the masculine energy should exist unmingled with it in any form.

Male and female represent the two sides of the great radical dualism. But, in fact, they are perpetually passing into one another. Fluid hardens to solid, solid rushes to fluid. There is no wholly masculine man, no purely feminine woman.

History jeers at the attempts of physiologists to bind great original laws by the forms which flow from them. They make a rule; they say from observation what can and cannot be. In vain! Nature provides exceptions to every rule. She sends women to battle, and sets Hercules spinning; she enables women to bear immense burdens, cold, and frost; she enables the man, who feels maternal love, to nourish his infant like a mother. Of late she plays still gayer pranks. Not only she deprives organizations, but organs, of a necessary end. She enables people to read with the top of the head, and see with the pit of the stomach. Presently she will make a female Newton, and a male Syren.[108]

---

106. The Muses were the Greek goddesses of poetry and the arts. Minerva: the goddess of wisdom.   107. "Liberty: Sequel to the Preceding" (1835).   108. Isaac Newton (1842–1727), English scientist. Sirens: Greek sea nymphs.

Man partakes of the feminine in the Apollo, woman of the Masculine as Minerva.

Let us be wise and not impede the soul. Let her work as she will. Let us have one creative energy, one incessant revelation. Let it take what form it will, and let us not bind it by the past to man or woman, black or white. Jove sprang from Rhea, Pallas from Jove.[109] So let it be.

If it has been the tendency of the past remarks to call woman rather to the Minerva side,—if I, unlike the more generous writer, have spoken from society no less than the soul,—let it be pardoned. It is love that has caused this, love for many incarcerated souls, that might be freed could the idea of religious self-dependence be established in them, could the weakening habit of dependence on others be broken up.

Every relation, every gradation of nature, is incalculably precious, but only to the soul which is poised upon itself, and to whom no loss, no change, can bring dull discord, for it is in harmony with the central soul.

If any individual live too much in relations, so that he becomes a stranger to the resources of his own nature, he falls after a while into a distraction, or imbecility, from which he can only be cured by a time of isolation, which gives the renovating fountains time to rise up. With a society it is the same. Many minds, deprived of the traditionary or instinctive means of passing a cheerful existence, must find help in self-impulse or perish. It is therefore that while any elevation, in the view of union, is to be hailed with joy, we shall not decline celibacy as the great fact of the time. It is one from which no vow, no arrangement, can at present save a thinking mind. For now the rowers are pausing on their oars, they wait a change before they can pull together. All tends to illustrate the thought of a wise contemporary. Union is only possible to those who are units. To be fit for relations in time, souls, whether of man or woman, must be able to do without them in the spirit.

It is therefore that I would have woman lay aside all thought, such as she habitually cherishes, of being taught and led by men. I would have her, like the Indian girl, dedicate herself to the Sun, the Sun of Truth, and go no where if his beams did not make clear the path. I would have her free from compromise, from complaisance, from helplessness, because I would have her good enough and strong enough to love one and all beings, from the fulness, not the poverty of being.

Men, as at present instructed, will not help this work, because they also are under the slavery of habit. I have seen with delight their poetic impulses. A sister is the fairest ideal, and how nobly Wordsworth, and even Byron, have written of a sister.

There is no sweeter sight than to see a father with his little daughter. Very vulgar men become refined to the eye when leading a little girl by the hand. At that moment the right relation between the sexes seems established, and you feel as if the man would aid in the noblest purpose, if you ask him in behalf of his little daughter. Once two fine figures stood before me, thus. The father of very intellectual aspect, his falcon eye softened by affection as he looked down on his fair child, she the image of himself, only more graceful and brilliant in expression. I was reminded of Southey's Kehama,[110] when lo, the dream was rudely broken. They were talking of education, and he said.

"I shall not have Maria brought too forward. If she knows too much, she will never find a husband; superior women hardly ever can."

---

109. In Greek myth, Rhea, the wife of Cronus, gave birth to Jove, from whose head Pallas Athena emerged. 110. Robert Southey (1774–1843), *The Curse of Kehama* (1810).

"Surely," said his wife, with a blush, "you wish Maria to be as good and wise as she can, whether it will help her to marriage or not."

"No," he persisted, "I want her to have a sphere and a home, and some one to protect her when I am gone."

It was a trifling incident, but made a deep impression. I felt that the holiest relations fail to instruct the unprepared and perverted mind. If this man, indeed, would have looked at it on the other side, he was the last that would have been willing to have been taken himself for the home and protection he could give, but would have been much more likely to repeat the tale of Alcibiades with his phials.

But men do *not* look at both sides, and women must leave off asking them and being influenced by them, but retire within themselves, and explore the groundwork of being till they find their peculiar secret. Then when they come forth again, renovated and baptized, they will know how to turn all dross to gold, and will be rich and free though they live in a hut, tranquil, if in a crowd. Then their sweet singing shall not be from passionate impulse, but the lyrical overflow of a divine rapture, and a new music shall be elucidated from this many-chorded world.

Grant her then for a while the armor and the javelin.[111] Let her put from her the press of other minds and meditate in virgin loneliness. The same idea shall reappear in due time as Muse, or Ceres,[112] the all-kindly, patient Earth-Spirit.

I tire every one with my Goethean illustrations. But it cannot be helped.

Goethe, the great mind which gave itself absolutely to the leadings of truth, and let rise through him the waves which are still advancing through the century, was its intellectual prophet. Those who know him, see, daily, his thought fulfilled more and more, and they must speak of it, till his name weary and even nauseate, as all great names have in their time. And I cannot spare the reader, if such there be, his wonderful sight as to the prospects and wants of women.

As his Wilhelm grows in life and advances in wisdom, he becomes acquainted with women of more and more character, rising from Mariana to Macaria.[113]

Macaria, bound with the heavenly bodies in fixed revolutions, the centre of all relations, herself unrelated, expresses the Minerva side.

Mignon, the electrical, inspired lyrical nature.

All these women, though we see them in relations, we can think of as unrelated. They all are very individual, yet seem nowhere restrained. They satisfy for the present, yet arouse an infinite expectation.

The economist Theresa, the benevolent Natalia, the fair Saint, have chosen a path, but their thoughts are not narrowed to it. The functions of life to them are not ends, but suggestions.

Thus to them all things are important, because none is necessary. Their different characters have fair play, and each is beautiful in its minute indications, for nothing is enforced or conventional, but everything, however slight, grows from the essential life of the being.

Mignon and Theresa wear male attire when they like, and it is graceful for them to do so, while Macaria is confined to her arm chair behind the green curtain, and the Fair Saint could not bear a speck of dust on her robe.

---

111. Traditional weapons of Minerva.   112. Roman goddess of agriculture.   113. Female characters in *Wilhelm Meister's Apprenticeship* (1795), by Johann Wolfgang von Goethe (1749–1832), as are Mignon, Theresa, and Natalia below.

All things are in their places in this little world because all is natural and free, just as "there is room for everything out of doors." Yet all is rounded in by natural harmony which will always arise where Truth and Love are sought in the light of freedom.

Goethe's book bodes an era of freedom like its own, of "extraordinary generous seeking," and new revelations. New individualities shall be developed in the actual world, which shall advance upon it as gently as the figures come out upon his canvass.

A profound thinker has said "no married woman can represent the female world, for she belongs to her husband. The idea of woman must be represented by a virgin."

But that is the very fault of marriage, and of the present relation between the sexes, that the woman does belong to the man, instead of forming a whole with him. Were it otherwise there would be no such limitation to the thought.

Woman, self-centred, would never be absorbed by any relation; it would be only an experience to her as to man. It is a vulgar error that love, *a* love to woman is her whole existence; she also is born for Truth and Love in their universal energy. Would she but assume her inheritance, Mary would not be the only Virgin Mother. Not Manzoni alone would celebrate in his wife the virgin mind with the maternal wisdom and conjugal affections. The soul is ever young, ever virgin.

And will not she soon appear? The woman who shall vindicate their birthright for all women; who shall teach them what to claim, and how to use what they obtain? Shall not her name be for her era Victoria, for her country and her life Virginia? Yet predictions are rash; she herself must teach us to give her the fitting name.

—1843

Things and Thoughts in Europe, No. XVIII

This letter will reach the United States about the 1st of January; and it may not be impertinent to offer a few New-Year's reflections. Every new year, indeed, confirms the old thoughts, but also presents them under some new aspects.

The American in Europe, if a thinking mind, can only become more American. In some respects it is a great pleasure to be here. Although we have an independent political existence, our position toward Europe, as to Literature and the Arts, is still that of a colony, and one feels the same joy here that is experienced by the colonist in returning to the parent home. What was but picture to us becomes reality; remote allusions and derivations trouble no more: we see the pattern of the stuff, and understand the whole tapestry. There is a gradual clearing up on many points, and many baseless notions and crude fancies are dropped. Even the post-haste passage of the business American through the great cities, escorted by cheating couriers, and ignorant *valets de place*,[1] unable to hold intercourse with the natives of the country, and passing all his leisure hours with his countrymen, who know no more than himself, clears his mind of some mistakes—lifts some mists from his horizon.

There are three species: first, the servile American—a being utterly shallow, thoughtless, worthless. He comes abroad to spend his money and indulge his tastes. His object in Europe is to have fashionable clothes, good foreign cookery, to know some

---

1. Guides.

titled persons, and furnish himself with coffee-house gossip, which he wins importance at home by retailing among those less traveled, and as uninformed as himself.

I look with unspeakable contempt on this class—a class which has all the thoughtlessness and partiality of the exclusive classes in Europe, without any of their refinement, or the chivalric feeling which still sparkles among them here and there. However, though these willing serfs in a free age do some little hurt, and cause some annoyance at present, it cannot last: our country is fated to a grand, independent existence, and as its laws develop, these parasites of a bygone period must wither and drop away.

Then there is the conceited American, instinctively bristling and proud of—he knows not what—He does not see, not he, that the history of Humanity for many centuries is likely to have produced results it requires some training, some devotion, to appreciate and profit by. With his great clumsy hands only fitted to work on a steam-engine, he seizes the old Cremona violin, makes it shriek with anguish in his grasp, and then declares he thought it was all humbug before he came, and now he knows it; that there is not really any music in these old things; that the frogs in one of our swamps make much finer, for *they* are young and alive. To him the etiquettes of courts and camps, the ritual of the Church, seem simply silly—and no wonder, profoundly ignorant as he is of their origin and meaning. Just so the legends which are the subjects of pictures, the profound myths which are represented in the antique marbles, amaze and revolt him; as, indeed, such things need to be judged of by another standard from that of the Connecticut Blue-Laws.[2] He criticises severely pictures, feeling quite sure that his natural senses are better means of judgment than the rules of connoisseurs—not feeling that to see such objects mental vision as well as fleshly eyes are needed, and that something is aimed at in Art beyond the imitation of the commonest forms of Nature.

This is Jonathan[3] in the sprawling state, the booby truant, not yet aspiring enough to be a good school-boy. Yet in his folly there is meaning; add thought and culture to his independence, and he will be a man of might: he is not a creature without hope, like the thick-skinned dandy of the class first specified.

The Artistes form a class by themselves. Yet among them, though seeking special aims by special means may also be found the lineaments of these two classes, as well as of the third, of which I am to speak.

3d. The thinking American—a man who, recognizing the immense advantage of being born to a new world and on a virgin soil, yet does not wish one seed from the Past to be lost. He is anxious to gather and carry back with him all that will bear a new climate and new culture. Some will dwindle; others will attain a bloom and stature unknown before. He wishes to gather them clean, free from noxious insects. He wishes to give them a fair trial in his new world. And that he may know the conditions under which he may best place them in that new world, he does not neglect to study their history in this.

The history of our planet in some moments seems so painfully mean and little, such terrible bafflings and failures to compensate some brilliant successes—such a crushing of the mass of men beneath the feet of a few, and these, too, of the least worthy—such a small drop of honey to each cup of gall, and, in many cases, so mingled, that it is never one moment in life purely tasted,—above all, so little

---

2. Laws prohibiting sales of goods on Sunday.   3. Conventional name for stereotypical American.

achieved for Humanity as a whole, such tides of war and pestilence intervening to blot out the traces of each triumph, that no wonder if the strongest soul sometimes pauses aghast! No wonder if the many indolently console themselves with gross joys and frivolous prizes. Yes! those men *are* worthy of admiration who can carry this cross faithfully through fifty years; it is a great while for all the agonies that beset a lover of good, a lover of men; it makes a soul worthy of a speedier ascent, a more productive ministry in the next sphere. Blessed are they who ever keep that portion of pure, generous love with which they began life! How blessed those who have deepened the fountains, and have enough to spare for the thirst of others! Some such there are; and, feeling that, with all the excuses for failure, still only the sight of those who triumph gives a meaning to life or makes its pangs endurable, we must arise and follow.

Eighteen hundred years of this Christian culture in these European Kingdoms, a great theme never lost sight of, a mighty idea, an adorable history to which the hearts of men invariably cling, yet are genuine results rare as grains of gold in the river's sandy bed! Where is the genuine Democracy to which the rights of all men are holy? where the child-like wisdom learning all through life more and more of the will of God? where the aversion to falsehood in all its myriad disguises of cant, vanity, covetousness, so clear to be read in all the history of Jesus of Nazareth? Modern Europe is the sequel to that history, and see this hollow England, with its monstrous wealth and cruel poverty, its conventional life and low, practical aims; see this poor France, so full of talent, so adroit, yet so shallow and glossy still, which could not escape from a false position with all its baptism of blood; see that lost Poland and this Italy bound down by treacherous hands in all the force of genius; see Russia with its brutal Czar and innumerable slaves; see Austria and its royalty that represents nothing, and its people who, as people, are and have nothing! If we consider the amount of truth that has really been spoken out in the world, and the love that has beat in private hearts—how Genius has decked each spring-time with such splendid flowers, conveying each one enough of instruction in its life of harmonious energy, and how continually, unquenchably the spark of faith has striven to burst into flame and light up the Universe—the public failure seems amazing, seems monstrous.

Still Europe toils and struggles with her idea, and, at this moment, all things bode and declare a new outbreak of the fire, to destroy old palaces of crime! May it fertilize also many vineyards!—Here at this moment a successor of St. Peter, after the lapse of near two thousand years, is called "Utopian" by a part of this Europe, because he strives to get some food into the mouths of the *leaner* of his flock. A wonderful state of things, and which leaves as the best argument against despair that men do not, *cannot* despair amid such dark experiences—and thou, my country! will thou not be more true? does no greater success await thee? All things have so conspired to teach, to aid! A new world, a new chance, with oceans to wall in the new thought against interference from the old!—Treasures of all kinds, gold, silver, corn, marble, to provide for every physical need! A noble, constant, starlike soul, an Italian, led the way to its shores, and, in the first days, the strong, the pure, those too brave, too sincere for the life of the Old World hastened to people them. A generous struggle then shook off what was foreign and gave the nation a glorious start for a worthy goal. Men rocked the cradle of its hopes, great, firm, disinterested men who saw, who wrote, as the basis of all that was to be done, a statement of the rights, the inborn rights of men, which, if fully interpreted and acted upon, leaves nothing to be desired.

Yet, oh Eagle, whose early flight showed this clear sight of the Sun, how often dost thou near the ground, how show the vulture in these later days! Thou wert to be the advance-guard of Humanity, the herald of all Progress; how often hast thou betrayed this high commission! Fain would the tongue in clear triumphant accents draw example from thy story, to encourage the hearts of those who almost faint and die beneath the old oppressions. But we must stammer and blush when we speak of many things. I take pride here that I may really say the Liberty of the Press works well, and that checks and balances naturally evolve from it which suffice to its government. I may say the minds of our people are alert, and that Talent has a free chance to rise. It is much. But dare I say that political ambition is not as darkly sullied as in other countries? Dare I say that men of most influence in political life are those who represent most virtue or even intellectual power? Is it easy to find names in that career of which I can speak with enthusiasm? Must I not confess in my country to a boundless lust of gain? Must I not confess to the weakest vanity, which bristles and blusters at each foolish taunt of the foreign press; and must I not admit that the men who make these undignified rejoinders seek and find popularity so? Must I not confess that there is as yet no antidote cordially adopted that will defend even that great, rich country against the evils that have grown out of the commercial system of the old world? Can I say our social laws are generally better, or show a nobler insight into the wants of man and woman? I do, indeed, say what I believe, that voluntary association for improvement in these particulars will be the grand means for my nation to grow and give a nobler harmony to the coming age. But it is only of a small minority that I can say they as yet seriously take to heart these things; that they earnestly meditate on what is wanted for their country,—for mankind,—for our cause is, indeed, the cause of all mankind at present. Could we succeed, really succeed, combine a deep religious love with practical development, the achievements of Genius with the happiness of the multitude, we might believe Man had now reached a commanding point in his ascent, and would stumble and faint no more. Then there is this horrible cancer of Slavery, and this wicked War,[4] that has grown out of it. How dare I speak of these things here? I listen to the same arguments against the emancipation of Italy, that are used against the emancipation of our blacks; the same arguments in favor of the spoliation of Poland as for the conquest of Mexico. I find the cause of tyranny and wrong everywhere the same—and lo! my Country the darkest offender, because with the least excuse, foresworn to the high calling with which she was called,—no champion of the rights of men, but a robber and a jailer; the scourge hid behind her banner; her eyes fixed, not on the stars, but on the possessions of other men.

How it pleases me here to think of the Abolitionists! I could never endure to be with them at home, they were so tedious, often so narrow, always so rabid and exaggerated in their tone.

But, after all, they had a high motive, something eternal in their desire and life; and, if it was not the only thing worth thinking of it was really something worth living and dying for to free a great nation from such a terrible blot, such a threatening plague. God strengthen them and make them wise to achieve their purpose!

---

4. Mexican-American War (1846–1848).

I please myself, too, with remembering some ardent souls among the American youth who, I trust, will yet expand and help to give soul to the huge, over fed, too hastily grown-up body. May they be constant. "Were Man but constant he were perfect!" it has been said; and it is true that he who could be constant to those moments in which he has been truly human—not brutal, not mechanical—is on the sure path to his perfection and to effectual service of the Universe.

It is to the youth that Hope addresses itself, to those who yet burn with aspiration, who are not hardened in their sins. But I dare not expect too much of them. I am not very old, yet of those who, in life's morning, I saw touched by the light of a high hope, many have seceded. Some have become voluptuaries; some mere family men, who think it is quite life enough to win bread for half a dozen people and treat them decently; others are lost through indolence and vacillation. Yet some remain constant. "I have witnessed many a shipwreck, yet still beat noble hearts."

I have found many among the youth of England, of France—of Italy also—full of high desire, but will they have courage and purity to fight the battle through in the sacred, the immortal band? Of some of them I believe it and await the proof. If a few succeed amid the trial, we have not lived and loved in vain.

To these, the heart of my country, a Happy New Year! I do not know what I have written. I have merely yielded to my feelings in thinking of America; but something of true love must be in these lines—receive them kindly, my friends; it is, by itself, some merit for printed words to be sincere.

—1848

from Summer on the Lakes, in 1843

Chapter I

Niagara, June 10, 1843.

Since you are to share with me such foot-notes as may be made on the pages of my life during this summer's wanderings, I should not be quite silent as to this magnificent prologue to the, as yet, unknown drama. Yet I, like others, have little to say, where the spectacle is, for once, great enough to fill the whole life, and supersede thought, giving us only its own presence. "It is good to be here," is the best, as the simplest, expression that occurs to the mind.

We have been here eight days, and I am quite willing to go away. So great a sight soon satisfies, making us content with itself, and with what is less than itself. Our desires, once realized, haunt us again less readily. Having "lived one day," we would depart, and become worthy to live another.

We have not been fortunate in weather, for there cannot be too much, or too warm sunlight for this scene, and the skies have been lowering, with cold, unkind winds. My nerves, too much braced up by such an atmosphere, do not well bear the continual stress of sight and sound. For here there is no escape from the weight of a perpetual creation; all other forms and motions come and go, the tide rises and recedes, the wind, at its mightiest, moves in gales and gusts, but here is really an incessant, an indefatigable motion. Awake or asleep, there is no escape, still this rushing round you and through you. It is in this way I have most felt the grandeur,—somewhat eternal, if not infinite.

At times a secondary music rises; the cataract seems to seize its own rhythm and sing it over again, so that the ear and soul are roused by a double vibration. This is some effect of the wind, causing echoes to the thundering anthem. It is very sublime, giving the effect of a spiritual repetition through all the spheres.

When I first came, I felt nothing but a quiet satisfaction. I found that drawings, the panorama, &c. had given me a clear notion of the position and proportions of all objects here; I knew where to look for everything, and everything looked as I thought it would.

Long ago, I was looking from a hill-side with a friend at one of the finest sunsets that ever enriched this world. A little cow-boy, trudging along, wondered what we could be gazing at. After spying about some time, he found it could only be the sunset, and looking, too, a moment, he said approvingly, "That sun looks well enough"; a speech worthy of Shakspeare's Cloten,[1] or the infant Mercury, up to everything from the cradle, as you please to take it.

Even such a familiarity, worthy of Jonathan, our national hero, in a prince's palace, or "stumping," as he boasts to have done, "up the Vatican stairs, into the Pope's presence, in my old boots," I felt here; it looks really *well enough*, I felt, and was inclined, as you suggested, to give my approbation as to the one object in the world that would not disappoint.

But all great expression, which, on a superficial survey, seems so easy as well as so simple, furnishes, after a while, to the faithful observer, its own standard by which to appreciate it. Daily these proportions widened and towered more and more upon my sight, and I got, at last, a proper foreground for these sublime distances. Before coming away, I think I really saw the full wonder of the scene. After awhile it so drew me into itself as to inspire an undefined dread, such as I never knew before, such as may be felt when death is about to usher us into a new existence. The perpetual trampling of the waters seized my senses. I felt that no other sound, however near, could be heard, and would start and look behind me for a foe. I realized the identity of that mood of nature in which these waters were poured down with such absorbing force, with that in which the Indian was shaped on the same soil. For continually upon my mind came, unsought and unwelcome, images, such as never haunted it before, of naked savages stealing behind me with uplifted tomahawks; again and again this illusion recurred, and even after I had thought it over, and tried to shake it off, I could not help starting and looking behind me.

As picture, the Falls can only be seen from the British side. There they are seen in their veils, and at sufficient distance to appreciate the magical effects of these, and the light and shade. From the boat, as you cross, the effects and contrasts are more melodramatic. On the road back from the whirlpool, we saw them as a reduced picture with delight. But what I liked best was to sit on Table Rock, close to the great fall. There all power of observing details, all separate consciousness, was quite lost.

Once, just as I had seated myself there, a man came to take his first look. He walked close up to the fall, and, after looking at it a moment, with an air as if thinking how he could best appropriate it to his own use, he spat into it.

This trait seemed wholly worthy of an age whose love of *utility* is such that the Prince Puckler Muskau[2] suggests the probability of men coming to put the bodies

---

1. An arrogant bully in *Cymbeline* (1623).   2. Herman von Puckler-Muskau (1785–1871), German travel writer.

of their dead parents in the fields to fertilize them, and of a country such as Dickens[3] has described; but these will not, I hope, be seen on the historic page to be truly the age or truly the America. A little leaven is leavening the whole mass for other bread.

The whirlpool I like very much. It is seen to advantage after the great falls; it is so sternly solemn. The river cannot look more imperturbable, almost sullen in its marble green, than it does just below the great fall; but the slight circles that mark the hidden vortex, seem to whisper mysteries the thundering voice above could not proclaim,—a meaning as untold as ever.

It is fearful, too, to know, as you look, that whatever has been swallowed by the cataract, is like to rise suddenly to light here, whether up-rooted tree, or body of man or bird.

The rapids enchanted me far beyond what I expected; they are so swift that they cease to seem so; you can think only of their beauty. The fountain beyond the Moss Islands, I discovered for myself, and thought it for some time an accidental beauty which it would not do to leave, lest I might never see it again. After I found it perma- nent, I returned many times to watch the play of its crest. In the little waterfall beyond, Nature seems, as she often does, to have made a study for some larger design. She delights in this,—a sketch within a sketch, a dream within a dream. Wherever we see it, the lines of the great buttress in the fragment of stone, the hues of the waterfall, copied in the flowers that star its bordering mosses, we are delighted; for all the linea- ments become fluent, and we mould the scene in congenial thought with its genius.

People complain of the buildings at Niagara, and fear to see it further deformed. I cannot sympathize with such an apprehension: the spectacle is capable to swallow up all such objects; they are not seen in the great whole, more than an earthworm in a wide field.

The beautiful wood on Goat Island is full of flowers; many of the fairest love to do homage here. The Wake-robin and May-apple are in bloom now; the former, white, pink, green, purple, copying the rainbow of the fall, and fit to make a garland for its presiding deity when he walks the land, for they are of imperial size, and shaped like stones for a diadem. Of the May-apple, I did not raise one green tent without finding a flower beneath.

And now farewell, Niagara. I have seen thee, and I think all who come here must in some sort see thee; thou art not to be got rid of as easily as the stars. I will be here again beneath some flooding July moon and sun. Owing to the absence of light, I have seen the rainbow only two or three times by day; the lunar bow not at all. However, the imperial presence needs not its crown, though illustrated by it.

General Porter[4] and Jack Downing were not unsuitable figures here. The former heroically planted the bridges by which we cross to Goat Island, and the Wake-robin- crowned genius has punished his termerity with deafness, which must, I think, have come upon him when he sank the first stone in the rapids. Jack seemed an acute and entertaining representative of Jonathan, come to look at his great water-privilege. He told us all about the Americanisms of the spectacle; that is to say, the battles that have been fought here. It seems strange that men could fight in such a place; but no temple can still the personal griefs and strifes in the breasts of its visiters.

---

3. Charles Dickens (1812–1870), *American Notes* (1842).   4. Peter Buell Porter (1773–1844), owner of Niagara Falls.

No less strange is the fact that, in this neighborhood, an eagle should be chained for a plaything. When a child, I used often to stand at a window from which I could see an eagle chained in the balcony of a museum. The people used to poke at it with sticks, and my childish heart would swell with indignation as I saw their insults, and the mien with which they were borne by the monarch-bird. Its eye was dull, and its plumage soiled and shabby, yet, in its form and attitude, all the king was visible, though sorrowful and dethroned. I never saw another of the family till, when passing through the Notch of the White Mountains,[5] at that moment striding before us in all the panoply of sunset, the driver shouted, "Look there!" and following with our eyes his upward-pointing finger, we saw, soaring slow in majestic poise above the highest summit, the bird of Jove.[6] It was a glorious sight, yet I know not that I felt more on seeing the bird in all its natural freedom and royalty, than when, imprisoned and insulted, he had filled my early thoughts with the Byronic "silent rages"[7] of misanthropy.

Now, again, I saw him a captive, and addressed by the vulgar with the language they seem to find most appropriate to such occasions,—that of thrusts and blows. Silently, his head averted, he ignored their existence, as Plotinus or Sophocles[8] might that of a modern reviewer. Probably, he listened to the voice of the cataract, and felt that congenial powers flowed free, and was consoled, though his own wing was broken.

The story of the Recluse of Niagara[9] interested me a little. It is wonderful that men do not oftener attach their lives to localities of great beauty,—that, when once deeply penetrated, they will let themselves so easily be borne away by the general stream of things, to live anywhere and anyhow. But there is something ludicrous in being the hermit of a show-place, unlike St. Francis in his mountain-bed, where none but the stars and rising sun ever saw him.

There is also a "guide to the falls," who wears his title labeled on his hat; otherwise, indeed, one might as soon think of asking for a gentleman usher to point out the moon. Yet why should we wonder at such, when we have Commentaries on Shakspeare, and Harmonies of the Gospels?[10]

And now you have the little all I have to write. Can it interest you? To one who has enjoyed the full life of any scene, of any hour, what thoughts can be recorded about it, seem like the commas and semicolons in the paragraph,—mere stops. Yet I suppose it is not so to the absent. At least, I have read things written about Niagara, music, and the like, that interested *me*. Once I was moved by Mr. Greenwood's remark, that he could not realize this marvel till, opening his eyes the next morning after he had seen it, his doubt as to the possibility of its being still there, taught him what he had experienced. I remember this now with pleasure, though, or because, it is exactly the opposite to what I myself felt. For all greatness affects different minds, each in "its own particular kind," and the variations of testimony mark the truth of feeling.

I will add a brief narrative of the experience of another here, as being much better than anything I could write, because more simple and individual.

"Now that I have left this 'Earth-wonder,' and the emotions it excited are past, it seems not so much like profanation to analyze my feelings, to recall minutely and accurately the effect of this manifestation of the Eternal. But one should go to such a scene prepared to yield entirely to its influences, to forget one's little self and one's

---

5. Crawford Notch in New Hampshire's White Mountains.   6. Roman sky god.   7. Thomas Moore (1779–1852), *Notices of the Life of Lord Byron* (1835).   8. Plotinus (c. 207–270) and Sophocles (d. 406 BC), Greek philosophers.   9. Francis Abbott (d. 1831).   10. Books that attempted to resolve scriptural discrepancies.

little mind. To see a miserable worm creep to the brink of this falling world of waters, and watch the trembling of its own petty bosom, and fancy that this is made alone to act upon him excites—derision?—No,—pity."

As I rode up to the neighborhood of the falls, a solemn awe imperceptibly stole over me, and the deep sound of the ever-hurrying rapids prepared my mind for the lofty emotions to be experienced. When I reached the hotel, I felt a strange indifference about seeing the aspiration of my life's hopes. I lounged about the rooms, read the stage-bills upon the walls, looked over the register, and, finding the name of an acquaintance, sent to see if he was still there. What this hesitation arose from, I know not; perhaps it was a feeling of my unworthiness to enter this temple which nature has erected to its God.

At last, slowly and thoughtfully I walked down to the bridge leading to Goat Island, and when I stood upon this frail support, and saw a quarter of a mile of tumbling, rushing rapids, and heard their everlasting roar, my emotions overpowered me, a choking sensation rose to my throat, a thrill rushed through my veins, "my blood ran rippling to my finger's ends." This was the climax of the effect which the falls produced upon me,—neither the American nor the British fall moved me as did these rapids. For the magnificence, the sublimity of the latter, I was prepared by descriptions and by paintings. When I arrived in sight of them I merely felt, "Ah, yes! here is the fall, just as I have seen it in picture." When I arrived at the Terrapin Bridge, I expected to be overwhelmed, to retire trembling from this giddy eminence, and gaze with unlimited wonder and awe upon the immense mass rolling on and on; but, somehow or other, I thought only of comparing the effect on my mind with what I had read and heard. I looked for a short time, and then with almost a feeling of disappointment, turned to go to the other points of view to see if I was not mistaken in not feeling any surpassing emotion at this sight. But from the foot of Biddle's Stairs, and the middle of the river, and from below the Table Rock, it was still "barren, barren all."And, provoked with my stupidity in feeling most moved in the wrong place, I turned away to the hotel, determined to set off for Buffalo that afternoon. But the stage did not go, and, after nightfall, as there was a splendid moon, I went down to the bridge, and leaned over the parapet, where the boiling rapids came down in their might. It was grand, and it was also gorgeous; the yellow rays of the moon made the broken waves appear like auburn tresses twining around the black rocks. But they did not inspire me as before. I felt a foreboding of a mightier emotion to rise up and swallow all others, and I passed on to the Terrapin Bridge. Everything was changed, the misty apparition had taken off its many-colored crown which it had worn by day, and a bow of silvery white spanned its summit. The moonlight gave a poetical indefiniteness to the distant parts of the waters, and while the rapids were glancing in her beams, the river below the falls was black as night, save where the reflection of the sky gave it the appearance of a shield of blued steel. No gaping tourists loitered, eyeing with their glasses, or sketching on cards the hoary locks of the ancient river-god. All tended to harmonize with the natural grandeur of the scene. I gazed long. I saw how here mutability and unchangeableness were united. I surveyed the conspiring waters rushing against the rocky ledge to overthrow it at one mad plunge, till, like toppling ambition, o'erleaping themselves, they fall on t'other side, expanding into foam ere they reach the deep channel where they creep submissively away.

Then arose in my breast a genuine admiration, and a humble adoration of the Being who was the architect of this and of all. Happy were the first discoverers of Niagara, those who could come unawares upon this view and upon that, whose feelings were entirely their own. With what gusto does Father Hennepin[11] describe "this great downfall of water," "this vast and prodigious cadence of water, which falls down after a surprising and astonishing manner, insomuch that the universe does not afford its parallel. 'Tis true Italy and Swedeland boast of some such things, but we may well say that they be sorry patterns when compared with this of which we do now speak."

—1844

Harriet Jacobs

1813–1897

The sexual and physical abuse that white masters perpetrated on enslaved African American women was made public in Harriet Jacobs's *Incidents in the Life of a Slave Girl* (1861). Addressing a nineteenth-century readership concerned with Victorian notions of propriety, Jacobs speaks directly to free women, anticipating their judgment by pointing out that even the socially constructed, male-conscripted roles of "free" women were denied to those enslaved:

> O, ye happy women, whose purity has been sheltered from childhood, who have been free to choose the objects of your affection, whose homes are protected by law, do not judge the poor desolate slave girl too severely! . . . I wanted to keep myself pure; and, under the most adverse circumstances, I tried hard to preserve my self-respect; but I was struggling alone in the powerful grasp of the demon Slavery; and the monster proved too strong for me. (p. 1018)

Denied a voice in society and literature, Jacobs creates one for herself by writing in a tradition previously available solely to black men: the slave narrative. She also subverts male-dominated genres, such as the sermon and the heroic quest, by relating the history of her struggle for liberty and equality as a spiritual autobiography, a courtly romance, and an epic.

Incidents changes many details to preserve Jacobs's identity and freedom from those who sought to bring her back to slavery, even after she had escaped to the North. The book begins with Linda Brent (Jacobs's alias) being born into slavery in South Carolina (actually Edenton, North Carolina), a status she was made painfully aware of after the death of her mother, Molly Horniblow. She was taken in by her mother's owner, Margaret Horniblow, who taught her to read and write. After Margaret's death, Jacobs was willed to Dr. James Norcom, whose continued sexual advances and assaults ruined her childhood and her hopes of being with the free African American man she loved. To escape Norcom (called Dr. Flint in *Incidents*), she entered into a relationship with Samuel Treadwell Sawyer, a "white unmarried gentleman" who according to Jacobs had no claim on her but kindness. Their two children, Joseph and Louisa Matilda, were born in 1829 and 1833, respectively. Two years after Louisa was born, Jacobs was forced into hiding to escape the sexual advances of Norcom, whom she had continuously fought off. After hiding for seven years in a cramped garret above a storeroom in her grandmother's house, Jacobs was able to escape to the North, alternating between New York and Massachusetts to escape her pursuers. By 1844, she was reunited with both of her children.

---

11. Louis Hennepin (1626–1705), Catholic priest and explorer.

Jacobs found employment as a nursemaid to the child of Nathaniel Parker Willis and Mary Stace Willis. In 1845, after Mary had passed away, Jacobs accompanied the Willis family to England to help care for the now motherless child. During her ten-month stay in the United Kingdom, Jacobs noted that "for the first time in my life I was in a place where I was treated according to my deportment, without reference to my complexion." Frederick Douglass, who was also in Britain at the time, had made similar comments about his treatment during his tour. Perhaps this experience provided for Jacobs, as it did for Douglass, a model for peaceful coexistence replacing the more blatant racism alive throughout America. The experience must have impressed upon her the notion that *Incidents* would appeal to a wide readership in Britain, as she returned many years later to secure a British publishing contract, which sadly proved unsuccessful. Nevertheless, her hope of a British readership was realized when a London edition was issued in 1862. Whether or not Douglass and Jacobs met during the 1840s in England is not known, but the two did meet at the end of the decade in Rochester, New York. Jacobs spent eighteen months working in an anti-slavery reading room and bookshop—run by her brother, John S. Jacobs, who had recently escaped from Norcom—that was housed in the same building as Douglass's abolitionist newspaper, *The North Star*. While living in Rochester, she also made the acquaintance of the abolitionist Amy Post, who along with the example of Douglass, inspired her to write *Incidents*, which was published in the same year the Civil War began. During the war, she returned to her hometown of Edenton, North Carolina, helping the newly freed men and women there. Her commitment to bringing about equality did not end with the Civil War. In the 1880s, she moved to Washington, DC, to help establish the National Association of Colored Women. She died there just three years before the turn of the century.

from Incidents in the Life of a Slave Girl

1

Childhood

I was born a slave; but I never knew it till six years of happy childhood had passed away. My father[1] was a carpenter, and considered so intelligent and skilful in his trade, that, when buildings out of the common line were to be erected, he was sent for from long distances, to be head workman. On condition of paying his mistress two hundred dollars a year, and supporting himself, he was allowed to work at his trade, and manage his own affairs. His strongest wish was to purchase his children; but, though he several times offered his hard earnings for that purpose, he never succeeded. In complexion my parents were a light shade of brownish yellow, and were termed mulattoes. They lived together in a comfortable home; and, though we were all slaves, I was so fondly shielded that I never dreamed I was a piece of merchandise, trusted to them for safe keeping, and liable to be demanded of them at any moment. I had one brother,[2] William, who was two years younger than myself—a bright, affectionate child. I had also a great treasure in my maternal grandmother,[3] who was a remarkable woman in many respects. She was the daughter of a planter in South Carolina, who, at his death, left her mother and his three children free, with money to go to St. Augustine, where they had relatives. It was during the Revolutionary War; and they were captured on their passage, carried back, and sold to different purchasers. Such was the story my grandmother used to tell me; but I do not remember all the particulars. She was a little girl when she was captured and sold to the keeper of a large hotel. I have often heard her tell how hard she fared during childhood.

1. Daniel Jacobs (d. 1826).   2. John S. Jacobs (c. 1815–1875).   3. Molly Horniblow (c. 1771–1853).

But as she grew older she evinced so much intelligence, and was so faithful, that her master and mistress could not help seeing it was for their interest to take care of such a valuable piece of property. She became an indispensable personage in the household, officiating in all capacities, from cook and wet nurse, to seamstress. She was much praised for her cooking; and her nice crackers became so famous in the neighborhood that many people were desirous of obtaining them. In consequence of numerous requests of this kind, she asked permission of her mistress to bake crackers at night, after all the household work was done; and she obtained leave to do it, provided she would clothe herself and her children from the profits. Upon these terms, after working hard all day for her mistress, she began her midnight bakings, assisted by her two oldest children. The business proved profitable; and each year she laid by a little, which was saved for a fund to purchase her children. Her master died, and the property was divided among his heirs. The widow had her dower in the hotel, which she continued to keep open. My grandmother remained in her service as a slave; but her children were divided among her master's children. As she had five, Benjamin, the youngest one, was sold, in order that each heir might have an equal portion of dollars and cents. There was so little difference in our ages that he seemed more like my brother than my uncle. He was a bright, handsome lad, nearly white; for he inherited the complexion my grandmother had derived from Anglo-Saxon ancestors. Though only ten years old, seven hundred and twenty dollars were paid for him. His sale was a terrible blow to my grandmother; but she was naturally hopeful, and she went to work with renewed energy, trusting in time to be able to purchase some of her children. She had laid up three hundred dollars, which her mistress one day begged as a loan, promising to pay her soon. The reader probably knows that no promise or writing given to a slave is legally binding; for, according to Southern laws, a slave, *being* property, can *hold* no property. When my grandmother lent her hard earnings to her mistress, she trusted solely to her honor. The honor of a slaveholder to a slave!

To this good grandmother I was indebted for many comforts. My brother Willie and I often received portions of the crackers, cakes, and preserves, she made to sell; and after we ceased to be children we were indebted to her for many more important services.

Such were the unusually fortunate circumstances of my early childhood. When I was six years old, my mother died; and then, for the first time, I learned, by the talk around me, that I was a slave. My mother's mistress was the daughter of my grandmother's mistress. She was the foster sister of my mother; they were both nourished at my grandmother's breast. In fact, my mother had been weaned at three months old, that the babe of the mistress might obtain sufficient food. They played together as children; and, when they became women, my mother was a most faithful servant to her whiter foster sister. On her death-bed her mistress promised that her children should never suffer for any thing; and during her lifetime she kept her word. They all spoke kindly of my dead mother, who had been a slave merely in name, but in nature was noble and womanly. I grieved for her, and my young mind was troubled with the thought who would now take care of me and my little brother. I was told that my home was now to be with her mistress; and I found it a happy one. No toilsome or disagreeable duties were imposed upon me. My mistress was so kind to me that I was always glad to do her bidding, and proud to labor for her as much as my young years would permit. I would sit by her side for hours, sewing diligently, with a heart as free from care as that of any free-born white child. When she thought I was tired, she would send me out to run and jump; and away I bounded, to gather berries or flowers to decorate her room. Those were happy days—too happy to last. The slave child had no thought for the morrow; but there came that blight, which too surely waits on every human being born to be a chattel.

When I was nearly twelve years old, my kind mistress sickened and died. As I saw the cheek grow paler, and the eye more glassy, how earnestly I prayed in my heart that she might live! I loved her; for she had been almost like a mother to me. My prayers were not answered. She died, and they buried her in the little churchyard, where, day after day, my tears fell upon her grave.

I was sent to spend a week with my grandmother. I was now old enough to begin to think of the future; and again and again I asked myself what they would do with me. I felt sure I should never find another mistress so kind as the one who was gone. She had promised my dying mother that her children should never suffer for any thing; and when I remembered that, and recalled her many proofs of attachment to me, I could not help having some hopes that she had left me free. My friends were almost certain it would be so. They thought she would be sure to do it, on account of my mother's love and faithful service. But, alas! we all know that the memory of a faithful slave does not avail much to save her children from the auction block.

After a brief period of suspense, the will of my mistress was read, and we learned that she had bequeathed me to her sister's daughter, a child of five years old. So vanished our hopes. My mistress had taught me the precepts of God's Word: "Thou shalt love thy neighbor as thyself." "Whatsoever ye would that men should do unto you, do ye even so unto them." But I was her slave, and I suppose she did not recognize me as her neighbor. I would give much to blot out from my memory that one great wrong. As a child, I loved my mistress; and, looking back on the happy days I spent with her, I try to think with less bitterness of this act of injustice. While I was with her, she taught me to read and spell; and for this privilege, which so rarely falls to the lot of a slave, I bless her memory.

She possessed but few slaves; and at her death those were all distributed among her relatives. Five of them were my grandmother's children, and had shared the same milk that nourished her mother's children. Notwithstanding my grandmother's long and faithful service to her owners, not one of her children escaped the auction block. These God-breathing machines are no more, in the sight of their masters, than the cotton they plant, or the horses they tend.

2

The New Master and Mistress

Dr. Flint, a physician in the neighborhood, had married the sister of my mistress, and I was now the property of their little daughter. It was not without murmuring that I prepared for my new home; and what added to my unhappiness, was the fact that my brother William was purchased by the same family. My father, by his nature, as well as by the habit of transacting business as a skilful mechanic, had more of the feelings of a freeman than is common among slaves. My brother was a spirited boy; and being brought up under such influences, he early detested the name of master and mistress. One day, when his father and his mistress both happened to call him at the same time, he hesitated between the two; being perplexed to know which had the strongest claim upon his obedience. He finally concluded to go to his mistress. When my father reproved him for it, he said, "You both called me, and I didn't know which I ought to go to first."

"You are *my* child," replied our father, "and when I call you, you should come immediately, if you have to pass through fire and water."

Poor Willie! He was now to learn his first lesson of obedience to a master. Grandmother tried to cheer us with hopeful words, and they found an echo in the credulous hearts of youth.

When we entered our new home we encountered cold looks, cold words, and cold treatment. We were glad when the night came. On my narrow bed I moaned and wept, I felt so desolate and alone.

I had been there nearly a year, when a dear little friend of mine was buried. I heard her mother sob, as the clods fell on the coffin of her only child, and I turned away from the grave, feeling thankful that I still had something left to love. I met my grandmother, who said, "Come with me, Linda;" and from her tone I knew that something sad had happened. She led me apart from the people, and then said, "My child, your father is dead." Dead! How could I believe it? He had died so suddenly I had not even heard that he was sick. I went home with my grandmother. My heart rebelled against God, who had taken from me mother, father, mistress, and friend. The good grandmother tried to comfort me. "Who knows the ways of God?" said she. "Perhaps they have been kindly taken from the evil days to come." Years afterwards I often thought of this. She promised to be a mother to her grandchildren, so far as she might be permitted to do so; and strengthened by her love, I returned to my master's. I thought I should be allowed to go to my father's house the next morning; but I was ordered to go for flowers, that my mistress's house might be decorated for an evening party. I spent the day gathering flowers and weaving them into festoons, while the dead body of my father was lying within a mile of me. What cared my owners for that? he was merely a piece of property. Moreover, they thought he had spoiled his children, by teaching them to feel that they were human beings. This was blasphemous doctrine for a slave to teach; presumptuous in him, and dangerous to the masters.

The next day I followed his remains to a humble grave beside that of my dear mother. There were those who knew my father's worth, and respected his memory.

My home now seemed more dreary than ever. The laugh of the little slave-children sounded harsh and cruel. It was selfish to feel so about the joy of others. My brother moved about with a very grave face. I tried to comfort him, by saying, "Take courage, Willie; brighter days will come by and by."

"You don't know any thing about it, Linda," he replied. "We shall have to stay here all our days; we shall never be free."

I argued that we were growing older and stronger, and that perhaps we might, before long, be allowed to hire our own time, and then we could earn money to buy our freedom. William declared this was much easier to say than to do; moreover, he did not intend to *buy* his freedom. We held daily controversies upon this subject.

Little attention was paid to the slaves' meals in Dr. Flint's house. If they could catch a bit of food while it was going, well and good. I gave myself no trouble on that score, for on my various errands I passed my grandmother's house, where there was always something to spare for me. I was frequently threatened with punishment if I stopped there; and my grandmother, to avoid detaining me, often stood at the gate with something for my breakfast or dinner. I was indebted to *her* for all my comforts, spiritual or temporal. It was *her* labor that supplied my scanty wardrobe. I have a vivid recollection of the linsey-woolsey dress given me every winter by Mrs. Flint. How I hated it! It was one of the badges of slavery.

While my grandmother was thus helping to support me from her hard earnings, the three hundred dollars she had lent her mistress were never repaid. When her mistress died, her son-in-law, Dr. Flint, was appointed executor. When grandmother applied to him for payment, he said the estate was insolvent, and the law prohibited payment. It did not, however, prohibit him from retaining the silver candelabra, which had been purchased with that money. I presume they will be handed down in the family, from generation to generation.

My grandmother's mistress had always promised her that, at her death, she should be free; and it was said that in her will she made good the promise. But when the estate was settled, Dr. Flint told the faithful old servant that, under existing circumstances, it was necessary she should be sold.

On the appointed day, the customary advertisement was posted up, proclaiming that there would be a "public sale of negroes, horses, &c." Dr. Flint called to tell my grandmother that he was unwilling to wound her feelings by putting her up at auction, and that he would prefer to dispose of her at private sale. My grandmother saw through his hypocrisy; she understood very well that he was ashamed of the job. She was a very spirited woman, and if he was base enough to sell her, when her mistress intended she should be free, she was determined the public should know it. She had for a long time supplied many families with crackers and preserves; consequently, "Aunt Marthy," as she was called, was generally known, and every body who knew her respected her intelligence and good character. Her long and faithful service in the family was also well known, and the intention of her mistress to leave her free. When the day of sale came, she took her place among the chattels, and at the first call she sprang upon the auction-block. Many voices called out, "Shame! Shame! Who is going to sell *you*, aunt Marthy? Don't stand there! That is no place for *you*." Without saying a word, she quietly awaited her fate. No one bid for her. At last, a feeble voice said, "Fifty dollars." It came from a maiden lady, seventy years old, the sister of my grandmother's deceased mistress. She had lived forty years under the same roof with my grandmother; she knew how faithfully she had served her owners, and how cruelly she had been defrauded of her rights; and she resolved to protect her. The auctioneer waited for a higher bid; but her wishes were respected; no one bid above her. She could neither read nor write; and when the bill of sale was made out, she signed it with a cross. But what consequence was that, when she had a big heart overflowing with human kindness? She gave the old servant her freedom.

At that time, my grandmother was just fifty years old. Laborious years had passed since then; and now my brother and I were slaves to the man who had defrauded her of her money, and tried to defraud her of her freedom. One of my mother's sisters, called Aunt Nancy, was also a slave in his family. She was a kind, good aunt to me; and supplied the place of both housekeeper and waiting maid to her mistress. She was, in fact, at the beginning and end of every thing.

Mrs. Flint, like many southern women, was totally deficient in energy. She had not strength to superintend her household affairs; but her nerves were so strong, that she could sit in her easy chair and see a woman whipped, till the blood trickled from every stroke of the lash. She was a member of the church; but partaking of the Lord's supper did not seem to put her in a Christian frame of mind. If dinner was not served at the exact time on that particular Sunday, she would station herself in the kitchen, and wait till it was dished, and then spit in all the kettles and pans that had been used for cooking. She did this to prevent the cook and her children from eking out their meagre fare with the remains of the gravy and other scrapings. The slaves could get nothing to eat except what she chose to give them. Provisions were weighed out by the pound and ounce, three times a day. I can assure you she gave them no chance to eat wheat bread from her flour barrel. She knew how many biscuits a quart of flour would make, and exactly what size they ought to be.

Dr. Flint was an epicure. The cook never sent a dinner to his table without fear and trembling; for if there happened to be a dish not to his liking, he would either order her to be whipped, or compel her to eat every mouthful of it in his presence. The poor, hungry creature might not have objected to eating it; but she did object to having her master cram it down her throat till she choked.

They had a pet dog, that was a nuisance in the house. The cook was ordered to make some Indian mush for him. He refused to eat, and when his head was held over it, the froth flowed from his mouth into the basin. He died a few minutes after. When Dr. Flint came in, he said the mush had not been well cooked, and that was the reason the animal would not eat it. He sent for the cook, and compelled her to eat it. He thought that the woman's stomach was stronger than the dog's; but her sufferings afterwards proved that he was mistaken. This poor woman endured many cruelties from her master and mistress; sometimes she was locked up, away from her nursing baby, for a whole day and night.

When I had been in the family a few weeks, one of the plantation slaves was brought to town, by order of his master. It was near night when he arrived, and Dr. Flint ordered him to be taken to the work house, and tied up to the joist, so that his feet would just escape the ground. In that situation he was to wait till the doctor had taken his tea. I shall never forget that night. Never before, in my life, had I heard hundreds of blows fall, in succession, on a human being. His piteous groans, and his "O, pray don't, massa," rang in my ear for months afterwards. There were many conjectures as to the cause of this terrible punishment. Some said master accused him of stealing corn; others said the slave had quarrelled with his wife, in presence of the overseer, and had accused his master of being the father of her child. They were both black, and the child was very fair.

I went into the work house next morning, and saw the cowhide still wet with blood, and the boards all covered with gore. The poor man lived, and continued to quarrel with his wife. A few months afterwards Dr. Flint handed them both over to a slave-trader. The guilty man put their value into his pocket, and had the satisfaction of knowing that they were out of sight and hearing. When the mother was delivered into the trader's hands, she said, "You *promised* to treat me well." To which he replied, "You have let your tongue run too far; damn you!" She had forgotten that it was a crime for a slave to tell who was the father of her child.

From others than the master persecution also comes in such cases. I once saw a young slave girl dying soon after the birth of a child nearly white. In her agony she cried out, "O Lord, come and take me!" Her mistress stood by, and mocked at her like an incarnate fiend. "You suffer, do you?" she exclaimed. "I am glad of it. You deserve it all, and more too."

The girl's mother said, "The baby is dead, thank God; and I hope my poor child will soon be in heaven, too."

"Heaven!" retorted the mistress. "There is no such place for the like of her and her bastard."

The poor mother turned away, sobbing. Her dying daughter called her, feebly, and as she bent over her, I heard her say, "Don't grieve so, mother; God knows all about it; and he will have mercy upon me."

Her sufferings, afterwards, became so intense, that her mistress felt unable to stay; but when she left the room, the scornful smile was still on her lips. Seven children called her mother. The poor black woman had but the one child, whose eyes she saw closing in death, while she thanked God for taking her away from the greater bitterness of life.

5

The Trials of Girlhood

During the first years of my service in Dr. Flint's family, I was accustomed to share some indulgences with the children of my mistress. Though this seemed to me no more than right, I was grateful for it, and tried to merit the kindness by the faithful discharge of my duties. But I now entered on my fifteenth year—a sad epoch in the life of a slave girl. My master began to whisper foul words in my ear. Young as I was, I could not remain ignorant of their import. I tried to treat them with indifference or contempt. The master's age, my extreme youth, and the fear that his conduct would be reported to my grandmother, made him bear this treatment for many months. He was a crafty man, and resorted to many means to accomplish his purposes. Sometimes he had stormy, terrific ways, that made his victims tremble; sometimes he assumed a gentleness that he thought must surely subdue. Of the two, I preferred his stormy moods, although they left me trembling. He tried his utmost to corrupt the pure principles my grandmother had instilled. He peopled my young mind with unclean images, such as only a vile monster could think of. I turned from him with disgust and hatred. But he was my master. I was compelled to live under the same roof with him—where I saw a man forty years my senior daily violating the most sacred commandments of nature. He told me I was his property; that I must be subject to his will in all things. My soul revolted against the mean tyranny. But where could I turn for protection? No matter whether the slave girl be as black as ebony or as fair as her mistress. In either case, there is no shadow of law to protect her from insult, from violence, or even from death; all these are inflicted by fiends who bear the shape of men. The mistress, who ought to protect the helpless victim, has no other feelings towards her but those of jealousy and rage. The degradation, the wrongs, the vices, that grow out of slavery, are more than I can describe. They are greater than you would willingly believe. Surely, if you credited one half the truths that are told you concerning the helpless millions suffering in this cruel bondage, you at the north would not help to tighten the yoke. You surely would refuse to do for the master, on your own soil, the mean and cruel work which trained bloodhounds and the lowest class of whites do for him at the south.

Every where the years bring to all enough of sin and sorrow; but in slavery the very dawn of life is darkened by these shadows. Even the little child, who is accustomed to wait on her mistress and her children, will learn, before she is twelve years old, why it is that her mistress hates such and such a one among the slaves. Perhaps the child's own mother is among those hated ones. She listens to violent outbreaks of jealous passion, and cannot help understanding what is the cause. She will become prematurely knowing in evil things. Soon she will learn to tremble when she hears her master's footfall. She will be compelled to realize that she is no longer a child. If God has bestowed beauty upon her, it will prove her greatest curse. That which commands admiration in the white woman only hastens the degradation of the female slave. I know that some are too much brutalized by slavery to feel the humiliation of their position; but many slaves feel it most acutely, and shrink from the memory of it. I cannot tell how much I suffered in the presence of these wrongs, nor how I am still pained by the retrospect. My master met me at every turn, reminding me that I belonged to him, and swearing by heaven and earth that he would compel me to submit to him. If I went out for a breath of fresh air, after a day of unwearied toil, his footsteps dogged me. If I knelt by my mother's grave, his dark shadow fell on me even there. The light heart which nature had given me became heavy with sad forebodings. The other slaves in my master's house noticed the change. Many of them pitied me; but none dared to ask the cause. They had no need to inquire. They knew too well the guilty practices under that roof; and they were aware that to speak of them was an offence that never went unpunished.

I longed for some one to confide in. I would have given the world to have laid my head on my grandmother's faithful bosom, and told her all my troubles. But Dr. Flint swore he would kill me, if I was not as silent as the grave. Then, although my grandmother was all in all to me, I feared her as well as loved her. I had been accustomed to look up to her with a respect bordering upon awe. I was very young, and felt shamefaced about telling her such impure things, especially as I knew her to be very strict on such subjects. Moreover, she was a woman of a high spirit. She was usually very quiet in her demeanor; but if her indignation was once roused, it was not very easily quelled. I had been told that she once chased a white gentleman with a loaded pistol, because he insulted one of her daughters. I dreaded the consequences of a violent outbreak; and both pride and fear kept me silent. But though I did not confide in my grandmother, and even evaded her vigilant watchfulness and inquiry, her presence in the neighborhood was some protection to me. Though she had been a slave, Dr. Flint was afraid of her. He dreaded her scorching rebukes. Moreover, she was known and patronized by many people; and he did not wish to have his villany made public. It was lucky for me that I did not live on a distant plantation, but in a town not so large that the inhabitants were ignorant of each other's affairs. Bad as are the laws and customs in a slaveholding community, the doctor, as a professional man, deemed it prudent to keep up some outward show of decency.

O, what days and nights of fear and sorrow that man caused me! Reader, it is not to awaken sympathy for myself that I am telling you truthfully what I suffered in slavery. I do it to kindle a flame of compassion in your hearts for my sisters who are still in bondage, suffering as I once suffered.

I once saw two beautiful children playing together. One was a fair white child; the other was her slave, and also her sister. When I saw them embracing each other, and heard their joyous laughter, I turned sadly away from the lovely sight. I foresaw the inevitable blight that would fall on the little slave's heart. I knew how soon her laughter would be changed to sighs. The fair child grew up to be a still fairer woman. From childhood to womanhood her pathway was blooming with flowers, and over-arched by a sunny sky. Scarcely one day of her life had been clouded when the sun rose on her happy bridal morning.

How had those years dealt with her slave sister, the little playmate of her childhood? She, also, was very beautiful; but the flowers and sunshine of love were not for her. She drank the cup of sin, and shame, and misery, whereof her persecuted race are compelled to drink.

In view of these things, why are ye silent, ye free men and women of the north? Why do your tongues falter in maintenance of the right? Would that I had more ability! But my heart is so full, and my pen is so weak! There are noble men and women who plead for us, striving to help those who cannot help themselves. God bless them! God give them strength and courage to go on! God bless those, every where, who are laboring to advance the cause of humanity!

6

The Jealous Mistress

I would ten thousand times rather that my children should be the half-starved paupers of Ireland than to be the most pampered among the slaves of America. I would rather drudge out my life on a cotton plantation, till the grave opened to give me rest, than to live with an unprincipled master and a jealous mistress. The felon's home in a penitentiary is preferable. He may repent, and turn from the error of his ways, and so find peace; but it is not so with a favorite slave. She is not allowed to have any pride of character. It is deemed a crime in her to wish to be virtuous.

Mrs. Flint possessed the key to her husband's character before I was born. She might have used this knowledge to counsel and to screen the young and the innocent among her slaves; but for them she had no sympathy. They were the objects of her constant suspicion and malevolence. She watched her husband with unceasing vigilance; but he was well practised in means to evade it. What he could not find opportunity to say in words he manifested in signs. He invented more than were ever thought of in a deaf and dumb asylum. I let them pass, as if I did not understand what he meant; and many were the curses and threats bestowed on me for my stupidity. One day he caught me teaching myself to write. He frowned, as if he was not well pleased; but I suppose he came to the conclusion that such an accomplishment might help to advance his favorite scheme. Before long, notes were often slipped into my hand. I would return them, saying, "I can't read them, sir." "Can't you?" he replied; "then I must read them to you." He always finished the reading by asking, "Do you understand?" Sometimes he would complain of the heat of the tea room, and order his supper to be placed on a small table in the piazza. He would seat himself there with a well-satisfied smile, and tell me to stand by and brush away the flies. He would eat very slowly, pausing between the mouthfuls. These intervals were employed in describing the happiness I was so foolishly throwing away, and in threatening me with the penalty that finally awaited my stubborn disobedience. He boasted much of the forbearance he had exercised towards me, and reminded me that there was a limit to his patience. When I succeeded in avoiding opportunities for him to talk to me at home, I was ordered to come to his office, to do some errand. When there, I was obliged to stand and listen to such language as he saw fit to address to me. Sometimes I so openly expressed my contempt for him that he would become violently enraged, and I wondered why he did not strike me. Circumstanced as he was, he probably thought it was better policy to be forbearing. But the state of things grew worse and worse daily. In desperation I told him that I must and would apply to my grandmother for protection. He threatened me with death, and worse than death, if I made any complaint to her. Strange to say, I did not despair. I was naturally of a buoyant disposition, and always I had a hope of somehow getting out of his clutches. Like many a poor, simple slave before me, I trusted that some threads of joy would yet be woven into my dark destiny.

I had entered my sixteenth year, and every day it became more apparent that my presence was intolerable to Mrs. Flint. Angry words frequently passed between her and her husband. He had never punished me himself, and he would not allow any body else to punish me. In that respect, she was never satisfied; but, in her angry moods, no terms were too vile for her to bestow upon me. Yet I, whom she detested so bitterly, had far more pity for her than he had, whose duty it was to make her life happy. I never wronged her, or wished to wrong her, and one word of kindness from her would have brought me to her feet.

After repeated quarrels between the doctor and his wife, he announced his intention to take his youngest daughter, then four years old, to sleep in his apartment. It was necessary that a servant should sleep in the same room, to be on hand if the child stirred. I was selected for that office, and informed for what purpose that arrangement had been made. By managing to keep within sight of people, as much as possible, during the day time, I had hitherto succeeded in eluding my master, though a razor was often held to my throat to force me to change this line of policy. At night I slept by the side of my great aunt, where I felt safe. He was too prudent to come into her room. She was an old woman, and had been in the family many years. Moreover, as a married man, and a professional man, he deemed it necessary to save appearances in some degree. But he resolved to remove the obstacle in the way of his scheme; and he thought he had planned it so that he should evade suspicion. He was well aware how much I prized my refuge by the side of my old aunt, and he determined to dispossess me of it. The first night the doctor had the little child in his room alone. The next morning, I was ordered to take my station as nurse the following night. A kind Providence interposed in my favor. During the day Mrs. Flint heard of this new arrangement, and a storm followed. I rejoiced to hear it rage.

After a while my mistress sent for me to come to her room. Her first question was, "Did you know you were to sleep in the doctor's room?"

"Yes, ma'am."

"Who told you?"

"My master."

"Will you answer truly all the questions I ask?"

"Yes, ma'am."

"Tell me, then, as you hope to be forgiven, are you innocent of what I have accused you?"

"I am."

She handed me a Bible, and said, "Lay your hand on your heart, kiss this holy book, and swear before God that you tell me the truth."

I took the oath she required, and I did it with a clear conscience.

"You have taken God's holy word to testify your innocence," said she. "If you have deceived me, beware! Now take this stool, sit down, look me directly in the face, and tell me all that has passed between your master and you."

I did as she ordered. As I went on with my account her color changed frequently, she wept, and sometimes groaned. She spoke in tones so sad, that I was touched by her grief. The tears came to my eyes; but I was soon convinced that her emotions arose from anger and wounded pride. She felt that her marriage vows were desecrated, her dignity insulted; but she had no compassion for the poor victim of her husband's perfidy. She pitied herself as a martyr; but she was incapable of feeling for the condition of shame and misery in which her unfortunate, helpless slave was placed.

Yet perhaps she had some touch of feeling for me; for when the conference was ended, she spoke kindly, and promised to protect me. I should have been much comforted by this assurance if I could have had confidence in it; but my experiences in slavery had filled me with distrust. She was not a very refined woman, and had not much control over her passions. I was an object of her jealousy, and, consequently, of her hatred; and I knew I could not expect kindness or confidence from her under the circumstances in which I was placed. I could not blame her. Slaveholders' wives feel as other women would under similar circumstances. The fire of her temper kindled from small sparks, and now the flame became so intense that the doctor was obliged to give up his intended arrangement.

I knew I had ignited the torch, and I expected to suffer for it afterwards; but I felt too thankful to my mistress for the timely aid she rendered me to care much about that. She now took me to sleep in a room adjoining her own. There I was an object of her especial care, though not of her especial comfort, for she spent many a sleepless night to watch over me. Sometimes I woke up, and found her bending over me. At other times she whispered in my ear, as though it was her husband who was speaking to me, and listened to hear what I would answer. If she startled me, on such occasions, she would glide stealthily away; and the next morning she would tell me I had been talking in my sleep, and ask who I was talking to. At last, I began to be fearful for my life. It had been often threatened; and you can imagine, better than I can describe, what an unpleasant sensation it must produce to wake up in the dead of night and find a jealous woman bending over you. Terrible as this experience was, I had fears that it would give place to one more terrible.

My mistress grew weary of her vigils; they did not prove satisfactory. She changed her tactics. She now tried the trick of accusing my master of crime, in my presence, and gave my name as the author of the accusation. To my utter astonishment, he replied, "I don't believe it; but if she did acknowledge it, you tortured her into exposing me." Tortured into exposing him! Truly, Satan had no difficulty in distinguishing the color of his soul! I understood his object in making this false representation. It was to show me that I gained nothing by seeking the protection of my mistress; that the power was still all in his own hands. I pitied Mrs. Flint. She was a second wife, many years the junior of her husband; and the hoary-headed miscreant was enough to try the patience of a wiser and better woman. She was completely foiled, and knew not how to proceed. She would gladly have had me flogged for my supposed false oath; but, as I have already stated, the doctor never allowed any one to whip me. The old sinner was politic. The application of the lash might have led to remarks that would have exposed him in the eyes of his children and grandchildren. How often did I rejoice that I lived in a town where all the inhabitants knew each other! If I had been on a remote plantation, or lost among the multitude of a crowded city, I should not be a living woman at this day.

The secrets of slavery are concealed like those of the Inquisition.[4] My master was, to my knowledge, the father of eleven slaves. But did the mothers dare to tell who was the father of their children? Did the other slaves dare to allude to it, except in whispers among themselves? No, indeed! They knew too well the terrible consequences.

My grandmother could not avoid seeing things which excited her suspicions. She was uneasy about me, and tried various ways to buy me; but the never-changing answer was always repeated: "Linda does not belong to *me*. She is my daughter's property, and I have no legal right to sell her." The conscientious man! He was too scrupulous to *sell* me; but he had no scruples whatever about committing a much greater wrong against the helpless young girl placed under his guardianship, as his daughter's property. Sometimes my persecutor would ask me whether I would like to be sold. I told him I would rather be sold to any body than to lead such a life as I did. On such occasions he would assume the air of a very injured individual, and reproach me for my ingratitude. "Did I not take you into the house, and make you the companion of my own children?" he would say. "Have I ever treated you like a negro? I have never allowed you to be punished, not even to please your mistress. And this is the recompense I get, you ungrateful girl!" I answered that he had reasons of his own for screening me from punishment, and that the course he pursued made my mistress hate me and persecute me. If I wept, he would say, "Poor child! Don't cry! don't cry! I will make peace for you with your mistress. Only let me arrange matters in my own way. Poor, foolish girl! you don't know what is for your own good. I would cherish you. I would make a lady of you. Now go, and think of all I have promised you."

I did think of it.

Reader, I draw no imaginary pictures of southern homes. I am telling you the plain truth. Yet when victims make their escape from this wild beast of Slavery, northerners consent to act the part of bloodhounds, and hunt the poor fugitive back into his den, "full of dead men's bones, and all uncleanness."[5] Nay, more, they are not only willing, but proud, to give their daughters in marriage to slave-holders. The poor girls have romantic notions of a sunny clime, and of the flowering vines that all the year round shade a happy home. To what disappointments are they destined! The young wife soon learns that the husband in whose hands she has placed her happiness pays no regard to his marriage vows. Children of every shade of complexion play with her own fair babies, and too well she knows that they are born unto him of his own household. Jealousy and hatred enter the flowery home, and it is ravaged of its loveliness.

Southern women often marry a man knowing that he is the father of many little slaves. They do not trouble themselves about it. They regard such children as property, as marketable as the pigs on the plantation; and it is seldom that they do not

4. Catholic tribunal that punished heresy.   5. Matthew 23.27.

make them aware of this by passing them into the slavetrader's hands as soon as possible, and thus getting them out of their sight. I am glad to say there are some honorable exceptions.

I have myself known two southern wives who exhorted their husbands to free those slaves towards whom they stood in a "parental relation;" and their request was granted. These husbands blushed before the superior nobleness of their wives' natures. Though they had only counselled them to do that which it was their duty to do, it commanded their respect, and rendered their conduct more exemplary. Concealment was at an end, and confidence took the place of distrust.

Though this bad institution deadens the moral sense, even in white women, to a fearful extent, it is not altogether extinct. I have heard southern ladies say of Mr. Such a one, "He not only thinks it no disgrace to be the father of those little niggers, but he is not ashamed to call himself their master. I declare, such things ought not to be tolerated in any decent society!"

10

A Perilous Passage in the Slave Girl's Life

After my lover[6] went away, Dr. Flint contrived a new plan. He seemed to have an idea that my fear of my mistress was his greatest obstacle. In the blandest tones, he told me that he was going to build a small house for me, in a secluded place, four miles away from the town. I shuddered; but I was constrained to listen, while he talked of his intention to give me a home of my own, and to make a lady of me. Hitherto, I had escaped my dreaded fate, by being in the midst of people. My grandmother had already had high words with my master about me. She had told him pretty plainly what she thought of his character, and there was considerable gossip in the neighborhood about our affairs, to which the open-mouthed jealousy of Mrs. Flint contributed not a little. When my master said he was going to build a house for me, and that he could do it with little trouble and expense, I was in hopes something would happen to frustrate his scheme; but I soon heard that the house was actually begun. I vowed before my Maker that I would never enter it. I had rather toil on the plantation from dawn till dark; I had rather live and die in jail, than drag on, from day to day, through such a living death. I was determined that the master, whom I so hated and loathed, who had blighted the prospects of my youth, and made my life a desert, should not, after my long struggle with him, succeed at last in trampling his victim under his feet. I would do any thing, every thing, for the sake of defeating him. What *could* I do? I thought and thought, till I became desperate, and made a plunge into the abyss.

And now, reader, I come to a period in my unhappy life, which I would gladly forget if I could. The remembrance fills me with sorrow and shame. It pains me to tell you of it; but I have promised to tell you the truth, and I will do it honestly, let it cost me what it may. I will not try to screen myself behind the plea of compulsion from a master; for it was not so. Neither can I plead ignorance or thoughtlessness. For years, my master had done his utmost to pollute my mind with foul images, and to destroy the pure principles inculcated by my grandmother, and the

---

6. Linda Brent has fallen in love with a free black man, but Dr. Flint has forbidden their marriage.

good mistress of my childhood. The influences of slavery had had the same effect on me that they had on other young girls; they had made me prematurely knowing, concerning the evil ways of the world. I knew what I did, and I did it with deliberate calculation.

But, O, ye happy women, whose purity has been sheltered from childhood, who have been free to choose the objects of your affection, whose homes are protected by law, do not judge the poor desolate slave girl too severely! If slavery had been abolished, I, also, could have married the man of my choice; I could have had a home shielded by the laws; and I should have been spared the painful task of confessing what I am now about to relate; but all my prospects had been blighted by slavery. I wanted to keep myself pure; and, under the most adverse circumstances, I tried hard to preserve my self-respect; but I was struggling alone in the powerful grasp of the demon Slavery; and the monster proved too strong for me. I felt as if I was forsaken by God and man; as if all my efforts must be frustrated; and I became reckless in my despair.

I have told you that Dr. Flint's persecutions and his wife's jealousy had given rise to some gossip in the neighborhood. Among others, it chanced that a white unmarried gentleman had obtained some knowledge of the circumstances in which I was placed. He knew my grandmother, and often spoke to me in the street. He became interested for me, and asked questions about my master, which I answered in part. He expressed a great deal of sympathy, and a wish to aid me. He constantly sought opportunities to see me, and wrote to me frequently. I was a poor slave girl, only fifteen years old.

So much attention from a superior person was, of course, flattering; for human nature is the same in all. I also felt grateful for his sympathy, and encouraged by his kind words. It seemed to me a great thing to have such a friend. By degrees, a more tender feeling crept into my heart. He was an educated and eloquent gentleman; too eloquent, alas, for the poor slave girl who trusted in him. Of course I saw whither all this was tending. I knew the impassable gulf between us; but to be an object of interest to a man who is not married, and who is not her master, is agreeable to the pride and feelings of a slave, if her miserable situation has left her any pride or sentiment. It seems less degrading to give one's self, than to submit to compulsion. There is something akin to freedom in having a lover who has no control over you, except that which he gains by kindness and attachment. A master may treat you as rudely as he pleases, and you dare not speak; moreover, the wrong does not seem so great with an unmarried man, as with one who has a wife to be made unhappy. There may be sophistry in all this; but the condition of a slave confuses all principles of morality, and, in fact, renders the practice of them impossible.

When I found that my master had actually begun to build the lonely cottage, other feelings mixed with those I have described. Revenge, and calculations of interest, were added to flattered vanity and sincere gratitude for kindness. I knew nothing would enrage Dr. Flint so much as to know that I favored another; and it was something to triumph over my tyrant even in that small way. I thought he would revenge himself by selling me, and I was sure my friend, Mr. Sands, would buy me. He was a man of more generosity and feeling than my master, and I thought my freedom could be easily obtained from him. The crisis of my fate now came so near that I was desperate. I shuddered to think of being the mother of children that should be owned by my old tyrant. I knew that as soon as a new fancy took him, his victims were sold far off to get rid of them; especially if they had children. I had seen several women sold, with his babies at the breast. He never allowed his offspring by slaves to remain long in sight of himself and his wife. Of a man who was not my master I could ask to have my children well supported; and in this case, I felt confident I should obtain the boon. I also felt quite sure that they would be made free. With all these thoughts revolving in my mind, and seeing no other way of escaping the doom I so much dreaded, I made a headlong plunge. Pity me, and pardon me, O virtuous reader! You never knew what it is to be a slave; to be entirely unprotected by law or custom; to have the laws reduce you to the condition of a chattel, entirely subject to the will of another. You never exhausted your ingenuity in avoiding the snares, and eluding the power of a hated tyrant; you never shuddered at the sound of his footsteps, and trembled within hearing of his voice. I know I did wrong. No one can feel it more sensibly than I do. The painful and humiliating memory will haunt me to my dying day. Still, in looking back, calmly, on the events of my life, I feel that the slave woman ought not to be judged by the same standard as others.

The months passed on. I had many unhappy hours. I secretly mourned over the sorrow I was bringing on my grandmother, who had so tried to shield me from harm. I knew that I was the greatest comfort of her old age, and that it was a source of pride to her that I had not degraded myself, like most of the slaves. I wanted to confess to her that I was no longer worthy of her love; but I could not utter the dreaded words.

As for Dr. Flint, I had a feeling of satisfaction and triumph in the thought of telling *him*. From time to time he told me of his intended arrangements, and I was silent. At last, he came and told me the cottage was completed, and ordered me to go to it. I told him I would never enter it. He said, "I have heard enough of such talk as that. You shall go, if you are carried by force; and you shall remain there."

I replied, "I will never go there. In a few months I shall be a mother."

He stood and looked at me in dumb amazement, and left the house without a word. I thought I should be happy in my triumph over him. But now that the truth was out, and my relatives would hear of it, I felt wretched. Humble as were their circumstances, they had pride in my good character. Now, how could I look them in the face? My self-respect was gone! I had resolved that I would be virtuous, though I was a slave. I had said, "Let the storm beat! I will brave it till I die." And now, how humiliated I felt!

I went to my grandmother. My lips moved to make confession, but the words stuck in my throat. I sat down in the shade of a tree at her door and began to sew. I think she saw something unusual was the matter with me. The mother of slaves is very watchful. She knows there is no security for her children. After they have entered their teens she lives in daily expectation of trouble. This leads to many questions. If the girl is of a sensitive nature, timidity keeps her from answering truthfully, and this well-meant course has a tendency to drive her from maternal counsels. Presently, in came my mistress, like a mad woman, and accused me concerning her husband. My grandmother, whose suspicions had been previously awakened, believed what she said. She exclaimed, "O Linda! has it come to this? I had rather see you dead than to see you as you now are. You are a disgrace to your dead mother." She tore from my fingers my mother's wedding ring and her silver thimble.

"Go away!" she exclaimed, "and never come to my house, again." Her reproaches fell so hot and heavy, that they left me no chance to answer. Bitter tears, such as the eyes never shed but once, were my only answer. I rose from my seat, but fell back again, sobbing. She did not speak to me; but the tears were running down her furrowed cheeks, and they scorched me like fire. She had always been so kind to me! So kind! How I longed to throw myself at her feet, and tell her all the truth! But she had ordered me to go, and never to come there again. After a few minutes, I mustered strength, and started to obey her. With what feelings did I now close that little gate, which I used to open with such an eager hand in my childhood! It closed upon me with a sound I never heard before.

Where could I go? I was afraid to return to my master's. I walked on recklessly, not caring where I went, or what would become of me. When I had gone four or five miles, fatigue compelled me to stop. I sat down on the stump of an old tree. The stars were shining through the boughs above me. How they mocked me, with their bright, calm light! The hours passed by, and as I sat there alone a chilliness and deadly sickness came over me. I sank on the ground. My mind was full of horrid thoughts. I prayed to die; but the prayer was not answered. At last, with great effort I roused myself, and walked some distance further, to the house of a woman who had been a friend of my mother. When I told her why I was there, she spoke soothingly to me; but I could not be comforted. I thought I could bear my shame if I could only be reconciled to my grandmother. I longed to open my heart to her. I thought if she could know the real state of the case, and all I had been bearing for years, she would perhaps judge me less harshly. My friend advised me to send for her. I did so; but days of agonizing suspense passed before she came. Had she utterly forsaken me? No. She came at last. I knelt before her, and told her the things that had poisoned my life; how long I had been persecuted; that I saw no way of escape; and in an hour of extremity I had become desperate. She listened in silence. I told her I would bear any thing and do any thing, if in time I had hopes of obtaining her forgiveness. I begged of her to pity me, for my dead mother's sake. And she did pity me. She did not say, "I forgive you;" but she looked at me lovingly, with her eyes full of tears. She laid her old hand gently on my head, and murmured, "Poor child! Poor child!"

17

The Flight

Mr. Flint[7] was hard pushed for house servants, and rather than lose me he had restrained his malice. I did my work faithfully, though not, of course, with a willing mind. They were evidently afraid I should leave them. Mr. Flint wished that I should sleep in the great house instead of the servants' quarters. His wife agreed to the proposition, but said I mustn't bring my bed into the house, because it would scatter feathers on her carpet. I knew when I went there that they would never think of such a thing as furnishing a bed of any kind for me and my little one. I therefore carried my own bed, and now I was forbidden to use it. I did as I was ordered. But now that I was certain my children were to be put in their power, in order to give them a stronger

---

7. As punishment, Brent has been sent to a plantation run by Dr. Flint's son.

hold on me, I resolved to leave them that night. I remembered the grief this step would bring upon my dear old grandmother; and nothing less than the freedom of my children would have induced me to disregard her advice. I went about my evening work with trembling steps. Mr. Flint twice called from his chamber door to inquire why the house was not locked up. I replied that I had not done my work. "You have had time enough to do it," said he. "Take care how you answer me!"

I shut all the windows, locked all the doors, and went up to the third story, to wait till midnight. How long those hours seemed, and how fervently I prayed that God would not forsake me in this hour of utmost need! I was about to risk every thing on the throw of a die; and if I failed, O what would become of me and my poor children? They would be made to suffer for my fault.

At half past twelve I stole softly down stairs. I stopped on the second floor, thinking I heard a noise. I felt my way down into the parlor, and looked out of the window. The night was so intensely dark that I could see nothing. I raised the window very softly and jumped out. Large drops of rain were falling, and the darkness bewildered me. I dropped on my knees, and breathed a short prayer to God for guidance and protection. I groped my way to the road, and rushed towards the town with almost lightning speed. I arrived at my grandmother's house, but dared not see her. She would say, "Linda, you are killing me;" and I knew that would unnerve me. I tapped softly at the window of a room, occupied by a woman, who had lived in the house several years. I knew she was a faithful friend, and could be trusted with my secret. I tapped several times before she heard me. At last she raised the window, and I whispered, "Sally, I have run away. Let me in, quick." She opened the door softly, and said in low tones, "For God's sake, don't. Your grandmother is trying to buy you and de chillern. Mr. Sands was here last week. He tole her he was going away on business, but he wanted her to go ahead about buying you and de chillren, and he would help her all he could. Don't run away, Linda. Your grandmother is all bowed down wid trouble now."

I replied, "Sally, they are going to carry my children to the plantation to-morrow; and they will never sell them to any body so long as they have me in their power. Now, would you advise me to go back?"

"No, chile, no," answered she. "When dey finds you is gone, dey won't want de plague ob de chillern; but where is you going to hide? Dey knows ebery inch ob dis house."

I told her I had a hiding-place, and that was all it was best for her to know. I asked her to go into my room as soon as it was light, and take all my clothes out of my trunk, and pack them in hers; for I knew Mr. Flint and the constable would be there early to search my room. I feared the sight of my children would be too much for my full heart; but I could not go out into the uncertain future without one last look. I bent over the bed where lay my little Benny and baby Ellen.[8] Poor little ones! fatherless and motherless! Memories of their father came over me. He wanted to be kind to them; but they were not all to him, as they were to my womanly heart. I knelt and prayed for the innocent little sleepers. I kissed them lightly, and turned away.

As I was about to open the street door, Sally laid her hand on my shoulder, and said, "Linda, is you gwine all alone? Let me call your uncle."

---

8. Brent has given birth to a daughter and a son, both the children of Mr. Sands.

"No, Sally," I replied, "I want no one to be brought into trouble on my account."

I went forth into the darkness and rain. I ran on till I came to the house of the friend who was to conceal me.

Early the next morning Mr. Flint was at my grandmother's inquiring for me. She told him she had not seen me, and supposed I was at the plantation. He watched her face narrowly, and said, "Don't you know any thing about her running off?" She assured him that she did not. He went on to say, "Last night she ran off without the least provocation. We had treated her very kindly. My wife liked her. She will soon be found and brought back. Are her children with you?" When told that they were, he said, "I am very glad to hear that. If they are here, she cannot be far off. If I find out that any of my niggers have had any thing to do with this damned business, I'll give 'em five hundred lashes." As he started to go to his father's, he turned round and added, persuasively, "Let her be brought back, and she shall have her children to live with her."

The tidings made the old doctor rave and storm at a furious rate. It was a busy day for them. My grandmother's house was searched from top to bottom. As my trunk was empty, they concluded I had taken my clothes with me. Before ten o'clock every vessel northward bound was thoroughly examined, and the law against harboring fugitives was read to all on board. At night a watch was set over the town. Knowing how distressed my grandmother would be, I wanted to send her a message; but it could not be done. Every one who went in or out of her house was closely watched. The doctor said he would take my children, unless she became responsible for them; which of course she willingly did. The next day was spent in searching. Before night, the following advertisement was posted at every corner, and in every public place for miles round:—

> $300 REWARD! Ran away from the subscriber, an intelligent, bright, mulatto girl, named Linda, 21 years of age. Five feet four inches high. Dark eyes, and black hair inclined to curl; but it can be made straight. Has a decayed spot on a front tooth. She can read and write, and in all probability will try to get to the Free States. All persons are forbidden, under penalty of the law, to harbor or employ said slave. $150 will be given to whoever takes her in the state, and $300 if taken out of the state and delivered to me, or lodged in jail.
>
> Dr. Flint.

39

The Confession[9]

For two years my daughter and I supported ourselves comfortably in Boston. At the end of that time, my brother William offered to send Ellen to a boarding school. It required a great effort for me to consent to part with her, for I had few near ties, and it was her presence that made my two little rooms seem home-like. But my judgment

---

9. After spending seven years concealed in her grandmother's attic, Brent has escaped to the north, where she works as a domestic, and has been joined by her daughter.

prevailed over my selfish feelings. I made preparations for her departure. During the two years we had lived together I had often resolved to tell her something about her father; but I had never been able to muster sufficient courage. I had a shrinking dread of diminishing my child's love. I knew she must have curiosity on the subject, but she had never asked a question. She was always very careful not to say any thing to remind me of my troubles. Now that she was going from me, I thought if I should die before she returned, she might hear my story from some one who did not understand the palliating circumstances; and that if she were entirely ignorant on the subject, her sensitive nature might receive a rude shock.

When we retired for the night, she said, "Mother, it is very hard to leave you alone. I am almost sorry I am going, though I do want to improve myself. But you will write to me often; won't you, mother?"

I did not throw my arms round her. I did not answer her. But in a calm, solemn way, for it cost me great effort, I said, "Listen to me, Ellen; I have something to tell you!" I recounted my early sufferings in slavery, and told her how nearly they had crushed me. I began to tell her how they had driven me into a great sin, when she clasped me in her arms, and exclaimed, "O, don't, mother! Please don't tell me any more."

I said, "But, my child, I want you to know about your father."

"I know all about it, mother," she replied; "I am nothing to my father, and he is nothing to me. All my love is for you. I was with him five months in Washington, and he never cared for me. He never spoke to me as he did to his little Fanny. I knew all the time he was my father, for Fanny's nurse told me so; but she said I must never tell any body, and I never did. I used to wish he would take me in his arms and kiss me, as he did Fanny; or that he would sometimes smile at me, as he did at her. I thought if he was my own father, he ought to love me. I was a little girl then, and didn't know any better. But now I never think any thing about my father. All my love is for you." She hugged me closer as she spoke, and I thanked God that the knowledge I had so much dreaded to impart had not diminished the affection of my child. I had not the slightest idea she knew that portion of my history. If I had, I should have spoken to her long before; for my pent-up feelings had often longed to pour themselves out to some one I could trust. But I loved the dear girl better for the delicacy she had manifested towards her unfortunate mother.

The next morning, she and her uncle started on their journey to the village in New York, where she was to be placed at school. It seemed as if all the sunshine had gone away. My little room was dreadfully lonely. I was thankful when a message came from a lady, accustomed to employ me, requesting me to come and sew in her family for several weeks. On my return, I found a letter from brother William. He thought of opening an anti-slavery reading room in Rochester, and combining with it the sale of some books and stationery; and he wanted me to unite with him. We tried it, but it was not successful. We found warm anti-slavery friends there, but the feeling was not general enough to support such an establishment. I passed nearly a year in the family of Isaac and Amy Post, practical believers in the Christian doctrine of human brotherhood. They measured a man's worth by his character, not by his complexion. The memory of those beloved and honored friends will remain with me to my latest hour.

41

Free at Last

Mrs. Bruce,[10] and every member of her family, were exceedingly kind to me. I was thankful for the blessings of my lot, yet I could not always wear a cheerful countenance. I was doing harm to no one; on the contrary, I was doing all the good I could in my small way; yet I could never go out to breathe God's free air without trepidation at my heart. This seemed hard; and I could not think it was a right state of things in any civilized country.

From time to time I received news from my good old grandmother. She could not write; but she employed others to write for her. The following is an extract from one of her last letters:—

> "Dear Daughter: I cannot hope to see you again on earth; but I pray to God to unite us above, where pain will no more rack this feeble body of mine; where sorrow and parting from my children will be no more.[11] God has promised these things if we are faithful unto the end. My age and feeble health deprive me of going to church now; but God is with me here at home. Thank your brother for his kindness. Give much love to him, and tell him to remember the Creator in the days of his youth,[12] and strive to meet me in the Father's kingdom. Love to Ellen and Benjamin. Don't neglect him. Tell him for me, to be a good boy. Strive, my child; to train them for God's children. May he protect and provide for you, is the prayer of your loving old mother."

These letters both cheered and saddened me. I was always glad to have tidings from the kind, faithful old friend of my unhappy youth; but her messages of love made my heart yearn to see her before she died, and I mourned over the fact that it was impossible. Some months after I returned from my flight to New England, I received a letter from her, in which she wrote, "Dr. Flint is dead. He has left a distressed family. Poor old man! I hope he made his peace with God."

I remembered how he had defrauded my grandmother of the hard earnings she had loaned; how he had tried to cheat her out of the freedom her mistress had promised her, and how he had persecuted her children; and I thought to myself that she was a better Christian than I was, if she could entirely forgive him. I cannot say, with truth, that the news of my old master's death softened my feelings towards him. There are wrongs which even the grave does not bury. The man was odious to me while he lived, and his memory is odious now.

His departure from this world did not diminish my danger. He had threatened my grandmother that his heirs should hold me in slavery after he was gone; that I never should be free so long as a child of his survived. As for Mrs. Flint, I had seen her in deeper afflictions than I supposed the loss of her husband would be, for she had buried several children; yet I never saw any signs of softening in her heart. The doctor had died in embarrassed circumstances, and had little to will to his heirs, except such property as he was unable to grasp. I was well aware what I had to expect from

10. Brent's employer.   11. Revelation 21.4.   12. Ecclesiastes 12.1.

the family of Flints; and my fears were confirmed by a letter from the south, warning me to be on my guard, because Mrs. Flint openly declared that her daughter could not afford to lose so valuable a slave as I was.

I kept close watch of the newspapers for arrivals; but one Saturday night, being much occupied, I forgot to examine the Evening Express as usual. I went down into the parlor for it, early in the morning, and found the boy about to kindle a fire with it. I took it from him and examined the list of arrivals. Reader, if you have never been a slave, you cannot imagine the acute sensation of suffering at my heart, when I read the names of Mr. and Mrs. Dodge,[13] at a hotel in Courtland Street. It was a third-rate hotel, and that circumstance convinced me of the truth of what I had heard, that they were short of funds and had need of my value, as *they* valued me; and that was by dollars and cents. I hastened with the paper to Mrs. Bruce. Her heart and hand were always open to every one in distress, and she always warmly sympathized with mine. It was impossible to tell how near the enemy was. He might have passed and repassed the house while we were sleeping. He might at that moment be waiting to pounce upon me if I ventured out of doors. I had never seen the husband of my young mistress, and therefore I could not distinguish him from any other stranger. A carriage was hastily ordered; and, closely veiled, I followed Mrs. Bruce, taking the baby again with me into exile. After various turnings and crossings, and returnings, the carriage stopped at the house of one of Mrs. Bruce's friends, where I was kindly received. Mrs. Bruce returned immediately, to instruct the domestics what to say if any one came to inquire for me.

It was lucky for me that the evening paper was not burned up before I had a chance to examine the list of arrivals. It was not long after Mrs. Bruce's return to her house, before several people came to inquire for me. One inquired for me, another asked for my daughter Ellen, and another said he had a letter from my grandmother, which he was requested to deliver in person.

They were told, "She *has* lived here, but she has left."

"How long ago?"

"I don't know, sir."

"Do you know where she went?"

"I do not, sir." And the door was closed.

This Mr. Dodge, who claimed me as his property, was originally a Yankee pedler in the south; then he became a merchant, and finally a slaveholder. He managed to get introduced into what was called the first society, and married Miss Emily Flint. A quarrel arose between him and her brother, and the brother cowhided him. This led to a family feud, and he proposed to remove to Virginia. Dr. Flint left him no property, and his own means had become circumscribed, while a wife and children depended upon him for support. Under these circumstances, it was very natural that he should make an effort to put me into his pocket.

I had a colored friend, a man from my native place, in whom I had the most implicit confidence. I sent for him, and told him that Mr. and Mrs. Dodge had arrived in New York. I proposed that he should call upon them to make inquiries

---

13. Brent's former mistress and her husband.

about his friends at the south, with whom Dr. Flint's family were well acquainted. He thought there was no impropriety in his doing so, and he consented. He went to the hotel, and knocked at the door of Mr. Dodge's room, which was opened by the gentleman himself, who gruffly inquired, "What brought you here? How came you to know I was in the city?"

"Your arrival was published in the evening papers, sir; and I called to ask Mrs. Dodge about my friends at home. I didn't suppose it would give any offence."

"Where's that negro girl, that belongs to my wife?"

"What girl, sir?"

"You know well enough. I mean Linda, that ran away from Dr. Flint's plantation, some years ago. I dare say you've seen her, and know where she is."

"Yes, sir, I've seen her, and know where she is. She is out of your reach, sir."

"Tell me where she is, or bring her to me, and I will give her a chance to buy her freedom."

"I don't think it would be of any use, sir. I have heard her say she would go to the ends of the earth, rather than pay any man or woman for her freedom, because she thinks she has a right to it. Besides, she couldn't do it, if she would, for she has spent her earnings to educate her children."

This made Mr. Dodge very angry, and some high words passed between them. My friend was afraid to come where I was; but in the course of the day I received a note from him. I supposed they had not come from the south, in the winter, for a pleasure excursion; and now the nature of their business was very plain.

Mrs. Bruce came to me and entreated me to leave the city the next morning. She said her house was watched, and it was possible that some clew to me might be obtained. I refused to take her advice. She pleaded with an earnest tenderness, that ought to have moved me; but I was in a bitter, disheartened mood. I was weary of flying from pillar to post. I had been chased during half my life, and it seemed as if the chase was never to end. There I sat, in that great city, guiltless of crime, yet not daring to worship God in any of the churches. I heard the bells ringing for afternoon service, and, with contemptuous sarcasm, I said, "Will the preachers take for their text, 'Proclaim liberty to the captive, and the opening of prison doors to them that are bound'?[14] or will they preach from the text, 'Do unto others as ye would they should do unto you'?"[15] Oppressed Poles and Hungarians could find a safe refuge in that city; John Mitchell[16] was free to proclaim in the City Hall his desire for "a plantation well stocked with slaves;" but there I sat, an oppressed American, not daring to show my face. God forgive the black and bitter thoughts I indulged on that Sabbath day! The Scripture says, "Oppression makes even a wise man mad;"[17] and I was not wise.

I had been told that Mr. Dodge said his wife had never signed away her right to my children, and if he could not get me, he would take them. This it was, more than any thing else, that roused such a tempest in my soul. Benjamin was with his uncle William in California, but my innocent young daughter had come to spend a vacation with me. I thought of what I had suffered in slavery at her age, and my heart was like a tiger's when a hunter tries to seize her young.

---

14. Isaiah 61.1.   15. Luke 6.31.   16. Irish nationalist and pro-slavery advocate (1815–1875).   17. Ecclesiastes 7.7.

Dear Mrs. Bruce! I seem to see the expression of her face, as she turned away discouraged by my obstinate mood. Finding her expostulations unavailing, she sent Ellen to entreat me. When ten o'clock in the evening arrived and Ellen had not returned, this watchful and unwearied friend became anxious. She came to us in a carriage, bringing a well-filled trunk for my journey—trusting that by this time I would listen to reason. I yielded to her, as I ought to have done before.

The next day, baby and I set out in a heavy snow storm, bound for New England again. I received letters from the City of Iniquity,[18] addressed to me under an assumed name. In a few days one came from Mrs. Bruce, informing me that my new master was still searching for me, and that she intended to put an end to this persecution by buying my freedom. I felt grateful for the kindness that prompted this offer, but the idea was not so pleasant to me as might have been expected. The more my mind had become enlightened, the more difficult it was for me to consider myself an article of property; and to pay money to those who had so grievously oppressed me seemed like taking from my sufferings the glory of triumph. I wrote to Mrs. Bruce, thanking her, but saying that being sold from one owner to another seemed too much like slavery; that such a great obligation could not be easily cancelled; and that I preferred to go to my brother in California.

Without my knowledge, Mrs. Bruce employed a gentleman in New York to enter into negotiations with Mr. Dodge. He proposed to pay three hundred dollars down, if Mr. Dodge would sell me, and enter into obligations to relinquish all claim to me or my children forever after. He who called himself my master said he scorned so small an offer for such a valuable servant. The gentleman replied, "You can do as you choose, sir. If you reject this offer you will never get any thing; for the woman has friends who will convey her and her children out of the country."

Mr. Dodge concluded that "half a loaf was better than no bread," and he agreed to the proffered terms. By the next mail I received this brief letter from Mrs. Bruce: "I am rejoiced to tell you that the money for your freedom has been paid to Mr. Dodge. Come home to-morrow. I long to see you and my sweet babe."

My brain reeled as I read these lines. A gentleman near me said, "It's true; I have seen the bill of sale." "The bill of sale!" Those words struck me like a blow. So I was *sold* at last! A human being *sold* in the free city of New York! The bill of sale is on record, and future generations will learn from it that women were articles of traffic in New York, late in the nineteenth century of the Christian religion. It may hereafter prove a useful document to antiquaries, who are seeking to measure the progress of civilization in the United States. I well know the value of that bit of paper; but much as I love freedom, I do not like to look upon it. I am deeply grateful to the generous friend who procured it, but I despise the miscreant who demanded payment for what never rightfully belonged to him or his.

I had objected to having my freedom bought, yet I must confess that when it was done I felt as if a heavy load had been lifted from my weary shoulders. When I rode home in the cars I was no longer afraid to unveil my face and look at people as they passed. I should have been glad to have met Daniel Dodge himself; to have had him seen me and known me, that he might have mourned over the untoward circumstances which compelled him to sell me for three hundred dollars.

---

18. New York City. See Genesis 18.20–26.

When I reached home, the arms of my benefactress were thrown round me, and our tears mingled. As soon as she could speak, she said, "O Linda, I'm *so* glad it's all over! You wrote to me as if you thought you were going to be transferred from one owner to another. But I did not buy you for your services. I should have done just the same, if you had been going to sail for California to-morrow. I should, at least, have the satisfaction of knowing that you left me a free woman."

My heart was exceedingly full. I remembered how my poor father had tried to buy me, when I was a small child, and how he had been disappointed. I hoped his spirit was rejoicing over me now. I remembered how my good old grandmother had laid up her earnings to purchase me in later years, and how often her plans had been frustrated. How that faithful, loving old heart would leap for joy, if she could look on me and my children now that we were free! My relatives had been foiled in all their efforts, but God had raised me up a friend among strangers, who had bestowed on me the precious, long-desired boon. Friend! It is a common word, often lightly used. Like other good and beautiful things, it may be tarnished by careless handling; but when I speak of Mrs. Bruce as my friend, the word is sacred.

My grandmother lived to rejoice in my freedom; but not long after, a letter came with a black seal. She had gone "where the wicked cease from troubling, and the weary are at rest."[19]

Time passed on, and a paper came to me from the south, containing an obituary notice of my uncle Phillip. It was the only case I ever knew of such an honor conferred upon a colored person. It was written by one of his friends, and contained these words: "Now that death has laid him low, they call him a good man and a useful citizen; but what are eulogies to the black man, when the world has faded from his vision? It does not require man's praise to obtain rest in God's kingdom." So they called a colored man a *citizen*! Strange words to be uttered in that region!

Reader, my story ends with freedom; not in the usual way, with marriage. I and my children are now free! We are as free from the power of slaveholders as are the white people of the north; and though that, according to my ideas, is not saying a great deal, it is a vast improvement in *my* condition. The dream of my life is not yet realized. I do not sit with my children in a home of my own. I still long for a hearthstone of my own, however humble. I wish it for my children's sake far more than for my own. But God so orders circumstances as to keep me with my friend Mrs. Bruce. Love, duty, gratitude, also bind me to her side. It is a privilege to serve her who pities my oppressed people, and who has bestowed the inestimable boon of freedom on me and my children.

It has been painful to me, in many ways, to recall the dreary years I passed in bondage. I would gladly forget them if I could. Yet the retrospection is not altogether without solace; for with those gloomy recollections come tender memories of my good old grandmother, like light, fleecy clouds floating over a dark and troubled sea.

—1861

---

19. Job 3.17.

Henry David Thoreau
1817–1862

Henry David Thoreau was born and lived most of his life in Concord, Massachusetts, where he was a friend of Ralph Waldo Emerson, Margaret Fuller, George Ripley, Nathaniel Hawthorne, and many of the other leading writers and intellectuals of his day. Concord was the site of one of the first battles of the American Revolution; at the North Bridge, in Emerson's words, "embattled farmers stood / And fired the shot heard round the world." Revolutionary ideals, already deeply undermined by the rapid spread of plantation slavery, were facing a stiff new challenge when Thoreau reached adulthood: Industrialization under capitalism was producing new kinds of inequality for workers in the rapidly growing new cities of the North. When Thoreau graduated from Harvard College in 1837, the young nation had just entered its second long economic depression in two decades. Hundreds of thousands of workers suddenly found themselves out of work, mired in deep poverty, and wondering whether the new American social order could deliver on its promises. Thoreau believed that in such a world, writers and artists had an especially important role to play. Their ministry was to remind a materialistic society of ideal truths and realities that had been forgotten in the competitive scramble for profit and prestige.

For the first decade of his life as a writer, Thoreau thought of himself mainly as a poet. His mentor, Emerson, wrote to Thomas Carlyle in England, saying, "I have a young poet in this village named Thoreau, who writes the truest verses." Thoreau's poetry was "the purest strain, the loftiest . . . that has yet pealed from this unpoetic American forest." At first, his themes and style were closely modeled after Emerson's Transcendentalist idealism, but he soon began to develop his own uniquely "wild" voice and practice, based on close observation and description of the human and natural environment through which he moved. Thoreau did not achieve the same kind of absolutely confident and single-minded formal invention that marks the work of Walt Whitman or Emily Dickinson. Nevertheless, at its best, his verse is firmly anchored in the physical specifics of New England. Its angular rhythms combine with insistent alliteration and an arresting vernacular to produce music that is quite new and powerful.

Thoreau's most dexterous and compelling verbal performance, a kind of long poem in prose, was *Walden; Or, Life in the Woods* (1854), the record of two years, two months, and two days during which he lived in a cabin on the shores of a small pond outside Concord. Thoreau explained: "I went to the woods because I wished to live deliberately, to front only the essential facts of life, and see if I could not learn what it had to teach, and not, when I came to die, discover that I had not lived." "Walking" (1855) provides a compressed statement of *Walden*'s pantheist creed: "In Wildness is the preservation of the World" (p. 1062). According to Thoreau's way of thinking, the divine was immanent in the natural world in the form of the transcendental or universal laws of nature ordained by God. The poet or writer, by walking in the woods and fields, could become sensitively attuned to such higher laws and use them to understand and reform a society that had backslid into avarice, greed, and hypocrisy. One way society demonstrated its degeneracy was in its treatment of the land; thus, "Walking" makes one of the earliest arguments for wilderness preservation and was long ago adopted as a manifesto by the American environmental movement.

During Thoreau's lifetime the main example of depths to which a materialistic society could slide was chattel slavery, the legal ownership of one human being by another. Following his belief in the priority of the individual conscience to social law, he frequently acted as a conductor on the Underground Railroad, concealing escaped slaves in his home and accompanying them to the next safe haven northward. Increasingly, he turned his rhetorical talents to supporting the abolitionist cause in essays that began as lectures. "Resistance to Civil Government" (1849), perhaps the most widely influential piece of Romantic political theory, has been cited as an inspiration by figures as significant as Martin Luther King and Mohandas Gandhi. Thoreau argues that "It is not desirable to cultivate a respect for the law, so much as for the right" (p. 1039) and therefore that "[u]nder a government which imprisons any unjustly, the true place for a just man is also a prison" (p. 1044). Tragically, Thoreau did not live to see the end of the Civil War and the emancipation of the slaves. He died of tuberculosis in Concord in the springtime in 1862. On his deathbed, asked if he could see the other side, he replied, "One world at a time."

Sympathy

Lately alas I knew a gentle boy,
Whose features all were cast in Virtue's mould,
As one she had designed for Beauty's toy,
But after manned him for her own stronghold.

On every side he open was as day,   5
That you might see no lack of strength within,
For walls and ports so only serve alway
For a pretence to feebleness and sin.

Say not that Caesar[1] was victorious,
With toil and strife who stormed the House of Fame   10
In other sense this youth was glorious,
Himself a kingdom wheresoe'er he came.

No strength went out to get him victory,
When all was income of its own accord;
For where he went none other was to see,   15
But all were parcel of their noble lord.

He forayed like the subtle haze of summer,
That stilly shows fresh landscapes to our eyes,
And revolutions works without a murmur,
Or rustling of a leaf beneath the skies.   20

So was I taken unawares by this,
I quite forgot my homage to confess;
Yet now am forced to know, though hard it is,
I might have loved him, had I loved him less.

---

1. Julius Caesar (100–44 BC), Roman emperor.

Each moment, as we nearer drew to each,   25
A stern respect withheld us farther yet,
So that we seemed beyond each other's reach,
And less acquainted than when first we met.

We two were one while we did sympathize
So could we not the simplest bargain drive;   30
And what avails it now that we are wise,
If absence doth this doubleness contrive?

Eternity may not the chance repeat,
But I must tread my single way alone,
In sad remembrance that we once did meet,   35
And know that bliss irrevocably gone.

The spheres henceforth my elegy shall sing,
For elegy has other subject none;
Each strain of music in my ears shall ring
Knell of departure from that other one.   40

Make haste and celebrate my tragedy;
With fitting strain resound ye woods and fields;
Sorrow is dearer in such case to me
Than all the joys other occasion yields.

Is't then too late the damage to repair?   45
Distance, forsooth, from my weak grasp hath reft
The empty husk, and clutched the useless tare,
But in my hands the wheat and kernel left.

If I but love that virtue which he is,
Though it be scented in the morning air,   50
Still shall we be truest acquaintances,
Nor mortals know a sympathy more rare.

—1840

Sic Vita[1]

I am a parcel of vain strivings tied
   By a chance bond together,
  Dangling this way and that, their links
   Were made so loose and wide,
     Methinks,   5
    For milder weather.

---

1. Sic vita fugit: so life departs (Latin).

A bunch of violets without their roots,
 And sorrel intermixed,
 Encircled by a wisp of straw
  Once coiled about their shoots,
   The law
   By which I'm fixed.

A nosegay which Time clutched from out
 Those fair Elysian fields,[2]
With weeds and broken stems, in haste,
 Doth make the rabble rout
  That waste
  The day he yields.   15

And here I bloom for a short hour unseen,
 Drinking my juices up,   20
Which have no root in the land
 To keep my branches green,
  But stand
  In a bare cup.

Some tender buds were left upon my stem   25
 In mimicry of life,
But ah! the children will not know
 Till time has withered them,
  The woe
  With which they're rife.   30

But now I see I was not plucked for nought,
 And after in life's vase
Of glass set while I might survive,
 But by a kind hand brought
  Alive   35
  To a strange place.

That stock thus thinned will soon redeem its hours,
 And by another year
Such as God knows, with freer air,
 More fruits and fairer flowers   40
  Will bear,
  While I droop here.

             —1841

---

2. A section of the Greek underworld reserved for the virtuous.

The Inward Morning

Packed in my mind lie all the clothes
    Which outward nature wears,
And in its fashion's hourly change
    It all things else repairs.

In vain I look for change abroad,   5
    And can no difference find,
Till some new ray of peace uncalled
    Illumes my inmost mind.

What is it gilds the trees and clouds,
    And paints the heavens so gay,   10
But yonder fast abiding light
    With its unchanging ray?

Lo, when the sun streams through the wood
    Upon a winter's morn,
Where'er his silent beams intrude   15
    The murky night is gone.

How could the patient pine have known
    The morning breeze would come,
Or humble flowers anticipate
    The insect's noonday hum?   20

Till the new light with morning cheer
    From far streamed through the aisles,
And nimbly told the forest trees
    For many stretching miles.

I've heard within my inmost soul   25
    Such cheerful morning news,
In the horizon of my mind
    Have seen such orient hues,

As in the twilight of the dawn,
    When the first birds awake,   30
Are heard within some silent wood,
    Where they the small twigs break,

Or in the eastern skies are seen,
    Before the sun appears,
The harbingers of summer heats   35
    Which from afar he bears.

—1842

Haze

Woof of the sun, ethereal gauze,
Woven of Nature's richest stuffs,
Visible heat, air-water, and dry sea,
Last conquest of the eye;
Toil of the day displayed, sun-dust,   5
Aerial surf upon the shores of earth,
Ethereal estuary, froth of light,
Breakers of air, billows of heat,
Fine summer spray on inland seas;
Bird of the sun, transparent-winged   10
Owlet of noon, soft-pinioned,
From heath or stubble rising without song;
Establish thy serenity o'er the fields.

                                                —1843

In the busy streets, domains of trade

In the busy streets, domains of trade,
Man is a surly porter, or a vain and hectoring bully,
Who can claim no nearer kindredship with me
Than brotherhood by law.

                                                —1906

Any fool can make a rule

Any fool can make a rule
And every fool will mind it.

                                                —1906

Wait not till slaves pronounce the word

            Spes sibi quisque
            Each one his own hope

Wait not till slaves pronounce the word
    To set the captive free,
Be free yourselves, be not deferred,
    And farewell slavery.

Ye are all slaves, ye have your price,   5
    And gang but cries to gang.
Then rise, the highest of ye rise,
    I hear your fetters clang.

Think not the tyrant sits afar
   In your own breasts ye have   10
The District of Columbia
   And power to free the Slave

The warmest heart the north doth breed,
   Is still too cold and far,
The colored man's release must come   15
   From outcast Africa.

Make haste & set the captive free!—
   Are ye so free that cry?
The lowest depths of slavery
   Leave freeedom for a sigh.   20

—1906

Ive seen ye, sisters, on the mountain-side

Ive seen ye, sisters, on the mountain-side
When your green mantles fluttered in the wind
Ive seen your foot-prints on the lakes smooth shore
Lesser than man's, a more ethereal trace,
I have heard of ye as some far-famed race—   5
Daughters of gods whom I should one day meet—
Or mothers I might say of all our race.
I reverence your natures so like mine
Yet strangely different, like but still unlike
Thou only stranger that hast crossed my path   10
Accept my hospitality—let me hear
The message which thou bring'st
   Made different from me
   Perchance thou't made to be
   The creature of a different destiny.   15
I know not who ye are that meekly stand
Thus side by side with man in every land.
When did ye form alliance with our race
Ye children of the moon who in placid nights
Vaulted upon the hills and sought this earth.   20
Reveal that which I fear ye can not tell
Wherein ye are not I, wherein ye dwell
Where I can never come.
What boots it that I do regard ye so
Does it make suns to shine or crops to grow?   25
What boots that I never should forget
Thee, I have sisters sitting for me yet

And what are sisters
The robust man who can so stoutly strive
In this bleak world is hardly kept alive.
And who is it protects ye smooths *your* way

—1906

I am the little Irish boy

I am the little Irish boy
  That lives in the shanty
I am four years old today
  And shall soon be one and twenty
  I shall grow up
  And be a great man
  And shovel all day
  As hard as I can.

  Down in the deep cut
  Where the men lived
  Who made the Rail road.

For supper
  I have some potatoe
  And sometimes some bread
  And then if it's cold
    I go right to bed.

  I lie on some straw
  Under my fathers coat

  My mother does not cry
  And my father does not scold
  For I am a little Irish Boy
  And I'm four years old.

  Every day I go to school
  Along the Railroad
  It was so cold it made me cry
  The day that it snowed.

  And if my feet ache
  I do not mind the cold
  For I am a little Irish boy
  & I'm four years old.

—1943

Poverty

If I am poor it is that I am proud,
If God has made me naked and a boor
He did not think it fit his work to shroud.

The poor man comes from heaven direct to earth
As stars drop down the sky and tropic beams.   5
The rich receives in our gross air his birth,
As from low suns are slanted golden gleams.

Men are by birth equal in this that given
Themselves and their condition they are even.
The less of inward essence is to leaven   10
The more of outward circumstance is given.

Yon sun is naked bare of satellite
Unless our earths and moons that office hold,
Though his perpetual day feareth no night
And his perennial summer dreads no cold.   15

Where are his gilded rays but in our sky?
His solid disk doth float far from us still,
The orb which through the central way doth fly
Shall naked seem though proudly circumstanced.

Ill leave my mineral wealth hoarded in earth,   20
Buried in seas in mines and ocean caves
More safely kept than is the merchant's worth,
Which every storm committeth to the waves.

—1943

I have seen some frozenfaced connecticut

I have seen some frozenfaced connecticut
Or Down east man in his crack coaster
With tort sail, with folded arms standing
Beside his galley with his dog & man
While his cock crowed aboard, scud thro the surf   5
By some fast anchored Staten island farm,
But just outside the vast and stirring line
Where the astonished Dutchman digs his clams
Or but half ploughs his cabbage garden plot
With unbroken steeds & ropy harness—   10
And some squat bantam whom the shore wind drownd
Feebly responded there for all reply,
While the triumphant Yankee's farm swept by.

—2001

Resistance to Civil Government

I heartily accept the motto, "That government is best which governs least;"[1] and I should like to see it acted up to more rapidly and systematically. Carried out, it finally amounts to this, which also I believe,—"That government is best which governs not at all;" and when men are prepared for it, that will be the kind of government which they will have. Government is at best but an expedient; but most governments are usually, and all governments are sometimes, inexpedient. The objections which have been brought against a standing army, and they are many and weighty, and deserve to prevail, may also at last be brought against a standing government. The standing army is only an arm of the standing government. The government itself, which is only the mode which the people have chosen to execute their will, is equally liable to be abused and perverted before the people can act through it. Witness the present Mexican war,[2] the work of comparatively a few individuals using the standing government as their tool; for, in the outset, the people would not have consented to this measure.

This American government,—what is it but a tradition, though a recent one, endeavoring to transmit itself unimpaired to posterity, but each instant losing some of its integrity? It has not the vitality and force of a single living man; for a single man can bend it to his will. It is a sort of wooden gun to the people themselves. But it is not the less necessary for this; for the people must have some complicated machinery or other, and hear its din, to satisfy that idea of government which they have. Governments show thus how successfully men can be imposed on, even impose on themselves, for their own advantage. It is excellent, we must all allow. Yet this government never of itself furthered any enterprise, but by the alacrity with which it got out of its way. *It* does not keep the country free. *It* does not settle the West. *It* does not educate. The character inherent in the American people has done all that has been accomplished; and it would have done somewhat more, if the government had not sometimes got in its way. For government is an expedient by which men would fain succeed in letting one another alone; and, as has been said, when it is most expedient, the governed are most let alone by it. Trade and commerce, if they were not made of india-rubber, would never manage to bounce over the obstacles which legislators are continually putting in their way; and, if one were to judge these men wholly by the effects of their actions and not partly by their intentions, they would deserve to be classed and punished with those mischievous persons who put obstructions on the railroads.

But, to speak practically and as a citizen, unlike those who call themselves no-government men, I ask for, not at once no government, but *at once* a better government. Let every man make known what kind of government would command his respect, and that will be one step toward obtaining it.

After all, the practical reason why, when the power is once in the hands of the people, a majority are permitted, and for a long period continue, to rule is not because they are most likely to be in the right, nor because this seems fairest to the minority, but because they are physically the strongest. But a government in which the majority rule in all cases cannot be based on justice, even as far as men understand it. Can there not be a government in which majorities do not virtually decide

---

1. Motto of the *Democratic Review*, a New York political magazine.   2. Mexican-American War (1846–1848).

right and wrong, but conscience?—in which majorities decide only those questions to which the rule of expediency is applicable? Must the citizen ever for a moment, or in the least degree, resign his conscience to the legislator? Why has every man a conscience, then? I think that we should be men first, and subjects afterward. It is not desirable to cultivate a respect for the law, so much as for the right. The only obligation which I have a right to assume is to do at any time what I think right. It is truly enough said that a corporation has no conscience; but a corporation of conscientious men is a corporation *with* a conscience. Law never made men a whit more just; and, by means of their respect for it, even the well-disposed are daily made the agents of injustice. A common and natural result of an undue respect for law is, that you may see a file of soldiers, colonel, captain, corporal, privates, powder-monkeys, and all, marching in admirable order over hill and dale to the wars, against their wills, ay, against their common sense and consciences, which makes it very steep marching indeed, and produces a palpitation of the heart. They have no doubt that it is a damnable business in which they are concerned; they are all peaceably inclined. Now, what are they? Men at all? or small movable forts and magazines, at the service of some unscrupulous man in power? Visit the Navy-Yard, and behold a marine, such a man as an American government can make, or such as it can make a man with its black arts,—a mere shadow and reminiscence of humanity, a man laid out alive and standing, and already, as one may say, buried under arms with funeral accompaniments, though it may be,—

> "Not a drum was heard, not a funeral note,
>   As his corse to the rampart we hurried;
> Not a soldier discharged his farewell shot
>   O'er the grave where our hero we buried."[3]

The mass of men serve the state thus, not as men mainly, but as machines, with their bodies. They are the standing army, and the militia, jailers, constables, *posse comitatus*,[4] etc. In most cases there is no free exercise whatever of the judgment or of the moral sense; but they put themselves on a level with wood and earth and stones; and wooden men can perhaps be manufactured that will serve the purpose as well. Such command no more respect than men of straw or a lump of dirt. They have the same sort of worth only as horses and dogs. Yet such as these even are commonly esteemed good citizens. Others—as most legislators, politicians, lawyers, ministers, and office-holders—serve the state chiefly with their heads; and, as they rarely make any moral distinctions, they are as likely to serve the devil, without *intending* it, as God. A very few—as heroes, patriots, martyrs, reformers in the great sense, and *men*—serve the state with their consciences also, and so necessarily resist it for the most part; and they are commonly treated as enemies by it. A wise man will only be useful as a man, and will not submit to be "clay," and "stop a hole to keep the wind away,"[5] but leave that office to his dust at least:—

> "I am too high-born to be propertied,
> To be a secondary at control,

<hr>

3. Charles Wolfe (1791–1823), "Burial of Sir John Moore at Corunna" (1817). 4. Sheriff's posse. 5. William Shakespeare (1564–1616), *Hamlet* (1603), 5.1.236–239.

> Or useful serving-man and instrument
> To any sovereign state throughout the world."[6]

He who gives himself entirely to his fellow-men appears to them useless and selfish; but he who gives himself partially to them is pronounced a benefactor and philanthropist.

How does it become a man to behave toward this American government today? I answer, that he cannot without disgrace be associated with it. I cannot for an instant recognize that political organization as *my* government which is the *slave's* government also.

All men recognize the right of revolution; that is, the right to refuse allegiance to, and to resist, the government, when its tyranny or its inefficiency are great and unendurable. But almost all say that such is not the case now. But such was the case, they think, in the Revolution of '75. If one were to tell me that this was a bad government because it taxed certain foreign commodities brought to its ports, it is most probable that I should not make an ado about it, for I can do without them. All machines have their friction; and possibly this does enough good to counterbalance the evil. At any rate, it is a great evil to make a stir about it. But when the friction comes to have its machine, and oppression and robbery are organized, I say, let us not have such a machine any longer. In other words, when a sixth of the population of a nation which has undertaken to be the refuge of liberty are slaves, and a whole country is unjustly overrun and conquered by a foreign army, and subjected to military law, I think that it is not too soon for honest men to rebel and revolutionize. What makes this duty the more urgent is the fact that the country so overrun is not our own, but ours is the invading army.

Paley, a common authority with many on moral questions, in his chapter on the "Duty of Submission to Civil Government,"[7] resolves all civil obligation into expediency; and he proceeds to say that "so long as the interest of the whole society requires it, that is, so long as the established government cannot be resisted or changed without public inconveniency, it is the will of God . . . that the established government be obeyed,—and no longer. This principle being admitted, the justice of every particular case of resistance is reduced to a computation of the quantity of the danger and grievance on the one side, and of the probability and expense of redressing it on the other." Of this, he says, every man shall judge for himself. But Paley appears never to have contemplated those cases to which the rule of expediency does not apply, in which a people, as well as an individual, must do justice, cost what it may. If I have unjustly wrested a plank from a drowning man, I must restore it to him though I drown myself. This, according to Paley, would be inconvenient. But he that would save his life, in such a case, shall lose it.[8] This people must cease to hold slaves, and to make war on Mexico, though it cost them their existence as a people.

In their practice, nations agree with Paley; but does any one think that Massachusetts does exactly what is right at the present crisis?

> "A drab of state, a cloth-o'-silver slut,
> To have her train borne up, and her soul trail in the dirt."[9]

---

6. Shakespeare, *King John* (1623), 5.1.79–82.   7. William Paley (1743–1805), *Principles of Moral and Political Philosophy* (1785).   8. Matthew 10.39.   9. Cyril Tourneur (c. 1575–1626), *The Revenger's Tragedy* (1607), 4.4.

Practically speaking, the opponents to a reform in Massachusetts are not a hundred thousand politicians at the South, but a hundred thousand merchants and farmers here, who are more interested in commerce and agriculture than they are in humanity, and are not prepared to do justice to the slave and to Mexico, *cost what it may*. I quarrel not with far-off foes, but with those who, near at home, co-operate with, and do the bidding of, those far away, and without whom the latter would be harmless. We are accustomed to say, that the mass of men are unprepared; but improvement is slow, because the few are not materially wiser or better than the many. It is not so important that many should be as good as you, as that there be some absolute goodness somewhere; for that will leaven the whole lump.[10] There are thousands who are *in opinion* opposed to slavery and to the war, who yet in effect do nothing to put an end to them; who, esteeming themselves children of Washington and Franklin,[11] sit down with their hands in their pockets, and say that they know not what to do, and do nothing; who even postpone the question of freedom to the question of free trade, and quietly read the prices-current along with the latest advices from Mexico, after dinner, and, it may be, fall asleep over them both. What is the price-current of an honest man and patriot to-day? They hesitate, and they regret, and sometimes they petition; but they do nothing in earnest and with effect. They will wait, well disposed, for others to remedy the evil, that they may no longer have it to regret. At most, they give only a cheap vote, and a feeble countenance and God-speed, to the right, as it goes by them. There are nine hundred and ninety-nine patrons of virtue to one virtuous man. But it is easier to deal with the real possessor of a thing than with the temporary guardian of it.

All voting is a sort of gaming, like checkers or backgammon, with a slight moral tinge to it, a playing with right and wrong, with moral questions; and betting naturally accompanies it. The character of the voters is not staked. I cast my vote, perchance, as I think right; but I am not vitally concerned that that right should prevail. I am willing to leave it to the majority. Its obligation, therefore, never exceeds that of expediency. Even voting *for the right* is *doing* nothing for it. It is only expressing to men feebly your desire that it should prevail. A wise man will not leave the right to the mercy of chance, nor wish it to prevail through the power of the majority. There is but little virtue in the action of masses of men. When the majority shall at length vote for the abolition of slavery, it will be because they are indifferent to slavery, or because there is but little slavery left to be abolished by their vote. *They* will then be the only slaves. Only *his* vote can hasten the abolition of slavery who asserts his own freedom by his vote.

I hear of a convention to be held at Baltimore, or elsewhere, for the selection of a candidate for the Presidency, made up chiefly of editors, and men who are politicians by profession; but I think, what is it to any independent, intelligent, and respectable man what decision they may come to? Shall we not have the advantage of his wisdom and honesty, nevertheless? Can we not count upon some independent votes? Are there not many individuals in the country who do not attend conventions? But no: I find that the respectable man, so called, has immediately drifted from his position, and despairs of his country, when his country has more reason to despair of him. He forthwith adopts one of the candidates thus selected as the only *available*

---

10. 1 Corinthians 5.6.   11. George Washington (1732–1799) and Benjamin Franklin (1706–1790), revolutionary leaders.

one, thus proving that he is himself *available* for any purposes of the demagogue. His vote is of no more worth than that of any unprincipled foreigner or hireling native, who may have been bought. O for a man who is a *man*, and, as my neighbor says, has a bone in his back which you cannot pass your hand through! Our statistics are at fault: the population has been returned too large. How many *men* are there to a square thousand miles in this country? Hardly one. Does not America offer any inducement for men to settle here? The American has dwindled into an Odd Fellow,[12]—one who may be known by the development of his organ of gregariousness, and a manifest lack of intellect and cheerful self-reliance; whose first and chief concern, on coming into the world, is to see that the almshouses are in good repair; and, before yet he has law-fully donned the virile garb,[13] to collect a fund for the support of the widows and orphans that may be; who, in short, ventures to live only by the aid of the mutual insurance company, which has promised to bury him decently.

It is not a man's duty, as a matter of course, to devote himself to the eradication of any, even the most enormous, wrong; he may still properly have other concerns to engage him; but it is his duty, at least, to wash his hands of it, and, if he gives it no thought longer, not to give it practically his support. If I devote myself to other pursuits and contemplations, I must first see, at least, that I do not pursue them sitting upon another man's shoulders. I must get off him first, that he may pursue his contemplations too. See what gross inconsistency is tolerated. I have heard some of my townsmen say, "I should like to have them order me out to help put down an insurrection of the slaves, or to march to Mexico;—see if I would go;" and yet these very men have each, directly by their allegiance, and so indirectly, at least, by their money, furnished a substitute. The soldier is applauded who refuses to serve in an unjust war by those who do not refuse to sustain the unjust government which makes the war; is applauded by those whose own act and authority he disregards and sets at naught; as if the state were penitent to that degree that it hired one to scourge it while it sinned, but not to that degree that it left off sinning for a moment. Thus, under the name of order and civil government, we are all made at last to pay homage to and support our own meanness. After the first blush of sin comes its indifference; and from immoral it becomes, as it were, *unmoral*, and not quite unnecessary to that life which we have made.

The broadest and most prevalent error requires the most disinterested virtue to sustain it. The slight reproach to which the virtue of patriotism is commonly liable, the noble are most likely to incur. Those who, while they disapprove of the character and measures of a government, yield to it their allegiance and support are undoubtedly its most conscientious supporters, and so frequently the most serious obstacles to reform. Some are petitioning the State to dissolve the Union, to disregard the requisitions of the President. Why do they not dissolve it themselves,—the union between themselves and the State,—and refuse to pay their quota into its treasury? Do not they stand in the same relation to the State that the State does to the Union? And have not the same reasons prevented the State from resisting the Union which have prevented them from resisting the State?

How can a man be satisfied to entertain an opinion merely, and enjoy *it*? Is there any enjoyment in it, if his opinion is that he is aggrieved? If you are cheated

---

12. The Odd Fellows were a secret fraternity.   13. Adult clothing.

out of a single dollar by your neighbor, you do not rest satisfied with knowing that you are cheated, or with saying that you are cheated, or even with petitioning him to pay you your due; but you take effectual steps at once to obtain the full amount, and see that you are never cheated again. Action from principle, the perception and the performance of right, changes things and relations; it is essentially revolutionary, and does not consist wholly with anything which was. It not only divides States and churches, it divides families; ay, it divides the *individual*, separating the diabolical in him from the divine.

Unjust laws exist: shall we be content to obey them, or shall we endeavor to amend them, and obey them until we have succeeded, or shall we transgress them at once? Men generally, under such a government as this, think that they ought to wait until they have persuaded the majority to alter them. They think that, if they should resist, the remedy would be worse than the evil. But it is the fault of the government itself that the remedy *is* worse than the evil. *It* makes it worse. Why is it not more apt to anticipate and provide for reform? Why does it not cherish its wise minority? Why does it cry and resist before it is hurt? Why does it not encourage its citizens to be on the alert to point out its faults, and *do* better than it would have them? Why does it always crucify Christ, and excommunicate Copernicus and Luther,[14] and pronounce Washington and Franklin rebels?

One would think, that a deliberate and practical denial of its authority was the only offence never contemplated by government; else, why has it not assigned its definite, its suitable and proportionate, penalty? If a man who has no property refuses but once to earn nine shillings for the State, he is put in prison for a period unlimited by any law that I know, and determined only by the discretion of those who placed him there; but if he should steal ninety times nine shillings from the State, he is soon permitted to go at large again.

If the injustice is part of the necessary friction of the machine of government, let it go, let it go: perchance it will wear smooth,—certainly the machine will wear out. If the injustice has a spring, or a pulley, or a rope, or a crank, exclusively for itself, then perhaps you may consider whether the remedy will not be worse than the evil; but if it is of such a nature that it requires you to be the agent of injustice to another, then, I say, break the law. Let your life be a counter-friction to stop the machine. What I have to do is to see, at any rate, that I do not lend myself to the wrong which I condemn.

As for adopting the ways which the State has provided for remedying the evil, I know not of such ways. They take too much time, and a man's life will be gone. I have other affairs to attend to. I came into this world, not chiefly to make this a good place to live in, but to live in it, be it good or bad. A man has not everything to do, but something; and because he cannot do *everything*, it is not necessary that he should do *something* wrong. It is not my business to be petitioning the Governor or the Legislature any more than it is theirs to petition me; and if they should not hear my petition, what should I do then? But in this case the State has provided no way: its very Constitution is the evil. This may seem to be harsh and stubborn and unconciliatory; but it is to treat with the utmost kindness and consideration the only spirit that can appreciate or deserves it. So is all change for the better, like birth and death, which convulse the body.

14. Copernicus (1473–1543), Polish astronomer; Martin Luther (1483–1546), German Protestant minister.

I do not hesitate to say, that those who call themselves Abolitionists should at once effectually withdraw their support, both in person and property, from the government of Massachusetts, and not wait till they constitute a majority of one, before they suffer the right to prevail through them. I think that it is enough if they have God on their side, without waiting for that other one. Moreover, any man more right than his neighbors constitutes a majority of one already.

I meet this American government, or its representative, the State government, directly, and face to face, once a year—no more—in the person of its tax-gatherer; this is the only mode in which a man situated as I am necessarily meets it; and it then says distinctly, Recognize me; and the simplest, the most effectual, and, in the present posture of affairs, the indispensablest mode of treating with it on this head, of expressing your little satisfaction with and love for it, is to deny it then. My civil neighbor, the tax-gatherer, is the very man I have to deal with,—for it is, after all, with men and not with parchment that I quarrel,—and he has voluntarily chosen to be an agent of the government. How shall he ever know well what he is and does as an officer of the government, or as a man, until he is obliged to consider whether he shall treat me, his neighbor, for whom he has respect, as a neighbor and well-disposed man, or as a maniac and disturber of the peace, and see if he can get over this obstruction to his neighborliness without a ruder and more impetuous thought or speech corresponding with his action. I know this well, that if one thousand, if one hundred, if ten men whom I could name,—if ten *honest* men only,—ay, if *one* HONEST man, in this State of Massachusetts, *ceasing to hold slaves*, were actually to withdraw from this copartnership, and be locked up in the county jail therefor, it would be the abolition of slavery in America. For it matters not how small the beginning may seem to be: what is once well done is done forever. But we love better to talk about it: that we say is our mission. Reform keeps many scores of newspapers in its service, but not one man. If my esteemed neighbor, the State's ambassador,[15] who will devote his days to the settlement of the question of human rights in the Council Chamber, instead of being threatened with the prisons of Carolina, were to sit down the prisoner of Massachusetts, that State which is so anxious to foist the sin of slavery upon her sister,—though at present she can discover only an act of inhospitality to be the ground of a quarrel with her,—the Legislature would not wholly waive the subject the following winter.

Under a government which imprisons any unjustly, the true place for a just man is also a prison. The proper place to-day, the only place which Massachusetts has provided for her freer and less desponding spirits, is in her prisons, to be put out and locked out of the State by her own act, as they have already put themselves out by their principles. It is there that the fugitive slave, and the Mexican prisoner on parole, and the Indian come to plead the wrongs of his race should find them; on that separate, but more free and honorable ground, where the State places those who are not *with* her, but *against* her,— the only house in a slave State in which a free man can abide with honor. If any think that their influence would be lost there, and their voices no longer afflict the ear of the State, that they would not be as an enemy within its walls, they do not know by how much truth is stronger than error, nor how much more eloquently and effectively he can combat injustice who has experienced a little in his own person. Cast your whole vote,

---

15. Samuel Hoar (1778–1856) was threatened with imprisonment in South Carolina while advocating the release of a group of black sailors.

not a strip of paper merely, but your whole influence. A minority is powerless while it conforms to the majority; it is not even a minority then; but it is irresistible when it clogs by its whole weight. If the alternative is to keep all just men in prison, or give up war and slavery, the State will not hesitate which to choose. If a thousand men were not to pay their tax-bills this year, that would not be a violent and bloody measure, as it would be to pay them, and enable the State to commit violence and shed innocent blood. This is, in fact, the definition of a peaceable revolution, if any such is possible. If the tax-gatherer, or any other public officer, asks me, as one has done, "But what shall I do?" my answer is, "If you really wish to do anything, resign your office." When the subject has refused allegiance, and the officer has resigned his office, then the revolution is accomplished. But even suppose blood should flow. Is there not a sort of blood shed when the conscience is wounded? Through this wound a man's real manhood and immortality flow out, and he bleeds to an everlasting death. I see this blood flowing now.

I have contemplated the imprisonment of the offender, rather than the seizure of his goods,—though both will serve the same purpose,—because they who assert the purest right, and consequently are most dangerous to a corrupt State, commonly have not spent much time in accumulating property. To such the State renders comparatively small service, and a slight tax is wont to appear exorbitant, particularly if they are obliged to earn it by special labor with their hands. If there were one who lived wholly without the use of money, the State itself would hesitate to demand it of him. But the rich man—not to make any invidious comparison—is always sold to the institution which makes him rich. Absolutely speaking, the more money, the less virtue; for money comes between a man and his objects, and obtains them for him; and it was certainly no great virtue to obtain it. It puts to rest many questions which he would otherwise be taxed to answer; while the only new question which it puts is the hard but superfluous one, how to spend it. Thus his moral ground is taken from under his feet. The opportunities of living are diminished in proportion as what are called the "means" are increased. The best thing a man can do for his culture when he is rich is to endeavour to carry out those schemes which he entertained when he was poor. Christ answered the Herodians according to their condition. "Show me the tribute-money," said he;—and one took a penny out of his pocket;—if you use money which has the image of Cæsar on it, and which he has made current and valuable, that is, *if you are men of the State*, and gladly enjoy the advantages of Cæsar's government, then pay him back some of his own when he demands it. "Render therefore to Cæsar that which is Cæsar's, and to God those things which are God's,"[16]—leaving them no wiser than before as to which was which; for they did not wish to know.

When I converse with the freest of my neighbors, I perceive that, whatever they may say about the magnitude and seriousness of the question, and their regard for the public tranquillity, the long and the short of the matter is, that they cannot spare the protection of the existing government, and they dread the consequences to their property and families of disobedience to it. For my own part, I should not like to think that I ever rely on the protection of the State. But, if I deny the authority of the State when it presents its tax-bill, it will soon take and waste all my property, and so harass me and my children without end. This is hard. This makes it impossible for a man to live honestly, and at the same time comfortably, in outward respects. It will not be

---

16. Matthew 22.16–21.

worth the while to accumulate property; that would be sure to go again. You must hire or squat somewhere, and raise but a small crop, and eat that soon. You must live within yourself, and depend upon yourself always tucked up and ready for a start, and not have many affairs. A man may grow rich in Turkey even, if he will be in all respects a good subject of the Turkish government. Confucius said: "If a state is governed by the principles of reason, poverty and misery are subjects of shame; if a state is not governed by the principles of reason, riches and honors are the subjects of shame."[17] No: until I want the protection of Massachusetts to be extended to me in some distant Southern port, where my liberty is endangered, or until I am bent solely on building up an estate at home by peaceful enterprise, I can afford to refuse allegiance to Massachusetts, and her right to my property and life. It costs me less in every sense to incur the penalty of disobedience to the State than it would to obey. I should feel as if I were worth less in that case.

Some years ago, the State met me in behalf of the Church, and commanded me to pay a certain sum toward the support of a clergyman whose preaching my father attended, but never I myself. "Pay" it said, "or be locked up in the jail." I declined to pay. But, unfortunately, another man saw fit to pay it. I did not see why the schoolmaster should be taxed to support the priest, and not the priest the schoolmaster; for I was not the State's schoolmaster, but I supported myself by voluntary subscription. I did not see why the lyceum should not present its tax-bill, and have the State to back its demand, as well as the Church. However, at the request of the selectmen, I condescended to make some such statement as this in writing:—"Know all men by these presents, that I, Henry Thoreau, do not wish to be regarded as a member of any incorporated society which I have not joined." This I gave to the town clerk; and he has it. The State, having thus learned that I did not wish to be regarded as a member of that church, has never made a like demand on me since; though it said that it must adhere to its original presumption that time. If I had known how to name them, I should then have signed off in detail from all the societies which I never signed on to; but I did not know where to find a complete list.

I have paid no poll-tax for six years. I was put into a jail once on this account, for one night; and, as I stood considering the walls of solid stone, two or three feet thick, the door of wood and iron, a foot thick, and the iron grating which strained the light, I could not help being struck with the foolishness of that institution which treated me as if I were mere flesh and blood and bones, to be locked up. I wondered that it should have concluded at length that this was the best use it could put me to, and had never thought to avail itself of my services in some way. I saw that, if there was a wall of stone between me and my townsmen, there was a still more difficult one to climb or break through before they could get to be as free as I was. I did not for a moment feel confined, and the walls seemed a great waste of stone and mortar. I felt as if I alone of all my townsmen had paid my tax. They plainly did not know how to treat me, but behaved like persons who are underbred. In every threat and in every compliment there was a blunder; for they thought that my chief desire was to stand the other side of that stone wall. I could not but smile to see how industriously they locked the door on my meditations, which followed them out again without let or hindrance, and *they* were really all that was dangerous. As they could not reach me,

---

17. Confucius (551–479 BC), *Analects*, 8.13.

they had resolved to punish my body; just as boys, if they cannot come at some person against whom they have a spite, will abuse his dog. I saw that the State was half-witted, that it was timid as a lone woman with her silver spoons, and that it did not know its friends from its foes, and I lost all my remaining respect for it, and pitied it.

Thus the State never intentionally confronts a man's sense, intellectual or moral, but only his body, his senses. It is not armed with superior wit or honesty, but with superior physical strength. I was not born to be forced. I will breathe after my own fashion. Let us see who is the strongest. What force has a multitude? They only can force me who obey a higher law than I. They force me to become like themselves. I do not hear of *men* being *forced* to live this way or that by masses of men. What sort of life were that to live? When I meet a government which says to me, "Your money or your life," why should I be in haste to give it my money? It may be in a great strait, and not know what to do: I cannot help that. It must help itself; do as I do. It is not worth the while to snivel about it. I am not responsible for the successful working of the machinery of society. I am not the son of the engineer. I perceive that, when an acorn and a chestnut fall side by side, the one does not remain inert to make way for the other, but both obey their own laws, and spring and grow and flourish as best they can, till one, perchance, overshadows and destroys the other. If a plant cannot live according to its nature, it dies; and so a man.

The night in prison was novel and interesting enough. The prisoners in their shirt-sleeves were enjoying a chat and the evening air in the doorway, when I entered. But the jailer said, "Come, boys, it is time to lock up;" and so they dispersed, and I heard the sound of their steps returning into the hollow apartments. My roommate was introduced to me by the jailer, as "a first-rate fellow and a clever man." When the door was locked, he showed me where to hang my hat, and how he managed matters there. The rooms were whitewashed once a month; and this one, at least, was the whitest, most simply furnished, and probably the neatest apartment in the town. He naturally wanted to know where I came from, and what brought me there; and, when I had told him, I asked him in turn how he came there, presuming him to be an honest man of course; and, as the world goes, I believe he was. "Why," said he, "they accused me of burning a barn; but I never did it." As near as I could discover, he had probably gone to bed in a barn when drunk, and smoked his pipe there; and so a barn was burnt. He had the reputation of being a clever man, had been there some three months waiting for his trial to come on, and would have to wait as much longer; but he was quite domesticated and contented, since he got his board for nothing, and thought that he was well treated.

He occupied one window, and I the other; and I saw that if one stayed there long, his principal business would be to look out the window. I had soon read all the tracts that were left there, and examined where former prisoners had broken out, and where a grate had been sawed off, and heard the history of the various occupants of that room; for I found that even here there was a history and a gossip which never circulated beyond the walls of the jail. Probably this is the only house in the town where verses are composed, which are afterward printed in a circular form, but not published. I was shown quite a long list of verses which were composed by some young men who had been detected in an attempt to escape, who avenged themselves by singing them.

I pumped my fellow-prisoner as dry as I could, for fear I should never see him again; but at length he showed me which was my bed, and left me to blow out the lamp.

It was like traveling into a far country, such as I had never expected to behold, to lie there for one night. It seemed to me that I never had heard the town clock strike before, nor the evening sounds of the village; for we slept with the windows open, which were inside the grating. It was to see my native village in the light of the Middle Ages, and our Concord was turned into a Rhine stream, and visions of knights and castles passed before me. They were the voices of old burghers that I heard in the streets. I was an involuntary spectator and auditor of whatever was done and said in the kitchen of the adjacent village inn,—a wholly new and rare experience to me. It was a closer view of my native town. I was fairly inside of it. I never had seen its institutions before. This is one of its peculiar institutions; for it is a shire town. I began to comprehend what its inhabitants were about.

In the morning, our breakfasts were put through the hole in the door, in small oblong-square tin pans, made to fit, and holding a pint of chocolate, with brown bread, and an iron spoon. When they called for the vessels again, I was green enough to return what bread I had left; but my comrade seized it, and said that I should lay that up for lunch or dinner. Soon after he was let out to work at haying in a neighboring field, whither he went every day, and would not be back till noon; so he bade me good-day, saying that he doubted if he should see me again.

When I came out of prison,—for some one interfered, and paid that tax,—I did not perceive that great changes had taken place on the common, such as he observed who went in a youth and emerged a tottering and gray-headed man; and yet a change had to my eyes come over the scene,—the town, and State, and country,—greater than any that mere time could effect. I saw yet more distinctly the State in which I lived. I saw to what extent the people among whom I lived could be trusted as good neighbors and friends; that their friendship was for summer weather only; that they did not greatly purpose to do right; that they were a distinct race from me by their prejudices and superstitions, as the Chinamen and Malays are; that in their sacrifices to humanity they ran no risks, not even to their property; that after all they were not so noble but they treated the thief as he had treated them, and hoped, by a certain outward observance and a few prayers, and by walking in a particular straight though useless path from time to time, to save their souls. This may be to judge my neighbors harshly; for I believe that many of them are not aware that they have such an institution as the jail in their village.

It was formerly the custom in our village, when a poor debtor came out of jail, for his acquaintances to salute him, looking through their fingers, which were crossed to represent the grating of a jail window, "How do ye do?" My neighbors did not thus salute me, but first looked at me, and then at one another, as if I had returned from a long journey. I was put into jail as I was going to the shoemaker's to get a shoe which was mended. When I was let out the next morning, I proceeded to finish my errand, and, having put on my mended shoe, joined a huckleberry party, who were impatient to put themselves under my conduct; and in half an hour,—for the horse was soon tackled,[18]—was in the midst of a huckleberry field, on one of our highest hills, two miles off, and then the State was nowhere to be seen.

This is the whole history of "My Prisons."

---

18. Harnessed.

I have never declined paying the highway tax, because I am as desirous of being a good neighbor as I am of being a bad subject; and as for supporting schools, I am doing my part to educate my fellow-countrymen now. It is for no particular item in the tax-bill that I refuse to pay it. I simply wish to refuse allegiance to the State, to withdraw and stand aloof from it effectually. I do not care to trace the course of my dollar, if I could, till it buys a man or a musket to shoot one with,—the dollar is innocent,—but I am concerned to trace the effects of my allegiance. In fact, I quietly declare war with the State, after my fashion, though I will still make what use and get what advantage of her I can, as is usual in such cases.

If others pay the tax which is demanded of me, from a sympathy with the State, they do but what they have already done in their own case, or rather they abet injustice to a greater extent than the State requires. If they pay the tax from a mistaken interest in the individual taxed, to save his property, or prevent his going to jail, it is because they have not considered wisely how far they let their private feelings interfere with the public good.

This, then, is my position at present. But one cannot be too much on his guard in such a case, lest his action be biased by obstinacy or an undue regard for the opinions of men. Let him see that he does only what belongs to himself and to the hour.

I think sometimes, Why, this people mean well, they are only ignorant; they would do better if they knew how: why give your neighbors this pain to treat you as they are not inclined to? But I think, again, This is no reason why I should do as they do, or permit others to suffer much greater pain of a different kind. Again, I sometimes say to myself, When many millions of men, without heat, without ill will, without personal feeling of any kind, demand of you a few shillings only, without the possibility, such is their constitution, of retracting or altering their present demand, and without the possibility, on your side, of appeal to any other millions, why expose yourself to this overwhelming brute force? You do not resist cold and hunger, the winds and the waves, thus obstinately; you quietly submit to a thousand similar necessities. You do not put your head into the fire. But just in proportion as I regard this as not wholly a brute force, but partly a human force, and consider that I have relations to those millions as to so many millions of men, and not of mere brute or inanimate things, I see that appeal is possible, first and instantaneously, from them to the Maker of them, and, secondly, from them to themselves. But if I put my head deliberately into the fire, there is no appeal to fire or to the Maker of fire, and I have only myself to blame. If I could convince myself that I have any right to be satisfied with men as they are, and to treat them accordingly, and not according, in some respects, to my requisitions and expectations of what they and I ought to be, then, like a good Mussulman[19] and fatalist, I should endeavor to be satisfied with things as they are, and say it is the will of God. And, above all, there is this difference between resisting this and a purely brute or natural force, that I can resist this with some effect; but I cannot expect, like Orpheus,[20] to change the nature of the rocks and trees and beasts.

I do not wish to quarrel with any man or nation. I do not wish to split hairs, to make fine distinctions, or set myself up as better than my neighbors. I seek rather, I may say, even an excuse for conforming to the laws of the land. I am but too ready to conform to them. Indeed I have reason to suspect myself on this head; and each year,

---

19. Muslim.   20. Legendary Greek musician.

as the tax-gatherer comes round, I find myself disposed to review the acts and position of the general and State governments, and the spirit of the people, to discover a pretext for conformity. I believe that the State will soon be able to take all my work of this sort out of my hands, and then I shall be no better a patriot than my fellow-countrymen. Seen from a lower point of view, the Constitution, with all its faults, is very good; the law and the courts are very respectable; even this State and this American government are, in many respects, very admirable and rare things, to be thankful for, such as a great many have described them; but seen from a point of view a little higher, they are what I have described them; seen from a higher still, and the highest, who shall say what they are, or that they are worth looking at or thinking of at all?

However, the government does not concern me much, and I shall bestow the fewest possible thoughts on it. It is not many moments that I live under a government, even in this world. If a man is thought-free, fancy-free, imagination-free, that which *is not* never for a long time appearing *to be* to him, unwise rulers or reformers cannot fatally interrupt him.

I know that most men think differently from myself; but those whose lives are by profession devoted to the study of these or kindred subjects content me as little as any. Statesmen and legislators, standing so completely within the institution, never distinctly and nakedly behold it. They speak of moving society, but have no resting-place without it. They may be men of a certain experience and discrimination, and have no doubt invented ingenious and even useful systems, for which we sincerely thank them; but all their wit and usefulness lie within certain not very wide limits. They are wont to forget that the world is not governed by policy and expediency. Webster[21] never goes behind government, and so cannot speak with authority about it. His words are wisdom to those legislators who contemplate no essential reform in the existing government; but for thinkers, and those who legislate for all time, he never once glances at the subject. I know of those whose serene and wise speculations on this theme would soon reveal the limits of his mind's range and hospitality. Yet, compared with the cheap professions of most reformers, and the still cheaper wisdom and eloquence of politicians in general, his are almost the only sensible and valuable words, and we thank Heaven for him. Comparatively, he is always strong, original, and, above all, practical. Still, his quality is not wisdom, but prudence. The lawyer's truth is not Truth, but consistency or a consistent expediency. Truth is always in harmony with herself, and is not concerned chiefly to reveal the justice that may consist with wrong-doing. He well deserves to be called, as he has been called, the Defender of the Constitution. There are really no blows to be given by him but defensive ones. He is not a leader, but a follower. His leaders are the men of '87.[22] "I have never made an effort," he says, "and never propose to make an effort; I have never countenanced an effort, and never mean to countenance an effort, to disturb the arrangement as originally made, by which the various States came into the Union." Still thinking of the sanction which the Constitution gives to slavery, he says, "Because it was a part of the original compact,—let it stand."[23] Notwithstanding his special acuteness and ability, he is unable to take a fact out of its

---

21. Daniel Webster (1782–1852), Massachusetts senator.   22. Framers of the Constitution.   23. Webster, "The Admission of Texas" (December 22, 1845).

merely political relations, and behold it as it lies absolutely to be disposed of by the intellect,—what, for instance, it behooves a man to do here in America to-day with regard to slavery,—but ventures, or is driven, to make some such desperate answer as the following, while professing to speak absolutely, and as a private man,—from which what new and singular code of social duties might be inferred? "The manner," says he, "in which the governments of those States where slavery exists are to regulate it is for their own consideration, under their responsibility to their constituents, to the general laws of propriety, humanity, and justice, and to God. Associations formed elsewhere, springing from a feeling of humanity, or any other cause, have nothing whatever to do with it. They have never received any encouragement from me, and they never will."[24]

They who know of no purer sources of truth, who have traced up its stream no higher, stand, and wisely stand, by the Bible and the Constitution, and drink at it there with reverence and humility; but they who behold where it comes trickling into this lake or that pool, gird up their loins once more, and continue their pilgrimage toward its fountain-head.

No man with a genius for legislation has appeared in America. They are rare in the history of the world. There are orators, politicians, and eloquent men, by the thousand; but the speaker has not yet opened his mouth to speak who is capable of settling the much-vexed questions of the day. We love eloquence for its own sake, and not for any truth which it may utter, or any heroism it may inspire. Our legislators have not yet learned the comparative value of free trade and of freedom, of union, and of rectitude, to a nation. They have no genius or talent for comparatively humble questions of taxation and finance, commerce and manufactures and agriculture. If we were left solely to the wordy wit of legislators in Congress for our guidance, uncorrected by the seasonable experience and the effectual complaints of the people, America would not long retain her rank among the nations. For eighteen hundred years, though perchance I have no right to say it, the New Testament has been written; yet where is the legislator who has wisdom and practical talent enough to avail himself of the light which it sheds on the science of legislation?

The authority of government, even such as I am willing to submit to,—for I will cheerfully obey those who know and can do better than I, and in many things even those who neither know nor can do so well,—is still an impure one: to be strictly just, it must have the sanction and consent of the governed. It can have no pure right over my person and property but what I concede to it. The progress from an absolute to a limited monarchy, from a limited monarchy to a democracy, is a progress toward a true respect for the individual. Is a democracy, such as we know it, the last improvement possible in government? Is it not possible to take a step further towards recognizing and organizing the rights of man? There will never be a really free and enlightened State until the State comes to recognize the individual as a higher and independent power, from which all its own power and authority are derived, and treats him accordingly. I please myself with imagining a State at last which can afford to be just to all men, and to treat the individual with respect as a neighbor; which even would not think it inconsistent with its own repose if a few were to live aloof from it, not meddling with it, nor embraced by it, who fulfilled all the duties of neigh-

---

24. [Thoreau's note] These extracts have been inserted since the Lecture was read.

bors and fellow-men. A State which bore this kind of fruit, and suffered it to drop off as fast as it ripened, would prepare the way for a still more perfect and glorious State, which also I have imagined, but not yet anywhere seen.

—1849

Walking

I wish to speak a word for Nature, for absolute freedom and wildness, as contrasted with a freedom and culture merely civil—to regard man as an inhabitant, or a part and parcel of Nature, rather than a member of society. I wish to make an extreme statement, if so I may make an emphatic one, for there are enough champions of civilization: the minister and the school committee and every one of you will take care of that.

I have met with but one or two persons in the course of my life who understood the art of Walking, that is, of taking walks,—who had a genius, so to speak, for *sauntering*: which word is beautifully derived "from idle people who roved about the country, in the Middle Ages, and asked charity, under pretence of going *à la Sainte Terre*," to the Holy Land, till the children exclaimed, "There goes a *Sainte-Terrer*," a Saunterer,—a Holy-Lander. They who never go to the Holy Land in their walks, as they pretend, are indeed mere idlers and vagabonds; but they who do go there are saunterers in the good sense, such as I mean. Some, however, would derive the word from *sans terre*, without land or a home, which, therefore, in the good sense, will mean, having no particular home, but equally at home everywhere. For this is the secret of successful sauntering. He who sits still in a house all the time may be the greatest vagrant of all; but the saunterer, in the good sense, is no more vagrant than the meandering river, which is all the while sedulously seeking the shortest course to the sea. But I prefer the first, which, indeed, is the most probable derivation. For every walk is a sort of crusade, preached by some Peter the Hermit[1] in us, to go forth and reconquer this Holy Land from the hands of the Infidels.

It is true, we are but faint-hearted crusaders, even the walkers, nowadays, who undertake no persevering, never-ending enterprises. Our expeditions are but tours, and come round again at evening to the old hearth-side from which we set out. Half the walk is but retracing our steps. We should go forth on the shortest walk, perchance, in the spirit of undying adventure, never to return,—prepared to send back our embalmed hearts only as relics to our desolate kingdoms. If you are ready to leave father and mother, and brother and sister, and wife and child and friends,[2] and never see them again,—if you have paid your debts, and made your will, and settled all your affairs, and are a free man, then you are ready for a walk.

To come down to my own experience, my companion and I, for I sometimes have a companion, take pleasure in fancying ourselves knights of a new, or rather an old, order,—not Equestrians or Chevaliers,[3] not Ritters[4] or Riders, but Walkers, a still more ancient and honorable class, I trust. The chivalric and heroic spirit which once belonged to the Rider seems now to reside in, or perchance to have

1. French priest (d. 1131), a leader of the first crusade in which European Christian armies attempted to capture Jerusalem. Infidel: unbeliever, i.e., Muslim.   2. Matthew 19.29.   3. Horse riders (French).   4. Riders (German).

subsided into, the Walker,—not the Knight, but Walker Errant.[5] He is a sort of fourth estate, outside of Church and State and People.[6]

We have felt that we almost alone hereabouts practised this noble art; though, to tell the truth, at least if their own assertions are to be received, most of my townsmen would fain walk sometimes, as I do, but they cannot. No wealth can buy the requisite leisure, freedom, and independence, which are the capital in this profession. It comes only by the grace of God. It requires a direct dispensation from Heaven to become a walker. You must be born into the family of the Walkers. *Ambulator nascitur, non fit.*[7] Some of my townsmen, it is true, can remember and have described to me some walks which they took ten years ago, in which they were so blessed as to lose themselves for half an hour in the woods; but I know very well that they have confined themselves to the highway ever since, whatever pretensions they may make to belong to this select class. No doubt they were elevated for a moment as by the reminiscence of a previous state of existence, when even they were foresters and outlaws.

> "When he came to grene wode,
>   In a mery mornynge,
> There he herde the notes small
>   Of byrdes mery syngynge.

> "It is ferre gone, sayd Robyn,
>   That I was last here;
> Me Lyste a lytell for to shote
>   At the donne dere."[8]

I think that I cannot preserve my health and spirits, unless I spend four hours a day at least—and it is commonly more than that—sauntering through the woods and over the hills and fields, absolutely free from all worldly engagements. You may safely say, A penny for your thoughts, or a thousand pounds. When sometimes I am reminded that the mechanics and shopkeepers stay in their shops not only all the forenoon, but all the afternoon too, sitting with crossed legs, so many of them,—as if the legs were made to sit upon, and not to stand or walk upon,—I think that they deserve some credit for not having all committed suicide long ago.

I, who cannot stay in my chamber for a single day without acquiring some rust, and when sometimes I have stolen forth for a walk at the eleventh hour of four o'clock in the afternoon, too late to redeem the day, when the shades of night were already beginning to be mingled with the daylight, have felt as if I had committed some sin to be atoned for,—I confess that I am astonished at the power of endurance, to say nothing of the moral insensibility, of my neighbors who confine themselves to shops and offices the whole day for weeks and months, ay, and years almost together. I know not what manner of stuff they are of,—sitting there now at three o'clock in the afternoon, as if it were three o'clock in the morning. Bonaparte may talk of the three-o'clock-in-the-morning courage,[9] but it is nothing to the courage which can sit down cheerfully at this hour in the afternoon over against one's self whom you have known all the morning, to starve

---

5. Medieval Knights Errant wandered in search of exploits. 6. The traditional three estates of pre-Revolutionary France. 7. A walker is born, not made (Latin). 8. *A Lytell Gest of Robyn Hode* (c. 1500). 9. Napoleon Bonaparte (1769–1821), emperor of France, said to have remarked that he almost never encountered courage at two in the morning.

out a garrison to whom you are bound by such strong ties of sympathy. I wonder that about this time, or say between four and five o'clock in the afternoon, too late for the morning papers and too early for the evening ones, there is not a general explosion heard up and down the street, scattering a legion of antiquated and house-bred notions and whims to the four winds for an airing,—and so the evil cure itself.

How womankind, who are confined to the house still more than men, stand it I do not know; but I have ground to suspect that most of them do not *stand* it at all. When, early in a summer afternoon, we have been shaking the dust of the village from the skirts of our garments, making haste past those houses with purely Doric or Gothic[10] fronts, which have such an air of repose about them, my companion whispers that probably about these times their occupants are all gone to bed. Then it is that I appreciate the beauty and the glory of architecture, which itself never turns in, but forever stands out and erect, keeping watch over the slumberers.

No doubt temperament, and, above all, age, have a good deal to do with it. As a man grows older, his ability to sit still and follow in-door occupations increases. He grows vespertinal[11] in his habits as the evening of life approaches, till at last he comes forth only just before sundown, and gets all the walk that he requires in half an hour.

But the walking of which I speak has nothing in it akin to taking exercise, as it is called, as the sick take medicine at stated hours,—as the swinging of dumbbells or chairs; but is itself the enterprise and adventure of the day. If you would get exercise, go in search of the springs of life. Think of a man's swinging dumbbells for his health, when those springs are bubbling up in far-off pastures unsought by him!

Moreover, you must walk like a camel, which is said to be the only beast which ruminates when walking. When a traveller asked Wordsworth's servant to show him her master's study, she answered, "Here is his library, but his study is out of doors."

Living much out of doors, in the sun and wind, will no doubt produce a certain roughness of character,—will cause a thicker cuticle to grow over some of the finer qualities of our nature, as on the face and hands, or as severe manual labor robs the hands of some of their delicacy of touch. So staying in the house, on the other hand, may produce a softness and smoothness, not to say thinness of skin, accompanied by an increased sensibility to certain impressions. Perhaps we should be more susceptible to some influences important to our intellectual and moral growth, if the sun had shone and the wind blown on us a little less; and no doubt it is a nice matter to proportion rightly the thick and thin skin. But methinks that is a scurf that will fall off fast enough,—that the natural remedy is to be found in the proportion which the night bears to the day, the winter to the summer, thought to experience. There will be so much the more air and sunshine in our thoughts. The callous palms of the laborer are conversant with finer tissues of self-respect and heroism, whose touch thrills the heart, than the languid fingers of idleness. That is mere sentimentality that lies abed by day and thinks itself white, far from the tan and callus of experience.

When we walk, we naturally go to the fields and woods: what would become of us, if we walked only in a garden or a mall?[12] Even some sects of philosophers have felt the necessity of importing the woods to themselves, since they did not go to the woods. "They planted groves and walks of Platanes," where they took *subdiales ambulationes*[13] in porticos open to the air. Of course it is of no use to direct our steps to the woods, if they

---

10. Architectural styles.   11. Active at evening.   12. A formal walkway.   13. Outdoor walks. Platanes: plane trees.

do not carry us thither. I am alarmed when it happens that I have walked a mile into the woods bodily, without getting there in spirit. In my afternoon walk I would fain forget all my morning occupations and my obligations to society. But it sometimes happens that I cannot easily shake off the village. The thought of some work will run in my head and I am not where my body is,—I am out of my senses. In my walks I would fain return to my senses. What business have I in the woods, if I am thinking of something out of the woods? I suspect myself, and cannot help a shudder, when I find myself so implicated even in what are called good works,—for this may sometimes happen.

My vicinity affords many good walks; and though for so many years I have walked almost every day, and sometimes for several days together, I have not yet exhausted them. An absolutely new prospect is a great happiness, and I can still get this any afternoon. Two or three hours' walking will carry me to as strange a country as I expect ever to see. A single farm-house which I had not seen before is sometimes as good as the dominions of the King of Dahomey.[14] There is in fact a sort of harmony discoverable between the capabilities of the landscape within a circle of ten miles' radius, or the limits of an afternoon walk, and the threescore years and ten of human life. It will never become quite familiar to you.

Nowadays almost all man's improvements, so called, as the building of houses, and the cutting down of the forest and of all large trees, simply deform the landscape, and make it more and more tame and cheap. A people who would begin by burning the fences and let the forest stand! I saw the fences half consumed, their ends lost in the middle of the prairie, and some worldly miser with a surveyor looking after his bounds, while heaven had taken place around him, and he did not see the angels going to and fro, but was looking for an old post-hole in the midst of paradise. I looked again, and saw him standing in the middle of a boggy stygian[15] fen, surrounded by devils, and he had found his bounds without a doubt, three little stones, where a stake had been driven, and looking nearer, I saw that the Prince of Darkness[16] was his surveyor.

I can easily walk ten, fifteen, twenty, any number of miles, commencing at my own door, without going by any house, without crossing a road except where the fox and the mink do: first along by the river, and then the brook, and then the meadow and the wood-side. There are square miles in my vicinity which have no inhabitant. From many a hill I can see civilization and the abodes of man afar. The farmers and their works are scarcely more obvious than woodchucks and their burrows. Man and his affairs, church and state and school, trade and commerce, and manufactures and agriculture, even politics, the most alarming of them all,—I am pleased to see how little space they occupy in the landscape. Politics is but a narrow field, and that still narrower highway yonder leads to it. I sometimes direct the traveller thither. If you would go to the political world, follow the great road,—follow that market-man, keep his dust in your eyes, and it will lead you straight to it; for it, too, has its place merely, and does not occupy all space. I pass from it as from a bean field into the forest, and it is forgotten. In one half-hour I can walk off to some portion of the earth's surface where a man does not stand from one year's end to another, and there, consequently, politics are not, for they are but as the cigar-smoke of a man.

The village is the place to which the roads tend, a sort of expansion of the highway, as a lake of a river. It is the body of which roads are the arms and legs,—a

14. West African country.   15. Dark. In Greek myth, the river Styx ran through the underworld.   16. Satan.

trivial or quadrivial[17] place, the thoroughfare and ordinary of travellers. The word is from the Latin *villa*, which, together with *via*, a way, or more anciently *ved* and *vella*, Varro[18] derives from *veho*, to carry, because the villa is the place to and from which things are carried. They who got their living by teaming were said *vellaturam facere*. Hence, too, the Latin word *vilis* and our vile, also *villain*.[19] This suggests what kind of degeneracy villagers are liable to. They are wayworn by the travel that goes by and over them, without traveling themselves.

Some do not walk at all; others walk in the highways; a few walk across lots. Roads are made for horses and men of business. I do not travel in them much, comparatively, because I am not in a hurry to get to any tavern or grocery or livery-stable or depot to which they lead. I am a good horse to travel, but not from choice a roadster. The landscape-painter uses the figures of men to mark a road. He would not make that use of my figure. I walk out into a Nature such as the old prophets and poets, Menu, Moses, Homer, Chaucer,[20] walked in. You may name it America, but it is not America: neither Americus Vespucius, nor Columbus,[21] nor the rest were the discoverers of it. There is a truer account of it in mythology than in any history of America, so called, that I have seen.

However, there are a few old roads that may be trodden with profit, as if they led somewhere now that they are nearly discontinued. There is the Old Marlborough Road, which does not go to Marlborough[22] now, methinks, unless that is Marlborough where it carries me. I am the bolder to speak of it here, because I presume that there are one or two such roads in every town.

The Old Marlborough Road

> Where they once dug for money,
> But never found any;
> Where sometimes Martial Miles[23]
> Singly files,
> And Elijah Wood,[24]
> I fear for no good:
> No other man,
> Save Elisha Dugan—
> O man of wild habits,
> Partridges and rabbits
> Who hast no cares
> Only to set snares,
> Who liv'st all alone,
> Close to the bone
> And where life is sweetest
> Constantly eatest.

---

17. A place where four roads meet.   18. Marcus Terrentius Varro (116–27 BC), Roman scholar.   19. Thoreau's fanciful etymologies and puns wander to the point that urban life is degraded and degrading.   20. Thoreau lists originators of Hindu, Hebrew, Greek, and English literatures.   21. Amerigo Vespucci (1454–1512) and Christopher Columbus (1451–1506), Italian explorers.   22. Massachusetts town southwest of Concord.   23. Myles Standish (c. 1584–1656), military leader of Pilgrims in New England.   24. A local inhabitant, as are the rest of the people named in Thoreau's poem.

When the spring stirs my blood
    With the instinct to travel,
    I can get enough gravel
On the Old Marlborough Road.
        Nobody repairs it,
        For nobody wears it;
        It is a living way,[25]
        As the Christians say.
Not many there be
    Who enter therein,
Only the guests of the
    Irishman Quin.
What is it, what is it
    But a direction out there,
And the bare possibility
    Of going somewhere?
        Great guide-boards of stone,
        But travellers none;
        Cenotaphs[26] of the towns
        Named on their crowns.
        It is worth going to see
        Where you *might* be.
        What king
        Did the thing,
        I am still wondering;
        Set up how or when,
        By what selectmen,
        Gourgas or Lee,
        Clark or Darby?
        They're a great endeavor
        To be something forever;
        Blank tablets of stone,
        Where a traveller might groan,
        And in one sentence
        Grave[27] all that is known
        Which another might read,
        In his extreme need.
        I know one or two
        Lines that would do,
        Literature that might stand
        All over the land
        Which a man could remember
        Till next December,
        And read again in the spring,
        After the thawing.

---

25. Hebrews 10.19–20.   26. Stone markers memorializing the dead.   27. Inscribe.

If with fancy unfurled
  You leave your abode,
You may go round the world
  By the Old Marlborough Road.

At present, in this vicinity, the best part of the land is not private property; the landscape is not owned, and the walker enjoys comparative freedom. But possibly the day will come when it will be partitioned off into so-called pleasure-grounds, in which a few will take a narrow and exclusive pleasure only,—when fences shall be multiplied, and man-traps and other engines invented to confine men to the *public* road, and walking over the surface of God's earth shall be construed to mean trespassing on some gentleman's grounds. To enjoy a thing exclusively is commonly to exclude yourself from the true enjoyment of it. Let us improve our opportunities, then, before the evil days come.

What is it that makes it so hard sometimes to determine whither we will walk? I believe that there is a subtle magnetism in Nature, which, if we unconsciously yield to it, will direct us aright. It is not indifferent to us which way we walk. There is a right way; but we are very liable from heedlessness and stupidity to take the wrong one. We would fain take that walk, never yet taken by us through this actual world, which is perfectly symbolical of the path which we love to travel in the interior and ideal world; and sometimes, no doubt, we find it difficult to choose our direction, because it does not yet exist distinctly in our idea.

When I go out of the house for a walk, uncertain as yet whither I will bend my steps, and submit myself to my instinct to decide for me, I find, strange and whimsical as it may seem, that I finally and inevitably settle southwest, toward some particular wood or meadow or deserted pasture or hill in that direction. My needle is slow to settle,—varies a few degrees, and does not always point due southwest, it is true, and it has good authority for this variation, but it always settles between west and south-southwest. The future lies that way to me, and the earth seems more unexhausted and richer on that side. The outline which would bound my walks would be, not a circle, but a parabola, or rather like one of those cometary orbits which have been thought to be non-returning curves, in this case opening westward, in which my house occupies the place of the sun. I turn round and round irresolute sometimes for a quarter of an hour, until I decide, for a thousandth time, that I will walk into the southwest or west. Eastward I go only by force; but westward I go free. Thither no business leads me. It is hard for me to believe that I shall find fair landscapes or sufficient wildness and freedom behind the eastern horizon. I am not excited by the prospect of a walk thither; but I believe that the forest which I see in the western horizon stretches uninterruptedly toward the setting sun, and there are no towns nor cities in it of enough consequence to disturb me. Let me live where I will, on this side is the city, on that the wilderness, and ever I am leaving the city more and more, and withdrawing into the wilderness. I should not lay so much stress on this fact, if I did not believe that something like this is the prevailing tendency of my countrymen. I must walk toward Oregon, and not toward Europe. And that way the nation is moving, and I may say that mankind progress from east to west. Within a few years we have witnessed the phenomenon of a southeastward migration, in the settlement of Australia; but this

tigers; but the traveller can lie down in the woods at night almost anywhere in North America without fear of wild beasts.

These are encouraging testimonies. If the moon looks larger here than in Europe, probably the sun looks larger also. If the heavens of America appear infinitely higher, and the stars brighter, I trust that these facts are symbolical of the height to which the philosophy and poetry and religion of her inhabitants may one day soar. At length, perchance, the immaterial heaven will appear as much higher to the American mind, and the intimations that star it as much brighter. For I believe that climate does thus react on man,—as there is something in the mountain air that feeds the spirit and inspires. Will not man grow to greater perfection intellectually as well as physically under these influences? Or is it unimportant how many foggy days there are in his life? I trust that we shall be more imaginative, that our thoughts will be clearer, fresher, and more ethereal, as our sky,—our understanding more comprehensive and broader, like our plains,—our intellect generally on a grander seale, like our thunder and lightning, our rivers and mountains and forests,—and our hearts shall even correspond in breadth and depth and grandeur to our inland seas. Perchance there will appear to the traveller something, he knows not what, of *læta* and *glabra*, of joyous and serene, in our very faces. Else to what end does the world go on, and why was America discovered?

To Americans I hardly need to say,—

"Westward the star of empire takes its way."[41]

As a true patriot, I should be ashamed to think that Adam in paradise was more favorably situated on the whole than the backwoodsman in this country.

Our sympathies in Massachusetts are not confined to New England; though we may be estranged from the South, we sympathize with the West. There is the home of the younger sons, as among the Scandinavians they took to the sea for their inheritance. It is too late to be studying Hebrew; it is more important to understand even the slang of to-day.

Some months ago I went to see a panorama of the Rhine. It was like a dream of the Middle Ages. I floated down its historic stream in something more than imagination, under bridges built by the Romans, and repaired by later heroes, past cities and castles whose very names were music to my ears, and each of which was the subject of a legend. There were Ehrenbreitstein and Rolandseck and Coblentz,[42] which I knew only in history. They were ruins that interested me chiefly. There seemed to come up from its waters and its vine-clad hills and valleys a hushed music as of Crusaders departing for the Holy Land. I floated along under the spell of enchantment, as if I had been transported to an heroic age, and breathed an atmosphere of chivalry.

Soon after, I went to see a panorama of the Mississippi, and as I worked my way up the river in the light of to-day, and saw the steamboats wooding up, counted the rising cities, gazed on the fresh ruins of Nauvoo,[43] beheld the Indians moving west across the stream, and, as before I had looked up the Moselle, now looked up the Ohio and the Missouri and heard the legends of Dubuque[44] and of Wenona's Cliff,[45]—still thinking

---

41. Paraphrases George Berkeley (1685–1753), "Verses on the Prospect of Planting Arts and Learning in America" (1752).   42. German city on the Rhine and Moselle rivers, near Ehrenbreitstein, a cliff. Rolandseck is a village nearby. 43. Illinois town, site of anti-Mormon riots.   44. Town in Iowa.   45. Winona, Minnesota, is at the base of high cliffs.

more of the future than of the past or present,—I saw that this was a Rhine stream of a different kind; that the foundations of castles were yet to be laid, and the famous bridges were yet to be thrown over the river; and I felt that *this was the heroic age itself*, though we know it not, for the hero is commonly the simplest and obscurest of men.

The West of which I speak is but another name for the Wild; and what I have been preparing to say is, that in Wildness is the preservation of the World. Every tree sends its fibers forth in search of the Wild. The cities import it at any price. Men plow and sail for it. From the forest and wilderness come the tonics and barks which brace mankind. Our ancestors were savages. The story of Romulus and Remus[46] being suckled by a wolf is not a meaningless fable. The founders of every state which has risen to eminence have drawn their nourishment and vigor from a similar wild source. It was because the children of the Empire were not suckled by the wolf that they were conquered and displaced by the children of the northern forests who were.

I believe in the forest, and in the meadow, and in the night in which the corn grows. We require an infusion of hemlock-spruce or arbor-vitæ in our tea. There is a difference between eating and drinking for strength and from mere gluttony. The Hottentots[47] eagerly devour the marrow of the koodoo and other antelopes raw, as a matter of course. Some of our Northern Indians eat raw the marrow of the Arctic reindeer, as well as various other parts, including the summits of the antlers, as long as they are soft. And herein, perchance, they have stolen a march on the cooks of Paris. They get what usually goes to feed the fire. This is probably better than stall-fed beef and slaughter-house pork to make a man of. Give me a wildness whose glance no civilization can endure,—as if we lived on the marrow of koodoos devoured raw.

There are some intervals which border the strain of the wood-thrush, to which I would migrate,—wild lands where no settler has squatted; to which, methinks, I am already acclimated.

The African hunter Cumming[48] tells us that the skin of the eland, as well as that of most other antelopes just killed, emits the most delicious perfume of trees and grass. I would have every man so much like a wild antelope, so much a part and parcel of Nature, that his very person should thus sweetly advertise our senses of his presence, and remind us of those parts of Nature which he most haunts. I feel no disposition to be satirical, when the trapper's coat emits the odor of musquash[49] even; it is a sweeter scent to me than that which commonly exhales from the merchant's or the scholar's garments. When I go into their wardrobes and handle their vestments, I am reminded of no grassy plains and flowery meads which they have frequented, but of dusty merchants' exchanges and libraries rather.

A tanned skin is something more than respectable, and perhaps olive is a fitter color than white for a man,—a denizen of the woods. "The pale white man!" I do not wonder that the African pitied him. Darwin the naturalist says, "A white man bathing by the side of a Tahitian was like a plant bleached by the gardener's art, compared with a fine, dark green one, growing vigorously in the open fields."[50]

Ben Jonson exclaims,—

"How near to good is what is fair!"[51]

---

46. Legendary twins who founded Rome.   47. The Khoikhoi people of south-western Africa.   48. R. G. Gordon-Cumming (1820–1866), travel writer.   49. Muskrat.   50. Charles Darwin (1809–1882), *The Voyage of the Beagle* (1839).   51. Ben Jonson (1572–1637), "Love Freed from Ignorance and Folly" (1611).

So I would say,—

"How near to good is what is *wild*!"

Life consists with wildness. The most alive is the wildest. Not yet subdued to man, its presence refreshes him. One who pressed forward incessantly and never rested from his labors, who grew fast and made infinite demands on life, would always find himself in a new country or wilderness, and surrounded by the raw material of life. He would be climbing over the prostrate stems of primitive forest-trees.

Hope and the future for me are not in lawns and cultivated fields, not in towns and cities, but in the impervious and quaking swamps. When, formerly, I have analyzed my partiality for some farm which I had contemplated purchasing, I have frequently found that I was attracted solely by a few square rods of impermeable and unfathomable bog,—a natural sink in one corner of it. That was the jewel which dazzled me. I derive more of my subsistence from the swamps which surround my native town than from the cultivated gardens in the village. There are no richer parterres[52] to my eyes than the dense beds of dwarf andromeda (*Cassandra calyculata*) which cover these tender places on the earth's surface. Botany cannot go farther than tell me the names of the shrubs which grow there,—the high-blueberry, panicled andromeda, lamb-kill, azalea, and rhodora,—all standing in the quaking sphagnum. I often think that I should like to have my house front on this mass of dull red bushes, omitting other flower plots and borders, transplanted spruce and trim box, even graveled walks,—to have this fertile spot under my windows, not a few imported barrow-fulls of soil only to cover the sand which was thrown out in digging the cellar. Why not put my house, my parlor, behind this plot, instead of behind that meager assemblage of curiosities, that poor apology for a Nature and Art, which I call my front-yard? It is an effort to clear up and make a decent appearance when the carpenter and mason have departed, though done as much for the passer-by as the dweller within. The most tasteful front-yard fence was never an agreeable object of study to me; the most elaborate ornaments, acorn tops, or what not, soon wearied and disgusted me. Bring your sills up to the very edge of the swamp, then (though it may not be the best place for a dry cellar), so that there be no access on that side to citizens. Front yards are not made to walk in, but, at most, through, and you could go in the back way.

Yes, though you may think me perverse, if it were proposed to me to dwell in the neighborhood of the most beautiful garden that ever human art contrived, or else of a dismal swamp, I should certainly decide for the swamp. How vain, then, have been all your labors, citizens, for me!

My spirits infallibly rise in proportion to the outward dreariness. Give me the ocean, the desert, or the wilderness! In the desert, pure air and solitude compensate for want of moisture and fertility. The traveller Burton[53] says of it,—"Your *morale* improves; you become frank and cordial, hospitable and single-minded. . . . In the desert, spirituous liquors excite only disgust. There is a keen enjoyment in a mere animal existence." They who have been traveling long on the steppes of Tartary[54] say,—"On re-entering cultivated lands, the agitation, perplexity, and turmoil of civilization oppressed and suffocated us; the air seemed to fail us, and we felt every moment as if about to die of

---

52. Gardens.   53. Richard Burton (1821–1890), travel writer.   54. A region of Kazakhstan.

asphyxia." When I would recreate myself, I seek the darkest wood, the thickest and most interminable, and, to the citizen, most dismal, swamp. I enter a swamp as a sacred place,—a *sanctum sanctorum*.[55] There is the strength, the marrow, of Nature. The wild-wood covers the virgin mould,—and the same soil is good for men and for trees. A man's health requires as many acres of meadow to his prospect as his farm does loads of muck. There are the strong meats on which he feeds. A town is saved, not more by the righteous men in it than by the woods and swamps that surround it. A township where one primitive forest waves above while another primitive forest rots below,—such a town is fitted to raise not only corn and potatoes, but poets and philosophers for the coming ages. In such a soil grew Homer and Confucius and the rest, and out of such a wilderness comes the Reformer eating locusts and wild honey.[56]

To preserve wild animals implies generally the creation of a forest for them to dwell in or resort to. So it is with man. A hundred years ago they sold bark in our streets peeled from our own woods. In the very aspect of those primitive and rugged trees there was, methinks, a tanning principle which hardened and consolidated the fibers of men's thoughts. Ah! already I shudder for these comparatively degenerate days of my native village, when you cannot collect a load of bark of good thickness, and we no longer produce tar and turpentine.

The civilized nations—Greece, Rome, England—have been sustained by the primitive forests which anciently rotted where they stand. They survive as long as the soil is not exhausted. Alas for human culture! little is to be expected of a nation, when the vegetable mould is exhausted, and it is compelled to make manure of the bones of its fathers. There the poet sustains himself merely by his own superfluous fat, and the philosopher comes down on his marrow-bones.

It is said to be the task of the American "to work the virgin soil," and that "agriculture here already assumes proportions unknown everywhere else." I think that the farmer displaces the Indian even because he redeems the meadow, and so makes himself stronger and in some respects more natural. I was surveying for a man the other day a single straight line one hundred and thirty-two rods[57] long, through a swamp at whose entrance might have been written the words which Dante read over the entrance to the infernal regions,—"Leave all hope, ye that enter,"[58]—that is, of ever getting out again; where at one time I saw my employer actually up to his neck and swimming for his life in his property, though it was still winter. He had another similar swamp which I could not survey at all, because it was completely under water, and nevertheless, with regard to a third swamp, which I did *survey* from a distance, he remarked to me, true to his instincts, that he would not part with it for any consideration, on account of the mud which it contained. And that man intends to put a girdling ditch round the whole in the course of forty months, and so redeem it by the magic of his spade. I refer to him only as the type of a class.

The weapons with which we have gained our most important victories, which should be handed down as heirlooms from father to son, are not the sword and the lance, but the bush-whack, the turf-cutter, the spade, and the bog hoe, rusted with the blood of many a meadow, and begrimed with the dust of many a hard-fought field. The very winds blew the Indian's cornfield into the meadow, and pointed out the way which

55. Holiest of holies (Latin).   56. Matthew 3.4.   57. A rod is 16.5 feet.   58. Dante Alighieri (1265–1321), *The Divine Comedy*.

touched is thenceforth palsied. Who would ever think of a *side* of any of the supple cat tribe, as we speak of a *side* of beef?

I rejoice that horses and steers have to be broken before they can be made the slaves of men, and that men themselves have some wild oats still left to sow before they become submissive members of society. Undoubtedly, all men are not equally fit subjects for civilization; and because the majority, like dogs and sheep, are tame by inherited disposition, this is no reason why the others should have their natures broken that they may be reduced to the same level. Men are in the main alike, but they were made several in order that they might be various. If a low use is to be served, one man will do nearly or quite as well as another; if a high one, individual excellence is to be regarded. Any man can stop a hole to keep the wind away,[65] but no other man could serve so rare a use as the author of this illustration did. Confucius says,—"The skins of the tiger and the leopard, when they are tanned, are as the skins of the dog and the sheep tanned." But it is not the part of a true culture to tame tigers, any more than it is to make sheep ferocious; and tanning their skins for shoes is not the best use to which they can be put.

When looking over a list of men's names in a foreign language, as of military officers, or of authors who have written on a particular subject, I am reminded once more that there is nothing in a name. The name Menschikoff, for instance, has nothing in it to my ears more human than a whisker, and it may belong to a rat. As the names of the Poles and Russians are to us, so are ours to them. It is as if they had been named by the child's rigmarole,—*Iery wiery ichery van, tittle-tol-tan.* I see in my mind a herd of wild creatures swarming over the earth, and to each the herdsman has affixed some barbarous sound in his own dialect. The names of men are, of course, as cheap and meaningless as *Bose* and *Tray,* the names of dogs.

Methinks it would be some advantage to philosophy if men were named merely in the gross, as they are known. It would be necessary only to know the genus and perhaps the race or variety, to know the individual. We are not prepared to believe that every private soldier in a Roman army had a name of his own,—because we have not supposed that he had a character of his own. At present our only true names are nicknames. I knew a boy who, from his peculiar energy, was called "Buster" by his playmates, and this rightly supplanted his Christian name. Some travellers tell us that an Indian had no name given him at first, but earned it, and his name was his fame; and among some tribes he acquired a new name with every new exploit. It is pitiful when a man bears a name for convenience merely, who has earned neither name nor fame.

I will not allow mere names to make distinctions for me, but still see men in herds for all them. A familiar name cannot make a man less strange to me. It may be given to a savage who retains in secret his own wild title earned in the woods. We have a wild savage in us, and a savage name is perchance somewhere recorded as ours. I see that my neighbor, who bears the familiar epithet William or Edwin, takes it off with his jacket. It does not adhere to him when asleep or in anger, or aroused by any passion or inspiration. I seem to hear pronounced by some of his kin at such a time his original wild name in some jaw-breaking or else melodious tongue.

Here is this vast, savage, hovering mother of ours, Nature, lying all around, with such beauty, and such affection for her children, as the leopard; and yet we are so early

---

65. William Shakespeare (1564–1616), *Hamlet* (1603), 5.1.236–237.

weaned from her breast to society, to that culture which is exclusively an interaction of man on man,—a sort of breeding in and in, which produces at most a merely English nobility, a civilization destined to have a speedy limit.

In society, in the best institutions of men, it is easy to detect a certain precocity. When we should still be growing children, we are already little men. Give me a culture which imports much muck from the meadows, and deepens the soil—not that which trusts to heating manures, and improved implements and modes of culture only!

Many a poor sore-eyed student that I have heard of would grow faster, both intellectually and physically, if, instead of sitting up so very late, he honestly slumbered a fool's allowance.

There may be an excess even of informing light. Niépce,[66] a Frenchman, discovered "actinism," that power in the sun's rays which produces a chemical effect,— that granite rocks, and stone structures, and statues of metal "are all alike destructively acted upon during the hours of sunshine, and, but for provisions of Nature no less wonderful, would soon perish under the delicate touch of the most subtle of the agencies of the universe." But he observed that "those bodies which underwent this change during the daylight possessed the power of restoring themselves to their original conditions during the hours of night, when this excitement was no longer influencing them." Hence it has been inferred that "the hours of darkness are as necessary to the inorganic creation as we know night and sleep are to the organic kingdom." Not even does the moon shine every night, but gives place to darkness.

I would not have every man nor every part of a man cultivated, any more than I would have every acre of earth cultivated: part will be tillage, but the greater part will be meadow and forest, not only serving an immediate use, but preparing a mould against a distant future, by the annual decay of the vegetation which it supports.

There are other letters for the child to learn than those which Cadmus[67] invented. The Spaniards have a good term to express this wild and dusky knowledge,—*Gramatica parda*, tawny grammar,—a kind of mother-wit derived from that same leopard to which I have referred.

We have heard of a Society for the Diffusion of Useful Knowledge.[68] It is said that knowledge is power; and the like. Methinks there is equal need of a Society for the Diffusion of Useful Ignorance, what we will call Beautiful Knowledge, a knowledge useful in a higher sense: for what is most of our boasted so-called knowledge but a conceit that we know something, which robs us of the advantage of our actual ignorance? What we call knowledge is often our positive ignorance; ignorance our negative knowledge. By long years of patient industry and reading of the newspapers—for what are the libraries of science but files of newspapers?—a man accumulates a myriad facts, lays them up in his memory, and then when in some spring of his life he saunters abroad into the Great Fields of thought, he, as it were, goes to grass like a horse and leaves all his harness behind in the stable. I would say to the Society for the Diffusion of Useful Knowledge, sometimes,—Go to grass. You have eaten hay long enough. The spring has come with its green crop. The very cows are driven to their country pastures before the end of May; though I have heard of one

---

66. Joseph Niépce (1765–1833), French photographer.   67. Legendary Greek inventor of the alphabet.   68. An English non-profit publisher of inexpensive books.

unnatural farmer who kept his cow in the barn and fed her on hay all the year round. So, frequently, the Society for the Diffusion of Useful Knowledge treats its cattle.

A man's ignorance sometimes is not only useful, but beautiful,—while his knowledge, so called, is oftentimes worse than useless, besides being ugly. Which is the best man to deal with,—he who knows nothing about a subject, and, what is extremely rare, knows that he knows nothing, or he who really knows something about it, but thinks that he knows all?

My desire for knowledge is intermittent, but my desire to bathe my head in atmospheres unknown to my feet is perennial and constant. The highest that we can attain to is not Knowledge, but Sympathy with Intelligence. I do not know that this higher knowledge amounts to anything more definite than a novel and grand surprise on a sudden revelation of the insufficiency of all that we called Knowledge before,—a discovery that there are more things in heaven and earth than are dreamed of in our philosophy.[69] It is the lighting up of the mist by the sun. Man cannot *know* in any higher sense than this, any more than he can look serenely and with impunity in the face of the sun: 'Ὡς τὶ νοῶν, ου κεινον νοήσεις—"You will not perceive that, as perceiving a particular thing," say the Chaldean Oracles.[70]

There is something servile in the habit of seeking after a law which we may obey. We may study the laws of matter at and for our convenience, but a successful life knows no law. It is an unfortunate discovery certainly, that of a law which binds us where we did not know before that we were bound. Live free, child of the mist,—and with respect to knowledge we are all children of the mist. The man who takes the liberty to live is superior to all the laws, by virtue of his relation to the law-maker. "That is active duty," says the Vishnu Purana,[71] "which is not for our bondage; that is knowledge which is for our liberation: all other duty is good only unto weariness; all other knowledge is only the cleverness of an artist."

It is remarkable how few events or crises there are in our histories, how little exercised we have been in our minds, how few experiences we have had. I would fain be assured that I am growing apace and rankly, though my very growth disturb this dull equanimity,—though it be with struggle through long, dark, muggy nights or seasons of gloom. It would be well if all our lives were a divine tragedy even, instead of this trivial comedy or farce. Dante, Bunyan,[72] and others appear to have been exercised in their minds more than we: they were subjected to a kind of culture such as our district schools and colleges do not contemplate. Even Mahomet,[73] though many may scream at his name, had a good deal more to live for, ay, and to die for, than they have commonly.

When, at rare intervals, some thought visits one, as perchance he is walking on a railroad, then, indeed, the cars go by without his hearing them. But soon, by some inexorable law, our life goes by and the cars return.

> "Gentle breeze, that wanderest unseen,
> And bendest the thistles round Loira of storms,
> Traveller of the windy glens,
> Why hast thou left my ear so soon?"

69. *Hamlet*, 1.5.166–167.   70. Mystical texts of second century AD.   71. Hindu scriptures.   72. John Bunyan (1628–1688), English preacher.   73. Muhammad (570–632), founder of Islam.

While almost all men feel an attraction drawing them to society, few are attracted strongly to Nature. In their relation to Nature men appear to me for the most part, notwithstanding their arts, lower than the animals. It is not often a beautiful relation, as in the case of the animals. How little appreciation of the beauty of the landscape there is among us! We have to be told that the Greeks called the world Κόσμος, Beauty, or Order, but we do not see clearly why they did so, and we esteem it at best only a curious philological fact.

For my part, I feel that with regard to Nature I live a sort of border life, on the confines of a world into which I make occasional and transient forays only, and my patriotism and allegiance to the state into whose territories I seem to retreat are those of a moss-trooper. Unto a life which I call natural I would gladly follow even a will-o'-the-wisp through bogs and sloughs unimaginable, but no moon nor firefly has shown me the causeway to it. Nature is a personality so vast and universal that we have never seen one of her features. The walker in the familiar fields which stretch around my native town sometimes finds himself in another land than is described in their owners' deeds, as it were in some faraway field on the confines of the actual Concord, where her jurisdiction ceases, and the idea which the word Concord suggests ceases to be suggested. These farms which I have myself surveyed, these bounds which I have set up, appear dimly still as through a mist; but they have no chemistry to fix them; they fade from the surface of the glass, and the picture which the painter painted stands out dimly from beneath. The world with which we are commonly acquainted leaves no trace, and it will have no anniversary.

I took a walk on Spaulding's Farm the other afternoon. I saw the setting sun lighting up the opposite side of a stately pine wood. Its golden rays straggled into the aisles of the wood as into some noble hall. I was impressed as if some ancient and altogether admirable and shining family had settled there in that part of the land called Concord, unknown to me,—to whom the sun was servant,—who had not gone into society in the village,—who had not been called on. I saw their park, their pleasure-ground, beyond through the wood, in Spaulding's cranberry-meadow. The pines furnished them with gables as they grew. Their house was not obvious to vision; the trees grew through it. I do not know whether I heard the sounds of a suppressed hilarity or not. They seemed to recline on the sunbeams. They have sons and daughters. They are quite well. The farmer's cart-path, which leads directly through their hall, does not in the least put them out,—as the muddy bottom of a pool is sometimes seen through the reflected skies. They never heard of Spaulding, and do not know that he is their neighbor,—notwithstanding I heard him whistle as he drove his team through the house. Nothing can equal the serenity of their lives. Their coat-of-arms is simply a lichen. I saw it painted on the pines and oaks. Their attics were in the tops of the trees. They are of no politics. There was no noise of labor. I did not perceive that they were weaving or spinning. Yet I did detect, when the wind lulled and hearing was done away, the finest imaginable sweet musical hum,—as of a distant hive in May, which perchance was the sound of their thinking. They had no idle thoughts, and no one without could see their work, for their industry was not as in knots and excrescences embayed.

But I find it difficult to remember them. They fade irrevocably out of my mind even now while I speak, and endeavor to recall them and recollect myself. It is only after a long and serious effort to recollect my best thoughts that I become again aware of their cohabitancy. If it were not for such families as this, I think I should move out of Concord.

was an early and clear voice in what would become a chorus of opposition to the growing destruction of nature for the sake of profits and in the name of progress.

The speed and intensity of the destruction was even more obvious in North America than in England. The American Revolution had released capitalism's truly dynamic potential, and during the next few decades, the rich forests and rivers of the eastern seaboard were cleared and dammed. Roads, canals, and railways were built from Georgia to Maine, integrating the United States into a single market and vastly accelerating economic expansion. The population more than doubled every two decades, as millions immigrated from Europe, following the promises of opportunity and free land. Soon, the vast forests and prairies west of the Appalachian and Alleghany ranges had been cleared and brought under the plow. Andrew Jackson enthusiastically cheered this process, and the violent displacement of Native Americans it entailed, in his 1830 address to Congress: "What good man would prefer a country covered with forests and ranged by a few thousand savages to our extensive Republic, studded with cities, towns, and prosperous farms . . . and filled with all the blessings of liberty, civilization, and religion?" (p. 1075). Like all such rhetorical questions, Jackson's was designed to preempt debate. Nevertheless, many did prefer forests to cities. Henry David Thoreau delivered his lecture "Walking" (1855) many times to large and approving crowds, asking his audience "to regard man as an inhabitant, or a part and parcel of Nature, rather than a member of society" (p. 1052). Thoreau believed life in the modern city was alienating and unhealthy and that "in Wildness is the preservation of the world."

Thoreau was no lone prophet of environmentalism. Concerns about the spiritual and physical effects of city life had spurred construction of Frederick Law Olmsted's Central Park in Manhattan. This was the largest public works project to date in the United States, employing tens of thousands of laborers who had been thrown out of work by the depression of 1837–1844. Other cities followed suit, and during his career Olmsted directed the construction of some of the most famous American landscapes, including Brooklyn's Prospect Park, Chicago's Riverside neighborhood, Atlanta's Druid Hills, Boston's Emerald Necklace, and Montreal's Mount Royal. All of Olmsted's projects set out to create opportunities for human enjoyment of beautiful settings; ironically, he was a pioneer of massive earth-moving projects, adapting the technology of mining to the building of "natural" landscapes. Other early environmentalists asked whether such technologies had not begun to seriously impact the environment as a whole. Vermont geographer George Perkins Marsh suggested, in his *Man and Nature; or, Physical Geography as Modified by Human Action* (1864), that "of all organic beings, man alone is to be regarded as essentially a destructive power" (p. 1081). Marsh drew on his extensive travels and historical research to describe a range of disturbing examples of human societies that had wholly destroyed the environments on which they had depended for their prosperity and even survival. As damage to the North American environment mounted, early travel writers and nature writers began to document and mourn the changes. Susan Fenimore Cooper's elegiac sketches of New England country life, especially in her influential collection *Rural Hours* (1850), launched one of the best-selling genres of the nineteenth century, women's regional writing. In magazine essays like "Otsego Leaves" (1878), Cooper connected the declining health of wild flora and fauna with the displacement of people from wholesome outdoor lives, capturing a widespread and building sense that capitalism was developing the nation into an intolerably mechanical and pallid future.

Andrew Jackson
1767–1845

Born in rural South Carolina to Irish immigrants, Andrew Jackson served as an officer's orderly during the American Revolution at age thirteen and was captured by the British along with his brother. Later, working as a lawyer, he often accepted land in payment of his fees and became one of the biggest landowners in Tennessee. He was active in the state militia, and when the War of 1812 broke out, his unit was ordered to retaliate against Creek Indians who had attacked a group of settlers in Alabama. The Battle of Horseshoe Bend in 1814 broke the organized military power of the Creeks and earned Jackson the nickname "Old Hickory." He cemented his reputation by defeating the British at New Orleans. Because of his experience as an "Indian killer," he was soon called into service again to subdue the Seminole, who were harassing the U.S. border with Spanish Florida. On his own authority, Jackson invaded, provoking international outrage that quieted only when Spain agreed to "sell" Florida to the United States for $5 million. A political career followed, culminating in his election to the presidency in 1828 as a candidate of the "common man."

Jackson immediately began to pursue an aggressive policy of Indian removal, forcing tribes east of the Mississippi to relocate to reservations in what is now Oklahoma. His addresses to Congress on the subject explain his policy in the language of paternalism, representing Native Americans as recalcitrant and irresponsible children for whom he feels only sympathy and concern. By the end of Jackson's two terms in office, at least 46,000 members of the Five Nations (the Cherokee, Creek, Chickasaw, Choctaw, and Seminole) had been forcibly removed from their homes. At least 4,000 Cherokee died of exposure, starvation, and disease on the forced march to the West that came to be known as the Trail of Tears. As a result, many millions of acres of the most fertile land in North America were made available for cotton production with slave labor. After leaving office, Jackson retired to his Tennessee plantation, where he died in 1845, just months after the annexation of the Republic of Texas, an act that would in turn precipitate the invasion of Mexico, the next step in America's "manifest destiny."

Message of the President of the United States to Both Houses of Congress at the Commencement of the Second Session of the Twenty-First Congress, December 7, 1830

It gives me pleasure to announce to Congress that the benevolent policy of the Government, steadily pursued for nearly 30 years, in relation to the removal of the Indians beyond the white settlements is approaching to a happy consummation. Two important tribes have accepted the provision made for their removal at the last session of Congress, and it is believed that their example will induce the remaining tribes also to seek the same obvious advantages.

The consequences of a speedy removal will be important to the United States, to individual States, and to the Indians themselves. The pecuniary advantages which it promises to the Government are the least of its recommendations. It puts an end to all possible danger of collision between the authorities of the General and State Governments on account of the Indians. It will place a dense and civilized population in large tracts of country now occupied by a few savage hunters. By opening the whole territory between Tennessee on the north and Louisiana on the south to the settlement of the whites it will incalculably strengthen the SW frontier and render the adjacent States strong enough to repel future invasions without remote aid. It will relieve the whole State of Mississippi and the western part of Alabama of Indian occupancy, and enable those States to advance rapidly in population, wealth, and power. It will separate the Indians from immediate contact with settlements of whites; free them from the power of the States; enable them to pursue happiness in their own way and under their own rude institutions; will retard the progress of decay, which is lessening their numbers, and perhaps cause them gradually, under the protection of the

Government and through the influence of good counsels, to cast off their savage habits and become an interesting, civilized, and Christian community. These consequences, some of them so certain and the rest so probable, make the complete execution of the plan sanctioned by Congress at their last session an object of much solicitude.

Toward the aborigines of the country no one can indulge a more friendly feeling than myself, or would go further in attempting to reclaim them from their wandering habits and make them a happy, prosperous people. I have endeavored to impress upon them my own solemn convictions of the duties and powers of the General Government in relation to the State authorities. For the justice of the laws passed by the States within the scope of their reserved powers they are not responsible to this Government. As individuals we may entertain and express our opinions of their acts, but as a Government we have as little right to control them as we have to prescribe laws for other nations.

With a full understanding of the subject, the Choctaw and the Chickasaw tribes have with great unanimity determined to avail themselves of the liberal offers presented by the act of Congress, and have agreed to remove beyond the Mississippi River. Treaties have been made with them, which in due season will be submitted for consideration. In negotiating these treaties they were made to understand their true condition, and they have preferred maintaining their independence in the Western forests to submitting to the laws of the States in which they now reside. These treaties, being probably the last which will ever be made with them, are characterized by great liberality on the part of the Government. They give the Indians a liberal sum in consideration of their removal, and comfortable subsistence on their arrival at their new homes. If it be their real interest to maintain a separate existence, they will there be at liberty to do so without the inconveniences and vexations to which they would unavoidably have been subject in Alabama and Mississippi.

Humanity has often wept over the fate of the aborigines of this country, and philanthropy has been long busily employed in devising means to avert it, but its progress has never for a moment been arrested, and one by one have many powerful tribes disappeared from the earth. To follow to the tomb the last of his race and to tread on the graves of extinct nations excite melancholy reflections. But true philanthropy reconciles the mind to these vicissitudes as it does to the extinction of one generation to make room for another. In the monuments and fortifications of an unknown people, spread over the extensive regions of the West, we behold the memorials of a once powerful race, which was exterminated or has disappeared to make room for the existing savage tribes. Nor is there any thing in this which, upon a comprehensive view of the general interests of the human race, is to be regretted. Philanthropy could not wish to see this continent restored to the condition in which it was found by our forefathers. What good man would prefer a country covered with forests and ranged by a few thousand savages to our extensive Republic, studded with cities, towns, and prosperous farms, embellished with all the improvements which art can devise or industry execute, occupied by more than 12,000,000 happy people, and filled with all the blessings of liberty, civilization, and religion?

The present policy of the Government is but a continuation of the same progressive change by a milder process. The tribes which occupied the countries now constituting the Eastern States were annihilated or have melted away to make room for the whites. The waves of population and civilization are rolling to the westward, and we now propose to acquire the countries occupied by the red men of the South and West by a fair exchange, and, at the expense of the United States, to send them to a land where their existence may be prolonged and perhaps made perpetual. Doubtless it will be painful to leave the graves of their fathers; but what do they more than our ancestors did or than our children are now doing? To better their condition in an unknown land our forefathers left all that was dear in earthly objects. Our children by thousands yearly leave the land of their birth to seek new homes in distant regions. Does Humanity weep at these painful separations from every thing, animate and inanimate, with which the young heart has become entwined? Far from it. It is rather a source of joy that our country affords scope where our young population may range unconstrained in body or in mind, developing the power and faculties of man in their highest perfection. These remove hundreds and almost thousands of miles at their own expense, purchase the lands they occupy, and support themselves at their new homes from the moment of their arrival. Can it be cruel in this Government when, by events which it can not control, the Indian is made discontented in his ancient home to purchase his lands, to give him a new and extensive territory, to pay the expense of his removal, and support him a year in his new abode? How many thousands of our own people would gladly embrace the opportunity of removing to the West on such conditions! If the offers made to the Indians were extended to them, they would be hailed with gratitude and joy.

And is it supposed that the wandering savage has a stronger attachment to his home than the settled, civilized Christian? Is it more afflicting to him to leave the graves of his fathers than it is to our brothers and children? Rightly considered, the policy of the General Government toward the red man is not only liberal, but generous. He is unwilling to submit to the laws of the States and mingle with their population. To save him from this alternative, or perhaps utter annihilation, the General Government kindly offers him a new home, and proposes to pay the whole expense of his removal and settlement.

In the consummation of a policy originating at an early period, and steadily pursued by every Administration within the present century—so just to the States and so generous to the Indians—the Executive feels it has a right to expect the cooperation of Congress and of all good and disinterested men. The States, moreover, have a right to demand it. It was substantially a part of the compact which made them members of our Confederacy. With Georgia there is an express contract; with the new States an implied one of equal obligation. Why, in authorizing Ohio, Indiana, Illinois, Missouri, Mississippi, and Alabama to form constitutions and become separate States, did Congress include within their limits extensive tracts of Indian lands, and, in some instances, powerful Indian tribes? Was it not understood by both parties that the power of the States was to be coextensive with their limits, and that with all convenient dispatch the General Government should extinguish the Indian title and remove every obstruction to the complete jurisdiction of the State governments over the soil? Probably not one of those States would have accepted a separate existence—certainly it would never have been granted by Congress—had it been understood that they were to be confined for ever to those small portions of their nominal territory the Indian title to which had at the time been extinguished.

It is, therefore, a duty which this Government owes to the new States to extinguish as soon as possible the Indian title to all lands which Congress themselves have included within their limits. When this is done the duties of the General Government in relation to the States and the Indians within their limits are at an end. The Indians may leave the State or not, as they choose. The purchase of their lands does not alter in the least their personal relations with the State government. No act of the General Government has ever been deemed necessary to give the States jurisdiction over the persons of the Indians. That they possess by virtue of their sovereign power within their own limits in as full a manner before as after the purchase of the Indian lands; nor can this Government add to or diminish it.

May we not hope, therefore, that all good citizens, and none more zealously than those who think the Indians oppressed by subjection to the laws of the States, will unite in attempting to open the eyes of those children of the forest to their true condition, and by a speedy removal to relieve them from all the evils, real or imaginary, present or prospective, with which they may be supposed to be threatened.

—1830

John Clare
1793–1864

John Clare might well have spent his life as a poor farm worker and lime burner in the village of Helpston, Northamptonshire. But as a young man, he immersed himself in the oral culture of ballads and songs and read widely in the formal poetic tradition. As a result, Clare developed a strong attachment to the landscape of his birth and wrote poems that document the fine detail of an English village's communal life on the land. The poems are purposely unconventional in their grammar, punctuation, and word choices, relying heavily on the dialect vocabulary of the rural poor. John Taylor, the publisher of John Keats, agreed to print Clare's first book, *Poems Descriptive of Rural Life and Scenery* (1820). However, Taylor heavily edited the poems, regularizing much of the spelling and syntax, and he added an introduction in which he framed the poems as the fascinating products of an almost childlike mind. The volume sold three thousand copies in its first year. Clare was lionized by London society; he toured from salon to salon in a green jacket and was introduced as "The Northamptonshire Peasant." His relationship with his elite readership, though, would always be strained and sometimes bitter. He recognized they were sentimentally consuming both his poems and his life as parts of a pastoral fantasy. At the same time, much of their wealth came from exploiting rural laborers like himself, along with the land he knew so much more closely than they did. Clare's lifetime spanned a period of large-scale enclosures mandated by Parliament. Large tracts of the English countryside had been held as commons for centuries, available to all for grazing, woodcutting, and even squatting. They were now being fenced off with hedges and sold to agricultural capitalists for development into large farms. Clare deplored this process, which he felt was destroying the integrity and interconnectedness of the land and the communities on it. Despite his financial dependence on the ruling-class buyers of his books, he denounced their greed in poems like "Helpstone":

> Accursed Wealth! o'erbounding human laws
> Of every evil thou remain'st the cause.
> Victims of want, those wretches such as me,
> Too truly lay their wretchedness to thee.

Clare's ambition to support himself as a poet was frustrated when he passed from vogue in London and sales of his books declined. Nevertheless, he continued to write, in increasingly elegiac tones, about his love for a way of living intimately on the land that was being destroyed by modernization. Eventually, he took refuge from that process in the Northamptonshire Lunatic Asylum, becoming increasingly depressed the longer he was away from his home at Helpston.

The Mores

Far spread the moorey ground a level scene
Bespread with rush and one eternal green
That never felt the rage of blundering plough
Though centurys wreathed springs blossoms on its brow
Still meeting plains that stretched them far away   5
In uncheckt shadows of green brown and grey
Unbounded freedom ruled the wandering scene
Nor fence of ownership crept in between
To hide the prospect of the following eye
Its only bondage was the circling sky   10
One mighty flat undwarfed by bush and tree
Spread its faint shadow of immensity
And lost itself which seemed to eke its bounds
In the blue mist the orisons[1] edge surrounds
Now this sweet vision of my boyish hours   15
Free as spring clouds and wild as summer flowers
Is faded all—a hope that blossomed free
And hath been once no more shall ever be
Inclosure came and trampled on the grave
Of labours rights and left the poor a slave   20
And memorys pride ere want to wealth did bow
Is both the shadow and the substance now
The sheep and cows were free to range as then
Where change might prompt nor felt the bonds of men
Cows went and came with evening morn and night   25
To the wild pasture as their common right
And sheep unfolded[2] with the rising sun
Heard the swains shout and felt their freedom won
Tracked the red fallow field and heath and plain
Then met the brook and drank and roamed again   30
The brook that dribbled on as clear as glass
Beneath the roots they hid among the grass
While the glad shepherd traced their tracks along
Free as the lark and happy as her song
But now alls fled and flats of many a dye   35
That seemed to lengthen with the following eye

---

1. Horizon's.   2. Left their pens.

Moors loosing from the sight far smooth and blea[3]
Where swopt the plover in its pleasure free
Are vanished now with commons wild and gay
As poets visions of lifes early day   40
Mulberry bushes where the boy would run
To fill his hands with fruit are grubbed and done
And hedgrow briars—flower lovers overjoyed
Came and got flower pots—these are all destroyed
And sky bound mores in mangled garbs are left   45
Like mighty giants of their limbs bereft
Fence now meets fence in owners little bounds
Of field and meadow large as garden grounds
In little parcels little minds to please
With men and flocks imprisoned ill at ease   50
Each little path that led its pleasant way
As sweet as morning leading night astray
Where little flowers bloomed round a varied host
That travel felt delighted to be lost
Nor grudged the steps that he had taen as vain   55
When right roads traced his journeys end again
Nay on a broken tree hed sit awhile
To see the mores and fields and meadows smile
Sometimes with cowslaps[4] smothered—then all white
With daiseys—then the summers splendid sight   60
Of corn fields crimson oer the 'headach'[5] bloomd
Like splendid armys for the battle plumed
He gazed upon them with wild fancys eye
As fallen landscapes from an evening sky
These paths are stopt—the rude philistines thrall   65
Is laid upon them and destroyed them all
Each little tyrant with his little sign
Shows where man claims earth glows no more divine
On paths to freedom and to childhood dear
A board sticks up to notice 'no road here'   70
And on the tree with ivy overhung
The hated sign by vulgar taste is hung
As tho the very birds should learn to know
When they go there they must no further go
This with the poor scared freedom bade good bye   75
And much the[y] feel it in the smothered sigh
And birds and trees and flowers without a name
All sighed when lawless laws enclosure came
And dreams of plunder in such rebel schemes
Have found too truly that they were but dreams   80

—1935

3. Blue-grey.   4. Primrose.   5. Poppy.

George Perkins Marsh
1801–1882

The product of one of Vermont's most eminent political dynasties, George Perkins Marsh was a gentleman philosopher who saw no borders between the various fields of human knowledge and undertaking. He attended Dartmouth College, where he excelled at foreign languages, learning at least six before he graduated in 1820. He followed family tradition by practicing law and winning elections, first to Vermont's state legislature and then to the U.S. Congress as a Whig, where he spoke out against slavery and the invasion of Mexico. He was also involved in a wide variety of business ventures: newspaper editing, sheep farming, lumber milling, marble quarrying, and more. Most were unsuccessful and entangled him in massive debts. At the same time, he practiced architecture, designing the Washington Monument, and he continued his study of languages, eventually learning more than twenty and becoming the foremost American scholar of Scandinavian languages. In 1849, President Zachary Taylor appointed him minister to Turkey, where he served for five years. Studying human social adaptations to this arid environment, Marsh formed a plan to naturalize camels as draft animals in the deserts of the American West. On his advice, Congress imported seventy-four camels to Texas, where the Army experimented with using them as military mounts. Returning to the United States, he taught philology, the science of linguistic evolution, at Columbia University and the Lowell Institute in Boston. He joined the anti-slavery Republican Party when it formed, and in 1861, President Abraham Lincoln named him minister to Italy. He remained there for twenty years, until his death in 1882, after which he was interred in the Protestant Cemetery in Rome.

During his long stay in Italy, Marsh studied deforestation and other forms of environmental degradation, and he wrote *Man and Nature; or, Physical Geography as Modified by Human Action* (1864), the first sustained environmentalist manifesto based on ecological insights into the interconnection of natural systems. He was the first to argue that human beings were "disturbing agent[s]" (p. 1081) who frequently changed what most scientists then thought of as steady natural states. Based on his observations of the Italian countryside and his experience of logging in Vermont, Marsh argued that the consequences of such disturbances could be devastating and persistent. However, his book received little attention until the 1930s, when Lewis Mumford, the pioneering historian of human geography, rediscovered it and called Marsh "the fountainhead of the conservation movement."

from Man and Nature; or, Physical Geography as Modified by Human Action

Destructiveness of Man

Man has too long forgotten that the earth was given to him for usufruct[1] alone, not for consumption, still less for profligate waste. Nature has provided against the absolute destruction of any of her elementary matter, the raw material of her works; the thunderbolt and the tornado, the most convulsive throes of even the volcano and the earthquake, being only phenomena of decomposition and recomposition. But she has left it within the power of man irreparably to derange the combinations of inorganic matter and of organic life, which through the night of aeons she had been pro-

---

1. Use, not ownership.

portioning and balancing, to prepare the earth for his habitation, when, in the fulness of time, his Creator should call him forth to enter into its possession.

Apart from the hostile influence of man, the organic and the inorganic world are, as I have remarked, bound together by such mutual relations and adaptations as secure, if not the absolute permanence and equilibrium of both, a long continuance of the established conditions of each at any given time and place, or at least, a very slow and gradual succession of changes in those conditions. But man is everywhere a disturbing agent. Wherever he plants his foot, the harmonies of nature are turned to discords. The proportions and accommodations which insured the stability of existing arrangements are overthrown. Indigenous vegetable and animal species are extirpated, and supplanted by others of foreign origin, spontaneous production is forbidden or restricted, and the face of the earth is either laid bare or covered with a new and reluctant growth of vegetable forms, and with alien tribes of animal life. These intentional changes and substitutions constitute, indeed, great revolutions; but vast as is their magnitude and importance, they are, as we shall see, insignificant in comparison with the contingent and unsought results which have flowed from them.

The fact that, of all organic beings, man alone is to be regarded as essentially a destructive power, and that he wields energies to resist which, nature—that Nature whom all material life and all inorganic substance obey—is wholly impotent, tends to prove that, though living in physical nature, he is not of her, that he is of more exalted parentage, and belongs to a higher order of existences than those born of her womb and submissive to her dictates.

There are, indeed, brute destroyers, beasts and birds and insects of prey—all animal life feeds upon, and, of course, destroys other life,—but this destruction is balanced by compensations. It is, in fact, the very means by which the existence of one tribe of animals or of vegetables is secured against being smothered by the encroachments of another; and the reproductive powers of species, which serve as the food of others, are always proportioned to the demand they are destined to supply. Man pursues his victims with reckless destructiveness; and, while the sacrifice of life by the lower animals is limited by the cravings of appetite, he unsparingly persecutes, even to extirpation, thousands of organic forms which he cannot consume. . . .

The earth was not, in its natural condition, completely adapted to the use of man, but only to the sustenance of wild animals and wild vegetation. These live, multiply their kind in just proportion, and attain their perfect measure of strength and beauty, without producing or requiring any change in the natural arrangements of surface, or in each other's spontaneous tendencies, except such mutual repression of excessive increase as may prevent the extirpation of one species by the encroachments of another. In short, without man, lower animal and spontaneous vegetable life would have been constant in type, distribution, and proportion, and the physical geography of the earth would have remained undisturbed for indefinite periods, and been subject to revolution only from possible, unknown cosmical causes, or from geological action.

But man, the domestic animals that serve him, the field and garden plants the products of which supply him with food and clothing, cannot subsist and rise to the full development of their higher properties, unless brute and unconscious nature be effectually combated, and, in a great degree, vanquished by human art. Hence, a certain measure of transformation of terrestrial surface, of suppression of natural, and stimulation of artificially modified productivity becomes necessary. This measure man has unfortunately exceeded. He has felled the forests whose network of fibrous roots bound the mould to the rocky skeleton of the earth; but had he allowed here and there a belt of woodland to reproduce itself by spontaneous propagation, most of the mischiefs which his reckless destruction of the natural protection of the soil has occasioned would have been averted. He has broken up the mountain reservoirs, the percolation of whose waters through unseen channels supplied the fountains that refreshed his cattle and fertilized his fields; but he has neglected to maintain the cisterns and the canals of irrigation which a wise antiquity had constructed to neutralize the consequences of its own imprudence. While he has torn the thin glebe[2] which confined the light earth of extensive plains, and has destroyed the fringe of semiaquatic plants which skirted the coast and checked the drifting of the sea sand, he has failed to prevent the spreading of the dunes by clothing them with artificially propagated vegetation. He has ruthlessly warred on all the tribes of animated nature whose spoil he could convert to his own uses, and he has not protected the birds which prey on the insects most destructive to his own harvests.

Purely untutored humanity, it is true, interferes comparatively little with the arrangements of nature, and the destructive agency of man becomes more and more energetic and unsparing as he advances in civilization, until the impoverishment, with which his exhaustion of the natural resources of the soil is threatening him, at last awakens him to the necessity of preserving what is left, if not of restoring what has been wantonly wasted. The wandering savage grows no cultivated vegetable, fells no forest, and extirpates no useful plant, no noxious weed. If his skill in the chase enables him to entrap numbers of the animals on which he feeds, he compensates this loss by destroying also the lion, the tiger, the wolf, the otter, the seal, and the eagle, thus indirectly protecting the feebler quadrupeds and fish and fowls, which would otherwise become the booty of beasts and birds of prey. But with stationary life, or rather with the pastoral state, man at once commences an almost indiscriminate warfare upon all the forms of animal and vegetable existence around him, and as he advances in civilization, he gradually eradicates or transforms every spontaneous product of the soil he occupies.

Human and Brute Action Compared

It has been maintained by authorities as high as any known to modern science, that the action of man upon nature, though greater in *degree*, does not differ in *kind*, from that of wild animals. It appears to me to differ in essential character, because, though it is often followed by unforeseen and undesired results, yet it is nevertheless guided by a self-conscious and intelligent will aiming as often at secondary and remote as at immediate objects. The wild animal, on the other hand, acts instinctively, and, so far as we are able to perceive, always with a view to single and direct purposes. The backwoodsman and the beaver alike fell trees; the man that he may convert the forest into an olive grove that will mature its fruit only for a succeeding generation, the beaver that he may feed upon their bark or use them in the construction of his habitation. Human differs from brute action, too, in its influence upon the material world, because it is not controlled by natural compensations and balances. Natural arrangements, once disturbed by man, are not restored until he retires from the field, and

---

2. Soil

leaves free scope to spontaneous recuperative energies; the wounds he inflicts upon the material creation are not healed until he withdraws the arm that gave the blow. On the other hand, I am not aware of any evidence that wild animals have ever destroyed the smallest forest, extirpated any organic species, or modified its natural character, occasioned any permanent change of terrestrial surface, or produced any disturbance of physical conditions which nature has not, of herself, repaired without the expulsion of the animal that had caused it.

The form of geographical surface, and very probably the climate of a given country, depend much on the character of the vegetable life belonging to it. Man has, by domestication, greatly changed the habits and properties of the plants he rears; he has, by voluntary selection, immensely modified the forms and qualities of the animated creatures that serve him; and he has, at the same time, completely rooted out many forms of both vegetable and animal being. What is there, in the influence of brute life, that corresponds to this? We have no reason to believe that in that portion of the American continent which, though peopled by many tribes of quadruped and fowl, remained uninhabited by man, or only thinly occupied by purely savage tribes, any sensible geographical change had occurred within twenty centuries before the epoch of discovery and colonization while, during the same period, man had changed millions of square miles, in the fairest and most fertile regions of the Old World, into the barrenest deserts.

The ravages committed by man subvert the relations and destroy the balance which nature had established between her organized and her inorganic creations; and she avenges herself upon the intruder, by letting loose upon her defaced provinces destructive energies hitherto kept in check by organic forces destined to be his best auxiliaries, but which he has unwisely dispersed and driven from the field of action. When the forest is gone, the great reservoir of moisture stored up in its vegetable mould is evaporated, and returns only in deluges of rain to wash away the parched dust into which that mould has been converted. The well-wooded and humid hills are turned to ridges of dry rock, which encumbers the low grounds and chokes the watercourses with its debris, and—except in countries favored with an equable distribution of rain through the seasons, and a moderate and regular inclination of surface—the whole earth, unless rescued by human art from the physical degradation to which it tends, becomes an assemblage of bald mountains, of barren, turfless hills, and of swampy and malarious plains. There are parts of Asia Minor, of Northern Africa, of Greece, and even of Alpine Europe, where the operation of causes set in action by man has brought the face of the earth to a desolation almost as complete as that of the moon; and though, within that brief space of time which we call "the historical period," they are known to have been covered with luxuriant woods, verdant pastures, and fertile meadows, they are now too far deteriorated to be reclaimable by man, nor can they become again fitted for human use, except through great geological changes, or other mysterious influences or agencies of which we have no present knowledge, and over which we have no prospective control. The earth is fast becoming an unfit home for its noblest inhabitant, and another era of equal human crime and human improvidence, and of like duration with that through which traces of that crime and that improvidence extend, would reduce it to such a condition of impoverished productiveness, of shattered surface, of climatic excess, as to threaten the depravation, barbarism, and perhaps even extinction of the species.

—1864

Susanna Moodie

1803–1885

Writing ran deep in the Strickland family into which Susanna was born in Suffolk, England. Six of the nine children of Thomas Strickland and Elizabeth Homer published works as diverse as a history of British queens, autobiographies, biographies, natural history, children's stories, and poetry. The parents instructed the older children in languages, literature, history, and math, and they, in turn, were responsible for educating the younger children. Susanna, the youngest of the family, was the first of the daughters to emigrate to Canada, following her marriage to a half-pay officer, John Dunbar Moodie, in April 1831. Dunbar had preferred South Africa but chose Canada in part to please his wife, who had read favorable accounts of the country. By the time the couple departed England, Susanna had already established herself as a literary presence, publishing volumes of poetry, children's stories, and works on slavery and abolition (a cause Susanna threw herself into in 1832). She had also contributed to journals such as *The Athenaeum* and *The Lady's Magazine.*

After arriving in Canada, she and her husband chose not to settle on the uncleared plot of land to which they were entitled (near Susanna's brother Samuel); instead, they purchased a piece of partly cleared land near Lake Ontario. Thus the Moodies did not experience life in the backwoods immediately and had to deal with what Susanna felt were maddening "Yankee" neighbors. Financial difficulty forced the Moodies to sell their farm and settle on the uncleared land near Susanna's brother (and, as of the summer of 1832, near her sister Catharine Parr Traill). Further financial difficulty and the inability to establish a workable farm required selling this property. The family moved to the growing town of Belleville, Ontario, where Susanna's husband was employed as a sheriff in January 1840. Here Susanna began work on her two-volume *Roughing It in the Bush*, published in London in 1852. The excerpts in this anthology capture Susanna's cultural and literary reflections on the country, as she responds to the new country, to her neighbors, and to the experience of living in a harsh climate and environment.

from Roughing It in the Bush; or, Life in Canada

Chapter 1: A Visit to Grosse Isle.[1]

As the sun rose above the horizon, all these matter-of-fact circumstances were gradually forgotten, and merged in the surpassing grandeur of the scene that rose majestically before me. The previous day had been dark and stormy; and a heavy fog had concealed the mountain chain, which forms the stupendous background to this sublime view, entirely from our sight. As the clouds rolled away from their grey, bald brows, and cast into denser shadow the vast forest belt that girdled them round, they loomed out like mighty giants—Titans of the earth, in all their rugged and awful beauty—a thrill of wonder and delight pervaded my mind. The spectacle floated dimly on my sight—my eyes were blinded with tears—blinded with the excess of beauty. I turned to the right and to the left, I looked up and down the glorious river; never had I beheld so many striking objects blended into one mighty whole! Nature had lavished all her noblest features in producing that enchanting scene.

---

1. Island in the St. Lawrence River, east of Quebec City.

The rocky isle in front, with its neat farm-houses at the eastern point, and its high bluff at the western extremity, crowned with the telegraph[2]—the middle space occupied by tents and sheds for the cholera patients, and its wooded shores dotted over with motley groups—added greatly to the picturesque effect of the land scene.[3] Then the broad, glittering river, covered with boats darting to and fro, conveying passengers from twenty-five vessels, of various size and tonnage, which rode at anchor, with their flags flying from the mast-head, gave an air of life and interest to the whole. Turning to the south side of the St. Lawrence, I was not less struck with its low fertile shores, white houses, and neat churches, whose slender spires and bright tin roofs shone like silver as they caught the first rays of the sun. As far as the eye could reach, a line of white buildings extended along the bank; their background formed by the purple hue of the dense, interminable forest. It was a scene unlike any I had ever beheld, and to which Britain contains no parallel. . . . .

"What sublime views of the north side of the river those *habitans*[4] of St. Thomas must enjoy," thought I. Perhaps familiarity with the scene has rendered them indifferent to its astonishing beauty.

Eastward, the view down the St. Lawrence towards the Gulf, is the finest of all, scarcely surpassed by anything in the world. Your eye follows the long range of lofty mountains until their blue summits are blended and lost in the blue of the sky. Some of these, partially cleared round the base, are sprinkled over with neat cottages; and the green slopes that spread around them are covered with flocks and herds. The surface of the splendid river is diversified with islands of every size and shape, some in wood, others partially cleared, and adorned with orchards and white farm-houses. As the early sun streamed upon the most prominent of these, leaving the others in deep shade, the effect was strangely novel and imposing. In more remote regions, where the forest has never yet echoed to the woodman's axe, or received the impress of civilisation, the first approach to the shore inspires a melancholy awe, which becomes painful in its intensity. . . . .

My day-dreams were dispelled by the return of the boat, which brought my husband and the captain from the island.

"No bread," said the latter, shaking his head; "you must be content to starve a little longer. Provision-ship not in till four o'clock." My husband smiled at the look of blank disappointment with which I received these unwelcome tidings. "Never mind, I have news which will comfort you. The officer who commands the station sent a note to me by an orderly, inviting us to spend the afternoon with him. He promises to show us everything worthy of notice on the island. Captain —— claims acquaintance with me; but I have not the least recollection of him. Would you like to go?"

"Oh, by all means. I long to see the lovely island. It looks a perfect paradise at this distance."

The rough sailor-captain screwed his mouth on one side, and gave me one of his comical looks, but he said nothing until he assisted in placing me and the baby in the boat.

"Don't be too sanguine, Mrs. Moodie; many things look well at a distance which are bad enough when near."

---

2. The first Canadian telegraph began operating in 1846.   3. Grosse Isle was used to quarantine cholera patients during an 1847 epidemic during which six thousand died.   4. Inhabitants.

I scarcely regarded the old sailor's warning, so eager was I to go on shore—to put my foot upon the soil of the new world for the first time. I was in no humour to listen to any depreciation of what seemed so beautiful.

It was four o'clock when we landed on the rocks, which the rays of an intensely scorching sun had rendered so hot that I could scarcely place my foot upon them. How the people without shoes bore it, I cannot imagine. Never shall I forget the extraordinary spectacle that met our sight the moment we passed the low range of bushes which formed a screen in front of the river. A crowd of many hundred Irish emigrants had been landed during the present and former day; and all this motley crew—men, women, and children, who were not confined by sickness to the sheds (which greatly resembled cattle-pens)—were employed in washing clothes, or spreading them out on the rocks and bushes to dry.

The men and boys were in the water, while the women, with their scanty garments tucked above their knees, were trampling their bedding in tubs, or in holes in the rocks, which the retiring tide had left half full of water. Those who did not possess washing-tubs, pails, or iron pots, or could not obtain access to a hole in the rocks, were running to and fro, screaming and scolding in no measured terms. The confusion of Babel[5] was among them. All talkers and no hearers—each shouting and yelling in his or her uncouth dialect, and all accompanying their vociferations with violent and extraordinary gestures, quite incomprehensible to the uninitiated. We were literally stunned by the strife of tongues. I shrank, with feelings almost akin to fear, from the hard-featured, sun-burnt harpies,[6] as they elbowed rudely past me.

I had heard and read much of savages, and have since seen, during my long residence in the bush, somewhat of uncivilised life; but the Indian is one of Nature's gentlemen—he never says or does a rude or vulgar thing. The vicious, uneducated barbarians who form the surplus of over-populous European countries, are far behind the wild man in delicacy of feeling or natural courtesy. The people who covered the island appeared perfectly destitute of shame, or even of a sense of common decency. Many were almost naked, still more but partially clothed. We turned in disgust from the revolting scene, but were unable to leave the spot until the captain had satisfied a noisy group of his own people, who were demanding a supply of stores.

And here I must observe that our passengers, who were chiefly honest Scotch labourers and mechanics from the vicinity of Edinburgh, and who while on board ship had conducted themselves with the greatest propriety, and appeared the most quiet, orderly set of people in the world, no sooner set foot upon the island than they became infected by the same spirit of insubordination and misrule, and were just as insolent and noisy as the rest.

While our captain was vainly endeavouring to satisfy the unreasonable demands of his rebellious people, Moodie[7] had discovered a woodland path that led to the back of the island. Sheltered by some hazel-bushes from the intense heat of the sun, we sat down by the cool, gushing river, out of sight, but, alas! not out of hearing of the noisy, riotous crowd. Could we have shut out the profane sounds which came to us on every breeze, how deeply should we have enjoyed an hour amid the tranquil beauties of that retired and lovely spot!

---

5. Genesis 11.8–9.   6. In Greek myth, birdlike servants of Zeus, the sky god.   7. Her husband.

The rocky banks of the island were adorned with beautiful evergreens, which sprang up spontaneously in every nook and crevice. I remarked many of our favourite garden shrubs among these wildings of nature. The fillagree, with its narrow, dark glossy-green leaves; the privet, with its modest white blossoms and purple berries; the lignum-vitæ, with its strong resinous odour; the burnet-rose, and a great variety of elegant unknowns.

Here, the shores of the island and mainland, receding from each other, formed a small cove, overhung with lofty trees, clothed from the base to the summit with wild vines, that hung in graceful festoons from the topmost branches to the water's edge. The dark shadows of the mountains, thrown upon the water, as they towered to the height of some thousand feet above us, gave to the surface of the river an ebon hue. The sunbeams, dancing through the thick, quivering foliage, fell in stars of gold, or long lines of dazzling brightness, upon the deep black waters, producing the most novel and beautiful effects. It was a scene over which the spirit of peace might brood in silent adoration; but how spoiled by the discordant yells of the filthy beings who were sullying the purity of the air and water with contaminating sights and sounds!

Chapter 12: The Charivari[8]

Yet, by what stern necessity were we driven forth to seek a new home amid the western wilds? We were not compelled to emigrate. Bound to England by a thousand holy and endearing ties, surrounded by a circle of chosen friends, and happy in each other's love, we possessed all that the world can bestow of good—but *wealth*. The half-pay of a subaltern officer, managed with the most rigid economy, is too small to supply the wants of a family; and if of a good family, not enough to maintain his original standing in society. True, it may find his children bread, it may clothe them indifferently, but it leaves nothing for the indispensable requirements of education, or the painful contingencies of sickness and misfortune. In such a case, it is both wise and right to emigrate; Nature points it out as the only safe remedy for the evils arising out of an over dense population, and her advice is always founded upon justice and truth.

Up to the period of which I now speak, we had not experienced much inconvenience from our very limited means. Our wants were few, and we enjoyed many of the comforts and even some of the luxuries of life; and all had gone on smoothly and lovingly with us until the birth of our first child. It was then that prudence whispered to the father, "You are happy and contented now, but this cannot always last; the birth of that child whom you have hailed with as much rapture as though she were born to inherit a noble estate, is to you the beginning of care. Your family may increase, and your wants will increase in proportion; out of what fund can you satisfy their demands? Some provision must be made for the future, and made quickly, while youth and health enable you to combat successfully with the ills of life. When you married for inclination, you knew that emigration must be the result of such an act of imprudence in over-populated England. Up and be doing, while you still possess the means of transporting yourself to a land where the industrious can never lack bread, and where there is a chance that wealth and independence may reward virtuous toil." . . .

---

8. Loud music from banging pots and pans, used to mock an unpopular marriage.

All was new, strange, and distasteful to us; we shrank from the rude, coarse familiarity of the uneducated people among whom we were thrown; and they in return viewed us as innovators, who wished to curtail their independence, by expecting from them the kindly civilities and gentle courtesies of a more refined community. They considered us proud and shy, when we were only anxious not to give offence. The semi-barbarous Yankee squatters, who had "left their country for their country's good," and by whom we were surrounded in our first settlement, detested us, and with them we could have no feeling in common. We could neither lie nor cheat in our dealings with them; and they despised us for our ignorance in trading and our want of smartness.

The utter want of that common courtesy with which a well-brought-up European addresses the poorest of his brethren, is severely felt at first by settlers in Canada. At the period of which I am now speaking, the titles of "sir" or "madam" were very rarely applied by inferiors. They entered your house without knocking; and while boasting of their freedom, violated one of its dearest laws, which considers even the cottage of the poorest labourer his castle, and his privacy sacred.

"Is your man to hum?"[9]—"Is the woman within?" were the general inquiries made to me by such guests, while my bare-legged, ragged Irish servants were always spoken to, as "sir" and "*mem*," as if to make the distinction more pointed.

Why they treated our claims to their respect with marked insult and rudeness, I never could satisfactorily determine, in any way that could reflect honour on the species, or even plead an excuse for its brutality, until I found that this insolence was more generally practised by the low, uneducated emigrants from Britain, who better understood your claims to their civility, than by the natives themselves. Then I discovered the secret.

The unnatural restraint which society imposes upon these people at home forces them to treat their more fortunate brethren with a servile deference which is repugnant to their feelings, and is thrust upon them by the dependent circumstances in which they are placed. This homage to rank and education is not sincere. Hatred and envy lie rankling at their heart, although hidden by outward obsequiousness. Necessity compels their obedience; they fawn, and cringe, and flatter the wealth on which they depend for bread. But let them once emigrate, the clog which fettered them is suddenly removed; they are free; and the dearest privilege of this freedom is to wreak upon their superiors the long-locked-up hatred of their hearts. They think they can debase you to their level by disallowing all your claims to distinction; while they hope to exalt themselves and their fellows into ladies and gentlemen by sinking you back to the only title you received from Nature—plain "man" and "woman." Oh, how much more honourable than their vulgar pretensions!

I never knew the real dignity of these simple epithets until they were insultingly thrust upon us by the working-classes of Canada.

But from this folly the native-born Canadian is exempt; it is only practised by the low-born Yankee, or the Yankeefied British peasantry and mechanics. It originates in the enormous reaction springing out of a sudden emancipation from a state of utter dependence into one of unrestrained liberty. As such, I not only excuse, but forgive it, for the principle is founded in nature; and, however disgusting and distaste-

---

9. Home.

ful to those accustomed to different treatment from their inferiors, it is better than a hollow profession of duty and attachment urged upon us by a false and unnatural position. Still it is very irksome until you think more deeply upon it; and then it serves to amuse rather than to irritate.

And here I would observe, before quitting this subject, that of all follies, that of taking out servants from the old country is one of the greatest, and is sure to end in the loss of the money expended in their passage, and to become the cause of deep disappointment and mortification to yourself.

They no sooner set foot upon the Canadian shores than they become possessed with this ultra-republican[10] spirit. All respect for their employers, all subordination, is at an end; the very air of Canada severs the tie of mutual obligation which bound you together. They fancy themselves not only equal to you in rank, but that ignorance and vulgarity give them superior claims to notice. They demand in terms the highest wages, and grumble at doing half the work, in return, which they cheerfully performed at home. They demand to eat at your table, and to set in your company; and if you refuse to listen to their dishonest and extravagant claims, they tell you that "they are free; that no contract signed in the old country is binding in 'Meriky[11];' that you may look out for another person to fill their place as soon as you like; and that you may get the money expended in their passage and outfit in the best manner you can."

Chapter 14: The Land-Jobber[12]

The knowledge of the causes which promote the rapid settlement of a new country, and of those in general which lead to the improvement of the physical condition of mankind, may be compared to the knowledge of a language. The inhabitant of a civilised and long-settled country may speak and write his own language with the greatest purity; but very few ever reflect on the amount of thought, metaphor, and ingenuity which has been expended by their less civilised ancestors in bringing that language to perfection. The barbarian first feels the disadvantage of a limited means of communicating his ideas, and with great labour and ingenuity devises the means, from time to time, to remedy the imperfections of his language. He is compelled to analyse and study it in its first elements, and to augment the modes of expression in order to keep pace with the increasing number of his wants and ideas.

A colony bears the same relation to an old-settled country that a grammar does to a language. In a colony, society is seen in its first elements, the country itself is in its rudest and simplest form. The colonist knows them in this primitive state, and watches their progress step by step. In this manner he acquires an intimate knowledge of the philosophy of improvement, which is almost unattainable by an individual who has lived from his childhood in a highly-complex and artificial state of society, where everything around him was formed and arranged long before he came into the world; he sees the *effects*, the *causes* existed long before his time. His place in society—his portion of the wealth of the country—his prejudices—his religion itself, if he has any, are all more or less hereditary. He is in some measure a mere machine, or rather a part of one. He is a creature of education, rather than of original thought.

---

10. Democratic.   11. America.   12. Real estate speculator.

The colonist has to create—he has to draw on his own stock of ideas, and to rouse up all his latent energies to meet all his wants in his new position. Thus his thinking principle is strengthened, and he is more energetic. When a moderate share of education is added to these advantages—for they are advantages in one sense—he becomes a superior being. . . .

Chapter 15: A Journey to the Woods

'Tis well for us poor denizens of earth
That God conceals the future from our gaze;
Or Hope, the blessed watcher on Life's tower,
Would fold her wings, and on the dreary waste
Close the bright eye that through the murky clouds
Of blank Despair still sees the glorious sun.

It was a bright frosty morning when I bade adieu to the farm,[13] the birthplace of my little Agnes, who, nestled beneath my cloak, was sweetly sleeping on my knee, unconscious of the long journey before us into the wilderness. The sun had not as yet risen. Anxious to get to our place of destination before dark, we started as early as we could. Our own fine team had been sold the day before for forty pounds; and one of our neighbours, a Mr. D——, was to convey us and our household goods to Douro for the sum of twenty dollars. During the week he had made several journeys, with furniture and stores; and all that now remained was to be conveyed to the woods in two large lumber-sleighs, one driven by himself, the other by a younger brother.

It was not without regret that I left Melsetter, for so my husband had called the place, after his father's estate in Orkney. It was a beautiful, picturesque spot; and, in spite of the evil neighbourhood, I had learned to love it; indeed, it was much against my wish that it was sold. I had a great dislike to removing, which involves a necessary loss, and is apt to give to the emigrant roving and unsettled habits. But all regrets were now useless; and happily unconscious of the life of toil and anxiety that awaited us in those dreadful woods, I tried my best to be cheerful, and to regard the future with a hopeful eye. . . .

The day was so bright for the time of year (the first week in February), that we suffered no inconvenience from the cold. Little Katie was enchanted with the jingling of the sleigh-bells, and, nestled among the packages, kept singing or talking to the horses in her baby lingo. Trifling as these little incidents were, before we had proceeded ten miles on our long journey, they revived my drooping spirits, and I began to feel a lively interest in the scenes through which we were passing.

The first twenty miles of the way was over a hilly and well-cleared country; and as in winter the deep snow fills up the inequalities, and makes all roads alike, we glided as swiftly and steadily along as if they had been the best highways in the world. Anon, the clearings began to diminish, and tall woods arose on either side of the path; their solemn aspect, and the deep silence that brooded over their vast solitudes, inspiring the mind with a strange awe. Not a breath of wind stirred the leafless branches, whose huge shadows reflected upon the dazzling white covering

---

13. Near Peterborough, Ontario.

of snow, lay so perfectly still, that it seemed as if Nature had suspended her operations, that life and motion had ceased, and that she was sleeping in her winding-sheet, upon the bier of death.

"I guess you will find the woods pretty lonesome," said our driver, whose thoughts had been evidently employed on the same subject as our own. "We were once in the woods, but emigration has stepped a-head of us, and made our'n a cleared part of the country. When I was a boy, all this country, for thirty miles on every side of us, was bush land. As to Peterborough, the place was unknown; not a settler had ever passed through the great swamp, and some of them believed that it was the end of the world."

"What swamp is that?" asked I.

"Oh, the great Cavan swamp. We are just two miles from it; and I tell you that the horses will need a good rest, and ourselves a good dinner, by the time we are through it. Ah, Mrs. Moodie, if ever you travel that way in summer, you will know something about corduroy roads.[14] I was 'most jolted to death last fall; I thought it would have been no bad notion to have insured my teeth before I left C——. I really expected that they would have been shook out of my head before we had done manœuvering over the big logs."

"How will my crockery stand it in the next sleigh?" quoth I. "If the road is such as you describe, I am afraid that I shall not bring a whole plate to Douro."

"Oh, the snow is a great leveller—it makes all rough places smooth. But with regard to this swamp, I have something to tell you. About ten years ago, no one had ever seen the other side of it; and if pigs or cattle strayed away into it, they fell prey to the wolves and bears, and were seldom recovered." . . .

When we reached Peterborough, Moodie wished us to remain at the inn all night, as we had still eleven miles of our journey to perform, and that through a blazed forest-road, little travelled, and very much impeded by fallen trees and other obstacles; but D—— was anxious to get back as soon as possible to his own home, and he urged us very pathetically to proceed.

The moon arose during our stay at the inn, and gleamed upon the straggling frame-houses which then formed the now populous and thriving town of Peterborough. We crossed the wild, rushing, beautiful Otonabee river by a rude bridge, and soon found ourselves journeying over the plains or level heights beyond the village, which were thinly wooded with picturesque groups of oak and pine, and very much resembled a gentleman's park at home.

Far below, to our right (for we were upon the Smith-town side) we heard the rushing of the river, whose rapid waters never receive curb from the iron-chain of winter. Even while the rocky banks are coated with ice, and the frost-king suspends from every twig and branch the most beautiful and fantastic crystals, the black waters rush foaming along, a thick steam rising constantly above the rapids, as from a boiling pot. The shores vibrate and tremble beneath the force of the impetuous flood, as it whirls round cedar crowned islands and opposing rocks, and hurries on to pour its tribute into the Rice Lake, to swell the calm, majestic grandeur of the Trent,[15] till its waters are lost in the beautiful bay of Quinté, and finally merged in the blue ocean of Ontario.

The most renowned of our English rivers dwindle into little muddy rills when compared with the sublimity of the Canadian waters. No language can adequately

---

14. Bumpy roads made by laying logs in mud.   15. River that flows into Lake Ontario.

express the solemn grandeur of her lake and river scenery; the glorious islands that float, like visions from fairy land, upon the bosom of these azure mirrors of her cloudless skies. No dreary breadth of marshes, covered with flags, hide from our gaze the expanse of heaven-tinted waters; no foul mud-banks spread their unwholesome exhalations around. The rocky shores are crowned with the cedar, the birch, the alder, and soft maple, that dip their long tresses in the pure stream; from every crevice in the limestone the hare-bell[16] and Canadian rose wave their graceful blossoms.

The fiercest droughts of summer may diminish the volume and power of these romantic streams, but it never leaves their rocky channels bare, nor checks the mournful music of their dancing waves.

Through the openings in the forest, we now and then caught the silver gleam of the river tumbling on in moonlight splendour, while the hoarse chiding of the wind in the lofty pines above us gave a fitting response to the melancholy cadence of the waters.

The children had fallen asleep. A deep silence pervaded the party. Night was above us with her mysterious stars. The ancient forest stretched around us on every side, and a foreboding sadness sunk upon my heart. Memory was busy with the events of many years. I retraced step by step the pilgrimage of my past life, until arriving at that passage in its sombre history, I gazed through tears upon the singularly savage scene around me, and secretly marvelled, "What brought me here?"

"Providence," was the answer which the soul gave. "Not for your own welfare, perhaps, but for the welfare of your children, the unerring hand of the Great Father has led you here. You form a connecting link in the destinies of many. It is impossible for any human creature to live for himself alone. It may be your lot to suffer, but others will reap a benefit from your trials. Look up with confidence to Heaven, and the sun of hope will yet shed a cheering beam through the forbidding depths of this tangled wilderness."

The road now became so bad that Mr. D—— was obliged to dismount, and lead his horses through the more intricate passages. The animals themselves, weary with their long journey and heavy load, proceeded at foot-fall. The moon, too, had deserted us, and the only light we had to guide us through the dim arches of the forest was from the snow and the stars, which now peered down upon us, through the leafless branches of the trees, with uncommon brilliancy.

"It will be past midnight before we reach your brother's clearing" (where we expected to spend the night), said D——. "I wish, Mr. Moodie, we had followed your advice, and staid at Peterborough. How fares it with you, Mrs. Moodie, and the young ones? It is growing very cold."

We were now in the heart of a dark cedar swamp, and my mind was haunted with visions of wolves and bears; but beyond the long, wild howl of a solitary wolf, no other sound awoke the sepulchral silence of that dismal-looking wood.

"What a gloomy spot!" said I to my husband. "In the old country, superstition would people it with ghosts."

"Ghosts! There are no ghosts in Canada!" said Mr. D——. "The country is too new for ghosts. No Canadian is afeard of ghosts. It is only in old countries, like your'n, that are full of sin and wickedness, that people believe in such nonsense. No human

---

16. Small, blue-flowered herb.

habitation has ever been erected in this wood through which you are passing. Until a very few years ago, few white persons had ever passed through it; and the Red Man would not pitch his tent in such a place as this. Now, ghosts, as I understand the word, are the spirits of bad men, that are not allowed by Providence to rest in their graves, but, for a punishment, are made to haunt the spots where their worst deeds were committed. I don't believe in all this; but, supposing it to be true, bad men must have died here before their spirits could haunt the place. Now, it is more than probable that no person ever ended his days in this forest, so that it would be folly to think of seeing his ghost."

This theory of Mr. D——'s had the merit of originality; and it is not improbable that the utter disbelief in supernatural appearances which is common to most native-born Canadians, is the result of the same very reasonable mode of arguing. The unpeopled wastes of Canada must present the same aspect to the new settler that the world did to our first parents after their expulsion from the Garden of Eden; all the sin which could defile the spot, or haunt it with the association of departed evil, is concentrated in their own persons. Bad spirits cannot be supposed to linger near a place where crime has never been committed. The belief in ghosts, so prevalent in old countries, must first have had its foundation in the consciousness of guilt.

—1852

Susan Fenimore Cooper
1813–1894

The second daughter of James Fenimore Cooper, Susan spent her childhood in Cooperstown, New York, the frontier settlement founded by her grandfather, Judge William Cooper. At thirteen, she was taken to Europe, where she lived the life of an international celebrity's daughter, developing polished social graces and aristocratic ways of thinking. The family returned to Cooperstown in 1833, when she was twenty, and she lived the rest of her long life there. She never married, dedicating herself instead to founding and maintaining an orphanage and other charities. She wrote a novel, *Elinor Wyllys; or, The Young Folk of Longbridge* (1846), as well as many short stories, children's stories, and articles for popular magazines. She was an articulate rural conservative on most of the political issues of the day. For instance, in her *Harper's New Weekly Magazine* article, "Female Suffrage. A Letter to the Christian Women of America" (1870), she argues that the "natural position of woman is clearly, to a limited degree, a subordinate one. Such it has always been throughout the world, in all ages, and in many widely different conditions of society." She goes on to say that women are physically and intellectually weaker than men, and that Christianity warrants male dominance.

She is best known for *Rural Hours* (1850), a record of her close observations of nature in and around her hometown, Cooperstown, New York. Four years before Thoreau's *Walden*, Cooper structured a book of nature writing about a specific locale by organizing it around the cycle of the seasons. William Cullen Bryant called it "a great book—the greatest of the season," and it has gone through many editions since. Like *Rural Hours*, the magazine piece collected in this anthology, "Otsego Leaves. Birds Then and Now" (1878), shows Cooper's intimate familiarity with the land and her vision of nature as a living community in which humans are merely one among many species of inhabitants. It also records her growing awareness of the devastation of that community by the rapid growth of human settlements.

Otsego[1] Leaves. Birds Then and Now

Any one who has had the happiness of living in a country-home, and on the same ground, during the last twenty years, must naturally have been led to observe the birds flitting about the gardens and lawns of the neighborhood. And it matters little whether that country-home be in a village or among open farms. Many birds are partial to a village-life. The gardens and fruit-trees are an attraction to them. Nay, there are some of the bird-folk who seem really to enjoy the neighborhood of man. Among these are the wrens, the robins, the cat-birds, and, to a certain extent, the hummingbirds. These lovely little creatures no doubt enjoy the Eden of the flower-garden, rather than the neighborhood of Adam and Eve.[2] They have no objection to the human race, however they endure our presence. And there can be no doubt that any ten acres of village-gardens will show you many more humming-birds during the midsummer hours between early dawn and the latest glimpse of twilight than can be found in the same extent of wood or meadow. These little creatures take especial delight in flitting about the flower-gardens in the evening, at the very moment when family groups gather on the verandas, and will often fly within arm's-length. They seem proudly conscious that their marvelous flight—rapid, is it not, beyond that of any other earthly creature?—will carry them half the length of the garden before that clumsy being, man, can rise to his feet. Who ever caught a humming-bird in flight? A humming-bird on the wing you may perhaps have captured; more than half their lives would seem to be passed on those quivering wings. They feed on the wing always. Of all the feathered tribe few so well deserve the epithet of birds of the air. Seldom do you see one at rest. While poising itself before some honey-yielding flower with that inconceivably rapid quivering of the wings, the humming-bird may occasionally be caught, but the achievement is not a common one. In actual flight it may be doubted if one ever was caught. Confident in their marvelous power of wing, they linger lovingly about the flower-garden while human forms are very near, and human voices are chatting in varied tones, and no doubt clearly heard by them. Few birds, excepting those belonging to the night, are out so late. They must have a large acquaintance among the fire-flies, the katydids, the gay moths, and the hooting owls. Doubtless the fragrance of the flowers, always more powerful in the dewy evening hours, proves the attraction. They do not, however, always visit the sweetest blossoms, they seldom poise before a rose or a lily, but they know very well that roses and lilies do not live alone; gathering about those queenly flowers, they will be sure to find a brilliant company yielding the sweets they seek. Whatever may be the cause, they are arrant little rovers, in the latest twilight and in the early moonlight. There are, indeed, few hours in the twenty-four when that silent sprite, the humming-bird, may not be found darting to and fro around our village homes.

That delightful singer, the merry house-wren, so delicate in form, so cheery in his ways, so lively, so fearless, so sweet and joyous in his song, is a fast friend of mankind, seeking from preference to build near us. It is a social little creature, often building within range of eye and hand, and almost cheating one into the fancy that his sole object is to sing for the amusement of his neighbors. He will begin a delightful strain close to a window, perched on a flowering shrub perchance, or swinging to and fro on a waving spray of some creeping vine, and sing half an hour away with little interrup-

---

1. Otsego County, location of Cooperstown.   2. Genesis 2.8–15.

counted by the score? *Now* you may sit on a garden-bench a long summer morning, and very possibly not see more than one oriole, one bluebird, one greenlet, one yellow-bird. Even the robins come hopping about the garden-walks by two and three, instead of the dozen who were formerly in sight at the same moment. And the humming-birds are very perceptibly less in numbers. One has to watch for them now in the summer twilight; presently you shall see little ruby-throat hovering alone about the honeysuckles; and perhaps, half an hour later, his wife, little green-breast, may come for a sip of sweets. But that is all. Rarely, indeed, do you see four or five quivering, darting, flashing about among the blossoms at the same moment, as one often saw them in past years.

The gregarious birds, too—the purple finches, the wax-wings, the red-wings—are only seen in small parties compared to the flocks that visited us twenty years ago.

And winter tells the same story. Not that the regular winter birds are so much less numerous than they were—probably there is little change among the sober snow-birds, the merry chickadees, or the winter-sparrows. These will probably gather about our doors in January in much the same groups and small flocks that we saw here formerly. The woodpeckers and the blue-jays are less numerous, however. The crows seem to hold their own, and in mild weather come flapping out of their favorite haunts in the woods, to take a look at the village. But winter offers a mode of guessing at the number of the summer population, which is a pretty fair test, so far as the tree-builders are concerned. When the leaves fall in November, the nests are revealed, and after snow has fallen, and each nest takes a tiny white dome, they become still more conspicuous. The Indian tribes count their people by so many lodges or *tepées*; in the same way, during the autumn and winter months, we may count the tree-building flock of the previous summer by their nests. And these tree-builders are probably a fair proportion of the whole summer flock, including those who build among the bushes or on the ground. It has often been a winter amusement of the writer, when walking through the village-streets, to count the birds'-nests in the different trees in sight. The trees are all familiar friends, and the nests of different kinds add no little to their interest. But, alas! every four or five winters one observes the number of nests diminishing. Among the maples and elms lining the streets, or standing on corners, or rooted on garden-lawns but overhanging the sidewalks, were certain individual trees which were apparently especial favorites; their gray limbs never failed to show year after year several of these white-domed nests. Here among the forked twigs of a young maple was the bold, rather coarsely-built nest of the robin, shreds of cloth or paper, picked up in the door-yards, hanging perhaps loosely from among the twigs. Yonder, on the drooping branch of an elm, near the churchyard-gate, was seen the long, closely-woven, pensile nest of the brilliant oriole. Here, again, not far from the town-pump—a primitive monument of civilization dating from the dark ages of village history, but still highly valued and much frequented by the present generation, although the little town now boasts its "Croton"[4]—a maple of good size was never without a nest in spite of the movement and noise about the pump. There were several of these trees which showed every year two or three nests; and one, a maple differing in no way from other maples so far as one could see, and standing near a corner before the door of a parsonage, the branches almost grazing the modest windows of the house, revealed every winter three, four, or even five, and one year six, nests

---

4. Croton Aqueduct supplies water to New York City.

on different branches, from the lowest to the highest. There were often two robins' nests, with the pendulous nest of the greenlet, and one of the goldfinch, and occasionally one of a summer yellow-bird, or of a small pewee. The tree is still standing, gay with brilliant coloring, gold and red in varied shades, at the moment we are writing; but, so far as one can see, there has been but one nest on its branches during this last summer. Such was the story told by the village-trees *then*; you were never out of sight of some one nest, and frequently half a dozen could be counted in near neighborhood. To-day it may be doubted if we have more than one-third of the number of these street-nests which could be counted twenty years ago.

This is a sad change. These are the facts which would seem to account for the diminished number of the summer flock. Young boys, scarcely old enough, one would think, to carry a gun, are allowed to shoot the birds with impunity in the spring, when they are preparing to build, or even when their eggs are actually in the nest. This should not be. The law against shooting certain birds at that season should be enforced. It is now a dead letter. Then, again, look at your daughter's hat. Dead birds cannot build nests; they cannot sing for our joy and their own delight; they are mute, but, unhappily, they are considered a pretty ornament when pinned down among ribbons, flowers, fruits, beads, and bugles, on that composite exaggeration to which Fashion, forsooth, has given the name, but not the uses, of a hat. All the smaller birds, with any beauty of plumage, are now murdered to satisfy this whim of Fashion. When we remember the millions of women, young girls, and children, in the country, and bear in mind that most American women require three or four hats in a year—some of them a score or two—we can imagine how many yellow-birds, ruby-throats, greenlets, etc., are required to pile up the holocaust. One sees sometimes even girls who are half-babies wearing a humming-bird in their tiny hats. Not long since the writer saw a pretty young girl wearing impaled on one side of her hat a Mexican humming-bird, on the other a fiery-crest kinglet, while the wing of a blue-jay stood boldly up behind. One frequently sees parts of two or thre different birds on the same hat—wings, or tails, or heads. Alas! why will our young maidens, pretty, and good, and kind-hearted in other matters, be so cruel to the birds? They would scold their little brothers for stealing nests or eggs, but they have no scruple whatever in wearing a dead bird in their hats!

A third cause of the lessened number of some species of our summer birds may be found in the fact that so many are now eaten at the South, by the caravan of travelers, when they are plump and in good condition from feeding on the many seeds and berries which form their usual winter harvest. "Small birds" are included in the bill-of-fare of every hotel in the warmer parts of the country from November to March. This is perfectly natural, and one has not a word to say against the dainty dish of "four-and-twenty rice-birds baked in a pie" to set before the invalid traveler. But the great number of this class of travelers now moving southward every winter has no doubt been one cause of diminishing the flock of our summer birds. Travelers who in January breakfast on robins and rice-birds in Florida cannot expect to hear them sing the next spring in their home-meadows.

But, whatever be the cause of this marked difference of numbers between the summer flocks *then* and *now*, that difference becomes a grief to us. We miss our bird-companions sadly; we miss them from their haunts about our village-homes; the ear pines for their music, the eye longs for the sight of their beautiful forms flitting gayly to and fro. Still more serious, however, is the practical consequence of this wholesale slaughter of the smaller birds. The increase of insects is a tremendous evil, but it is the inevitable result of destroying the birds.

Remember that the plague of grasshoppers, so fearful at the West, is attributed entirely by some persons to the reckless slaughter of the prairie-hens shot by tens of thousands by covetous speculators, who send them now to Europe.

—1878

Charles Sangster
1822–1893

Charles Sangster came from Loyalist stock and spent the majority of his life in and around his birthplace, Kingston, Ontario, until moving to Ottawa in 1868 to work for the newly formed national postal system. His writing reflects his sense of connection with the area: His poetry is infused with the sights and sounds of the region, and his goal was to produce "Canadian" verse. His poems are pastoral and patriotic, recording the rich natural majesty of Canada as they pay tribute to the mounting sense of national spirit that led to confederation in 1867.

After emigrating from Scotland and fighting in the American Revolution, Sangster's grandfather settled in Prince Edward Island. His son, Sangster's father, left the island and set-tled in the Kingston area, where, because of his military service as a shipbuilder, he was enti-tled to a plot of land. He died when Charles was two years old, and his wife raised the five children. Economic difficulty forced Charles to quit school at age fifteen, when he found his first job, making rifle cartridges for the military. He was also employed by a number of period-icals, working as editor, reporter, and proofreader.

With little formal education, Sangster viewed himself (later in life) as "a self made and pretty much a self taught man." By age seventeen, Sangster had composed a long poem, *The Rebel* (1839), which, in its elevated diction and handling of iambic tetrameter, demonstrated signs of real poetic skill. His first volume of poetry, *The St. Lawrence and the Saguenay, and Other Poems*, published in Canada and America in 1856, was viewed by many critics as the most important North American book to appear to date—even earning him the title of "the Wordsworth of Canada." The title poem was praised for its technical virtuosity, as well as its awareness of a wide range of authors, from William Wordsworth and Alfred Lord Tennyson to Henry Wadsworth Longfellow and John Greenleaf Whittier. The poem follows the journey of the speaker down the St. Lawrence and Saguenay rivers. Indebted to Byron's *Childe Harold's Pilgrimage* (1812–1818) and Wordsworth's *Prelude* (1850) and *The River Duddon* (1820), this account of a physical journey into the interior of the continent is matched by a spiritual jour-ney, as Sangster reflects on the presence of the divine in nature.

from *The St. Lawrence and the Saguenay*

[The Thousand Islands]

III

The bark leaps love-fraught from the land; the sea
Lies calm before us. Many an isle is there,   20
Clad with soft verdure[1]; many a stately tree

---

1. Greenery.

Uplifts its leafy branches through the air;
The amorous current bathes the islets fair,
As we skip, youth-like, o'er the limpid[2] waves;
White cloudlets speck the golden atmosphere,   25
Through which the passionate sun looks down, and graves
His image on the pearls that boil from the deep caves,

IV

And bathe the vessel's prow. Isle after isle
Is passed, as we glide tortuously through
The opening vistas, that uprise and smile   30
Upon us from the ever-changing view.
Here nature, lavish of her wealth, did strew
Her flocks of panting islets on the breast
Of the admiring River, where they grew,
Like shapes of Beauty, formed to give a zest   35
To the charmed mind, like waking Visions of the Blest.

V

The silver-sinewed arms of the proud Lake,
Love-wild, embrace each islet tenderly,
The zephyrs[3] kiss the flowers when they wake
At morn, flushed with a rare simplicity;   40
See how they bloom around yon birchen tree,
And smile along the bank, by the sandy shore,
In lovely groups—a fair community!
The embossed rocks glitter like golden ore,
And here, the o'eraching trees form a fantastic bower.   45

VI

Red walls of granite rise on either hand,
Rugged and smooth; a proud young eagle soars
Above the stately evergreens, that stand
Like watchful sentinels on these God-built towers;
And near yon beds of many-colored flowers   50
Browse two majestic deer, and at their side
A spotted fawn all innocently cowers;
In the rank brushwood it attempts to hide,
While the strong-antlered stag steps forth with lordly stride,

VII

And slakes his thirst, undaunted, at the stream.   55
Isles of o'erwhelming beauty! surely here

---

2. Clear.   3. Breezes.

The wild enthusiast might live, and dream
His life away. No Nymphic trains[4] appear,
To charm the pale Ideal Worshipper
Of Beauty; nor Neriads[5] from the deeps below;   60
Nor hideous Gnomes,[6] to fill the breast with fear:
But crystal streams through endless landscapes flow,
And o'er the clustering Isles the softest breezes blow.

—1856

⁓ END OF TRANSATLANTIC EXCHANGES ⁓

Frederick Douglass
1818–1895

In the poem "Douglass," the early twentieth-century poet Paul Laurence Dunbar honored and
invoked the abolitionist movement's foremost speaker:

> Ah, Douglass, we have fall'n on evil days,
> Such Days as thou, not even thou didst know,
> When thee, the eyes of that harsh long ago
> Saw, salient, at the cross of devious ways,
> And all the country heard thee with amaze.

Although Frederick Douglass did tirelessly lecture, edit, and publish to advocate for African
American civil liberties, there are few monuments to him in verse, stone, or metal. Dunbar's
1903 poem, with its suggestion that much work remains to be done in the cause Douglass represented, still rings true over a hundred years later. The exclusivity of many historical accounts
of the movement to abolish slavery is one of the reasons that many African American abolitionists have yet to be fully recognized for their contributions to the struggle. The second half
of the twentieth century and the first part of the twenty-first have given rise to accounts of abolition's history that restore figures like Douglass to the positions of international eminence they
held during the movement.

Douglass sought to erase what the writers W. E. B. Du Bois and Charles Chesnutt referred
to as the "color line." Born Frederick Augustus Bailey, Douglass was the son of an enslaved
African American woman, Harriet Bailey, and a European-American man whose identity
remains unknown. During his childhood, he often suffered from a lack of food and clothing
during the cold Maryland winters, and he endured the loss of his mother when he was only
seven. More change was in store for Douglass, for Aaron Anthony sold him to the Aulds of
Baltimore. After Mr. Auld forbade his wife to teach Douglass any more reading and writing
skills, the young child cleverly challenged white schoolchildren to alphabet-reciting contests
to continue on his path to literacy. Forced to leave Baltimore for life on an Auld family farm
in St. Michael's, Douglass labored under the cruel lash of Edward Covey, an overseer and "slave

---

4. Processions of beautiful women.   5. Sea nymphs.   6. Small people.

breaker." After witnessing and experiencing Covey's unjust infliction of pain on others, Douglass was singled out by Covey for a more severe punishment than he had yet received. Fighting for his life and liberty, the sixteen-year-old Douglass overpowered Covey, who never dared to touch him again. This scene, vividly described in Douglass's autobiography, mirrors earlier scenes of deliverance from bondage in the autobiographies of Olaudah Equiano and Ukawsaw Gronniosaw and also serves as a metaphor for Douglass's lifelong struggle for life and liberty, proving that the pen is mightier than the whip. Douglass continued to teach himself to read and write, as did other African Americans, by working in Fell's Point and other shipyards; according to Douglass, "the shipyard was more to us than to many others. It was our schoolhouse, where we learned to write and to count. Its timber and boards were our first copy-books and the white carpenters writing 'larboard' and 'starboard' with chalk were our unconscious teachers."

After escaping to the North, Douglass published his autobiography in 1845. It sold over 35,000 copies. He then traveled abroad that same year to spread the gospel of freedom and to be out of the reach of the Aulds and others who might try to force him back into bondage in the South through the Fugitive Slave Act. Douglass toured England, Scotland, and Ireland, where his abolitionist lectures met with thunderous applause. Due to his speeches and autobiography he emerged as the most important transatlantic abolitionist of his time, uniting those who supported the cause in both countries. As present-day scholar Alasdair Pettinger has argued, Douglass met with an especially enthusiastic response in Scotland. The slaveholding South and the notion of a Southern gentleman were to a degree modeled on Scotland and the actions of heroes in Sir Walter Scott's novels and poems; some plantations even took their names from these works. However, by assuming the name Douglass from Scott's *Lay of the Last Minstrel* and proving that Scotland was mostly comprised of abolitionists, Frederick Douglass was able to rupture and subvert the supposed transatlantic continuities between Scotland and the South. He started a campaign to send back money supplied by America's Southern Presbyterians in support of the Free Church of Scotland, which had seceded from the English-controlled Church. Douglass's eloquence and wit proved a successful combination in his addresses on this issue. He pointed out the hypocrisy of the endeavor by recreating for his audience the hypothetical response of a "Christian" slaveholder who had just been asked to contribute funds to the Free Church of Scotland: "I'll tell you what I will do. I have a fine young Negro who is to be sold, and I will sell him tomorrow and give you a contribution to the cause of freedom." The response was such that all over Edinburgh there was graffiti that read "Send Back the Money"; this slogan was even cut into the grass on the prominent hillside, Arthur's Seat.

Although the money was never sent back, the number of Scottish, English, and Irish anti-slavery societies started alone was high enough to mark the trip as a success. These societies raised enough money for Douglass to purchase his freedom and start the African American newspaper *The North Star*, for which he wrote the novella *The Heroic Slave* (1853). The paper took its name from Polaris, the star above the Big Dipper that sailors had long used to point vessels north and that African Americans escaping bondage in the Southern states used to guide them to the Northern states and Canada, where slavery was outlawed. According to Paul Gilroy's *The Black Atlantic* (1993), Douglass's "consciousness of race, self, and society were profoundly changed by being outside America." The exposure to the longstanding abolitionism of Scotland, Ireland, and England, where Parliament outlawed the slave trade in 1807 and freed the slaves in British colonies in 1833, caused Douglass to break with the European American abolitionists in New England who sought to control him. The financial backing he secured during the trip gave him the means to advocate freedom independently and to found black-based initiatives.

After publishing a new version of his autobiography in 1855, Douglass renewed his efforts overseas by returning to Britain in 1859–1860, on the eve of Civil War in America. The trip was important to counteract the work of pro-slavery ministers from America who had tried to garner support in the United Kingdom. Commenting on the noticeable differences from his first trip, he pointed out that "American prejudice might be found on the streets of Liverpool and in nearly all . . . commercial towns." Returning to America, Douglass pressed President Abraham Lincoln to allow African American platoons to fight for the North and demanded that the President's successor, Andrew Johnson, give African American men the right to vote. Douglass's advocacy for the oppressed did not cease, as he lobbied against the oppression of African Americans, of the Irish by the English, and of women. He continued this work almost literally until the moment of his death on February 20, 1895.

The Meaning of July Fourth for the Negro: Speech at Rochester, New York, July 5, 1852[1]

Mr. President, Friends and Fellow Citizens:

He who could address this audience without a quailing sensation, has stronger nerves than I have. I do not remember ever to have appeared as a speaker before any assembly more shrinkingly, nor with greater distrust of my ability, than I do this day. A feeling has crept over me quite unfavorable to the exercise of my limited powers of speech. The task before me is one which requires much previous thought and study for its proper performance. I know that apologies of this sort are generally considered flat and unmeaning. I trust, however, that mine will not be so considered. Should I seem at ease, my appearance would much misrepresent me. The little experience I have had in addressing public meetings, in country school houses, avails me nothing on the present occasion.

The papers and placards say that I am to deliver a Fourth of July Oration. This certainly sounds large, and out of the common way, for me. It is true that I have often had the privilege to speak in this beautiful Hall, and to address many who now honor me with their presence. But neither their familiar faces, nor the perfect gage I think I have of Corinthian Hall seems to free me from embarrassment.

The fact is, ladies and gentlemen, the distance between this platform and the slave plantation, from which I escaped, is considerable—and the difficulties to be overcome in getting from the latter to the former are by no means slight. That I am here to-day is, to me, a matter of astonishment as well as of gratitude. You will not, therefore, be surprised, if in what I have to say I evince no elaborate preparation, nor grace my speech with any high sounding exordium. With little experience and with less learning, I have been able to throw my thoughts hastily and imperfectly together; and trusting to your patient and generous indulgence, I will proceed to lay them before you.

This, for the purpose of this celebration, is the Fourth of July. It is the birthday of your National Independence, and of your political freedom. This, to you, is what the Passover[2] was to the emancipated people of God. It carries your minds back to the day, and to the act of your great deliverance; and to the signs, and to the wonders, associated with that act, and that day. This celebration also marks the beginning of another year of your national life; and reminds you that the Republic of America is now 76 years old. I am glad, fellow-citizens, that your nation is so young. Seventy-six

1. Speech organized by the Rochester Ladies' Anti-slavery Society.   2. Jewish celebration of Moses leading the Israelites out of slavery in Egypt.

years, though a good old age for a man, is but a mere speck in the life of a nation. Three score years and ten is the allotted time for individual men; but nations number their years by thousands. According to this fact, you are, even now, only in the beginning of your national career, still lingering in the period of childhood. I repeat, I am glad this is so. There is hope in the thought, and hope is much needed, under the dark clouds which lower above the horizon. The eye of the reformer is met with angry flashes, portending disastrous times; but his heart may well beat lighter at the thought that America is young, and that she is still in the impressible stage of her existence. May he not hope that high lessons of wisdom, of justice and of truth, will yet give direction to her destiny? Were the nation older, the patriot's heart might be sadder, and the reformer's brow heavier. Its future might be shrouded in gloom, and the hope of its prophets go out in sorrow. There is consolation in the thought that America is young.—Great streams are not easily turned from channels, worn deep in the course of ages. They may sometimes rise in quiet and stately majesty, and inundate the land, refreshing and fertilizing the earth with their mysterious properties. They may also rise in wrath and fury, and bear away, on their angry waves, the accumulated wealth of years of toil and hardship. They, however, gradually flow back to the same old channel, and flow on as serenely as ever. But, while the river may not be turned aside, it may dry up, and leave nothing behind but the withered branch, and the unsightly rock, to howl in the abyss-sweeping wind, the sad tale of departed glory. As with rivers so with nations.

Fellow-citizens, I shall not presume to dwell at length on the associations that cluster about this day. The simple story of it is, that, 76 years ago, the people of this country were British subjects. The style and title of your "sovereign people" (in which you now glory) was not then born. You were under the British Crown. Your fathers esteemed the English Government as the home government; and England as the fatherland. This home government, you know, although a considerable distance from your home, did, in the exercise of its parental prerogatives, impose upon its colonial children, such restraints, burdens and limitations, as, in its mature judgment, it deemed wise, right and proper.

But your fathers, who had not adopted the fashionable idea of this day, of the infallibility of government, and the absolute character of its acts, presumed to differ from the home government in respect to the wisdom and the justice of some of those burdens and restraints. They went so far in their excitement as to pronounce the measures of government unjust, unreasonable, and oppressive, and altogether such as ought not to be quietly submitted to. I scarcely need say, fellow-citizens, that my opinion of those measures fully accords with that of your fathers. Such a declaration of agreement on my part would not be worth much to anybody. It would certainly prove nothing as to what part I might have taken had I lived during the great controversy of 1776. To say now that America was right, and England wrong, is exceedingly easy. Everybody can say it; the dastard,[3] not less than the noble brave, can flippantly discant on[4] the tyranny of England towards the American Colonies. It is fashionable to do so; but there was a time when, to pronounce against England, and in favor of the cause of the colonies, tried men's souls.[5] They who did so were accounted in their day plotters of mischief, agitators and rebels, dangerous men. To side with the right against the wrong, with the weak against the strong, and with the

---

3. Despicable person.   4. Comment on.   5. Paraphrases Thomas Paine (1737–1809), *The American Crisis* (1780–1783).

oppressed against the oppressor! here lies the merit, and the one which, of all others, seems unfashionable in our day. The cause of liberty may be stabbed by the men who glory in the deeds of your fathers. But, to proceed.

Feeling themselves harshly and unjustly treated, by the home government, your fathers, like men of honesty, and men of spirit, earnestly sought redress. They petitioned and remonstrated; they did so in a decorous, respectful, and loyal manner. Their conduct was wholly unexceptionable. This, however, did not answer the purpose. They saw themselves treated with sovereign indifference, coldness and scorn. Yet they persevered. They were not the men to look back.

As the sheet anchor takes a firmer hold, when the ship is tossed by the storm, so did the cause of your fathers grow stronger as it breasted the chilling blasts of kingly displeasure. The greatest and best of British statesmen admitted its justice, and the loftiest eloquence of the British Senate came to its support. But, with that blindness which seems to be the unvarying characteristic of tryants, since Pharaoh and his hosts were drowned in the Red Sea,[6] the British Government persisted in the exactions complained of.

The madness of this course, we believe, is admitted now, even by England; but we fear the lesson is wholly lost on our present rulers.

Oppression makes a wise man mad. Your fathers were wise men, and if they did not go mad, they became restive under this treatment. They felt themselves the victims of grievous wrongs, wholly incurable in their colonial capacity. With brave men there is always a remedy for oppression. Just here, the idea of a total separation of the colonies from the crown was born! It was a startling idea, much more so than we, at this distance of time, regard it. The timid and the prudent (as has been intimated) of that day were, of course, shocked and alarmed by it.

Such people lived then, had lived before, and will, probably, ever have a place on this planet; and their course, in respect to any great change (no matter how great the good to be attained, or the wrong to be redressed by it), may be calculated with as much precision as can be the course of the stars. They hate all changes, but silver, gold and copper change! Of this sort of change they are always strongly in favor.

These people were called Tories in the days of your fathers; and the appellation, probably, conveyed the same idea that is meant by a more modern, though a somewhat less euphonious[7] term, which we often find in our papers, applied to some of our old politicians.

Their opposition to the then dangerous thought was earnest and powerful; but, amid all their terror and affrighted vociferations against it, the alarming and revolutionary idea moved on, and the country with it.

On the 2d of July, 1776, the old Continental Congress, to the dismay of the lovers of ease, and the worshipers of property, clothed that dreadful idea with all the authority of national sanction. They did so in the form of a resolution; and as we seldom hit upon resolutions, drawn up in our day, whose transparency is at all equal to this, it may refresh your minds and help my story if I read it.

"Resolved, That these united colonies are, and of right, ought to be free and Independent States; that they are absolved from all allegiance to the British

---

6. Exodus 14.21–28.   7. Euphonious: pleasant sounding. The term Douglass refers to may be "toady" or "hunker," a label for conservative democrats.

Crown; and that all political connection between them and the State of Great Britain is, and ought to be dissolved."[8]

Citizens, your fathers made good that resolution. They succeeded; and to-day you reap the fruits of their success. The freedom gained is yours; and you, therefore, may properly celebrate this anniversary. The 4th of July is the first great fact in your nation's history—the very ring-bolt in the chain of your yet undeveloped destiny.

Pride and patriotism, not less than gratitude, prompt you to celebrate and to hold it in perpetual remembrance. I have said that the Declaration of Independence is the ringbolt to the chain of your nation's destiny; so, indeed, I regard it. The principles contained in that instrument are saving principles. Stand by those principles, be true to them on all occasions, in all places, against all foes, and at whatever cost.

From the round top[9] of your ship of state, dark and threatening clouds may be seen. Heavy billows, like mountains in the distance, disclose to the leeward huge forms of flinty rocks! That bolt drawn, that chain broken, and all is lost. Cling to this day—cling to it, and to its principles, with the grasp of a storm-tossed mariner to a spar at midnight.

The coming into being of a nation, in any circumstances, is an interesting event. But, besides general considerations, there were peculiar circumstances which make the advent of this republic an event of special attractiveness.

The whole scene, as I look back to it, was simple, dignified and sublime. The population of the country, at the time, stood at the insignificant number of three millions. The country was poor in the munitions of war. The population was weak and scattered, and the country a wilderness unsubdued. There were then no means of concert and combination, such as exist now. Neither steam nor lightning had then been reduced to order and discipline. From the Potomac to the Delaware was a journey of many days. Under these, and innumerable other disadvantages, your fathers declared for liberty and independence and triumphed.

Fellow Citizens, I am not wanting in respect for the fathers of this republic. The signers of the Declaration of Independence were brave men. They were great men, too—great enough to give frame to a great age. It does not often happen to a nation to raise, at one time, such a number of truly great men. The point from which I am compelled to view them is not, certainly, the most favorable; and yet I cannot contemplate their great deeds with less than admiration. They were statesmen, patriots and heroes, and for the good they did, and the principles they contended for, I will unite with you to honor their memory.

They loved their country better than their own private interests; and, though this is not the highest form of human excellence, all will concede that it is a rare virtue, and that when it is exhibited it ought to command respect. He who will, intelligently, lay down his life for his country is a man whom it is not in human nature to despise. Your fathers staked their lives, their fortunes, and their sacred honor, on the cause of their country. In their admiration of liberty, they lost sight of all other interests.

They were peace men; but they preferred revolution to peaceful submission to bondage. They were quiet men; but they did not shrink from agitating against

---

8. Declaration of Independence (1776); see p. 130.   9. A platform at the top of a ship's mast.

oppression. They showed forbearance; but that they knew its limits. They believed in order; but not in the order of tyranny. With them, nothing was "settled" that was not right. With them, justice, liberty and humanity were "final"; not slavery and oppression. You may well cherish the memory of such men. They were great in their day and generation. Their solid manhood stands out the more as we contrast it with these degenerate times.

How circumspect, exact and proportionate were all their movements! How unlike the politicians of an hour! Their statesmanship looked beyond the passing moment, and stretched away in strength into the distant future. They seized upon eternal principles, and set a glorious example in their defence. Mark them!

Fully appreciating the hardships to be encountered, firmly believing in the right of their cause, honorably inviting the scrutiny of an on-looking world, reverently appealing to heaven to attest their sincerity, soundly comprehending the solemn responsibility they were about to assume, wisely measuring the terrible odds against them, your fathers, the fathers of this republic, did, most deliberately, under the inspiration of a gloroius patriotism, and with a sublime faith in the great principles of justice and freedom, lay deep, the corner-stone of the national super-structure, which has risen and still rises in grandeur around you.

Of this fundamental work, this day is the anniversary. Our eyes are met with demonstrations of joyous enthusiasm. Banners and pennants were exultingly on the breeze. The din of business, too, is hushed. Even Mammon[10] seems to have quitted his grasp on this day. The ear-piercing fife and the stirring drum unite their accents with the ascending peal of a thousand church bells. Prayers are made, hymns are sung, and sermons are preached in honor of this day; while the quick martial tramp of a great and multitudinous nation, echoed back by all the hills, valleys and mountains of a vast continent, bespeak the occasion one of thrilling and universal interest—a nation's jubilee.

Friends and citizens, I need not enter further into the causes which led to this anniversary. Many of you understand them better than I do. You could instruct me in regard to them. That is a branch of knowledge in which you feel, perhaps, a much deeper interest than your speaker. The causes which led to the separation of the colonies from the British crown have never lacked for a tongue. They have all been taught in your common schools, narrated at your firesides, unfolded from your pulpits, and thundered from your legislative halls, and are as familiar to you as household words. They form the staple of your national poetry and eloquence.

I remember, also, that, as a people, Americans are remarkably familiar with all facts which make in their own favor. This is esteemed by some as a national trait—perhaps a national weakness. It is a fact, that whatever makes for the wealth or for the reputation of Americans and can be had cheap! will be found by Americans. I shall not be charged with slandering Americans if I say I think the American side of any question may be safely left in American hands.

I leave, therefore, the great deeds of your fathers to other gentlemen whose claim to have been regularly descended will be less likely to be disputed than mine!

My business, if I have any here to-day, is with the present. The accepted time with God and His cause is the ever-living now.

---

10. Personification of greed.

> Trust no future, however pleasant,
>   Let the dead past bury its dead;
> Act, act in the living present,
>   Heart within, and God overhead.[11]

We have to do with the past only as we can make it useful to the present and to the future. To all inspiring motives, to noble deeds which can be gained from the past, we are welcome. But now is the time, the important time. Your fathers have lived, died, and have done their work, and have done much of it well. You live and must die, and you must do your work. You have no right to enjoy a child's share in the labor of your fathers, unless your children are to be blest by your labors. You have no right to wear out and waste the hard-earned fame of your fathers to cover your indolence. Sydney Smith[12] tells us that men seldom eulogize the wisdom and virtues of their fathers, but to excuse some folly or wickedness of their own. This truth is not a doubtful one. There are illustrations of it near and remote, ancient and modern. It was fashionable, hundreds of years ago, for the children of Jacob to boast, we have "Abraham to our father," when they had long lost Abraham's faith and spirit.[13] That people contented themselves under the shadow of Abraham's great name, while they repudiated the deeds which made his name great. Need I remind you that a similar thing is being done all over this country to-day? Need I tell you that the Jews are not the only people who built the tombs of the prophets, and garnished the sepulchers of the righteous? Washington could not die till he had broken the chains of his slaves.[14] Yet his monument is built up by the price of human blood, and the traders in the bodies and souls of men shout— "We have Washington to our *father*."—Alas! that it should be so; yet so it is.

> The evil that men do, lives after them,
> The good is oft interred with their bones.[15]

Fellow-citizens, pardon me, allow me to ask, why am I called upon to speak here to-day? What have I, or those I represent, to do with your national independence? Are the great principles of political freedom and of natural justice, embodied in that Declaration of Independence, extended to us? and am I, therefore, called upon to bring our humble offering to the national altar, and to confess the benefits and express devout gratitude for the blessings resulting from your independence to us?

Would to God, both for your sakes and ours, that an affirmative answer could be truthfully returned to these questions! Then would my task be light, and my burden easy and delightful. For *who* is there so cold, that a nation's sympathy could not warm him? Who so obdurate and dead to the claims of gratitude, that would not thankfully acknowledge such priceless benefits? Who so stolid and selfish, that would not give his voice to swell the hallelujahs of a nation's jubilee, when the chains of servitude had been torn from his limbs? I am not that man. In a case like that, the dumb might eloquently speak, and the "lame man leap as an hart."[16]

But such is not the state of the case. I say it with a sad sense of the disparity between us. I am not included within the pale of this glorious anniversary! Your high

---

11. Henry Wadsworth Longfellow (1807–1882), "A Psalm of Life" (1838); see p. 906.   12. English satirist (1771–1845).   13. Luke 3.8.   14. George Washington's will insisted that his slaves be freed after his wife's death.   15. William Shakespeare (1567–1616), *Julius Caesar* (1623), 3.2.76.   16. Isaiah 35.6.

independence only reveals the immeasurable distance between us. The blessings in which you, this day, rejoice, are not enjoyed in common.—The rich inheritance of justice, liberty, prosperity and independence, bequeathed by your fathers, is shared by you, not by me. The sunlight that brought light and healing to you, has brought stripes[17] and death to me. This Fourth of July is *yours*, not *mine*. *You* may rejoice, *I* must mourn. To drag a man in fetters into the grand illuminated temple of liberty, and call upon him to join you in joyous anthems, were inhuman mockery and sacrilegious irony. Do you mean, citizens, to mock me, by asking me to speak to-day? If so, there is a parallel to your conduct. And let me warn you that it is dangerous to copy the example of a nation whose crimes, towering up to heaven, were thrown down by the breath of the Almighty, burying that nation in irrevocable ruin! I can to-day take up the plaintive lament of a peeled and woe-smitten people!

"By the rivers of Babylon, there we sat down. Yea! we wept when we remembered Zion. We hangd our harps upon the willows in the midst thereof. For there, they that carried us away captive, required of us a song; and they who wasted us required of us mirth, saying, Sing us one of the songs of Zion. How can we sing the Lord's song in a strange land? If I forget thee, O Jerusalem, let my right hand forget her cunning. If I do not remember thee, let my tongue cleave to the roof of my mouth."[18]

Fellow-citizens, above your national, tumultuous joy, I hear the mournful wail of millions! whose chains, heavy and grievous yesterday, are, to-day, rendered more intolerable by the jubilee shouts that reach them. If I do forget, if I do not faithfully remember those bleeding children of sorrow this day, "may my right hand forget her cunning, and may my tongue cleave to the roof of my mouth!" To forget them, to pass lightly over their wrongs, and to chime in with the popular theme, would be treason most scandalous and shocking, and would make me a reproach before God and the world. My subject, then, fellow-citizens, is American slavery. I shall see this day and its popular characteristics from the slave's point of view. Standing there identified with the American bondman, making his wrongs mine, I do not hestitate to declare, with all my soul, that the character and conduct of this nation never looked blacker to me than on this 4th of July! Whether we turn to the declarations of the past, or to the professions of the present, the conduct of the nation seems equally hideous and revolting. America is false to the past, false to the present, and solemnly binds herself to be false to the future. Standing with God and the crushed and bleeding slave on this occasion, I will, in the name of humanity which is outraged, in the name of liberty which is fettered, in the name of the constitution and the Bible which are disregarded and trampled upon, dare to call in question and to denounce, with all the emphasis I can command, everything that serves to perpetuate slavery—the great sin and shame of America! "I will not equivocate; I will not excuse"[19]; I will use the severet language I can command; and yet not one word shall escape me that any man, whose judgment is not blinded by prejudice, or who is not at heart a slave-holder, shall not confess to be right and just.

But I fancy I hear some one of my audience say, "It is just in this circumstance that you and your brother abolitionists fail to make a favorable impression on the public mind. Would you argue more, and denounce less; would you persuade more, and rebuke less; your cause would be much more likely to succeed." But, I submit, where all is plain

---

17. Lacerations from whippings.   18. Psalms 137.1–6.   19. William Lloyd Garrison (1805–1879), *The Liberator*, January 1, 1831; see p. 249.

there is nothing to be argued. What point in the anti-slavery creed would you have me argue? On what branch of the subject do the people of this country need light? Must I undertake to prove that the slave is a man? That point is conceded already. Nobody doubts it. The slaveholders themselves acknowledge it in the enactment of laws for their government. They acknowledge it when they punish disobedience on the part of the slave. There are seventy-two crimes in the State of Virginia which, if committed by a black man (no matter how ignorant he be), subject him to the punishment of death; while only two of the same crimes will subject a white man to the like punishment. What is this but the acknowledgment that the slave is a moral, intellectual, and responsible being? The manhood of the slave is conceded. It is admitted in the fact that Southern statute books are covered with enactments forbidding, under severe fines and penalties, the teaching of the slave to read or to write. When you can point to any such laws in reference to the beasts of the field, then I may consent to argue the manhood of the slave. When the dogs in your streets, when the fowls of the air, when the cattle on your hills, when the fish of the sea, and the reptiles that crawl, shall be unable to distinguish the slave from a brute, *then* will I argue with you that the slave is a man!

For the present, it is enough to affirm the equal manhood of the Negro race. Is it not astonishing that, while we are ploughing, planting, and reaping, using all kinds of mechanical tools, erecting houses, constructing bridges, building ships, working in metals of brass, iron, copper, silver and gold; that, while we are reading, writing and ciphering, acting as clerks, merchants and secretaries, having among us lawyers, doctors, ministers, poets, authors, editors, orators and teachers; that, while we are engaged in all manner of enterprises common to other men, digging gold in California, capturing the whale in the Pacific, feeding sheep and cattle on the hill-side, living, moving, acting, thinking, planning, living in families as husbands, wives and children, and, above all, confessing and worshipping the Christian's God, and looking hopefully for life and immortality beyond the grave, we are called upon to prove that we are men!

Would you have me argue that man is entitled to liberty? that he is the rightful owner of his own body? You have already declared it. Must I argue the wrongfulness of slavery? Is that a question for Republicans? Is it to be settled by the rules of logic and argumentation, as a matter beset with great difficulty, involving a doubtful application of the principle of justice, hard to be understood? How should I look to-day, in the presence of Americans, dividing, and subdividing a discourse, to show that men have a natural right to freedom? speaking of it relatively and positively, negatively and affirmatively. To do so, would be to make myself ridiculous, and to offer an insult to your understanding.—There is not a man beneath the canopy of heaven that does not know that slavery is wrong *for him*.

What, am I to argue that it is wrong to make men brutes, to rob them of their liberty, to work them without wages, to keep them ignorant of their relations to their fellow men, to beat them with sticks, to flay their flesh with the lash, to load their limbs with irons, to hunt them with dogs, to sell them at auction, to sunder their families, to knock out their teeth, to burn their flesh, to starve them into obedience and submission to their masters? Must I argue that a system thus marked with blood, and stained with pollution, is *wrong*? No! I will not. I have better employment for my time and strength than such arguments would imply.

What, then, remains to be argued? Is it that slavery is not divine; that God did not establish it; that our doctors of divinity are mistaken? There is blasphemy in the thought. That which is inhuman, cannot be divine! *Who* can reason on such a proposition? They that can, may; I cannot. The time for such argument is passed.

At a time like this, scorching irony, not convincing argument, is needed. O! had I the ability, and could reach the nation's ear, I would, to-day, pour out a fiery stream of biting ridicule, blasting reproach, withering sarcasm, and stern rebuke. For it is not light that is needed, but fire; it is not the gentle shower, but thunder. We need the storm, the whirlwind, and the earthquake. The feeling of the nation must be quickened; the conscience of the nation must be roused; the propriety of the nation must be startled; the hypocrisy of the nation must be exposed; and its crimes against God and man must be proclaimed and denounced.

What, to the American slave, is your 4th of July? I answer; a day that reveals to him, more than all other days in the year, the gross injustice and cruelty to which he is the constant victim. To him, your celebration is a sham; your boasted liberty, an unholy license; your national greatness, swelling vanity; your sounds of rejoicing are empty and heartless; your denunciation of tyrants, brass fronted impudence; your shouts of liberty and equality, hollow mockery; your prayers and hymns, your sermons and thanksgivings, with all your religious parade and solemnity, are, to Him, mere bombast, fraud, deception, impiety, and hypocrisy—a thin veil to cover up crimes which would disgrace a nation of savages. There is not a nation on the earth guilty of practices more shocking and bloody than are the people of the United States, at this very hour.

Go where you may, search where you will, roam through all the monarchies and despotisms of the Old World, travel through South America, search out every abuse, and when you have found the last, lay your facts by the side of the everyday practices of this nation, and you will say with me, that, for revolting barbarity and shameless hypocrisy, America reigns without a rival.

Take the American slave-trade, which we are told by the papers, is especially prosperous just now. Ex-Senator Benton[20] tells us that the price of men was never higher than now. He mentions the fact to show that slavery is in no danger. This trade is one of the peculiarities of American institutions. It is carried on in all the large towns and cities in one-half of this confederacy; and millions are pocketed every year by dealers in this horrid traffic. In several states this trade is a chief source of wealth. It is called (in contradistinction to the foreign slave-trade) *"the internal slave-trade."* It is, probably, called so, too, in order to divert from it the horror with which the foreign slave-trade is contemplated. That trade has long since been denounced by this government as piracy. It has been denounced with burning words from the high places of the nation as an execrable traffic. To arrest it, to put an end to it, this nation keeps a squadron, at immense cost, on the coast of Africa. Everywhere, in this country, it is safe to speak of this foreign slave-trade as a most inhuman traffic, opposed alike to the laws of God and of man. The duty to extirpate and destroy it, is admitted even by our doctors of divinity. In order to put an end to it, some of these last have consented that their colored brethren (nominally free) should leave this country, and establish themselves on the western coast of Africa! It is, however, a notable fact that, while so much execration is poured out by Americans upon all those engaged in the foreign slave-trade, the men engaged in the slave-trade between the states pass without condemnation, and their business is deemed honorable.

---

20. Thomas Hart Benton (1782–1858) declared his opposition to slavery in 1849.

Behold the practical operation of this internal slave-trade, the American slave-trade, sustained by American politics and American religion. Here you will see men and women reared like swine for the market. You know what is a swine-drover? I will show you a man-drover. They inhabit all our Southern States. They perambulate the country, and crowd the highways of the nation, with droves of human stock. You will see one of these human flesh jobbers,[21] armed with pistol, whip, and bowie-knife, driving a company of a hundred men, women, and children, from the Potomac to the slave market at New Orleans. These wretched people are to be sold singly, or in lots, to suit purchasers. They are food for the cotton-field and the deadly sugar-mill. Mark the sad procession, as it moves wearily along, and the inhuman wretch who drives them. Hear his savage yells and his blood-curdling oaths, as he hurries on his affrighted captives! There, see the old man with locks thinned and gray. Cast one glance, if you please, upon that young mother, whose shoulders are bare to the scorching sun, her briny tears falling on the brow of the babe in her arms. See, too, that girl of thirteen, weeping, yes! weeping, as she thinks of the mother from whom she has been torn! The drove moves tardily. Heat and sorrow have nearly consumed their strength; suddenly you hear a quick snap, like the discharge of a rifle; the fetters clank, and the chain rattles simultaneously; your ears are saluted with a scream, that seems to have torn its way to the centre of your soul! The crack you heard was the sound of the slave-whip; the scream you heard was from the woman you saw with the babe. Her speed had faltered under the weight of her child and her chains! that gash on her shoulder tells her to move on. Follow this drove to New Orleans. Attend the auction; see men examined like horses; see the forms of women rudely and brutally exposed to the shocking gaze of American slave-buyers. See this drove sold and separated forever; and never forget the deep, sad sobs that arose from that scattered multitude. Tell me, citizens, where, under the sun, you can witness a spectacle more fiendish and shocking. Yet this is but a glance at the American slave-trade, as it exists, at this moment, in the ruling part of the United States.

I was born amid such sights and scenes. To me the American slave-trade is a terrible reality. When a child, my soul was often pierced with a sense of its horrors. I lived on Philpot Street, Fell's Point, Baltimore, and have watched from the wharves the slave ships in the Basin, anchored from the shore, with their cargoes of human flesh, waiting for favorable winds to waft them down the Chesapeake. There was, at that time, a grand slave mart kept at the head of Pratt Street, by Austin Woldfolk. His agents were sent into every town and county in Maryland, announcing their arrival, through the papers, and on flaming "hand-bills," headed cash for Negroes. These men were generally well dressed men, and very captivating in their manners; ever ready to drink, to treat, and to gamble. The fate of many a slave has depended upon the turn of a single card; and many a child has been snatched from the arms of its mother by bargains arranged in a state of brutal drunkenness.

The flesh-mongers gather up their victims by dozens, and drive them chained, to the general depot at Baltimore. When a sufficient number has been collected here, a ship is chartered for the purpose of conveying the forlorn crew to Mobile, or to New Orleans. From the slave prison to the ship, they are usually driven in the darkness of night; for since the anti-slavery agitation, a certain caution is observed.

---

21. Slave traders.

In the deep, still darkness of midnight, I have been often aroused by the dead, heavy footsteps, and the piteous cries of the chained gangs that passed our door. The anguish of my boyish heart was intense; and I was often consoled, when speaking to my mistress in the morning, to hear her say that the custom was very wicked; that she hated to hear the rattle of the chains and the heart-rending cries. I was glad to find one who sympathized with me in my horror.

Fellow-citizens, this murderous traffic is, to-day, in active operation in this boasted republic. In the solitude of my spirit I see clouds of dust raised on the high-ways of the South; I see the bleeding footsteps; I hear the doleful wail of fettered humanity on the way to the slave-markets, where the victims are to be sold like *horses, sheep, and swine*, knocked off to the highest bidder. There I see the tenderest ties ruthlessly broken, to gratify the lust, caprice and rapacity of the buyers and sell-ers of men. My soul sickens at the sight.

> Is this the land your Fathers loved,
>   The freedom which they toiled to win?
> Is this the earth whereon they moved?
>   Are these the graves they slumber in?[22]

But a still more inhuman, disgraceful, and scandalous state of things remains to be presented. By an act of the American Congress, not yet two years old, slavery has been nationalized in its most horrible and revolting form. By that act, Mason and Dixon's line has been obliterated; New York has become as Virginia; and the power to hold, hunt, and sell men, women and children, as slaves, remains no longer a mere state institution, but is now an institution of the whole United States.[23] The power is co-extensive with the star-spangled banner, and American Christianity. Where these go, may also go the merciless slave-hunter. Where these are, man is not sacred. He is a bird for the sportsman's gun. By the most foul and fiendish of all human decrees, the lib-erty and person of every man are put in peril. Your broad republican domain is hunt-ing ground for *men*. Not for thieves and robbers, enemies of society, merely, but for men guilty of no crime. Your law-makers have commanded all good citizens to engage in this hellish sport. Your President, your Secretary of State, your *lords, nobles,* and ecclesiastics enforce, as a duty you owe to your free and glorious country, and to your God, that you do this accursed thing. Not fewer than forty Americans have, within the past two years, been hunted down and, without a moment's warning, hurried away in chains, and consigned to slavery and excruciating torture. Some of these have had wives and children, dependent on them for bread; but of this, no account was made. The right of the hunter to his prey stands superior to the right of marriage, and to *all* rights in this republic, the rights of God included! For black men there is neither law nor justice, humanity nor religion. The Fugitive Slave *Law* makes mercy to them a crime; and bribes the judge who tries them. An American judge gets ten dollars for every victim he consigns to slavery, and five, when he fails to do so. The oath of any two villains is sufficient, under this hell-black enactment, to send the most pious and exemplary black man into the remorseless jaws of slavery! His own testimony is noth-ing. He can bring no witnesses for himself. The minister of American justice is bound

22. John Greenleaf Whittier (1807–1892), "Stanzas for the Times" (1835).   23. Fugitive slave laws required northerners to return escaped slaves to their masters.

by the law to hear but *one side*; and *that* side is the side of the oppressor. Let this damning fact be perpetually told. Let it be thundered around the world that in tyrant-killing, king-hating, people-loving, democratic, Christian America the seats of justice are filled with judges who hold their offices under an open and palpable *bribe*, and are bound in deciding the case of a man's liberty, *to hear only his accusers!*

In glaring violation of justice, in shameless disregard of the forms of administering law, in cunning arrangement to entrap the defenceless, and in diabolical intent this Fugitive Slave Law stands alone in the annals of tyrannical legislation. I doubt if there be another nation on the globe having the brass and baseness to put such a law on the statute-book. If any man in this assembly thinks differently from me in this matter, and feels able to disprove my statements, I will gladly confront him at any suitable time and place he may select.

I take this law to be one of the grossest infringements of Christian Liberty, and, if the churches and ministers of our country were not stupidly blind, or most wickedly indifferent, they, too, would so regard it.

At the very moment that they are thanking God for the enjoyment of civil and religious liberty, and for the right to worship God according to the dictates of their own consciences, they are utterly silent in respect to a law which robs religion of its chief significance and makes it utterly worthless to a world lying in wickedness. Did this law concern the *"mint, anise, and cummin"*[24]—abridge the right to sing psalms, to partake of the sacrament, or to engage in any of the ceremonies of religion, it would be smitten by the thunder of a thousand pulpits. A general shout would go up from the church demanding *repeal, repeal, instant repeal!*—And it would go hard with that politician who presumed to solicit the votes of the people without inscribing this motto on his banner. Further, if this demand were not complied with, another Scotland would be added to the history of religious liberty, and the stern old covenanters[25] would be thrown into the shade. A John Knox[26] would be seen at every church door and heard from every pulpit, and Fillmore[27] would have no more quarter than was shown by Knox to the beautiful, but treacherous, Queen Mary of Scotland.[28] The fact that the church of our country (with fractional exceptions) does not esteem "the Fugitive Slave Law" as a declaration of war against religious liberty, implies that that church regards religion simply as a form of worship, an empty ceremony, and not a vital principle, requiring active benevolence, justice, love, and good will towards man. It esteems sacrifice above mercy; psalm-singing above right doing; solemn meetings above practical righteousness. A worship that can be conducted by persons who refuse to give shelter to the houseless, to give bread to the hungry, clothing to the naked, and who enjoin obedience to a law forbidding these acts of mercy is a curse, not a blessing to mankind. The Bible addresses all such persons as "scribes, pharisees, hypocrites, who pay the tithe of *mint, anise, and cummin,* and have omitted the weightier matters of the law, judgment, mercy, and faith."

But the church of this country is not only indifferent to the wrongs of the slave, it actually takes sides with the oppressors. It has made itself the bulwark of American slavery, and the shield of American slave-hunters. Many of its most eloquent Divines,[29]

---

24. Matthew 23.25.   25. Adherents to the Scottish "National Covenant" of 1638; zealots.   26. Scottish preacher (1513–1572).   27. President Millard Fillmore (1800–1874) signed the Fugitive Slave Act into law.   28. Mary, Queen of Scots (1542–1587) imprisoned Knox for treason.   29. Ministers.

who stand as the very lights of the church, have shamelessly given the sanction of religion and the Bible to the whole slave system. They have taught that man may, properly, be a slave; that the relation of master and slave is ordained of God; that to send back an escaped bondman to his master is clearly the duty of all the followers of the Lord Jesus Christ; and this horrible blasphemy is palmed off upon the world for Christianity.

For my part, I would say, welcome infidelity! welcome atheism! welcome anything! in preference to the gospel, *as preached by those Divines*! They convert the very name of religion into an engine of tyranny and barbarous cruelty, and serve to confirm more infidels, in this age, than all the infidel writings of Thomas Paine, Voltaire, and Bolingbroke[30] put together have done! These ministers make religion a cold and flinty-hearted thing, having neither principles of right action nor bowels of compassion. They strip the love of God of its beauty and leave the throne of religion a huge, horrible, repulsive form. It is a religion for oppressors, tyrants, man-stealers, and *thugs*. It is not that *"pure and undefiled religion"*[31] which is from above, and which is *"first pure, then peaceable, easy to be entreated,* full of mercy and good fruits, *without partiality, and without hypocrisy."*[32] But a religion which favors the rich against the poor; which exalts the proud above the humble; which divides mankind into two classes, tyrants and slaves; which says to the man in chains, *stay there;* and to the oppressor, *oppress on;* it is a religion which may be professed and enjoyed by all the robbers and enslavers of mankind; it makes God a respecter of persons, denies his fatherhood of the race, and tramples in the dust the great truth of the brotherhood of man. All this we affirm to be true of the popular church, and the popular worship of our land and nation—a religion, a church, and a worship which, on the authority of inspired wisdom, we pronounce to be an abomination in the sight of God. In the language of Isaiah, the American church might be well addressed, "Bring no more vain oblations; incense is an abomination unto me: the new moons and Sabbaths, the calling of assemblies, I cannot away with; it is iniquity, even the solemn meeting. Your new moons, and your appointed feasts my soul hateth. They are a trouble to me; I am weary to bear them; and when ye spread forth your hands I will hide mine eyes from you. Yea! when ye make many prayers, I will not hear. Your hands are full of blood; cease to do evil, learn to do well; seek judgment; relieve the oppressed; judge for the fatherless; plead for the widow."[33]

The American church is guilty, when viewed in connection with what it is doing to uphold slavery; but it is superlatively guilty when viewed in its connection with its ability to abolish slavery.

The sin of which it is guilty is one of omission as well as of commission. Albert Barnes[34] but uttered what the common sense of every man at all observant of the actual state of the case will receive as truth, when he declared that "There is no power out of the church that could sustain slavery an hour, if it were not sustained in it."

Let the religious press, the pulpit, the Sunday School, the conference meeting, the great ecclesiastical, missionary, Bible and tract associations of the land array their immense powers against slavery, and slave-holding; and the whole system of crime and blood would be scattered to the winds, and that they do not do this involves them in the most awful responsibility of which the mind can conceive.

---

30. Thomas Paine (1737–1809), American revolutionary; Voltaire (1694–1778), French philosopher; Henry St. John Bolingbroke (1678–1751), English politician. 31. James 1.27. 32. James 3.17. 33. Isaiah 1.13–17. 34. American minister and author (1798–1870).

In prosecuting the anti-slavery enterprise, we have been asked to spare the church, to spare the ministry; but *how*, we ask, could such a thing be done? We are met on the threshold of our efforts for the redemption of the slave, by the church and ministry of the country, in battle arrayed against us; and we are compelled to fight or flee. From *what* quarter, I beg to know, has proceeded a fire so deadly upon our ranks, during the last two years, as from the Northern pulpit? As the champions of oppressors, the chosen men of American theology have appeared—men honored for their so-called piety, and their real learning. The Lords of Buffalo, the Springs of New York, the Lathrops of Auburn, the Coxes and Spencers of Brooklyn, the Gannets and Sharps of Boston, the Deweys of Washington,[35] and other great religious lights of the land have, in utter denial of the authority of *Him* by whom they professed to be called to the ministry, deliberately taught us, against the example of the Hebrews, and against the remonstrance of the Apostles, *that we ought to obey man's law before the law of God.*

My spirit wearies of such blasphemy; and how such men can be supported, as the "standing types and representatives of Jesus Christ," is a mystery which I leave others to penetrate. In speaking of the American church, however, let it be distinctly understood that I mean the *great mass* of the religious organizations of our land. There are exceptions, and I thank God that there are. Noble men may be found, scattered all over these Northern States, of whom Henry Ward Beecher, of Brooklyn; Samuel J. May, of Syracuse; and my esteemed friend (Rev. R. R. Raymond)[36] on the platform, are shining examples; and let me say further, that, upon these men lies the duty to inspire our ranks with high religious faith and zeal, and to cheer us on in the great mission of the slave's redemption from his chains.

One is struck with the difference between the attitude of the American church towards the anti-slavery movement, and that occupied by the churches in England towards a similar movement in that country. There, the church, true to its mission of ameliorating, elevating and improving the condition of mankind, came forward promptly, bound up the wounds of the West Indian slave, and restored him to his liberty. There, the question of emancipation was a high religious question. It was demanded in the name of humanity, and according to the law of the living God. The Sharps, the Clarksons, the Wilberforces, the Buxtons, the Burchells, and the Knibbs[37] were alike famous for their piety and for their philanthropy. The anti-slavery movement *there* was not an anti-church movement, for the reason that the church took its full share in prosecuting that movement; and the anti-slavery movement in this country will cease to be an anti-church movement, when the church of this country shall assume a favorable instead of a hostile position towards that movement.

Americans! your republican politics, not less than your republican religion, are flagrantly inconsistent. You boast of your love of liberty, your superior civilization, and your pure Christianity, while the whole political power of the nation (as embodied in the two great political parties) is solemnly pledged to support and perpetuate the enslavement of three millions of your countrymen. You hurl your anathemas at the crowned headed tyrants of Russia and Austria and pride yourselves on your Democratic institutions, while you yourselves consent to be mere *tools* and *body-guards* of the tyrants of Virginia and Carolina. You invite to your shores fugitives of oppression from abroad,

---

35. Douglass lists pro-slavery ministers.   36. Henry Ward Beecher (1813–1887), Samuel J. May (1797–1871), and Robert Raikes Raymond (c. 1819–1890), prominent abolitionist ministers.   37. British abolitionist leaders.

honor them with banquets, greet them with ovations, cheer them, toast them, salute them, protect them, and pour out your money to them like water; but the fugitives from your own land you advertise, hunt, arrest, shoot, and kill. You glory in your refinement and your universal education; yet you maintain a system as barbarous and dreadful as ever stained the character of a nation—a system begun in avarice, supported in pride, and perpetuated in cruelty. You shed tears over fallen Hungary,[38] and make the sad story of her wrongs the theme of your poets, statesmen, and orators, till your gallant sons are ready to fly to arms to vindicate her cause against the oppressor; but, in regard to the ten thousand wrongs of the American slave, you would enforce the strictest silence, and would hail him as an enemy of the nation who dares to make those wrongs the subject of public discourse! You are all on fire at the mention of liberty for France or for Ireland; but are as cold as an iceberg at the thought of liberty for the enslaved of America. You discourse eloquently on the dignity of labor; yet, you sustain a system which, in its very essence, casts a stigma upon labor. You can bare your bosom to the storm of British artillery to throw off a three-penny tax on tea; and yet wring the last hard earned farthing from the grasp of the black laborers of your country. You profess to believe "that, of one blood, God made all nations of men to dwell on the face of all the earth,"[39] and hath commanded all men, everywhere, to love one another; yet you notoriously hate (and glory in your hatred) all men whose skins are not colored like your own. You declare before the world, and are understood by the world to declare that you *"hold these truths to be self-evident, that all men are created equal; and are endowed by their Creator with certain inalienable rights; and that among these are, life, liberty, and the pursuit of happiness["]*[40]; and yet, you hold securely, in a bondage which, according to your own Thomas Jefferson, *"is worse than ages of that which your fathers rose in rebellion to oppose,"*[41] *a seventh part* of the inhabitants of your country.

Fellow-citizens, I will not enlarge further on your national inconsistencies. The existence of slavery in this country brands your republicanism as a sham, your humanity as a base pretense, and your Christianity as a lie. It destroys your moral power abroad; it corrupts your politicians at home. It saps the foundation of religion; it makes your name a hissing and a bye-word to a mocking earth. It is the antagonistic force in your government, the only thing that seriously disturbs and endangers your *Union*. It fetters your progress; it is the enemy of improvement; the deadly foe of education; it fosters pride; it breeds insolence; it promotes vice; it shelters crime; it is a curse to the earth that supports it; and yet you cling to it as if it were the sheet anchor of all your hopes. Oh! be warned! be warned! a horrible reptile is coiled up in your nation's bosom; the venomous creature is nursing at the tender breast of your youthful republic; *for the love of God, tear away*, and fling from you the hideous monster, and *let the weight of twenty millions crush and destroy it forever!*

But it is answered in reply to all this, that precisely what I have now denounced is, in fact, guaranteed and sanctioned by the Constitution of the United States; that, the right to hold, and to hunt slaves is a part of that Constitution framed by the illustrious Fathers of this Republic.

Then, I dare to affirm, notwithstanding all I have said before, your fathers stooped, basely stooped

38. Conquered by Russia in 1849.   39. Acts 17.26.   40. Declaration of Independence (1776); see p. 130.   41. Thomas Jefferson (1743–1836), Letter to Nicholas Demeunier, June 26, 1776.

To palter with us in a double sense:
And keep the word of promise to the ear,
But break it to the heart.[42]

And instead of being the honest men I have before declared them to be, they were the veriest imposters that ever practised on mankind. This is the inevitable conclusion, and from it there is no escape, but I differ from those who charge this baseness on the framers of the Constitution of the United States. It is a slander upon their memory, at least, so I believe. There is not time now to argue the constitutional question at length; nor have I the ability to discuss it as it ought to be discussed. The subject has been handled with masterly power by Lysander Spooner, Esq., by William Goodell, by Samuel E. Sewall, Esq., and last, though not least, by Gerrit Smith, Esq.[43] These gentlemen have, as I think, fully and clearly vindicated the Constitution from any design to support slavery for an hour.

Fellow-citizens! there is no matter in respect to which the people of the North have allowed themselves to be so ruinously imposed upon as that of the pro-slavery character of the Constitution. In that instrument I hold there is neither warrant, license, nor sanction of the hateful thing; but interpreted, as it ought to be interpreted, the Constitution is a glorious liberty document. Read its preamble, consider its purposes. Is slavery among them? Is it at the gateway? or is it in the temple? it is neither. While I do not intend to argue this question on the present occasion, let me ask, if it be not somewhat singular that, if the Constitution were intended to be, by its framers and adopters, a slaveholding instrument, why neither slavery, slaveholding, nor slave can anywhere be found in it. What would be thought of an instrument, drawn up, legally drawn up, for the purpose of entitling the city of Rochester to a tract of land, in which no mention of land was made? Now, there are certain rules of interpretation for the proper understanding of all legal instruments. These rules are well established. They are plain, commonsense rules, such as you and I, and all of us, can understand and apply, without having passed years in the study of law. I scout the idea that the question of the constitutionality, or unconstitutionality of slavery, is not a question for the people. I hold that every American citizen has a right to form an opinion of the constitution, and to propagate that opinion, and to use all honorable means to make his opinion the prevailing one. Without this right, the liberty of an American citizen would be as insecure as that of a Frenchman. Ex-Vice-President Dallas[44] tells us that the constitution is an object to which no American mind can be too attentive, and no American heart too devoted. He further says, the Constitution, in its words, is plain and intelligible, and is meant for the home-bred, unsophisticated understandings of our fellow-citizens. Senator Berrien[45] tells us that the Constitution is the fundamental law, that which controls all others. The charter of our liberties, which every citizen has a personal interest in understanding thoroughly. The testimony of Senator Breese, Lewis Cass,[46] and many others that might be named, who are everywhere esteemed as sound lawyers, so regard the constitution. I take it, therefore, that it is not presumption in a private citizen to form an opinion of that instrument.

---

42. William Shakespeare (1564–1616), *Macbeth* (1603), 5.8.19–22.   43. American abolitionists.   44. George Mifflin Dallas (1792–1864).   45. John Berrien (1781–1856) of Georgia.   46. Sidney Breese (1800–1878) of Illinois; Lewis Cass (1782–1866) of Michigan.

Now, take the Constitution according to its plain reading, and I defy the presentation of a single pro-slavery clause in it. On the other hand, it will be found to contain principles and purposes, entirely hostile to the existence of slavery.

I have detained my audience entirely too long already. At some future period I will gladly avail myself of an opportunity to give this subject a full and fair discussion.

Allow me to say, in conclusion, notwithstanding the dark picture I have this day presented, of the state of the nation, I do not despair of this country. There are forces in operation which must inevitably work the downfall of slavery. "The arm of the Lord is not shortened,"[47] and the doom of slavery is certain. I, therefore, leave off where I began, with hope. While drawing encouragement from "the Declaration of Independence," the great principles it contains, and the genius of American Institutions, my spirit is also cheered by the obvious tendencies of the age. Nations do not now stand in the same relation to each other that they did ages ago. No nation can now shut itself up from the surrounding world and trot round in the same old path of its fathers without interference. The time was when such could be done. Long established customs of hurtful character could formerly fence themselves in, and do their evil work with social impunity. Knowledge was then confined and enjoyed by the privileged few, and the multitude walked on in mental darkness. But a change has now come over the affairs of mankind. Walled cities and empires have become unfashionable. The arm of commerce has borne away the gates of the strong city. Intelligence is penetrating the darkest corners of the globe. It makes its pathway over and under the sea, as well as on the earth. Wind, steam, and lightning are its chartered agents. Oceans no longer divide, but link nations together. From Boston to London is now a holiday excursion. Space is comparatively annihilated.—Thoughts expressed on one side of the Atlantic are distinctly heard on the other.

The far off and almost fabulous Pacific rolls in grandeur at our feet. The Celestial Empire, the mystery of ages, is being solved. The fiat of the Almighty, "Let there be Light,"[48] has not yet spent its force. No abuse, no outrage whether in taste, sport or avarice, can now hide itself from the all-pervading light. The iron shoe, and crippled foot of China[49] must be seen in contrast with nature. Africa must rise and put on her yet unwoven garment. "Ethiopia shall stretch out her hand unto God."[50] In the fervent aspirations of William Lloyd Garrison, I say, and let every heart join in saying it:

> God speed the year of jubilee
>   The wide world o'er!
> When from their galling chains set free,
> Th' oppress'd shall vilely bend the knee,
> And wear the yoke of tyranny
>   Like brutes no more.
> That year will come, and freedom's reign,
> To man his plundered rights again
>   Restore.
>
> God speed the day when human blood
>   Shall cease to flow!

---

47. Isaiah 59.1.   48. Genesis 1.3.   49. Chinese practice of binding feet tightly to prevent growth.   50. Psalm 68.31.

In every clime be understood,
The claims of human brotherhood,
And each return for evil, good,
    Not blow for blow;
That day will come all feuds to end,
And change into a faithful friend
    Each foe.

God speed the hour, the glorious hour,
    When none on earth
Shall exercise a lordly power,
Nor in a tyrant's presence cower;
But to all manhood's stature tower,
    By equal birth!
That hour will come, to each, to all,
And from his prison-house, to thrall
    Go forth.

Until that year, day, hour, arrive,
With head, and heart, and hand I'll strive,
To break the rod, and rend the gyve,
The spoiler of his prey deprive—
So witness Heaven!
And never from my chosen post,
Whate'er the peril or the cost,
Be driven.

—1852

The Heroic Slave

Part I

Oh! child of grief, why weepest thou?
    Why droops thy sad and mournful brow?
Why is thy look so like despair?
    What deep, sad sorrow lingers there?

The State of Virginia is famous in American annals for the multitudinous array of her statesmen and heroes. She has been dignified by some the mother of statesmen. History has not been sparing in recording their names, or in blazoning their deeds. Her high position in this respect, has given her an enviable distinction among her sister States. With Virginia for his birth-place, even a man of ordinary parts, on account of the general partiality for her sons, easily rises to eminent stations. Men, not great enough to attract special attention in their native States, have, like a certain distinguished citizen in the State of New York, sighed and repined that they were not born in Virginia. Yet not all the great ones of the Old Dominion have, by the fact of their birth-place, escaped undeserved obscurity. By some strange neglect, *one* of the truest, manliest, and bravest of her children,—one who, in after years, will, I think, command the pen of genius to set his merits forth, holds now no higher place in the records of that grand old Commonwealth than is held by a horse or an ox. Let those account for it who can, but there stands the fact, that a man who loved liberty as well as did Patrick Henry,[1]—who deserved it as much as Thomas Jefferson,[2]—and who fought for it with a valor as high, an arm as strong, and against odds as great, as he who led all the armies of the American colonies through the great war for freedom and independence,[3] lives now only in the chattel records[4] of his native State.

Glimpses of this great character are all that can now be presented. He is brought to view only by a few transient incidents, and these afford but partial satisfaction. Like a guiding star on a stormy night, he is seen through the parted clouds and the howling tempests; or, like the gray peak of a menacing rock on a perilous coast, he is seen by the quivering flash of angry lightning, and he again disappears covered with mystery.

Curiously, earnestly, anxiously we peer into the dark, and wish even for the blinding flash, or the light of northern skies to reveal him. But alas! he is still enveloped in darkness, and we return from the pursuit like a wearied and disheartened mother, (after a tedious and unsuccessful search for a lost child,) who returns weighed down with disappointment and sorrow. Speaking of marks, traces, possibles, and probabilities, we come before our readers.

In the spring of 1835, on a Sabbath morning, within hearing of the solemn peals of the church bells at a distant village, a Northern traveller through the State of Virginia drew up his horse to drink at a sparkling brook, near the edge of a dark pine forest. While his weary and thirsty steed drew in the grateful water, the rider caught the sound of a human voice, apparently engaged in earnest conversation.

Following the direction of the sound, he descried, among the tall pines, the man whose voice had arrested his attention. "To whom can he be speaking?" thought the traveller. "He seems to be alone." The circumstance interested him much, and he became intensely curious to know what thoughts and feelings, or, it might be, high aspirations, guided those rich and mellow accents. Tieing his horse at a short distance from the brook, he stealthily drew near the solitary speaker; and, concealing himself by the side of a huge fallen tree, he distinctly heard the following soliloquy:—

"What, then, is life to me? it is aimless and worthless, and worse than worthless. Those birds, perched on yon swinging boughs, in friendly conclave, sounding forth their merry notes in seeming worship of the rising sun, though liable to the sportsman's fowling-piece, are still my superiors. They *live free*, though they may die slaves. They fly where they list by day, and retire in freedom at night. But what is freedom to me, or I to it? I am a *slave*,—born a slave, an abject slave,—even before I made part of this breathing world, the scourge was platted for my back; the fetters were forged for my limbs. How mean a thing am I. That accursed and crawling snake, that miserable reptile, that has just glided into its slimy home, is freer and better off than I. He escaped my blow, and is safe. But here am I, a man,—yes, *a man!*—with thoughts and wishes, with powers and faculties as far as angel's flight above that hated reptile,—yet he is my superior, and scorns to own me as his master, or to stop to take my blows. When he saw

---

1. Patrick Henry (1736–1799), American revolutionary.   2. Thomas Jefferson (1743–1826), third U.S. president.   3. George Washington (1732–1799), first U.S. president.   4. Records of slave and cattle sales.

my uplifted arm, he darted beyond my reach, and turned to give me battle. I dare not do as much as that. I neither run nor fight, but do meanly stand, answering each heavy blow of a cruel master with doleful wails and piteous cries. I am galled with irons; but even these are more tolerable than the consciousness, the *galling* consciousness of cowardice and indecision. Can it be that I *dare* not run away? *Perish the thought*, I *dare* do any thing which may be done by another. When that young man struggled with the waves *for life*, and others stood back appalled in helpless horror, did I not plunge in, forgetful of life, to save his? The raging bull from whom all others fled, pale with fright, did I not keep at bay with a single pitchfork? Could a coward do that? *No,—no,—*I wrong myself,—I am no coward. *Liberty* I will have, or die in the attempt to gain it. This working that others may live in idleness! This cringing submission to insolence and curses! This living under the constant dread and apprehension of being sold and transferred, like a mere brute, is *too* much for me. I will stand it no longer. What others have done, I will do. These trusty legs, or these sinewy arms shall place me among the free. Tom escaped; so can I. The North Star[5] will not be less kind to me than to him. I will follow it. I will at least make the trial. I have nothing to lose. If I am caught, I shall only be a slave. If I am shot, I shall only lose a life which is a burden and a curse. If I get clear, (as something tells me I shall,) liberty, the inalienable birth-right of every man, precious and priceless, will be mine. My resolution is fixed. *I shall be free.*"

At these words the traveller raised his head cautiously and noiselessly, and caught, from his hiding-place, a full view of the unsuspecting speaker. Madison (for that was the name of our hero) was standing erect, a smile of satisfaction rippled upon his expressive countenance, like that which plays upon the face of one who has but just solved a difficult problem, or vanquished a malignant foe; for at that moment he was free, at least in spirit. The future gleamed brightly before him, and his fetters lay broken at his feet. His air was triumphant.

Madison was of manly form. Tall, symmetrical, round, and strong. In his movements he seemed to combine, with the strength of the lion, a lion's elasticity. His torn sleeves disclosed arms like polished iron. His face was "black, but comely."[6] His eye, lit with emotion, kept guard under a brow as dark and as glossy as the raven's wing. His whole appearance betokened Herculean strength: yet there was nothing savage or forbidding in his aspect. A child might play in his arms, or dance on his shoulders. A giant's strength, but not a giant's heart was in him. His broad mouth and nose spoke only of good nature and kindness. But his voice, that unfailing index of the soul, though full and melodious, had that in it which could terrify as well as charm. He was just the man you would choose when hardships were to be endured, or danger to be encountered,—intelligent and brave. He had the head to conceive, and the hand to execute. In a word, he was one to be sought as a friend, but to be dreaded as an enemy.

As our traveller gazed upon him, he almost trembled at the thought of his dangerous intrusion. Still he could not quit the place. He had long desired to sound the mysterious depths of the thoughts and feelings of a slave. He was not, therefore, disposed to allow so providential an opportunity to pass unimproved. He resolved to hear more; so he listened again for those mellow and mournful accents which, he says, made such an impression upon him as can never be erased. He did not have to wait long. There

---

5. Polaris, the star slaves used to find their way north.   6. Song of Solomon 1.5.

came another gush from the same full fountain; now bitter, and now sweet. Scathing denunciations of the cruelty and injustice of slavery; heart-touching narrations of his own personal suffering, intermingled with prayers to the God of the oppressed for help and deliverance, were followed by presentations of the dangers and difficulties of escape, and formed the burden of his eloquent utterances; but his high resolution clung to him,—for he ended each speech by an emphatic declaration of his purpose to be free. It seemed that the very repetition of this, imparted a glow to his countenance. The hope of freedom seemed to sweeten, for a season, the bitter cup of slavery, and to make it, for a time, tolerable; for when in the very whirlwind of anguish,—when his heart's cord seemed screwed up to snapping tension, hope sprung up and soothed his troubled spirit. Fitfully he would exclaim, "How can I leave her? Poor thing! what can she do when I am gone? Oh! oh! 'tis impossible that I can leave poor Susan!"

A brief pause intervened. Our traveller raised his head, and saw again the sorrow-smitten slave. His eye was fixed upon the ground. The strong man staggered under a heavy load. Recovering himself, he argued thus aloud: "All is uncertain here. To-morrow's sun may not rise before I am sold, and separated from her I love. What, then, could I do for her? I should be in more hopeless slavery, and she no nearer to liberty,—whereas if I were free,—my arms my own,—I might devise the means to rescue her."

This said, Madison cast around a searching glance, as if the thought of being overheard had flashed across his mind. He said no more, but, with measured steps, walked away, and was lost to the eye of our traveller amidst the wildering woods.

Long after Madison had left the ground, Mr. Listwell (our traveller) remained in motionless silence, meditating on the extraordinary revelations to which he had listened. He seemed fastened to the spot, and stood half hoping, half fearing the return of the sable preacher to his solitary temple. The speech of Madison rung through the chambers of his soul, and vibrated through his entire frame. "Here is indeed a man," thought he, "of rare endowments,—a child of God,—guilty of no crime but the color of his skin, hiding away from the face of humanity, and pouring out his thoughts and feelings, his hopes and resolutions to the lonely woods; to him those distant church bells have no grateful music. He shuns the church, the altar, and the great congregation of christian worshippers, and wanders away to the gloomy forest, to utter in the vacant air complaints and griefs, which the religion of his times and his country can neither console nor relieve. Goaded almost to madness by the sense of the injustice done him, he resorts hither to give vent to his pent up feelings, and to debate with himself the feasibility of plans, plans of his own invention, for his own deliverance. From this hour I am an abolitionist. I have seen enough and heard enough, and I shall go to my home in Ohio resolved to atone for my past indifference to this ill-starred race, by making such exertions as I shall be able to do, for the speedy emancipation of every slave in the land.

Part II

"The gaudy, babbling and remorseful day
Is crept into the bosom of the sea;
And now loud-howling wolves arouse the jades
That drag the tragic melancholy night;
Who with their drowsy, slow, and flagging wings

Clip dead men's graves, and from their misty jaws
Breathe foul contagions, darkness in the air."

Shakspeare.[7]

Five years after the foregoing singular occurence, in the winter of 1840, Mr. and Mrs. Listwell sat together by the fireside of their own happy home in the State of Ohio. The children were all gone to bed. A single lamp burnt brightly on the centre-table. All was still and comfortable within; but the night was cold and dark; a heavy wind sighed and moaned sorrowfully around the house and barn, occasionally bringing against the clattering windows a stray leaf from the large oak trees that embowered their dwelling. It was a night for strange noises and for strange fancies. A whole wilderness of thought might pass through one's mind during such an evening. The smouldering embers, partaking of the spirit of the restless night, became fruitful of varied and fantastic pictures, and revived many bygone scenes and old impressions. The happy pair seemed to sit in silent fascination, gazing on the fire. Suddenly this *reverie* was interrupted by a heavy growl. Ordinarily such an occurrence would have scarcely provoked a single word, or excited the least apprehension. But there are certain seasons when the slightest sound sends a jar through all the subtle chambers of the mind; and such a season was this. The happy pair started up, as if some sudden danger had come upon them. The growl was from their trusty watch-dog.

"What can it mean? certainly no one can be out on such a night as this," said Mrs. Listwell.

"The wind has deceived the dog, my dear; he has mistaken the noise of falling branches, brought down by the wind, for that of the footsteps of persons coming to the house. I have several times to-night thought that I heard the sound of footsteps. I am sure, however, that it was but the wind. Friends would not be likely to come out at such an hour, or such a night; and thieves are too lazy and self-indulgent to expose themselves to this biting frost; but should there be any one about, our brave old Monte, who is on the lookout, will not be slow in sounding the alarm."

Saying this they quietly left the window, whither they had gone to learn the cause of the menacing growl, and re-seated themselves by the fire, as if reluctant to leave the slowly expiring embers, although the hour was late. A few minutes only intervened after resuming their seats, when again their sober meditations were disturbed. Their faithful dog now growled and barked furiously, as if assailed by an advancing foe. Simultaneously the good couple arose, and stood in mute expectation. The contest without seemed fierce and violent. It was, however, soon over,—the barking ceased, for, with true canine instinct, Monte quickly discovered that a friend, not an enemy of the family, was coming to the house, and instead of rushing to repel the supposed intruder, he was now at the door, whimpering and dancing for the admission of himself and his newly made friend.

Mr. Listwell knew by this movement that all was well; he advanced and opened the door, and saw by the light that streamed out into the darkness, a tall man advancing slowly towards the house, with a stick in one hand, and a small bundle in the other. "It is a traveller," thought he, "who has missed his way, and is coming to inquire

7. William Shakespeare (1564–1616), *Henry VI*, part 2 (1594), 4.1.1–7.

the road. I am glad we did not go to bed earlier,—I have felt all the evening as if somebody would be here to-night."

The man had now halted a short distance from the door, and looked prepared alike for flight or battle. "Come in, sir, don't be alarmed, you have probably lost your way."

Slightly hesitating, the traveller walked in; not, however, without regarding his host with a scrutinizing glance. "No, sir," said he "I have come to ask you a greater favor."

Instantly Mr. Listwell exclaimed, (as the recollection of the Virginia forest scene flashed upon him,) "Oh, sir, I know not your name, but I have seen your face, and heard your voice before. I am glad to see you. *I know all.* You are flying for your liberty,—be seated,—be seated,—banish all fear. You are safe under my roof."

This recognition, so unexpected, rather disconcerted and disquieted the noble fugitive. The timidity and suspicion of persons escaping from slavery are easily awakened, and often what is intended to dispel the one, and to allay the other, has precisely the opposite effect. It was so in this case. Quickly observing the unhappy impression made by his words and action, Mr. Listwell assumed a more quiet and inquiring aspect, and finally succeeded in removing the apprehensions which his very natural and generous salutation had aroused.

Thus assured, the stranger said, "Sir, you have rightly guessed, I am, indeed, a fugitive from slavery. My name is Madison,—Madison Washington my mother used to call me. I am on my way to Canada, where I learn that persons of my color are protected in all the rights of men; and my object in calling upon you was, to beg the privilege of resting my weary limbs for the night in your barn. It was my purpose to have continued my journey till morning; but the piercing cold, and the frowning darkness compelled me to seek shelter; and, seeing a light through the lattice of your window, I was encouraged to come here to beg the privilege named. You will do me a great favor by affording me shelter for the night."

"A resting-place, indeed, sir, you shall have; not, however, in my barn, but in the best room of my house. Consider yourself, if you please, under the roof of a friend; for such I am to you, and to all your deeply injured race."

While this introductory conversation was going on, the kind lady had revived the fire, and was diligently preparing supper; for she, not less than her husband, felt for the sorrows of the oppressed and hunted ones of earth, and was always glad of an opportunity to do them a service. A bountiful repast was quickly prepared, and the hungry and toil-worn bondman was cordially invited to partake thereof. Gratefully he acknowledged the favor of his benevolent benefactress; but appeared scarcely to understand what such hospitality could mean. It was the first time in his life that he had met so humane and friendly a greeting at the hands of persons whose color was unlike his own; yet it was impossible for him to doubt the charitableness of his new friends, or the genuineness of the welcome so freely given; and he therefore, with many thanks, took his seat at the table with Mr. and Mrs. Listwell, who, desirous to make him feel at home, took a cup of tea themselves, while urging upon Madison the best that the house could afford.

Supper over, all doubts and apprehensions banished, the three drew around the blazing fire, and a conversation commenced which lasted till long after midnight.

"Now," said Madison to Mr. Listwell, "I was a little surprised and alarmed when I came in, by what you said; do tell me, sir, *why* you thought you had seen my face before, and by what you knew me to be a fugitive from slavery; for I am sure that I never was before in this neighborhood, and I certainly sought to conceal what I supposed to be the manner of a fugitive slave."

Mr. Listwell at once frankly disclosed the secret; describing the place where he first saw him; rehearsing the language which he (Madison) had used; referring to the effect which his manner and speech had made upon him; declaring the resolution he there formed to be an abolitionist; telling how often he had spoken of the circumstance, and the deep concern he had ever since felt to know what had become of him; and whether he had carried out the purpose to make his escape, as in the woods he declared he would do.

"Ever since that morning," said Mr. Listwell, "you have seldom been absent from my mind, and though now I did not dare to hope that I should ever see you again, I have often wished that such might be my fortune; for, from that hour, your face seemed to be daguerreotyped[8] on my memory."

Madison looked quite astonished, and felt amazed at the narration to which he had listened. After recovering himself he said, "I well remember that morning, and the bitter anguish that wrung my heart; I will state the occasion of it. I had, on the previous Saturday, suffered a cruel lashing; had been tied up to the limb of a tree, with my feet chained together, and a heavy iron bar placed between my ankles. Thus suspended, I received on my naked back forty stripes, and was kept in this distressing position three or four hours, and was then let down, only to have my torture increased; for my bleeding back, gashed by the cow-skin, was washed by the overseer with old brine, partly to augment my suffering, and partly, as he said, to prevent inflammation. My crime was that I had stayed longer at the mill, the day previous, than it was thought I ought to have done, which, I assured my master and the overseer, was no fault of mine; but no excuses were allowed. 'Hold your tongue, you impudent rascal,' met my every explanation. Slave-holders are so imperious when their passions are excited, as to construe every word of the slave into insolence. I could do nothing but submit to the agonizing infliction. Smarting still from the wounds, as well as from the consciousness of being whipt for no cause, I took advantage of the absence of my master, who had gone to church, to spend the time in the woods, and brood over my wretched lot. Oh, sir, I remember it well, and can never forget it."

"But this was five years ago; where have you been since?"

"I will try to tell you," said Madison. "Just four weeks after that Sabbath morning, I gathered up the few rags of clothing I had, and started, as I supposed, for the North and for freedom. I must not stop to describe my feelings on taking this step. It seemed like taking a leap into the dark. The thought of leaving my poor wife and two little children caused me indescribable anguish; but consoling myself with the reflection that once free, I could, possibly, devise ways and means to gain their freedom also, I nerved myself up to make the attempt. I started, but ill-luck attended me; for after being out a whole week, strange to say, I still found myself on my master's grounds; the third night after being out, a season of clouds and rain set in, wholly preventing me from seeing the North Star, which I had trusted as my guide, not dreaming that clouds might intervene between us.

"This circumstance was fatal to my project, for in losing my star, I lost my way; so when I supposed I was far towards the North, and had almost gained my freedom,

---

8. Photographically imprinted.

I discovered myself at the very point from which I had started. It was a severe trial, for I arrived at home in great destitution; my feet were sore, and in travelling in the dark, I had dashed my foot against a stump, and started a nail, and lamed myself. I was wet and cold; one week had exhausted all my stores; and when I landed on my master's plantation, with all my work to do over again,—hungry, tired, lame, and bewildered,—I almost cursed the day that I was born. In this extremity I approached the quarters. I did so stealthily, although in my desperation I hardly cared whether I was discovered or not. Peeping through the rents of the quarters, I saw my fellow-slaves seated by a warm fire, merrily passing away the time, as though their hearts knew no sorrow. Although I envied their seeming contentment, all wretched as I was, I despised the cowardly acquiescence in their own degradation which it implied, and felt a kind of pride and glory in my own desperate lot. I dared not enter the quarters,—for where there is seeming contentment with slavery, there is certain treachery to freedom. I proceeded towards the great house, in the hope of catching a glimpse of my poor wife, whom I knew might be trusted with my secrets even on the scaffold. Just as I reached the fence which divided the field from the garden, I saw a woman in the yard, who in the darkness I took to be my wife; but a nearer approach told me it was not she. I was about to speak; had I done so, I would not have been here this night; for an alarm would have been sounded, and the hunters been put on my track. Here were hunger, cold, thirst, disappointment, and chagrin, confronted only by the dim hope of liberty. I tremble to think of that dreadful hour. To face the deadly cannon's mouth in warm blood unterrified, is, I think, a small achievement, compared with a conflict like this with gaunt starvation. The gnawings of hunger conquers by degrees, till all that a man has he would give in exchange for a single crust of bread. Thank God, I was not quite reduced to this extremity.

"Happily for me, before the fatal moment of utter despair, my good wife made her appearance in the yard. It was she; I knew her step. All was well now. I was, however, afraid to speak lest I should frighten her. Yet speak I did; and, to my great joy, my voice was known. Our meeting can be more easily imagined than described. For a time hunger, thirst, weariness, and lameness were forgotten. But it was soon necessary for her to return to the house. She being a house-servant, her absence from the kitchen, if discovered, might have excited suspicion. Our parting was like tearing the flesh from my bones; yet it was the part of wisdom for her to go. She left me with the purpose of meeting me at midnight in the very forest where you last saw me. She knew the place well, as one of my melancholy resorts, and could easily find it, though the night was dark.

"I hastened away, therefore, and concealed myself, to await the arrival of my good angel. As I lay there among the leaves, I was strongly tempted to return again to the house of my master and give myself up; but remembering my solemn pledge on that memorable Sunday morning, I was able to linger out the two long hours between ten and midnight. I may well call them long hours. I have endured much hardship; I have encountered many perils; but the anxiety of those two hours, was the bitterest I ever experienced. True to her word, my wife came laden with provisions, and we sat down on the side of a log, at that dark and lonesome hour of the night. I cannot say we talked; our feelings were too great for that; yet we came to an understanding that I should make the woods my home, for if I gave myself up, I should be whipped and sold away; and if I started for the North, I should leave a wife doubly dear to me. We mutually determined, therefore, that I should remain in the vicinity. In the dismal swamps I lived, sir, five long years,—a cave for my home during the day. I wandered about at night with the wolf and the bear,—sustained by the promise that my good Susan would meet me in the pine woods at least once a week. This promise was redeemed, I assure you, to the letter, greatly to my relief. I had partly become contented with my mode of life, and had made up my mind to spend my days there; but the wilderness that sheltered me thus long took fire, and refused longer to be my hiding-place.

"I will not harrow up your feelings by portraying the terrific scene of this awful conflagration. There is nothing to which I can liken it. It was horribly and indescribably grand. The whole world seemed on fire, and it appeared to me that the day of judgment had come; that the burning bowels of the earth had burst forth, and that the end of all things was at hand. Bears and wolves, scorched from their mysterious hiding-places in the earth, and all the wild inhabitants of the untrodden forest, filled with a common dismay, ran forth, yelling, howling, bewildered amidst the smoke and flame. The very heavens seemed to rain down fire through the towering trees; it was by the merest chance that I escaped the devouring element. Running before it, and stopping occasionally to take breath, I looked back to behold its frightful ravages, and to drink in its savage magnificence. It was awful, thrilling, solemn, beyond compare. When aided by the fitful wind, the merciless tempest of fire swept on, sparkling, creaking, cracking, curling, roaring, out-doing in its dreadful splendor a thousand thunderstorms at once. From tree to tree it leaped, swallowing them up in its lurid, baleful glare; and leaving them leafless, limbless, charred, and lifeless behind. The scene was overwhelming, stunning,—nothing was spared,—cattle, tame and wild, herds of swine and of deer, wild beasts of every name and kind,—huge night-birds, bats, and owls, that had retired to their homes in lofty tree-tops to rest, perished in that fiery storm. The long-winged buzzard, and croaking raven mingled their dismal cries with those of the countless myriads of small birds that rose up to the skies, and were lost to the sight in clouds of smoke and flame. Oh, I shudder when I think of it! Many a poor wandering fugitive, who, like myself, had sought among wild beasts the mercy denied by our fellow men, saw, in helpless consternation, his dwelling-place and city of refuge reduced to ashes forever. It was this grand conflagration that drove me hither; I ran alike from fire and from slavery."

After a slight pause, (for both speaker and hearers were deeply moved by the above recital,) Mr. Listwell, addressing Madison, said, "If it does not weary you too much, do tell us something of your journeyings since this disastrous burning,—we are deeply interested in everything which can throw light on the hardships of persons escaping from slavery; we could hear you talk all night; are there no incidents that you could relate of your travels hither? or are they such that you do not like to mention them."

"For the most part, sir, my course has been uninterrupted; and, considering the circumstances, at times even pleasant. I have suffered little for want of food; but I need not tell you how I got it. Your moral code may differ from mine, as your customs and usages are different. The fact is, sir, during my flight, I felt myself robbed by society of all my just rights; that I was in an enemy's land, who sought both my life and my liberty. They had transformed me into a brute; made merchandise of my body, and, for all the purposes of my flight, turned day into night,—and guided by my own necessities, and in contempt of their conventionalities, I did not scruple to take bread where I could get it."

"And just there you were right," said Mr. Listwell; "I once had doubts on this point myself, but a conversation with Gerrit Smith,[9] (a man, by the way, that I wish you could see, for he is a devoted friend of your race, and I know he would receive you gladly,) put an end to all my doubts on this point. But do not let me interrupt you."

"I had but one narrow escape during my whole journey, " said Madison.

"Do let us hear of it," said Mr. Listwell.

"Two weeks ago," continued Madison, "after travelling all night, I was overtaken by daybreak, in what seemed to me an almost interminable wood. I deemed it unsafe to go farther, and, as usual, I looked around for a suitable tree in which to spend the day. I liked one with a bushy top, and found one just to my mind. Up I climbed, and hiding myself as well I could, I, with this strap, (pulling one out of his old coat-pocket,) lashed myself to a bough, and flattered myself that I should get a *good night's* sleep that day; but in this I was soon disappointed. I had scarcely got fastened to my natural hammock, when I heard the voices of a number of persons, apparently approaching the part of the woods where I was. Upon my word, sir, I dreaded more these human voices than I should have done those of wild beasts. I was at a loss to know what to do. If I descended, I should probably be discovered by the men; and if they had dogs I should, doubtless, be 'treed.' It was an anxious moment, but hardships and dangers have been the accompaniments of my life; and have, perhaps, imparted to me a certain hardness of character, which, to some extent, adapts me to them. In my present predicament, I decided to hold my place in the tree-top, and abide the consequences. But here I must disappoint you; for the men, who were all colored, halted at least a hundred yards from me, and began with their axes, in right good earnest, to attack the trees. The sound of their laughing axes was like the report of as many well-charged pistols. By and by there came down at least a dozen trees with a terrible crash. They leaped upon the fallen trees with an air of victory. I could see no dog with them, and felt myself comparatively safe, though I could not forget the possibility that some freak or fancy might bring the axe a little nearer my dwelling than comported with my safety.

"There was no sleep for me that day, and I wished for night. You may imagine that the thought of having the tree attacked under me was far from agreeable, and that it very easily kept me on the look-out. The day was not without diversion. The men at work seemed to be a gay set; and they would often make the woods resound with that uncontrolled laughter for which we, as a race, are remarkable. I held my place in the tree till sunset,—saw the men put on their jackets to be off. I observed that all left the ground except one, whom I saw sitting on the side of a stump, with his head bowed, and his eyes apparently fixed on the ground. I became interested in him. After sitting in the position to which I have alluded ten or fifteen minutes, he left the stump, walked directly towards the tree in which I was secreted, and halted almost under the same. He stood for a moment and looked around, deliberately and reverently took off his hat, by which I saw that he was a man in the evening of life, slightly bald and quite gray. After laying down his hat carefully, he knelt and prayed aloud, and such a prayer, the most fervent, earnest, and solemn, to which I think I ever listened. After reverently addressing the Almighty, as the all-wise, all-good, and the common Father of all mankind, he besought God for grace, for strength, to bear up under, and to endure, as a good soldier, all the hardships and trials which beset the journey of life, and to enable him to live in a manner which accorded

9. Prominent abolitionist (1797–1874).

with the gospel of Christ. His soul now broke out in humble supplication for deliverance from bondage. 'O thou,' said he, 'that hearest the raven's cry, take pity on poor me! O deliver me! O deliver me! in mercy, O God, deliver me from the chains and manifold hardships of slavery! With thee, O Father, all things are possible. Thou canst stand and measure the earth. Thou hast beheld and drove asunder the nations,—all power is in thy hand,—thou didst say of old, "I have seen the affliction of my people, and am come to deliver them,"—Oh look down upon our afflictions, and have mercy upon us.' But I cannot repeat his prayer, nor can I give you an idea of its deep pathos. I had given but little attention to religion, and had but little faith in it; yet, as the old man prayed, I felt almost like coming down and kneel by his side, and mingle my broken complaint with his.

"He had already gained my confidence; as how could it be otherwise? I knew enough of religion to know that the man who prays in secret is far more likely to be sincere than he who loves to pray standing in the street, or in the great congregation. When he arose from his knees, like another Zacheus,[10] I came down from the tree. He seemed a little alarmed at first, but I told him my story, and the good man embraced me in his arms, and assured me of his sympathy.

"I was now about out of provisions, and thought I might safely ask him to help me replenish my store. He said he had no money; but if he had, he would freely give it me. I told him I had *one dollar*; it was all the money I had in the world. I gave it to him, and asked him to purchase some crackers and cheese, and to kindly bring me the balance; that I would remain in or near that place, and would come to him on his return, if he would whistle. He was gone only about an hour. Meanwhile, from some cause or other, I know not what, (but as you shall see very wisely,) I changed my place. On his return I started to meet him; but it seemed as if the shadow of approaching danger fell upon my spirit, and checked my progress. In a very few minutes, closely on the heels of the old man, I distinctly saw *fourteen men*, with something like guns in their hands."

"Oh! the old wretch!" exclaimed Mrs. Listwell, "he had betrayed you, had he?"

"I think not," said Madison, "I cannot believe that the old man was to blame. He probably went into a store, asked for the articles for which I sent, and presented the bill I gave him; and it is so unusual for slaves in the country to have money, that fact, doubtless, excited suspicion, and gave rise to inquiry. I can easily believe that the truthfulness of the old man's character compelled him to disclose the facts; and thus were these blood-thirsty men put on my track. Of course I did not present myself ; but hugged my hiding-place securely. If discovered and attacked, I resolved to sell my life as dearly as possible.

"After searching about the woods silently for a time, the whole company gathered around the old man; one charged him with lying, and called him an old villain; said he was a thief; charged him with stealing money; said if he did not instantly tell where he got it, they would take the shirt from his old back, and give him thirty-nine lashes.

"'I did *not* steal the money,' said the old man, 'it was given me, as I told you at the store; and if the man who gave it me is not here, it is not my fault.'

"'Hush! you lying old rascal; we'll make you smart for it. You shall not leave this spot until you have told where you got that money.'

"They now took hold of him, and began to strip him; while others went to get . sticks with which to beat him. I felt, at the moment, like rushing out in the midst of

---

10. Luke 19.1–10.

them; but considering that the old man would be whipped the more for having aided a fugitive slave, and that, perhaps, in the *melée* he might be killed outright, I disobeyed this impulse. They tied him to a tree, and began to whip him. My own flesh crept at every blow, and I seem to hear the old man's piteous cries even now. They laid thirty-nine lashes on his bare back, and were going to repeat that number, when one of the company besought his comrades to desist. 'You'll kill the d—d old scoundrel! You've already whipt a dollar's worth out of him, even if he stole it!' 'O yes,' said another, 'let him down. He'll never tell us another lie, I'll warrant ye!' With this, one of the company untied the old man, and bid him go about his business.

"The old man left, but the company remained as much as an hour, scouring the woods. Round and round they went, turning up the underbrush, and peering about like so many bloodhounds. Two or three times they came within six feet of where I lay. I tell you I held my stick with a firmer grasp than I did in coming up to your house tonight. I expected to level one of them at least. Fortunately, however, I eluded their pursuit, and they left me alone in the woods.

"My last dollar was now gone, and you may well suppose I felt the loss of it; but the thought of being once again free to pursue my journey, prevented that depression which a sense of destitution causes; so swinging my little bundle on my back, I caught a glimpse of the *Great Bear* (which ever points the way to my beloved star,)[11] and I started again on my journey. What I lost in money I made up at a hen-roost that same night, upon which I fortunately came."

"But you did'nt eat your food raw? How did you cook it?" said Mrs. Listwell.

"O no, Madam," said Madison, turning to his little bundle:—"I had the means of cooking." Here he took out of his bundle an old-fashioned tinder-box, and taking up a piece of a file, which he brought with him, he struck it with a heavy flint, and brought out at least a dozen sparks at once. "I have had this old box," said he, "more than five years. It is the *only* property saved from the fire in the dismal swamp. It has done me good service. It has given me the means of broiling many a chicken!"

It seemed quite a relief to Mrs. Listwell to know that Madison had, at least, lived upon cooked food. Women have a perfect horror of eating uncooked food.

By this time thoughts of what was best to be done about getting Madison to Canada, began to trouble Mr. Listwell; for the laws of Ohio were very stringent against any one who should aid, or who were found aiding a slave to escape through that State. A citizen, for the simple act of taking a fugitive slave in his carriage, had just been stripped of all his property, and thrown penniless upon the world. Notwithstanding this, Mr. Listwell was determined to see Madison safely on his way to Canada. "Give yourself no uneasiness," said he to Madison, "for if it cost my farm, I shall see you safely out of the States, and on your way to a land of liberty. Thank God that there is *such* a land so near us! You will spend to-morrow with us, and to-morrow night I will take you in my carriage to the Lake. Once upon that, and you are safe."

"Thank you! thank you," said the fugitive; "I will commit myself to your care."

For the *first* time during *five* years, Madison enjoyed the luxury of resting his limbs on a comfortable bed, and inside a human habitation. Looking at the white sheets, he said to Mr. Listwell, "What, sir! you don't mean that I shall sleep in that bed?"

"Oh yes, oh yes."

---

11. Two stars in the Big Dipper point to the North Star.

After Mr. Listwell left the room, Madison said he really hesitated whether or not he should lie on the floor; for that was *far* more comfortable and inviting than any bed to which he had been used.

We pass over the thoughts and feelings, the hopes and fears, the plans and purposes, that revolved in the mind of Madison during the day that he was secreted at the house of Mr. Listwell. The reader will be content to know that nothing occurred to endanger his liberty, or to excite alarm. Many were the little attentions bestowed upon him in his quiet retreat and hiding-place. In the evening, Mr. Listwell, after treating Madison to a new suit of winter clothes, and replenishing his exhausted purse with five dollars, all in silver, brought out his two-horse wagon, well provided with buffaloes,[12] and silently started off with him to Cleveland. They arrived there without interruption, a few minutes before sunrise the next morning. Fortunately the steamer Admiral lay at the wharf, and was to start for Canada at nine o'clock. Here the last anticipated danger was surmounted. It was feared that just at this point the hunters of men might be on the look-out, and, possibly, pounce upon their victim. Mr. Listwell saw the captain of the boat; cautiously sounded him on the matter of carrying liberty-loving passengers, before he introduced his precious charge. This done, Madison was conducted on board. With usual generosity this true subject of the emancipating queen welcomed Madison, and assured him that he should be safely landed in Canada, free of charge. Madison now felt himself no more a piece of merchandise, but a passenger, and, like any other passenger, going about his business, carrying with him what belonged to him, and nothing which rightfully belonged to anybody else.

Wrapped in his new winter suit, snug and comfortable, a pocket full of silver, safe from his pursuers, embarked for a free country, Madison gave every sign of sincere gratitude, and bade his kind benefactor farewell, with such a grip of the hand as bespoke a heart full of honest manliness, and a soul that knew how to appreciate kindness. It need scarcely be said that Mr. Listwell was deeply moved by the gratitude and friendship he had excited in a nature so noble as that of the fugitive. He went to his home that day with a joy and gratification which knew no bounds. He had done something "to deliver the spoiled out of the hands of the spoiler," he had given bread to the hungry, and clothes to the naked; he had befriended a man to whom the laws of his country forbade all friendship,—and in proportion to the odds against his righteous deed, was the delightful satisfaction that gladdened his heart. On reaching home, he exclaimed, "*He is safe,—he is safe,—he is safe*,"—and the cup of his joy was shared by his excellent lady. The following letter was received from Madison a few days after.

"WINDSOR, CANADA WEST, DEC. 16, 1840.

My dear Friend,—for such you truly are:—

Madison is out of the woods at last; I nestle in the mane of the British lion, protected by his mighty paw from the talons and the beak of the American eagle. I AM FREE, and breathe an atmosphere too pure for *slaves*, slave-hunters, or slave-holders. My heart is full. As many thanks to you, sir, and to your kind lady, as

---

12. Buffalo robes.

there are pebbles on the shores of Lake Erie; and may the blessing of God rest upon you both. You will never be forgotten by your profoundly grateful friend,

MADISON WASHINGTON."

Part III

—His head was with his heart,
And that was far away!
Childe Harold. [13]

Just upon the edge of the great road from Petersburg, Virginia, to Richmond, and only about fifteen miles from the latter place, there stands a somewhat ancient and famous public tavern, quite notorious in its better days, as being the grand resort for most of the leading gamblers, horse-racers, cock-fighters, and slave-traders from all the country round about. This old rookery, the nucleus of all sorts of birds, mostly those of ill omen, has, like everything else peculiar to Virginia, lost much of its ancient consequence and splendor; yet it keeps up some appearance of gaiety and high life, and is still frequented, even by respectable travellers, who are unacquainted with its past history and present condition. Its fine old portico looks well at a distance, and gives the building an air of grandeur. A nearer view, however, does little to sustain this pretension. The house is large, and its style imposing, but time and dissipation, unfailing in their results, have made ineffaceable marks upon it, and it must, in the common course of events, soon be numbered with the things that were. The gloomy mantle of ruin is, already, outspread to envelop it, and its remains, even but now remind one of a human skull, after the flesh has mingled with the earth. Old hats and rags fill the places in the upper windows once occupied by large panes of glass, and the moulding boards along the roofing have dropped off from their places, leaving holes and crevices in the rented wall for bats and swallows to build their nests in. The platform of the portico, which fronts the highway is a rickety affair, its planks are loose, and in some places entirely gone, leaving effective mantraps in their stead for nocturnal ramblers. The wooden pillars, which once supported it, but which now hang as encumbrances, are all rotten, and tremble with the touch. A part of the stable, a fine old structure in its day, which has given comfortable shelter to hundreds of the noblest steeds of "the Old Dominion" at once, was blown down many years ago, and never has been, and probably never will be, rebuilt. The doors of the barn are in wretched condition; they will shut with a little human strength to help their worn out hinges, but not otherwise. The side of the great building seen from the road is much discolored in sundry places by slops poured from the upper windows, rendering it unsightly and offensive in other respects. Three or four great dogs, looking as dull and gloomy as the mansion itself, lie stretched out along the door-sills under the portico; and double the number of loafers, some of them completely rum-ripe, and others ripening, dispose themselves like so many sentinels about the front of the house. These latter understand the science of scraping acquaintance to perfection. They know every-body, and almost every-body knows them. Of course, as their title implies, they have no regular employment. They are (to use an expressive phrase) *hangers on*, or still better, they are what sailors would denominate

---

13. George Gordon, Lord Byron (1788–1824), *Childe Harold's Pilgrimage* (1812–1818), 4.141.141–142.

holders-on to the slack, in every-body's mess, and in nobody's watch. They are, however, as good as the newspaper for the events of the day, and they sell their knowledge almost as cheap. Money they seldom have; yet they always have capital the most reliable. They make their way with a succeeding traveller by intelligence gained from a preceding one. All the great names of Virginia they know by heart, and have seen their owners often. The history of the house is folded in their lips, and they rattle off stories in connection with it, equal to the guides at Dryburgh Abbey.[14] He must be a shrewd man, and well skilled in the art of evasion, who gets out of the hands of these fellows without being at the expense of a treat.

It was at this old tavern, while on a second visit to the State of Virginia in 1841, that Mr. Listwell, unacquainted with the fame of the place, turned aside, about sunset, to pass the night. Riding up to the house, he had scarcely dismounted, when one of the half dozen bar-room fraternity met and addressed him in a manner exceedingly bland and accommodating.

"Fine evening, sir."

"Very fine," said Mr. Listwell. "This is a tavern, I believe?"

"O yes, sir, yes; although you may think it looks a little the worse for wear, it was once as good a house as any in Virginy. I make no doubt if ye spend the night here, you'll think it a good house yet; for there aint a more accommodating man in the country than you'll find the landlord."

Listwell. "The most I want is a good bed for myself, and a full manger for my horse. If I get these, I shall be quite satisfied."

Loafer. "Well, I alloys like to hear a gentleman talk for his horse; and just becase the horse can't talk for itself. A man that don't care about his beast, and don't look arter it when he's travelling, aint much in my eye anyhow. Now, sir, I likes a horse, and I'll guarantee your horse will be taken good care on here. That old stable, for all you see it looks so shabby now, once sheltered the great *Eclipse*, when he run here agin *Batchelor* and *Jumping Jemmy*. Them was fast horses, but he beat 'em both."

Listwell. "Indeed."

Loafer. "Well, I rather reckon you've travelled a right smart distance to-day, from the look of your horse?"

Listwell. "Forty miles only."

Loafer. "Well! I'll be darned if that aint a pretty good *only*. Mister, that beast of yours is a singed cat, I warrant you. I never see'd a creature like that that was'nt good on the road. You've come about forty miles, then?"

Listwell. "Yes, yes, and a pretty good pace at that."

Loafer. "You're somewhat in a hurry, then, I make no doubt? I reckon I could guess if I would, what you're going to Richmond for? It would'nt be much of a guess either; for it's rumored hereabouts, that there's to be the greatest sale of niggers at Richmond to-morrow that has taken place there in a long time; and I'll be bound you're a going there to have a hand in it."

Listwell. "Why, you must think, then, that there's money to be made at that business?"

Loafer. "Well, 'pon my honor, sir, I never made any that way myself; but it stands to reason that it's a money making business; for almost all other business in Virginia

---

14. Scottish monastery, location of Sir Walter Scott's tomb.

is dropped to engage in this. One thing is sartain, I never see'd a nigger-buyer yet that had'nt a plenty of money, and he was'nt as free with it as water. I has known one on 'em to treat as high as twenty times in a night; and, ginerally speaking, they's men of edication, and knows all about the government. The fact is, sir, I alloys like to hear 'em talk, bekase I alloys can learn something from them."

  Listwell. "What may I call your name, sir?"

  Loafer. "Well, now, they calls me Wilkes. I'm known all around by the gentlemen that comes here. They all knows old Wilkes."

  Listwell. "Well, Wilkes, you seem to be acquainted here, and I see you have a strong liking for a horse. Be so good as to speak a kind word for mine to the hostler to-night, and you'll not lose anything by it."

  Loafer. "Well, sir, I see you don't say much, but you I've got an insight into things. It's alloys wise to get the good will of them that's acquainted about a tavern; for a man don't know when he goes into a house what may happen, or how much he may need a friend." Here the loafer gave Mr. Listwell a significant grin, which expressed a sort of triumphant pleasure at having, as he supposed, by his tact succeeded in placing so fine appearing a gentleman under obligations to him. The pleasure, however, was not mutual; for there was something so insinuating in the glance of this loquacious customer, that Mr. Listwell was very glad to get quit of him, and to do so more successfully, he ordered his supper to be brought to him in his private room, private to the eye, but not to the ear. This room was directly over the bar, and the plastering being off, nothing but pine boards and naked laths separated him from the disagreeable company below,—he could easily hear what was said in the bar-room, and was rather glad of the advantage it afforded, for, as you shall see, it furnished him important hints as to the manner and deportment he should assume during his stay at that tavern.

  Mr. Listwell says he had got into his room but a few moments, when he heard the officious Wilkes below, in a tone of disappointment, exclaim, "Whar's that gentleman?" Wilkes was evidently expecting to meet with his friend at the bar-room, on his return, and had no doubt of his doing the handsome thing. "He has gone to his room," answered the landlord, "and has ordered his supper to be brought to him."

  Here some one shouted out, "Who is he, Wilkes? Where's he going?"

  "Well, now, I'll be hanged if I know; but I'm willing to make any man a bet of this old hat agin a five dollar bill, that that gent is as full of money as a dog is of fleas. He's going down to Richmond to buy niggers, I make no doubt. He's no fool, I warrant ye."

  "Well, he acts d—d strange," said another, "anyhow. I likes to see a man, when he comes up to a tavern, to come straight into the bar-room, and show that he's a man among men. Nobody was going to bite him."

  "Now, I don't blame him a bit for not coming in here. That man knows his business, and means to take care on his money," answered Wilkes.

  "Wilkes, you're a fool. You only say that, becase you hope to get a few coppers out on him."

  "You only measure my corn by your half-bushel, I won't say that you're only mad becase I got the chance of speaking to him first."

  "O Wilkes! you're known here. You'll praise up any body that will give you a copper; besides, 'tis my opinion that that fellow who took his long slab-sides up stairs, for all the world just like a half-scared woman, afraid to look honest men in the face, is a *Northerner,* and as mean as dish-water."

"Now what will you bet of that," said Wilkes.

The speaker said, "I make no bets with you, 'kase you can get that fellow up stairs there to say anything."

"Well," said Wilkes, "I am willing to bet any man in the company that *that* gentleman is a *nigger*-buyer. He did'nt tell me so right down, but I reckon I knows enough about men to give a pretty clean guess as to what they are arter."

The dispute as to *who* Mr. Listwell was, what his business, where he was going, etc., was kept up with much animation for some time, and more than once threatened a serious disturbance of the peace. Wilkes had his friends as well as his opponents. After this sharp debate, the company amused themselves by drinking whiskey, and telling stories. The latter consisting of quarrels, fights, *rencontres*,[15] and duels, in which distinguished persons of that neighborhood, and frequenters of that house, had been actors. Some of these stories were frightful enough, and were told, too, with a relish which bespoke the pleasure of the parties with the horrid scenes they portrayed. It would not be proper here to give the reader any idea of the vulgarity and dark profanity which rolled, as "a sweet morsel," under these corrupt tongues. A more brutal set of creatures, perhaps, never congregated.

Disgusted, and a little alarmed withal, Mr. Listwell, who was not accustomed to such entertainment, at length retired, but not to sleep. He was *too* much wrought upon by what he had heard to rest quietly, and what snatches of sleep he got, were interrupted by dreams which were anything than pleasant. At eleven o'clock, there seemed to be several hundreds of persons crowding into the house. A loud and confused clamour, cursing and cracking of whips, and the noise of chains startled him from his bed; for a moment he would have given the half of his farm in Ohio to have been at home. This uproar was kept up with undulating course, till near morning. There was loud laughing,—loud singing,—loud cursing,—and yet there seemed to be weeping and mourning in the midst of all. Mr. Listwell said he had heard enough during the forepart of the night to convince him that a buyer of men and women stood the best chance of being respected. And he, therefore, thought it best to say nothing which might undo the favorable opinion that had been formed of him in the barroom by at least one of the fraternity that swarmed about it. While he would not avow himself a purchaser of slaves, he deemed it not prudent to disavow it. He felt that he might, properly, refuse to cast such a pearl before parties which, to him, were worse than swine. To reveal himself, and to impart a knowledge of his real character and sentiments would, to say the least, be imparting intelligence with the certainty of seeing it and himself both abused. Mr. Listwell confesses, that this reasoning did not altogether satisfy his conscience, for, hating slavery as he did, and regarding it to be the immediate duty of every man to cry out against it, "without compromise and without concealment," it was hard for him to admit to himself the possibility of circumstances wherein a man might, properly, hold his tongue on the subject. Having as little of the spirit of a martyr as Erasmus,[16] he concluded, like the latter, that it was wiser to trust the mercy of God for his soul, than the humanity of slave-traders for his body. Bodily fear, not conscientious scruples, prevailed.

In this spirit he rose early in the morning, manifesting no surprise at what he had heard during the night. His quondam[17] friend was soon at his elbow, boring him with

---

15. Battles.   16. Desiderius Erasmus (1466–1536), German religious reformer.   17. Former.

all sorts of questions. All, however, directed to find out his character, business, residence, purposes, and destination. With the most perfect appearance of good nature and carelessness, Mr. Listwell evaded these meddlesome inquiries, and turned conversation to general topics, leaving himself and all that specially pertained to him, out of discussion. Disengaging himself from their troublesome companionship, he made his way towards an old bowling-alley, which was connected with the house, and which, like all the rest, was in very bad repair.

On reaching the alley Mr. Listwell saw, for the first time in his life, a slave-gang on their way to market. A sad sight truly. Here were one hundred and thirty human beings,—children of a common Creator—guilty of no crime—men and women, with hearts, minds, and deathless spirits, chained and fettered, and bound for the market, in a christian country,—in a country boasting of its liberty, independence, and high civilization! Humanity converted into merchandise, and linked in iron bands, with no regard to decency or humanity! All sizes, ages, and sexes, mothers, fathers, daughters, brothers, sisters,—all huddled together, on their way to market to be sold and separated from home, and from each other *forever*. And all to fill the pockets of men too lazy to work for an honest living, and who gain their fortune by plundering the helpless, and trafficking in the souls and sinews of men. As he gazed upon this revolting and heart-rending scene, our informant said he almost doubted the existence of a God of justice! And he stood wondering that the earth did not open and swallow up such wickedness.

In the midst of these reflections, and while running his eye up and down the fettered ranks, he met the glance of one whose face he thought he had seen before. To be resolved, he moved towards the spot. It was MADISON WASHINGTON! Here was a scene for the pencil! Had Mr. Listwell been confronted by one risen from the dead, he could not have been more appalled. He was completely stunned. A thunderbolt could not have struck him more dumb. He stood, for a few moments, as motionless as one petrified; collecting himself, he at length exclaimed, "*Madison! is that you?*"

The noble fugitive, but little less astonished than himself, answered cheerily, "O yes, sir, they've got me again."

Thoughtless of consequences for the moment, Mr. Listwell ran up to his old friend, placing his hands upon his shoulders, and looked him in the face! Speechless they stood gazing at each other as if to be doubly resolved that there was no mistake about the matter, till Madison motioned his friend away, intimating a fear lest the keepers should find him there, and suspect him of tampering with the slaves.

"They will soon be out to look after us. You can come when they go to breakfast, and I will tell you all."

Pleased with this arrangement, Mr. Listwell passed out of the alley; but only just in time to save himself, for, while near the door, he observed three men making their way to the alley. The thought occurred to him to await their arrival, as the best means of diverting the ever ready suspicions of the guilty.

While the scene between Mr. Listwell and his friend Madison was going on, the other slaves stood as mute spectators,—at a loss to know what all this could mean. As he left, he heard the man chained to Madison ask, "Who is that gentleman?"

"He is a friend of mine. I cannot tell you now. Suffice it to say he is a friend. You shall hear more of him before long, but mark me! whatever shall pass between that gentleman and me, in your hearing, I pray you will say nothing about it. We are all chained here together,—ours is a common lot; and that gentleman is not less *your* friend than *mine*." At these words, all mysterious as they were, the unhappy company gave signs of satisfaction and hope. It seems that Madison, by that mesmeric power which is the invariable accompaniment of genius, had already won the confidence of the gang, and was a sort of general-in-chief among them.

By this time the keepers arrived. A horrid trio, well fitted for their demoniacal work. Their uncombed hair came down over foreheads "*villainously low*," and with eyes, mouths, and noses to match. "Hallo! hallo!" they growled out as they entered. "Are you all there!"

"All here," said Madison.

"Well, well, that's right! your journey will soon be over. You'll be in Richmond by eleven to-day, and then you'll have an easy time on it."

"I say, gal, what in the devil are you crying about?" said one of them. "I'll give you something to cry about, if you don't mind." This was said to a girl, apparently not more than twelve years old, who had been weeping bitterly. She had, probably, left behind her a loving mother, affectionate sisters, brothers, and friends, and her tears were but the natural expression of her sorrow, and the only solace. But the dealers in human flesh have *no* respect for such sorrow. They look upon it as a protest against their cruel injustice, and they are prompt to punish it.

This is a puzzle not easily solved. *How* came he here? what can I do for him? may I not even now be in some way compromised in this affair? were thoughts that troubled Mr. Listwell, and made him eager for the promised opportunity of speaking to Madison.

The bell now sounded for breakfast, and keepers and drivers, with pistols and bowie-knives gleaming from their belts, hurried in, as if to get the best places. Taking the chance now afforded, Mr. Listwell hastened back to the bowling-alley. Reaching Madison, he said, "Now *do* tell me all about the matter. Do you know me?"

"Oh, yes," said Madison, "I know you well, and shall never forget you nor that cold and dreary night you gave me shelter. I must be short," he continued, "for they'll soon be out again. This, then, is the story in brief. On reaching Canada, and getting over the excitement of making my escape, sir, my thoughts turned to my poor wife, who had well deserved my love by her virtuous fidelity and undying affection for me. I could not bear the thought of leaving her in the cruel jaws of slavery, without making an effort to rescue her. First, I tried to get money to buy her; but oh! the process was *too slow*. I despaired of accomplishing it. She was in all my thoughts by day, and my dreams by night. At times I could almost hear her voice, saying, 'O Madison! Madison! will you then leave me here? can you leave me here to die? No! no! you will come! you will come!' I was wretched. I lost my appetite. I could neither work, eat, nor sleep, till I resolved to hazard my own liberty, to gain that of my wife! But I must be short. Six weeks ago I reached my old master's place. I laid about the neighborhood nearly a week, watching my chance, and, finally, I ventured upon the desperate attempt to reach my poor wife's room by means of a ladder. I reached the window, but the noise in raising it frightened my wife, and she screamed and fainted. I took her in my arms, and was descending the ladder, when the dogs began to bark furiously, and before I could get to the woods the white folks were roused. The cool night air soon restored my wife, and she readily recognized me. We made the best of our way to the woods, but it was now *too* late,—the dogs were after us as though they would have torn us to pieces. It was all over with me now! My old master and his two sons ran out with loaded rifles, and before we were out of gunshot, our ears were assailed with 'Stop! stop! or be shot down.' Nevertheless we ran on. Seeing that we gave no heed to their calls, they fired, and my poor wife fell by my side dead, while I received but a slight flesh wound. I now became desperate, and stood my ground, and awaited their attack over her dead body. They rushed upon me, with their rifles in hand. I parried their blows, and fought them 'till I was knocked down and overpowered."

"Oh! it was madness to have returned," said Mr. Listwell.

"Sir, I could not be free with the galling thought that my poor wife was still a slave. With her in slavery, my body, not my spirit, was free. I was taken to the house,—chained to a ring-bolt,—my wounds dressed. I was kept there three days. All the slaves, for miles around, were brought to see me. Many slave-holders came with their slaves, using me as proof of the completeness of their power, and of the impossibility of slaves getting away. I was taunted, jeered at, and berated by them, in a manner that pierced me to the soul. Thank God, I was able to smother my rage, and to bear it all with seeming composure. After my wounds were nearly healed, I was taken to a tree and stripped, and I received sixty lashes on my naked back. A few days after, I was sold to a slave-trader, and placed in this gang for the New Orleans market."

"Do you think your master would sell you to me?"

"O no, sir! I was sold on condition of my being taken South. Their motive is revenge."

"Then, then," said Mr. Listwell, "I fear I can do nothing for you. Put your trust in God, and bear your sad lot with the manly fortitude which becomes a man. I shall see you at Richmond, but don't recognize me." Saying this, Mr. Listwell handed Madison ten dollars; said a few words to the other slaves; received their hearty "God bless you," and made his way to the house.

Fearful of exciting suspicion by too long delay, our friend went to the breakfast table, with the air of one who half reproved the greediness of those who rushed in at the sound of the bell. A cup of coffee was all that he could manage. His feelings were too bitter and excited, and his heart was too full with the fate of poor Madison (whom he loved as well as admired) to relish his breakfast; and although he sat long after the company had left the table, he really did little more than change the position of his knife and fork. The strangeness of meeting again one whom he had met on two several occasions before, under extraordinary circumstances, was well calculated to suggest the idea that a supernatural power, a wakeful providence, or an inexorable fate, had linked their destiny together; and that no efforts of his could disentangle him from the mysterious web of circumstances which enfolded him.

On leaving the table, Mr. Listwell nerved himself up and walked firmly into the bar-room. He was at once greeted again by that talkative chatter-box, Mr. Wilkes.

"Them's a likely set of niggers in the alley there," said Wilkes.

"Yes, they're fine looking fellows, one of them I should like to purchase, and for him I would be willing to give a handsome sum."

Turning to one of his comrades, and with a grin of victory, Wilkes said, "Aha, Bill, did you hear that? I told you I know'd that gentleman wanted to buy niggers, and would bid as high as any purchaser in the market."

"Come, come," said Listwell, "don't be too loud in your praise, you are old enough to know that prices rise when purchasers are plenty."

"That's a fact," said Wilkes, "I see you knows the ropes—and there's not a man in old Virginy whom I'd rather help to make a good bargain than you, sir."

Mr. Listwell here threw a dollar at Wilkes, (which the latter caught with a dexterous hand,) saying, "Take that for your kind good will." Wilkes held up the dollar to his right eye, with a grin of victory, and turned to the morose grumbler in the corner who had questioned the liberality of a man of whom he knew nothing.

Mr. Listwell now stood as well with the company as any other occupant of the bar-room.

We pass over the hurry and bustle, the brutal vociferations of the slave-drivers in getting their unhappy gang in motion for Richmond; and we need not narrate every application of the lash to those who faltered in the journey. Mr. Listwell followed the train at a long distance, with a sad heart; and on reaching Richmond, left his horse at a hotel, and made his way to the wharf in the direction of which he saw the slave-coffle[18] driven. He was just in time to see the whole company embark for New Orleans. The thought struck him that, while mixing with the multitude, he might do his friend Madison one last service, and he stept into a hardware store and purchased three strong *files*. These he took with him, and standing near the small boat, which lay in waiting to bear the company by parcels to the side of the brig that lay in the stream, he managed, as Madison passed him, to slip the files into his pocket, and at once darted back among the crowd.

All the company now on board, the imperious voice of the captain sounded, and instantly a dozen hardy seamen were in the rigging, hurrying aloft to unfurl the broad canvas of our Baltimore-built American Slaver. The sailors hung about the ropes, like so many black cats, now in the round-tops, now in the cross-trees, now on the yard-arms; all was bluster and activity. Soon the broad fore topsail, the royal and top gallant sail were spread to the breeze. Round went the heavy windlass, clank, clank went the fall-bit,—the anchors weighed, jibs, mainsails, and topsails hauled to the wind, and the long, low, black slaver, with her cargo of human flesh, careened and moved forward to the sea.

Mr. Listwell stood on the shore, and watched the slaver till the last speck of her upper sails faded from sight, and announced the limit of human vision. "Farewell! farewell! brave and true man! God grant that brighter skies may smile upon your future than have yet looked down upon your thorny pathway."

Saying this to himself, our friend lost no time in completing his business, and in making his way homewards, gladly shaking off from his feet the dust of Old Virginia.

Part IV

Oh, where's the slave so lowly
Condemn'd to chains unholy,
 Who could he burst
 His bonds at first
Would pine beneath them slowly?
 Moore.[19]

---

18. A group of chained slaves.   19. Thomas Moore (1779–1852), *Irish Melodies* (1808–1834), vol. 6.

—Know ye not
Who would be free, *themselves* must strike the blow.
Childe Harold.[20]

What a world of inconsistency, as well as of wickedness, is suggested by the smooth and gliding phrase, AMERICAN SLAVE TRADE; and how strange and perverse is that moral sentiment which loathes, execrates, and brands as piracy and as deserving of death the carrying away into captivity men, women, and children from the *African coast*; but which is neither shocked nor disturbed by a similar traffic, carried on with the same motives and purposes, and characterized by even *more* odious peculiarities on the coast of our MODEL REPUBLIC. We execrate and hang the wretch guilty of this crime on the coast of Guinea, while we respect and applaud the guilty participators in this murderous business on enlightened shores of the Chesapeake. The inconsistency is so flagrant and glaring, that it would seem to cast a doubt on the doctrine of the innate moral sense of mankind.

Just two months after the sailing of the Virginia slave brig, which the reader has seen move off to sea so proudly with her human cargo for the New Orleans market, there chanced to meet, in the Marine Coffee-house at Richmond, a company of *ocean birds*, when the following conversation, which throws some light on the subsequent history, not only of Madison Washington, but of the hundred and thirty human beings with whom we last saw him chained.

"I say, shipmate, you had rather rough weather on your late passage to Orleans?" said Jack Williams, a regular old salt, tauntingly, to a trim, compact, manly looking person, who proved to be the first mate of the slave brig in question.

"Foul play, as well as foul weather," replied the firmly knit personage, evidently but little inclined to enter upon a subject which terminated so ingloriously to the captain and officers of the American slaver.

"Well, betwixt you and me," said Williams, "that whole affair on board of the Creole was miserably and disgracefully managed. Those black rascals got the upper hand of ye altogether; and, in my opinion, the whole disaster was the result of ignorance of the real character of darkies in general. With half a dozen *resolute* white men, (I say it not boastingly,) I could have had the rascals in irons in ten minutes, not because I'm so strong, but I know how to manage 'em. With my back against the *caboose*, I could, myself, have flogged a dozen of them; and had I been on board, by every monster of the deep, every black devil of 'em all would have had his neck stretched from the yard-arm. Ye made a mistake in yer manner of fighting 'em. All that is needed in dealing with a set of rebellious *darkies*, is to show that yer not afraid of 'em. For my own part, I would not honor a dozen niggers by pointing a gun at one on 'em,—a good stout whip, or a stiff rope's end, is better than all the guns at Old Point to quell a *nigger* insurrection. Why, sir, to take a gun to a *nigger* is the best way you can select to tell him you are afraid of him, and the best way of inviting his attack."

This speech made quite a sensation among the company, and a part of them indicated solicitude for the answer which might be made to it. Our first mate replied, "Mr. Williams, all that you've now said sounds very well *here* on shore, where, per-

---

20. George Gordon, Lord Byron (1788–1824), *Childe Harold's Pilgrimage* (1812–1818), 2.76.

haps, you have studied negro character. I do not profess to understand the subject as well as yourself; but it strikes me, you apply the same rule in dissimilar cases. It is quite easy to talk of flogging niggers here on land, where you have the sympathy of the community, and the whole physical force of the government, State and national, at your command; and where, if a negro shall lift his hand against a white man, the white community, with one accord, are ready to unite in shooting him down. I say, in such circumstances, it's easy to talk of flogging negroes and of negro cowardice; but, sir, I deny that the negro is, naturally, a coward, or that your theory of managing slaves will stand the test of *salt* water. It may do very well for an overseer, a contemptible hireling, to take advantage of fears already in existence, and which his presence has no power to inspire; to swagger about whip in hand, and discourse on the timidity and cowardice of negroes; for they have a smooth sea and a fair wind. It is one thing to manage a company of slaves on a Virginia plantation, and quite another thing to quell an insurrection on the lonely billows of the Atlantic, where every breeze speaks of courage and liberty. For the negro to act cowardly on shore, may be to act wisely; and I've some doubts whether *you*, Mr. Williams, would find it very convenient were you a slave in Algiers, to raise your hand against the bayonets of a whole government."

"By George, shipmate," said Williams, "you're coming rather *too* near. Either I've fallen very low in your estimation, or your notions of negro courage have got up a button-hole too high. Now I more than ever wish I'd been on board of that luckless craft. I'd have given ye practical evidence of the truth of my theory. I don't doubt there's some difference in being at sea. But a nigger's a nigger, on sea or land; and is a coward, find him where you will; a drop of blood from one on 'em will skeer a hundred. A knock on the nose, or a kick on the shin, will tame the wildest 'darkey' you can fetch me. I say again, and will stand by it, I could, with half a dozen good men, put the whole nineteen on 'em in irons, and have carried them safe to New Orleans too. Mind, I don't blame you, but I do say, and every gentleman here will bear me out in it, that the fault was somewhere, or them niggers would never have got off as they have done. For my part I feel ashamed to have the idea go abroad, that a ship load of slaves can't be safely taken from Richmond to New Orleans. I should like, merely to redeem the character of Virginia sailors, to take charge of a ship load on 'em to-morrow."

Williams went on in this strain, occasionally casting an imploring glance at the company for applause for his wit, and sympathy for his contempt of negro courage. He had, evidently, however, waked up the wrong passenger; for besides being in the right, his opponent carried that in his eye which marked him a man not to be trifled with.

"Well, Sir," said the sturdy mate, "you can select your own method for distinguishing yourself;—the path of ambition in this direction is quite open to you in Virginia, and I've no doubt that you will be highly appreciated and compensated for all your valiant achievements in that line; but for myself, while I do not profess to be a giant, I have resolved never to set my foot on the deck of a slave ship, either as officer, or common sailor again; I have got enough of it."

"Indeed! indeed!" exclaimed Williams, derisively.

"Yes, *indeed*," echoed the mate; "but don't misunderstand me. It is not the high value that I set upon my life that makes me say what I have said; yet I'm resolved never to endanger my life again in a cause which my conscience does not approve. I dare say *here* what many men *feel*, but *dare not speak*, that this whole slave-trading business is a disgrace and scandal to Old Virginia."

"Hold! hold on! shipmate," said Williams, "I hardly thought you'd have shown your colors so soon,—I'll be hanged if you're not as good an abolitionist as Garrison[21] himself."

The mate now rose from his chair, manifesting some excitement. "What do you mean, sir," said he, in a commanding tone. *"That man does not live who shall offer me an insult with impunity."*

The effect of the words was marked; and the company clustered around. Williams, in an apologetic tone, said, "Shipmate! keep your temper. I meant no insult. We all know that Tom Grant is no coward, and what I said about your being an abolitionist was simply this: you *might* have put down them black mutineers and murderers, but your conscience held you back."

"In that, too," said Grant, "you were mistaken. I did all that any man with equal strength and presence of mind could have done. The fact is, Mr. Williams, you underrate the courage as well as the skill of these negroes, and further, you do not seem to have been correctly informed about the case in hand at all."

"All I know about it is," said Williams, "that on the ninth day after you left Richmond, a dozen or two of the niggers ye had on board, came on deck and took the ship from you;—had her steered into a British port, where, by the by, every wooly head of them went ashore and was free. Now I take this to be a discreditable piece of business, and one demanding explanation."

"There are a great many discreditable things in the world," said Grant. "For a ship to go down under a calm sky is, upon the first flush of it, disgraceful either to sailors or caulkers. But when we learn, that by some mysterious disturbance in nature, the waters parted beneath, and swallowed the ship up, we lose our indignation and disgust in lamentation of the disaster, and in awe of the Power which controls the elements."

"Very true, very true," said Williams, "I should be very glad to have an explanation which would relieve the affair of its present discreditable features. I have desired to see you ever since you got home, and to learn from you a full statement of the facts in the case. To me the whole thing seems unaccountable. I cannot see how a dozen or two of ignorant negroes, not one of whom had ever been to sea before, and all of them were closely ironed between decks, should be able to get their fetters off, rush out of the hatchway in open daylight, kill two white men, the one the captain and the other their master, and then carry the ship into a British port, where every 'darkey' of them was set free. There must have been great carelessness, or cowardice somewhere!"

The company which had listened in silence during most of this discussion, now became much excited. One said, I agree with Williams; and several said the thing looks black enough. After the temporary tumultuous exclamations had subsided,—

"I see," said Grant, "how you regard this case, and how difficult it will be for me to render our ship's company blameless in your eyes. Nevertheless, I will state the facts precisely as they came under my own observation. Mr. Williams speaks of 'igno-

---

21. William Lloyd Garrison (1805–1879), American abolitionist.

rant negroes,' and, as a general rule, they are ignorant; but had he been on board the *Creole* as I was, he would have seen cause to admit that there are exceptions to this general rule. The leader of the mutiny in question was just as shrewd a fellow as ever I met in my life, and was as well fitted to lead in a dangerous enterprise as any one white man in ten thousand. The name of this man, strange to say, (ominous of greatness,) was MADISON WASHINGTON. In the short time he had been on board, he had secured the confidence of every officer. The negroes fairly worshipped him. His manner and bearing were such, that no one could suspect him of a murderous purpose. The only feeling with which we regarded him was, that he was a powerful, good-disposed negro. He seldom spake to any one, and when he did speak, it was with the utmost propriety. His words were well chosen, and his pronunciation equal to that of any schoolmaster. It was a mystery to us *where* he got his knowledge of language; but as little was said to him, none of us knew the extent of his intelligence and ability till it was too late. It seems he brought three files with him on board, and must have gone to work upon his fetters the first night out; and he must have worked well at that; for on the day of the rising, he got the irons *off eighteen* besides himself.

"The attack began just about twilight in the evening. Apprehending a squall, I had commanded the second mate to order all hands on deck, to take in sail. A few minutes before this I had seen Madison's head above the hatchway, looking out upon the white-capped waves at the leeward. I think I never saw him look more good-natured. I stood just about midship, on the larboard[22] side. The captain was pacing the quarter-deck on the starboard side, in company with Mr. Jameson, the owner of most of the slaves on board. Both were armed. I had just told the men to lay aloft, and was looking to see my orders obeyed, when I heard the discharge of a pistol on the starboard side; and turning suddenly around, the very deck seemed covered with fiends from the pit. The nineteen negroes were all on deck, with their broken fetters in their hands, rushing in all directions. I put my hand quickly in my pocket to draw out my jack-knife; but before I could draw it, I was knocked senseless to the deck. When I came to myself, (which I did in a few minutes, I suppose, for it was yet quite light,) there was not a white man on deck. The sailors were all aloft in the rigging, and dared not come down. Captain Clarke and Mr. Jameson lay stretched on the quarter-deck,—both dying,—while Madison himself stood at the helm unhurt.

"I was completely weakened by the loss of blood, and had not recovered from the stunning blow which felled me to the deck; but it was a little too much for me, even in my prostrate condition, to see our good brig commanded by a *black murderer*. So I called out to the men to come down and take the ship, or die in the attempt. Suiting the action to the word, I started aft. You murderous villain, said I, to the imp at the helm, and rushed upon him to deal him a blow, when he pushed me back with his strong, black arm, as though I had been a boy of twelve. I looked around for the men. They were still in the rigging. Not one had come down. I started towards Madison again. The rascal now told me to stand back. 'Sir,' said he, 'your life is in my hands. I could have killed you a dozen times over during this last half hour, and could kill you now. You call me a *black murderer*. I am not a murderer. God is my witness that LIBERTY, not *malice*, is the motive for this night's work. I have done no more to those dead men yonder, than they would have done to me in like circumstances. We have

---

22. Port, or left, side.

struck for our freedom, and if a true man's heart be in you, you will honor us for the deed. We have done that which you applaud your fathers for doing, and if we are murderers, *so were they.*'

"I felt little disposition to reply to this impudent speech. By heaven, it disarmed me. The fellow loomed up before me. I forgot his blackness in the dignity of his manner, and the eloquence of his speech. It seemed as if the souls of both the great dead (whose names he bore) had entered him. To the sailors in the rigging he said: 'Men! the battle is over,—your captain is dead. I have complete command of this vessel. All resistance to my authority will be in vain. My men have won their liberty, with no other weapons but their own BROKEN FETTERS. We are nineteen in number. We do not thirst for your blood, we demand only our rightful freedom. Do not flatter yourselves that I am ignorant of chart or compass. I know both. We are now only about sixty miles from Nassau.[23] Come down, and do your duty. Land us in Nassau, and not a hair of your heads shall be hurt.'

"I shouted, *Stay where you are, men,*—when a sturdy black fellow ran at me with a handspike, and would have split my head open, but for the interference of Madison, who darted between me and the blow. 'I know what you are up to,' said the latter to me. 'You want to navigate this brig into a slave port, where you would have us all hanged; but you'll miss it; before this brig shall touch a slave-cursed shore while I am on board, I will myself put a match to the magazine, and blow her, and be blown with her, into a thousand fragments. Now I have saved your life twice within these last twenty minutes,—for, when you lay helpless on deck, my men were about to kill you. I held them in check. And if you now (seeing I am your friend and not your enemy) persist in your resistance to my authority, I give you fair warning YOU SHALL DIE.'

"Saying this to me, he cast a glance into the rigging where the terror-stricken sailors were clinging, like so many frightened monkeys, and commanded them to come down, in a tone from which there was no appeal; for four men stood by with muskets in hand, ready at the word of command to shoot them down.

"I now became satisfied that resistance was out of the question; that my best policy was to put the brig into Nassau, and secure the assistance of the American consul at that port. I felt sure that the authorities would enable us to secure the murderers, and bring them to trial.

"By this time the apprehended squall had burst upon us. The wind howled furiously,—the ocean was white with foam, which, on account of the darkness, we could see only by the quick flashes of lightning that darted occasionally from the angry sky. All was alarm and confusion. Hideous cries came up from the slave women. Above the roaring billows a succession of heavy thunder rolled along, swelling the terrific din. Owing to the great darkness, and a sudden shift of the wind, we found ourselves in the trough of the sea. When shipping a heavy sea over the starboard bow, the bodies of the captain and Mr. Jameson were washed overboard. For awhile we had dearer interests to look after than slave property. A more savage thunder-gust never swept the ocean. Our brig rolled and creaked as if every bolt would be started, and every thread of oakum would be pressed out of the seams. To the pumps! to the pumps! I cried, but not a sailor would quit his grasp. Fortunately this squall soon passed over, or we must have been food for sharks.

---

23. Capital of the Bahamas.

"During all the storm, Madison stood firmly at the helm,—his keen eye fixed upon the binnacle.[24] He was not indifferent to the dreadful hurricane; yet he met it with the equanimity of an old sailor. He was silent but not agitated. The first words he uttered after the storm had slightly subsided, were characteristic of the man. 'Mr. mate, you cannot write the bloody laws of slavery on those restless billows. The ocean, if not the land, is free.' I confess, gentlemen, I felt myself in the presence of a superior man; one who, had he been a white man, I would have followed willingly and gladly in any honorable enterprise. Our difference of color was the only ground for difference of action. It was not that his principles were wrong in the abstract; for they are the principles of 1776. But I could not bring myself to recognize their application to one whom I deemed my inferior.

"But to my story. What happened now is soon told. Two hours after the frightful tempest had spent itself, we were plump at the wharf in Nassau. I sent two of our men immediately to our consul with a statement of facts, requesting his interference in our behalf. What he did, or whither he did anything, I don't know; but, by order of the authorities, a company of *black* soldiers came on board, for the purpose, as they said, of protecting the property. These impudent rascals, when I called on them to assist me in keeping the slaves on board, sheltered themselves adroitly under their instructions only to protect property,—and said they did not recognize *persons as property*. I told them that by the laws of Virginia and the laws of the United States, the slaves on board were as much property as the barrels of flour in the hold. At this the stupid blockheads showed their *ivory*, rolled up their white eyes in horror, as if the idea of putting men on a footing with merchandise were revolting to their humanity. When these instructions were understood among the negroes, it was impossible for us to keep them on board. They deliberately gathered up their baggage before our eyes, and, against our remonstrances, poured through the gangway,—formed themselves into a procession on the wharf,—bid farewell to all on board, and, uttering the wildest shouts of exultation, they marched, amidst the deafening cheers of a multitude of sympathizing spectators, under the triumphant leadership of their heroic chief and deliverer, MADISON WASHINGTON."

—1853

Letter to the Editor of *The Times* [1]

Sir, —I take up my pen to lay before you a few facts respecting an unjust proscription by which I find myself subjected on board the steamship Cambria, to sail from this port at 10 o'clock to-morrow morning for Boston, United States.

On the 4th of March last, in company with Mr. George Monbay, of the Hall of Commerce, London, I called upon Mr. Ford, the London agent of the Cunard line of steamers, for the purpose of securing a passage on board the steam ship Cambria to Boston, United States. On inquiring the amount of the passage I was told 40*l*. 19s. I inquired further, if a second class passage could be obtained. He answered no, there was but one fare, all distinctions having been abolished. I then gave him 40*l*. 19s and

---

24. Compass case.

1. The editors wish to thank Alan J. Rice, University of Central Lancashire, for bringing this letter and the responses to it to their attention.

received from him in return a ticket entitling me to berth No. 72 on board the steam-ship Cambria, at the same time asking him if my colour would prove any barrier to my enjoying all the rights and privileges enjoyed by other passengers. He said, 'No.' I then left the office, supposing all well, and thought nothing more of the matter until this morning, when in company with a few friends, agreeably to public notice, I went on board the Cambria with my luggage, and on inquiring for my berth, found, to my surprise and mortification, that it had been given to another passenger, and was told that the agent in London had acted without authority in selling me the ticket. I expressed my surprise and disappointment to the captain, and inquired what I had better do in the matter. He suggested my accompanying him to the office of the agent in Water street, Liverpool, for the purpose of ascertaining what could be done. On stating the fact of my having purchased the ticket of the London agent, Mr. M'Iver (the Liverpool agent) answered that the London agent, in selling me the ticket, had acted without authority, and that I should not go on board the ship unless I agreed to take my meals alone, not to mix with the saloon company, and to give up the berth for which I had paid. Being without legal remedy, and anxious to return to the United States, I have felt it due to my own rights as a man, as well as to the honour and dig-nity of the British public, to lay these facts before them, sincerely believing that the British public will pronounce a just verdict on such proceedings. I have travelled in this country 19 months, and have always enjoyed equal rights and privileges with other passengers, and it was not until I turned my face towards America that I met anything like proscription on account of my colour.

    Yours respectfully,
    FREDERICK DOUGLASS
Brown's Temperance Hotel, Liverpool, April 3
The Times, Tuesday April 6, 1847

—1847

CONTEMPORARY RESPONSE

The Times

1847

As Alan Rice and Martin Crawford have pointed out in *Liberating Sojourn: Frederick Douglass & and Transatlantic Reform* (1999), the ocean, ports, and maritime tradition pro-vided Douglass "with his route to liberty when in 1838, dressed in sailor's clothes and with a free black sailor's papers, he escaped northward by ferry and train." In *The Heroic Slave* (1853), Douglass wrote that one "cannot write the bloody laws of slavery on those restless billows. The ocean, if not the land, is free" (p. 1146). However, on his first trip to Britain, the reverse was true: He was forced to cross the Atlantic in steerage so as to not offend racist passengers. During his return trip to America, he was once again forced out of the cabin his ticket entitled him to; recounting the experience, Douglass noted that it was "rather hard after having enjoyed nearly two years of equal social privileges in England, often dining with gentleman of great literary, social, political, and religious eminence— never during the whole time, having met with a single word, look, or gesture which gave me the slightest reason to think my color was an offense to anybody—now to be cooped up in the stern of the *Cambria*." He protested this discrimination in his letter to *The Times* of London, which sparked a furious debate in the pages of the paper.

Editorial

The tyranny complained of in a letter signed "FREDERICK DOUGLASS", which appeared in our paper of Tuesday, ought not to be allowed to pass in this country without some public expression of disapprobation and disgust at a proceeding wholly repugnant to our English notions of justice and humanity. A highly respectable gentleman of colour, after visiting England, being about to return to America, had taken and paid for a berth in the steamship Cambria, when, on going on board with his luggage, he is informed that the accommodation he had purchased for himself has been allotted to another passenger. On seeking for an explanation of this piece of manifest dishonesty, for it is certainly dishonest to take a sum of money and refuse to perform the condition on which it has been received, the aggrieved person was told that if he wished to go by the ship he must take his meals alone, forego mixing with the company in the saloon, and relinquish to another the berth he had paid to secure. The plain fact of the matter appears to be, that Mr. DOUGLASS being a man of colour, was not allowed to go out on an equal footing with the rest of the passengers on board the Cambria. It signifies very little to us how contemptible the Americans may make themselves by the prejudices they act upon in their own country, and it concerns, perhaps, none but themselves, that they should present the anomaly of a nation talking largely of equality and liberality while practically drawing one of the meanest and most senseless distinctions that it is possible to conceive. The shame is theirs alone of giving the lie to their own boasted theory of freedom both in action and opinion, by the habitual exercise of the most despotic restraint over the former in the case of the coloured population, and the subjugation of the latter in their own case to a most paltry prejudice.

We are unfortunately compelled to witness in some points a deviation on the part of America from those general principles of enlightenment which are acknowledged by the people of every other civilized nation in the world. We, however, are not in any way bound to tolerate the introduction into this country of any of the degrading peculiarities of society in the United States, nor can we observe with calm indifference any tendency to import among us prejudices utterly at variance with our feelings and character. We therefore do not refrain from expressing our most intense disgust at the conduct of the agents of the Cambria, in having succumbed to a miserable and unmeaning assumption of skin-deep superiority by the American portion of their passengers. We do not know who the over-sensitive individuals may have been that feared contamination in taking out a person of colour as a fellow passenger in the Cambria, but we cannot believe them to have been superior either in education, position, or refinement, either natural or acquired, to the average run of our English colonial governors. The latter—although acting as the representatives of HER MAJESTY—do not refuse to receive at their tables this class of gentlemen when American nicety will not admit even into equal participation of the advantages of a public conveyance, which is free to all except in the land making special claim to freedom.

It is one of the most inexcusable aggravations of the gross injustice of the case we have been alluding to, that the ship in which Mr. DOUGLASS has paid for the berth, he was not allowed to occupy, on account of his colour, belongs to a partly English company, which draws an immense sum of English money annually for its conveyance of the mail, and is otherwise greatly indebted to English connexion. Common decency should have taught the agents of the Cambria not to offend our notices of justice and common sense for the sake of truckling[1] to an unworthy prejudice of our transatlantic neighbours. Mr. DOUGLASS had, by his sojourn and reception in this country, earned at least some title to be regarded as not unfit to mix in the society of a vessel accessible to the public in general. The breach of the contract entered into with him seems to us as dishonourable, as the prejudice against him is ignorant and contemptible.

Thursday, April 8, 1847

To the Editor of *The Times*

Sir, —I regret to find that a letter signed 'Frederick Douglass' has been published, in which my name is mixed up in a manner that appears to me to be very extraordinary and unjustifiable. Having been absent from Liverpool for a week on business, I had not an earlier opportunity of noticing this, which I shall now do as briefly as possible.

The first time Mr. Frederick Douglass saw or met with me was not, as he states, *before*, but *after*, he had agreed with my people to arrangements and accommodation for his passage on board the Cambria, with which he expressed his dissatisfaction to me, but the contrary. Mr. Douglass had no conversation whatever with me except in the presence of three or four other individuals, and the whole point of my remarks amounted to this—that he (Mr. Douglass) when coming from the United States some months ago in the same vessel, the Cambria, as a steerage passenger, was invited by some of the cabin passengers to enter the saloon, and was the cause, whether intentionally or unintentionally on his part, of producing, by the observations he made use of, serious disturbance on board, which required the authority of the captain to quell, in order to restore peace and safety. Under these circumstances I told Mr. Douglass that had he entered into the arrangements which had been completed, I should undoubtedly have considered it my duty to require of him, before allowing him to embark, a distinct pledge that he would neither of himself, nor at the desire of others, follow such a course as was likely to lead to a repetition of such scenes of confusion as had formerly occurred. I added that, from the conversation that had just taken place between us, it was unnecessary I should act or say more upon the subject. I moreover told him that I should have taken the same course had his name been John Jones, or anything else, instead of Frederick Douglass, or had he been the whitest man in the world. These were my words.

All I find fault with is, that Mr. Frederick Douglass has withheld the entire conversation which took place between us, and by suppressing the most material facts and giving a spurious version had misled the public.

---

1. Pandering, appeasing.

I admit, to the fullest extent, my accountability for what was actually done, or actually said, to Mr. Douglass by my people; but, he having so commenced by interpreting the conversation I myself had with him, I shall not discuss through the press, either now or again, his allegations as to what took place with others.

I am, Sir, your most obedient servant

CHAS MAC. IVER

British and North American Royal Mail Company, Liverpool April 12, 1847

Tuesday, April 13, 1847

To the Editor of *The Times*

Sir, —My accidental absence from town for a couple of days has occasioned my seeing at the same time your journal of the 7th and 8th inst.,[1] the former of which contains a letter from Mr. F Douglass and the latter some observations of your own on the subject of that communication.

You are pleased to speak 'of your intense disgust at the conduct of the agents of the Cambria:' expressions in my opinion equally unmerited and strong.

Allow me, as one of the principal proprietors in the Cunard Company, and as the person responsible for the directions given to its subordinate agents in this country, to place the matter fairly before your readers.

So far as we ourselves are concerned, it is really a matter of perfect indifference whether the passengers conveyed by our vessels are black, white, or copper-coloured. Non olet mummus: the fare of one man is as good as that of another. But if there exists, as I distinctly affirm that there does, an absolute and invincible disgust on the part of the great majority of white men, and particularly of white women, not less in England than in America, to come into close contact with blackamores, are we the proper parties to be blamed for this aversion and loathing? Can it be expected by any reasonable being that the proprietors of a mere carrying trade shall utterly annihilate, not their profits only, but whatever they many be, of a very great proportion of their customers? It is no longer back than the 7th of November last, that 43 first-class berths having been engaged on board this very vessel, it so happened that the 44th and 45th were taken by a black gentleman and his wife, also a black woman. On these circumstances becoming known only three days before the ship sailed, and on the London agents, who were without specific instructions on the matter, having refused to cancel the two last issued tickets, no less than 29 out of 43 berths were thrown up, and the company sustained a loss exceeding 1,100*l*. Of the parties thus throwing up their berths, I took the trouble to ascertain that 10 only were American, and the remaining 19, English. Are we, I repeat it, to blame for refusing to renew the costly experiment? When the sight and smell of the majority of your countrymen are so much altered as that their eyes can regale upon the colour, and their noses agreeably imbibe the odour of a negro, we shall gladly welcome the change. Until then we are compelled by our own interests as a commercial company to place upon the issue of tickets to blacks such restrictions and conditions as were specifically state to Mr. Douglass.

---

1. Just passed.

Of Mr. Douglass's letter I do not wish to say a word in disparagement. He has stated the matter plainly, simply, and without exaggeration; though he ought, I must add, not to have omitted mentioning that the ticket was originally issued by a mere lad in the absence of the senior clerk, and that the instant the circumstance was discovered he was pressed to receive back the money which had been thus improperly taken.

I am, Sir, your faithful servant,
CHARLES M. BURROP,
(Of Asgill, Virginia, United States,)
Head manager of the Cunard Company of Liners
Maidenhead, Berkshire, April 8.

Tuesday, April 13, 1847

To the Editor of *The Times*

Sir, —Observing in *The Times* of this day a letter signed "Charles M. Burrop, of Asgill, Virginia, United States, Head Manager of the Cunard Company of Liners," I beg to inform you that no such person, or any other individual in the United States, holds any share or interest in the steam ships alluded to, and that the statements set forth in that letter are entirely untrue.

No one can regret more than I do the unpleasant circumstances respecting Mr. Douglass's passage; but I can assure you that nothing of the kind will again take place in the steam-ships with which I am connected.

I am, Sir, your obedient servant,
S. CUNARD
22, Duke-street, St. James's, April 13.

Tuesday, April 13, 1847

To the Editor of *The Times*

Sir, —As Mr. MacIver, in his letter contained in your impression of this day, has brought a charge against Frederick Douglass of having created a disturbance on board the Cambria during his passage in that vessel to this country, I beg to hand you a correct account of the circumstances, as detailed by him at a meeting held at Cork on the 20th of October, 1845.

I am, your obedient servant,
PETER J. BOLTON
27, New Bread-street, April 13.

"I will briefly tell you what passed during my voyage to this country, which will illustrate the feelings of our people towards the black man. I took passage at Boston, or rather my friend Mr. Buffum, the gentleman who lived in the same town with me, went to Boston from Lynn to learn if I could have a cabin passage on board the vessel. He was answered that I could not, that it would give offence to the majority of the American passengers. Well, I was compelled to take a steerage passage, good enough for me. I suffered no inconvenience from the place—I kept myself in the forecastle cabin, and walked about on the forward deck. Walking about there from day to day my presence soon excited the interest of the persons on the quarter-deck, and my character and situation were made known to several gentlemen of distinction on board, some of whom became interested in me. In four or five days I was very well known to the passengers, and there was quite a curiosity to hear me speak on the subject of slavery—I did not feel at liberty to go on the quarter-deck—the captain at last invited me to address the passengers on slavery. I consented—commenced—but soon observed a determination on the part of some half a dozen to prevent my speaking, who I found were slave-owners. I had not uttered more than a sentence before up started a man from Connecticut, and said, 'That's a lie.' I proceeded without taking notice of him, then shaking his fist, he said again, 'That's a lie.' Some said I should not speak, others that I should—I wanted to inform the English, Scotch, and Irish on board on slavery—I told them blacks were not considered human beings in America. Up started a slave-owner from Cuba, 'Oh,' said he, 'I wish I had you in Cuba!' 'Well,' said I, 'ladies and gentlemen, since what I have said has been pronounced lies, I will read, not what I have written, but what the southern legislators themselves have written—I mean the law.['] I proceeded to read—this raised a general clamour, for they did not wish the laws exposed. They hated facts—they knew that the people of these countries who were on the deck would draw their own inferences from them. Here a general hurry ensued—'Down with the nigger,' said one; 'He shan't speak,' said another. I sat with my arms folded, feeling no way anxious for my fate; I never saw a more barefaced attempt to put down the freedom of speech than upon this occasion. Now came the captain—he was met by one of the other party, who put out his fist at him—the captain knocked him down; instead of his bowie, the fallen man drew out his card, crying, 'I'll meet you at Liverpool.' 'Well,['] said the captain, 'and I'll meet you.' The captain, restored order, and proceeded to speak:—'I have done all I could from the commencement of the voyage to make the voyage agreeable to all. We have had a little of everything on board. We have had all sorts of discussions, religious, moral, and political, we have had singing and dancing, everything that we could have, except an anti-slavery speech, and since there was a number of ladies and gentlemen interested in Mr. Douglass, I requested him to speak. Now, those who are not desirous to hear him, let them go to another part of the vessel.['] 'Gentlemen,' he said, 'you have behaved derogatory to the character of gentlemen and Christians,' 'Mr. Douglass,' said he, 'go on, pitch into them like bricks!' (Laughter.) However, this excitement was such that I was not allowed to go on. The agitation, however, did not cease, for the question was discussed to the moment we landed at Liverpool. The captain threatened the disturbers with putting them in irons if they did not become quiet—these men disliked the irons—were quieted by the threat; yet this infamous class have put the irons on the black."

Wednesday, April 14, 1847

Herman Melville
1819–1891

Herman Melville was born in New York, the third child of Allan Gansevoort, a prosperous importer, and his wife, Maria, the daughter of a Revolutionary hero. When Melville was eleven years old, his father went bankrupt and then died a year later. To help support his seven siblings, Melville went to work, first on his uncle's farm and later as a bank clerk, a bookkeeper, and a teacher. At nineteen, he signed on as a cabin boy on the *St. Lawrence*, a merchant ship on the New York to Liverpool route. His next voyage was aboard the whaling ship *Acushnet* of New Bedford, Massachusetts, bound for the South Seas. He later wrote, "A whale-ship was my Yale College and my Harvard." As a common deckhand, Melville suffered brutal working conditions and mixed with men of all races, most of them from the bottom rungs of society. He described his crewmates as the "meanest mariners, and renegades, and castaways." He also saw in them "high qualities" and "tragic graces" of courage, strength, and solidarity.

After deciding that conditions on the *Acushnet* were unbearable, Melville and a fellow sailor, Richard Greene, jumped ship and lived among Polynesian natives, the Typee, in the Marquesas Islands. The sight of French warships menacing islanders led Melville to a political epiphany he later described in his popular first novel, *Typee* (1846): "The fiend-like skill we display in the invention of all manner of death dealing engines, the vindictiveness with which we carry on our wars, and the misery and desolation that follow in their train, are enough of themselves to distinguish the white civilized man as the most ferocious animal on the face of the earth." By contrast, he described the Typee tribe in idyllic terms, as a kind of natural democracy: "The natives appeared to form one household, whose members were bound together by the ties of strong affection. The love of kindred I did not so much perceive, for it seemed blended in the general love; and there all were treated as brothers and sisters." Melville worked his way home gradually on a series of ships, participating in at least two mutinies, one of which landed him in jail for a time in Tahiti. After enlisting in the U.S. Navy in Hawaii, he witnessed the corporal punishment of sailors. He later described this practice graphically in *White-Jacket* (1850), a novel that was said to have helped force the outlawing of flogging on U.S. ships. He arrived home in New York in 1844 and turned to writing to make a living, perhaps inspired by the success of Richard Henry Dana's 1840 account of his shipboard experiences, *Two Years before the Mast*.

From the beginning, Melville's writing career was shaped not just by the need to make a living in the North's biggest new city but also by the radical convictions he developed during his travels. His familiarity with the racism and violence of imperial expansion, and his experience of oppression on shipboard, provided him with material for the two autobiographical novels that established him as an author, *Typee* (1846) and *Omoo* (1847). His later, more wholly invented fictions combine to form a sweeping critique of nineteenth-century society. He attacks slavery in *Mardi* (1849), the mistreatment of immigrants in *Redburn* (1849), military discipline in *White-Jacket* (1850), the exploitation of women workers in "The Paradise of Bachelors and the Tartarus of Maids" (1855), and the compulsive irrationality of the profit system in *Moby Dick* (1851). His early works sold well, but as he became more politically forthright, he alienated the bourgeois readers of magazines and novels, and he sometimes saw his work censored by timid editors. He wrote to his friend Nathaniel Hawthorne, "Try to get a living by the Truth, and go to the Soup Societies." Melville's response to this truth was to write stories that were inconspicuously subversive, especially by creating unreliable but congenial narrators who would win the sympathies of American readers and then lead them through situations that revealed their shared weaknesses.

One of his most successful stories in this vein is "Bartleby, the Scrivener: A Story of Wall Street" (1853), the story of a Wall Street lawyer who advertises for a scrivener, a worker who would copy legal briefs and other documents by hand. A pale, quiet man, Bartleby, is hired and at first he works efficiently. But one day the lawyer asks him to proofread a document, and Bartleby replies, "I would prefer not to." By expressing a personal preference, he reveals the truth of the situation in the office. He declares a one-man strike that reveals the emptiness of the lawyer's professions of human sympathy for his workers. As the story becomes increasingly absurd, it shows how the relationship between boss and worker, the most fundamental social relationship under capitalism, reduces to an exchange of money for labor, and when this fails, nothing is left.

Bartleby, the Scrivener

A Story of Wall Street

I am a rather elderly man. The nature of my avocations for the last thirty years has brought me into more than ordinary contact with what would seem an interesting and somewhat singular set of men, of whom as yet nothing that I know of has ever been written:—I mean the law-copyists or scriveners. I have known very many of them, professionally and privately, and if I pleased, could relate divers histories, at which good-natured gentlemen might smile, and sentimental souls might weep. But I waive the biographies of all other scriveners for a few passages in the life of Bartleby, who was a scrivener the strangest I ever saw or heard of. While of other law-copyists I might write the complete life, of Bartleby nothing of that sort can be done. I believe that no materials exist for a full and satisfactory biography of this man. It is an irreparable loss to literature. Bartleby was one of those beings of whom nothing is ascertainable, except from the original sources, and in his case those are very small. What my own astonished eyes saw of Bartleby, *that* is all I know of him, except, indeed, one vague report which will appear in the sequel.

Ere introducing the scrivener, as he first appeared to me, it is fit I make some mention of myself, my *employées*, my business, my chambers, and general surroundings; because some such description is indispensable to an adequate understanding of the chief character about to be presented.

Imprimis[1]: I am a man who, from his youth upwards, has been filled with a profound conviction that the easiest way of life is the best. Hence, though I belong to a profession proverbially energetic and nervous, even to turbulence, at times, yet nothing of that sort have I ever suffered to invade my peace. I am one of those unambitious lawyers who never addresses a jury, or in any way draws down public applause; but in the cool tranquillity of a snug retreat, do a snug business among rich men's bonds and mortgages and title-deeds. All who know me, consider me an eminently *safe* man. The late John Jacob Astor,[2] a personage little given to poetic enthusiasm, had no hesitation in pronouncing my first grand point to be prudence; my next, method. I do not speak it in vanity, but simply record the fact, that I was not unemployed in my profession by the late John Jacob Astor; a name which, I admit, I love to repeat, for it hath a rounded

---

1. In the first place (Latin).   2. Fur trader and real estate tycoon (1763–1848).

and orbicular sound to it, and rings like unto bullion. I will freely add, that I was not insensible to the late John Jacob Astor's good opinion.

Some time prior to the period at which this little history begins, my avocations had been largely increased. The good old office, now extinct in the State of New York, of a Master in Chancery,[3] had been conferred upon me. It was not a very arduous office, but very pleasantly remunerative. I seldom lose my temper; much more seldom indulge in dangerous indignation at wrongs and outrages; but I must be permitted to be rash here and declare, that I consider the sudden and violent abrogation of the office of Master in Chancery, by the new Constitution, as a——premature act; inasmuch as I had counted upon a life-lease of the profits, whereas I only received those of a few short years. But this is by the way.

My chambers were up stairs at No.—Wall-street. At one end they looked upon the white wall of the interior of a spacious sky-light shaft, penetrating the building from top to bottom. This view might have been considered rather tame than otherwise, deficient in what landscape painters call "life." But if so, the view from the other end of my chambers offered, at least, a contrast, if nothing more. In that direction my windows commanded an unobstructed view of a lofty brick wall, black by age and everlasting shade; which wall required no spy-glass to bring out its lurking beauties, but for the benefit of all near-sighted spectators, was pushed up to within ten feet of my window panes. Owing to the great height of the surrounding buildings, and my chambers being on the second floor, the interval between this wall and mine not a little resembled a huge square cistern.

At the period just preceding the advent of Bartleby, I had two persons as copyists in my employment, and a promising lad as an office-boy. First, Turkey; second, Nippers; third, Ginger Nut. These may seem names, the like of which are not usually found in the Directory. In truth they were nicknames, mutually conferred upon each other by my three clerks, and were deemed expressive of their respective persons or characters. Turkey was a short, pursy[4] Englishman of about my own age, that is, somewhere not far from sixty. In the morning, one might say, his face was of a fine florid hue, but after twelve o'clock, meridian—his dinner hour—it blazed like a grate full of Christmas coals; and continued blazing—but, as it were, with a gradual wane—till 6 o'clock, P.M. or thereabouts, after which I saw no more of the proprietor of the face, which gaining its meridian with the sun, seemed to set with it, to rise, culminate, and decline the following day, with the like regularity and undiminished glory. There are many singular coincidences I have known in the course of my life, not the least among which was the fact, that exactly when Turkey displayed his fullest beams from his red and radiant countenance, just then, too, at that critical moment, began the daily period when I considered his business capacities as seriously disturbed for the remainder of the twenty-four hours. Not that he was absolutely idle, or averse to business then; far from it. The difficulty was, he was apt to be altogether too energetic. There was a strange, inflamed, flurried, flighty recklessness of activity about him. He would be incautious in dipping his pen into his inkstand. All his blots upon my documents, were dropped there after twelve o'clock, meridian. Indeed, not only would he be reckless and sadly given to making blots in the afternoon, but some days he went further, and was rather noisy. At such times, too, his face flamed with augmented blazonry, as if cannel coal[5] had been

---

3. A court that tried property disputes.   4. Breathless and obese.   5. A bright-burning form of coal.

heaped on anthracite. He made an unpleasant racket with his chair; spilled his sand-box; in mending his pens, impatiently split them all to pieces, and threw them on the floor in a sudden passion; stood up and leaned over his table, boxing his papers about in a most indecorous manner, very sad to behold in an elderly man like him. Nevertheless, as he was in many ways a most valuable person to me, and all the time before twelve o'clock, meridian, was the quickest, steadiest creature too, accomplishing a great deal of work in a style not easy to be matched—for these reasons, I was willing to overlook his eccentricities, though indeed, occasionally, I remonstrated with him. I did this very gently, however, because, though the civilest, nay, the blandest and most reverential of men in the morning, yet in the afternoon he was disposed, upon provocation, to be slightly rash with his tongue, in fact, insolent. Now, valuing his morning services as I did, and resolved not to lose them; yet, at the same time made uncomfortable by his inflamed ways after twelve o'clock; and being a man of peace, unwilling by my admonitions to call forth unseemly retorts from him; I took upon me, one Saturday noon (he was always worse on Saturdays), to hint to him, very kindly, that perhaps now that he was growing old, it might be well to abridge his labors; in short, he need not come to my chambers after twelve o'clock, but, dinner over, had best go home to his lodgings and rest himself till tea-time. But no; he insisted upon his afternoon devotions. His countenance became intolerably fervid, as he oratorically assured me—gesticulating with a long ruler at the other end of the room—that if his services in the morning were useful, how indispensable, then, in the afternoon?

"With submission, sir," said Turkey on this occasion, "I consider myself your right-hand man. In the morning I but marshal and deploy my columns; but in the afternoon I put myself at their head, and gallantly charge the foe, thus!"—and he made a violent thrust with the ruler.

"But the blots, Turkey," intimated I.

"True,—but, with submission, sir, behold these hairs! I am getting old. Surely, sir, a blot or two of a warm afternoon is not to be severely urged against gray hairs. Old age—even if it blot the page—is honorable. With submission, sir, we *both* are getting old."

This appeal to my fellow-feeling was hardly to be resisted. At all events, I saw that go he would not. So I made up my mind to let him stay, resolving, nevertheless, to see to it, that during the afternoon he had to do with my less important papers.

Nippers, the second on my list, was a whiskered, sallow, and, upon the whole, rather piratical-looking young man of about five and twenty. I always deemed him the victim of two evil powers—ambition and indigestion. The ambition was evinced by a certain impatience of the duties of a mere copyist, an unwarrantable usurpation of strictly professional affairs, such as the original drawing up of legal documents. The indigestion seemed betokened in an occasional nervous testiness and grinning irritability, causing the teeth to audibly grind together over mistakes committed in copying; unnecessary maledictions, hissed, rather than spoken, in the heat of business; and especially by a continual discontent with the height of the table where he worked. Though of a very ingenious mechanical turn, Nippers could never get this table to suit him. He put chips under it, blocks of various sorts, bits of pasteboard, and at last went so far as to attempt an exquisite adjustment by final pieces of folding blotting-paper. But no invention would answer. If, for the sake of easing his back, he brought the table lid at a sharp angle well up towards his chin, and wrote there like a man using the steep roof of a Dutch house for his desk:—then he declared that it stopped the circulation in his arms. If now he low-ered the table to his waistbands, and stooped over it in writing, then there was a sore aching in his back. In short, the truth of the matter was, Nippers knew not what he wanted. Or, if he wanted any thing, it was to be rid of a scrivener's table altogether. Among the manifestations of his diseased ambition was a fondness he had for receiving visits from certain ambiguous-looking fellows in seedy coats, whom he called his clients. Indeed I was aware that not only was he, at times, considerable of a ward-politician, but he occasionally did a little business at the Justices' courts, and was not unknown on the steps of the Tombs.[6] I have good reason to believe, however, that one individual who called upon him at my chambers, and who, with a grand air, he insisted was his client, was no other than a dun, and the alleged title-deed, a bill. But with all his failings, and the annoyances he caused me, Nippers, like his compatriot Turkey, was a very useful man to me; wrote a neat, swift hand; and, when he chose, was not deficient in a gentlemanly sort of deportment. Added to this, he always dressed in a gentlemanly sort of way; and so, incidentally, reflected credit upon my chambers. Whereas with respect to Turkey, I had much ado to keep him from being a reproach to me. His clothes were apt to look oily and smell of eating-houses. He wore his pantaloons very loose and baggy in summer. His coats were execrable; his hat not to be handled. But while the hat was a thing of indifference to me, inasmuch as his natural civility and deference, as a dependent Englishman, always led him to doff it the moment he entered the room, yet his coat was another matter. Concerning his coats, I reasoned with him; but with no effect. The truth was, I suppose, that a man with so small an income, could not afford to sport such a lus-trous face and a lustrous coat at one and the same time. As Nippers once observed, Turkey's money went chiefly for red ink. One winter day I presented Turkey with a highly-respectable looking coat of my own, a padded gray coat, of a most comfortable warmth, and which buttoned straight up from the knee to the neck. I thought Turkey would appreciate the favor, and abate his rashness and obstreperousness of afternoons. But no. I verily believe that buttoning himself up in so downy and blanket-like a coat had a pernicious effect upon him; upon the same principle that too much oats are bad for horses. In fact, precisely as a rash, restive horse is said to feel his oats, so Turkey felt his coat. It made him insolent. He was a man whom prosperity harmed.

Though concerning the self-indulgent habits of Turkey I had my own private sur-mises, yet touching Nippers I was well persuaded that whatever might be his faults in other respects, he was, at least, a temperate young man. But indeed, nature herself seemed to have been his vintner, and at his birth charged him so thoroughly with an irritable, brandy-like disposition, that all subsequent potations were needless. When I consider how, amid the stillness of my chambers, Nippers would sometimes impa-tiently rise from his seat, and stooping over his table, spread his arms wide apart, seize the whole desk, and move it, and jerk it, with a grim, grinding motion on the floor, as if the table were a perverse voluntary agent, intent on thwarting and vexing him; I plainly perceive that for Nippers, brandy and water were altogether superfluous.

It was fortunate for me that, owing to its peculiar cause—indigestion—the irri-tability and consequent nervousness of Nippers, were mainly observable in the morn-ing, while in the afternoon he was comparatively mild. So that Turkey's paroxysms only coming on about twelve o'clock, I never had to do with their eccentricities at

---

6. Nippers is performing legal services for poor convicts. The Tombs: a New York prison.

one time. Their fits relieved each other like guards. When Nippers' was on, Turkey's was off; and *vice versa*. This was a good natural arrangement under the circumstances.

Ginger Nut, the third on my list, was a lad some twelve years old. His father was a carman, ambitious of seeing his son on the bench instead of a cart, before he died. So he sent him to my office as student at law, errand boy, and cleaner and sweeper, at the rate of one dollar a week. He had a little desk to himself, but he did not use it much. Upon inspection, the drawer exhibited a great array of the shells of various sorts of nuts. Indeed, to this quick-witted youth the whole noble science of the law was contained in a nut-shell. Not the least among the employments of Ginger Nut, as well as one which he discharged with the most alacrity, was his duty as cake and apple purveyor for Turkey and Nippers. Copying law papers being proverbially a dry, husky sort of business, my two scriveners were fain to moisten their mouths very often with Spitzenbergs[7] to be had at the numerous stalls nigh the Custom House and Post Office. Also, they sent Ginger Nut very frequently for that peculiar cake—small, flat, round, and very spicy— after which he had been named by them. Of a cold morning when business was but dull, Turkey would gobble up scores of these cakes, as if they were mere wafers—indeed they sell them at the rate of six or eight for a penny—the scrape of his pen blending with the crunching of the crisp particles in his mouth. Of all the fiery afternoon blunders and flurried rashnesses of Turkey, was his once moistening a ginger-cake between his lips, and clapping it on to a mortgage for a seal. I came within an ace of dismissing him then. But he mollified me by making an oriental bow, and saying—"With submission, sir, it was generous of me to find you in stationery on my own account."

Now my original business—that of a conveyancer and title hunter,[8] and drawer-up of recondite documents of all sorts—was considerably increased by receiving the master's office. There was now great work for scriveners. Not only must I push the clerks already with me, but I must have additional help. In answer to my advertisement, a motionless young man one morning, stood upon my office threshold, the door being open, for it was summer. I can see that figure now—pallidly neat, pitiably respectable, incurably forlorn! It was Bartleby.

After a few words touching his qualifications, I engaged him, glad to have among my corps of copyists a man of so singularly sedate an aspect, which I thought might operate beneficially upon the flighty temper of Turkey, and the fiery one of Nippers.

I should have stated before that ground glass folding-doors divided my premises into two parts, one of which was occupied by my scriveners, the other by myself. According to my humor I threw open these doors, or closed them. I resolved to assign Bartleby a corner by the folding-doors, but on my side of them, so as to have this quiet man within easy call, in case any trifling thing was to be done. I placed his desk close up to a small side-window in that part of the room, a window which originally had afforded a lateral view of certain grimy back-yards and bricks, but which, owing to subsequent erections, commanded at present no view at all, though it gave some light. Within three feet of the panes was a wall, and the light came down from far above, between two lofty buildings, as from a very small opening in a dome. Still further to a satisfactory arrangement, I procured a high green folding screen, which might entirely isolate Bartleby from my sight, though not remove him from my voice. And thus, in a manner, privacy and society were conjoined.

---

7. Apples.   8. A lawyer who handles property sales.

At first Bartleby did an extraordinary quantity of writing. As if long famishing for something to copy, he seemed to gorge himself on my documents. There was no pause for digestion. He ran a day and night line, copying by sun-light and by candle-light. I should have been quite delighted with his application, had he been cheerfully industrious. But he wrote on silently, palely, mechanically.

It is, of course, an indispensable part of a scrivener's business to verify the accuracy of his copy, word by word. Where there are two or more scriveners in an office, they assist each other in this examination, one reading from the copy, the other holding the original. It is a very dull, wearisome, and lethargic affair. I can readily imagine that to some sanguine temperaments it would be altogether intolerable. For example, I cannot credit that the mettlesome poet Byron would have contentedly sat down with Bartleby to examine a law document of, say five hundred pages, closely written in a crimpy hand.

Now and then, in the haste of business, it had been my habit to assist in comparing some brief document myself, calling Turkey or Nippers for this purpose. One object I had in placing Bartleby so handy to me behind the screen, was to avail myself of his services on such trivial occasions. It was on the third day, I think, of his being with me, and before any necessity had arisen for having his own writing examined, that, being much hurried to complete a small affair I had in hand, I abruptly called to Bartleby. In my haste and natural expectancy of instant compliance, I sat with my head bent over the original on my desk, and my right hand sideways, and somewhat nervously extended with the copy, so that immediately upon emerging from his retreat, Bartleby might snatch it and proceed to business without the least delay.

In this very attitude did I sit when I called to him, rapidly stating what it was I wanted him to do—namely, to examine a small paper with me. Imagine my surprise, nay, my consternation, when without moving from his privacy, Bartleby in a singularly mild, firm voice, replied, "I would prefer not to."

I sat awhile in perfect silence, rallying my stunned faculties. Immediately it occurred to me that my ears had deceived me, or Bartleby had entirely misunderstood my meaning. I repeated my request in the clearest tone I could assume. But in quite as clear a one came the previous reply, "I would prefer not to."

"Prefer not to," echoed I, rising in high excitement, and crossing the room with a stride. "What do you mean? Are you moon-struck? I want you to help me compare this sheet here—take it," and I thrust it towards him.

"I would prefer not to," said he.

I looked at him steadfastly. His face was leanly composed; his gray eye dimly calm. Not a wrinkle of agitation rippled him. Had there been the least uneasiness, anger, impatience or impertinence in his manner; in other words, had there been any thing ordinarily human about him, doubtless I should have violently dismissed him from the premises. But as it was, I should have as soon thought of turning my pale plaster-of-paris bust of Cicero[9] out of doors. I stood gazing at him awhile, as he went on with his own writing, and then reseated myself at my desk. This is very strange, thought I. What had one best do? But my business hurried me. I concluded to forget the matter for the present, reserving it for my future leisure. So calling Nippers from the other room, the paper was speedily examined.

---

9. Roman orator (106–42 BC).

A few days after this, Bartleby concluded four lengthy documents, being quadruplicates of a week's testimony taken before me in my High Court of Chancery. It became necessary to examine them. It was an important suit, and great accuracy was imperative. Having all things arranged I called Turkey, Nippers and Ginger Nut from the next room, meaning to place the four copies in the hands of my four clerks, while I should read from the original. Accordingly, Turkey, Nippers and Ginger Nut had taken their seats in a row, each with his document in hand, when I called to Bartleby to join this interesting group.

"Bartleby! quick, I am waiting."

I heard a slow scrape of his chair legs on the uncarpeted floor, and soon he appeared standing at the entrance of his hermitage.

"What is wanted?" said he mildly.

"The copies, the copies," said I hurriedly. "We are going to examine them. There"—and I held towards him the fourth quadruplicate.

"I would prefer not to," he said, and gently disappeared behind the screen.

For a few moments I was turned into a pillar of salt,[10] standing at the head of my seated column of clerks. Recovering myself, I advanced towards the screen, and demanded the reason for such extraordinary conduct.

"*Why* do you refuse?"

"I would prefer not to."

With any other man I should have flown outright into a dreadful passion, scorned all further words, and thrust him ignominiously from my presence. But there was something about Bartleby that not only strangely disarmed me, but in a wonderful manner touched and disconcerted me. I began to reason with him.

"These are your own copies we are about to examine. It is labor saving to you, because one examination will answer for your four papers. It is common usage. Every copyist is bound to help examine his copy. Is it not so? Will you not speak? Answer!"

"I prefer not to," he replied in a flute-like tone. It seemed to me that while I had been addressing him, he carefully revolved every statement that I made; fully comprehended the meaning; could not gainsay the irresistible conclusion; but, at the same time, some paramount consideration prevailed with him to reply as he did.

"You are decided, then, not to comply with my request—a request made according to common usage and common sense?"

He briefly gave me to understand that on that point my judgment was sound. Yes: his decision was irreversible.

It is not seldom the case that when a man is browbeaten in some unprecedented and violently unreasonable way, he begins to stagger in his own plainest faith. He begins, as it were, vaguely to surmise that, wonderful as it may be, all the justice and all the reason is on the other side. Accordingly, if any disinterested persons are present, he turns to them for some reinforcement for his own faltering mind.

"Turkey," said I, "what do you think of this? Am I not right?"

"With submission, sir," said Turkey, with his blandest tone, "I think that you are."

"Nippers," said I, "what do *you* think of it?"

"I think I should kick him out of the office."

---

10. Genesis 19.26.

(The reader of nice perceptions will here perceive that, it being morning, Turkey's answer is couched in polite and tranquil terms, but Nippers replies in ill-tempered ones. Or, to repeat a previous sentence, Nippers's ugly mood was on duty, and Turkey's off.)

"Ginger Nut," said I, willing to enlist the smallest suffrage in my behalf, "what do *you* think of it?"

"I think, sir, he's a little *luny*," replied Ginger Nut, with a grin.

"You hear what they say," said I, turning towards the screen, "come forth and do your duty."

But he vouchsafed no reply. I pondered a moment in sore perplexity. But once more business hurried me. I determined again to postpone the consideration of this dilemma to my future leisure. With a little trouble we made out to examine the papers without Bartleby, though at every page or two, Turkey deferentially dropped his opinion that this proceeding was quite out of the common; while Nippers, twitching in his chair with a dyspeptic nervousness, ground out between his set teeth occasional hissing maledictions against the stubborn oaf behind the screen. And for his (Nippers's) part, this was the first and the last time he would do another man's business without pay.

Meanwhile Bartleby sat in his hermitage, oblivious to every thing but his own peculiar business there.

Some days passed, the scrivener being employed upon another lengthy work. His late remarkable conduct led me to regard his ways narrowly. I observed that he never went to dinner; indeed that he never went any where. As yet I had never of my personal knowledge known him to be outside of my office. He was a perpetual sentry in the corner. At about eleven o'clock though, in the morning, I noticed that Ginger Nut would advance toward the opening in Bartleby's screen, as if silently beckoned thither by a gesture invisible to me where I sat. The boy would then leave the office jingling a few pence, and reappear with a handful of ginger-nuts which he delivered in the hermitage, receiving two of the cakes for his trouble.

He lives, then, on ginger-nuts, thought I; never eats a dinner, properly speaking; he must be a vegetarian then; but no; he never eats even vegetables, he eats nothing but ginger-nuts. My mind then ran on in reveries concerning the probable effects upon the human constitution of living entirely on ginger-nuts. Ginger-nuts are so called because they contain ginger as one of their peculiar constituents, and the final flavoring one. Now what was ginger? A hot, spicy thing. Was Bartleby hot and spicy? Not at all. Ginger, then, had no effect upon Bartleby. Probably he preferred it should have none.

Nothing so aggravates an earnest person as a passive resistance. If the individual so resisted be of a not inhumane temper, and the resisting one perfectly harmless in his passivity; then, in the better moods of the former, he will endeavor charitably to construe to his imagination what proves impossible to be solved by his judgment. Even so, for the most part, I regarded Bartleby and his ways. Poor fellow! thought I, he means no mischief; it is plain he intends no insolence; his aspect sufficiently evinces that his eccentricities are involuntary. He is useful to me. I can get along with him. If I turn him away, the chances are he will fall in with some less indulgent employer, and then he will be rudely treated, and perhaps driven forth miserably to starve. Yes. Here I can cheaply purchase a delicious self-approval. To befriend Bartleby; to humor him in his strange wilfulness, will cost me little or nothing, while I lay up in my soul what will eventually prove a sweet morsel for my conscience. But this mood was not invariable with me. The passiveness of Bartleby sometimes irritated me. I felt strangely goaded on to encounter him in new opposition, to elicit some angry spark from him answerable to my own. But indeed I might as well have essayed to strike fire with my knuckles against a bit of Windsor soap. But one afternoon the evil impulse in me mastered me, and the following little scene ensued:

"Bartleby," said I, "when those papers are all copied, I will compare them with you."

"I would prefer not to."

"How? Surely you do not mean to persist in that mulish vagary?"

No answer.

I threw open the folding-doors near by, and turning upon Turkey and Nippers, exclaimed:

"Bartleby a second time says, he won't examine his papers. What do you think of it, Turkey?"

It was afternoon, be it remembered. Turkey sat glowing like a brass boiler, his bald head steaming, his hands reeling among his blotted papers.

"Think of it?" roared Turkey; "I think I'll just step behind his screen, and black his eyes for him!"

So saying, Turkey rose to his feet and threw his arms into a pugilistic position. He was hurrying away to make good his promise, when I detained him, alarmed at the effect of incautiously rousing Turkey's combativeness after dinner.

"Sit down, Turkey," said I, "and hear what Nippers has to say. What do you think of it, Nippers? Would I not be justified in immediately dismissing Bartleby?"

"Excuse me, that is for you to decide, sir. I think his conduct quite unusual, and indeed unjust, as regards Turkey and myself. But it may only be a passing whim."

"Ah," exclaimed I, "you have strangely changed your mind then—you speak very gently of him now."

"All beer," cried Turkey; "gentleness is effects of beer—Nippers and I dined together to-day. You see how gentle I am, sir. Shall I go and black his eyes?"

"You refer to Bartleby, I suppose. No, not to-day, Turkey," I replied; "pray, put up your fists."

I closed the doors, and again advanced towards Bartleby. I felt additional incentives tempting me to my fate. I burned to be rebelled against again. I remembered that Bartleby never left the office.

"Bartleby," said I, "Ginger Nut is away; just step round to the Post Office, won't you? (it was but a three minutes walk) and see if there is any thing for me."

"I would prefer not to."

"You will not?"

"I prefer not."

I staggered to my desk, and sat there in a deep study. My blind inveteracy returned. Was there any other thing in which I could procure myself to be ignominiously repulsed by this lean, penniless wight?—my hired clerk? What added thing is there, perfectly reasonable, that he will be sure to refuse to do?

"Bartleby!"

No answer.

"Bartleby," in a louder tone.

No answer.

"Bartleby," I roared.

Like a very ghost, agreeably to the laws of magical invocation, at the third summons, he appeared at the entrance of his hermitage.

"Go to the next room, and tell Nippers to come to me."

"I prefer not to," he respectfully and slowly said, and mildly disappeared.

"Very good, Bartleby," said I, in a quiet sort of serenely severe self-possessed tone, intimating the unalterable purpose of some terrible retribution very close at hand. At the moment I half intended something of the kind. But upon the whole, as it was drawing towards my dinner-hour, I thought it best to put on my hat and walk home for the day, suffering much from perplexity and distress of mind.

Shall I acknowledge it? The conclusion of this whole business was, that it soon became a fixed fact of my chambers, that a pale young scrivener, by the name of Bartleby, had a desk there; that he copied for me at the usual rate of four cents a folio (one hundred words); but he was permanently exempt from examining the work done by him, that duty being transferred to Turkey and Nippers, out of compliment doubtless to their superior acuteness; moreover, said Bartleby was never on any account to be dispatched on the most trivial errand of any sort; and that even if entreated to take upon him such a matter, it was generally understood that he would prefer not to—in other words, that he would refuse point-blank.

As days passed on, I became considerably reconciled to Bartleby. His steadiness, his freedom from all dissipation, his incessant industry (except when he chose to throw himself into a standing revery behind his screen), his great stillness, his unalterableness of demeanor under all circumstances, made him a valuable acquisition. One prime thing was this,—*he was always there*;—first in the morning, continually through the day, and the last at night. I had a singular confidence in his honesty. I felt my most precious papers perfectly safe in his hands. Sometimes to be sure I could not, for the very soul of me, avoid falling into sudden spasmodic passions with him. For it was exceeding difficult to bear in mind all the time those strange peculiarities, privileges, and unheard of exemptions, forming the tacit stipulations on Bartleby's part under which he remained in my office. Now and then, in the eagerness of dispatching pressing business, I would inadvertently summon Bartleby, in a short, rapid tone, to put his finger, say, on the incipient tie of a bit of red tape with which I was about compressing some papers. Of course, from behind the screen the usual answer, "I prefer not to," was sure to come; and then, how could a human creature with the common infirmities of our nature, refrain from bitterly exclaiming upon such perverseness—such unreasonableness. However, every added repulse of this sort which I received only tended to lessen the probability of my repeating the inadvertence.

Here it must be said, that according to the custom of most legal gentlemen occupying chambers in densely-populated law buildings, there were several keys to my door. One was kept by a woman residing in the attic, which person weekly scrubbed and daily swept and dusted my apartments. Another was kept by Turkey for convenience sake. The third I sometimes carried in my own pocket. The fourth I knew not who had.

Now, one Sunday morning I happened to go to Trinity Church, to hear a celebrated preacher, and finding myself rather early on the ground, I thought I would walk round to my chambers for a while. Luckily I had my key with me; but upon applying it to the lock, I found it resisted by something inserted from the inside. Quite surprised, I called out; when to my consternation a key was turned from within; and thrusting his lean visage at me, and holding the door ajar, the apparition of Bartleby appeared, in his shirt sleeves, and otherwise in a strangely tattered dishabille, saying quietly that he was sorry, but he was deeply engaged just then, and—preferred not admitting me at present. In a brief word or two, he moreover added, that perhaps I had better walk round the block two or three times, and by that time he would probably have concluded his affairs.

Now, the utterly unsurmised appearance of Bartleby, tenanting my law-chambers of a Sunday morning, with his cadaverously gentlemanly *nonchalance*, yet withal firm and self-possessed, had such a strange effect upon me, that incontinently I slunk away from my own door, and did as desired. But not without sundry twinges of impotent rebellion against the mild effrontery of this unaccountable scrivener. Indeed, it was his wonderful mildness chiefly, which not only disarmed me, but unmanned me, as it were. For I consider that one, for the time, is a sort of unmanned when he tranquilly permits his hired clerk to dictate to him, and order him away from his own premises. Furthermore, I was full of uneasiness as to what Bartleby could possibly be doing in my office in his shirt sleeves, and in an otherwise dismantled condition of a Sunday morning. Was any thing amiss going on? Nay, that was out of the question. It was not to be thought of for a moment that Bartleby was an immoral person. But what could he be doing there?—copying? Nay again, whatever might be his eccentricities, Bartleby was an eminently decorous person. He would be the last man to sit down to his desk in any state approaching to nudity. Besides, it was Sunday; and there was something about Bartleby that forbade the supposition that he would by any secular occupation violate the proprieties of the day.

Nevertheless, my mind was not pacified; and full of a restless curiosity, at last I returned to the door. Without hindrance I inserted my key, opened it, and entered. Bartleby was not to be seen. I looked round anxiously, peeped behind his screen; but it was very plain that he was gone. Upon more closely examining the place, I surmised that for an indefinite period Bartleby must have ate, dressed, and slept in my office, and that too without plate, mirror, or bed. The cushioned seat of a rickety old sofa in one corner bore the faint impress of a lean, reclining form. Rolled away under his desk, I found a blanket; under the empty grate, a blacking box and brush; on a chair, a tin basin, with soap and a ragged towel; in a newspaper a few crumbs of ginger-nuts and a morsel of cheese. Yes, thought I, it is evident enough that Bartleby has been making his home here, keeping bachelor's hall all by himself. Immediately then the thought came sweeping across me, What miserable friendlessness and loneliness are here revealed! His poverty is great; but his solitude, how horrible! Think of it. Of a Sunday, Wall-street is deserted as Petra[11]; and every night of every day it is an emptiness. This building too, which of week-days hums with industry and life, at nightfall echoes with sheer vacancy, and all through Sunday is forlorn. And here Bartleby makes his home; sole spectator of a solitude

11. Ancient city in present-day Jordan.

which he has seen all populous—a sort of innocent and transformed Marius[12] brooding among the ruins of Carthage!

For the first time in my life a feeling of overpowering stinging melancholy seized me. Before, I had never experienced aught but a not-unpleasing sadness. The bond of a common humanity now drew me irresistibly to gloom. A fraternal melancholy! For both I and Bartleby were sons of Adam. I remembered the bright silks and sparkling faces I had seen that day, in gala trim, swan-like sailing down the Mississippi of Broadway; and I contrasted them with the pallid copyist, and thought to myself, Ah, happiness courts the light, so we deem the world is gay; but misery hides aloof, so we deem that misery there is none. These sad fancyings—chimeras, doubtless, of a sick and silly brain—led on to other and more special thoughts, concerning the eccentricities of Bartleby. Presentiments of strange discoveries hovered round me. The scrivener's pale form appeared to me laid out, among uncaring strangers, in its shivering winding sheet.

Suddenly I was attracted by Bartleby's closed desk, the key in open sight left in the lock.

I mean no mischief, seek the gratification of no heartless curiosity, thought I; besides, the desk is mine, and its contents too, so I will make bold to look within. Every thing was methodically arranged, the papers smoothly placed. The pigeon holes were deep, and removing the files of documents, I groped into their recesses. Presently I felt something there, and dragged it out. It was an old bandanna handkerchief, heavy and knotted. I opened it, and saw it was a savings' bank.

I now recalled all the quiet mysteries which I had noted in the man. I remembered that he never spoke but to answer; that though at intervals he had considerable time to himself, yet I had never seen him reading—no, not even a newspaper; that for long periods he would stand looking out, at his pale window behind the screen, upon the dead brick wall; I was quite sure he never visited any refectory or eating house; while his pale face clearly indicated that he never drank beer like Turkey, or tea and coffee even, like other men; that he never went any where in particular that I could learn; never went out for a walk, unless indeed that was the case at present; that he had declined telling who he was, or whence he came, or whether he had any relatives in the world; that though so thin and pale, he never complained of ill health. And more than all, I remembered a certain unconscious air of pallid—how shall I call it?—of pallid haughtiness, say, or rather an austere reserve about him, which had positively awed me into my tame compliance with his eccentricities, when I had feared to ask him to do the slightest incidental thing for me, even though I might know, from his long-continued motionlessness, that behind his screen he must be standing in one of those dead-wall reveries of his.

Revolving all these things, and coupling them with the recently discovered fact that he made my office his constant abiding place and home, and not forgetful of his morbid moodiness; revolving all these things, a prudential feeling began to steal over me. My first emotions had been those of pure melancholy and sincerest pity; but just in proportion as the forlornness of Bartleby grew and grew to my imagination, did that same melancholy merge into fear, that pity into repulsion. So true it is, and so terrible too, that up to a certain point the thought or sight of misery enlists our best affections; but, in certain special cases, beyond that point it does not. They err who would assert that invariably this is owing to the inherent selfishness of the human heart. It rather

---

12. Gaius Marius (157–86 BC), Roman general.

proceeds from a certain hopelessness of remedying excessive and organic ill. To a sensitive being, pity is not seldom pain. And when at last it is perceived that such pity cannot lead to effectual succor, common sense bids the soul be rid of it. What I saw that morning persuaded me that the scrivener was the victim of innate and incurable disorder. I might give alms to his body; but his body did not pain him; it was his soul that suffered, and his soul I could not reach.

I did not accomplish the purpose of going to Trinity Church that morning. Somehow, the things I had seen disqualified me for the time from church-going. I walked homeward, thinking what I would do with Bartleby. Finally, I resolved upon this;—I would put certain calm questions to him the next morning, touching his history, &c., and if he declined to answer them openly and unreservedly (and I supposed he would prefer not), then to give him a twenty dollar bill over and above whatever I might owe him, and tell him his services were no longer required; but that if in any other way I could assist him, I would be happy to do so, especially if he desired to return to his native place, wherever that might be, I would willingly help to defray the expenses. Moreover, if, after reaching home, he found himself at any time in want of aid, a letter from him would be sure of a reply.

The next morning came.

"Bartleby," said I, gently calling to him behind his screen.

No reply.

"Bartleby," said I, in a still gentler tone, "come here; I am not going to ask you to do any thing you would prefer not to do—I simply wish to speak to you."

Upon this he noiselessly slid into view.

"Will you tell me, Bartleby, where you were born?"

"I would prefer not to."

"Will you tell me *any thing* about yourself?"

"I would prefer not to."

"But what reasonable objection can you have to speak to me? I feel friendly towards you."

He did not look at me while I spoke, but kept his glance fixed upon my bust of Cicero, which as I then sat, was directly behind me, some six inches above my head.

"What is your answer, Bartleby?" said I, after waiting a considerable time for a reply, during which his countenance remained immovable, only there was the faintest conceivable tremor of the white attenuated mouth.

"At present I prefer to give no answer," he said, and retired into his hermitage.

It was rather weak in me I confess, but his manner on this occasion nettled me. Not only did there seem to lurk in it a certain calm disdain, but his perverseness seemed ungrateful, considering the undeniable good usage and indulgence he had received from me.

Again I sat ruminating what I should do. Mortified as I was at his behavior, and resolved as I had been to dismiss him when I entered my office, nevertheless I strangely felt something superstitious knocking at my heart, and forbidding me to carry out my purpose, and denouncing me for a villain if I dared to breathe one bitter word against this forlornest of mankind. At last, familiarly drawing my chair behind his screen, I sat down and said: "Bartleby, never mind then about revealing your history; but let me entreat you, as a friend, to comply as far as may be with the usages of this office. Say now you will help to examine papers to-morrow or next day: in short, say now that in a day or two you will begin to be a little reasonable:—say so, Bartleby."

"At present I would prefer not to be a little reasonable," was his mildly cadaverous reply.

Just then the folding-doors opened, and Nippers approached. He seemed suffering from an unusually bad night's rest, induced by severer indigestion than common. He overheard those final words of Bartleby.

"*Prefer not*, eh?" gritted Nippers—"I'd *prefer* him, if I were you, sir," addressing me—"I'd *prefer* him; I'd give him preferences, the stubborn mule! What is it, sir, pray, that he *prefers* not to do now?"

Bartleby moved not a limb.

"Mr. Nippers," said I, "I'd prefer that you would withdraw for the present."

Somehow, of late I had got into the way of involuntarily using this word "prefer" upon all sorts of not exactly suitable occasions. And I trembled to think that my contact with the scrivener had already and seriously affected me in a mental way. And what further and deeper aberration might it not yet produce? This apprehension had not been without efficacy in determining me to summary measures.

As Nippers, looking very sour and sulky, was departing, Turkey blandly and deferentially approached.

"With submission, sir," said he, "yesterday I was thinking about Bartleby here, and I think that if he would but prefer to take a quart of good ale every day, it would do much towards mending him, and enabling him to assist in examining his papers."

"So you have got the word too," said I, slightly excited.

"With submission, what word, sir," asked Turkey, respectfully crowding himself into the contracted space behind the screen, and by so doing, making me jostle the scrivener. "What word, sir?"

"I would prefer to be left alone here," said Bartleby, as if offended at being mobbed in his privacy.

"*That's* the word, Turkey," said I—"*that's* it."

"Oh, *prefer?* oh yes—queer word. I never use it myself. But, sir, as I was saying, if he would but prefer—"

"Turkey," interrupted I, "you will please withdraw."

"Oh certainly, sir, if you prefer that I should."

As he opened the folding-doors to retire, Nippers at his desk caught a glimpse of me, and asked whether I would prefer to have a certain paper copied on blue paper or white. He did not in the least roguishly accent the word prefer. It was plain that it involuntarily rolled from his tongue. I thought to myself, surely I must get rid of a demented man, who already has in some degree turned the tongues, if not the heads of myself and clerks. But I thought it prudent not to break the dismission at once.

The next day I noticed that Bartleby did nothing but stand at his window in his dead-wall revery. Upon asking him why he did not write, he said that he had decided upon doing no more writing.

"Why, how now? what next?" exclaimed I, "do no more writing?"

"No more."

"And what is the reason?"

"Do you not see the reason for yourself," he indifferently replied.

I looked steadfastly at him, and perceived that his eyes looked dull and glazed. Instantly it occurred to me, that his unexampled diligence in copying by his dim window for the first few weeks of his stay with me might have temporarily impaired his vision.

I was touched. I said something in condolence with him. I hinted that of course he did wisely in abstaining from writing for a while; and urged him to embrace that opportunity of taking wholesome exercise in the open air. This, however, he did not do. A few days after this, my other clerks being absent, and being in a great hurry to dispatch certain letters by the mail, I thought that, having nothing else earthly to do, Bartleby would surely be less inflexible than usual, and carry these letters to the post-office. But he blankly declined. So, much to my inconvenience, I went myself.

Still added days went by. Whether Bartleby's eyes improved or not, I could not say. To all appearance, I thought they did. But when I asked him if they did, he vouchsafed no answer. At all events, he would do no copying. At last, in reply to my urgings, he informed me that he had permanently given up copying.

"What!" exclaimed I; "suppose your eyes should get entirely well—better than ever before—would you not copy then?"

"I have given up copying," he answered, and slid aside.

He remained as ever, a fixture in my chamber. Nay—if that were possible—he became still more of a fixture than before. What was to be done? He would do nothing in the office: why should he stay there? In plain fact, he had now become a millstone to me, not only useless as a necklace, but afflictive to bear. Yet I was sorry for him. I speak less than truth when I say that, on his own account, he occasioned me uneasiness. If he would but have named a single relative or friend, I would instantly have written, and urged their taking the poor fellow away to some convenient retreat. But he seemed alone, absolutely alone in the universe. A bit of wreck in the mid Atlantic. At length, necessities connected with my business tyrannized over all other considerations. Decently as I could, I told Bartleby that in six days' time he must unconditionally leave the office. I warned him to take measures, in the interval, for procuring some other abode. I offered to assist him in this endeavor, if he himself would but take the first step towards a removal. "And when you finally quit me, Bartleby," added I, "I shall see that you go not away entirely unprovided. Six days from this hour, remember."

At the expiration of that period, I peeped behind the screen, and lo! Bartleby was there.

I buttoned up my coat, balanced myself; advanced slowly towards him, touched his shoulder, and said, "The time has come; you must quit this place; I am sorry for you; here is money; but you must go."

"I would prefer not," he replied, with his back still towards me.

"You *must*."

He remained silent.

Now I had an unbounded confidence in this man's common honesty. He had frequently restored to me sixpences and shillings carelessly dropped upon the floor, for I am apt to be very reckless in such shirt-button affairs. The proceeding then which followed will not be deemed extraordinary.

"Bartleby," said I, "I owe you twelve dollars on account; here are thirty-two; the odd twenty are yours.—Will you take it?" and I handed the bills towards him.

But he made no motion.

"I will leave them here then," putting them under a weight on the table. Then taking my hat and cane and going to the door I tranquilly turned and added—"After you have removed your things from these offices, Bartleby, you will of course lock the door—since every one is now gone for the day but you—and if you please, slip your key underneath the mat, so that I may have it in the morning. I shall not see you again; so good-bye to you. If hereafter in your new place of abode I can be of any service to you, do not fail to advise me by letter. Good-bye, Bartleby, and fare you well."

But he answered not a word; like the last column of some ruined temple, he remained standing mute and solitary in the middle of the otherwise deserted room.

As I walked home in a pensive mood, my vanity got the better of my pity. I could not but highly plume myself on my masterly management in getting rid of Bartleby. Masterly I call it, and such it must appear to any dispassionate thinker. The beauty of my procedure seemed to consist in its perfect quietness. There was no vulgar bullying, no bravado of any sort, no choleric hectoring, and striding to and fro across the apartment, jerking out vehement commands for Bartleby to bundle himself off with his beggarly traps. Nothing of the kind. Without loudly bidding Bartleby depart—as an inferior genius might have done—I *assumed* the ground that depart he must; and upon that assumption built all I had to say. The more I thought over my procedure, the more I was charmed with it. Nevertheless, next morning, upon awakening, I had my doubts,—I had somehow slept off the fumes of vanity. One of the coolest and wisest hours a man has, is just after he awakes in the morning. My procedure seemed as sagacious as ever,—but only in theory. How it would prove in practice—there was the rub. It was truly a beautiful thought to have assumed Bartleby's departure; but, after all, that assumption was simply my own, and none of Bartleby's. The great point was, not whether I had assumed that he would quit me, but whether he would prefer so to do. He was more a man of preferences than assumptions.

After breakfast, I walked down town, arguing the probabilities *pro* and *con*. One moment I thought it would prove a miserable failure, and Bartleby would be found all alive at my office as usual; the next moment it seemed certain that I should find his chair empty. And so I kept veering about. At the corner of Broadway and Canal-street, I saw quite an excited group of people standing in earnest conversation.

"I'll take odds he doesn't," said a voice as I passed.

"Doesn't go?—done!" said I, "put up your money."

I was instinctively putting my hand in my pocket to produce my own, when I remembered that this was an election day. The words I had overheard bore no reference to Bartleby, but to the success or non-success of some candidate for the mayoralty. In my intent frame of mind, I had, as it were, imagined that all Broadway shared in my excitement, and were debating the same question with me. I passed on, very thankful that the uproar of the street screened my momentary absent-mindedness.

As I had intended, I was earlier than usual at my office door. I stood listening for a moment. All was still. He must be gone. I tried the knob. The door was locked. Yes, my procedure had worked to a charm; he indeed must be vanished. Yet a certain melancholy mixed with this: I was almost sorry for my brilliant success. I was fumbling under the door mat for the key, which Bartleby was to have left there for me, when accidentally my knee knocked against a panel, producing a summoning sound, and in response a voice came to me from within—"Not yet; I am occupied."

It was Bartleby.

I was thunderstruck. For an instant I stood like the man who, pipe in mouth, was killed one cloudless afternoon long ago in Virginia, by summer lightning; at his own warm open window he was killed, and remained leaning out there upon the dreamy afternoon, till some one touched him, when he fell.

"Not gone!" I murmured at last. But again obeying that wondrous ascendancy which the inscrutable scrivener had over me, and from which ascendancy, for all my chafing, I could not completely escape, I slowly went down stairs and out into the street, and while walking round the block, considered what I should next do in this unheard-of perplexity. Turn the man out by an actual thrusting I could not; to drive him away by calling him hard names would not do; calling in the police was an unpleasant idea; and yet, permit him to enjoy his cadaverous triumph over me,—this too I could not think of. What was to be done? or, if nothing could be done, was there any thing further that I could *assume* in the matter? Yes, as before I had prospectively assumed that Bartleby would depart, so now I might retrospectively assume that departed he was. In the legitimate carrying out of this assumption, I might enter my office in a great hurry, and pretending not to see Bartleby at all, walk straight against him as if he were air. Such a proceeding would in a singular degree have the appearance of a home-thrust. It was hardly possible that Bartleby could withstand such an application of the doctrine of assumptions. But upon second thoughts the success of the plan seemed rather dubious. I resolved to argue the matter over with him again.

"Bartleby," said I, entering the office, with a quietly severe expression, "I am seriously displeased. I am pained, Bartleby. I had thought better of you. I had imagined you of such a gentlemanly organization, that in any delicate dilemma a slight hint would suffice—in short, an assumption. But it appears I am deceived. Why," I added, unaffectedly starting, "you have not even touched that money yet," pointing to it, just where I had left it the evening previous.

He answered nothing.

"Will you, or will you not, quit me?" I now demanded in a sudden passion, advancing close to him.

"I would prefer *not* to quit you," he replied, gently emphasizing the *not*.

"What earthly right have you to stay here? Do you pay any rent? Do you pay my taxes? Or is this property yours?"

He answered nothing.

"Are you ready to go on and write now? Are your eyes recovered? Could you copy a small paper for me this morning? or help examine a few lines? or step round to the post-office? In a word, will you do any thing at all, to give a coloring to your refusal to depart the premises?"

He silently retired into his hermitage.

I was now in such a state of nervous resentment that I thought it but prudent to check myself at present from further demonstrations. Bartleby and I were alone. I remembered the tragedy of the unfortunate Adams and the still more unfortunate Colt in the solitary office of the latter[13]; and how poor Colt, being dreadfully incensed by Adams, and imprudently permitting himself to get wildly excited, was at

---

13. A widely publicized murder case that occurred near Wall Street in 1841.

unawares hurried into his fatal act—an act which certainly no man could possibly deplore more than the actor himself. Often it had occurred to me in my ponderings upon the subject, that had that altercation taken place in the public street, or at a private residence, it would not have terminated as it did. It was the circumstance of being alone in a solitary office, up stairs, of a building entirely unhallowed by humanizing domestic associations—an uncarpeted office, doubtless, of a dusty, haggard sort of appearance;—this it must have been, which greatly helped to enhance the irritable desperation of the hapless Colt.

But when this old Adam of resentment rose in me and tempted me concerning Bartleby, I grappled him and threw him. How? Why, simply by recalling the divine injunction: "A new commandment give I unto you, that ye love one another."[14] Yes, this it was that saved me. Aside from higher considerations, charity often operates as a vastly wise and prudent principle—a great safeguard to its possessor. Men have committed murder for jealousy's sake, and anger's sake, and hatred's sake, and selfishness' sake, and spiritual pride's sake; but no man that ever I heard of, ever committed a diabolical murder for sweet charity's sake. Mere self-interest, then, if no better motive can be enlisted, should, especially with high-tempered men, prompt all beings to charity and philanthropy. At any rate, upon the occasion in question, I strove to drown my exasperated feelings towards the scrivener by benevolently construing his conduct. Poor fellow, poor fellow! thought I, he don't mean any thing; and besides, he has seen hard times, and ought to be indulged.

I endeavored also immediately to occupy myself, and at the same time to comfort my despondency. I tried to fancy that in the course of the morning, at such time as might prove agreeable to him, Bartleby, of his own free accord, would emerge from his hermitage, and take up some decided line of march in the direction of the door. But no. Half-past twelve o'clock came; Turkey began to glow in the face, overturn his inkstand, and become generally obstreperous; Nippers abated down into quietude and courtesy; Ginger Nut munched his noon apple; and Bartleby remained standing at his window in one of his profoundest dead-wall reveries. Will it be credited? Ought I to acknowledge it? That afternoon I left the office without saying one further word to him.

Some days now passed, during which, at leisure intervals I looked a little into "Edwards on the Will," and "Priestley on Necessity."[15] Under the circumstances, those books induced a salutary feeling. Gradually I slid into the persuasion that these troubles of mine touching the scrivener, had been all predestinated from eternity, and Bartleby was billeted upon me for some mysterious purpose of an all-wise Providence, which it was not for a mere mortal like me to fathom. Yes, Bartleby, stay there behind your screen, thought I; I shall persecute you no more; you are harmless and noiseless as any of these old chairs; in short, I never feel so private as when I know you are here. At last I see it, I feel it; I penetrate to the predestinated purpose of my life. I am content. Others may have loftier parts to enact; but my mission in this world, Bartleby, is to furnish you with office-room for such period as you may see fit to remain.

I believe that this wise and blessed frame of mind would have continued with me, had it not been for the unsolicited and uncharitable remarks obtruded upon me by my

14. John 13.34.   15. Jonathan Edwards (1703–1758), *Freedom of the Will* (1754), and Joseph Priestley (1733–1804), *Doctrine of Philosophical Necessity Illustrated* (1777).

professional friends who visited the rooms. But thus it often is, that the constant friction of illiberal minds wears out at last the best resolves of the more generous. Though to be sure, when I reflected upon it, it was not strange that people entering my office should be struck by the peculiar aspect of the unaccountable Bartleby, and so be tempted to throw out some sinister observations concerning him. Sometimes an attorney having business with me, and calling at my office, and finding no one but the scrivener there, would undertake to obtain some sort of precise information from him touching my whereabouts; but without heeding his idle talk, Bartleby would remain standing immovable in the middle of the room. So after contemplating him in that position for a time, the attorney would depart, no wiser than he came.

Also, when a Reference[16] was going on, and the room full of lawyers and witnesses and business was driving fast; some deeply occupied legal gentlemen present, seeing Bartleby wholly unemployed, would request him to run round to his (the legal gentleman's) office and fetch some papers for him. Thereupon, Bartleby would tranquilly decline, and yet remain idle as before. Then the lawyer would give a great stare, and turn to me. And what could I say? At last I was made aware that all through the circle of my professional acquaintance, a whisper of wonder was running round, having reference to the strange creature I kept at my office. This worried me very much. And as the idea came upon me of his possibly turning out a long-lived man, and keep occupying my chambers, and denying my authority; and perplexing my visitors; and scandalizing my professional reputation; and casting a general gloom over the premises; keeping soul and body together to the last upon his savings (for doubtless he spent but half a dime a day), and in the end perhaps outlive me, and claim possession of my office by right of his perpetual occupancy: as all these dark anticipations crowded upon me more and more, and my friends continually intruded their relentless remarks upon the apparition in my room; a great change was wrought in me. I resolved to gather all my faculties together, and for ever rid me of this intolerable incubus.

Ere revolving any complicated project, however, adapted to this end, I first simply suggested to Bartleby the propriety of his permanent departure. In a calm and serious tone, I commended the idea to his careful and mature consideration. But having taken three days to meditate upon it, he apprised me that his original determination remained the same; in short, that he still preferred to abide with me.

What shall I do? I now said to myself, buttoning up my coat to the last button. What shall I do? what ought I to do? what does conscience say I *should* do with this man, or rather ghost? Rid myself of him, I must; go, he shall. But how? You will not thrust him, the poor, pale, passive mortal,—you will not thrust such a helpless creature out of your door? you will not dishonor yourself by such cruelty? No, I will not, I cannot do that. Rather would I let him live and die here, and then mason up his remains in the wall. What then will you do? For all your coaxing, he will not budge. Bribes he leaves under your own paper-weight on your table; in short, it is quite plain that he prefers to cling to you.

Then something severe, something unusual must be done. What! surely you will not have him collared by a constable, and commit his innocent pallor to the common jail? And upon what ground could you procure such a thing to be done?—a

---

16. A hearing.

vagrant, is he? What! he a vagrant, a wanderer, who refuses to budge? It is because he will *not* be a vagrant, then, that you seek to count him *as* a vagrant. That is too absurd. No visible means of support: there I have him. Wrong again: for indubitably he *does* support himself, and that is the only unanswerable proof that any man can show of his possessing the means so to do. No more then. Since he will not quit me, I must quit him. I will change my offices; I will move elsewhere; and give him fair notice, that if I find him on my new premises I will then proceed against him as a common trespasser.

Acting accordingly, next day I thus addressed him: "I find these chambers too far from the City Hall; the air is unwholesome. In a word, I propose to remove my offices next week, and shall no longer require your services. I tell you this now, in order that you may seek another place."

He made no reply, and nothing more was said.

On the appointed day I engaged carts and men, proceeded to my chambers, and having but little furniture, every thing was removed in a few hours. Throughout, the scrivener remained standing behind the screen, which I directed to be removed the last thing. It was withdrawn; and being folded up like a huge folio, left him the motionless occupant of a naked room. I stood in the entry watching him a moment, while something from within me upbraided me.

I re-entered, with my hand in my pocket—and—and my heart in my mouth.

"Good-bye, Bartleby; I am going—good-bye, and God some way bless you; and take that," slipping something in his hand. But it dropped upon the floor, and then,—strange to say—I tore myself from him whom I had so longed to be rid of.

Established in my new quarters, for a day or two I kept the door locked, and started at every footfall in the passages. When I returned to my rooms after any little absence, I would pause at the threshold for an instant, and attentively listen, ere applying my key. But these fears were needless. Bartleby never came nigh me.

I thought all was going well, when a perturbed looking stranger visited me, inquiring whether I was the person who had recently occupied rooms at No.— Wall-street.

Full of forebodings, I replied that I was.

"Then sir," said the stranger, who proved a lawyer, "you are responsible for the man you left there. He refuses to do any copying; he refuses to do any thing; he says he prefers not to; and he refuses to quit the premises."

"I am very sorry, sir," said I, with assumed tranquillity, but an inward tremor, "but, really, the man you allude to is nothing to me—he is no relation or apprentice of mine, that you should hold me responsible for him."

"In mercy's name, who is he?"

"I certainly cannot inform you. I know nothing about him. Formerly I employed him as a copyist; but he has done nothing for me now for some time past."

"I shall settle him then,—good morning, sir."

Several days passed, and I heard nothing more; and though I often felt a charitable prompting to call at the place and see poor Bartleby, yet a certain squeamishness of I know not what withheld me.

All is over with him, by this time, thought I at last, when through another week no further intelligence reached me. But coming to my room the day after, I found several persons waiting at my door in a high state of nervous excitement.

"That's the man—here he comes," cried the foremost one, whom I recognized as the lawyer who had previously called upon me alone.

"You must take him away, sir, at once," cried a portly person among them, advancing upon me, and whom I knew to be the landlord of No.—Wall-street. "These gentlemen, my tenants, cannot stand it any longer; Mr. B——" pointing to the lawyer, "has turned him out of his room, and he now persists in haunting the building generally, sitting upon the banisters of the stairs by day, and sleeping in the entry by night. Every body is concerned; clients are leaving the offices; some fears are entertained of a mob; something you must do, and that without delay."

Aghast at this torrent, I fell back before it, and would fain have locked myself in my new quarters. In vain I persisted that Bartleby was nothing to me—no more than to any one else. In vain:—I was the last person known to have any thing to do with him, and they held me to the terrible account. Fearful then of being exposed in the papers (as one person present obscurely threatened) I considered the matter, and at length said, that if the lawyer would give me a confidential interview with the scrivener, in his (the lawyer's) own room, I would that afternoon strive my best to rid them of the nuisance they complained of.

Going up stairs to my old haunt, there was Bartleby silently sitting upon the banister at the landing.

"What are you doing here, Bartleby?" said I.

"Sitting upon the banister," he mildly replied.

I motioned him into the lawyer's room, who then left us.

"Bartleby," said I, "are you aware that you are the cause of great tribulation to me, by persisting in occupying the entry after being dismissed from the office?"

No answer.

"Now one of two things must take place. Either you must do something, or something must be done to you. Now what sort of business would you like to engage in? Would you like to re-engage in copying for some one?"

"No; I would prefer not to make any change."

"Would you like a clerkship in a dry-goods store?"

"There is too much confinement about that. No, I would not like a clerkship; but I am not particular."

"Too much confinement," I cried, "why you keep yourself confined all the time!"

"I would prefer not to take a clerkship," he rejoined, as if to settle that little item at once.

"How would a bar-tender's business suit you? There is no trying of the eyesight in that."

"I would not like it at all; though, as I said before, I am not particular."

His unwonted wordiness inspirited me. I returned to the charge.

"Well then, would you like to travel through the country collecting bills for the merchants? That would improve your health."

"No, I would prefer to be doing something else."

"How then would going as a companion to Europe, to entertain some young gentleman with your conversation,—how would that suit you?"

"Not at all. It does not strike me that there is any thing definite about that. I like to be stationary. But I am not particular."

"Stationary you shall be then," I cried, now losing all patience, and for the first time in all my exasperating connection with him fairly flying into a passion. "If you do not go away from these premises before night, I shall feel bound—indeed I *am* bound—to—to—to quit the premises myself!" I rather absurdly concluded, knowing not with what possible threat to try to frighten his immobility into compliance. Despairing of all further efforts, I was precipitately leaving him, when a final thought occurred to me—one which had not been wholly unindulged before.

"Bartleby," said I, in the kindest tone I could assume under such exciting circumstances, "will you go home with me now—not to my office, but my dwelling— and remain there till we can conclude upon some convenient arrangement for you at our leisure? Come, let us start now, right away."

"No: at present I would prefer not to make any change at all."

I answered nothing; but effectually dodging every one by the suddenness and rapidity of my flight, rushed from the building, ran up Wall-street towards Broadway, and jumping into the first omnibus was soon removed from pursuit. As soon as tranquillity returned I distinctly perceived that I had now done all that I possibly could, both in respect to the demands of the landlord and his tenants, and with regard to my own desire and sense of duty, to benefit Bartleby, and shield him from rude persecution. I now strove to be entirely care-free and quiescent; and my conscience justified me in the attempt; though indeed it was not so successful as I could have wished. So fearful was I of being again hunted out by the incensed landlord and his exasperated tenants, that, surrendering my business to Nippers, for a few days I drove about the upper part of the town and through the suburbs, in my rockaway[17]; crossed over to Jersey City and Hoboken, and paid fugitive visits to Manhattanville and Astoria. In fact I almost lived in my rockaway for the time.

When again I entered my office, lo, a note from the landlord lay upon the desk. I opened it with trembling hands. It informed me that the writer had sent to the police, and had Bartleby removed to the Tombs as a vagrant. Moreover, since I knew more about him than any one else, he wished me to appear at that place, and make a suitable statement of the facts. These tidings had a conflicting effect upon me. At first I was indignant; but at last almost approved. The landlord's energetic, summary disposition, had led him to adopt a procedure which I do not think I would have decided upon myself; and yet as a last resort, under such peculiar circumstances, it seemed the only plan.

As I afterwards learned, the poor scrivener, when told that he must be conducted to the Tombs, offered not the slightest obstacle, but in his pale unmoving way, silently acquiesced.

Some of the compassionate and curious bystanders joined the party; and headed by one of the constables arm in arm with Bartleby, the silent procession filed its way through all the noise, and heat, and joy of the roaring thoroughfares at noon.

The same day I received the note I went to the Tombs, or to speak more properly, the Halls of Justice. Seeking the right officer, I stated the purpose of my call, and was informed that the individual I described was indeed within. I then assured the functionary that Bartleby was a perfectly honest man, and greatly to be compassionated, however unaccountably eccentric. I narrated all I knew, and closed by suggesting the

---

17. Carriage.

idea of letting him remain in as indulgent confinement as possible till something less harsh might be done—though indeed I hardly knew what. At all events, if nothing else could be decided upon, the alms-house must receive him. I then begged to have an interview.

Being under no disgraceful charge, and quite serene and harmless in all his ways, they had permitted him freely to wander about the prison, and especially in the inclosed grass-platted yards thereof. And so I found him there, standing all alone in the quietest of the yards, his face towards a high wall, while all around, from the narrow slits of the jail windows, I thought I saw peering out upon him the eyes of murderers and thieves.

"Bartleby!"

"I know you," he said, without looking round,—"and I want nothing to say to you."

"It was not I that brought you here, Bartleby," said I, keenly pained at his implied suspicion. "And to you, this should not be so vile a place. Nothing reproachful attaches to you by being here. And see, it is not so sad a place as one might think. Look, there is the sky, and here is the grass."

"I know where I am," he replied, but would say nothing more, and so I left him.

As I entered the corridor again, a broad meat-like man, in an apron, accosted me, and jerking his thumb over his shoulder said—"Is that your friend?"

"Yes."

"Does he want to starve? If he does, let him live on the prison fare, that's all."

"Who are you?" asked I, not knowing what to make of such an unofficially speaking person in such a place.

"I am the grub-man. Such gentlemen as have friends here, hire me to provide them with something good to eat."

"Is this so?" said I, turning to the turnkey.

He said it was.

"Well then," said I, slipping some silver into the grub-man's hands (for so they called him). "I want you to give particular attention to my friend there; let him have the best dinner you can get. And you must be as polite to him as possible."

"Introduce me, will you?" said the grub-man, looking at me with an expression which seemed to say he was all impatience for an opportunity to give a specimen of his breeding.

Thinking it would prove of benefit to the scrivener, I acquiesced; and asking the grub-man his name, went up with him to Bartleby.

"Bartleby, this is Mr. Cutlets; you will find him very useful to you."

"Your sarvant, sir, your sarvant," said the grub-man, making a low salutation behind his apron. "Hope you find it pleasant here, sir; nice grounds—cool apartments, sir—hope you'll stay with us some time—try to make it agreeable. May Mrs. Cutlets and I have the pleasure of your company to dinner, sir, in Mrs. Cutlets' private room?"

"I prefer not to dine to-day," said Bartleby, turning away. "It would disagree with me; I am unused to dinners." So saying he slowly moved to the other side of the inclosure, and took up a position fronting the dead-wall.

"How's this?" said the grub-man, addressing me with a stare of astonishment. "He's odd, aint he?"

"I think he is a little deranged," said I, sadly.

"Deranged? deranged is it? Well now, upon my word, I thought that friend of yourn was a gentleman forger; they are always pale and genteel-like, them forgers. I can't help pity 'em—can't help it, sir. Did you know Monroe Edwards?"[18] he added touchingly, and paused. Then, laying his hand pityingly on my shoulder, sighed, "he died of consumption at Sing-Sing.[19] So you weren't acquainted with Monroe?"

"No, I was never socially acquainted with any forgers. But I cannot stop longer. Look to my friend yonder. You will not lose by it. I will see you again."

Some few days after this, I again obtained admission to the Tombs, and went through the corridors in quest of Bartleby; but without finding him.

"I saw him coming from his cell not long ago," said a turnkey, "may be he's gone to loiter in the yards."

So I went in that direction.

"Are you looking for the silent man?" said another turnkey passing me. "Yonder he lies—sleeping in the yard there. 'Tis not twenty minutes since I saw him lie down."

The yard was entirely quiet. It was not accessible to the common prisoners. The surrounding walls, of amazing thickness, kept off all sounds behind them. The Egyptian character of the masonry weighed upon me with its gloom. But a soft imprisoned turf grew under foot. The heart of the eternal pyramids, it seemed, wherein, by some strange magic, through the clefts, grass-seed, dropped by birds, had sprung.

Strangely huddled at the base of the wall, his knees drawn up, and lying on his side, his head touching the cold stones, I saw the wasted Bartleby. But nothing stirred. I paused; then went close up to him; stooped over, and saw that his dim eyes were open; otherwise he seemed profoundly sleeping. Something prompted me to touch him. I felt his hand, when a tingling shiver ran up my arm and down my spine to my feet.

The round face of the grub-man peered upon me now. "His dinner is ready. Won't he dine to-day, either? Or does he live without dining?"

"Lives without dining," said I, and closed the eyes.

"Eh!—He's asleep, aint he?"

"With kings and counsellors,"[20] murmured I.

There would seem little need for proceeding further in this history. Imagination will readily supply the meagre recital of poor Bartleby's interment. But ere parting with the reader, let me say, that if this little narrative has sufficiently interested him, to awaken curiosity as to who Bartleby was, and what manner of life he led prior to the present narrator's making his acquaintance, I can only reply, that in such curiosity I fully share, but am wholly unable to gratify it. Yet here I hardly know whether I should divulge one little item of rumor, which came to my ear a few months after the scrivener's decease. Upon what basis it rested, I could never ascertain; and hence, how true it is I cannot now tell. But inasmuch as this vague report has not been without a certain strange suggestive interest to me, however sad, it may prove the same with some others; and so I will briefly mention it. The report was this: that Bartleby had been a subordinate clerk in the Dead Letter Office at Washington, from which he had been suddenly removed by a change in the administration. When I think over this rumor, hardly can I express the emotions which seize me.

---

18. A notorious financial swindler.   19. A prison in Ossining, New York.   20. Job 3.14.

Dead letters! does it not sound like dead men? Conceive a man by nature and misfortune prone to a pallid hopelessness, can any business seem more fitted to heighten
it than that of continually handling these dead letters, and assorting them for the
flames? For by the cart-load they are annually burned. Sometimes from out the
folded paper the pale clerk takes a ring:—the finger it was meant for, perhaps, moulders in the grave; a bank-note sent in swiftest charity:—he whom it would relieve,
nor eats nor hungers any more; pardon for those who died despairing; hope for those
who died unhoping; good tidings for those who died stifled by unrelieved calamities.
On errands of life, these letters speed to death.

Ah Bartleby! Ah humanity!

—1853

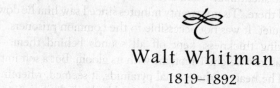

Walt Whitman
1819–1892

"I greet you at the beginning of a great career," wrote Ralph Waldo Emerson to Walt Whitman
after reading *Leaves of Grass* (1855), which Emerson hailed as the "most extraordinary piece of
wit and wisdom that America has yet contributed." Although it seems like Emerson is qualify-
ing his praise by noting that the book is the best America has yet produced, he is also alluding
to the achievement of Whitman's *Leaves* as a work that rivals its British predecessors and contemporaries. Americans were very slow to recognize one of their greatest poets, and even
Emerson eventually distanced himself from the radically innovative poet. Thanks to an 1868
British edition of *Leaves* (edited by W. M. Rossetti), the most resounding praise of Whitman
originated from his transatlantic contemporaries and successors: Gerard Manley Hopkins,
Algernon Charles Swinburne, Alfred Lord Tennyson, and Oscar Wilde. The book and its
author had humble beginnings, but were to eventually achieve an afterlife of fame that is alive
and well to this very day.

Born to a poor family in Long Island, New York, Whitman was never able to afford college. His university was the city, to which his family moved closer in search of work after failing to earn a living on the farm where the poet was born. He attended public schools until
age twelve or so, by which point he was working for a doctor and lawyer whose son introduced
him to the novels of Sir Walter Scott. Whitman was able to get his hands on books by type-
setting them and reviewing them for local newspapers—such as the *Brooklyn Daily Eagle*,
which he would edit from 1846 to 1848. He also spent three months in New Orleans writing
for *The Crescent*. By working for over ten newspapers, he received a thorough education in
the poetry of his British and American contemporaries and learned enough about the book
trade to embark upon his own venture. His work as a compositor gave him the skills to set the
type for *Leaves of Grass*, for which he wrote many anonymous reviews. His knowledge about
what would encourage the success of a book shows in his reprinting (without permission)
Emerson's praise of the book, as well as in the very appearance of the book itself. The material form of the book exemplified the title, with its green binding and front cover in which
the title appears to have grown there organically from the roots that dangle from the letters.
As the title indicates, the book was meant to be a text of nature. The double meaning of the
word "Leaves" refers to both the leaves (pages) of a book and the leaves of a tree, and the title

intimates that the book is a natural one, a text read on the veins of a leaf and a book with pages made of grass. In creating a book with this title and material form, Whitman was participating in a transatlantic conversation begun by British Romantic poets who referred to nature as a divine text and continued by American Transcendentalists and poets who wrote about the forests, mountains, and streams of America as living words in the Bible of landscape. William Wordsworth wrote about "God who made the book of the world," Henry David Thoreau about going into the woods to hear the gospel according to the moment, and Whitman about grass as the "handkerchief of the Lord, / . . . designedly dropt, / Bearing the owner's name . . . in the corners" and as "a uniform hieroglyphic . . . / Growing among black folks as among white" (p. 1182).

It is no coincidence that the grass mentioned in the poem grows on both sides of the "color line," as Whitman supported abolitionism in his poetry, politics, and actions. In 1848, he was fired from his job at the *Brooklyn Daily Eagle* for his anti-slavery views. During the Civil War, he served as a nurse to the Northern troops. His poetry of this time depicted the battlefields as places of great suffering. In addition to writing about landscapes, Whitman expanded the uses of this metaphor to cityscapes and seascapes, singing of New York's streets and shores skirted by Atlantic waters. Although much of his poetry is about New York, he does not limit himself merely to the local. His poetry expands from the world of New York City to encompass other states and nations as well as themes of the cosmic and transcendent. It not only discusses the external world but also delves into the internal space of identity, spirituality, and sexuality. The allusions and references to the autoerotic and homoerotic in his verse on the one hand opened up new topics for poets, but on the other they cost him dearly in terms of professional and personal relationships. Once Emerson and his fellow Transcendentalists picked up on what was deemed to be impropriety in Whitman's works, they were quick to distance themselves from him. After the Civil War, Whitman was fired from his position as clerk to the Secretary of the Interior because *Leaves of Grass* was viewed as going against "the rules of decorum and propriety prescribed by a Christian Civilization." Further judgments of Whitman and his book were to be leveled at him throughout his life. In 1880, a Boston district attorney held that *Leaves* violated the "Public Statutes respecting obscene literature." However, by the time Whitman had settled in Camden, New Jersey (where he remained from 1874 until his death), he had drawn to himself a circle of admirers—including the Canadian R. M. Bucke, his biographer and one of his literary executors—and several visitors from overseas, including writers Oscar Wilde and Bram Stoker. After Whitman's death, his poetry continued to influence eminent writers, including Wallace Stevens, William Carlos Williams, Ezra Pound, Hart Crane, and Allen Ginsberg.

Song of Myself[1]

I celebrate myself,
And what I assume you shall assume,
For every atom belonging to me as good belongs to you.

I loafe and invite my soul,
I lean and loafe at my ease .... observing a spear of summer grass.   5

Houses and rooms are full of perfumes .... the shelves are crowded with perfumes,
I breathe the fragrance myself, and know it and like it,
The distillation would intoxicate me also, but I shall not let it.

---

1. In the 1855 edition of *Leaves of Grass*, "Song of Myself" was untitled; it received its current title in the 1881 "deathbed" edition.

The atmosphere is not a perfume .... it has no taste of the distillation .... it is
    odorless,
It is for my mouth forever .... I am in love with it, 10
I will go to the bank by the wood and become undisguised and naked,
I am mad for it to be in contact with me.

The smoke of my own breath,
Echos, ripples, and buzzed whispers .... loveroot, silkthread, crotch and vine,
My respiration and inspiration .... the beating of my heart .... the passing of
    blood and air through my lungs, 15
The sniff of green leaves and dry leaves, and of the shore and darkcolored
    sea-rocks, and of hay in the barn,
The sound of the belched words of my voice .... words loosed to the eddies of the
    wind,
A few light kisses .... a few embraces .... a reaching around of arms,
The play of shine and shade on the trees as the supple boughs wag,
The delight alone or in the rush of the streets, or along the fields and hillsides, 20
The feeling of health .... the full-noon trill .... the song of me rising from bed
    and meeting the sun.

Have you reckoned a thousand acres much? Have you reckoned the earth much?
Have you practiced so long to learn to read?
Have you felt so proud to get at the meaning of poems?

Stop this day and night with me and you shall possess the origin of all poems, 25
You shall possess the good of the earth and sun .... there are millions of suns left,
You shall no longer take things at second or third hand .... nor look through the
    eyes of the dead .... nor feed on the spectres in books,
You shall not look through my eyes either, nor take things from me,
You shall listen to all sides and filter them from yourself.

I have heard what the talkers were talking .... the talk of the beginning and
    the end,
But I do not talk of the beginning or the end. 30

There was never any more inception than there is now,
Nor any more youth or age than there is now;
And will never be any more perfection than there is now,
Nor any more heaven or hell than there is now. 35

Urge and urge and urge,
Always the procreant urge of the world.

Out of the dimness opposite equals advance .... Always substance and increase,
Always a knit of identity .... always distinction .... always a breed of life.
To elaborate is no avail .... Learned and unlearned feel that it is so. 40

Sure as the most certain sure .... plumb in the uprights, well entretied,[2] braced in
    the beams,
Stout as a horse, affectionate, haughty, electrical,
I and this mystery here we stand.

Clear and sweet is my soul .... and clear and sweet is all that is not my soul.

Lack one lacks both .... and the unseen is proved by the seen,   45
Till that becomes unseen and receives proof in its turn.

Showing the best and dividing it from the worst, age vexes age,
Knowing the perfect fitness and equanimity of things, while they discuss I am
    silent, and go bathe and admire myself.

Welcome is every organ and attribute of me, and of any man hearty and clean,
Not an inch nor a particle of an inch is vile, and none shall be less familiar than
    the rest.   50

I am satisfied .... I see, dance, laugh, sing;
As God comes a loving bedfellow and sleeps at my side all night and close on
    the peep of the day,
And leaves for me baskets covered with white towels bulging the house with
    their plenty,
Shall I postpone my acceptation and realization and scream at my eyes,
That they turn from gazing after and down the road,   55
And forthwith cipher and show me to a cent,
Exactly the contents of one, and exactly the contents of two, and which is ahead?

Trippers and askers surround me,
People I meet .... the effect upon me of my early life .... of the ward and city I
    live in .... of the nation,
The latest news .... discoveries, inventions, societies .... authors old and new,   60
My dinner, dress, associates, looks, business, compliments, dues,
The real or fancied indifference of some man or woman I love,
The sickness of one of my folks—or of myself .... or ill-doing .... or loss or lack
    of money .... or depressions or exaltations,
They come to me days and nights and go from me again,
But they are not the Me myself.   65

Apart from the pulling and hauling stands what I am,
Stands amused, complacent, compassionating, idle, unitary,
Looks down, is erect, bends an arm on an impalpable certain rest,
Looks with its sidecurved head curious what will come next,
Both in and out of the game, and watching and wondering at it.   70

---

2. Cross-braced.

Backward I see in my own days where I sweated through fog with linguists and
    contenders,
I have no mockings or arguments .... I witness and wait.

I believe in you my soul .... the other I am must not abase itself to you,
And you must not be abased to the other.

Loafe with me on the grass .... loose the stop from your throat,   75
Not words, not music or rhyme I want .... not custom or lecture, not even the best,
Only the lull I like, the hum of your valved voice.

I mind how we lay in June, such a transparent summer morning;
You settled your head athwart my hips and gently turned over upon me,
And parted the shirt from my bosom-bone, and plunged your tongue to my
    barestript heart,
And reached till you felt my beard, and reached till you held my feet.   80

Swiftly arose and spread around me the peace and joy and knowledge that pass
    all the art and argument of the earth;
And I know that the hand of God is the elderhand of my own,
And I know that the spirit of God is the eldest brother of my own,
And that all the men ever born are also my brothers .... and the women my
    sisters and lovers,
And that a kelson[3] of the creation is love;   85
And limitless are leaves stiff or drooping in the fields,
And brown ants in the little wells beneath them,
And mossy scabs of the wormfence, and heaped stones, and elder and mullen
    and pokeweed.

A child said, What is the grass? fetching it to me with full hands;   90

How could I answer the child? .... I do not know what it is any more than he.

I guess it must be the flag of my disposition, out of hopeful green stuff woven.

Or I guess it is the handkerchief of the Lord,
A scented gift and remembrancer designedly dropped,
Bearing the owner's name someway in the corners, that we may see and remark,
    and say Whose?
    95

Or I guess the grass is itself a child .... the produced babe of the vegetation.

Or I guess it is a uniform hieroglyphic,
And it means, Sprouting alike in broad zones and narrow zones,
Growing among black folks as among white,
Kanuck, Tuckahoe, Congressman, Cuff,[4] I give them the same, I receive them
    the same.
    100

---

3. A beam bracing the keel of a ship.   4. Kanuck, a Canadian; Tuckahoe, a Virginian; Cuff, a black person.

And now it seems to me the beautiful uncut hair of graves.

Tenderly will I use you curling grass,
It may be you transpire from the breasts of young men,
It may be if I had known them I would have loved them;
It may be you are from old people and from women, and from offspring taken
    soon out of their mothers' laps,   105
And here you are the mothers' laps.

This grass is very dark to be from the white heads of old mothers,
Darker than the colorless beards of old men,
Dark to come from under the faint red roofs of mouths.

O I perceive after all so many uttering tongues!   110
And I perceive they do not come from the roofs of mouths for nothing.

I wish I could translate the hints about the dead young men and women,
And the hints about old men and mothers, and the offspring taken soon out of
    their laps.

What do you think has become of the young and old men?
And what do you think has become of the women and children?   115

They are alive and well somewhere;
The smallest sprout shows there is really no death,
And if ever there was it led forward life, and does not wait at the end to
    arrest it,
And ceased the moment life appeared.

All goes onward and outward .... and nothing collapses,   120
And to die is different from what any one supposed, and luckier.

Has any one supposed it lucky to be born?
I hasten to inform him or her it is just as lucky to die, and I know it.

I pass death with the dying, and birth with the new-washed babe .... and am
    not contained between my hat and boots,
And peruse manifold objects, no two alike, and every one good,   125
The earth good, and the stars good, and their adjuncts all good.

I am not an earth nor an adjunct of an earth,
I am the mate and companion of people, all just as immortal and fathomless as
    myself;
They do not know how immortal, but I know.

Every kind for itself and its own .... for me mine male and female,   130
For me all that have been boys and that love women,
For me the man that is proud and feels how it stings to be slighted,
For me the sweetheart and the old maid .... for me mothers and the mothers of
    mothers,
For me lips that have smiled, eyes that have shed tears,
For me children and the begetters of children.   135

Who need be afraid of the merge?
Undrape .... you are not guilty to me, nor stale nor discarded,
I see through the broadcloth and gingham whether or no,
And am around, tenacious, acquisitive, tireless .... and can never be shaken away.

The little one sleeps in its cradle,   140
I lift the gauze and look a long time, and silently brush away flies with my hand.

The youngster and the redfaced girl turn aside up the bushy hill,
I peeringly view them from the top.

The suicide sprawls on the bloody floor of the bedroom.
It is so .... I witnessed the corpse .... there the pistol had fallen.   145

The blab of the pave .... the tires of carts and sluff of bootsoles and talk of the
    promenaders,
The heavy omnibus, the driver with his interrogating thumb, the clank of the
    shod horses on the granite floor,
The carnival of sleighs, the clinking and shouted jokes and pelts of snowballs;
The hurrahs for popular favorites .... the fury of roused mobs,
The flap of the curtained litter—the sick man inside, borne to the hospital,   150
The meeting of enemies, the sudden oath, the blows and fall,
The excited crowd—the policeman with his star quickly working his passage to
    the centre of the crowd;
The impassive stones that receive and return so many echoes,
The souls moving along .... are they invisible while the least atom of the stones
    is visible?
What groans of overfed or half-starved who fall on the flags[5] sunstruck or in fits, 155
What exclamations of women taken suddenly, who hurry home and give birth to
    babes,
What living and buried speech is always vibrating here .... what howls restrained
    by decorum,
Arrests of criminals, slights, adulterous offers made, acceptances, rejections with
    convex lips,
I mind them or the resonance of them .... I come again and again.

The big doors of the country-barn stand open and ready,   160
The dried grass of the harvest-time loads the slow-drawn wagon,
The clear light plays on the brown gray and green intertinged,
The armfuls are packed to the sagging mow:
I am there .... I help .... I came stretched atop of the load,
I felt its soft jolts .... one leg reclined on the other,   165
I jump from the crossbeams, and seize the clover and timothy,
And roll head over heels, and tangle my hair full of wisps.

---

5. Paving stones.

Alone far in the wilds and mountains I hunt,
Wandering amazed at my own lightness and glee,
In the late afternoon choosing a safe spot to pass the night,   170
Kindling a fire and broiling the freshkilled game,
Soundly falling asleep on the gathered leaves, my dog and gun by my side.

The Yankee clipper is under her three skysails .... she cuts the sparkle and scud,
My eyes settle the land .... I bend at her prow or shout joyously from the deck.

The boatmen and clamdiggers arose early and stopped for me,   175
I tucked my trowser-ends in my boots and went and had a good time,
You should have been with us that day round the chowder-kettle.

I saw the marriage of the trapper in the open air in the farwest .... the bride was
      a red girl,
Her father and his friends sat near by crosslegged and dumbly smoking .... they had
      moccasins to their feet and large thick blankets hanging from their shoulders;
On a bank lounged the trapper .... he was dressed mostly in skins .... his luxuriant
      beard and curls protected his neck,   180
One hand rested on his rifle .... the other hand held firmly the wrist of the
      red girl,
She had long eyelashes .... her head was bare .... her coarse straight locks
      descended upon her voluptuous limbs and reached to her feet.

The runaway slave came to my house and stopped outside,
I heard his motions crackling the twigs of the woodpile,
Through the swung half-door of the kitchen I saw him limpsey and weak,   185
And went where he sat on a log, and led him in and assured him,
And brought water and filled a tub for his sweated body and bruised feet,
And gave him a room that entered from my own, and gave him some coarse
      clean clothes,
And remember perfectly well his revolving eyes and his awkwardness,
And remember putting plasters on the galls of his neck and ankles;   190
He staid with me a week before he was recuperated and passed north,
I had him sit next me at table .... my firelock leaned in the corner.

Twenty-eight young men bathe by the shore,
Twenty-eight young men, and all so friendly,
Twenty-eight years of womanly life, and all so lonesome.   195

She owns the fine house by the rise of the bank,
She hides handsome and richly drest aft the blinds of the window.

Which of the young men does she like the best?
Ah the homeliest of them is beautiful to her.

Where are you off to, lady? for I see you,   200
You splash in the water there, yet stay stock still in your room.

Dancing and laughing along the beach came the twenty-ninth bather,
The rest did not see her, but she saw them and loved them.

The beards of the young men glistened with wet, it ran from their long hair,
Little streams passed all over their bodies.   205

An unseen hand also passed over their bodies,
It descended tremblingly from their temples and ribs.

The young men float on their backs, their white bellies swell to the sun .... they
    do not ask who seizes fast to them,
They do not know who puffs and declines with pendant and bending arch,
They do not think whom they souse with spray.   210

The butcher-boy puts off his killing-clothes, or sharpens his knife at the stall in
    the market,
I loiter enjoying his repartee and his shuffle and breakdown.[6]
Blacksmiths with grimed and hairy chests environ the anvil,
Each has his main-sledge .... they are all out .... there is a great heat in the fire.

From the cinder-strewed threshold I follow their movements,   215
The lithe sheer of their waists plays even with their massive arms,
Overhand the hammers roll—overhand so slow—overhand so sure,
They do not hasten, each man hits in his place.

The negro holds firmly the reins of his four horses .... the block swags underneath
    on its tied-over chain,
The negro that drives the huge dray of the stoneyard .... steady and tall he stands
    poised on one leg on the stringpiece,[7]   220
His blue shirt exposes his ample neck and breast and loosens over his hipband,
His glance is calm and commanding .... he tosses the slouch of his hat away from
    his forehead,
The sun falls on his crispy hair and moustache .... falls on the black of his polish'd
    and perfect limbs.

I behold the picturesque giant and love him .... and I do not stop there,
I go with the team also.   225

In me the caresser of life wherever moving .... backward as well as forward slueing,
To niches aside and junior bending.

Oxen that rattle the yoke or halt in the shade, what is that you express in your
    eyes?
It seems to me more than all the print I have read in my life.

---

6. Popular dances.   7. A beam that secures a load.

My tread scares the wood-drake and wood-duck on my distant and daylong
    ramble, 230
They rise together, they slowly circle around.
    .... I believe in those winged purposes,
And acknowledge the red yellow and white playing within me,
And consider the green and violet and the tufted crown intentional;
And do not call the tortoise unworthy because she is not something else, 235
And the mockingbird in the swamp never studied the gamut, yet trills pretty
    well to me,
And the look of the bay mare shames silliness out of me.

The wild gander leads his flock through the cool night,
Ya-honk! he says, and sounds it down to me like an invitation;
The pert may suppose it meaningless, but I listen closer, 240
I find its purpose and place up there toward the November sky.

The sharphoofed moose of the north, the cat on the housesill, the chickadee,
    the prairie-dog,
The litter of the grunting sow as they tug at her teats,
The brood of the turkeyhen, and she with her halfspread wings,
I see in them and myself the same old law. 245

The press of my foot to the earth springs a hundred affections,
They scorn the best I can do to relate them.

I am enamoured of growing outdoors,
Of men that live among cattle or taste of the ocean or woods,
Of the builders and steerers of ships, of the wielders of axes and mauls, of the
    drivers of horses, 250
I can eat and sleep with them week in and week out.

What is commonest and cheapest and nearest and easiest is Me,
Me going in for my chances, spending for vast returns,
Adorning myself to bestow myself on the first that will take me,
Not asking the sky to come down to my goodwill, 255
Scattering it freely forever. . . .

I am of old and young, of the foolish as much as the wise,
Regardless of others, ever regardful of others,
Maternal as well as paternal, a child as well as a man,
Stuffed with the stuff that is coarse, and stuffed with the stuff that is fine,
One of the great nation, the nation of many nations—the smallest the same
    and the largest the same, 330
A southerner soon as a northerner, a planter nonchalant and hospitable,
A Yankee bound my own way .... ready for trade .... my joints the limberest
    joints on earth and the sternest joints on earth,
A Kentuckian walking the vale of the Elkhorn in my deerskin leggings,

A boatman over the lakes or bays or along coasts .... a Hoosier, a Badger, a
    Buckeye,[8]
A Louisianian or Georgian, a poke-easy from sandhills and pines,   335
At home on Canadian snowshoes or up in the bush, or with fishermen off
    Newfoundland,
At home in the fleet of iceboats, sailing with the rest and tacking,
At home on the hills of Vermont or in the woods of Maine or the Texan ranch,
Comrade of Californians .... comrade of free northwesterners, loving their big
    proportions,
Comrade of raftsmen and coalmen—comrade of all who shake hands and
    welcome to drink and meat;   340
A learner with the simplest, a teacher of the thoughtfulest,
A novice beginning experient of myriads of seasons,
Of every hue and trade and rank, of every caste and religion,
Not merely of the New World but of Africa Europe or Asia .... a wandering savage,
A farmer, mechanic, or artist .... a gentleman, sailor, lover or quaker,   345
A prisoner, fancy-man, rowdy, lawyer, physician or priest.
I resist anything better than my own diversity,
And breathe the air and leave plenty after me,
And am not stuck up, and am in my place.

The moth and the fisheggs are in their place,   350
The suns I see and the suns I cannot see are in their place,
The palpable is in its place and the impalpable is in its place.

These are the thoughts of all men in all ages and lands, they are not original
    with me,
If they are not yours as much as mine they are nothing or next to nothing,
If they do not enclose everything they are next to nothing,   355
If they are not the riddle and the untying of the riddle they are nothing,
If they are not just as close as they are distant they are nothing.

This is the grass that grows wherever the land is and the water is,
This is the common air that bathes the globe.

This is the breath of laws and songs and behaviour,   360
This is the tasteless water of souls .... this is the true sustenance,
It is for the illiterate .... it is for the judges of the supreme court .... it is for the
    federal capitol and the state capitols,
It is for the admirable communes of literary men and composers and singers and
    lecturers and engineers and savans,
It is for the endless races of working people and farmers and seamen.

This is the trill of a thousand clear cornets and scream of the octave flute
    and strike of triangles.   365

---

8. Residents of Indiana, Wisconsin, and Ohio, respectively.

I play not a march for victors only .... I play great marches for conquered and
    slain persons.

Have you heard that it was good to gain the day?
I also say it is good to fall .... battles are lost in the same spirit in which they are
    won.

I sound triumphal drums for the dead .... I fling through my embouchures[9] the
    loudest and gayest music to them,
Vivas to those who have failed, and to those whose war-vessels sank in the sea,
    and those themselves who sank in the sea,   370
And to all generals that lost engagements, and all overcome heroes, and the
    numberless unknown heroes equal to the greatest heroes known.

This is the meal pleasantly set .... this is the meat and drink for natural hunger,
It is for the wicked just the same as the righteous .... I make appointments with all,
I will not have a single person slighted or left away,
The keptwoman and sponger and thief are hereby invited .... the heavy-lipped
    slave is invited .... the venerealee is invited,   375
There shall be no difference between them and the rest.

This is the press of a bashful hand .... this is the float and odor of hair,
This is the touch of my lips to yours .... this is the murmur of yearning,
This is the far-off depth and height reflecting my own face,
This is the thoughtful merge of myself and the outlet again.   380

Do you guess I have some intricate purpose?
Well I have .... for the April rain has, and the mica on the side of a rock has.

Do you take it I would astonish?
Does the daylight astonish? or the early redstart twittering through the woods?
Do I astonish more than they?   385

This hour I tell things in confidence,
I might not tell everybody but I will tell you.

Who goes there! hankering, gross, mystical, nude?
How is it I extract strength from the beef I eat?

What is a man anyhow? What am I? and what are you?   390
All I mark as my own you shall offset it with your own,
Else it were time lost listening to me.

I do not snivel that snivel the world over,
That months are vacuums and the ground but wallow and filth,

---

9. Mouthpieces of trumpets.

That life is a suck and a sell, and nothing remains at the end but threadbare
    crape and tears.   395

Whimpering and truckling fold with powders for invalids .... conformity goes to the
    fourth-removed,[10]
I cock my hat as I please indoors or out.

Shall I pray? Shall I venerate and be ceremonious?

I have pried through the strata and analyzed to a hair,
And counselled with doctors and calculated close and found no sweeter fat than
    sticks to my own bones.   400

In all people I see myself, none more and not one a barleycorn less,
And the good or bad I say of myself I say of them.

And I know I am solid and sound,
To me the converging objects of the universe perpetually flow,
All are written to me, and I must get what the writing means.   405

And I know I am deathless,
I know this orbit of mine cannot be swept by a carpenter's compass,
I know I shall not pass like a child's carlacue cut with a burnt stick at night.

I know I am august,
I do not trouble my spirit to vindicate itself or be understood,   410
I see that the elementary laws never apologize,
I reckon I behave no prouder than the level I plant my house by after all.

I exist as I am, that is enough,
If no other in the world be aware I sit content,
And if each and all be aware I sit content.   415

One world is aware, and by far the largest to me, and that is myself,
And whether I come to my own today or in ten thousand or ten million years,
I can cheerfully take it now, or with equal cheerfulness I can wait.

My foothold is tenoned and mortised[11] in granite,
I laugh at what you call dissolution,   420
And I know the amplitude of time.

I am the poet of the body,
And I am the poet of the soul.

The pleasures of heaven are with me, and the pains of hell are with me,
The first I graft and increase upon myself .... the latter I translate into a new
    tongue.   425

---

10. A distant relation.   11. Tightly fitted joints used in carpentry.

I am the poet of the woman the same as the man,
And I say it is as great to be a woman as to be a man,
And I say there is nothing greater than the mother of men.

I chant a new chant of dilation or pride,
We have had ducking and deprecating about enough,   430
I show that size is only development.

Have you outstript the rest? Are you the President?
It is a trifle .... they will more than arrive there every one, and still pass on.

I am he that walks with the tender and growing night;
I call to the earth and sea half-held by the night.   435

Press close barebosomed night! Press close magnetic nourishing night!
Night of south winds! Night of the large few stars!
Still nodding night! Mad naked summer night!

Smile O voluptuous coolbreathed earth!
Earth of the slumbering and liquid trees!   440
Earth of departed sunset! Earth of the mountains misty-topt!
Earth of the vitreous pour of the full moon just tinged with blue!
Earth of shine and dark mottling the tide of the river!
Earth of the limpid gray of clouds brighter and clearer for my sake!
Far-swooping elbowed earth! Rich apple-blossomed earth!   445
Smile, for your lover comes!

Prodigal! you have given me love! .... therefore I to you give love!
O unspeakable passionate love!

Thruster holding me tight and that I hold tight!
We hurt each other as the bridegroom and the bride hurt each other.   450

You sea! I resign myself to you also .... I guess what you mean,
I behold from the beach your crooked inviting fingers,
I believe you refuse to go back without feeling of me;
We must have a turn together .... I undress .... hurry me out of sight of the land,
Cushion me soft .... rock me in billowy drowse,   455
Dash me with amorous wet .... I can repay you.

Sea of stretched ground-swells!
Sea breathing broad and convulsive breaths!
Sea of the brine of life! Sea of unshovelled and always-ready graves!
Howler and scooper of storms! Capricious and dainty sea!   460
I am integral with you .... I too am of one phase and of all phases.

Partaker of influx and efflux .... extoler of hate and conciliation,
Extoler of amies[12] and those that sleep in each others' arms.

---

12. Friends, comrades (French).

I am he attesting sympathy;
Shall I make my list of things in the house and skip the house that supports
    them?   465

I am the poet of commonsense and of the demonstrable and of immortality;
And am not the poet of goodness only .... I do not decline to be the poet of
    wickedness also.

Washes and razors for foofoos .... for me freckles and a bristling beard.

What blurt is it about virtue and about vice?
Evil propels me, and reform of evil propels me .... I stand
    indifferent,   470
My gait is no faultfinder's or rejecter's gait,
I moisten the roots of all that has grown.

Did you fear some scrofula out of the unflagging pregnancy?
Did you guess the celestial laws are yet to be worked over and rectified?

I step up to say that what we do is right and what we affirm is right .... and
    some is only the ore of right,   475
Witnesses of us .... one side a balance and the antipodal side a balance,
Soft doctrine as steady help as stable doctrine,
Thoughts and deeds of the present our rouse and early start.

This minute that comes to me over the past decillions,
There is no better than it and now.   480

What behaved well in the past or behaves well today is not such a wonder,
The wonder is always and always how there can be a mean man or an infidel.

Endless unfolding of words of ages!
And mine a word of the modern .... a word en masse.

A word of the faith that never balks,   485
One time as good as another time .... here or henceforward it is all the same to me.

A word of reality .... materialism first and last imbueing.
Hurrah for positive science! Long live exact demonstration!
Fetch stonecrop and mix it with cedar and branches of lilac;
This is the lexicographer or chemist .... this made a grammar of the old
    cartouches,[13]   490
These mariners put the ship through dangerous unknown seas,
This is the geologist, and this works with the scalpel, and this is a mathematician.

Gentlemen I receive you, and attach and clasp hands with you,
The facts are useful and real .... they are not my dwelling .... I enter by them to
    an area of the dwelling.

---

13. Scroll-like tablets used for inscribing hieroglyphics.

I am less the reminder of property or qualities, and more the reminder of life,   495
And go on the square for my own sake and for others' sakes,
And make short account of neuters and geldings, and favor men and women fully
    equipped,
And beat the gong of revolt, and stop with fugitives and them that plot and
    conspire.

Walt Whitman, an American, one of the roughs, a kosmos,
Disorderly fleshy and sensual .... eating drinking and breeding,   500
No sentimentalist .... no stander above men and women or apart from them ....
    no more modest than immodest.

Unscrew the locks from the doors!
Unscrew the doors themselves from their jambs!

Whoever degrades another degrades me .... and whatever is done or said returns
    at last to me,
And whatever I do or say I also return.   505

Through me the afflatus[14] surging and surging .... through me the current and
    index.

I speak the password primeval .... I give the sign of democracy;
By God! I will accept nothing which all cannot have their counterpart of on the
    same terms.

Through me many long dumb voices,

Voices of the interminable generations of slaves,   510
Voices of prostitutes and of deformed persons,
Voices of the diseased and despairing, and of thieves and dwarfs,
Voices of cycles of preparation and accretion,
And of the threads that connect the stars—and of wombs, and of the fatherstuff,
And of the rights of them the others are down upon,   515
Of the trivial and flat and foolish and despised,
Of fog in the air and beetles rolling balls of dung.

Through me forbidden voices,
Voices of sexes and lusts .... voices veiled, and I remove the veil,
Voices indecent by me clarified and transfigured.   520

I do not press my finger across my mouth,
I keep as delicate around the bowels as around the head and heart,
Copulation is no more rank to me than death is.

I believe in the flesh and the appetites,
Seeing hearing and feeling are miracles, and each part and tag of me is a
    miracle.   525

---

14. Divine wind.

Divine am I inside and out, and I make holy whatever I touch or am touched from;
The scent of these arm-pits is aroma finer than prayer,
This head is more than churches or bibles or creeds.

If I worship any particular thing it shall be some of the spread of my body;
Translucent mould of me it shall be you,   530
Shaded ledges and rests, firm masculine coulter,[15] it shall be you,

Whatever goes to the tilth[16] of me it shall be you,
You my rich blood, your milky stream pale strippings of my life;
Breast that presses against other breasts it shall be you,
My brain it shall be your occult convolutions,   535
Root of washed sweet-flag, timorous pond-snipe, nest of guarded duplicate eggs,
    it shall be you,
Mixed tussled hay of head and beard and brawn it shall be you,
Trickling sap of maple, fibre of manly wheat, it shall be you;
Sun so generous it shall be you,
Vapors lighting and shading my face it shall be you,   540
You sweaty brooks and dews it shall be you,
Winds whose soft-tickling genitals rub against me it shall be you,
Broad muscular fields, branches of liveoak, loving lounger in my winding paths,
    it shall be you,
Hands I have taken, face I have kissed, mortal I have ever touched, it shall be you.

I dote on myself .... there is that lot of me, and all so luscious,   545
Each moment and whatever happens thrills me with joy.

I cannot tell how my ankles bend .... nor whence the cause of my faintest wish,
Nor the cause of the friendship I emit .... nor the cause of the friendship I take again.

To walk up my stoop is unaccountable .... I pause to consider if it really be,
That I eat and drink is spectacle enough for the great authors and schools,   550
A morning-glory at my window satisfies me more than the metaphysics of books.

To behold the daybreak!
The little light fades the immense and diaphanous shadows,
The air tastes good to my palate.

Hefts of the moving world at innocent gambols, silently rising, freshly exuding,   555
Scooting obliquely high and low.

Something I cannot see puts upward libidinous prongs,
Seas of bright juice suffuse heaven.

The earth by the sky staid with .... the daily close of their junction,
The heaved challenge from the east that moment over my head,   560
The mocking taunt, See then whether you shall be master!

---

15. Blade of a plow.   16. Tilling, plowing.

Dazzling and tremendous how quick the sunrise would kill me,
If I could not now and always send sunrise out of me.

We also ascend dazzling and tremendous as the sun,
We found our own my soul in the calm and cool of the daybreak.   565
My voice goes after what my eyes cannot reach,
With the twirl of my tongue I encompass worlds and volumes of worlds.

Speech is the twin of my vision .... it is unequal to measure itself.

It provokes me forever,
It says sarcastically, Walt, you understand enough .... why don't you let it
     out then?   570

Come now I will not be tantalized .... you conceive too much of articulation.

Do you not know how the buds beneath are folded?
Waiting in gloom protected by frost,
The dirt receding before my prophetical screams,
I underlying causes to balance them at last,   575
My knowledge my live parts .... it keeping tally with the meaning of things,
Happiness .... which whoever hears me let him or her set out in search of this day.

My final merit I refuse you .... I refuse putting from me the best I am.

Encompass worlds but never try to encompass me,
I crowd your noisiest talk by looking toward you.   580

Writing and talk do not prove me,
I carry the plenum[17] of proof and every thing else in my face,
With the hush of my lips I confound the topmost skeptic.

I think I will do nothing for a long time but listen,
And accrue what I hear into myself .... and let sounds contribute toward me.   585

I hear the bravuras of birds .... the bustle of growing wheat .... gossip of
     flames .... clack of sticks cooking my meals.

I hear the sound of the human voice .... a sound I love,
I hear all sounds as they are tuned to their uses .... sounds of the city and sounds
     out of the city .... sounds of the day and night;
Talkative young ones to those that like them .... the recitative of fish-pedlars
     and fruit-pedlars .... the loud laugh of workpeople at their meals,
The angry base of disjointed friendship .... the faint tones of the sick,   590
The judge with hands tight to the desk, his shaky lips pronouncing a death-
     sentence,
The heave'e'yo of stevedores unlading ships by the wharves .... the refrain of the
     anchor-lifters;

---

17. A full space.

The ring of alarm-bells .... the cry of fire .... the whirr of swift-streaking engines
    and hose-carts with premonitory tinkles and colored lights,
The steam-whistle .... the solid roll of the train of approaching cars;
The slow-march played at night at the head of the association, 595
They go to guard some corpse .... the flag-tops are draped with black muslin.

I hear the violincello or man's heart's complaint,
And hear the keyed cornet or else the echo of sunset.

I hear the chorus .... it is a grand-opera .... this indeed is music!

A tenor large and fresh as the creation fills me, 600
The orbic flex of his mouth is pouring and filling me full.

I hear the trained soprano .... she convulses me like the climax of my love-grip;
The orchestra whirls me wider than Uranus flies,
It wrenches unnamable ardors from my breast,
It throbs me to gulps of the farthest down horror, 605
It sails me .... I dab with bare feet .... they are licked by the indolent waves,
I am exposed .... cut by bitter and poisoned hail,
Steeped amid honeyed morphine .... my windpipe squeezed in the fakes of death,
Let up again to feel the puzzle of puzzles,
And that we call Being. 610

To be in any form, what is that?
If nothing lay more developed the quahaug and its callous shell were enough.

Mine is no callous shell,
I have instant conductors all over me whether I pass or stop,
They seize every object and lead it harmlessly through me. 615

I merely stir, press, feel with my fingers, and am happy,
To touch my person to some one else's is about as much as I can stand. . . .

Swift wind! Space! My Soul! Now I know it is true what I guessed at;
What I guessed when I loafed on the grass, 710
What I guessed while I lay alone in my bed .... and again as I walked the beach
    under the paling stars of the morning.

My ties and ballasts leave me .... I travel .... I sail .... my elbows rest in the
    sea-gaps,
I skirt the sierras .... my palms cover continents,
I am afoot with my vision.

By the city's quadrangular houses .... in log-huts, or camping with lumbermen, 715
Along the ruts of the turnpike .... along the dry gulch and rivulet bed,
Hoeing my onion-patch, and rows of carrots and parsnips .... crossing savannas
    .... trailing in forests,
Prospecting .... gold-digging .... girdling the trees of a new purchase,
Scorched ankle-deep by the hot sand .... hauling my boat down the shallow river;

Where the panther walks to and fro on a limb overhead .... where the buck turns
    furiously at the hunter,   720
Where the rattlesnake suns his flabby length on a rock .... where the otter is
    feeding on fish,
Where the alligator in his tough pimples sleeps by the bayou,
Where the black bear is searching for roots or honey .... where the beaver pats
    the mud with his paddle-tail;
Over the growing sugar .... over the cottonplant .... over the rice in its low
    moist field;
Over the sharp-peaked farmhouse with its scalloped scum and slender shoots
    from the gutters;   725
Over the western persimmon .... over the longleaved corn and the delicate
    blueflowered flax;
Over the white and brown buckwheat, a hummer and a buzzer there with the rest,
Over the dusky green of the rye as it ripples and shades in the breeze;
Scaling mountains .... pulling myself cautiously up .... holding on by low
    scragged limbs,
Walking the path worn in the grass and beat through the leaves of the brush; 730
Where the quail is whistling betwixt the woods and the wheatlot,
Where the bat flies in the July eve .... where the great goldbug drops through
    the dark;
Where the flails keep time on the barn floor,
Where the brook puts out of the roots of the old tree and flows to the meadow,
Where cattle stand and shake away flies with the tremulous shuddering of
    their hides,   735
Where the cheese-cloth hangs in the kitchen, and andirons straddle the
    hearth-slab, and cobwebs fall in festoons from the rafters;
Where triphammers crash .... where the press is whirling its cylinders;
Wherever the human heart beats with terrible throes out of its ribs;
Where the pear-shaped balloon is floating aloft .... floating in it myself and
    looking composedly down;
Where the life-car is drawn on the slipnoose .... where the heat hatches
    pale-green eggs in the dented sand,   740
Where the she-whale swims with her calves and never forsakes them,
Where the steamship trails hindways its long pennant of smoke,
Where the ground-shark's fin cuts like a black chip out of the water,
Where the half-burned brig is riding on unknown currents,
Where shells grow to her slimy deck, and the dead are corrupting below; 745
Where the striped and starred flag is borne at the head of the regiments;
Approaching Manhattan, up by the long-stretching island,
Under Niagara, the cataract falling like a veil over my countenance;
Upon a door-step .... upon the horse-block of hard wood outside,
Upon the race-course, or enjoying pic-nics or jigs or a good game of base-ball, 750
At he-festivals with blackguard jibes and ironical license and bull-dances[18] and
    drinking and laughter,

---

18. All-male dances.

At the cider-mill, tasting the sweet of the brown sqush[19] .... sucking the juice
    through a straw,
At apple-pealings, wanting kisses for all the red fruit I find,
At musters and beach-parties and friendly bees and huskings and house-raisings;
Where the mockingbird sounds his delicious gurgles, and cackles and screams
    and weeps,   755
Where the hay-rick stands in the barnyard, and the dry-stalks are scattered, and
    the brood cow waits in the hovel,
Where the bull advances to do his masculine work, and the stud to the mare,
    and the cock is treading the hen,
Where the heifers browse, and the geese nip their food with short jerks;
Where the sundown shadows lengthen over the limitless and lonesome prairie,
Where the herds of buffalo make a crawling spread of the square miles far and near;   760
Where the hummingbird shimmers .... where the neck of the longlived swan is
    curving and winding;
Where the laughing-gull scoots by the slappy shore and laughs her near-human
    laugh;
Where beehives range on a gray bench in the garden half-hid by the high weeds;
Where the band-necked partridges roost in a ring on the ground with their
    heads out;
Where burial coaches enter the arched gates of a cemetery;   765
Where winter wolves bark amid wastes of snow and icicled trees;
Where the yellow-crowned heron comes to the edge of the marsh at night and
    feeds upon small crabs;
Where the splash of swimmers and divers cools the warm noon;
Where the katydid works her chromatic reed on the walnut-tree over the well;
Through patches of citrons and cucumbers with silver-wired leaves,   770
Through the salt-lick or orange glade .... or under conical firs;
Through the gymnasium .... through the curtained saloon .... through the office
    or public hall;
Pleased with the native and pleased with the foreign .... pleased with the new
    and old,
Pleased with women, the homely as well as the handsome,
Pleased with the quakeress as she puts off her bonnet and talks melodiously,   775
Pleased with the primitive tunes of the choir of the whitewashed church,
Pleased with the earnest words of the sweating Methodist preacher, or any
    preacher .... looking seriously at the camp-meeting;
Looking in at the shop-windows in Broadway the whole forenoon .... pressing
    the flesh of my nose to the thick plate-glass,
Wandering the same afternoon with my face turned up to the clouds;
My right and left arms round the sides of two friends and I in the middle;   780
Coming home with the bearded and dark-cheeked bush-boy .... riding behind
    him at the drape of the day;
Far from the settlements studying the print of animals' feet, or the moccasin print;
By the cot in the hospital reaching lemonade to a feverish patient,

---

19. Mash.

By the coffined corpse when all is still, examining with a candle;
Voyaging to every port to dicker and adventure;   785
Hurrying with the modern crowd, as eager and fickle as any,
Hot toward one I hate, ready in my madness to knife him;
Solitary at midnight in my back yard, my thoughts gone from me a long while,
Walking the old hills of Judea with the beautiful gentle god by my side;
Speeding through space .... speeding through heaven and the stars,   790
Speeding amid the seven satellites and the broad ring and the diameter of eighty
    thousand miles,
Speeding with tailed meteors .... throwing fire-balls like the rest,
Carrying the crescent child that carries its own full mother in its belly;
Storming enjoying planning loving cautioning,
Backing and filling, appearing and disappearing,   795
I tread day and night such roads.

I visit the orchards of God and look at the spheric product,
And look at quintillions ripened, and look at quintillions green.

I fly the flight of the fluid and swallowing soul,
My course runs below the soundings of plummets.   800

I help myself to material and immaterial,
No guard can shut me off, no law can prevent me.

I anchor my ship for a little while only,
My messengers continually cruise away or bring their returns to me.

I go hunting polar furs and the seal .... leaping chasms with a pike-pointed
    staff .... clinging to topples of brittle and blue.   805

I ascend to the foretruck .... I take my place late at night in the crow's nest ....
    we sail through the arctic sea .... it is plenty light enough,
Through the clear atmosphere I stretch around on the wonderful beauty,
The enormous masses of ice pass me and I pass them .... the scenery is plain
    in all directions,
The white-topped mountains point up in the distance .... I fling out my fancies
    toward them;
We are about approaching some great battlefield in which we are soon to be
    engaged,   810
We pass the colossal outposts of the encampments .... we pass with still feet
    and caution;
Or we are entering by the suburbs some vast and ruined city .... the blocks and
    fallen architecture more than all the living cities of the globe.

I am a free companion .... I bivouac by invading watchfires.

I turn the bridegroom out of bed and stay with the bride myself,
And tighten her all night to my thighs and lips.   815

My voice is the wife's voice, the screech by the rail of the stairs,
They fetch my man's body up dripping and drowned.

I understand the large hearts of heroes,
The courage of present times and all times;
How the skipper saw the crowded and rudderless wreck of the steamship, and
    death chasing it up and down the storm,   820
How he knuckled tight and gave not back one inch, and was faithful of days
    and faithful of nights,
And chalked in large letters on a board, Be of good cheer, We will not desert you;
How he saved the drifting company at last,
How the lank loose-gowned women looked when boated from the side of their
    prepared graves,
How the silent old-faced infants, and the lifted sick, and the sharp-lipped
    unshaved men;   825
All this I swallow and it tastes good .... I like it well, and it becomes mine,
I am the man .... I suffered .... I was there.

The disdain and calmness of martyrs,
The mother condemned for a witch and burnt with dry wood, and her children
    gazing on;
The hounded slave that flags in the race and leans by the fence, blowing and
    covered with sweat,   830
The twinges that sting like needles his legs and neck,
The murderous buckshot and the bullets,
All these I feel or am.

I am the hounded slave .... I wince at the bite of the dogs,
Hell and despair are upon me .... crack and again crack the
    marksmen,   835
I clutch the rails of the fence .... my gore dribs thinned with the ooze of my skin,
I fall on the weeds and stones,
The riders spur their unwilling horses and haul close,
They taunt my dizzy ears .... they beat me violently over the head with their
    whip-stocks.

Agonies are one of my changes of garments;   840
I do not ask the wounded person how he feels .... I myself become the
    wounded person,
My hurt turns livid upon me as I lean on a cane and observe.

I am the mashed fireman with breastbone broken .... tumbling walls buried
    me in their debris,
Heat and smoke I inspired.... I heard the yelling shouts of my comrades,
I heard the distant click of their picks and shovels;   845
They have cleared the beams away .... they tenderly lift me forth.

I lie in the night air in my red shirt .... the pervading hush is for my sake,
Painless after all I lie, exhausted but not so unhappy,
White and beautiful are the faces around me .... the heads are bared of their
    fire-caps,
The kneeling crowd fades with the light of the torches.   850

Distant and dead resuscitate,
They show as the dial or move as the hands of me .... and I am the clock myself.

I am an old artillerist, and tell of some fort's bombardment .... and am there again.

Again the reveille of drummers .... again the attacking cannon and mortars
    and howitzers,
Again the attacked send their cannon responsive.   855

I take part .... I see and hear the whole,
The cries and curses and roar .... the plaudits for well aimed shots,
The ambulanza slowly passing and trailing its red drip,
Workmen searching after damages and to make indispensible repairs,
The fall of grenades through the rent roof .... the fan-shaped
    explosion,   860
The whizz of limbs heads stone wood and iron high in the air.

Again gurgles the mouth of my dying general .... he furiously waves with his hand,
He gasps through the clot .... Mind not me .... mind .... the entrenchments.

I tell not the fall of Alamo .... not one escaped to tell the fall of Alamo,
The hundred and fifty are dumb yet at Alamo.   865

Hear now the tale of a jetblack sunrise,
Hear of the murder in cold blood of four hundred and twelve young men.[20]
Retreating they had formed in a hollow square with their baggage for breastworks,
Nine hundred lives out of the surrounding enemy's nine times their number was
    the price they took in advance,
Their colonel was wounded and their ammunition gone,   870
They treated for an honorable capitulation, received writing and seal, gave up
    their arms, and marched back prisoners of war.

They were the glory of the race of rangers,
Matchless with a horse, a rifle, a song, a supper, or a courtship,
Large, turbulent, brave, handsome, generous, proud and affectionate,
Bearded, sunburnt, dressed in the free costume of hunters,   875
Not a single one over thirty years of age.

The second Sunday morning they were brought out in squads and massacred ....
    it was beautiful early summer,
The work commenced about five o'clock and was over by eight.

None obeyed the command to kneel,
Some made a mad and helpless rush .... some stood stark and straight,   880
A few fell at once, shot in the temple or heart .... the living and dead lay together,
The maimed and mangled dug in the dirt .... the new-comers saw them there;
Some half-killed attempted to crawl away,
These were dispatched with bayonets or battered with the blunts of muskets;

---

20. Massacre at Goliad, March 27, 1836, during the Mexican-American War.

A youth not seventeen years old seized his assassin till two more came to
    release him,   885
The three were all torn, and covered with the boy's blood.

At eleven o'clock began the burning of the bodies;
And that is the tale of the murder of the four hundred and twelve young men,
And that was a jetblack sunrise. . . .

Somehow I have been stunned. Stand back!   955
Give me a little time beyond my cuffed head and slumbers and dreams and gaping,
I discover myself on a verge of the usual mistake.

That I could forget the mockers and insults!

That I could forget the trickling tears and the blows of the bludgeons and
    hammers!
That I could look with a separate look on my own crucifixion and bloody
    crowning!   960

I remember .... I resume the overstaid fraction,
The grave of rock multiplies what has been confided to it .... or to any graves,
The corpses rise .... the gashes heal .... the fastenings roll away.

I troop forth replenished with supreme power, one of an average unending
    procession,
We walk the roads of Ohio and Massachusetts and Virginia and Wisconsin and
    New York and New Orleans and Texas and Montreal and San Francisco
    and Charleston and Savannah and Mexico,   965
Inland and by the seacoast and boundary lines .... and we pass the boundary lines.

Our swift ordinances are on their way over the whole earth,
The blossoms we wear in our hats are the growth of two thousand years.

Eleves[21] I salute you,
I see the approach of your numberless gangs .... I see you understand yourselves
    and me,   970
And know that they who have eyes are divine, and the blind and lame are
    equally divine,
And that my steps drag behind yours yet go before them,
And are aware how I am with you no more than I am with everybody.

The friendly and flowing savage .... Who is he?
Is he waiting for civilization or past it and mastering it?   975

Is he some southwesterner raised outdoors? Is he Canadian?
Is he from the Mississippi country? or from Iowa, Oregon or California? or from
    the mountains? or prairie life or bush-life? or from the sea?

---

21. Students (French).

Wherever he goes men and women accept and desire him,
They desire he should like them and touch them and speak to them and stay
    with them.

Behaviour lawless as snow-flakes .... words simple as grass .... uncombed head
    and laughter and naivete;   980
Slowstepping feet and the common features, and the common modes and
    emanations,
They descend in new forms from the tips of his fingers,
They are wafted with the odor of his body or breath .... they fly out of the glance
    of his eyes.

Flaunt of the sunshine I need not your bask .... lie over,
You light surfaces only .... I force the surfaces and the depths also.   985

Earth! you seem to look for something at my hands,
Say old topknot! what do you want?

Man or woman! I might tell how I like you, but cannot,
And might tell what it is in me and what it is in you, but cannot,
And might tell the pinings I have .... the pulse of my nights and days.   990

Behold I do not give lectures or a little charity,
What I give I give out of myself.

You there, impotent, loose in the knees, open your scarfed chops till I blow grit
    within you,
Spread your palms and lift the flaps of your pockets,
I am not to be denied .... I compel .... I have stores plenty and to spare,   995
And any thing I have I bestow.

I do not ask who you are .... that is not important to me,
You can do nothing and be nothing but what I will infold you.

To a drudge of the cottonfields or emptier of privies I lean .... on his right cheek
    I put the family kiss,
And in my soul I swear I never will deny him.   1000

On women fit for conception I start bigger and nimbler babes,
This day I am jetting the stuff of far more arrogant republics.

To any one dying .... thither I speed and twist the knob of the door,
Turn the bedclothes toward the foot of the bed,
Let the physician and the priest go home.   1005

I seize the descending man .... I raise him with resistless will.

O despairer, here is my neck,
By God! you shall not go down! Hang your whole weight upon me.

I dilate you with tremendous breath .... I buoy you up;
Every room of the house do I fill with an armed force .... lovers of me, bafflers
    of graves: 1010
Sleep! I and they keep guard all night;
Not doubt, not decease shall dare to lay finger upon you,
I have embraced you, and henceforth possess you to myself,
And when you rise in the morning you will find what I tell you is so.

I am he bringing help for the sick as they pant on their backs,   1015
And for strong upright men I bring yet more needed help.

I heard what was said of the universe,
Heard it and heard of several thousand years;
It is middling well as far as it goes .... but is that all?

Magnifying and applying come I,   1020
Outbidding at the start the old cautious hucksters,
The most they offer for mankind and eternity less than a spirt of my own
    seminal wet,
Taking myself the exact dimensions of Jehovah and laying them away,
Lithographing Kronos and Zeus his son, and Hercules his grandson,
Buying drafts of Osiris and Isis and Belus and Brahma and Adonai,   1025
In my portfolio placing Manito loose, and Allah on a leaf, and the crucifix
    engraved,
With Odin, and the hideous-faced Mexitli, and all idols and images,[22]
Honestly taking them all for what they are worth, and not a cent more,
Admitting they were alive and did the work of their day,
Admitting they bore mites as for unfledged birds who have now to rise and fly
    and sing for themselves,   1030
Accepting the rough deific sketches to fill out better in myself .... bestowing
    them freely on each man and woman I see,
Discovering as much or more in a framer framing a house,
Putting higher claims for him there with his rolled-up sleeves, driving the mallet
    and chisel;
Not objecting to special revelations .... considering a curl of smoke or a hair on
    the back of my hand as curious as any revelation;
Those ahold of fire-engines and hook-and-ladder ropes more to me than the gods
    of the antique wars,   1035
Minding their voices peal through the crash of destruction,
Their brawny limbs passing safe over charred laths .... their white foreheads
    whole and unhurt out of the flames;
By the mechanic's wife with her babe at her nipple interceding for every person
    born;
Three scythes at harvest whizzing in a row from three lusty angels with shirts
    bagged out at their waists;

---

22. Whitman lists gods from many of the world's religions.

The snag-toothed hostler with red hair redeeming sins past and to come,   1040
Selling all he possesses and traveling on foot to fee lawyers for his brother and
    sit by him while he is tried for forgery:
What was strewn in the amplest strewing the square rod about me, and not filling
    the square rod then;
The bull and the bug never worshipped half enough,
Dung and dirt more admirable than was dreamed,
The supernatural of no account .... myself waiting my time to be one of the
    supremes,   1045
The day getting ready for me when I shall do as much good as the best, and be
    as prodigious,
Guessing when I am it will not tickle me much to receive puffs out of pulpit
    or print;
By my life-lumps! becoming already a creator!
Putting myself here and now to the ambushed womb of the shadows! . . .

I do not despise you priests;
My faith is the greatest of faiths and the least of faiths,
Enclosing all worship ancient and modern, and all between ancient and modern,
Believing I shall come again upon the earth after five thousand
    years,   1095
Waiting responses from oracles .... honoring the gods .... saluting the sun,
Making a fetish of the first rock or stump .... powowing with sticks in the circle
    of obis,[23]
Helping the lama[24] or brahmin as he trims the lamps of the idols,
Dancing yet through the streets in a phallic procession .... rapt and austere in the
    woods, a gymnosophist,[25]
Drinking mead from the skull-cup .... to shasta[26] and vedas admirant .... minding
    the koran,   1100
Walking the teokallis,[27] spotted with gore from the stone and knife—beating the
    serpent-skin drum;
Accepting the gospels, accepting him that was crucified, knowing assuredly that
    he is divine,
To the mass kneeling—to the puritan's prayer rising—sitting patiently in a pew,
Ranting and frothing in my insane crisis—waiting dead-like till my spirit arouses
    me;
Looking forth on pavement and land, and outside of pavement and land,   1105
Belonging to the winders of the circuit of circuits.

One of that centripetal and centrifugal gang,
I turn and talk like a man leaving charges before a journey.

Down-hearted doubters, dull and excluded,
Frivolous sullen moping angry affected disheartened atheistical,   1110

---

23. West African witchcraft and sorcery.   24. A Buddhist monk.   25. Hindu ascetic.   26. Shastras and Vedas, Hindu
sacred writings.   27. Aztec temple.

I know every one of you, and know the unspoken interrogatories,
By experience I know them.

How the flukes splash!
How they contort rapid as lightning, with spasms and spouts of blood!

Be at peace bloody flukes of doubters and sullen mopers,   1115
I take my place among you as much as among any;
The past is the push of you and me and all precisely the same,
And the day and night is for you and me and all,
And what is yet untried and afterward is for you and me and all.

I do not know what is untried and afterward,   1120
But I know it is sure and alive, and sufficient.

Each who passes is considered, and each who stops is considered, and not a
      single one can it fail.
It cannot fail the young man who died and was buried,
Nor the young woman who died and was put by his side,
Nor the little child that peeped in at the door and then drew back and was
      never seen again,   1125
Nor the old man who has lived without purpose, and feels it with bitterness
      worse than gall,
Nor him in the poorhouse tubercled by rum and the bad disorder,
Nor the numberless slaughtered and wrecked .... nor the brutish koboo,[28] called
      the ordure of humanity,
Nor the sacs merely floating with open mouths for food to slip in,
Nor any thing in the earth, or down in the oldest graves of the earth,   1130
Nor any thing in the myriads of spheres, nor one of the myriads of myriads
      that inhabit them,
Nor the present, nor the least wisp that is known. . . .

I am the teacher of athletes,
He that by me spreads a wider breast than my own proves the width of my own,
He most honors my style who learns under it to destroy the teacher.

The boy I love, the same becomes a man not through derived power but in his
      own right,
Wicked, rather than virtuous out of conformity or fear,   1235
Fond of his sweetheart, relishing well his steak,
Unrequited love or a slight cutting him worse than a wound cuts,
First rate to ride, to fight, to hit the bull's eye, to sail a skiff, to sing a song or
      play on the banjo,
Preferring scars and faces pitted with smallpox over all latherers and those that
      keep out of the sun.

---

28. Sumatran native.

I teach straying from me, yet who can stray from me?   1240
I follow you whoever you are from the present hour;
My words itch at your ears till you understand them.

I do not say these things for a dollar, or to fill up the time while I wait for
     a boat;
It is you talking just as much as myself .... I act as the tongue of you,
It was tied in your mouth .... in mine it begins to be loosened.   1245

I swear I will never mention love or death inside a house,
And I swear I never will translate myself at all, only to him or her who privately
     stays with me in the open air.

If you would understand me go to the heights or water-shore,
The nearest gnat is an explanation and a drop or the motion of waves a key,
The maul the oar and the handsaw second my words.   1250

No shuttered room or school can commune with me,
But roughs and little children better than they.

The young mechanic is closest to me .... he knows me pretty well,
The woodman that takes his axe and jug with him shall take me with him all day,
The farmboy ploughing in the field feels good at the sound of my voice,   1255
In vessels that sail my words must sail .... I go with fishermen and seamen, and
     love them,
My face rubs to the hunter's face when he lies down alone in his blanket,
The driver thinking of me does not mind the jolt of his wagon,
The young mother and old mother shall comprehend me,
The girl and the wife rest the needle a moment and forget where they are,   1260
They and all would resume what I have told them.

I have said that the soul is not more than the body,
And I have said that the body is not more than the soul,
And nothing, not God, is greater to one than one's-self is,
And whoever walks a furlong without sympathy walks to his own funeral,
     dressed in his shroud,   1265
And I or you pocketless of a dime may purchase the pick of the earth,
And to glance with an eye or show a bean in its pod confounds the learning of
     all times,
And there is no trade or employment but the young man following it may
     become a hero,
And there is no object so soft but it makes a hub for the wheeled universe,
And any man or woman shall stand cool and supercilious before a million
     universes.   1270

And I call to mankind, Be not curious about God,
For I who am curious about each am not curious about God,
No array of terms can say how much I am at peace about God and about death.

I hear and behold God in every object, yet I understand God not in the least, 1275
Nor do I understand who there can be more wonderful than myself.

Why should I wish to see God better than this day?
I see something of God each hour of the twenty-four, and each moment then,
In the faces of men and women I see God, and in my own face in the glass;
I find letters from God dropped in the street, and every one is signed by God's name,
And I leave them where they are, for I know that others will punctually come
forever and ever. 1280

And as to you death, and you bitter hug of mortality .... it is idle to try to alarm me.
To his work without flinching the accoucheur[29] comes,
I see the elderhand pressing receiving supporting,
I recline by the sills of the exquisite flexible doors .... and mark the outlet, and
mark the relief and escape.

And as to you corpse I think you are good manure, but that does not
offend me, 1285
I smell the white roses sweetscented and growing,
I reach to the leafy lips .... I reach to the polished breasts of melons.

And as to you life, I reckon you are the leavings of many deaths,
No doubt I have died myself ten thousand times before.

I hear you whispering there O stars of heaven, 1290
O suns .... O grass of graves .... O perpetual transfers and promotions .... if
you do not say anything how can I say anything?

Of the turbid pool that lies in the autumn forest,
Of the moon that descends the steeps of the soughing twilight,
Toss, sparkles of day and dusk .... toss on the black stems that decay in the muck,
Toss to the moaning gibberish of the dry limbs. 1295

I ascend from the moon .... I ascend from the night,
And perceive of the ghastly glitter the sunbeams reflected,
And debouch[30] to the steady and central from the offspring great or small.

There is that in me .... I do not know what it is .... but I know it is in me.

Wrenched and sweaty .... calm and cool then my body becomes; 1300
I sleep .... I sleep long.

I do not know it .... it is without name .... it is a word unsaid,
It is not in any dictionary or utterance or symbol.

Something it swings on more than the earth I swing on,
To it the creation is the friend whose embracing awakes me. 1305

---

29. Midwife.   30. Pour forth.

Perhaps I might tell more .... Outlines! I plead for my brothers and sisters.

Do you see O my brothers and sisters?
It is not chaos or death .... it is form and union and plan .... it is eternal life ....
    it is happiness.

The past and present wilt .... I have filled them and emptied them,
And proceed to fill my next fold of the future.   1310

Listener up there! Here you .... what have you to confide to me?
Look in my face while I snuff the sidle of evening,
Talk honestly, for no one else hears you, and I stay only a minute longer.

Do I contradict myself?
Very well then .... I contradict myself;   1315
I am large .... I contain multitudes.

I concentrate toward them that are nigh .... I wait on the door-slab.

Who has done his day's work and will soonest be through with his supper?
Who wishes to walk with me?

Will you speak before I am gone? Will you prove already too late?   1320

The spotted hawk swoops by and accuses me .... he complains of my gab and
    my loitering.

I too am not a bit tamed .... I too am untranslatable,
I sound my barbaric yawp over the roofs of the world.

The last scud of day holds back for me,
It flings my likeness after the rest and true as any on the shadowed wilds,   1325
It coaxes me to the vapor and the dusk.

I depart as air .... I shake my white locks at the runaway sun,
I effuse my flesh in eddies and drift it in lacy jags.

I bequeath myself to the dirt to grow from the grass I love,
If you want me again look for me under your bootsoles.   1330

You will hardly know who I am or what I mean,
But I shall be good health to you nevertheless,
And filter and fibre your blood.
Failing to fetch me at first keep encouraged,
Missing me one place search another,   1335
I stop some where waiting for you [31]

                                                     —1855

---

31. There is no period at the end of this poem in the 1855 *Leaves of Grass*.

Frances Ellen Watkins Harper
1825–1911

In the last line of the first stanza of "Ethiopia," Frances Ellen Watkins Harper alludes to Psalm 68, a central part of African American theology of liberation.

> Yes! Ethiopia yet shall stretch
>   Her bleeding hands abroad
> Her cry of agony shall reach
>   The burning throne of God! . . .
> Redeemed from dust and freed from chains
>   Her sons shall lift their eyes
> From cloud-capt hills and verdant plains
>   Shall shouts of triumph rise.

In this work, Harper sets up a transatlantic African identity, as all the people whose roots are in Africa are eventually freed through God's will. "Ethiopia" was to help bring this prophecy to fruition; like many of her other poems, it was published in abolitionist papers.

    Unlike Harriet Jacobs, Frederick Douglass, and other African American abolitionists who were born into slavery, Harper was born "free" in the slave state of Maryland. Orphaned at a young age, Harper's early years centered around her uncle, William Watkins, and his school, where she was educated. Her academic excellence led to her being the first woman teacher in the African Methodist Episcopal Church of Ohio's Union Seminary. After teaching at another institution in Pennsylvania, Harper decided to lead and enrich people in another way: by devoting her time and energy to the abolition of slavery. And it is in the service of this cause that she penned a poem in response to Harriet Beecher Stowe's *Uncle Tom's Cabin* (1852) entitled "Eliza Harris" (1853). Her time spent teaching served her well, as she would teach Americans about the evils of slavery and the necessity of emancipation, lecturing in many cities throughout the autumn of 1854. Her activism brought her into contact with several abolitionists of international fame, including Frederick Douglass and William Lloyd Garrison, in whose journals her poems found a home and a national audience. She also traveled to Canada, the terminus of the Underground Railroad, to garner support for the movement. She grew increasingly radical in her politics and supported John Brown, who was sentenced to death for gathering together a militia to attack West Virginia's Harper's Ferry and to free slaves, an action condemned by many moderates who considered themselves abolitionists. Through her efforts, money was raised for Brown's imprisoned helpers and their families. Her poem "Bury Me in a Free Land" (1872), which she wrote as part of a letter to one of the incarcerated men, later gained a wider audience in the *Liberator*. This poem speaks to the horrible legalized violence of slavery—"I could not rest, if I saw the lash / Drinking . . . blood at each fearful gash"—and addresses the hypocrisy of the government in legally punishing Brown and his followers but not the cruelty of masters and overseers. Her advocacy was key to mobilizing support for the Civil War, after which she was able to hear the "shouts of triumph rise" from the mouths of former slaves.

    During the time leading up to (as well as the time after) the Civil War, Harper's life was devoted to unifying humanity in the cause of equal rights. Prior to the war, she had published abolitionist poems in the *Anglo-American Magazine* and had worked with feminists such as Sojourner Truth and Elizabeth Cady Stanton to bring about universal suffrage (the right for all people to vote). When various civil rights groups began to factionalize over whether black men or white women should be enfranchised first, she reminded them, as did Sojourner Truth, that they were leaving black women out of the picture and that we "are all bound up together in one great bundle of humanity." While the Civil War was being waged, Frances married Fenton Harper. By 1864, he was dead, only four years after they were wed. During the next seven years, Harper actively lectured to provide for herself and her then fatherless child, Mary. Once again she devoted herself to overcoming divisions, this time between the North and the newly freed South as well as between African Americans and European Americans, noting that between "the white people and the colored there is a community of interests, and the sooner they find it out, the better it will be for both parties."

As always, Harper continued to accomplish her ends through publication. In 1869, she published a novel, *Minnie's Sacrifice*, and a collection of poems, *Moses: A Story of the Nile*. Another collection simply entitled *Poems* appeared in 1871. A year later, she distilled her experience in and knowledge of the South during Reconstruction in *Sketches of Southern Life*. By this time, she was living in Philadelphia. She also returned to publishing in newspapers, contributing to a column called "Fancy Sketches." She remained incredibly prolific throughout the remaining years of the nineteenth century and published many more novels and collections of poetry. By the time of her death in 1911, she had lived though slavery, the Civil War, and Reconstruction; had seen the nineteenth century wane and the twentieth wax; and had earned many honors and distinctions by working toward equality through unity to the last. Thanks to her own efforts and those of other abolitionists, she was granted what she had in earlier life so fervently hoped for:

> I ask no monument, proud and high,
> To arrest the gaze of the passers by
> All that my yearning spirit craves
> Is—*Bury me not in a land of slaves!*

The Slave Mother

Heard you that shriek? It rose
   So wildly on the air,
It seemed as if a burdened heart
   Was breaking in despair.

Saw you those hands so sadly clasped—   5
   The bowed and feeble head—
The shuddering of that fragile form—
   That look of grief and dread?

Saw you the sad, imploring eye?
   Its every glance was pain,   10
As if a storm of agony
   Were sweeping through the brain.

She is a mother, pale with fear,
   Her boy clings to her side,
And in her kirtle[1] vainly tries   15
   His trembling form to hide.

---

1. Gown.

He is not hers, although she bore
   For him a mother's pains;
He is not hers, although her blood
   Is coursing through his veins!   20

He is not hers, for cruel hands
   May rudely tear apart
The only wreath of household love
   That binds her breaking heart.

His love has been a joyous light   25
   That o'er her pathway smiled,
A fountain gushing ever new,
   Amid life's desert wild.

His lightest word has been a tone
   Of music round her heart,   30
Their lives a streamlet blent in one—
   Oh, Father! must they part?

They tear him from her circling arms.
   Her last and fond embrace.
Oh! never more may her sad eyes   35
   Gaze on his mournful face.

No marvel, then, these bitter shrieks
   Disturb the listening air;
She is a mother, and her heart
   Is breaking in despair.   40

—1854

Learning to Read

Very soon the Yankee teachers
   Came down and set up school;
But, oh! how the Rebs[1] did hate it—
   It was agin' their rule.

Our masters always tried to hide   5
   Book learning from our eyes;
Knowledge didn't agree with slavery—
   'Twould make us all too wise.

But some of us would try to steal
   A little from the book,   10
And put the words together,
   And learn by hook or crook.

---

1. Confederate Army during the Civil War.

I remember Uncle Caldwell,
    Who took pot liquor[2] fat
And greased the pages of his book,
    And hid it in his hat

And had his master ever seen
    The leaves upon his head,   15
He'd have thought them greasy papers,
    But nothing to be read.   20

And there was Mr. Turner's Ben,
    Who heard the children spell,
And picked the words right up by heart,
    And learned to read 'em well.

Well, the Northern folks kept sending   25
    The Yankee teachers down;
And they stood right up and helped us,
    Though Rebs did sneer and frown.

And, I longed to read my Bible,
    For precious words it said;   30
But when I begun to learn it,
    Folks just shook their heads,

And said there is no use trying,
    Oh! Chloe, you're too late;
But as I was rising sixty,   35
    I had no time to wait.

So I got a pair of glasses,
    And straight to work I went,
And never stopped till I could read
    The hymns and Testament.   40

Then I got a little cabin
    A place to call my own—
And I felt as independent
    As the queen upon her throne.

—1872

Free Labor

I wear an easy garment,
    O'er it no toiling slave
Wept tears of hopeless anguish,
    In his passage to the grave.

---

2. Broth.

And from its ample folds
  Shall rise no cry to God,
Upon its warp and woof[1] shall be
  No stain of tears and blood.

Oh, lightly shall it press my form,
  Unladen with a sigh,
I shall not 'mid its rustling hear,
  Some sad despairing cry.

This fabric is too light to bear
  The weight of bondsmen's tears,
I shall not in its texture trace
  The agony of years.

Too light to bear a smothered sigh,
  From some lorn woman's heart,
Whose only wreath of household love
  Is rudely torn apart.

Then lightly shall it press my form,
  Unburdened by a sigh;
And from its seams and folds shall rise,
  No voice to pierce the sky,

And witness at the throne of God,
  In language deep and strong,
That I have nerved Oppression's hand,
  For deeds of guilt and wrong.

—1874

An Appeal to My Country Women

You can sigh o'er the sad-eyed Armenian
  Who weeps in her desolate home.
You can mourn o'er the exile of Russia
  From kindred and friends doomed to roam.

You can pity the men who have woven
  From passion and appetite chains
To coil with a terrible tension
  Around their heartstrings and brains.

You can sorrow o'er little children
  Disinherited from their birth,
The wee waifs and toddlers neglected,
  Robbed of sunshine, music and mirth.

---

1. The vertical and horizontal threads in a woven garment.

For beasts you have gentle compassion;
   Your mercy and pity they share.
For the wretched, outcast and fallen   15
   You have tenderness, love and care.

But hark! from our Southland are floating
   Sobs of anguish, murmurs of pain,
And women heart-stricken are weeping
   Over their tortured and their slain.   20

On their brows the sun has left traces;
   Shrink not from their sorrow in scorn.
When they entered the threshold of being
   The children of a King were born.

Each comes as a guest to the table   25
   The hands of our God has outspread,
To fountains that ever leap upward,
   To share in the soil we all tread.

When we plead for the wrecked and fallen,
   The exile from far-distant shores,
Remember that men are still wasting   30
   Life's crimson around our own doors.

Have ye not, oh, my favored sisters,
   Just a plea, a prayer or a tear,
For mothers who dwell 'neath the shadows   35
   Of agony, hatred and fear?

Men may tread down the poor and lowly,
   May crush them in anger and hate,
But surely the mills of God's justice
   Will grind out the grist of their fate.   40

Oh, people sin-laden and guilty,
   So lusty and proud in your prime,
The sharp sickles of God's retribution
   Will gather your harvest of crime.

Weep not, oh my well-sheltered sisters,   45
   Weep not for the Negro alone,
But weep for your sons who must gather
   The crops which their fathers have sown.

Go read on the tombstones of nations
   Of chieftains who masterful trod,   50
The sentence which time has engraven,
   That they had forgotten their God.

'Tis the judgment of God that men reap
    The tares[1] which in madness they sow,
Sorrow follows the footsteps of crime,
    And Sin is the consort of Woe.

—1894

Thomas D'Arcy McGee
1825–1868

Born in Ireland, McGee was an active supporter of the national liberation movements that eventually freed much of Ireland from the yoke of English rule. Throughout his active political and journalistic careers he stirred controversy, shifting ideological positions several times, embarrassing and outraging allies. He was elected a member of Assembly in 1858, changed political parties to great advantage, served as minister of agriculture, and helped build the foundation for Canadian Confederation in 1867. His reversal of opinion late in life—denouncing the Irish Republicanism he vocally advocated in his youth—led to his assassination in Ottawa on April 7, 1868 at the hands of the Fenians, a secret society founded in the United States in 1858 that lobbied and protested politically (sometimes violently) for Irish freedom.

McGee was one of over ninety thousand Irish immigrants who came to North America in 1842—the largest number in a single year prior to the great famine of 1845–1850. The "Great Hunger," caused by a potato fungus that was inadvertently carried from North America to Europe, saw the population of Ireland fall from eight to six and a half million people. Half died of starvation, and half left Ireland for destinations around the globe. McGee arrived in Boston and began working for a Catholic newspaper. He would spend the majority of his life working in different capacities for a number of newspapers in America, Canada, and Ireland, even establishing his own: the *New York Nation*, the *American Celt* (Boston), and *The New Era* (Montreal). The steady stream of poetry and essays he produced on political and cultural topics, as well as the numerous nonfiction volumes (histories of Ireland, the Irish in North America, and Catholics in North America, among others), reveals a capacious mind. *The Mental Outfit of the New Dominion* (1867), published in the year of Canadian Confederation, attempts to establish a national literature and to parry the cultural thrust of American literature and culture into pre-Confederation Canada, revealing McGee's worries about the dangers of "the Americanization of the future inhabitants of Canada West."

The Mental Outfit of the New Dominion

Before the Montreal Literary Club,
November 4th, 1867

Mr. President and Gentlemen:

    I propose . . . to consider now, on the eve of our first Dominion Parliament, with what intellectual forces and appliances, with what quantity and kind of men-

---

1. Weeds.

tal common stock, we are about to set up for ourselves a distinct national existence in North America. . . .

Regarding the New Dominion as an incipient new nation, it seems to me that our mental self-reliance is an essential condition of our political independence; I do not mean a state of public mind puffed up on small things; an exaggerated opinion of ourselves and a barbarian depreciation of foreigners; a controversial state of mind; or a merely imitative apish civilization. I mean a mental condition, thoughtful and true; national in its preferences, but catholic[1] in its sympathies; gravitating inward, not outward; ready to learn from every other people on one sole condition, that the lesson when learned has been worth acquiring. In short, I would desire to see, Gentlemen, our new national character distinguished by a manly modesty as much as by mental independence; by the conscientious exercise of the critical faculties, as well as by the zeal of the inquirer. . . .

God speed the trowel and the plumb-line, as well as the loom, the plough and the anvil. But dream not . . . that great cities are built chiefly by stone-masons. Let me give you an illustration of the contrary fact. Take Boston and Montreal, for example, in their actual relations. Boston has some advantages in size and wealth, but it has another and a nobler sort of superiority; it is the vicinage of native poets like Longfellow and Lowell[2]; or orators like Wendell Phillips; of a sort of Leipsig[3] commerce in books, if not the largest in quantity, the most valuable in quality, of any carried on in the New World. Take a thousand of the most intelligent of our citizens, and you will find that Boston books and Boston utterances sway the minds of one-half of them; while Montreal is, I fear, absolutely unknown and unfelt, as an intellectual community in Boston and elsewhere. Far be it from me to disparage our own city; I cordially concur in the honest pride of every inhabitant, in the strong masonry and fine style of our new edifices. But if "stone walls do not a prison make,"[4] still less do they make a capital—a ruling city—a seat of light and guidance, and authority, to a nation or a generation. When the Parliamentary Buildings were finished at Ottawa, one of the first problems was to regulate the heating apparatus, in short to make them habitable for half the year; and this precisely is the problem with us in relation to another and equally necessary kind of plenishing and furnishing, for town and country. It remains for us to learn whether we have the internal heat, and light, to stand alone, and go alone—as go we must, either alone or with a master, leading us by the hand. . . .

Our reading supplies are, as you know, drawn chiefly from two sources; first, books, which are imported from the United States, England and France—a foreign supply likely long to continue foreign. The second source is our newspaper literature, chiefly supplied . . . from among ourselves, but largely supplemented by English and American journals.

I shall not be accused of flattering anyone when I say that I consider our press tolerably free from the licence which too often degrades and enfeebles the authority of the free press of the United States. Ours is chiefly to blame for the provincial narrowness of its views; for its localism and egotism; for the absence of a large and gen-

---

1. All-embracing.   2. Henry Wadsworth Longfellow (1807–1882) and James Russell Lowell (1819–1891), American poets.
3. Industrial and cultured German city.   4. Richard Lovelace (1618–1657), "To Althea, From Prison" (1649).

erous catholicity of spirit; both in the selection of its subjects and their treatment; for a rather servile dependence for its opinions of foreign affairs, on the leading newspapers of New York and London. . . .

This newspaper literature forms by much the largest part of our general reading. There are in the four united provinces about one hundred and thirty journals, of which thirty at least are published daily. . . .

As to the other branch of supply I believe our booksellers have nothing to complain of. The sale of books is on the increase, though not at all so largely as the sale of newspapers. Our books are mainly English or American reprints of English originals. In point of price the editions are not so far apart as they were on the other side of the Civil War. As to the classes of books most in request, I have been informed by one of our members well informed on the matter, that the sales may be divided somewhat in these proportions: religious books, 18 per cent.; poetical works, 10 per cent.; books on historical, scientific and literary subjects 28 per cent.; and works of fiction 44 per cent. My obliging informant (Mr. Samuel Dawson[5]) adds in relation to the comparative money value of the several classes of books most in demand, the historical, scientific and literary works would represent about 45 per cent., the works of fiction 22, the poetical 15, and the religious 18 per cent. of the whole. We thus have this striking result that, whereas the works of fiction are, in volume, nearly one-half of all the reading done among us, in cost they come to less than one-fourth what is expended for other and better books. . . .

Mention must be made, Gentlemen, of those institutions of learning, and those learned professional classes which ought, and doubtless do, leaven the whole lump of our material progress. We have already twelve Universities in the Dominion—perhaps more than enough, though dispersed at long distances—as from Windsor and Fredericton to Cobourg and Toronto. . . .

Of the learned professions which represent in the world to a large extent these native colleges and universities, there are, probably, in the Dominion above 3,000 clergyman, 2,500 medical men, and perhaps (this is a guess) from 500 to 600 lawyers; say, apart from collegiate professors, 6,000 essentially "educated men." The special requirements of this large body of men, in languages, laws, history, dialectics, chemistry, and *belles lettres*, ought surely not to be confined solely within the rigid limits of professional occupation; but ought, at least occasionally, to flow out in secular channels for the benefit of lay societies, and the general elevation of the public taste. . . .

From all these sources—our numerous reading classes—our colleges—our learned professions—we ought to be able to give a good account of the mental outfit of the new Dominion. Well, then, for one of those expected to say what he thinks in these matters, I must give it as my opinion that we have as yet but few possessions in this sort that we can call our own. We have not produced in our Colonial era any thinker of the reputation of Jonathan Edwards, or Benjamin Franklin; nor any native poet of the rank of Garcilaso de la Vega—the Spanish American.[6] The only sustained poems we have of which the scenes are laid within the Dominion are both by Americans, Longfellow's "Evangeline" and Mr. Street's "Frontenac"—the latter much

---

5. A Montreal bookseller.   6. Jonathan Edwards (1703–1758), American minister; Benjamin Franklin (1706–1790), American statesman; Garcilaso de la Vega (1503–1536), Spanish poet.

less read than it deserves. One original humourist we have had, hardly of the highest order, however, in the late Judge Haliburton[7]; one historian of an undoubtedly high order, in the late Mr. Garneau; one geologist, Sr. William Logan; but, as yet, no poet, no orator, no critic, of either American or European reputation.

About a century ago an eminent French writer raised a doubt as to whether any German could be a literary man. Not, indeed, to answer that, but many others, arose as a golden cloud that gifted succession of poets, critics, and scholars, whose works have placed the German language in the vanguard of every department of human thought. Thirty years ago a *British Quarterly Review* asked: "Who reads an American book?" Irving had answered that long ago; but Longfellow, Cooper, Emerson, Prescott, Hawthorne, Holmes, and many another, has answered the taunt triumphantly since. Those Americans might, in turn, taunt us to-day with "Who reads a Canadian book?" I should answer frankly, very few, for Canadian books are exceedingly scarce. Still, we are not entirely destitute of resident writers. Dr. Dawson has given the world a work on his favourite science, which has established his name as an authority: Dr. Daniel Wilson's[8] speculations and researches on Prehistoric Man have received the approval of high names; Mr. Alpheus Todd has given us a masterly and original treatise on Parliamentary Government, which will be read and quoted wherever there is constitutional government in the world; Heavysege, Sangster, and McLachlan, are not without honour. An amiable friend of mine, Mr. J. LeMoine of Quebec, has given the world many "Maple Leaves" worthy of all praise—the only thoroughly Canadian book in point of subject which has appeared of late days, and for which, I am ashamed to say, the author has not received that encouragement his labours deserve. If he were not an enthusiast he might well have become a misanthrope, as to native literature, at least. Another most deserving man in a different walk—a younger man—but a man of very untired industry and laudable ambition—Mr. Henry J. Morgan, now of Ottawa, announces a new book of reference, *The Bibliotheca Canadensis*,[9] which I trust will repay him for the enormous labour of such a compilation. . . .

I believe the existence of a recognized literary class will by and by be felt as a state and social necessity. The books that are made elsewhere, even in England, are not always the best fitted for us; they do not always run on the same mental gauge, nor connect with our trains of thought; they do not take us up at the by-stages of cultivation at which we have arrived, and where we are emptied forth as on a barren, pathless, habitationless heath. They are books of another state of society, bearing traces of controversies, or directed against errors or evils which for us hardly exist, except in the pages of these exotic books. Observe, I do not object to such books, especially when truthfully written; but it seems to me we do much need several other books calculated to our own meridian, and hitting home to our own society, either where it is sluggish or priggish, or wholly defective in its present style of culture.

If English-made books do not mortice[10] closely with our Colonial deficiencies, still less do American national books. I speak not here of such literary universalists as Irving, Emerson and Longfellow; but of such American nationalists as Hawthorne, Bancroft, Brownson, Draper, and their latter prose writers generally.

---

7. Thomas Chandler Haliburton (1796–1865).   8. Archaeologist and President of University of Toronto (1816–1892).
9. *Bibliography of Canadian Literature* (1867).   10. Fit.

Within the last few years, especially since the era of the Civil War, there has been a craving desire to assert the mental independence of America as against England; to infuse an American philosophy of life, and philosophy of government, into every American writing and work of art. Mr. Bancroft's oration on the death of Mr. Lincoln was an example fo this new spirit; and Dr. Draper's *Civil Policy of America* affords another illustration. It is a natural ambition for them to endeavour to Americanize their literature more and more; all nations have felt the same ambition, earlier or later; so Rome wearied of borrowing from the Greeks, and so Germany revolted a century ago against French philosophy, French romances and a Frenchified drama; so the sceptre of mind passed for a time from Berlin to Weimar, and of late only by annexation has it gone back to Berlin. No one complains of this revolution. As long as justice, and courtesy, and magnanimity are not sacrificed to an intolerant nationalism, the growth of new literary States must be to the increase of the universal literary Republic. . . .

It is quite clear to me that if we are to succeed with our new Dominion, it can never be by accepting a ready-made easy literature, which assumes Bostonian culture to be the worship of the future, and the American democratic system to be the manifestly destined form of government for all the civilized world, new as well as old. . . .

It is usual to say of ourselves, Gentlemen, that we are entering on a new era. It may be so, or it may be only the mirage of an era painted on an exhalation of self-opinion. Such eras, however, have come for other civilized States, why not for us also? There came for Germany the Swabian era, the era of Luther, and the era of Goethe; for modern Italy the age of Leo X; for France the age of Louis XIV; in our own history there have been an Elizabethan and a Georgian era; and perhaps there is at hand an American era, in ideas, in manners, and in politics. How far we, who are to represent British ethics and British culture in America—we, whose new Constitution solemnly proclaims "the well-understood principles of the British Constitution"; how far we are to make this probable next era our own—either by adhesion or resistance—is what, Gentlemen, we must all determine for ourselves, and so fare forth, for the Dominion. . . .

—1867

Emily Dickinson
1830–1886

"I must tell you about the *character* of Amherst," writes Mabel Loomis Todd of Emily Dickinson in 1881:

> It is a lady whom all the people call the *Myth*. . . . She has not been outside her house in fifteen years, except once to see a new church, when she crept out at night, & viewed it by moonlight. No one who calls upon her mother & sister ever sees her, but

she allows little children once in a great while, & one at a time, to come in, when she gives them cake or candy, or some nicety, for she is very fond of little ones. But more often she lets down the sweetmeat by a string, out of a window, to them. She dresses wholly in white, & her mind is said to be perfectly wonderful. She writes finely, but no one *ever* sees her. [Her sister] invited me to come & sing to her mother sometime. . . . People tell me the *myth* will hear every note—she will be near, but unseen. . . . Isn't that like a book? So interesting.

An aspiring novelist, Todd had moved to Amherst, Massachusetts, where her husband had taken up an astronomy professorship at Amherst College. The couple was welcomed into the Dickinson household, and within a year Dickinson and Todd began a friendship that was almost entirely textual since Todd, as she writes above, never saw Dickinson; the two corresponded only. Todd captures—albeit melodramatically—the dominant image of Dickinson as a quiet, reclusive genius that has colored popular perception of the poet since her poetry was first published in 1890, four years after her death. The circumstances of Dickinson's life, however, have yielded more fanciful and negative images as well, also suggested in Todd's account: The poet is often represented as an anti-social creature of the night, a madwoman living in the attic.

Dickinson's poetry reveals the degree to which she shunned public life: "How dreary— to be—Somebody! / How public—like a Frog— / To tell one's name." The extent of her literary production was unknown to her family. After her death, her sister found 900 poems neatly bundled together with twine in a bureau drawer. Eleven poems were published in her lifetime, and while the poetry presented in this anthology remained unpublished, Dickinson was engaged in a deeply personal poetic project that was transatlantic in scope. In the close to 1,800 poems she penned, Dickinson attempts to make sense of the literary, political, and cultural worlds that surrounded her. She ranged from the classics to the Bible and through the Renaissance to Romantic and Victorian writers. To the editor of the *Atlantic* (and her future publisher), Thomas Wentworth Higginson, Dickinson wrote in April 1862, "For Poets—I have Keats—and Mr and Mrs Browning. For Prose—Mr Ruskin—Sir Thomas Browne—and the Revelations."

Born in Amherst, Dickinson's father was a lawyer who eventually held a seat in Congress. The Dickinson household was prominent politically and socially, and their home was filled with regular visitors. One has a sense in Dickinson's poetry of the sounds of dinner-table debates and mirth carrying up to her as she writes in her second-floor bedroom. Educated at Amherst College, Dickinson went on to Mount Holyoke Female Seminary in 1847 but left after one year. She did not fit spiritually with the school's Christian ideology, and as a friend recounts, when the principal asked students who wanted to be Christians to stand, Dickinson was the only one to remain seated. Following her departure from the Seminary, Dickinson began to withdraw more from social life, spending her time in her father's house with the exception of a few trips: to Washington and Philadelphia in 1855, and to Boston in 1864–1865 (presumably to visit a doctor for treatment of exotropia, an outward-turning eye, which caused decreased vision and sensitivity to light). She does not seem to have left her father's property after this time or to have greeted many visitors, although she corresponded steadily with friends, family, other writers, and editors. Dickinson does seem to have had several romantic attachments, and there has been much speculation about the identity (male and female) of these individuals.

Dickinson honed her skill as a poet throughout the 1850s and 1860s, and her self-training bore fruit in 1862 when she penned 366 poems. Impressed and encouraged by Higginson's article on the craft of writing in the *Atlantic*, Dickinson wrote him, asking him to judge the merit of her work. The two corresponded steadily, with Dickinson figuring him as a mentor from whom she sought guidance (advice, however, to which she never yielded). Higginson was one of the few visitors Dickinson greeted in person. Judging from a letter to his wife on August 16,

1870, Dickinson was as intense in person as she is on the page: "I never was with any one," he wrote, "who drained my nerve power so much. Without touching her, she drew from me. I am glad not to live near her."

Despite his personal reservations, Higginson saw some skill in Dickinson's poetry. Of "I died for Beauty—but was scarce," (#449) he remarks: "one can no more criticize a faulty rhyme here and there than a defect of drawing in one of Blake's pictures." Similarly, the British author Christina Rossetti wrote in a letter of December 1890, "There is a book I might have shown you . . . Poems by Emily Dickinson lately sent me from America—but perhaps you know it. She *had* (for she is dead) a wonderful Blakean gift, but therewithal a startling recklessness of poetic ways of means." Surely the "recklessness" Rossetti has in mind refers to the compressed poetic diction (often witty and punning) and the startling punctuation (inspired by the informality of letters). But the brevity of Dickinson's verse is not the product of spontaneous or careless composition— a flurry of words and dashes committed to the page quickly. Rather, as her manuscripts suggest, Dickinson crafted each carefully, weighing choices in diction, line length, and stanza division.

Rossetti also seems to have registered the visionary quality of Dickinson's work, which like Blake's, is built upon a deeply personal mythology. The sweep of her poems as a whole can be seen as a project on the scale of William Wordsworth's *Prelude* (1850)—to record her interior life, the development of her poetic self:

> The Poets light but Lamps—
> Themselves—go out—
> The Wicks they stimulate—
> If vital Light
>
> Inhere as do the Suns—
> Each Age a Lens
> Disseminating their
> Circumference— (#883)

Writing for Dickinson was both meditative and visceral. She saw her poetry as lyrical, a vehicle for exploring her identity: personal, public, spiritual, and feminine. She often refers to her style as song-like, writing in one letter that her "business is to sing." And on the occasion of her father's passing, she writes of her desire to mourn in the third person: "Let Emily sing for you because she cannot pray." At the same time, poetry should stir a physical reaction. In a letter describing an 1870 meeting with Dickinson, Higginson records her saying, "If I read a book [and] it makes my whole body so cold no fire ever can warm me I know *that* is poetry. If I feel physically as if the top of my head were taken off, I know *that* is poetry. These are the only ways I know it. Is there any other way?"

84: Her breast is fit for pearls

Her breast is fit for pearls,
But I was not a "Diver"—
Her brow is fit for thrones
But I have not a crest.
Her heart is fit for *home*—   5
I—a Sparrow—build there
Sweet of twigs and twine
My perennial nest.

—1894

216: Safe in their Alabaster Chambers [1; *version B*]

Safe in their Alabaster Chambers—
Untouched by morning
And untouched by Noon—
Sleep the meek members of the Resurrection—
Rafter of satin,   5
And Roof of stone.

Light laughs the breeze
In her Castle above them—
Babbles the Bee in a stolid Ear,
Pipe the Sweet Birds in ignorant cadence—   10
Ah, what sagacity perished here!

—1862

216: Safe in their Alabaster Chambers [2; *version E*]

Safe in their Alabaster Chambers—
Untouched by Morning—
And untouched by Noon—
Lie the meek members of the Resurrection—
Rafter of Satin—and Roof of Stone!   5

Grand go the Years—in the Crescent—above them—
Worlds scoop their Arcs—
And Firmaments—row—
Diadems—drop—and Doges—surrender—
Soundless as dots—on a Disc of Snow—   10

—1890

249: Wild nights—Wild nights!

Wild nights—Wild nights!
Were I with thee
Wild Nights should be
Our luxury!

Futile—the winds—   5
To a Heart in port—
Done with the Compass—
Done with the Chart!

Rowing in Eden—
Ah, the Sea!
Might I but moor—tonight—   10
In Thee!

—1891

280: I felt a Funeral, in my Brain

I felt a Funeral, in my Brain,
And Mourners to and fro
Kept treading—treading—till it seemed
That Sense was breaking through—

And when they all were seated,   5
A Service, like a Drum—
Kept beating—beating—till I thought
My Mind was going numb—

And then I heard them lift a Box
And creak across my Soul   10
With those same Boots of Lead, again,
Then Space—began to toll,

As all the Heavens were a Bell,
And Being, but an Ear,
And I, and Silence, some strange Race   15
Wrecked, solitary, here—

And then a Plank in Reason, broke,
And I dropped down, and down—
And hit a World, at every plunge,
And Finished knowing—then—[1]   20

—1896

303: The Soul selects her own Society—

The Soul selects her own Society—
Then—shuts the Door—
To her divine Majority—
Present no more—

Unmoved—she notes the Chariots—pausing—   5
At her low Gate—
Unmoved—an Emperor be kneeling
Upon her Mat—

---

1. In a manuscript, Dickinson added a final line: "Crash—Got through—".

I've known her—from an ample nation—
Choose One—
Then—close the Valves of her attention—   10
Like Stone—

—1890

341: After great pain, a formal feeling comes—

After great pain, a formal feeling comes—
The Nerves sit ceremonious, like Tombs—
The stiff Heart questions 'was it He, that bore,'
And 'Yesterday, or Centuries before'?

The Feet, mechanical, go round—   5
Of Ground, or Air, or Ought—
A Wooden way
Regardless grown,
A Quartz contentment, like a stone—

This is the Hour of Lead—   10
Remembered, if outlived,
As Freezing persons, recollect the Snow—
First—Chill—then Stupor—then the letting go—

—1929

435: Much Madness is divinest Sense—

Much Madness is divinest Sense—
To a discerning Eye—
Much Sense—the starkest Madness—
'Tis the Majority
In this, as All, prevail—   5
Assent—and you are sane—
Demur—you're straightway dangerous—
And handled with a Chain—

—1890

441: This is my letter to the World

This is my letter to the World
That never wrote to Me—
The simple News that Nature told—
With tender Majesty

Her Message is committed   5
To Hands I cannot see—
For love of Her—Sweet—countrymen—
Judge tenderly—of Me

—1890

443: I tie my Hat—I crease my Shawl—

I tie my Hat—I crease my Shawl—
Life's little duties do—precisely—
As the very least
Were infinite—to me—

I put new Blossoms in the Glass—   5
And throw the old—away—
I push a petal from my Gown
That anchored there—I weigh
The time 'twill be till six o'clock
I have so much to do—   10
And yet—Existence—some way back—
Stopped—struck—my ticking—through—
We cannot put Ourself away
As a completed Man
Or Woman—When the Errand's done   15
We came to Flesh—upon—
There may be—Miles on Miles of Nought—
Of Action—sicker far—
To simulate—is stinging work—
To cover what we are   20
From Science—and from Surgery—
Too Telescopic Eyes
To bear on us unshaded—
For their—sake—not for Ours—
'Twould start them—   25
We—could tremble—
But since we got a Bomb—
And held it in our Bosom—
Nay—Hold it—it is calm—

Therefore—we do life's labor—   30
Though life's Reward—be done—
With scrupulous exactness—
To hold our Senses—on—

—1929

465: I heard a Fly buzz—when I died—

I heard a Fly buzz—when I died—
The Stillness in the Room
Was like the Stillness in the Air—
Between the Heaves of Storm—

The Eyes around—had wrung them dry—   5
And Breaths were gathering firm
For that last Onset—when the King
Be witnessed—in the Room—

I willed my Keepsakes—Signed away
What portion of me be   10
Assignable—and then it was
There interposed a Fly—

With Blue—uncertain—stumbling Buzz—
Between the light—and me—
And then the Windows failed—and then   15
I could not see to see—

—1896

518: Her sweet Weight on my Heart a Night

Her sweet Weight on my Heart a Night
Had scarcely deigned to lie—
When, stirring, for Belief's delight,
My Bride had slipped away—

If 'twas a Dream—made solid—just   5
The Heaven to confirm—
Or if Myself were dreamed of Her—
The power to presume—

With Him remain—who unto Me—
Gave—even as to All—   10
A Fiction superseding Faith—
By so much—as 'twas real—

—1945

569: I reckon—When I count at all—

I reckon—When I count at all—
First—Poets—Then the Sun—
Then Summer—Then the Heaven of God—
And then—the List is done—

But, looking back—the First so seems   5
To Comprehend the Whole—
The Others look a needless Show—
So I write—Poets—All—

Their Summer—lasts a Solid Year—
They can afford a Sun   10
The East—would deem extravagant—
And if the Further Heaven—

Be Beautiful as they prepare
For Those who worship Them—
It is too difficult a Grace—   15
To justify the Dream—

                                                                —1929

613: They shut me up in prose—

They shut me up in prose—
As when a little Girl
They put me in the Closet—
Because they liked me "still"—

Still! Could themself have peeped—   5
And seen my Brain—go round—
They might as wise have lodged a Bird
For Treason—in the Pound—

Himself has but to will
And easy as a Star   10
Abolish his Captivity—
And laugh—No more have I—

                                                                —1935

668: "Nature" is what we see—

"Nature" is what we see—
The Hill—the Afternoon—
Squirrel—Eclipse—the Bumble bee—
Nay—Nature is Heaven—
Nature is what we hear—   5
The Bobolink—the Sea—
Thunder—the Cricket—
Nay—Nature is Harmony—
Nature is what we know—

Yet have no art to say—
So impotent Our Wisdom is
To her Simplicity

—1914

709: Publication—is the Auction

Publication—is the Auction
Of the Mind of Man—
Poverty—be justifying
For so foul a thing

Possibly—but We—would rather   5
From Our Garret go
White—Unto the White Creator—
Than invest—Our Snow—

Thought belong to Him who gave it—
Then—to Him Who bear
It's Corporeal illustration—Sell
The Royal Air—

In the Parcel—Be the Merchant
Of the Heavenly Grace—
But reduce no Human Spirit   15
To Disgrace of Price—

—1929

712: Because I could not stop for Death—

Because I could not stop for Death—
He kindly stopped for me—
The Carriage held but just Ourselves—
And Immortality.

We slowly drove—He knew no haste   5
And I had put away
My labor and my leisure too,
For His Civility—

We passed the School, where Children strove
At Recess—in the Ring—   10
We passed the Fields of Gazing Grain—
We passed the Setting Sun—

Or rather—He passed Us—
The Dews drew quivering and Chill—
For only Gossamer, my Gown—   15
My Tippet—only Tulle—

We paused before a House that seemed
A Swelling of the Ground—
The Roof was scarcely visible—
The Cornice—in the Ground—   20

Since then—'tis Centuries—and yet
Feels shorter than the Day
I first surmised the Horses' Heads
Were toward Eternity—

                                                          —1890

754: My Life had stood—a Loaded Gun—

My Life had stood—a Loaded Gun—
In Corners—till a Day
The Owner passed—identified—
And carried Me away—

And now We roam in Sovereign Woods—   5
And now We hunt the Doe—
And every time I speak for Him
The Mountains straight reply—

And do I smile, such cordial light
Upon the Valley glow—   10
It is as a Vesuvian face
Had let its pleasure through—

And when at Night—Our good Day done—
I guard My Master's Head—
'Tis better than the Eider-Duck's   15
Deep Pillow—to have shared—

To foe of His—I'm deadly foe—
None stir the second time—
On whom I lay a Yellow Eye—
Or an emphatic thumb—   20

Though I than He—may longer live
He longer must—than I—
For I have but the power to kill,
Without—the power to die—

                                                          —1929

790: Nature—the Gentlest Mother is

Nature—the Gentlest Mother is,
Impatient of no Child—
The feeblest—or the Waywardest—
Her Admonition mild—

In Forest—and the Hill—   5
By Traveller—be heard—
Restraining Rampant Squirrel—
Or too impetuous Bird—

How fair Her Conversation—
A Summer Afternoon—
Her Household—Her Assembly—   10
And when the Sun go down—

Her Voice among the Aisles
Incite the timid prayer
Of the minutest Cricket—
The most unworthy Flower—   15

When all the Children sleep—
She turns as long away
As will suffice to light Her lamps—
Then bending from the Sky—   20

With infinite Affection—
And infiniter Care—
Her Golden finger on Her lip—
Wills Silence—Everywhere—

                                                              —1891

970: Color—Caste—Denomination—

Color—Caste—Denomination—
These—are Time's Affair—
Death's diviner Classifying
Does not know they are—

As in sleep—All Hue forgotten—
Tenets—put behind—   5
Death's large—Democratic fingers
Rub away the Brand—

If Circassian—He is careless—
If He put away

Chrysalis of Blonde—or Umber—
Equal Butterfly—   10

They emerge from His Obscuring—
What Death—knows so well—
Our minuter intuitions—
Deem unplausible   15

—1929

986: A narrow Fellow in the Grass

A narrow Fellow in the Grass
Occasionally rides—
You may have met Him—did you not
His notice sudden is—

The Grass divides as with a Comb—   5
A spotted shaft is seen—
And then it closes at your feet
And opens further on—

He likes a Boggy Acre
A Floor too cool for Corn   10
Yet when a Boy, and Barefoot—
I more than once at Noon
Have passed, I thought, a Whip lash
Unbraiding in the Sun
When stooping to secure it   15
It wrinkled, and was gone—

Several of Nature's People
I know, and they know me—
I feel for them a transport
Of cordiality—   20

But never met this Fellow
Attended, or alone
Without a tighter breathing
And Zero at the Bone—

—1866

1129: Tell all the truth but tell it slant—

Tell all the truth but tell it slant—
Success in Circuit lies
Too bright for our infirm Delight
The Truth's superb surprise

As Lightning to the Children eased
With explanation kind
The Truth must dazzle gradually
Or every man be blind—

—1945

1249: The Stars are old, that stood for me—

The Stars are old, that stood for me—
The West a little worn—
Yet newer glows the only Gold
I ever cared to earn—
Presuming on that lone result   5
Her infinite disdain
But vanquished her with my defeat
'Twas Victory was slain.

—1914

1545: The Bible is an antique Volume—

The Bible is an antique Volume—
Written by faded Men
At the suggestion of Holy Spectres—
Subjects—Bethlehem—
Eden—the ancient Homestead—   5
Satan—the Brigadier—
Judas—the Great Defaulter—
David—the Troubadour—
Sin—a distinguished Precipice
Others must resist—   10
Boys that "believe" are very lonesome—
Other Boys are "lost"—
Had but the Tale a warbling Teller—
All the Boys would come—
Orpheus' Sermon captivated—   15
It did not condemn—

—1924

1593: There came a Wind like a Bugle—

There came a Wind like a Bugle—
It quivered through the Grass
And a Green Chill upon the Heat
So ominous did pass
We barred the Windows and the Doors   5

As from an Emerald Ghost—
The Doom's Electric Moccasin
That very instant passed—
On a strange Mob of panting Trees
And Fences fled away   10
And Rivers where the Houses ran
Those looked that lived—that Day—
The Bell within the steeple wild
The flying tidings told—
How much can come   15
And much can go,
And yet abide the World!

—1891

⟍ A SHEAF OF POEMS ⟍

Canadian Poets of Confederation

In the introduction to the first published anthology of Canadian poetry, *Selections from the Canadian Poets* (1864), Edward Hartley Dewart writes that "a national literature is essential in the formation of national character" but that

> there is probably no country in the world, making equal pretension to intelligence and progress, where the claims of native literature are so little felt, and where every effort in poetry has been met with so much coldness and indifference, as in Canada.

The 1860s saw a shift in the reception (and production) of Canadian literature that Dewart writes of. By 1867, a collection of poets, loosely identified as the Poets of Confederation began to change the landscape of Canadian poetry. The dates 1864–1867 are important because they help to explain the cool reception of, and hint at the content and form of, pre-Confederation poetry.

Before 1867, Canadian poetry was steeped in the conventions and traditions of eighteenth-century British verse (such as the balanced meter and rhyme scheme of Oliver Goldsmith's "The Deserted Village" [p. 75], for instance). Drawing on the epic, many poems offer a survey—topographical, cultural, and historical—of the Maritime provinces that are rooted in the literary, historical, and mythological landscape of British literature. Thus the coldness and indifference Dewart writes about may, in part, stem from the often-formulaic worldview and narrative voices of these poems. Politically, much of this early Canadian verse is Loyalist, and while warming (nostalgically) to thoughts and images of England, poets such as Joseph Stansbury and Margaret Blennerhasset disparage America, attacking republican politics and Jeffersonian democracy. Their verse, however, is shaped by the very British literature that American writers had been distancing themselves from for some years.

The date of Dewart's anthology, 1864, marks a threshold. English Canadian literature begins to shift in form and content from the eighteenth century to the British Romantics. Indeed, it also signals the date at which authors and critics feel that there is a discernible national literature. In 1867, for instance, Henry J. Morgan published *Bibliotheca Canadensis, or a Manual of Canadian Literature*, the first comprehensive history of Canadian literature (French and English). In spirit and letter, Morgan presents a literature he believes is distinct from American literature—the quality of which, however, is questioned by an anonymous review of

Morgan's book in the Boston periodical *The North American Review* in 1868: "the current literature of the English side of the colonies is, as might be expected, still crude and provincial. . . .
Canada is too much engrossed with the development of her material resources to find leisure
for much else." The verse of the Poets of Confederation suggests otherwise. Drawing on the
Romantic poets' abiding interest in exploring physical and psychological landscapes in rural
and urban settings, they explore the politics, history, and culture of Canada.

Charles G. D. Roberts
1860–1943

A poet, school teacher, university professor, and short story writer, Charles G. D. Roberts lived
and worked in Canada, America, and Britain. The son of a minister, Roberts spent his childhood rambling the countryside near his home in Sackville, New Brunswick, Canada. The
scenes of the Tantramar area, with its wetlands, marshes, and fertile farmland, influenced his
writing and nationalist politics. His first collection of verse, *Orion and Other Poems* (1880),
invests the Canadian landscape with the symbols and images of the British Romantics; the volume gained national attention. Poet Archibald Lampman wrote in 1891 that "it was like a
voice from some new paradise of art calling us to be up and doing," while Roberts himself
described the book as the "work of practically a schoolboy, drunk with the music of Keats,
Shelley, Tennyson, and Swinburne."

In 1883, Roberts joined the literary magazine *The Week*, promoting the work of Lampman
and Bliss Carman. However, Roberts left after one year because his intense nationalism clashed
with the beliefs of the journal's editor, who felt Canada should be annexed to the United
States. Roberts's work is patriotic, always mindful of what he sees as a distinctly Canadian (and
Maritimes) ethos: the relationship of civilization and wilderness. Roberts served as a war correspondent during World War I for the British and Canadian armies, and his popularity following the war was immense. The patriotism of his writing made him a national figure; he toured
widely reading his work and was knighted in 1935.

The Tantramar Revisited

Summers and summers have come, and gone with the flight of the swallow;
Sunshine and thunder have been, storm, and winter, and frost;
Many and many a sorrow has all but died from remembrance,
Many a dream of joy fall'n in the shadow of pain.
Hands of chance and change have marred, or molded, or broken,   5
Busy with spirit or flesh, all I most have adored;
Even the bosom of Earth is strewn with heavier shadows,—
Only in these green hills, aslant to the sea, no change!
Here where the road that has climbed from the inland valleys and woodlands,
Dips from the hilltops down, straight to the base of the hills,—   10
Here, from my vantage-ground, I can see the scattering houses,
Stained with time, set warm in orchards, meadows, and wheat,

Dotting the broad light slopes outspread to southward and eastward,
Wind-swept all day long, blown by the southeast wind.

Skirting the sunbright uplands stretches a riband of meadow,   15
Shorn of the laboring grass, bulwarked well from the sea,
Fenced on its seaward border with long clay dikes from the turbid
Surge and flow of the tides vexing the Westmoreland shores.[1]
Yonder, toward the left, lie broad the Westmoreland marshes,—
Miles on miles they extend, level, and grassy, and dim,   20
Clear from the long red sweep of flats to the sky in the distance,
Save for the outlying heights, green-rampired Cumberland Point[2];
Miles on miles outrolled, and the river-channels divide them,—
Miles on miles of green, barred by the hurtling gusts.

Miles on miles beyond the tawny bay is Minudie.   25
There are the low blue hills; villages gleam at their feet.
Nearer a white sail shines across the water, and nearer
Still are the slim, gray masts of fishing boats dry on the flats.
Ah, how well I remember those wide red flats, above tide-mark
Pale with scurf of the salt, seamed and baked in the sun!   30
Well I remember the piles of blocks and ropes, and the net-reels
Wound with the beaded nets, dripping and dark from the sea!
Now at this season the nets are unwound; they hang from the rafters
Over the fresh-stowed hay in upland barns, and the wind
Blows all day through the chinks, with the streaks of sunlight, and sways them   35
Softly at will; or they lie heaped in the gloom of a loft.

Now at this season the reels are empty and idle; I see them
Over the lines of the dikes, over the gossiping grass.
Now at this season they swing in the long strong wind, thro' the lonesome
Golden afternoon, shunned by the foraging gulls.   40
Near about sunset the crane will journey homeward above them;
Round them, under the moon, all the calm night long,
Winnowing soft gray wings of marsh-owls wander and wander,
Now to the broad, lit marsh, now to the dusk of the dike.
Soon, thro' their dew-wet frames, in the live keen freshness of morning,   45
Out of the teeth of the dawn blows back the awakening wind.
Then, as the blue day mounts, and the low-shot shafts of the sunlight
Glance from the tide to the shore, gossamers jewelled with dew
Sparkle and wave, where late sea-spoiling fathoms of driftnet
Myriad-meshed, uploomed sombrely over the land.   50

Well I remember it all. The salt raw scent of the margin;
While, with men at the windlass,[3] groaned each reel, and the net,
Surging in ponderous lengths, uprise and coiled in its station;
Then each man to his home,—well I remember it all!

---

1. In New Brunswick.   2. Nova Scotia, which is also the location of Minudie (line 25).   3. Winch for raising the anchor.

Yet, as I sit and watch, this present peace of the landscape,—   55
Stranded boats, these reels empty and idle, the hush,
One gray hawk slow-wheeling above yon cluster of haystacks,—
More than the old-time stir this stillness welcomes me home.

Ah the old-time stir, how once it stung me with rapture,—
Old-time sweetness, the winds freighted with honey and salt!   60
Yet will I stay my steps and not go down to the marsh-land,—
Muse and recall far off, rather remember than see,—
Lest on too close sight I miss the darling illusion,
Spy at their task even here the hands of chance and change.

—1887

The Skater

My glad feet shod with the glittering steel
I was the god of the winged heel.

The hills in the far white sky were lost;
The world lay still in the wide white frost;

And the woods hung hushed in their long white dream   5
By the ghostly, glimmering, ice-blue stream.

Here was a pathway, smooth like glass,
Where I and the wandering wind might pass

To the far-off palaces, drifted deep,
Where Winter's retinue rests in sleep.   10

I followed the lure, I fled like a bird,
Till the startled hollows awoke and heard

A spinning whisper, a sibilant twang,
As the stroke of the steel on the tense ice rang;

And the wandering wind was left behind   15
As faster, faster I followed my mind;

Till the blood sang high in my eager brain,
And the joy of my flight was almost pain.

Then I stayed the rush of my eager speed
And silently went as a drifting seed,—   20

Slowly, furtively, till my eyes
Grew big with the awe of a dim surmise,

And the hair of my neck began to creep
At hearing the wilderness talk in sleep.

Shapes in the fir-gloom drifted near.   25
In the deep of my heart I heard my fear;

And I turned and fled, like a soul pursued,
From the white, inviolate solitude.

—1896

from Ave!
(An Ode for the Shelley Centenary, 1892)

I

O tranquil meadows, grassy Tantramar,
    Wide marshes ever washed in clearest air,
Whether beneath the sole and spectral star
    The dear severity of dawn you wear,
Or whether in the joy of ample day   5
    And speechless ecstasy of growing June
You lie and dream the long blue hours away
        Till nightfall comes too soon,
Or whether, naked to the unstarred night,
You strike with wondering awe my inward sight,—   10

II

You know how I have loved you, how my dreams
    Go forth to you with longing, though the years
That turn not back like your returning streams
    And fain would mist the memory with tears,
Though the inexorable years deny   15
    My feet the fellowship of your deep grass,
O'er which, as o'er another, tenderer sky,
        Cloud phantoms drift and pass,—
You know my confident love, since first, a child,
Amid your wastes of green I wandered wild.   20

III

Inconstant, eager, curious, I roamed;
    And ever your long reaches lured me on;
And ever o'er my feet your grasses foamed,
    And in my eyes your far horizons shone.

But sometimes would you (as a stillness fell   25
    And on my pulse you laid a soothing palm),
Instruct my ears in your most secret spell;
    And sometimes in the calm
Initiate my young and wondering eyes
Until my spirit grew more still and wise.   30

IV

Purged with high thoughts and infinite desire
    I entered fearless the most holy place,
Received between my lips the secret fire,
    The breath of inspiration on my face.
But not for long these rare illumined hours,   35
    The deep surprise and rapture not for long.
Again I saw the common, kindly flowers,
      Again I heard the song
Of the glad bobolink,[1] whose lyric throat
Pealed like a tangle of small bells afloat. . . .   40

XI

Therefore with no far flight, from Tantramar
    And my still world of ecstasy, to thee,
Shelley, to thee I turn, the avatar[2]
    Of Song, Love, Dream, Desire and Liberty;
To thee I turn with reverent hands of prayer   105
    And lips that fain would ease my heart of praise,
Whom chief of all whose brows prophetic wear
      The pure and sacred bays
I worship, and have worshipped since the hour
When first I felt thy bright and chainless power.   110

XII

About thy sheltered cradle, in the green
    Untroubled groves of Sussex, brooded forms
That to the mother's eye remained unseen,—
    Terrors and ardours, passionate hopes, and storms
Of fierce retributive fury, such as jarred   115
    Ancient and sceptred creeds, and cast down kings,
And oft the holy cause of Freedom marred,
      With lust of meaner things,
With guiltless blood, and many a frenzied crime
Dared in the face of unforgetful Time. . . .   120

---

1. Songbird.   2. Human incarnation.

XV

And thou, thenceforth the breathless child of change,
    Thine own Alastor, on an endless quest
Of unimagined loveliness, didst range,
    Urged ever by the soul's divine unrest.
Of that high quest and that unrest divine   145
    Thy first immortal music thou didst make,
Inwrought with fairy Alp, and Reuss, and Rhine,[3]
        And phantom seas that break
In soundless foam along the shores of Time,
Prisoned in thine imperishable rhyme.   150

XVI

Thyself the lark melodious in mid-heaven;
    Thyself the Protean[4] shape of chainless cloud,
Pregnant with elemental fire, and driven
    Through deeps of quivering light, and darkness loud
With tempest, yet beneficent as prayer;   155
    Thyself the wild west wind, relentless strewing
The withered leaves of custom on the air,
        And through the wreck pursuing
O'er lovelier Arnos,[5] more imperial Romes,
Thy radiant visions to their viewless homes. . . .   160

XX

Thou on whose lips the word of Love became
    A rapt evangel to assuage all wrong,
Not Love alone, but the austerer name
    Of Death engaged the splendours of thy song.
The luminous grief, the spacious consolation   195
    Of thy supreme lament, that mourned for him
Too early haled to that still habitation
        Beneath the grass-roots dim,—
Where his faint limbs and pain-o'erwearied heart
Of all earth's loveliness became a part,   200

XXI

But where, thou sayest, himself would not abide,—
    Thy solemn incommunicable joy
Announcing Adonais has not died,
    Attesting Death to free but not destroy,
All this was as thy swan-song mystical.   205
    Even while the note serene was on thy tongue

---

3. Rivers originating in Switzerland.   4. In Greek myth, Proteus, god of the sea, was a shape-changer.   5. Italian river.

Thin grew the veil of the Invisible,
    The white sword nearer swung,—
And in the sudden wisdom of thy rest
Thou knewest all thou hadst but dimly guessed.   210

XXII

—Lament, Lerici,[6] mourn for the world's loss!
    Mourn that pure light of song extinct at noon!
Ye waves of Spezzia[7] that shine and toss
    Repent that sacred flame you quenched too soon!
Mourn, Mediterranean waters, mourn   215
    In affluent purple down your golden shore!
Such strains as his, whose voice you stilled in scorn,
    Our ears may greet no more,
Unless at last to that far sphere we climb
Where he completes the wonder of his rhyme!   220

                         —1892

Bliss Carman
1861–1929

Descended from American Loyalists who left America following the War of Independence, Bliss Carman was a distant relative of Ralph Waldo Emerson and cousin of Charles G. D. Roberts. Born in Fredericton, New Brunswick, Canada, Carman was educated at the University of New Brunswick, Oxford, and Edinburgh. Perhaps one of his most important educational experiences was a two-year stint at Harvard. Although Carman left Harvard without taking a degree, he was bolstered by the support and advice of the Transcendentalist poet Richard Hovey and decided to devote his life to art. Carman did, however, try his hand at teaching, law, and real estate. Following his spell at Harvard, he worked as a journalist and columnist while trying to eke out a living as a working poet.

    His 1893 collection of verse, *Low Tide on Grand Pré*, explored the fragility of human life and was well received on both sides of the Atlantic. Carman's verse is indebted to the British and American Romantics, combining the pantheism of William Wordsworth, the Transcendentalism of Emerson, and the mysticism of Percy Bysshe Shelley and Edgar Allan Poe, creating a sense in his verse of feeling at one (or always striving to) with the natural universe. His Anglicanism gave way to a more naturalistic faith, and his poetry explores spiritual and psychological landscapes as they take root in physical ones, often drawing on the scenery of the Maritime Provinces. During his lifetime, Carman was the most popular of the Poets of Confederation.

---

6. In Italy near site of Percy Bysshe Shelley's drowning.   7. Gulf of Spezzia, Italy.

By the Aurelian Wall

In Memory of John Keats

By the Aurelian Wall,
Where the long shadows of the centuries fall
From Caius Cestius'[1] tomb,
A weary mortal seeking rest found room
For quiet burial,   5

Leaving among his friends
A book of lyrics.
Such untold amends
A traveller might make
In a strange country, bidden to partake   10
Before he farther wends[2];

Who shyly should bestow
The foreign reed-flute they had seen him blow
And finger cunningly,
On one of the dark children standing by,   15
Then lift his cloak and go.

The years pass. And the child
Thoughtful beyond his fellows, grave and mild,
Treasures the rough-made toy,
Until one day he blows it for clear joy,   20
And wakes the music wild.

His fondness makes it seem
A thing first fashioned in delirious dream,
Some god had cut and tried,
And filled with yearning passion, and cast aside   25
On some far woodland stream,—

After long years to be
Found by the stranger and brought over sea,
A marvel and delight
To ease the noon and pierce the dark blue night,   30
For children such as he.

He learns the silver strain
Wherewith the ghostly houses of gray rain
And lonely valleys ring,
When the untroubled whitethroats[3] make the spring   35
A world without a stain;

---

1. Keats is buried in the Protestant Cemetery in Rome near the grave of this ancient Roman politician.   2. Goes on his way.   3. English songbird.

Then on his river reed,
With strange and unsuspected notes that plead
Of their own wild accord
For utterances no bird's throat could afford,   40
Lifts it to human need.

His comrades leave their play,
When calling and compelling far away
By river-slope and hill,
He pipes their wayward footsteps where he will,   45
All the long lovely day.

Even his elders come.
"Surely the child is elvish," murmur some,
And shake the knowing head;
"Give us the good old simple things instead,   50
Our fathers used to hum."

Others at the open door
Smile when they hear what they have hearkened for
These many summers now,
Believing they should live to learn somehow   55
Things never known before.

But he can only tell
How the flute's whisper lures him with a spell,
Yet always just eludes
The lost perfection over which he broods;   60
And how he loves it well.

Till all the country-side,
Familiar with his piping far and wide,
Has taken for its own
That weird enchantment down the evening blown,—   65
Its glory and its pride.

And so his splendid name,
Who left the book of lyrics and small fame
Among his fellows then,
Spreads through the world like autumn—who knows when?—   70
Till all the hillsides flame.

Grand Pré[4] and Margaree[5]
Hear it upbruited from the unresting sea;
And the small Gaspareau,[6]

---

4. Carman's home on the Bay of Fundy, Nova Scotia.   5. In Cape Breton, Nova Scotia.   6. Village in Nova Scotia.

Whose yellow leaves repeat it, seems to know 75
A new felicity.

Even the shadows tall,
Walking at sundown through the plain, recall
A mound the grasses keep,
Where once a mortal came and found long sleep 80
By the Aurelian Wall.

—1898

Low Tide on Grand Pré[1]

The sun goes down, and over all
   These barren reaches by the tide
Such unelusive glories fall,
   I almost dream they yet will bide
   Until the coming of the tide.

And yet I know that not for us,
   By any ecstasy of dream,
He lingers to keep luminous
   A little while the grievous stream,
   Which frets, uncomforted of dream— 10

A grievous stream, that to and fro
   Athrough the fields of Acadie[2]
Goes wandering, as if to know
   Why one beloved face should be
   So long from home and Acadie. 15

Was it a year or lives ago
   We took the grasses in our hands,
And caught the summer flying low
   Over the waving meadow lands,
   And held it there between our hands? 20

The while the river at our feet—
   A drowsy inland meadow stream—
At set of sun the after-heat
   Made running gold, and in the gleam
   We freed our birch upon the stream. 25

---

1. Nova Scotian town at the head of the Bay of Fundy, which has a fifty-foot tide. 2. First French colony in North America, settled 1604.

There down along the elms at dusk
  We lifted dripping blade to drift,
Through twilight scented fine like musk,
  Where night and gloom awhile uplift,
  Nor sunder soul and soul adrift.

And that we took into our hands
  Spirit of life or subtler thing—
Breathed on us there, and loosed the bands
  Of death, and taught us, whispering,
  The secret of some wonder-thing.

Then all your face grew light, and seemed
  To hold the shadow of the sun;
The evening faltered, and I deemed
  That time was ripe, and years had done
  Their wheeling underneath the sun.

So all desire and all regret,
  And fear and memory, were naught;
One to remember or forget
  The keen delight our hands had caught;
  Morrow and yesterday were naught.

The night has fallen, and the tide. . . .
  Now and again comes drifting home,
Across these aching barrens wide,
  A sigh like driven wind or foam:
  In grief the flood is bursting home.

—1887

A More Ancient Mariner

The swarthy bee is a buccaneer,
A burly velveted rover,
Who loves the booming wind in his ear
As he sails the seas of clover.

A waif of the goblin pirate crew,
With not a soul to deplore him,
He steers for the open verge of blue
With the filmy world before him.

His flimsy sails abroad on the wind
Are shivered with fairy thunder;
On a line that sings to the light of his wings
He makes for the lands of wonder.

He harries the ports of Hollyhocks,
And levies on poor Sweetbriar;
He drinks the whitest wine of Phlox,   15
And the Rose is his desire.

He hangs in the Willows a night and a day;
He rifles the Buckwheat patches;
Then battens his store of pelf[1] galore
Under the tautest hatches.   20

He woos the Poppy and weds the Peach,
Inveigles[2] Daffodilly,
And then like a tramp abandons each
For the gorgeous Canada Lily.

There's not a soul in the garden world   25
But wishes the day were shorter,
When Mariner B. puts out to sea
With the wind in the proper quarter.

Or, so they say! But I have my doubts;
For the flowers are only human,   30
And the valor and gold of a vagrant bold
Were always dear to woman.

He dares to boast, along the coast,
The beauty of Highland Heather,—
How he and she, with night on the sea,   35
Lay out on the hills together.

He pilfers every port of the wind,
From April to golden autumn;
But the thieving ways of his mortal days
Are those his mother taught him.   40

His morals are mixed, but his will is fixed;
He prospers after his kind,
And follows an instinct, compass-sure,
The philosophers call blind.

And that is why, when he comes to die,   45
He'll have an earlier sentence
Than someone I know who thinks just so,
And then leaves room for repentance.

He never could box the compass round;
He doesn't know port from starboard;   50

---

1. Treasure.   2. Wins by guile.

But he knows the gates of the Sundown Straits,
Where the choicest goods are harbored.

He never could see the Rule of Three,
But he knows the rule of thumb
Better than Euclid's,[3] better than yours,   55
Or the teachers' yet to come.

He knows the smell of the hydromel[4]
As if two and two were five;
And hides it away for a year and a day
In his own hexagonal hive.   60

Out in the day, hap-hazard, alone,
Booms the old vagrant hummer,
With only his whim to pilot him
Throught the splendid vast of summer.

He steers and steers on the slant of the gale,   65
Like the fiend or Vanderdecken[5];
And there's never an unknown course to sail
But his crazy log can reckon.

He drones along with his rough sea-song
And the throat of a salty tar,   70
This devil-may-care, till he makes his lair
By the light of a yellow star.

He looks like a gentleman, lives like a lord,
And works like a Trojan hero;
Then loafs all winter upon his hoard,   75
With the mercury at zero.

—1894

Archibald Lampman
1861–1899

Like his Romantic hero, John Keats, Archibald Lampman died at a young age. Lampman's health suffered throughout his life from the lingering effects of the rheumatic fever he contracted at age seven, and he was just thirty-eight when he passed away. Lampman attended the renowned private school at Rice Lake, Canada, modeled after the English preparatory school system and run by Frederick William Barron, a Cambridge graduate. Well versed in Latin,

3. Greek mathematician (325–263 BC).   4. Honey mixed with water.   5. Legendary sea-captain, also known as the Flying Dutchman.

Greek, and the Bible, Lampman next attended Trinity College at the University of Toronto, his Anglican minister father's alma mater.

During Lampman's childhood, the family moved regularly as his father's pastoral appointments required. The poetry Lampman began to write at university grew out of his experiences in a number of varied but equally beautiful regions of Canada: western and central Ontario, Ottawa, and the Gatineau hills near the Ontario–Quebec border. Lampman is a member of a group of poets commonly called the "group of the sixties" but more often "the poets of Confederation," which included Bliss Carman, Charles G. D. Roberts, and Duncan Campbell Scott. All four poets were born in the early 1860s and shared a key interest in writing about nature. Lampman's interest in the British Romantics surfaced early: In 1880–1881, he published an article on Percy Bysshe Shelley and friendship in the university newspaper, *Rouge et Noir*. Soon after that, he began to publish poetry. Upon graduation, he tried his hand at teaching, cautioning a friend, "never descend to the abyss of pedagogy if there is another path open in any direction to thee in this life," and then became a clerk in the post office in Ottawa in January 1883. Lampman traveled widely in the areas surrounding Ottawa, often hiking and canoeing with his good friend Roberts, but rarely ventured out of the province or the country.

Lampman's last years were productive. Between 1892 and 1893, he, along with Duncan Campbell Scott and William Wilfred Campbell, published a weekly column in the Toronto *Globe*. Lampman wrote close to ninety columns on a wide array of literary and cultural topics and numerous authors (including Shelley, Alfred Lord Tennyson, and Matthew Arnold), and he wrote over three hundred poems in the 1890s, only half of which were published during his lifetime. Of the Romantics, Keats in particular influenced him: "Keats has always had such a fascination for me and so permeated my whole mental outfit that I have an idea that he has found a sort of faint reincarnation in me."

The City at the End of Things

Beside the pounding cataracts[1]
Of midnight streams unknown to us
'Tis builded in the leafless tracts
And valleys huge of Tartarus.[2]
Lurid and lofty and vast it seems;   5
It hath no rounded name that rings,
But I have heard it called in dreams
The City of the End of Things.

Its roofs and iron towers have grown
None knoweth how high within the night,   10
But in its murky streets far down
A flaming terrible and bright
Shakes all the stalking shadows there,
Across the walls, across the floors,
And shifts upon the upper air   15
From out a thousand furnace doors;
And all the while an awful sound
Keeps roaring on continually,
And crashes in the ceaseless round

---

1. Waterfalls or rapids.   2. A region of Hades, the Greek underworld, reserved for the wicked.

Of a gigantic harmony.   20
Through its grim depths re-echoing
And all its weary height of walls,
With measured roar and iron ring,
The inhuman music lifts and falls.
Where no thing rest and no man is,   25
And only fire and night hold sway;
The beat, the thunder and the hiss
Cease not, and change not, night nor day.
And moving at unheard commands,
The abysses and vast fires between,   30
Flit figures that with clanking hands
Obey a hideous routine;
They are not flesh, they are not bone,
They see not with the human eye,
And from their iron lips is blown   35
A dreadful and monotonous cry;
And whoso of our mortal race
Should find that city unaware,
Lean Death would smite him face to face,
And blanch[3] him with its venomed air: 40
Or caught by the terrific spell,
Each thread or memory snapt and cut,
His soul would shrivel and its shell
Go rattling like an empty nut.
It was not always so, but once,   45
In days that no man thinks upon,
Fair voices echoed from its stones,
The light above it leaped and shone:
Once there were multitudes of men,
That built that city in their pride,   50
Until its might was made, and then
They withered age by age and died.
By now of that prodigious race,
Three only in an iron tower,
Set like carved idols face to face,   55
Remain the masters of its power;
And at the city gate a fourth,
Gigantic and with dreadful eyes,
Sits looking toward the lightless north,
Beyond the reach of memories;   60
Fast rooted to the lurid floor,
A bulk that never moves a jot,
In his pale body dwells no more,
Or mind or soul,—an idiot!

---

3. Scald.

But sometime in the end those three   65
Shall perish and their hands be still,
And with the master's touch shall flee
Their incommunicable skill.
A stillness absolute as death
Along the slacking wheels shall lie,   70
And, flagging at a single breath,
The fires that moulder out and die.
The roar shall vanish at its height,
And over that tremendous town
The silence of eternal night   75
Shall gather close and settle down.
All its grim grandeur, tower and hall,
Shall be abandoned utterly,
And into rust and dust shall fall
From century to century;   80
Nor ever living thing shall grow,
Nor trunk of tree, nor blade of grass;
No drop shall fall, no wind shall blow,
Nor sound of any foot shall pass:
Alone of its accursèd state,   85
One thing the hand of Time shall spare,
For the grim Idiot at the gate
Is deathless and eternal there.

—1899

The Frogs

I

Breathers of wisdom won without a quest,
    Quaint uncouth dreamers, voices high and strange,
    Flutists of lands where beauty hath no change,
And wintry grief is a forgotten guest,
Sweet murmurers of everlasting rest,   5
    For whom glad days have ever yet to run,
    And moments are as aeons,[1] and the sun
But ever sunken half-way toward the west.

Often to me who heard you in your day,
    With close wrapt ears, it could not choose but seem   10
That earth, our mother, searching in what way,
    Men's hearts might know her spirit's inmost dream,
        Ever at rest beneath life's change and stir,
        Made you her soul, and bade you pipe for her.

---

1. Eons, ages.

II

In those mute days when spring was in her glee,   15
    And hope was strong, we knew not why or how,
    And earth, the mother, dreamed with brooding brow,
Musing on life, and what the hours might be,
When love should ripen to maternity,
    Then like high flutes in silvery interchange   20
    Ye piped with voices still and sweet and strange,
And ever as ye piped, on every tree

The great buds swelled; among the pensive woods
    The spirits of first flowers awoke and flung
From buried faces the close fitting hoods,   25
    And listened to your piping till they fell,
    The frail spring-beauty with her perfumed bell,
The wind-flower, and the spotted adder-tongue.

III

All the day long, wherever pools might be
    Among the golden meadows, where the air   30
    Stood in a dream, as it were moorèd there
Forever in a noon-tide reverie,
Or where the birds made riot of their glee
    In the still woods, and the hot sun shone down,
    Crossed with warm lucent shadows on the brown   35
Leaf-paven pools, that bubbled dreamily.

Or far away in whispering river meads
    And watery marshes where the brooding noon,
    Full with the wonder of its own sweet boon,
Nestled and slept among the noiseless reeds,   40
    Ye sat and murmured, motionless as they,
    With eyes that dreamed beyond the night and day.

IV

And when day passed and over heaven's height,
    Thin with the many stars and cool with dew,
    The fingers of the deep hours slowly drew   45
The wonder of the ever-healing night,
No grief or loneliness or wrapt delight
    Or weight of silence ever brought to you
    Slumber or rest; only your voices grew
More high and solemn; slowly with hushed flight   50

Ye saw the echoing hours go by, long-drawn,
   Nor ever stirred, watching with fathomless eyes,
   And with your countless clear antiphonies[2]
Filling the earth and heaven, even till dawn,
   Last-risen, found you with its first pale gleam,   55
   Still with soft throats unaltered in your dream.

V

And slowly as we heard you, day by day,
   The stillness of enchanted reveries
   Bound brain and spirit and half-closèd eyes,
In some divine sweet wonder-dream astray;   60
To us no sorrow or upreared dismay
   Nor any discord came, but evermore
   The voices of mankind, the outer roar,
Grew strange and murmurous, faint and far away.

Morning and noon and midnight exquisitely,   65
   Wrapt with your voices, this alone we knew,
Cities might change and fall, and men might die,
   Secure were we, content to dream with you,
      That change and pain are shadows faint and fleet,
      And dreams are real, and life is only sweet.   70

—1888

The Railway Station

The darkness brings no quiet here, the light
   No waking: ever on my blinded brain
   The flare of lights, the rush, and cry, and strain,
The engines' scream, the hiss and thunder smite:
I see the hurrying crowds, the clasp, the flight,   5
   Faces that touch, eyes that are dim with pain:
   I see the hoarse wheels turn, and the great train
Move labouring out into the bourneless night.

So many souls within its dim recesses,
   So many bright, so many mournful eyes: 10
Mine eyes that watch grow fixed with dreams and guesses;
   What threads of life, what hidden histories,
What sweet or passionate dreams and dark distresses,
   What unknown thoughts, what various agonies!

—1888

---

2. Alternating responses between two singers.

Voices of Earth

We have not heard the music of the spheres,
The song of star to star, but there are sounds
More deep than human joy and human tears,
That Nature uses in her common rounds;
The fall of streams, the cry of winds that strain   5
The oak, the roaring of the sea's surge, might
Of thunder breaking afar off, or rain
That falls by minutes in the summer night.
These are the voices of earth's secret soul,
Uttering the mystery from which she came.   10
To him who hears them grief beyond control,
Or joy inscrutable without a name,
Wakes in his heart thoughts bedded there, impearled,
Before the birth and making of the world.

—1899

Temagami[1]

Far in the grim Northwest beyond the lines
That turn the rivers eastward to the sea,
Set with a thousand islands, crowned with pines,
Lies the deep water, wild Temagami:
Wild for the hunter's roving, and the use   5
Of trappers in its dark and trackless vales,
Wild with the trampling of the giant moose,
And the weird magic of old Indian tales.
All day with steady paddles toward the west
Our heavy-laden long canoe we pressed: 10
All day we saw the thunder-travelled sky
Purpled with storm in many a trailing tress,
And saw at eve the broken sunset die
In crimson on the silent wilderness.

—1943

Duncan Campbell Scott
1862–1947

At age twenty-one, Duncan Campbell Scott met the poet Archibald Lampman, who pressed him to write poetry. An accomplished pianist and amateur photographer, in 1879 Scott began working for the Department of Indian Affairs (a ministry in which he eventually became Deputy Superintendent), his dream of pursuing a medical career quashed by lack of family

---

1. Lake north of North Bay, Ontario.

financial support. Lampman's influence and Scott's employment shaped the latter's poetry, although it would take ten years before his first volume of verse appeared as *The Magic House and Other Poems* (1893). Scott's interest in Native issues surfaces in his poetry, as he attempts to render portraits of the First Nations in distinctly Canadian terms. At the same time, the influences of English Romantic and Victorian writers shows in his 1898 collection, *Labour and the Angel*. Scott was a versatile writer, and his renown as a poet was matched by his skill as a short story writer. He also published two biographies and wrote regularly for American and Canadian newspapers and journals. Scott achieved a level of literary notoriety, earning several honorary doctorates and election to the Royal Society of Canada.

The Onondaga[1] Madonna

She stands full-throated and with careless pose,
This woman of a weird and waning race,
The tragic savage lurking in her face,
Where all her pagan passion burns and glows;
Her blood is mingled with her ancient foes,   5
And thrills with war and wildness in her veins;
Her rebel lips are dabbled with the stains
Of feuds and forays and her father's woes.

And closer in the shawl about her breast,
The latest promise of her nation's doom,   10
Paler than she her baby clings and lies,
The primal warrior gleaming from his eyes;
He sulks, and burdened with his infant gloom,
He draws his heavy brows and will not rest.

—1898

Night Hymns on Lake Nipigon

Here in the midnight, where the dark mainland and island
Shadows mingle in shadow deeper, profounder,
Sing we the hymns of the churches, while the dead water
    Whispers before us.

Thunder is travelling slow on the path of the lightning;   5
One after one the stars and the beaming planets
Look serene in the lake from the edge of the storm-cloud,
    Then have they vanished.

While our canoe, that floats dumb in the bursting thunder,
Gathers her voice in the quiet and thrills and whispers,   10
Presses her prow in the star-gleam, and all her ripple
    Lapses in blackness.

---

1. Native tribe of Lake Ontario region.

Sing we the sacred ancient hymns of the churches,
Chanted first in old-world nooks of the desert,
While in the wild, pellucid Nipigon[1] reaches   15
    Hunted the savage.

Now have the ages met in the Northern midnight,
And on the lonely, loon-haunted Nipigon reaches
Rises the hymn of triumph and courage and comfort,
    Adeste Fideles.[2]   20

Tones that were fashioned when the faith brooded in darkness,
Joined with sonorous vowels in the noble Latin,
Now are married with the long-drawn Ojibwa,[3]
    Uncouth and mournful.

Soft with the silver drip of the regular paddles   25
Falling in rhythm, timed with the liquid, plangent[4]
Sounds from the blades where the whirlpools break and are carried
    Down into darkness;

Each long cadence, flying like a dove from her shelter
Deep in the shadow, wheels for a throbbing moment,   30
Poises in utterance, returning in circles of silver
    To nest in the silence.

All wild nature stirs with the infinite, tender
Plaint of a bygone age whose soul is eternal,
Bound in the lonely phrases that thrill and falter   35
    Back into quiet.

Back they falter as the deep storm overtakes them,
Whelms them in splendid hollows of booming thunder,
Wraps them in rain, that, sweeping, breaks and onrushes
    Ringing like cymbals.   40

—1905

Ode for the Keats[1] Centenary

Read at the Hart House Theatre
before the University of Toronto, February 23, 1921.

The Muse is stern unto her favoured sons,
Giving to some the keys of all the joy
Of the green earth, but holding even that joy

---

1. Lake in western Ontario; pellucid: clear.   2. O come all ye faithful (Latin).   3. Native tribe of Ontario.   4. Loud, reverberating.
1. John Keats (1795–1821), English poet.

Back from their life;
Bidding them feed on hope,   5
A plant of bitter growth,
Deep-rooted in the past;
Truth, 'tis a doubtful art
To make Hope sweeten
Time as it flows;   10
For no man knows
Until the very last,
Whether it be a sovereign herb that he has eaten,
Or his own heart.

O stern, implacable Muse,   15
Giving to Keats so richly dowered,
Only the thought that he should be
Among the English poets after death;
Letting him fade with that expectancy,
All powerless to unfold the future!   20
What boots it that our age has snatched him free
From thy too harsh embrace,
Has given his fame the certainty
Of comradeship with Shakespeare's?
He lies alone   25
Beneath the frown of the old Roman stone
And the cold Roman violets;
And not our wildest incantation
Of his most sacred lines,
Nor all the praise that sets   30
Towards his pale grave,
Like oceans towards the moon,
Will move the Shadow with the pensive brow
To break his dream,
And give unto him now   35
One word!—

When the young master reasoned
That our puissant[2] England
Reared her great poets by neglect,
Trampling them down in the by-paths of Life   40
And fostering them with glory after death,
Did any flame of triumph from his own fame
Fall swift upon his mind; the glow
Cast back upon the bleak and aching air
Blown around his days—?   45
Happily so!

---

2. Powerful.

But he, whose soul was mighty as the soul
Of Milton, who held the vision of the world
As an irradiant orb self-filled with light,
Who schooled his heart with passionate control 50
To compass knowledge, to unravel the dense
Web of this tangled life, he would weigh slight
As thistledown blown from his most fairy fancy
That pale self-glory, against the mystery,
The wonder of the various world, the power 55
Of "seeing great things in loneliness."[3]

Where bloodroot in the clearing dwells
Along the edge of snow;
Where, trembling all their trailing bells,
The sensitive twinflowers blow; 60

Where, searching through the ferny breaks,
The moose-fawns find the springs;
Where the loon[4] laughs and diving takes
Her young beneath her wings;

Where flash the fields of arctic moss 65
With myriad golden light;
Where no dream-shadows ever cross
The lidless eyes of night;

Where, cleaving a mountain storm, the proud
Eagles, the clear sky won, 70
Mount the thin air between the loud
Slow thunder and the sun;

Where, to the high tarn[5] tranced and still
No eye has ever seen,
Comes the first star its flame to chill 75
In the cool deeps of green;—
Spirit of Keats, unfurl thy wings,
Far from the toil and press,
Teach us by these pure-hearted things,
Beauty in loneliness. 80

Where, in the realm of thought, dwell those
Who oft in pain and penury[6]
Work in the void,
Searching the infinite dark between the stars,

---

3. Keats, letter to B. R. Haydon, Dec. 22, 1818: "I feel in myself all vices of the Poet. . . . I value more the Privilege of seeing great things in loneliness than the fame of a Prophet."   4. Aquatic bird.   5. Small mountain lake.   6. Poverty.

The infinite little of the atom,   85
Gathering the tears and terrors of this life,
Distilling them to a medicine for the soul;
(And hated for their thought
Die for it calmly;
For not their fears,   90
Nor the cold scorn of men,
Fright them who hold to truth:)
They brood alone in the intense serene
Air of their passion,
Until on some chill dawn   95
Breaks the immortal form foreshadowed in their dream,
And the distracted world and men
Are no more what they were.
Spirit of Keats, unfurl thy deathless wings,
Far from the wayward toil, the vain excess,   100
Teach us by such soul-haunting things
Beauty in loneliness.

The minds of men grow numb, their vision narrows,
The clogs of Empire and the dust of ages,
The lust of power that fogs the fairest pages,   105
Of the romance that eager life would write,
These war on Beauty with their spears and arrows.
But still is Beauty and of constant power;
Even in the whirl of Time's most sordid hour,
Banished from the great highways,   110
Affrighted by the tramp of insolent feet,
She hangs her garlands in the by-ways;
Lissome[7] and sweet
Bending her head to hearken and learn
Melody shadowed with melody,   115
Softer than shadow of sea-fern,
In the green-shadowed sea:
Then, nourished by quietude,
And if the world's mood
Change, she may return   120
Even lovelier than before.—

The white reflection in the mountain lake
Falls from the white stream
Silent in the high distance;
The mirrored mountains guard   125
The profile of the goddess of the height,

---

7. Lithe, flexible.

Floating in water with a curve of crystal light;
When the air, envious of the loveliness,
Rushes downward to surprise,
Confusion plays in the contact,   130
The picture is overdrawn
With ardent ripples,
But when the breeze, warned of intrusion,
Draws breathless upward in flight,
The vision reassembles in tranquillity,   135
Reforming with a gesture of delight,
Reborn with the rebirth of calm.

Spirit of Keats, lend us thy voice,
Breaking like surge in some enchanted cave
On a dream-sea-coast,   140
To summon Beauty to her desolate world.
For Beauty has taken refuge from our life
That grew too loud and wounding;
Beauty withdraws beyond the bitter strife,
Beauty is gone, (Oh where?)   145
To dwell within a precinct of pure air
Where moments turn to months of solitude;
To live on roots of fern and tips of fern,
On tender berries flushed with the earth's blood.
Beauty shall stain her feet with moss   150
And dye her cheek with deep nut-juices,
Laving her hands in the pure sluices
Where rainbows are dissolved.
Beauty shall view herself in pools of amber sheen
Dappled with peacock-tints from the green screen   155
That mingles liquid light with liquid shadow.
Beauty shall breathe the fairy hush
With the chill orchids in their cells of shade,
And hear the invocation of the thrush
That calls the stars into their heaven,   160
And after even
Beauty shall take the night into her soul.
When the thrill voice goes crying through the wood,
(Oh, Beauty, Beauty!)
Troubling the solitude   165
With echoes from the lonely world,
Beauty will tremble like a cloistered thing
That hears temptation in the outlands singing,
Will steel her dedicated heart and breathe
Into her inner ear to firm her vow:—   170
"Let me restore the soul that ye have marred.

O mortals, cry no more on Beauty,
Leave me alone, lone mortals,
Until my shaken soul comes to its own,
Lone mortals, leave me alone!"
(Oh Beauty, Beauty, Beauty!)
All the dim wood is silent as a dream
That dreams of silence.

—1921

⟶ END OF A SHEAF OF POEMS ⟵

Timeline

1767–1867

Abbreviations: b for birth, d for death

1767   Andrew Jackson b
       Oliver Goldsmith, *The Vicar of Wakefield*
       Britain: The Townshend Acts; first iron-railed railroads built

1768   Mary Robinson b
       Oliver Goldsmith, *The Good-Natured Man*
       Samson Occom, *A Short Narrative of My Life*
       Britain: *Encyclopædia Britannica* project begun (concludes 1771); Sir Joshua
       Reynolds elected first President of the Royal Academy; Coal Heavers' Case: armed
       miners protest reduced wages with violence; James Cook departs to map South
       Pacific, under Royal Society commission

1769   Napoleon b
       Britain: Royal Academy of Arts (painting, sculpture, architecture) formally
       founded; James Watt invents the steam engine; Arkwright invents water frame,
       mechanizing textile production
       Canada: Nova Scotia and Prince Edward Island become separate colonies

1770   William Wordsworth b
       Ludwig van Beethoven b
       Oliver Goldsmith, *The Deserted Village*
       Britain: Lord Frederick North becomes Prime Minister (until 1782); spinning
       jenny invented, allowing for increased production of yarn, by James Hargreaves

1771   Robert Owen b
       Sir Walter Scott b
       Dorothy Wordsworth b
       Henry Mackenzie, *The Man of Feeling*
       Britain: World's first water-powered cotton mill in operation

1772   Samuel Taylor Coleridge b
       Charlotte Dacre b
       Anna Laetitia Barbauld, *Poems* (dated 1773)

Britain: Mansfield Decision concludes there is no legal basis for slavery; James
Burgh, *Political Disquisitions*, seeks to replace Parliament with a U.S.-style assembly;
Daniel Rutherford discovers nitrogen

1773   Anna Laetitia Barbauld (with John Aikin), *Miscellaneous Pieces in Prose*
Hannah More, *The Search After Happiness*
Henry Mackenzie, *The Man of the World*
Phillis Wheatley, *Poems on Various Subjects*
Britain: Regulating Act of Lord North controls powers of East India Company
(founded in 1600) in India
U.S.: Boston Tea Party (American revolt against British taxes); Massachusetts
slaves petition for freedom

1774   Robert Southey b
Oliver Goldsmith (Irish) d
John Wesley, *Thoughts upon Slavery*
Hannah More, *The Inflexible Captive*
Johann Wolfgang von Goethe, *The Sorrows of Young Werther*
John Woolman, *The Journal of John Woolman*
Joseph Priestley isolates oxygen
Britain: Perpetual copyright abolished
U.S.: Tensions increase between American Colonists and British government;
importation of slaves prohibited by Continental Congress
Canada: Quebec Act, British attempt to secure support from colonists in Canada,
protects language and religious freedom of French Canadians

1775   Joseph Priestley, *Hartley's Theory of the Human Mind*
Mercy Otis Warren, *The Group*
Joseph Mallord William Turner (painter) b
Britain: James Watts perfects steam engine
U.S.: War with Britain begins (lasts until 1783); George Washington becomes
commander of American military; British defeated at Lexington, victorious at
Bunker Hill; Philadelphia Quakers organize first anti-slavery society; 800 slaves
promised freedom for joining British troops comprise "Ethiopian Regiment";
Loyalists from New England settle in Nova Scotia and Quebec
Canada: Population is 85,000 people (approximately 10,000 Americans)

1776   Robert Hutchinson Rose b
Thomas Paine, *Common Sense*
Adam Smith, *Enquiry into the Wealth of Nations*
Richard Price, *On Civil Liberty*
Edward Gibbon, *Decline and Fall of the Roman Empire*
U.S.: American Declaration of Independence

1777   Hannah More, *Percy and Essay on Various Subjects, Principally Designed for Young
Ladies*
James Cook, *Voyage towards the South Pole in 1772–5*
U.S.: Vermont's constitution abolishes slavery; New York allows permit-holding,
property-owning, resident black males to vote

1778   William Hazlitt b
        Jean Jacques Rousseau d
        Anna Laetitia Barbauld, *Lessons for Children*
        Frances Burney, *Evelina*
        Clara Reeve, *The Old English Baron*
        James Cook discovers Hawaii, maps Pacific coast of America
        Britain: Pitt introduces laws to control slave trade; Catholic Relief Act lifts
        property and economic restrictions

1779   Thomas Moore b
        Hannah More, *The Fatal Falsehood*

1780   Frances Trollope b
        William Ellery Channing b
        Britain: Society for Constitutional Information founded, calling for vote and par-
        liamentary reform; Gordon Riots in response to Roman Catholic Relief Act (1778)
        U.S.: Pennsylvania legalizes interracial marriage; African Americans in
        Massachusetts rally against "taxation without representation"

1781   Anna Laetitia Barbauld, *Hymns in Prose for Children*
        Immanuel Kant, *Critique of Pure Reason*
        Jean-Jacques Rousseau, *Confessions*
        J. C. Friedrich Schiller, *The Robbers*
        Britain/U.S.: The *Zong* Incident: captain of the slave ship *Zong* throws 133
        enslaved Africans into shark-infested waters, hoping to collect insurance; British
        defeated by Continental Army at Yorktown, Virginia

1782   Fanny Burney, *Cecilia*
        William Cowper, *Poems*
        Michel Guillaume Jean de Crèvecoeur, *Letters from an American Farmer*
        Hannah More, essay on "Sensibility" in *Sacred Dramas*
        Britain: Gilbert's Act helps people find work near their homes; Irish gain legislative
        independence
        U.S.: Fighting in American War of Independence ceases
        Canada: Mass immigration of United Empire Loyalists to Maritime colonies from
        U.S.; North West Company (fur traders) founded

1783   Washington Irving b
        Andrews Norton b
        William Blake prints *Poetical Sketches*
        Hugh Blair, *Lectures on Rhetoric and Belles Lettres*
        Olaudah Equiano publicizes *Zong* incident of 1781, which is brought to trial
        Britain: William Pitt becomes Prime Minister (1783–1801, 1804–1806); Treaty of
        Versailles, peace with U.S.; Britain cedes land west of Mississippi River
        U.S.: Massachusetts legislature grants black male taxpayers voting rights
        U.S./Canada: 80,000 Loyalists emigrate to Canada

1784   Phillis Wheatley d
        Samuel Johnson d
        Charlotte Smith, *Elegiac Sonnets, and Other Poems*, volume II

Sir William Jones, *A Discourse on the Institution of a Society for Inquiring into the History, Civil and Natural, the Antiquities, Arts, Sciences, and Literature of Asia*
James Ramsay, *Essay on the Treatment and Conversion of African Slaves*
Immanuel Kant, *What Is Enlightenment?*
John Wesley founds Methodism
Britain: India Act, Crown guides Indian politics, rather than East India Company; Edmund Cartwright invents the power loom (first run by water, then steam)
U.S.: American War of Independence formally ends; Benjamin Franklin invents bifocal glasses
Canada: New Brunswick becomes colony

1785   David Walker b
        William Cowper, *The Task*
        William Paley, *Principles of Moral and Political Philosophy*
        Della Crusca (Robert Merry), *The Florence Miscellany*
        Ann Yearsley, *Poems, on Several Occasions*
        Britain: Parliament regulates trade with Ireland

1786   Hannah More, *The Bas Bleu; or Conversation*
        Robert Burns, *Poems Chiefly in the Scottish Dialect*
        William Beckford, *Vathek*
        Thomas Clarkson, *An Essay on the Slavery and Commerce of the Human Species*
        Philip Freneau, *Poems*
        U.S.: Shay's Rebellion

1787   Alexander Hamilton and James Madison, *The Federalist Papers* (1787–1788)
        Thomas Jefferson, *Notes on the State of Virginia*
        W. A. Mozart, *Don Giovanni*
        Britain: Society for the Abolition of the British Slave Trade formed
        U.S.: Constitutional Convention convenes in Philadelphia; Congress bans slavery in the Northwest Territories; free African Americans in Rhode Island establish African Union Society to establish free slaves in Sierra Leone; Northwest/Freedom Ordinance established organized regions of country around the Great Lakes
        Canada/U.S.: blacks from U.S. and Nova Scotia resettle in Sierra Leone

1788   Lord Byron b
        William Blake starts his method of relief etch printing
        Mary Wollstonecraft, *Mary, a Fiction* and *Original Stories from Real Life*
        Hannah More, *Thoughts on the Importance of the Manners of the Great to General Society* and *Slavery, A Poem*
        Charlotte Smith, *Emmeline*
        Thomas Clarkson, *Impolicy of the Slave Trade*
        Ann Yearsley, *A Poem on the Inhumanity of the Slave Trade*
        Britain: The Dolben Act dictates more humane conditions on slave ships; first British (penal) colony settled in Australia; uncertain mental fitness of King George III leads to Regency Crisis; employment Law stipulates that chimney sweepers be eight years old; liberal, literary journal *Analytical Review* founded
        Canada: British trader John Meares establishes a trading post at Nootka Sound, British Columbia
        France: Friends of the Negro, abolitionist movement formed

1789   Catharine Maria Sedgwick b
        James Fenimore Cooper b
        Leigh Hunt b
        Jeremy Bentham, *Principles of Morals and Legislation*
        W. L. Bowles, *Sonnets*
        William Blake, *Songs of Innocence* and *Book of Thel*
        Olaudah Equiano, *The Interesting Narrative of the Life of Olaudah Equiano*
        Ann Radcliffe, *The Castles of Athlyn and Dunbane*
        Charlotte Smith, *Ethelinda, or The Recluse of the Lake*
        Erasmus Darwin, *The Botanic Garden*
        Britain: William Wilberforce introduces slave trade resolutions in Parliament;
        Dolben Act (1788) renewed annually; beginning of peasant's revolts
        U.S.: George Washington elected President
        Canada: Explorer and fur trader Alexander Mackenzie canoes the Mackenzie River
        from Canadian prairies to the Arctic Ocean (1,000 miles)
        France: Storming of the Bastille and formation of French National Assembly: com-
        mencement of French Revolution; *Declaration of the Rights of Man and of the Citizen*

1790   Fitz-Greene Halleck b
        Benjamin Franklin d
        William Blake working on *Marriage of Heaven and Hell*
        Edmund Burke, *Reflections on the Revolution in France*
        Mary Wollstonecraft, *Vindication of the Rights of Men*
        Joanna Baillie, *Poems*
        Immanuel Kant, *The Critique of Judgement*
        Judith Sargent Murray, *On the Equality of the Sexes*
        Helen Maria Williams, *Julia: A Novel* and *Letters from France*
        Ann Radcliffe, *A Sicilian Romance*
        Britain: Henry James Pye becomes Poet Laureate, replacing Thomas Warton;
        J. M. W. Turner's paintings exhibited for first time at the Royal Academy
        U.S.: Pennsylvania abolitionists petition Congress; first census: 3,929,214

1791   Lydia Huntley Sigourney b
        John Wesley d
        Thomas Paine, *Rights of Man*, volume I
        Edmund Burke, *Letter to a Member of the National Assembly*
        William Gilpin, *Observations on the River Wye*
        Elizabeth Inchbald, *A Simple Story*
        Ann Radcliffe, *The Romance of the Forest*
        Susanna Rowson, *Charlotte: A Tale of Truth*
        Britain: Birmingham riots, a protest of Bastille Day; William Wilberforce's aboli-
        tion motion rejected
        Canada: Constitutional Act creates Upper Canada and Lower Canada as separate
        legislative bodies, using the St. Lawrence River to divide the two regions
        France: Massacre of Champ de Mars, protestors (60 killed, 200 injured) call for
        king's abdication; Olympe de Gouges publishes *Declaration of the Rights of Woman*
        San Domingo: 100,000 slaves revolt (1791–1803)

1792   Percy Bysshe Shelley b
        Samson Occom d
        Thomas Paine, *Rights of Man*, volume II; Paine flees Britain for France
        Mary Wollstonecraft, *A Vindication of the Rights of Woman*
        Britain: King Goerge III orders Royal proclamation against sedition; Thomas Paine
        on trial for treason; Libel Act calls for jury, not judge trial, to decide libel; first use
        of gas lights
        Denmark: Begins abolition of slave trade (to 1803)
        France: "September Massacres," execution of 12,000 political prisoners; King Louis
        XVI tried for treason

1793   John Clare b
        Felicia Dorothea Hemans b
        William Godwin, *An Enquiry Concerning the Principles of Political Justice and Its
        Influence on General Virtue and Happiness*
        William Blake, *America* and *Visions of the Daughters of Albion*
        William Wordsworth, *An Evening Walk* and *Descriptive Sketches*
        Anna Laetitia Barbauld, *Sins of Government, Sins of the Nation*
        Britain: Aliens Act passes, regulating activities and employment of foreigners;
        declares war on France
        U.S.: First fugitive slave law passed by Congress; invention of cotton gin
        Canada: Upper Canada Parliament abolishes bringing slaves into colony
        France: Louis XVI and Marie Antoinette executed, Reign of Terror begins; declares
        war on Britain, Spain, Dutch Republic; Revolutionary Tribunal orders execution of
        17,000 people from 1793 to 1794

1794   William Cullen Bryant b
        Oliver Goldsmith (Canadian) b
        William Blake, *Songs of Innocence and of Experience*; *Europe: A Prophecy*; *The First
        Book of Urizen*
        Mary Wollstonecraft, *An Historical and Moral View of the Origin and Progress of the
        French Revolution*
        William Godwin, *Caleb Williams*
        Ann Radcliffe, *Mysteries of Udolpho*
        Britain: Joseph Priestley emigrates to the U.S.; habeas corpus, right to fair legal
        dealings, is suspended
        U.S.: Congress prohibits slave trade with other countries; printers in New York
        strike for better wages, fewer hours (first union to strike)
        France: Maximilien Robespierre, leader of revolution, executed; French National
        Convention abolishes slavery, but Napoleon reverses decision in 1802

1795   John Keats b
        Thomas Carlyle b
        Britain: "The Gagging Acts," or "Two Bills"—Seditious Meetings and Treasonable
        Practices Bills—introduced, banning mass meetings and the political lecture

1796   Thomas Chandler Haliburton b
        Robert Burns d
        Fanny Burney, *Camilla*
        Samuel Taylor Coleridge, *Poems on Various Subjects*

Mary Hays, *Memoirs of Emma Courtney*
Matthew Lewis, *The Monk*
U.S.: Lucy Terry Prince, an African American, argues in front of Supreme Court, the first woman to do so; court upholds her African American family's claim to land against a white man's attempt to steal it; Joshua Johnson, first African American portrait painter to be recognized in America, sets up studio in Maryland
France: Napoleonic War begins (ends in 1815)

1797   Mary Shelley b
Sojourner Truth b
Mary Wollstonecraft d
Olaudah Equiano d
Edmund Burke d
Britain: Tax on newspapers increased to repress radical publications; Bank of England begins to issue paper banknotes
France: Napoleon invades Austria and Venice

1798   William Apess b
Joanna Baillie, *Plays on the Passions*, volume I
Jeremy Bentham, *Political Economy*
William Godwin, *Memoirs of the Author of A Vindication of the Rights of Woman*
Thomas Malthus, *An Essay on the Principle of Population*
Wordsworth and Coleridge, *Lyrical Ballads*
Coleridge writing *Kubla Khan*; Wordsworth writing *The Prelude*
Britain: Nelson wins Battle of the Nile
U.S.: Congress passes Alien and Sedition Acts, prohibiting anti-government behavior and legalizing deportation; Georgia last state to abolish slave trade
France: Storming of the Bastille; Napoleon invades Egypt
Ireland: Rebellion sees 100,000 revolt (25,000 die) and Irish Parliament abolished

1799   Amos Bronson Alcott b
Britain: Trade unions suppressed
France: Napoleon appointed First Consul
Italy: Allessandro Volta invents first electric battery

1800   William Cowper d
Mary Robinson d
Maria Edgeworth, *Castle Rackrent*
Maria Robinson, *Lyrical Tales*
Second edition of *Lyrical Ballads* includes Wordsworth's "Preface"
Britain: Act of the Union with Ireland
U.S.: Illegal for citizens to export slaves; Library of Congress founded; seat of government moves from Philadelphia to Washington; census: 5,308,000

1801   George Perkins Marsh b
Quobna Ottobah Cugoano d
Maria Edgeworth, *Belinda*
Britain: First census (England and Wales: 8,893,000; Scotland: 1,608,000); Union with Ireland; Britain adopts national flag

1802   Harriet Martineau b
        George Ripley b
        Samuel Taylor Coleridge, *Poems*
        Walter Scott, *Ministrelsy of the Scottish Border*
        Britain: *Edinburgh Review* begins publication; John Constable's paintings first
        exhibited at Royal Academy
        Britain: First factory legislation
        Britain/France: Peace of Amiens
        San Domingo (Haiti): Toussaint L'Ouverture installed as governor after slave-
        holders overthrown

1803   Susanna Moodie b
        Joseph Howe b
        Ralph Waldo Emerson b
        Orestes Brownson b
        Sophia Ripley b
        Britain: Declares war against France; sugar (major import) prices rise; General
        Enclosure Act
        U.S.: Purchases Louisiana from France
        France/Canada: Napoleonic Code becomes basis for law in France and Canada

1804   Nathaniel Hawthorne b
        Elizabeth Palmer Peabody b
        Amelia Opie, *Adeline Mowbray*
        Ludwig van Beethoven, *Eroica* symphony
        Britain: Spain declares war
        U.S.: Lewis and Clark expedition to Pacific (Oregon); Noah Webster publishes his
        first dictionary
        France: Napoleon becomes Emperor

1805   William Lloyd Garrison b
        Sir Walter Scott, *The Lay of the Last Minstrel*
        Britain: Battle of Trafalgar, Nelson defeats French fleet; John Dalton publishes
        table of elements

1806   Walter Scott, *Ballads and Lyrical Pieces*
        Lady Morgan, *The Wild Irish Girl*
        Britain: Blockade of France
        U.S.: Lewis and Clark, crossing America, reach the Pacific coast

1807   John Greenleaf Whittier b
        Henry Wadsworth Longfellow b
        Frederic Henry Hedge b
        Lord Byron, *Hours of Idleness*
        Charles and Mary Lamb, *Tales from Shakespeare*
        William Wordsworth, *Poems in Two Volumes*
        Britain: Abolition of slave trade with Slave Trade Act
        U.S.: Congress attempts to outlaw importation of slaves; first voyage of steamboat,
        the *Cleremont*, on Hudson River

1808   Henry Reed b
        Sir Walter Scott, *Marmion*
        Johann Wolfgang Von Goethe, *Faust,* part I
        Ludwig Van Beethoven, *Symphonies* V and VI
        France: Napoleon invades Spain

1809   Edgar Allan Poe b
        Fanny Kemble b
        Lord Tennyson b
        Isaac Hunt d
        Thomas Paine d
        Hannah More, *Coelebs in Search of a Wife*
        Canada: John Molson builds *Accommodation*, Canada's first steamship
        France: Napoleon captures Vienna, imprisons the Pope
        South America: Independence movements (1809–1825)

1810   Margaret Fuller b
        Elizabeth Gaskell b
        William Wordsworth, *Guide to the Lakes*
        Britain: Regency begins, George III deemed insane
        U.S.: Census: 7,240,000
        Spain/Mexico: War of Independence from Spain (until 1821)
        Portugal: Under British pressure, begins to abolish slave trade

1811   Jane Austen, *Sense and Sensibility*
        Mary Brunton, *Self Control*
        Britain: Parliament makes slave trading a felony; Prince of Wales made regent to
        replace George III, who is suffering from insanity; Luddite rioters in Manchester
        (until 1815) smash machines and weaving frames; second Census: England and
        Wales, 10,165,000; Scotland, 1,806,000
        Canada: Hudson's Bay Company grants 70,000 square mile land grant to Lord
        Selkirk, to start colony at Red River, Manitoba

1812   Robert Browning b
        Charles Dickens b
        Benjamin Drew b
        Joel Barlow d
        Lord Byron, *Childe Harold* (Cantos I and II)
        Britain: Anti-Luddite law (see 1811) includes capital punishment for frame-breaking
        U.S.: Declares war on Britain, lasts until 1815
        Canada: Start of war in 1812 (ends in 1815; called the "British-American" war in
        Britain) between British-Canadians and Americans; Battle of Queenston Heights,
        an important victory over the Americans; population of Upper Canada is 100,000
        (80% of U.S. origin)

1813   Susan Fenimore Cooper b
        Harriet Jacobs b
        Christopher Pearse Cranch b
        Michel Guillaume Jean de Crèvecoeur d
        Jane Austen, *Pride and Prejudice*

Lord Byron, *The Bride of Abydos, The Corsair, The Giaour*
Percy Shelley, "Queen Mab"
Robert Southey becomes Poet Laureate
Sweden: Abolishes slave trade

1814   Sir Walter Scott, *Waverley*
William Wordsworth, *The Excursion*
Britain: Elgin Marbles displayed at British Museum
U.S.: British burn the White House; Britain and United States sign peace agreement
France: Treaty of Paris reinstates French slave trade (until 1819); Battle of
Waterloo; Napoleon exiled to Elba

1815   Elizabeth Cady Stanton b
Jane Austen, *Emma*
William Wordsworth, *Poems*
Britain: Corn Laws prevent inexpensive imports
Canada: Treaty of Ghent ratified, ending the War of 1812
France: Napoleon's forces defeated at Battle of Waterloo, ending Napoleonic War
started in 1796

1816   Charlotte Brontë b
Lord Byron, *Childe Harold* (Cantos III and IV)
Samuel Tayor Coleridge, *Christabel; Kubla Khan: A Vision; The Pains of Sleep*
Percy Bysshe Shelley, *Alastor*
Britain: Economic depression
U.S.: First Seminole War (1816–1818) between federal troops and Native
Americans assisted by runaway slaves
Barbados: Slave revolt

1817   Henry David Thoreau b
Timothy Dwight d
Jane Austen d
Lord Byron, *Manfred*
Samuel Tayor Coleridge, *Sibylline Leaves* and *Biographia Literaria*
John Keats, *Poems*
Britain: *Blackwood's Magazine* established (Tory periodical); Princess Charlotte dies
U.S.: Construction on Erie Canal begins

1818   Emily Brontë b
Frederick Douglass b
Karl Marx b
Jane Austen, *Northanger Abbey* and *Persuasion* (posthumous publication)
William Hazlitt, *Lectures on the English Poets*
John Keats, *Endymion*
Susan Ferrier, *Marriage*
Thomas Love Peacock, *Nightmare Abbey*
Mary Shelley, *Frankenstein*
U.S.: President granted power to use armed ships to stop slave ships in Africa

1819   George Eliot b
        Walt Whitman b
        Herman Melville b
        George Eliot b
        Lord Byron, *Don Juan* (Cantos I and II)
        Percy Bysshe Shelley, *Mask of Anarchy*
        Britain: Peterloo Massacre in Manchester; Parliament passes Six Acts, to suppress
        future civil disorder; Queen Victoria born
        U.S.: First steam ship, the *Savannah*, crosses Atlantic from Savannah, Georgia, to
        Liverpool; Florida acquired from Spain

1820   Anne Brontë b
        Frederick Engels b
        Charles King Newcomb b
        William Parsons Atkinson b
        Washington Irving, *The Sketch Book*
        John Keats, *Lamia, Isabella, the Eve of St. Agnes, and Other Poems*
        Percy Bysshe Shelley, *Prometheus Unbound*
        James Mill, *Essay on Government*
        Britain: *London Magazine* begins publication; George III d, George IV (formerly the
        Prince of Wales) begins reign; Cato Street conspiracy, a plot to kill cabinet members,
        is thwarted
        U.S.: Missouri Compromise, Maine enters Union as a free state, Missouri as a slave
        state (1821), outlaws slavery in all new states of Northern Plains; census: 9,634,000

1821   John Keats d
        Charles Baudelaire b
        Napoleon d
        Lord Byron, *Don Juan* (Cantos III and IV)
        Thomas De Quincey, *Confessions of an English Opium-Eater*
        William Hazlitt, *Table Talk*
        Percy Bysshe Shelley, *Adonais* and *Epipsychidion*
        Britain: Legislation regarding free trade passed in Britain; third census, population
        of England and Wales is 12,000,000, Scotland, 2,092,000
        U.S.: First all–African American acting troupe performs as African Grove Theater,
        New York City; syllabary for written form of Cherokee language invented by
        Sequoyah (George Guess); opening of Santa Fe Trail (1821–1822)
        Canada: Founding of McGill University in Montreal; Hudson's Bay Company (fur
        traders founded in 1670) merged with North West Companies
        Spain/Mexico: Treaty of Córdoba marks Mexican independence

1822   Charles Sangster b
        Percy Bysshe Shelley d
        Lord Byron, *Don Juan* (Cantos VI–XIV)
        Franz Schubert, *Unfinished Symphony*
        Britain: Period of university reform begins; St David's College, Lampeter, founded

1823   James Fenimore Cooper, *The Pioneers*
        Charles Lamb, *Essays of Elia*
        U.S.: Monroe Doctrine sees government rebuffing interference by European
        governments

1824   Lord Byron d
Susanna Rowson d
Lord Byron, *Don Juan* (Cantos XV–XVI)
Letitia Landon, *The Improvisatrice*
France: Charles X crowned King of France

1825   Thomas D'Arcy McGee b
Frances Ellen Watkins Harper b
Charlotte Dacre d
Anna Laetitia Barbauld d
William Hazlitt, *Spirit of the Age*
Britain: Railroad begins, steam train begins operation from Stockton to Darlington;
changes to Child Labor Acts, designed to improve conditions in factories; trade
unions legalized; bank crisis
U.S.: Erie canal opens way from Great Lakes to Atlantic; Thomas Cole establishes
Hudson River school of landscape painting

1826   Thomas Jefferson d
John Adams d
Elizabeth Barrett Browning, *Essay on Mind and Other Poems*
U.S.: Nashoba, colony for free African Americans, established on the outskirts of
Memphis, Tennessee

1827   William Blake d
Ludwig van Beethoven d
David Cusick, *Sketches of Ancient History of the Six Nations*
John Clare, *The Shepherd's Calendar*
U.S.: Cherokee Nation establishes its constitution (1827–1828) and composes
Memorials (1828–1830) and founds newspaper, *The Cherokee Phoenix*; railroad
constructed in Baltimore and Ohio

1828   Felicia Hemans, *Records of Woman*
Samuel Taylor Coleridge, *Poetical Works*
Britain: University College, London, founded

1829   Milcah Martha Moore d
William Apess, *A Son of the Forest*
David Walker, *Appeal*
Britain: Catholic Emancipation Act passed, lifting political and economic restric-
tions; William Austin Burt patents "Typographer," early typewriter; Robert Peel
founds Metropolitan Police in London
U.S.: Andrew Jackson pushes Native Americans further west and encourages
European Americans to settle on their ancestral lands; European Americans riot in
Cincinnati, burning homes of African Americans, who flee to Canada
Canada: Welland Canal opens, linking Lakes Erie and Ontario

1830   Emily Dickinson b
William Hazlitt d
David Walker d
Charles Lyell, *Principles of Geology* (1830–1833)

Lord Tennyson, *Poems, Chiefly Lyrical*
Britain: George IV dies, William IV crowned; first long-distance railway operates Manchester to Liverpool; start of cholera epidemic; Royal Geographic Society founded
U.S.: Indian Removal Act passed by Congress, sanctioning removal by force of eastern tribes to lands west of the Mississippi River; First National Negro Convention in Philadelphia; census: 12,866,000
France: Louis Philippe becomes King

1831   Maria W. Stewart, *Religion and the Pure Principles of Morality*
Britain: Riots against mechanized agriculture; Peasants' Revolt (also called Tyler's Rebellion) over poll tax levied to finance overseas military operations; fourth census (England and Wales: 13,897,000; Scotland: 2,364,000)
U.S.: Nat Turner leads slave revolt in Virginia, 3,000 militia men respond, killing African Americans whether involved or not; abolitionist journal *The Liberator* started by William Lloyd Garrison
Jamaica: Large slave revolt

1832   Sir Walter Scott d
Philip Morin Freneau d
Johann Wolfgang von Goethe d
Lord Tennyson, *Lady of Shalott*
Britain: Reform Bill grants vote to more people throughout the United Kingdom
Canada: Cholera epidemic (also in 1834, 1849, 1854)
Scotland: Durham University founded

1833   Hannah More d
Robert Browning, *Pauline*
Thomas Carlyle, *Sartor Resartus*
Charles Lamb, *Essays of Elia*
Lord Tennyson, *Poems*
Britain: The British Emancipation Act bans slavery in colonies, with a six-year phase-out: some 800,000 slaves freed and owners compensated; Factory Act limits child labor; *Royal William* is first ship to cross Atlantic under steam power

1834   Samuel Taylor Coleridge d
Charles Lamb d
Catharine Maria Sedgwick, *A Reminiscence of Federalism*
Britain: Abolishes slavery in its colonies; Poor Law abolishes prior employment protections, including minimum wages

1835   William Cobbett d
Felicia Dorothea Hemans d
Alexis de Tocqueville, *Democracy in America*
Britain: Municipal Reform Act
U.S.: Second Seminole War (1835–1842)

1836   William Godwin d
James Madison d
Charles Dickens, *Pickwick Papers*

Ralph Waldo Emerson, *Nature*
Thomas Babington Macaulay, *Minutes on Indian Education*
Britain: Economic recession (until 1842)
U.S.: The Transcendental Club begins to meet in Massachusetts, inaugurating
American Transcendentalism
Canada: First railroad opens

1837   Charles Dickens, *Oliver Twist*
Victor Séjour, *The Mulatto*
Britain: William IV d, Victoria succeeds to throne
Canada: Rebellions in Upper Canada led by William Lyon Mackenzie, attempting
to form a republican government

1838   Elizabeth Barrett Browning, *The Seraphim and Other Poems*
Britain: Chartist Movement founded, seeking social and political reform;
Immediate Abolition Act ends slavery, overturning the stipulations of the British
Emancipation Act (1833)
Britain/Canada: Durham Report recommends union of Upper and Lower Canada,
to quell political unease; fifth census (England and Wales: 15,914,000; Scotland:
2,620,000)
U.S.: Federal troops force Cherokees from their ancestral lands to travel west on
the "Trail of Tears"
U.S./Canada: Underground Railroad helps escaped slaves from the American south
to freedom in the Northeast states and Canada

1839   William Apess d
Caroline Stansbury Kirkland, *A New Home—Who'll Follow?*
Britain: Wars with China, takes Hong Kong
U.S.: Off the eastern seaboard, Cinque leads slave revolt on the *Amistad*, Spanish
ship
France: Louis Daguerre invents early form of photography

1840   Percy Bysshe Shelley, *A Defence of Poetry*
U.S.: Census: 17,000,000

1841   Thomas Bangs Thorpe, *The Big Bear of Arkansas*
Canada: Queen's University founded (Kingston); city of Halifax incorporated

1842   William Ellery Channing d
Robert Hutchinson Rose d
Britain: Parliament rejects Chartist petition; Chartist uprisings (Plug Riots);
Parliament passes Coal Mines Act, regulating work underground by children and
women
Canada: Population 450,000

1843   Robert Southey d
Thomas Carlyle, *Past and Present*
Margaret Fuller, *The Great Lawsuit*
Britain: William Wordsworth named Poet Laurete

1844   Joseph Priestley d
        U.S.: Telegraph invented by Samuel Morse; death of Joseph Smith, founder of the
        Mormon Church (Church of Latter-Day Saints)
        Canada: First edition of newspaper *Globe* (Toronto); New Brunswick passes Indian
        Act, sees Crown land sold to form Indian Reservations

1845   Andrew Jackson d
        Frederick Douglass, *Narrative of the Life of Frederick Douglass, an American Slave*
        Frederick Engels, *The Condition of the Working Class in England in 1844*
        Britain: Repeal of the Corn Laws; sewing machine patented
        Ireland: Famine (until 1850)
        U.S.: Texas annexed; journalist John O'Sullivan coins phrase "Manifest Destiny";
        rules of baseball established

1846   U.S.: War waged against Mexico (1846–1848), gains the Southwest through treaty
        of Guadalupe Hidalgo; 49th parallel set as international border between U.S. (at
        Oregon) and Canada
        Canada: First telegraph

1847   Henry Wadsworth Longfellow, *Evangeline*
        U.S.: Mormons settle in Salt Lake, Utah, led by Brigham Young
        Britain/Canada: Franklin Expedition (mapping Northwest Passage from Europe to
        Asia) of two ships, 128 men, disappears
        Canada: Ryerson report recommends a government-supported school system based
        on Christian faith

1848   Karl Marx and Frederick Engels, *The Communist Manifesto*
        U.S.: Women's rights convention at Seneca Falls; California Gold Rush
        (1848–1849)
        Canada: "Responsible government" established (government must answer to House
        of Commons); Fraser Gold Rush (British Columbia)
        France, Italy, Germany, Hungary: Revolutions of 1848

1849   Edgar Allan Poe d
        U.S.: Harriet Tubman escapes slavery and conducts Underground Railroad
        Canada: Crown colony establishes Vancouver Island; Gold Rush to Fraser

1850   William Wordsworth d
        Margaret Fuller d
        Nathaniel Hawthorne, *The Scarlet Letter*
        William Wordsworth, *The Prelude*
        Lord Tennyson, *In Memoriam*; becomes Poet Laurete
        U.S.: Fugitive Slave Act (strengthening of the 1793 legislation): legally compels
        citizens of free states to return escaped slaves to slaveholders; *Harper's Magazine*
        founded; census: 23,192,000

1851   Mary Shelley d
        James Fenimore Cooper d
        Joanna Baillie d
        Herman Melville, *Moby Dick*

Britain: Sixth census (England and Wales: 17,928,000; Scotland: 2,889,000)
U.S.: Women's Rights Conference in Ohio, Sojourner Truth delivers speech; New York *Times* established; Sioux give land in Iowa to government
Canada: Population approximately 2,400,000 people

1852   Thomas Moore d
Bishop Newman, *The Idea of a University*
Harriet Beecher Stowe, *Uncle Tom's Cabin*
Britain: Roget's *Thesaurus* published

1853   William Wells Brown, *Clotel*
Fanny Fern (Sarah Willis Parton), *Fresh Leaves*
J. M. Whitfield, *America and Other Poems*

1854   Henry Reed d
Leigh Hunt d
Charles Dickens, *Hard Times*
Frances Ellen Watkins Harper, *Poems on Miscellaneous Subjects*
Henry David Thoreau, *Walden*
Britain: Crimean War (Britain and France declare war on Russia—ends 1856)
U.S.: Republican Party founded, bringing together anti-slavery parties; Kansas-Nebraska Act repeals Missouri Compromise
Canada/U.S.: Reciprocity treaty controls or eliminates duties on goods between the two countries

1855   Frederick Douglass, *My Bondage, My Freedom*
Walt Whitman, *Leaves of Grass*
U.S./Canada: First train crosses suspension bridge at Niagara Falls

1856   Britain: Crimean War ends
Canada: Grand Trunk Railroad completed, stretching across southern Ontario

1857   Elizabeth Barrett Browning, *Aurora Leigh*
U.S.: Supreme Court rules in Dred Scott case to deny citizenship to African Americans
Canada: Ottawa selected as national capital

1858   Robert Owen d
Abraham Lincoln, *A House Divided*
Britain: Queen Victoria proclaims permanent British rule of India
U.S./Canada/Britain: Transatlantic cable (New York/Newfoundland/Ireland) completed but fails after 27 days of operation
Canada: Colony of British Columbia established

1859   Washington Irving d
Lydia Maria Child, *Letter to Mrs. M. J. C. Mason*
Charles Darwin, *Origin of Species*
Charles Dickens, *Tale of Two Cities*
George Eliot, *Adam Bede*
Harriet Adams Wilson, *Our Nig*
U.S.: Drilling for oil begins, Pennsylvania

1860   Charles G. D. Roberts b
        Andrews Norton d
        Charles Dickens, *Great Expectations*
        Harriett Prescott Spofford, *Circumstance*
        U.S.: Pony Express runs from Missouri to California: South Carolina secedes from
        Union; census: 31,443,000

1861   Archibald Lampman b
        Bliss Carman b
        Sophia Ripley d
        Oliver Goldsmith (Canadian) d
        Rebecca Harding Davis, *Life in the Iron Mills*
        Harriet Jacobs, *Incidents in the Life of a Slave Girl*
        U.S: Civil War begins (lasts until 1865)
        Canada: Cariboo Gold Rush (British Columbia)

1862   Duncan Campbell Scott b
        Henry David Thoreau d
        U.S.: Slavery banned in District of Columbia and U.S. territories by Congress

1863   Frances Trollope d
        U.S.: Emancipation Proclamation

1864   John Clare d
        Nathaniel Hawthorne d
        Matthew Arnold, *The Function of Criticism at the Present Time*
        U.S.: Fugitive Slave Law repealed
        Canada: Charlottetown Conference meets to discuss confederation of colonies
        France: Louis Pasteur invents pasteurization

1865   Thomas Chandler Haliburton d
        Lydia Huntley Sigourney d
        Matthew Arnold, *Essays in Criticism*
        Lewis Carroll, *Alice's Adventures in Wonderland*
        Britain: Lord John Russell becomes Prime Minister
        U.S.: Civil War ends with surrender of Confederate army; "Black Codes" issued
        in Southern states, limiting African American civil liberties; President Lincoln
        assassinated

1866   John Greenleaf Whittier, *Snow-Bound: A Winter Idyl*
        U.S.: Civil Rights Act passed by Congress to grant African Americans citizenship
        and reverse "Black Codes"; Fenian raids on Canada; Ku Klux Klan founded;
        Society for the Prevention of Cruelty to Animals (SPCA) founded
        U.S./Britain: Completion of two functioning transatlantic cables

1867   Catharine Maria Sedgwick d
        Fitz-Greene Halleck d
        Karl Marx, *Das Kapital*
        Britain: Suffrage extended by Parliamentary Reform Act
        U.S.: Reconstruction Act grants the vote to African American males
        Canada: British North America Act leads to Confederation of Canada

A Glossary of Literary and Cultural Terms

Accent: The **stress** (that is, emphasis) placed on a syllable when pronounced (represented with —).

Accentual-Syllabic Verse: Verse with a relatively regular number of syllables and balance of stressed and unstressed syllables. See **quantitative verse**.

Accentual Verse: Also called accentual-alliterative verse. Poetry of four heavy **accents**, two before and two after a mid-line pause (**caesura**) that is often combined with **alliteration** (**assonance** and **consonance**). Used in many Old English texts, such as *Beowulf* and the following line from Cædmon's "Hymn" :

> – – / /   – / – /
> He *a*erest sceop   *a*elda *bea*rnum
> [He first created   for men's sons]

See **meter, foot**.

Agon: From the Greek for competition or contest, the term refers in Greek tragedy to the conflict that drives the play and can be applied more widely to **narratives**. See **antagonist, protagonist**.

Alexandrine: A verse of **iambic hexameter**—of six feet, each with a **stress** on the second of the two beats of the iamb. In "An Essay on Criticism," Alexander Pope writes the following **couplet**—the first in pentameter, the second, hexameter:

> A needless alexandrine ends the song
> that like a wounded snake, drags its slow length along. (2.356–357)

See **meter, foot**.

Allegory: A **narrative** that stands as an extended **symbol** or **metaphor**. Characters, setting, and images convey a literal and a figurative meaning, allowing the narrative to be read at two levels. Coleridge's "Rime of the Ancient Mariner" has been read as a religious or spiritual allegory about brotherly love and the Fall of humanity, as well as a personal allegory of Coleridge's life. See **metaphor**.

Alliteration: The repetition of the same sound in a series of words. The repetition is often of consonants (**consonance**) as in Coleridge's "Kubla Khan"—"Five miles meandering in a *mazy motion*"—but can include repeated vowel sounds (**assonance**).

Alliterative Verse: See **accentual verse, meter**.

1278

Allusion: Reference to a person, place (real or imagined), historical event, or work of art, literature, or music. Allusion can take the form of intertextuality—a dialogue between two or more literary works achieved through specific quotation, paraphrase, or parody.

Amplification: An expanded repetition; the second instance elaborates upon the first.

Analogy: A comparison founded between two objects, places, people, ideas, or works of art that share a common feature. One is used to highlight a quality in the other.

Anapest (Anapestic): A metrical **foot** of two unstressed syllables, followed by a stressed. See **meter.**

Anaphora: The exact repetition of a series of words at the beginning of a series of lines of verse or sentences.

Antagonist: A central character in a narrative, often opposed to the **protagonist**, the **agon** of which anchors the plot. An antagonist, however, is not necessarily a simple villain.

Anthropomorphism: The representation of an object or animal in human form, or as having human characteristics to animals and inanimate objects. See **personification.**

Antithesis: The contrast or opposition of two ideas.

Aphorism: A short, concise statement that offers a supposed truth, of known authorship. See **proverb.**

Apostrophe: A **figure of speech** in which a speaker directly addresses a deceased or imagined person, idea, or abstraction.

Approximate Rhyme: See **near rhyme.**

Archaism: An obsolete phrase or word; or an appeal to a lost semantic sense of a word.

Archetype: In literature, the original model of a genre or form, and a symbol or myth that has historically and culturally become associated with an idea. In psychology, Jung argues that archetypes comprise the collective unconscious of humanity, only surfacing in unconscious ways.

Assonance: Repetition of vowel sounds. See **alliteration, consonance.**

Aubade: A poem about dawn. See **nocturne.**

Ballad: Historically, a song passed down orally through the generations, but during the Romantic period, a brief verse narrative, possibly set to music. Typically, it can have a narrative structure of **ballad stanzas, refrains** or **incremental repetition,** and **dialogue.**

Ballad Stanza: Four-line stanza typically found in a **ballad,** with a rhyme scheme of *abcb* (although rhymes may be a mix of **near** and **perfect** rhyme), written in alternating **iambic tetrameter** and **trimeter.**

Bard: Used to refer to a poet, but derived from early Celtic poets who recited poems of heroism.

Bathos: A shift from the serious to the ridiculous.

Blank Verse: Unrhymed iambic pentameter, but has come to refer to any unrhymed verse.

Blazon (du Corps): In heraldry, a description of a coat of arms. In literature, the term can be applied to a list of objects or items (even of the body—"corps" is French for body). In "The Stolen White Girl" (1868) the American poet John Rollin Ridge (1827–1867) writes of "Her sweet eye of blue, and her soft silken hair, / Her beautiful waist, and her bosom of white" (lines 18–19).

Bon Mot: From the French for "good word," a witty or clever remark.

Broadside: A single-page publication, typically printed on one side, that was sold cheaply.

Burlesque: Comedy that distorts and ridicules through low, often bawdy, humour. More specifically, a form of writing that offers a **parody** and **travesty** of another work, or of a person. See **caricature**.

Cacophony: A number of disharmonious and discordant sounds.

Caesura: Pause in a line of poetry based on speaking rhythm of the words and punctuation, not meter.

Canon: Generally, the corpus of works in literature acknowledged as defining a literary or national culture; and the entire body of writing of an individual author.

Canto: A division in a long poem—comprised, for instance, of many **stanzas**.

Caricature: From "to load" in Italian, a distorted portrait that typically exaggerates several physical features of a person.

Carpe Diem: Latin for "seize the day," the motto encourages one to live life fully immediately.

Chapbook: A small, inexpensive pamphlet of popular literature.

Chartism: British social and political reform movement, taking its name from the *People's Charter* of 1838, which called for a reorganized parliamentary system and universal suffrage for all men over twenty-one.

Chiasmus: A form of repetition in which the second instance is inverted; "ask not what your *country* can do for *you*; but what *you* can do for your *country*."

Classicism: Drawing on the art and culture of ancient Rome and Greece, an ideal in art and literature that encourages balance, clarity, decorum, order, reason, simplicity, and unity in form and content. This artistic style was often appealed to in the eighteenth century—often viewed as the opposite of Romantic ideas of art.

Cliché: An expression made tired and trite through over-use and over-familiarity.

Closet Drama: A drama intended for private reading, not public performance, that is structured as a play with acts, scenes, and dialogue and is often written in verse.

Cockney: Term for a person from East London, noted for a thick accent, rich **dialect**, and **slang**.

Comedy: Now refers to a humorous and entertaining literary work, but originally referred to drama—such as the romantic comedies of Shakespeare and ancient comedy.

Common Meter: Ballad stanza form consisting of a quatrain (rhyming *abab* or *abcb*) in alternating iambic tetrameter and trimeter.

Conceit: An extended metaphor that centers on a sustained and elaborate comparison of two ideas, images, places, or people (among other topics).

Confederation: The British North America Act of 1867 united the province of Canada (Quebec and Ontario) with the colonies of Nova Scotia and New Brunswick as a Dominion (a wholly self-governing political entity of the British empire).

Connotation: An idea, association, or meaning suggested by a word other than its **denotation**, or accepted meaning.

Consonance: Repetition of consonant sounds. See **alliteration, assonance**.

Continental Congress: The federal legislature of the thirteen U.S. colonies, and later the U.S., between 1774 and 1789.

Corn Laws: A series of laws passed in the early nineteenth century that levied import tariffs on foreign grants, in an effort to protect British farmers.

Couplet: A pair of verse lines that **rhyme**.

Dactyl (Dactylic): Metrical **foot** of one stressed and two unstressed syllables:

$$\overset{-}{ec} - \overset{/}{sta} - \overset{/}{sy}$$

See **meter**.

Deism: The spiritual belief that reason will guide human beings, as will the Bible, which is viewed more metaphorically than literally, leading people to act virtuously.

Denotation: The dictionary definition, or commonly accepted meaning, of a word. See **connotation**.

Dénouement: From the French for "unknotting," the coming undone of the **plot** threads of a **narrative**.

Dialect: A regional subset of a national language that can vary widely in grammar, pronunciation, syntax, and vocabulary.

Dialogue: An exchange or conversation involving more than one person. See **monologue**.

Diction: Word choice—either an author's or a character's within a literary text.

Didactic: Instructive or persuasive on a moral or practical point.

Dimeter: A verse line of two feet. See **meter, foot**.

Discourse: The words of a narrative, not its plot. More generally, the language associated with a field of knowledge.

Dissenter: Starting in the mid-1640s, a person who opposed the teaching and rules of the Anglican Church.

Dissenting Academy: A nonconformist training school for ministers in Daventry, England. Attended by Joseph Priestley.

Dissonance: Sound that is harsh and discordant.

Dramatic Irony: A disparity that occurs when an audience member or reader knows more about characters in a work of fiction or drama than the characters know of themselves.

Dramatic Monologue: A verse monologue, in which a single figure speaks to a quiet audience and unintentionally reveals information about himself or herself.

Dystopia: From the Greek for "bad place," a harsh and difficult place to live—environmentally, politically, socially. See **utopia**.

Edition: The form of a published book, including its physical construction (binding, cover) as well as its contents.

Elegiac Stanza: A **quatrain**, in **iambic pentameter**, with the rhyme *abab*.

Elegy: From the Greek for "lament," a poem about death or significant loss.

Elision: The omission of part of a word, by substituting an apostrophe for a removed letter. See Robert Burns, "To a Mouse," p. 282.

Emphasis: Emotional or physical stress or weight placed on a word through figurative language, punctuation.

Enclosed Rhyme: A couplet that is surrounded by an enclosing set of rhyming lines: *abba*.

End Rhyme: **Rhyme** in which the sound of the ends of two words match, typically in two or more lines of verse, such as the opening lines of Blake's "The Ecchoing Green": "The Sun does *arise*, / And make happy the *skies*." Two rhyming lines immediately following one another form a **couplet**, such as the closing lines of Shakespeare's sonnet "Shall I Compare thee to a summer's day?": "So long as man can breathe or eyes can *see*, / So long lives this, and this gives life to *thee*."

End-Stopped Line: A verse line in which meaning is self-contained and is marked by a physical pause or end.

English Sonnet: A fourteen-line poem consisting of three quatrains and a couplet, with a rhyme scheme *abab cdcd efef gg*. The logical or narrative structure of the poem often matches the stanza units. See **sonnet**.

Enjambment: From the French for "striding over," a thought or sentiment in verse that covers over from one line to a second, in contrast to an **end-stopped line**; also called a run-on line.

Enlightenment: During the seventeenth and eighteenth centuries, an intellectual and philosophical movement that valued human reason and logic over organized religion as a means to acquiring knowledge and finding happiness.

Epic: Long narrative poem that treats grand characters and events in a formal style. Historically, an epic was a long narrative poem, composed in an elevated style, about a serious subject or one of national import in which the fate of a nation or humanity rests with a hero, but the term is now also applied to works of a large scale or that address a weighty topic.

Epic Simile: Also called a Homeric simile, a sustained simile in which the **vehicle** (the object, person, or idea appealed to in order to convey an idea or image) is associated with the **tenor** (the object, person, or idea described). In the famous phrase "O, my luve is like a red, red rose" from Robert Burns's "A Red, Red Rose" (p. 288), "my luve" is the tenor, "rose," the vehicle. See **metaphor**.

Epigram: A short poem that is humorous or witty.

Epigraph: In literature, a quotation at the beginning of a work (or part of a work) that acts as a motto.

Epilogue: The concluding section of a literary work or play.

Epiphany: From the Greek for "showing forth" or "manifestation," a moment, in a literary work, in which a character has a revelation—gains new insight.

Episode: An incident in a literary work.

Episodic Structure: A series of episodes arranged to form a sustained story.

Epistle/Epistolary: A letter; a series of letters.

Epistolary Novel: A novel structured as a series of exchanged letters.

Epitaph: Inscription on a tombstone or memorial.

Epithet: A phrase used to describe a person.

Etymology: The study of the historical derivation of words.

Eulogy: A statement praising a deceased person.

Euphemism: Replacement of a harsh, rude, or sexual word with a more polite one.

Euphony: Melodious and harmonious sound. See **cacophony**.

Eye Rhyme: Words that may appear to rhyme because of their similar spelling, but do not when pronounced: cough/bough. See **rhyme**.

Fable: Short, allegorical prose or verse narrative with a moral.

Falling Meter: See **meter**.

Feminine Ending: A verse line that ends with an extra, unstressed syllable (often in the form of an **iambic** or **anapestic** foot).

Feminine Rhyme: A rhyme of a stressed and unstressed syllable of two **feminine endings**.

Fiction: Generally, any imagined work or **narrative** in prose, verse, or drama, but used more specifically to refer to prose works (novels, short stories).

Figurative Language: Language that uses **figures of speech** to draw out **metaphoric** meaning and **connotations**, beyond the **denotative** meanings of the words.

Figure of Speech: A phrase that connotes rather than denotes—that involves a metaphoric use of language to establish an association, connection, or image in the reader's mind.

First-Person Narration: A narrative told by a single figure—either the author or a character in a literary work—whose sense of events is limited to what he or she knows and experiences directly.

Folk Song: A song of unknown origin handed down between generations in a specific community.

Foot: A rhythmic unit in metrical verse, comprised of stressed (–) and unstressed (/) syllables. Metrical feet include: iamb (– /), trochee (/ –), anapest (/ / –), dactyl (/ – –), spondee (– –), and the less common, pyrrhic (/ /). The feet of a line can be measured accordingly: monometer (one), dimeter (two), trimeter (three), tetrameter (four), pentameter (five), hexameter (six), heptameter (seven), and octameter (eight). See **meter**.

Foreshadow: Future-looking information in a narrative that hints of events or action to come.

Fourteener: A verse line of fourteen syllables, usually written in **iambic heptameter**.

Frame Narrative: A narrative that encases another, the larger story offering context or background for the enclosed one.

Free Verse: From the French *vers libre*, verse that lacks regular meter and line length and does not rhyme.

Genre: From the French for "kind" or "type," the categorization of literary works based on historical convention or some element of content or form. Broader historically distinctions have been made between the larger modes of prose, verse, and drama and between the classical modes of comedy, epic, lyric, pastoral, satire, and tragedy but extend to classification based on style and specific convention: the gothic or romance, for instance.

Gloss; Glossary: An explanatory note (such as Coleridge's marginal glosses in "The Rime of the Ancient Mariner," p. 465); a list of explained and defined words.

Gothic: Historically refers to the Goths, a German tribe, who warred with the Roman Empire and were seen as savage and barbaric. In the middle ages, gothic castles and cathedrals included architectural features such as pointed arches and vaults, spires and towers, and flying buttresses, and they were often dark, mysterious buildings. In literature, the term refers to a set of aesthetic conventions that includes the supernatural, mysterious settings and characters, and suspense.

Gothic Novel and **Gothic Romance**: Fiction first made popular in the late eighteenth century that includes several of a small cluster of set conventions: the supernatural, dark and dangerous settings, heroes and heroines separated but (often) reunited, and atmospheres of terror, horror, mystery, and suspense. See **romance**.

Great Awakening: A period of social and spiritual change in the U.S. during the 1730s and 1740s that saw Jonathan Edwards and George Whitfield call for people to return to their Calvinist roots.

Heptameter: A verse line of seven metrical feet. See **meter, foot**.

Heroic Couplet: A balanced **couplet**, written in **iambic pentameter**.

Hexameter: A verse line of six metrical feet. See **meter, foot**.

Homily: A sermon or speech offering personal or spiritual guidance and advice.

Hymn: Song of praise, in verse.

Hyperbole: A **figure of speech** that overstates and exaggerates for ironic or comic effect.

Iamb (or **Iambic**): A metrical foot of one unstressed and one stressed foot. See **meter, foot**.

Idyll: Short narrative, often in verse, that extols the pleasures of **pastoral** landscapes.

Image: A visual or mental picture of an object, person, or place (among others) that appeals to the senses.

Imperfect Rhyme: See **near rhyme.**

Industrial Revolution: Starting in the mid-seventeenth century, the rise of the mechanization of agricultural and industrial production through new technologies (such as steam).

Innuendo: A remark or physical action that insinuates a belittling or sexual meaning.

Interlocking Rhyme: A rhyme that spans two or more stanzas, connecting them, such as *abba bccb*.

Internal Rhyme: A repetition of similar or matching sound in a single line of verse. In "Rime of the Ancient Mariner," Coleridge writes: "The ship drove *fast*, loud roared the *blast* (line 49, p. 467). See **rhyme.**

Intertextuality: See **allusion.**

Irony: An incongruity between appearance and reality, or between expectation and reality. **Verbal irony** is the divergence between what an author or character says, on the one hand, and believes to be true, on the other. **Situational irony** arises from an event, involving a discrepancy between reality and appearance (an event that is opposite to what was anticipated). **Dramatic irony** involves a reader's or audience's awareness of the falsity or inaccuracy of characters' words or actions, which will return to haunt them.

Italian Sonnet: Also called a Petrarchan sonnet (after the fourteenth-century Italian poet Petrarch who popularized it), a fourteen-line poem, consisting of one **octave** and one **sestet**, with a rhyme scheme of *abbaabba cdecde* (or *cdcdcd*). The logical or narrative structure of the poem often matches the stanza units. See **sonnet**.

Jargon: Diction specific to a discipline, trade, or profession, as in sports jargon, medical jargon.

Lay: A form of **ballad** that originated in twelfth- and thirteenth-century France, adapted in literature to describe a short song or verse narrative—such as those of Sir Walter Scott (p. 459).

Leitmotif: The repetition of a **motif** (a recurring **theme** through **images**, **symbols**, and **metaphors**, among other literary devices) that stirs associations across the literary work, unifying it.

Libertine: A free thinker, who believes in being free from the restraints of social and religious norms and morals.

Literal: From the Latin for "letter," the concise meaning of a word in simple terms.

Loyalist: A colonist in British North America who remained a devoted subject of the British Crown; many fled to Canada from the U.S.

Lyric: A short poem capturing the thoughts and emotions of one narrator (who is not necessarily the poet) that focuses on personal impression and imagery rather than **narrative**.

Manuscript: A handwritten document.

Marginalia: Comments and annotations recorded in the margins of the page. See **gloss**.

Masculine Ending: A **rhyme** that ends on a **stressed syllable** (an **iamb**, for instance).

Masculine Rhyme: A rhyme of stressed one-syllable words.

Metaphor: A figure of speech that associates two separate images, ideas, people, places, or objects, employing one to represent the other. The image, idea, person, place, or object used to describe is the **vehicle**. That which is represented is the **tenor**. See **allegory**.

Meter: The musical beats of poetry; or the rhythmic pattern of words and their produced stressed and unstressed syllables in a regular sequence with a discernible pattern of accents, or feet. Meter can rise, ending with a heavy stress (**iambic** and **anapestic**), and fall (**trochaic** and **dactylic**). Meter can be made up of feet of varying lengths:

one foot: monometer
two feet: dimeter
three feet: trimeter

four feet: tetrameter
five feet: pentameter
six feet: hexameter
seven feet: heptameter (or a **fourteener**)
eight feet: octameter

The traditional feet of English meter include: iamb (or iambic), one unstressed syllable and one stressed; anapest (or anapestic), two unstressed, followed by one stressed; trochee (trochaic): a metrical foot of one stressed and one unstressed; and, a less common foot, pyrrhic (pyrrhic): two unstressed.

Metonymy: A figure of speech in which an idea or object stands for another idea or object associated with the former.

Mimesis: The act of imitating, or fashioning one's writing style after a model.

Mock Epic: An epic that subverts the convention of the form by taking a trivial rather than a serious subject as its focus, presented in ridiculous rather than elevated terms.

Monody: A poem of lamentation, often sung by one person for another.

Monologue: Extended **narrative** by one speaker. See **dialogue**.

Motif: Unifying or recurring **theme** in a literary work.

Muse: In Greek mythology, the nine daughters of Zeus, each charged with overseeing an art or science. More generally, a source of inspiration appealed to (sometimes directly in a literary work) by artists for creative assistance.

Mysticism: Belief in spiritual or divine knowledge through extrasensory knowledge, through intuition and meditation, for instance, rather than the five senses.

Myth: From the Greek for "narrative" or "plot," a narrative that explains a natural or supernatural occurrence or being, the creation of the world, or history of a people.

Narrative: A story or account of a story, real or imagined, that includes character, setting, and plot.

Narrative Poem: A poem that tells a story.

Narrator: A speaker of a narrative, not necessarily the author or a character in the text. The point of view of the narrator can be: first person, a participant in the narrative; or third person, with an omniscient (all-knowing) or limited understanding of surrounding events and characters.

Naturalism: Nineteenth-century literary movement, influenced by evolutionary and scientific thinking, that valued realism based on detailed, objective description.

Near Rhyme: Also called slant rhyme, off rhyme, approximate rhyme, or imperfect rhyme. See **rhyme**.

Negative Capability: A phrase used by John Keats to indicate an artistic quality possessed by Shakespeare, whom he saw as writing intuitively and organically, and was able to be "in uncertainties, mysteries, doubts, without any irritable reaching after fact and reason." An ability to resist formal categories and rational explanations of uncertain or ambiguous situations or ideas.

Neologism: A freshly coined word, or the innovative use of an existing word. See "liberticide" in Shelley's "Sonnet: England in 1819," p. 684.

Nocturne: An artistic work that involves the nocturnal—nighttime. See **aubade**.

Novel: An extended work of fiction, written in prose. During the Romantic period, the term had a more limited definition than it does in the twentieth and twenty-first centuries. The form arose in the eighteenth century, with the **picaresque** novel (a tale of a rogue's adventures), the **sentimental** novel (a story of exalted emotion, coupled with the virtue of feeling and proper moral conduct), and the **epistolary** novel (an exchange of letters). The Romantic period drew a distinction between the **romance** novel (see **romance**) and **realistic** novel (that explores the psychology and feelings of characters).

Novella: From the Italian for "a little new thing," a short prose narrative—of about one hundred pages or less (longer than a short story, and not as long as a novel).

Octameter: A line of verse with eight feet. See **meter, foot**.

Octave: A stanza of eight lines, usually comprised of two **quatrains**, that form part of a **sonnet**.

Ode: Written in an elevated style, a long **lyric** poem that is serious and meditative in tone and addresses a matter of great importance. See Keats's "Ode to a Nightingale," for instance, p. 781.

Off Rhyme: See **near rhyme**.

Omniscient Narrator: The speaker of a narrative who knows and recounts experiences and emotions belonging to other characters, and events beyond his or her direct knowledge.

Onomatopoeia: A word that, when pronounced, sounds like what it signifies: *buzz, hiss*.

Organic and **Organicism**: The natural or innate unfolding of form and content in a literary work—that the two function as a unified whole.

Orientalism: Cultural and historical ideas, images, and representations of the Oriental world (the Far East to the Middle East) by the Occidental world (U.S. and Europe). The twentieth-century literary critic Edward Said explores the concept at length in *Orientalism* (1978), arguing that the Orient is misrepresented by false images, which contributed to the colonization of East by West.

Ossian: Ancient Celtic poet, who James Macpherson (1736–1796) claimed to have translated from the original Gaelic. The translations influenced writers from Scott to Goethe.

Oxymoron: From the Greek for "pointedly foolish," a figure of speech that opposes two contradictory ideas.

Palimpsest: A writing surface on which two layers of writing appear, the latter not fully erasing the former.

Panegyric: A laudatory literary work, praising a person, event, or idea.

Pantheism: From the Greek for "all" and "god," the belief that God, nature, and the universe are all one.

Pantisocracy: Name of a commune Samuel Taylor Coleridge and Robert Southey planned to establish in Pennsylvania.

Paradox: Seemingly false or contradictory statement that yields truth.

Paraphrase: Restatement in one's own words of a part or all of a literary text.

Parody: The imitation of another literary text's or author's distinct characteristics through exaggeration and distortion.

Pastoral: From the Latin for "shepherd," a text with a rural setting, and, more specifically during the Romantic period, with shepherds and country life.

Pathos: Pity, sympathy, or compassion for the suffering and the vulnerable.

Pentameter: Verse line of five feet. See **meter, foot**.

Perfect Rhyme: Rhyme of stressed and identical sounds.

Persona: From the Latin for "mask," the speaker of a text who may or may not be the author.

Personification: Figure of speech in which human attributes are given to the nonhuman.

Peterloo: Modeled after Napoleon's "Waterloo," name of a massacre in Manchester, England, in which government troops violently dispersed, injured, and killed protestors seeking Parliamentary reform.

Petrarchan Sonnet: See **Italian sonnet**.

Picturesque: Idealized landscape in painting or writing that captures a stock or popular setting (ruined buildings, quaint cottage, babbling brook).

Plagiarism: From the Latin for "kidnapping," the representation of another's ideas or words as one's own.

Poet Laureate: State or royally appointed poet who composes verse for special occasions. In England, the first Poet Laureate was John Dryden, appointed in 1670. The title has become more honorary in the nineteenth through twenty-first centuries.

Poetry: Figurative rich language, written in verse form, in which the denotative and connotative senses as well as the sound of language are appealed to for musical, rhetorical, rhythmic, and metaphoric effect.

Prose: Ordinary written expression, presented in grammatical and syntactical order.

Prosody: Study of **meter**.

Protagonist: The central character in a narrative, whose emotions, actions, and words center around an **agon**, a key conflict, which the **antagonist** is at odds with.

Proverb: Aphorism of unknown authorship.

Pseudonym: Fictitious name assumed by an author.

Pun: Play on words through sense or sound (homonym) that slips between multiple meanings of a word.

Puritanism: Protestant movement in England and North America that valued the direct experience of God, rejecting the mediating influence of the clergy.

Pyrrhic: A foot of two unstressed feet (not a common foot in English verse). See **meter, foot**.

Republican: The political belief that power rests with the people and that the state should protect the liberties of each individual.

Quantitative Verse: Poetry based not on stresses but on the number of syllables; the opposite of **accentual-syllabic verse**.

Quatrain: Four-line stanza.

Refrain: A recurring line or lines in verse, either exactly or with minor variation.

Rhetoric: Greek for "orator" (*rhetor*), the art of persuasion in speaking, but also now applied to writing.

Rhetorical Figure: An ornamented figure of speech, the arrangement of which, through word choice and order, sound, repetition, or semantics, is designed to enhance literal and figurative meaning.

Rhetorical Question: A question raised for dramatic effect and not to evoke an answer (which is often self-evident).

Rhyme: The repetition of similar or matching sounds in two or more words. The rhyming sound does not have to be spelled similarly in each word, but can rhyme with consonants or vowels, to create **consonance** and **assonance** (bouquet/weigh), respectively. (Indeed, **eye rhyme** exists when words may appear to rhyme because of their similar spelling, but do not when pronounced: cough/bough). **End rhyme** is the most common form of rhyme in English poetry, as in the following lines from Coleridge's "Rime of the Ancient Mariner":

> The Bridegroom's doors are opened wide,
> And I am next of *kin*;
> The guests are *met*, the feast is *set*:
> May'st hear the merry *din*.' (lines 5–8)

Kin/din in lines 6 and 8 are end rhymes (and also exact or perfect rhyme); while met/set in line 7 is an example of **internal rhyme**. An end rhyme that ends with a strong **stress**, single-syllable word (as in kin/din) is an example of **masculine rhyme**. **Feminine rhyme**, on the other hand, involves a stressed word or sound followed by a matching unstressed sound.

Rhythm: From the Greek word for "flow," the measured flow of words, the **stressed** and **unstressed** parts of the words forming a pattern of beats, when spoken aloud.

Rising Meter: See **meter**.

Romance: A Medieval narrative of adventure, usually involving a knight, a damsel in distress, frustrated love, a quest, and, ultimately, triumph. The term has since been adopted: in the Romantic period, a work of adventure, often including the supernatural. See **gothic romance**.

Run-on Line: See **enjambment**.

Satire: The ridicule of vice or imperfection for the purposes of reforming the shortcoming.

Scansion: The analysis of the meter in verse in order to determine stressed and unstressed syllables.

Sensibility: Relating to emotion and feeling. In late eighteenth-century British literature, a movement that saw authors focusing on the interior and emotions of characters.

Sestet: A six-line stanza.

Shakespearean Sonnet: See **English sonnet**.

Simile: A **figure of speech** that compares two objects, persons, or places (among other things), using *as*, *as if*, or *like*. See **metaphor**.

Situational Irony: An incongruity between an actual event and one that was expected. See **irony**.

Slang: Informal vocabulary or diction choice that is considered base or substandard, even pro-fane, by common educational and cultural standards.

Slant Rhyme: See **near rhyme**.

Sonnet: From the Italian for "little song," a poem of fourteen lines with a fixed form in rhyme and stanza structure. See **English sonnet** and **Italian sonnet**.

Spenserian Stanza: Nine-line **stanza** developed by Edmund Spenser in *The Faerie Queene* (1590–1596), eight of **iambic pentameter**, and the last of **iambic hexameter**, rhyming *abab-bcbcc*. Used by Percy Bysshe Shelley in "Adonais" (1821) and John Keats in "The Eve of St. Agnes," p. 769.

Spondee: A metrical foot of two stressed syllables. See **meter, foot**.

Spontaneity: Impulsively or naturally occurring. A touchstone of Romanticism, the belief in the virtue of the organic and uncultivated. Wordsworth: "Poetry is the spontaneous overflow of powerful feelings" (pp. 405, 410).

Stanza: A group of lines in verse set off from other lines and other stanzas. Stanzas can vary in length (see **octave**, **quatrain**, **sestet**, **Spenserian stanza**, **tercet**).

Stress; Unstress: The accent or emphasis, heavy (stressed) or light (unstressed), of a syllable in verse. See **meter**.

Sublime: An elevating quality in a literary work, whether in content (noble subject matter) or in form (stylized and poetic language).

Syllabic Verse: Verse with a fixed syllable count, regardless of stresses.

Symbol: Something (an object, place, person, idea) that while conveying meaning itself also suggests or signifies a secondary idea. See **allegory.**

Syncopation: A musical term that indicates the stressing of a normally unaccented beat, which can be used to describe some shifts in the rhythm of poetry.

Synecdoche: A figure of speech in which a part of an idea, object, or person stands for the whole.

Synesthesia: A mixing together, or confusion, of the five senses—seeing a sound, for instance.

Tenor: The part of a **metaphor** that is described or represented by the vehicle.

Tercet: A **stanza** of three lines.

Terza Rima: **Tercet**-based verse with **interlocking rhyme** (*aba bcb cdc*), such as Shelley's "Ode to the West Wind," p. 694.

Tetrameter: A verse line of four feet. See **meter, foot.**

Theme: A main point of a literary work; a subject or idea, or abstract concept, that emerges in a literary work.

Third-Person Narrator: A speaker of a narrative who is not a participant in the events related.

Topographical Poem: A poem that surveys the topography—the landscape—of a region.

Tragedy: Serious literary work—originally referring to a dramatic form—that focuses on the downfall of or disasters faced by a protagonist.

Tragic Irony: Irony freighted with foreboding—reader awareness of impeding disaster for a character.

Transcendentalism: A philosophical and literary movement in nineteenth-century America that sought a form of spirituality focused on nature through individual intuition and conscience, rather than rational thought, in an effort to find moral truths in nature and not in a specific organized religion.

Travesty: **Burlesque** that deflates a dignified person or subject through ridicule, **hyperbole,** or **parody** and renders it not just common, but base and gross.

Trimeter: A verse line of three feet. See **meter, foot.**

Trochee (Trochaic): A metrical foot of one stressed and one unstressed foot. See **meter, foot.**

Trope: A **figure of speech** that twists the meaning of a word to give it a **metaphoric** sense.

Utopia: From the Greek for "good place" and "no place," an Edenic, ideal place that does not exist in reality. See **dystopia.**

Vehicle: One part of a metaphor. Aspects or details of the vehicle are attributed to the **tenor** (the person, object, or place described).

Verbal Irony: A disparity between a speaker's or author's implicit meaning and that made explicit. See **irony**.

Verisimilitude: The appearance of reality.

Vignette: A short story, or a sketch of a person.

Villanelle: A nineteen-line poem, consisting of five **tercets** (*aba*) and one **quatrain** (*abaa*), governed by the repetition of two rhymes and two refrains, based on lines 1 and 3: thus line 1 is repeated as lines 6, 12, and 18; and line 3, as 9, 15, and 19.

Zeugma: From the Greek for "a yoking," the application of one word to two (or more) words— in at least one case illogically or against the idiomatic grain of the word; such as in Byron's *Don Juan* (1819–1824): "The loud tempests *raise* / The *waters*, and *repentance* for past sinning" (5.44–45).

Selected Bibliography of Transatlantic Romanticism

Internet Resources

American Studies Hypertexts ~ http://xroads.virginia.edu/~HYPER/hypertex.html
American Transcendentalism Web ~ http://www.vcu.edu/engweb/transcendentalism
American Verse Project ~ http://www.hti.umich.edu/a/amverse/
The Bluestocking Archive ~ http://www.faculty.umb.edu/elizabeth_fay/toc.html
British Poetry 1780–1910: A Hypertext Archive of Scholarly Editions ~ http://etext.lib.
    virginia.edu/britpo.html
British Women Playwrights around 1800 ~ http://www.etang.umontreal.ca/bwp1800/
British Women Romantic Poets ~ http://digital.lib.ucdavis.edu/projects/bwrp/
The EServer ~ http://eserver.org/
Library of Congress American Memory Collections ~ http://memory.loc.gov/ammem
Making of America at Cornell ~ http://cdl.library.cornell.edu/moa/moa_browse.html
Making of America at Michigan ~ http://www.hti.umich.edu/m/moagrp/
NINES (Network Interface for Nineteenth-Century Electronic Scholarship) ~
    http://www.nines.org/
Representative Poetry Online ~ http://eir.library.utoronto.ca/rpo
Romantic Chronology ~ http://english.ucsb.edu:591/rchrono
Romantic Circles ~ http://www.rc.umd.edu
Romanticism on the Net ~ http://www.ron.umontreal.ca
Romantics Unbound ~ http://www.romanticsunbound.net/
SSAWW Archive of Nineteenth-Century American Women Writers ~
    http://www.lehigh.edu/~dek7/SSAWW/eTextLib.htm
The Star Project (Scotland's Transatlantic Relations) ~ http://www.star.ac.uk/index.html
Voice of the Shuttle ~ http://vos.ucsb.edu
William Blake Archive ~ http://www.blakearchive.org/
Women Romantic-Era Writers ~ http://www.bbk.ac.uk/english/ac/wrew.htm
Women Writers Project ~ http://www.wwp.brown.edu/

Studies of Transatlantic Romanticism

Almeida, Joselyn, "The Sight of a New World: Discovery and Romanticism," *The Wordsworth Circle*, 2001.
Andrews, Stuart, "Fellow Pantisocrats: Brissot, Cooper, and Imlay," *Symbiosis*, 1997.
Appiah, Kwame Anthony, "Against National Culture," *Text and Nation: Cross-Disciplinary Essays on Cultural and National Identities*, eds. Laura Garcia-Moreno and Peter C. Pfeiffer, 1996.

Atchison, Erin, "Transporting Elizabeth's Piano: Literature and the Piano in the Early American Republic," *Symbiosis*, 2004.

Austin, Allan D., *African Muslims in Antebellum America*, 1997.

Barnes, James J., *Authors, Publishers and Politicians: The Quest for an Anglo-American Copyright Agreement, 1815–1854*, 1974.

Barth, J. Robert, and Elizabeth C. Nordbeck, "Coleridge's Orthodoxy in Transcendentalist New England," *The Wordsworth Circle*, 2001.

Bauer, Ralph, "Notes on the Comparative Study of the Colonial Americas," *Early American Literature*, 2003.

Beer, Janet, and Bridget Bennett, eds., *Special Relationships: Anglo-American Affinities and Antagonisms, 1854–1939*, 2002.

Berlin, Ira, "From Creole to African: Atlantic Creoles and the Origins of African-American Society in Mainland North America," *How Did American Slavery Begin*, ed. Edward Countryman, 1999.

Blake, David, and Elliott Gruner, "Redeeming Captivity: The Negative Revolution of Blake's *Visions of the Daughters of Albion*," *Symbiosis*, 1997.

Brantley, Richard, *Anglo-American Antiphony: The Late Romanticism of Tennyson and Emerson*, 1994.

———, *Coordinates of Anglo-American Romanticism: Wesley, Edwards, Carlyle, and Emerson*, 1993.

———, *Experience and Faith: The Late-Romantic Imagination of Emily Dickinson*, 2004.

Buell, Lawrence, *Emerson*, 2003.

———, "Postcolonial Anxiety in Classic U.S. Literature," *Postcolonial Theory and the United States: Race, Ethnicity, and Literature*, eds. Amritjit Singh and Peter Schmidt, 2000.

Castillo, Susan, "Imperial Pasts and Dark Futurities: Freneau and Brackenridge's 'The Rising Glory of America,'" *Symbiosis*, 2002.

Chai, Leon, *The Romantic Foundations of the American Renaissance*, 1987.

Christianson, Frank, "From Sympathy to Altruism: Philanthropic Fiction in a Transatlantic Context," *Symbiosis*, 2004.

Clark, Jennifer, "Poisoned Pens: The Anglo-American Relationship and the Paper War," *Symbiosis*, 2002.

Coronato, Rocco, "Inducting Pocohontas," *Symbiosis*, 1998.

Culler, Jonathan, "Comparative Literature and the Pieties," *Profession*, 1986.

Cutler, Edward S., *Recovering the New: Transatlantic Roots of Modernism*, 2003.

Desmond, Jane C., and Virginia R. Dominguez, "Resituating American Studies in a Critical Internationalism," *American Quarterly*, 1996.

Dimock, Wai-Chee, "Literature for the Planet," *PMLA*, 2001.

Duffy, John J., *Coleridge's American Disciples: The Selected Correspondence of James Marsh*, 1973.

Durey, Michael, *Transatlantic Radicals and the Early American Republic*, 1997.

Eagleton, Terry, Fredric Jameson, and Edward W. Said, *Nationalism, Colonialism and Literature*, 1990.

Ellison, Julie, *Cato's Tears and the Making of Anglo-American Emotion*, 2000.

Fender, Stephen, *Sea Changes: British Emigration and American Literature*, 1992.

———, ed., *Americans and European National Identities: Faces in the Mirror*, 1996.

Finnerty, Páraic, "The Daisy and the Dandy," *Symbiosis*, 2005.

Flynn, Christopher, "'No Other Island in the World': *Mansfield Park*, North America and Post-Imperial Malaise," *Symbiosis*, 2000.

Frank, Armin Paul, and Christel-Maria Maas, *Transnational Longfellow*, 2005.

Frank, Armin Paul, and Kurt Mueller-Vollmer, *The Internationality of National Literatures in Either America: Transfer and Transformation*, 2000.

Fulford, Timothy, "Romantic Indians and Colonial Politics: The Case of Thomas Campbell," *Symbiosis*, 1998.

Gardner, Jared, *Master Plots: Race and the Founding of an American Literature, 1787–1845*, 1998.

Gerzina, Gretchen Holbrook, "Mobility in Chains: Freedom of Movement in the Early Black Atlantic," *South Atlantic Quarterly*, 2001.

Gidley, Mick, and Robert Lawson-Peebles, eds., *Views of American Landscapes*, 1989.

Gifford, Henry, *Comparative Literature*, 1969.

Giles, Paul, *Transatlantic Insurrections*, 2001.

———, "Transnationalism and Classic American Literature," *PMLA*, 2003.

———, *Virtual Americas: Transnational Fictions and the Transatlantic Imaginary*, 2002.

Gilroy, Paul, *The Black Atlantic*, 1993.

Goddu, Teresa, *Gothic America: Narrative, History, and Nation*, 1997.

Goodman, Russell B., *American Philosophy and the Romantic Tradition*, 1990.

Graver, Bruce, "George Ticknor, Robert Southey, and *The Poem of the Cid*," *The Wordsworth Circle*, 2001.

Gravil, Richard, "'The Discharged Soldier' and 'The Runaway Slave': Wordsworth and the Definition of Walt Whitman," *Symbiosis*, 1997.

———, "Emily Dickinson (and Walt Whitman): The Escape from 'Locksley Hall,'" *Symbiosis*, 2003.

———, "Regicide and Ethnic Cleansing: or, Edmund Burke in Wish-ton-Wish," *Symbiosis*, 2000.

———, *Romantic Dialogues: Anglo-American Continuities, 1776–1862*, 2000.

Green, David Bonnell, "William Wordsworth and Lydia Huntley Sigourney," *The New England Quarterly*, 1964.

Grey, Robin, *The Complicity of Imagination: The American Renaissance, Contests of Authority, and Seventeenth-Century English Culture*, 1997.

Gross, Robert A., "The Transnational Turn: Rediscovering American Studies in a Wider World," *Journal of American Studies*, 2000.

Guarneri, Carl, *The Utopian Alternative: Fourierism in Nineteenth-Century America*, 1991.

Halliwell, Martin, *Romantic Science and the Experience of Self: Transatlantic Crosscurrents from William James to Oliver Sacks*, 1999.

Harding, Walter, *Emerson's Library*, 1967.

Henderson, Mae G., ed., *Borders, Boundaries and Frames: Essays in Cultural Criticism and Cultural Studies*, 1995.

Hertz, Robert, "English and American Romanticism," *Personalist*, 1965.

Heydt-Stevenson, Jillian, and Jeffrey N. Cox, eds., "Romantic Cosmopolitanism," a special issue of *European Romantic Review*, 2005.

Hoeveler, Diane Long, and Tamar Heller, eds., *Approaches to Teaching Gothic Fiction: The British and American Traditions*, 2003.

Hollock, John, *The American Byron: Homosexuality and the Fall of Fitz-Greene Halleck*, 2000.

Holman, Rupert, "Nathaniel Hawthorne at Greenwich," *Symbiosis*, 2001.

Hook, Andrew, *Scotland and America, 1750–1835*, 1975.

Howard, Leon, *Literature and the American Tradition*, 1960.

Jones, Catherine A., "Hawthorne's Scotland: Memory and Imagination," *Symbiosis*, 2000.

Kadir, Djelal, ed., "America and Its Studies," Introduction to special issue "America: The Idea, the Literature," *PMLA*, 2003.

Karbiener, Karen, "Cross-Cultural Confessions: America Passes Judgment on Thomas De Quincey," *Symbiosis*, 1999.

Kaufman, Will, and Heidi Macpherson, eds., *Transatlantic Studies*, 2000.

———, eds., *New Perspectives in Transatlantic Studies*, 2002.

Keach, William, "A Transatlantic Romantic Century," *European Romantic Review*, 2000.

Kennedy, J. Gerald, and Liliane Weissberg, eds., *Romancing the Shadow: Poe and Race*, 2001.

Kerr, Howard, John W. Crowley, and Charles L. Crow, *The Haunted Dusk: American Supernatural Fiction, 1820–1920*, 1983.

Koenig-Woodyard, Chris, and Joel Pace, "Coleridge and Divine Providence," *The Wordsworth Circle*, 2001.

Lauter, Paul, "American Studies and Ethnic Studies at the Borderlands Crossroads," *From Walden Pond to Jurassic Park: Activism, Culture and American Studies*, 2001.

———, "The Literatures of America: A Comparative Discipline," *Redefining American Literary History*, eds. A. LaVonne Brown Ruoff and Jerry Ward, 1990.

Lee, Sohui, "The Guillotine and the American Public: A Godwinian Reading of *The Scarlet Letter*," *Symbiosis*, 2000.

Lenz, Gunter H., "Toward a Dialogics of International American Culture Studies: Transnationality, Border Discourses, and Public Culture," *Amerikastudien/American Studies*, 1999.

Logan, Deborah, "Harriet Martineau and the Martyr Age of the United States," *Symbiosis*, 2001.

Lopez, Debbie, "Liberties with Lamia: The 'Gordian Knot' of Relations Between Keats and Hawthorne," *Symbiosis*, 1998.

Maertz, Gregory, ed., *Cultural Interactions in the Romantic Age*, 1998.

Mahoney, John, *Wordsworth and the Critics*, 2001.

Makdisi, Saree, *Romantic Imperialism*, 1998.

Mandell, Laura, ed., "The Poetess Tradition," introduction to special issue "The Transatlantic Poetess," *Romanticism on the Net*, 2003.

Manning, Susan, *Fragments of Union: Making Connections in Scottish and American Writing*, 2002.

———, *The Puritan-Provincial Vision: Scottish and American Literature in the Nineteenth Century*, 1990.

Marx, Leo, *The Machine in the Garden: Technology and the Pastoral Ideal in America*, 1964.

Mazzeo, Tilar J., "The Impossibility of Being Anglo-American: The Rhetoric of Emigration and Transatlanticism in British Romantic Culture, 1791–1833," *European Romantic Review*, 2005.

McGuire, Ian, "Culture and Antipathy: Arnold, Emerson, and *Democratic Vistas*," *Symbiosis*, 2001.

McKusick, James, "From Coleridge to John Muir: The Romantic Origins of Environmentalism," *The Wordsworth Circle*, 1995.

———, *Green Writing: Romanticism and Ecology*, 2000.

———, "Stepping Westward," introduction to "Transatlantic Romanticism," a special issue of *The Wordsworth Circle*, 2001.

Miller, J. Hillis, "English Romanticism, American Romanticism: What's the Difference?" *Theory Now and Then*, 1991.

Miller, Perry, "Thoreau in the Context of International Romanticism," *The New England Quarterly*, 1961.

Mills, Nicolaus, *American and English Fiction in the Nineteenth Century: An Anti-Genre Critique and Comparison*, 1973.

Moldenhauer, Joseph, "*Walden* and Wordsworth's *Guide to the Lake District*," *Studies in the American Renaissance*, 1990.

Mulvey, Christopher, *Anglo-American Landscapes: A Study of Anglo-American Travel Literature*, 1983.

———, *Transatlantic Manners: Social Patterns in Nineteenth-Century Anglo-American Travel Literature*, 1990.

Murphy, Geraldine, "Olaudah Equiano, Accidental Tourist," *Eighteenth-Century Studies*, 1994.

Muthyala, John, "Rewording America: The Globalization of American Studies," *Cultural Critique*, 2001.

Nash, Roderick, ed., *S. T. Coleridge: Interviews and Recollections*, 2000.

Newman, Lance, *Our Common Dwelling: Henry Thoreau, Transcendentalism, and the Class Politics of Nature*, 2005.

Newman, Lance, Joel Pace, and Chris Koenig-Woodyard, eds., *Sullen Fires Across the Atlantic: Essays in Romanticism*. Romantic Circles Praxis Series (http://www.rc.umd.edu/praxis), forthcoming 2005.

Oliver, Susan, "Transatlantic Influences in Periodical Editing: From Francis Jeffrey's *Edinburgh Review* to Horace Greeley's *New-York Tribune*," *Symbiosis*, 2005.

Ortega, Julio, "Transatlantic Translations," *PMLA*, 2003.

Pace, Joel, "'Lifted to Genius?': Wordsworth in Emerson's Nurture and *Nature*," *Symbiosis*, 1998.

———, "Wordsworth and America: Reception and Reform," *The Cambridge Companion to Wordsworth*, ed. Stephen Gill, 2003.

Pace, Joel, and Matthew Scott, eds., *Wordsworth in American Literary Culture*, 2005.

Pace, Joel, Chris Koenig-Woodyard, and Lance Newman, eds., "Transatlantic Romanticism," a special issue of *Romanticism on the Net*, forthcoming 2006.

Pease, Donald, "National Narratives, Postnational Narration," *Modern Fiction Studies*, 1997.

Pease, Donald, and Robyn Wiegman, eds., *The Futures of American Studies*, 2002.

Potkay, Adam, and Sandra Burr, eds., *Black Atlantic Writers of the Eighteenth Century: Living the New Exodus in England and the Americas*, 1995.

Power, Julia, *Shelley in America in the Nineteenth Century*, 1940.

Raven, James, *London Booksellers and American Customers: Transatlantic Literary Community and the Charleston Library Society, 1748–1811*, 2002.

Reynolds, David, *Beneath the American Renaissance*, 1988.

Rice, Alan J., and Martin Crawford, *Liberating Sojourn: Frederick Douglass and Transatlantic Reform*, 1999.

Richardson, Alan, and Sonia Hofkosh, eds., *Romanticism, Race, and Imperial Culture, 1780–1834*, 1996.

Richardson, Jr., Robert D., "Liberal Platonism and Transcendentalism: Shaftesbury, Schleiermacher, Emerson," *Symbiosis*, 1997.

Roach, Joseph, *Cities of the Dead: Circum-Atlantic Performance*, 1996.

Robertson, Fiona, "British Romantic Columbiads," *Symbiosis*, 1998.

Roessel, David, *In Byron's Shadow: Modern Greece in the English and American Imagination*, 2002.

Ronda, Bruce A., ed., *The Letters of Elizabeth Palmer Peabody*, 1984.

Rowe, John Carlos, "Nineteenth-Century United States Literary Culture and Transnationality," *PMLA*, 2003.

———, "Postnationalism, Globalism, and the New American Studies," *Cultural Critique*, 1998.

Said, Edward, *Orientalism*, 1978.

Sattelmeyer, Robert, *Thoreau's Reading*, 1988.

Smith, Lorrie, "'Walking' from England to America: Re-Viewing Thoreau's Romanticism," *The New England Quarterly*, 1985.

Stafford, Fiona, *The Last of the Race: The Growth of a Myth from Milton to Darwin*, 1994.

Steinman, Lisa, "Transatlantic Cultures: Godwin, Brown, and Mary Shelley," *The Wordsworth Circle*, 2001.

Sutton, Emma, "Foreign Bodies: Mark Twain, Music and Anglo-American Identity," *Symbiosis*, 2004.

Swyderski, Ann, "Dickinson's Enchantment: the Barrett Browning Fascicles," *Symbiosis*, 2003.

Tanner, Tony, "Notes for a Comparison between American and European Romanticism," *Journal of American Studies*, 1968.

Tatsumi, Takayuki, "Literary History on the Road: Transatlantic Crossings and Transpacific Crossovers," *PMLA*, 2004.

Taylor, Clare, *British and American Abolitionists: An Episode in Transatlantic Understanding*, 1974.

Thomas, Gordon K., "'And When America Was Free': Thomas Paine and the English Romantics," *Charles Lamb Bulletin*, 1990.

Thomas, Helen, *Romanticism and Slave Narratives: Transatlantic Testimonies*, 2000.

Vallins, David, "Self-Reliance: Individualism in Emerson and Coleridge," *Symbiosis*, 2001.

Vansickle, Eugene S., "A Transnational Vision for African Colonization: John H. B. Latrobe and the Future of Maryland in Liberia," *Journal of Transatlantic Studies*, 2003.

Verhoeven, W. M., "'New Philosophers' in the Backwoods: Romantic Primitivism in the 1790s Novel," *The Wordsworth Circle*, 2001.

———, *Revolutionary Histories: Transatlantic Cultural Nationalism, 1775–1815*, 2002.

Verhoeven, W. M., and Beth Dolan Kautz, eds., *Revolutions and Watersheds: Transatlantic Dialogues 1775–1815*, 1999.

Voller, Jack G., *The Supernatural Sublime: The Metaphysics of Terror in Anglo-American Romanticism*, 1994.

Ware, Tracy, ed., *A Northern Romanticism: Poets of the Confederation*, 2000.

Weisbuch, Robert, *Atlantic Double-Cross: American Literature and British Influence in the Age of Emerson*, 1986.

Wellek, Rene, "The Name and Nature of Comparative Literature," *Discriminations: Further Concepts of Criticism*, 1970.

Wilkson, Rob, et al., eds., *Global/Local: Cultural Production and the Transnational Imaginary*, 1996.

Wilson, Eric, "Coleridge, Emerson, and Electromagnetic Hermeticism," *The Wordsworth Circle*, 2001.

Wind, Astrid, "'Adieu to all': The Death of the American Indian at the Turn of the Eighteenth Century," *Symbiosis*, 1998.

———, "Irish Legislative Independence and the Politics of Staging American Indians in the 1790s," *Symbiosis*, 2001.

Wood, Marcus, *Blind Memory: Visual Representations of Slavery in England and America, 1780–1865*, 2000.

———, *The Poetry of Slavery: An Anglo-American Anthology, 1764–1865*, 2004.

———, *Slavery, Empathy, and Pornography*, 2003.

Worth, Tim, "'An Extraordinary Species of Tyranny': Fanny Trollope and the *Domestic Manners of the Americans*," *Symbiosis*, 2001.

Yellin, Jean Fagan, and John Van Horne, eds., *The Abolitionist Sisterhood*, 1994.

Credits

Texts

Apess, William, "An Indian's Looking Glass for the White Man," copyright © 1992 by the University of Massachusetts Press. Reprinted by permission.

Atkinson, William Parson, letter to William Wordsworth, reprinted by the kind permission of the Trustees of Dove Cottage, with special thanks to Jeff Cowton, Robert Woof, and Jonathan Wordsworth. Dove Cottage Manuscript: A/Atkinson/1, 25 May 1845.

Clare, John, "The Mores," reprinted courtesy of Curtis Brown Group Ltd.

Dickinson, Emily, reprinted by permission of the publishers and the Trustees of Amherst College from *The Poems of Emily Dickinson: Variorum Edition*, Ralph W. Franklin, ed., Cambridge, Mass.: The Belknap Press of Harvard University Press, Copyright © 1998 by the President and Fellows of Harvard College. Copyright © 1951, 1955, 1979, 1983 by the President and Fellows of Harvard College.

Keats, John, reprinted by permission of the publisher from *The Letters of John Keats, 1814–1821, Volumes I and II*, edited by Hyder Edward Rollins, Cambridge, Mass.: Harvard University Press, Copyright © 1958 by the President and Fellows of Harvard College.

Occom, Samson, "A Short Narrative of My Life," reprinted courtesy of Dartmouth College Library.

Thoreau, Henry David, "Sympathy" and "Poverty," reprinted courtesy of Morgan Library.

Thoreau, Henry David, "I have seen some frozen faced Connecticut," reprinted courtesy of Princeton University Library.

Illustrations

Bierstadt, Albert, *Emigrants Crossing the Plains*, 1867. Oil on canvas. National Heritage & Western Heritage Museum, Oklahoma City, OK.

Blake, William, title page, *America*, 1793. Fitzwilliam Museum, University of Cambridge, UK/ The Bridgeman Art Library International Ltd.

Blake, William, "The Tyger," *Songs of Innocence and Experience*, 1794. Fitzwilliam Museum, University of Cambridge, UK/ The Bridgeman Art Library International Ltd.

Church, Frederic Edwin, *Niagara*, 1857. The National Gallery of Scotland.

Constable, John, *Branch Hill Pond, Hampstead*, 1825. The Cleveland Museum of Fine Arts, Leonard C. Hanna, Jr., Fund, 1972.48.

Equiano, Olaudah, frontispiece, *The Interesting Narrative of the Life of Olaudah Equiano*, 1789. British Library.

Fuller, Margaret, from *Portrait Gallery of Eminent Men and Women of Europe and America. . . . With Biographies. By E. A. D.*, 1872–1874. British Library.

Hunt, Isaac, title page of *The Political Family*, 1775. Courtesy, American Antiquarian Society.

Turner, Joseph Mallord William (British, 1775–1851), *Slave Ship (Slavers Throwing Overboard the Dead and the Dying, Typhoon Coming On)*, 1840. Oil on canvas. 90.8 x 122.6 cm (35³/₄ x 48¹/₄ in.) Henry Lillie Pierce Fund. Courtesy, Museum of Fine Arts, Boston.

Index